THE
BIBLE
READER'S
COMPANION

THE
BIBLE
READER'S
COMPANION

LAWRENCE O. RICHARDS

HALO PRESS

The chart on page 44 is taken from *The Bible Knowledge Commentary*, John F. Walvoord and Roy B. Zuck, eds., © 1985 by Scripture Press Publications, Inc. The art on page 205 is taken from *The 365-Day Devotional Commentary*, by Lawrence O. Richards, © 1990 by Scripture Press Publications, Inc. The chart on page 590 is taken from *The Teacher's Commentary*, by Lawrence O. Richards, © 1987 by Scripture Press Publications, Inc. Used by permission

Unless otherwise noted, Scripture quotations are from the *Holy Bible, New International Version*, © 1973, 1978, 1984, International Bible Society. Used by permission of Zondervan Bible Publishers. Other quotations are from *New American Standard Bible* (NASB), © the Lockman Foundation 1960, 1962, 1963, 1968, 1971, 1972, 1973, 1975, 1977; J.B. Phillips: *The New Testament in Modern English*, Revised Edition, (PH), © J.B. Phillips, 1958, 1960, 1972, permission of Macmillan Publishing Co. and Collins Publishers; the *Jerusalem Bible* (JB), published and copyrighted 1966, 1967, and 1968, by Darton, Longman & Todd Ltd. and Doubleday & Co., Inc. and used by permission of the publisher; and the *Authorized (King James) Version* (KJV).

Library of Congress Cataloging-in-Publication Data

Richards, Larry. 1931–
   The Bible reader's companion / by Larry Richards.
     p.   cm.
   Includes bibliographical references and index.
   ISBN 0-89693-039-4
   1. Bible—Outlines, syllabi, etc. I. Title.
BS592.R53   1991
220'.02–dc20   90-44915
                                              CIP

© 1991 SP Publications, Inc. All rights reserved. Printed in the United States of America.
This edition published by Ottenheimer Publishers, Inc.
Halo Press is a trademark of Ottenheimer Publishers, Inc.
10 Church Lane, Baltimore, Maryland 21208, USA
BI068D

Contents

PREFACE

The Bible is exciting. But sometimes it's hard to understand the message of a passage you read or study. There are commentaries. But these are usually long and filled with complicated discussion. There are Bible dictionaries. But these discuss topics, not the particular passage you want to understand. There are expository dictionaries of Bible words, Bible handbooks, and many other tools. But none give you the instant access to just the information you need to understand and to apply the specific message of every chapter of God's Word.

That's why this book is special: a companion you'll want by your side as you read the Word of God for your own enrichment, or as you prepare to teach others. It truly is a guide to *every chapter of the Bible!* At the top of each page you'll find the message of a chapter of the Bible summarized, a key verse identified, and a personal application suggested. You'll also find a list of key concepts found in that chapter, with arrows (») identifying the pages on which each truth is carefully explained!

There's also a special INSIGHT section for each chapter. The insight section gives fascinating information on Bible customs and archeology, defines Bible words, explains key Bible truths, solves apparent conflicts, and in many additional ways enriches your understanding of Scripture. There are also carefully researched illustrations, so you can see as well as read about the biblical world! You'll see the kind of jewelry Isaac gave to his bride Rebekah, examine the sturdy walls of Jericho, and find out what the "sounding brass" Paul alludes to in 1 Corinthians 13 really was!

There's never been a Bible study help quite like *The Bible Reader's Companion.* And you'll never find a simpler, easier to use, yet more complete and fact-filled single volume Bible study help.

That's why I'm so excited that Victor Books has decided to let me share with you this product of many years of study. The Bible truly is an exciting Book. The more I explore it, the more deeply I realize how vital, alive, and life-changing all of Scripture—not just those familiar passages most of us know so well—truly are. *Every chapter* is a very special message from God to you and me. And if this book helps you to appreciate each chapter of God's Word better, and helps you better hear His living voice, the purpose that Victor Books and I have in publishing it will be fulfilled.

Larry Richards

The Bible

The Bible is the world's best-selling book. It has been translated into more languages than any other book in history. And it has been honored over the ages as a unique book—a book given by God Himself, containing a timeless message for all human beings, everywhere. Other religions have sacred books. But none compares with the Bible. It is a unique book. This collection of 66 works by many different authors, written and compiled over a span of some 1,600 years, is the only book that can support a claim to have been inspired by God Himself. It is the only book that accurately conveys the message God intends to communicate to humanity—and to you and me. How important, then, that you and I read Scripture carefully and intelligently. How important that we have some grasp of how each of the over 1,100 chapters of the Bible fits into the whole. How important to sense the contribution each chapter makes to our understanding of God, and to deepening our relationship with Him.

A Word from God

The prophets and writers whose works are recorded in our Bible were convinced of one thing. Their message was not of their own invention. What they communicated was the very Word of God.

Affirmations like these lead us to see Scripture in a unique light. The Bible is not speculation, but revelation. It is not simply inspiring, but inspired. As such the Bible is an authoritative word from God, and has been recognized as authoritative by believers from the beginning.

Revelation

Hebrew and Greek words translated "revelation" mean "to uncover, expose, disclose, or make known." According to Scripture, God has made known information that mankind needs to know, and has also made Himself known to us in that information, and in the person of Jesus Christ. Key Verse: "No eye has seen, no ear has heard, no mind has conceived what God has prepared for those who love Him—but God has revealed it to us by His Spirit" (1 Cor. 2:9-10).

Inspiration

This word renders a Greek term meaning "God-breathed." God so carried along the writers of Scripture that what they wrote were the very words God intended to use to convey His message to humankind. Thus the words of the Bible, not the writers, are said to be inspired. Key Verse: "All Scripture is God-breathed and is useful for teaching, rebuking, correcting and training in righteousness, so that the man of God may be thoroughly equipped for every good work" (2 Tim. 3:16-17).

While this high view of the Bible is the traditional one, held by believers since the beginning, the past century has seen the emergence of other views. Some suggest that the Bible is simply a record of man's search for God, not of God's revelation to man. In this view Scripture is no more than an account of the efforts of religious people to probe ultimate questions. Another contemporary view holds that the Bible is a report of human experience with God. The human authors struggled to put what they experienced into words, and often adopted miraculous language to describe rather ordinary events. God thus didn't really free Israel from slavery by a series of miraculous acts. But the Israelites found freedom so wonderful that they used the language of miracles to express their awe. An even newer view holds that most of the Old Testament is a reconstruction of Israel's history by a Jewish priestly class that wanted support for its superior social position in postexilic society. In the same way, the Gospels are supposed to be a reconstruction by the church leaders of Jesus' life, intended to support their notion that the simple rabbi from Nazareth was divine.

These and other theories, which in effect rob Scripture of its authority, fall short in many ways. First, they rest on speculation, without sound historical support. In contrast, archeological finds have consistently shown not only the details of Scripture but also the broad portrayals of ancient cultures to be stunningly accurate. Second, the notion that Scripture is a human invention collapses when tested by prophecy. Scores of detailed predictions, often made hundreds or even thousands of years before the event described, make clear a supernatural source. As God says through Isaiah, "I am God, and there is no other; I am God, and there is none like Me. I make known the end from the beginning, from ancient times what is still to come" (Isa. 46:9-10). When we add to this the internal consistency of the Bible, despite its many writers who lived at different times and places, and the testimony of millions whose lives have been transformed by this Book of books, the truth is utterly clear. The Bible is the Word of God. It is completely reliable, and is vitally relevant to our lives.

And so, again, we see why it is so important to have a grasp of every chapter of the Bible, rather than simply know more familiar parts. The Scripture in its entirety is the Word of God, and in every part God speaks to us as His people.

What's in the Bible?

The Bible is a rich, complex book. It reflects the personalities of the writers and the literary styles of their times. It contains historical narrative, poetry, philosophy, pithy proverbs, prophetic denunciation, instruction and teaching, sermons and exhortations, predictions concerning the future, and grand apocalyptic visions. The Bible reports God's momentous interventions in history, introduces us to saints and sinners, and provides instruction in godly living. The Bible explains the origin of the universe, affirms the uniqueness of mankind, accounts for the presence of evil and suffering in our world, unveils the future, and in its exalted revelation of God calls us to faith. In Scripture we are confronted with our own imperfection, our sins, and the fleeting nature of our days on earth. Yet through Scripture we come in contact with a God of power and wisdom, of love and justice. Through Scripture we sense His overwhelming compassion for the lost, His awesome and costly commitment to our salvation, and the wonder of His invitation to us to become children of God through faith in Christ. No more wonderful, no more important volume has ever been produced.

No wonder we want to read the Bible with understanding. No wonder we want to know the message of every chapter of the wonderful Word of God!

THE BIBLE: A LIBRARY OF BOOKS ABOUT GOD

THE OLD TESTAMENT BOOKS

Narrative: Books that Relate Israel's History

Genesis	(Creation story: ?) (Abraham's family: 2165–1885 B.C.)	Judges	(Years of Apostasy: 1375?–1043 B.C.)
Exodus	(Deliverance: 1446 B.C.)	1–2 Samuel	(The monarchy established: 1043–970 B.C.)
Leviticus	(Worship instruction: 1445 B.C.)	1–2 Kings	(Monarchy to Babylonian Captivity: 970–586 B.C.)
Numbers	(Wilderness wandering: 1445–1406 B.C.)	1–2 Chronicles	(Monarchy to Babylonian Captivity: 970–586 B.C.)
Deuteronomy	(Moses' last sermons: 1406 B.C.)	Ezra	(Return from Captivity: 538–455 B.C.)
Joshua	(Conquest of Canaan: 1406–1385? B.C.)	Nehemiah	(Rebuilding Jerusalem: 446–430 B.C.)

Wisdom Literature: Practical Advice for Godly Living

Proverbs	Principles learned from experience (O.T. period)

Worship Literature: Guidance for Public and Private Worship

Psalms	Personal experience with God (O.T. period)

Prophets: Call to Repentance and Visions of the Future

Isaiah	(Early 8th century B.C.)	Jonah	(Early 8th century B.C.)
Jeremiah	(Early 6th century B.C.)	Micah	(Mid 8th century B.C.)
Lamentations	(Early 6th century B.C.)	Nahum	(Late 7th century B.C.)
Ezekiel	(Early 6th century B.C.)	Habakkuk	(Late 7th century B.C.)
Daniel	(Mid 6th century B.C.)	Zephaniah	(Late 7th century B.C.)
Hosea	(Mid 8th century B.C.)	Haggai	(Late 6th century B.C.)
Joel	(Late 9th century B.C.)	Zechariah	(Late 6th century B.C.)
Amos	(Early 8th century B.C.)	Malachi	(Early 5th century B.C.)
Obadiah	(Date unknown)		

Biography: Stories of Bible People

Ruth	(1100 B.C.?)	Esther	(477 B.C.?)

Philosophy: Examining Life's Ultimate Concerns

Job	Why do the godly suffer? (2100 B.C.?)	Song of Songs	Celebrating sexuality (925 B.C.?)
Ecclesiastes	What gives life meaning? (935 B.C.?)		

THE NEW TESTAMENT BOOKS

The Gospels: Four Portraits of Jesus Christ's Life on Earth (A.D. 4–33)

Matthew	Jesus as the promised Messiah of the O.T.	Luke	Jesus as an ideal human being.
Mark	Jesus as the One busy doing God's work.	John	Jesus as the eternal Son of God, become man.

Narrative History: The Early Years of Christ's Church

Acts — The spread of the church through the Roman Empire (A.D. 33–60)

Epistles: Letters Instructing Young Churches in Christian Faith and Life, Written between A.D. 40–90

Letters by Paul

Romans	The Gospel and righteousness.	Ephesians	The church as Christ's living body.
1 Corinthians	Solving relationship problems.	Philippians	Keys to joy in the Christian life.
2 Corinthians	Principles of spiritual leadership.	Colossians	Dynamic spirituality explained.
Galatians	Salvation by faith alone.		

More Letters by Paul

1 Thessalonians	Missionary ministry and our hope.	2 Timothy	Guidance for dealing with false teachers.
2 Thessalonians	Christ's second coming.	Titus	Guidance for another young leader.
1 Timothy	Guidance for a young minister.	Philemon	An appeal for a runaway slave.

Letters by Other Leaders of the Early Church that Explain Christian Faith and Life

Hebrews	Christ fulfills the Old Testament faith.	1 John	Love and obedience in Christian life.
James	Living the life of faith every day.	2–3 John	Personal letters of encouragement.
1 Peter	Christian suffering and submission.	Jude	A warning against false teachers.
2 Peter	Scoffers and Christ's second coming.		

Prophecy: An Apocalyptic Vision of History's End and God's Final Judgment of Sinful Humanity

Revelation — Final judgment and eternity described.

Preserved, for Us to Read

The earliest parts of the Bible were written some 3,400 years ago! And it is certain that traditions and possibly documents included in Scripture go back another 400 or 500 years. How can we have confidence in such an old book? Wouldn't corruptions have distorted the original text? However wonderful it might be to have a Word from God today, what basis is there for assuming that what we read in our English versions accurately relates God's message?

The story of the transmission and translation of the Bible is an exciting one, and confirms our confidence in Scripture. The people of Israel from the first looked on the first books of the Bible as God's inspired Word, and were careful to preserve it. Scribes took pains to copy the text accurately, even counting the letters in each line, on each page, and in each book, to make sure that the middle letter was the same as in the original. For hundreds of years the earliest text of the Old Testament available was copied in about A.D. 1100. Then, with the discovery of the Dead Sea Scrolls, texts of Old Testament books dating as early as 200 B.C. — some 1,300 years older! — were found. When compared, scholars discovered that these texts were virtually identical. And none of the changes that did creep in over that awesome span of years made any material difference in the meaning or message of the books!

Similarly one well-respected New Testament scholar has estimated that all the truly disputed words found in the Greek New Testament could be printed on one half of one page in a Greek New Testament. And not one Christian doctrine would be called into question.

Thus the preservation of the text of the Bible confirms our conviction that Scripture is the Word of God. God not only gave us His Word, but has guarded it, so that today we too can read the Bible, and hear His living voice.

And so read the Bible we must! And what better way is there to read than to read each chapter with understanding. And to apply what God has to say in each chapter to our own lives, so that we might respond to Him in faith and love.

This is the whole purpose of this *Bible Reader's Companion*. Whatever chapter you may turn to in the Scripture, you'll find information to help you better understand what you read, and insights to help you apply what you read to yourself. Ultimately, this is the reason God had for giving us His Word. He wants us to know Him. He wants us to respond to Him — first by exercising a saving faith in Christ, and then by setting out daily to do those things His Word tells us please Him best.

The World of the Old Testament

Old Testament events are set in the cradle of ancient civilizations, the broad area known as the "Fertile Crescent." That crescent is anchored in the north in Mesopotamia. It sweeps upward, following the courses of the Tigris and Euphrates Rivers, and then bends to follow the shoreline of the Mediterranean southward. There it encompasses Canaan, an area archeologists today call Syria/Palestine. The Fertile Crescent continues southward along the Mediterranean into Egypt, and there finds its southern anchor in the rich farmlands that lie along the River Nile (see map on p. 23).

In the 2,000 years before Christ that are reflected in the Old Testament's story of the Jewish people, a series of great empires flourished in the north and in the south. Abraham was born in the north, when Ur was a rich and powerful city-state. In the centuries that followed, other Mesopotamian city-states extended their power across the north and along the Mediterranean. Among the ancient Mesopotamian world powers that play a vital role in sacred history are the Assyrian Empire of the 700s B.C., the Babylonian Empire of the 600s B.C., and the Persian Empire of the 500s B.C. Meanwhile, in Egypt, a series of great dynasties flourished, their power and influence in the Middle East alternately waxing and waning.

Syria/Palestine served as a land bridge between the great powers of the north and south. All too frequently it served also as their battleground. At nearly all times, the smaller states of the area were forced to deal with one or the other of the great powers as they sought to establish their influence in the Middle East, or to dominate the area.

Yet when Abraham came into Canaan around the year 2100 B.C., the land was at peace. Pioneers from many different areas—the Hittites of the far north, the Philistines from the upper Mediterranean, Hivites, Jebusites, Amorites, and others—had established smaller city-states in fertile Canaan. Each city-state was independent, controlling only a local area. In Abraham's time the populated areas were largely limited to valley lands: the hill country was unsettled, and it was there that Abraham, his son Isaac, and his grandson Jacob lived nomadic lives. They farmed some of the lowlands in season, and as summer's heat dried the grasses there they led their flocks and herds up into the verdant highlands.

Canaan, now known as Palestine, or Israel, is a land of great geographic and climatic contrasts. A belt of low-lying, fertile land lies along its border with the Mediterranean. This meets a range of wooded hills that soar upward to become rounded mountains, dotted with meadow-like valleys that lie below rocky ridges. Farther to the east the mountains fall sharply away into the deep Jordan rift valley. Set like a jewel in the upper end of this valley is the Sea of Galilee, which empties into the Jordan River. That river drops rapidly into a broad valley opposite the heights of Jerusalem and Jericho, which controls the passes leading into the highlands.

This varied topography makes Palestine a land of varied climates and crops. Grain can be grown in the lowlands and mountain meadows. Oranges, figs, olives, and other fruit trees flourish in their own ranges. Grapes thrive, and on terraced hillsides every kind of vegetable and melon can be grown. Truly the land when visited by Abraham was a land of "milk and honey": a rich, fertile, beautiful, and varied land. It was this land that God promised to give to Abraham and to his descendants. It was in this land that

God did plant His people. And it is this land, once so rich and beautiful, that was devastated by centuries of warfare as the descendants of Abraham so persistently turned away from God.

A Brief History of Israel

The Old Testament has two major divisions. The first 11 chapters of Genesis deal with the whole human race, and with questions of origin. There we are told that God created this universe, and that human beings are special within it. There we learn of the Fall which introduced sin into the world, of judgment, and of the hope of redemption. Once these basic themes are established, the Book of Genesis introduces us to Abraham — and the rest of the Old Testament tells the story of this one man and his descendants. Yet the story is important to all of us. It was through this man and his descendants that God chose to reveal Himself to all mankind. And it was through this man and his descendants, the Jewish people, that Christ came to win redemption for us all.

For some 200 years, between about 2090 and 1875 B.C., the children and grandchildren of Abraham lived a nomadic life in Palestine. Then they moved to Egypt, where the Israelites remained for over 400 years. Originally welcomed, in time the descendants of Abraham were enslaved. As their bondage became more and more bitter, they cried out to the God of their forefathers for deliverance. That deliverance came in the person of Moses, a Jewish child who had been brought up as Pharaoh's daughter's foster son. Around 1450 B.C. Moses confronted a new Pharaoh, and by a series of devastating miraculous judgments forced the Egyptians to release his people. The Israelites, whose numbers had grown to between 2 and 3 million while in Egypt, were led into the Sinai peninsula. There God gave Moses a Law that called Israel to become a worshiping and just moral community.

Moses and the Exodus generation died before Abraham's offspring returned to Canaan. But their children did return. Under Joshua the Israelites invaded Canaan around 1400 B.C., defeated the combined Canaanite forces, and established a dominant presence in that land. Yet the story of the next 400 years is dark. The Israelites fell into a pattern of apostasy, followed by domination by foreign enemies, followed by repentance and then relief won by charismatic leaders called Judges. The "dark days of the judges" demonstrate a principle stated when the Law was originally given. Obedience to God's Law would bring Israel blessing; disobedience would ensure defeat.

The era of the Judges ended at last as Israel adopted a monarchic form of government, about 1040 B.C. The first king, Saul, was severely flawed, and failed to honor the Lord. He was replaced by David, a military and political genius who was wholly devoted to God. Under David the territory controlled by Israel was expanded 10 times over. Nearly all the land promised to Abraham was occupied by this generation! David also established an effective bureaucracy, established Jerusalem as the political and religious capital of Israel, and led a spiritual reformation. And God promised David that history's ultimate Ruler, destined to lead God's people to ultimate victory and establish an everlasting kingdom, would come from his line.

The era of David and Solomon was Israel's Golden Age. The great powers in both north and south were weak during the tenth century B.C. Israel not only extended its territory, but dominated nearby nations and controlled trade routes that brought the nation vast wealth. For the first time, under Solomon, Israel set out to sea, in a joint trading venture with the maritime city-state of Tyre, exporting grain and copper smelted for Israel's ore. At home Solomon engaged in ambitious building projects. He constructed a stunning temple to the Lord in Jerusalem, a magnificent palace for himself, and fortified a number of strategic cities. These decades were a golden literary age as well. David reformed worship, and added dozens of psalms to Israel's worship liturgy. Solomon collected proverbs, and wrote the penetrating philosophical analysis of life's meaning found in Ecclesiastes, as well as the delicately erotic Song of Songs.

Solomon, David's son, successfully maintained the kingdom David built. But on Solomon's death in 930 B.C., the nation was divided into two rival kingdoms: Israel in the north, and Judah in the south. The Northern Kingdom, where a corrupt religious system was established by its first king, was ruled by an unbroken succession of godless rulers. Despite the efforts of prophets God sent to His people in Israel, the apostate nation was ultimately invaded by Assyria and its people taken into captivity in 722 B.C.

Judah, ruled by descendants of David, fared better. Several of its kings were truly godly individuals, who struggled against the tendency to idolatry that troubled the Southern as well as Northern Kingdom. Ultimately, however,

A relief in the palace of Sennacherib shows Assyrian forces attacking the fortress of Lachish in Judah during the campaign which marked the end of the Northern Kingdom's separate existence.

Judah too descended into apostasy, again despite the powerful preaching of a series of prophets whose messages are preserved in the Old Testament. The end came as Babylon, which supplanted Assyria as the dominant world power at the end of the seventh century B.C., razed Jerusalem in 586 B.C. and burned the beautiful temple erected there by Solomon.

After the destruction of Jerusalem the remaining population of Judah was deported to Babylon. This period, known as the Exile, or the Captivity, led to radical changes in Jewish faith and life. Prior to the Babylonian Captivity Jewish religion had honored the Old Testament Law, but had emphasized temple worship and sacrifice. Life in Babylon was not hard, but separation from the Promised Land had a traumatic effect on the Jewish people. Intense self-examination led to the conviction that God's people had strayed from His Law. Out of this grew a strong popular movement that emphasized the study of the Old Testament and application of its laws to every aspect of Jewish life. The synagogue was developed as a house of worship and study, and scribes—men like Ezra (cf. Ezra 7:10), who dedicated themselves to study and to teach God's Law—began to play an increasingly significant role in Jewish religion.

When the Persian Cyrus overcame the Babylonian Empire in 539 B.C., and replaced it with the Medo-Persian, he reversed the Babylonian policy of deporting conquered peoples from their homeland. The Jewish people were permitted to return home, and were even encouraged to rebuild the Jerusalem temple! Not many did. Many had settled into a comfortable and prosperous life in Babylon, even as many of the Israelites deported in 722 B.C. had found homes in major cities dominated by Assyria. Thus while the Old Testament's focus is on Judea and Jerusalem, many times more Jews lived in the cities of the East than in the Jewish homeland! It has been estimated that by the time of the New Testament 1 in 5 of the population of Babylon and other Eastern cities may have been Jewish! And 1 in 10 of the population of the Roman Empire in the time of Christ may well have been Jews!

Back in the homeland, however, the little group of some 50,000 struggled to survive. Settled within just a few miles of Jerusalem, in the now tiny district of Judea, the returned exiles succeeded only in laying the foundation of a new temple. Then, 18 years later, exhorted by the Prophets Haggai and Zechariah, temple building was resumed, and the house of worship finished. Jerusalem itself still lay in ruins, until Nehemiah, who had achieved high status in the Persian court, came as its governor to rebuild the city walls. The last historical books of the Old Testament tell of his and Ezra the scribe's struggle to move God's people to keep His Law. The last book of Old Testament prophecy, Malachi, written about 435 B.C., suggests that those efforts too fell short.

And so the Old Testament closes on a dark note, and yet one of hope. God, who had acted in history past to rescue His people from Egyptian bondage, to bring them into the Promised Land, to judge them when they sinned, and to preserve generations that trusted in Him, must surely act again. Surely God would keep His ancient promises. He would send the Deliverer, the Descendant promised to David, who would not only restore Israel's ancient glory, but would restore all her people to a vibrant and holy relationship with Israel's God.

Through the next 400 years God's people preserved this ancient hope. A hope that suddenly flowered and bore fruit when an angel appeared to a young country woman named Mary, and announced that she would bear a Son whose name would be Jesus. This Son would save His people from their sins and raise up again the fallen royal house of David, Israel's greatest king.

Major Themes of the Old Testament

The history of God's Old Testament people is significant, for in many ways the history of Israel is the record of God's revelation of Himself to humanity. In God's promises to Abraham we meet a God who chooses to commit Himself unconditionally to bless human beings, and who will accept our faith in place of a righteousness we do not have. In the Exodus miracles we see a God who not only can but also will act in history, to break the bonds that hold man captive. In the Law given Moses we see God's moral character, and hear His call to us to live holy and righteous lives. In the sacrificial system that Moses initiated we sense the terrible fact that sinners deserve death—and discover with relief that God in grace will accept a substitute. In the history of Israel we see underlined again and again the truth that obedience leads to divine blessing, while disobedience brings judgment and misery. Yet even in the most corrupt of times God refreshes with reminders of His firm intention to do man good. The prophets who warned of imminent judgment still concluded with bright visions of the future. Jeremiah encourages a people about to be led into Captivity with the message that God has not deserted them, even though they have abandoned God. The day is coming, Jeremiah proclaims, when God will make a New Covenant with the people of Israel (Jer. 31–32). Under the gracious provisions of that New Covenant God's people will no longer stray, for God will give each of His own a new heart: a heart that responds joyfully to Him.

Thus in every way the themes that we can trace through the Old Testament harmonize perfectly with the themes developed in the New. In each Testament we meet a God of love, of faithfulness, of grace. In each we see His deep concern for humankind, expressed in provisions He has made for our salvation and our blessing. And in each we find emphasized the importance of a responsive faith: a faith which relies on God completely, takes Him at His word, and expresses itself in a committed effort to do that which pleases the One we have come to know and to love.

In all these ways, as well as in the Old Testament's promise of a coming Saviour and Lord, whom we recognize in Jesus Christ, the Old Testament is a rich resource for Christian as well as Jew, a foundation document on which we rest our understanding of God, and our faith in Him.

Life in Old Testament Times

Our brief survey of Israel's history reminds us that life in any age is hazardous. Our present generation has lived with terrorism and the threat of atomic war. But each generation of Israelites lived with a similar threat of devastation by hostile nations whose armies lay just over the horizon. Even so, life for most of God's Old Testament people fell into a familiar pattern. Israel was an agricultural nation, a people of the land. There were artisans and small shopkeepers in large cities, like Jerusalem and Samaria. There were potters, leatherworkers, stonemasons, and builders. But there was no merchant class: no venturesome travelers who led caravans to far-off lands, or set out in little ships to engage in trade along the Mediterranean or Gulf coasts. Most

of the people in Israel farmed. They built cisterns to catch and hold water on rocky, terraced hillsides, where they grew vegetables and tended vineyards. Or they raised grain or flax on the plains, olives in the highlands, and watched the flocks of sheep and goats that ranged the open lands. Life fell into a repeated cycle governed by the agricultural year: planting and harvest, rainy and dry seasons, a time to reap barley, and a time to reap wheat. A time to press the juice of grapes, a time to press the oil from olives. And, at regular intervals, times to go up to Jerusalem to offer thanks to God, who had given Israel the land, and who in His goodness sent the rains that sustained life.

The men of Israel worked the fields, joined by the women at harvesttime. The women carried out the necessary household tasks. They ground the grain to be mixed with a bit of olive oil and formed into flat cakes of bread. They dried the flax, pounded out its fibers, and fashioned them into thread. Or they carded the wool of sheep, twisted it into thread, and from these two materials made clothing for the family. The women cared for the young children, prepared the family food, and in these ways were partners with their men in the family farm or the cottage industry that provided them with a living, with enough extra to bring God a thank offering, and a bit more to set aside for the poor, the widow, the orphan, and the stranger in their land.

The typical Israelite lived in what archeologists today call a "four-room house" (see p. 20). This small dwelling was typically home for some 6 to 8 persons. Through much of the Old Testament era many Israelites lived in

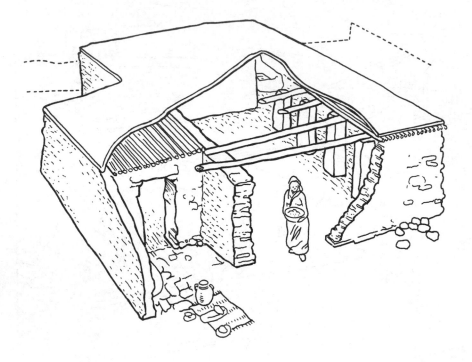

Most Old Testament men and women lived in a "four-room house" like the one shown here. Cooking and much of the work was done outdoors.

small mini-villages, clusters of 8 to 10 of these dwellings set in the hills around larger towns. Water was collected during the rainy season in a series of cisterns, hollowed out of the ground and sealed with plaster, with the last and largest of the cisterns dug out under the floor of the house itself. The typical size of the family that lived in such a house has been computed by calculating the amount of water the cistern system holds, and the amount of water needed to sustain an individual through the dry season. Based on the height of the ceilings of these houses, it has been suggested that the typical Israelite man in the time of the Judges or of David was probably about 5 foot 2 inches tall.

It was thus that most of the men and women of the Old Testament lived, far from the center of political and religious activity in Jerusalem, as the centuries flowed. The majority of men and women of that time had as little influence on the great events that shaped their times as you and I do today. Jerusalem was as far away from them as Washington, D.C. is from us, even though men in each capital make decisions that shape all citizens' lives. Yet the ordinary people of old, like us today, were involved in the greatest issues of all. Then, as now, the individual was called to live a godly life: to bring up a family, to do justice, and to seek to influence his society for good.

Old Testament Law distributed responsibility for the society throughout Israel. There was no national police force, and no system of national courts. Local elders heard disputes and criminal cases. Individuals with relevant information were responsible to testify, and elders pronounced the penalties established in God's Law. As long as the majority in a community were faithful to God and to His Law, justice would be done in the land. The Prophet Micah reflects this theme, as he cries out in God's name, "He has showed you, O man, what is good. And what does the Lord require of you? To act justly and to love mercy and to walk humbly with your God" (Micah 6:8).

God's Old Testament people often did walk humbly with God. Many an individual resisted the lure of pagan worship to remain faithful to the Lord. They lived humbly, seeking to follow the precepts God had laid down in His Word. They lived in faith, depending on God for the rains that made their land fertile, and for protection from foreign enemies and from natural disasters such as earthquakes and locust invasions. They brought up their children to know and honor God, and they faithfully brought their offerings to Jerusalem, to take part in the great festivals of worship that recalled His past faithfulness, and celebrated His continuing commitment to His people.

As we study the Old Testament we are often impressed with the flaws that corrupted the Israelites, and brought divine judgment on so many generations. But we must never forget that even in the darkest of times, men and women of faith lived out quiet lives, honoring God, and keeping the flame of faith alive. History — even sacred history — reports the great events that shape national experience, and tends to neglect the individual. So even when the text of Scripture draws our attention to these great events, and reveals the dark stain of sin that mars the history of Israel, we must not be misled, or overlook the godly Jews. At all times God has maintained a people for His name. In every era the Old Testament describes there were godly Jews, whose lives of quiet faith testify to God's wisdom and His grace in choosing Israel as a people for His name.

Reading the Old Testament

In reading the Old Testament we need to remember that we hold a very human document as well as the living Word of God. The Old Testament is the story of a people, and of God's work in the history of a chosen nation. Yet it is also the story of men and women of faith. It is the story of heroes and heroines, like Abraham, Moses, Joshua, Deborah, Gideon, David, Esther, and a host of others. As fascinating as that history and its heroes may be, the Old Testament is also a witness to the primacy of faith in God. Looking back we can appreciate the course of sacred history, and understand how God was working through its flow. No single generation of Old Testament believers understood God's overall purposes as we do today. And yet in each generation thousands of individuals never mentioned on the sacred page lived and died in faith, secure in the hope that God was at work, and that He would do His work well.

What an example they are for you and me today. We too are unnoticed by the world, yet vitally important to the Lord. We too can live in faith and hope, and seek to honor God in all we do. And the great truths revealed in the Old Testament, and taken to heart by many of His Old Testament people, will help us to do just this.

Genesis

The first words we read express the great value of this exciting Old Testament book: "In the beginning God."

Genesis takes us back beyond recorded history, and by revelation unveils the origin both of the universe and of the human race. The thrust of the Genesis message is that to understand who we are and where we came from, we must begin with God.

There are really only two ways to understand origins. A person can see everything as the product of random chance operating in an impersonal universe, or as the craftsman-like work of a Person. Genesis unhesitatingly affirms this second position. It traces the Creation of the universe to a personal God. It portrays human beings as unique, special creations of this God. It explains the origin of sin and evil. It affirms man's moral responsibility, and lays a foundation for a doctrine of redemption.

Genesis explains the origins of the Hebrews; a people chosen by God to serve as a channel of blessing for the whole world. Special promises given to Abraham, the father of the chosen race, are evidence that God has a continuing purpose for human beings, and is working out this purpose in history.

Genesis lays the foundation for understanding all Scripture, for the whole Bible speaks from the context defined in this first book. God is. God cares uniquely about human beings. God must and will judge sin, but God also has set in motion a process that brings even sinners back to Him. In a grand plan for the benefit of our race, set in motion in the call of Abraham, God has revealed the wonder of His endless, redeeming love.

GENESIS AT A GLANCE

KEY PEOPLE

Adam *The first man, whose disobedience corrupted the race.*

Eve *The first woman, whose temptation opened the door to sin.*

Noah *The ark builder, whose obedience delivered his family.*

Abraham *The patriarch, whose trust in God serves as Scripture's prime example of saving faith in God.*

Isaac *Abraham's son who inherited the covenant promise.*

Jacob *Isaac's son who continued the covenant line. His name was changed to Israel, and his sons founded the tribes that make up the Jewish people.*

Joseph *Jacob's son, who brought his family to Egypt and safety.*

KEY EVENTS

Creation (Gen. 1). *God shapes the material universe in seven days.*

Creation of man (Gen. 2). *God creates man and woman in His image.*

Fall of man (Gen. 3). *Adam's disobedience introduces sin into the race.*

The Flood (Gen. 6–8). *God judges sinful human society, destroying nearly all life on earth by a great Flood.*

The Abrahamic Covenant (Gen. 12; 15). *God gives Abraham special and binding promises that affect his offspring and all mankind.*

Abraham's trip to Canaan (Gen. 12). *Abraham leaves his home at God's command and goes to Canaan, the Promised Land.*

Jacob's family moves to Egypt (Gen. 46). *The Children of Israel settle in Egypt, where they will multiply in safety.*

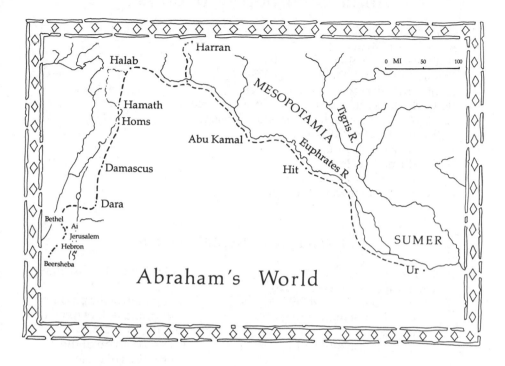

Halab
Harran
0 MI 50 100
MESOPOTAMIA
Hamath
Homs
Tigris R.
Abu Kamal
Euphrates R.
Damascus
Hit
Dara
Bethel
Ai
Jerusalem
Hebron
Beersheba
SUMER
Ur

Abraham's World

The map border is from an inlaid Sumerian war memorial, 2500 B.C.

WHERE THE ACTION TAKES PLACE

The only fixed location for early Genesis is Mt. Ararat, where Noah's ark came to rest after the great Flood. Then, about 2100 B.C., Abraham left Ur in the Mesopotamian Valley, where great ancient empires grew, to go to Canaan, until about 1875 B.C., when Joseph, then vizier of Egypt, resettled them in Goshen.

Date and Authorship. Genesis is the first of five books ascribed to Moses. The great lawgiver, whom God used to break bonds of slavery in Egypt, led the Hebrew people to the very edge of Canaan. On the way Moses met with God on Mt. Sinai to receive the laws that shaped the lifestyle of God's Old Testament people. While the date of the Exodus is disputed, most conservative scholars agree with tradition and believe Moses led the Israelites out of Egypt about 1450 B.C. Moses led the Hebrew people for some 40 years, and recorded in five books of narrative and legislation the revelations he received from the Lord. Most agree that Moses relied on stories told and retold by Israelites in Egypt, and possibly on written sources, for his stories of the patriarchs. Yet one of the most striking features of the Genesis narrative is the accuracy with which Moses related customs no longer practiced in his time. There is no doubt that the rest of Scripture, and Christ Himself, views Genesis and Moses' other books as God's Word, a completely accurate and reliable account of what actually happened in ancient times (cf. Matt. 19:4-6; John 8:56-58; Rom. 5:12-15).

THEOLOGICAL OUTLINE OF GENESIS

I. CREATION — 1–2
  A. Of the Universe — 1
  B. Of Human Beings — 2
II. CHOICE AND CONSEQUENCES — 3–11
  A. Sin and Personal Consequences — 3–4
  B. Wickedness and Universal Consequences — 5–9
  C. Disobedience and International Consequences — 10–11
III. COVENANT OF PROMISE — 12–50
  A. Made with Abraham — 12–25
  B. Confirmed to Isaac — 26–27
  C. Confirmed to Jacob/Israel — 28–36
  D. Worked out through Joseph — 37–50

CONTENT OUTLINE OF GENESIS

I. Primeval Events (1:1–11:32)
  A. Creation Overview (1:1–2:3)
  B. Creation Detail (2:4–4:26)
    1. Creation of man, woman (2:4-25)
    2. Temptation and Fall (3:1-7)
    3. Impact of sin (3:8–4:26)
      a. On Adam, Eve (3:8-24)
      b. On their offspring (4:1-18)
      c. On society (4:19-26)
  C. Man's Early History (5:1–11:32)
    1. Adam to Noah (5:1-32)
    2. Corruption of the race (6:1-8)
    3. Noah's survival of the Flood (6:9–8:22)
    4. God's covenant with Noah (9:1-17)
    5. The curse on Canaan (9:18-29)
    6. Nations springing from Noah's sons (10:1-32)
    7. Origin of languages (11:1-9)
    8. From Shem to Abram (11:10-32)
II. Patriarchal Narratives (12:1–50:26)
  A. The Story of Abraham (12:1–25:18)
    1. Making of the Covenant (12:1–15:21)
    2. Provision of the promised seed, and tests of Abraham's faith (16:1–22:19)
    3. Transmission of the promises to Isaac (22:20–25:11)
    4. The history of Ishmael (25:12-18)
  B. The Story of Jacob (25:19–35:29)
    1. Transmission of the blessing to Jacob rather than Esau (25:19–28:22)
    2. Jacob's sojourn in Paddan Aram (29:1–30:43)
    3. Jacob's return (31–35)
  C. The History of Esau (36:1–37:1)
  D. The Story of Joseph (37:2–50:26)
    1. Joseph sold to Egypt (37:2-36)
    2. Corruption of Judah (38:1-30)
    3. Rise of Joseph in Egypt (39:1–41:57)
    4. The move to Egypt (42:1–47:31)
    5. The Covenant story to be continued (48:1–50:26)

Chapter summary. God exercises His creative power and, by merely speaking, brings the universe into being. He focuses His attention on Planet Earth, carefully shapes it to support life, and populates it with living creatures. Finally God creates humankind in His own image, and sets man to rule over His Creation. The chapter emphasizes the awesome power of our Creator, and yet reminds us that human beings are the clear focus of God's loving concern.

Outline
Place
Finder

CREATION
CHOICE
COVENANT

Yet God's revelation of Himself is the heart of this chapter. His majestic name is found no less than 32 times, usually the subject of some active verb. He speaks, makes, separates, sets the sun and stars in the heavens, and blesses. He demonstrates His trustworthiness in the regularity of day following night, and season succeeding season. He displays His love and unselfishness by sharing His likeness with human beings. In everything we are reminded that God is a Person — vastly intelligent, but also caring and warm. The Creation story, like Creation itself, reveals our God.

Key verse. 1:27: God affirms our significance.

Personal application. God has shared His own image with you.

Key concepts. Creation »p. 430. Dominion »p. 352. Trinity »p. 797. Image of God »p. 28. Holy Spirit »p. 73. Heavens »p. 437.

INSIGHT

"**In the beginning.**" The two-word Heb. phrase *(re'sit)* occurs 51 times in the O. T., and indicates the launching of a series of events. God's creative acts set history in motion, and determined its flow toward an intended end. From the very beginning God has known, and indeed controls, the end (cf. Prov. 8:23; Isa. 41:4, 20, 26). What a reminder that God is sovereign. And what reassurance.

Creation myths. Ancient explanations of the universe ranged from the Mesopotamian claim that matter represents the corpse of a slain deity, Tiamat, to the Greek conviction that the physical universe preexisted the gods. Only Genesis exalts God above His Creation. And only Genesis gives human beings a central place in Creation, as persons made in God's image who are deeply loved by Him. Thus the biblical view of Creation has always been radical — and remains in direct conflict with the modern notion that everything is the product of chance evolution.

The creative "days." Sincere Christians hold differing views. Some hold each "day" represents a geologic era — a vast period of time. Some hold the days are symbolic, or are seven literal days Moses spent on Mt. Sinai (cf. Ex. 32:16), during which God showed Moses how He created all things. Still others assume seven literal days, separated by long ages, while yet another group argues for seven consecutive days.

There is no certain resolution of the conflict. But it may well miss the point. We must focus on the fact that God created, not on disputes over how long it took Him. Our world is no product of blind chance. A living Person lovingly, carefully designed all that is. We live in a personal rather than impersonal universe, and because of this, we have hope. God is! As we commit ourselves to Him, our emptiness will be filled, and we will find life's meaning.

"**Be fruitful and increase.**" Christians have sometimes argued that Adam and Eve's fall was sexual: that they abandoned celibacy, and this was the "original sin." But Gen. 1:28 makes it clear that God intended a sinless Adam and Eve to have children and "increase in number." Human sexuality was invented by God Himself, and is intended as a gift. Within the framework of marriage (Gen. 2) sexual expression is a joyful affirmation of a couple's intimacy, and every pleasure is blessed by God Himself. Sex »p. 836.

"**Very good.**" God evaluated each of the first five days' creative work and called it "good" (attractive, useful, desirable, morally right). The work of creating man is called "very good."

Outline
Place
Finder

CREATION
CHOICE
COVENANT

Chapter summary. God rests from His creative work (2:1-3), and the author returns to look in depth at the creation of mankind. This is not a second Creation account, but a close-up look at the most significant of God's works (vv. 4-7). Note how carefully God shapes Eden, to permit Adam to use those capacities of personhood the Lord shared with him, such as: a love of beauty (v. 9), delight in meaningful work (v. 15), moral responsibility (vv. 16-17), and even a capacity for invention (vv. 19-20). Yet despite these fulfilling gifts, Adam gradually realizes something is lacking, and so God makes Eve, a "suitable helper" for him (vv. 18, 20). God's method, taking a rib from Adam, teaches that man and woman share a common identity: they are equals, each fully participating in God's gift of His image and likeness (vv. 21-23). Yet they are different, so that a man and woman can bond together as husband and wife, and so meet each other's deepest needs for intimacy, lifelong commitment, and mutual support (vv. 24-25).

Key verse. 2:23: Woman shares fully in all that man is.

Personal application. What needs can be met only by the life-long commitment God intended marriage to be?

Key concepts. Sabbath »p. 71. Marriage »p. 801. Shame »p. 356. Women »pp. 394, 723. Work »p. 28.

INSIGHT

Eden. Eden lay somewhere along the Tigris/Euphrates Rivers, possibly in the mountains of Armenia. In later Scriptures Eden stands for a "delightful place" (cf. Isa. 51:3; Ezek. 28:13; Joel 2:3).

Dust and breath. The Creation account reminds us that we human beings are spiritual as well as biological creatures. When God breathed life into Adam, He made him a spiritual being. Man is no animal, but is God's direct, special creation.

Adam/mankind. "Adam" is a Heb. word, the name of the first man, but also the Bible's term for humanity. Man alone was: (1) directly, personally shaped by the Lord and given breath by Him, Gen. 2:7, (2) created in God's image and likeness, 1:26-27 »p. 28, (3) granted the right to rule Creation as God's representative, 1:26, 28-30, (4) morally responsible to obey God's commands, 2:16-17, and (5) given a nature which requires intimate, lifelong relationships with others as well as with God. Thus persons have infinite worth and value.

Flesh. The Heb. term, *basar*, has a wide variety of meanings, ranging from the physical body, to the self, to all living creatures, to family relationships. Yet when used of human nature, "flesh" draws attention to our mortal life; the life we presently live in the material universe. Thus 2:24's affirmation that a married couple become "one flesh" implies more than sexual union. It indicates that God intends a husband and wife to share the joys and sorrows that life in this world holds. To be "one flesh" is to be bonded together in a loving, supportive union that not only lasts but becomes deeper and more significant as the years pass. See also »pp. 458, 743.

Marriage. The phrase "suitable helper" has often been misunderstood, and used to support a distorted view of marriage. Helper here is *'ezer*, and means "a support," "a helper," or "an assistant." It does not imply subordination, for the same word is used to describe God as man's helper. The concept strongly supports equality of women. Only one who is "bone of my bones and flesh of my flesh," and thus fully shares the human identity, could possibly meet anyone's deeper needs. In its original conception, then, marriage was the union of equals, each respecting as well as caring for the other, and each committed to be the other's helper.

Adam's rib. A lovely Jewish tradition notes that God did not take Eve from Adam's foot, lest he try to dominate her, or from his head, lest she see herself as above him. Instead God took Eve from Adam's rib, that the two might go through life side by side.

Chapter summary. The innocence and harmony of original Creation are shattered when Adam and Eve choose to disobey God, with consequences that affect the entire human race. The story of the Fall is Scripture's explanation for the sin and evils that mar society, corrupt personal and international relationships, and doom us to biological and spiritual death. The chapter explores temptation (3:1-6), the impact of sin on relationship with God (vv. 7-12) and with other persons (vv. 12-13). It records God's devastating judgment on man and woman, and the impact of human sin on nature itself (vv. 14-20). Adam and Eve are exiled from Eden (vv. 21-24). But first God Himself provides them with coverings of skin: Scripture's first word of a forgiveness won through the shedding of blood (v. 21).

Outline
Place
Finder

CREATION
CHOICE
COVENANT

Key verse. 3:10: Sin alienates us from God and His love.

Personal application. Sin does have consequences. Only by fleeing to God rather than from Him can we find help.

Key concepts. Curse »p. 138. Death »p. 741. Sacrifice »pp. 78, 862. Satan »pp. 501, 655. Temptation »pp. 655, 871.

INSIGHT

Temptation. Satan's devious enticement of Eve reminds us that we cannot be forced to sin. But we are vulnerable to temptation. Satan first misrepresented God's word (3:1; cf. 2:16-17), then directly denied it (3:4), and finally questioned God's motives (v. 5). Her confidence in God thus undermined, Eve relied on what seemed pleasurable to her physical senses, and what seemed desirable to her human understanding (v. 6)—and sinned. To overcome temptation we need to know God's Word accurately, trust His judgment completely, and obey in the full assurance that what God chooses for us is both right and best.

Know. The fruit forbidden Adam and Eve is on the "tree of the knowledge of good and evil" (v. 17). The Heb. word here, *yada'*, suggests a wide range of ideas. But basic to them is both the capacity to make distinctions and to experience. As long as Adam and Eve "knew" only good, they remained innocent, choosing and experiencing only what was right in God's sight. They did not even see opportunities to do wrong! The Fall introduced the capacity to see evil choices as well as good ones, and with it the desire to try both! How urgently you and I today need to know good. But not to know evil.

"I was afraid" (3:10). How stunning this reaction of Adam's is. He has walked and talked with God. He has known God's love in a deeply personal way. Yet now, aware of his guilt, Adam runs from God and tries to hide. Adam's reaction helps us understand our own

sense of alienation from God when we sin. But God's search for Adam and Eve reminds us that, even when we sin, God does not abandon us. He continues to care. We need to remember this, and when we fall, we need to hurry to Him rather than run away.

"She gave me" (3:12). It's so hard to take responsibility for our own acts. Adam tries to blame God, who put the woman there, and Eve, who gave him the fruit. And Eve tries to blame the serpent (v. 13). Sin not only alienated Adam from God: it introduced hostility into his relationship with Eve as well! The only way we can keep our relationship with God and others pure is to accept responsibility for our sins and failures, and rely on forgiving love to heal the damage done.

"Pains in childbearing" (3:16). Some take this to refer to the introduction of a monthly, rather than a more widely spaced, menstrual cycle.

"He will rule" (3:16). Male dominance in the family is a consequence of sin. Why perpetuate it in the Christian home? » p. 801.

Expelled from Eden (3:21-24). Banishment from Eden was not punishment. It was for Adam's and Eve's benefit. How terrible if they had been forced to live forever (v. 22), and see the anguish and suffering their sin brought on their descendants! Biological death is in fact a gift of grace. In the resurrection we will shed the stain of sin that keeps us company here, and know the full extent of the redeeming love of God.

Outline
Place
Finder

CREATION
CHOICE
COVENANT

Chapter summary. The consequences of the Fall now work themselves out in the descendants of Adam and Eve. Cain murders his brother, Abel (4:1-18). Lamech breaks the pattern of monogamous marriage by taking two wives (vv. 19-22), and justifies his murder of a young man "for injuring me" (vv. 23-24), making the bent of sinful human society all too clear. But another son is born to Adam and Eve, Seth, and at least some in his line "call on the name of the Lord" (vv. 25-26). Centuries pass. God keeps track of the godly line (5:1-31), which culminates in a man named Noah (v. 32).

Key verse. 5:3: Adam's children bear his likeness.

Personal application. How will your children be like you?

Key concepts. Anger »pp. 72, 196, 359. Genealogy »p. 264. Marriage »pp. 26, 801. Polygamy »p. 41. Murder »pp. 114, 607.

INSIGHT

Significance. God had warned Adam that the very day he ate the forbidden fruit he would "surely die" (2:17). The act of sin brought immediate spiritual death. Genesis 4 demonstrates the reality of the spiritual death that grips our race. In the murder committed by Cain, and the arrogant selfishness of Lamech, we see the first hint of the crime and the injustice that corrupt human society.

Cain's offering. Why was Cain's offering unacceptable? Cain brought vegetables that he had grown. Genesis 4:7 indicates that Cain knew it was "right" to sacrifice an animal as an offering to God (cf. 3:21). Cain may have brought his best. But we are sinners, whose access to God calls for blood sacrifice.

"Cain was very angry" (4:5). Cain's anger shows how intent he was on having his own way rather than submitting to God. Anger is a destructive emotion. We can never excuse attacks on others by saying, "I have a bad temper." We need to acknowledge anger as a sin, and consciously submit to God's will.

Why did God protect Cain? Cain feared he would be killed for murdering his brother. God marked Cain instead. Why? Perhaps to demonstrate that no one who lives away "from the Lord's presence" can be the source of a just society.

Cainite civilization. Gen. 4:20-22 pictures a developed culture, with leisure time for music, and a technology capable of smelting metal ores. But no matter how great human achievements in the material realm, humanity is spiritually crippled. Lamech's poetic defense of his murderous revenge reminds us that sinful man is still incapable of shaping a world of love, harmony, and peace.

"The likeness of God" (5:1-2). "Image" and "likeness" (*selem, demut*) are found together in passages where the essential nature of man is taught (cf. 1:26). Together these make a theological statement: to understand human nature we must see man as originally created, gifted with the "image-likeness" of God. We must not compare our nature with that of any animal, but only with God. What is this image-likeness? What sets us apart is that we share with God attributes of personhood. Like Him, we have a capacity to think, to feel, to choose. This image-likeness makes each human being of worth and value in God's eyes. We are like Him, and God cares for each one of us. Verses 1-3 remind us, however, that the image which reflected God so well in Adam was warped and twisted in the Fall. Adam passed to us, not the unflawed image-likeness of God, but his own imperfection. Today we are still like God in many respects. But we are also like Adam, in desperate need of Christ and His transforming touch.

Long lives? (Gen. 5) Many cultures have stories of long lives for ancestors who lived prior to a great flood. Some have suggested that heavy cloud cover then (cf. 2:5-6) may have cut off the radiation we know today is associated with aging.

Painful toil (5:29). The curse on nature (3:17-19) helps shape the O. T.'s view of work. Some passages suggest work can be productive and satisfying. But many reflect the fact that work can be drudgery: unending, unpleasant toil that brings neither fulfillment nor profit. At its best, work reflects the joy God found in creating. At its worst, it reminds us of the burden of Adam's Fall.

Chapter summary. The corruption of human civilization became so great that God resolved on cataclysmic judgment. The Flood, which wiped out all human life except for righteous Noah and his family, serves as a powerful biblical statement of God's commitment to judge sin at history's end. The preservation of Noah and his family is an equally powerful statement of God's commitment to save those who respond to Him in obedient faith. These chapters explain God's determination to act (6:1-8), relate Noah's 120-year stuggle to build a great ship (vv. 9-22), and describe Flood results (7:1-24).

Outline
Place
Finder

CREATION
CHOICE
COVENANT

Key verse. 7:4: God will surely judge man's wickedness.

Personal application. Obedience is costly. But disobedience costs far more!

Key concepts. Clean animals »p. 82. Evil »pp. 72, 662. Holy Spirit »p. 73. Demons »p. 659, 895.

INSIGHT

"Sons of God." This obscure passage (6:1-4) has been taken as intermarriage between the "godly line of Seth" and the line of Cain. But Jewish commentators saw it as forbidden intercourse between fallen angels and human women, which produced a race of Nephilim (giants). »p. 331.

Wickedness and violence. These two words are used to characterize the sins that brought on the Genesis Flood. Wickedness is *rasah'*, criminal acts committed against others that violate their rights and profit from others' pain. Violence is *hamas*, willfully destructive acts intended to damage others. When any society is marked by continual expressions of wickedness and violence, that society is in peril of divine judgment.

Noah. Noah is to be honored for his persistent faithfulness. He labored 120 years constructing a great ship on a waterless plain (cf. 6:3). He must have suffered merciless ridicule from his neighbors, none of whom responded to his warnings of judgment to come. Yet his trust in God did not waver, nor did his obedience. It's when our faith is tested, often by years of working and waiting, that the quality of that faith is displayed.

The ark. The ark was half again as long as a football field, with proportions that match modern cargo vessels. It was large enough for its cargo and the food they required. First Peter 3 views it as a symbol of salvation: God's agency to carry the believer safely through judgment to a new world.

"Kind." The ark did not contain every breed of animal, but prototype "kinds." A single pair of cattle carried the genes that provide for the wide variation within this animal class that we see in the Brahma, the Longhorn, and other cattle. The biblical account of Creation confronts the notion that all animal life evolved from single-celled ancestors, but has no quarrel with evolutionists' account of variation within species.

The Flood. Christians who hold a high view of Scripture debate whether the Genesis Flood was a universal flood, that covered the entire surface of the globe, or a limited flood affecting only areas of human population. Verses that state "all the high mountains under the entire heavens" were covered (7:19-20) and that "every living [breathing] thing" on earth perished (vv. 21-23) support a worldwide cataclysm. But what about the fact that there is not enough water on our planet and in the atmosphere to cover such mountains as Everest? Those who hold the universal view believe that the Flood changed the face of the earth, causing the sea beds to indent, and thrusting mountains up higher than before. Whatever our view, it is clear that the account of the Flood makes a powerful theological statement. It affirms that God is the moral Ruler of this universe, who has and who will exercise His obligation to judge sin. Second Peter 3 reminds those who scoff at the idea of final judgment that God acted in the time of Noah to judge wicked and violent human beings. The God whose hatred of sin is revealed in the Flood will not let our sins go unpunished.

Outline
Place
Finder

CREATION
CHOICE
COVENANT

Chapter summary. Gradually the waters of the great Flood subside. Noah and his family begin life in a fresh new world with sacrifice and worship (8:1-22). God introduces human government by making human beings responsible to resist evil in society (9:1-7), and commits Himself to never again destroy all life by floodwaters (vv. 8-17). The earth was cleansed. But the little family carried the fallen human nature and the sin which almost immediately expressed itself in the drunkenness of Noah and the immorality of his son, Ham (vv. 18-29).

Key verse. 9:6: God institutes human government when He makes man responsible to punish evildoers.

Personal application. What contribution can I make to creating a more just, righteous society?

Key concepts. Image and likeness »p. 28. Murder »p. 114. Human government »p. 750. Covenant »p. 35. Sacrifice »pp. 78, 862. Curse »pp. 138–139. Bless »p. 49. Accountability »p. 503.

INSIGHT

How long was the Flood? Gen. 7–8 give specifics. The animals entered May 10 (7:8-9). The rain began May 17 (v. 11) and the water rose till June 26 (v. 12). The ark did not touch land until Oct. 13 (8:4). Mountaintops were seen on Jan. 1 (v. 4), ark doors finally opened on April 1 (v. 13). The land was dry enough for Noah's family to exit May 27 (v. 14) one year and 10 days after the Flood began.

"A pleasing aroma" (8:21). The phrase means that Noah's offering was accepted by God. All too often the sacrifices of God's O.T. people were not acceptable, because of their sin. »p. 555.

"Food for you" (9:1-4). In the original Creation man and animals were given green plants for food (cf. 1:29-30). Only now, after the Flood, are living creatures given for food, with the single condition that the blood not be eaten with the flesh. This is consistent with the small number of animals taken into the ark. Before this all animals lived on vegetation rather than meat!

Capital punishment. The text quotes God as commanding capital punishment for murder. The reason given is that God made man in His own image. It is important to understand that the death sentence is neither retribution, nor simply preventative. Because we bear God's image, each human being is irreplaceable. Every human life is so significant that no penalty less than death provides an adequate measure of its value. Only by decreeing capital punishment as a penalty for murder can society affirm the ultimate worth and value of each individual citizen. See »p. 114. Most scholars

see the responsibility to impose the death penalty for murder as the institution of human government, for it implies that society is obligated to restrain individuals from sin.

Rainbow. The rainbow is described as a "sign" of God's covenant with Noah. In the O.T. a covenant is a promise stated in a legally binding form: a binding promise made openly before witnesses. Today the rainbow makes us witnesses with all the rest of mankind to God's firm commitment never again to destroy all life on earth by a flood. Let the next rainbow you see remind you that God has kept His promise for millenniums. He will keep every promise He makes to you and me.

Ham's sin (9:18-23). The sin is much debated, as the phrase "uncover the nakedness of" is used of illicit sexual relationships (cf. Lev. 18, KJV). Here the text suggests that Ham's sin was one of ridiculing the father he should have honored (cf. Ex. 20:12). The flaws in Noah and Ham remind us that however perfect the environment, the root of sin is planted deeply within the human personality. The cause of our failures lies within us.

The curse on Canaan (9:25). The curse here is a prediction, not a malicious wish. Once this passage was used to support slavery in the United States. The argument is doubly flawed: the curse is pronounced against Canaan, just one of Ham's sons. Canaan's descendants are described in Gen. 10 as the peoples who lived in that land in the days of Abram and later when Joshua invaded that land. The ancestors of Africa's black races are represented by Cush (Ethiopia) and Mizraim (Egypt).

Outline
Place
Finder

CREATION
CHOICE
COVENANT

Chapter summary. The "table of nations" (Gen. 10) traces the relationships between the peoples known to ancient Israel, and explains their link to the sons of Noah (see map). The peoples are classified by language, land, and treaty links as well as ethnically.

But how did the race of man, springing afresh from a single family, become so divided? The story of the Tower of Babel explains (11:1-9). God introduced the languages that divide our race as an act of judgment when the early descendants of Noah arrogantly attempted to "reach the heavens."

With this explanation offered, the chapter gives an account of the descendants of Shem, the line from which Abram, and ultimately Christ, sprang (vv. 10-32). With the end of this chapter we reach one of Scripture's great turning points. God is about to choose a single family, through whom the fallen race of man will ultimately be redeemed.

Key verse. 11:7: Judgment may take many different forms.

Personal application. International and interpersonal divisions too are a consequence of sin.

INSIGHT

Table of nations. Careful study has identified many of the peoples listed in Gen. 10. The modern name of selected peoples is identified below.

Tower of Babel. Steplike tower mounds, called ziggurats, are associated with worship in South America as well as in the ancient Middle East. The phrase "with a tower that reaches to the heavens" (11:4) may refer to the shrine usually placed atop ziggurats.

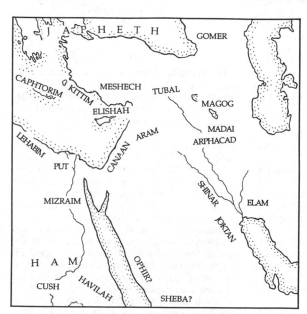

Identity of peoples
OF JAPHETH
Gomer = Cimmerians
Madai = Medes
Javan = Greeks
Ashkenaz = Scythians
Elishah = Crete
Tarshish = W. Spain
Kittim = Cyprus

OF HAM
Cush = Ethiopia
Mizraim = Egypt
Lehabites = Lybians
Caphtorim = Cretans
Hittites, etc. = Pre-Israelite
inhabitants of Canaan

OF SHEM (SEMITES)
Eber = Hebrews
Aram = Syrians
(in third millennium, north:
in second, next to Canaan)
Arphaxad = N. Iraq?

Map showing general location of ancient peoples named in Genesis 11.

Outline
Place
Finder

CREATION
CHOICE
COVENANT

Chapter summary. God makes Abram unconditional promises telling him what "I will" do (12:1-3). These promises, soon confirmed by a legal covenant (see Gen. 15), define the unique relationship with God to be enjoyed by Abram and his offspring. In a first great act of faith, Abram leaves his homeland to travel to an unknown land (12:4-9). Though a man of faith, Abram is far from perfect. He moves to Egypt without divine direction, and there fear leads him to lie about his relationship with his half sister/wife Sarai (vv. 10-16). Yet God protects Abram, and he and his own are sent from Egypt back to Canaan (12:17-20).

Key verses. 12:2-3: God's "I will" commitment to Abram.

Personal application. Consider how to imitate Abram's faith in God, and avoid his lapses.

INSIGHT

Tracing the promises. Each of the "I will" promises of God has been or is being fulfilled.

"*I will make you into a great nation.*" Jewish and Arab peoples are descended from Abraham. See Gen. 21:18; 25:13-18. Despite the later Babylonian Captivity, recent studies estimate as many as 1 in 10 persons in the first-century Roman Empire were Jews!

"*I will bless you.*" Abraham lived a long life (25:7), and was blessed with great wealth (13:2). Best of all, God forgave and protected him (12:17; 20), and Abraham was granted an intimate personal relationship with the Lord (15:6; 18:17-19).

"*I will make your name great.*" Adherents of three world religions honor Abraham (see next page).

"*And you will be a blessing.*" God's revelation to man came through Abraham's descendants.

"*I will bless those who bless you, and whoever curses you I will curse.*" God has judged nations hostile to the Jewish people. See Isa. 10:9-19; Jer. 50; Obad.; Nahum.

"*All peoples on earth will be blessed through you.*" Jesus, God's Son, who offers salvation to all who believe, was Abraham's Descendant. His work of redemption is the blessing God showers on all peoples everywhere. See Matt. 1; Gal. 3:15-18.

"*To your offspring I will give this land*" (12:7). Despite centuries of exile, prophets predict the

Illustration: *Abram's travels. It was 500 miles on foot from Ur to Canaan. We know the road; rainfall patterns of the era show only one route could have been followed. In Canaan Abram still lived as a nomad, in tents.*

ultimate possession of Palestine by the Jewish people. See Deut. 30:1-5; Jer. 31:23-28; Zech. 8:7-8; 10:6-10. Many see the young Jewish state of Israel (founded 1948) as preparation for fulfillment of the ancient promises.

Canaan. Ancient name of Palestine, meaning *land of purple*. See Joshua Intro.

Canaanites. A variety of ethnic groups that established small city-states in Canaan at the end of the third millennium B.C. See Gen. 15.

Did Pharaoh have sex with Sarai? No. A period of purification that might last for months was typical when a bride entered a ruler's harem (see Es. 2:12 for the practice in the later Persian era). God protected Sarai from Abram's lack of faith.

Abraham

Abram, whose name God later changed to Abraham, was born in one of the fabled cities of the ancient world, Ur. In Abram's day, 4,100 years ago, Ur was center of a rich Sumerian culture; a city lying along the Euphrates that boasted monumental architecture, vast wealth, comfortable homes, music, and art. There Abram "worshiped other gods" (Josh. 24:2). But when God spoke to him, Abram left his civilization, traveled to Canaan, and there lived a nomadic life in tents for nearly a hundred years!

Abram exchanged the fading glory of this world for a personal relationship with God—and won undying fame. Today Abram is revered by adherents of three great world religions: Judaism, Islam, and Christianity. The Old Testament recognizes him as father of God's chosen people, the Jews. And the New Testament honors him as the spiritual ancester of all "who . . . walk in the footsteps of the faith that our father Abraham had" (Rom. 4:12).

What is the importance of Abraham to us today? First, we cannot begin to understand the Old Testament until we see it as the outworking in history of the promises that God gave this towering figure. Second, as we meditate on stories of Abraham's life, we find many principles we can apply today to enrich our personal relationship with the Lord.

Abraham's clothing reflects the patterns and style of garments worn in Ur in the third millennium B.C.

Outline
Place
Finder

CREATION
CHOICE
COVENANT

Chapter summary. God told Abram to leave his family and go to Canaan (12:1), but Abram brought his nephew Lot. Yet separation from Lot was necessary to ensure Abram's son alone would inherit his material and spiritual blessings. Soon herds grown too great to share grass and water cause family conflict, and force the necessary separation (13:1-13). God invites Abram to travel through the whole land, saying "I will give [it] to you and your offspring forever" (vv. 14-18). When Lot is taken by raiding armies from the north, Abram routs the superior force in a night attack (14:1-16). Abram accepts the blessing of Melchizedek, a type of Christ (vv. 17-20), but rejects the king of Sodom's offer of wealth, lest Sodom rather than God be credited with enriching him (vv. 21-24).

Key verses. 13:15; 14:22-23: God's commitment, and Abram's response.

Personal application. Abram's surrender of his right as eldest to first choice diffused family conflict. Despite Lot's bad choice and its consequence, Abram remained loyal and rescued him. What attitudes of Abram can we apply in our own family life?

INSIGHT

Negev. The word means "south," and identifies the dry plains area between Egypt and Palestine.

Bethel. A highland city north of Jerusalem, associated with worship from the time of Abraham. After the death of Solomon, a worship center was set up there by an apostate king to rival the established worship center at Jerusalem. »p. 230.

Plain of the Jordan. The rich flat plain at the southern end of the Jordan Valley. Apparently in ancient times it was irrigated, as was the Nile Valley. Lot was dazzled by the land's fertility but did not consider the character of the evil men of Sodom (see Gen. 19). Who we choose as neighbors is more important than the looks of the neighborhood!

Kedorlaomer (Kedor-LAY-oh-mr). The peoples named in Gen. 14:1-7 lived north of Palestine. Though there is no secular mention of the persons, the name contains authentic Elamite name elements. In this early period warring kings tended to raid for booty and prisoners rather than to occupy land.

Melchizedek (mel-KIZ-a-deck). This king of Salem (later renamed Jerusalem) serves as a type of Christ. His name means "king of peace" and he was also a priest. Abraham recognized his priestly authority in accepting a blessing from him (14:19) and in giving him a tithe of everything (v. 20). Psalm 110:4 identifies the Messiah (God's promised Saviour) as a "priest forever, in the order of Melchizedek." The writer of Hebrews uses this verse to dem-

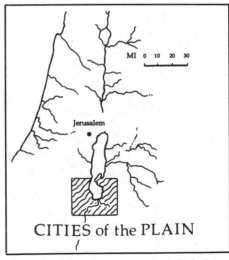

CITIES of the PLAIN

onstrate Jesus' superiority as our High Priest to the high priests of the O.T. system (Heb. 4:14–5:10).

A tenth (tithe). The percent of one's yearly income the O.T. sets aside for God. »p. 103. While no N.T. passage teaches tithing, the practice antedates the Mosaic Law, and may serve as a good rule of thumb for believers today. For N.T. giving, see 2 Cor. 8–9.

"Blessed be." A formula used under inspiration to confer prophetic blessing on others. The act of blessing usually implies spiritual superiority. »p. 49.

Chapter summary. This is a key chapter in the history of salvation. A childless, aged Abram believes God's promise that a son of his own will be his heir. God credits Abram's faith as the righteousness no human being has (15:1-6). So a trusting Abram will know his descendants will one day own all of Canaan (vv. 7-8), God enters into the most binding of ancient legal contracts, a "covenant of blood" (vv. 9-21).

Key verse. 15:6: God imputes righteousness to the believer.

Personal application. Trust all God's promises completely.

Key concepts. Abrahamic Covenant »p. 32. Righteousness »p. 734. Belief, faith »pp. 458, 740.

INSIGHT

Abram's heir. Documents found by archeologists reveal that in Abram's day a childless couple might adopt a servant, who would care for them in their old age, and inherit their estate. But if a son was born to the family, this right of the adopted servant was set aside (15:1-3).

Abram believed God (15:4-6). The Heb. word here is 'aman, in verb form means "to be certain." It focuses our attention on the absolute trustworthiness of the object of Abram's faith, and expresses Abram's own firm conviction that God's promise to him was reliable. Abram's belief in God is held up in Scripture as an example of saving faith. Abram examined the circumstances, recognized the human impossibility of fathering a child with Sarai, and yet remained convinced that God could and would do what He promised. Romans 4:18-21 reminds us that a similar faith-won righteousness is credited to us when we too are "fully persuaded that God [has] power to do what He [has] promised" us in Christ.

"How can I know?" (15:7-8) Abram believed God for the impossible, that he would have a son. He wavered when God added that He would give Canaan to Abram's offspring! We too may exercise a faith that brings us into personal relationship with God — yet fail to keep on trusting Him after! Let's trust God with our salvation, and everything else!

Imputation. This theological term is rooted in the N.T. parallel of the phrase "credited to him for righteousness." The Gk. word used to describe what happened here is logizomai, "to reckon." In ordinary speech it was an accounting term that meant "to make an entry in the account book." O.T. and N.T. teach the doctrine of imputation that God looked in our account book, saw we were not righteous, but in grace chose to accept faith in Him in place of righteousness. And so for those who have a faith like Abram's God writes "righteous" over our accounts, and cancels the record of all our sins.

Covenant. The Heb. word, brit, has a wide variety of applications. Between two businessmen a "covenant" is a contract. In a country it is a "constitution." Between two nations it's a treaty. The best single definition is, a covenant is "a legally binding, formal expression of intent." In Abram's time there were several types of covenants, including a covenant formalized by eating together (covenants of "bread" or "salt"). But the most binding of all covenants was the "covenant of blood," formalized by passing through the divided halves of sacrificial animals. It was this covenant God made with Abram. Heb. 6:13-20 explains. God wanted Abram, and us, to know that when God makes a promise, we "may be greatly encouraged." God will never break His promises. He will never go back on His word. Several critical covenants are identified in Scripture: notably the Abrahamic »p. 32, the Mosaic »p. 62, the Davidic »p. 370, and the New »p. 466. Each states God's intentions clearly. Each makes clear what God most certainly will do.

Abram's deep sleep (15:12). Usually covenants were confirmed by both parties. This implied that each accepted obligations related to carrying out the intentions the covenant expressed. How significant Abram's deep sleep becomes. God alone passed between the parts of the sacrificed beasts. Abram has no part in making the covenant, so nothing Abram does can cause it to be canceled. You and I contributed nothing to our salvation: Jesus did it all. All we must do, all we can do, is put our trust in God. He will keep His covenant promise to save us for Jesus' sake.

Outline
Place
Finder

CREATION
CHOICE
COVENANT

Chapter summary. Sarai urges Abram to follow an accepted custom and father a child with her maidservant, Hagar (16:1-4). But Hagar's pregnancy creates intense jealousy. Only God's intervention prevents Hagar from running away (vv. 7-16). Years later, when Abram is 99, God introduces circumcision as a sign of covenant relationship (17:1-14). God also announces that His promise of countless descendants will not be fulfilled through Hagar's son Ishmael, but through a child to be borne by Sarah, who is now 90 (vv. 15-27). Today, some 4,000 years later, the rite of circumcision is still practiced by the descendants of Abraham!

Key verse. 17:19: God is a God of the impossible.

Personal application. It's a mistake to limit God.

Key concepts. Angel of the Lord »p. 358. Almighty »p. 208. Blessing »pp. 49, 358. Appearance of God to man »pp. 56, 814.

INSIGHT

Hagar. The relationship of Sarai, Hagar, and Abram seems strange to us. But by ancient custom it was lawful for a barren wife to give a slave to her husband. Any children born were considered the wife's rather than the servant's (cf. 16:2). Documents of the era also show that Abram quoted a point of law in verse 6: the wife did have a legal right in that era to mistreat her slave, though there were limits to what she could do. The story illustrates the wisdom of God's marital ideal. Even when it was "legal" to have a woman other than one's wife, the practice created strife.

Ishmael. God promised to multiply this son's descendants too. God did, for Ishmael is the father of the Arab peoples. The modern strife between Israel and the Palestinians is one consequence of Abram's and Sarai's decision not to wait for God to act. There is a fine line between acting in faith, and self-effort.

"The God who sees me" (16:6-16). What a message for you and me in this passage. When life becomes too painful to bear, we can find strength in remembering what Hagar discovered. The Lord is "the God who sees me." When we sense this, when we know the Lord is aware of our pain and need, our strength will

be renewed. For God not only sees us, He sees the future. He promised Hagar that a bright future for her unborn son lay ahead. We too have hope for tomorrow, whatever our pain today.

Abram to Abraham (17:1-5). Abram means "father," while Abraham means "father of a multitude." What faith it must have taken for the aged Abram, parent of a single child, to announce that change of name! Faith is like this. It enables us to act as if the "not yet" were "now," in full assurance that it soon will be!

Circumcision. The rite involves removing the flap of skin that covers the tip of the male's penis. This is done the eighth day of a Jewish boy's life. Circumcision was the physical mark of participation in the covenant which God made with Abraham and his descendants. One who did not consider covenant relationship with God important enough to identify himself or his children with the covenant people, and thus did not practice circumcision, "will be cut off from his people; he has broken My covenant" (v. 14). Both testaments, however, testify that the physical sign is no more than a formality. It symbolizes a readiness to respond to God that is spoken of as "circumcision of the heart" (Deut. 10:16; Phil. 3:3). »p. 126.

Abraham's visitors were welcomed with food, probably spread on a tanned hide "table." Hospitality had high priority through O.T. times.

Chapter summary. Three angels are shown hospitality by Abraham (18:1-8). They confirm God's promise that Sarah will have a son, though Sarah scoffs (vv. 9-15). Leaving, one angel tells Abraham the Lord is about to destroy wicked Sodom and Gomorrah (vv. 16-21). In one of the Old Testament's great intercessory prayers, Abraham begs God to spare any righteous in these cities (vv. 22-33). The scene shifts to Sodom. There two angels are welcomed by Lot, whose house is soon surrounded by a mob intent on homosexual rape (19:1-5). Nothing Lot says dissuades them, and Lot himself is saved only by divine intervention (vv. 6-11). Lot flees the city (vv. 12-22), which is destroyed as soon as he is safe (vv. 23-29). Lot and two daughters survive, but are reduced to living in a cave. There the girls make Lot drunk to become pregnant by their father (vv. 30-38).

Outline
Place
Finder

CREATION
CHOICE
COVENANT

Key verse. 18:23: Prayer is an appeal to God's character.

Personal application. Always expect God to do the good and right thing, even when judgment is most severe.

Key concepts. Prayer »p. 181. Choice of individuals »p. 797.

INSIGHT

Hospitality. In lands without motels or hotels travelers were dependent on hospitality. It was considered a good deed in biblical times to feed and house strangers. The lengths to which a host would go to serve and protect such guests is shown in Gen. 24:15-31 and 19:1-8. Rom. 12:13 says, "Share with God's people who are in need. Practice hospitality."

Angel of the Lord. This phrase is thought by many to indicate an appearance of God Himself in human form. Note that the text indicates that when this angel spoke, "the Lord said" (Gen. 18:17, 20), and that Abraham is speaking to God as he begs for the lives of any innocent in Sodom (v. 27). Cf. 22:11-12.

"I have chosen him" (18:19). Here is a verse worth memorizing. We have been chosen to direct our children into God's ways!

Abraham's prayer (18:20-33). Abraham shows a sensitive concern for the innocent. He begs God to spare the wicked cities of the plain for 50, then 45, and finally even 10 righteous. God was even more sensitive than Abraham. Only one righteous person lived in Sodom—Lot—and God withheld the fires of judgment until that one was safe! What confidence this gives us as we pray for others. God cares for them even more than we do, and will do even more for them than we ask.

Sodom and Gomorrah. Many believe that these "cities of the plain" lie beneath the southern end of the Dead Sea. The area had great deposits of highly flammable bitumen. This and a geologically unstable land mass

were doubtless agencies God used to cause the fiery holocaust of Gen. 19.

Homosexuality. Every biblical reference to homosexuality indicates it is not an "alternate lifestyle," but gross sin. Lev. 18:22-23 forbids homosexual acts and calls them "detestable." Rom. 1:24-27 speaks of homosexual desire as "shameful lusts" and calls homosexual acts "indecent," a "perversion," and "the degrading of their bodies." The Christian must take a stand with God's Word, to reject homosexuality as a personal option and boldly identify it as wickedness and sin.

Lot. Lot's experience stands as a warning to all. He chose to live in the valley because of the material advantages it provided (Gen. 13:10-11). At first he pitched a tent outside the city (v. 12). This chapter tells us he had moved into the city (19:3). Second Peter 2:7-8 tells us Lot was a "righteous man," who was "distressed by the filthy lives" of Sodom's citizens. But even so Lot preferred to stay there and make a profit than to leave, and thus take a stand against evil. Lot's willingness to compromise his convictions robbed him of influence with the men of Sodom (Gen. 19:6-9). His lack of integrity is also revealed in his daughters' incestuous plan following the destruction of the city. And what did Lot gain by compromising his convictions? The wealth and ease for which he sold them out? Not at all. Our last glimpse of Lot shows him destitute and drunk, lying senseless in a mountain cave.

Outline
Place
Finder

CREATION
CHOICE
COVENANT

Chapter summary. Abraham's faith wanes and he again lies about his relationship with Sarah, and again is protected by God (20:1-18). As promised, Sarah gives joyful birth to a son, Isaac (21:1-7). Strife again erupts in the family, and Sarah insists Abraham send Ishmael and Hagar away (vv. 8-13). Hagar and the teenage Ishmael set out alone into the desert, where God intervenes to provide water (vv. 14-21). After Abraham peacefully resolves a dispute with a Philistine city (vv. 22-34), he experiences the ultimate test of his faith. God tells Abraham to offer his son Isaac as a sacrifice (Gen. 22).

Key verse. 22:5: Abraham did not know how, but he was sure that God would preserve Isaac's life!

Personal application. Even giants of faith like Abraham stumbled at times. Don't be too hard on yourself.

Key concepts. Dreams »p. 99. Fear of God »p. 387. Tests »p. 748.

INSIGHT

Abimelech. The name means "My father [is] king" and was apparently a hereditary title rather than a personal name (cf. Gen. 26). This is the earliest mention of "Philistines" in Canaan's coastal area (21:32; 26:1). These "sea peoples" from Crete were probably few in number, as archeologists have traced a great influx some 800 years later. »p. 169. Some claim the Bible is wrong to place Philistines in Canaan at this time. But pioneers from many ancient lands established early settlements there.

Fear. Abraham explains his lie about his relationship with Sarah (cf. 12:10-13). He thought the people of Gerar didn't fear God, and thus could not be trusted! Whether the people feared God or not, God was there! Abraham could have trusted the Lord, even if he didn't trust Philistines. Fear of others still makes fools of God's people.

Ishmael sent away. Well-established custom in the Patriarchal Age protected the rights of any child born to a man by a slave woman. Though the son of the wife was a man's legal heir, his child by a concubine was guaranteed an inheritance. Sarah's demand that Abraham send Ishmael away was doubly distressing. Abraham loved Ishmael. And he believed that sending Ishmael away was morally wrong. Only God's direct intervention, and God's promise to guarantee Ishmael's future, finally moved Abraham to banish Hagar and his son. Abraham would surely understand the pain of those who lose their children through divorce. How desperately we need to remember that God cares for our loved ones, even when we cannot.

"God opened her eyes" (21:19). God did not create a spring when Hagar and Ishmael seemed about to die. He enabled her to see a well of water that was already there! In hard times you and I simply need to ask God to show us the solution He has already provided.

"Your only son" (22:1-2). God did not intend for Abraham to sacrifice Isaac. The command was a test: a test of how far Abraham would trust the Lord with his most precious possession. Yet the story is also prophetic. God, who was too kind to take Abraham's son, was willing to surrender His Son, His only Son, whom He loves, to win our salvation. In the test of Abraham we see foreshadowed the ultimate test of God's own love. And the proof that God's love for us is real.

"We will come back to you" (22:5). These words affirm Abraham's faith. God had said His promises to Abraham would be kept in Isaac's offspring. Heb. 11:19 says Abraham "reasoned that God could raise the dead" if need be to keep His word! Let's be like Abraham, sure that God will provide. Let's trust God completely, even rising early (Gen. 22:3) to keep the most difficult of His commands.

Lambs. Throughout the O.T. the lamb is the preferred sacrificial animal. It is the animal most frequently specified in the levitical law of sacrifice. »pp. 82–83. So it's fitting that the innocent, harmless lamb is the O.T.'s prime sacrificial symbol. Jesus, the innocent Lamb of God, offered Himself as a sacrifice for us. He took our place, as the ram of Gen. 22 took the place of Isaac. Through His suffering, the sinless Son of God purged our sins and made us clean (John 1:29, 36; 1 Peter 1:19).

Chapter summary. Sarah dies and is buried (Gen. 23). The story is immediately followed by the report of finding a bride for her son, Isaac (Gen. 24). Placed side by side, these stories remind us of the continuity of sacred history. One generation dies; another takes its place. Each generation has its role in carrying out God's grand plan of redemption.

Particularly notable in Genesis 24 is the quiet faith of the unnamed servant, and clear evidence that God actively arranges circumstances so that His purposes are fulfilled.

Key verse. 24:27: Be aware of the kindnesses of God in the circumstances of your own life.

Personal application. Prayer and providence operate in harmony. Ask God for guidance, and expect Him to supervise the circumstances of your life.

Key concepts. Prayer »pp. 181, 608, 609. Providence »p. 324.

Outline
Place
Finder

CREATION
CHOICE
COVENANT

INSIGHT

Hittites. The great Hittite Empire lay far to the north of Canaan. These ethnic Hittites were the descendants of pioneers from the north who had settled in Canaan long before, and had established small city-states.

"An alien and a stranger" (23:4). A resident alien (*ger*) had limited rights, but not the right to own land. This in part explains the exorbitant price (equivalent to perhaps $50,000!) charged Abraham for a burial plot.

"I give you the field" (23:11). The offer was not sincere, but part of a well-established negotiating ritual followed in the patriarchal era. The reference to "the trees within the borders of the field" adds another authentic touch. Hittite land contracts characteristically specify trees.

But Rabbi Mose Besden suggests the offer to give Abraham the land was an attempt to get him to identify with the people of the land, rather than maintain his identity as an alien and stranger. Abraham's purchase meant Sarah would be buried in Jewish soil, and thus identified forever with the promises God made to Abraham and his descendants.

A wife for Isaac (24:1-4). The O.T. consistently calls for God's people to marry within the family of faith (cf. Deut. 7:3-4; 1 Kings 11:4; Ezra 9). Paul emphasizes the same thought when he says a person one marries "must belong to the Lord" (1 Cor. 7:39). Both partners in marriage must be committed to the Lord if they are to experience the blessings God intends to bring through marriage—and if each is to be responsive to God's known will.

The servant. The servant of Gen. 24 has

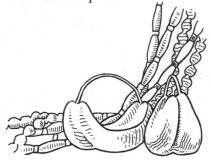

Illustration. *Gold jewelry from the third millennium* B.C. *indicates how the gifts given Rebekah may have looked.*

drawn much attention. Some, noting he is never named, consider him a type of the Holy Spirit. Others assume he is Eliezer, Abraham's chief steward. If so, he is one of Scripture's most admirable men. His own hope of inheriting Abraham's wealth was dashed by the birth of Isaac (15:2). Yet here he faithfully carries out a mission that calls for selfless service to the one who supplanted him! To set self aside to serve others is a singular spiritual achievement.

Answered prayer. Gen. 24 tells us the servant prayed three times: to request a sign (vv. 12-13), to praise God for leading (vv. 26-27), and to give thanks for the fulfillment of his mission (v. 52). Note the change of posture. He stands to make his request, bows his head at evidence of God's leading, but bows "down to the ground" when it is clear God enabled him to complete his assignment. Answers to prayer deepen our awe of God too. As we see God work in our lives, we are moved to praise and to worship.

Outline
Place
Finder

CREATION
CHOICE
COVENANT

Chapter summary. Abraham dies, and his two sons, Isaac and Ishmael, bury him (25:9). After taking brief note of Ishmael's line (vv. 12-18), the text focuses on Isaac and the twin sons born to him (vv. 19-34). Which son will carry the covenant promises of God into the future? The vigorous outdoorsman Esau? Or his quiet younger brother, Jacob? After reporting an incident which shows Isaac repeating his father's sins (26:1-35), Genesis tells of Jacob's deceitful theft of the parental blessing Isaac intended to go to Esau (27:1-40). This act makes Esau so furious he determines to murder Jacob when their father dies, so Jacob is forced to flee to the distant home of his uncle, Laban (vv. 41-46).

Key verse. 25:32: Those who cannot see beyond the moment forfeit their future.

Personal application. It's not necessary to lie or cheat to obtain the blessings God has promised to us. Only to wait.

Key concepts. Fear »p. 363. Guilt »pp. 79, 739. Blessing »p. 49. Firstborn »p. 134. God's choice of individuals »p. 797.

INSIGHT

"The Lord said" (25:23). Rom. 9 points out that before Jacob and Esau were born God chose Jacob to carry on the covenant line. The choice did not depend on the actions of either. Some argue this isn't fair. Yet neither deserved God's gift: both Esau and Jacob made bad choices! Be glad God isn't "fair" with us, but instead sovereignly showers us with His grace.

Selling birthrights. A custom that had the force of law in the biblical world decreed that a man's first son by a lawful wife inherited the major share of tangible and intangible property. This was his "birthright." Documents from the patriarchal era show that some actually did sell their birthrights, taking an immediate gain in place of the prospect of a future inheritance. So the account of Esau's sale of his birthright for a bowl of stew accurately mirrors patriarchal times.

In Esau's case, it does more. The intangible asset associated with his birthright was the covenant promise God made to Abraham and his offspring. These promises meant nothing to Esau, a man caught up completely in the affairs of this life. We may not admire the young Jacob. But we must give him credit for valuing spiritual things.

Guilt. A fearful Isaac tried to pass his wife off as his sister, as Abraham had done. Abimelech's horror when he realized Rebekah was married (26:10) reveals an important truth. God plants a moral sense, an awareness of right and wrong, in human nature itself. All

sin. Yet an inner witness to righteousness and guilt shine in every age. Conscience, »p. 738.

Favoritism. Gen. 27 contains an ugly but too typical portrait of parental favoritism. Isaac favored Esau; Rebekah, Jacob. Rebekah's scheming to advance Jacob was foolish as well as wrong. God had promised, "the older will serve the younger" (25:23). Rebekah had no need to lie and cheat to gain what she wanted. The story is rich in irony. In choosing deceit, Rebekah so provoked Esau's hostility that Jacob, her favorite, was forced to flee. All her conniving did was deprive her of her son for 20 years of her life! Ends never justify adopting sinful means.

Isaac's blessing. Documents from Nuzi in central Mesopotamia show that a father's oral blessing had the force of a will, and would stand up in court. Isaac's blessing was important!

The blessing Isaac pronounced incorporated elements of the original Abrahamic Covenant (cf. 27:29 with 12:3). It's clear that for Isaac, the most important thing he had to hand down to his son was his relationship with God.

"He will be blessed" (27:33). With Isaac's realization that he had been tricked came a flash of insight. He favored Esau, but God had chosen Jacob. And so at last Isaac submits to God's will, and confirms the blessing given Jacob. He does have a blessing for Esau (vv. 39-40): material prosperity. Esau was angry with his brother, but actually received everything he ever cared about!

Chapter summary. Isaac blesses Jacob and sends him to his mother's relatives to find a wife (28:1-9). God appears to Jacob at Bethel, to confirm transmission of His covenant with Abraham to Jacob (vv. 10-15). Awed, Jacob commits himself to the Lord (vv. 16-22). In Paddan Aram, Jacob finds his uncle Laban, and falls in love with his cousin Rachel (29:1-15). He works seven years as payment of the traditional bridal price, but Laban tricks Jacob into marrying his other daughter, Leah (vv. 16-25). Laban gives Jacob his beloved Rachel in return for seven more years of labor (vv. 26-30), and thus Jacob begins a tension-filled marriage to two wives (vv. 31-35).

Outline
Place
Finder

CREATION
CHOICE
COVENANT

Key verse. 28:15: We can claim this promise, as God's New Covenant people.

Personal application. Keep on trusting when life takes unexpected turns.

Key concepts. Anoint »p. 187. Anger »pp. 72, 196. Tithe »p. 103.

INSIGHT

"Esau then realized" (28:8). Was Esau insensitive, or were Isaac and Rebekah at fault? Most children do want to please their parents (cf. v. 9). Parents are responsible to counsel and to guide.

"I will give" (28:13-15). The promise made to Jacob takes the same form as those originally made to Abraham. God states, unconditionally, what He will do (cf. 12:1-3). This is the most awesome aspect of the scene, not the drawing back of the veil that separates the natural and supernatural realms. God makes "I will" promises to mere human beings. He chooses to be with us, to watch over us wherever we go, and never to leave us till He has accomplished all He has promised (28:15).

"If God" (28:20-22). How do we explain Jacob's apparently conditional commitment to God? The Ramban, a rabbi of old, suggested the Hebrew *im* means "when" here, as in 29:15 and Num. 36:4. "When" rather than "if" transforms Jacob's response from an expression of doubt to an affirmation of faith. But even if *im* here is "if," it need not express doubt. Instead it may express the excitement of a sudden realization that came to the empty-handed Jacob: "If God is with me, and brings me back to the homeland safely, then I'll be able to worship here again!"

You and I need just such a faith that accepts the promises of God, and because we realize that God is with us, see a bright new future ahead.

Rachel's price (29:18). It was customary in O.T. times for the groom to pay the father of his bride in money or cattle. This was not "buying and selling" women. The bride price acknowledged the fact that the father was losing a productive member of his family, and also showed that the husband placed a high value on his wife-to-be. Jacob had no wealth when he came to Laban. But his offer to work seven years for Rachel was high and reflected his deep love for her.

"Laban gave" (29:24). In biblical times the father of the bride gave her a dowry. Tablets found in excavations at Nuzi mention the gift of a maidservant to the bride by her father.

Laban's trick. Laban's substitution of Leah for Rachel reminds us of Jacob's own substitution for his brother Esau! At last Jacob must have grasped how it felt to be deceived and cheated.

At times God must teach us the hard way to be sensitive to others. This was not an easy lesson for Jacob to learn, but it was a vital one.

Polygamy. Monogamy is the biblical ideal for marriage. »pp. 26, 801. Yet the O.T. contains reports of multiple wives for the patriarchs, and later for Israel's and Judah's kings. Scripture also tells how David committed adultery, and how Judas betrayed Jesus. Such things are reports of what did happen, not examples of what should happen.

The story of Jacob's marriages reminds us of the wisdom of God's original design. How deeply it hurt Leah to be married to a man who did not love her. How tragic the pain felt by childless Rachel, and Leah's attempt to get back at her sister through her own ability to bear children. God's way really is always best.

Chapter summary. These chapters mark Jacob's decision to return to the land God promised to give to Abraham's, and now to his, descendants. Competition between Rachel and Leah for Jacob's love intensifies, as each gives Jacob her maid as a secondary wife (30:1-24). Jacob continues to supervise Laban's herds, but now for wages (vv. 25-36). When Jacob's personal herds increase Laban becomes hostile (30:37–31:2). Jacob consults with his wives, and they agree to return to Canaan (vv. 3-21). Jacob slips off with his family and flocks, but Laban pursues. God warns Laban in a dream not to harm Jacob, and after a painful confrontation, Jacob and his family continue on toward the Promised Land (vv. 22-55).

Key verse. 31:31: Being without God is being at risk!

Personal application. When others try to victimize us, we can trust God. But we may have to leave!

INSIGHT

Illustration. *The "household gods" (teraphim) mentioned in these chapters probably looked much like these figurines. Texts from Mesopotamia sites suggest Jacob was adopted when he married Laban's daughters. If sons were later born to Laban, each would have an equal share of Laban's estate. But one son would be given the household gods, which signified headship of the family. Rachel's theft may have been an assertion of her husband's (and later her son's?) headship of the entire family.*

Other contributions of archeology. Many details in these chapters are illustrated by texts found at Nuzi, Mari, Ugarit, and elsewhere. Records of lawsuits quote contracts much like the one Jacob had with Laban, including payment for loss caused by wild animals. It's interesting that spring shearing was the time work contracts were entered into. When Jacob left Laban (Gen. 31:3, 21) he had completed his contract period, and not entered into an-

other! Though Laban "changed [Jacob's] wages ten times," Jacob had apparently learned to act honestly and with integrity.

"Treat me with honor" (31:20). Painful reality has a way of changing our expectations. Earlier Leah had hoped desperately that giving Jacob a son would lead him to love her (29:32). With the third son she hoped that Jacob would "become attached to" her (v. 34). With her sixth son, she hoped only that her husband would treat her with honor (30:20). Leah never knew the love she hoped for. Yet God did bless her, and 6 of Jacob's 12 sons—ancestors of 6 of Israel's 12 tribes—were her offspring. Life has meaning, even when hopes are unfulfilled.

"Fresh cut branches." There was no magic in Jacob's placement of stripped branches in the breeding area (30:34-43), even though herdsmen in eighteenth-century Europe superstitiously followed the practice. In Gen. 31:8-10 God caused animals to be born with markings.

"Rachel and Leah replied" (31:4-21). Jacob did not decide to return to Canaan and command his wives to tag along. He was careful to obtain their wholehearted agreement. What a blow to the "man the master" view of the biblical family!

"My children . . . my flocks" (31:43). Laban's answer to Jacob's accusation of unfairness was, "I had the (legal) right!" For 20 years Laban had shown himself to be unjust, deceitful, and greedy. Legalities never make wronging others right.

This heap of stones (31:51-54). It was common in O.T. times to set up a visible symbol as a "witness" to agreements.

Outline
Place
Finder

CREATION
CHOICE
COVENANT

Chapter summary. As Jacob nears home, he is filled with memories of his treatment of Esau and Esau's murderous anger. He sends a message to Esau, calling himself "your servant Jacob" (32:1-8). Just before reaching Canaan Jacob begs God for help — and sends a series of "gifts" on ahead to his brother (vv. 9-21). That night Jacob wrestles with God, and his name is changed to Israel (vv. 22-32). Esau actually welcomes him, and a relieved Jacob worships God (33:1-20). But when Jacob's daughter is raped by a young Canaanite, her brothers practice deceit and exact bloody revenge (34:1-31).

Key verse. 32:11-12: To counter fear remember God's grace.

Personal application. Pray, plan, and proceed.

Key concepts. Fear »p. 363. Prayer »pp. 608–609, 894.

INSIGHT

Jacob prays. Jacob was terrified as the little company neared Canaan. The story alternates reports of Jacob's prayers and his plans (plan, 32:7-8; pray, vv. 9-12; plan, vv. 13-21; pray, vv. 22-32; plan, vv. 33:1-3). Jacob was wise to bathe his plans in prayers. We do well to follow the same pattern of plan, pray — and proceed in faith.

Jacob's prayer (32:9-12). Jacob has matured. He has obeyed God's command (v. 9). He acknowledges his own unworthiness (v. 10). He admits his fears, to himself and to God (v. 11). He shows concern for others (v. 11). And Jacob's final thought is one of confidence, based on God's commitment to him (v. 12). If we deal with our fears as Jacob did with his, we too will overcome.

"Israel." The new name Jacob won means the struggles with God." The word we take as "struggle" is found in only one other text: Hosea 12:4-5. Some suggest it may imply "persevere." Jacob has learned not to resist God, but to struggle with Him. How important not only to be on God's side, but to persevere in this commitment.

"Bless me" (32:26). In what sense was the name "Israel" a blessing? In giving Jacob the name Israel, God revealed to Jacob something of what he had become — and what he would continue to be. What name does God intend to bless you with?

"I already have plenty" (33:9). Jacob, who now realizes that Esau has reason to hate him (33:20), is stunned when instead Esau welcomes Jacob home! Let's not credit Esau with a forgiving spirit. There is a simple explanation, cast in Esau's own words. Esau had been angry because he feared that in taking his birthright and blessing Jacob had doomed him to poverty. In fact Esau prospered materially, as shown by the 400 retainers who came with

him to meet Jacob. Esau no longer cared what his brother had taken, for spiritual blessings had no meaning to this totally worldly man.

The man who is satisfied with the good things this world has to offer will never realize that he has missed the most important things of all.

Rape (Gen. 34). The casual way in which the son of Shechem's ruler violated Israel's daughter Dinah reminds us how uncertain life was in biblical times. The subsequent offer of marriage was not motivated by morality, but by passion: Shechem "has his heart set on your daughter" (v. 8). It would have meant the corruption of the covenant line, and abandonment of the covenant promises that Jacob had given so much to retain.

Sometimes there are no easy ways out when life is unfair. Every human society shows similar evidence of sin's impact, and the godly as well as ungodly individual is vulnerable.

Deceit. Again sins of the father are imitated in his offspring. Dinah's brothers promise to "settle among you" — if the men of Shechem accept circumcision. When the men were still disabled by the pain of the operation, Simeon and Levi, Dinah's full brothers, murdered them all and then stripped Shechem of its wealth. The rape was terrible. But the vengeance was even more so. We can never justify sinning by the fact that we have been sinned against.

"We are few in number" (34:30). Jacob was frightened by his sons' violence. As a family of less than 70 persons they were vulnerable to the far more numerous people of Canaan. His fear lays the foundation for the next sweeping section of Genesis — the story of Joseph, whom God used to prepare a place for the Israelites in Egypt, a land where they would be protected, and would grow in number.

Outline
Place
Finder

CREATION
CHOICE
COVENANT

Chapter summary. Jacob returns to Bethel, where God had revealed Himself to him. Jacob settles there, and builds an altar (35:1-15), a memorial to the God who called him, who gave him a new name, and who confirmed transmission of the promises given Abraham to Jacob/Israel's children. Rachel dies in giving birth to Benjamin (vv. 16-20). Jacob finds his father, Isaac, in time to join Esau in burying him (vv. 21-29). All of chapter 36 is devoted to a genealogical record of Esau's line. Esau was rejected as far as the covenant is concerned, but not forgotten.

Key verse. 35:3: Our experience with God enables us to influence our family and others.

Personal application. Knowing God gives life meaning, even though we may experience tragedies.

Key concepts. God's appearances »p. 56. Abrahamic Covenant »p. 32. Idolatry »p. 433. Altar »p. 79. Genealogy »p. 264.

INSIGHT

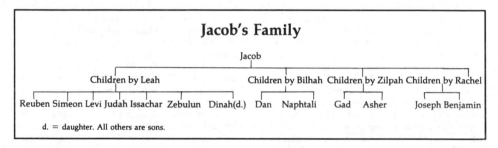

Jacob's Family

Jacob

Children by Leah — Children by Bilhah — Children by Zilpah — Children by Rachel

Reuben Simeon Levi Judah Issachar Zebulun Dinah(d.) — Dan Naphtali — Gad Asher — Joseph Benjamin

d. = daughter. All others are sons.

Chart. *The Covenant promises were passed from Abraham to Isaac to Jacob, and then to the sons of Jacob/Israel, shown here with the mothers to whom each was born.*

Bethel. The name *Bethel* means "house of God." There Jacob worshiped "El Bethel," the "God of the house of God," who had appeared to him. Centuries later wicked King Jeroboam I established a worship center here, to compete with Jerusalem where God's temple stood. Corruption is sure to follow when we honor the place or tradition more than the Lord. It is the God who revealed Himself in the place who is significant, not the place.

Foreign gods (35:2). Bethel marks Israel's total commitment to God. Jacob/Israel's commitment is marked by remembrance of what God has said, by erection of an altar for public worship, and insistence that his family purify itself from idolatry. Idols brought along from their old life in Paddan Aram were buried. A new life was to begin. Let's be sure that we too bury the baggage of the old life we lived before we knew Christ.

Death and sin. Three events remind us that even full commitment to the Lord does not insulate from pain. Jacob's beloved Rachel dies giving birth (35:16-18). Reuben, Jacob's oldest son, sins sexually with Bilhah, Jacob's concubine and the mother of his sons Dan and Napthali (v. 22). And Jacob's father, Isaac, dies (vv. 27-29). At times those who are the most committed to the Lord seem to be the most severely tested. Yet every life knows just such pain. How gracious of God to wait until Jacob has found the strength that commitment brings before permitting such suffering.

Esau's genealogy. The appearance of Esau's genealogy here follows an established pattern. Before continuing the story of the chosen line, the author of Genesis ties up loose ends by telling what happened to Jephthah and Ham (Gen. 10), to Ishmael (Gen. 25), and now to Esau (Gen. 36). These genealogies are more than a literary device. They remind us that even those not in the covenant line are remembered by God. His love follows them through the ages, even as it follows us.

Chapter summary. Joseph, Israel's favorite son, innocently provokes the hostility of his older brothers (37:1-11). The brothers plot against Joseph, and at the last moment determine to sell him to slave traders rather than kill him (vv. 12-28). Joseph's blood-stained robe is brought to an unconsolable Israel as evidence Joseph is dead (vv. 29-35). The traders sell Joseph to a high Egyptian official (v. 36).

Meanwhile Judah too has troubles. When he fails to marry a widowed daughter-in-law to a younger son, as custom requires, she disguises herself as a prostitute (38:1-16). Judah makes her pregnant, and then is exposed as the father (vv. 17-30). Standing side by side, the two stories contrast the suffering of innocent Joseph and the troubles Judah brought on himself. Both the innocent and the guilty may suffer. But the truth that God has a purpose in the suffering of the innocent will be revealed as the story of Joseph unfolds.

Outline
Place
Finder

CREATION
CHOICE
COVENANT

Key verse. 37:11: Jealousy stimulates many an evil act.

Personal application. It is better to suffer innocently than as a consequence of wrong and foolish choices.

INSIGHT

Innocence. Joseph was innocent, but totally naive. We look at Joseph, and are amazed that he never suspected his honest report of his brothers' failings (37:2), his father's open favoritism (vv. 3-4), and his narration of his dreams (vv. 5-11) would make his brothers jealous. But Joseph was only 17. It is often a quality of the virtuous to expect others to be as generous and good as they are.

Innocence is attractive, and to be cultivated. But we need to guard against a naïveté that unwittingly provokes hostility.

Joseph's dreams. These dreams, as many others recorded in Scripture, were prophetic revelations from God. »p. 99.

Ishmaelites. An ancient trade route led past Dothan; a highway linking Egypt with Damascus and the north. It would not be unusual for a caravan of Arab traders to pass by the place where Joseph was sold by his brothers. Egyptian lists of house slaves mention many with Semitic names. Another authentic touch is the fact that 20 pieces of silver was the standard price for a slave in the early second millennium B.C. (cf. Lev. 27:5).

Joseph's silence. Many take Joseph as a type of Christ: an innocent person who suffered because of the wickedness of others, and through whom the chosen people were delivered from certain death. Joseph's silence as his brothers debate his fate (Gen. 37:12-35) prefigures the silence of Christ before His judges (cf. Isa. 53:7; 1 Peter 2:23).

Levirate marriage. Ancient custom called for a man to marry the childless widow of his brother. The first son of such a union was considered the child of the dead brother, to carry on the dead man's line and inherit his property. This custom underlies the story of Judah's relationship with Tamar, the childless widow of his firstborn.

Birth control? Some have erroneously taught that the judgment of Onan for "spilling his seed on the ground" suggests divine displeasure of birth control methods. In the context of the story it's clear that Onan's sin lay in his unwillingness to father a child for his dead brother, not for using this early birth-control method.

Prostitution. Two kinds of prostitution are mentioned in the O.T.: professional prostitution for money, and cult prostitution performed as an element in pagan worship. »p. 135. Both are wrong, but Scripture takes a more serious view of cult prostitution. The incident here describes professional prostitution (cf. 38:16), and suggests prostitutes wore distinctive dress and were easily recognized (vv. 14-15).

Judah's wrong choices. Gen. 38 shows Judah separated from the family, married a Canaanite, failed to keep his word to Tamar, hired a prostitute, and showed himself unforgiving and harsh. Note that it was after Judah's wife died and he recovered from his grief (v. 12) that he hired a prostitute. We can sympathize with the pressures that lead to wrong choices. But we must not give in to them.

Outline
Place
Finder

CREATION
CHOICE
COVENANT

Chapter summary. In Egypt Joseph becomes supervisor of his master's estate (39:1-6). But when Joseph resists efforts of his master's wife to seduce him, she falsely accuses him and Joseph is imprisoned (vv. 7-20). God is with Joseph; soon he is running the prison for the warden (vv. 21-23). This brings him in contact with two high officials, whose prophetic dreams Joseph correctly interprets (40:1-23). Two years later Pharaoh is troubled by repeated dreams, and one official remembers Joseph (41:1-13). Joseph is called and, giving full credit to God, explains that the dream warns of seven years of famine to follow seven years of plenty. Joseph adds his own advice on how to meet the crisis (vv. 14-40). Pharaoh, convinced of Joseph's wisdom, grants him wide powers to supervise storage of grain in preparation for the coming famine (vv. 41-57).

Key verses. 39:21; 41:16: God acts for us, whether we are in prison or stand before world rulers.

Personal application. Proving our faithfulness in small things is the very best preparation for greatness.

Key concepts. Dreams »p. 99. Egypt »p. 421.

INSIGHT

Illustration. *Every detail concerning the court of Egypt rings absolutely true. The chief butler and chief baker were high government officials. The reference to "all kinds of baked goods" (40:17) is illuminated by an Egyptian document that lists 38 types of cake and 57 kinds of bread made by the royal kitchens! Joseph's investment with signet ring, court dress (expressly intended by the Egyptian word translated "fine linen," 41:42), and the gold collar (chain) for his neck are established by documents and tomb paintings as appropriate to the creation of a vizier—the highest Egyptian official below Pharaoh himself.*

Other details. Other details mark the story as an authentic portrayal of Egyptian custom. The honors granted Joseph (41:43), and giving him an Egyptian name (v. 45) are well attested.

Potiphar's wife. The contrast between Judah (39:15-16) and Joseph is powerful. Both were tempted sexually. Judah sought illicit sex, while Joseph refused the repeated efforts of his master's wife to seduce him. Joseph reminds us that we can never say our sex drive made us sin. The choice is ours, to play the part of Judah or Joseph.

Joseph in prison. God was with Joseph in prison as well as in Potiphar's house. Yet in each setting Joseph clearly set to work with a will to be helpful. The conviction that God is with us in every circumstance frees us to keep on doing our best, however great our setbacks. Joseph's faithfulness prepared him for the sudden advancement he experienced. If we cannot be faithful in small things, we cannot expect great things to follow.

Famines in Egypt. Egyptian records tell of famines lasting many years, caused by droughts at the headwaters of the Nile. Egyptian agriculture depended on annual floods along the Nile that deposited rich new soil and made irrigation possible. In this element too the authenticity of the biblical account has full historic support.

Chapter summary. When the predicted famine strikes, peoples from all over the Mediterranean world come to Egypt for grain (cf. 41:57). Among the supplicants are Joseph's brothers (42:1-7). A strange sequence of events follows, in which Joseph seems to toy cruelly with his brothers (42:8–43:34). In fact Joseph's actions test his brothers' sincerity, and drive them to search their consciences for a reason why God would place them in such a precarious relationship with Egypt's ruler. A final test, which puts Joseph's brother Benjamin in danger of becoming Joseph's slave, reveals the change that has taken place in the brothers (44:1-26). Judah, whose flaws were revealed in chapter 38, shows that he has been cleansed of the jealousy that led the brothers to sell Joseph, and now thinks more of his father's grief than of consequences to himself (44:27-34). God, who was at work in Joseph all these years, has been at work in Joseph's brothers too! Deeply moved, Joseph stuns his brothers by revealing who he is, and explains that God has exalted him to power in Egypt in order to preserve all their lives (45:1-20). The brothers return home and tell the joyful news to Jacob, who is thrilled that he will see his favorite son again (vv. 21-28).

Outline
Place
Finder

CREATION
CHOICE
COVENANT

Key verse. 42:22: Everyone must give an accounting for his or her sins. Sin has consequences.

Personal application. Expect God to change the hearts of those who sin against you, even as He has been changing you.

Key concepts. Test (for quality) »pp. 276, 452. Sin »p. 362. Providence »p. 322.

INSIGHT

Mysteries of providence. Joseph could not grasp the purpose God had in mind when the Lord permitted his captivity. But the story helps us remember that God sees the whole picture. The Lord weaves the history of individuals, families, and nations into a single tapestry. We each play our part, and each of us must trust God with the whole — even when our part seems painful at the time.

Joseph's actions. We are never told Joseph's motives for the "games" he played with his 11 brothers. We can only deduce his reasons from Joseph's own character, and from the results of his actions. From Joseph's character we determine that his acts were not vindictive; he had a redemptive goal in mind. From the results, we can sense what that goal is, and perhaps assume that Joseph was guided in his actions by God. Joseph's "games" first caused his brothers to examine their consciences, and openly admit their earlier sin in selling Joseph into slavery. Those same "games" also revealed the change of heart that God had worked in the brothers. That change

of heart, expressed in Judah's touching and selfless appeal (44:21-34), must have melted any residue of hostility Joseph felt, and freed him to forgive his brothers completely.

Reconciliation, where hurt has been given and received, calls for confession by the offender. But the person hurt must be willing to forgive. The story in these chapters shows how Joseph and his brothers were both prepared by the Lord for a reconciliation that would unite the little family of Israel as one.

"God sent me ahead" (45:4-7). The reunion answered a question that must have troubled Joseph deeply during his years as a slave and a prisoner. Why did God do this to me? It is not often that a believer is given a clear answer. God had used his brothers' jealousy — and Joseph's own early innocence — to preserve all their lives.

Joseph's story is an important reminder for you and me. Even when we do not know "why," we must remain confident that God is at work in every experience of our lives. Even the painful ones.

Outline
Place
Finder

CREATION
CHOICE
COVENANT

Chapter summary. The little family that journeys to Egypt, with Joseph and his two sons, totals 70 direct descendants of Abraham and Isaac (46:1-27). After an emotional reunion with Joseph (vv. 28-34), Jacob meets Pharaoh, and the family is granted land and employment in Egypt's richest district (47:1-12). Meanwhile Joseph administers Egypt, and with the stored grain purchases all privately held land in the country (vv. 13-26). Jacob dies in Egypt, but asks that his body be buried in Canaan with that of his father and grandfather (vv. 27-31). Just before his death, Jacob blesses and adopts Joseph's two sons as his own (48:1-22). Later when the tribe of Levi is set aside to serve God, there will still be 12 tribes to inherit the Promised Land.

Key verses. 48:3-4: As Jacob/Israel nears the end of his life his focus remains on the future. God will keep His promise, and give his descendants the Promised Land.

Personal application. When traveling in your Egypt, don't lose sight of the land God has promised you.

Key concepts. Covenant »pp. 32, 35. Blessing »p. 49.

INSIGHT

"**Seventy in all**" (**46:27**). The number is significant. In Egypt the descendants of Israel multiplied, and when the time came to return to Canaan the Israelites were numerous enough to establish themselves in the land.

Aliens in Egypt. The Egyptians were noted for welcoming foreigners who crossed their borders. Ancient records suggest they were quick to take advantage of any special skills such visitors possessed. Thus Pharaoh's willingness to employ Joseph's brothers is not at all a special or unusual case (47:6).

Goshen. This district lay in Egypt's delta region, which was especially fertile. The generosity of this particular gift undoubtedly did reflect Pharaoh's affection for Joseph.

Joseph's purchase. There is no question that Egypt's Pharaohs were considered owners of all the land and properties of Egypt. The story of Joseph's purchase, though not independently attested in any known Egyptian record, gives a basis for what is known to be later legal theory.

The independence of the priests of Egypt, also mentioned here, is also well attested, as is the 20 percent tax levy on produce harvested in Egypt.

"**Do not bury me in Egypt**" (**47:29-30**). Jacob identified himself fully with the promises and purposes of God. His roots were in Canaan, and his vision of the future was bound up in the ideal of a Jewish homeland to be established there. What a reminder that when death comes, we too look backward—and ahead. We remember who we are as God's people, and we look ahead joyfully to all that relationship with Him promises (cf. 48:3-4).

The adoption of Joseph's sons. Jacob's adoption of Manasseh and Ephraim had lasting consequences. First, it made it possible to set aside the tribe of Levi to serve God, and still maintain a 12-tribe division of the Promised Land. Second, it changed the structure of tribal authority. Reuben, though firstborn, forfeited his birthright by his sin with Bilhah (cf. 35:22; 49:4). Ephraim, Joseph's second son, was given Reuben's tribal headship (1 Chron. 5:1-2). Joseph was fully repaid for his suffering. He was raised to personal power, received the predicted homage of his brothers, and saw his two sons adopted and given a prominent place as founders of two of the future nation's strongest tribes.

God's goodness (**48:11**). Jacob expresses the wonder of something we all experience. God is so good. He showers blessings on us that we never expected, and that we surely do not deserve.

Chapter summary. Jacob gathers his sons to bless them (49:1-28) just before he dies (vv. 29-33). This blessing is prophetic, and predicts "what will happen to you in days to come" (v. 1). Jacob is embalmed at Joseph's orders, and taken back to Canaan for burial (50:1-14).

Outline
Place
Finder

CREATION
CHOICE
COVENANT

With their father dead, Joseph's brothers fear that he will take revenge for their mistreatment of him as a youth. Joseph, however, has recognized the hand of God, and gently promises to provide for his brothers and their families (vv. 15-21). Many years later Joseph asks that his bones be taken to Canaan when God visits Israel and brings them home (vv. 22-26).

Key verse. 50:25: God may delay, but He will surely act.

Personal application. How can you best follow Joseph's example of willingness to forgive despite mistreatment?

INSIGHT

Blessing. The Heb. root (brk) occurs 415 times, highlighting the importance of blessing in O.T. thought. Jacob's blessing is prophetic: it is revelation as well as a father's vision of his children's future. The *Theological Wordbook of the Old Testament* notes that "blessing" means "to endue with power for success, prosperity, fecundity, longevity, etc." More than a wish, the blessing was viewed as an actual transfer of a special gift or power from a father or someone in authority. But the relationship with God of those in Scripture who pronounce blessings on others is the source of its power. »pp. 127, 358.

The scepter (49:10). This verse is recognized as one of the earliest messianic prophecies. »p. 431. David of Judah established the royal line from which Christ came. The scepter did "not depart" from Judah, as an unbroken line of David's descendants stretch from that great king to Jesus, born some 1,000 years later! Many versions read "till Shiloh comes." The Aramaic Targum takes Shiloh as a name of the Messiah. The niv takes the Heb. word as a verb rather than a name, and translates "until He comes to whom it belongs." In either case the clear reference is to Jesus, to whom all

Illustration. *Wall painting from the tomb of Rekhmire (2100 b.c.) portrays stages in Egyptian embalming. Corpses were carefully preserved because the Egyptians believed life after death depended on existence of the physical body. In contrast, the Jews buried the body as soon after death as possible, with no attempt at preservation. Only Jacob and Joseph were embalmed, for transportation of the corpses back to the Promised Land. For the O.T. view of resurrection, »p. 522.*

authority in heaven and on earth belong (cf. Ezek. 21:25-27; Rev. 19:16).

Joseph's brothers (50:15-21). Earlier Joseph had freely forgiven his brothers (45:1-15). But they still felt guilt, and thus fear. Joseph had experienced the grace of God, and thus was able to be gracious to his brothers. Knowing God's grace, we must not only forgive others, but do them good (50:21).

"God will surely come to your aid" (50:22-26). The phrase is repeated twice in verses 24-25. Joseph died confident that God would bring the people of Israel back to the land that He had promised to give Abraham's offspring. In life and in death we have this same certain hope. God will keep His promises to us.

Exodus

As Exodus begins, the descendants of Abraham, Isaac, and Jacob are trapped in Egypt, enslaved by a Pharaoh who no longer remembers or cares about the help given his people by Joseph some 430 years earlier. Exodus tells the exciting tale of the chosen people's deliverance, and stands as the Old Testament's boldest image of redemption. Through God's direct action, His covenant people are released from bondage and granted freedom, that they might know and worship Him.

Exodus also introduces one of the Bible's most revered characters: Moses. Though born a slave, Moses grew up in Egypt's royal palace. As an adult he identified with his helpless people and determined to free them. After 80 years God fulfilled Moses' early dream: Moses was commissioned to win the release of the Jewish people, and to lead them to the Promised Land.

Exodus also tells how God through Moses gave His chosen people a Law intended to guide their relationship with Him, and with one another. That Law, as summed up in ten basic commandments, has served the civilized world as a basic moral code to this very day. As developed in Exodus and in other books of Moses, God's Law defined a just, moral way of life for his Old Testament people. Its concern for the poor and oppressed, its concepts of a criminal justice system, its ecological concern for the land, and its emphasis on equality for all are unmatched in ancient or modern legal codes. All this, and a unique design for worship that provides access to God for penitent sinners, is introduced in Exodus. Without doubt this book is foundational for both the Jewish and Christian view of who God is, for our understanding of morality, and for an introduction to the nature of worship. And with all this, Exodus stands as one of the greatest adventure stories of all times.

EXODUS AT A GLANCE

KEY PEOPLE

Moses   *The deliverer, lawgiver, and leader of the Jews during the Exodus.*
Aaron   *The brother of Moses, who was appointed as Israel's high priest.*
Miriam   *The sister of Moses, a prophetess in her own right.*
Pharaoh   *The arrogant young ruler of Egypt, who fought against God despite crushing miracles of divine judgment.*

KEY EVENTS

Moses' discovery (Ex. 1).   *Moses is found in a bullrush boat and adopted by an Egyptian princess.*
Moses' call (Ex. 3–4).   *Eighty years later a now-humbled Moses is commissioned by God to free the enslaved Israelites.*
The ten plagues (Ex. 7–11).   *God brings devastating judgments on Egypt to force Pharaoh to let His people go.*
The Passover instituted (Ex. 12).   *God commands His people to keep a commemorative annual feast to remember redemption.*
The Ten Commandments (Ex. 20).   *The foundations of Western morality are laid in ten basic principles given Moses at Mount Sinai.*
Tabernacle (tent) worship (Ex. 25–27).   *The design for a special structure where God is to be worshiped is revealed by Moses.*

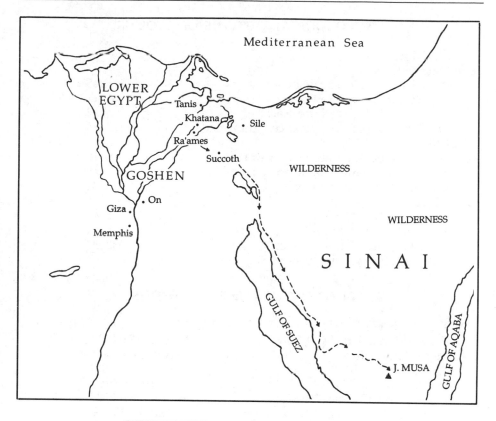

WHERE THE ACTION TAKES PLACE

The adventure begins in Egypt. There Israelite slaves labor at Pharaoh's building projects, constructing store cities at Rameses and Pithom. The scene shifts to the Sinai peninsula, where Moses flees after killing an Egyptian. There, near Mt. Sinai, God appears to Moses, and commissions him to rescue His people. After a series of confrontations with Pharaoh, Moses leads the freed Israelites out of Egypt, across the Red (or "Reed") Sea, and back to Mt. Sinai. While the people camp before the mountain, God gives Moses the Ten Commandments, and outlines the Law Israel is to live by in the Promised Land.

Date and Authorship. Exodus is the second of five books in the Pentateuch, whose traditional author is Moses. While many moderns deny Mosaic authorship, their arguments have been effectively countered by conservative scholars (see introduction to Genesis, page 23). If we go by the dates provided within the Old Testament itself, the birth of Moses would have taken place about 1527 B.C., his flight to Midian about 1486 B.C., and his confrontation with Pharaoh in 1447 B.C. This would make Thutmose III the Pharaoh that Moses fled, and whose long reign (1483 B.C.–1450 B.C.) kept Moses in exile for 40 years (cf. Ex. 2:23 with 4:19). The Pharaoh of the Exodus would thus be Amenhotep II, and the confrontation would have taken place between a venerable Moses and an arrogant youngster, just raised to power.

THEOLOGICAL OUTLINE OF EXODUS

CONTENT OUTLINE OF EXODUS

Outline
Place
Finder

Chapter summary. Jacob and their descendants. The family has grown "greatly" in its 430-some year sojourn in Egypt (1:1-7). The Egyptians, threatened by their sheer numbers, enslave the Israelites and work them ruthlessly (vv. 8-14). But the Jews, toughened by the harsh treatment, keep on multiplying! So Pharaoh commands the Hebrew midwives to put to death any boy children who are born to the Israelites—history's first recorded pogrom intended to wipe out the Jewish race (vv. 15-19). When this fails Pharaoh commands everyone to throw Jewish male infants into the river Nile (vv. 20-22). This Exodus 1 sketch of the grim bondage of the Jews in Egypt serves as background to the great Exodus story of redemption. And it provides us with insight into the forbidding and ugly nature of the spiritual bondage from which God is equally committed to free all who believe.

SLAVERY
DELIVERANCE
LAW
ACCESS

Key verse. 1:14: Sin too is a harsh taskmaster that ruthlessly uses us but fails to offer any real reward.

Personal application. Why remain in bondage to persons or practices who do not really care about you, when God does?

Key concepts. Slavery »pp. 90, 685. Egypt »p. 420. Israel »p. 745.

INSIGHT

The Israelites. It's sometimes hard to know just what the Bible refers to by "Israel." But context will usually tell you whether it refers to (1) the patriarch Jacob, whose name was changed to Israel; (2) the descendants of Jacob's 12 sons, who are known as the "Children of Israel" or Israelites; (3) the united nation of Israel formed of these people about 1040 B.C. and ruled by Saul, David, and Solomon; (4) the Northern of two kingdoms into which the nation split in 930 B.C.; (5) the reunited peoples envisioned by the prophets, who are to be regathered and redeemed at history's end; (6) the Jewish race and/or religion of the N.T. era; or (7) spiritually sensitive and redeemed individuals, of both Jewish and Gentile descent.

How numerous? Three Heb. verbs in Ex. 1:7 emphasize the multiplication of the Israelites. Given 430 years in Egypt (see intro), and the 603,550 men of military age reported in the Ex. census (Num. 1:46), the total number Moses led was probably between 2 and 3 million persons!

Bitter lives (1:14). Some suggest that the root translated "bitter" actually means "strong." Pharaoh intended slavery to crush the spirit of the Jewish people, and to cause many to die. Instead the harsh treatment toughened them. Difficult experiences can have this result in our lives too, if we meet them with faith and determination.

"Hebrew midwives" (1:15-21). The midwives Pharaoh threatened have names which archeology has shown were common Semitic names in the second millennium B.C. It is likely, given the Egyptian dependence on bureaucracy, that Shiphrah and Puah headed a midwives agency that served Jews and Egyptians. They failed to obey the king's command to kill Hebrew boy babies, and were blessed by God. Some have seen a moral contradiction here, and argue that God blessed the two for lying to Pharaoh. It is far more likely that they told the exact truth—and had instructed their staff to be sure to arrive late when called to aid a Hebrew mother!

The courage and ingenuity of the midwives thwarted this second plan of Pharaoh to reduce the numbers of the Jewish people.

Drowning Hebrew boys. The continued rise in the Jewish population led Pharaoh to institute a third plan. He commanded the whole population (*kol 'ammo*) to drown any boy children born to the Jews. The policy would reduce the number of slaves available for work in labor camps. But as a "final solution," it would in time eliminate the troublesome race.

The horror of this story reminds us of the suffering experienced by our Jewish friends across the millenniums, and should make us more sensitive. The steadfastness of the Jews despite pogrom and holocaust is a witness to the grace and covenant faithfulness of God.

Chapter summary. An infant destined to deliver the Jewish people is hidden in a basket-boat, where he is found and adopted by Pharaoh's daugher (2:1-10). As an adult, Moses chooses to stand with his Hebrew brothers (vv. 11-14). He is forced to flee for his life to the central Sinai Peninsula, inhabited by nomadic Midianites (vv. 15-22). In Egypt, intense suffering moves the Hebrew slaves to cry out to God (vv. 23-25). God appears to Moses in a burning bush (3:1-6), to announce to the now reluctant hero that he is to go to Pharaoh "to bring My people . . . out of Egypt" (vv. 7-11). God tells Moses His own personal and redemptive name, Yahweh (the LORD), and promises Moses success and plunder (vv. 12-22). The deliverance God is about to work will establish for all time the redemptive meaning of the name Yahweh, "the name by which I am to be remembered from generation to generation."

Key verse. 3:15: God's redemptive name is ours, forever.

Personal application. Though our dreams of being used by God have faded, they may yet come true!

Key concepts. Holy »p. 81. Fear of God »p. 387. Call on God »p. 361. Angel of the Lord »p. 37. Abraham »pp. 32–33.

INSIGHT

Moses' birth. The story of Moses' discovery by an Egyptian princess rings true. Egyptian art shows royal ladies and their attendants going down to the Nile to bathe.

Moses' choice. Moses made a difficult choice. Heb. 11:24-25 says he "refused to be known as the son of Pharaoh's daughter" but "chose to be mistreated along with the people of God rather than to enjoy the pleasures of sin for a short time." This is a choice each of us must make at some point in life.

Midianites. The Midianites were nomads in this era, with no settled territory. Archeologists have found evidence of consistent use of the Sinai Peninsula by nomadic groups, where the text places Moses during his 40 years of exile.

God's name (3:13-15). The "what" (Heb. *mah*) raises the issue of God's nature rather than a title. God answers by calling Himself YHWH, usually rendered Yahweh or, mistakenly, Jehovah. The name is rooted in the Hebrew verb "to be," and may be understood as "He Who Is," or "The One Who Is Always Present." God's O.T. people had heard the name, but had not experienced its meaning. In the series of terrible judgments about to fall on Egypt, and in the miraculous release of the Israelites, God's people were about to experience Him as One who is present, and present in power! We too are to consider Him present with us, and count on Him to exercise His

power for us. In English versions God's special name is found wherever LORD is found.

Illustration. *(Opposite page) Moses hides his face as he stands barefoot before the burning bush from which God speaks, as Mount Sinai looms in the distance (above). The very ground itself was made holy by the living presence of God. Moses is reluctant now, but rather than rebuke him, God promises to be with him, and describes the ultimate victory he will win (3:18-22).*

Moses

For 40 years Moses lived as a prince in Egypt; for 40 years he was an outcast in Midian; for 40 years he led the people of Israel on their trek to freedom. In the first 40 years Moses learned leadership skills, in the next 40, humility, and during the last 40 years he accomplished his life work.

Moses' contributions are varied. He authored the bulk of the first five books of the Old Testament, the fundamental historical revelation out of which all Scripture grows. As God's agent, Moses won the release of the Jewish people from Egypt. Moses delivered to Israel a code of laws unmatched for its high moral and spiritual tone, which has shaped the West's concept of the duty man owes to God and to his fellowman. As God's agent, Moses also conveyed the design of a religious system offering sinners a way to approach God and to worship Him.

Moses is also a very human hero. He was a man deeply aware of his inadequacies, a "very humble man, more humble than anyone else on the face of the earth" (Num. 12:3). He expressed that humility in his glad submission to God's will, and won praise as "faithful in all God's house" (Heb. 3:2). Moses felt deeply the stress of leading a great and unruly people. Yet his firm commitment to his calling, his reliance on prayer, and his total trust in God remain an example every spiritual leader would do well to follow.

Passages that reveal Moses the man, and contain rich lessons for us to apply to our own lives, include: Ex. 3–4 (Moses' sense of inadequacy); 5:22–6:12 (Moses' frustration and despair); Ex. 7–11 (Moses' boldness in confronting Pharaoh); Ex. 16 (Moses' frustration with an unresponsive people); Ex. 32 (Moses' anger over the golden calf incident); Num. 11 (Moses' expression of his doubts to God); Num. 16 (Moses' prayer for rebellious Israel); Num. 27 (Moses' prayer for guidance, and sharing of authority); Deut. 3:21-29 (Moses' open admission of personal sin); Deut. 11 (Moses' deep sense of God's love).

Chapter summary. Moses is given miraculous powers to authenticate him as God's messenger (4:1-9). But Moses remains reluctant, provoking God's anger (vv. 10-17). Promised the help of his brother Aaron, Moses sets out for Egypt. But he is threatened with death until his sons are circumcised (vv. 18-26). Moses and Aaron are welcomed by the elders of Israel, who believe their signs (vv. 27-31). But Pharaoh shows utter contempt for the God of his slaves (5:1-3). The workload of the Hebrew slaves is increased. Unable to meet unrealistic quotas, the slaves are beaten unmercifully (vv. 4-18). They blame Moses and Aaron (vv. 19-21) — and Moses complains bitterly to God (vv. 22-23).

Key verse. 4:12: With God's help we can do anything.

Personal application. We can carry humility too far.

Key concepts. Aaron »p. 70. Redemption »p. 791. Circumcision »p. 36. Knowing God »pp. 461, 813. Miracles »p. 57.

INSIGHT

Moses' signs (4:1-9). The miraculous signs given Moses were proof that God actually had appeared to him. These signs were intended to convince Moses' fellow Hebrews (v. 5), not Pharaoh. Miracles confirm faith, but are rejected by those who choose not to believe. »p. 679.

I can't (4:10-12). Our "I can'ts" are as foolish as Moses'. God, who created us, can overcome every human weakness. Moses had God's promise, "I will help you speak and teach you what to say." Whatever God asks us to do, He commits Himself to help us succeed.

"Please send someone else" (4:13). We can carry humility too far. There's a time to set modesty and fears aside, and respond to God.

God's anger. Moses surely provoked God. But even in anger, God was gracious! He gave Moses his brother Aaron to serve as spokesman. How wonderful that God does not strike out at us when we provoke Him, but provides more grace, that we might ultimately obey.

Pharaoh's hard heart. Many are troubled by statements in Exodus that God hardened Pharaoh's heart (4:21). If God made Pharaoh resist Him, it wasn't fair to punish the ruler and Egypt for that sin! The text does say God hardened Pharaoh's heart (4:21; 7:3; 14:4). It also says Pharaoh hardened his own heart (8:32; 9:34-35). Also, how God hardened Pharaoh's heart is important. God did not change Pharaoh's natural tendency, nor did God force Pharaoh to act against his will. It was God's act of self-revelation that hardened the heart of Pharaoh. A similar self-revelation caused the Hebrew elders to believe (4:30-31).

God still hardens and softens hearts — by the same means. He reveals Himself to us in Christ. Those who choose to believe are softened, and respond to the Lord. Those who choose not to believe are hardened, and refuse to respond. Each freely choses his or her own reaction to God's self-revelation. And each, like Pharaoh, is fully responsible for his or her own choice.

"God of the Hebrews." Pharaoh's question, "Who is the Lord?" (5:2) drips with sarcasm and contempt. In ancient times gods and goddesses were measured by the power of the people who worshiped them. As Egypt was a world power, its deities were thought of as most potent. To Pharaoh's way of thinking, the God of Hebrew slaves must be weak and contemptible. Only by mighty acts of power would the Lord be established in every mind as the greatest God of all.

Bricks without straw. Chopped straw was an essential ingredient in Egyptian brick-making. Straw contains a chemical which causes bricks to harden more quickly, and strengthens them.

"Why?" (5:19-23) Moses' confrontation with Pharaoh served only to increase the burden on Israel. The Jews were angry and hostile toward Moses. Moses was equally upset with God (vv. 22-23). Instead of rescue, obeying God's command seemed to have made the situation worse! Don't be surprised if obedience doesn't bring immediate relief or instant change in our difficult situations. God has His own purposes in what happens, and often things appear to get worse before they get better. It's all right at such times to complain to God. Just be sure to keep on obeying Him all the same.

Chapter summary. God explains His purpose in permitting Pharaoh to resist (6:1-7), and commits Himself to bring His people to the land promised Abraham so long ago (v. 8). But the discouraged Israelites are too crushed to hope (vv. 9-12). The flow of the story is broken by a list of the heads of the tribal families (vv. 13-27). God then prepares the hesitant Moses for further rejection by telling him how Pharaoh will react—and promising to free Israel through "mighty acts of judgment" (7:1-5). Just as God predicted, the first miracles Moses performs are duplicated by Egypt's magicians, and a hard-hearted Pharaoh refuses to listen (vv. 6-24). The stage is now set for a devastating series of divine judgments, which will force Pharaoh to capitulate to the God of his slaves.

Outline
Place
Finder

SLAVERY
DELIVERANCE
LAW
ACCESS

Key verse. 6:5: God doesn't forget His commitment to us.

Personal application. Expect reversals on the way to success.

Key concepts. Redeem »p. 791. Genealogy »p. 264. Prophet »p. 131.

INSIGHT

"**I am the LORD.**" Ex. 6:3's affirmation that God did not make Himself known to the patriarchs by the name YAHWEH ("the LORD") has been taken as an error in Scripture. Genesis does use this name! But as the great Jewish rabbi Rashi explains, the text means "I did not make Myself known, I did not allow My real character to be recognized." While the four-letter name YHWH appears in Genesis, its true significance was only revealed in the acts of power by which God intervened in Egypt to free Israel. From this time on, God's people will know not only what God's name is, but what that name means!

"**Outstretched arm**" (6:6). Heb. is a language of graphic images. Such phrases as "outstretched arm" and "mighty hand" (v. 1) are not used in an anthropomorphic sense, as though God had hands and arms, but to suggest His ability to act powerfully in the physical universe. In the Exodus events God did display awesome power as well as loving commitment to His covenant people.

Unbelief (6:9-11). Moses' report of God's promise to use His power to free Israel was met with unbelief. The circumstances were just too cruel to permit hope. Even Moses hesitates, and again complains about his "faltering" speech. The old saying, "it's always darkest before the dawn," seems trite. But it's true. However cruel the circumstances, we can trust God, who truly has a "mighty hand" and "outstretched arm."

The genealogy (6:13-27). Some claim this and similar "third person" sections in the Pentateuch prove Moses did not author these books. But study of comparative literature of the ancient world shows that using the third person in narratives was one established convention. Historical records of Egypt's kings, the Greek historian Xenophon, and even Julius Caesar, use similar literary devices.

But why is this genealogy placed here? Likely because Aaron is about to take a more visible role in the story. The genealogy emphasizes Aaron, and serves to establish his credentials as a true Jew and descendant of the patriarchs.

Miracles. In Exodus the miraculous signs are events which in their nature, extent, and/or timing are recognized by observers as supernatural in character. God did use natural phenomenon such as locust swarms and winds in causing the miracle. But the devastating nature of the events and their appearance at Moses' command, as well as their removal at his word, made the supernatural character of the events clear to all. It is foolish to argue that in a "pre-scientific age" people could not tell the difference between natural and supernatural events. They obviously could make distinctions—and the Egyptians ultimately did!

Magic. The magicians of Egypt duplicated Moses' first miracles by their "secret arts." Two possibilities exist. First, that their "miracles" were based on deception and illusion, as are the tricks of modern magicians. Second, the Egyptian priest/magicians were empowered by some demonic source (cf. Matt. 24:24; 2 Thes. 2:9; Rev. 13:13). In ancient times magic was viewed as a way of manipulating gods or supernatural beings, and the magician was held in awe for his special powers.

Chapter summary. Now God brings on Egypt a devastating series of miraculous plagues: of frogs (8:1-15), of gnats (vv. 16-19), of flies (vv. 20-32), of anthrax (?) (9:1-7), of boils (vv. 8-12), of hail (vv. 13-34), of locusts (10:1-20), of darkness (vv. 21-29), and ultimately God announces that on one terrible night He will bring death to the firstborn in every Egyptian home (11:1-10). As these plagues bombard Egypt, Pharaoh wavers in frustration and anger. He pledges to release the Jews, goes back on his word, and despite the urging of his terrified advisers, determines to battle this God of his Hebrew slaves to the very end. That end is more terrible than Pharaoh can imagine, and stands forever as a warning to those who intend harm to God's own.

Key verse. 9:16: God is glorified even in those who reject Him.

Personal application. God is just as able to act for us as He was able to act for the Israelites enslaved in Egypt.

INSIGHT

Illustration. *The gods and goddesses of Egypt were exposed as powerless by the devastating plagues that God brought on the Hebrews' oppressors. Three reasons for the plagues are given in Exodus: so Israel might know that "I am the Lord your God" (6:7); that Egypt might learn that "I am the Lord" (7:5); and as a "judgment on all the gods of Egypt" (12:12). It was clearly futile to depend on the gods that Egypt counted on to bring greatness and to ensure a life after death. Soon the limits of Egyptian magic were reached and the sorcerers admitted Moses' works were performed by God. Even this "expert" testimony was rejected by Pharaoh.*

God's distinction (8:22-23). God's protection of Goshen from plagues that struck the rest of Egypt drives home an important truth. God does treat His own differently. Even if believer and unbeliever both experience tragedy, God's purpose in our suffering is different!

Grace and judgment (9:15-19). Any of the plagues could have wiped out all life in Egypt. God's restraint demonstrated grace—and also gave an opportunity for

Pharaoh to demonstrate his rebellious character. God "raised up" (permitted Pharaoh to become and continue as) Egypt's ruler to demonstrate His power to the whole earth. The events also demonstrate the hardness of the sinful human heart, and the grace of God, who did not destroy the nation that oppressed His people.

Pharaoh's confessions of sin (9:27). The awesome judgments led Pharaoh to a grudging acknowledgment of his sin in resisting God's known will. The confession was meaningless, because as soon as the pressure was removed, Pharaoh went back to his old ways. Saying "I did wrong" is useless unless it leads to a choice of what is right.

Egypt ruined (10:7). Pharaoh kept to his disastrous course even after his land was ruined by the devastating plagues. We can't expect a knowledge of consequences to lead every individual to reform. Sin makes people do foolish things.

Gold and silver (11:2-3). In the end God's people were paid for their centuries of labor in the service of Egypt!

Death of the firstborn (11:4-10). It would be wrong to suppose that Pharaoh alone was responsible for Israel's suffering, or that it was unjust to take the firstborn of every Egyptian family. Every member of an oppressive majority is in some respect responsible for the suffering of those who are discriminated against. The Egyptians formed no committees to free the Hebrew slaves: they were glad someone else was doing the hard work!

The passage reminds us that there is such a thing as corporate responsibility for social evils.

Outline
Place
Finder

SLAVERY
DELIVERANCE
LAW
ACCESS

Chapter summary. The month God strikes the firstborn of Egypt is established as the beginning of the Hebrew religious year (12:1-2). Moses tells each Jewish family to select a year-old lamb on the 10th, care for it till the 14th, and then kill the lamb. The blood is to be sprinkled on the doorframe of the home, and the lamb roasted and eaten (vv. 3-11). That very night God will strike Egypt's firstborn, but will pass over the blood-marked homes of the Israelites (vv. 12-13). For all time Jewish families are to hold a commemorative meal on that date, as culmination of a seven-day Passover season (vv. 14-20). The elders quickly convey Moses' orders. Death does spare the Israelites, as the silence of the night is broken by Egyptian wails (vv. 21-30). Terrified, Pharaoh and all the Egyptians urge the Israelites to leave, pressing wealth on them (vv. 31-32). Exactly 430 years after entering Egypt, the bonds of the Hebrew people are shattered, and they depart, free (vv. 33-42). The chapter closes with additional instructions for keeping Passover (vv. 43-51).

Key verses. 12:26-27: Let's tell our children what God means to us.

Personal application. Keep on remembering what God does for you.

Key concepts. Blood »p. 85. Eat »p. 664.

INSIGHT

Pharaoh's firstborn. The Dream Stela of Thutmose IV contains an inscription which suggests that this son of Amenhotep II was not the crown prince, but a son who did not expect to be raised to the throne until given a stunning dream which predicted his elevation.

Passover. The name comes from the Hebrew word *pasah*, which means "to pass over." The word became the name of one of the O.T.'s most important annual festivals, instituted to commemorate God's grace in sparing Jewish sons the night He struck Egypt's homes with death. Israel was given explicit instructions on keeping this annual feast, at which each family reenacted events of that significant night and ate the special Passover meal together (cf. Lev. 23:5-8; Num. 28:16-25; Deut. 16:1-8). This festival took place in the month of Abib (March/April). The festival was not kept faithfully in Israel. Its celebration is often associated with revival (cf. Josh. 5:10-12; 2 Kings 23:21-23; 2 Chron. 30:1; Ezra 6:19-22).

As a symbol of redemption that links life and the shedding of blood, Passover speaks to us of Christ, our Passover Lamb, who was sacrificed for us (1 Cor. 5:7).

"Hyssop" (12:22). The plant was chosen for its thick roots, which make it a good sprinkler.

"Our homes" (12:24-27). Passover is identified in v. 14 as a commemorative feast. The Heb. word is *zikkaron*. It is used of events,

places, and objects which are intended to make God's historic acts especially real to His worshipers. Thus the father tells the youngest son, when he asks the ritual question, "What does this ceremony mean?" that it marks the time when God passed over "our" homes! Through the worship experience, the people of God unite with their ancestors, and realize in a fresh way that they were there, present when God acted for them. In the same way, the Communion service is a *zikkaron* for Christians. It brings us back to the cross, and to the realization that by faith we were present when Jesus died, and that the death He suffered was for us.

Unleavened bread. Bread made without yeast speaks of purity. Yet the significance of such bread is as an aid to remembering the haste with which Israel finally left Egypt; so quickly there was no time for bread to rise.

Eating the sacrifice. In the ancient world a person who ate a meal as a guest came under the protection of his or her host. Many of the O.T.'s sacrifices call for the worshiper and his family to eat part of the animal that has been offered to God. Thus symbolically God has become the host at the sacrificial meal, and the believer rejoices not only in God's provision, but in this evidence that he and his family have been placed under the protection of the Creator of the universe.

Outline
Place
Finder

SLAVERY
DELIVERANCE
LAW
ACCESS

Chapter summary. Moses decrees that in remembrance of God sparing Israel's firstborn, all firstborn persons and animals are to be considered His (13:1-16). The Israelites avoid the shorter but fortified route to Canaan along the Mediterranean coast, and instead travel toward the Sinai (vv. 17-19). They are led by a cloudy-fiery pillar, visible evidence of God's guiding presence (vv. 20-22). But the pillar leads them into an apparent trap — and Moses is told that Pharaoh has sent a chariot army to recapture his slaves (14:1-9). The approach of the Egyptian army creates panic (vv. 10-20), until Moses parts the sea so his people can cross (vv. 21-22). The pursuing Egyptians rush in after them, and are destroyed when the waters rush back at Moses' command (vv. 23-31). The triumphant Israelites join Moses in a song of praise (15:1-21). But in just three days, when the water supply runs out, the Hebrews have forgotten all God's miracles and grumble (vv. 22-27).

Key verses. 14:13-14: Stand firm. God does fight for us.

Personal application. Remembering what God has done for us can increase our faith when we are in difficult situations.

Key concepts. Light »p. 685. Leading »p. 720. Firstborn »p. 134. Covenant love »p. 351. Consecration »p. 391. Women »p. 723.

INSIGHT

Consecrate. In most places this means "set apart to God," or "consider this God's."

Redeem. To redeem means to buy at a price. The firstborn of ritually clean animals (»p. 82) were sacrificed. A fixed money price was paid for firstborn sons. The Levites were later set aside to serve God, to redeem the firstborn of the Exodus generation (cf. Num. 3:11-13).

Philistine country. Archeologists have found the coastal highway that led from Egypt into Canaan through Philistine territory was heavily fortified. God led His people by a different route because they were not ready to face war. When approaching any objective we need to keep in mind the readiness of all involved.

The cloudy-fiery pillar. This symbol of God's guidance stayed with the Israelites all during the wilderness wanderings. The fact that such visible evidence of God's presence failed to produce a confident faith when dangers arose helps us sense how spiritually weak the Exodus generation was — and helps us understand the necessity that lay behind the introduction of God's Law (»p. 61).

"Stand firm" (14:13). Faith sees overwhelming danger as another opportunity for God to act.

The route of the Exodus. The route followed by the fleeing Israelites is much debated, as is the body of water indicated by the Heb.

Yam Suph. It is almost certainly not the Red Sea. Most translate the name "Sea of Reeds," and believe it refers to one of a string of marshy lakes that lie across the proposed central route of the Exodus (see map, p. 51). Because most of the place names given that trace the Exodus route are lost in antiquity, the debate over the route of the Exodus and thus the exact location of the Yam Suph is unlikely to be resolved. The message of the passage, however, is dramatic and clear. When God's people follow His leading, He does act on our behalf. The most overwhelming odds are nothing to Him. The believer who is in God's will need only be still: "The Lord will fight for you."

Moses' song (15:1-18). The song (psalm) recorded here celebrates God's victory over the Egyptians. It is more than a song, however. It is a teaching tool. Words set to music are more easily remembered. Let's remember the power of songs — and be sure that the music our children listen to promotes godliness rather than the attitudes and values of a lost world.

Marah and Elim. How easy it is to forget that God is with us when difficulties arise. Israel shows no depth of understanding, and none of the faith that seemed to bloom when the Egyptian army was destroyed. A faith that depends on circumstances is a weak faith indeed.

Chapter summary. On the journey to Sinai events illustrate the Israelites' need for Law. They complain angrily about food; yet God supplies meat and manna (16:1-35). They quarrel with Moses and question God's commitment; yet God supplies water (17:1-7). Despite the people's lack of faith, God gives them victory in a battle with Amalekites (vv. 8-16). Moses meets his father-in-law, Jethro, who expresses faith in God (18:1-12). Jethro also suggests that Moses distribute the burden of judging his contentious people (vv. 13-27). Israel's unresponsiveness to pure grace sets the scene for the introduction of Law, which will set up clear standards and provide a basis for discipline.

Outline
Place
Finder

SLAVERY
DELIVERANCE
LAW
ACCESS

Key verse. 17:2: We need to trust God, not test Him.

Personal application. A mature faith responds to God gladly, and thus has no need for an external law.

Key concepts. Testing »p. 125. Rebellion »p. 101. Manna »p. 99.

INSIGHT

Permissiveness. Permissive child-rearing is no longer popular. We've learned that letting children do what they want, without correction, brings disaster! How then do we explain God's "permissive" treatment of Israel on the route to Mt. Sinai? It demonstrated that the people could not trust God, despite constant evidences of His power and love. It demonstrated the need for Law. This people needed clear standards and discipline when they disobeyed. It demonstrated God's fairness. He did not punish the most rebellious act before there were clear standards of right and wrong.

Short memories (16:1-3). Two months before the Israelites were crying out for deliverance from cruel slave drivers. Here they speak about sitting around "pots of meat" and eating "all the food we wanted." Don't idealize the past. Each time of life has its own tribulations. Just trust God. He is able to deliver us from them all.

Grumbling. The phrase "grumble against" (Heb. *lon 'al*) occurs seven times in five verses of chapter 16 (vv. 2, 7-9, 12) and in 17:3. It indicates a specific event: a prevailing attitude expressed in bitter complaint or hostility. Ultimately grumbling is against God, for He is sovereign and in control of our circumstances (16:8). Fail to see God in our circumstances, and we become negative. Trust God to work, and we are filled with optimism and hope.

Manna »p. 99. God's instructions for gathering manna were specific. The fact that some "paid no attention" to these instructions is another illustration of Israel's careless and rebellious attitude toward God (cf. 16:20, 27). God is committed to helping His people be holy.

Law was introduced to discipline Israel, and help them grow toward this goal.

Sabbath. The seventh day of the week (Saturday) was recognized as a holy day by Israel before it was included in Moses' list of 10 commandments (20:8-11).

Testing God (17:1-7). The Heb. word here, *nissah*, means to test or prove. The idea is to subject to a trial, in order to determine whether a person is loyal or trustworthy. It is appropriate for God to test us, as He did Abraham (Gen. 22:1). Such tests strengthen us, as they confirm our loyalty to the Lord, or correct us, by showing some flaw in our commitment. It is never appropriate for us to test God. Our relationship with Him is rooted in faith's firm conviction that God is God, and the one truly trustworthy Being in the universe. It is not only a lack of faith to test God. It is also arrogance.

Upraised hands (17:8-16). Moses' upraised hands symbolized dependence on the Lord. God protected Israel from unhealthy pride in the victory by showing that the battle was won only with divine aid. Our successes reflect what God is doing through us, not what we have accomplished on our own.

Shared responsibility (18:13-27). The appointment of judges for tens, fifties, hundreds, and thousands illustrates a basic principle of the O.T. legal justice system. Elders in little towns or villages were responsible to serve as judges and administer God's Law fairly. This sharing of responsibility meant that all citizens had immediate access to justice, and that every case would be heard first by people who knew the individuals involved personally.

Outline
Place
Finder

SLAVERY
DELIVERANCE
LAW
ACCESS

Chapter summary. After a three-month journey the Israelites camp in front of Mt. Sinai (19:1-2). There God offers to make a covenant with the people which offers many benefits—but which obligates them to obey (vv. 3-6). The people immediately agree (vv. 7-8). Preparations are made for the appearance of God at Sinai (vv. 9-15). When the appointed day comes, the Lord descends to the mountaintop in fire, accompanied by thunder, lightning, and a terrifying earthquake (vv. 16-19). The awesome display accentuates the holiness of God, as does the warning that no one but Moses must approach the mountain on which His presence now rests (vv. 20-25). The stage is now set for God's revelation of the Law, those religious and moral standards which if lived by will shape Israel into a just and holy people, who reflect the character of their God.

Key verse. 19:6: God wants His people to be holy.

Personal application. Don't treat God lightly, for He is awesome in His holiness and elemental power.

Key concept. Consecration »p. 391.

INSIGHT

Mount Sinai. Most believe that Mount Sinai is Jabel el Mussa, which lies near the east end of the Sinai Peninsula (see map, p. 51).

Covenantal structure. Yahweh's words here, and later the structure of the Book of Deuteronomy (see p. 116), reflect a distinctive covenant form from the mid second millennium B.C. This is a covenant made between a superior—a ruler, or king—and his people. Such covenants refer to what the ruler has done for his people (cf. 19:4), and explain the responsibilities of the people to their ruler and the ruler to his people (cf. vv. 5-6). Such covenants served as the constitution of nations. Thus what we see here is the birth of Israel as a nation under God: a nation which is to look to God as its Sovereign, Protector, Ruler, and Lord.

"Now if" (19:5). God forces no one into a relationship with Him. Commitment is voluntary, and we are free—though foolish!—to reject His invitation. But if we do accept God's offer, we become responsible to obey.

The Mosaic Covenant. Biblical covenants (*brit*) make statements about what God intends or is committed to do. While the Mosaic or Law Covenant shares this essential characteristic with other biblical covenants, it is also different from them. The original covenant God made with Abraham contained a number of "I will" statements made by the Lord (Gen. 12). These promises were given formal and legal force in a "covenant of blood" (Gen. 15). At that time God caused Abraham to fall asleep, and the Lord alone passed between the parts of sacrificed animals. God thus showed He would keep His promises to Abraham *no matter what Abraham might do!*

Other covenants, such as the Davidic Covenant (»p. 370) and the New Covenant (»p. 466), are also one-party commitments. God will do what He has promised without reference to how human beings behave.

What sets the Mosaic (Law) Covenant apart is that what God says He will do does hinge on how His people behave. If God's people love and obey Him, the Mosaic Covenant guarantees that God will bless and protect them. If, on the other hand, God's people turn aside to worship pagan deities and forsake God's righteous ways, then God will discipline and punish them. Here alone what God does is in response to choices made by the people of Israel.

There are other differences between the Mosaic and other covenants. The others speak of what God will do at history's end. This covenant tells what God will do for each generation as history unfolds. The others are permanent covenants. The Mosaic is a temporary covenant, in force only until Jesus, the promised Redeemer, arrived (Gal. 3:15-25). Today God's O.T. Law continues to reveal the holy nature of the Lord, and His moral standards. But today God's Holy Spirit enables us to live a life of love that even more perfectly displays the character of our Lord. »p. 759.

Chapter summary. The critical list of basic spiritual and moral commandments is introduced: "And God spoke all these words." These principles for living in harmonious relationship with God and with one's fellowman are no mere human invention. While they provide moral guidance for all, they are specifically intended for the covenant community: for men and women who share a common relationship with God (20:1-17).

The awesome quaking of the smoking Mt. Sinai underscores the fact that it is God Himself who speaks to Israel from heaven (vv. 18-22), and that no fictional god of man's fabrication is to be given a place beside the Lord (v. 23). God also tells Israel to use only simple altars of sacrifice, to further set His worship apart from pagan worship (vv. 24-26). See page 64 for a discussion of each of the Ten Commandments.

Outline
Place
Finder

SLAVERY
DELIVERANCE
LAW
ACCESS

Key verse. 20:1: God has revealed His moral standards.

Personal application. Consistently violating any commandment indicates we are not living in fellowship with the Lord.

INSIGHT

The Ten Commandments. For a discussion of each of the Ten Commandments, see p. 64.

Which ten? Jewish, Protestant, and Catholic believers agree that there are Ten Commandments. But they do not agree on how to divide the list given in Exodus 20. In Judaism, verse 2 is taken as the first commandment, and verses 3-6 the second. Protestants view verse 3 as the first. Catholics take verses 3-6 together as the first commandment, and divide verse 17 into two parts, which they count as the 9th and 10th commandments. If you should come across lists that differ, this is the reason why.

"Thou shalt . . . Thou shalt not." Ancient codes state their laws in conditional form: "if you do this, this must happen." Israel's code alone lays down principles as absolutes. These things are to be done, not because of consequences, but because they are right.

Thus in the Ten Commandments we have a unique revelation of the character of God Himself. He is the kind of person who believes it is right to refrain from murder, from adultery, from stealing, etc. He is a person who considers human beings important, and calls on us to treat each other with respect!

"Thou shalt not." Eight of the ten commandments are expressed as negatives. But each negative implies not just one but a range of positive commands. In saying, "Thou shalt not steal," the command implies that we shall be honest, respect others' property rights, earn by our own labors what we possess, etc. Thus the stern negative in a few brief words suggests a host of positive attitudes and behaviors.

"You." Each command is expressed in the second person singular. While God may be speaking to the community of Israel collectively, He also speaks to each individual personally. When God says, "you," He means "you"—and "me." No one can escape the impact of that "you." Each one of us is responsible to respond with obedience to the God who created humankind, and who redeems His covenant people.

Are the Ten Commandments for Christians? It's true that the Ten Commandments were given specifically to Israel. It's also true that they are part of a law system which the N.T. says we, who are under grace, are no longer under (Rom. 6:14). Our relationship with God doesn't depend on keeping an external list of laws, but rather on responding to the promptings of the Spirit within us.

But in a deeper sense, the Ten Commandments are for us. The commandments reveal God as a deeply moral and loving Person. How could we, who claim Him as Father, not try to be like Him? The commandments point the way. The Ten Commandments also provide a vision of a just and moral human society. How could we, who are called to love others and seek the best for them, fail to live by these commandments and hold them up as an ideal for all?

In Christ we are freed from the futile search for a salvation we earn by trying to keep God's Law. In Christ we are freed to express the reality of a salvation we have received as a free gift. And one way we express our salvation is by living a life that's in full harmony with the standards God revealed in the Ten Words spoken from Mt. Sinai (cf. Rom. 8:3-4).

The Ten Commandments

THE TWO TABLETS OF LAW

THE FIRST TABLET

"No other gods" (20:3). God must be given absolute priority. This commandment is key to all the others. Unless we commit ourselves to God, and to God alone, our hearts will be drawn away from the righteousness the Ten Commandments decree. For ancient Israel "other gods" were often pagan idols. For us "other gods" may be the pursuit of wealth or pleasure. If our commitment to the Lord is complete, keeping the rest of the commandments will follow naturally.

"You shall not make . . . an idol" (20:4). God is Spirit. So cutting any image for use in worship must corrupt our grasp of His nature as Yahweh. God's "jealousy" (v. 5) reflects a passionate concern for us to know and worship Him as He truly is. The reference to "punishing the children for the sin of the fathers" reminds us that the consequences of a flawed understanding of God persist for generations. If we know and worship God in His spiritual nature we protect our descendants from the sins, and subsequent punishments, that grow wherever men fail to know and love the Lord.

"You shall not misuse the name of the Lord" (20:7). The "name" of the Lord, Yahweh, occurs 6,828 times in the O.T.! This is the personal name of Israel's God. It is never used of a pagan deity. Thus God's "name" conveys His uniqueness; the very essence of who He is. The Heb. word trans. "misuse" in the NIV, and "in vain" in other versions, means "nothingness," or "an insubstantial thing." We are never to speak of the Lord or use His name as if He were unreal or unimportant. We are to speak of Him with respect, as the One who has absolute priority in our lives.

"Remember the Sabbath Day by keeping it holy" (20:8-11). This is the only command of the Decalogue not repeated in the N.T., which establishes Sunday as the Christian's day of worship. The pattern of six days of work and one of rest was established by God Himself in the Creation, and God's O.T. people were to honor Him by refraining from work on the seventh day.

THE SECOND TABLET

"Honor your father and your mother" (20:12). An intensive form of the word "honor" is used here, and the command might well be trans. "show respect." Parents are God's instruments in a child's life, to meet his or her physical needs, and to introduce the child to God's ways. The spiritual priority of parents is seen in the fact that many of Israel's religious ceremonies, such as the Passover meal, were conducted within the family. And Deut. 6 and 11 fix responsibility for nurture in the home. It's significant that in a predominantly male O.T. world "mother" is given equal status, and even listed first in the Heb. text of Lev. 19:3.

"You shall not murder" (20:13). "Murder" is more accurate here than "kill." The Heb. *rasah* is a unique word with no parallel in other societies of the 2nd millennium B.C. It identifies "personal killings," and includes premeditated murders performed with hostile intent and accidental killings or manslaughter. Within the covenant community great care is to be taken, so that no one loses his or her life even by accident.

The term *rasah* is not applied to killings in war or to judicial executions. »pp. 114, 128.

"You shall not commit adultery" (20:14). The integrity of relationships is critical in the covenant community; the faithfulness of a man and woman to each other reflects the faithfulness of God to His people. In other ancient Near Eastern societies adultery was considered a "great sin" against the spouse. Scripture sees it as a sin against God, a denial of the covenant structure that binds a people to the Lord. It's no wonder that idolatry is frequently portrayed as spiritual adultery, a sin against the bond of intimacy that exists between the Lord and Israel.

"You shall not steal" (20:15). The command prohibits stealing of any kind. The concern here is not so much for the rights of the individual to property, as for the destructive impact of stealing on relationships within the covenant community. Thus the penalty for theft in the O.T. is not jail, but restitution, by paying back at least twice what was stolen (cf. 22:9). Payment made to the victim is intended to restore harmony by balancing the books, and is not punitive.

"You shall not give false testimony against your neighbor" (20:16). The commandment includes, but goes beyond, testimony given in court. False testimony is any malicious statement intended to degrade or harm another. The reputation of others as well as their property is to be guarded by all.

"You shall not covet" (20:17). To want anything which God has chosen to give another reveals a failure to give God priority in our lives.

64

Chapter summary. The ancient rabbis counted 613 specific laws in the Pentateuch. Here, within a section called the Book of the Covenant (20:22–23:13), a number of these 613 rulings are listed. They illustrate, and thus help to explain, the implications of the basic Ten Commandments for members of the covenant community. The laws in these can be grouped by general content: there are laws governing treatment of Hebrew servants (21:1-11), governing compensation for personal injury (vv. 12-36), governing restitution for violation of property rights (22:1-15), and laws that deal with various responsibilities individuals have as members of the covenant community (vv. 16-31). The important truths this collection of laws illustrates are, first, that God is deeply concerned with every aspect of the believer's lifestyle. And, second, the basic Ten Commandments have the broadest possible application. We are to be sensitive to their implications for every choice we make, and for every law our society enacts.

Outline
Place
Finder

SLAVERY
DELIVERANCE
LAW
ACCESS

Key verse. 22:31: God's laws point the way to holiness.

Personal application. Look for unexpected ways God's Ten Commandments can be expressed in personal and social life.

Key concepts. Slavery »p. 90. Widows »p. 126. Lend »p. 129.

INSIGHT

"The laws" (21:1). Here the Heb. *mispatim* means "guiding decisions." These are illustrative laws, intended to provide future generations of judges with precedents that can serve as guides for their decisions.

"Hebrew servant" (21:2-11). Slaves in the ancient Near East had few if any personal rights. But under the Law no one could be sold into perpetual slavery: a seven-year term was fixed. There is a key difference also in the intent. The seven-year term was an apprenticeship. During it the slave learned from his master, and was given capital for a fresh start (see Deut. 15:12-18).

This does not apply to daughters for the text assumes she will become a slave-wife, and thus be treated as one of the family.

"An eye for an eye, a tooth for a tooth" (21:12-35). This principle does not call for a person who injures another to be mutilated. Injury cases were settled by establishing money damages. What the principle does is *limit the penalty which can be imposed.* In the ancient world blood feuds were common, and an injury to a family member often led to escalating attacks by the victim's family, intent on revenge. The "eye for an eye" rules out revenge and requires the victim to settle for fair compensation. In modern terms, if someone dents your car's fender, don't try to stick the person or his insurance company for a new car!

Crime and punishment (22:1-15). Individuals are responsible for damage to the property of others. If property is misappropriated or stolen, the victim has a right to have his property returned and to an additional payment (see vv. 4, 7). This points up a basic difference between biblical and modern criminal justice theory. Our justice system assumes that a crime is committed against society, and that the state has a right to punish the criminal. The biblical system assumes that a crime is committed against the victim, and that the victim should be compensated.

In the biblical system, only deliberate murder is so terrible a crime that no money compensation can make adequate restitution (21:12).

"My anger will be aroused" (22:24). A person's character is shown not so much in whether he ever becomes angry, but by what makes him angry. This passage reminds us that God is angered by those actions which harm others: mistreating or oppressing an alien (v. 21), taking advantage of a widow or orphan (v. 22), squeezing the poor (vv. 25-27). Let's not become hardened against those on whom God has compassion.

Outline
Place
Finder

SLAVERY
DELIVERANCE
LAW
ACCESS

Chapter summary. The "Covenant Code" continues, with laws that call for justice (23:1-9) and keeping the Sabbath (vv. 10-13). God establishes three annual religious holidays, during which "all the men" are to appear at the worship center (vv. 14-19). But relationship with God is not just a matter of moral and religious duty. There is mutual commitment: God will protect and bless His people (vv. 20-31) if they remain separate and committed to Him (vv. 32-33).

Moses' report is welcomed enthusiastically, and the people promise to do "everything the Lord has said" (24:1-3). This commitment is confirmed by a solemn sacrifice, with the blood sprinkled on the people (vv. 4-8). God invites the elders to a significant meal in His presence (»p. 59), and Moses goes up to the mountaintop to commune with God for 40 days (vv. 9-18).

Key verse. 24:3: This promise is one we must keep.

Personal application. God never invites our allegiance without giving us far more than we can possibly give Him.

Key concepts. Sabbath »p. 71. Work »p. 28. Healing »p. 784. Festivals »p. 89.

INSIGHT

"Justice" (23:1-8). The O.T. justice system required each individual to tell what he or she knew to establish the facts of a case. The O.T. warns against shading testimony to side with the crowd, against accepting a bribe (to side with the wealthy), and against showing favoritism to the poor. The only way a just society can be maintained is to be partial only to the truth!

"Aliens" (23:9). O.T. laws are extremely sensitive to the foreigner or alien, called a *zar*, one who is not related to Abraham's family, or a *ger*, one who is not a member of the covenant community. While Israel was to drive pagan peoples from their lands, resident aliens were to be treated with kindness. The rights of such persons are listed in Ex. 22:21; 23:9; Lev. 19:33-34; Deut. 10:18-19; 24:14, 17-18. But while living in Israel aliens were required to live according to God's Law (Lev. 24:22; 25:35; Deut. 14:29; 24:19; 26:11-15).

Sabbath for the land (23:10-13). The meaning of the root from which "Sabbath" is derived is "rest." A unique concept in O.T. Law is that the land, like people and animals, requires a rest. Thus every seventh year landowners were to leave their fields unplanted and orchards untended. Any crop that grew "of itself" was to be harvested by the poor, not the landowner. It was Israel's failure to give the land its Sabbaths for 490 years that fixed the length of the Babylonian Captivity (2 Chron. 36:21).

"You must demolish them" (23:24). The O.T. frequently calls for the extermination of the peoples who inhabited the Promised Land. Archeologists have learned much about the degraded Canaanite religion of the era, which incorporated repugnant sexual practices and cult prostitution, and even child sacrifice. The often repeated command to wipe out the Canaanites commissioned Israel as agents of divine judgment on gross sin, and protected God's own people from temptation.

"Sickness" (23:25-26). The O.T. covenant with Israel contains a unique guarantee: if Israel obeys, God will take away sickness and give His people large families and a full life span. Some have applied His promise to Christians, and assume that sickness is evidence of disobedience or a lack of faith. But the New Covenant under which we live contains no such guarantee (Jer. 31:31-34). Even in O.T. times, the promise was contingent on obedience of the nation, not of individuals. The great comfort Scripture offers us is the teaching that God is able to take our difficulties and use them for our good. Job suffered painful boils. And the Apostle Paul, whose faith was surely strong, prayed for a healing God chose not to grant (2 Cor. 12:7-10). God does what is best for His children today too. But remember: what God considers "best" for us is spiritual maturity. If He uses sickness to strengthen us, that experience, though unpleasant, is "good" (Rom. 8:28-29).

The Tabernacle

God has taught Israel Ten Commandments that sum up the spiritual and moral requirements for fellowship with Him (Ex. 20–23). God now gives Moses plans for a portable worship center, the tabernacle. God will put His presence there: the tabernacle will be the one place on earth where God's people can meet with and worship the Lord.

God also provides a priesthood to serve at the tabernacle. With God's laws defined and accepted by God's people, the possibility of lawbreaking becomes a fearful reality. And sins, whether of rebellion or unintentional error, shatter a believer's fellowship with the Lord. So God establishes a priesthood commissioned to offer sacrifices for sin, so that fellowship can be restored, and forgiven sinners can have access to the Lord again. Thus the tabernacle not only stands for access to God in Israel's religion, but also for atonement and reconciliation.

The Book of Hebrews tells us that every detail of the tabernacle's design and every item of its furniture has significance. Each symbolizes some spiritual reality. Thus the one door that opens onto the temple court testifies to the fact that there is only one way to approach God. And the altar of sacrifice, placed just inside that door, informs us that we must come with a sacrifice, the blood of a substitute. In the Exodus chapters that follow, the tabernacle blueprint and each item of furniture is carefully discussed.

Outline
Place
Finder

SLAVERY
DELIVERANCE
LAW
ACCESS

Chapter summary. During the 40 days Moses spends on Mt. Sinai with God (24:18), the Lord instructs Moses to invite the Israelites to contribute materials for the tabernacle (25:1-8). He emphasizes the importance of making the tabernacle and its furnishings "exactly like the pattern I will show you" (v. 9). God then goes on to describe a portable chest, called the ark of the covenant (vv. 10-22), a golden table (vv. 23-30), and golden lamp (menorah) (vv. 31-40) to be placed within the tabernacle. He describes the tabernacle itself in great detail (26:1-37), and then gives plans for an altar for burnt offerings (27:1-8) to stand in an enclosed courtyard (vv. 9-19). In the tabernacle, the menorah is to be kept burning (vv. 20-21).

Key verse. 25:9: Always follow God's instructions exactly.

Personal application. Christ is the reality to which the symbolic elements of the tabernacle point.

INSIGHT

Giving. A basic principle of giving is established in 25:2. Offerings to the Lord are to be voluntary and spontaneous. The Hebrew text reads literally, "whose heart urges him to give." Wanting to is still basic in dedicating anything to the Lord. This principle is emphasized in 1 Chron. 29:5; 1 Cor. 9:17; 2 Cor. 9:7; and 1 Peter 5:2.

Where did the Israelites obtain the wealth indicated in the next verses? From the Egyptians, who pressed gold and silver on the departing Israelites in their eagerness to see them go! And so another principle of giving is illustrated. We give only what God has seen to it we have been given!

The materials (25:3-7). Many have looked for symbolic significance in the metals, colors, and precious stones contributed. Thus some suggest gold represents God's glory; silver, redemption; and bronze, judgment. Similarly purple is seen as the color of royalty, scarlet of sacrifice, etc. While there are biblical associations that make such interpretations possible, the meaning of the colors and metals is never explained in either O.T. or N.T. On the other hand the significance of the tabernacle design and of its furniture is much easier to establish.

The ark. This gold-covered wooden chest was about 3'9" long and 2'3" wide and high. It is spoken of in 22 different ways in the O.T.: as the ark, the ark of the covenant, the ark of the Lord, the ark of God, the ark of the testimony, the ark of the covenant of God, etc. It rested in the innermost room of the tabernacle, and was the most sacred item in O.T. religion.

The ark was hollow, and later served as the repository for the stone tablets God gave Moses on which the Lord Himself engraved the Ten Commandments. It also would hold a

container of manna and Aaron's rod that budded (cf. Num. 17).

The deepest significance of the ark, however, is found in its cover. Made of pure gold, and featuring models of two of the angels that guard the holiness of God (cherubim, »p. 491), the cover was the symbolic throne of God. God spoke to Moses from above this cover, called the "mercy seat." And it was here that once a year the high priest sprinkled sacrificial blood for the forgiveness of all the sins of Israel (cf. Lev. 16, »p. 84).

The ark was carefully preserved and later was transferred to Jerusalem, and then placed in the innermost room of Solomon's temple. It disappears from history after the destruction of that temple in 586 B.C.

"The table" (25:23-30). A low, gold-covered table was to be placed in the first room of the tabernacle. It had a solid gold top, and special golden dishes and bowls were placed on it. This table held loaves of bread, called the "Bread of the Presence." A dozen loaves were placed on the table each Sabbath, in two rows of six (cf. Lev. 24:5-9). These were very large loaves, each made of some seven quarts of flour! No wonder they once fed not only David but also his soldiers (cf. 1 Sam. 21:1-6).

There is some debate whether the bread respresents offerings to the Lord, or is symbolic of divine provision. It is best to take the showbread as symbolic of Christ, the Bread of Life (John 6), and to see in the great size of the loaves the generous provision God has made for us in our Lord.

A golden table for showbread was also found in the temple. It may be this table that is carved on the Arch of Titus, which shows Roman soldiers carrying away the temple treasures after the fall of Jerusalem in A.D. 70.

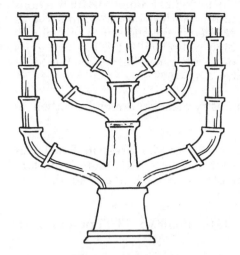

Illustration. *No one is sure just what the seven-branched lamp that stood in the tabernacle looks like. This representation of the ancient "tree of light" stands outside modern Israel's Knesset (parliament).*

"**The lampstand**" (25:31-40). A seven-branched stand which held flowerlike lamps filled with pure olive oil stood opposite the bread-laden table. Jewish interpreters see in the menorah a symbol of the chosen people, hammered out of the seed of Abraham, intended to serve as a tree of light, calling mankind back to Eden and God's tree of life. Christians note that there were no windows in the tabernacle, and that only the lamps supported on this stand shed light. To most this suggests God's presence with us, the only true source of light, and thus it points to Christ, the light of the world (John 1:6-9).

Again the text emphasizes, "see that you make them according to the pattern shown you." We can see reality only in the light God provides.

"**The tabernacle**" (26:1-37). The tabernacle was to be constructed of several layers of curtains laid over an intricate wooden frame. There were no windows, and the interior was completely secluded. The outside entrance was covered with a drapery hanging, and inside another drapery, a special, heavy veil divided the interior of the tabernacle into two sections. The outer room, where the lampstand and table of showbread were, was called the holy place. The inner section was the most holy place. This inner room could be entered only once a year, on the Day of Atonement. Only the high priest could enter this room, and he must always come with sacrificial blood.

The tabernacle and its carefully divided rooms communicated a unique message. God was present with His people. But God could not be approached freely. The N.T. explains the symbolism of the inner veil: "the Holy Spirit was showing by this that the way into the most holy place had not yet been disclosed" (Heb. 9:8). How significant then the report in the Gospels that the moment Christ died, the veil of the temple was torn from top to bottom (Matt. 27:51). Through the death of Christ all who believe have immediate, free access into the very presence of God.

The altar of burnt offering (27:1-8). This was the one altar in ancient Judaism on which burnt offerings were to be made. The altar was a 4'6" bronze-covered hollow cube, with bronze extensions on each corner that looked something like a short animal horn. A bronze grate was set inside the altar, with wood beneath it and sacrificed animals laid on it.

Most significantly, other passages tell us that this portable altar was placed just inside the one door that led into the courtyard. Anyone who wished to approach God must do so by way of sacrifice.

Both the single door entering into the courtyard and the placement of the altar have significance to Christians. Jesus said "I am the door," and made it clear that "no one comes to the Father but by Me." The popular notion that there are many roads to God, and that the one God goes by many names, is simply false. If a person wishes access to God, he must come through Jesus Christ. And he must come through Christ crucified; Christ, the true sacrifice, whose blood purchased salvation for you and me.

"**The courtyard**" (27:9-19). The courtyard that contained the tabernacle was large, some 150 feet long by 75 feet wide. Even more significant, the single entrance to the courtyard was wide—some 30 feet wide! There may be only one door. But that door is wide and welcoming. There's room for whosoever will to come.

Permanent light (27:20-21). Inside, the lights that symbolize God's presence are kept burning to remind us there's a welcome here for you and me.

Outline
Place
Finder

SLAVERY
DELIVERANCE
LAW
ACCESS

Chapter summary. On Mt. Sinai God continues His instructions to Moses. Moses is to set Aaron and his sons apart to serve as priests (28:1). God gives a detailed description of the ritual garments to be worn by the high priest (vv. 2-43). He also gives detailed instructions for a consecration ceremony which is to set them aside for their ministry (29:1-46).

Key verse. 28:29: Priestly ministry means representing others to God.

Personal application. The most splendid dress in Israel was worn by the ministering priest, for there is no more important ministry than to represent others to God, and lead them to worship Him.

Key concepts. Leading »p. 131. Anoint »p. 187. Priesthood »p. 81. Consecration »p. 391.

INSIGHT

Illustration. *Aaron's jeweled breastpiece held the Urim and Thummim that guided Israel (below).*

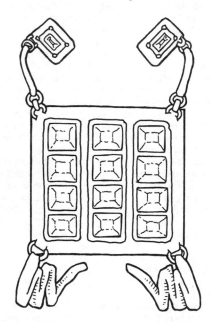

Aaron. Aaron, the brother of Moses, was the first high priest. His descendants alone were to serve as priests in Israel's religion. Thus Aaron is the O.T.'s representative priest, as Moses is its representative prophet. The Aaronic priesthood served throughout Israel's history, till it was supplanted by Jesus' high priesthood (Heb. 7).

The ephod. The vest worn by the high priest was ornate. Stones set in two shoulder clasps, on which the names of Israel's tribes were engraved, seem its most important feature. In wearing it the high priest accepted a role as representative of the whole people. What he did, he did for them as well as for God.

Ordinary priests wore simple, thigh-length ephods made of fine white linen when they ministered (Ex. 39:27; 1 Sam. 2:18; 2 Sam. 6:14).

"The breastpiece" (28:15-30). The breastpiece was a finely fashioned purse. It was fastened to the ephod with chains of gold, and decorated with four rows of jewels, each of which represented one of Israel's tribes. There is special significance in wearing the name of Israel's tribes over the high priest's heart. One representing others to God must care about them deeply, even as God Himself cares. Worship may have ceremonial expressions. But it can deteriorate to mere ritual.

Urim and Thummim. The breastpiece is called the "breastpiece for making decisions" because it contained these mysterious objects. Most believe that the Urim and Thummim were colored stones representing "yes" or "no" and "maybe." When God's O.T. people needed guidance, the high priest had means at hand for discerning God's will. God does not want us to wander hopelessly through life. In every era He is committed to directing His own into His chosen path.

Consecration. The lengthy consecration ceremony God ordained for dedicating Aaron's family to the priesthood reminds us of a basic O.T. truth. No one and no thing is set apart to God without being cleansed by sacrificial blood. Only the cleansing work of God can fit a human being to approach Him, or to serve Him.

70

Chapter summary. Still on Mt. Sinai, God gives Moses the design of an altar for burning incense (30:1-10). He demands "atonement money" from each adult male (vv. 11-16), and gives instructions for making a large basin in which the priests who offer sacrifices can wash (vv. 17-21). Formulas are given for an anointing oil to be used only by priests (vv. 22-33) and a special incense to be used only in worship (vv. 34-38). Moses is then told that God has specially gifted individuals with the skills needed to construct the worship center (31:1-11). Moses' last message from the mount concerns Sabbath: "You must observe My Sabbaths" (vv. 12-18).

Outline
Place
Finder

SLAVERY
DELIVERANCE
LAW
ACCESS

Key verse. 31:3: God's Spirit gives many kinds of gifts.

Personal application. Look at every talent you have as a gift from God, and use it for His glory.

INSIGHT

Furnishings. Two more items of furniture for the tabernacle are described. The altar of incense, which represents prayer, is set inside the holy place (30:1-10). A basin for washing is placed in the court between the altar of sacrifice and the entrance to the tabernacle. The washing here represents maintaining personal purity after sacrifice has been offered. Those who are cleansed by Christ are to keep themselves clean when they seek to approach the Lord.

The ransom (30:11-16). The underlying reason for this tax, which was continued in the days of the temple, is not clearly specified. But several elements of its collection are fascinating. Each adult over 20 (which in Scripture is the age of military enlistment) paid the tax. The amount was small, being approximately .2 ounce, or 5.7 grams. Thus everyone was able to pay it. Yet the rich were not to pay more than the poor: each Israelite approached God on an equal basis spiritually, whatever his material condition. Centuries later Jesus pointed out that rulers collect taxes from aliens, not their own family members (Matt. 17:25). The ransom paid by each Israelite was a witness to the need of each for redemption. It isn't physical descent from Abraham but a faith like Abraham's that counts with God.

"Anointing oil" (30:22-33). Olive oil was used as a base for perfumes and fragrant lotions that were used by men and women alike. These were not just cosmetic, but also were soothing in Palestine's dry climate. Oil was also used in compounding medicines. The use here, however, is ritual: to set aside individuals and objects as sacred. No one could use an oil made from this formula for other than a sacred purpose.

"Incense" (30:34-38). Incense was burned at parties or in the home on special occasions. But the special incense used in worship was to be used for no ordinary or common purpose.

Spiritual gifts (31:1-11). Lists of spiritual gifts given in the N.T. are representative, not complete. This passage emphasizes the role of the Holy Spirit in enabling artisans to construct the tabernacle. God gives us many different kinds of abilities and skills. We need to recognize Him as the source of each talent we have, and dedicate it to His glory.

Sabbath. The O.T. commands only that no one work on the seventh day, and that it be kept holy. Yet the central significance of the Sabbath is seen both in O.T. history and also in modern Judaism. The name "Sabbath" comes from a root meaning "rest." It suggests not merely physical rest, but an inner rest that is restored by contemplating the Lord and His goodness.

Three great acts of God are associated with Sabbath. The Creation story tells us God rested on the seventh day, and Ex. 20:8-11 takes this as the basis of the command to Israel to rest. The people of God are to enter the rest He experienced when all His works were finished (cf. Heb. 3–4). Sabbath also is a symbol of God's covenant relationship with Israel, which is rooted in deliverance from Egypt (cf. Deut. 5:15). Israel is to keep the Sabbath because Israel is a redeemed people, that live in constant affirmation of that redemption. Finally, Sabbath is a reminder of the bond between God and Israel expressed in the Law (Ex. 31:12-17). Sabbath is celebration, a reminder that Israel is God's, and God is Israel's God. The mutual commitment that exists between God and His own is expressed in keeping the Sabbath holy. Thus for Israel the seventh day of the week spoke of Creation, of redemption, and of covenant ties. And observing the Sabbath was an expression of love for and obedience to Israel's wonderful God.

Outline
Place
Finder

SLAVERY
DELIVERANCE
LAW
ACCESS

Chapter summary. Israel's desperate need for the priesthood and tabernacle system is driven home by a terrible incident. In the very shadow of rumbling Mt. Sinai, the people urge Aaron to make an idol, and they worship it (32:1-16). When Moses sees, he angrily breaks the stone tablets of Law God had given him, and calls the Levites to kill the idolaters (vv. 17-29). Later Moses begs God to forgive Israel (32:30–33:6). The Lord continues to meet with Moses (vv. 7-11), and even permits Moses a glimpse of His essential glory (vv. 12-23). God gives Moses new stone tablets (34:1-9), and reaffirms His covenant relationship with Israel. God also reemphasizes laws that call for worship of the Lord alone (vv. 10-28). The transforming impact of intimate relationship with God is visibly reflected in Moses' radiant face (vv. 29-35).

Key verse. 33:16: God's presence sets His people apart.

Personal application. Sin must be dealt with immediately.

Key concepts. Prayer »p. 181. Evil »p. 662. Anger »pp. 196, 359. Compassion »p. 440. Forgiveness »pp. 357, 633.

INSIGHT

Moses' prayer (32:11-14). Moses rightly did not base his prayer for Israel on any human merit. He asked God to consider His own glory (vv. 11-12) and act according to His own faithfulness (v. 13). God's commitment to us flows from His character. Did God "relent"? (v. 14) Did Moses persuade God to change His mind? Not really (see v. 10). God's anger was real. But His words constitute a test of Moses. Did Moses care more about God's honor and God's people than the prospect of personal glory? When our motives are right, our prayers too will be powerful!

Anger (32:19). Anger is a physical and emotional reaction. The O.T. speaks of both justified and unjustified human anger (cf. also 1 Sam. 20:34). Some, like Moses, are angered by the things that anger God: injustice, idolatry, and betrayal. In others anger is an expression of pride, or a reaction at being confronted with a personal sin. Either kind of anger is dangerous, for it can lead us to act hastily. Ps. 37:8 warns that anger "leads only to evil." For help in dealing with anger, »p. 196.

Kill "brother and friend and neighbor" (32:27). Moses' command was judicial. Thus this killing is not identified as rasah ("murder") in the Heb. text. By implication the Levites killed only those who were actively engaged in the idolatry. No one who was guilty, however dear, could be spared.

"Evil" (32:12-13, 22). The Heb. word (ra') means "to act wickedly," "to be bad," and "to do harm." In the first sense evil is an act that violates God's standards for human beings. In the second sense, evil is a consequence of wicked acts. It is the tragedy, the suffering, the physical and emotional distress that results from wrong moral choices. God does not do evil in the sense of making wrong moral choices. But as moral Ruler God does do evil to (bring disaster on) evildoers! We do live in a moral universe, and our sinful acts have consequences for us and others.

God's face. Chapter 33 uses "face" in two senses. "Face-to-face" is an idiom implying direct communication. But to "see God's face" means to gaze on God in His essential splendor. No one has seen God in this sense, for as 1 Tim. 6:16 says He "lives in unapproachable light." The graphic image of God showing Moses His "back" suggests that Moses saw something of God's essence, but not enough to overwhelm him.

For a discussion of God's "glory," see »p. 74.

Moses' radiant face (34:29-35). The key to this passage is the fact that Moses' face shone only after meeting with God, and that the glow faded when Moses was out of His presence. Paul applies the story to Christian experience in 2 Cor. 3:12-18. The radiance represents the transforming power of God's presence in the believer's life. The fading glory shows that without His presence, no transformation can take place. How we need to stay close to the Lord today!

Chapter summary. In Exodus 25–27 Moses carefully recorded the blueprints God gave him for the design of the tabernacle and its furnishings. Now Moses describes the construction of the tabernacle and repeats, almost word for word, material in the earlier chapters. The repetition serves as a reminder. The tabernacle, and the sacrifices offered there, were central in Israel's faith. They spoke then and today of worship, and of access to God even for those who had sinned.

Here then we find again Sabbath regulations (35:1-3), a list of materials (vv. 4-29), enablement of gifted craftsmen (35:30–36:7), construction of the tabernacle (vv. 8-38), the ark (37:1-9), the table for showbread (vv. 10-16), the lampstand (vv. 17-24), the altar of incense (vv. 25-29), the altar of burnt offering (38:1-8), the courtyard (vv. 9-20), and finally, a summary of the materials used (vv. 21-31).

Key verse. 36:1: The Lord must give us not only directions, but also the ability to do His work.

Personal application. It is important to know exactly what God wants. It is even more important to do it!

Key concepts. Tabernacle »p. 67. Freewill offerings »p. 73. Sabbath »pp. 71, 664.

INSIGHT

"**From what you have**" **(35:5).** We sometimes dream of what we would give to God if we were wealthy. Moses' instructions to Israel are a healthy reminder. We can give only from what we have. When we give willingly, we please God and find joy in giving.

"**More than enough**" **(36:6).** The invitation to give was extended to all. The response was so great that Moses had to stop the outpouring of gifts. Today too, if all would give of what they have, there would be more than enough to do all God commands.

"**The Spirit of God.**" Those chosen to serve God were equipped for service by the Holy Spirit. What does the Bible tell us about the Spirit? The Holy Spirit is not an "influence," but a Person. Christ used the personal pronoun "He" in speaking of the Spirit (John 14:17, 26; 16:13-15). The Bible says that the Spirit knows and understands (Rom. 8:27; 1 Cor. 2:11), acts and chooses (12:11), loves (Rom. 15:30), teaches (John 14:26), intercedes (Rom. 8:26), convicts (John 16:7-8), bears witness (15:26), and guides (16:13). These are acts of a Person, not an impersonal influence.

The Spirit is identified as God. He is called eternal (Heb. 9:14), the Spirit of the Lord (Isa. 11:2), and the Spirit of God (Gal. 4:6). He is omnipresent (Ps. 139:7), an agent in Creation (Gen. 1:2; Ps. 104:30), and works miracles

(Matt. 12:28). The Holy Spirit is the One who brings us new life (John 3:6), and enables us to live a victorious Christian life (Rom. 8:11). The Holy Spirit is also the divine agent of revelation, who "carried along" the writers of Scripture (2 Peter 1:21).

The Bible uses a number of different words in speaking of the Holy Spirit's work in the life of a believer. Among them are filling, receiving, and anointing. The Christian is baptized with the Spirit on conversion (cf. 1 Cor. 12:13), and thus united to Jesus and all other believers. The image of the Holy Spirit filling Bezalel and Oholiab, thus enabling them to construct the tabernacle, prefigures many of His works for us. Today the Holy Spirit is the Source of our spiritual vitality and our joy (John 7:37-38). He helps us understand what Jesus taught (14:25-26; 1 Cor. 2:10, 12-14), guides us (Rom. 8:4-5), assists us in prayer (v. 26), and transforms us toward Christ's likeness (2 Cor. 3:18). When we respond to His inner promptings He creates the spiritual fruit of love, joy, peace, etc. in our characters (Gal. 5:22-23). How freeing to realize that the God who calls us to serve Him steps into our lives and enables us to do His will. Like Bezalel and Oholiab, you and I will be able to carry out God's commands fully, because He is present within us to help.

Outline
Place
Finder

SLAVERY
DELIVERANCE
LAW
ACCESS

Chapter summary. Moses describes the crafting of the high priest's garments—the ephod (39:1-7), the purselike breastpiece (vv. 8-21), and other garments (vv. 22-31). Again the chapter repeats almost word-for-word instructions recorded earlier (cf. Ex. 28). Moses then inspects the work, for it is vital that God's commands be carried out exactly (39:32-43). The ark is now set up in its enclosure and consecrated (40:1-33). Then, symbolizing both God's acceptance of their work and God's living presence with His people, a cloud covered the entire worship center, and God's glory settled within the tabernacle.

Key verse. 39:43: Let's check the work we do for the Lord carefully. He deserves our best.

Personal application. There's great satisfaction in doing God's work in His way.

Key concepts. Priesthood »p. 81. Tabernacle »p. 67. Anoint »p. 187.

INSIGHT

Priestly garments. See discussion on p. 70.

Aaron's "crown" (39:30). What older English versions called a "crown" or "diadem" is correctly rendered by the NIV as a gold "plate." This flat piece of gold, engraved with HOLY TO THE LORD, was worn on Aaron's turban (headdress). Every thought of Israel's worship leader was to be focused on the Lord.

Inspect the work (39:42-43). This section of Exodus describing construction of the tabernacle suggests a pattern for us to follow. First, be sure we have understood God's instructions clearly. Second, carry them out exactly. Finally, inspect what we've done to be sure. Let's show this kind of care in doing God's work.

"The glory of the Lord" (40:34-36). In the O.T. the "glory of the Lord" is associated with His self-revelation. The awesome holiness of God as He makes His presence known in the world is underscored by images of splendor, fire, and cloud (cf. 16:10; 2 Chron. 7:1-2). Psalm 19:1 reminds us, however, that the visible images are not necessary for us to sense God's glory. "The heavens declare the glory of God," that psalm reminds us. God's very goodness, expressed in mercy and compassion, expresses His glory (Ex. 33:10, 20-22). And judgment as well as redemption display God's glory (14:4; Num. 14:21-23). We can say then that any act of intervention in the material universe has the impact of revealing something of God's nature and character, and thus shows His glory.

What is our response to such revelations of God to be? We are to "glory in His holy name" (1 Chron. 16:10), worshiping and praising Him for who He is (cf. v. 28; Ps. 29:1).

Leviticus

The Israelites are camped on the plains below a smouldering Mt. Sinai. A few short months ago God freed this people from slavery by mighty acts of power. He guided them deep into the desolate Sinai Peninsula, and there He gave them commandments they promised to obey. God also gave Moses specific plans for a portable worship center, the tabernacle. Those plans were followed exactly, and now a splendid tent-church stands in the center of Israel's camp, and Aaron and his sons have been ordained as priests.

The Book of Leviticus is actually a manual, a how-to guide for the new priesthood, explaining the duties of priest and people as they worship God at His tabernacle. In general, the first half of the book covers sacrifices and duties of priests, and the second half states principles of personal as well as ritual holiness. What is most striking is that powerful revelation about relationship with God is implied in all the Leviticus details. We realize that God has chosen to dwell with His people in a tabernacle that symbolizes both His presence and His power. We realize God's presence has an awesome impact: those with whom God dwells must be a different, holy people! Every ritual and moral regulation of Leviticus is designed to drive this truth home. If God is with us, we must be wholly set apart to Him. We also realize through the emphasis on sacrifice that we stand before God as sinners. Only a people cleansed by sacrificial blood can draw near to the Lord to worship Him and to celebrate His presence. The frequent focus of Leviticus on ritual matters may seem foreign to you and me. But the underlying message of this manual of O.T. worship shines bright, and is relevant to us today.

LEVITICUS AT A GLANCE

KEY PEOPLE

Moses *The deliverer, lawgiver, and leader of the Jews during the Exodus, who writes down the instructions given in this worship manual.*
Aaron *The brother of Moses, appointed as Israel's high priest.*
Nadab, Abihu *Sons of Aaron who show contempt for God's instructions.*
Eleazar, Ithamar *The surviving sons of Aaron, who serve as priests.*

KEY EVENTS
Priests begin their ministry (Lev. 9).
Nadab, Abihu are killed (Lev. 10). *God's judgment on these sons of Aaron which drives home the importance of holiness in those who stand in God's presence.*

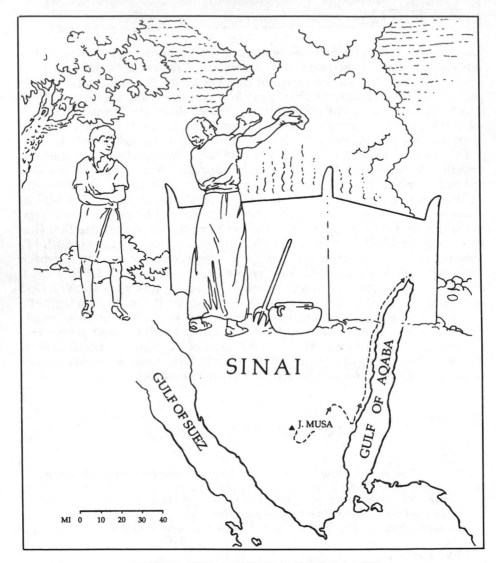

WHERE THE ACTION TAKES PLACE

The Israelites are camped before Mt. Sinai. There they receive detailed rules for holy living, and for offering the sacrifices required to stay in fellowship with God. Here a priest burns choice parts of a sin offering, required from all who sinned unintentionally or were ritually unclean.

Date and Authorship. Leviticus is the third of five books written by Moses. For a discussion of Mosaic authorship, see page 23. This worship manual was probably written during the months that the Israelites were camped on the plains below Mt. Sinai, approximately 1445 B.C.

THEOLOGICAL OUTLINE OF LEVITICUS

I. HOW TO MAKE OFFERINGS		1–10
A. The Sacrifices Required	1–7	
B. The Priests Ordained	8–10	
II. HOW TO KEEP RITUALLY CLEAN		11–15
III. HOW TO MAKE ATONEMENT FOR ALL		16
IV. HOW TO LIVE HOLY LIVES		17–22
A. Rules for Everyone	17–20	
B. Rules for Priests	21–22	
V. HOW TO WORSHIP GOD		23–27
A. Celebrating His Presence	23:1–24:9	
B. Serving His Purposes	24:10–27:34	

CONTENT OUTLINE OF LEVITICUS

I. Rules for Sacrifice (1:1–7:38)
  A. Burnt Offerings (1:1-17)
  B. Grain Offerings (2:1-16)
  C. Fellowship Offerings (3:1-17)
  D. Sin Offerings (4:1–5:13)
  E. Guilt Offerings (5:14–6:7)
  F. Additional Rules (6:8–7:38)
II. Consecration of Priests (8:1–10:20)
  A. The Ceremony (8:1-13)
  B. Required Offerings (8:14–9:24)
  C. Nadab and Abihu (10:1-7)
  D. More Rules for Priests (10:8-20)
III. Clean and Unclean Defined (11:1–15:33)
  A. Clean Animals (11:1-47)
  B. Purifying Mothers (12:1-8)
  C. Rules for Skin Diseases and Mildew (13:1–14:57)
  D. Rules for Bodily Discharges (15:1-33)

IV. The Day of Atonement (16:1-34)
V. Rules for Holy Living (17:1–22:33)
  A. Rules for Eating (17:1-16)
  B. Rules for Sexual Expression (18:1-30)
  C. Rules for Daily Living (19:1-37)
  D. Penalties for Specific Sins (20:1-27)
  E. Rules for Priests (21:1–22:33)
VI. Worship Festivals (23:1-44)
VII. Worship as Obedience (24:1–27:34)
  A. Seriousness of Worship (24:1-23)
  B. Compassion as Worship (25:1-55)
  C. Rewards and Punishments (26:1-46)
  D. Commitment as Worship (27:1-34)

Outline
Place
Finder

OFFERINGS
CLEANNESS
ATONEMENT
HOLINESS
WORSHIP

Chapter summary. God gives Moses rules for bringing different types of offerings (see chart below). The rules in 1:1–6:7 are for the people. Additional rules for the priests are found in 6:8–7:38. Many of the offerings are voluntary. But the sin offering (4:1–5:13) and the guilt offering (6:1-7) are mandatory. Anyone who is guilty of ritual or moral offense must confess his fault, and bring an animal to be sacrificed by the priests. In the sacrificial system of Israel the Old Testament believer was able to confess sins and find forgiveness, to express thanks, and experience intimate fellowship with God.

Key verse. 5:6: Seeking forgiveness is a must now as then.

Personal application. God still invites His people to draw near for cleansing and for worship.

Key concepts. Atonement »pp. 69, 84. Forgiveness »p. 357. Blood »p. 85.

INSIGHT

Unintentional sins (4:2). Individuals could find atonement only for unintentional sins. But on the annual Day of Atonement, the high priest made a unique sacrifice for all the sins of God's people (see Lev. 16). There really is a difference between sins we commit unintentionally and conscious, willful disobedience of God's commands.

"He must confess" (5:5-6). Confession of sins is not optional. To live in fellowship with God, we must seek and accept forgiveness when we fail.

Guilt (5:15). Moderns think of "guilt" as a matter of feelings. The Bible treats guilt as a fact. In the O.T. guilt (Heb., *'asam*) has three aspects. (1) There is an act which brings guilt. (2) There is the condition of guilt which follows the act. (3) There is punishment appropriate to the act. In any verse "guilt" may focus attention on any one of these three aspects. But always each of the elements is implied.

In the N.T., guilt is a judicial concept. The Greek word groups are drawn from the courts, and emphasize liability to punishment. The guilty person has been accused, tried, and convicted.

Both Testaments view acts which bring guilt as offenses against God. But God is loving, and has made a way for guilty sinners to escape punishment and be restored to fellowship with Him. This is the triumphant message of Leviticus, whose sacrifices foreshadow the sacrifice of Jesus, the One whose blood cleanses us from every sin (Heb. 9:11-28).

"Restitution" (6:1-7). Sins against others also are sins against God. Thus the person who stole or defrauded another had to bring a guilt offering to God as a penalty. This was done only after he or she made restitution to the person harmed! This principle underlies Jesus' command to "leave your gift at the altar" if you remember your brother has something against you, and be reconciled before you worship (Matt. 5:23-24). To worship God, we must be right with Him—and with others too!

SACRIFICES BROUGHT BY INDIVIDUAL ISRAELITES

Name	Contents	Practice	Significance
Burnt offering Lev. 1; 6:8-13	A bull, ram, he-goat, or (for the poor) a male dove or young pigeon without defect.	Offerer lays hands on head of sacrifice. He kills, cuts up, and washes sacrifice. Priest pours blood on the altar, burns carcass.	This voluntary offering symbolizes complete surrender to God.
Grain (meal) offering Lev. 2; 6:14-23	Grain, flour, or bread, with olive oil and salt but never with any yeast.	Food prepared by offerer. Priest burns a handful, keeps the rest for his food.	This voluntary offering accompanies most burnt offerings and symbolizes devotion to God.
Fellowship (peace) offering Lev. 3; 7:11-36	Any unblemished animal from herd or flock.	Offerer lays hands on head of sacrifice. He kills it. Priest throws blood on the altar. Part is eaten by worshiper and his family.	The meal following this voluntary offering symbolizes fellowship with God, and thanksgiving for blessing.
Sin offering Lev. 4:1–5:13; 6:24-30; 12:6-8; 14:12-14	Specific animal required depends on status and position. The very poor are allowed to bring an offering of fine flour.	Offerer lays hands on head of sacrifice. He kills it. Priest pours blood on the altar. Best of the carcass is burned, the rest goes to the priest.	For sin or ritual uncleanness. The hands on the head signify identification of the offerer with the sacrifice that made atonement for him.
Guilt offering Lev. 5:14–6:7; 7:1-6; 14:12-18	Valuable ram or lamb without defect.	Offerer makes restitution plus one-fifth. He then lays hands on head of sacrifice, kills it. Priest pours blood on the ground around the altar. Best parts burned.The priest receives the rest	This offering was required when a person violated the rights of another, as by theft. It was also required when healed from leprosy, as God had been deprived a worshiper while the person was diseased.

Chapter summary. Aaron and his sons are ordained as priests as the entire assembly looks on (8:1-4). Aaron is dressed in his splendid garments (vv. 5-9), the worship center and its equipment is consecrated with special anointing oil (vv. 10-13), and solemn sacrifices are offered (vv. 14-29). Then Aaron and his sons are dedicated with anointing oil and blood, and they are required to stay in the tabernacle court for seven days (vv. 30-36). The ordination service was designed to impress on the people and on Aaron's sons the supreme significance of their role in Israel's worship of God.

Key verse. 8:34: Priests require atonement before they can make atonement for others.

Personal application. It is special indeed to serve the Lord.

Key concepts. Aaron »p. 70. Anoint »p. 187. Atonement »pp. 69, 84.

INSIGHT

Illustration. *Aaron is shown dressed in the high priest's regalia. Each of his garments was designed by the Lord, and each has spiritual significance. See the discussion on page 70.*

Ordination. This historic act forever set the priesthood apart from all other Israelites. Even after the time of Jesus only those who could prove their descent from Aaron by complete genealogical records were permitted to serve in the priesthood. And the wife of a priest was required to be a pure-blooded Israelite from a family without blemish. Today every believer is a priest, an adopted member of God's family (1 Peter 2:5). There is no greater heritage than this!

Ear, thumb, toe (8:22-23). Some have suggested that touching these parts of the body with blood symbolizes the need for priests to be ever ready to hear God's voice, ever ready to serve Him, and ever ready to follow Him.

"Do not leave" (8:33). Part of the ceremony of ordination involved restricting Aaron and his sons to the court of the tabernacle for seven days. The act symbolized setting the priests apart from the rest of the people, and setting them apart to God. But it suggests even more. Only those who live daily in the very presence of God can serve the Lord effectively. We must remain close to Him if we are to have a ministry to others.

Chapter summary. Newly ordained, the priests begin their ministry. They make the required sin offering, and also all the voluntary offerings permitted in the Law (9:1-21). The sacrifices complete, Aaron turns and blesses the people (v. 22). The fire that supernaturally consumes the sacrifices indicates acceptance of Israel's worship and confirms the blessing announced by Aaron (vv. 23-24).

But when Aaron's sons, Nadab and Abihu, offer incense that has not been kindled from the altar, supernatural fire consumes them! Priests, whose duty is to guard the holiness of the nation, must show themselves holy by strict obedience to God's Word (10:1-5). Aaron and his remaining sons are not allowed to engage in traditional mourning rites (vv. 6-7), but are to go about their duties (vv. 8-20).

Outline
Place
Finder

OFFERINGS
CLEANNESS
ATONEMENT
HOLINESS
WORSHIP

Key verse. 10:3: All who approach God must honor Him by obeying.

Personal application. God is not to be taken, or treated, lightly.

Key concepts. Holy »p. 86. Priesthood »pp. 858, 880.

INSIGHT

No wine (10:8-11). Wine is forbidden lest it impair a priest's judgment, and bring on him the fate that met Nadab and Abihu. Priests are to distinguish between the clean and unclean, and to teach Israel how to please God. This high calling requires every faculty be alert.

The Bible does not condemn the drinking of wine, but warns against excess. Drunkenness is condemned in the O.T., often. This command forbidding priests to drink when serving God has implications for us. We need our faculties clear at all times if we are to distinguish between right and wrong. If we are to influence others, it's best not to drink at all.

Holy. The Heb. word translated "holy" is *qadas*. It means to be dedicated, or set apart. Applied to persons, places, or things, it means being set apart for the service of God, and thus sacred, removed from the realm of the ordinary. Everything associated with worship in the O.T. is set apart in this way, and thus is sacred. Since the holy is God's realm, and God is to be honored supremely, everything associated with the holy was to be treated with the utmost respect and care. Nadab and Abihu showed contempt for God by failing to follow His instructions on how to burn incense. Such contempt could not be overlooked, and the fire that consumed them taught Israel a vital lesson. God is holy, and they must always honor Him. Rituals must be performed as God ordained, and moral choices made as God directs.

We no longer worship God with O.T. rituals. But the fact that even ritual was regarded as holy because of its association with God is a healthy reminder for us today. In all we do, we are to remember the holiness of God, and show Him the utmost respect.

The priesthood. Lev. 9–10 identify several priestly ministries. Priests were to officiate at sacrifices and offerings, and thus lead in worship. They were to "distinguish between the holy and the profane" (10:10). They were to teach the Israelites God's decrees (v. 11). But there is more. The priests were to diagnose diseases that made worshipers ceremonially unclean (Lev. 13–14). They offered ritual purification to those who recovered (Lev. 14). They examined all sacrificial animals to be sure they were healthy and flawless (22:17-21). Priests established the value of all goods that were dedicated to God (Lev. 27). They supervised care of the tabernacle and later of the temple (Num. 3; 4). Priests announced the beginning of all religious festivals (Lev. 25:9). They served on a sort of supreme court convened to hear difficult cases (Deut. 17:11). They used the Urim and Thummim to convey God's answer to questions posed by the nation's leaders (Num. 27:21). And priests accompanied the army, to exhort trust in God (Deut. 20:1-4). In short, the priests served as the guardian of Israel's faith. Their duties were not just ritual, but called for involvement with ordinary Israelites in all aspects of their lives and relationship with the Lord.

We who are in Christ are all called to His royal priesthood and can find insight into modern ministry by meditating on the calling of O.T. priests.

81

Chapter summary. This chapter introduces the concept of ritual "cleanness" and "uncleanness." In Israel a person in an unclean condition was disqualified from taking part in worship (see INSIGHT, below). Animals and objects as well as people were unclean, and transmitted that condition to all who came in contact with them.

Here Moses lists criteria for distinguishing between clean and unclean animals. Only clean animals were to be eaten by God's Old Testament people, or offered in sacrifice. Classes of animals considered are: domesticated and wild animals (11:1-8, 26-28), fish and water creatures (vv. 9-12), birds (vv. 13-19), flying insects (vv. 20-23), and creatures which "move about on the ground" (vv. 24-31). Detailed rules are given for cleansing whatever comes in contact with an unclean creature (vv. 32-47).

Key verse. 11:44: Keeping laws of ritual cleanness was an expression of consecration to God.

Personal application. Our daily choices today are to reflect personal dedication to the holy God.

INSIGHT

Clean, unclean. The Heb. root meaning "clean" (*t-h-r*) is found 204 times in the O.T., and the root meaning "unclean" or "defiled" (*t-m-'*) 279 times. These words describe a state or condition that affects a person's relationship with God.

In Lev., clean and unclean are ritual terms. An "unclean" person could not take part in worship or eat sacrificed meat (Num. 5:1-4). In some cases an unclean person was to be isolated from others (Lev. 13:45-46). As the next chapters of Lev. show, rules of ritual cleanness and uncleanness focus on the basic experiences of life—birth, death, sex, health, and food. In setting up these rules, God showed He was concerned about every aspect of His people's life and that people are to relate all things in life to the Lord.

Later the prophets of Israel applied the image of ritual uncleanness to moral issues. They boldly announced that sin defiles, thus cutting sinners off from God. The psalmist says of Israel, "they defiled (*t-m-'*) themselves by what they did" (Ps. 106:39). Thus the imagery of uncleanness has great spiritual significance, and powerfully communicates the truth that sin separates us from God. Only a cleansed sinner can approach the Lord.

Why no bacon? Many have tried to show that concern for His people's health underlies God's rules in this chapter. Even today some will argue that eating pork is "unhealthy."

One wild notion I've heard argued fiercely holds that pigs do not eliminate impurities and so store excrement in their cells. Thus pork is actually "dirty" and thus, unclean!

Aside from being false, such reasoning misses the point. In the N.T. Paul says no food is "unclean in itself" (Rom. 14:14). The ritual regulations had a spiritual purpose. They were intended to set Israel apart as God's people, and to help His people be aware of Him in everything they did.

Cleansing. Ritual uncleanness was not a permanent condition. Individuals who became defiled in some way could be restored to a clean condition. This restoration typically involved (1) a period of time during which a person was unclean, and (2) washing with water or purification by a blood sacrifice.

When the O.T. prophets applied the imagery of ritual uncleanness to moral issues, they also applied the imagery of cleansing. Sin defiled God's people. But they could be cleansed of their sins, and made right with God again. So Jeremiah cries out God's good news: "I will cleanse them from all the sin they have committed against Me" (33:8), and Isaiah says, "Though your sins are like scarlet, they shall be as white as snow" (1:18).

What good news for us! Sin need not cut us off from God forever. We can come to Him for cleansing and find it in the blood of His Son (Heb. 9:22).

Chapter summary. Regulations concerning uncleanness (»p. 82) are carefully spelled out in these chapters. None of the issues found here involve willful sin on the part of the worshiper, and with each definition of uncleanness, a process of restoration to the clean state is explained. The rulings here concern childbirth (12:1-8), infectious skin diseases (KJV, "leprosy") (13:1-46), mildew on garments (vv. 47-59), and mildew in buildings (14:33-57). Thorough instructions are given for cleansing after a person has been healed of a skin disease (vv. 1-32). The regulations conclude with a discussion of bodily discharges which make a person ritually unclean.

These include discharges linked with disease, such as from a boil (15:1-15), and those related to sex, as a man's emission of semen or a woman's menstrual flow (vv. 16-33).

Outline
Place
Finder

OFFERINGS
CLEANNESS
ATONEMENT
HOLINESS
WORSHIP

Key verses. 14:19-20: God provides cleansing from all that defiles.

Personal application. Be sensitive to anything that interrupts fellowship with the Lord, and hurry back to Him.

Key concepts. Clean, unclean »p. 82. Priesthood »p. 81.

INSIGHT

Childbirth (12:6-7). Why must a sin offering be made after the birth of a child? Not as some have supposed because sex is somehow polluting. Rather the mother has brought another human being flawed by sin into the world (cf. Ps. 51:5). But note that the mother also brings a burnt offering, which symbolizes complete surrender to God. What a lovely expression of the wonderful truth that God in His grace forgives sinners, and welcomes their commitment to Him.

"Two doves" (12:8). In these chapters God shows special sensitivity to the poor who are unable to offer the more expensive lamb cleansings called for (cf. also 14:21-22). Mary herself was able only to bring this offering of the poor after the birth of Jesus (Luke 2:24). So this law expresses God's concern for the poor. And it tells us that God placed His own Son in a poor family rather than a family of wealth.

Leprosy. The Heb. sara'at and Gk. lepra are translated "leprosy" in older English versions. They are actually general terms for any disease that causes skin eruptions or sores. What we know as "leprosy" is Hansen's disease. This would be only one type of sara'at. The NIV

rendering of this word as "infectious skin disease" best captures the word's meaning.

The priest's role. Priests did not serve as doctors, or have any role in curing disease. The priest was to identify disorders that made a person ritually unclean, and to certify his or her recovery from that condition. For a discussion of the priest's role in O.T. religion, see »p. 81.

Isolation (13:45-46). The isolation of persons with infectious skin diseases from others did have public health benefits. By quarantining such persons "outside the camp," the community was protected from diseases like measles, scarlet fever, and small pox, which were likely to cause epidemics. Other rulings have similar advantages, as those which call for washing of anything touched by a person with a disease that causes a bodily discharge (cf. 15:1-12). While the primary purpose of rules relating to uncleanness is spiritual (see »p. 82), it should not surprise us that they have additional benefits. God is deeply concerned with our total well-being. Anyone who follows biblical guidelines for spiritual well-being will also enjoy better physical health.

Chapter summary. God gives Moses specific details of a ritual of blood atonement to be followed by the high priest just once a year. Only on this day is he allowed to enter the inner room of the tabernacle, the "most holy place" (16:1-19). The effect of the sacrifice is expressed in the living goat that symbolically carries Israel's sins away into the wilderness (vv. 20-22). All other sacrifices only provided forgiveness for unintentional sins. This sacrifice alone is "for *all the sins* of the Israelites" (v. 34, italics added). The solemnity of the day is underlined by the fact that it is the only Old Testament holy day on which all are to "deny yourselves" (fast) (v. 31).

Key verse. 16:34: God does forgive *all* our sins.

Personal application. Sense the awe with which the high priest approached the most holy place and meditate on Calvary, where atonement was made for us by Jesus Christ.

INSIGHT

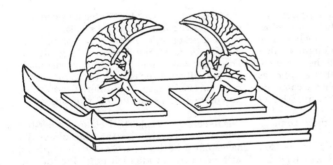

Mercy seat (shown). The cover of the ark of the covenant, which two gold angels sheltered with their wings. Here once a year sacrificial blood was sprinkled by the high priest. God accepted the blood, and forgave "all the sins" of His people.

Atonement. The Heb. word, *kippur*, is used in Scripture in a special way. It is intimately associated with sin, guilt, and forgiveness, and involves the offering of a blood sacrifice. The sacrifice in some way deals with the guilt so that God forgives, and the person or group is reconciled to the Lord.

The best way to view atonement is in relation to the death of Christ. The N.T. teaches that He died to pay for our sins, taking the punishment that we deserved and that God, as a just Judge, must require. Christ thus atoned for our sins. He won us both forgiveness and righteous standing with God. O.T. sacrifices were not adequate to win anyone forgiveness, but did cover the sins of the O.T. saint until Christ died to provide a basis for their forgiveness. See Rom. 3:23; Heb. 9:23–10:14.

Atonement for the altar? In the O.T., places, objects, and persons must be ritually as well as morally pure to be in the presence of Israel's holy God. Sacrificial blood was used to purify any object or person used in rituals of divine worship. The writer of Hebrews sees this as an object lesson, intended to drive home an important spiritual truth: "the Law requires that nearly everything be cleansed with blood, and without the shedding of blood there is no forgiveness" (Heb. 9:22).

Atonement in ancient cultures. Most ancient cultures had some concept of atonement. But these were shaped by a society's view of its gods. Most saw the gods as capricious rather than just, and as a result tended to see atoning sacrifices as bribes intended to prevent or to end divine punishment arbitrarily inflicted by offended deities.

Chapter summary. These chapters launch the fourth major section of Leviticus, which lists rules for holy living. These moral rules focus on personal relationships. First, however, Moses reminds Israel that God has given them the blood of animals to make atonement. All sacrifices are to be made to God at the tabernacle (17:1-9), and blood is to be used for no other purpose than sacrifice (vv. 10-16). God's standards are high. But He is a forgiving God, who accepts the sinner who comes with blood to confess and to be restored.

Moses then goes on to list sexual relationships which defile the individual and pollute the land (18:1-28). Anyone who makes a practice of these forbidden sins is to be "cut off from their people" (vv. 29-30).

Key verses. 17:11; 18:29: Atonement is blood bought.

Personal application. As God's purified people it is up to us to choose purity in our personal relationships.

Key concepts. Adultery »pp. 64, 388. Atonement »pp. 69, 84. Homosexuality »p. 37. Marriage »p. 26. Sex »p. 836.

Outline
Place
Finder

OFFERINGS
CLEANNESS
ATONEMENT
HOLINESS
WORSHIP

INSIGHT

Blood. The Heb. word *dam* is found 360 times in the O.T. Most refer either to the violent shedding of blood in war or crime, or to animal blood shed in making a sacrifice. Lev. 17:11 and Deut. 12:23 make it clear that blood is a sacred fluid. It represents life itself. On the altar, shed blood pictures a substitute making the offerer right with God.

The N.T. focuses our attention on the "blood of Christ," and does so in the context of Calvary. Here we discover that the sacrifices of ancient times foreshadowed Christ's self-sacrifice. The blood spilled on the altar defined for Israel and for us the meaning of Jesus' death. He gave up His life as a substitute for us, that our sins might be atoned for. Passages that teach this wonderful truth include Rom. 3:23; 5:9; Eph. 1:7; 2:3; Col. 1:20; Heb. 9:12, 14; 1 John 1:7; and Rev. 1:5.

Spiritual adultery (17:7). Adultery is engaging in sexual intercourse with someone other than your spouse. Adultery is condemned in Scripture, as is sexual intercourse prior to marriage. This verse establishes an early link between adultery and prostitution and idolatry; a link powerfully developed by the prophets. As adultery violates a person's covenant commitment to his or her spouse, so idolatry violated the Israelites' covenant commitment to God. Each is to be an exclusive relationship. Each calls for total commitment. Idolatry like adultery is a terrible violation of intimacy that shakes the very foundations of relationship.

The revulsion implied in images like prostitution and adultery as used to depict idolatry reminds us that we are to be faithful in our own marriages. And that we are to be utterly faithful in our commitment to the Lord.

"Do as they do" (18:2-3). One of the most common excuses for sexual looseness is, "everyone else does it." While particularly strong in high school, where many teens are ridiculed for being virgins, our society pressures young and older adults by making sexual promiscuity seem "normal." God reminded Israel that as His people, they were not to do as the people of Egypt, where they had lived, do. They were not to do as the people of Canaan, where they would live, do. "Everybody else does it" has never been a valid excuse. Because we are God's people, we are to do as He says, not follow the practices of pagans.

"Molech" (18:21). The reference is to a *m-l-k* sacrifice, not a pagan deity. This was a child sacrifice, offered to any pagan deity from whom a person hoped to derive some benefit.

"Detestable" (18:22). The word used here to describe homosexual acts is *'ebah*. It expresses strong revulsion, and is used of practices that are morally rather than ritually disgusting to God. Prov. 6:17-19 lists seven other *'ebahs*, including "hands that shed innocent blood," a heart that devises wicked schemes," and "feet that are quick to rush into evil." To God, homosexuality is hardly an "alternative lifestyle."

Outline
Place
Finder

OFFERINGS
CLEANNESS
ATONEMENT
HOLINESS
WORSHIP

Chapter summary. Now Israel's holy God issues a number of moral directives. Interspersed with them are commands with symbolic rather than explicit moral import. Thus the decrees forbidding mixing animals, crops, and material in clothing (19:19) are a token reminding Israel that they are a distinctive people, who are never to mix the practices God ordains with the practices of other nations (see also vv. 27-28).

Key verse. 19:2: Remembering God is holy is still the strongest motivation we can have to be holy too.

Personal application. Holiness is a positive, active trait. It is displayed more in what we do than in what we don't do.

Key concepts. Vengeance »pp. 428, 748. Neighbor »p. 661. Love »p. 690.

INSIGHT

"Holy" (19:2). The commands that follow the affirmation, "I am holy," are moral rather than ceremonial in character. They speak of such things as theft, fraud, lying, revenge, honesty in court, and so on. Regularly in this chapter we see the repeated refrain, "I am the Lord." The force of the introductory and repeated sayings is to link the commands directly to God's own moral nature. God is committed to doing what is good and right, and He expects those who worship Him to have the same commitment. Isaiah says, "The holy God will show Himself holy by His righteousness" (5:16).

This reminds us that holiness is a positive and not a negative trait. The truly holy person does refrain from doing evil. He or she is also committed to doing good! Seen in this light, holiness is one of the most attractive of God's qualities. And a quality that makes us attractive to others.

Reaping (19:9-10). The holy person leaves some crops in the field for the poor to gather.

Hired men (19:13). Day laborers depended on what they earned each day to feed themselves and their families. A person who held wages overnight might make a family go hungry.

No partiality (19:15). Only when persons tell the truth in court, and are unswayed by either sympathy or potential rewards, can a just moral society emerge.

Endangering life (19:16). This is the logical positive implication of the commandment, "Do not kill." The O.T. illustrates this command in other places, by calling for a parapet around the flat roof of houses, and by requiring cisterns or other open holes to be covered. It's not enough to intend no harm. We are to take great care to guard against accidents. Again we see that holiness is active, and that it

is our moral responsibility to do good.

Hate (19:17). The Heb. word *sane'* pictures an attitude or emotional response. This emotion has a destructive impact when focused on another person. It is linked with conflict (Prov. 10:12) and violence (29:10). It spills over into antagonistic acts (10:19), and is condemned in the N.T. as the antithesis of love and godliness (1 John 2:9-11; 3:14-15). In Lev. 19:17 God commands His people, "Do not hate your brother in your heart."

The illustration given is important, for it again helps us see the active nature of holiness. A person who hates another might not step in to rebuke him when he sins, secretly hoping that his faults would bring disaster. The believer, however, will love, and moved by love rebuke his brother, hoping to help him avoid the harm that follows close behind every sin.

The aged (19:32). Respect for older adults is emphasized in this and other Bible passages. Sixty was generally the point at which a person was thought to enter old age (27:1-8). Older men served together as community elders. In the ideal vision of community life in the Pentateuch, these elders had great responsibility for maintaining the community's commitment to God. It was assumed that experience had given them wisdom, and the story of Rehoboam's refusal to listen to the older men's advice drives home the point that it is perilous to ignore an older person's advice (1 Kings 12:6-20). A similar attitude is reflected in the N.T. (1 Tim. 5:1-2). Paul points out another advantage of choosing older people for spiritual leadership. The community has had a chance to observe the older person for years, and his or her character is well known (vv. 9-11; cf. 3:1-12).

"Dishonest standards" (19:35-36). See the illustration on page 87.

Chapter summary. Moses now recapitulates subjects dealt with in earlier chapters (esp. 18–19). Here the consequences of disregarding various regulations are spelled out.

The chapter looks at two kinds of sins: offenses against true religion (20:2-6, 27), and offenses against family (vv. 9-21). Both deserve the death penalty, because they are crimes that threaten the very existence of God's people as a covenant community. But the emphasis here too is on exhortations to live a holy life (vv. 7-8, 22-26).

A feature of the chapter is the expectation that the community will act against one who violates these laws. It is everyone's task to maintain purity among the people of God.

Outline
Place
Finder

OFFERINGS
CLEANNESS
ATONEMENT
HOLINESS
WORSHIP

Key verse. 20:22: The community that permits individuals to sin will itself be judged.

Personal application. We cannot impose our standards on a secular society, but must encourage enactment of just laws.

Key concepts. Adultery »pp. 64, 85, 388. Magic »p. 57.

INSIGHT

"Put to death" (20:2). This is not a violation of the Ten Commandments, for the sixth commandment is against murder, a personal crime. Putting to death those whose sins threaten the existence of the covenant community is not murder, but a judicial act.

"Cut him off" (20:3). In this verse the phrase indicates execution. In others it may mean an early death, or ostracism from the community.

Illustration. *Lev. 19:35 (p. 86) calls for "honest scales and honest weights." These were stones of various sizes, to be placed in balancing scales.*

In early times there was no common standard of weights and measures. Archeologists have found recovered weights that vary several grams or even ounces. A dishonest person would buy with heavier weights, and then switch to lighter weights to sell.

"Set My face against" (20:6). This means "be hostile to," or "take action against."

"Curse his father or mother" (20:9). Here and in 24:11 we have a special use of "curse." This is no uttering of casual oaths, or mere angry words. This is a *qalal* curse, linked in pagan thought with magic intended to harm others. The sin thus is doubly terrible. It appealed to spiritual powers other than God or was an attempt to use God's name in magic. And it was an offense against parents, whom God's people are to honor.

Separation (20:22-26). The call to holiness again emphasizes the fact that Israel is to be different from other peoples and "set apart" to God. One key O.T. term, *badal*, means to remove something from something else, so making a distinction between them. This thought is clearly seen in verses 24-25. In O.T. times separation was carried out by isolation of God's people as a separate nation.

It was maintained by ritual and moral standards that differentiated the Israelites from all pagan peoples, and supported by bans against intermarriage and other close contact with non-Israelites.

Yet underlying separation from others was the dynamic of separation to God. Only complete commitment to Him could maintain God's people as a holy nation. For only God could make His people holy in the dynamic, positive sense of holiness seen here in Lev.

Chapter summary. Moses now turns to the priests, with moral and ritual regulations that relate specifically to them. The standard for priests is higher because the priest serves God in the tabernacle, and thus comes closer to the Lord.

Priests are not to touch any dead body except that of a near relative (21:1-6). The high priest, who comes closest to God of all, is not even to enter a place where a body lies (vv. 10-12). Priests may not marry divorced or loose women (vv. 7-8, 13-15). And no priest with a physical defect may officiate at sacrifices or offerings (vv. 16-24).

Moses carefully defines who are considered members of priestly families and thus eligible to eat the priest's portion of food offered in sacrifice (cf. chart, pp. 78–79) (22:1-16). The special instructions to the priests conclude with a discussion of what makes a sacrifice unacceptable to the Lord (vv. 17-33).

Key verse. 22:32: Those God makes holy must be holy.

Personal application. The nearer a person is to the Lord, the more responsible he or she is to live a holy life.

Key concepts. Priesthood »p. 81. Sacrifice »pp. 78, 555. Worship »p. 380. Divorce »p. 136. Clean, unclean »p. 82, 617.

INSIGHT

The dead (21:1-4). In Israel anyone who touched a dead body became ceremonially unclean, until he or she had washed and a certain period of time had passed (cf. 11:39-40; Num. 9:6-7). While unclean, no person could approach God. Priests were not allowed to defile themselves in this way for anyone but a member of their immediate family. The high priest could not even do this, for he must always be available to approach God on behalf of the people (cf. Lev. 21:11-12).

Divorced women (21:7-8, 13-15). The prohibition reminds us that in O.T. times those who divorced would normally remarry. See divorce, »p. 136. The Aramaic O.T. uses a word in v. 7 that may indicate "deserted," and thus left without a paper legalizing the divorce. If this is the meaning, even priests could marry legally divorced women, but the high priest could marry only a "virgin from his own people" (v. 14).

The emphasis on the purity of the priest's line was carried to extremes in N.T. times. Then priests were not allowed to marry a woman unless she could show by her genealogy that she was of pure Israelite stock. Many priests insisted on marrying only the daughters of other priests. The genealogies of priests were the most strictly maintained in Israel, and they wanted to be sure their children would qualify to serve at the temple.

Blemishes (21:16-21; 22:17-22). The lists of physical defects that disqualify priests and sacrificial animals are similar. Together they remind us that God requires our very best. To offer less than the best of our people to serve God, or to bring less than the best of our possessions, is to treat God with contempt.

Acceptable worship. In defining what was unacceptable in the O.T. worship system, the Bible helps us to better understand the nature of worship itself. Neither priests nor sacrifices with defects were acceptable to God. Malachi offers us a picture of a later generation that "despised" God's name, and showed their disrespect by bringing crippled and diseased animals for sacrifice. The prophet says sarcastically, "Try offering them to your governor! Would he be pleased with you?" Malachi gives God's verdict: "I will accept no offering from your hands. My name will be great among the nations" (Mal. 1:6-11).

Acceptable worship then recognizes the greatness of God. Acceptable worship honors God, both by being our best for Him, and bringing our best to Him. If we approach worship with an attitude of awe and respect; if we come with a pure heart and mind; if we bring God the best of whatever we may have—then our worship is acceptable. For such worship alone shows due respect for our God.

Chapter summary. Moses now focuses on worship, launching this topic with a summary of the special occasions on which God's O.T. people gathered for worship (Lev. 23). Here attention is focused on the Lord Himself, a theme developed in the subsequent mention of perpetual offerings (24:1-9), and underlined by the death penalty inflicted when a young man blasphemed and used God's name in a curse (see 20:9, »p. 87).

Outline
Place
Finder

OFFERINGS
CLEANNESS
ATONEMENT
HOLINESS
WORSHIP

Key verse. 23:2: How good to join others in worship.

Personal application. Worship is partly expressed in church, but mainly in the way we live our daily lives.

Key concepts. Worship »p. 88. Capital punishment »pp. 30, 114.

ISRAEL'S RELIGIOUS CALENDAR

Festival	Date	Meaning
Passover	14 Nisan (Mar/Apr)	A memorial festival, celebrated in the home. Each family ate a Passover meal symbolizing their solidarity with the Exodus generation the night God struck the Egyptians and passed over Jewish homes (see Ex. 12). This was the first day of the religious year, for it marked God's redemption of His people from slavery in Egypt.
Unleavened Bread	15–21 Nisan (Mar/Apr)	A week-long period marked by sacrifices, during which the people ate bread made without yeast, as a reminder of their forefather's hasty departure from Egypt (see Ex. 12:34).
Firstfruits	16 Nisan (Mar/Apr)	A celebration of thanksgiving, held at harvesttime, during which the first newly ripened barley was presented to the Lord. The symbolism foreshadows the resurrection of Jesus, called a firstfruit in 1 Cor. 15:20-23.
Pentecost (Weeks)	5 Sivan (May/Jun)	New grain is offered in thanksgiving to the Lord, and special sacrifices are offered. It is significant the Holy Spirit came on the Day of Pentecost, and 3,000 were converted. These first Christians were representative of the millions God will harvest from our lost race as His own.
Trumpets (Rosh Hashanah)	1 Tishri (Sept/Oct)	This day of rest was the first day in Israel's civil year. "Rosh Ha-SHA-nah" means "head of the year," i.e., new year.
Day of Atonement (Yom Kippur)	10 Tishri (Sept/Oct)	On this solemn day of fasting and prayer the high priest entered the innermost room of the sanctuary and made atonement for "all the sins" of the people of Israel (see Lev. 16). "Yom Kippur" means "Day of Atonement."
Tabernacles (Succoth)	15–21 Tishri (Sept/Oct)	During this week the people of Israel lived outside in shelters made of branches. No work was done during this time, and the family was to relive the days of ancient Israel's travel through the wilderness. Following the solemn Day of Atonement, this relaxing week symbolized the rest and joy that follows our salvation. "Succoth" means "shelters," or "lean-tos." This festival was concluded with a solemn assembly and sacrifice on 22 Tishri.

NOTE: Later other festivals celebrating God's work in Israel's history were added by the Jews. Hanukkah, the Feast of Dedication or Feast of Lights, is held the 25th of Kislev (Nov/Dec). This festival marks God's miraculous supply of purified oil to burn in the newly rededicated temple in the time of the Maccabees. Purim, which celebrates the salvation of the Jewish people through the intervention of Queen Esther, is held the 14th of Adar (Feb/Mar).

Chapter summary. Worship is more than celebrating God's presence. It is also serving God's purpose. Moses now gives Israel unique regulations: choices that Israel will choose to make if they truly honor God, and share His concern for the land and its people. The first choice is to observe a Sabbatical year, by giving the land a rest from cultivation every seventh year (25:1-7). The second is to observe a Year of Jubilee every 50 years, at which time all land "sold" to a new owner is returned to the family which held it originally (vv. 8-34). With these laws, God makes special provision for the poor and oppressed, including introduction of a unique kind of "slavery" intended to guarantee future "freedom"! This chapter is a key to understanding the ways in which God's Old Testament Law provided for the poor and fought oppression.

Key verses. 25:36-37: Help, do not take advantage of, the poor.

Personal application. The godly help the less fortunate.

INSIGHT

"**The land**" (25:23-24). When Israel entered the Promised Land, it was distributed by lot, with each family receiving a portion. This land was to be held in perpetuity by the original family: it was a grant given them personally by God, who owned the land. This concept underlies the Jubilee principle found in this chapter.

Poverty. O.T. law makes special provision for the poor, and does not assume that poverty is "their own fault." Here is how law provides for the poor, as seen in this and other O.T. passages. (1) Judges were required not to favor the wealthy in civil cases (19:15). (2) Family land could not be lost permanently, but every 50 years was to be returned to the original owners. This meant every half-century all Israelites were recapitalized, and given the means to support themselves (Lev. 25). (3) The poor were to gather crops from others' lands during the Sabbatical year, when no crop could be cultivated or harvested by the owner (Ex. 23:10-11). (4) During regular harvests the poor were allowed in the fields, to gather anything that fell to the ground or was left on a tree after one picking of fruit (vv. 10-11; Lev. 19:10). (5) Loans to poor Israelites were to carry no interest, and sales of food were to include no profit (25:35-37). (6) Every seventh year any outstanding debt still owed was to be forgiven completely (Deut. 15:7-11). (7) Regular collections were made every third year of a tithe on crops. Food gathered was to be stored locally, for distribution to the needy (14:28-29). (8) A person truly poverty-stricken could sell himself as a temporary slave to a fellow Israelite. At the end of just seven years

he was to be freed, and provided with enough resources to give him a fresh start (Lev. 25:39-54; Deut. 15:12-18). By this means the temporary slave could pay off old debts, live for seven years as a "trainee" in the employ of a successful Israelite, and then have help to get himself on his own feet.

This unique system demonstrates God's deep concern for the poor and oppressed. It challenges us to find ways to help them become self-supporting.

Slavery. Seen in its context as a way to help the poor, O.T. slavery was not the oppressive institution we have learned to hate. Yes, a slave was subject to his master's will. But the condition was temporary, it carried many benefits, and the slave was guaranteed humane treatment by his master (25:42-43).

This ideal was not always realized. Jeremiah speaks of those who pressed their fellow Jews into permanent slavery (cf. Jer. 34). Documents from the first century show that inhabitants of Jerusalem paid 40 times as much for a Gentile as a Jewish slave, because the Jewish slave would have to be released. Despite such practices, slavery in Israel was very different from that institution in other lands, and was intended to aid the poor.

Redemption. To "redeem" means to buy back. The right to buy back family land or persons sold to another is affirmed in this chapter. When an individual had no resources with which to redeem his land or himself, a near relation had the right to redeem for him. Christ had to become a true human being so that as our Near Kinsman, He could pay the price that bought us back for God.

90

Chapter summary. Our worship, and our decision to serve God's purposes, are to be made spontaneously and freely. Why then does Leviticus 26 catalog rewards for obedience (vv. 1-13), and terrible disasters sure to follow failure to respond to God? (vv. 14-39) First, because there are consequences to every choice we make, and God wants us to realize what these are ahead of time. The second reason is seen in verses 40-46. When in the future Israel would reject God and suffer those consequences, the Lord wanted each generation to realize that they had not been rejected completely.

The book concludes with a discussion of voluntary offerings freely vowed to God (27:1-25), and a discussion of tithes, which are in effect the "rent" Israel pays to God as owner of the Promised Land (vv. 26-34).

Outline
Place
Finder

OFFERINGS
CLEANNESS
ATONEMENT
HOLINESS
WORSHIP

Key verse. 26:44: Knowing God does not reject us completely is important when we fall, and to keep us from falling.

Personal application. How gladly we serve God when we realize He is committed to us completely.

Key concepts. Covenant »pp. 35, 62. Vow »p. 96. Tithe »p. 103.

INSIGHT

"Enemies" (26:7-13). The Heb. words for "enemy" emphasize both hatred and hostile acts. They are primarily used in the O.T. of relations between Israel and the surrounding pagan nations. This chapter promises Israel victory over enemies when faithful to the Lord, and defeat when the nation abandons Him. Because of the surrounding nations' paganism and God's commitment to His people, "enemy" is primarily theological rather than political.

Though God is hostile to nations hostile toward His people, God is God of the whole earth. Thus He at times uses enemy nations to discipline His own people. God calls Assyria the "rod of My anger, in whose hand is the club of My wrath" (Isa. 10:5). Centuries later, Habakkuk realized that God was raising up the Babylonians to discipline His own sinning people (Hab. 1:12). Thus the O.T. sees God's hand in international events, and relates war and peace to the commitment to their Lord.

"Confess" (26:40). It's a mistake to see painful events in Scripture or in our lives merely as punishment from God. Suffering that comes as a consequence of our own sins is intended to be instructive. It is intended to force us to face our guilt and responsibility, and turn to God in honest confession. So never feel, whatever may happen, that it's too late for you. Remember that God's door is always open to anyone willing to acknowledge their sins. Any pain you may have suffered was not intended to crush you, but to turn you back to Him, so He might lift you up.

Not reject completely (26:44). If you're far from God, it is you who has moved! And if you turn around, you'll find Him right there, waiting to welcome you home.

Valuing persons (27:1-8). A money value was set on persons an individual might dedicate to the Lord. These prices say nothing about the intrinsic value of the person as a human being. Instead they represent the value of the individual in terms of his or her potential economic contribution to the household. Thus there is no contradiction between the high value Israel was to place on older persons (»p. 86), and the much lower cash value of the older person given on this list.

We can gain fascinating insights from this price list. For instance, full maturity seems to be counted from age 20. And old age seems to begin at 60. The economic contribution of an adult woman to the household is assumed to be 3/5 the contribution of an adult man. Below that age, the contribution is about 1/2 as great.

At times it may be appropriate to measure persons by what they do in a society. But it is much more important for you and me to measure persons by their intrinsic value to God. If we do, we will realize each individual has infinite worth and value, as a person for whom Christ willingly died.

Numbers

Numbers is a book of transition. The Israelites have been freed from slavery in Egypt and given God's Law at Sinai (Ex., Lev.). This is their past. Their future is in the land God promised long ago to give Abraham's descendants (Gen.). Numbers tells the story of the journey from Sinai to Canaan, the last stage of the long trail that leads from slavery to rest in the Promised Land. As we read Numbers we see that the journey was filled with tests and challenges. And we realize that these could be met successfully only by an obedience that grows out of a vital, living faith. The failure of the Exodus generation to meet those tests successfully is reflected in the Hebrew name for the book, *bemidbar*, "in the wilderness."

Numbers is a historical report of ancient Israel's experience. But it can also be read as an analogy of Christian experience. We too are a redeemed people on a journey to God's Promised Land. Our journey too is filled with tests and challenges. And for us too, only a faith that responds obediently to the Lord can preserve us from disasters along the way.

The Book of Numbers teaches us much about God. He is with His people as they travel. His holiness is expressed in His demand for obedience. Yet His holiness is tempered by mercy and grace. The wonderful truth we realize as we travel with ancient Israel is that God remains constant and faithful in His commitment to His own. When sinning and when obedient, in success and in failure, God stays with us. He is committed to bring us at last to His own Promised Land.

NUMBERS AT A GLANCE

KEY PEOPLE

Moses   *The deliverer, lawgiver, and leader of the Jews during the Exodus.*
Aaron   *The brother of Moses, appointed as Israel's high priest.*
Joshua   *One of two spies who urged Israel to trust God, destined to succeed Moses as leader of the Israelites.*
Caleb   *The second faithful spy, with Joshua the only individual to survive the wilderness wanderings.*
Balaam   *A pagan prophet who unsuccessfully tried to curse God's people.*

KEY EVENTS

The first census (Num. 1).   *The number of men of military age leaving Egypt is established. "Numbers" takes its English name from two censuses.*
Twelve spies enter Canaan (Num. 13).   *They establish the fruitfulness of the Promised Land, and also the military might of its inhabitants.*
The people rebel (Num. 14).   *The fearful Israelites refuse to attack Canaan, and are condemned to wander in the wilderness.*
Balaam tries to curse Israel (Num. 22–24).   *God turns the pagan seer's curses into blessings.*
The second census (Num. 26).   *The first generation has died, but a new generation just as numerous takes its place, and will inherit Canaan.*

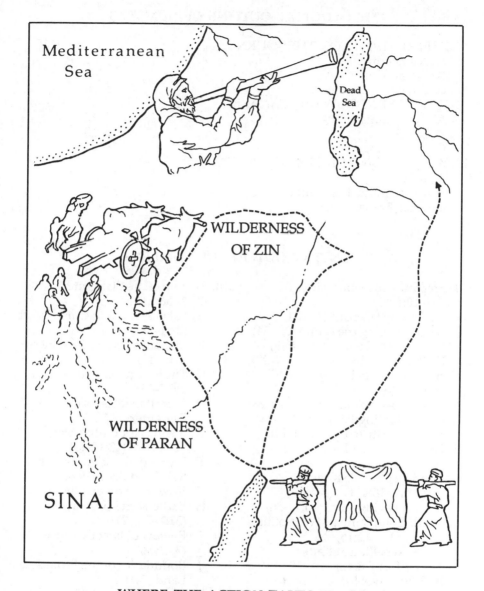

WHERE THE ACTION TAKES PLACE

Numbers takes place "on the road." Numbers 1:1–10:10 reports preparations for leaving Sinai. Numbers 10:11–21:35 tells about the journey from Sinai to the plains of Moab. Numbers 22:1–36:13 relates three events that took place on those plains. The illustration shows the Levites carrying the portable tabernacle on the journey (see 3:21–4:49).

Date and Authorship. The traditional authorship of Moses is supported in this book by the phrase "The Lord said to Moses," which is repeated throughout it. The book covers events that spanned 39 years, 1445–1406 B.C.

THEOLOGICAL OUTLINE OF NUMBERS

CONTENT OUTLINE OF NUMBERS

Chapter summary. Moses now prepares the Israelites to move on. A military census is taken by tribe of all adult men able to fight (1:1-44), except for the Levites (vv. 45-54). The tabernacle is placed in the center of the camp, and each tribe is assigned a place around it (2:1-34). God then claims the Levites as His own, in place of the Israelite firstborn whose lives He spared in Egypt (cf. Ex. 12) (3:1-51). Each Levite family is then assigned special duties at the tabernacle when camped, and other duties when on the journey (4:1-49). In serving God, the Levites served all Israel, for the tabernacle they cared for was at the center of Israel's life with God, as well as at the center of the camp.

Outline
Place
Finder

PREPARATION
JOURNEYING
WAITING

Key verses. 3:12-13: Those spared from death belong to God.

Personal application. God claims our service that others might be blessed.

Key concepts. Tabernacle »p. 67. Priesthood »p. 81. Passover »p. 59.

INSIGHT

The census (Num. 1). Given some 603,000 men of military age, Keil and Delitzsch calculated that there must be at least an equal number of women, and at least 2 children per family. Thus they assume there must have been at least 2 million people who set out from Sinai on the journey to Canaan!

"Listing every man by name" (1:2). What a reminder that every individual is important. God not only knows our names, but expects every one of us to be enlisted in His army! Reaching the world for Christ is not the calling of the clergy. It is the commission of every believer!

Israel's camp (Num. 2). The tribes were arranged in a boxlike square. The tabernacle stood in the center, with the tents of three tribes each set to the north, south, east, and west. The Levite clans were arranged in the same boxlike fashion, with a different clan camped to the north, south, east, and west in between the other tribes and the tabernacle. The structure of the camp reminds us that God is to be at the center of all our lives.

"Firstborn" (3:13). Firstborn (*bakar*) occurs 158 times in the O.T. The firstborn son had a special position in the ancient family. He was given a double portion of any inheritance, and had a right to the father's intangible property (position, etc.). Because God spared the Israelites' firstborn when He destroyed the firstborn of Egypt on the first Passover, the Lord claims all firstborn males as His own special possession. While firstborn animals were sacrificed, firstborn children were redeemed (Ex. 13:2-15). The rite reminds us that when God has

the right of ownership He gives life, rather than takes it.

This chapter tells how God took the Levites in place of the firstborn of the Exodus generation (Num. 3:1-45). The imagery conveys another beautiful truth. Those who belong to God are drawn close to Him, and given the privilege of service. God takes the life He saves, and makes it the most meaningful life of all!

Levites. The Levites descended from Levi, the third of six sons born to Jacob by his wife Leah. This whole tribe was set aside to serve God and care for the Hebrews' worship center. One family of Levites, Aaron's, had the right to serve as priests. The other families ministered to the priests and maintained the tabernacle. The Levites were not given a tribal allotment in Canaan, but were scattered in cities throughout the lands of the other tribes. God was their special portion, and they were to be supported from the tithes and offerings given to God by the other tribes. There is a lovely interplay of gifts here. Israel gives God the Levites. God gives the Levites to the sons of Aaron to assist them in their priestly duties. And, of course, the priesthood is itself a gift from God to Israel, for the priests enable the people to have access to God. Every gift given is returned, and multiplied. Just as everything we give God today is generously given back to enrich our lives.

"From thirty" (4:3). Twenty was old enough to fight. But a man had to be 30 to serve in the tabernacle. Everyone is to be involved in the struggle. But maturity is called for when it comes to spiritual leadership.

Outline
Place
Finder

PREPARATION
JOURNEYING
WAITING

Chapter summary. With the camp organized, God turns to issues of purity. These serve as reminders to Israel that on the way, each must remain in fellowship with God. And that each has the opportunity for the utmost personal dedication. Those who are "unclean" are sent outside the camp (5:1-4). A test for unfaithfulness in a wife affirms God's active presence in searching out and punishing hidden sins (vv. 5-31), and laws governing the Nazarite vow remind each Israelite of his or her opportunity for complete commitment to the Lord (6:1-21). The chapter concludes with the blessing the priests are to pronounce on Israel: a blessing rooted in God's personal commitment to His people (vv. 22-27).

Key verses. 6:24-26: God's presence is itself our blessing.

Personal application. We must be pure to live close to God and know His blessing.

Key concepts. Clean, unclean »pp. 82, 505, 617. Adultery »pp. 64, 388. Blessing »p. 127.

INSIGHT

"Where I dwell" (5:1-6). There were public health reasons for isolating persons with communicable diseases from the majority. But the central reason given here is ceremonial and thus educational. God's people must learn that nothing which hinders worship or service must exist where God dwells. What a lesson for us. God has taken up residence in the heart of every believer. We are to be morally pure, because He is with us, and within us (cf. 2 Cor. 6:14-18).

Hidden sins (5:5-31). The significance of the test for an unfaithful wife is revealed in verses 5-10. These state that a person who wrongs others "in any way" must confess his sin and make restitution. Adultery is the classic hidden sin, for it is never committed where others can witness it! The prescribed ritual is not magical. Rather the call for a jealous husband to take his suspected wife to "stand before the Lord" (v. 16) acts out the belief that God is present among His people. The whole ritual is an affirmation of faith, and in response to that faith God promises to act. He will clear an innocent woman and visibly judge a guilty one. The ritual is thus communication between God and His people. The jealous husband speaks to God, and in response God speaks to the husband. What is more, God speaks to the whole community. He reminds His people that sins have consequences, and that the sinner must bear the consequences even of hidden sins.

Abdomen swell and thigh waste away (5:22, 27). The phrase does not describe a deadly disease, but rather was a way the Hebrews spoke of childlessness and miscarriage. O.T. Heb. is notably delicate in the language used to speak of sex, even though sexual matters are treated quite openly.

Nazarite vow. An ordinary person could dedicate himself or herself to a life of special holiness, vowing not to drink alcohol or touch grape products, by letting his or her hair grow uncut, and by staying away from dead bodies. This vow was for a limited period, at the end of which special sacrifices were to be offered. The Nazarite vow conveyed several powerful messages to Israel. While God's people were all holy, individuals had the opportunity for personal commitment to an even more holy lifestyle. This opportunity was open to all. The extensive regulations concerning the Nazarite make it clear that commitment to God is an exceptionally serious matter, not to be entered into or broken lightly.

Today every Christian is holy through his or her participation in Christ. And each of us is invited to make a personal commitment to live the most holy life possible, in honor of our Lord.

Other vows. A vow is a dedication of one's self or one's possessions to the Lord. Other passages speak of dedicating loved ones or possessions to God (cf. Lev. 27). A special feature of O.T. vows is found in Num. 30:3-9, where the law permits a husband or father to overrule a woman's vow, if he does so when he first hears of it. Still, vows were voluntary, and every Israelite had the opportunity to thus express his or her gratitude to God.

"The Lord bless you" (6:24-26). The oldest recovered verse of the O.T. is found engraved on thin metal foil.

Chapter summary. The leaders of each tribe, as representatives of the people, brought gifts at the dedication of the tabernacle (7:1-9). They also brought sacrifices at the dedication of the altar (vv. 10-89). A purified people want to give their best to God, and have that privilege!

Now, just before the Israelites set out on their journey, Aaron is reminded to set up the candlestick so that it lights the area in front of it, perhaps symbolic of the fact that our most important use of Scripture is to light the way before us, so we will journey safely (8:1-4). The Levites are purified and dedicated to the service to which God has called them (vv. 5-26).

Outline
Place
Finder

PREPARATION
JOURNEYING
WAITING

Key verse. 8:15: Purified and dedicated, the Levites are allowed to do their work.

Personal application. We must be purified and dedicated before we try to do God's work.

Key concepts. Sacrifice »pp. 76, 84. Levites »p. 95. Lamp »p. 376.

INSIGHT

Interpretation. We look for the meaning of O.T. events and institutions in the historical setting itself. Here the key question is, "What did this mean to the people of that generation?" At the same time, we know from the N.T. that these historic events had additional significance. Paul says in 1 Cor. 10:11 that "these things happened to [the Exodus generation] as examples, and were written down as warnings for us." Thus it is possible when applying the narrative passages of the O.T. to see symbolism in historic events that speaks to our own life and experience. Here the key question is, "What does this suggest to you and me?" Perhaps no book is as rich in "example" material as the Book of Numbers.

It is important when reading and applying the Bible to remember that interpretation comes first, and then application. And that the usefulness of our application of a passage depends on how well we interpret that passage and see its meaning in the original historic context.

"The first day" (7:12). For 12 days, 1 after the other, a different leader brought his offering for the dedication of the altar. And each offering was exactly the same! Yet the description is repeated, word for word, a dozen times. Why? Perhaps as a reminder that every gift we gladly bring to the Lord is recorded in heaven, with our name. What you give to the Lord is special because you give it, not because it is better than or different from what others may bring.

Facing forward (8:2). It's good perhaps to look back, and to understand our past in the light shed by God's Word. But Scripture, which the Psalms frequently represent as a lamp or light, is really intended to shed light in front of us, to guide us on our life's journey. Keep studying the Word. But keep Scripture facing forward, so you can apply its principles to the choices you make in daily life.

"The Levites will be Mine" (8:14). What does God do with this tribe that He claims as His? He gives them special work to do. Some view heaven as a place where the redeemed stand idle, strumming harps. But throughout the O.T. those who have been closest to God have been the most active! Heaven will be filled with work and worship. And those committed to work and worship experience a foretaste of heaven now!

"They must retire" (8:23-26). God wants us to make room for the next generation. But the call to retire here is not an invitation to become idle. The O.T. says specifically, "they may assist." But then the passage adds, "but they themselves must not do the work."

How we struggle to hold on to power, long after it's time for us to turn responsibility over to others. How hard it is to realize that the most important role for the spiritually mature is one of advising. It is more important to enable others to do God's work than to do that work ourselves.

Outline
Place
Finder

PREPARATION
JOURNEYING
WAITING

Chapter summary. A year has passed since the Israelites escaped from Egypt. Now the people are told to celebrate the Passover, the Jewish festival of freedom (9:1-5). The importance of this meal and the associated sacrifices is seen in a unique regulation: even those who are ceremonially unclean are to take part (vv. 6-13), and even a resident alien may celebrate this solemn rite that speaks so clearly of redemption (v. 14).

Before telling of the Israelites' departure from Sinai, Moses mentions two things. The cloudy-fiery pillar that represented God's presence showed Israel when to move on and when to remain camped (vv. 15-23). Two silver trumpets were formed for signaling (10:1-10). Communication, from God and between believers, is vital for a journey to God's Promised Land.

With the organization of the camp complete, the Israelites left Sinai, setting out on a journey which promised them victory — but which, because of their own disobedience, would lead to disaster (vv. 11-36).

Key verse. 9:8: Don't act without knowing what the Lord commands.

Personal application. God's Spirit is our pillar of cloud.

Key concepts. Passover »p. 59. Unclean »p. 82. Tabernacle »p. 67.

INSIGHT

"Wait" (9:8). This is one of the most difficult of spiritual disciplines, but one of the most important. God does guide us, and we need to find out what the Lord wants rather than make hasty decisions. If we are uncertain, it's best to wait, to pray, and to expect God to lead.

"The alien and the native-born" (9:14). Israel's worship was an expression of a unique covenant relationship that existed between God and the descendants of Abraham, Isaac, and Jacob. Why then is the alien who "wants to" to be permitted to celebrate Passover? Because Passover symbolizes redemption, God's great act of deliverance from a slavery that in its brutal oppression represents the grip of sin on all our lives. God's salvation is available to all humankind.

When and where (9:17). The pillar of cloud told Israel when to set out. And the same verse tells us the cloud told Israel where to camp. Divine guidance is not only a matter of where we are to go, but also a matter of timing. Again we see how important it is to be sensitive to God, and let Him lead us.

"Remembered by the Lord" (10:9). The silver trumpets were for communication within the camp, and also for communication with God. In time of danger, blowing on the trumpets was in effect a prayer for God's help.

"Remembered by the Lord" is a promise of help. In Scripture "remember" is not a word describing a mental process, but a word describing divine action. Thus to say God remembered someone's sin means that He acted to punish those sins. To say God remembered His covenant means He acted on the covenant promises, and came to His people's aid.

There are many special phrases in the Bible that feature "remember." The psalmist is thrilled that God "remembers we are dust" (Ps. 103:14), which means that He considers our weakness, and is merciful rather than judging us as our sins deserve. Perhaps most wonderful of all is the statement in Heb. 8:12 that God forgives our wickedness, and "will remember their sins no more." Because Jesus has paid for our sins, we have no fear of God acting against us. Because of Christ, God is on our side.

"You can be our eyes" (10:31). What a strange thing to say, in view of the fact that God's pillar of cloud told Israel when to go and where to camp. But perhaps it's not strange after all. Moses was a great man, but still just a man. And it is hard to depend completely on God, without resting just a little on human resources. The text reports what Moses said, but there is no hint of criticism here or elsewhere. God does remember our frailty, and in His grace makes allowances for us all.

Chapter summary. On the journey to Sinai (Ex. 16–18) God dealt graciously with Israel's sins. But at Sinai the Israelites were given the divine Law. Now, on the journey away from Sinai, they are held responsible for every act! Thus when the people complain, fire threatens the camp (11:1-3). When the people demand meat, God provides quail—but with them a severe plague (vv. 4-35). When Miriam and Aaron oppose their brother Moses, God strikes Miriam with leprosy (12:1-16). Leaders and the people must learn to obey God, not to rebel against the divine order. We should see these judgments as instruction, and thus unusual expressions of grace. Very soon God will call the whole nation to enter Canaan. If Israel has learned its lesson, and obeys, all will be well.

Outline
Place
Finder

PREPARATION
JOURNEYING
WAITING

Key verse. 11:17: Great leaders want to share responsibility.

Personal application. Don't make these mistakes yourself.

Key concepts. God's anger »p. 65. Prophet »p. 131.

INSIGHT

Manna. The sweet, seedlike particles of manna were the basic food of Israel during its 40 years in the wilderness (see Ex. 16:14-36; Ps. 78:24-31). This bread from heaven that sustained life demonstrated God's daily care for His people, and proved that the Lord was continually with them. Manna had to be gathered daily, and so also symbolized man's need for constant dependence on the Lord. Jesus drew on the rich symbolism of manna in identifying Himself as the true bread, who gives and who sustains spiritual life (John 6:25-59).

The bitter complaints of the Israelites about manna were a rejection of God and of His provision for them. It was this rejection that aroused God's anger, and led to judgment.

Moses' prayer (11:10-15). There is a basic difference between Moses' complaint and that of the people. Moses complained to God. The people complained about God. In going directly to the Lord with his feelings, Moses honored God and demonstrated deep trust in Him. We need to recall this prayer of Moses when we are discouraged or upset. At such times, we too should bring our complaints to the Lord, confident He will act.

"They will help" (11:17). This greatest of O.T. leaders showed no jealousy when God took "of the Spirit that is on you" and empowered a number of the congregation's elders. In fact Moses rebuked Joshua when he was upset (v. 29), and wished all God's people could be so blessed. It is a sign of spiritual insecurity and spiritual immaturity to want to be a congregation's only, or most important, leader. The mature leader is eager to see others develop and

use their spiritual gifts, and is not fearful about losing his position.

Why only Miriam? (12:10) Only Miriam was stricken with leprosy. Some feminists have seen this as an affront; an example of chauvinism in the Bible. Not at all. The reason Aaron was spared had nothing to do with his sex. It was because Aaron was high priest, and according to Lev. 21:10-12, was not allowed to become ceremonially unclean for any reason. The high priest represented the people of Israel to God, and he must always be available to minister in that capacity. So only Miriam was stricken by leprosy, not because she was a woman or because her sin was any worse than Aaron's, but because God in grace refused to deprive His people of the high priest's ministry.

Visions and dreams (12:6). The O.T. mentions several kinds of dreams (*halom*), including the ordinary dream we're familiar with (Job 7:14; Ecc. 5:3). This verse, however, suggests dreams were often used to communicate God's revelations to His prophets. The O.T. mentions different kinds of revelatory dreams. In some God seemed to speak directly (as Gen. 20:3-7; Matt. 2:12-23). In others information was communicated in symbols (as Gen. 40–41; Dan. 2). God even spoke to pagans in dreams, as to Pharaoh (Gen. 40–41) and Nebuchadnezzar (Dan. 2). Are there revelatory dreams today? Not ordinarily. As Heb. says, God who once spoke in dreams has now spoken to us by His Son. We have in Jesus a full and complete revelation of the love, and the will, of God.

Outline
Place
Finder

PREPARATION
JOURNEYING
WAITING

Chapter summary. God has led Israel to the southern border of Canaan. Moses is told to send out spies to explore and report on the Promised Land (13:1-3). He sends one leader from each tribe (vv. 4-20). The spies return laden with evidence of Canaan's fertility—and information (vv. 21-25). The land is rich, but the people there are powerful (vv. 26-29). One of the spies, Caleb, enthusiastically suggests the Israelites attack, but most of the other spies are terrified by the "great size" of the Canaanites, and cry out, "We can't attack."

Key verse. 13:30: "We can do it" remains ever true.

Personal application. It's not the facts, but how we interpret them that counts.

INSIGHT

Illustration. *13:23. Canaan was so fertile in the Exodus era that it took two men to carry a single cluster of grapes.*

Canaan. A man riding a train in Palestine in the 1930s looked at the dry, desolate countryside, and scoffed. "And the Bible calls this a land of milk and honey!"

His fellow passenger looked up. He reached into his bag, drew out a Bible, and opened it to Deut. 28, which predicts the devastation of the land and the people which would surely follow disobedience. The land of Canaan, modern Palestine, is gradually being restored to fruitfulness. But it is not yet the beautiful land that it was in Moses' day. Archeologists have helped us realize what a truly rich land Canaan was. The plains along the Mediterranean were well-watered and fertile. The hills of the mid-second millennium B.C. were wooded and green. Quiet meadows covered with grasses and wildflowers dotted mountain valleys in the central highlands. Up there plateaus were covered with grass, and shepherds led their flocks across the hills in the summer-

time. Though there were a number of city-states in low-lying areas, the population was still sparse in the hills. Crops of all sorts flourished, providing everything an agricultural people might need. The land was rich and beautiful, ready, waiting for its occupation by the people of God. It's no wonder that biblical Canaan has served as a symbol of rest and peace in Christian hymns and poetry and that it serves in Scripture as a symbol of the peace believers experience when they trust fully in the Lord.

Facts, and perspective (13:30-31). Caleb and the other spies possessed the same facts about Canaan and its inhabitants. But their perspective was different. An old chorus sums up the difference. "Others saw the giants. Caleb saw the Lord." We should face difficulties realistically. But most of all we need to remain aware of God, and share Caleb's confidence that "we can certainly do it" with His help.

Chapter summary. Numbers 14 marks a dramatic turning point in the experience of the Exodus generation. The terrified Israelites angrily reject Moses' plea for trust in God, and are ready to kill Moses when God intervenes (14:1-11). Moses begs God not to wipe out the camp (vv. 12-19). Though God relents, that entire generation is doomed to wander in the desert for 40 years, until all over 20 years of age die (vv. 20-35). But the spies whose pessimistic report caused the rebellion are struck down immediately (vv. 36-38). When Moses reports God's verdict, the people refuse to accept it. They rush to attack Canaan in their own strength, and are beaten back (vv. 39-45). The events reported in this crucial Old Testament chapter serve throughout Scripture as a symbol of unbelief and rebellion, and of opportunities lost. What a warning for us, not to let hardness caused by unbelief keep us from responding to God (cf. Heb. 3–4).

Outline
Place
Finder

PREPARATION
JOURNEYING
WAITING

Key verse. 14:24: Following God wholeheartedly brings great reward.

Personal application. Failure to obey God reveals a lack of faith in God.

Key concepts. Unbelief »p. 857. Prayer »p. 181. Forgiveness »p. 357. Glory of God »p. 74.

INSIGHT

Contempt for God (14:11). This underlies the reaction of Israel to the spies' report. The pillar of cloud and the daily gift of manna were proof of God's presence with the Exodus generation, and of His provision for them. Our own fear of the future and pessimism reflect the attitude the Israelites display so clearly (vv. 1-4). These attitudes are possible only if we ignore God's power or question His love, and thus show contempt for the Lord as He has revealed Himself to us.

Moses' prayer (14:13-19). As in earlier prayers, Moses bases his appeal for mercy not on any merit in Israel, but on God's own character. God cannot abandon His people: to abandon them would be to fail in the eyes of others. Besides, the Lord is by nature a God of love and forgiveness, who deals justly, but remembers mercy.

This prayer should comfort us in times of personal failure. God will not abandon us: He has committed Himself to us publicly in the Gospel. Besides, God is loving and merciful. We may be disciplined but we will not be rejected.

"Nevertheless" (14:21). Forgiveness restores harmony in our relationship with God. But forgiveness does not mean we avoid the consequences of our actions. The person who robs a bank can't just say, "Sorry," or "I was converted and now I'm right with God" and expect to get off scot-free. He still must stand trial and serve time in jail. Forgiveness or no, there is a price

to pay for wrongdoing. Our sins, even though God forgives us, have built-in consequences too.

This is what we discover in the judgment God announces. Don't mistake Israel's years of wilderness wanderings as punishment. They are consequences. No generation unable to trust God enough to obey could succeed in conquering the Promised Land. The unbelief and rebellion of the Exodus generation disqualified them as conquerers, even though God forgave their sins.

We Christians are guaranteed forgiveness in Christ. But let's never assume we can sin with impunity. Every sin has consequences, which even the forgiven cannot avoid.

Age of accountability? Theologians have asked when a person becomes accountable for his personal sins. Surely toddlers of 1 or 2 aren't accountable. But what about children of 8 or 11? The Bible does not answer that question. But it's suggestive that it was only those "twenty years and older" who were condemned to die in the wilderness. Apparently God is extremely gracious, and in this case fixed responsibility on only those who were clearly and unmistakably adult.

Caleb and Joshua. No one has to follow the crowd. These two men held fast to the Lord against the crowd, and were blessed. God knows when we take a stand for Him. And He rewards.

Outline
Place
Finder

PREPARATION
JOURNEYING
WAITING

Chapter summary. God gives Moses additional instructions on offerings, to be followed "after you enter the land" (15:1-21). God draws a clear distinction between unintentional sins committed in ignorance (vv. 22-29), and conscious, "defiant" sins (vv. 30-31). Underlining the seriousness of defiant sins, God commands that a Sabbath-breaker be stoned to death by the whole assembly (vv. 32-36), and calls for tassels to be worn on Jews' clothing as ever-present reminders of God's commandments (vv. 37-41). Despite the stoning's grim reminder of the seriousness of sin, rebellion again breaks out. A family of Levites leads a demand that others in the community be given priestly prerogatives, and challenges Moses' leadership (16:1-15). God shows His choice of Moses and Aaron by opening a fissure in the earth that swallows up one group (vv. 16-34), and fire flares from the Lord to consume others who presumed to act as priests (vv. 35-40). But the very next day the community dares to accuse Moses of killing the Lord's people (v. 41). Again only Moses' prayers and Aaron's priestly action avoids complete disaster, though 14,700 of the Israelites die.

Key verse. 15:30: The person who sins defiantly must be cut off.

Personal application. Don't expect to sin willfully and avoid severe consequences.

INSIGHT

"After you enter" (15:2, 18). These instructions to be followed "after you enter" are to be spoken "to the Israelites." Why? To assure them that despite their lapse, God remains committed to them!

Defiant sins (15:30). These are sins committed with a full knowledge of God's will. Israel's refusal to enter Canaan was a defiant sin. So are the other sins in these two chapters: gathering wood on the Sabbath, and demanding priestly prerogatives. Persons who sin defiantly are to be "cut off" from Israel. Here the defiant sinners were executed.

This should not lead us to the conclusion that Christians who sin willfully can be lost. Lev. 16 reminds us that the sacrifice offered by the high priest on the Day of Atonement covered "all sins." These incidents instead drive home the point that willful sin cannot be tolerated in a believing community.

The Sabbath-breaker (15:32-36). The "whole assembly" was told to stone the Sabbath-breaker. Each individual is responsible to keep the community pure and holy.

Tassels. The tassels attached to clothing were more than reminders of God's Law. The blue thread suggested that each person had priestly responsibility for the purity of the camp, for the high priest's clothing was of blue (cf. Ex. 39:22).

Moses' leadership challenged. Truth can be applied—and misapplied. Here the truth that all God's people are holy, and that the Lord is with each individual, is taken to imply that Moses' leadership is flawed. Today all believers have spiritual gifts. Yet God still appoints leaders who are to be honored, especially when they are godly individuals.

Treating God with contempt (16:30). This phrase from Num. 14 appears again here. It means to know what God's will is—and willfully refuse to abide by it. Korah did not rebel against Moses, but against the divine order laid down in Law concerning the priesthood.

"You have killed the Lord's people" (16:41). Every spiritual leader knows that ridiculous charges are sometimes made against him, and that the most foolish rumors are frequently repeated. It should be a comfort to see the same thing happen to Moses. Moses killed the Lord's people? It was obviously God who made the ground open up, and God whose fire burned the 250 who wanted to be priests. The spiritually blind and insensitive will always misinterpret the work of God, and lay foolish charges against God's own. We can ignore them. If they do harm, God will judge them in His time.

Chapter summary. With Korah's rebellion put down, God acts to confirm His call of Aaron's family alone to the priesthood. Leaders of each tribe and Aaron, representing the tribe of Levi, lay a staff before the Lord. Overnight Aaron's staff buds, and bears fruit (17:1-13).

Outline
Place
Finder

PREPARATION
JOURNEYING
WAITING

With the privileged role of the priests and Levites established, Moses gives Aaron instructions about the care of the sanctuary (18:1-7), and the Lord instructs Moses concerning the tithe that the other tribes are to pay for the Levites support in the Promised Land (vv. 8-32).

Key verse. 18:7: Serving God is a privilege, not a chore.

Personal application. Serve God cheerfully in whatever place He gives you, aware that the opportunity to serve is a wonderful gift.

Key concepts. Priesthood »pp. 81, 858. Offerings »p. 78.

INSIGHT

Tithing. Num. 18 mentions the tithe which was paid to the Levites and priests, and used, along with food from various freewill offerings, for their support. The subject of tithing is less clear than it may seem.

Lev. 27:30-33 says that a tenth of all that the land produces is to be "holy to the Lord." The underlying concept is that the tithe is "rent" which Israel owes to God for the use of His land. Num. 18 tells us that the tithe was to be used to maintain the Levites, who would receive no tribal lands when Canaan was conquered. Deut. 12:5-14 and 14:22-26 announce that tithes are to be brought to a central sanctuary, to be established in Canaan. These passages also introduce another tithe: 10 percent which was to be collected every third year and stored locally. This tithe was to be distributed to the poor and needy. Thus there were at least two tithes collected in Israel: one annual tithe, and an extra tithe every third year.

Those who tithed not only kept a divine commandment, they also expressed confidence in God's ability to provide for them. As God said through Malachi centuries later, calling on His people to obey the law of the tithe, "See if I will not throw open the floodgates of heaven, and pour out so much blessing that you will not have room enough for it" (3:10).

The tithe was owed God, as rent for the property each family lived on in the Promised Land. But it is important to remember that the godly Jew went beyond the tithe in expressing gratitude to God. A number of the offerings described in Lev. 1–5 are freewill offerings: voluntary gifts, contributed gladly out of a sense of love and not of duty.

No N.T. passage imposes the tithe as an obligation on Christians. There the principles that are to guide our giving are rooted in the concept underlying the O.T.'s freewill offerings, not the concept of the tithe. »p. 781.

Outline
Place
Finder

PREPARATION
JOURNEYING
WAITING

Chapter summary. Death now stalks all the Israelites, for the years of wandering are nearly over. Moses reminds Israel that touching a dead body brings uncleanness. But the ashes of a special sacrifice, mixed in water, provides ceremonial cleansing (19:1-22). Moses himself is affected by the stress of his constant struggle with his rebellious people. When water runs out, Moses disobeys God. Rather than speak to a rock from which water poured earlier (cf. Ex. 17:1-7), Moses strikes the rock with his rod (Num. 20:1-11). Even Moses must bear the consequences of disobedience. He will not live to bring God's people into the Promised Land (vv. 12-13). The Moabites refuse Israel access to the direct route to Canaan (vv. 14-21), and shortly afterward Aaron, Moses' brother and Israel's high priest, dies (vv. 22-29).

Key verse. 20:12: Any act of disobedience indicates a lack of trust in God.

Personal application. Let nothing distract you from the path of obedience.

Key concept. Uncleanness »p. 82.

INSIGHT

The red heifer (Num. 19). The passage does not describe a sacrifice. The animal is killed and burned (*sarap*) outside the camp, not by the altar (cf. Lev. 1–4). The Heb. word is used only of nonsacrificial burning. Also here only the blood is burned, and other materials associated with cleansing (cf. 14:4; Ps. 51:7) are added. The whole purpose is to produce ashes to be mixed with water that will symbolize cleansing, and further drive home to Israel the necessity of being ceremonially clean when approaching God.

Travel narratives. This chapter introduces a third and last travel narrative. Israel moved from the Red Sea to Sinai (Ex. 13–19), and from Sinai to Kadesh (Num. 11–12). This one brings us from Kadesh to the plains across the Jordan from Canaan (Num. 20–21). The first journey began with victory over Egypt, and ended with a hostile and disgruntled Israel camped at Sinai. The second began with divine leading, but ends in rebellion at Kadesh Barnea (Num. 14). This one begins on the dark note of death, but ends with glorious victories over powerful enemies! The destiny of the new generation of Israelites is very different from that of the first.

Moses' disobedience (20:1-13). What did Moses do? God told him to bring his rod and speak to the rock. Instead Moses spoke (angrily) to the people, and hit the rock with his rod. Verse 12 calls this a lack of trust. Why? Because "faith" or "trust" is essentially an appropriate response to God's Word, whether that response is to claim a divine promise, or obey a divine command. Moses did not obey, and thus his response was as much unbelief as was the people's earlier refusal to enter Canaan! (Num. 14) Thus too the punishment was the same: Moses, like the rest of the Exodus generation's adults, would die before God's people entered the Promised Land.

Striking the rock. Some see symbolic significance in God's command to speak to rather than strike the rock. They believe the rock represents Christ (cf. 1 Cor. 10:4). Christ was struck with death one time only, for that was sufficient to provide salvation. For Moses to strike the rock again was to symbolically question the sufficiency of Christ's one sacrifice.

Edom. The Edomites were descended from Esau, and thus were closely related to the Israelites, who were offspring of Esau's brother, Jacob. Despite Israel's unwillingness to battle these close relatives (cf. Num. 20:14-21; Jud. 11:17-18), later Edomites were persistently hostile to Israel. The prophets predicted that God would judge Edom for its hostility toward Israel (Jer. 49:7-22; Ezek. 25:12-14; Joel 3:19; Amos 9:12; Obad.).

"The king's highway" (20:17). This major trade route, that served the ancient world for millenniums, ran through Moabite territory.

"Gathered to his people" (20:26). This beautiful image of death is found frequently in the O.T. (cf. Gen. 25:8, 17; 35:29; 49:33; Num. 31:2). It suggests an early conviction that death is not the end, but that when a person dies he or she is reunited with other members of his family.

Chapter summary. The chapter marks the end of the journeys of the Israelites. Soon the last of the rebellious generation will be gone, and the victorious note sounded in this chapter will swell to become a symphony of triumph. We sense the future in the Israelites' victory over Arad (21:1-3), and see remnants of the past in the grumbling that moved God to send poisonous serpents among His people (vv. 4-9). But the sound of victory swells even louder, as Israel moves on toward Canaan, and defeats the people of Ammon and Bashon (vv. 10-35).

Outline
Place
Finder

PREPARATION
JOURNEYING
WAITING

Key verse. 21:34: Fear is an enemy that denies us victory.

Personal application. Concentrate on what God has done for you in the past, and you will not shrink from future challenges.

INSIGHT

Illustration. *Where the* KJV *reads "fiery serpents" the Aramaic O.T. has* kwawatha kharmaney, *the cockatrice. These shiny reddish colored snakes are extremely poisonous and aggressive as well. During the First World War the British army had many problems with these snakes, in the same area the ancient Israelites were passing through.*

Interestingly, a copper serpent has been found by archeologists in a Midianite worship center dating from at least 1150 B.C.

Total destruction (21:2). The theme of total destruction is sounded frequently in the story of the Conquest of Canaan. This was ordained by God as a punishment for the gross immorality and idolatry practiced by the Canaanites, and to protect the Israelites from corruption.

Look and live (21:4-9). Jesus drew an analogy between His cross and the bronze snake Moses raised on a pole (cf. John 3:14-15). The link between these two events is expressed in verse 15. The person who believed God's Word enough to look to the source of healing was saved.

The secret of the healing power of the bronze snake lay not in magic but in faith. Just as the secret of our appropriation of the healing power of Jesus lies in believing God's Word about the meaning of Christ's death.

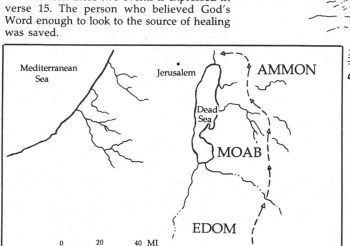

The map shows the final stages of Israel's journey. The people are now camped across the Jordan River from Canaan, in the territory of the defeated Ammonites.

Outline
Place
Finder

PREPARATION
JOURNEYING
WAITING

Chapter summary. Israel's military success terrifies the Moabites. King Balak and the Midianites hire Balaam, a seer with a reputation for supernatural powers, to curse Israel (22:1-7). Balaam is told by God not to respond to Balak's summons (vv. 8-13). But when Balak promises Balaam great wealth, Balaam asks again, and is given permission to go (vv. 14-20). On the way Balaam's donkey sees an invisible angel waiting to kill Balaam, and balks (vv. 21-27). The donkey is given the power of speech, and Balaam is suddenly able to see the angel standing there with drawn sword (vv. 28-34). Balaam is warned again to speak only what God tells him to say, and continues on to meet Balak (vv. 35-41).

Key verse. 22:19: When we already know what God's will is, it is wrong to go back to see "what else" He may say.

Personal application. Don't let your prayers deteriorate into asking God for permission to do something you already know is not His will.

INSIGHT

Balaam. Num. makes no editorial comments about Balaam. Some have noted he sought God's instruction (22:8, 19) and his pious remarks about speaking only what God told him (vv. 18, 38), and assumed he was a true prophet. Contradicting this view, the N.T. pictures Balaam as a greedy person who "loved the wages of wickedness" (2 Peter 2:15). A good indicator of Balaam's true character is seen in the advice he gave Balak after his attempts to curse Israel failed. The Midianites followed that advice, and set young women to seduce Israelite men into sexual adventures and idolatry, assuming that if Israel could be corrupted, God Himself would curse His people (cf. 31:16).

Against this background, we can see Balaam's pious talk for what it is: an attempt to impress others with his supposed special spiritual powers. His frequent references to money can be understood not as a rejection of wealth, but as a sly attempt to inflate the price of his services!

Watch out for people like Balaam.

God spoke through a donkey too (22:21-30). Some argue that Balaam must have been a pious person, because God did speak through him. The incident with Balaam's donkey reminds us that God can speak even through an ass! Other passages teach us the same truth. God even spoke through Caiaphas, the high priest who was Christ's active enemy, when Caiaphas uttered a prophetic statement about the meaning of Jesus' death (John 11:50-52). Being used by God is not proof of personal holiness.

Balaam's curse (22:6). Balak wanted Balaam to "put a curse on Israel." The word for curse here is 'arar. In pagan thought this curse had the magical ability to render an enemy powerless. Balak was hoping that Balaam would be able through magic to neutralize Israel's military might, and thus permit the Midianites to defeat them. The mention of "divination" (v. 7) and "sorcery" (24:1) tell us that Balaam's basic reliance was not on God, but on occult powers to which he appealed. Deut. 18 makes it clear that any appeal to the occult is "detestable" to the Lord.

God's directive and permissive will (22:12, 20). When Balak's representatives first appeared, God very clearly told Balaam, "Do not go with them." This was God's directive will: what He instructed Balaam to do. When Balaam went back to see "what else" God would say when the second delegation came, Balaam was permitted to go with them.

The problem here is, of course, that Balaam's second appeal was in essence a request for God to change His mind! Balaam knew God's directive will. He simply did not want to obey it.

You and I are often in Balaam's situation. We know what God wants. But we want something else so badly that we keep going back to the Lord, asking Him to change His mind. Later, when things go wrong, we're likely to say as Balaam did after being warned by the donkey, "I did not realize" (v. 34). But this is the worst kind of lie—a lie we tell ourselves. Down deep we knew all along what God really wanted us to do!

Let's learn from Balaam not to deceive ourselves, and to choose God's directive will, rather than settle merely for permission.

Chapter summary. Balaam calls for multiple sacrifices and appeals to God to curse Israel (23:1-5). But Balaam is forced to pronounce an oracle of blessing, not a curse (v. 10). Balak is furious, for instead of weakening Israel by a curse, Balaam had strengthened his enemy with the blessing (vv. 11-12). Balaam tries to work his sorcery a second (vv. 13-26) and a third time (vv. 27-30)—with the same results.

Now Balaam gives up, but at the sight of the Israelite camp spread across the plain, he is moved by God's Spirit to utter yet another blessing (24:1-9). At this Balak can no longer contain his anger, and orders Balaam to go home (vv. 10-14). Before he goes, however, Balaam utters a final prediction that includes one of the O.T.'s earliest predictions of the Messiah (vv. 15-19), and warns of the devastation to strike Israel's enemies (vv. 20-25).

Outline
Place
Finder

PREPARATION
JOURNEYING
WAITING

Key verse. 23:21: We are protected by the presence of God.

Personal application. God is fully capable of protecting His own from those who are eager to do us harm.

Key concepts. Blessing »p. 127. Curse »p. 138. Messiah »p. 350.

INSIGHT

Seven altars (23:1-2). A Babylon tablet tells of the same ritual described here. It was used by diviners, who used magic in an attempt to learn or shape the future. Thus Balaam's actions clearly have roots in pagan religion.

Oracle. The Heb. term, *ne'um,* means "an utterance." It is used when God is the originator of the message, and stresses divine origin and authority. God used the hostile Balaam to deliver His own message of blessing on the nation of Israel.

"He has blessed" (23:19-20). The ancient pagans saw offerings as bribes; attempts to manipulate their gods and goddesses. This explains the persistent attempts of Balak and Balaam to win God over by repeating the multiple sacrifices. God announces through Balaam that He cannot be manipulated. Unlike a human being, He does not change His mind once He has made a promise, or speak and fail to act. What an important truth for us to remember. God has made a commitment to us in Jesus, and nothing—no one—can move Him to go back on His word.

"No misfortune" (23:21-22). In the second oracle Balaam identifies the source of Israel's blessing. It is the living presence of God Himself among them. When others attack God's people, they attack God! And no one can prevail against Him.

Blessed, and cursed (24:9). Balaam's third attempt to curse Israel again turns into a blessing. Verse 9 is an obvious reference to the original Abrahamic Covenant (Gen. 12:1-3). God continues to bless those who bless His people, and condemn those who curse them.

"A star will come out of Jacob" (24:17). This reference to a coming royal Person has been taken as a reference to Jesus, based on Revelation 22:16. Some believe that it is the verse that led the magi of N.T. times to realize that the star of Bethlehem indicated the Christ Child's birth (cf. Matt. 2:2).

"Amalek" (24:20). The Amalakites were a people of the Sinai who were utterly hostile to Israel (cf. Ex. 17:8-16; Num. 14:43-45; Jud. 6:3, 33). They were defeated by both Saul and David (1 Sam. 15:18; 30:17), but were not wiped out until the time of Hezekiah (1 Chron. 4:43).

Kenites. This people, linked to Moses by marriage (Jud. 1:16; 4:11) remained friendly to Israel. In the end they would be subdued by the neighboring Israelite tribe of Asher. Thus both hostile and friendly peoples would ultimately submit to Israel, the people who have God as their King.

Outline
Place
Finder

PREPARATION
JOURNEYING
WAITING

Chapter summary. This chapter records the last act of rebellion of the generation that left bondage in Egypt some 40 years before. Balaam had tried unsuccessfully to curse Israel (Num. 23–24). But before he returned home he advised Balak to corrupt Israel, so that God would curse them Himself (cf. 31:16). So Balak set young women to seduce the Israelites and lead them into idolatry (25:1-3). God commanded that all who joined in this apostasy be killed (vv. 4-5). When an Israelite openly brought a Midianite woman into the camp, Phinehas, a priest, executed them both, stopping a plague that killed some 24,000 (vv. 6-9). Phinehas was rewarded for his zeal (vv. 10-13), and Israel was told to view the Midianites as enemies (vv. 16-17).

Key verse. 25:11: Caring about God's honor wins rewards.

Personal application. We remain vulnerable to sin, even as we near the end of life's journey.

Key concepts. Idolatry »p. 433. Adultery »pp. 64, 85. Priest »p. 81.

INSIGHT

A turning point. This chapter serves as a turning point in the Exodus narrative. Up to this time, the Israelites have been dominated by the generation that left Egypt. The sexual immorality and spiritual corruption described here sum up the unbelief, the rebelliousness, the perverse unwillingness to trust or obey God, that has marked this generation from the first. There was no way that God could bring such a people into the Promised Land, or bless them as He yearned to do.

But the very next chapter, which begins "after the plague" (26:1), tells us that "not one" adult of that first generation, except the faithful Caleb and Joshua, was still alive (v. 65). Chapter 25 is a tombstone, engraved with the last sin of a rebellious generation. From now on, we will see a marked spirit of obedience dominating God's people. And we will see this, the new generation, claim by obedience blessings the first generation never knew.

Baal of Peor. Baal means "owner," or "master," and in paganism, "god." Pagan deities were thought to own territory they controlled, thus the god of Peor was worshiped in Peor as the controlling deity of that locality. How different from our God, who created the entire universe, who fills it, and who is in control of all things, everywhere.

"Expose them in broad daylight" (25:4). When sins are exposed, and punishment is public, other members of the community are warned, and God is honored as holy. Those who think they protect God's reputation by covering up the sins of Christian leaders are wrong.

"Each of you" (25:5). It's easy, when we know wrongdoing is taking place, to say "Why doesn't somebody do something?" This verse reminds us we are the somebody God expects to act. The purity of the believing community is the responsibility of "each of you."

"Zeal" (25:11). The Heb. *qana'* is an intense love, an emotion that involves a high level of commitment. It was thus an intense concern for the honor of God, and commitment to Him, that moved Phinehas to kill the man who openly brought the Midianite woman into his tent for sex. The killing was not, however, a personal killing, but the judicial act of a priest commissioned to maintain the holiness of God's O.T. people. Phinehas' action stopped a plague that killed thousands, and won his family a secure future in the priesthood. Care intensely about God's honor, and God will honor you.

"Zimri" (25:14). The text identifies Zimri as "the leader of a Simeonite family." As family leadership in Israel was inherited by the oldest living family member, Zimri must have been a member of the first Exodus generation. His act reflects that generation's contempt for God, and his death reflects its fate.

108

Chapter summary. As the Israelites wait for word to conquer Canaan, Moses takes a second military census. He finds that all adult members of the Exodus generation except Caleb and Joshua have died, and that the new generation can field nearly as many fighting men as the old (26:1-65). There has been no loss in numbers, and an immeasurable growth in morale!

While still waiting, five daughters of a man named Zelophehad raise an important question about the inheritance rights of women (27:1-11). The way this question is resolved suggests how much of Old Testament case law developed.

Finally, God tells Moses that he will soon die, and has him appoint Joshua the leader of Israel in his place (vv. 12-23).

Outline
Place
Finder

PREPARATION
JOURNEYING
WAITING

Key verse. 26:51: We lose nothing through waiting.

Personal application. Every Christian is counted with this second, faithful generation—or the first, untrusting one.

Key concepts. Women »p. 394. Laying on hands »p. 836.

INSIGHT

Census results. Num. reports two censuses, taken 40 years apart. The total count is quite close, some 603,550 in the first Exodus generation compared to 601,730 in the second. However, larger population shifts are shown within tribes, very likely reflecting which tribes' members were more faithful during the journey from Sinai to Canaan.

Tribe	First Census	Second Census
Reuben	46,500	43,730
Simeon	59,300	22,200
Gad	45,650	40,500
Judah	74,600	76,500
Issachar	54,400	64,300
Zebulun	57,400	60,500
Ephraim	40,500	32,500
Manasseh	32,200	52,700
Benjamin	35,400	45,600
Dan	62,700	64,400
Asher	41,500	53,400
Naphtali	53,400	45,400
Levi	22,000	23,000

Each tribe's allotment of land depended on the numbers established in this census. You and I may be unfaithful in our relationship with God, and it will not diminish the strength of His army. But it will diminish the size of our inheritance.

Zelophehad's daughters (27:1-4). Normally daughters received their share of the family estate in the form of a dowry given them when they married. Sons later divided the estate on the death of the father. Because of the dowry, O.T. inheritance laws did not actually discriminate against women. They were given their share of the father's estate when they left home, and after marriage became members of the husband's family.

Making law. The story of Zelophehad's daughters illustrates how O.T. law was made. Here was a case where no precedent existed. The problem was taken to Moses, who inquired of God for a ruling. The ruling given by the Lord then served as a precedent for judges to use in settling other, similar cases. For other examples of this process, see Num. 15:32-36; Lev. 24:10-23.

"Joshua" (27:12-23). Joshua will succeed Moses, but not replace him! Joshua has been Moses' assistant from the beginning (cf. Ex. 17:9; 24:13; 32:17; Num. 11:28). Now God tells Moses to appoint Joshua as his successor and "give him some of your authority" (27:20). That "some" is important. God spoke to Moses face-to-face, and granted him the power to work miracles. Joshua will seek God's will by going to the high priest, and using the Urim and Thummim (cf. Ex. 28:30). He will be guided by the sacred lot, not face-to-face communication. And though Joshua will see Jericho's walls fall down, he will perform no personal miracles as Moses did. Yet Joshua, not Moses, will lead the Israelites to victory in Canaan.

We can rejoice in any leadership role we may be given. We need not envy others with greater prominence or authority. All we need to do is be available to God, and let Him use us as He will.

Outline
Place
Finder

PREPARATION
JOURNEYING
WAITING

Chapter summary. Moses is told to remind the Israelites again of the regular offerings they are to make, and of the offerings to be made on special religious holidays (Num. 28–29). These instructions confirm God's intention to bring His people into the land that lies just across the Jordan. God will bring His people to their new home, for they must worship Him there.

What a parallel to our own experience. We can worship the Lord on our spiritual journey, here and now. But we know that God will bring us safely to Him at life's end, and that we will worship Him perfectly in heaven.

Key verse. 28:2: We must not neglect worship.

Personal application. Worship is to be both regular and special!

Key concepts. Festivals »p. 89. Offerings »p. 78.

INSIGHT

Offerings. The material here duplicates regulations found in other passages, such as Ex. 29 and Lev. 23. But the thrust here is unique. These chapters identify offerings to be made through the course of a year for the nation as a whole. Other passages speak of individual sacrifices, but these are the required national offerings. Again, they are given here during Israel's waiting time as an encourager of faith. God will bring His people into the land, and they will worship Him there, year after year after year.

How many? If we total the required offerings, we find that the yearly national offerings must include 113 bulls, 32 rams, and 1,086 lambs, plus over a ton of flour and about 1,000 containers of oil and wine. And this is in addition to the offerings to be made by leaders and individuals! What this means is that God will not only bring Israel into Canaan, but will also make them so prosperous that they will have plenty from which to make offerings to the Lord.

Worship. The English word "worship" comes from the Saxon "worth-ship," meaning worthy of worship. Several biblical words are translated worship. In the O.T., *sahah* means to fall prostrate out of respect, and *'asab* means to serve. This last word is associated with the priests' and Levites' work at the tabernacle, and later the temple. The N.T. parallel term is *latreuo*, which is the worshipful service a Christian expresses by praise and a holy life.

The most common N.T. word for worship is *prokyneo*, which means to bow down to. A study of this word's 60 appearances in the N.T. shows that worship is always to be directed to God, and that both public and private expressions of devotion and praise fall into this category.

Undoubtedly the most powerful images of worship in Scripture are found in the Psalms, but even more so in the Book of Revelation. Here we sense the awe of the believer as every capacity is focused on God and who He is. Here too we sense the true meaning of worship, as praise and adoration of God for who He by His very nature is:

You are worthy, our Lord and God,
>to receive glory and honor and power,
>>for You created all things,
and by Your will they were created
>and have their being (4:11).

>Praise and glory
and wisdom and thanks and honor
>and power and strength
be to our God forever and ever.
>Amen! (7:12)

It is this spirit of worship that was to be expressed in the festivals of the O.T. It is this spirit of worship that is to be expressed in our churches, and in our hearts.

Chapter summary. The long years of wandering are nearly over, and Israel is about to engage in a struggle for the Promised Land. Moses may very well have brought up the question of vows here, especially vows made by women, because many women would feel pressure to make vows in hope God would protect their loved ones in battle (30:1-16).

Immediately after, God sends a small army of 12,000 to battle the much larger Midianite forces (31:1-6). They wiped out the Midianites, and killed Balaam as well (cf. Num. 22–24). The Midianite women who had seduced the Israelites at Peor were also killed (31:7-24), and the spoil was divided between the fighting men and the rest of the community (vv. 25-48). This victory was won without the loss of a single Israelite. In thanksgiving, the soldiers dedicated to God their share of the gold taken, some 420 pounds (vv. 49-54). This total victory over the Midianites, won with only a small force, was clear and powerful evidence that God was on the side of His people.

Key verses. 31:49-50: It's appropriate to thank God.

Personal application. God helps those He calls.

Key concepts. Vows »p. 96. War »p. 133. Extermination »p. 66.

INSIGHT

Vows. A vow typically involved promising to give something to God, or promising not to do something. Either might have an economic impact on the family, and so the husband and father, who was responsible for the family's well-being, had the right to override vows made by a wife or daughter.

"He confirms them by saying nothing" (30:14). This principle has found its way into English law, so that if someone remains silent about something he or she is assumed to consent to it. The spiritual principle is even more important, however. If we know of something wrong, we are to speak up about it. We can't give assent to sin by saying nothing about it.

"Phinehas" (31:6). In Israel, priests accompanied the army to encourage the soldiers. Phinehas, who had been so zealous for God when an Israelite dared bring a Midianite woman into the camp (25:10-13), was a good choice for chaplain! The silver trumpets mentioned here were used to call God to the aid of His people (10:1-10).

"Balaam" (31:8, 16). Balaam had wanted money from Balak, and he got it. Not for cursing Israel, but for devising the plan to corrupt them. He had very little time to enjoy his new wealth! He was killed along with the Midianites.

Unclean (31:19-24). There was nothing morally wrong in killing the Midianites, who had

clearly demonstrated their hostility to God and His people. The touching of any dead body, however, made an Israelite ceremonially unclean, and he or she must be purified before appearing at the tabernacle to worship the Lord. See Deut. 20, »p. 133.

"Not one is missing" (31:49). Some commentators take this as "an obvious indication of the unrealistic character of the story." But it was not "unrealistic" for God to give His people just this kind of encouragement before leading them to battle in Canaan itself. God is gracious, as well as all-powerful. What could have served better to strengthen the faith of the Israelites for the struggle ahead than this amazing evidence of God's grace and His power.

Why should the soldiers donate gold as "an atonement"? (31:48-50) The word *atone* means "to cover," and it is used in the O.T. of covering men's sins, as well as when dedicating objects or persons to God. The context here suggests that the motive for the gold offering was gratitude: no Israelite soldier lost his life. Yet the soldiers had made serious mistakes, especially in permitting the women who corrupted Israel on the plains of Moab to live. The gold offering was an atonement, in that it recognized both the guilt of the offerer and the grace of God, and expressed thanks to Him for that grace.

Outline
Place
Finder

PREPARATION
JOURNEYING
WAITING

Chapter summary. After the war with Moab and the Midianites two tribes appeal to Moses to let them occupy the conquered lands east of the Jordan (32:1-5). Moses is upset, fearing that their motives are wrong, and that God will punish Israel as He did when their fathers rebelled 40 years earlier at Kadesh (vv. 6-15). But when the Reubenites and Gadites volunteer to send every man to fight with the other tribes for Canaan, Moses' fears are relieved. And he gives them the Transjordan lands they requested (vv. 16-30). So Reuben and Gad, joined by Manasseh, settle their families and herds in the Transjordan, in preparation for the invasion of Canaan.

Key verse. 32:17: The two tribes' commitment is complete.

Personal application. We should not sit back comfortably while brothers and sisters fight spiritual battles alone.

INSIGHT

Cause and effect (32:15). The Bible assumes that moral principles govern events on earth. God is the ultimate, though often the indirect, cause of events in history, and in our personal lives. Because we human beings have freedom to make moral choices, we too have a causal impact on what happens. Thus Moses warns that "if you turn away from following [God] . . . you will be the cause of their destruction." The choices made by that generation have the power to shape history, for God will act according to the righteousness or unrighteousness of those choices. Moderns view cause and effect in mechanical, rather than moral perspective. Israel was weak in the time of the Judges because the Philistines had iron and Israel didn't. The Bible, however, teaches that Israel was weak because the people abandoned God and their law, and tells the story of a national resurgence under the godly David—in spite of the iron technology of the Philistines! What a lesson for us to remember. We do live in a moral universe. And the moral choices a person makes are the primary human cause of events, for a moral God shapes history according to His righteousness and His ends.

"We are ready" (32:17). The literal meaning of the Heb. translated "ready" is "hurrying." The rest of the verse is stunning, for the Transjordan tribes volunteered to "go before" the rest of the Israelites. That is, they were ready to be in the first wave of the attack, and take the highest number of casualties!

Was the request right? Christians debate whether the request of these tribes for land outside of Canaan was in God's will. Some say these tribes symbolize materialistic Christians. Calvin emphasized the fact their request enlarged the land possessed by God's people.

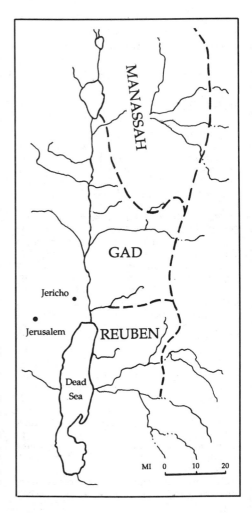

Chapter summary. For a moment Moses looks back, and lists the stopping places of the Israelites on their long journey to Canaan (33:1-49). But then God directs the attention of His people ahead, to the coming Conquest. When Israel invades, the symbols of pagan religion are to be destroyed, the land is to be divided by lot, and the present inhabitants driven out (vv. 50-56). God carefully defines the boundaries of Canaan, which nine and a half tribes will inherit (34:1-15). Finally God selects the leaders who will supervise the casting of lots for the distribution of tribal territories to clans and families (vv. 16-29). There is no question here of "if we win the land." Israel is to prepare for victory, for with God's help, victory is assured.

Outline
Place
Finder

PREPARATION
JOURNEYING
WAITING

Key verse. 33:54: We are to take possession of what God gives us.

Personal application. Don't miss God's blessings by failing to reach out and by faith take what He promises.

INSIGHT

Stages in the journey (33:1-49). Forty-two places are listed, in six groups of seven. Most locations are unknown, as place names survive only when the site is settled continuously. Most of these are unmarked sites in the wilderness. Many have sought spiritual significance by comparing the groups of seven. The thrust of the list, however, is to remind Israel that God directed each step of the journey, and had brought them to the camp they now occupied, ready to conquer Canaan.

What happened at these sites? Here are passages that report events at several of the listed sites:

vv. 3-5	Ex. 12:37	v. 17	Num. 11:35
v. 6	Ex. 13:20	vv. 31-33	Deut. 10:6-7
vv. 7-8	Ex. 14:2ff	v. 36	Num. 20:1
v. 8	Ex. 15:22ff	vv. 37-39	Num. 20:22ff
v. 9	Ex. 15:27	v. 40	Num. 21:1-3
vv. 10-12	Ex. 16:1	v. 41	Num. 21:4
v. 14	Ex. 17:1	v. 43	Num. 21:10
v. 15	Ex. 19:2	v. 44	Num. 21:11

"High places" (33:52). Pagan peoples in the biblical world chose hilltop sites for worship. In cities, they typically used a raised platform. Thus the "high places" mentioned so frequently in the O.T. are outdoor worship centers, where the rites practiced frequently involved immorality.

Typically these centers featured altars, where sacrifices or incense were burned, and symbolic stone pillars and wooden poles, as well as idols and various equipment like censors, bowls, and tongs.

As this chapter states, God commanded the Israelites to demolish the Canaanite high places. Sacrifice and worship in Israel was to be conducted only at the central worship center—now the tabernacle, and later the temple built by Solomon. But in times of religious apostasy, Israel worshiped at local high places. While some worshiped the Lord at such sites (cf. 1 Sam. 9:12-27; 2 Chron. 33:17), more often the Israelites worshiped pagan deities (cf. Jud. 6:25-28; 2 Kings 23:13). The command to desecrate all cult centers in Canaan was intended to protect God's people from the temptation to take part in pagan worship.

The Israelites did in fact succumb to temptation, and centuries later were driven from the Promised Land. Thus God did "do to you" what He planned to do to the original Canaanites: drive them from the land because of gross sin.

Take the gift (33:53). The command, "take possession" really does go with the statement, "I have given." We can do nothing to earn salvation, yet we must take the gift God has provided in Christ. It's the same with other things in the spiritual life. Did God give Israel the Promised Land? Yes, but they had to fight for it. Will God take care of us and meet our needs? Yes, but we need to work at the job He provides. Has God given us spouses to love? Yes, but we must work at enriching the relationship. Acting on God's promises, reaching out to possess what He has given us, is an act of faith. To sit, wait, and expect God to drop things in our laps, is unbelief, and will never be rewarded.

Boundaries of Canaan. See map on page 153.

113

Outline
Place
Finder

PREPARATION
JOURNEYING
WAITING

Chapter summary. Moses continues laying down principles for the occupation of Canaan. He has spoken about driving out the Canaanites (33:50-56), defined the boundaries of Canaan (34:1-15), and selected men to supervise distribution (vv. 16-29). Now Moses sets aside 48 towns for the Levites within the other tribes' territories (35:1-8). He establishes "cities of refuge," and rules for dealing with homicide, so the Promised Land will not be defiled by blood guilt (vv. 9-34). This chapter thus becomes a key to understanding the Old Testament's outlook on murder and capital punishment. Finally, Moses rules that the land of one tribe must not be transferred to another: tribal and family lands are to be held by the original owners forever. The time of waiting is nearing its end. The time has not been wasted. It has been used to plan ahead for the occupation of Canaan, which must surely come.

Key verse. 35:33: A human life has no price tag.

Personal application. We must be committed to affirming the value of human life—but in the way God has ordained.

INSIGHT

Levitical towns (35:1-8). The 48 towns to be given the Levites were scattered throughout the territories of the other tribes. How significant! As God's servants, the Levites shared teaching duties with the priests. No tribe in Israel was to be without its teachers, so that all might know the Law of the Lord.

"Cities of refuge" (35:9-15). The cities of refuge (the levitical towns indicated by a star on the map) were placed so that no Israelite would be more than a day's journey from sanctuary. God has ordained that murderers be punished, but that no one be punished until his guilt or innocence can be established.

Capital punishment (35:31). In other ancient cultures a murderer could avoid another penalty by paying a ransom to the victim's family. The Koran (2:173-174) permits this even when a killing is premeditated! The O.T., however, says, "Do not accept a ransom for the life of a murderer, who deserves to die. He must surely be put to death."

The rationale for this ruling is rooted in the O.T.'s vision of man's nature. God made human beings in His own image and likeness. This makes each individual not only special, but makes his or her life of ultimate value. The demand for capital punishment in the case of murder is intended to uphold the value of life. Only a society which requires the murderer be put to death shows a proper respect for the sanctity of human life.

Manslaughter (35:22-25). The Heb. word *rasah* means a personal killing, but includes what we would call premeditated murder, manslaughter, and even accidental homicides.

This passage makes it clear that God expects His people to examine intent in the case of a homicide. Killings involving hostility are to be treated very differently than those which are the result of accidents. The passage makes it very clear that hostile intent must be established by witnesses before anyone can be put to death, and that it is necessary to have more than one witness (v. 30).

Both kinds of *rasah* pollute the land (cause it to become unclean, and thus unacceptable to God). So both call for atonement. But only the murderer, who kills with hostile intent, is to be executed. The person who kills accidentally is permitted to live untouched in a city of refuge until the natural death of the current high priest.

"The avenger of blood" (35:25). There was no police force in ancient Israel. A close relative thus became responsible to serve as the "avenger of blood," and execute the divine sentence on a murderer. The cities of refuge were necessary, lest an angry relative take revenge on a person who killed a loved one inadvertently. This wise and humane system not only protected the innocent, but also secured Israel from the dangerous rounds of blood feuds common in many societies.

"Zelophehad's daughters" (36:1-13). An earlier ruling gave the five daughers of Zelophehad the right to inherit their father's lands, as he had no male offspring (cf. Num. 27). The additional ruling found here required them to marry within their own tribe, so that tribal lands would not be transferred out of the family.

LEVITICAL CITIES OF REFUGE

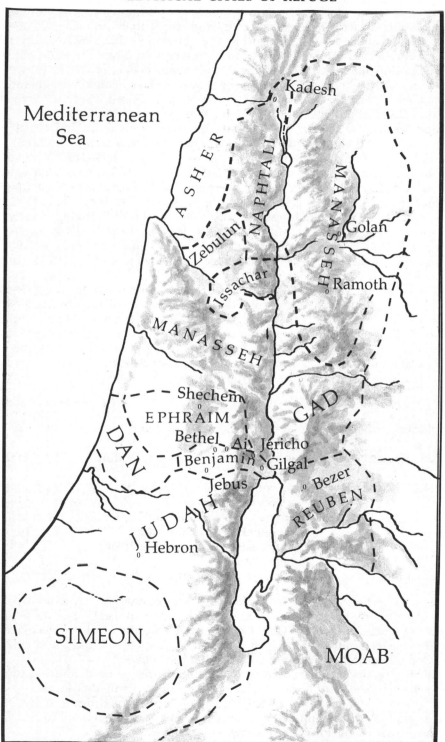

Deuteronomy

As Deuteronomy opens, the people of Israel are camped on plains just across the Jordan River from Canaan. All in the generation that saw so many miracles when God broke the bonds of their slavery in Egypt are gone, victims of their unwillingness to trust the Lord. A new generation has grown to maturity during 40 years of wilderness wanderings. This new generation, which has "held fast to the Lord" (Deut. 4:4), is poised, eager to cross the Jordan River and challenge the entrenched power of the Canaanites.

But Moses, the leader whose piety and commitment to God Israel has come to trust, is about to die. It will be a new leader, Joshua, who takes the armies of the Lord into battle across the river. Moses, aware of his personal destiny, assembles the people he has led and loved to hear his final words. These words, captured for us on the pages of Deuteronomy, sum up the central truths and basic principles Moses has come to understand through his many years of intimate relationship with the Lord. Speaking under the inspiration of God's Spirit, Moses rehearses the history of God's saving work for Israel. He explains the motives that lie behind God's choice of Israel and God's gift of the Law. And Moses goes on to review and to add to earlier instructions for holy living.

Perhaps the most unusual feature of Deuteronomy is its form. Moses adopts as a pattern for his message the Hittite type of suzerainty treaty. This treaty type was not used after 1200 B.C., a fact which supports Mosaic authorship of the book. The treaty structure invites us to see Deuteronomy as a national constitution: a binding agreement made between God as the nation's ruler, and Israel as His people. The well-known treaty format, and its match to the Book of Deuteronomy, is:

Treaty format	Intent	Deuteronomy passage
Historical prologue	Defines relationship of ruler to subjects	1:6–3:29
Basic stipulations	Defines general principles guiding behavior	5:1–11:32
Detailed stipulations	Lists some specific rules to be followed	12:1–26:19
Document clause	Citizens ratify constitution	27:1-26
Blessings	Lists benefits of relationship	28:1-14
Curses	Lists penalties for breaking treaty regulations	28:15-68
Recapitulation	Reviews and sums up the treaty	29:1–30:10

Understood within this treaty structure, we see that in Deuteronomy Moses is reminding Israel of a great and wonderful truth. Israel is God's people, and the Lord God is their King. God's people owe the Lord their allegiance, for He has committed Himself to them. As the Israelites prove good citizens of God's kingdom, divine blessings will surely flow.

What a reminder for us, who acknowledge Christ as Lord, and rightly see ourselves as the people of the King. The relevance of this great book to Christians is shown in the fact that it is quoted some 80 times in the New Testament! We can confidently expect to find special insights into our relationship with God in Deuteronomy.

DEUTERONOMY AT A GLANCE

KEY PEOPLE
Moses *The deliverer, lawgiver, and leader of the Jews during the Exodus.*

KEY EVENTS
Moses' final address *The entire book is composed of Moses' sermons.*

KEY WORDS AND THEMES
Covenant *Found some 27 times. Twenty-four times Israel is called to keep, observe, follow, and obey its requirements (cf. 4:2; 5:29; 6:2; 7:9, 11-12; etc.).*
Love *Found 20 times, of God's love 7 times (cf. 4:37; 7:8, 13; 23:5); of love for God 11 times (cf. 6:5; 7:9; 10:12; 13:3; etc.), and 2 times a call to love the alien (10:18-19).*
Listen/obey *The same root word in Hebrew, this call is heard 18 times (4:30; 5:1; 9:1; 20:3, etc.).*
Fear/revere the Lord *Found 20 times (4:10; 13:4; 17:19; etc.).*
Remember *Found 15 times, recall of what God has done is to help us make wise choices today (5:15; 15:15; 24:18, 22; etc.).*
God's choice of and concern for Israel *These are seen in His redemption of Israel from slavery (5:6; 6:12; 7:8; 8:14; 9:26; 13:5; 15:15; 21:8; 24:18), His sovereign and free choice of Israel (4:27; 7:6-7; 10:15; 14:2) to be His own (4:20; 7:6; 14:2; 26:18; 28:9) holy (7:6; 14:2, 21; 26:19; 28:9) and treasured people (7:6; 14:2; 26:18).*

WHERE THE ACTION TAKES PLACE

The Book of Deuteronomy is a book of sermons Moses delivered to Israel while the people were camped east of the Jordan River, on the plains of Moab (see map, p. 112).

Date and Authorship. The treaty format of the book demonstrates the unity of Deuteronomy and supports the conservative view that this too is a book of Moses. The sermons would have been given about 1406 B.C., just prior to the Conquest of Canaan.

THEOLOGICAL OUTLINE OF DEUTERONOMY

CONTENT OUTLINE OF DEUTERONOMY

I. Moses' First Sermon: What God Has Done (1:1–4:43)
  A. God's Help and Israel's Rebellion (1:1–3:29)
    1. Horeb to Hamath (1:1-46)
    2. Through Transjordan (2:1-25)
    3. Conquest of Transjordan (2:26–3:11)
    4. Distribution of the Transjordan (3:12-17)
    5. Preparations to invade Canaan (3:18-29)
  B. The New Generation's Responsibility (4:1-43)
    1. Listen, obey (4:1-14)
    2. Reject idolatry (4:15-31)
    3. Live as God's chosen people (4:32-43)
II. Moses' Second Address: Life under the Covenant (4:44–28:68)
  A. Introduction (4:44-49)
  B. Complete Commitment to Yahweh in Personal Devotion (5:1–11:32)
    1. Obey out of love (5:1–6:3)
    2. Remember God always (6:4-25)
    3. Reject competing faiths (7:1-26)
    4. Do not forget, but fear the Lord always (8:1–10:11)
    5. Love and obey God only (10:12–11:32)
  C. Complete Commitment to God's Law As It Defines a Holy Lifestyle (12:1–26:19)
    1. Worship God rightly (12:1–16:17)
      a. At His appointed place (12:1-32)
      b. Rejecting other gods (13:1-18)
      c. When ritually clean (14:1-21)
      d. With tithes (14:22-29)
      e. By doing justice (15:1-23)
      f. At annual festivals (16:1-17)
    2. Follow godly leaders (16:18–18:22)
      a. Who judge impartially (16:18-20)
      b. Who execute idolaters (16:21–17:7)
      c. Who follow God's Law (17:8-13)
      d. Follow kings who are God's appointees (17:14-20)
      e. Priests/Levites, for God has chosen them (18:1-8)
      f. Rejecting the occult (18:9-13)
      g. Heeding authenticated prophets of God (18:14-22)
    3. Apply criminal law carefully (19:1-21)
    4. Go to war with confidence in the Lord (20:1-20)
    5. Keep all God's laws and apply them as precedents (21:1–25:19)
    6. Pay tithes regularly (26:1-15)
    7. And obey always (26:16-19)
  D. Reconfirm the Covenant in the Promised Land (27:1-26)
  E. Expect Blessing If You Obey (28:1-14)
  F. Expect Disaster If You Disobey (28:15-68)
III. Moses' Third Sermon: A Review of the Covenant (29:1–30:20)
  A. A Historical Review (29:1-9)
  B. Exhortation to Commit (29:10-15)
  C. Punishment for Disobedience (29:16-29)
  D. Repentance and Forgiveness (30:1-10)
  E. An Appeal to Choose Life (30:11-20)
IV. The Last Acts and Death of Moses (31:1–34:12)
  A. Joshua Confirmed as New Leader (31:1-8)
  B. Law to Be Read to All Israel (31:9-13)
  C. Moses Predicts Rebellion (31:14-29)
  D. Moses Teaches a Song of Instruction (31:30–32:47)
  E. Moses to Die on Mt. Nebo (32:48-52)
  F. Moses Blesses Israel (33:1-29)
  G. The Death of Moses (34:1-12)

Chapter summary. These chapters contain the bulk of Moses' first sermon to the Israelites assembled on the plains of Moab and eager to conquer Canaan (1:1-5). They lay the historical basis for the relationship between God and Israel defined in Deuteronomy.

That basis, Moses says, is the covenant promises God made to Abraham (vv. 6-8), confirmed in all God has done to keep those promises. Thus the theme of these chapters is the faithfulness of God—and His demand for a faithful people. Though Moses carefully appointed leaders (vv. 9-18), Israel rebelled against the Lord at Kadesh, and was condemned to wander in the wilderness (1:19–2:1). Even there God watched over Israel and defeated their enemies (2:2–3:11). God sealed His commitment by giving Israel the Transjordan (vv. 12-20). But God showed the necessity of total faithfulness. He refused to let Moses enter Canaan for a single act of disobedience (vv. 21-27).

God will be faithful Joshua will lead Israel to victory (vv. 28-29). Yet to have God's help, Israel must be faithful to God.

Key verses. 1:30, 43; 2:7: God's love is seen most clearly against the backdrop of human failure.

Personal application. Look back and see what lessons God has taught you as you lived your life with Him.

Key concepts. Prayer conditions »p. 894. Fear »p. 363.

Outline
Place
Finder

CONSIDER
COVENANT
COMMIT
CONCLUSION

INSIGHT

Leaders (1:13-17). Leaders must be wise, respected, impartial, fearless, and humble.

Israel's fear (1:29-31). It was futile and foolish. God would have fought for them, as He already had fought for them. When you and I look ahead, let's remember all God has done for us before, and be released from fear of the future.

Arrogance (1:43). At heart, arrogance or pride is a denial of God's involvement in our lives, or a refusal to obey Him. Each shows that we, the mere creature, consider ourselves greater or wiser than the Creator. This attitude is the root from which rebellion, like the rebellion of Israel at Kadesh Barnea, grows. Ps. 10:4 says that "in his pride the wicked does not seek [God]; in all his thoughts there is no room for God." Pride puts us in danger of disaster, as it did the Exodus generation. But pride also puts us in serious danger of divine judgment. Twice Isaiah says, "The eyes of the arrogant man will be humbled and the pride of men brought low; the Lord alone will be exalted in that day" (Isa. 2:11, 17). So remember that God is. And respond wholeheartedly to Him.

"We went on past" (2:8). The people of Edom were spared because of their family relationship to Israel through Esau (v. 8). But note another reason: God had already provided everything Israel required (v. 7). When we trust God to provide, we can be content with the "enough" we have, without wanting extras possessed by others.

Archeological notes (2:10-12, 20-23). These verses use non-Hebrew names for peoples who once possessed the land. The name Anak goes back in Egyptian texts to 2100 and 2000 B.C., and is found in Gen. 6:4. The term is either an ethnic designation or a word meaning "giants."

"Completely destroyed them" (2:34). The text emphasizes Israel's commission to totally destroy or drive the Canaanites from the Promised Land.

Moses' request refused (3:23-29). Moses' many prayers for Israel were successful (cf. Num. 14:11-20; 16:22). But his personal appeal to enter Canaan was rejected, and Moses was told, "Do not speak to Me any more about this matter" (Deut. 3:26). The words "any more" imply that Moses was persistent in prayer, and remind us that persistence isn't enough. We must be in tune with God's will.

"Because of you" (3:26). Moses may simply have referred to the stress Israel's rebelliousness caused, that led him to sin. Num. 20:12 makes it clear Moses was judged for his own failure to trust and obey.

119

Outline
Place
Finder

CONSIDER
COVENANT
COMMIT
CONCLUSION

Chapter summary. Moses has reviewed the history of God's role in Israel's immediate history. Now he defines appropriate response. Israel is to accept God's Law as the foundation of her national life (4:1-8). She must never forget that it was God who gave the Law, or turn away from Him to idolatry (vv. 9-24). God's Law not only defines a godly lifestyle: it serves as the basis for future judgment (vv. 25-31). God has chosen Israel and powerfully demonstrated His love (vv. 32-38). Thus God must be acknowledged and His decrees kept, that the future of Israel may be secured (vv. 39-40). Moses then identifies the six cities of refuge (cf. Num. 35), and introduces his review of the contents of God's Law (Deut. 4:44-49).

Key verse. 4:40: Law brings blessing to those who keep it.

Personal application. Be clear about who God is.

Key concepts. Love »p. 529. Know »p. 27. Anger of God »pp. 65, 72. Idolatry »p. 433. Evil »p. 72. Fear of God »p. 387. Remember »p. 98. Power »p. 430. Law »pp. 63–64.

INSIGHT

Law (4:1). In the O.T. "law" is *torah*. The Heb. word means "teaching." Torah is broadly applied to Moses' writings, the Ten Commandments, the entire O.T., to the over 600 specific rulings the rabbis have identified in the O.T. In Deut. 4 we find the most common derived meaning of *torah*. "Law" is that body of specific instruction given to Israel through Moses, including the Ten Commandments but also many additional rulings intended to shape Israel's personal, civil, international, and religious way of life. Law, given by God Himself, demonstrates the intimacy that existed between God and His people (v. 7). It was a ground for Israel's boasts about God, for its righteousness displayed His character, and its stipulations are far superior to the other ancient law codes (v. 8).

Righteousness (4:8). The Law is remarkable for its "righteous decrees." The Heb. words translated "righteous" imply a moral and ethical norm against which human behavior can be measured. This verse makes it clear: that standard is expressed in the practical, detailed rulings found in the body of Law given Israel by God, through Moses. When we say God is righteous, we make a claim that He is absolutely righteous, and that all He does is in harmony with the ultimate standard of His own character. But to say that a person is "righteous" is using the term in a relative way. The righteous person is not sinless, but conducts his or her life in accord with the standard of behavior laid down in the Law.

Idol or image (4:16). The word *pesel* was a sculptured object of wood or stone, sometimes overlaid with precious metals, that developed the meaning "idol." Here "shape" is *tabnit*, which means a construction, and is used of idols that have human or animal form. Israel is to remember that God never appeared to them in such form when giving the Law. Nothing but God in heaven and earth could have rescued Israel from Egypt, to be His inheritance. He alone must be worshiped.

Heart and soul (4:29). Heart (*leb*) and soul (*nepes*) overlap in Heb. But when together, the heart suggests man's intellect and will, and the soul, man's emotions and desires. Israel will seek God and obey Him, He will restore, for God is merciful (v. 31).

Only Israel (4:32-34). Don't draw back from the biblical conviction that there is one road to God. God spoke to Israel alone, of all peoples of the world. Christ invites all to come to God, and only those who come by Christ can come to know God.

"Acknowledge" (4:39). Most O.T. passages using this word focus on the believer's response to God. Two elements are always present. First, there is knowledge of who God is, gained from revelation. Second, there is a personal commitment to God. Where such commitment is lacking, "there is no faithfulness, no love. . . . There is only cursing, lying and murder, stealing and adultery" (Hosea 4:1-2). When we do know God, and "take to heart" who He is, we will "keep His decrees and commands." Then and only then will it go well with us, and with our society.

Chapter summary. Moses restates the Ten Commandments, found first in Exodus 20 (Deut. 5:1-21). For a discussion of their nature and of each commandment, see pages 63–64. Moses reminds Israel of the initial awe felt by the Exodus generation at Sinai (vv. 22-27). Yet that awe faded quickly, and Israel fell away (vv. 28-29). Moses stayed there and spoke with the Lord: the laws Moses gives are God's laws (vv. 30-31). And now Israel must keep "all the way" marked out by those laws if the people are to prosper and remain in the land God is about to give them (vv. 32-33). These pointed remarks introduce a statement of love that motivated God to give the Law, and the only motive that will enable Israel to keep the Law: a love for Him.

Outline
Place
Finder

CONSIDER
COVENANT
COMMIT
CONCLUSION

Key verse. 5:2: God's standards are for every generation.

Personal application. Let's never forget who God is, lest we neglect trying to please Him and lose our way in life.

Key concepts. Always »p. 129. Blasphemy »p. 64. Father »p. 140. Fear »p. 363. Murder »p. 114. Name »p. 64. Redemption »p. 90. Remember (by God) »p. 98. Testimony »p. 132.

INSIGHT

Today (5:1). The Heb. word "today" (*hayyom*) is found 58 times in Deut. and "this very day" (*hayyom hazze*) a dozen, for some 70 times in all! Today is a vital concept, for it reminds Israel and us that we are always in the presence of God. What happened to the forefathers lies in the past, but its meaning is as present for us now as is God Himself. For the individual as well as the nation Israel, the Law that Moses conveys here has vital, current meaning. It is God's Word to His people now, as well as yesterday and forever.

The writer to the Hebrews picks up this thought in chapters 3 and 4. Because it is always "today" in our relationship with God, we too can enter the Promised Land of God's rest. But we too must respond when we hear God's voice speaking to us. The central obligation of the believer is to listen to God in each "today," and trust God so much that we respond in obedience.

Responding to God (5:1). If we wonder what it means to respond to God's voice, this same verse tells us. Note the active verbs. We are to hear God's words, we are to learn their meaning, and we are to be sure to follow them. If we do this, our todays will be rich in experience of the presence of the living God.

Moses' role (5:22-32). Moses reminds Israel that God spoke directly to the whole people. Only the fear of the first Exodus generation led to Moses' appointment as mediator. Thus in several ways Israel can be absolutely sure that the Law is from God. (1) God spoke the

Ten Commandments to all, and the rest of the Law can be traced back to these basic religious and moral principles. (2) Moses alone spent 40 days on Sinai, speaking with God face-to-face. Since it is clear from this that God is the Author of the Law Moses transmitted, Israel must respect and obey that Law as God's own words. Moses was a mediator of the Law, but is not its author.

Awe of God (5:25). This verse pictures the terror that Israel felt at God's appearance on Mt. Sinai. It's fascinating that Israel experienced that fear as terror: the people were concerned God would strike out at them. But God saw that fear as a positive thing! When the Israelites feared God, they were inclined to keep His commandments (v. 29). And then all would "go well" for the Israelites and their children.

A fear of God that exists as terror of Him is foolish, for God loves us. But a failure to fear God in a healthy way, remembering with a sense of awe just who He is, is even more foolish. Only when we respect God enough to respond to Him is our future secure.

That you may live long (5:32-33). This theme is found often in Deut. God gave Israel the Law as a gift of love. Only if they lived in fellowship with Him could they prosper in His land. And the Law showed Israel how to remain in fellowship. The principle, if not Mosaic Law, is surely for us today. If we are to be blessed, we must live close to the Lord. We can only stay close by being responsive and obedient.

Chapter summary. This is one of the central chapters in the Old Testament. It contains a call not just to respect and obey God (6:1-3), but to love God completely (vv. 4-9). The call is so central to Old Testament religion that it is celebrated in Judaism as the *shema*, a confession of faith repeated in synagogue services across the world for untold centuries.

The words lead directly into the Old Testament's central prescription for the communication of faith across the generations (vv. 5-9; see opposite page). The chapter continues by returning to these themes. God will bless Israel with prosperity. When this happens Israel is to remember Him, and to serve Him by doing "what is right and good" in His sight (vv. 10-19). In the future Israel is to rehearse the wonderful acts of deliverance by which God proved His love for His people—and which should awaken their love for Him (vv. 20-25).

Key verse. 6:5: Jesus called this the first and great command.

Personal application. Love God, and you will want to do what is right and good, in order to please Him.

Key concepts. Trinity »p. 797. Love and obedience »p. 126. Father's role »p. 592. Children »p. 378.

INSIGHT

"Go well with you" (6:1-3). Again the emphasis is placed on God's motives in giving Israel the Law. God is eager that Israel will experience blessing, and blessing can only come by response to the known will of God.

No Trinity? (6:4) Does the O.T. affirmation, "the Lord is One," contradict the N.T. teaching that God is One, but at the same time a Trinity composed of Father, Son, and Holy Spirit? The Heb. word for "one" is *'ehad*. It means one, but can indicate a composite unity, as one cluster made up of several grapes (Num. 13:23) or a whole people assembled as one congregation (Jud. 20:1). To say that God is *'ehad* does not teach the doctrine of the Trinity. But neither does it contradict it. »p. 797.

How do the rabbis understand 6:4? One Midrash suggests the two names of God here suggest compassion and raw power. Their linkage here reminds Israel that no matter what terrible things may happen, God is a God of compassion and even what seems evil is intended for good. Another Midrash sees in it a historical statement. Then only Israel acknowledged the God of the covenant. But one day God will be "one," in the sense that all will recognize Israel's God as God and find peace in Him. However we understand the opening verse of the *shema*, the next verse is clear. Complete love for Him is the duty, and destiny, of the redeemed.

Nurturing children (6:5-8). The Scripture's basic principles are laid out here. Parents are to love God themselves and take His words to heart. They are then to talk about His words in the context of daily life, and so make them real to their boys and girls. »p. 123.

"Upon your hearts" (6:6). The words convey a very different view of the O.T. than the legalistic. The O.T. believer was to consider, meditate on, and remain conscious of God's words. In this process God's words would shape the believer's entire outlook on life and his or her attitudes toward others.

The danger of prosperity (6:10-12). God is about to give Israel a material prosperity for which the people never worked. This is intended as a blessing. Yet this blessing brings the danger that when physical wants are satisfied, the spiritual source of blessings will be forgotten. John Wesley urged the early Methodists to work hard and make all the money they could, but then to give it away! He felt that only in this way could they remain godly.

A family faith (6:20-25). The passage pictures the family sharing the annual Passover meal. »p. 59. The intimate image of that meal, the father sharing with the children, all sensing solidarity with the redeemed of every Jewish generation, is perhaps the clearest model of religious nurture in either Testament.

Learning God's Law

The Old Testament ideal is that of a community committed to live out love for God and others. The family was to be the focus of nurture. And the focus of the family was father and mother who loved God and took His words to heart (Deut. 6:5-6). Mothers and daughters worked together in the home, while sons worked with fathers. Parents had many opportunities to impress God's words on their offspring, explaining the things they did and the choices they made as responses to God's Word.

God's words were talked about "when you sit at home and when you walk along the road, when you lie down and when you get up." Everyday experience thus was the context for learning the meaning of Scripture, as learning God's Law took place in the classroom of life. The modeling of committed parents, the intimacy of family love, and the opportunity to see the implications of God's Laws as they were followed, together constituted the most powerful educational design ever devised. Philo, writing in New Testament times, says children "are taught, so to speak, from their swaddling clothes by their parents, by their teachers, and by those who bring them up, even before instruction in the sacred laws and unwritten customs, to believe in God, the One Father and Creator of the world" (*Leg. ad Caium*, 31).

Boys began formal schooling between ages five and seven, under a teacher paid by a tax on all with children. The children learned to read and write, but the center of the curriculum was memorizing the most important biblical laws, learning how to live godly lives, and knowing the "deeds of the forefathers."

The children also participated in the worship of the community. They joined in many of the annual festivals: eating the Passover meal; searching the house for leaven before the seven days of the Feast of Unleavened Bread; sleeping outdoors during the week-long Feast of Booths. Each week on the Sabbath they shared the weekly day of rest, and watched as the men assembled to discuss the Torah. And they watched as the mystery of sacrifice was repeated. They saw adults confess sins, and rejoice in the cleansing that permitted them to join others in the worship of God. And so the children grew. And even in the darkest of times, many came to know, love, trust, and obey the Lord.

123

Outline
Place
Finder

CONSIDER
COVENANT
COMMIT
CONCLUSION

Chapter summary. Moses requires Israel to adopt a policy of extermination in the coming war for Canaan. The pagan religion that corrupts Canaan must be rooted out, so that Israel can live in the land as a people set apart to God alone (7:1-6). The reason for God's choice of Israel is a mystery, but the fact is that God in love has chosen and redeemed His people (vv. 7-10). Thus they must follow Him completely (v. 11). If Israel loves God and responds with obedience, He will pour out on the chosen people blessings of prosperity, health, and success (vv. 12-16).

But first, Israel must fight for her land. The people are encouraged to remember what God did to Pharaoh and all Egypt, and trust Him. Israel's faithful God will lead His people to total victory (vv. 17-26).

Key verse. 7:9: Know God, and experience His faithfulness.

Personal application. God chooses us to love Him.

Key concepts. Faithfulness »p. 140. Sickness »p. 66. God's love »pp. 351, 529. Commandment »p. 749. Extermination »p. 66.

INSIGHT

"Sacred stones" (7:5). The Heb. word *massebot* denotes stone pillars set up at pagan worship centers. They may have been phallic symbols linked to cult fertility worship. Asherah poles bear the name of a pagan goddess, and may have been wooden images in her likeness.

God's choice of Israel (7:7-9). These verses make a critical theological point. They clearly affirm God's freedom in making choices, by showing that they are internally motivated. God did not choose Israel, or make any other choice, because it was required by the merits or actions of those chosen. No necessity of any kind impelled God to choose. Rather God's choices were spontaneous acts, motivated only by His own loving character.

God's free choice of Israel is frequently affirmed in the O.T. (cf. Deut. 7:6; 14:2; 18:5; 21:5; Ps. 33:12; Isa. 14:1; 41:8-9; 44:1; 45:4; Ezek. 20:5). The O.T. also speaks of God choosing individuals: Abraham (Gen. 18:19; Neh. 9:7), Moses (Ps. 106:23), and David (1 Sam. 16:9-12; 1 Kings 8:16; Ps. 78:70). These choices too were free choices, which God made simply because He chose to.

But a free and spontaneous choice is not a capricious choice! Once such a choice is made, God does not change His mind. And so the text links God's choice both to His love and to "the oath He swore to your forefathers" (Deut. 7:8). God chooses out of love, and when He has made His choice, He is faithful to us to the end.

What an encouragement for us today. Our own relationship with God is not rooted in

what we do, but in God's love. It is all of grace. And now that we know God through Christ, we can be utterly confident that God will remain committed to us, and bring us ultimately to be with Him.

"Those who hate Him" (7:10). Here as in other passages "hate" means "decisively reject."

Blessed with wealth (7:13). The O.T. places wealth within the context of Israel's covenant relationship with God. God committed Himself to give His O.T. people "abundant prosperity" if Israel worshiped and served Him alone (cf. 28:11). This commitment to the nation was also made to individuals. So the psalmist celebrates, thankful that "wealth and riches are in the house" of a man who fears God (Ps. 112:1-6). So one basic thread in O.T. teaching on wealth, reflected here in Deut. 7, does picture prosperity as a blessing granted to those who faithfully worship and serve God.

This theme was distorted in later Judaism, and in Christ's day the possession of great wealth was taken as *prima facie* evidence of godliness! Yet there are other teachings on wealth in the O.T. Wealth may be a blessing, but 8:17-18 warns that the wealthy man is likely to forget God. Wealth can lead a person into sin (Hosea 12:8), and even a man "without [spiritual] understanding" can have wealth (Ps. 49:20). Wealth can be a blessing to us too. But riches without spiritual insight bring everlasting ruin (52:5-7).

Chapter summary. This powerful chapter focuses our attention on remembering and forgetting. It reminds us that trials make us depend on God, while in prosperity we too often forget Him.

Israel is urged to remember all that God has done for them, and to learn the lesson of dependence His discipline and mercy have taught (8:1-5). Thoroughly trained by God, Israel is now about to take possession of a "good land," poetically described (vv. 6-9). But the very richness of the land holds hidden danger. Israel must "be careful" in the coming prosperity not to forget the Lord (vv. 10-13). Ease and plenty often lead to pride, and to a neglect of God. If this happens, and Israel turns to paganism, the nation will be destroyed (vv. 14-20).

Outline
Place
Finder

CONSIDER
COVENANT
COMMIT
CONCLUSION

Key verse. 8:18: In every circumstance, remember God.

Personal application. Prosperity conceals spiritual snares.

Key concepts. Remember »p. 98. Bread »pp. 605, 683. Discipline »pp. 387, 866. Humble »p. 259. Wealth »p. 124.

INSIGHT

To humble (8:2, 16). God's provision of manna in the wilderness was intended to educate Israel. The people needed to learn that their very existence depended not on their own efforts, but on God meeting their needs. Each morning God must speak a fresh word and provide that day's manna. Jesus quoted this verse to overcome Satan's first temptation (Matt. 4; Luke 4). Though hungry, Jesus chose to await a word from God, knowing that responding to God is more essential to life than food itself! It is this truth that the wilderness experience, with its severe deprivations countered time after time by divine provision, was intended to teach.

Testing (8:2). The phrase "in order to know what was in your heart" helps us understand the nature of testing. The Heb. words translated "test" in the O.T. are *nasah, sarap,* and *bahan.* The word used here, *nasah,* indicates an attempt to prove the existence of a particular quality in someone or something. *Sarap* means "to refine," usually indicating the purifying result of divine judgment. *Bahan* focuses attention on an examination to prove the existence of some spiritual quality, such as integrity. Underlying the use of each of these words is the conviction that even when a test involves difficulty or suffering, God intends His tests of our faith to bring us something good. The Israelites Moses addresses passed God's test, and proved they were ready to enter the Promised Land. Each test we experience is intended to prepare us not for more suffering, but for greater blessings to come.

Canaan (8:8-9). The description of mid-second millennium B.C. is accurate, even to the hidden deposits of metal ores.

"Praise the Lord" (8:10). This verse is the source of the Jewish utterance of the three traditional blessings as a grace said after meals. The first blessing praises God as King of the universe for nourishing the entire world. The second praises God for giving His people a land on which to grow food. And the third blessing calls on the worshiper not to forget Jerusalem, the city of God's presence.

Forgetting (8:11). This verse describes the essential nature of forgetting: it is summed up in "failing to observe His commands, His laws and His decrees." Thus forgetting is not just a failure to remember. Forgetting is a failure to give the lessons of the past a significant place in our present. Forgetting is a neglect of the meaning of things we remember, so that we fail to experience God as a real and living Person now, or fail to guide present choices by truths we have learned in the past. Thus Moses is saying that if Israel forgets the lessons taught in the wilderness, fails to depend completely on God, fails to worship Him, and fails to respond to His Word, the disaster that will surely follow will wipe out all the blessings that remembering God brings.

"Ability to produce wealth" (8:18). There is no such thing as a "self-made man." Some like to boast of their accomplishments, yet the intelligence, the health, the drive that make accomplishment possible, all come from God. All we are and all we have is ultimately His gift. And this is something we need to remember, and never forget.

Chapter summary. God's goodness is grasped against the back-drop of sin and failure. Moses develops this theme, guarding against the common assumption that if we are blessed by God, we are deserving. Israel will conquer Canaan, not because the Israelites are righteous, but because the Canaanites are wicked, and God is faithful to His promise to Abraham (9:1-6). In great detail Moses reminds Israel of the golden calf incident, to dem-onstrate that victory in Canaan is a triumph of God's grace, not an indication of Israel's moral superiority (9:7–10:11). Moses then concludes with a powerful call to Israel to respond to God's love, and hold fast to Him always (vv. 12-22).

Key verses. 10:20-21: God is to be Israel's praise.

Personal application. Remember that all the good we have and are is an expression of God's grace, and praise Him.

Key concepts. Unbelief »p. 857. Righteous »p. 120. Fear of God »p. 387. Heart, soul »p. 120. Prayer »p. 181. Alien »p. 66.

INSIGHT

Illustration. *The "calf of Dan" is a small cast image dating to the 2nd millennium B.C. It may have been a cult object used by Israelites, or by the Canaanites. The storm god of the Canaanites was often portrayed standing on the back of a bull. Thus the golden calf of the Exodus symbolized the pres-ence of a deity, and clearly implied paganism.*

Loving God (10:12-13). "Love" in Scripture is more than an emotion or feeling. God's love finds expression in saving acts performed for His people. Those acts reveal not only His power, but His faithfulness, compassion, and commitment to His own. We know God through His acts, as those are recorded and explained for us in Scripture.

These critical verses remind us that those who truly love God express their love in ac-tion too. They "walk in all His ways," they

"serve the Lord your God with all your heart and with all your soul." They "observe the Lord's commands and decrees." We respond to God's loving acts performed for us by per-forming loving acts for Him!

This theme of love, woven so vividly into Deut., reminds us that for the O.T. saint God's Law was to be a source of joy. Just as today a caress is a joyful way to express love to our spouse, so obeying God is still a joyful way for us to express love to our Lord.

Circumcision of the heart (10:16). Physical circumcision was the O.T.'s outward sign of one's covenant relationship with God through His people, Israel. »p. 36. Here Moses applies the image of circumcision to teach that for a true covenant relationship with God, one's in-ward attitude is critical. Only those whose hearts are in tune with God are truly members of God's covenant people. Thus the Apostle Paul says "a man is a Jew if he is one inward-ly; and circumcision is circumcision of the heart, by the Spirit, not by the written code" (Rom. 2:29). Those with circumcized hearts are identified by their love for God, and for others.

"The fatherless and the widows" (10:18). In the O.T., the fatherless and the widow sym-bolize, often with the alien, those who are so-cially powerless. They are poor and weak, for there is no man to protect or provide for them. Thus O.T. Law lays a special emphasis on the attitude of the godly toward them. They are to be treated justly in the courts (24:17; 27:19), and lack of concern for them is a sign of a corrupt society (Job 31:17; Ps. 94:6; Isa. 1:17, 23; Zech. 7:10).

Chapter summary. With this chapter we reach the end of Moses' statement of the basic principles guiding those in covenant relationship with God. The chapter has a typical form. Moses states God's requirements (11:1, 8, 13) and then applies and illustrates them (vv. 2-7, 9-12, 14-17). The chapter, and this section of Deuteronomy, concludes with a summary that draws together basic commands found in earlier chapters. When we see these together, we realize again that the believer's ongoing relationship with God is marked by two things: love and obedience. Those who love and obey the Lord will surely enjoy His blessings, and most important of all, will experience daily fellowship with their Lord.

Outline
Place
Finder

CONSIDER
COVENANT
COMMIT
CONCLUSION

Key verse. 11:1: This is the whole duty of those who know God.

Personal application. Staying close to God guarantees blessing, but straying means sure distress.

Key concepts. Heart, soul »p. 120. Covenant »pp. 32, 35, 62.

INSIGHT

Love God (11:1). And keep His requirements. The events of the Exodus (vv. 2-7) had their impact on the present generation. God's acts of deliverance and judgment trained up an obedient generation, prepared to trust and obey God, and thus experience His blessing. Remember that everything God has done in your life prepares you to love Him and live for Him today—and tomorrow.

Observe the commands (11:8). This second requirement anticipates the future. We obey not only because of past experiences with God, but because we know that obedience will bring us into "a land flowing with milk and honey." Today's obedience is a doorway to tomorrow's blessings.

"Be careful" (11:16). The third requirement is in the form of a condition. The experience of future blessing hinges on Israel's willingness to hold fast to the Lord, and to teach future generations to know Him (vv. 14-17). The true source of every blessing is God, and God alone. How vital then that we remain close to Him!

Blessing. To "bless" is to give success, prosperity, and a long life. A life filled with blessing is rich, fulfilling, and abundant. The O.T. sees God as the source of all blessedness, and notes that He blesses "the righteous" (Ps. 5:12).

This blessing is provided within the context of a unique relationship. God made a commitment to Abraham to bless his offspring (Gen. 12; 17). But each generation and each Israelite had to personally accept that relationship by faith, and by faith choose to follow the moral and religious pathway God laid down in Moses' Law. God still stands poised to pour out blessings on His people. But we too must choose the path that leads to blessing. As Deut. 11:26-28 says, there is blessing "if you obey the commands of the Lord your God" but a "curse if you disobey . . . and turn from the way" (curse »p. 138).

Gerizim and Ebal (11:29). When Israel crossed the Jordan they were to act out all Moses had taught. Part of the people would stand on Mt. Gerizim, and pronounce the blessings to be won by obedience. And part would stand on Mt. Ebal and pronounce the curses that disobedience would surely bring. The two Mounts chosen have different geological structures that graphically illustrate God's point. Gerizim is fruitful and green. Ebal is sterile and barren. Let's choose the fruitfulness of a life committed to God rather than the barren slopes ever associated with disobedience.

Summing up. The last verses of this chapter pick up and reflect the emphasis on love, Law, and obedience found throughout this section of Deuteronomy. To review these themes, compare:

11:18 with 6:8
11:19 with 4:9-10; 6:7
11:20 with 6:9
11:21 with 4:40; 6:2
11:22 with 6:17
11:23 with 4:38; 9:1
11:24 with 1:7-8
11:25 with 2:25; 7:23-24

Outline
Place
Finder

CONSIDER
COVENANT
COMMIT
CONCLUSION

Chapter summary. Deuteronomy 5–11 stated principles underlying the covenant relationship between God and Israel. Deuteronomy 12–26 lists specific commands that are to shape Israel's lifestyle. As we might expect, the first subject taken up, in 12:1–16:18, is worship. For Israel's relationship with God, like our own, is the central issue in life.

Moses tells the people that after they enter Canaan God will choose a single site for worship, and that only there may sacrifices be offered (12:1-14). Animals may be killed at any location for food, as long as their blood is not eaten (vv. 15-16), but an animal offered to God must be killed only at Israel's one place of worship (vv. 17-28). This command not only affirms the unity of Israel's one God, it is intended to protect Israel from adopting pagan practices, and must be obeyed (vv. 29-32).

A religious leader who calls Israel to worship other gods must be put to death, even if he performs miracles or predicts the future (13:1-5). Even members of one's immediate family must be exposed (vv. 6-12), and a town that turns to idolatry must be wiped out (vv. 13-18). The penalty may seem harsh, but the destiny of the nation depends on each citizen's faithfulness to God.

Key verse. 12:4: We can worship God only in His way.

Personal application. God deserves our total allegiance.

Key concepts. Blood »pp. 85, 766. Prophet »p. 131. Sacrifice »pp. 28, 78. Jerusalem »p. 205.

INSIGHT

Pagan worship sites. Postholes with the rotted wood of Asherah poles, upright sacred stones, and altars have been found at many places in Israel. These cult symbols were to be destroyed to protect Israel from temptation, and make it impossible for pagans to contact their gods.

"Sacrifices" (12:5-6). All the offerings listed in Lev. 1–7 are mentioned here. All worship involving sacrifice of any kind must be conducted at Israel's central sanctuary.

"The place the Lord your God will choose" (12:5). The primary reference is to Jerusalem, where David brought God's ark and Solomon built God's temple. Many believe that up until that time, the tabernacle served as a central sanctuary. Where it stood was, in effect, the place God chose to be worshiped. Before David's time that place moved, with the tabernacle, from Shechem (Josh. 24:1) to Bethel (Jud. 20:18) to Shiloh (1 Sam. 1:3; 4:3-4).

Repetition? Repetition is a literary device found often in the O.T. When instructions are repeated, as 12:20-28 repeats verses 15-18, the intent is to emphasize the importance of the teaching.

Child sacrifice (12:31). In O.T. Law child sacrifice is a capital offense (Lev. 18:21; 20:2-5).

Purge evil (13:5). This is a repeated theme in Deut., found here and in 17:7, 12; 19:19; 21:21; 22:21-22, 24; and 24:7. In each case except 19:19 it deals with the death penalty. The whole community, including every individual, was responsible to maintain religious and moral purity.

Justified killing. Both Deut. 12 and 13 touch on offenses which call for the death penalty. In Heb. there are two words for killing. *Rasah* is a personal killing. Depending on the circumstances we would call it murder, manslaughter, or accidental homicide. The other Heb. word, *harag*, looks at killing simply as an event. Usually it is used of the violent killing of a person by other human beings. These killings may be unjustified, as was Cain's killing of his brother Abel (Gen. 4:25; cf. also 1 Sam. 22:21; 1 Kings 18:13), or they may be justified, as was the killing of the prophets of Baal at Elijah's command (19:1; cf. Ex. 13:15). Deut. 13 is a key passage that develops the biblical view that some offenses committed by human beings not only deserve, but require, that the offender be judicially killed. Thus vv. 8-9 say, "you must certainly put him to death [*harag*]."

Chapter summary. These chapters continue the theme of worship under the Mosaic Covenant, introduced in Deuteronomy 12. Israel is to eat only clean foods (14:1-21) and to pay required tithes (vv. 22-29). But worship has person-to-person as well as person-to-God aspects. Israelites worship God by being sensitive to the poor and canceling debts the seventh year (15:1-11). Israelites worship by freeing Hebrew slaves after six years of service (vv. 12-18) as well as by setting every firstborn animal apart to God (vv. 19-23). Finally Israel is to worship as a gathered community, assembling to celebrate God's goodness at the three important Festivals of Passover, Weeks, and Tabernacles (16:1-17).

Outline
Place
Finder

CONSIDER
COVENANT
COMMIT
CONCLUSION

Key verses. 15:4-5: A right relationship with God will transform society.

Personal application. Worship goes beyond Sunday.

Key concepts. Clean, unclean »p. 82. Tithe »p. 103. God's choice of Israel »p. 124. Brotherly love »pp. 690, 867. Slavery »p. 90. Work »p. 28. Passover »p. 59. Poor and oppressed »p. 90.

INSIGHT

Mourning (14:1-3). Pagan mourning rites are not appropriate for a people whom God has chosen. Our relationship with God makes death a different kind of event than for those who do not know Him.

Why two sets of dishes? (14:21b) No one knows the reason for the command not to cook a young goat in its mother's milk. But the orthodox Jew keeps two sets of dishes, one for meat and one for milk products, lest this command be violated by chance.

Always (14:23). Different Heb. constructions are used that cast "always" as either "for all time" or as "continually." Israel was commanded to do two things "for all time." God's people were always "to keep all My commandments" (5:29) and always to "revere the Lord your God" (14:23).

The third-year tithe (14:28). Some believe this is a separate tithe, in addition to the one to be paid at the central sanctuary. It was to be used to provide food for the poor.

"There should be no poor" (15:4). There is no conflict between verses 4 and 11, which says "there will always be poor people in the land." The land itself was rich, so poverty was not necessary. The problem then, as now, was with people who piled up more than they needed at the expense of others.

Lending, borrowing. The O.T. teaching on this topic is unique. Israel had no credit economy. A person borrowed to meet serious personal or family needs. Those with enough were commanded to lend to fellow Israelites.

And, every seventh year, the debts of a person unable to repay a loan were to be automatically canceled: God's own bankruptcy plan! The land of Israel produced plenty for all. Only if the people who benefited from God's largess were unwilling to share it would poverty stalk that good land.

The warning in 15:9 against harboring the "wicked thought" of refusing to help a poor brother is significant. Poverty in any land is the result of sin, and the "hardhearted" and "tightfisted" will face the judgment of God.

The pierced ear (15:16-17). In Scripture the ear represents a person's capacity to perceive and respond. So the pierced ear symbolizes the servant's choice to open his ear, and respond obediently to his master for life. What a picture of the believer, who is to keep spiritual ears open to God, and respond obediently to His Word.

Slavery (15:12-18). Laws governing slavery in Israel, and the implications of the system, are discussed on »p. 90 (Lev. 25).

Joy and mourning (16:14). The verse portrays religious festivals as a time of joy, even for orphans and widows. The Talmud sees an important principle in this verse, and rules that even the traditional seven days of mourning (*shiva*) observed for the newly dead must be set aside, and the mourner join in the festivities of the holy days. Even personal tragedy can be transcended in celebrating what God has done for His people. And what He most surely will do.

Chapter summary. Moses now turns to governing the new nation, with particular attention to its leaders, its justice system, and its conduct of war. This section of the detailed code regulating life under the Law covenant runs from 16:18 to 20:20.

Moses begins by calling for incorruptible judges, who will be impartial in their rulings (16:18-20). These judges must be committed enough to the Law that they will put idolaters to death, if sufficient evidence of the crime exists (16:21–17:7). Complicated legal cases can be referred to a court of priests and Levites, whose decision will be final (vv. 8-13). When in time Israel is ruled by a king, that king must be one of their own people, be humble, and subject himself to God's Law (vv. 14-20).

The detailed regulations in this chapter, though specific to ancient Israel's situation, provide many insights into qualities to be desired in spiritual leaders in any time.

Key verse. 17:9: Leaders must be willing to be led by God.

Personal application. We proclaim God's Law, not remake it.

Key concepts. Priesthood »p. 81. Polygamy »p. 41. Legal justice system »p. 132. Accountability »pp. 495, 503. Judges »p. 158.

INSIGHT

"Judges . . . in every town" (16:18). There is great significance in calling for judges "in every town." First, everyone is likely to know the character of a lifelong neighbor, so truly impartial, unbribable officials can be selected. Second, local judges will know the character of witnesses and of those who are accused, and be better able to ferret out the true facts of a case. The same principle is reflected in Paul's instructions on choosing local church elders (cf. 1 Tim. 3; Titus 1).

Investigation and conviction (17:4-6). All in Israel were responsible for the purity of the community. Even rumors were to be reported to local judges, who then investigated. Those with knowledge were to testify, and in the case of guilt, were to be first to participate in carrying out the court's sentence. The Christian citizen must never plead, "I don't want to be involved."

A supreme court (17:9). Local judges might determine the facts, but not be expert enough in the Law to make a ruling. So Moses provides for a higher, final court of priests and judges. This system was adopted by Jehoshaphat (872–848 B.C., 2 Chron. 19:5-11). The same system was followed in N.T. times. Each town had local judges, but the Jerusalem Sanhedrin was Judaism's supreme court.

Israel's king. In biblical times the king (Heb. *melek*) was a person who was responsible for all the functions of modern governments. He made laws, was the chief executive, and also served as chief judge. In early Israel these functions were decentralized. God was acknowledged as King, and His Law was the divine legislation applied by local officials. This Deut. passage looks forward to a time when Israel would have a human king, and sets out two guidelines for the king's rule.

First, the king is to remain a man of the people. This is to be symbolized by repudiation of the symbols of power adopted by Oriental potentates: a large military establishment (17:16), a harem (v. 17a), and amassing great personal wealth (v. 17b). Only a king who was and remained humble could serve both the people and God.

Second, the king is to have a personal copy of God's Law, and "read it all the days of his life" (v. 19). This has powerful symbolic meaning. In the ancient Near East vassal kings were provided with copies of treaties between their people and the "great king" over them. The personal copy of God's Law maintained by the king affirmed his role as a secondary ruler, under God as Israel's true and great King.

Again there is a parallel with modern spiritual leadership. Christian leaders are also to be men of the people, who reject symbols which might exalt them over those they serve. We too lead others "under God," and have no authority except that which comes from understanding His Word.

Chapter summary. Along with local elders, the priests and legal experts who comprised the supreme court, and the king, Israel had other leaders. These included the ordinary priests and Levites who served brief shifts at the central sanctuary (18:1-8), and most notably, the prophets who served as God's contemporary spokesmen to His people. Israel was not to seek supernatural guidance from an occult source (vv. 9-13), for God would give any direction needed beyond that provided in Scripture through His prophets (vv. 14-22). The true prophet of God could be recognized by three tests: he was a Jew (v. 15), he would speak in the name of the Lord (v. 20), and what he predicted would surely come to pass (v. 22).

Outline
Place
Finder

CONSIDER
COVENANT
COMMIT
CONCLUSION

Key verse. 18:14: God is committed to guide His own.

Personal application. It's up to us to discern whether any message is from God or not.

INSIGHT

Offerings (18:4). The priests and Levites were dependent on the rest of Israel for their support. The priests were due a definite tithe, plus a portion of most sacrifices. But these ministers were also to be given "the firstfruits" of crops. No definite amount is set here. First-century rabbis held that a generous man would give a thirtieth of the crop. A fortieth or fiftieth was typical, while less than a sixtieth marked a man as greedy and avaricious. The measure people use in giving still serves as an indication of character.

The occult (18:9-15). Underlying all occult practices — whether palm reading, astrology, consulting mediums, channeling, sorcery, or black magic — is the belief that supernatural powers can be consulted or manipulated to man's advantage. Each of these practices is an abomination, for it involves acknowledging a power other than God. In the covenant community this was active rebellion against the Lord. Even for those outside the covenant community, occult practices were "detestable," for they represented a rejection of what could be known about God through creation in favor of the demonic or the unreal. This utter condemnation remains a stern warning to modern Christians that a believer can have nothing to do with anything linked to the occult.

"A prophet like me" (18:15). While this passage lays a foundation for the ministry of many prophets in Israel, later Judaism saw in its singular form a prophecy of a coming individual. In Acts 3:22-23 Peter announces that expected Prophet is none other than Jesus.

Prophets in Israel. Moses is the prototype prophet. He was commissioned as God's spokesman and communicated the Word of God that was to shape Israel's lifestyle in the Promised Land. While Moses left the written Law to guide Israel, the Lord was committed to provide supernatural guidance in specific situations not covered by Law. Later prophets stopped wars, gave kings military as well as moral guidance, confronted those who did wrong, and announced divine judgment. The prophets served as the conscience of the nation, as well as visionaries whose predictions about the future were intended to shape contemporary attitudes and acts. The office of prophet was not hereditary, nor was it limited to men (cf. Ex. 15:20; Jud. 4:4; 2 Chron. 34:22; Neh. 6:14). These messengers were called from all walks of life to what was, most often, a thankless and dangerous ministry. Only a deep sense of divine calling could move the true prophet to risk speaking an unpopular word in times of royal or national apostasy. The primary focus of every prophet's ministry was to the people of his or her own time. Yet "prophet" most often calls to our mind prediction of future events. The most famous O.T. prophecies are predictions of events hundreds or even thousands of years beyond the prophet's era. Yet the O.T. prophets characteristically also produced an authenticating sign: a miracle, or a near-term prophecy that came true. Thus Elijah announced that no rain would fall in Israel except at his command — and none fell for over three years. And Jeremiah, contradicted by the false prophet Hananiah, announced that Hananiah would die within a year — and he did. Thus each generation had evidence that the prophets among them did speak with God's own authority. And each generation was responsible to respond to the prophetic word and be blessed, or to reject that word and suffer the consequences of disobeying God.

Outline
Place
Finder

CONSIDER
COVENANT
COMMIT
CONCLUSION

Chapter summary. Moses concludes his exposition of laws that structure national life with a word about criminal justice, and about the conduct of war. The ultimate crime against others, murder, is to be dealt with decisively, but with scrupulous care that no innocent person is punished (19:1-14). Especially important is the fact that evidence against a person must be absolutely conclusive, and that one who lies in court becomes liable to the punishment he hoped to inflict on the accused (vv. 15-21).

The laws on war are unique too. It is a privilege to fight the Lord's battles, and anyone who fears, and thus does not trust God, is automatically excused from the army (20:1-9). The enemy must be given the opportunity to make peace, and only if they refuse are they to be engaged in battle (vv. 10-15). This humane law does not apply, however, to the holy war for the Promised Land Israel is about to engage in, for if Canaanites remain in the land they will corrupt the faith of Israel (vv. 16-18). And even in the heat of battle no land is to be so devastated that it will not produce crops after the war is over (vv. 19-20).

Key verse. 19:3: Society is to guard each man's rights.

Personal application. We must take an active role in seeking justice: freedom for the innocent, and punishment for the guilty.

Key concepts. Legal justice system »p. 130. Accountability »pp. 495, 503. Destruction of the Canaanites »p. 66.

INSIGHT

"**Build roads**" (19:3). What a stunning command. The nation is responsible to make sure a person who kills another accidentally can quickly reach sanctuary in one of the cities of refuge. »p. 114. Any righteous society must have mechanisms to guard the innocent against improper punishment.

Criminal justice. Deut. 17 describes the legal systems' structures. »p. 130. This passage lays down a central principle. Justice involves making sure the guilty are punished. But justice is just as concerned with making sure the innocent are protected. We see this in the setting aside of cities of refuge, and building roads to them (vv. 3, 6). We see it also in the requirement for more than one witness to establish guilt (v. 15), and in the penalty for perjury (vv. 18-19). It is better to let a guilty man escape punishment for lack of conclusive evidence than to take a chance that an innocent man might be wrongly condemned.

Elders. The elders mentioned here and the "judges" of 16:18 are the same. These were older, respected men, who heard and decided local civil and criminal cases. The N.T. "elder" parallels the O.T. "elder." Each is chosen for his character and commitment to God's Word

rather than wealth, popularity, or other outstanding gifts.

Moving boundary stones (19:14). Perhaps the injunction is repeated here to remind us that when we threaten a person's livelihood, we threaten his life.

"**Testimony**" (19:15). A witness ('ed) was a person with firsthand knowledge, who could report what he saw or heard (cf. Lev. 5:1). The O.T. speaks of legal testimony advanced by a witness in court in both civil and criminal matters. The witness must speak the truth. And any witness who has personal knowledge of a matter before a court must come forward with his or her testimony. These elements of O.T. Law emphasize the personal responsibility of every citizen to maintain a just and moral society. A person who lies in giving testimony becomes vulnerable to the punishment that would have been inflicted on the accused if he were guilty. Such punishment is intended to deter others from lying in their court cases.

"**A thorough investigation**" (19:18). Under O.T. Law the witness as well as the accused are to be examined thoroughly. Thus the rights of the accused as well as the victim are protected in law.

Illustration. *Israelite warriors of the second millennium B.C. battle Canaanites in a hand-to-hand struggle featuring weapons of the era: bow and arrows, javelins, and swords.*

God and war in O.T. times. The O.T. holds out the bright vision of a future without war (cf. Isa. 2:3-5; Micah 4:1-5; Zech. 14). Yet war was a grim reality in the ancient world. The Heb. language has two primary words for war: the root *laham,* to fight or wage war, is found 490 times in the O.T., while *seba'ot,* armies, is linked no less than 285 times with God's name. While the "Lord of Armies" is intended to symbolize God's unmatched power, "God of Armies" does link the Lord firmly with the wars fought by His people.

Psalm 44 reminds Israel, "It was not by their sword they won the land" but that "through [God's] name we trample our foes." David praised God as the One "who trains my hands for war, my fingers for battle" (144:1). War, as well as peace, is associated with Israel's God.

The biblical identification of God with war is rooted in His covenant relationship with His people. Under the covenant God was obligated to come to their aid when they were faithful to Him. The O.T. also teaches that many of Israel's wars were judicial, undertaken to punish evildoers (cf. Deut. 7:1-2; 20:16-17). This is particularly true of the wars of extermination Israel launched against the Canaanites. The Lord also called other nations to go to war with Israel when His own people sinned (cf. Isa. 63:10; Amos 3:14-15).

When the Prophet Habakkuk cried out to God about the injustices he saw in the Jewish homeland (Hab. 1:1-4), he was told that God was raising up the Babylonians to punish his people (vv. 5-11). Habakkuk understood, but remained disturbed. How could God use such an ungodly instrument? (vv. 13-17) In response God showed His prophet that the warlike course entered on by Babylon held the seeds of its own future destruction (2:1-20). A constant process of judgment is taking place in world history, as successive waves of oppressors fall and are replaced. God thus uses cycles of war and peace to purge social evils, and war—as terrible as it is—is an instrument of judgment in His hand. This theme is developed in major O.T. passages, among them Isa. 13–23; Jer. 46–51; Ezek. 25–32, and Amos 1–2.

God is the God of Armies, then, in a distinctive sense. As long as man's society is corrupted by sin, purging wars will take place. One day God will establish peace over the whole earth. Yet even that peace will be achieved only through His Messiah's personal involvement in a terrible final war, through which the rebellion of mankind is at last put down (cf. Isa. 13:4; 24:21-23; 29:5-8; Micah 4:1-5, 13).

Outline
Place
Finder

CONSIDER
COVENANT
COMMIT
CONCLUSION

Chapter summary. The focus of Moses' detailed description of covenant life under divine Law shifts again to concentrate on rulings governing family and social relationships. This theme will be maintained through Deuteronomy 25. Here Moses writes about unsolved murders, and how to deal with the guilt that the entire community bears when the killer is not known (21:1-9). Humane concern is reflected in the relatively gentle treatment of non-Canaanite (cf. 20:16) women taken as captives in warfare (21:10-14). The rights of the firstborn son, even if his mother is not the father's favorite wife, are protected (vv. 15-17). In Roman law, the father was assumed to be the giver of life, and thus had the right to execute his children. Here Moses restricts the parents' rights over their children to disciplining them, for God is the Giver of life and parents do not have the right to take their children's lives (vv. 18-21).

Key verse. 21:17: Law, not personal preference, governs.

Personal application. There is no "right" to be inconsiderate.

Key concepts. Guilt »pp. 79, 739. Firstborn »p. 95. Birthright »p. 40. Divorce »p. 136. Elders »p. 132. God's choice of Israel »p. 124.

INSIGHT

Corporate responsibility (21:1-9). O.T. Law makes the community responsible to execute a murderer. But what if the killer isn't known? There are two theories as to why the elders of the nearest city bear guilt. The first is that they are unable to carry out their responsibility in seeing that the killer is punished. The second is stated beautifully by Rabbi Shlomo Riskin, chief rabbi of Efrat and dean of Ohr Tora institutions in Israel today: "Whenever a man is murdered, the responsibility rests not only on the murderer, but also on the elders and sages of the nearest city. Even though the leaders themselves committed no murderous act, the corpse attests to the tragedy of human and social failures which the elders failed to halt before the ultimate fate of violent death. . . .

"Justifications can always be found, but the Torah finds the leaders guilty, and demands that the elders of the city closest to the discovered corpse go through an atonement ritual" (*Jerusalem Post*, Jan. 6, 1990).

Cultural background. The Code of Hammurabi, as well as Hittite laws, also made the nearest city responsible to pay when a traveler was robbed, and to compensate the family of a murdered man. Corporate responsibility was a basic principle of ancient law.

Captive wives (21:10-14). Sensitivity to the grief of a woman captured in war, and her subsequent legal status as a wife rather than slave, stands in sharp contrast to the brutal practices of other ancient armies. The ritual shaving and putting on new clothing is symbolic, perhaps of purification, but surely of a change in status.

Love and hate (21:15). The Heb. text reads love and hate where the NIV has "love" and "does not love." This is an accurate translation, for in Heb. "hate" may cover the entire range of meanings from intense animosity, to a rather indifferent failure to prefer.

Firstborn rights (21:16). The ruling which protects the right of the actual firstborn to a larger share of his father's estate illustrates a vital principle. God's people are not free to do whatever they may want. We are free to do what is right. The godly individual subordinates personal feelings and chooses what is virtuous.

The city gates (21:19). The gates are mentioned here, because this was the public place in the ancient world where the elders of a community gathered to administer the Law (cf. 22:15; 25:7; Ruth 4:1-2, 11; Job 29:7; Ps. 127:5).

The stubborn son (21:18-21). There is no record of such a charge being brought in Israel. Yet the existence of this law underlines the importance of family discipline in the social order. When both parents found a child uncontrollable, the city elders were to serve as judges.

Jesus prefigured (21:22-23). Gal. 3:13 quotes this verse, whose Heb. construction is strongly emphatic. Jesus bore God's curse for us.

Outline
Place
Finder

CONSIDER
COVENANT
COMMIT
CONCLUSION

Chapter summary. Old Testament sections containing specific laws frequently seem to lack organizing principles. Rulings with no obvious relationship to one another will be grouped in one small section, and this may be followed by a group of rulings which do have cohesiveness. This is true in these two chapters of Deuteronomy covenant stipulations. Here miscellaneous laws reflect God's concern for the individual (22:1-12), discuss marital relations (vv. 13-30), and identify those who cannot take part in Israel's worship (23:1-8). With them are specific regulations for preserving the cleanness of men on military expeditions (vv. 9-14), followed by more miscellaneous laws (vv. 15-25). They remind us that God was concerned with every aspect of His people's relationship with Him and others.

Key verse. 23:14: God moves about the believer's camp.

Personal application. Look for ways to honor God.

Key concepts. Eunuch »p. 715. Brotherly love »pp. 690, 867.

INSIGHT

"Do not ignore" (22:1-4). The key teaching here is that we are responsible to help others whenever aware of their need. Looking the other way, or hesitating to become involved, has no place in a biblical way of life.

Slacks? (22:5) This verse has sometimes been taken to rule out the wearing of slacks by women. Hardly. In biblical times both men and women wore loose-fitting robes—but designed differently for each of the sexes. The point of the verse is that we are not to confuse the sexes; each person is to gladly identify himself or herself as a man or woman. Each is to take pride in the person he or she is.

Proof of virginity (22:13-21). The "proof" was once thought to be blood from the girl's broken hymen, found on the marital bed. It is much better to take the Heb. *betulim* as "female adolescence" rather than "virginity." Thus the "proof" would be menstrual blood. The fact of menstruation would show that the girl was not pregnant when she married.

Rape (22:23-27). Any woman who had sex with a man in a city was assumed to have consented, since she could have cried out, and in the densely populated towns of biblical times would surely have been heard and rescued. But any who had sex in the countryside was presumed innocent. This presumption of innocence is significant, as in most cases of rape in our day attorneys typically argue that the women in some way invited the attack. Here the O.T. that some claim is "chauvinistic" is more sensitive to women than modern law!

Sexual fidelity. O.T. marriage laws empha-size fidelity and monogamy in a profligate pagan world. The penalties may seem harsh. But the principle of loyalty they accentuated remains vital for God's people.

Prostitution (23:17-18). Two types of prostitution were familiar in O.T. times. One was secular: a business transaction, sex for hire. The Heb. word is *taznut,* trans. "harlotry" in some versions, and illustrated in Gen. 34:31. There was also religious prostitution, and a cult prostitution was called *qades.* In *qades* male prostitutes (Deut. 23:17; 1 Kings 14:24; 15:12; 22:46; 2 Kings 23:7) or female prostitutes (Deut. 23:17; Hosea 4:14) engaged in sex with worshipers to stimulate pagan deities to those sex acts believed to make croplands and herds fertile. The death penalty was not imposed for secular prostitution, though it was called for in the case of religious prostitution. The Bible's strong negative view of prostitution is reflected in Deut. 23:18's prohibition against using the earnings of a prostitute to pay a vow to God. The act and its profits are detestable.

Wages/earnings. In all cultures wages involved exchanging money for services rendered. The N.T. points out that the wage sin pays is death (Rom. 6:23). In contrast, eternal life is God's gift.

Runaway slaves (23:15-16). Slaves from other nations could find refuge in Israel, which had known slavery itself in Egypt. This attitude toward the helpless contrasts with other ancient law codes. Under Hammurabi's Code, anyone harboring a runaway slave was subject to death.

Outline
Place
Finder

CONSIDER
COVENANT
COMMIT
CONCLUSION

Chapter summary. Chapter 24 continues to list miscellaneous regulations showing Israel how to live in covenant relationship with God. Here too laws are not linked in common categories, but illustrate the biblical principle that God is involved in every aspect of the believer's life. He is concerned about our marriages, our work, our sickness, the need that causes us to borrow, our relationship with the poor, and everything else in our lives.

Key verse. 24:10: Even the poor deserve respect.

Personal application. Help every person maintain his or her self-respect by treating them with sensitivity.

Key concepts. Fatherless/widows »p. 126. Lend/borrow »p. 129.

INSIGHT

"Divorce" (24:1-4). This is the O.T.'s primary passage on divorce. But its focus is on the remarriage which typically followed divorce rather than on divorce itself. The cause of divorce ("something indecent") is unclear, and has been argued futilely by ancient rabbis and modern theologians. What is clear is (1) divorce was an issue decided by the couple involved. The husband writes the divorce decree, rather than elders or a priestly court. (2) It was expected that a divorced person would remarry, as marriage was considered the normal state for an adult in ancient Israel. (3) Once a divorced wife remarried, there was no chance of a return to the first husband. Thus the integrity of the second marriage was protected.

This procedure does not mean that divorce was common in Israel, or that divorce for any and every cause was encouraged. Probably the greatest deterrent to divorce was the fact that the husband, when he gave his wife the written release, also had to return her dowry, and perhaps pay other money costs! Jesus explained this clause in O.T. Law by saying that God permitted divorce "because your hearts were hard" (Matt. 19:8). This is best understood as recognition that sin so damages some marriages that the relationship becomes destructive. In such cases, where God's intention to bless through the marriage cannot be achieved because of the hardness of human hearts, divorce is permitted.

This provision in no way changes the biblical ideal of lifelong marriage, or Scripture's condemnation of divorces motivated by lust (cf. Mal. 2:14, 16).

Marriage and war (24:5). Newlyweds were among those exempt from military service. Strikingly, the reason given is not that the family line be preserved, but that he "bring happiness to the wife he has married." Again we see the unusual sensitivity of the O.T. to women, as well as to other humanitarian concerns.

Debt and security. Several rulings here deal with the issue of debt, and security offered by the debtor to guarantee repayment. O.T. Law did not permit Israelites to charge each other interest, which in other contemporary cultures typically ran to 50 percent! O.T. Law did, however, permit taking items as security against repayment.

But even here, rulings protected the debtor. No millstone could be taken in an effort to pressure repayment, for the family depended on millstones to grind grain for daily bread (v. 6). A debtor might sell himself as a slave voluntarily to pay a debt (cf. Ex. 21:2-11), but he could not be enslaved against his will (Deut. 24:7). Even a cloak given as a pledge had to be returned at night, as cloaks were typically used as blankets when the poor slept (vv. 11-13). Thus the rights of the poor who were forced to borrow were carefully protected in law.

Don't "take" (24:11). Other verses in this passage protect the poor from those who might demand something essential to life in order to pressure repayment of a debt. This verse reminds us that self-respect is also essential to an individual's life. The person who makes a loan must wait until whatever is offered in pledge is brought to him, voluntarily. He cannot enter the poor man's house and take something of value from him. Others deserve respect, whatever their social status!

Daily pay (24:15). Wage earners in O.T. times depended on daily earnings to buy food for themselves and their families. There were no checking or savings accounts or credit cards. Thus workmen were to be paid daily, so they could meet their daily needs.

"You were slaves" (24:18, 22). We must never suppose we are better than others. To preserve us from pride and insensitivity, we must remember we too were slaves to sin till Jesus saved us.

Chapter summary. The covenant section of Deuteronomy concludes with additional miscellaneous laws (25:1-19), and two rituals of thanksgiving to be performed when Israel has occupied the Promised Land (26:1-15). A final exhortation reflects the tone of the opening of Deuteronomy's extended call to covenant living (cf. Deut. 5–11). Israel is God's treasured possession. As Israel responds to God heart and soul, in willing obedience, the Lord will set her "in praise, fame and honor high above all the nations" (v. 19).

Outline
Place
Finder

CONSIDER
COVENANT
COMMIT
CONCLUSION

Key verse. 26:18: Keep God's commandments.

Personal application. What a joy to be able to declare before the Lord that we have done what is right in His eyes.

Key concepts. Wicked »pp. 29, 350. Heart, soul »p. 120. Legal justice system »pp. 130, 132.

INSIGHT

Flogging (25:1-3). Wrongdoers were not imprisoned in Israel. Rather they were forced to make restitution to those they harmed, and make a guilt offering as a penalty. At times wrongdoers might be flogged. Other cultures also had the 40-lash limit. In later Judaism, the Jews reduced the limit to 39, lest someone miscount and strike one blow more than the Law allowed. Paul was beaten to the limit of this Law five times (2 Cor. 11:24).

Muzzling the ox (25:4). Oxen were used to thresh grain. They were hitched to a heavy sledge, and driven back and forth over grain stalks. Workers tossed the crushed material into the air, to be separated by winds that carried away lighter chaff and let heavier grain fall in heaps. This ruling suggests that the ox that does the heavy work of threshing has a right to munch on the stalks and any grain it might contain. Paul refers to this verse, using a familiar form of argument which reasons from a lesser issue to a similar, but greater issue. In 1 Cor. 9:9 he argues that the principle of the unmuzzled ox implies the right of spiritual leaders to be supported by those who benefit from their labors.

Levirate marriage (25:5-10). The practice of marrying a childless widow to one of her husband's brothers was not limited to Israel, but has been practiced in ancient Mesopotamia, India, Africa, and South America. The practice underlies the story of Onan, in Gen. 38. Its purpose was to maintain the line of the dead husband. The ruling against sexual intercourse with a brother's wife in Lev. 18:16 and 20:21 implies a "living" brother. While a male relative was expected to take the husband's role, an individual had the right to refuse. However, significant social pressure was exercised to get the relative to change his mind (Deut. 25:7-10). It is valid for others to add the weight of public opinion to the "should" side.

Mutilation (25:11-12). This is the only instance in the O.T. of mutilation being prescribed for an offense. This contrasts with Islamic law, which demands mutilation for many offenses. Why here? Perhaps because the act described might threaten the capacity of the man involved to have children and thus maintain his own family line.

Differing weights. See Lev. 19:36. »p. 87.

"I declare today" (26:3-10). This affirmation is a unique confession of faith: a statement of the individual's solidarity with the historic Jewish people. That people descended from a "wandering Aramean" (the patriarch Jacob) who entered Egypt as a tiny family, became a great people there, cried out to the Lord, and were delivered from servitude by great miracles and wonders, and then were brought by Him into the Promised Land. The confession, to be made each year as Israelites presented the firstfruits of the land's rich crops to the Lord, reaffirmed the identity of the individual Jew as a member of the chosen people, whose identity is firmly rooted in sacred history. We each need this strong sense of a personal identity that is rooted in God's acts for us in history. You and I might affirm that our father was a sinner, lost and alienated. We wandered in a barren land until God acted, in justice and grace, and through His crucified Son invited us to believe and so be adopted into His family. This, above all, is who we are: sons and daughters of God through faith in Jesus Christ.

Outline
Place
Finder

CONSIDER
COVENANT
COMMIT
CONCLUSION

Chapter summary. Moses' sermon on covenant life now draws to a close. Following the traditional suzerainty covenant form (see intro.), Moses prepares the people for the decision they must soon make. When the people enter Canaan, an altar is to be built on Mt. Ebal, with the words of God's Law written on its stones (27:1-8: see illustration, p. 139). There an impressive ceremony is intended to drive home critical truth. If Israel fully obeys the Lord, the nation will be blessed (28:1-14). But if Israel does not obey, terrible curses (disasters) will overtake the nation (vv. 15-68). This extended "disaster" section provides a preview of what actually did happen to ancient Israel, it served as the source of the prophets' interpretation of history.

Key verse. 28:1: Blessings do follow obedience.

Personal application. Every choice has consequences.

Key concepts. Altar »p. 79. Cause/effect »p. 112. Law »pp. 120, 145. Blessing »p. 127.

INSIGHT

Illustration (Opposite page). *Remains of a gigantic altar have been found by archeologists on Mt. Ebal. The tiny altar in the foreground is the tabernacle's altar of sacrifice, which gives some idea of the size of the Ebal altar. It is not certain that the remains are of the Ebal altar mentioned in Deut. 27:1-8.*

"Pronounce curses" (27:13). The distinctive word for curse used here (*me'erah*) means a binding act. This noun and its verb (*'arar*) do more than define the consequences of wrong acts. They serve as a judicial announcement of punishments that God has already imposed. The person or thing cursed is in some significant way bound, weakened, limited, and unable to do what it otherwise could. Here, as in other violations of divine law, the curse is not pronounced after the act, but is linked with the act, so one is "automatically" cursed when he or she sins. How futile to think, as some do, that "I will be safe, even though I persist in going my own way" (29:19).

The captivity (28:15-68). This passage outlines the increasingly severe judgments future generations can expect if they persist in violating God's statutes, and in turning away from Him to idolatry. The culminating judgment is captivity: "You will be uprooted from the land" and "then the Lord will scatter you among all nations" (vv. 63-64). This ultimate punishment is graphically described in verses 64-68, and is found frequently in the prophets.

Among the prophetic warnings rooted in this Deut. passage are: Isa. 5:13; Jer. 13:19; 46:19; Ezek. 12:3-11; Amos 5:27; 6:7; 7:11-17; etc. These warnings became more frequent as the rest of the judgments found in Deut. 28 were imposed—and ignored by Israel.

What did actually happen? Centuries after Moses wrote the words of warning, the people of Israel were divided into two nations, north and south. The Northern Kingdom, called Israel, was crushed and its people taken into captivity by the Assyrians in 722 B.C. The Southern Kingdom, Judah, survived only until 586 B.C., when after a series of deportations the Babylonians finally destroyed Jerusalem.

A token population returned to settle Jerusalem and part of Judea some 70 years later, but the majority of the Jews remained in foreign lands through the N.T. era. Then in A.D. 70, Jerusalem was again razed, this time by the Romans, and up until 1948 the Jewish people had no national homeland. The terrible persecutions suffered by the Jews, culminating in the Nazi holocaust of the '30s and '40s, add their testimony to the ancient words of Moses: "Among those nations you will find no repose, no resting place for the sole of your foot. There the Lord will give you an anxious mind, eyes weary with longing, and a despairing heart. You will live in constant suspense, filled with dread both night and day, never sure of your life." Yet how good to know that God has preserved His exiled people and, as Moses later promises, will yet regather and restore them as His own.

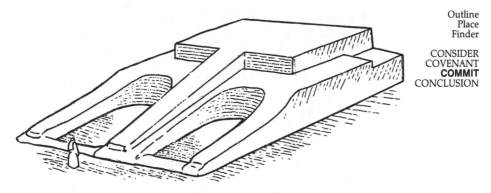

Outline
Place
Finder

CONSIDER
COVENANT
COMMIT
CONCLUSION

Chapter summary. Moses' third and last sermon is found in these two chapters. He has described the nature of covenant relationship with God carefully. Now this generation must make a decision. Moses reminds the people of what God has done (29:1 8). A decision to accept the covenant will confirm this generation as the people of the true God (vv. 9-15). But commitment to God must be irrevocable, or judgment will surely follow (vv. 16-29). As long as Israel remains faithful to God, or if a future generation turns back to Him heart and soul after straying, God will restore and bless (30:1-10). Thus the choice Israel faces is a choice between God and emptiness: between blessing and disaster, between life and death (vv. 11-20). And so Moses' sermons conclude with an invitation as meaningful today as it was then: "Now choose life, so that you and your children may live."

Key verse. 30:20: What is God to His people? Life!

Personal application. Every day we choose life and blessing by following the guidelines provided in God's Word.

INSIGHT

Curse (29:21). A different word is found here: *'alah.* This "curse" is a solemn warning, a preview of what must come if wrong choices are made. Such a "curse" is in many ways a blessing! Only if we know the consequences of our wrong choices are we likely to avoid them.

"You" (29:12-13). The Law covenant was made with the Exodus generation, who represented all Israel. Yet again and again in the O.T. we see new generations gathered "in order to enter into a covenant with the Lord your God." These events are for "covenant renewal" (cf. Josh. 24): events at which a new generation consciously and solemnly accepts for itself the benefits and obligations of covenant relationship with God.

What a reminder for you and me. The Gospel is for all—yet you and I claim it by faith for ourselves. Christ is Lord of all—yet you and I must choose to acknowledge Him as Lord in all that we do. For every individual there are those solemn moments when God speaks, and says, "You."

"Secret things" (29:29). Most commentators understand the "secret things" to refer to events known only to God. Why and how are these contrasted here with the "things which have been revealed" which belong to us? God is telling Israel not to concern itself with the future, which they cannot know or control. Instead Israel is to concern itself with the laws God has given. If Israel concentrates on keeping the Law the future will take care of itself!

Returning to God (30:1-2). The Heb. word is *sub.* The same term is used in the O.T.'s covenant vocabulary for turning away, and turning back to God. The choice is always open to us. The direction in which we turn is the most critical issue in life.

Outline
Place
Finder

CONSIDER
COVENANT
COMMIT
CONCLUSION

Chapter summary. The last four chapters of Deuteronomy depict the conclusion of Moses' life, and his last acts on behalf of the Israelites he has led so faithfully for 40 years. First he publicly commissions Joshua as his successor (31:1-8). Moses completes the writing of the Law, and commands that it be read to all Israel every seven years, at the Feast of Tabernacles (vv. 9-13). God tells Moses that in the future Israel will surely corrupt themselves with foreign gods and experience disastrous judgments (vv. 14-18). Moses is to teach Israel a "song": a poem that will be passed from generation to generation (vv. 19-29). In essence this song summarizes Israel's relationship with God: its origin in God's love (32:1-14), its sins against Him that bring national disasters (vv. 15-35), and its hope for restoration when the nation turns back to her compassionate Lord (vv. 36-43). With the song taught, Moses again exhorts obedience (vv. 44-47). Then, that very day, Moses is told to climb Mt. Nebo. From its heights Moses will be able to see the distant land across the Jordan River that has been the goal of his long journey. And there on Mt. Nebo Moses will die (vv. 48-52).

Key verse. 32:29: He who wounds heals.

Personal application. God is always faithful to discipline us when we sin and to restore us when we turn back to Him.

Key concepts. Love/obedience »p. 126. Death »p. 741. Commandment »p. 749. Abandon »p. 366. Idolatry »p. 433.

INSIGHT

"Strong and courageous" (31:6-7, 23). These two words are spoken again and again to Joshua, and appear again in the Book of Joshua (1:6, 9). Each time the exhortation is linked with promises: God will be with Joshua, and will surely enable Israel to conquer Canaan. God has given us promises too. But like Joshua, we must be strong and courageous to claim them.

"Moses wrote down this Law" (31:9). Anyone who views Scripture as God's inspired Word must accept the Pentateuch as Moses' work.

Covenant renewal (31:10-13). Many see in the command to read the Law to all every seventh year a call to Israel to regularly renew its commitment to God. Mention of children is significant: they not only need to know the Law. They also need to see their parents make overt commitment to God.

The song (31:19). Moses speaks of the song as a "witness against" Israel. It follows an ancient Middle East pattern of an indictment, or *rib*, and also serves as a summary of the covenant detailed in the rest of Deut. Through the song Israel would see the validity of God's later charges against His people and admit guilt.

The song analyzed. *Rib* pattern elements found in Deut. 32 include an introduction (vv. 1-4), interrogation (vv. 5-6), statement of God's mighty acts for Israel (vv. 7-14), direct charges (vv. 15-18), and sentence (vv. 19-25). But now the song departs from the secular pattern! Because God is compassionate, sinning Israel will be restored (vv. 26-38), and a delivered people will again worship the Lord (vv. 39-43). What a difference it makes when God is the One who charges us with fault. He does so to bring us to Himself, that He might forgive, and lift us up.

Faithfulness (32:4). As an attribute of God, "faithfulness" expresses the total dependability of God's character and His utter commitment to keeping all His promises.

God as Father (32:6). The added words "your Creator," remind us that in the O.T. God is viewed as Father in a limited sense. He is Father in the sense of Originator, the One who gives existence. Only in the N.T. is the more personal sense of Father found.

Unmixed blessing? (32:15-18) These verses remind us of Luther's observation: "A full stomach does not promote piety, for it stands secure and neglects God."

Chapter summary. Moses is about to take his last, long journey up Mt. Nebo to glimpse the Promised Land and die.

But first, as the spiritual father of Israel, Moses pronounces a blessing on the 12 tribes (33:1-5). In that time, such a blessing had special legal and prophetic significance. Moses' blessing takes the form of praise, prayers, predictions, and commands for each tribe (vv. 6-25). Often these reflect the earlier blessing given the tribal ancestors by Jacob (cf. Gen. 49). Now another writer takes up the story, and in simple yet powerful words sketches Moses' final journey (Deut. 34:1-8), and pens the great leader's epitaph (vv. 9-12).

Outline
Place
Finder

CONSIDER
COVENANT
COMMIT
CONCLUSION

Key verses. 34:10-12: God's great men deserve honoring.

Personal application. How will we be remembered at life's end?

Key concept. Blessing »p. 49.

INSIGHT

Blessings for the twelve tribes (33:6-25). For *Reuben:* Survival. The census lists in Num. 1 and 26 show a slight decline in numbers, but later the tribe suffered severely from attacks by Ammonites.

For *Judah:* Succor. Jacob (Gen. 49) singled out Judah as the future bearer of the royal scepter. Moses prays God will come to Judah's aid.

For *Levi:* Skill. Levi possesses the priesthood and the mission of serving God. How greatly this people needed every possible skill in carrying out its ministry, and encouraging devotion in Israel as a whole.

For *Benjamin:* Security. The tribe, which with Judah remained faithful to David's house at the time of the division of the kingdom in 730 B.C., is pictured as especially precious to God, and shielded by Him.

For *Joseph:* Superabundance. This is the longest of the blessings, and features a five times repetition of the Heb. word *meged,* which indicates the choicest of gifts, the richest yield of crops, and an overflowing abundance. After the division of Solomon's kingdom, the tribe of Joseph's son Ephraim emerged as the most powerful in the Northern Kingdom.

For *Zebulun* and *Issachar:* Success. These tribes later gained wealth and material success, some of which was obtained by trade.

For *Gad:* Superiority. The Heb. is obscure, but the text suggests military success and leadership.

For *Dan:* Springing. The text makes a simple but symbolic statement, perhaps suggesting an aggressive character for this tribe that was settled in Galilee.

For *Naphtali:* Satiation. Naphtali too is destined to abound with plenty.

For *Asher:* Strength. The strength is economic, symbolized by dipping one's feet in (olive) oil. This Eastern idiom simply means "let him be prosperous." Interestingly, a recent scam based on the assumption that this verse predicts petroleum will be found in Asher's tribal area took hundreds of thousands of dollars from gullible Christian investors.

Mt. Nebo. The promontory of Pisgah is 2,740 feet above sea level. It lies just 12 miles east of the place where the Jordan empties into the Dead Sea, itself 1,292 feet below sea level. Looking toward Canaan Moses would have seen the snowy peak of 9,232-foot Mt. Hermon over a hundred miles to the north, as well as the rocky highland and lush Jordan Valley of the Promised Land. Though Moses wanted to enter that land himself, he must have taken great comfort from the knowledge that soon the people he had led and loved would enter and possess it.

Moses' heritage (34:10-12). No epitaph can sum up the significance of Moses in sacred history. But these verses sum up the reverence with which he is still viewed by Jew and Christian alike.

Joshua

Joshua is the Old Testament's book of triumph and victory. It tells the story of the Israelites' conquest of Canaan under Joshua, the nation's spiritual and military leader. But the story told in this powerful Old Testament book began hundreds of years before the events it records.

Around 2100 B.C. God spoke to a man named Abram, who then lived in the fabled city of Ur, in Mesopotamia. God made wonderful promises to Abram, promises that were passed on to his son Isaac and grandson Jacob. God promised that He would have a special relationship with the descendants of these men, honored as the patriarchs, and that Abram's offspring would be given the fertile land of Canaan. The three patriarchs lived a nomadic life in Canaan, but the 12 sons of Jacob moved to Egypt in a time of terrible famine. The little family stayed there for some 400 years, and their numbers increased. The 70 who entered Egypt multiplied to become millions. But in Egypt they were enslaved. God, remembering His ancient promises, sent Moses to lead the Israelites to freedom. Their freedom was won through miracles God performed, and the Exodus generation was led by Moses to Mt. Sinai. There God gave Israel a Law that showed His chosen people how to love Him and one another. But the Exodus generation refused to trust God. Because of their rebellion, all the adults who left Egypt died during 40 years of wandering in the desert. But their children learned from the Exodus generation's experiences. The new generation did trust God, and was fully committed to obey Him. It is this new and committed generation that we read about in the Book of Joshua. It is this new, obedient generation who wins by warfare the land God promised to Abraham so long ago.

The Book of Joshua has long been a favorite of believers. We love its stories: of Rahab, who chose to side with God against her own city, and whose faith saved her life. Of Jericho, and the puzzling command to march silently around the fortress city, waiting for God to tumble its massive walls. But most of all, Joshua reminds us of the faithfulness of God, who keeps all His promises. And Joshua reminds us of the need for obedience, if we are to claim God's promises to us, and know spiritual victory in our own day.

JOSHUA AT A GLANCE

KEY PEOPLE
Moses   *The deliverer, lawgiver, and leader of the Jews during the Exodus.*
Joshua   *The successor of Moses and leader of the armies of Israel.*
Caleb   *A bold warrior whose faith in God is as unshakable in his old age as when he urged Israel to attack Canaan 40 years earlier.*

KEY EVENTS
Crossing the Jordan (Josh. 3).
The battle for Jericho (Josh. 6).   *Israel obeys God's strange command—and watches awestruck as the walls of the fortress city crumble.*
Sin at Ai (Josh. 7).   *One man's sin costs the lives of 36 soldiers, and teaches Israel a grim lesson on the necessity of total obedience.*
The land divided (Josh. 13–19).   *Tribes and families are assigned land by lot.*
Joshua says farewell (Josh. 23–24).   *Joshua urges victorious Israel to keep on serving and obeying God.*

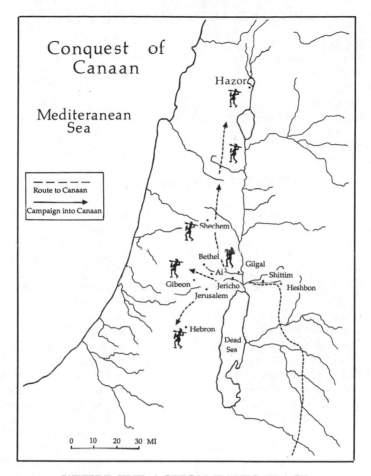

WHERE THE ACTION TAKES PLACE

The events reported in Joshua take place in Canaan. The Israelite forces crossed the Jordan opposite Jericho, a strategic city that controlled the passes leading up into Canaan's central highlands. From the base camp at Gilgal Joshua launched two major campaigns. The first struck south, to defeat a coalition of kings of the Amorite city-states of Jerusalem, Hebron, Jamut, Lachish, and Eglon. The other struck north, against a more powerful mixed Canaanite force from Hazor, Madon, and other northern cities. These campaigns ended organized Canaanite resistance. But only part of the Promised Land was occupied by Israel at this time. Tribal groups were to drive out the remaining Canaanites when they needed land for expansion. *Major cities are indicated on the map. Arrows trace the course of central, southern, and northern campaigns. Figures show the sites of major battles.*

Date and Authorship. No author is named, but Joshua may have written this report of the Conquest. The invasion and conquest of Canaan probably took place between 1406 B.C. and 1399 B.C., with Joshua's farewell speech given at the covenant renewal ceremony of 1385 B.C.

THEOLOGICAL OUTLINE OF JOSHUA

CONTENT OUTLINE OF JOSHUA

Chapter summary. From the beginning Joshua served as Moses' assistant and Israel's leader in battle (cf. Ex. 17:9). Now this man, whom some believe was an officer in Pharaoh's army before the Exodus, is to be Moses' successor. Joshua will be the spiritual and military leader of God's people during the conquest of Canaan, the Promised Land. It's appropriate then that the book opens with a description of God's preparation of Joshua for his role. That preparation opens with a promise (1:1-5), for all God's work in us is rooted in grace. Joshua is to be "strong and courageous," and claim the promise by carefully following God's Law (vv. 6-8). As Joshua walks the path Law defines, the Lord will be with him wherever he goes (v. 9).

Ready now, Joshua orders the people to prepare to break camp in three days (vv. 10-11), and reminds the Transjordan tribes of their promise to fight with their brothers (vv. 12-15; cf. Num. 32). The tribes reiterate their commitment to the Conquest, and acknowledge Joshua's leadership under God (Josh. 1:16-18). Joshua, spiritually prepared and recognized now as the successor of Moses, is ready to lead Israel to victory.

Key verse. 1:9: God's command and presence are enough.

Personal application. A knowledge of God's promises still gives us the courage we need to obey His Word.

INSIGHT

Servant (1:1). The word identifying Moses as God's servant is the participle of *sarat*, to serve or minister. It indicates that the person served (here, God) is of high rank, it suggests a close relationship between the servant and the one served, and it casts the work of the servant as of the greatest importance. Being "the servant of the Lord" is the highest rank.

The Promised Land (1:3-4). Two sets of boundaries are identified in Scripture. One sets out the full extent of the land to be possessed, and is stated in 1:4 and many other passages (cf. Gen. 15:18; Num. 13:21; 34:1-12; Deut. 1:7; 11:24; 1 Kings 4:21; Amos 6:14). The other defines the land historically possessed by Israel, implied here in Josh. 1:3 ("where you set your foot") and in other passages as "from Dan to Beersheba" (2 Sam. 24:2-8). God has more for Israel than she has ever been able to possess.

Obeying all the Law (1:7). The dominant theological theme in Deut. and in Josh. is obedience to the Law. And the theme is woven on past these early times throughout Israel's history (cf. Deut. 4:44; Josh. 1:7; 22:2, 4-5; Jud. 2:20; 1 Sam. 12:14-15; 1 Kings 2:3-4; 11:9-13, 31-39; 2 Kings 17:7-20; 21:2-15; 22:11-20). Theologians have defined three functions of O.T. Law. One: Law reveals the character of the God who gave it. Two: Law serves as a standard against which human behavior can be measured, and by which all can be judged. And three: Law guides choices, enabling the believer to please God and thus to enjoy His blessing here and now. It is this "third function of the Law" that is highlighted in this and other O.T. passages. Biblical history demonstrates the fact that when God's O.T. people kept His Law, the Lord blessed them and enabled them to succeed. It also documents Israel's failures, and shows that when the Law was abandoned, national disaster followed. For more on Law, see »pp. 120, 376, 606, 790.

Model leaders. Moses is the unique leader of Israel, the prototype prophet who prefigures Jesus Christ. But Joshua is a model for all leaders of the O.T. era. What do we learn of leadership from him? First, the mission of O.T. leaders was to enable Israel to claim and hold the land promised by God (1:2-4). Second, the effectiveness of O.T. leaders depended on the divine presence, for it was God who gave victory (v. 5). Third, prime responsibility of the leader was personal commitment to "be careful to obey all the Law My servant Moses gave you" (v. 7). Fourth, the chief characteristic of the leader was strength and courage, for many times it would seem risky to obey God completely, and yet obedience was essential.

Outline
Place
Finder

PREPARATION
WARFARE
ALLOTMENT
FAREWELL

Chapter summary. Two spies are sent to explore Jericho (2:1). They are discovered, but are hidden by an innkeeper/prostitute named Rahab (vv. 2-7). Her actions are explained as a faith-response to God, which contrasts with the fear-response of her fellow Canaanites (vv. 8-11). Rahab's faith is honored, and she and her family are promised safety when the Israelites over-throw Jericho (vv. 12-22). In the spies' report, the terror felt by the people of Jericho is taken as evidence that God has indeed "given the whole land into our hands" (vv. 23-24).

Yet Israel's faith needs strengthening, and God provides a sign. Joshua tells Israel that when priests carry the ark of God into the Jordan River, then in flood stage, its waters will dry up (3:1-13). This miracle happens, and the whole people cross the riverbed "on dry ground" (vv. 14-17). A confident Israel and the fearful Canaanites are about to meet in the Conquest's first battle, each freshly aware that God is with Israel.

Key verse. 2:11: There's a great difference between knowing God and knowing about Him.

Personal application. Rahab reminds us that it is what we do that demonstrates the reality of our faith.

Key concepts. Ark of covenant »p. 68. Faith »pp. 35, 458.

INSIGHT

A prostitute named Rahab. Many believe that Rahab maintained a small inn, and that one of the services offered was prostitution.

Rahab. Rahab is one of three women mentioned in the lineage of Christ (Matt. 1:5). She is commended in Heb. 11:31 for her faith, and in James 2:25 for expressing her faith in her acts. Some commentators have become involved in lengthy debates over Rahab's lie to the ruler of Jericho (cf. 2:4-5), arguing on the one hand that she should be excused because of the extreme circumstances, and others roundly condemning her because lies are never justified. The debate, however, misses the point. Rahab was a woman from a pagan culture, in which prostitute inn-keepers were considered respectable, in whom faith was newly born. Like the rest of us, Rahab was a sinner who made wrong and unwise choices. And like all of God's redeemed she was saved despite, rather than because of, her personal moral qualities. What sets Rahab apart is that when she heard of God, she chose to commit herself to Him. Her faith response to the Lord, not her past, or her lie, won her both salvation and praise. Her acceptance into the people of God and her role as an ancestress of Jesus Christ reminds us that the God who forgives our past gives us a new character—and a new future as well.

"Our hearts sank" (2:11). Rahab describes the fear response to God that gripped the others in Jericho, and which contrasts with her own faith response. It is never enough to believe that God exists. That knowledge can terrorize as well as transform. The issue is, what will we do with our knowledge of God. Rahab made the right choice: she would turn to Him and trust Him. We need to help others who say "I believe" see that "believing" is not faith until it becomes personal commitment.

Shittim. The name means "acacia tree," and was a site about seven miles east of the Jordan River. Jericho lay about seven miles west.

Stopping the Jordan's waters. The Jordan is a narrow stream except when it's at flood stage. Even in flood, however, landslides up-river have cut off the river's waters opposite Jericho as recently as the 19th century. However, the text makes it very clear that whatever stopped the river waters in Joshua's day was a miracle. God may have used natural means, but the supernatural is attested by: (1) foretelling the event (3:13-14); (2) the exact timing of the event (v. 15); (3) the amount of water held back "in a heap" for most of a day (v. 16); (4) the fact that the drained river bottom immediately became as firm as "dry ground" (v. 17); and the timing of the return of the waters with when the priests carrying the ark left the riverbed (4:18). God strengthens our faith before He tests us.

Chapter summary. Joshua commemorates God's miraculous parting of the waters of the Jordan River by erecting a heap of 12 stones taken from the stream bed (4:1-5). The "memorial" (Heb. *zikkaron*) is a witness, a visible symbol that will enable future generations to sense the wonder of what God did in bringing Israel into the Promised Land (vv. 6-9). The miracle, witnessed by all Israel, also confirms Joshua's appointment as leader and enables him to command the people's respect (vv. 10-16). When the priests leave the riverbed, the waters of the Jordan return to full flood stage (vv. 17-18). The dozen stones are set up at Gilgal, where Israel camps, to remind present and future generations of the power of the Lord (vv. 19-24). But now, before the Conquest can continue, the people must be spiritually prepared. Joshua has all the men circumcised (5:1-9), and when this important sign of covenant relationship with God is completed, the Israelites celebrate their first Passover in Canaan (vv. 10-12). When Israel is prepared, a supernatural visitor appears to Joshua as "Commander of the Lord's army," to give Joshua the strangest orders ever recorded in the annals of warfare (vv. 13-15).

Key verse. 4:24: God's wonders promote faith.

Personal application. We prepare for spiritual warfare by making sure of our relationship with God.

Key concepts. Ark of covenant »p. 68. Passover »p. 59. Manna »p. 99. Circumcision »pp. 36, 126. Priests »p. 81. War »p. 133.

INSIGHT

Memorial (4:7). The *zikkaron* "memorial" or "remembrance" is one of the most powerful of O.T. religious concepts. It is applied to this heap of stones, but also to the Passover festival itself. Thus a "memorial" is any symbolic item or event intended to help God's people identify with a work of God on their behalf. The heap of stones would help future generations sense that God had parted the waters of the Jordan for them, as well as that first generation. The Passover supper would help them sense the wonder of God's redemption, as He saved them from death as well as Israel's first-born in Egypt. We Christians have a *zikkaron* too: instituted when Jesus said, "This is My body." When we take part in the Lord's Supper we are present at the cross: we identify ourselves with Christ's sacrifice, and claim the benefits of salvation for ourselves.

Revered (4:14). Joshua was revered because the miracle was taken as evidence of his closeness to God. We need leaders we can revere, not because they perform miracles, but because they are marked by an intimate personal relationship with God.

The reproach of Egypt (5:9). The reproach of Egypt was the social shame of slavery. The circumcision of this generation in obedience to God's ancient command came at a time when the new generation was about to take its place as a nation in its own right. The social shame which was attached to circumcision as the mark of a slave race was about to be replaced by the pride of becoming a race of conquerors.

The manna stopped (5:12). God had not stopped supplying the daily need of His people. He was about to supply their needs in a different way—from the produce of their own land. Let's remember when the manna stops for us, it is not a sign that we have been abandoned by God. It is simply a sign that something new, and better, lies ahead.

Commander of the army (5:14). The phrase, "prince of the host of Yahweh" is found only here and in Dan. 8:11, where the prince is God Himself. This, plus the call for Joshua to take off his shoes, with many O.T. references to an "Angel of the Lord" who is God Himself (»p. 37), suggests that it is God who appears to command Israel's armies.

Outline
Place
Finder

PREPARATION
WARFARE
ALLOTMENT
FAREWELL

Chapter summary. Joshua is told to lead his people in a silent circuit of Jericho for six consecutive days. On the seventh day the people are to march around the city seven times, and then at a signal everyone is to shout. Then, God promised, "the walls will collapse" and the city will fall (6:1-5). The people follow the strange instructions (vv. 6-14), and on the seventh day, the walls fall (vv. 15-21). Rahab and her family are saved. But the rest of the population is killed, Jericho's wealth is dedicated to God (vv. 22-25), and Joshua places a curse on any who might try to rebuild the fallen Canaanite stronghold (vv. 26-27).

Key verse. 6:2: God gives the victory.

Personal application. We aren't to judge the reasonableness of God's commands. We're to obey them.

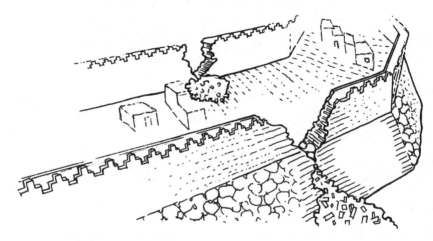

INSIGHT

Illustration. *The rugged walls of Jericho featured a stone base 11 feet high, topped by 35 feet of smooth stone sloping upward at 35 degrees to join the towering main walls. Direct assault would have been nearly impossible, and a protracted siege would have permitted the other Canaanite tribes to mobilize and attack Israel. God's intervention, which toppled the walls, made that strategically important quick victory possible.*

Jericho archeology. Archeologists have disagreed on the dating of the ruins of Jericho. Initially John Garstang dated the ruins of what is known as City IV, an occupation level that shows destruction due to warfare, at about 1400 B.C., which fits with the biblical date of the Exodus. Later Kathleen Kenyon argued that the data implies a 1250 B.C. date for City IV, which does not fit the traditional date of the Exodus and Conquest at all. Most recently, British scholar John J. Bimson and others have reexamined the data and Ken-

yon's arguments, and shown that a 15th century B.C. date actually is indicated. While the date of the Exodus continues to be debated by scholars, the weight of the evidence now firmly supports 1400 B.C. and the internal chronology of Scripture.

Destroyed every living thing (6:21). The extermination of the people of Jericho has been objected to on humanitarian grounds. Yet 400 years earlier God told Abraham that Israel could not inherit Canaan "for the sin of the Ammorites has not yet reached its full measure" (Gen. 15:16). Like the Genesis Flood and the fiery destruction of Sodom and Gomorrah, Israel's extermination of the Canaanites was a judicial act. They were to be destroyed because their sins were so great and their religious corruption so complete that extermination was just (cf. »p. 66).

Joshua's curse (6:26-27). Joshua's prophetic curse came true (cf. 1 Kings 16:34; »p. 138).

Chapter summary. After the victory at Jericho, Joshua sends spies to Ai (7:1-2). Because of their report, he sends only a small force to attack the city of Ai (vv. 3-4). But the men of Ai route the Israelite force, killing 36 (v. 5). A grim Joshua (vv. 6-9) is told that the defeat was caused by the disobedience of one man, who violated God's command and took treasure from Jericho (vv. 10-13). The next morning the guilty man, Achan, is exposed. He confesses (vv. 14-21), and the stolen treasure is unearthed in Achan's tent. The guilty Achan and his family are stoned to death (vv. 22-26). With the sin purged, Israel easily defeats Ai (8:1-25), and this time the plunder is distributed to the Israelites. The king of Ai, the last survivor of the city, is executed (vv. 26-29). Jericho has demonstrated that obedience brings victory. Ai has shown that disobedience leads to defeat. With these vital spiritual lessons deeply impressed on Israel, the people gather on Mount Ebal and Mount Gerizim, to hear the Law recited, as Moses had commanded before the people invaded the Promised Land (vv. 30-35; cf. Deut. 27).

Outline
Place
Finder

PREPARATION
WARFARE
ALLOTMENT
FAREWELL

Key verse. 7:21: Values nothing more than doing God's will.

Personal application. We can't expect spiritual victories if we consciously disobey the Lord.

INSIGHT

"Devoted" (7:1). The term (*haram*) indicates anything dedicated to God. Devoted objects, such as the gold and silver of Jericho, were purified by fire and became part of the tabernacle treasures. Cities and enemies "devoted" to God were under a ban, and were to be completely destroyed.

"I will not be with you" (7:12). Joshua rightly interpreted the defeat at Ai as withdrawal of divine aid. But Joshua did not understand why until God unveiled the sin that caused it. When we experience reverses we too often ask, "why?" (v. 7) The reason for reverses is not always sin. But it is still wise for us to examine our hearts.

"Come forward" (7:14). This descriptive phrase suggests how the guilty person was discovered. It is most likely the Urim and Thummim (»p. 70) were used by the high priest to indicate "yes" or "no" as tribes, then clans, then families, and finally individuals came forward to determine the guilty man.

A **"disgraceful thing"** (7:15). The Heb. phrase is *nabalah beyisrael*. It comes from the same root as *nabal*, which is often translated "fool" but which indicates the gross immorality of one who denies God and remains closed to Him. To commit a "disgraceful thing in Israel" is to defy the standards of the believing community and selfishly gratify one's own perverted desires.

Achan's sons and daughters (7:24-26). Why were Achan's family members executed for Achan's sin? Some have argued the reason is a "Hebrew concept of corporate personality." A more likely reason is suggested by verse 21: the items were hidden "inside my tent." Family members must have known what their father did, and where the stolen wealth was hidden.

Was the death penalty merited? Certainly, for Achan's act had affected the well-being of the entire Hebrew community and led to the death of 36 Israelite soldiers at the hands of the men of Ai.

Ai's location. Ai has long been assumed to be identified with the ruins of Et-Tell. But the findings of archeologists simply do not fit with the story in Joshua or any dating of the Conquest, for Et-Tell was unoccupied between 2400 B.C. and 1220 B.C., when it was merely a tiny, unwalled village. Recent suggestions that Et-Tell is not the site of Ai have gained support, and no one is sure just where Ai lay.

Thirty thousand? (8:3) Many believe the force of "best fighting men" (i.e., "best men") numbered 30 rather than 30,000. The reason is that the Heb. word *'elep*, which means "thousand," also can be translated "officer" or "chief." Only a small force would have been required to take an Ai empty of defenders, and set the city afire.

149

Outline
Place
Finder

PREPARATION
WARFARE
ALLOTMENT
FAREWELL

Chapter summary. News of the Israelites' victories in central Canaan mobilizes the other city-states to united action (9:1-2). But the nearby Gibeonites rely on deceit in a desperate effort to survive. Pretending to come from a great distance, delegates offer to become a subject people out of respect for Israel's God (vv. 3-13). The Israelites failed to seek divine guidance. They were taken in, and concluded a peace treaty—only to learn three days later that the Gibeonites were near neighbors (vv. 14-17). Because the peace treaty was sworn to in the Lord's name, it could not be broken. The Gibeonites survived, but as virtual slaves of the Israelites (9:18-27).

Key verse. 9:14: Don't make the mistake Israel did!

Personal application. A person who gives his or her word is bound to keep it, even when a promise is made unwisely.

Key concepts. Covenant »p. 35. Leading »p. 131.

INSIGHT

Gibeon. The Gibeonites occupied four cities (v. 17) in Canaan's central highlands, just six miles from Jerusalem. Archeological studies suggest their combined population was only about 7,500 people.

"We are your servants" (9:8). Most scholars take this statement as a polite form of address. Others see it as expressing a willingness to be subject to Joshua and Israel.

Make a treaty (9:6, 11). The Heb. word is *brit,* "covenant." The linkage of "make a covenant" and "we are your servants" in v. 11 indicates that the Gibeonites expected to be subject to Israel and were willing to make a treaty which spelled out their subordination. This treaty, however, would have definite advantages for the Gibeonites. This type of ancient treaty obligated subject people to pay tribute and recognize their partner's authority, but it also obligated the superior nation to protect the subordinate from enemies.

Inquire of the Lord. God gives general guidance to His people through Scripture. But for us as well as ancient Israel, specific situational guidance is also available. In O.T. times this was provided by prophets and by use of the Urim and Thummim, worn by the high priest. Joshua failed to seek God's guidance, but relied on evidence available to his senses—the worn clothing, cracked wineskins, and moldy bread. What a reminder that we must rely not on our own understanding but seek guidance from the Lord.

The whole assembly grumbled (9:18). This grumbling is different from that of the first Exodus generation (cf. Ex. 16:2, 8). Then Israel complained against the Lord. Here they complain against the leaders, because they are prevented from carrying out God's command to exterminate Canaan and make no peace treaty with them (cf. Ex. 23:32-33; Deut. 7:2, 16; 20:11, 15). The people were finally convinced by the argument that no oath made in God's name could be broken, even if it was entered into foolishly.

Slavery for the Gibeonites. The treaty had established Israel as suzerain, and Gibeon as a subject people. Joshua was thus within his rights to condemn the Gibeonites to perpetual slavery as "woodcutters and water carriers." What happened to the Gibeonites? This small group of Canaanite people survived through the era of the Judges into the period of the Kings. Some 400 years after the treaty was made, King Saul rashly tried to exterminate them. Later they demanded David surrender seven of Saul's descendants to be hanged to expiate Saul's violation of the ancient treaty. David felt obligated to comply (cf. 2 Sam. 21). Even an ancient oath, sworn in God's name, must be honored by future generations.

Chapter summary. A coalition of Canaanite kings now attacks Gibeon, which calls on Joshua to honor his treaty obligations and provide help (10:1-6). The Israelite attack, after an all-night march, puts the enemy to flight. God turns this into a decisive defeat by hurtling hailstones on the fleeing Canaanites (vv. 7-11), and by extending daylight a full 24 hours so Israel's enemy can be exterminated (vv. 12-15). The captured kings are executed (vv. 16-28) and key cities of the south are destroyed (vv. 29-39). Joshua's decisive action has crushed the ability of the south to resist, and subdues the entire region.

Success of the southern campaign motivates all the north to unite, and a large, well-equipped army moves out against the Israelites (11:1-6). Again Joshua attacks suddenly. The enemy army is destroyed, and Joshua moves against the most powerful northern cities (vv. 7-15). Though battles are fought for "a long time," the campaign is a success and at last "the land had rest from war" (vv. 16-23). The account of the Conquest concludes with a list of defeated Canaanite kings and territories (12:1-24).

Outline
Place
Finder

PREPARATION
WARFARE
ALLOTMENT
FAREWELL

Key verse. 11:15: Total obedience brought total victory.

Personal application. Don't expect to win spiritual victories quickly, or without effort. But do expect victory.

INSIGHT

Joshua's march (10:7). The distance between Gilgal and Gibeon is about 18 miles, and could have been covered in about 10 hours.

The sun stood still (10:12-14). Some dismiss the description as poetic hyperbole, but conservatives have always held to a historic intervention by God. Many have, however, debated what the text actually describes. (1) Some suggest an eclipse divided the normal day and thus seemed to double it. (2) Some believe the light was prolonged by a "miraculous suspension of the revolution of the earth upon its axis." (3) Some suggest a comet flew near the earth, slowing the earth's rotation, or shedding unexpected light. The text makes it clear that what happened was a miracle, an intervention by God on behalf of Israel in answer to Joshua's prayer. The physical means God employed are irrelevant to the passage's portrayal of God's personal involvement in Israel's struggle for the land.

Triumph (10:24). The image of the victor's feet placed on the neck of defeated enemies is also seen in David's psalm of praise to God who "armed me with strength for battle; You made my adversaries bow at my feet" (Ps. 18:39).

Hazor (11:1). Hazor was 10 times the size of any Canaanite city of the era, covering some 175 acres and protected by great earthen walls. The city is mentioned in Egyptian docu-ments of about 1900 B.C., and Mesopotamian documents of 1700 B.C. In Joshua's time it probably had 40,000 inhabitants, with a similar number of horses.

"Suddenly" (11:7). Josephus says the northern coalition army had 300,000 infantry, 10,000 cavalry, and 20,000 war chariots. These chariots would have been of wood, armored with bits of iron and possibly equipped with iron blades attached to their wheels. The geography of the site, with the description of Joshua's attack, suggested to John Garstang that the chariots had been disassembled for transportation through the mountains to the flat plains of Merom, and had not been put back together when Joshua attacked "suddenly."

Hamstrung horses (11:6). Cutting the tendon in one of the rear legs of a horse made it useless in war. God's command to hamstring enemy chariot horses and to burn captured chariots was intended to drive home a vital message. Victory did not depend on superior armament, but on God's help.

Only Hazor (11:13). The lengthy war (v. 18), which took some five years (cf. 14:10), saw only Hazor razed in the north. Frequent mention of "the hill country" (11:16-23) is consistent with later reports. The military campaign crippled organized Canaanite resistance, but Israel's control was largely limited to Canaan's hill country.

Chapter summary. Though large areas of Canaan remain unoccupied, it is time for Joshua to divide the land among the nine and a half tribes who will settle west of the Jordan (13:1-7). The text reviews the inheritance of the Transjordan tribes (vv. 8-33). Then Joshua gives a detailed description of the allotment of the other tribes in Canaan proper (14:1–19:51). But first Joshua tells of the request of that grand old warrior, Caleb, who 45 years earlier spied out Canaan with Joshua and urged Israel to take the land then (cf. Num. 14). Caleb, now 85, asks for Hebron, a fertile but strongly fortified hilltop site occupied by Anakites (giants). "The Lord helping me," Caleb proclaims, "I will drive them out" (14:6-15). The spirit of Caleb, which has enabled Israel to triumph over the Canaanites, will permit each tribe to occupy all its territory as its population expands, if only Israel will continue to trust.

Key verse. 18:6: Land division was not by chance, for God controlled the lot.

Personal application. David reflects on God's sovereignty in his life in Psalm 16, saying, "Lord, You have assigned me my portion and my cup. . . . The boundary lines have fallen for me in pleasant places." Let us rejoice in the good God gives us.

INSIGHT

Large areas to be taken (13:1). Joshua has succeeded as a leader. He completely obeyed Moses' commands (11:15), and though much of Canaan has not been taken, he is now to divide it among the Israelites. Joshua is the model of a successful leader, and a challenge to the leaders who will follow. Only by obeying the Lord as fully as Moses did can Israel hope to take the yet unoccupied territory. No leader's task is ever finished. Each generation has new challenges to faith. The only thing of value we can pass on to others is that faithfulness to God which brings victory.

The remaining land (13:2-5). The territories described lie outside Canaan's highlands. These were rich lands, thickly settled by the Canaanites, and adaptable to chariot warfare.

The allotment (15:1). The distribution of the land by lot has great significance. Apparently the same process was used to determine clan and family lands within tribes. As God controlled the fall of the lot, each family felt that God had personally granted its holdings. These family lands were not to be sold, but could be leased for a maximum of 50 years before being returned to the original owners (cf. Lev. 25). The tithes paid on produce of the land were a rightful return to God, the land's owner. Throughout the O.T., there runs the deep feeling that an individual's land testifies to his personal relationship with God and that possession of the Promised Land is a witness to Israel's unique position as God's chosen.

Map (opposite page). The map shows the territories allotted to Israel's tribes. The shaded areas represent land actually occupied at the time of the Conquest. Most of the cities named in the carefully defined description of tribal allotments cannot be placed with any certainty today. Key cities which can be definitely located within tribal areas are shown on the map.

Manasseh's folly (17:12-13). The decision of the tribe of Manasseh to subject the Canaanites in their territory to forced labor rather than drive them out prefigures the failure of Israel as a whole to follow Moses' instructions after the death of Joshua. This failure led to religious and moral corruption as Canaanite practices were adopted, and resulted in centuries of oppression, described in the next book of the O.T., Judges.

Manasseh's complaint (17:14-18). These verses further display the deterioration of faith. The people of Manasseh complain they do not have enough territory, and demand more of the conquered lands. They want an easy life, without challenges. Joshua tells them to take the land they need from the Canaanites. But the Manassates object that they are unable to defeat forces with chariots of iron. How quickly we forget! May God give us the courage to keep on believing when life keeps on raising up new challenges for you and me.

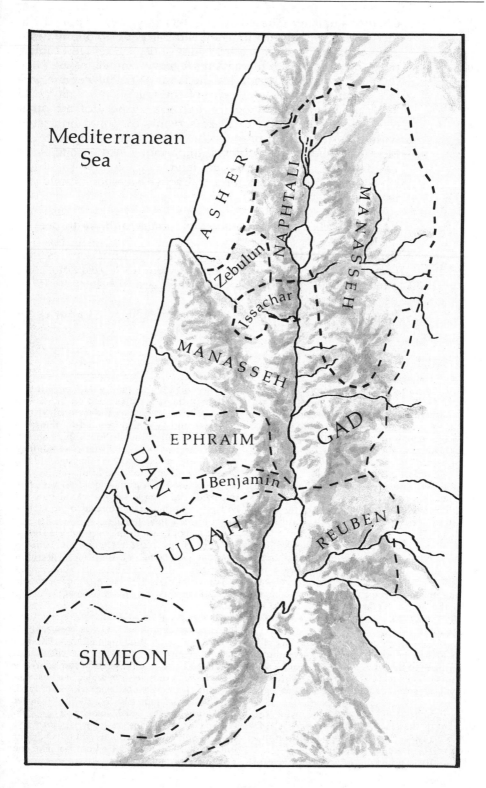

Mediterranean
Sea

ASHER

Zebulun

NAPHTALI

Issachar

MANASSEH

MANASSEH

EPHRAIM

GAD

DAN

Benjamin

JUDAH

REUBEN

SIMEON

Chapter summary. These two chapters serve as an appendix to the allotment of the land. They show a people continuing to obey the Lord, first by establishing cities of refuge—centers which were central to the nation's legal system (chap. 20). Then the people make provision for the landless Levites, whose welfare depends on the generosity of the landed tribes. Some 48 levitical cities are scattered through the territory of the other tribes, giving all access to these servants of God who shared with the priests the duty of teaching God's Law (chap. 21). The message of these two chapters is important. Obedience to God's Word enabled Israel to take the land. Only continuing obedience to a law which calls for a distinctive national lifestyle will maintain her there.

Key verse. 20:2: A victorious people must continue to obey.

Personal application. The time of greatest spiritual peril is after some significant victory is won, and we tend to relax our commitment to depend on and obey the Lord.

Key concepts. Legal justice system »pp. 130, 132. Capital punishment »pp. 29, 114. Levites »p. 95.

INSIGHT

Cities of refuge (20:2). The importance of a biblical theme is frequently demonstrated by its repetition. This principle marks cities of refuge as of great importance, for extended instructions about them are found in Ex. 21, Num. 35, Deut. 4, 19, and here in Josh. 20. Legal principles laid down for flight to a city of refuge define elements that were to characterize Israel's entire legal system. There was to be quick access to the legal system's protection, illustrated by the placement of the cities and the fact that roads were to be constructed to them. There was careful examination for guilt or innocence under strict rules of evidence. Motive or the lack of motive was to be weighed, and multiple witnesses were required for conviction. When evidence was lacking, the accused was to be given the benefit of the doubt. While the guilty were to be strictly punished, the innocent were to be safeguarded.

Conditions in modern society are very different from conditions in ancient agricultural Israel. But the humane legal principles imbedded in the laws relating to the cities of refuge can still serve as guidelines to what is right and just.

Location (20:7-9). For a map showing the location of the cities of refuge see page 115.

A gift (21:3). The closer we are to God, the more merciful we are to others.

A spiritual principle. A unique feature of

Israelite religion was that, while the spiritual welfare of the tribes depended on the service of the priests and Levites, the material welfare of priests and Levites depended on the spiritual state of the other tribes! This is shown throughout the O.T., for in times of spiritual renewal the tithes were paid that enabled the priests and Levites to serve at the temple. But often in times of spiritual decline tithes were not paid, and temple service was abandoned as God's ministers were forced to work their fields to feed their families.

God's people are to take care of the clergy. But the clergy must maintain the people's spiritual well-being, or they too will suffer materially.

The cities (21:4-41). The location of the 48 levitical cities is shown on the map on page 115.

A summary (21:43-45). These verses sum up the message of Joshua: God has been faithful. He has kept every promise, and given His people rest. However, another theme emerges in Joshua and will be developed in Judges. While God has been completely faithful, Israel has fallen short of complete obedience (cf. 13:1-6; 15:63; 16:10; 17:12-13; Jud. 1:19, 21, 27-35). Whatever the future holds for Israel, no one will be able to blame God for failing to keep His promises. How true this is today. God is faithful. Only our unfaithfulness can keep us from claiming the rest that He provides.

154

Outline
Place
Finder

PREPARATION
WARFARE
ALLOTMENT
FAREWELL

Chapter summary. With the land conquered, the men of the tribes whose lands lie east of the Jordan return home. But just over the Jordan they stop to build an altar. The action scandalizes the other tribes, who see the act as apostasy. This chapter tells the story of that event, and in the process shows how Israel, now settled in her land, can deal with the disputes which must surely come.

The story is introduced with a summary of Joshua's commendation and release of eastern tribes (22:1-8). The chapter shifts to narrative form, and tells of the construction of an altar, the dismay this created, and Israel's readiness to launch a holy war against the supposed apostates (vv. 9-12). But first a delegation led by Phinehas the priest is sent to see if conflict can be avoided (vv. 13-15). Adopting the formal legal style of accusation (vv. 16-20), defense (vv. 21-29), and resolution (vv. 30-34), the story shows how a people committed to God can work out differences. With harmony restored Israel is ready to settle down and enjoy the land God has so generously provided.

Key verse. 22:31: Resolve, don't retain, doubts.

Personal application. Love for God and others often calls for confrontation, not to condemn, but to express concern.

Key concepts. Altar »p. 79. Love, obedience »p. 126. Tabernacle »p. 67. Heart and soul »p. 120. Blessing »p. 49.

INSIGHT

Background. When the Israelites approached Canaan they were opposed by peoples who lived east of the Jordan. They defeated these people, but two and a half of Israel's tribes asked for their rich grasslands, ideal for raising cattle, as their inheritance. Moses gave them the land, but only on condition that all their fighting men cross the Jordan and fight the Canaanites with the other tribes. This condition was accepted, and for at least five years the men of Reuben, Gad, and the half-tribe of Manasseh, remained faithful to their commitment (cf. Num. 32). Josh. 22:1-8 reports Joshua's discharge of these faithful soldiers.

The altar (22:10-11). Mosaic Law commanded that sacrifices be made only at the altar of Israel's central sanctuary (cf. Deut. 12), which at that time stood in the tabernacle court. Building another altar, of the unique design that God required for altars of sacrifice (cf. Ex. 20:24-26), seemed an act of open defiance of the divine Law. The fact that the tribes west of the Jordan were willing to go to war over this issue shows how dedicated the people were at that time to obeying God completely.

The reconciliation process. The chapter illustrates a process for reconciling differences that can be applied today as well as in ancient

Israel. (1) The Israelites immediately sent a delegation to investigate the issue, (vv. 13-14). Rather than gossip or slander, the Israelites were dedicated to dealing with the issue and finding a way to maintain harmony. (2) The delegation stated its fears plainly, and urged repentance (vv. 15-20). Even though the delegation had prejudged the Transjordan tribes, they were eager to restore relationship with God and brotherhood. (3) Though innocent, the Transjordan tribes listened without defensiveness (vv. 15-20). (4) The Transjordan tribes then explained fully, expressing their concern that the accusers might reject them in the future, (vv. 21-29). Now it was the accusers' turn to accept implied criticism. And they did! In a controversy very seldom is one side completely right, and the other completely wrong! When we confront others, we must be willing to deal with our own faults as well as theirs. (5) Each side joyfully accepted the explanation of the other (vv. 30-34), and the issue was put to rest, never to be raised again.

If we would follow these steps—investigate, confront honestly, listen, see our own faults, accept what others say about their motives, rejoice in restored harmony, and never again raise an issue once dealt with—we too would know harmony in our homes and churches.

Outline
Place
Finder

PREPARATION
WARFARE
ALLOTMENT
FAREWELL

Chapter summary. The Book of Joshua closes with two farewell addresses by Joshua. The first, a farewell speech to the leaders, is Joshua's final testimony to God's faithfulness. But it is also a grim warning of the dangers of abandoning God (chap. 23). God has been, is, and will be faithful to His promise and drive out the remaining Canaanites—if Israel obeys (23:1-11). But God will also be faithful to His words of warning. If Israel turns to other gods, the Lord will bring on His people all the evil He has threatened (vv. 12-16). Like Deuteronomy 28, Joshua 23 sets forth an Old Testament theology of history, in which all events are linked to Israel's response to God and His Law.

The final chapter relates a ceremony of covenant renewal, held at Shechem during one of Joshua's last years. It follows the familiar pattern of Hittite suzerainty treaties, a pattern established in Deuteronomy itself (»p. 116). Here is Joshua's last introduction of God as King (24:2), his final recounting of God's relationship with Israel (vv. 2-13), his statement of God's requirements (vv. 14, 16, 18, 21, 23-24), his appeal to witnesses (vv. 22, 27), and his recitation of blessings and curses (vv. 19-20). As the grand old man of Israel calls on his people to choose whom they will serve, we sense our own need for fresh and constant devotion to the Lord.

At last Joshua dies (vv. 28-33). Israel is settled in the land. But the grim vision of the future he shared in his farewell address (23:15-16) will all too soon come to pass.

Key verse. 24:15: Each must choose someone to serve.

Personal application. When we choose complete commitment to the Lord, we shape our family's future as well as our own.

Key concepts. Father »p. 392. Law »p. 145. Separation »p. 87. Anger of God »pp. 65, 72. Mosaic Covenant »p. 62.

INSIGHT

Be strong (23:6). Doing what is right in God's sight rather than following the crowd is one mark of a godly person.

Separation (23:12-13). Joshua calls for complete separation from the Canaanites, knowing that Israel was more likely to be tempted to follow pagan gods than to convert pagans! The process described is "ally yourself," then "intermarry" and then "associate." The meaning of "associate" is defined in verse 7: "invoke the names of their gods or swear by them." Today we're not to cut ourselves off from unbelievers (cf. 1 Cor. 5:9-11). But we're to be careful that friendships do not lead to alliance, intermarriage, and "associating."

"I" (24:3-13). The basis for any relationship with God is found in what He has done for us, not in what we supposedly can do for Him.

Note in these verses all that God has done for Israel: "I took Abraham" (v. 3), "I gave him Isaac" (v. 3), "I sent Moses and Aaron" (v. 5), "I afflicted the Egyptians" (v. 5), "I brought you out" (v. 5), "I brought you to the land" (v. 8), "I gave them into your hands" (v. 11), "I sent the hornet ahead of you" (v. 12), "So I gave you a land" (v. 13). For us too relationship with the Lord is founded on what He has done for us, in Christ. If God spoke the message of Joshua to modern Christians, what "I" statements might He make?

The choice (24:14-15). The choice is never between serving God and personal freedom. The choice is always between God and other masters—whether pagan gods, our sinful passions, or wealth, success, and power.

Judges

The Book of Judges picks up the story of an Israel at rest—and takes us into the tormented centuries that followed. When the leaders who served with Joshua died, the commitment of the Israelites to the Lord relaxed. Rather than drive out the remaining Canaanites as the Lord commanded, the Israelites set defeated foes to forced labor, or simply refused to attack enemy strongholds. Soon Israelites were intermarrying with the people of the land, and many adopted pagan gods and customs.

This grim Old Testament book traces the spiritual and political deterioration of Israel. The bulk of the book tracks seven patterned cycles that characterized the era. The cycles involve: Sin, as the Israelites turn to idolatry and abandon God's Law; Servitude, as God permits an enemy to oppress his people; Supplication, as a desperate Israel turns back to God, confessing its sin and begging for help; Salvation, in the person of a charismatic leader (a judge) who defeats the oppressors; and Silence, a period of rest during which the judge helps Israel remain faithful to the Lord. The tragedy is that this cycle is repeated over and over again, with each swing downward more serious and each oppression more severe. Yet the book is bright with a special kind of hope. Despite repeated failures, God remains willing to give His straying people repeated fresh chances, and to send them deliverer after deliverer.

The "Judges" from whom this book takes its name were charismatic leaders who led rebellions against foreign oppressors and afterward served as spiritual and political leaders of the nation or one or more of its tribal areas. Like the later kings, a "judge" exercised powers we associate with all three branches of government: legislative, administrative, and judicial.

JUDGES AT A GLANCE

KEY PEOPLE

Othniel *The first judge, whose story first reveals the cyclical pattern (3:7-11).*

Deborah *The only woman judge, whose bold leadership encouraged her general, Barak, to win a great victory over resurgent Canaanites (4–5).*

Gideon *The reluctant warrior whose growing faith was demonstrated by the discharge of his army, so he could battle the Midianites with a mere 300 men (6–8).*

Jephthah *An outcast who returned to lead the Israelites who rejected him to a great, but personally costly, victory (10:6–12:7).*

Samson *Though gifted with great physical strength, this judge proved a moral weakling, and failed to deliver his people, though he killed many of their enemies (13–16).*

KEY EVENTS

God's help withdrawn (2:1-4). *The Angel of the Lord announces that because of Israel's sin God will no longer drive out the Canaanites.*

Micah's idolatry (17:1–18:31). *One man's story illustrates the loss of Israel's knowledge of God during this period.*

The Levite's concubine (19:1–20:48). *The tribe of Dan's determination to protect a community guilty of gang rape and murder leads to civil war, and demonstrates Israel's moral and civil decline.*

Stories of some of the most familiar of
Bible heroes are found in the Book of
Judges. Deborah, whose presence gave
General Barak courage to face a superi-
or force; Samson, whose God-given
strength enabled him to defeat a Philistine army single-handedly; Gideon,
whose faith was encouraged by answers
to prayer, and who led a mere 300 men
armed with torches and trumpets to
victory over a great army. We read
these stories, and many others, in this
adventurous Old Testament book.

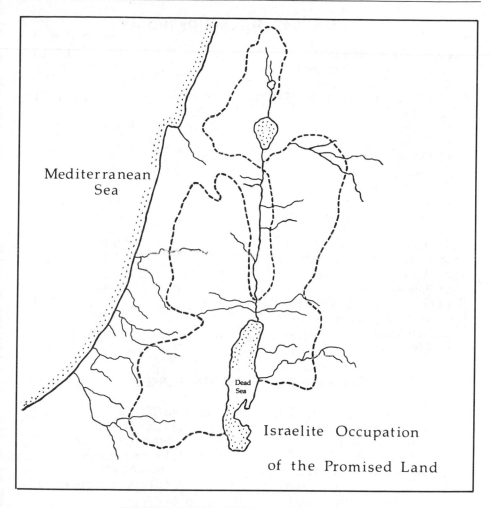

Mediterranean
Sea

Dead
Sea

Israelite Occupation

of the Promised Land

WHERE THE ACTION TAKES PLACE

All the action in Judges takes place in the hill country of Canaan, which is still held by the nearly powerless Israelite tribes. The map locates the seat of Israel's judges, and shows the direction from which each oppressor's assault came. During this era the tribes were not united. Enemy peoples typically overran only a few of the tribal areas, and judges served their own districts rather than all the land occupied by Israel.

Date and Authorship. The events reported here probably took place between 1390 B.C. and 1050 B.C. While the years specified for the Judges' rule total 410, the discrepancy is explained by overlap of their ministries. This same feature makes it difficult to fix dates for the rule of any given judge. The author of the book is unknown, though a Talmudic tradition credits Samuel.

THEOLOGICAL OUTLINE OF JUDGES

I. CAUSES OF DECLINE		1:1–3:6
A. Incomplete Obedience	1:1-36	
B. Active Disobedience	2:1–3:6	
II. CHARACTERS OF THE PERIOD		3:7–16:31
A. Othniel	3:7-11	
B. Ehud	3:12-30	
C. Shamgar	3:31	
D. Deborah, Barak	4–5	
E. Gideon	6–8	
F. Abimelech	9	
G. Tola	10:1-2	
H. Jair	10:3-5	
K. Jephthah	10:6–12:7	
L. Ibzan	12:8-10	
M. Elon	12:11-12	
N. Abdon	12:13-15	
O. Samson	13–16	
III. CONSEQUENCES OF THE DECLINE		17–21
A. Lost Knowledge of God	17–18	
B. Immorality	19	
C. Civil War	20–21	

CONTENT OUTLINE OF JUDGES

I. Incomplete Conquest (1:1–2:5)
  A. Conquest of Southern Canaan (1:1-21)
  B. Capture of Bethel (1:22-26)
  C. Unoccupied Lands (1:27-36)
  D. Judgment for the Broken Covenant (2:1-5)

II. History of the Period (2:6–16:31)
  A. The Period Explained (2:6–3:6)
  B. Othniel vs. Aram (3:7-11)
  C. Ehud vs. Moab (3:12-30)
  D. Shamgar vs. Philistines (3:31)
  E. Deborah, Barak (1:4–5:31)
    1. Battle with the Canaanites (4:1-24)
    2. Deborah's song of triumph (5:1-31)
  F. Gideon vs. Midianites (6:1–8:35)
  G. Abimelech and Civil War (9:1-57)

  H. Tola (10:1-2)
  I. Jair (10:3-5)
  J. Jephthah (10:6–12:7)
    1. Vs. Ammonites (10:6–11:40)
    2. Ephraimite jealousy (12:1-7)
  K. Ibzan (12:8-10)
  L. Elon (12:11-12)
  M. Abdon (12:13-15)
  N. Samson vs. Philistines (13:1–16:31)

III. Appendixes (17:1–21:25)
  A. Micah's Idol (17:1-13)
  B. Migration of the Danites (18:1-31)
  C. Rape at Gibeah (19:1-30)
  D. War with the Benjamites (20:1-48)
  E. Wives for the Benjamites (21:1-25)

Chapter summary. Joshua, the faithful associate of Moses and leader of Israel during the Conquest, is dead (1:1). His victories ended organized resistance to the Hebrew invasion. But Joshua did not exterminate the Canaanites. Each tribe is now responsible to carry out the policy of extermination which serves as a divine judgment on the sinful practices of the Canaanites and as protection from the Canaanites' corrupting influence.

Outline
Place
Finder

CAUSES
CHARACTERS
CONSEQUENCES

The tribe of Judah responds to the challenge and continues the battle to purify Canaan (vv. 2-19a). But even Judah is unable to drive out the Canaanites in the lowlands, because they have war chariots (v. 19b). Hebron was given to Caleb (v. 20). Now, with this first subtle indication of a failure of faith, the text darkens. The Benjamites defeat the Jebusites, but fail to dislodge them from Jerusalem (v. 21). There are other victories (vv. 22-27). But there are also defeats—and direct disobedience! When tribes became strong they instead pressed "the Canaanites into forced labor" (v. 28). As faith and commitment wane, tribe after tribe follows this policy, in direct violation of God's command (cf. Ex. 23:32-33; 34:10-16). A flawed faith and disobedience are the direct causes of the spiritual and political darkness about to descend on God's chosen people.

Key verse. 1:28: Don't change God's policies. Follow them.

Personal application. Incomplete obedience robs you of rest.

INSIGHT

Adoni-Bezek (1:5). This is a title, "lord of Bezek," not a name. The "kings" he had defeated and disgraced by mutilating them in such a way they could not fight, were undoubtedly leaders of smaller local communities he may have raided again and again over a period of years. This is the only instance of Israel treating an enemy in this way, and even Adoni-Bezek acknowledged the justice of his being paid back "in kind" for his barbarity.

Perizzites (1:5). Recent etymological studies suggest this is not an ethnic term but means "hill dwellers." In apposition "Canaanite" may mean "coastal peoples." Thus Judah's conquests demonstrate God's ability to give His people victory over all peoples of the land.

"Jerusalem" (1:8). Jerusalem has been occupied almost continuously for at least 5,000 years! The apparent conflict between v. 8 and v. 21 is easily resolved. The city was taken and burned, but was not occupied by the Israelites. Later the surviving Jebusites returned and rebuilt their city—something that happens in every war. Jerusalem remained a Jebusite stronghold to the time of David, 400 years later!

"Iron chariots" (1:19). The first Egyptian war chariots were lightweight vehicles. They were used to carry archers, who fought at long distances, or in pursuit of a fleeing enemy. Heavier, three-man chariots were used in Mesopotamia. The Canaanite chariots mentioned here are defined by their iron studwork as the heavier Mesopotamian type. These chariots, often equipped with blades attached to the wheels, were used to charge infantry and scatter the enemy. Such chariots were ineffective in hill country, but on flat plains were terrifying instruments. In Judges, chariots represent the military superiority of the enemy: a superiority which should have called Israel to greater reliance on God, but instead led to a failure to complete her mission of conquest. Spiritually, chariots stand for any overwhelming challenge that we may flee from in fear, but can overcome by faith and confidence in God (cf. Jud. 4).

"Forced labor" (1:28). The most critical failure of the post-Joshua era was the practice of letting defeated Canaanites remain in the land, in direct disobedience to God's command. The Israelites asked the fateful question "How can we make a profit?" rather than "How can we please God?" You and I too are always vulnerable to the temptation to do what seems to offer a short-term profit rather than remain committed to what God says is right.

Outline
Place
Finder

CAUSES
CHARACTERS
CONSEQUENCES

Chapter summary. Israel's disobedience brings a judgment announced by the Angel of the Lord. God will no longer drive out the Canaanites, but will permit them to remain in the land as a snare, to test Israel's obedience (2:1-5). The writer now gives an overview of the era of the Judges: A new generation that does not know God turns to idolatry (vv. 6-13). In anger God permits enemies to oppress them (vv. 14-15). But then God raises up judges, who deliver them during their own lifetimes (vv. 16-18). But when a judge dies, Israel returns to idolatry (v. 19). As the cycle of broken covenant, oppression, deliverance, and subsequent denial continues, Israel finds itself a stranger in its own land, subject to those foreigners whose daughters and whose gods they prefer to obeying the Lord (2:20–3:6). The chapter concludes with the story of two judges who illustrate the deadly cycle: Othniel (vv. 7-11) and Ehud (vv. 12-30).

Key verse. 3:6: The choice of evil always has consequences.

Personal application. God sees the long-term results of our choices while we do not. How wise then to trust what Scripture says, and be guided always by God's Word.

Key concepts. Angel of the Lord »p. 37. Evil »p. 72. Testing »p. 125. Anger of God »pp. 65, 72. Holy Spirit »pp. 73, 744.

INSIGHT

"**A snare**" (2:3). The word means a net the victim triggers by touching a spring. Israel did not drive out the Canaanites or break down their altars. The religion of these people would be the spring which triggered God's judgment of His faithless people. God doesn't "entrap" us. Our own acts cause judgment to fall.

"**The people wept aloud**" (2:4). Don't mistake the meaning of tears. They may be superficial, expressing sorrow for the consequence but not for the act! Israel's tears were superficial, for the people went on to even greater disobedience. When tears represent repentance, they are followed by a change of life, not repeated sins.

Knowing God (2:10). People who do not know God still feel a need for some kind of supernatural aid. Recent research suggests 30 to 40 percent of American adolescents have some degree of involvement in the occult. If we fail to reach the next generation, our nation's sins may also trigger divine judgment.

Baal and Ashtoreth. In Canaanite mythology Baal (which means "master" or "owner") was the god of storm and rain. He thus controlled the fertility of the land, and was widely worshiped in the ancient Near East. Baal was thought to be excited by violence and by sex, and thus rites honoring him often featured acts intended to stimulate his emotions and

lead him to similar acts in the heavens, which were thought to bring rain to earth. Thus in Elijah's time the priests of Baal cut themselves, hoping the smell of blood would rouse him and attract his attention. Cult prostitutes and orgies were elements in Canaanite worship.

Ashtoreth was Baal's consort, also known under the names Astarte, Ishtar (in Babylon), and Anath (in Ugarit, in North Syria). She was the goddess of war and fertility, and was Baal's female counterpart in Canaanite religion's erotic rites. Rather than exterminate this degraded religion, the Israelites adopted it and/or many of its features, thus breaking their covenant with God and stimulating God's anger.

Return to God? (2:16) No mention is made of this element here, yet its constant emphasis in later stories of the Judges makes it clear. God's people had to turn to Him before He could help.

Aram Naharaim (3:8). The area lies to the north of Canaan, while Othniel lived in Judah, in south Canaan. This suggests how completely Cushan (the next word is descriptive, and means "the double wicked") was able to dominate the Israelites.

"**Eighty years**" (3:30). Only Ehud brought the land peace for two generations. The limit of the other Judges' impact was 40 years, one generation. How important to pass our faith to our children!

Chapter summary. Israel has again turned to idolatry, and experienced its consequences in two decades of oppression by the Canaanites, united again under the leadership of resurgent Hazor (cf. Josh. 11). This time a woman, Deborah, identified both as a prophetess and a judge, is the agent of God's deliverance (Jud. 4:1-5). She accompanies a reluctant general, Barak; directs the battle; and Barak's 10,000 rout a much larger Canaanite force (vv. 6-16). In the confusion the Canaanite commander, Sisera, escapes, only to be killed in an exhausted sleep by a woman whose family has long been allied to Israel (vv. 17-24). Deborah's song, long recognized as one of the most powerful poems of antiquity, celebrates the Hebrew victory. The song calls on all to extol God (5:1-5), expresses the excited joy of the people (vv. 6-11), contrasts those tribes who responded to the call to battle with those who did not (vv. 12-18), and exalts God as the One whose intervention caused the victory (vv. 19-23). The poem closes with a vivid description of Sisera's death and the growing anxiety of his mother when he fails to return in triumph when expected (vv. 24-31).

Outline
Place
Finder

CAUSES
CHARACTERS
CONSEQUENCES

Key verse. 4:15: Why fear chariots of iron?

Personal application. God works deliverance through those who trust Him, whatever their sex.

INSIGHT

Deborah. Deborah illustrates an important truth. Even in a male-oriented society, women with exceptional personal and spiritual qualities can rise to leadership. Deborah's impact is only partly explained by her call as a prophetess. Jud. 5:6-7 describes a total breakdown of Hebrew society, which Deborah's vigorous leadership was able to repair. She instilled pride and confidence in her people, settled their disputes, and was able to rally an army of 10,000 willing to face an overwhelming force of Canaanites. The respect in which Deborah was held is reflected in Barak, her general's, unwillingness to face the enemy unless she was present. While this reaction suggests a limited faith in God, it also demonstrates the dominant role in the society that Deborah had achieved. Deborah's acceptance as the leader of ancient Israel, when such roles were not extended to women, reminds us that what qualifies an individual for leadership is not his or her sex, but his or her relationship with God, and call by Him to ministry.

"Jabin" (4:1). Jabin is most likely a dynastic title. Hazor heads a coalition of Canaanite peoples who have dominated the Hebrews for some 20 years!

Kenites. The nomadic group of which Heber, husband of Jael was a member, had been associated with Israel from the time of Exodus (Num. 24:21-22). They settled in Judah, and then near Jericho (Jud. 1:14-16), though Heber's tent was located by the Sea of Galilee in territory controlled by Jabin.

The Lord (4:14). The text emphasizes Barak's force numbered 10,000, because the Canaanite force was much larger. Battlefields identified lie several miles apart along the Kishon River (4:16; 5:19). Deborah's song suggests the Lord won the battle by causing a downpour, which turned the plains by the river into a sea of mud, making Sisera's chariots useless (cf. v. 4).

Jael. Custom then decreed that giving a person food or drink symbolized offering them protection. But note that Jael was alone, and that Sisera's request might well be taken as a demand conveying an implied threat. Jael would surely have been able to drive the tent peg through Sisera's temple. In O.T. times, taking down and putting up the tent, including driving tent pegs in hard ground, was the job of nomadic women!

Lingering (5:13-18). Only four of Israel's tribes contributed troops, while others "lingered" at home. This may suggest that only the involved tribes had been oppressed by the Canaanites. But it reminds us that when we fail to join in fighting the Lord's battles, we betray our brothers and sisters—and miss the blessing of seeing God work.

Chapter summary. The Israelites are crushed by Midianites, nomadic raiders who invade each year at harvesttime (6:1-10). God appears to a reluctant Gideon and calls him to be Israel's deliverer (vv. 11-24). Gideon fulfills his first mission, to destroy the town's Baal shrine, which is on his own father's land (vv. 25-32). Then, filled with God's Spirit and encouraged by two miraculous signs, Gideon calls out an army to resist the Midianites (6:33–7:1). But God tells Gideon the army is too large, and systematically reduces his force to a mere 300 men (vv. 2-8). Encouraged by yet another sign (vv. 9-15), Gideon sets his men around the Midianite camp with torches and rams' horn trumpets. At 10:00 that night the trumpets sound! The confused Midianites, seeing only blurred figures stumbling in the dark outside their tents, strike out in panic and kill each other (vv. 16-22). As the Midianites flee, the rest of Israel rallies and cuts down the stragglers (vv. 23-25). In the wake of the battle Gideon diffuses tribal jealousy (8:1-3), disciplines the elders of an Israelite town that refused to help his forces (vv. 4-17), executes two Midianite kings (vv. 18-21), and rejects Israel's appeal that he accept the throne (vv. 22-27). For the rest of Gideon's long life the Israelites continue to serve the Lord (vv. 28-35).

Key verse. 6:16: Numbers don't count.

Personal application. One individual willing to obey God can still have an impact on his or her entire society.

Key concepts. Angel of the Lord »p. 37. God's appearances »p. 56. Miracle »p. 57. High places »p. 113. Baal »p. 162. Abandon »p. 188. Holy Spirit »pp. 73, 759. Dreams »p. 99. King »p. 130.

INSIGHT

Gideon. One hundred verses are taken to tell of Gideon. There are many spiritual lessons to be learned from a study of Gideon.

Midian. These nomadic peoples came from south of Edom; the Amalekites south of Judah. Their superiority rested in part on history's first documented use of the camel in warfare. A camel could carry 400 pounds plus its rider, could travel a week without drinking, and with only a rider could cover as much as a hundred miles a day! Thus the Midianites could strike in force long before Israel could assemble an army. The annual invasion of these nomadic peoples at harvesttime suggests they raided primarily to take Israel's crops. Israel's flight to caves (6:4) and the murder of Gideon's brothers (8:19) suggests brutal killing of any Israelites they found during their raids.

"You have not listened" (6:7-10). Israel's impoverishment was a consequence of abandoning God. Before God can help anyone who is being disciplined for sin, that person must accept responsibility for his or her acts, and repent.

"The Lord has abandoned us" (6:13). The Heb. word (*natas*) indicates a withdrawal. God did not reject His people, but stood back while they experienced the consequences of their idolatry. We can't expect God to act for us while we sin. He may well stand back and let us experience sin's consequences. But He will never reject us, as the call of Gideon to deliver Israel demonstrates!

"Go in the strength you have" (6:14). You and I have the same strength Gideon did. It's found in verse 12. "The Lord is with you, mighty warrior." We may be as weak as Gideon evidently felt. But if the Lord is with us, we have strength enough.

"A sign" (6:17). The word for "sign" here means a miracle that will confirm and substantiate that which a spokesman says is a message from God. Asking for a sign was not an act of unbelief.

Illustration. *In ancient times grain was threshed on hilltops, where wind could blow the lighter chaff away from the heavier kernels. But winepresses were cut into the sides of hills. The fact that Gideon was threshing in a winepress suggests he was trying to hide from spying eyes, and shows the pervasive fear Israel felt of the invading Midianites.*

"An ephah of flour" (6:19). The word for "offering" is used of voluntary gifts presented to God. Gideon's gift of 40 pounds of flour in time of famine shows Gideon's request for a sign was an act of faith. He honored his visitor with a very generous offering.

Gideon's fear (6:22). God told Moses, "No one may see Me and live" (Ex. 33:20). Gideon recognized the angel as a manifestation of God and was afraid. But the Ex. 33 passage means seeing God in His essential glory, not in another form.

Tear down the altar of Baal (6:25). God cannot work for us while our hearts are turned in another direction. The use of the bull to tear down the altar is significant. The bull was the sacred animal of the Canaanite cult. The bull was then sacrificed to the Lord, burned on a fire kindled from the Asherah pole. The false faith was thus symbolically rejected. When we turn to the Lord, we must also symbolically burn the remnants of everything that earlier kept us from worshiping Him.

"Jerub-baal" (6:32). The name meaning "let Baal contend" later shifted subtly in meaning, to mark Gideon as "Baal-fighter."

The Spirit "came upon" Gideon (6:34). The Heb. verb means "to clothe with." One poet captured the sense in suggesting that Gideon was a "glove the Spirit wore." The presence of God's Spirit and His possession of Gideon was the key to the victory that followed. It is the same today. God, working in and through us, enables us to overcome.

The Abiezrites (6:34). How striking that his fellow townsmen (cf. v. 11), who had been ready to kill Gideon, were now the first to follow him. It must have encouraged Gideon. And it reminds us that when we take a stand for God even those who are hostile to us may be influenced in the end.

The fleece (6:36-40). Most commentators take Gideon's request for two additional signs as evidence of a "weak faith" (cf. Matt. 12:38;

1 Cor. 1:22-23). But note that *before* Gideon asked for a sign, he had obeyed God's commands to tear down the altar of Baal, and call out the Israelites to war. Gideon had demonstrated his faith by obedience, and God honored that faith by giving him a reassuring sign. We too may have doubts and fears at times. But as long as we faithfully obey God, we can hardly be charged with "weak faith."

Lapping the water (7:5). The 300 apparently reached down to cup water in their hands as they passed through the stream. A few, so eager to do God's work that they cannot stop even to drink, will win greater victories than many who are fearful or uncommitted.

Barley (7:13). Barley was the food of the poor, and the round loaf represented oppressed Israel. Note that Gideon did not ask for this sign, but that it was given to encourage him. How gracious God is to us, to strengthen us for our challenges.

Humility (8:1-3). Gideon wisely gave credit to those who demanded it. Let your deeds speak for themselves—and let others praise themselves all they wish (cf. also Prov. 15:1).

Succoth and Peniel (8:13-17). When God is at work, not to join in is the same as supporting the other side.

Gideon as king? (8:22-27) Gideon's pious rejection of royal authority probably should not be taken at face value. Why? (1) Often acceptance of offers was expressed as an initial, polite refusal, as Gen. 23:11 and 2 Sam. 24:22-23. (2) Gideon's use of the ephod-oracle (Jud. 8:27), of jewelry and royal clothing (v. 26), and gathering of a harem (v. 30) all fit practices of ancient monarchs. (3) Perhaps decisive is the name given Abimelech, one of his sons. The name means, "my father is king" (v. 31). Abimelech even assumes that a son of Gideon should succeed him (9:2).

Rest for 40 years (8:28). Whatever his flaws, Gideon was a man of honor, who kept Israel faithful to the Lord for 40 years.

Outline
Place
Finder

CAUSES
CHARACTERS
CONSEQUENCES

Chapter summary. Chapter 9 contains the story of an ambition-driven pseudo-king. Abimelech, the son of Gideon, conspired with the Canaanite population of his mother's hometown, Shechem. They financed the murder of Gideon's 70 other sons and then proclaimed Abimelech king (9:1-6). Jotham, the youngest son of Gideon, escaped the massacre and shouted out a prophetic parable to the Shechemites. If they "acted honorably and in good faith," may they prosper. But if in choosing Abimelech they did wrong, may the wicked city and the evil king destroy each other (vv. 7-20). As Jotham predicted, selfish passions led to conflict. Abimelech died in a war that ruined Shechem (vv. 21-56).

Chapter 10 briefly mentions two judges, Tola (10:1-2) and Jair (vv. 3-5). It then prepares us to meet a man who, like Abimelech, was born out of wedlock and rejected by his brothers. Again Israel is crushed under foreign enemies because of its sin (vv. 6-14). Again God confronts His people, and they repent (vv. 15-18). The stage is now set for the appearance of Jephthah, whose childhood rejection did not turn him from God, and whose stressful life has prepared him for leadership.

Key verse. 9:19: No good comes from dishonorable acts.

Personal application. Ambition must be subject to the will of God, or it corrupts.

INSIGHT

Shechem. Reference to Baal-Berith ("Baal of the Covenant") in 8:33 suggests Shechem was a member of a league of Canaanite cities existing within Israelite territory. Abimelech's reference to Gideon as Jerub-Baal ("Baal fighter") indicates that he was promising to support Baal worship, as does the contribution from the Baal temple treasury of funds to hire the killers of Gideon's 70 other sons.

Ambition. Abimelech was ready to use religion—even pagan religion—to advance his ambition. Ambition for self-advancement is still a snare (James 3:14, 16). Like Paul we must "make it our ambition" to lead a quiet life, that wins respect (1 Thes. 4:11-12).

Concubine. Abimelech's mother was a concubine (8:31). Such a woman, who had often been a slave, was considered married to her husband rather than a mistress. But those in such a "second class" marriage had less rights than regular wives.

Anoint (9:8). This implies no divine recognition, unless when carried out by a prophet. »p. 187.

Parables. In both Testaments a parable is an illustration, created by setting a concrete situation alongside an abstract concept. Here the "trees" are the people of Shechem, who want a king. The "thornbush" is Abimelech. This bush was useless, producing no crop. It was also dangerous, a menace because its dry branches frequently started fires. This powerful imagery predicted Abimelech would destroy both Shechem and himself.

Other images in the O.T. share this parable-like quality (cf. 2 Sam. 12:1-7; Isa. 5:1-7). But the most familiar parables of Scripture are those told by Jesus, who illustrated spiritual truths drawing on familiar sights like the flowers of the field, the birds of the air, the sower going out to sow his fields, banquets, and the practices of rulers.

"An evil spirit" (9:23-25). The hostility that developed between Shechem and Abimelech was a consequence of God's judicial action, but was also a natural expression of each party's character.

The bone of contention was the Shechemites habit of robbing travelers. As petty ruler of the area, Abimelech expected to collect tolls in return for safe conduct.

"God repaid" (9:56-57). The story is tragic and foolish. Abimelech gained nothing from his wickedness but a few years' rule of a tiny district in Israelite territory populated mostly by Canaanites and an early death, the just judgment of God. How meaningless ambition for advancement or wealth is in the final analysis.

Chapter summary. Jephthah ("Jeff-tha"), like Abimelech (Jud. 9), was rejected by his brothers (11:1-2). But Jephthah struck out on his own, gathered bold followers, and founded a settlement (v. 3). Later, when his father's people beg him to return as commander of their army, he demonstrates in words (vv. 4-11) and in his letter to the Ammonite enemy (vv. 12-28) a clear knowledge of and firm faith in God. Empowered by the Spirit, Jephthah makes a vow to the Lord, and wins a great victory (vv. 29-33). But when Jephthah returns home, his daughter runs to greet him—and he realizes he must surrender her to the Lord to fulfill his vow (vv. 34-40). Jephthah's victory makes the Ephraimites jealous, and a bloody civil war follows (12:1-6). Jephthah's brief rule lasts only six years (v. 7), as other judges emerge to lead various tribes (vv. 8-15).

Outline
Place
Finder

CAUSES
CHARACTERS
CONSEQUENCES

Key verse. 11:36: One's word to God must be kept.

Personal application. A difficult childhood need not ruin our adult life. We can still know God, and be used by Him.

Key concepts. Vow »p. 96.

INSIGHT

Contrast. Like Abimelech, Jephthah was illegitimate, rejected by his brothers. Seeing the two side by side reminds us that our choices, not our environment, shape the persons we become. Abimelech chose to reject God and use pagan religion for personal advancement. Jephthah sought no revenge, but struck out on his own. His deep personal faith is expressed in words to the elders of Gilead (cf. 11:9-11), the letter to the Ammonite ruler (vv. 12-27), in his vow before the battle (vv. 30-31), and in the surrender of his only daughter to the Lord (vv. 35-40). Our choices, not our environment, set the course of our lives.

"Ammonites" (10:17). These peoples lay east of the Jordan. They attacked the tribe of Gad, which occupied the central Transjordan.

"Head" (11:8). The word "head" (*rosh*) could be used of civil as well as military leaders. Jephthah negotiated until the meaning was clear: lifetime leadership of the district.

Jephthah's letter (11:14-27). Jephthah relied on sacred history to demonstrate Israel's right to the disputed land. He claimed the land as a divine gift, which showed Yahweh's generosity in contrast to the stinginess of the Ammonite god, who did not provide them enough territory (cf. v. 24). Jephthah uses irony here. Yet he clearly saw his role as defender of territory provided by God, and he expected God to provide the victory.

"300 years" (11:26). This fits with other dates given in Scripture that fix the Conquest around 1400 B.C.

Jephthah's vow (11:30-31). Iron Age houses stabled animals on a ground-level floor or in the courtyard. Jephthah had an animal sacrifice in mind when he made his vow.

Was Jephthah's daughter sacrificed? (11:34-37) Some argue yes. But it seems unlikely, for these reasons: (1) Child sacrifice was against Mosaic Law (Lev. 18:21; 20:2-5; Deut. 12:31), and Jephthah's letter indicates he knew the O.T. (2) The daughter mourned her perpetual virginity, not her coming death (Jud. 11:37-39). (3) The law of vows, Lev. 27, permits monetary redemption of persons vowed to God (vv. 1-8), but specifies that any person "devoted" to God cannot be redeemed (vv. 28-29). Jephthah apparently saw his vow in this light, and thus committed her not to death but to lifelong service of God at the tabernacle. (4) No priest would officiate at a human sacrifice, and priests alone could offer sacrifices. (5) The statement "and she was a virgin" follows "he did to her as he had vowed," 11:39, implying not execution but lifelong service. It is inconceivable that Jephthah would have literally sacrificed his daughter in an act he knew to be repugnant to God.

Civil war (12:1-6). The Ephraimites were the largest and leading tribe in the north. Resentment of Jephthah's victory impelled them to cross the Jordan to discipline Jephthah. He was less diplomatic than Gideon (cf. 8:1-3), and gave the Ephraimites a severe beating.

Outline
Place
Finder

CAUSES
CHARACTERS
CONSEQUENCES

Chapter summary. The familiar story of Samson begins with Israel again apostate, and this time oppressed by Philistines. Samson's birth is announced by an angel, and he is brought up as a Nazarite (13:1-25). Samson is gifted with great physical strength as well as godly parents. But as an adult he insists on marriage to a Philistine woman (14:1-11). Tricked, a furious Samson leaves the marriage feast, and when his bride is given to another, this powerful man launches a one-man vendetta against Israel's enemies (14:12–15:8). Threatened by war, the men of Judah turn Samson over to his enemies—and he slaughters their entire army single-handedly (vv. 9-20). Samson is finally betrayed by his passion for Delilah and his hair, the symbol of his Nazarite vow, is cut off (16:1-19). Drained of his supernatural strength, Samson is blinded and set to work grinding grain for the Philistines (vv. 20-21). Later Samson is brought into a Philistine temple to be ridiculed. But his hair has grown back, and his strength has returned. With one final, mighty effort, Samson dislodges the pillars that hold up the temple, and dies with hundreds of his enemies (vv. 22-31). He is the only judge who failed to deliver his people. Though a man of great physical strength, his moral and spiritual weakness doomed him.

Key verse. 14:7: A leader must put his people first.

Personal application. Samson was ruled by his physical desires. Let's not make the same mistake, but subject our bodies to God.

Key concepts. Angel of the Lord »p. 37. Nazarite »p. 96. Vengeance »p. 428. Philistines »p. 185.

INSIGHT

Philistines (13:1). The 40-year oppression was the longest on record in Judges. During this era the Philistines (see »p. 185), whose major settlements lay along the seacoast, established outposts and villages as far east as the Jordan Valley, threatening the very existence of Israel as a separate people! In view of this threat, Samson's preoccupation with personal affronts and vengeance is a grim commentary on his character.

Godly parents (13:1-24). Manoah and his wife display qualities of truly godly parents. They believe the promise of a son. They ask God "to teach us how to bring up the boy who is to be born" (v. 8). Yet Samson was far from the godly, dedicated person we might expect to come from such a home. In a way, this story is a blessing for all godly parents whose children disappoint. We can do our best, and even do everything "right," and still see our children make wrong choices. Each person is responsible to God for the choices he or she makes, and there is nothing we can do

to force a son or daughter in the right direction. Samson was even given the Spirit of God (v. 25), and still made poor and selfish decisions! Don't be overcome with guilt over a prodigal child. That child has made his or her own choices, and God may yet bring him or her home.

"I have seen" (14:1-4). Samson's character is revealed in this one phrase. The sight of the Philistine girl—her physical appearance and not her character—excited his desires. God did use his sudden passion, as verse 4 notes. God can use our weaknesses for His purposes too. But this does not excuse them.

He scooped out and ate (14:9). The Nazarite was forbidden to even "go near" a dead body (Num. 6:6). We characteristically focus on his bravery in facing and killing the lion with his bare hands. We might better ponder Samson's casual scooping of honey out of the carcass of the lion he killed. This is a further indication of his careless attitude toward spiritual things.

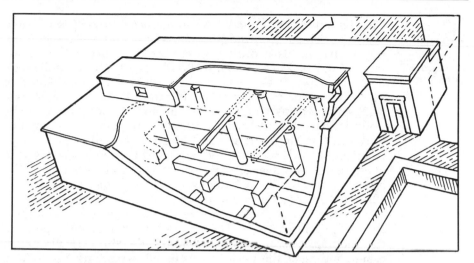

Banquets (14:10). The Heb. word for banquet is *misteh*, which means "drink" as well as "feast." Ancient banquets were festive occasions, at which the drinking of wine had an important place (John 2:1-11). While a banquet might be held to mark a child's coming of age (Gen. 21:8) or a son's return (Luke 15:23), the most common occasion for celebration was the wedding. Wedding feasts typically lasted several days, during which the bride and groom were honored with much music, dancing, and laughter. Good-natured word games were played, riddles asked, and the cares of daily life were generally set aside.

Riddles (14:12). The ancient world enjoyed word games and riddles, though in Heb. culture riddles seemed to probe life's more important questions (1 Kings 10:1; Ps. 49:4). The wager made Samson's riddle serious indeed: linen garments were expensive, and a person usually would have only one set of "Sunday Best," which the word for "clothes" here implies. Samson's unfriendly challenge led to threats against his bride, and ultimately to many deaths. How much better it would have been if Samson had called out troops and faced the Philistines in battle.

Ashkelon (14:19). Samson went to a city 23 miles distant to obtain the clothing to pay off his wager. In those days this was a long journey, and the 30 deaths were not connected to Samson's wager with the Philistines.

Vengeance (15:3-19). Samson's angry departure confused his bride's parents and, not wishing to waste the banquet (?), they married her to another. The story now traces what commonly happens when a person decides to take revenge: hostilities escalate, as more and more harm is done.

Perhaps the Philistine oppressors of Israel deserved what happened. But note that in each instance Samson is acting for himself, not

Illustration. *Temples of the era show common characteristics: a covered part looking out on a courtyard, separated by wooden pillars set on stone bases that support the roof. Officials assembled below, crowds of ordinary folk gathered on the roof. The weight of the crowd on the roof would make the structure unstable. Samson used his returned strength to slide the pillars off their stone bases and topple the structure. In this final act, all Samson thought of was "revenge on the Philistines for my two eyes," rather than the glory of the God whose servant he claimed to be.*

his people. His motive was to get revenge (v. 7) rather than deliver Israel. Obsession with personal revenge is not for those who, like Israel's Judges and Christian leaders, are called to serve others.

"Your servant" (15:18). Samson saw himself as God's servant, yet saw no conflict with this and his subsequent visit to a prostitute (16:1). This moral weakness made him vulnerable to his later betrayal by Delilah.

"The city gate" (16:3). The description gives us some measure of Samson's amazing strength. The width of principle gates to Palestinian cities was typically 13 to 14 feet. They were thick, of solid wood studded with metal. Samson tore out the whole construction, including the gate posts, and carried the entire structure some 38 miles, uphill, to Hebron!

"Delilah" (16:4). Samson had been a user of women, motivated by sensual passion. Now he met a woman who was a user of men. Samson wanted sex: Delilah wanted money, and was willing to use sex. The price the Philistines offered for the secret of Samson's strength was princely: some 28 pounds of silver from each of the five Philistine rulers, a fortune in those days. But the measure of a man or a woman is not the price of betrayal. The measure is whether one is willing to betray at all!

Outline
Place
Finder

CAUSES
CHARACTERS
CONSEQUENCES

Chapter summary. Judges now shifts focus, to look at undated events which sum up the spiritual, moral, and social deterioration that took place during an era when "everyone did as he saw fit" (17:6; 21:25). Judges 17 tells of Micah, an individual who steals (vv. 1-4), sets up a shrine in his house featuring silver idols, ordains a son as a priest until he hires a Levite (vv. 5-12), and expects God to bless him for his piety (v. 13). The irony is that each of Micah's acts directly disobeys commands found in the Mosaic Law—and Micah does not know!

Judges 18 adds to the story. Some of the tribe of Dan plan to move north. An advance party passes Micah's house, obtains the blessing of his priest, and later locates a likely place to settle (18:1-10). Later the larger group stops again at Micah's house, steals the objects from his shrine, and invites the Levite to come with them as tribal priest (vv. 11-26). The men of Dan then take the peaceful city their spies located, set up Micah's idols in a tribal worship center, and make the Levite's sons hereditary priests. Like Micah, the Danites do not know, or do not care, that their worship is in direct violation of Old Testament Law. The message of these two chapters is clear. During the age of the Judges, the knowledge of God and His will was lost, diluted by Canaanite concepts which found their way into the religious consciousness of Israel.

Key verse. 17:13: One who thinks "I know" can be wrong.

Personal application. Let's check all our ideas about God and His ways against what God has revealed in His Scriptures.

Key concepts. Idolatry »p. 433. Levites »p. 95.

INSIGHT

"Curse" (17:2). Here the "curse" was a semi-magical utterance intended to protect property. It frightened the superstitious Micah, who returned his mother's property. Her "blessing" was probably intended to nullify the curse.

The idol (17:3). The consecrated silver was used to make an idol in direct violation of the commandment, "You shall not make for yourself an idol in the form of anything" (Ex. 20:4).

"A shrine" (17:5). The Heb. says a "house of God." But O.T. Law said worship of the Lord was to be conducted only at a central sanctuary, wherever the tabernacle, and later where the temple, stood (cf. Deut. 12). Only there were sacrifices to be made (Lev. 1–7).

A priest (17:5). Only a direct descendant of Aaron was to serve God as a priest in Israel (Num. 3–4). Thus when Micah ordained his son he again violated the Law. He even violated it when he hired a Levite to be his priest.

"My father" (17:10). Often in Scripture "father" is used in direct address to indicate respect. Those with spiritual as well as governmental authority might be addressed as "my father" (cf. 18:19; 2 Kings 2:12; 6:21). Micah's promise that the Levite would be "my father and priest" is a promise that, though the priest is hired by Micah, the priest will be acknowledged as the one having spiritual authority.

"Now . . . the Lord will be good to me" (17:13). Micah now had the external elements he felt were necessary to obtain God's blessing: a shrine, idols, a Levite to pray for him, etc. How many today rely on religious trappings in a vain effort to please God and obtain His blessing!

"600 men" (18:11). At the time of the Conquest, Dan numbered 64,400 fighting men. Either the tribe has been seriously reduced, or only a small group intends to move north.

"What else do I have?" (18:24) Micah's anguish as the Danites march off with his idols and his priest shows how sincere he was in his belief. People who are sincere in their effort to win heaven, but reject God's plan of salvation through Jesus, remain just as lost as the person who ridicules belief in an afterlife.

Chapter summary. An incident that took place during the era of the Judges is described, without reference to date. It shows the moral deterioration of the period.

Outline
Place
Finder

CAUSES
CHARACTERS
CONSEQUENCES

A Levite sets out to be reconciled with his concubine, who has left him and returned to her father's house (19:1-3). The Levite is welcomed, and after several days of merrymaking, sets out for home about 3:00 in the afternoon (vv. 4-10). As night approaches, the Levite insists on stopping in Gibeah, because it is an Israelite rather than a Canaanite village (vv. 11-14). Finally one man shows them hospitality (vv. 15-22), but that night the men of the city determine on the homosexual rape of the visitor (v. 22). Finally the Levite thrusts his concubine outside, and the Gibeahites rape and brutalize her all night (vv. 23-26). The next morning the Levite finds her dead outside the front door (vv. 27-28). He takes the body, and when he reaches home cuts the body into 12 parts, sending a section to each tribe as gruesome evidence of the Gibeahites' sin (vv. 29-30).

Though the next chapters tell of the Israelites' outrage, the husband's cruel disregard of his concubine is as revealing as the brutality of the men of Gibeah. How Israel has fallen from the ideal of a covenant community marked by love for all!

Key verse. 19:12: A wrong choice made for the right reasons.

Personal application. Commitment to God is a nation's one sure barrier against moral corruption and insensitivity.

Key concepts. Levites »p. 95. Concubine »p. 166. Hospitality »p. 37. Israel »p. 53.

INSIGHT

Unfaithful? (19:2) The Septuagint (the Jewish translation of the O.T. into Greek) says that she "was angry with" him, not "was unfaithful to" him. This is supported by her husband's effort to "persuade her" to return. The Heb. has "speak to her heart," that is, kindly.

"Two donkeys" (19:3). The husband's consideration is reflected in bringing two donkeys. Normally the wife would expect to walk, and only the husband would ride. These opening touches suggest an honest affection for the concubine, which makes the events that follow even more stunning.

Jebus, Gibeah (19:11-12). The cities are only two miles apart. The close proximity of Israelite and Canaanite settlements show the intermixture that God warned Moses against (Deut. 20:16-18).

No one took them home (19:15). This comment shows the breakdown of a basic morality that infused not only Israelite but also Canaanite culture. The custom of hospitality imposed a moral obligation to welcome and care for strangers. The Levite should have been warned by this sign that his little group was not safe in Gibeah.

Homosexual rape (19:22). The sin that brought judgment on Sodom (Gen. 19) is now practiced in Israel itself, showing ultimate moral degradation.

"My virgin daughter" (19:24). In ancient society the host was morally obligated to protect a guest at any cost. The offer of the daughter is hardly moral by any standards, but the host saw it as the lesser of two moral evils.

The concubine (19:25). Fear may have moved the Levite to send his concubine outside. But we can offer no excuse.

"Get up; let's go" (19:28). These unfeeling words contrast with the earlier sensitivity shown by the Levite. Perhaps they suggest the ultimate in moral decline: a society in which rape and sexual promiscuity aren't viewed as all that bad. The Canaanite attitude toward sex has corrupted the people of God, as Hollywood seeks to corrupt us.

Outline
Place
Finder

CAUSES
CHARACTERS
CONSEQUENCES

Chapter summary. The last two chapters of Judges continue the theme introduced in Judges 17, describing events that reflect the spiritual, moral, and social conditions of the era.

Evidence of the Gibeahite's rape and murder of the Levite's concubine causes consternation among the tribes (20:1-3). The tribes gather, and determine that Gibeah must be destroyed and its people executed (vv. 4-11). But the Benjamites choose to defend their fellow tribesmen, and civil war breaks out (vv. 12-18). The allied forces are defeated in two battles, driving them back to God and confession of sins (vv. 19-28). The next battle is decisive, and only 600 Benjamite men survive (vv. 29-48). At this point the Israelites realize that an entire tribe is in danger of extermination. Four hundred brides are provided by razing the city of Jabesh Gilead, which had sent no one in response to the call to arms against Gibeah (21:1-14). Brides for the remaining 200 men were provided by letting the Benjamites "steal" them from marriageable young women who danced in fields during the annual Festival of Tabernacles (vv. 15-25).

The chapter shows that social anarchy as well as spiritual and moral decline follow when a nation turns its back on God.

Key verse. 20:28b: Evil must be purged, whatever the cost.

Personal application. Society must take a stand against great evils, even though there is always a cost.

INSIGHT

The assembly (20:1). The phrase "before the Lord" indicates the tribes came together to serve as a judicial court that would make its determination according to divine Law.

"Lewd and disgraceful" (20:6). The Levite uses two significant terms. "Lewd" is *zimma*, used often of sexual perversions worthy of death (cf. Lev. 18:17; 19:29). "Disgraceful" is *nebala*, a strong term for active moral rebellion against the divine standards, as in rape (2 Sam. 13:14), homosexual acts (Jud. 19:23-24) and general promiscuity (Deut. 22:21). While the Levite was mute about his own role in the affair, the acts of the Gibeahites merited death under O.T. Law (cf. Jud. 20:13).

The Benjamites' response (20:14). By coming to the aid of Gibeah rather than joining in the punishment of that city the tribe identified with the wicked men and merited their punishment.

Slings (20:16). The sling, like the one which David used to kill Goliath, was an impressive weapon, capable of hurling one-pound weights accurately at a speed of 90 miles an hour!

"Burnt offerings" (20:26-28). This type of voluntary offering signified full surrender to God (Lev. 1:1-17). It suggests that the community's worship was marked by repentance and recommitment. Now spiritually prepared, God promised victory.

"Phinehas" (20:28). Mention of this contemporary of Joshua's (Josh. 22) suggests that the events described in Judges 19–21 took place relatively early in the period.

All towns put to the sword (20:48). The Israelites had set out to punish Gibeah. The defeats administered by the Benjamites, with loss of life, now led to what we must consider revenge killings, as the towns and families of theBenjamite warriors are utterly destroyed.

The incident illustrates the author's theme: that anarchy reigned during the period. Just as there was no one able to command the Gibeahites to deal justly with visitors, and no one to command the Benjamites to take sides against their brothers, so now there was no one to restrain them from taking violent revenge. "Everyone did as he saw fit."

Extermination? (21:3) Extermination had never been intended. Now, with only 600 men left, the others felt obligated to provide Jewish wives so the Benjamites could fulfill their God-given destiny in the land. Jabesh Gilead was under the ban (*herem*) for failing to contribute troops. The city was destroyed, and 400 virgin wives offered to the surviving Benjamites.

Stolen wives (21:15-25). It is easier to find a way around the letter of a law than its spirit.

172

Ruth

Ruth is one of the Old Testament's warmest and most encouraging books. This brief book takes its name from the main character, a Moabite woman who chose to commit herself to her Hebrew mother-in-law and to Israel's God.

The story is set in the difficult days of the Judges, which were marred by appalling spiritual, moral, and social decline. Yet, as the story unfolds, we discover that within the corrupt society there were still true believers: simple folk who tried honestly to love and serve God, and to live generously with their neighbors. The unveiling of Ruth, of her mother-in-law Naomi, and of her husband-to-be, Boaz, reminds us that the true sacred history is not learned so much in the annals of heroes and kings, as in the daily lives of godly women and men. The Book of Ruth should be required reading for any who study the era of the Judges, for it brings much-needed balance to our impression of that age of spiritual disarray.

The Book of Ruth also makes distinctive theological and historical contributions. Theologically it provides a clear picture of the kinsman-redeemer, an individual who through relationship is able to intervene on a family member's behalf. In this role Boaz prefigures Jesus Christ, who became a real human being so that He might be our kinsman, and qualify as our Redeemer. Historically Ruth is an ancestress of David the king, who also prefigures Jesus, the ultimate Ruler of God's kingdom. How stunning that God called a Moabite woman, not one of the chosen people, for this significant role. What clear evidence that, in ancient times as in ours, God's love reaches out to all.

RUTH AT A GLANCE

KEY PEOPLE

Ruth   *A Moabite widow who allied herself with God's people out of love for her Hebrew mother-in-law, and whose gracious character won her renewed hope and a place among the people of God.*

Naomi   *A Hebrew woman who knew tragedy, but rediscovered happiness through the faithfulness of Ruth, her Moabite daughter-in-law.*

Boaz   *A godly Hebrew man, a relative of Naomi, who accepted a kinsman's responsibility and married Ruth, to the benefit of all three.*

KEY EVENTS

Ruth's choice (1:11-18).   *Ruth chose to return with Naomi to her people, even though she had no prospect of remarriage in Israel, a foreign land.*

Ruth's labors (2:1-13).   *Ruth was willing to work, which brought her to the attention of Boaz.*

Boaz's choice (3:11).   *Boaz responded to Ruth's invitation and good reputation by arranging to marry her.*

Obed's birth (4:13-22).   *The child of Ruth and Boaz became the grandfather of David, Israel's greatest king.*

WHERE THE ACTION TAKES PLACE

The family of Naomi is driven by famine from the Jewish homeland to Moab. During the 10 years there Naomi's husband and two married sons die. Naomi then returns home, to the Bethlehem area, accompanied by her daughter-in-law, Ruth. The rest of the story takes place near Bethlehem, destined to be the birthplace of King David as well as of Jesus Christ.

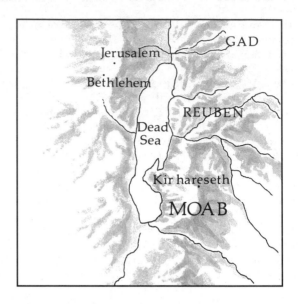

Date and Authorship. The events take place "in the days when the Judges ruled" (Ruth 1:1). The genealogy may suggest a date near the end of the era, but because Hebrew genealogies characteristically skip generations, this is uncertain. Ruth appears in the earliest Jewish lists of sacred writings, and is placed with the historical books, which are the oldest in the Old Testament canon. The names of the men in Naomi's family, most of the unique words and constructions, as well as familiarity with details of antique customs, support an early date for the book's composition. An early but unsupported rabbinic tradition identifies Samuel as the author of Ruth, as well as of Judges and the books that bear his name.

OUTLINE OF RUTH

I. The Family Moves to Moab		1:1-5
II. Naomi Returns to Judah		1:6-22
A. Ruth's Choice	1:6-18	
B. Naomi's Despair	1:19-22	
III. Ruth Gleans in Boaz's Field		2:1-23
A. Ruth's Dependability	2:1-3	
B. Ruth's Reputation	2:4-12	
C. Boaz's Kindness	2:13-16	
D. Naomi's Reaction	2:17-23	
IV. Boaz Redeems and Marries Ruth		3:1–4:22
A. Naomi's Plan	3:1-5	
B. Boaz's Response	3:6-18	
C. Boaz Redeems Ruth	4:1-12	
D. The Birth of Obed	4:13-17	
E. The Genealogy of David	4:18-22	

Chapter summary. In the days of the Judges a famine in Judah drives a Jewish family to Moab. The two sons marry there, but within a decade the father and both sons die (1:1-5). When news comes that the famine in Judah has ended, the widow Naomi decides to return home. Despite the affection that exists between the women, Naomi urges her daughters-in-law to remain in Moab and find other husbands (vv. 6-13). But one of the two, Ruth, is determined to stay with Naomi, and makes one of the most famous pledges to be found in any literature (vv. 14-18). The two women return to Judah, but there, in the familiar setting, a bitter and despondent Naomi is overcome by a renewed sense of her loss (vv. 19-22).

Key verses. 1:16-17: Friendship has no greater example.

Personal application. Let's be the kind of persons who draw others to us, and through our friendship, to our God.

INSIGHT

"Famine" (1:1). Agriculture in Palestine depends on regular rainfall, so any failure of the rains brings famine (cf. Gen. 26:1; 2 Sam. 21:1; 1 Kings 18:2). The Law covenant identifies famine as one of the judgments God will bring on His people when they are unfaithful (Deut. 28:23-24). Given the characteristics of the era, it's clear the family of Naomi fled during a time when most in the district had turned to Baal worship.

This makes the steadfast faith of Naomi and of the godly Boaz even more striking. They remind us that whatever the condition of our society, we and our family can remain committed to God.

"Bethlehem" (1:1). The name means "house of bread," or "granary." How ironic that an area named for its fertility is stricken by famine. The God who blesses is able also to judge.

Names (1:2). Heb. names are significant, for (1) they have meanings that often reflect the nature or character of the place or person named, and (2) they can often be used to define historical setting. Here Elimelech means "My God is King," Mahlon means "sickly," and Chilion "failing," or "wasting away." Each name has been found at Ugarit, so they fit the era of the Judges when Scripture says the events took place.

Was it unlawful to marry Moabite wives? (1:4) The law against intermarriage is directed against the Canaanites (Deut. 7:3). Moabites were not Canaanites, though there was a prohibition against too quickly admitting offspring of such a marriage to the congregation (23:3). The Jewish Midrash implies that even this prohibition related only to women who wed Moabite males.

God came "to the aid of His people" (1:6). The Heb. says that God "visited" His people. This word is typically used of divine activity. God does act, either to help or to punish, His own.

"Am I going to have any more sons?" (1:11) Naomi's reasoning depends on one of the ancient customs reflected in the Book of Ruth. In the ancient Middle East a childless widow would expect to marry her husband's brother. Naomi reminded her daughters-in-law that she had no more sons to give them. Even if she had more, why should young women wait for sons to grow up? Their best chance was to stay in their homeland and find new husbands.

Ruth's profession (1:16-17). Ruth's famous expression of commitment to her mother-in-law not only shows loyalty to a friend, but also clear theological insight. Ruth said, "Your people will be my people" before saying, "And your God my God." In O.T. times God had a covenant relationship with Israel alone. By identifying herself with the covenant people, Ruth qualified herself to claim Israel's God as her own.

In Bethlehem (1:19-21). Rather than make Naomi happy, familiar surroundings and old friends made Naomi's distress more intense. We can understand why. Going back home after the death of a loved one is likely to make us feel our loss. Our home seems so empty, the silence deafening. Suddenly we are weighed down by grief, for the one thing that is missing—our loved one—is what made the house "home." For Naomi, who had left Bethlehem with a husband and two sons, the return brutally drove home the extent of her loss.

"The Almighty" (1:21). The meaning of the Heb. *sadday* is uncertain. Most theories focus on one of two themes: power or compassion. Naomi feels crushed by God's power, all the more puzzling because the Lord is compassionate. The rest of the story shows that God truly is compassionate, as Naomi's bitterness is replaced by unexpected joy.

Chapter summary. Naomi and Ruth were now in the position of the "widow and fatherless" in Israel: they had no one to care for them, and no means of support. As it was the beginning of barley harvest, Ruth volunteered to go into the fields to collect whatever the workers missed. Without planning it, she began work in a field belonging to Boaz, a relative of Naomi's dead husband (2:1-3). When Boaz arrived, he welcomed her and invited her to keep working in his fields. He also told his workmen to make sure they left stalks of grain for her to gather (vv. 4-16). With this help, Ruth was able to gather about 40 pounds of grain (vv. 17-18), an unusually large amount for a gleaner. Naomi immediately saw the significance, and realized that someone had purposely helped her (v. 19). When Naomi discovered the man was Boaz, a near relative and thus qualified to be a kinsman-redeemer, Naomi told Ruth to continue working in Boaz's fields (vv. 20-23). Naomi already had begun to hope—and to plan.

Key verse. 1:12: God is a rewarder of those who seek Him.

Personal application. For us as well as for Ruth, a good reputation opens the door to a happier future.

INSIGHT

"Boaz" (2:1). Boaz is introduced as a relative of Naomi's deceased husband. This is important, for if he had been her relative, Boaz would not have qualified as a "kinsman-redeemer" (see below).

Gleaning (2:2-3). O.T. Law gave the poor the right to gather any produce left in field or orchard after the harvesters made one sweep (cf. Lev. 19:9-10; 23:22; Deut. 24:19). Ruth's reference to whoever is kind enough to let her glean (the meaning of "in whose eyes I find favor") reminds us that not everyone followed the Law!

Chance, or sovereign grace? (2:3) The expression trans. "it turned out" is found only here and in Ecc. 2:14ff. Ruth did not intentionally stop at the field of Boaz. But God intended that she should.

A pious greeting (2:4). Often pious expressions become part of the language, and lose their original meaning. "Good-bye" originally meant "God be with you." But we can hardly deduce piety from a person's use of "good-bye" today! In Boaz's case we perhaps can. Though the greeting may have been conventional, it is not recorded elsewhere in Scripture nor attested in archeological finds.

A deserved reputation (2:6, 10-11, 13). In a small community the story of Ruth and Naomi would be common knowledge, the focus of much conversation (cf. v. 11). Now events showed Ruth hardworking (v. 7), respectful (v. 10), modest, and grateful (v. 13). The reputation we earn opens— or closes—the door of opportunity.

Boaz's blessing (2:12). Boaz blesses Ruth, in a statement which may be taken as a prayer. "Reward" here is *maskoret*, a word which means "wages." Boaz believes that Ruth deserves the best for her piety and choice of Israel's God, and is convinced that a just God will see that she is well rewarded. Boaz, who utters this prayer, is the means by which it is answered. God often uses one who prays as His agent to answer that prayer.

"Told the men not to touch you" (2:9; cf. v. 22). Again we sense that Naomi, Ruth, and Boaz live in an oasis of peace in a turbulent, sinful society. Ruth was apparently in danger of being raped while working in the fields. Among his many kindnesses (cf. vv. 8-9, 14-15, 18, 21), Boaz personally warned his workers—not just their supervisors—that Ruth was not to be touched.

"The Lord" (2:20). Naomi sensed God's hand in Ruth's experience, and saw it as evidence of the Lord's continuing care. When we are burdened with grief, awareness of even little things God does for us can bring praise and release.

Kinsman-redeemer (2:20). The Heb. is *go'el*. Like other words from the root *g'l*, it indicates fulfilling one's responsibilities as a kinsman. O.T. family law gave the kinsman the right to redeem a relation from slavery, or buy back his fields (Lev. 25). Here another duty of the kinsman is in view: the obligation of the next of kin to marry a childless widow and have a child, which would be considered the offspring of the dead husband. In this way the dead husband's line would be carried on, and his property preserved. This "family law" with its implied responsibility to aid a near relative, prefigures the ministry of Jesus. In taking on human nature He became our near kinsman, and accepted the obligation to redeem us despite the terrible cost (»pp. 90, 791).

Chapter summary. Ruth works in Boaz's fields through the six weeks of the barley and wheat harvests. Naomi then instructs her to approach Boaz, and following an ancient custom, ask him to marry her as kinsman-redeemer (3:1-9). Boaz agrees, providing an even closer relative will not marry her (vv. 10-18). The very next morning Boaz obtains a release of the other's right of redemption (4:1-8). He publicly announces his marriage to Ruth, making the relationship official (vv. 9-12). In due time Ruth bears a son, to be cared for by a joyful Naomi (vv. 13-17), and who becomes the grandfather of David, Israel's greatest king (vv. 18-22).

Key verse. 4:22: How unexpectedly personal events influence national history!

Personal application. Our tragedies too can turn into triumphs, as we trust God and keep on doing our best.

INSIGHT

Night threshing? (3:2) Grain was threshed by tossing the crushed stalks into the air, for the wind to separate from the kernels of grain. Boaz did this *hallayiah,* in "the evening," not night. One commentator says the wind blows during this season from about four till shortly after dark.

Sleeping out (3:4). Boaz probably slept at the threshing floor to guard the grain. As reference to eating and drinking suggests (v. 7), the conclusion of the harvest was a time for partying. In pagan societies it was also an immoral time. There is, however, no suggestion of moral looseness in the events that follow.

Spread your garment over me (3:9). The source of the custom is lost in antiquity, though it is clear from the context Ruth was inviting Boaz to marry her. The same metaphor, suggesting the protection of a wife by her husband, is found in Ezek. 16:8, and apparently was used by Arabs as late as the 1800s. Some understand "skirt" to read "wings," picking up the image of Boaz's blessing in Ruth 2:12 which asks the Lord to bless Ruth, for she has "come to take refuge" under His "wings." What a beautiful image of the peace and security human beings are intended to find in the Lord, and in marriage.

Ruth's "kindness" (3:10). The Heb. word is *hesed,* often translated "loving-kindness," and used to describe God's faithfulness to His covenant promises. In this context Boaz praises Ruth for her loyalty to family, first in staying with her mother-in-law, and second in seeking marriage within the family structure rather than to one of the many "young men" who would have been delighted to marry her. The delicate interplay here suggests that Boaz was significantly older, and that Ruth was not only an admirable but a desirable younger woman.

"A woman of noble character" (3:11). The Heb. uses a term translated "mighty" when describing a warrior, or "wealthy" when describing an ordinary person. It suggests special attainment in the area of endeavor being discussed. Used of Ruth, it affirms that the whole community sees her as an "ideal bride" or a "bride worth winning."

Boaz's gift (3:15). The six "measures" were probably six *seah,* about 88 pounds of grain. Ruth was strong as well as beautiful.

"The town gate" (4:1). In O.T. times the town gate was an open space where people tended to gather. The local elders met there to judge civil and criminal cases brought to them. And business transactions were completed there, in the open and before witnesses. While written records were kept in ancient times, there was also great dependence on eyewitnesses, who would be able to attest to any agreement during the participant's lifetime. Thus we see Boaz approaching the other kinsman at the gate, holding his discussion with him in the open, and calling on bystanders to witness the other's repudiation of his right to serve as Ruth's kinsman-redeemer.

"Endanger my own estate" (4:6). The nearer relative gave this reason for not redeeming the land and widow of Elimelech's son. What did he mean? The best explanation seems to be that if he paid the price for the land, and took on the added expense of caring for a wife, he would be overextended financially.

Loosing the sandal (4:7). The verse contains an editor's note which explains an early custom which was no longer practiced and thus was unfamiliar. The inclusion of this and other early practices attests to the antiquity of the story.

"Naomi took the child" (4:16). The child born to Ruth and Boaz was apparently raised by Naomi, a replacement for the sons she lost. The Lord gave Naomi a family again: not only a daughter-in-law who loved her, but a grandson to care for and raise in hope, for through him her husband's and sons' line would be continued.

1 Samuel

The Books of 1 and 2 Samuel trace the most exciting period in Israel's history. God had fulfilled His covenant commitments to Abraham. After breaking the slave bonds of Abraham's descendants, the Lord brought them safely into Canaan, the Promised Land. But there Israel proved faithless, again and again abandoning God for the idols and debased practices of the pagans who shared the land with them. For 400 years, during the time of the Judges, Israelite strength continued to wane. Then, suddenly, under a leader appointed by God, a stunning transformation took place. Over the space of some 50 years Israel was converted from an oppressed minority in Canaan into a powerful nation. First and 2 Samuel record the key events of these critical years, and focus our attention on one of the most beloved of biblical heroes: David, the shepherd boy who became Israel's greatest king.

The story of the birth of the Hebrew monarchy is told through the lives of three men: Samuel, the last judge; Saul, Israel's first and failed king; and David, whose personal gifts and courageous faith in God catapulted him to greatness. Through the stories of these men the author of 1 and 2 Samuel gives us deep insights into the religious, social, and political condition of the times. He also, without preaching, underlines foundational spiritual truths which shape not only the course of history, but also the direction of our individual lives. As we study 1 Samuel we learn from the experiences of one of the Bible's truly great men. And we better understand the way that God works through all who trust, and are eager to respond to Him.

---

1 SAMUEL AT A GLANCE

KEY PEOPLE
Samuel *Israel's last judge, who supervised the founding of the monarchy.*
Saul *Israel's first king, whose flawed character and unwillingness to trust God led to the rejection of his family as hereditary rulers.*
David *The "man after God's heart" whose faith and devotion to God, with many special personal qualities, lifted him from shepherd boy to lead his people to nationhood and greatness.*

KEY EVENTS
Philistines defeated at Mizpah (1 Sam. 7). *The revival and victory led by Samuel prepares the way for the monarchy.*
The people demand a king (1 Sam. 8). *The people's motive is wrong, but God's timing calls for a national renewal.*
Saul, the first king, fails to trust God (1 Sam. 13; 15). *Despite early successes, Saul's moral and spiritual flaws lead to his rejection.*
Samuel secretly anoints David (1 Sam. 16). *God prepares the man for the task before He asks the man to perform it.*
David kills Goliath (1 Sam. 17). *The stunning victory leads to rapid advancement for David, and earns the jealous hostility of a rapidly deteriorating King Saul.*
David flees Saul (1 Sam. 21). *David becomes a fugitive, but during these years draws together a band of bold followers who later become key military leaders and advisers.*
Saul killed in battle (1 Sam. 31). *The death of Saul marks the end of David's years as a fugitive, and provides the opportunity for his rise to power.*

WHERE THE ACTION TAKES PLACE

Nearly all the events reported in 1 Samuel take place in the hill country of Palestine. Even during the years covered in this book, the Israelites were more a loose confederation of peoples than a unified nation. Saul (above) was more a chieftan than a king. Ruins that have been identified as his "fortress at Gibeah" (also shown above) show how small his "palace" really was, and remind us that the organization of the Israelite kingdom and the launching of its golden age was the work of the spiritual David, not of the unworthy Saul.

Date and Authorship. In the Hebrew canon the Books of 1 and 2 Samuel were a single book: the Book of Samuel. First Samuel is organized around the history of three men: Samuel, Israel's last judge; Saul, who ruled from about 1050–1010 B.C.; and David, whose rule extended from 1010 to 970 B.C. While the dates of the principle characters are relatively fixed, there is no agreement on a date for authorship of the books. A Jewish tradition suggests Samuel was the principle author, and that after his death his work was carried on and completed by the Prophets Nathan and Gad (cf. 1 Chron. 29:29). The tradition is a late one, however, and there is no certainty about who labored to give us these vital books.

A NOTE ON THE ORGANIZATION OF 1 SAMUEL

The plan of 1 Samuel 15–2 Samuel 8 has been clarified by the discovery of parallels with the Hittite "Apology of Hattusilus." This document is a 13th century B.C. defense of a new Hittite dynasty. Similarities suggest that one of our author's primary purposes in recording the history of the era was to firmly establish the legitimacy of David and his line, and defend their continuing right to the throne. The literary parallels include: a detailed description of why the previous ruler was disqualified; an emphasis on events leading up to the ruler taking the throne; an affirmation of the new ruler's piety; and a summary of the king's reign showing that God confirmed His choice by blessing the nation. Such parallels between biblical and secular documents do not challenge our belief in the inspiration of Scripture, but rather help us better understand the cultural setting within which God spoke, and thus the author's intent.

THEOLOGICAL OUTLINE OF 1 SAMUEL

CONTENT OUTLINE OF 1 SAMUEL

Chapter summary. The first chapters of 1 Samuel are set in the days of the Judges. While conditions reflect the spiritual and moral decline of the times, the central figure of this chapter, Hannah is one of those godly individuals whose faith remains strong however dark society.

Hannah comes with her husband on his annual pilgrimage to worship God at the tabernacle, then at Shiloh (1:1-5). This time Hannah's childlessness, made more bitter by the ridicule of her husband's other wife, drives Hannah to despairing prayer (vv. 6-10). In her anguish she vows that if God gives her a son, she will dedicate the boy to serve God (v. 11). Her fervent prayer is first misunderstood, and then blessed by the old priest, Eli, and Hannah suddenly finds her heart at rest (vv. 12-19). Hannah has a son, Samuel (v. 20), and when he is three she leaves him at the tabernacle to learn to serve God (vv. 21-28). Fulfilling her vow brings Hannah great joy, which she reveals in one of Scriptures' most delightful poems of praise (2:1-11).

Outline
Place
Finder

SAMUEL
SAUL
DAVID

Key verse. 1:11: Willingness to surrender brings blessing.

Personal application. The most difficult situation can be transformed by bringing it to the Lord in prayer.

Key concepts. God's blessing »p. 127. Vow »p. 96.

INSIGHT

A sinful society. Social conditions are shown by Eli's assumption that the woman outside the tabernacle was drunk (1:14), the corrupt priests (2:22), withdrawal of prophets (3:1), and Philistine oppression (4:1, 17).

A pious family. Elkanah, Hannah's husband, was a Levite (1 Chron. 6:26, 33) living in the tribal territory of Ephraim (1 Sam. 1:1). His piety is shown in his coming "year after year" to worship God and offer sacrifice.

Two wives. As childless Hannah is identified as Elkanah's "first wife," it seems likely that he only took a second wife to produce children, a course of action legitimized in Deut. 21:15-17. His continuing deep love for Hannah shows he was not moved by lust to take a second wife.

God and childbearing (1:5). Repeated O.T. sayings that God closes and opens wombs (cf. Gen. 30:2, 22; 33:5; Ps. 127:3) remind us that God is sovereign in the conception of children. Abortion, which takes a life God has given, is a denial of this awe-inspiring truth.

Hannah's prayer (1:10-11; 2:1-10). We have many models of prayer in the O.T. Among the greatest are: Gen. 18:16-33; Ex. 32:11-14; Num. 14:11-19; 2 Sam. 7:18-29; 12:13-23; 1 Kings 8:22-53; 2 Kings 19:14-19; 2 Chron. 20:6-12; and Ezra 9:5-15.

Certain principles underlie O.T. prayer. God is acknowledged as Creator, Redeemer, and Covenant-giver. This provides the O.T. saint with a context in which a deeply personal relationship can be established. In this relationship, prayer is free and spontaneous. Emotions are expressed without hesitation, and requests are made with the abandon of a child who realizes he or she is completely dependent on another—and that this Other cares.

Bargaining with God? (1:11) Hannah's emotional plea included a vow to give the son she yearned for to God, to serve Him as a Nazarite (cf. Num. 6). Was this offering God a "payoff"? While it might be so understood, the biblical vow is better seen as an expression of thanksgiving, offered to God in the expectation that He intends to bless the worshiper. At the same time, a vital spiritual principle infuses Hannah's promise. Before we are ready to receive many of God's blessings, we must commit them to Him. Surrender purifies and prepares us so we are not harmed by God's good gifts.

A sovereign, gracious God (2:1-11). Hannah's prayer celebrates God's sovereignty, expressing her personal joy (vv. 1-3), sharing her personal testimony (vv. 4-9), and concluding with a prophetic affirmation that God will judge the earth through a coming King He will anoint.

Outline
Place
Finder

SAMUEL
SAUL
DAVID

Chapter summary. An aged Eli is high priest when Hannah fulfills her vow, and leaves three-year-old Samuel at the tabernacle (chap. 1). Eli's sons are immoral and corrupt, and while Eli rebukes them, he fails to discipline them (2:12-26). At last a prophet approaches Eli with the grim message that God will act where Eli has not: his sons will die, and his line be set aside (vv. 27-36). With the promise that God will rise up a "faithful priest" (v. 35), the focus shifts to the boy Samuel, to report his call by God to the prophetic office (3:1-10). Samuel's first mission is to tell Eli that the time is near when his family will be punished (vv. 11-14). How hard it must be for Samuel to bring grim news to one he'd come to love, who was his mentor. But Samuel does convey the word of the Lord, and Eli humbly submits to God's judgment (vv. 15-18).

Key verse. 2:30: One's response to God is critical.

Personal application. Hearing God speak, and then doing as He says, is the key to spiritual achievement.

Key concepts. Priesthood »p. 81. Ephod »p. 70. Prophet »p. 131. Offerings »p. 79. Appearance of God to man »p. 81. Guilt »p. 79.

INSIGHT

Eli's sons. They are described in Heb. by the expression "sons of Beliel," which is associated with both idolatry and immorality (Deut. 13:13; Jud. 19:22). Their contempt for the Lord was shown in open violation of the Law's ritual (1 Sam. 2:17; cf. Lev. 7:14) and moral (1 Sam. 2:22) provisions. Eli's rebuke was only a slap on the wrist, when the two son's behavior called for execution (cf. 2:25).

"Man of God" (2:27). This phrase is often used in the O.T. of a prophet who delivers God's message. It emphasizes the message, rather than the character of the messenger, as contemporary use of the phrase tends to do.

"Samuel" (3:1). The author's alternation between Eli's sons and Samuel is intended to present a sharp contrast. It legitimizes Samuel's lifelong mission as God's agent during the transformation of Israel into a monarchy. It also drives home a vital spiritual principle, expressed in 2:30. Eli's sons and Samuel were both placed in a position of privilege. One honored God, and was honored by Him. The others despised God, and were set aside. Let's not treat our spiritual privileges lightly.

What happened to Eli's family? His two sons were killed in battle (4:17). Many descendants were massacred at Nob (22:11-19), and the high priesthood was transferred to the family of Zadok by Solomon (1 Kings 2:26-27, 35).

How old was Samuel when God spoke to him? (3:1) The Heb. word trans. "boy" here is the same used to describe David when he killed Goliath (17:33). It mean's "young person," and suggests that Samuel was probably in his early teens when the incident described took place.

Cursing God (3:13). The Septuagint states this is the sin of the two sons of Eli. The Heb. text, with restraint, simply says they "made themselves contemptible." In either case, the point is that their sins were not unintentional. The sons acted arrogantly, in full knowledge that what they did was wrong, and that they were showing utter contempt for God and His Law. Even a priest's unintentional sin could be atoned for by a sacrifice (cf. Lev. 4:3-12). But there was no sacrifice prescribed for any person's willful violation of God's laws.

Samuel's test (3:11-17). The first message that Samuel was to deliver served as a severe test. He had a close, affectionate relationship with Eli. Would he pass on the message of impending doom with total honesty? In his test, Samuel prefigures the ministry of many of the prophets who will follow him. Most of the O.T. prophets were called to warn Israel of coming divine judgments! Prophets were not especially popular in their own time!

"From Dan to Beersheba" (3:20). The distance is only about 150 miles, from north to south. But the common expression meant "everywhere in Israel."

Chapter summary. The Philistines dominate Canaan during this period (cf. Jud. 13–16). But now the Israelites determine to resist, and are defeated in battle (1 Sam. 4:1-2). The army sends for the ark, superstitiously expecting this symbol of God's presence will guarantee victory (vv. 3-9). Instead the Israelite forces are crushed, Eli's two sons are killed, and the holy ark is captured (vv. 10-11). When Eli hears the news, he faints, falls, and is killed (vv. 12-22). In one day Israel has lost a war, its high priest, and its symbol of relationship with God!

Meanwhile the Philistines place the ark before an idol of their god as a token of his superiority (5:1-2). But the idol falls to the ground before the ark, and its head and hands break off (vv. 3-5). Even more troubling, the people in the city where the ark rests are stricken with painful tumors. Wherever they move the ark, the Philistines find themselves afflicted (vv. 6-12). Israel mourns its loss. But God defends His own!

Outline
Place
Finder

SAMUEL
SAUL
DAVID

Key verse. 4:3: God, not religious relics, is what counts.

Personal application. Never suppose when you suffer loss that God has been defeated.

Key concepts. Philistines »p. 185. Ark »p. 68. Covenant »p. 35.

INSIGHT

"Returned to camp" (4:3). The initial battle was a defeat, but not a disaster. There was no rout; the army "returned to camp."

Bringing the ark (4:3). Pagan armies frequently carried idols, supposing that their gods would guarantee victory (cf. 2 Sam. 5:21; 1 Chron. 14:12). The Israelite adoption of this superstitious practice is a further indication of the deterioration of faith, for God is by nature omnipresent, always present to enable us as long as we are in right relationship with Him. In looking to the ark for deliverance, significant though it was in O.T. religion, God's people were depending on "it" rather than on God for deliverance. The fact that their attitude was essentially pagan is reflected in the response of the Philistines (cf. 1 Sam. 4:7-9). The incident reminds us how important it is for us to have an accurate concept of God, that we may base our actions on truth.

"Shiloh" (4:3). Excavations suggest that Shiloh was destroyed about 1050 B.C. It seems possible the Philistines razed the city after the battle described in this chapter (cf. Jer. 7:12).

Interpreting events (4:21-22). Eli's dying daughter-in-law understandably saw the defeat, the death of Eli and his two sons, and the capture of the ark as a total disaster. In fact, these events were purging judgments, which ended a dark era and ushered in an age of hope. It's helpful to remember the battle of

Aphek when things look darkest. God may be preparing a great and good work.

"Dagon" (5:2). Dagon was once thought to be a "fish god." Further discoveries in Ugarit indicate Dagon was the father of Baal, a Canaanite fertility deity. The name Dagon seems linked to Semitic words for "grain" or "rain," and his temples are frequently mentioned in Scriptures dealing with this era (cf. Josh. 19:27; Jud. 16:23; 1 Chron. 10:10). The worship of Dagon was persistent in the area: a temple of Dagon in Ashdod was destroyed by the Maccabean leader, Jonathan, in 167 B.C.

The idol fell (5:2-4). The ark was placed next to the idol of Dagon. One commentator suggests this was to honor Yahweh, on the supposition that He had abandoned Israel "to acknowledge the power and superiority of their god." But the prostrate position of the idol before the ark discovered the next morning indicates submission — something the Philistines were not ready to admit. They sat Dagon back up, and the Heb. emphasizes they got up *early* the next morning to see what had happened. The idol was again fallen, with hands and head broken off. In Canaanite mythology as learned at Ugarit, enemy heads and hands were trophies taken by the goddess Anat. The imagery was clear: Yahweh and Dagon had fought, and Yahweh was triumphant!

"Tumors" (5:6). Many believe boils to be swellings associated with bubonic plague.

Outline
Place
Finder

SAMUEL
SAUL
DAVID

Chapter summary. After seven months of torment, the Philistines are desperate to be rid of the ark. But they want to dispose of it in a way that will not further anger Israel's God. The solution is to cast gold offerings in the shape of tumors and of mice, to indicate respect for the Lord (6:1-6). But the Philistines also devise a test. The ark is placed in a cart pulled by two cows with calves, who normally would not leave their offspring (vv. 7-9). The cows, lowing in protest, act against nature and head directly for Israelite territory! Now the Philistines know: God did cause the plagues that have struck them (vv. 10-18). In Israel the ark is received with joy, but when a number of Israelites fail to show respect and peer inside, 70 die (6:19–7:1). These events stimulated a true revival (vv. 2-7). When the Philistines launch an attack against a gathering of God's people for worship, God intervenes and the Philistine forces are slaughtered (vv. 8-13a). Throughout Samuel's years as judge, God aids Israel against the Philistines (vv. 13b-17).

Key verse. 6:6: Some people do learn from history after all!

Personal application. Keep the focus of your faith on the Lord, and not symbols.

Key concepts. Altar »p. 79. Baals »p. 162. Holy »p. 73.

INSIGHT

A guilt offering (6:4). In O.T. Law a person who committed an offense against another was required to pay back what had been taken, plus an additional amount as reparation (cf. Ex. 21:34; Lev. 5:16, 18). Only by such a humble confession of error and symbolic repayment could the Philistines hope for relief from divine judgment.

Why gold mice? Some suggest mice were the carriers of bubonic plague, which caused the tumors. It seems probable that a swarm of mice did overrun Philistia, but unlikely that the Philistines would have seen the cause/effect link.

Why did God "strike down" 70 Israelites? The ark was no idol, but a holy object. By peering into it, the curious people of Beth Shemesh failed to show respect for God. Num. 4 gives explicit instructions for the priests to cover the ark and other holy objects before the Levites were even permitted to carry them.

How can a rock be a witness? (6:18) The idea of a natural object serving as a witness to a historic act is found often in the O.T. (for stones of witness, see Gen. 31:52; Josh. 24:27). Such objects do witness, for later generations can touch, feel, and see them as they recall what took place there, thus solidly anchoring their faith in history. Ours is not a religion of myths and made-up stories. Ours is a faith that rests on what God has actually done in space and time.

"Twenty years" (7:2). The 20-year period has been variously understood, as the total time the ark was at Kiriath Jearim, as 20 years of Philistine oppression, or as 20 years between the events of chapters 5–7 and the battle at Mizpah.

Why did the Philistines attack? Other O.T. passages relate crying out to the Lord with undertaking a holy war (cf. Josh. 24:7; Jud. 3:9; 6:6-7; 1 Sam. 12:8, 10). The Philistines may have seen the great prayer meeting Samuel called as a prelude to an Israelite attack, and struck first.

"Subdued" (7:13). The Israelite victory threw the Philistines back and secured the borders of Israelite territory. As 1 Sam. goes on to show, it did not shift the balance of power or change the basic Philistine military superiority.

"Over Israel" (7:15-17). The circuit covered by Samuel is limited to central Palestine, with no city lying more than 10 miles from Jerusalem. This reminds us of the severely weakened state of Israel in the era, and sets the stage for the stunning surge of Israelite power under David.

The Philistines

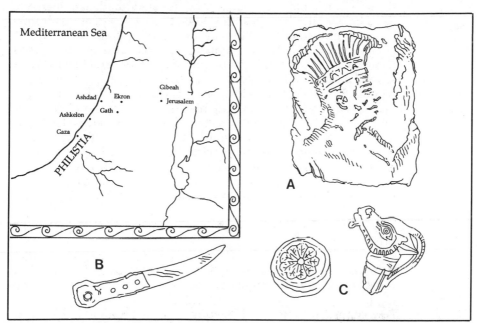

A) A cult stand used in Philistine worship. B) A Philistine knife with an iron blade and ivory handle. C) Gold earrings found at a Philistine site.

A large body of sea peoples, who originated in ancient Crete, flooded the coastal plains of Palestine around 1200 B.C. Representatives of the race had settled in Canaan centuries before (cf. Gen. 21:22-34). But during the era of the Judges a major invasion of the eastern Mediterranean took place. Ancient records tell of an incursion into Egypt in the time of Pharaoh Merneptah (1236–1223 B.C.), and of a massive land and sea invasion of the Nile Delta in the eighth year of Rameses III (1198–1166 B.C.). The sea peoples were thrown back, but established major cities in Palestine at Ashdod, Ashkelon, Ekron, Gath, and Gaza (see map, above). These settlers put great pressure on the Israelites, pushing their settlements deeper and deeper into the central highlands occupied by Israelites.

At this time the Philistines possessed two great advantages: a superior material culture, and a unified system of government. The Philistines knew the secret of working iron, which rested on advanced technology capable of focusing the intense heat required to smelt iron ore. Archeological digs of sites in Israel dating from before 1000 B.C. show that only those occupied by Philistines contained iron tools or weapons. Thus iron proved a "secret weapon" which kept Israel subservient to the Philistines for centuries. Also Israel was disorganized, while the Philistines operated with a ruling counsel.

Though David later administered crushing defeats to the Philistines, and won the secret of working iron, historical books tell of hostilities between Israel and the Philistines in the time of Jehoram (853–841 B.C.; 2 Chron. 21:16), of Uzziah (780–741 B.C.; 2 Chron. 26:6-7), and of Hezekiah (715–687 B.C.; 2 Kings 18:8). The Philistine presence was maintained on Palestine's coastal plains until they were finally crushed by the Babylonians.

Outline
Place
Finder

SAMUEL
SAUL
DAVID

Chapter summary. These critical chapters begin the transformation of Israel into a monarchy. Moses had predicted that one day Israel would have a king (Deut. 17:14-20). Yet at this historic moment, Israel's motive in demanding a king is wrong (1 Sam. 8:1-5). God tells Samuel, now old and about to pass from the scene, to warn His people. But when Israel insists on a king, Samuel is told to honor their request (vv. 6-22). Now the scene shifts, and we meet a young Saul, setting off in search of lost donkeys (9:1-5). Saul and his servant come to Samuel for help (vv. 6-14), and Samuel recognizes Saul as God's choice for the throne (vv. 15-20). The youthful Saul is appropriately humble, and stunned to be the guest of honor at a banquet planned long before he appeared at Samuel's door. Tension builds, as the next morning Samuel sends the servant on ahead, to share with Saul alone a message from God (vv. 21-27).

Key verse. 8:20: It is the glory of the believer not to be like all other people.

Personal application. Our motives in prayer are as important as the character of the things we ask for.

Key concepts. Judge »p. 158. King »p. 130. Man of God »p. 182.

INSIGHT

Samuel's sons (8:1-3). The sons violated the most basic provisions in O.T. Law concerning doing justice (cf. Ex. 18:21; 23:2, 6, 8; Deut. 16:19; 24:17). It's popular to suggest that Samuel like Eli (1 Sam. 2) must have been to blame, and that perhaps he gave so much time to his ministry he neglected his family. But God's own people Israel, whom He loved, cared for, and disciplined, also strayed. We do not blame God for the sinful choices of His children. Let's not be too quick to blame godly parents for the sinful choices of *their* children.

Reasons for a king, now (8:4-6). Samuel was old. His sons weren't suitable to succeed him. Israel wanted to be like other nations. Israel wanted a military commander to "fight our battles" (v. 20). What was wrong with this thinking? At each point it shows lack of trust in God. Israel was not to be like other nations, for God was her King, and God led Israel in battle. Each reason given by Israel for a king shows a disregard of or implicit rejection of God. Let's not seek our own solutions when we come to a critical point in our lives. Let's do what Israel did not. Turn to God in prayer and ask Him for His solution.

"Saul" (9:2). Saul is described as physically impressive, a trait perhaps required for Israel to accept him. Yet the mystery remains. Why did God choose Saul, who despite a promising beginning proved to be flawed and failed

critical spiritual tests? The answer may lie in Israel's request for a ruler to "fight our battles." Saul did succeed as a military leader. Israel had placed no value on spiritual leadership—and so God gave them just what they asked for: a man with military skills but no spiritual depth.

Sharing in God's suffering (8:8). Samuel felt the anguish of rejection. Though God reminded Samuel that the request for a king was rejection of the Lord, not of Samuel, God comforted His servant with the reminder that He had felt the same rejection "from the day I brought them up out of Egypt." Serving God thrusts us into caring deeply for people who will surely disappoint and hurt us. But let's remember that it is God's suffering we share—and that through suffering Christ has redeemed the world.

"High place" (9:13). Canaanite worship centers, constructed on hilltops and also called "high places" were to be destroyed. »p. 113. Until the construction of the temple by Solomon, Israelites worshiped at high places of their own (cf. 1 Kings 3:4-5).

The banquet (9:24). The meal, which Samuel had known the future king would attend before he met Saul, anticipates a "coronation banquet" (cf. 11:15; 16:1-33; 1 Kings 1:9). The Heb. "invited" used to describe the guests may be a technical term also related to coronation of kings (cf. 1:41, 49; Zeph. 1:7).

Chapter summary. Samuel privately anoints Saul as king of Israel (10:1), and makes predictions that will confirm Saul as God's choice (vv. 2-7). Samuel also gives Saul specific instructions to be followed at an undefined future time when Saul finds himself at Gilgal (v. 8). Saul returns home, and says nothing about the private anointing (vv. 9-16). Samuel calls an assembly of all Israel. There, perhaps by use of Urim and Thummim, Saul is publicly identified as God's choice for Israel's king (vv. 17-24). Though most are pleased with Saul because of his impressive height, some complain (vv. 26-27). Saul goes back home and keeps on working his fields, until Jabesh Gilead is besieged by Ammonites. Then, empowered by God's Spirit, Saul calls out Israel's militia (11:1-7). The people respond in force. Saul leads a surprise night attack, and crushes the Ammonite invaders (vv. 8-11). Ecstatic at the victory, the Israelites are ready to execute those who earlier questioned the choice of Saul. But Saul credits God with the rescue of Israel and refuses to spoil the occasion with the blood of any of his own people (vv. 12-13). The victorious crowd travels to Gilgal, where the authority of Saul is gladly reaffirmed (vv. 14-15).

Outline
Place
Finder

SAMUEL
SAUL
DAVID

Key verse. 10:6: God equips even flawed individuals to serve Him effectively.

Personal application. Let's not only begin well—let's persist in doing well till the end.

Key concepts. Prophet »p. 131. Urim and Thummim »p. 70.

INSIGHT

Anoint (10:1). The act of pouring oil is mentioned 69 times in the O.T. In most cases it has ritual significance, in setting something (as the altar, Ex. 29:36) or someone (as priests, 28:41; kings, and even prophets, 1 Kings 19:16) apart for the service of God.

"Gibeah of God" (10:5). The Philistine outpost here, just three miles north and east of Jerusalem, shows how deeply the Philistines had penetrated into Israel, despite defeats during Samuel's rule.

"A procession of prophets" (10:5). This is the first mention in the O.T. of a group of prophets. Some say Samuel began schools to train prophets.

"Changed into a different person" (10:6). Some take this as conversion. Others see it as equipping a humble individual (cf. v. 22) to become a bold military leader (cf. 11:6-8).

"Who is their father?" (10:12) This reply was in answer to the doubt of some onlookers that Saul could be a prophet, even though he joined the group in prophesying. It reminded the hesitant that God sovereignly chooses His prophets without regard to ancestry.

"Besieged" (11:1). Nahash, whose name means "serpent," apparently besieged the city because he was unwilling to take the losses associated with direct attack, or because he hoped to provoke a general war with supposedly disorganized Israel.

Why gouge out the right eye? (11:2) In ancient warfare soldiers fought behind shields, with only their right eyes exposed.

330,000. This force is approximately half the number available when Israel first attacked Canaan and reflects the decline in the Judges era.

"Surrender"? (11:10) The Heb. reads "go out" to you. It was understood by the Ammonites to mean surrender. But the same Heb. term is used of "going out" to offer battle!

Saul's great promise (11:13). Saul demonstrated appropriate piety in crediting God with the victory and great wisdom in refusing to punish those who had scoffed at him earlier. But as the pressures of leadership grew, Saul's flaws were clearly revealed. A good beginning is never enough. It's lifelong follow-through that counts.

Outline
Place
Finder

SAMUEL
SAUL
DAVID

Chapter summary. At Gilgal, Samuel gives an address which marks the end of his career as political though not spiritual leader of Israel (cf. 12:23-24). Samuel is innocent of injustice and of using his office for personal gain (vv. 1-5). But Israel has a history of rebellion against God (vv. 6-11). This has culminated in the rejection of God implied in her request for a human king (v. 12). Even so, God will bless if the king and Israel fear, serve, and obey the Lord (vv. 13-15). A terrible storm reveals God's continuing power to act, and awes the people, underlining Samuel's words of warning (vv. 16-22, 25).

In the second year of Saul's reign, the Philistines mobilize for a major war effort (13:1-5). Rather than trust God, Israel hides in terror (vv. 6-7). Saul, as previously arranged (cf. 10:8), waits at Gilgal for the prophet to appear and sacrifice to the Lord (13:8). As more of his tiny standing army deserts each day, Saul can stand it no longer. Rather than wait, Saul violates God's Law and steps into the role of a priest (vv. 9-10). Samuel angrily rejects Saul's excuses, and the king is forced to retreat, leaving the Philistines free to raid at will (vv. 11-18). The desperate condition of the Israelites is explained in part by the Philistine possession of one of the ancient world's greatest military secrets: the capacity to work iron (vv. 19-22) (cf. »p. 185).

Key verses. 12:14; 13:13: God's commands must be given priority in any situation.

Personal application. Stressful and uncertain times test our trust in God, not our strength of character.

INSIGHT

Samuel blameless (12:1-5). The situation is formal, with Samuel implying and refuting charges, and all Israel, with God, serving as witnesses who testify to his innocence. The testimony to Samuel contrasts with testimony the prophet is about to give about Israel.

"But . . . you" (12:12). Historically Israel had abandoned God, but after punishment, repented, cried out to Him, and was delivered (cf. vv. 9-11). This generation was more wicked, because when threatened by the Ammonites they begged Samuel for a king rather than repent and turn to God!

God is faithful, anyway (12:14-15). The call for a king was a rejection of God—but God did not reject Israel. If the people would show reverence for (fear of) God by serving and obeying Him, God would bless. The very faithfulness of God to His covenant promises should move us to trust, and to obey.

"As for me" (12:23). Samuel would no longer give political leadership. But his spiritual influence would persist. When our children are grown and we no longer exert control over them, we can still pray for them, and exert a powerful moral example.

No fear of God (13:5-7). "Fear" of God is that reverential awe that considers Him both real and present. Israel's terrified flight from the army of Philistia showed that they considered their human foes more "real," and thus more powerful, than their God!

Saul's response (13:8-12). Saul could have set the spiritual tone and called Israel back to faith by his example. Instead the stress made him anxious, and in direct disobedience to Scripture he chose to officiate at a sacrifice, rather than wait for Samuel, an ordained priest (cf. 10:8).

"Foolishly" (13:13). The word indicates a moral corruption, not merely a mistake or miscalculation. Saul's disobedience mirrored the unbelief and historic wickedness of God's people, and disqualified him from permanent leadership.

600 men (13:15). Why does the text make a point of Saul's 600 men? Because this is twice the number with which Gideon defeated another massed enemy force. The difference? Gideon had faith.

Chapter summary. Saul's son Jonathan shows the faith his father lacks. He successfully attacks a Philistine detachment (14:1-14). The Philistines panic, and as word spreads, those who had hidden in fear find courage and harry the now fleeing enemy (vv. 15-23). Saul unwisely forbids his men to eat, but Jonathan, who has not heard, gains fresh strength by eating honey (vv. 24-30). The exhausted Israelites break into the Philistine stores, and sin by eating meat with the blood in it (vv. 31-36; cf. Gen. 9:4; Lev. 17:10). When God will not answer Saul's inquiry, Saul concludes someone has sinned and discovers that Jonathan violated his command. The rigid Saul, who himself willfully disobeyed God's wise command, is now ready to execute Jonathan for unintentionally violating Saul's own foolish ruling! Only the people's intervention saves the young man's life (vv. 37-47). Despite continual skirmishes with the Philistines, God sends Saul to war against the Amalekites. Saul again willfully disobeys a direct command of God (15:1-17). Saul's growing pride and arrogance brings his final rejection by God (vv. 18-34). Saul will rule till he dies, but no son will succeed him.

Outline
Place
Finder

SAMUEL
SAUL
DAVID

Key verse. 14:6: A son's faith puts his father to shame.

Personal application. Disobedience brings discipline.

INSIGHT

Faith (14:6). Jonathan's faith was exhibited in his confidence that God could save—and in his asking God for a sign before he attacked (vv. 10-12). But it is wise to wait for guidance before we act, to make sure that what we plan is in harmony with His will.

"Panic" (14:15). Jonathan's victory was hardly enough to shake the confidence of the Philistines. But an earthquake, sent by God, did! Let's do what we can, and expect God to make the most of it!

No time for faith (14:19). Saul's statement to the priest, "withdraw your hand," probably relates to using Urim and Thummim to inquire into God's will. In essence Saul was saying, "There's no time to inquire of God." The incident is another indication of Saul's growing arrogance and indifference to the Lord.

God is silent (14:37). When Saul did at last inquire concerning God's will, no answer was given. Don't disobey God persistently, and then expect Him to come running on call.

"What sin has been committed" (14:38). Saul did not ask "what sin?" but "who sinned?" The lot indicated Jonathan, for he had violated the king's command, though unintentionally. In O.T. Law no unintentional sin merits death. To demand full payment from those who break our commands, but ignore our own violation of God's commands, is blindness and arrogance.

Saul's flaws. Chapter 15 reveals the developed flaws in Saul's character that serve as warnings to believers today. Once humble (v. 17), power made him so arrogant that he disobeyed God in the name of piety (vv. 21-23). Yet Saul was so insecure that his disobedience was committed out of fear of the people he supposedly led (v. 24). Even when Saul was forced to admit his guilt to Samuel, he was more concerned about how things appeared to the people than he was with the reality of his relationship with God (vv. 30-31). The pride that so often accompanies promotion just as frequently masks fear of what others think. Only by remaining humbly dependent on God, can we be safe from the flaws that brought down Israel's first king.

Did God make a mistake? (15:11, 35) Some have taken the phrase "God was grieved" He had made Saul king as an admission of error, as if God had not known how Saul would turn out. But the Heb. word *niham* can mean emotional involvement and anguish over a situation affecting others, as well as indicate a change of mind, as it does in verse 29 where Samuel asserts that God does not "change His mind." God made Saul king, and Saul was an effective military leader. The fact that Saul's flaws endangered the nation was a matter of deep divine regret, but no indication that God had made a mistake.

Outline
Place
Finder

SAMUEL
SAUL
DAVID

Chapter summary. God sends Samuel to Bethlehem to anoint a new king of Israel (16:1-5). There, to Samuel's surprise, a handsome but unimpressive young shepherd, David, is identified as God's choice (vv. 6-13). As Saul now suffers from deep depressions, David gains experience at court as a harp player, for David's music soothes the troubled king (vv. 14-23). Then, suddenly, David's character and his courageous faith are displayed. Israel is again invaded by the Philistines. As sometimes happened in ancient warfare, a Philistine war hero, Goliath, challenges Israel to provide a man to meet him in single combat. Goliath, a giant over nine feet tall, is so impressive none in Israel dare respond (17:1-11). But David, bringing supplies from home for his three brothers, isn't awed. In what is undoubtedly history's most famous battle, young David, confident that God will help him, kills the giant Philistine with his sling (vv. 12-51). David's victory leads to a rout of the Philistines, and causes Saul to wonder about David's family line (vv. 52-58).

Key verses. 16:7; 17:37: A heart for God is displayed in one's actions, not in a person's appearance.

Personal application. David's confidence came from the belief that he was on God's side, not that God was on his.

Key concepts: Anoint »p. 187. Holy Spirit »p. 73. God's choice of individual »p. 797. Philistines »p. 185.

INSIGHT

The whole truth? (16:2-3) Samuel rightly feared Saul would kill him if he heard Samuel anointed another king of Israel. God instructs Samuel to say he has come to sacrifice. We are not obligated to reveal everything we intend when if all were known another might be moved to sin.

"The heart" (16:7). In Heb. the heart (*leb*) represents the inner man, the real self. My Uncle Paul married a frail, unattractive woman weakened by constant bouts with arthritis. He met her at church, came to admire her, and fell in love with her inner beauty rather than her outward appearance. How important it is to learn the lesson God taught Samuel.

The Spirit departed (16:14). In the O.T. most comings of the Spirit on a person are to empower him or her for a specific task. Only in 10:6, 10 and 11:6 is Saul described as flooded with the Spirit. Here, after his rejection by God, we are told the Holy Spirit has departed permanently.

David in court (16:15-23). Some take this passage as a "separate tradition" about David's introduction to Saul's court that conflicts with 17:55-58. Why, if Saul knew David as his harpist, would he ask Abner about the family of "that young man"? The conflict is only appar-

ent. After David's victory over Goliath, he was seen in a totally different light than he had been as a harpist. Saul had no reason to remember details about the family of a mere harpist, but wanted to learn all he could about the emergent military hero!

Why bring food? (17:17) The "army" of Israel was really a volunteer militia. Each man provided his own food and weapons. The 40-day stalemate probably meant many were running out of food.

Saul and David (17:33-38). Saul was a warrior, the largest man in the Israelite forces (cf. 10:23), and the logical opponent of Goliath. David is described as a "lad," untrained, and so small that Saul's armor made it difficult for David even to "walk around" (17:38-39). The text, however, sets out the real contrast between the two. David had total confidence in God as the Lord of armies, and advanced fearlessly for the honor of God's name (vv. 45-47). By abandoning God Saul had lost the moral and spiritual force so vital to leading. David displayed the very strengths Saul lacked.

Victory symbols (17:54). The verse implies that David kept Goliath's head. Though grizzly, this symbol of victory would remind David and his people of the power of faith.

David

Illustration. *David, shown playing a kinnor, a twelve-stringed, hand-held instrument translated "harp" in many English versions. Despite his military and political achievements, David is best remembered as the "sweet singer of Israel," who authored psalms and songs in praise of God.*

The young shepherd boy who became Israel's greatest king is known for many outstanding achievements. As soldier, he expanded the territory held by Israel some 10 times over (cf. map, p. 202) and reorganized the army. As king, David created an effective central government. As spiritual leader, he established Jerusalem as the national religious center, and restructured the worship of his people. He also contributed many of the psalms and hymns used in public worship. His vigor and piety, and his unmatched impact on the history of the Jewish people, mark David as Israel's ideal king. The era of David and Solomon was unquestionably Israel's golden age.

But David is honored more for what he represents than what he accomplished. David is the prophetic prototype of a Ruler to descend from him, destined to establish God's kingdom worldwide. Through this promised Ruler, whom the Bible identifies as Jesus Christ, God's people will ultimately be led to eternal victory and peace.

Yet David's greatest appeal lies not in his theological significance but in his human qualities. The Bible contains more stories about David than any other person except for Jesus Christ. David's appeal is understandable. David is the poor boy who makes good; the humble person who overcomes tremendous odds through trust in God. David is the saint who stumbles and falls, yet through confession is cleansed to walk even closer to the Lord. David is the man who suffers rejection, and yet finds comfort and hope in the Lord. Through it all David shares his deepest feelings freely in his psalms, teaching us that we too can be honest with God, teaching us that God is a sure foundation for our hopes, our confidence in this life and the next.

Favorite stories about David include his victory over Goliath (1 Sam. 17), his friendship with the noble Jonathan (chap. 20), his refusal to take Saul's life (chaps. 24; 26), his willingness to listen to the beautiful and assertive Abigail (chap. 25), his transportation of the ark to Jerusalem (2 Sam. 6), and his repentance when confronted concerning his sin with Bathsheba (chaps. 11–12). In coming to know David well, we learn about our own weakness and how to love God better than before.

Outline
Place
Finder

SAMUEL
SAUL
DAVID

Chapter summary. The winsome David quickly wins the friendship of Jonathan, Saul's oldest son (18:1-4). His successes in battle win popular approval, and also followers at court, who must already have begun to lose confidence in the erratic Saul (v. 5). When Saul hears songs of praise that exalt David more than him, he becomes both angry and jealous (vv. 6-9). Twice, in fits of anger, Saul hurls the spear that serves him as a scepter at David, but misses (vv. 10-11). When Saul gives David a dangerous military command, David wins a string of victories that impresses and further frightens the king (vv. 12-15). Finally Saul offers David his younger daughter, who is in love with the handsome young captain, asking as a dowry only tokens to prove David has killed a hundred Philistines (vv. 16-25). David brings twice the number of tokens, and the frustrated king, who had hoped David would be killed, is forced to keep his word and marry Michal to the man he increasingly feared (vv. 26-30).

Key verse. 18:15: Insecure people fear the successful.

Personal application. Don't be surprised when others are jealous and hostile at your success.

Key concepts. Anger »pp. 72, 196. Envy »p. 864.

INSIGHT

"Jonathan" (18:1). Saul's son Jonathan is one of the O.T.'s most admirable characters. Though he soon realizes that David is destined to follow his father on the throne, Jonathan boldly defends David as a loyal servant of the king (chap. 19). When forced to take sides, Jonathan chooses to support David, and faces his father's fury in order to save David's life (chap. 20). When we remember that Jonathan would normally have succeeded Saul as Israel's king, his friendship for David is especially impressive. The O.T. contains no finer example of what it means to be a friend. The story of how David returned Jonathan's friendship is found in 2 Sam. 9.

"Saul's officers" (18:5). These are court officials. The phrase suggests that many influential persons formed a "David party" and became his supporters (cf. vv. 16, 28).

"Singing and dancing" (18:6-7). Celebration usually followed battlefield victories (cf. Ex. 15:20; Jud. 11:34). The praise of David shows his popularity, and explains why Saul began to hate and fear him. The weak man, and Saul was morally weak, naturally responds with hostility when others are honored.

Saul's fears (18:12). Let's rejoice when we see that God is with a brother or sister. To react with hostility or envy is evidence that our own relationship with God is flawed.

David led them (18:16). The Heb. says "going out" and "coming in" "before" Israel. David's military command called for being in the thick of the fighting (cf. 2 Sam. 5:24).

"The king's son-in-law" (18:18). The chapter continues to emphasize the role (cf. vv. 21-23, 26-27). Membership in the royal family was indeed special. David's refusal not only showed humility, but also may have reflected the fact that he lacked the wealth needed to provide the bride price expected for the daughter of a king (cf. vv. 23-24).

A hundred foreskins (18:24). Jewish men were circumcised, but the Philistines were not. If David presented the king with a hundred penises with the flap of skin that covers the tip unremoved, Saul would know the dead really were Philistines.

A price for the bride (18:24). Don't get the idea that women were sold! The "bride price" paid to the father as compensation for the loss of his daughter was in fact a cultural affirmation of her worth and value. In return the father gave his daughter a dowry, which might be money, goods, land, slaves, etc. This remained hers, and if the marriage was ever dissolved, the dowry belonged to the bride. Thus the exchange of gifts showed that both the father and the groom valued the woman, and was far from treating her as property.

Outline
Place
Finder

SAMUEL
SAUL
DAVID

Chapter summary. Saul now tries openly to have David killed, but Jonathan affects a brief reconciliation (19:1-7). When war breaks out and David again proves himself a hero, Saul's old hostility and madness return. David's wife helps him flee (vv. 8-17), and God Himself intervenes when Saul sends men to capture David (vv. 18-24). Jonathan, who has apparently been absent from court, simply cannot believe Saul plans to murder David (20:1-3). The two devise a plan to discover Saul's intentions, and Jonathan promises to report to his friend (vv. 4-10). Going out into a field where they will be unobserved, the two make a formal commitment to each other. Jonathan explicitly acknowledges David as future king, and David binds himself to deal kindly with Jonathan and his descendants (vv. 11-23). When Saul's behavior at a ceremonial meal David would normally attend reveals Saul does intend to kill David, father and son have an angry confrontation (vv. 24-34). The loyal Jonathan warns David as promised, and the grief-stricken friends part (vv. 35-42).

Key verse. 20:42: Friendship tested is friendship proved.

Personal application. In times of stress it's vital to have, and to be, a friend.

Key concepts. Kill »p. 64. Covenant »p. 64.

INSIGHT

Jonathan's role (19:1-7). The Heb. emphasizes Jonathan's offer: I myself will speak to "my father" about you. Jonathan's open advocacy of David was courageous, for it meant taking sides with David against the king.

"Michal" (19:11-17). Michal is a tragic character. She loved David, and helped him escape. But her father never considered her feelings (cf. 18:20-21), and after David fled married her to another (25:44). Years later when David took the throne, he demanded the return of Michal, but his action was politically motivated (cf. 2 Sam. 3:13-16). Now bitter, she showed her contempt for David and the Lord when she saw David praising God ecstatically (6:17-23). Life was unfair to Michal. But it was also unfair to David. Unlike her husband, Michal failed to seek comfort in her relationship with God, and succumbed to bitterness.

Michal's lies (19:14, 17). The text reports, but does not evaluate, Michal's lies.

Michal's "idol" (19:13). The Heb. word is *teraphim*, found 15 times in the O.T. In Gen. 31:19 these are small "household gods." They were also found in Micah's neighborhood shrine (Jud. 17:5; 18:17-18). Some think the teraphim were like cultic face masks found at Hazor, but no one is sure today.

"Prophesying" (19:18-24). The verb in v. 20 indicates the true prophets were delivering prophetic oracles. »p. 131. But the hithpael verb form that describes the assassins sent by Saul, and Saul himself, implies that they were *behaving like prophets.* The text implies that they seemed "high," or elated, and shouted out in ecstasy. Some commentators thus take the answer to the question, "Is Saul also among the prophets?" to be, "No, he's just acting like they do sometimes."

How could David's brother "order" him? (20:29) After a father's death or incapacitation, the oldest brother became the head of the family.

"The Lord be with you as He has been with my father" (20:13). This wish is explicit recognition David will be king. Jonathan now shifts from being the king's son and David's superior to one who asks favors from David (vv. 14-15). His request reflects the common practice of new rulers to kill all members of the previous ruling family.

Jonathan's anger (20:30-34). Jonathan was publicly humiliated by Saul, but his anger reflects his shame at Saul's unfair treatment of his friend. What a contrast with Saul's anger at his son, for siding with a man Saul was mistreating (v. 30). A person's character is shown by the persons and values he or she loves—and by the behaviors that he or she hates.

Outline
Place
Finder

SAMUEL
SAUL
DAVID

Chapter summary. David is now a fugitive. On the run, he stops at Nob where the tabernacle stands, and asks the priest Ahimelech for food and a weapon (21:1-9). David goes to the Philistine city of Gath, but is recognized and has to pretend madness to escape (vv. 10-15). As followers trickle in to join David's growing band, he moves his family to Moab (22:1-4).

David himself returns to Judah (v. 5). Meanwhile Doeg, an Edomite who witnessed Ahimelech aid David, informs Saul (vv. 6-10). Saul refuses to listen to Ahimelech's reasonable explanation. Instead the paranoid ruler sees the priest's innocent acts as evidence of a conspiracy. Saul orders the whole clan of priests killed, and wipes out their families as well (vv. 11-19). Only one priest, Abiathar, survives. When he brings the news to David, David blames himself, and offers Abiathar refuge (vv. 20-23).

Key verse. 22:10: No act can be understood until we know a person's motives.

Personal application. When we're tempted to deceive, let's look for some other way out.

Key concepts. Holy »pp. 81, 86. Covenant »p. 35. Priest »p. 81.

INSIGHT

"Consecrated bread" (21:3-6). This "show-bread" was placed before God within the tabernacle, and was to be eaten only by priests (Ex. 25:30; Lev. 24:5-9). But Jesus commended Ahimelech's act as an illustration of the principle underlying His own act of healing on the Sabbath (Matt. 12:3-4; Mark 2:23-28). That principle is that the moral obligation to preserve and enrich human life supersedes ceremonial obligations. Let's remember that caring for others has priority with God.

"Holiness" and women (21:4-5). The priest referred to ritual cleanness, not moral purity, when he asked if David's men had not had intercourse with women the preceding night. David reminded Ahimelech that when on a military mission the Israelites were especially careful to maintain a ritually holy state (cf. Deut. 23:9-10).

David in Gath (21:10-15). David was foolish to take the sword of Goliath—and then try to hide in Gath, Goliath's hometown (17:4). The incident is evidence that under great stress David was not thinking straight; something that may in part excuse his deceit of Ahimelech and his failure at the time to realize that Doeg would surely report what took place.

David was not viewed as king of Israel. Here the Heb. word has the sense of "local chieftain." David writes of this experience in Pss. 34 and 56.

Why Moab? (22:3-4) David had family ties to Moab (cf. Ruth 1:4-18). The king of Moab might also have hoped to weaken Israel by supporting this rival of King Saul.

Saul's complaint (22:6-8). Though David was a fugitive, Saul felt he was being persecuted. As he saw it, his son was disloyal, his subjects refused to aid him, and David was conspiring against him. The wicked tend to see their own motives and character in others. But what are we to do if we actually are persecuted? Read Psalm 57, which was written by David during this time, and see.

Execution of the priests (22:11-19). The unjust killing of the 85 priests at Nob was a partial fulfillment of the judgment predicted to strike the family of Eli (cf. 2:27-36). The act was so repulsive that Saul's Hebrew officials disobeyed the king's direct orders.

Abiathar. The one priest who escaped brought with him the ephod, which he used to seek God's guidance for David during the fugitive years (cf. 30:7-8). When David came to power he shared high priestly authority with Zadok (1 Kings 1:7). In the end Abiathar joined the rebellion of David's son, Absalom. In view of his past service David did not execute him, but rather exiled him (2:26-27).

"I am responsible" (22:22). David may have known Doeg would tell Saul, but could not have known that Saul would dare murder an entire clan of priests. Yet David had lied, and lies have consequences we cannot foretell.

Outline
Place
Finder

SAMUEL
SAUL
DAVID

Chapter summary. When the Philistines attack an Israelite settlement at Keilah, David leads his men to the rescue (23:1-6). But Saul hears David is at Keilah, and mounts an expedition against it (vv. 7-8). God leads David out of the city into the hills, and at last Saul returns home (vv. 9-14). This enables Jonathan to slip away for a last visit with his friend (vv. 15-18). Residents of the wilderness where David is hiding volunteer to scout for Saul, and Saul sets out again to hunt David down (vv. 19-25). This time David escapes only because a Philistine raid forces Saul to call off the hunt (vv. 26-29). The intense pressure on David makes his next act even more stunning. David and his men are hiding in a cave when Saul enters, alone. Saul can be killed easily, but David refuses to touch him (24:1-7). Later, outside the cave, David shows the king a piece of his own robe which David cut off. Humbled at this further evidence of David's loyalty and piety, the king admits that he knows David is destined to be king (vv. 8-20). David promises to spare Saul's offspring, and Saul returns home . . . for a time. David, knowing Saul's character, returns to his stronghold (vv. 21-22).

Key verse. 24:10: Respect the God-given office, if not the man.

Personal application. The really important time to resist temptation to do wrong is when it's most difficult.

Key concepts. Ephod »p. 70. Inquire of God »p. 131. Righteous »p. 120.

INSIGHT

Abiathar and the ephod (23:6). The priest who alone survived Saul's massacre of his clan (chap. 22) had brought the ephod, used by the high priest to determine God's will in specific situations. David now used the ephod to determine if he should fight the Philistines, and to encourage his men by assuring them God would fight for them. How ironic that in killing priests who had not conspired with David, Saul placed in David's hand a vital spiritual resource that permitted David to escape him again and again! God is still able to take plans laid against us, and turn them to our advantage.

"Ziph" (23:14). The hilly, wilderness area of Ziph lies about 13 miles S.E. of Keilah. David apparently set up a series of camps, and planned to move between them to avoid a battle with Saul and David's own fellow countrymen.

"Jonathan" (23:15-18). This is the last meeting of the two friends. Jonathan's encouragement "in Yahweh" was a prediction that God would save David, that he would be king, and that Jonathan would willingly take second place to David in his kingdom. For other

encouragement in the Lord, see Isa. 35:3; Jer. 23:1-14.

Discouraged? To sense David's emotions during his years as a fugitive, we can read Pss. 54, 56–57, 63, 138, and 142. No one under great stress for such a long time could avoid discouragement. David needed the encouragement offered by his friend, Jonathan. And he needed to express his feelings to God, and draw strength from the Lord. Don't feel guilty if you react as David did when you find yourself under stress.

Why conscience-stricken? Clothing in O.T. times carried symbols of one's rank. Thus Jonathan's act of giving David his clothes might be understood as surrendering his right of royal succession (cf. 18:4). David was conscience-stricken because he felt his act might be misunderstood as a symbolic tearing of Saul's kingdom from him by force. David later explained his act as a way to convince Saul that David intended him no harm (24:11).

David's commitment (24:10). You and I too must trust God enough not to take hostile actions against enemies, even when we have opportunity.

Outline
Place
Finder

SAMUEL
SAUL
DAVID

Chapter summary. Samuel dies, and David leads his men to the wilderness country of Maon, near a great ranch owned by the wealthy Nabal, whose name means "fool" (25:1-3, »p. 353). At sheepshearing time David sends a delegation to ask politely for a small portion of food for his men, in view of their past favors to Nabal's herdsmen (vv. 1-9; cf. vv. 15-16). Nabal ridicules David and sends them away with nothing. Furious, David orders his men to get weapons, and leads them against the feasting Nabal (vv. 10-13). But Nabal's terrified men appeal to Abigail, their master's beautiful and intelligent wife (vv. 14-17). Abigail acts quickly and intercepts the increasingly angry David with a generous gift of food (vv. 18-22). She apologizes humbly for her surly husband, and wisely points out that revenge against Nabal would be unwise for one who hopes to be the future ruler of Judah (vv. 23-34). David's anger subsides, and he leads his men home. When Abigail tells Nabal, Nabal has a stroke, and David invites the willing widow to join him as his wife (vv. 35-43).

Key verses. 25:30-31: A man of faith seeks no vengeance.

Personal application. Diffuse others' anger, and your own.

Key concepts. Women »pp. 163, 394. Vengeance »p. 428.

INSIGHT

Nabal's wealth (25:2). Compare with Job, the richest of his time, with 7,000 sheep (Job 1:2).

A polite request (25:4-8). David's request was modest, polite, and appropriate. David's reference to himself as "your son" showed both humility and respect.

Anger rehearsed (25:12-13, 21-22). David's reaction to the insult was understandable. The more he thought about what Nabal had said, the angrier he became, and the more justified he felt in taking revenge. All of us know times when some incident serves as the last straw. How much we need the perspective that Abigail brought to David at that time!

Abigail's solution (25:18-32). David's anger was understandable, but not justified. Abigail showed great sensitivity in helping David with his anger. Note: *She brought David food, and in this acted to correct the situation that had made David angry. Where an injustice has been committed, we must try to correct it. *She asked David for forgiveness. This is a godly alternative to striking out in an attempt to obtain revenge. *She pointed out the consequences of acting in anger. David would be guilty of shedding blood needlessly. And later, when David became king, his action might erode the confidence and support of the people of Judah. *She also urged David to leave vengeance in God's hands. God, who

rights all wrongs, would care for David—and take care of all David's enemies. Impressed by the words of this bold and yet humble woman, David blessed her for keeping him from acting hastily.

Nabal "becomes like a stone" (25:37). This is a common Aramaic idiom meaning he had a heart attack or stroke and became paralyzed.

Nabal and Saul. Some commentators note a similarity between Nabal and Saul. Each is hostile to a loyal and honest David. Each goes against the advice of family and retainers. Each ultimately is struck down by God, not by David. Samuel even told Saul he acted foolishly, using the same Hebrew letters that make up Nabal's name (13:13). The evil each did David returned to condemn him. What a lesson for us. Let's let our enemies' own acts condemn them, rather than take revenge.

David's marriage to Abigail (25:40-43). David's marriage to Abigail was legitimate in that culture even though David had another wife. The marriage undoubtedly reflected David's respect for this unusual and beautiful woman.

Michal (25:44). There is no cause/effect relationship between Saul's marriage of Michal to Paltiel and David's marriage to Abigail. The author is writing about marriages and simply notes this event, so significant later (2 Sam. 3:13-16).

Chapter summary. When Ziphite scouts locate David, Saul mounts another expedition against his fugitive son-in-law. This time David takes the initiative, watches Saul's camp, and slips in at night among the sleeping army (26:1-8). For a second time David refuses to kill his helpless king (cf. chap. 24). Instead he takes Saul's spear and water bottle, and then shouts to the king from a safe distance (26:9-12). Again the humbled king blesses David and promises in return that he will not harm David (vv. 13-25). Saul may be sincere when he makes his promise, but David realizes the erratic ruler is sure to change his mind. Depressed and discouraged, David leads his force to Gath, where he volunteers to serve Achish, the Philistine ruler, as a mercenary (27:1-4). David is given the town of Ziklag, from which he raids Israel's traditional enemies (vv. 5-9). David's accurate but vague reports of raiding "south of" various Judean locations convinces Achish that David has cut all ties with his people, and will now serve Philistine interests (vv. 10-12).

Outline
Place
Finder

SAMUEL
SAUL
DAVID

Key verse. 27:1: The faith of the greatest saints may falter.

Personal application. One of our most difficult challenges is to keep on doing the right thing while waiting for God to act.

INSIGHT

"The desert" (26:3). The Heb. term does not necessarily mean a sandy waste, as today. It does indicate land that can't be farmed: a wilderness area of any sort.

"Abishai" (26:7). This outstanding warrior was a nephew of David (1 Chron. 2:16), who becomes a prominent warrior (cf. 2 Sam. 2:18-24; 10:9-10; 18:2-14; 20:6-10; 21:16-17). Though faithful, his bloodthirstiness contrasts sharply with the restraint shown by David here (cf. 3:30, 39; 16:5-11). It is not enough to be brave. We must be wise and humane.

Sovereignty. The biblical doctrine of sovereignty affirms that God is in charge. As other doctrines, this one is to shape behavior, not simply to be believed. David shows us one practical implication in vv. 9-11. God made Saul king, God alone has the right to deal the blow that removes him (cf. 25:38; 2 Sam. 12:15). Let's show our own belief in God's sovereignty by refusing to take illegitimate or sinful steps, even to right a wrong.

"Go serve other gods" (26:19). David feels being cut off from his own people and their worship is the same as telling him to deny Yahweh and go serve other gods. This is the most devastating impact to David of Saul's hostility and his fugitive state.

Saul's promise (26:21). Saul may have been sincere, but David has learned a vital lesson. Sincerity when a promise is made is no guarantee a promise will be kept! Saul had made

that promise before, and broken it (cf. 19:6). We must judge whether or not a promise is valid on the basis of a person's actions, not his words. Many a battered wife returns to a repentant husband who promises, again and again, not to beat her. She relies on his sincerity and believes his words. How we need to learn a lesson from David here!

Great saints falter (27:1). David's depression followed the "high" of his bold venture into Saul's camp. We are often most vulnerable to a "down" after some significant success. It's then too we are likely to repeat David's mistake of failing to remember God is sovereign. Let's not be too hard on ourselves when sometimes we forget to trust. Even great saints falter.

Mercenaries (27:2-3). In O.T. times bands of foreigners led by a captain were often hired by rulers as mercenary troops (cf. 2 Sam. 15:18-22).

"Ziklag" (27:6). The town lies about 25 miles S.W. of Gath, and at the Conquest was originally given to Judah (cf. Josh. 15:31; 19:5). There David had freedom to act independently.

"Negev" (27:10). Negev means "the south." The peoples David raided were remnants of those who God had told Israel to drive from the land (cf. Josh. 13:2-3). David's policy of extermination reflects that instituted for the holy war. »p. 66.

Outline
Place
Finder

SAMUEL
SAUL
DAVID

Chapter summary. The Philistines prepare a mass invasion of Israelite territory. Achish tells David and his 600 men to report for duty (28:1-2). It seems David will now be forced to fight the very people he expects one day to rule!

In Israel, Saul is terrified. The Philistines are coming, and God does not answer his frantic pleas for guidance (vv. 3-6). Desperate, Saul orders his men to locate a spiritist. He will try to raise the dead Samuel's spirit (vv. 7-11). The spiritist is amazed when Samuel actually appears, only to predict a Philistine victory and the death of Saul and his sons (vv. 12-19). Saul collapses. Finally, at the urging of his men, he eats a little food. Then Saul goes out into the night to meet his destiny (vv. 20-25).

Key verse. 28:6: Why should God answer a king who has shown he will not obey anyway?

Personal application. Stay close to the Lord, so that when you need His help most, it will be available.

Key concepts. Leading »p. 70. Occult »p. 131. Resurrection »p. 522.

INSIGHT

"Achish's bodyguard" (28:2). David's flight from Judah in a moment of despair has placed him in a position where he is expected to fight against his own people. The promise that if he fights well he will become Achish's bodyguard is ironic. At home David would be king of Israel. Now it seems he is destined to guard the life of one of Israel's fiercest enemies! A failure to trust God may seem insignificant for a time, but has long-term consequences.

The occult (28:3). Saul's exile of spiritists and mediums from Israel was in obedience to O.T. commands (cf. Deut. 18:9-13; Ex. 22:18; Lev. 19:31). His consulting a spiritist at Endor shows how driven Saul was by anxiety and fear.

The results show the futility of all such appeals to the occult. Samuel tells Saul only what he had told the king while he was alive: God had taken the kingdom from Saul to give to David. In the same way, in Jesus' parable Abraham tells a rich man that it would be futile to send the dead Lazarus to warn his brothers. If they do not believe the word given by Moses, they would not believe a voice from beyond the grave (Luke 16:27-31). There is no good or helpful information to be obtained through *any* occult means.

Life after death. Some have questioned whether Samuel really appeared to Saul, arguing for a pyschological phenomenon or demonic impersonation. However, the text indicates the apparition really was Samuel, who God permitted to speak from beyond the grave. Evidence: *the spiritist's surprise (v. 12), *Saul's recognition (v. 14), *the accurate prediction (v. 19), *the testimony of the text (vv. 12, 15-16).

The event is one of the O.T.'s clearest affirmations that there is conscious, personal life after death.

Why consult Samuel? (28:16) Samuel's question implies, "What can I do?" Samuel is God's spokesman, and has already told Saul that God has turned away from him. Saul's situation is a result of his own unfaithfulness to the Lord, and there is nothing anyone can do for him now.

How often moms and dads foolishly protect their children from the consequences of wrong actions. We must all learn that sinful choices will ultimately put us in a situation where no one can help.

Was Saul a believer? (28:19) Many scholars take Samuel's prediction that "tomorrow you and your sons will be with me" as evidence that Saul was a true believer, whose salvation is not in question. Like some Christians Saul chose to be disobedient despite having an authentic faith. Saul's fate warns us not to disobey God lightly, for God certainly disciplines believers who do.

"Saul fell full length" (28:20). What an image! The king, who stood a head taller than any other Israelite (9:2), lies prostrate and helpless on the ground. It is spiritual stamina that is rooted in faith and expressed as obedience that gives any believer strength to stand.

Chapter summary. The Philistine commanders force Achish to send David away, fearing he will turn on them when the battle begins (29:1-11). When David's men reach home, they find Amalekites have raided Ziklag and taken their families captive (30:1-5). For the first time, David is blamed by his bitter men (v. 6). After seeking divine guidance, David leads his men in pursuit. They overtake the Amalekites and after a fierce, all-day battle, rescue their families and recover all their goods, with much additional plunder (vv. 7-20). David divides the plunder fairly (vv. 21-25), and as part of his campaign to be recognized as king he sends gifts to various cities in Judah (vv. 26-31).

Outline
Place
Finder

SAMUEL
SAUL
DAVID

Key verse. 30:6: David does not lose faith in God.

Personal application. We do pay a price for making bad choices.

Key concepts. Ephod »p. 70.

INSIGHT

Philistine fears (29:1-7). The fear of the army commanders that David might turn on them in the heat of battle has precedent. In an earlier battle Hebrews, who like David lived in Philistine controlled territory, were in the Philistine army, but turned on them in battle with Israel (cf. 14:21).

Head to head (29:4). There's a pun here in the original. Achish promised to make David his bodyguard, which in Heb. is "keeper of the head." The Philistine commanders sarcastically observed that David might very well regain Saul's favor by keeping heads—theirs!

Was David disappointed? (29:8) Most have taken David's apparent disappointment when told by Achish he could not march up to battle with the Philistine army as deceitful. There is, however, another possibility. In speaking of "my lord the king" David might really have meant Saul, not Achish! He may very well have planned to turn on the Philistines in the heat of battle, and by this strategy win the war for Israel!

"The Amalekites" (30:1). Saul had been told to wipe out the Amalekites, but failed (1 Sam. 15). In the years that followed this semi-nomadic people became strong enough to raid again. Again we see a common theme: disobedience always has its consequences. The call for all Philistine men to report for the war with Israel left the south, and Ziklag, exposed. The Amalekites were quick to respond.

David's distress (30:3-6). David's men had followed him into Philistia. But now they blamed David for the loss of wives and children. This was David's first experience with the most painful of a leader's disappoint-ments: the failure of followers to be loyal. In view of his own fierce loyalty to Saul this was especially bitter for David. How important when human beings disappoint us to have the kind of relationship with God David exhibit-ed. He "found strength in the Lord his God."

"The ephod" (30:7-8). The vestlike ephod of the high priest contained means used to determine the will of God. When David inquired whether he should pursue the raiders, the answer was yes. It would seem so obvious that David should at least try to overtake the enemy that we wonder why he waited to inquire formally about God's will. The answer is perhaps given in Josh. 9, where Joshua made an equally "obvious" choice—and was wrong! Time spent seeking God's will is never wasted.

"Too exhausted" (30:10). David and his men had crossed some 50 miles of difficult territory between Aphek (29:1) and Ziklag carrying all their weapons. Then they set out on a forced march to overtake the raiders who captured their families. No wonder a full third of his hardened men could not take the pace and were too exhausted to go on.

Four hundred rode off (30:16-18). David's sudden attack was devastating. It's ironic that "only" 400 Amalekites escaped the attack. Why? Because David had "only" 400 exhausted Israel-ites to lead against them in the first place.

"The plunder" (30:26-31). Each of the towns mentioned is in southern Judah, in the general area of Hebron. Later David was crowned king of Judah in Hebron (2 Sam. 2:4). Always politically sensitive, David used every oppor-tunity to prepare for his future, illustrating a principle Jesus expressed in Luke 16:9.

Outline
Place
Finder

SAMUEL
SAUL
DAVID

Chapter summary. The battle at Mount Gilboa results in a complete Philistine victory. David's friend Jonathan, with two of Saul's other sons, is killed, and Saul is critically wounded (31:1-3). Rather than be captured and made the object of ridicule, Saul falls on his sword (vv. 4-6). The now leaderless Israelites abandon whole towns in a desperate haste to escape (v. 7). When Saul's body is found, the Philistines take his head and nail his body to a wall at Beth Shan (vv. 8-10). In a heroic act men from Jabesh Gilead recover the bodies of Saul and his sons, burn them, and bury their bones in a safe place (vv. 11-13). Israel's first king, crowned by a people eager for someone to fight their battles for them, has failed and by his disobedience to God led them to a crushing defeat.

Key verse. 31:7: Trust placed in mere men is always misplaced.

Personal application. Those who follow flawed leaders will experience defeat with them.

INSIGHT

"Uncircumcised fellows" (31:4). The phrase is one of contempt. Saul did not expect such an enemy to torment or ridicule him, the king of Israel.

Suicide (31:4). The text describes but does not evaluate Saul's act. There are only a few other incidents of suicide described in Scripture (cf. Jud. 9:54; 16:30). The general attitude expressed in the Bible is that life is a gift of God and, as David once said, only God is competent to determine when one's life is to end (cf. 26:10).

A discrepancy? The accounts of Saul's death given here and in 2 Samuel 1 seem to conflict. This has led some to propose two contradictory "traditions" and others to claim the differences prove that Scripture is not without error. But the "conflict" may well be only apparent!

First Sam. 31 says Saul was critically wounded, and fell on his own sword. Second Sam. 1 contains a young man's report that he saw Saul, "in the throes of death," leaning on his spear with the Philistines almost on him. Saul requested the young man to kill him, which he did, taking Saul's crown as evidence of his deed.

There are two possibilities. First, the young man is lying in hopes that David will reward him for killing Saul. Second, that Saul's attempt at suicide failed, and that though near death he had not yet died when he asked the young man to dispatch him. Either of these two reasonable options removes the apparent "conflict," and reminds us that Scripture is reliable in all things, as well as authoritative in matters of faith and morals.

Aftermath (31:7). The defeat at Gilboa wiped out the earlier gains Saul had made in his war with the Philistines. The towns now reoccupied by the Philistines restored the situation to what it had been 40 years earlier. The Philistines controlled the rich plain of Jezreel and the region along the Jordan itself.

Saul's weapons (31:10). It was common practice for people of the ancient Near East to put trophies of war in the houses of their gods (cf. 17:54; 21:9).

"Jabesh Gilead" (31:11-13). At the beginning of his reign, Saul had rescued Jabesh Gilead from besieging Ammonites (11:1-15). The men of that city now repaid Saul by stealing his body from the Philistines, burning it, and hiding his bones. They also rescued the bodies of Saul's sons.

This final act reminds us that King Saul, while a flawed ruler, had served his people well, battling their enemies, and doing all he could to protect them. But Saul was far more a weak man than a bad one. If he had only been able to trust God enough to obey Him, those weaknesses could have been overcome in time.

Saul remains one of the most powerful O.T. examples for believers. We are each flawed, and each has his or her own weaknesses. As events will show, David certainly did! Yet if our hearts are constantly turned to God, the Lord can protect us from our weaknesses even as He uses our strengths. The wonderful word for us in the story of Saul is, "You and I do not have to end our life as Saul did, a failure." We can make different choices, and succeed in this world!

2 Samuel

Second Samuel continues the story of Israel's emergence as a unified and powerful nation under David, her greatest king. In the Hebrew O.T. it forms a single book with 1 Samuel (see p. 179). Second Samuel picks up the story of David after the death of Saul, and follows him for some 40 years.

David's years of waiting are over. He now throws himself into the task of building a great kingdom. He takes Jerusalem, a city on the border between north and south, and makes it his capital. He organizes and trains a powerful military, and establishes the bureaucracy necessary to any central government. Yet God still has priority in the life of the warrior king. He moves the ark of God to Jerusalem, reorganizes public worship, and writes many of the hymns himself. David's accomplishments establish him as one of the most creative and effective rulers of all time, while his deep personal relationship with God makes him a model for saints of every era.

---

2 SAMUEL AT A GLANCE

KEY PEOPLE
David   *Israel's greatest king, whose gifts and piety enable him to forge a new nation and reorganize its worship of the Lord.*
Bathsheba   *The beautiful and innocent woman with whom David commits adultery.*
Nathan   *The bold prophet who confronts David and leads him to repent.*
Absalom   *The son who breaks David's heart and leads a rebellion against his own father.*
Joab   *David's cousin and the grim army commander who, despite his loyalty to David, brings grief after grief to the king.*

KEY EVENTS
Coronation (2 Sam. 2; 5).   *David crowned king of Judah and later of Israel too.*
David takes Jerusalem (2 Sam. 5).   *The city becomes the political and religious capital of the United Hebrew Kingdom.*
David given covenant promises by God (2 Sam. 7).   *The promises to David will later be fulfilled in Christ!*
David sins with Bathsheba, and repents (2 Sam. 11–12).   *Psalm 51 commemorates the event, and serves as a model of confession for us today.*
Absalom rebels (2 Sam. 15–19).   *The civil war that results will lead in time to the division of the United Kingdom.*

Date and Authorship. The events span 40 years, 1010 B.C. and 970 B.C. The author of 2 Samuel is not identified, though some credit the Prophets Gad and Nathan.

THEOLOGICAL OUTLINE OF 2 SAMUEL

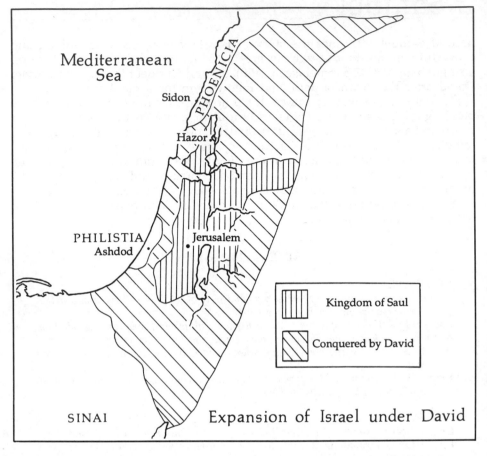

In 40 years David multiplies the territory controlled by Israel tenfold, and makes his nation a dominant Middle Eastern power.

CONTENT OUTLINE OF 2 SAMUEL

I. David's Triumphs (1:1–10:19)
  A. Saul's Death (1:1-27)
  B. David Anointed King of Judah (2:1-7)
  C. Civil War Exists with Israel, Ruled by a Son of Saul (2:8–4:12)
  D. David Becomes King of All Israel (5:1-5)
  E. David Takes Jerusalem (5:6-16)
  F. David Defeats the Philistines (5:17-25)
  G. David Brings the Ark to Jerusalem (6:1-23)
  H. God Promises to Establish David's Kingdom (7:1-29)
  I. David Defeats Enemies (8:1-18)
  J. David Keeps His Promise to Jonathan (9:1-13)
  K. David Defeats the Ammonites (10:1-19)
II. David's Troubles (11:1–20:26)
  A. Personal and Moral (11:1–12:31)
  B. Family (13:1–18:33)
  C. Nation (19:1–20:26)
III. David's Trials (21:1–24:25)
  A. Famine (21:1-14)
  B. Warfare (21:15-22)
  C. Praise (22:1-51)
  D. Confidence (23:1-7)
  E. Control (23:8-39)
  F. Census (24:1-25)

Outline
Place
Finder

TRIUMPHS
TROUBLES
TRIALS

Chapter summary. David learned of Saul's death from an Amalekite who claimed to have dispatched the wounded king, and who brought Saul's crown to David, expecting a reward. David executed him for daring to lay a hand on the Lord's anointed (1:1-16). David then led his band in mourning Israel's loss of the great warrior and his son, Jonathan (vv. 17-27).

With the proprieties observed, David moved quickly to establish himself as king of Judah (2:1-4). His praise for the men of Jabesh Gilead for burying Saul was honest, yet also shows how David tried to establish support in the north (vv. 5-7). But in the north Saul's army commander, Abner, threw his support to Saul's son, Ish-Bosheth (vv. 8-11). No pitched battles were fought, but skirmishes like the one in which Joab's brother Asahel was killed, were common (vv. 12-32). The impasse lasted for many years, but it became clear that David's strength was increasing, while Abner's northern forces became weaker.

Key verse. 1:23: In death forget flaws to celebrate strengths.

Personal application. Abner's personal ambition stood in the way of David and Israel's destiny. Don't let your ambition block the fulfillment of others' potential.

INSIGHT

The Amalekite (1:1-15). David was legally bound to execute the Amalekite. Saul was not killed in battle, but afterward. Thus innocent blood had been shed, and the land had incurred blood guilt. Since the Amalekite confessed to killing Saul, no witnesses were necessary. David as the king's son-in-law was responsible to see his killer punished.

The execution was also wise politically. It showed that no one who killed a king of Israel could expect a reward (cf. 4:9-11).

David's lament (1:17-27). David's poem celebrates the positive qualities of Saul and the benefits of his rule. It is appropriate to speak only well of the dead.

A pure friendship (1:26). Recent suggestions that David and Jonathan had a homosexual relationship are uncalled for. Homosexuality is strongly condemned in both O.T. and N.T. (»p. 37). David is portrayed as (too!) enthusiastically heterosexual in orientation. The Hebrew word for "love" is not primarily sexual, but is used to express affection in a wide variety of relationships. The contrast with the "love of women" includes that of a mother for her children, and a wife for her husband. There is no basis to suppose the friendship of Jonathan and David was less than pure.

David's letter (2:4-7). The letter was intended to show that, though David was a man of Judah, his heart was for all Israel. But for Abner's influence in the north David's overtures might have won him the throne more quickly.

A contradiction? (2:10-11) How could David rule Judah for seven years if Ish-Bosheth, Saul's son, ruled only two during the same period? Abner sequestered Saul's son for five years while he fought the Philistines for some level of control over the area occupied by the northern tribes. With this accomplished, he brought out Ish-Bosheth and had him crowned as a puppet ruler. As events prove, Abner was the real power in the north.

Ish-Bosheth. The name, meaning "man of shame" was originally Ish-Baal, "man of baal," or Esh-Baal, "Baal exists" (cf. 1 Chron. 8:33). In Canaanite religion Baal is the name of a major deity, but the Heb. baal also is the common term for "lord" or "master." When Saul gave his son this name he may well have intended the Baal to be religiously neutral or to refer to Yahweh. It seems likely that later, when wicked rulers in both the north and south actively promoted Baal worship in Israel, pious scribes substituted "shame" where "Baal" occurred in earlier proper names.

"This will end in bitterness" (2:26). It seems that both north and south tried to keep the sputtering civil war between them from breaking out in a general conflict. Not only did each side realize the "enemy" was a "brother." Each side must also have known that one day the issue would be resolved by reunion. Neither wanted a bloody war that would embitter families in each region.

Outline
Place
Finder

TRIUMPHS
TROUBLES
TRIALS

Chapter summary. When Abner is insulted by his puppet king Ish-Bosheth, he decides to defect to David and bring all Israel with him (3:1-12). David first demands the return of Michal, Saul's daughter and his own wife (vv. 13-16). Abner now actively lobbies for the north to recognize David, reminding the tribes of something he had conveniently ignored: that the Lord had promised David would be king (vv. 17-18). Abner and David meet and reach agreement, but the vengeful Joab goes behind David's back and murders Abner (vv. 19-27). Though David does not punish Joab, he publicly curses him and forces Joab to show respect at Abner's funeral (vv. 28-39). Meanwhile two soldiers murder Ish-Bosheth and bring his head to David, expecting a reward. Instead David executes them, as he should. The way is clear for David to become king of a united Hebrew people.

Key verses. 3:9-10: Abner delayed doing what he knew was right.

Personal application. The disobedience of others may block us for a time, but God's good purposes for us *will* be realized.

INSIGHT

Why the fuss over a concubine? (3:6-8) The "offense" Ish-Bosheth accused Abner of was political, not personal or moral. In that day taking the king's concubine (»p. 166) was tantamount to claiming a right to his throne.

Abner's oath (3:9-11). Abner's open declaration is triply revealing. He was confident in his power: Ish-Bosheth could do nothing. He was sure of his influence with the northern tribes. They would do what he said. And he had known all along that it was God's will for David to be king. His quest for personal power moved him to resist God's known will, and was the cause of a lengthy, bloody civil war. Joab was wrong to murder him. But Abner's own choices led directly to his death.

Michal (3:13-17). We should not understand David's insistence on the return of Michal as an indication of love. His restored marriage to Saul's daughter made him again Saul's son-in-law, and strengthened David's claim to the throne. The tears of her husband Paltiel suggest their marriage had been a happy one, and that Michal is again treated as a political pawn (»p. 193).

Was David's remarriage to Michal legal? Yes, in that he had never given her the "bill of divorce" required by Deut. 24:1. Thus her relationship with Paltiel was not, technically, marriage, and vv. 2-3 do not apply. Also, contemporary laws in other Near East societies held a husband who returned from exile or captivity should recover a remarried wife.

Joab's rebuke (3:24). Joab's rebuke of David suggests that David's military commander,

though faithful to him, had a strong personal power base, as Abner did. Through David's life Joab remained a faithful but independent and vexatious supporter.

"Hebron" (3:27). Hebron was a city of refuge, in which killers were safe from those set to avenge a relative's death. It may be significant that Joab took Abner "aside into the gateway." There, just outside the city confines, he might explain the act as lawful revenge for the killing of his brother Asahel (v. 30). Since Asahel was killed in battle, Abner believed no legitimate basis for vengeance existed, and having made a pact with David felt safe. David may well not have punished the murder of Abner not only because Joab and his family were so influential (v. 39), but also because the legal situation was not at all clear-cut. So David settled for a verbal reprimand (v. 29) and public mourning over Abner's death (vv. 31-34). In view of the serious way in which O.T. peoples viewed curses, in laying a curse against Joab David *did* punish him.

The murder of Ish-Bosheth (4:7-11). The killers claim to have acted out of piety and in harmony with God's will. However, their timing—after the death of Abner—and their haste to bring the victim's head to David make their real motives clear. They expected a reward from David, whose way is now cleared to become king. David, however, executes them for the murder of an "innocent man." Though not the Lord's anointed, as Saul was, the killing of any innocent person requires the death sentence (»p. 114).

Jerusalem

David's capture of Jerusalem, reported in 2 Samuel 5, is significant on many levels. At the time, making it his capital was a brilliant political move. The site lies on the border between Judah and the northern tribes, and symbolized his concern for the whole Hebrew people. David soon moved the ark to Jerusalem, thus making it the religious as well as political capital (2 Sam. 6), and further unifying a people whose common bond was essentially religious.

But Jerusalem has significance that extends far beyond David's time. Moses had predicted that one day God would "put His name" on a particular place. The phrase means to "identify Himself with." And for nearly 3,000 years, for Jews and for Christians, Jerusalem has been identified as God's city. The temple Moses predicted was built there by Solomon, and a rebuilt temple stood on the same site in the time of Christ. Much of the ministry of Jesus took place in Jerusalem, and it was just outside this city's walls that Christ died, was buried, and rose to life again.

Yet the lasting significance of Jerusalem rests on more than its role in sacred history. Jerusalem is a major topic of Old and New Testament prophecy. In the Old Testament Jerusalem is the focus of divine judgment (cf. Isa. 22; 29; Jer. 4–6). Yet while the immediate future of Jerusalem is dark (Zeph. 3:1-7), her bright destiny is assured (vv. 8-20). God will purify the city, forgive her sins, and "the Lord, the King of Israel," will be with it. The oppressors will be dealt with, the Jewish people brought home, and "I will give you honor and praise among all the peoples of the earth when I restore your fortunes before your very eyes." Jerusalem will be the site of the Messiah's return and capital of the worldwide kingdom He establishes (Isa. 66; Joel 3; Zech. 14). And in the New Testament, in Revelation, the name of earthly Jerusalem is preserved in a heavenly city that will serve as capital of the eternal, re-created universe (Rev. 21).

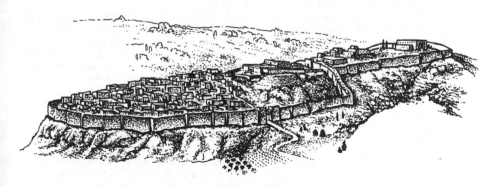

Archeologist's reconstruction of Jerusalem in the time of David and Solomon.

Outline
Place
Finder

TRIUMPHS
TROUBLES
TRIALS

Chapter summary. The tribes of Israel now make David king. He is the only viable military leader with a proven record of victories in past campaigns (5:1-5). One of David's first acts is to take the strategic city of Jerusalem, and make it his capital (vv. 6-16; see p. 205). The Philistines recognize the threat David poses as Israel's king. They organize a preemptive strike intended to kill him before he can weld Israel together (v. 17). David, guided by God, deals the Philistines a series of quick defeats, foreshadowing the end of that sea people's military and technological dominance. David at last is in command of his people, and immediately reveals the vigor that will mark his actions throughout his long future reign.

Key verse. 5:10: When God's time comes, things move quickly.

Personal application. Wait patiently, but be ready to act.

Key concepts. Philistines »p. 185.

INSIGHT

The choice of David (5:1-3). With Abner and Ish-Bosheth dead, Israel had two major reasons to turn to David. He was a proven military man, a motive that reflects Israel's earlier demand for a king (cf. 1 Sam. 8). But David also was known as God's choice to "shepherd" Israel. At last Israel's and God's will were in harmony. The great things that follow David's recognition as king remind us that success can come only when our will is in harmony with the known will of God.

The "blind and the lame" (5:6). The hilltop fortress was thought to be so impregnable it could be defended by persons who were lame and blind. The shouts of defiance may merely have been typical prebattle rhetoric, but do reflect the Jebusites' feelings of security. Rabbinic writers have not taken the words literally, but suggest they refer to the defenders' idols.

David apparently took the fortress by direct assault. The six-month period implied in v. 5 is too short to have taken it by cutting off the city's water supply, as some have understood reference to the rock well shaft in v. 8.

"Hiram" (5:11). Other states now recognized the renewed independence of Israel and opened official relations. David developed especially friendly ties with Tyre, which traded building supplies for agricultural products during the reigns of both David and his son Solomon.

Why did David take more wives? (5:13) The mention of more wives follows reference to Hiram of Tyre, because marriages formed a keystone in ancient treaty relationships between states. It seems likely David married

several foreign wives, as Solomon did after him, to cement international relationships. This was not only unwise, but violated a clear provision of Deuteronomic law: the king of Israel "must not take many wives" (Deut. 17:17). The dire prediction that doing so would lead to idolatry was fulfilled in Solomon (cf. 1 Kings 11).

The Philistine response (5:17). Some have suggested the full-scale invasion was mounted to punish David for his failure to act as a vassal of the ruler of Gath (cf. 1 Sam. 27). It is more likely this was a preemptive strike, intended to keep Israel helpless by finding and killing her brilliant general, and now king, David.

David, however, sought guidance from God, and led his people to two decisive victories. The Philistine defeats must have been much more crushing than the text relates, for next David is pictured leading his forces against other enemies (2 Sam. 8; 10). The victories also enabled Israel to break the Philistines iron monopoly, which had explained in part their military superiority. According to 2 Sam. 21 there were other future battles against the Philistines. But these two initial victories secured and extended David's western border.

"David did as the Lord commanded him" (5:25). What a summary of the difference between David and Saul. Each was an effective military leader. Each had the opportunity to be great. But where Saul disobeyed the Lord's commands, David did as the Lord commanded. It is this that enables us too to reach the full potential of the gifts and abilities God has given us.

Chapter summary. David leads an honor guard to escort the ark of the covenant, Israel's most holy object, from its resting place near Kiriath Jearim (1 Sam. 7:1) to Jerusalem (2 Sam. 6:1-5). But on the way a man named Uzzah innocently touches the ark, and is struck dead! David, angry and afraid, temporarily leaves the ark by the house of a man named Obed-Edom, and goes back to Jerusalem (vv. 6-11). But when God blesses Obed-Edom, David decides to try again. This time Levites carry the ark, as Moses' law demands, and it is brought successfully to Jerusalem (vv. 6:12-13). David strips off his royal robes and, wearing the simple linen garment of a servant in God's tabernacle, he leads the joyful procession into the city, shouting and singing (vv. 14-19). At home after the celebration David is confronted by a contemptuous Michal, who scorns him for taking off his royal robes to dance and sing like a commoner. David bluntly tells his princess bride that he will continue to praise God enthusiastically, and be honored by those with the spiritual insight she lacks (vv. 20-23).

Outline
Place
Finder

TRIUMPHS
TROUBLES
TRIALS

Key verse. 6:21: Celebrate God wholeheartedly and freely.

Personal application. Don't let others dampen your enthusiasm for the Lord.

Key concepts. Ephod »p. 70. Ark of the covenant »p. 68.

INSIGHT

"The ark" (6:1-2). The presence of the ark in Jerusalem was essential if the city was to be the religious as well as political capital of Israel. The ark was the most holy object in Israel's religion, the specific locus of God's presence with His people. »p. 68.

Why did Uzzah die? (6:6-7) Uzzah touched the ark. This would not have happened if David had followed the clear O.T. Law concerning its transport (cf. Num. 4:5-6; 7:9). What has troubled believers is that Uzzah's intent was excellent: he sought only to save the ark from harm. Was his death fair?

The point, however, is that God is holy. This is emphasized in the text's description of the ark (2 Sam. 6:2). God is holy, awesome, and never to be taken lightly, whatever one's motives. Uzzah's death served as a vital lesson for all Israel.

"**David was angry**" (6:8). David already held God in awe, so he needed no reminder of the Lord's presence and power. Very seldom does the O.T. portray God as the object of human anger (cf. Gen. 4:5; Jonah 4:1). In most cases such anger reflects an inability or unwillingness to understand what God intends.

"**David was afraid**" (6:9). This is a much more common reaction. In this case, David was unable to take any more risks with the ark, and left it where it stood. In our own case, we are much wiser to respond to an unexpected disaster with trust. We do not need to be afraid of God. We have overwhelming evidence of God's love.

Carrying the ark (6:12). When next David tries to bring the ark to Jerusalem, he has Levites carry it. Evidently David consulted the writings of Moses to learn how it should be transported.

The sequence here is important. There was a disaster. David was angry and frightened. But he went home and searched the Scriptures. God's Word offers more than comfort. It provides correction and guidance. Let's look there *before* we act, and avoid the kind of disaster that confused David.

David's ephod. The term is usually used of linen garments worn by priests or Levites when serving God. Some take the "ephod" here to be a diaper-like wrap. Others see it as a short tunic, and understand Michal's contempt as evidence that David inadvertently exposed himself while dancing enthusiastically. It is much better to understand Michal's reaction as disgust that David would forget his royal position and act like a commoner.

Chapter summary. David desires to build a temple to house the ark of the covenant (7:1-2). God speaks to Nathan the prophet, rejecting David's plan (vv. 3-7). But in the kind of wordplay the Hebrew people love, God promises to build David's "house" — not a residence, but his family line (vv. 8-16). God promises that David's son will succeed him and he will build the temple/house David yearns to provide (v. 12). Then, in a statement that echoes throughout all time, God promises to maintain David's house/line forever. God will discipline kings in that line who do wrong. But there will come a time when David's throne is "established forever." This great promise, the Davidic Covenant, is echoed by the prophets, and is fulfilled in Jesus Christ, David's Descendant and Lord of an eternal kingdom.

In response, all David can do is fall on his knees and praise God, expressing faith in God as Sovereign Lord, and praying that the Lord will do as He has said (vv. 18-29).

Key verse. 7:16: Jesus will reign!

Personal application. We express faith in God when we ask Him to keep His promises.

Key concepts. Ark »p. 68. Tabernacle »p. 67. Prayer »p. 181. Davidic Covenant »pp. 270, 370. Almighty »p. 175.

INSIGHT

Nathan. This is the first mention of a prophet who plays a key role through the rest of David's reign (cf. 2 Sam. 12; 1 Kings 1; 1 Chron. 17). Nathan's original reaction to David's request is a personal opinion, based on Nathan's awareness of David's piety and the nature of the request. The fact that God later spoke at night suggests a dream. »p. 99.

There's a lesson here. Believers rightly make most decisions based on a general understanding of God's will and a desire to honor Him. But we must always be ready to listen to a corrective word from God, whether the Spirit speaks in our heart or by a trusted friend.

Why couldn't David build a temple? The Bible gives three reasons. A tent was perfectly fitting (v. 6). God hadn't asked for a temple (v. 7). And, as a "man of blood," David was not the person to build the temple (cf. v. 5 with 1 Chron. 22:8; 28:3). This is symbolically significant. The temple speaks of universal peace achieved by knowledge of God. It was not fitting for it to be built by a warrior.

Remember (7:8-9). The past is a foundation for the future. God who has been faithful in our yesterdays will surely be with us in our tomorrows.

How has the Davidic Covenant been fulfilled? The text promises David's house and kingdom will endure, and his throne will be established forever. An unbroken rule is not implied, but an unbroken line is. There must always be someone with a right to Israel's throne. Before Jesus' birth the angel told Mary "the Lord God will give Him the throne of His father David, and His kingdom will never end" (Luke 1:32-33). The promises to David thus are confirmed to Jesus, who maintains a permanent right to the eternal kingdom He will establish at His return.

Father, son (7:14). The terms as used here do not imply physical descent, but do suggest three other concepts. God adopts the Davidic line and so maintains a parental interest in it. God establishes a covenant with David's line and so has a superior's right to direct and discipline. God by royal grant places David's line over His people and land.

"Sovereign Lord." This, uttered seven times in David's prayer (vv. 18-29) is literally *Yahweh Elohim*, "Yahweh, God." Sovereignty is implied in the use of the phrase in Ezekiel.

A lack of faith? David's fervent requests to God to keep promises that David says he is confident will be kept seems strange at first. Why ask for what you have been given? Actually the prayer reminds us that we too are to pray "in God's will." Asking what we know God wants to give us is an expression of dependence, not unbelief.

Chapter summary. David defeats the surrounding nations in turn (8:1-14). His significant conquests expand and secure his borders, and also gain control of trade routes, which will pour wealth into the kingdom of his son Solomon. At home David lays a foundation for a national administration (vv. 15-18). He also searches for a child of Jonathan, in order to fulfill his promise to his dead friend (9:1-13).

Outline
Place
Finder

TRIUMPHS
TROUBLES
TRIALS

The text now gives details of an Ammonite war only mentioned in 8:12. David is not an aggressor, but the friend of a king who had been Saul's enemy (cf. 1 Sam. 11:1-11). Yet when David's delegation offering condolences at the old king's death is humiliated, David is forced to act. No nation can let such an insult pass without implying weakness (10:1-5). Despite being outnumbered by the Ammonites and their Aramean mercenaries, Israel wins that war (vv. 6-14). The army then goes on to defeat a new Aramean force (vv. 15-19). David's acts may seem brutal (8:2), but in destroying the capacity of foreign nations to make war, David brings peace to Israel.

Key verse. 8:15: David's first duty was to his own people.

Personal application. We should try to "show kindness" to all, though not everyone will permit us to do so.

INSIGHT

Moabite execution (8:2). No other ancient record of such a method for selecting prisoners for execution exists. In view of David's links with Moab (cf. Ruth 4:21-22), he must have taken this action to destroy the capacity of Moab to make further war on Israel.

"Became famous" (8:13). The campaign must have been particularly difficult and David's personal role prominent for the famous slayer of Goliath to become even more of a military celebrity.

David's officials (8:15-18). A longer list is found in 20:23-26. This may reflect an earlier stage in David's development of a government.

"Show kindness" (9:1). The Heb. means "loyal love." David intended to keep the promise he made to Jonathan (cf. 1 Sam. 20:14-15). David went further than his promise required in granting Mephibosheth Saul's lands.

The king's table (9:10). Eating at the king's table was a mark of honor. Here it probably implies that Mephibosheth lived in Jerusalem, with all his personal expenses met by the king. The idea that David wanted to keep an eye on this descendant of Saul, and that the honor was little more than house arrest in disguise, is unlikely. Given the military role expected of ancient kings, Mephibosheth's crippled legs would disqualify him.

"A dead dog" (9:8). To call others a dog was a term of contempt. To call oneself a dog or the stronger "dead dog" was an expression of humility before a superior. In O.T. times dogs were not kept as pets, but were barely tolerated scavengers. Many see a theological cast to Mephibosheth's story. Each human being is crippled by sin and unworthy. Yet God's loyal love makes us rich, and calls us to live in His presence.

Loyal love for foreigners (10:2). The concept of loyal love links this story with chapter 9. In the case of Mephibosheth, David's expression of loyal love was humbly accepted. When David sought to express loyal love to the Ammonites, David's initiative was decisively rejected. When the magnitude of the insult was realized, rather than apologize the Ammonites prepared for war. In context, the story is told to show that David did not initiate the wars he won, but fought out of necessity. Yet those who seek symbolic meaning may find it. Each person is invited to experience God's kindness and loyal love. Those who humbly accept, like Mephibosheth, are blessed. Those who show contempt for God's initiative and remain hostile to Him will be destroyed.

"His people" (8:15). The history of David's wars is put in perspective by chapter 10, and by this verse. David's first responsibility was to do what is just and right for his own people. This is also God's primary concern.

209

Chapter summary. These chapters begin the report of David's troubles and reveal the flawed, human side of this essentially godly man. David is troubled with temptation when he sees an innocent Bathsheba bathing at night in her own courtyard. He takes her and she becomes pregnant (11:1-5). To hide his deed David recalls her soldier husband, Uriah, from the front. But that gallant officer will not sleep with his wife while his companions are still in the field. So David gives orders that he is to be given an assignment which will lead to his death (vv. 6-25). Uriah is killed and David marries Bathsheba (vv. 26-27).

Nathan the prophet uses a parable to reveal the magnitude of David's sin, and boldly announces the divine punishment (12:1-12). David, with deep feeling revealed in Psalm 51, his public admission of the deed, confesses "I have sinned against the Lord" (v. 13). David is forgiven, but the child of Bathsheba dies despite David's desperate fasting and prayers (vv. 14-23). The extent of God's grace is revealed in the fact that David and Bathsheba, whose relationship was launched in sin but has been cleansed by divine forgiveness, have another son. And this child, Solomon, is destined to succeed David as Israel's king (vv. 24-25). God's grace is also revealed in the military victory won by Joab during this time (vv. 26-31).

Key verse. 12:9: The question still is, why do we sin, in view of all God has done for us?

Personal application. Gratitude to God and self-interest both urge us to resist temptations.

Key concepts. Parables »p. 166. Confession of sin »p. 892. Children »p. 378. Fasting »p. 378. Prayer »p. 181.

INSIGHT

Bathsheba innocent (11:1-5). Some have tried to cast Bathsheba as a temptress. But the text affirms the innocence of Bathsheba. Note *David as king should have been at war. *Bathsheba was bathing after David was in bed. *Bathsheba was in her own courtyard, and could only be seen from the palace roof. *David took the initiative to find out who she was. *David sent for her. As a woman alone she had no way to reject the demands of a king, who in the ancient Near East had the power of life and death. In essence Bathsheba was forced to come to David's bed, in what was essentially rape.

The Hittite. Probably a professional soldier, Uriah had married a Jewess and served faithfully in Israel's army. Uriah is identified as a Hittite and thus was a resident alien in Israel. By O.T. Law the *gur*, or resident alien, was granted most of the rights and obligations of a Hebrew. »p. 66. David was legally as well as

morally obligated to treat him much better than he did.

David like Saul? (11:14) In ordering Joab to expose Uriah to danger the king was using a means Saul had used in an effort to be rid of David himself (cf. 1 Sam. 18:24-25). What then is the difference between the failed Saul and David? Each succumbed to temptation and sinned terribly. The difference is that when found out, Saul made excuses and begged Samuel not to expose him before his people. He was more concerned with public opinion than with his relationship with God (cf. 15:15-24). In contrast David was so concerned with his relationship with the Lord that he took the initiative and made a public confession, which we can read in Ps. 51.

All human beings are flawed, and any of us may fall short. How we resist temptation and how we deal with our sins are both indicators of godliness.

Illustration. *Homes within Jerusalem's walls were built on hillsides. The homes of the more well-to-do featured a walled inner court off which rooms opened. Bathsheba would have been within the inner court, invisible to all except a person walking on the palace roof above. To avoid even this possibility Bathsheba apparently chose to bathe at night, when all were asleep (11:1-4).*

Bathsheba mourned (11:26). As a time of mourning was prescribed, this tells us little of the relationship of Uriah and Bathsheba.

Nathan's parable (12:1-6). Nathan's parable was intended to jolt David, by making him angry about an injustice, and thus able to sense the anger God felt at his sin. It's not enough for us to agree intellectually that we have sinned. We need to sense the horror of our sin, to see it as God does. By shifting David's viewpoint Nathan enabled the king to see his sin for what it was.

"You killed him" (12:9). It was an Ammonite sword that struck Uriah, but David who killed him. One O.T. law calls for building a wall around the flat roof of the house, where people gathered on summer evenings to work or talk (Deut. 22:8). This law grows from the command, "Thou shalt not kill," and suggests that each of us must do all we can to actively protect human life. David's intent, and his orders, placed Uriah in danger of being killed, and he thus was guilty of murder.

"Calamity" (12:7-12). David's sin was against the sanctity of the family. His punishment reflects that. Again and again David's family is marred by strife, which culminates in the rebellion of David's much loved son Absalom.

Why should the child die for the parent's sins? (12:15) If the child had lived, each time his parents saw him he would have reminded them of their sin. What a terrible burden for a child to bear! He would also have been a symbol of the sin itself, to David and to his nation. Yet God had forgiven the sin, and it was sent away. »p. 357. David and his people must live in the light of forgiveness, not in dark shadow cast by past sins. As for the child, it was no punishment for him to go to paradise and await final redemption with all God's saints.

David's reaction to terminal illness (12:15-23). David prayed fervently while life remained, waiting to see if God would graciously spare his child's life. When death came, David worshiped and then went on with his life. What a model for us. Because we care deeply for our loved ones, we are certainly to pray for their recovery. Yet we know that all die, so in prayer for the seriously ill we can never be sure of God's will. If our loved ones recover, we will rejoice. If not, we are to adopt David's wise attitude, accept the will of God, and get on with our lives, comforted by the fact that while our dear one will not come to us, we "will go to him."

Outline
Place
Finder

TRIUMPHS
TROUBLES
TRIALS

Chapter summary. The troubles predicted by Nathan the prophet now strike David's family. His son Amnon rapes his half sister, Tamar (13:1-19). Tamar's brother Absalom counsels her to keep the matter quiet, but determines to kill Amnon (vv. 20-22). He conceals his intention for two years, and then invites his unsuspecting victim and the rest of the king's sons to a feast. There his servants kill Amnon, and Absalom takes refuge in a foreign country (vv. 23-39). Absalom is now next in line for the throne, but in exile. Joab, who has thrown his political support to Absalom, engineers a recall (14:1-23). But David refuses to see his son for two years. Finally Absalom forces Joab to intercede, and David welcomes Absalom home (vv. 24-33).

Key verse. 13:21: Just being angry is no way to deal with sin.

Personal application. When our children do wrong we need to take sides—against them.

INSIGHT

Political overtones. The Tamar/Amnon/Absalom story is not simply a tale of lust and a brother's revenge. Amnon, as David's oldest son (3:2-5), was first in line for the throne. Kileab had apparently died, so Absalom was next in line after Amnon. Rivalry already existed between Amnon and Absalom! We need to understand the political implications of the events to fully understand the story.

Amnon's frustration (13:2). Amnon's frustration was lust mixed with hatred, not love. Today we realize that rape is not so much a sex act as an expression of hostility and aggression. Tamar's beauty, mixed with Amnon's hostility to Absalom, made Amnon fixate on "doing" something to her.

Jonadab (13:3). This cousin of Amnon and Absalom is described as "shrewd." The Heb. word might be translated "crafty." He clearly understands the motivations of the royal princes (cf. vv. 32-33). Like all too many "friends," Jonadab is always ready to ingratiate himself by finding a way for others to do what they want to do, whether it is right or not. Don't mistake the Jonadabs you know for friends. A true friend will rebuke us when we're wrong (cf. Prov. 27:6).

Could Amnon have married Tamar? (13:13) O.T. Law forbids marriage between siblings (cf. Lev. 18:9, 11; 20:17; Deut. 27:22). Yet Gen. 20:12 might serve as a precedent. Rabbinic writers suggest Tamar was illegitimate, and marriage could have taken place. The point, however, is that Amnon did not want to marry Tamar. He wanted to humiliate her and thus get at her brother Absalom.

David's inaction. While this rape was not a capital crime, Amnon's rape of an unattached virgin called for forced marriage and the payment of a bride price (cf. Deut. 22:28-29). Though furious, for some reason David did not take this (or any other!) action. Too many parents intervene to protect sons and daughters from the consequences of their wrong actions. Only by dealing appropriately with wrongdoing can further wrongs be prevented.

Tamar (13:20). Tamar is truly a victim here. "Desolate" implies childless, and perhaps even an early death. She may have known Absalom intended revenge, but revenge is small comfort. No one involved seems to have tried to take any steps to console her. Later Absalom named his daughter Tamar. He apparently had some affection for his sister, but not enough to console her while he carried out his plan for revenge and political advancement.

"Geshur" (13:37). The king was Absalom's grandfather (cf. 3:3).

A legal parallel? (14:1-14) The fictitious story does not fit Absalom's case, which involved premeditated murder with known hostile intent (13:32). David could only have responded as he did because he wanted his son to return so badly (cf. vv. 37-39). Be careful when others find reasons for you to do what you badly want to do.

God devises ways (14:14). God has two ways to deal with sin. One is the way of forgiveness, which requires us to acknowledge our sin and repent. The other is the way of punishment, which requires payment of the penalty law requires. David recalled his banished son, but did not do it in God's way. Don't weakly overlook someone's sins and then claim you are being like God. You're not.

Chapter summary. Absalom now begins a four-year campaign to supplant David on the throne. Knowing the south is loyal, he focuses on winning the allegiance of the northern tribes (15:1-6). When Absalom judges the time is right, he summons his supporters and is acclaimed king in Hebron, the site where David was crowned King of Judah (vv. 7-12; cf. 5:3). David immediately flees Jerusalem with a few supporters (15:13-23). David sends the ark back to Jerusalem, and arranges for several loyal men to pretend support for Absalom (vv. 24-37). On the way Ziba provides David with food, and David is cursed by one of Saul's relatives, Shimei (16:1-14). Still decisive, though shaken by events and uncertain of God's intentions, David hurries toward lands he had hidden in as a fugitive from Saul.

Meanwhile Absalom enters Jerusalem. He publicly sleeps with his father's concubines. Now there can be no turning back. The act declares Absalom's firm intention to wrest the throne from his father, and fully commits his followers (vv. 15-23).

Outline
Place
Finder

TRIUMPHS
TROUBLES
TRIALS

Key verses. 15:25-26: David is ready to accept God's will.

Personal application. Troubles must never cause us to doubt God.

INSIGHT

Politicians (15:1-7). Absalom is a model of the insincere politician. He relied on pomp (v. 1), criticism of the present administration (vv. 2-3), campaign promises (v. 4), and personal charm (vv. 5-6) to seek an office he wanted for personal reasons, not the public good. Watch out for the person who says what he thinks the majority wants to hear, rather than speaking honestly and boldly.

"Hebron" (15:7). Absalom probably picked Hebron for practical as well as symbolic reasons. David's move of the capital to Jerusalem could hardly have been popular in Hebron.

"Ittai" (15:19). The loyalty of foreign mercenary troops who had been employed only recently contrasts with the readiness of David's own people to turn against him. The contrast must have made David feel the pain of his people's rejection even more deeply. "Yesterday" here means "a short time ago." The mention of Gath does not imply these Gittites were Philistines, but only that they had formerly been employed by Achish.

Submission (15:25-26). Sending the ark back to Jerusalem, David confessed both his willingness to submit to God's will, and his uncertainty about his fate. David sinned terribly with Bathsheba, and failed to discipline his sons, as Eli (1 Sam. 2) and Samuel (8:1-3) had done before him. His doubts are powerfully expressed in Ps. 3 written during his flight from Absalom. Only a clear conscience can keep God's children from tormenting doubts about the future.

Don't give up (15:27-37). David's actions remind us not to give up when we have doubts. He creates a spy network, arranges for couriers to bring him news, and infiltrates his adviser Hushai to sabotage Absalom's plans. Being uncertain about God's will for the future does not mean we should hesitate to prepare for it!

"Hushai" (15:37). "Friend of David" was a court title, indicating he was an official adviser of the king. Hushai was loyal to David, but the word "friend" here does not indicate affection.

"Ziba" (16:1-4). Ziba showed confidence in David when he supplied his column with food. He also lied about Mephibosheth. The fact that David believed the lie may suggest he was aware of the dissatisfaction with his rule that Absalom had capitalized on (cf. 15:2-3).

"Shimei" (16:5-14). Shimei's accusation may indicate that the execution of seven of Saul's relatives happened before Absalom's rebellion (cf. chap. 21). Even so, cursing David was a crime under O.T. Law (Ex. 22:28).

Ahithophel's advice (16:15-23). Concubines were secondary, but still lawful, wives. The point was to make a public, unmistakable statement that a complete break between Absalom and David existed. Now Absalom's followers need not fear Absalom would have a change of heart.

Outline
Place
Finder

TRIUMPHS
TROUBLES
TRIALS

Chapter summary. Absalom now occupies Jerusalem, and must determine what to do next. Ahithophel urges him to pursue David immediately with a small, mobile force, before David can reach safety and raise an army (17:1-4). Hushai plays on Absalom's fears, reminding him of David's prowess as a warrior. Absalom will want an army at his back before he faces David (vv. 5-14). Hushai's delaying tactics work. David is informed and escapes (vv. 15-29). David raises an army (18:1-3), and in the ensuing battle Absalom is killed by Joab, against David's express orders (vv. 4-18). When David hears of the great "victory" and of Absalom's death, he is overcome with grief (vv. 19-33).

Key verse. 17:14: God works through man's decisions.

Personal application. Grief awaits the parents who fail to correct and control their children.

INSIGHT

Two plans (17:1-14). The core of Ahithophel's plan was to kill only David. With David gone, his supporters would have no choice but to rally to Absalom. Without a civil war the nation would remain united and all David's gains would be preserved. Hushai proposed that a mass attack be made on David and his supporters, and that they all be wiped out. It assumed that David would be unable to raise an army, and that Absalom would enjoy absolute numerical superiority.

The fact that all the men of Israel agree, with the effectiveness of Absalom's earlier criticism of David's administration (cf. 15:3), suggests there was considerable unhappiness with David's later leadership. The most successful general will lose troops. And continual warfare must place a strain on the local economy, if for no other reason than that men are not available to plant and harvest crops. This interpretation is supported by Hushai's phrase, "from Dan to Beersheba," an expression meaning the whole nation.

Psalm 3:2. David's descriptive words further support this view. He says, "Many are saying of me, 'God will not deliver him.'" Many apparently lost confidence in David's integrity through the affair with Bathsheba and the bitter struggle between royal brothers.

How dangerous it is to judge another's relationship with God! Even those who openly fail can be forgiven, and given a fresh start.

Inquire of God? It is significant that neither Absalom nor any other adviser thought of asking God for guidance, even though the ark, the high priest, and ephod used in inquiring of God were present in Jerusalem. Absalom's failure suggests he ignored God

completely in his plan to seize the throne.

Ahithophel's suicide (17:23). Ahithophel knew all was lost when his counsel was rejected. Later Jewish religious writings condemn suicide, but Ahithophel's burial in his father's tomb suggests no social stigma was attached in David's time.

Thousands and hundreds (18:1). These are military units, which may or may not have included full complements of men.

David's withdrawal (18:2-3). The war was over David. If he were killed, the lives of his supporters might be forfeit. It was wiser to have him stay behind the lines.

Absalom's death (18:9-15). Joab, as before, acts in what he thinks are the king's best interests, despite orders to the contrary (cf. 3:22-27). He tries to bribe a soldier to kill Absalom, but when the soldier wisely refuses Joab himself stabs Absalom. Once Joab committed himself fully, his soldiers finish off the king's son. Absalom deserves death, and his killing undoubtedly saves the kingdom future strife.

Absalom's monument (18:18). The verse is another of those "conflicts" in Scripture, which reports Absalom had three sons (14:27), and that he was buried under a "heap of stones" (18:17). First, the stone pillar (*massebot*) was not a tombstone but a monument. And second, Absalom had no *surviving* son to "carry on the memory of my name." Apparently only his daughter Tamar lived to adulthood.

"My son, my son" (18:33). Every parent can understand David's anguish and grief. While we must let our children go when they become adults, and let them be responsible for their own choices, our pain when they make bad choices is very real.

Chapter summary. David remains lost in grief over his dead son, Absalom, until Joab rebukes him. David must remember the risks taken by those who supported him, and show his appreciation (19:1-8). Meanwhile the rebels have a change of heart. They belatedly remember how David has protected his people from their enemies, and talk about inviting him back. David arranges for the elders of Judah to accompany him and heads for Jerusalem (vv. 9-18). He is met by Shimei, who begs for mercy (vv. 18-23), and by Mephibosheth, who explains why he had not come with David earlier (vv. 24-30). David also rewards an early supporter, Barzillai (vv. 31-40).

But now the northern tribes become upset that an honor guard from Judah has returned David to Jerusalem (vv. 41-43). The jealousy leads to open conflict, and the northern tribesmen again rebel (20:1-2). Joab murders Amasa, whom David has appointed the new commander of his forces, and taking personal command again, pursues the leaders of the new revolt. He puts this rebellion down (vv. 3-22), and is restored to command of all David's forces. David reorganizes his government (vv. 23-26). His throne has been saved.

Outline
Place
Finder

TRIUMPHS
TROUBLES
TRIALS

Key verse. 19:43: Jealousy creates strife.

Personal application. Keep your focus on major issues, and don't be sidetracked by personal jealousy or pride.

INSIGHT

Exaggeration (19:1-8). Joab exaggerates, but is correct. Sometimes our public responsibilities mean we must put aside personal griefs.

Politics again (19:9-15). David woos the leaders of Judah, even promising command of the militia to Amasa, an influential southerner who had been on Absalom's side. The strategy did get Judah to act, but had long-term negative impact. Jealousy had existed between the northern and southern tribes from the time of the Judges (cf. Jud. 8:1; 12:1). There had been persistent strife between Judah and the north during the seven years David ruled Judah alone. By encouraging Judah to act alone David exacerbated the situation, which in some 50 years would lead to a permanent division of the kingdom. We may win our point by dividing rather than uniting others. But in the long run playing one group off against another leads to disaster.

"Mephibosheth" (19:21-30). Jonathan's son may well have told the truth, but it is difficult to know. On the other hand, Ziba's help was positive proof of commitment to David. Ziba surely would have been punished by Absalom, and the situation looked most dark for David at the time. What David did was probably the only thing he could have done.

"Sheba" (20:1-2). There seems to have been no great support for Sheba, who is finally captured hiding in a small city (vv. 14-22). Most likely the northern tribesmen simply went home, grumbling, to see what happened.

Amasa and Joab (20:4-7). We need to make a distinction between professional soldiers and militia in David's kingdom. In time of war all able-bodied men were expected to report, and became a citizen army. At the same time David had a smaller professional corp of "Kerethites and Pelethites" and "mighty warriors." We can add to the mercenary forces like that led by Ittai, that were typically employed as king's bodyguards (cf. 15:18-21). Apparently Joab had been "supreme commander" of all forces. David's act in making Amasa commander of militia diminished Joab's role, though it does not imply Amasa replaced Joab completely. Amasa failed to raise troops to pursue Sheba in the three days David had given him. This may have provided Joab with an excuse for killing him, but David later reminds Solomon that Joab had shed (innocent) blood in peacetime in killing both Amasa and Abner (1 Kings 2:5). Joab regained control of the militia and other forces (2 Sam. 20:23), though Benaiah was made commander of David's professional army, and thus served as a counterweight to Joab.

Outline
Place
Finder

TRIUMPHS
TROUBLES
TRIALS

Chapter summary. Chapters 21–24 relate six undated incidents representing David's trials. First mentioned is a three-year famine. David learns that this is a consequence of Saul's efforts to wipe out the Gibeonites, in violation of a treaty Joshua had made hundreds of years earlier (21:1-2; cf. Josh. 9). In reparation, the Gibeonites demand the right to execute seven of Saul's male descendants (vv. 3-14). The executions end the famine. A second trial is continuing warfare with the Philistines (vv. 15-22). The lengthy wars destroyed the capacity of the Philistines to ever again mount a serious threat to Israel. A third trial noted here is Saul's active hostility to David (22:1). Rather than dwell on the pain, David writes a psalm of praise, celebrating God as Fortress and Deliverer (vv. 2-51). Trials are always difficult as we experience them. But later they bring fresh appreciation of the goodness of our God.

Key verse. 22:2: What God was to David, He is for us.

Personal application. Don't resent trials, for they remind us to depend on God. And afterward to celebrate His goodness.

Key concepts. Covenant »p. 35. Philistines »p. 185.

INSIGHT

Why did David let the Gibeonites execute Saul's descendants? The famine was clearly a divine punishment (Deut. 28:47-48), and Saul's family was responsible. The reparation demanded was legal (cf. Num. 35:31). Yet the O.T. prohibits punishment of a son for his father's sins (Deut. 24:16; cf. Ezek. 18:1-4, 14-17). Perhaps the answer is found in the reference to Saul's "blood-stained house" (2 Sam. 21:1). The seven adult male descendants of Saul may very well have had a part in the war against the Gibeonites.

Who killed Goliath? (21:19) The verse says Elhanan did. But 1 Sam. 17 tells the familiar story of how *David* killed Goliath! The apparent conflict is resolved in 1 Chron. 20:5. That passage tells us Elhanan killed the *brother* of Goliath. Apparently our text omitted "brother." Jewish tradition says Elhanan and David are the same person, and this view is supported by evidence that a Hebrew king's "throne name" (i.e., David) might be different than his personal name (i.e., Elhanan).

Praise. This psalm is a beautiful example of praise, which is perhaps best understood as acknowledging God or confessing Him. This psalm contains both descriptive praise, which focuses on what God is like, and declarative praise, which announces what He has done. Examples of descriptive praise are found in vv. 2-3, 29, 31-32, 47-48. Examples of declarative praise are found in vv. 7, 13-20, 34-37, 40, 44, and 51.

"My fortress" (22:2-3). Imagery is a major characteristic of the Heb. language and especially of Heb. poetry. Here parallel images—fortress, rock, stronghold, shield—are repeated to convey the sense of security David finds in his relationship with God. The ancient "fortress" was a walled city, a sophisticated construction of defensive barriers that kept out all but the most persistent of enemies. Typically it featured high, thick stone walls, often constructed above a *glasis*, a sharply angled, smooth stone slope. In a land of mostly unwalled villages, the population hurried to a walled "fortress" city for security when an enemy attacked.

Analysis. David's praise is stimulated by his experience with Saul, but is placed here because it sums up a lifetime of experiencing God's grace. God is David's Deliverer (vv. 2-4). However extreme the danger (vv. 5-6) David can call out to God in his distress (v. 7). And God, the awesome God of the universe, responds (vv. 8-16). God "reaches down" to rescue David from powerful foes for, wonder of wonder, God delights "in me" (vv. 17-20). David has loved and honored God, and God has been faithful to him in return (vv. 21-28). With the resources God supplies David has been victorious (vv. 29-46). All this is from God, whose unfailing kindness David praises with his whole heart (vv. 47-51).

Chapter summary. The survey of six trials faced by David continues, but not in any particular order. David faces and comes to terms with death (23:1-7). David is served by a number of "mighty men" (war heroes) (vv. 8-39). This is a blessing but also a trial. David's own rise after killing Goliath, and the history of the ancient world, reminds us how often military heroes took the throne from their kings! Finally David, his kingdom secure, determines to take a census of his fighting men (24:1-10). The reason this decision displeased God is not stated, but most assume the census expressed pride or reliance on military might rather than the Lord. David is allowed to choose his punishment, and selects a plague (vv. 11-14). God stops when David sacrifices on what became the site of Solomon's temple (vv. 15-25).

Outline
Place
Finder

TRIUMPHS
TROUBLES
TRIALS

Key verse. 24:14: We can expect mercy from God.

Personal application. Our choice of good or evil affects others as well as ourselves.

Key concepts. Davidic Covenant »p. 374. Holy Spirit »pp. 73, 759. Messiah »p. 431. Altar »p. 79.

INSIGHT

David's last words (23:1-7). An "oracle" is a prophetic utterance, here expressed in David's formal "last words." Theologically, the oracle looks forward to ultimate triumph over evil to be won through David's house (i.e., his Descendant, the Messiah). At the same time, the oracle is a unique *personal* confession of faith. Near the end of his life, David looks ahead and expresses confidence that God will "bring to fruition my salvation" and will "grant me my every desire" (v. 5). For the believer death is no end, but a new beginning.

Inspiration (23:2). David's affirmation, "the Spirit of the Lord spoke through me; His word was on my tongue," is a beautiful expression of the biblical doctrine of "inspiration." This doctrine holds not that the biblical writers were inspired, but that the words they communicated were the very words the Holy Spirit intended to use to accurately convey God's message to man. The doctrine is developed in 2 Tim. 3:16-17, which pictures the biblical writers as "borne along" as a sailing boat is by the wind, and in 2 Peter 1:20-21 as well as Acts 4:25. The Bible is the Lord's message, Spirit-guided, so that we have in Scripture a reliable and relevant word of God.

"The Thirty" (23:24). This was apparently an elite corps, perhaps David's bodyguard. The fact that 37 persons are listed in this chapter may be accounted for by supposing new individuals were added when one of the group was killed. Or the Three, experts in single combat (vv. 1-12), with the commanders Abishai and Benaiah (vv. 18, 20), were not counted among the 30.

Loyalty (23:13-17). David's sentimental longing for a drink from a familiar spring moved three of his men to get it for him! The story illustrates the bonds of loyalty that existed between David and his men. Only a leader who inspired such loyalty could be safe from a possible coup. When David poured out the gift he was not rejecting it. He was saying that such commitment is deserved by God alone, and thus honored their act.

God "incited" David (24:1). Counting Israel was not wrong in itself, but was indicative of the pride felt by the resurgent nation and by David. The attitude existed in David's heart: God's "inciting" moved him to reveal the attitude by an action. Sins of attitude may be denied, but once acted on, guilt is undeniable. The act of pride, seen as wrong even by the insensitive Joab (v. 3), led to the Prophet Gad's announcement of judgment. David chose wisely. God is more merciful than nature or human beings!

"The threshing floor" (24:18-25). The land David purchased became the site of the temple to be built by Solomon (1 Chron. 22:1). According to 2 Chron. 3:1 this is also the very spot where Abraham came to offer up his son Isaac (Gen. 22:2, 14). Thus the temple mount links Abraham, David, and ultimately, Jesus.

217

1 Kings

For the first time in history the Hebrew people seem about to fulfill the destiny implicit in God's ancient promises to Abraham (Gen. 12). The traditional great powers of the ancient Near East, the Hittites and Assyria in the north and Egypt in the south, are dormant. Under David the Hebrews, an oppressed minority in Canaan, have become a powerful, united nation, master of a spreading empire. That destiny shines brightly under Solomon, David's brilliant son and successor. But on Solomon's death, economic stress and tribal rivalries tear the nation apart. Within a few hundred years both northern and southern halves of the now divided nation are crushed by foreign powers, and the Jewish people scattered in pagan lands.

This brief overview helps us sense the theme of the history contained in 1 and 2 Kings, which are a single book in the Hebrew Old Testament. The author, writing during the last grim years of the south's existence as an independent nation, traces the causes of the twin nations' decline. God's people, despite revivals in the south, and despite the emergence of a vital prophetic ministry in both Hebrew kingdoms, have been unfaithful to the Lord. The people worshiped pagan gods and abandoned the principles of righteousness expressed in Moses' Law. Because Israel in the north and Judah in the south abandoned God, the Lord withdrew His protection. He permitted the ruin of the Promised Land, and the fateful scattering of His chosen people.

Archeology has proven the report of events in the Books of Kings is accurate. But these books are more than history. They are a theological testimony: historic evidence that failure to live in covenant relationship with God brings personal and national disaster. The books serve Christians today in this same way. The Books of Kings remind us of God's grace, of the many chances He gives us to respond to Him, and of the judgment that must fall if we do not.

---

1 KINGS AT A GLANCE

KEY PEOPLE

Solomon   *David's brilliant successor, who builds the Jerusalem temple and brings vast wealth to Israel, and contributes to three O.T. books.*

Rehoboam   *Solomon's foolish son who loses the northern half of his kingdom.*

Jeroboam   *First ruler of the north (Israel), who sets up a religious system that counterfeits Mosaic Law and permanently corrupts that land.*

Ahab   *Evil king of Israel who actively promotes Baal in Israel.*

Elijah   *The bold but sensitive prophet who struggles to resist Ahab and Jezebel, and finally triumphs in a historic confrontation with the priests of Baal on Mt. Carmel.*

KEY EVENTS

Solomon dedicates the temple (1 Kings 8–9).

Israel rebels against Rehoboam (1 Kings 12).   *After this tragic division of Solomon's kingdom, not one godly king rules in the north!*

Ahab of Israel promotes Baal worship (1 Kings 16).   *He and his foreign bride Jezebel seek to stamp out worship of the Lord in Israel.*

Elijah emerges as God's champion (1 Kings 17–19).   *In a series of conflicts Elijah thwarts the efforts of Ahab and Jezebel to establish Baalism.*

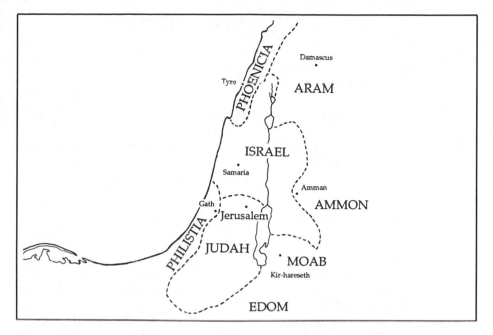

WHERE THE ACTION TAKES PLACE

After the division of Solomon's kingdom action alternates between the south (Judah) and the north (Israel), with mentions of two major foreign enemies: Syria (Aram) and Assyria.

Date and Authorship. Jewish tradition says that Jeremiah wrote 1 and 2 Kings. They were written in his time (around 580 B.C.) using source documents mentioned in the text (cf. 1 Kings 4:9-11; 11:41; 14:29).

1 Kings chapter	Date	King of Israel	King of Judah	Prophet	Major foreign enemy
1–11	970	S O L O M O N			
12–14	930	Jeroboam I	Rehoboam	Ahijah	
15	913		Abijah		
	911		Asa		
	910	Nadab			
	909	Baasha			
16	886	Elah			
	885	Zimri			
	885	Tibni			
	885	Omri			
	881				Ben-Hadad I (Syria)
17–21	874	Ahab	Jehoshaphat	Elijah	
	860				Ben-Hadad II
22	853	Ahaziah			Shalmaneser III (Assyria)

Rulers, prophets, and enemies of the two Hebrew kingdoms, with their dates, and with a chapter-by-chapter match to 1 Kings.

THEOLOGICAL OUTLINE OF 1 KINGS

I. THE KINGDOM UNITED — 1–11
II. THE KINGDOM DIVIDED — 12–16
III. KINGDOMS IN CONFLICT — 17–22

CONTENT OUTLINE OF 1 KINGS

I. The United Kingdom (1:1–11:43)
  A. Solomon Becomes King
    (1:1–2:12)
  B. Solomon Secures the Throne
    (2:13–3:28)
  C. Solomon Organizes His
    Kingdom (4:1-34)
  D. Solomon's Construction Plans
    (5:1–8:66)
    1. Prepares to build temple
      (5:1-18)
    2. Builds temple (6:1-38)
    3. Builds other buildings
      (7:1-12)
    4. Equips the temple (7:13-51)
    5. Dedicates the temple
      (8:1-66)
      a. Moves in the ark
        (8:1-11)
      b. Addresses his people
        (8:12-21)
      c. Prays to God (8:22-53)
      d. Blesses the assembly
        (8:54-66)
  E. Solomon's Era Summarized
    (9:1–11:43)
    1. God's appearances (9:1-9)
    2. Business and building
      (9:10-24)
    3. Sacrifices (9:25)
    4. Trade (9:26-28)
    5. Royal visits (10:1-13)
    6. Wealth and splendor
      (10:14-29)
    7. Many wives (11:1-13)
    8. Enemies (11:14-40)
    9. Death of Solomon (11:41-43)
II. The Divided Kingdom
  (12:1–16:34)
  A. The Division (12:1–14:31)
    1. The ten northern tribes
      secede (12:1-24)

2. Jeroboam I rules Israel;
  sets up false religion
  (12:25-33)
3. Unnamed prophet pre-
  dicts Jeroboam's judgment
  (13:1-34)
4. Ahijah prophesies against
  Jeroboam (14:1-20)
5. Rehoboam rules in Judah
  (14:21-31)
  B. Kings of the South and North
    (15:1–16:34)
    1. Abijah (Judah) (15:1-8)
    2. Asa (Judah) (15:9-24)
    3. Nadab (Israel) (15:25-31)
THE SECOND DYNASTY IN ISRAEL
    4. Baasha (15:32–16:7)
    5. Elah (16:8-14)
THE THIRD DYNASTY IN ISRAEL
    6. Zimri and Tibni (16:15-22)
    7. Omri (16:23-28)
    8. Ahab (16:29-34)
III. Man's Kingdom and God's King-
  dom in Conflict: Ahab vs. Elijah
  (17:1–22:40)
  A. Elijah's Famine (17:1–19:21)
    1. Elijah's call (17:1-6)
    2. Elijah and the widow
      (17:7-24)
    3. Elijah and Obadiah
      (18:1-15)
    4. Elijah vs. the prophets of
      Baal (18:16-46)
    5. Elijah flees Jezebel
      (19:1-9a)
    6. God speaks to Elijah
      (19:9b-18)
    7. Elijah commissions Elisha
      (19:19-21)
  B. Ahab's Failures (20:1–22:40)
IV. The Divided Kingdom
  (Continued) (22:41-53)

Chapter summary. David is old, about to die. And he has not yet publicly announced who will succeed him. Adonijah, David's oldest living son, decides to take matters into his own hands. With the support of General Joab and Abiathar the priest, he plans to proclaim himself king (1:1-9). But the Prophet Nathan hears, and goes to Bathsheba. Bathsheba makes a touching appeal to David (vv. 10-21), then Nathan enters to report what Adonijah is up to (vv. 22-27). Stirred to action at last, David has Solomon publicly anointed and acclaimed king (vv. 28-40). The noise of the celebration in Jerusalem reaches the spot where Adonijah is plotting with his supporters. When a messenger reports that Solomon is now king, Adonijah's guests, fearful and uncertain, all scurry away (vv. 41-49). Adonijah himself hurries to the altar to seek sanctuary (vv. 50-53).

Outline
Place
Finder

UNITED
DIVIDED
CONFLICT

Key verse. 1:30: David keeps his promises—at last.

Personal application. Don't delay making your intentions known.

Key concepts. Anoint »p. 187. Altar »p. 79.

INSIGHT

David's feebleness (1:1-4). Though only 70 (cf. 2 Sam. 5:4-5), David is feeble and withdrawn. Some suggest the stress of his constant struggles with Saul and foreign enemies took their toll. Others emphasize David's family problems: especially the rebellion and death of his favorite son Absalom (2 Sam. 15–18). The weakness of the once-decisive David created a power vacuum, and Adonijah determined to establish himself as king.

Adonijah's supporters. David's wishes and God's will for Solomon to succeed were known (cf. 2 Sam. 12:24-25; 1 Chron. 22:9-10; 28:4-7). How did Adonijah find supporters? General Joab had always been loyal to David, but not to David's desires (cf. 2 Sam. 3:22-39; 18:1-18). He may well have planned this coup. Abiathar, originally David's chief priest (1 Sam. 22:2-22), later seems to have been displaced by Zadok (1 Chron. 16:39). Perhaps jealousy motivated him. How dangerous self-will and pride are to doing God's will!

Not invited (1:10). The feast Adonijah prepared was certainly part of an anointing and enthroning ceremony. The failure to invite Nathan, Bathsheba, and Solomon had special significance. A host was obligated to protect his guests. By not inviting these three Adonijah expressed his intent to do away with them.

Solomon. God's early declaration of special love for Solomon (2 Sam. 12:24-25) and his intent to give Solomon the throne conveys a

wonderful message. David and Bathsheba truly were forgiven, and the proof lies in God's exaltation of their son. No wonder the name chosen means "peace" (*shalom*). When we accept God's forgiveness, we can count on God's grace enriching our future.

Bathsheba. The text reveals a truly loving relationship between David and the woman he betrayed (2 Sam. 11–12). David had acknowledged his sin, and not only God but also Bathsheba had forgiven him. Together they had four sons, and in his old age concern for Bathsheba's safety (1 Kings 1:21) helped shake David from his lethargy. What hope this promises for hurting couples today. If we acknowledge our sins against each other, and accept forgiveness, the love of husbands and wives still can be restored.

Let your intentions be known. When David made known his intention for Solomon to follow him on the throne, the population of Jerusalem accepted his choice enthusiastically. When David had been silent, there had been only confusion. Let's not make people guess what we wish, or what we plan to do. Only clear communication of intentions and desires can maintain harmony.

Adonijah's fear (1:50-53). Adonijah's fear also shows that he had intended to kill his rival, Solomon, when he took the throne. Solomon was gracious not to execute Adonijah, and wise to make his continued safety depend on good behavior!

Outline
Place
Finder

UNITED
DIVIDED
CONFLICT

Chapter summary. David instructs Solomon to be strong, to remain faithful to the Lord, and to keep Moses' commandments (2:1-4). David also reminds Solomon of acts performed by Joab and Shimei that have not been punished (vv. 5-9). David then dies, and all acknowledge Solomon as king (vv. 10-11).

Shortly after, Adonijah asks to marry David's nurse, Abishag. As she had the status of a secondary wife of David (cf. 1:2-4), Solomon realizes Adonijah still seeks the throne, and executes him for treason (2:13-25). Solomon exiles Abiathar the priest for supporting Adonijah (vv. 26-27). Joab, who conspired with Adonijah, knows he must be next. His execution clears David's line of any responsibility for two murders Joab committed earlier (vv. 28-34). Shimei, who had cursed David, is promised immunity as long as he stays in Jerusalem, and takes a solemn oath. When he violates the oath, he too is executed (vv. 34-46a). All threats to David's line disposed of, Solomon's throne is secure (v. 46b).

Key verses. 2:2-3: It takes strength to follow the Lord's ways.

Personal application. Prepare for the future by taking care of problems you have left unresolved.

Key concepts. Law »p. 145. Heart & soul »p. 120.

INSIGHT

David's charge (2:1-4). David's charge to Solomon is expanded in 1 Chron. 22:6-13; 28:9. David's concern that Solomon might not "be strong" was rooted in his feeling that Solomon was "young and inexperienced" (22:5). We feel this way as our sons and daughters mature. Yet each of us must let go, having encouraged them to be committed to the Lord.

"Be strong" (2:2). Strength of character is indicated by commitment to God's ways, despite pressures from within, or from others.

"Joab" (2:5-6). Why hadn't David punished Joab for the two murders he mentions?(cf. 2 Sam. 3:22-39; 20:1-10) Some suggest loyalty to a man who had been loyal to him. But it is best to see that in each case Joab might argue technicalities: that he killed Abner outside a city of refuge as his family's "avenger of blood," and had killed Amasa for failing to obey orders to recall the army within three days. Solomon would not have to argue these cases, for Joab had conspired against David's known successor with Adonijah.

"Adonijah" (2:13-25). The Greek historian Herodotus says that among the Persians a new king inherited the previous king's harem, and that to possess the harem was taken as title to the throne. While no such custom is expressed in Scripture, Absalom's earlier public appropriation of his father's concubines did symbolize his determination to take David's

throne (2 Sam. 16:21-23). Solomon rightly took Adonijah's request for Abishag, who had been David's concubine, »p. 166, as an indication he was still plotting rebellion.

Bathsheba. As queen mother, Bathsheba now had a very influential role. It was not unusual for a supplicant to enlist the queen mother's aid in seeking a favor from the king. It is interesting to speculate if Bathsheba was so naive that she did not realize the implications of Adonijah's request. Perhaps she did, and was glad to let Adonijah condemn himself.

Abiathar. The divine curse on Eli's family, mentioned in 2:27 is found in 1 Sam. 2:36.

Shimei. Shimei was a member of Saul's clan who had openly supported Absalom's rebellion (cf. 1 Sam. 16:5-14). David had not punished Shimei when he was restored to the throne, but this member of the Saulite family did represent a threat to the Davidic dynasty. Solomon acted with restraint in restricting Shimei to Jerusalem, and obtaining an oath from him. When Shimei violated his oath, there could be no doubt his punishment was just.

Solomon. Solomon showed himself wise and patient. He acted decisively when necessary, and showed restraint when this was the better course. How we need God's help to discern which course we should follow in making our decisions!

Chapter summary. Two chapters provide a general summary of Solomon's rule, and God's faithfulness to this descendant of David. Early in his reign Solomon demonstrates love for God by lavish sacrifices (3:1-4). When God appears to Solomon in a dream, the king asks for wisdom to govern wisely (vv. 5-9). Pleased, God promises Solomon not only wisdom but also riches and honor (vv. 10-15). The gift of wisdom is displayed when Solomon discerns which of two claimants is the real mother of an infant (vv. 16-28), and in a reorganization of the government which sets up administrative districts that ignore old tribal boundaries (4:1-19). The gift of wealth is displayed in the extent of his daily provisions (vv. 20-23), and expansion of the standing army (vv. 24-28). And the gift of honor is seen in a worldwide reputation for intellectual accomplishment (vv. 29-34).

Outline
Place
Finder

UNITED
DIVIDED
CONFLICT

Key verse. 3:13: Solomon asked wisely, and so God blessed.

Personal application. When our priorities are right, we can expect God to give us additional gifts.

Key concepts. High places »p. 113. Dreams »p. 99. Wisdom »p. 387.

INSIGHT

Solomon's alliances (3:1). In ancient times treaties between nations often involved marriages between the royal houses. Why is this seemingly thrown in here, with no apparent reason? Because Solomon's policy of cementing foreign relations by marriages was against God's expressed will (Deut. 17:17).

Great strengths are no guarantee against failure.

Gibeon. Gibeon was an important "high place" (worship center) because the tabernacle was there at the time (1 Chron. 16:39-40), though David had moved the ark of the covenant into Jerusalem (2 Sam. 6). When Solomon completed the temple every excuse for worship at a high place ceased.

"Burnt offerings" (3:4). This offering was voluntary, showing thanksgiving and dedication. »p. 78.

God's promises (3:10-14). Solomon requested true wisdom, not just intelligence. The Heb. concept of wisdom always involves the ability to "distinguish between right and wrong." God responded with three unconditional and one conditional promises. Solomon was guaranteed wisdom, wealth, and honor. He was promised long life "if you will walk in My ways." We too are given unconditional promises. Yet some blessings remain conditional on our obedience.

How did prostitutes have access to the king? (3:16-28) In many ancient societies it was customary for a day to be set aside for ordinary people to bring matters to the king (cf. 2 Kings 8:1-6).

Solomon's administrative districts (4:1-19). These districts do not follow the old tribal boundaries. Many believe this was deliberate. In the time of the Judges and even in David's day a strong sense of tribal loyalty existed, just as during America's Civil War many felt more loyalty to their home state than to the Union. Solomon may have been trying to weaken the tribal system in order to strengthen the central government.

Solomon's court (4:20-23). The provisions described here would have fed some 4,000 to 5,000 people though some estimates run as many as 14,000! The figures suggest Solomon developed a large, complex bureaucracy, and the land was wealthy enough to support it.

Solomon's intellectual prowess (4:29-34). The ancient world produced many kinds of literature and much inquiry into what we would call "the sciences." Solomon created proverbs (cf. Prov.), love poetry (Song), and philosophical inquiry (Ecc.). To say that Solomon "named" (1 Kings 4:33, NIV, "described") plants and animals means that he mastered zoology and biology.

Outline
Place
Finder

UNITED
DIVIDED
CONFLICT

Chapter summary. Solomon strengthens relations with Tyre and contracts for materials with which to build the temple that David had dreamed of erecting (5:1-12). Solomon drafts thousands of Israelite workers (vv. 13-18), and in the fourth year of his reign (968 B.C.), begins construction (6:1-7). The structure is magnificent, of the best marble and cedar wood, richly adorned with gold overlay and furnished with gold furniture (vv. 8-36). The project takes seven years, but at last the building is complete (vv. 37-38). Illustration, p. 283.

Key verse. 5:5: Solomon honors God first with his best.

Personal application. Careful preparation is called for when we undertake any task.

INSIGHT

Illustration. *Stoneworkers detach great blocks of marble for the temple foundations (5:17-18). Holes are drilled in the rock, and wooden wedges inserted. Soaked in water, these expand and split the rock along predetermined lines. Working only with such simple tools, ancient stone masons created multiton blocks of rock so perfectly crafted that they fit together without the need for mortar, and so exact that the thinnest knife could not be inserted between the blocks.*

David and Hiram (5:1-6). David had developed close commercial relationships with Tyre (cf. 2 Sam. 5:11). Solomon's note about the temple begins, "You know," suggesting that David had shared his dream of building a temple with Hiram as well, and that the two may have been friends. Solomon's promise to pay "whatever wages you set" suggests a continuing bond of trust between two rulers.

Solomon carefully nurtures his relationship with Hiram, who will supply not only the wood, but the skilled craftsmen to train Solomon's people in the skills needed to build the temple.

Solomon's workers (5:13-17). In addition to slave labor, Solomon relied on the *corvee* to provide workers. This practice was common in ancient times, and involved claiming a person's labor as sort of a personal tax. By alternating shifts Solomon was able to maintain agricultural production at home, while keeping work moving on his massive construction project. Not many years ago some rural counties in the Midwest had a form of corvee: farmers would keep the roadsides mowed in return for a reduction of local taxes.

King Solomon's gold (6:20-22, 30). The text calls for almost 25 U.S. tons of gold; gold worth nearly three *billion* dollars even at the old, fixed price of $35 an ounce! Some have found this incredible, even the product of an "exuberant imagination!" But there is external evidence that ancient Middle Eastern kings collected vast amounts of gold, and specific evidence of Solomon's lavish use of gold in decorating his temple.

First Kings 14:25-26 tells us that Pharaoh Shishak of Egypt attacked Jerusalem and carried off the temple treasures, including King Solomon's gold. He was followed to the throne of Egypt just a year or so later by Osorkon I. Soon Osorkon erected a granite pillar at Bubastis describing his own magnificent gift to the gods of his land. That gift? Tons of silver—and of gold. The report of Solomon's use of tons of gold in decorating his temple is no product of anyone's imagination. We even know what happened to the gold, just five or so years after it was taken to Egypt. It was dedicated to Egypt's deities by Osorkon, the son of Shishak.

Chapter summary. An enthusiastic builder, Solomon not only builds a magnificent temple for the Lord, but goes on to construct a grand personal palace and national administrative center (7:1-12). Yet vast wealth and skills are poured out in equipping the temple. A skilled Israelite foundryman is brought from Tyre (vv. 13-14) to make massive bronze fixtures for the temple court (vv. 15-47) and delicate gold within (vv. 48-51).

Outline
Place
Finder

UNITED
DIVIDED
CONFLICT

Key verse. 7:51: David's dedication outlived him.

Personal application. Commitment to God is expressed in careful preparation for worship, not just attendance.

INSIGHT

Illustration. *Archeological finds give us some insight into what various equipment for Solomon's temple may have looked like. For instance, the ten-wheeled bronze stands for lavers, which held water in which the priests might wash, may well have been a much larger model of the wheeled stand at the right, used to hold a basin in a pagan temple. The stand was found at Ekron, and dates from the 12th century* B.C.

The temple plan. The plan of the temple, and its furnishings, is modeled on the plan God gave Moses for a portable worship center. This tent worship center, called the tabernacle, is described on pages 67–68, and the significance of each item of furniture is explained. Temple furnishings, while on a much grander scale, had the same spiritual significance as each corresponding item in the tabernacle.

Solomon's palace. The project took 13 years, compared to the 7 years it took to build the temple. We should not conclude, however, that Solomon spent more money and effort on this personal home and national administrative center. Temple construction apparently involved a "crash" approach, and the palace a lesser priority. Often what we get done first is more important to us than what we put off till later.

"Huram" (7:13). In the description of Huram, the word *zur* may have been confused with the Aramaic word *zaiar*. If so the text would indicate Huram's father was an artist, not a man of Tyre. However, in ancient times Tyre was known for its brasswork, its builders and designers.

"The pillars" (7:15-22). The two 27-foot-high pillars, some 6 feet around, were given names that mean "he shall uphold" (*yakin*) and "may strength be in him" (*boaz*). The symbolism of these impressive pillars which stood in front of the temple has been much debated. Perhaps, however, they were to serve as a reminder to Solomon and to his royal offspring of David's final advice, recorded in 2:2-4. If Solomon would only be strong and obey the Lord, the Lord would surely keep His promise and uphold the Davidic dynasty.

The metal sea (7:23-26). It would be difficult even with modern techniques to cast a massive, one-piece metal bowl like the one described here. It was intended to hold water for the priests' required ceremonial washings. Two different figures are given for the amount of water it held: 2,000 baths here, and 3,000 in 2 Chron. 4:5. As Heb. numbers were written in a kind of shorthand, the discrepancy is easily explained as a later error in transmission. If 2,000 is the correct number, the bowl held some 11,500 gallons. If 3,000 is correct, it held about 17,500!

David's last gift (7:51). David had devoted his last years to assembling building materials and collecting wealth for the temple (1 Chron. 29). His last great gift to God outlives him.

Outline
Place
Finder

UNITED
DIVIDED
CONFLICT

Chapter summary. When the temple is complete, Solomon calls all Israel together (8:1-2). As the ark of the covenant is placed in the temple's inner room, a cloud symbolizing God's presence fills the temple (vv. 3-13). Solomon blesses the people in God's name (v. 14) and, after giving a word of personal testimony (vv. 15-21), offers one of the Old Testament's most notable prayers (vv. 22-53). He acknowledges that God is too great to be contained in any structure (8:22-28). Yet Solomon asks God to be aware of prayers directed to Him at the temple whether the worshiper comes for help or for forgiveness (vv. 29-53). Solomon again blesses the people, and reminds them that their hearts must be "fully committed to the Lord our God" (vv. 54-61). The temple is then dedicated (vv. 62-66).

Key verses. 8:27-28: God is transcendent, yet is with us.

Personal application. Come to God freely, whatever your need. He will hear from heaven, forgive, and act.

Key concepts. Ark »p. 68. Covenant »pp. 35, 62. Abandon »p. 188. Prayer »p. 181.

INSIGHT

"The seventh month" (8:2). The seventh-month festival was Booths, which celebrated the end of the wilderness wanderings. It was also a harvest festival (cf. Deut. 12:8-11). This thanksgiving feast was an appropriate time to dedicate the temple.

The cloud (8:12-13). Solomon recognized the significance of the cloud that filled the temple. It was a visible manifestation of God's personal presence with His people (cf. Ex. 19:9; 20:21; Lev. 16:2), and thus the divine stamp of approval on the temple project.

Solomon's personal testimony (8:15-21). Timing the dedication for the Feast of Booths served as a public testimony to God's faithfulness. Solomon added his own personal testimony, God was not only faithful to Israel; He was faithful to Solomon, who succeeded David as God had pledged. Church history witnesses to God's faithfulness. You and I can testify to God's faithfulness to us as individuals. Like Solomon, we need to testify publicly.

Solomon's prayer (8:22-53). Unlike pagans, Solomon did not suppose God would actually live in the temple. Israel could always reach God through the temple, however long the distance between them. Solomon foresaw five situations in which Israel would have a special need for confidence that God would hear, and answer. (1) He asks that when a court case is in doubt the truth will come out (vv. 31-32); (2) that when Israel sins, is defeated in battle, and repents, God will forgive and restore (vv.

33-34); (3) that when Israel sins, is punished by drought, and repents, God will forgive and teach His people the right way to live (vv. 35-36); (4) that when Israel sins in any way and seeks forgiveness, God will forgive and act for them (vv. 37-40); and (5) that foreigners may have this same privilege of having prayers answered by Him (vv. 41-43). Whatever our failures, and whatever disasters may result, God will welcome us home.

Affliction (8:35). The Heb. word 'anah means to afflict, oppress, humble. It is linked with poverty and defenselessness, a truly terrible condition. While affliction is a punishment from God, it is also a gift. This verse tells us it is intended to help people "turn from their sin." When we understand this, we will be able to say with the psalmist, "It was good for me to be afflicted so that I might learn Your decrees" (Ps. 119:71).

God and man (8:56-61). Solomon's charge to his people links two great truths that we too must live by. On the one hand all is of grace: "Not one word has failed of all the good promises" of God. On the other hand, "Your hearts must be fully committed to the Lord our God, to live by His decrees." There is no conflict between faith and works, between God's sovereignty and human responsibility. God is ever ready to pour His grace out on an undeserving people. Yet it is obedience that brings us to the streambed from which His grace overflows.

Solomon

Archeologists have unearthed many of Solomon's ambitious building projects. This detail is of the typical "double entry" city gates of Megiddo, a fortress city that controlled two vital trade routes. Extensive digging at Megiddo makes it one of the best known of Solomon's efforts. Building techniques used there have enabled scholars to identify other ruins as Solomonic.

Solomon was undoubtedly one of the greatest rulers of the ancient world. Most rulers counted on conquest to win a reputation. Solomon's 40-year reign was unmarred by war, and his fame rests on creative and constructive accomplishments. Solomon's temple was one of the world's wonders in its day, as was his palace. He built extensively throughout his kingdom, and was one of the most effective diplomats of any era. He dominated Middle Eastern land trade routes, and was the only Israelite king to ever successfully launch a fleet of trading ships (10:22). All these activities brought him vast wealth, which he spent lavishly to strengthen and beautify his kingdom. Solomon's era was also a golden age for literature. Solomon himself contributed love poetry (Songs), philosophy (Ecc.), and pithy proverbs rich in practical "how-to" advice on life in general (Prov.). His reputation brought visitors from all over the world to consult him (cf. 10:1-13).

Yet Solomon emerges as one of Scripture's most puzzling as well as most gifted personalities. His early years are marked by a zeal seldom matched in Hebrew rulers. Even before God appeared to Solomon, the young king offered thousands of freewill offerings, symbolic of dedication (3:1-5). Then he selflessly requested the wisdom needed to "distinguish between right and wrong" in governing God's people (vv. 8-9). He showed total commitment to finishing God's temple. And his prayer at its dedication (8:22-53) demonstrates a deep insight into the nature of God's relationship with believers. That prayer also contains one of Scripture's earliest and most powerful expressions of the truth that the Lord is God of all peoples, not only the chosen race (vv. 41-43). Yet Solomon, for all his early zeal and wisdom, violated God's special rules for kings (cf. Deut. 17:16-17). In cementing treaties with foreign nations he "married many wives," and in his passion for them not only permitted them to worship their pagan deities but also began to worship them himself. The Book of Ecclesiastes records the confusion and emptiness of Solomon's last years, and demonstrates again that even the most vast human intelligence is not a substitute for simple faith.

Outline
Place
Finder

UNITED
DIVIDED
CONFLICT

Chapter summary. The main highlights of Solomon's long reign are summed up in these three chapters. The account begins with a second appearance of God to Solomon, reaffirming promises, but also warning Solomon. He and his sons must carefully keep God's commandments (9:1-9). The source of Solomon's vast labor force is revealed (vv. 10-24), and his faithfulness in worship is underscored (v. 25). We are also told how Solomon was able to train crews for his sea trading ventures (vv. 26-28). The fame won by Solomon's intellectual achievements is illustrated by the visit of the Queen of Sheba, who travels over 1,000 miles to question him (10:1-13). His overwhelming wealth is illustrated and its sources are identified (vv. 14-29). But then, suddenly, the bright picture of unbroken success is overshadowed by tragedy. Solomon's passion for his foreign wives becomes so great that they influence Solomon to turn away from God, and join them (11:1-8). His betrayal of the God who has appeared to Solomon twice calls for judgment. The kingdom will be divided (vv. 9-13). So, near the end of Solomon's reign, foreign (vv. 14-25) and domestic enemies arise (vv. 26-39). As he nears the end of his life Solomon becomes the desolate man revealed in Ecclesiastes, and futilely tries to overturn the will of God by attempts on the life of Jeroboam, destined to rule 10 of Israel's 12 tribes when the kingdom divides (v. 40). After a spectacular but unfulfilling reign, Solomon, history's wisest man but most foolish lover, dies (vv. 41-43).

Key verses. 9:6-7: Success and failure depend on spiritual rather than material considerations.

Personal application. Our greatest strengths are meaningless unless we remain faithful to the Lord.

INSIGHT

God's second appearance (9:2). The text places the appearance of God to Solomon about his 24th year. Why then? The text says Solomon had "achieved all he had desired to do." As long as he was striving toward a goal, Solomon was spiritually secure. His life had meaning and purpose, and he felt the need to rely on God. But when all was accomplished, and Solomon in effect "retired," he was in great spiritual danger. God's appearance to Solomon at this spiritual crossroads was a gracious warning to him—and to us. Let's make it our goal to serve God daily, in whatever work we do, and in whatever relationships we may develop.

"Integrity of heart" (9:4). The O.T. suggests six things to do with all our heart that will keep our hearts pure. These are (1) Serve Him (Deut. 11:13); (2) Keep His Word (26:16); (3) Love Him (30:6); (4) Follow Him (1 Sam. 12:14); (5) Seek Him (2 Chron. 15:12); and (6) Praise Him (Ps. 86:12).

The consequences of disobedience (9:6-9). God's warning was a shout to gain Solomon's attention, not a whisper. The threatened consequences are frightening, as three Heb. words reveal. *Karat* ("cut off," v. 7) is a drastic term used of serious offenses that banish offenders from God's presence. *Sillah* ("reject," v. 7) is the word for divorce, and implies great grief in the shattering of an intimate relationship. *Masai* and *seninah* ("byword" and "object of ridicule," v. 7) describe a stunning misfortune which exposes one to the ridicule of others. It truly is costly for anyone who turns away from the Lord.

"Slave labor" (9:15-23). Throughout the era of the Judges and even into the early monarchy, centers existed where survivors of the original inhabitants of Canaan still lived (cf. Gen. 15:19; Jud. 3:1-5). Solomon now enslaved them and put them to work on his building projects, using Israelites to supervise their work and man his army.

Solomon's ships (9:26-28). Israel was a rich agricultural land, and its people have been men and women of the land. The land has always maintained a strong grip on the Jewish psyche. The Arabians might leave home to travel with trade caravans—but not the Jew. The fact that Solomon built a fleet and manned it with Jewish sailors gives us insight into the visionary character of his rule. Solomon was not a traditionalist!

"Sheba" (10:1). Sheba probably lay in southwest Arabia (modern Yemen). It was fertile, but also a center of trade, with route leading to Africa, India, and the Mediterranean coast. It is not at all surprising word of Solomon reached Sheba.

The queen's questions (10:3). The Heb. calls these "hard questions," or "riddles." Our impression is that the Queen determined to test Solomon. We might say she was on a "fact-finding junket," and after a careful examination of his bureaucracy was overwhelmed.

The exchange of gifts (10:10-13). It is likely that the exchange of "gifts" is a polite way of describing a trade agreement.

Who was the Queen, really? Romantic legends have grown up around the visit of the Queen of Sheba. The Talmud casts her as a witch, who seduced Solomon. Some Jewish legends say that the gift "desired and asked for" (v. 13) was a son, which Solomon provided. Most likely the Queen was simply an active ruler, who went on a long journey to satisfy her curiosity and to negotiate trade agreements with the wealthy kingdom.

Solomon's gold (10:14-15). The text puts Solomon's annual income from trade at about four and one half tons of gold. More came from taxes on the caravans that passed along major trade routes Solomon controlled by selling franchises on government trade monopolies, and by gifts brought by those seeking an audience with Solomon (v. 25). Some have doubted that the vast amounts of gold credited to Solomon could be correct. »p. 224.

Solomon's chariots (10:26-29). The development of a chariot army violated laws laid down for kings in Deut. 17. This most likely was to keep Israel from relying on military might, for chariots were the most powerful weapon system known in the ancient world. At one time it was thought some of the stables for Solomon's chariot army had been uncovered at Megiddo. Later studies indicate this particular ruin was probably a warehouse rather than stables. For some reason Solomon is not rebuked for this sin. Perhaps this is because the law he did violate, marrying foreign wives, led to such deadly consequences. Every sin is important. Yet those which can harm us or others greatly are more serious.

Disaster by degrees (11:1-13). Solomon did not wake up one morning and decide, "I guess I'll go worship a foreign god." Instead Solomon's decline was by slow degrees: he married foreign wives. He loved them. He let them worship their gods. He built houses of worship for his wives' gods. He became accustomed to idolatry, and only then did he slip into the practice of idolatry himself.

What a warning this is for us. The first step of disobedience leads slowly, but inexorably, to more and greater sins. Let's not take that first step, but obey God fully.

Don't let familiarity rob you of your awareness that sin is sin, and wrongdoing is wrong, whatever the circumstances.

"Held fast to them in love" (11:2). These words indicate a strong emotional attachment, the kind of commitment one wants to see in marriage. But Solomon was committed to the wrong women! And in order to bond to them he willingly broke his close connection with the Lord.

Let's not be the slaves of our emotions. We can and must choose what to love. And we must love nothing or no one more than the Lord.

"Ashtoreth" (11:5-8). This Canaanite deity was a fertility goddess. »p. 162. Her worship involved fertility rites, in which Solomon must have taken some part. Solomon's decline was moral as well as spiritual. Don't expect to maintain high moral standards unless you maintain complete commitment to God as an anchor.

God who had appeared to him twice (11:9-10). The simple phrase reminds us of the high privileges enjoyed by Solomon. The closer one has been to God, the more terrible disobedience becomes.

Three adversaries (11:14-40). After Solomon abandoned God, three enemies emerged to make his last years stressful. Hadad, a member of Edom's royal family, was intensely hostile to Israel (cf. 2 Sam. 8:13-14), and encouraged resistance to Solomon's occupying forces while preparing for rebellion. Rezon, a military officer in the Syrian forces defeated by David, seized Damascus and threatened Solomon's control of vital trade routes. Jeroboam, an ambitious Israelite, stirred up unrest in Israel itself. Solomon must have known intense frustration as all he had built seemed in danger of falling apart. How foolish he had been to abandon the Lord for idolatry.

God and Jeroboam (11:27-39). The Prophet Ahijah tells Jeroboam he will rule 10 of Israel's tribes. If he will be faithful to God, his own dynasty will be confirmed, as David's was. The question now is, will Jeroboam learn from Solomon's fall? The safest way to learn is from experience—the experience of someone else!

Outline
Place
Finder

UNITED
DIVIDED
CONFLICT

Chapter summary. Solomon is succeeded by his son, Rehoboam (12:1). But Jeroboam leads a delegation of the 10 tribes to demand that the heavy taxes imposed by Solomon be reduced (vv. 2-4). Rehoboam foolishly disregards the advice of his older counselors, and threatens to make the tax burden even heavier (vv. 5-15). At this the northern tribesmen return home, and when Rehoboam tries to collect taxes, his representatives are stoned (vv. 16-19). When the northern tribes acclaim Jeroboam king, Rehoboam raises an army (vv. 20-21). But the army is disbanded when the Prophet Shemaiah forbids civil war (vv. 22-24). In the meantime Jeroboam sets out on a course of outright disobedience, ignoring the conditional promise given him years earlier by the Lord (cf. 11:38). He decides that he must keep his citizens from going up to Jerusalem to worship the Lord. So he institutes a worship system that mimics the pattern given Moses, and gives lip service to the worship of Yahweh (12:25-33). This apostate system, with its illegitimate priesthood, illicit sacrifices and festivals, and images of bulls, will be maintained by every succeeding northern king and for centuries will cause Israel to sin.

Key verse. 12:24: Rehoboam was foolish, but not disobedient.

Personal application. It is as foolish for ordinary people as for kings to disregard God's promise and act out of fear.

Key concepts. Israel »p. 53. Calf »p. 126. Worship »p. 88.

INSIGHT

Taxes (12:4). Despite the wealth of Israel in Solomon's day not everyone experienced prosperity. The need for exports to pay for Solomon's building materials, and for workers to staff his projects, placed a heavy burden on the average person.

Counsel of others (12:6-11). In critical times it is wise to get advice from others. If we seek advice from several sources, someone is likely to suggest the best way to deal with our situation. But it is up to us to decide which advice to follow! Here many persons make their mistake. As this biblical incident illustrates, we need to seek God's guidance when facing any critical decision. »p. 720.

The kingdom divides (12:16). From this point on, in 730 B.C., the Heb. people were divided into two, often mutually hostile, kingdoms. The North, composed of 10 tribal groups, is known as Israel, while the South, taking in the territory originally given the tribe of Judah, is known as Judah (see p. 219).

Jeroboam's fears (12:26-27). Jeroboam had a purely political motive in setting up Yahweh worship centers at Bethel and Dan. He failed to take God's promise to him into account

(11:38), because he could not imagine that theological unification of the Hebrew people would not lead to political reunification. Human wisdom often dictates one course while faith calls us to risk another. How much wiser it is to follow the path illuminated by faith.

Dan and Bethel. These two sites were chosen because they had historic associations with worship of the Lord (cf. Jud. 18:27-31; Gen. 28:16-22; 35:1-4). However, God expressed His intention to establish a worship center, and that lay in Jerusalem.

The calves (12:28). These were not idols, but were intended to replace the ark of the covenant as symbols of God's presence. Ancient Middle Eastern faiths frequently envisioned deities as seated or standing on cattle.

Israel's worship system. The elements of the system Jeroboam designed were maintained by all the kings of Israel. It was characterized by shrines at Bethel and Dan, a non-Aaronic priesthood, festivals counterfeiting those the O.T. commanded. The Prophet Amos cried out over a century later, "Go to Bethel and sin" (Amos 4:4). Worship in the North could never be acceptable to God.

Chapter summary. Jeroboam, Israel's king, has set up his own state church as a rival to Jerusalem, despite the fact his system violates Moses' Law. These chapters announce the divine condemnation of Jeroboam and of his apostate religion.

God sends a prophet from Judah to the worship center at Bethel. There, as Jeroboam presents an offering, the man of God loudly condemns the altar and predicts its destruction (13:1-6). On the way home the man of God violates God's command, and is killed by a lion (vv. 7-32). The incident is a stern warning against ignoring God's Word. But Jeroboam will not change his ways (vv. 33-34). Later, when a son of Jeroboam falls ill, the Prophet Ahijah announces doom for Jeroboam and all his offspring (14:1-20). Judah too apostatizes under Rehoboam. She is punished by an Egyptian invasion that strips Solomon's glorious temple of its gold (vv. 21-31, »p. 224).

Outline
Place
Finder

UNITED
DIVIDED
CONFLICT

Key verse. 13:33: Some sins demand judgment.

Personal application. Each of us is responsible to respond to God's will as we understand it, whatever others may say.

Key concepts. Altar »p. 79. Man of God »p. 182. Prophet »p. 131. Prophecy »p. 434. Prostitution »pp. 45, 146.

INSIGHT

Authenticating signs (13:1-6). Immediately fulfilled predictions and miracles authenticated the messages delivered by O.T. prophets. Here we find both: the altar splits open as predicted (v. 5), and Jeroboam's arm withers and is restored (vv. 4, 6).

Why was the man of God from Judah killed? Commentators have puzzled over this story. Some have seen it as a parable concerning revelation: how can we recognize a true word from God? Yet the man from Judah had already demonstrated that his word from God was authentic, so no question about revelation remained. The key to interpretation seems to lie in 13:33: "Even after this, Jeroboam did not change his evil ways." The man of God from Judah died for violating the command of God. Despite this omen, Jeroboam persisted in his ways. And he found many eager to be priests, in clear violation of God's word.

Lessons for living. (1) Note that God did not send the "old prophet" of Israel, but a prophet of Judah. Could the old prophet have been jealous, and lied on purpose? Watch out for jealousy! (2) The man of God from Judah faithfully delivered God's message—but was easily led to disobey God's word to him. Being used by God does not release us from the need for personal obedience. (3) The man of Judah mistook another's word for that of God. Each of us is responsible to God for our choices. We must accept that responsibility, and act on what we believe God's will to be.

Why did Jeroboam's wife bring only bread? (14:1-3) Bread was the correct gift. In the East those seeking healing brought food, whether rich or poor.

"Ahijah" (14:2). It is possible that Jeroboam sent his wife to Ahijah because Ahijah had announced God would give him the 10 northern tribes (cf. 11:34-40). We tend to consult with folks who tell us what we want to hear. But Ahijah's message was one of devastating judgment. The word we hear from God doesn't depend on the messenger, but on our own actions. We're rewarded as we deserve.

Why Abijah? (14:12-13) The death of the only son of Jeroboam, the only one in Jeroboam's house in whom the Lord had found anything good is illuminated by Isaiah 57:1-2. "The righteous perish, and no one ponders it in his heart; devout men are taken away, and no one understands that the righteous are taken away to be spared from evil. Those who walk uprightly enter into peace; they find rest as they lie in death."

Judah's sins (14:21-24). Rehoboam permitted and perhaps promoted the idolatry that Solomon's wives had reintroduced. Reference to cult prostitutes shows the extent to which old Canaanite practices corrupted biblical religion.

Outline
Place
Finder

UNITED
DIVIDED
CONFLICT

Chapter summary. The division of Solomon's empire into two competing kingdoms is complete. The author of Kings now provides a quick survey of the rulers of both kingdoms between 913 B.C. and 874 B.C. In Judah, Rehoboam is succeeded by a wicked son, Abijah (15:1-8). In just three years he gives way to Asa, Judah's first godly king. Asa's 41-year reign is marked by strife, but also by one of those religious revivals stimulated by Judah's all-too-infrequent pious rulers (vv. 9-24). In Israel, Jeroboam's dynasty is brought to a bloody end as Baasha assassinates Nadab (vv. 25-32). Baasha's evil rule lasts 24 years (15:33–16:7), but his son Elah is assassinated in turn by Zimri (vv. 8-14). Zimri rules seven days, then commits suicide when the army commander, Omri, takes the capital (vv. 15-20). Civil war ensues, and finally the forces of Omri defeat those of another claimant to the throne, Tibni (vv. 21-24). Omri ruled 12 years (vv. 25-28) and was succeeded by his son, Ahab (vv. 29-34). Religious revival has brought stability to Judah. In the North, abandoning God has unleashed evil.

Key verse. 15:14: One thing in life seems most important.

Personal application. No society that abandons God's moral standards can avoid wickedness and strife.

INSIGHT

"**Abijah**" **(15:1-8).** Abijah might be called one of Judah's "forgettable" kings. How much better to be memorable, as David was, for lifelong dedication to God.

"**Asa**" **(15:9-24).** Asa is the first truly pious ruler of Judah. Each pious king's rule was characterized by a religious revival and God's

blessing. For an overview of revivalism, »p. 233.

The "**stone curtain**" **(15:17).** Over 2,500 years ago Baasha of Israel tried to wall Israel off so none of his people could leave or enter "the territory of Judah." A comparison of the relative forces raised in Judah when the kingdom divided (2 Chron. 11:1) and a few years later (13:3) indicates that many in the North actually moved to Judah in order to worship God correctly. The "stone curtain," like the modern iron curtain, was intended not for defense, but to keep citizens in!

Assassination. The prevalence of assassination in the North stands in contrast to David's restraint in refusing to kill Saul when he had the opportunity (1 Sam. 24; 26). In abandoning God, the kings of Israel destroyed respect for the throne, and sealed their own destruction!

Illustration. *The famous Moabite stone, a stela erected by Mesha, king of Moab after the death of Ahab, tells of Moab's conquest by Omri and later battle for freedom in the time of his successor Ahab. Assyrian records reflect the respect he won, for decades later they identify Palestine as bit-Humria, the House of Omri. Excavations in Samaria show the extent of the capital Omri established. Yet Omri is dismissed in the O.T. account with a few scant verses that mention his evil ways. What man considers historically important is less important ultimately than relationship with God.*

Revivals in Judah

Many differences between the history of Israel and Judah hinge on the fact that one kingdom's course was altered again and again by religious revivals. The Northern Kingdom survived just over 200 years. During that time it was governed by nine dynasties and 20 different kings. Each of Israel's kings is dismissed with the grim note that he "did evil" in God's eyes. Many prophets were active in Israel during its two-century existence, but the course chosen by the rulers was reflected in the lives of Israel's citizens. In the end the North was invaded by Assyria, and its population deported from the Promised Land.

Judah maintained its independent existence for nearly 350 years. During that time it was ruled by 19 kings, all belonging to one dynastic family, that of David. Though less exposed to military pressure from the north, Judah struggled with the same local enemies as her sister kingdom. Judah also struggled against the same religious influences, and all too often a generation or two succumbed and turned to paganism. But eight of Judah's kings are identified as "good" in the Old Testament. And four led notable religious revivals. These revivals came at critical junctures, and were keys to preserving the nation. Each godly king who brought revival enjoyed a long reign.

Asa (910–869 B.C.). About to be invaded by Egypt, Asa's prayer of humble dependence on God is answered with a great victory. Afterward the Prophet Azariah urges Asa to cleanse Judah of idolatry, and repair the temple altar in Jerusalem. Thousands move from Israel to Judah to participate in a great revival worship festival (1 Kings 15:9-24; 2 Chron. 14:2–16:4).

Jehoshaphat (872–848 B.C.). The crisis in his time is religious, as Ahab and Jezebel in the North attempt to install Baal as Israel's national deity. Jehoshaphat trusts God when attacked by a combined Moabite/Ammonite force. He removes the shrines that dot his land, and sends out itinerant Levites to teach God's Law throughout his land (1 Kings 22:41-50; 2 Chron. 17–20).

Hezekiah (715–686 B.C.). Hezekiah rules during the years Assyria crushes Israel. The Assyrians also invade Judah, and destroy her fortified defensive cities. But Hezekiah has spiritually prepared his people. He has reopened the closed temple, restored public worship there, and begun to hold the ancient festivals commanded in Moses' Law. He too has tried to cleanse the land of high places where idolatrous worship takes place. God answers Hezekiah's prayer, and the Assyrians withdraw (2 Kings 18–20; 2 Chron. 29–32).

Josiah (640–609 B.C.). This last and most zealous of Judah's godly kings lives in the turbulent days when Assyria is crushed by rising Babylonian power. Josiah too, vigorously destroys pagan altars and worship centers. With total dedication, and guided by rediscovered lost books of Scripture, Josiah recalls the Levites to serve at the temple, and reinstitutes the Passover celebration. With similar zeal Josiah seeks to wipe out paganism in his land (2 Kings 22:1–23:20; 2 Chron. 34–35).

Each revival is stimulated by the personal commitment to God of a single influential individual. You and I may not be rulers, but we can take the lead in commitment and be used by God to influence others. Each revival involved a purging of everything that competed for the people's religious allegiance. Each revival featured the purification and restoration of worship. Each revival was marked by a humble dependence on God to act. And the greatest revivals were stimulated and guided by God's Word.

Outline
Place
Finder

UNITED
DIVIDED
CONFLICT

Chapter summary. The division of Judah and Israel, and the hostility between the two kingdoms, is merely background for the real conflict. And that is the never-ending struggle between the kingdom of God and the kingdom of Satan. First Kings 17–22 focuses squarely on this struggle, with the Prophet Elijah representing Yahweh, and Israel's King Ahab, a savage paganism. We are hurtled, with no introduction, into the middle of this ferocious spiritual war.

Elijah announces that no rain will fall in Israel except at his word (17:1), and promptly the prophet disappears into the desert, where he is fed by ravens (vv. 2-6). When the drought dries up the brook by which Elijah is camped, he leaves Israel for Zarephath, in Sidon (vv. 7-9). There Elijah miraculously extends the dwindling food supply of a widow and her son. When the son dies, Elijah restores him to life (vv. 10-24). These miracles remind us that in the invisible war God is concerned with preserving individuals, despite hardships national judgment may bring.

Key verse. 17:24: Not just the act but its character marks the man of God.

Personal application. However great the issue, never lose concern for individuals who are affected.

INSIGHT

Background. Ahab (873–851 B.C.) was one of Israel's strongest kings. He maintained military superiority over Syria, and in a vital battle with the Assyrians at Qarqar in 854 B.C., Ahab supplied the largest single force to the allied Palestinian forces that threw them back. Yet Ahab was an essentially weak individual. Spurred on by his strong-willed wife Jezebel, Ahab established Baal worship and licentious Asherah rites in Samaria itself, and set out to make his virulent form of Baal worship the official religion of Israel. No wonder 16:33 says that "Ahab did more to provoke the Lord . . . to anger than did all the kings of Israel before him."

Elijah. God's champion is Elijah, one of the O.T.'s most human and fascinating prophets. As God's spokesman, Elijah announces a devastating drought. He also defeats the prophets of Baal in a public contest between the gods. This pivotal event holds the wavering population of Israel back from full commitment to Baal, and forces the people to acknowledge Yahweh's superiority. In a final confrontation Elijah announces Ahab's coming death.

Other prophets of the Lord play a role in the conflict between God and Satan, but Elijah's role is central. As a human being Elijah reminds us that it takes courage for the believer to take a stand for God, and that commitment is often lonely. Yet Elijah also reminds us that one person who does stand up for the Lord really can hold back the forces of evil.

Drought (17:1). Drought was an appropriate weapon in this conflict. Baal and Asherah (»p. 162) were nature deities, supposed to control the rains and the fertility of the ground. By announcing a drought in the name of the Lord, Elijah demonstrated conclusively that Yahweh, not Baal, is supreme.

"Zarephath" (17:9). The town to which God sent Elijah was in Jezebel's homeland! What a message this teaches us. When Baalism entered Israel, the result was a devastating drought that crippled the land. But when Yahweh's prophet entered a foreign land, he brought hope to a starving widow and even restored her son to life!

One indication of the validity of our faith is its impact on individuals. Today as in Elijah's day the messenger of God must bring compassion and healing as well as truth.

Daily supply. How significant that the prophet did not bring a massive food supply. The little that the widow had proved always to be enough. God stretched supplies to meet daily needs. It is the same for us today. Jesus calls us to depend on Him for "daily bread" (Matt. 6:11). How good to know that we can.

Chapter summary. Three years of drought have drained the land of Israel of its vitality, and the next battle in the invisible war for the hearts of God's people is about to take place. God sends Elijah to Ahab (18:1). On the way he meets Obadiah, a court official who has remained faithful to the Lord, and arranges a meeting with the king (vv. 2-15). Elijah challenges Ahab to call the prophets of Baal and Asherah to a now-famous contest at Mount Carmel. The prophets, trailed by crowds of people, come from all over the land (vv. 16-19). There Elijah cries out to the wavering people of Israel to follow the deity who is truly God. Baal does not respond to the cries of his prophets. But the Lord does answer Elijah, with fire from heaven that consumes his sacrifice. Now the people decide! "The Lord, He is God!" (vv. 20-39) At Elijah's command they enthusiastically slaughter the prophets of Baal (v. 40). A tiny cloud appears on the horizon, and soon a heavy rain falls at last on the parched land. God's people, though not the king and queen, have acknowledged Him again. And He is quick to bless them.

Outline
Place
Finder

UNITED
DIVIDED
CONFLICT

Key verse. 18:24: Answers still mark the Lord as God.

Personal application. We must trust God if He is to bless us.

Key concepts. Baal »p. 162. Prophet »p. 131. Sacrifice »pp. 28, 78.

INSIGHT

"Horses and mules" (18:5). Ahab's concern was military. At Qarqar he supplied 2,000 chariots to the combined forces. The famine was so great he feared he would have to kill his horses, and strip himself of military might.

"Obadiah" (18:4). How could Obadiah be a worshiper of the Lord and still serve the corrupt royal house of Ahab? Shouldn't he have taken a stand against Jezebel's murder of God's prophets, even if it cost him his own life? Some have thought so. Yet Obadiah was able to use his position to save the lives of a hundred prophets! It's easy to criticize those who have difficult moral decisions to make. But each individual must be guided by his or her own sense of God's leading. What may appear to us to be "compromise" may instead be a courageous decision to follow a difficult and dangerous course.

Sincerely wrong. The willingness of Ahab to summon Baal's prophets, and the loud prayers of the prophets of Baal, suggest Ahab and his prophets had a sincere faith in Baal. But the test is whether one's god is real.

Shouting for Baal (18:26-29). Elijah's ridicule was based on pagan theology. Myths associated with Middle Eastern gods pictured them engaged in the same kind of activities as humans. The taunts picture Baal as a disinter-

ested god: too busy with his own affairs to be troubled by the cries of his servants. The prophets of Baal cut themselves because their myths pictured the god as being aroused by the odor of blood.

Water in a drought? (18:33) Some have ridiculed the Elijah story, saying there would be no water available in a three-year drought. There are, however, springs on Mount Carmel and in the Kishon Valley below that do not depend on rainfall.

Proof, positive. The people of Israel definitely had wavered between the religion of Baal so aggressively supported by Ahab and Jezebel, and the religion of Yahweh (v. 21). The fire from heaven, which recalls an incident reported in Lev. 9:23-26, compelled belief. The killing of the prophets of Baal was also evidence: evidence that the people were ready to turn back to God.

Prayer (18:42). Facedown on one's knees was the posture for fervent prayer.

Go, before the rain stops you (18:44). Elijah had announced the rains would return, and prayed to that end. He did not expect sprinkles, but a downpour, and told Ahab to hurry. What an example for us. If we have a prayer meeting for rain, we'd better bring an umbrella.

Outline
Place
Finder

UNITED
DIVIDED
CONFLICT

Chapter summary. When Jezebel hears of the events on Mt. Carmel (1 Kings 18) she is unawed, and threatens Elijah's life. Suddenly, inexplicably, Elijah is terrified, and flees (19:1-5a). God's response to His troubled prophet encourages all who suffer depression or despair. God gives Elijah strength to flee (vv. 5b-8), speaks gently (vv. 9-13), listens to Elijah's doubts and fears (v. 14), gives Elijah tasks to do (vv. 15-17), encourages him (v. 18), and also gives him a companion who will be his friend as well as student (vv. 19-21). What a reminder that God is aware of our frailty.

Key verse. 19:18: We are never really alone.

Personal application. When you fear or fail, don't be harder on yourself than God is.

Key concepts. Survivors »p. 427. Anoint »p. 187. Angel of the Lord »p. 37.

INSIGHT

"Jezebel" (19:1-2). Jezebel's words are a challenge; a threat opening formal hostilities. Had the queen wished, she might have sent soldiers to arrest Elijah rather than mere messengers. Jezebel is unquestionably the moral power behind the weak Ahab. With her prophets killed, and her husband humbled, Jezebel seems to say to Elijah, "Now you have to face *me!*"

No matter how many victories we win in our personal and spiritual life, there is always a new foe to overcome. Strangely, we are most vulnerable to fear during the letdown that always seems to follow a triumph.

Despair (19:4). Researchers say that over 50 percent of the women in the U.S. have serious problems with depression. So many of us can understand the darkness that seemed to settle over Elijah and make him wish he were dead. What makes this scene so helpful is that there seems no reason for Elijah's despair. Like many who suffer from depression today, Elijah had experienced many and great blessings. All too often when such unexplainable bouts come, things are made worse by the feeling that one shouldn't be depressed. If this ever happens to you, remember Elijah — and remember that God isn't angry with Elijah, but gently helps him deal with his emotions.

God's remedy for depression. Doctors today believe that most depression is chemically based rather than psychological. Whatever the basis of depression, God's way of dealing with Elijah helps us see how to help ourselves. Note these steps: (1) Don't blame yourself. God didn't blame, and was even willing to provide nourishment so His prophet could run away (vv. 7-8). (2) Express your feelings. Elijah needed to talk, even though what he says seems only loosely related to the fear that triggered his bout of depression. You can express your feelings freely to the Lord, or find someone willing to serve as God's listening post (v. 10). (3) Remember God speaks to the hurting in gentle whispers. Don't imagine God is angry or disgusted with you (vv. 11-14). (4) Return to work. Inactivity feeds depression. God had a task for Elijah that would give him a renewed sense of purpose (vv. 15-17). (5) Reality-test your perceptions. Anyone who is feeling despair will have his or her view of things colored by the emotion. Elijah felt alone, but God told His prophet he was one of thousands who worship Him. Let facts shape your feelings, rather than letting your feelings distort the facts (v. 18). (6) Share with a friend. If you have no close friends, ask the Lord to give you a companion. Loneliness and depression often walk hand in hand (vv. 19-21).

Ministering to the depressed. If you have a friend or loved one who suffers from depression, you can apply the principles above to help them.

Elijah's tasks. The men Elijah was sent to anoint played critical roles in Israel's immediate future. Hazael of Syria (Aram) became a chief foe of Israel (2 Kings 8:7-15). Jehu wiped out the family of Ahab and the Baal cult in Israel, though for political rather than religious reasons (cf. 9:1-13). And Elisha, Elijah's successor, nourished the return to Yahweh that Elijah's public triumph over the priests of Baal stimulated.

Chapter summary. God continues to demonstrate His power to Ahab by giving Israel victories over the Syrian enemy. The famine which has just ended has weakened Israel. Ben-Hadad of Syria seizes the opportunity to march against Samaria, Ahab's capital, and demands abject surrender (20:1-9). Ahab refuses (vv. 10-12), and a prophet promises Israel victory (v. 13). Ahab asks the prophet instructions, and when he follows them, Israel is victorious (vv. 14-21). The next year when Syria invades again, the same prophet promises another victory (vv. 22-30). Again Israel is victorious, but Ahab foolishly makes a treaty with the defeated Ben-Hadad and lets him live (vv. 31-34). Now another prophet reenacts Ahab's sin in releasing the enemy of God's people, and announces that Ahab himself will die in Ben-Hadad's place (vv. 35-42). Rather than repent, a sullen and angry Ahab returns to Samaria (v. 43).

Outline
Place
Finder

UNITED
DIVIDED
CONFLICT

Key verse. 20:43: Reactions display basic attitudes.

Personal application. Be aware of how God's goodness to you can honor Him in the eyes of others.

INSIGHT

Ben-Hadad. The name is a dynastic rather than a personal name. This ruler is most likely Ben-Hadad II. Probable dates of the kings of Syria (Aram, Damascus) are Ben-Hadad I (885–860 B.C.), Ben-Hadad II (860–842 B.C.), Hazael (841–802 B.C.), and Ben-Hadad III (802–780? B.C.). During this era Israel and Syria were trade rivals, and frequently at war.

Why abject surrender? (20:4) Ahab's submission to Ben-Hadad's demand for his wealth, his women, and his children shows how greatly the three-year famine had depleted Israel's military power. Ben-Hadad then added to his demands, in an obvious effort to provoke war. Some speculate Ben-Hadad feared that Israel might ally itself with Assyria.

Proverbial wisdom (20:11). The preference in the ancient Middle East for proverbs is reflected in Ahab's classic reply to Ben-Hadad's demand. The Heb. is emphatic: "Tell him" means repeat exactly.

God's prophet (20:13). Elijah's defeat of the prophets of Baal at Carmel (chap. 18) established the Lord's superiority. Now a prophet's promise indicates God is willing to exercise His power for His people. Other lessons are taught in the passage. When a desperate Ahab asks for and follows the prophet's plan, Israel is victorious. As always, obedience leads to success. Later the prophet predicts another Syrian defeat, because they have no respect for God. The lessons? God has power to act for His people. God intends to act for His people. Obedience brings blessing. Disdain for God brings destruction. Will Ahab learn?

Why did Ahab spare Ben-Hadad? (20:31-34) At this time Assyria, under Shalmaneser III, was exerting tremendous pressure on Syria-Palestine. Ahab may well have wanted a relatively strong Aram as a buffer between Israel and Assyria. Later Ahab did join a coalition that defeated the Assyrians at Qarqar. If this was Ahab's motive, it indicates that he had not learned the spiritual lessons taught in recent events. Ahab was still not ready to rely on the Lord.

"Sons of the prophets" (20:35). The phrase has stimulated much debate. Some think the phrase indicates a kind of guild of prophets. Some think it indicates a sort of seminary, in which young men studied to become prophets. Others think it does no more than indicate adherents; persons who were followers of and studied under the prophets. It seems clear that in this text, one "son of the prophets" had and exercised the prophetic gift. Most see Samuel, some 200 years before these events, as the first "president" of such a group, and see Elijah and Elisha presiding over other such companies (cf. 2 Kings 2:3, 5, 7, 16; 4:38).

Mercy? (20:40) Irony dominates this passage. Ben-Hadad assumes the kings of Israel are merciful, and his life is spared. When one of Ahab's own soliders (so Ahab supposed) appeals for Ahab's judgment in his case, Ahab coldly condemns him! Clearly it was not mercy that moved Ahab to spare Ben-Hadad. And just as clearly the king who did himself what he condemned in others deserved no mercy from God (cf. Matt. 5:7).

Outline
Place
Finder

UNITED
DIVIDED
CONFLICT

Chapter summary. The spiritual conflict that raged in the time of Elijah demanded decision. At Mt. Carmel and in the war with Syria God revealed His power. Now Ahab reveals his response. Ahab is driven by a desire to possess a nearby vineyard, which the owner, Naboth, will not sell (21:1-6). Jezebel promises to get the vineyard for Ahab anyway. She arranges false witnesses who accuse Naboth of blasphemy and treason (vv. 7-14). When Naboth is dead, Ahab hurries off to take possession of the vineyard. He is met by Elijah, who announces God's judgment on the king and his house (vv. 15-26). But when Ahab humbles himself, God promises that the predicted disasters will not fall until the king is dead (vv. 27-29). In the invisible war, each person must choose good or evil, and face the consequences.

Key verses. 21:25-26: One's character is expressed in the pattern of his or her choice.

Personal application. When a choice is demanded, let's be guided by God's Word and do what is right.

Key concepts. Evil »p. 72. Fasting »p. 442. Humble »p. 259.

INSIGHT

"Jezreel" (21:1). Ahab had a home in Jezreel in addition to his palace in the capital city of Samaria.

Why did Naboth refuse? (21:3) Ahab seems willing to pay a fair price for Naboth's land. But Naboth refused because the vineyard was an ancestral holding, and as such Moses' Law stated that it could not be sold (cf. Lev. 25). Ahab's response was to sulk, leading Jezebel to scorn him as weak.

Jezebel's plan (21:7-14). The Heb. reads literally, "You now; you are going to perform majesty over Israel." The saying seems to indicate that she will show Ahab how to magnify himself by having his way in Israel. Her use of the king's seal indicates that she had his authority for her plot against Naboth. Ahab lent her his full support.

Legal background. The "day of fasting" Jezebel called for suggests that she had the elders call an assembly to identify the cause of some recent disaster or difficulty (cf. Joel 1:14-18). Some suggest that the charge made by the two "scoundrels" was that Naboth went back on a pledge made in God's name to sell his land to the king. Failure to keep an oath made in God's name would be blasphemy. In that case, after Naboth's execution, the king could legally have taken possession of the property in dispute. Second Kings 9:26 adds that Naboth's sons were killed at the same time. With no heir left alive, there seemingly was no one left to dispute Ahab's claim to the land.

"Elijah" (21:17). Again Elijah himself is called to confront Ahab. The charge "you" murdered Naboth and seized his property makes it clear Ahab was a party to Jezebel's plot all along.

"Dogs" (21:19). Dogs were scavengers, who traveled in packs, and were held in contempt in the Middle East. The prediction that dogs would lick Ahab's and Jezebel's blood was equivalent to calling the king and queen garbage! The fulfillment of the prediction is reported in 22:38 and 2 Kings 9:36-37.

Ahab's character (21:20, 25-26). These verses sum up Ahab's character. God revealed Himself to Ahab in many ways, from severe judgments to acts of great grace. Neither moved the king, who "sold himself to do evil." While we are each faced with many different choices every day, there is a basic choice which sets the direction of our lives, and shapes our daily decisions. That choice is whether or not to commit ourselves to God and His ways. There is no middle ground, and this one decision is decisive in shaping our character.

"Jezebel" (21:25). Who we pick as a life partner does make a difference! So choose to be close only to those who urge you on to do good, not evil.

Ahab's repentance (21:27-28). Even though the outward signs of repentance did not signal a true change of heart in Ahab's case, the Lord was gracious and delayed judgment. Think what true repentance might have won!

Outline
Place
Finder

UNITED
DIVIDED
CONFLICT

Chapter summary. Ahab and King Jehoshaphat of Judah meet, probably to discuss the new international situation after the battle of Qarqar. Ahab feels he must occupy the strategic city of Ramoth Gilead, ceded to him by Ben-Hadad earlier (chap. 20), but never surrendered by the Arameans (22:1-3). Ahab asks Jehoshaphat's help, but Judah's king wants to consult the Lord. Ahab's prophets, members of the corrupted Yahweh cult established by Jeroboam (chap. 12), predict success. But Jehoshaphat wants to hear from a true prophet, and Micaiah is called (22:4-14). Micaiah's initial endorsement of Ahab's prophets' words drips so heavily with sarcasm that Ahab demands he tell the truth. Micaiah explains that a "lying spirit" has moved Ahab's prophets to predict victory, and that God does not intend Israel's king to survive this battle (vv. 15-28). Ahab goes into battle in disguise, but is mortally wounded by a "random" arrow (vv. 29-36). When his gory carriage is washed, dogs lick the wicked king's blood, as Elijah had predicted (vv. 37-40; cf. 21:19). The chapter closes with a brief mention of Jehoshaphat of Judah (22:41-50), and Ahab's successor, Ahaziah (vv. 51-53).

Key verse. 22:7: Important decisions call for guidance.

Personal application. God's spokesmen are often outnumbered. But that is no reason not to speak out with the truth.

INSIGHT

Jehoshaphat. Much more is told of this godly king of Judah in 2 Chron. 17–20. His only flaw seems to have been a penchant for joint ventures with the wicked kings of Israel.

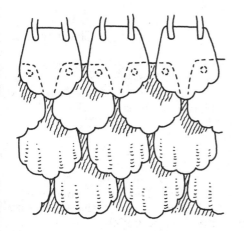

Illustration. *Ancient armor featured metal scales sewn on heavy cloth shirts. It was most vulnerable at the armpit, where there was space between sections. Ahab was probably struck here.*

Ramoth Gilead. The city was a key administrative center in Solomon's time (4:13), lost to Syria in the time of Omri, and ceded back to Ahab after a decisive victory over Ben-Hadad (20:34). As it controlled passes leading into Israel's heartland, Ahab felt compelled to occupy it, though the Syrians were not willing to let it go without a battle.

Ahab's prophets. These prophets were part of the corrupt state religion established by Israel's first king, Jeroboam I (chap. 12). Though nominally dedicated to the Lord, Israel's state religion was never recognized as valid by God. »p. 230. The fact that Ahab's prophets predicted what he wanted to hear, but that Micaiah "never prophesies anything good about me, but always bad," shows us that a "lying spirit" always animated those prophet's words.

Did God Himself lie to Ahab? Not at all. He did permit Ahab's prophets to lie in His name. God in fact clearly revealed to Ahab the source of his prophets' predictions, and the truth about what would happen to him in the coming battle. Ahab's death resulted from refusing to believe the truth, not from a failure to know it. Let's be careful not to blame God for the consequences of our own fully conscious choices.

2 Kings

Second Kings traces the history of the Divided Hebrew Kingdoms, Israel in the north, and Judah in the south, from about 850 B.C. to the destruction of Israel in 722 B.C. and of Judah in 586 B.C. For a general introduction see p. 218. The chart shows the rulers, prophets, and enemies of the kingdoms.

2 Kings chapter	Date	King of Israel	King of Judah	Prophet	Major foreign enemy
1	853	Ahaziah	Jehoshaphat		Assyria:
	859				Shalmaneser III
2–8	852	Joram			
8	848		Jehoram	Elisha	
	841		Ahaziah		Syria: Hazael
9–10	841	Jehu			
11	841	Athaliah			Syria:
					Ben-Hadad III
12	835		Joash	Joel?	
13	814	Jehoahaz			
	802				
	798	Jehoash			
14	796		Amaziah		
14–15	792	Jeroboam II	Uzziah	Micah	
				Amos	
				Jonah	
15	753	Zechariah			
	752	Shallum			
	752	Menahem		Hosea	Assyria:
	745				Tiglath-
					Pileser III
	742	Pekahiah			
	740	Pekah	Jotham	Micah	
16	735		Ahaz		
17	732	Hoshea			
	727				Shalmaneser V
	722	FALL OF NORTHERN KINGDOM			Sargon II
	705				Sennacherib
18–20	716		Hezekiah	Isaiah	
21	698		Manasseh		
	642		Amon		
22–23	640		Josiah	Habakkuk	
				Nahum	
				Zephaniah	
	605		FIRST DEPORTATION	Daniel	Babylon: Nebuchadnezzar
	608		Jehoahaz	Jeremiah	
24	608		Jehoiakim	Ezekiel	
24–25	598		Jehoiachin		
	598		Zedekiah		
	586		JERUSALEM'S FALL		

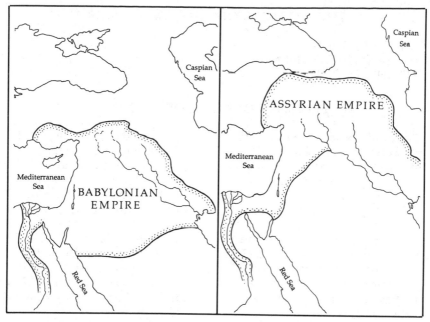

Assyrian Empire, 800 B.C.

Babylonian Empire, 538 B.C.

WHERE THE ACTION TAKES PLACE

Events in Israel and Judah were dramatically affected by emerging northern powers. The Assyrian Empire, pressing westward, was held back in the time of Ahab (map left, above). But within 50 years Syria was reduced to vassal status, and by 722 B.C. Israel no longer existed as a nation. But Assyria suffered a stunning fall to the Babylonians, who took Nineveh in 612 B.C., and by 605 B.C. dominated Judah and began to resettle its population.

---

2 KINGS AT A GLANCE

KEY PEOPLE

Elisha *This prophet succeeded Elijah. His ministry focused on rebuilding faith in the Northern Kingdom.*

Jehu *An army commander, he wiped out the family of Ahab, and became king.*

Joash *The only member of the Davidic line to survive assassination by his own grandmother, he became a godly king of Judah.*

Hezekiah *The godly king of Judah for whom God intervened to throw back the invading forces of the Assyrian, Sennacherib.*

Josiah *The last godly king of Judah, whose revival could not delay the fall of Judah beyond his own death.*

KEY EVENTS

The fall of Israel, 722 B.C. (2 Kings 17). *The legacy of an unbroken string of evil rulers in the North is exiled from the Promised Land.*

The fall of Jerusalem, 586 B.C. (2 Kings 25). *Judah, whose people followed the idolatrous lead of Israel, shares the northern nation's fate.*

THEOLOGICAL OUTLINE OF 2 KINGS

CONTENT OUTLINE OF 2 KINGS

Chapter summary. Elijah has been a fierce warrior in the conflict between God and evil during the reign of Ahab (1 Kings 17–21). He has defeated that king's attempt to establish Baal as Israel's national deity. But Elijah is not the man to rebuild the faith of Israel's masses. When Ahaziah, Ahab's son, consults a foreign deity, Elijah announces God's judgment: the king will die (2 Kings 1:1-8). Ahaziah sends soldiers to arrest Elijah, but the prophet calls down fire from heaven and kills a first and second delegation (vv. 9-12). The commander of the third troop begs for their lives. Instructed by an angel, Elijah goes with this troop and personally delivers God's message to Ahaziah: "You will surely die." Elijah, tuned to conflict rather than nurture, has served God's purpose well. But he is not the prophet needed now that victory is won (vv. 13-18).

Outline
Place
Finder

FAITH-BUILDING
DOWNFALL
DECLINE

Key verse. 1:15: Check motives before acting.

Personal application. Let's be sure when we confront or strike out at others that we're acting in faith rather than fear.

Key concepts. Man of God »p. 182.

INSIGHT

Ahaziah. First Kings 22:51-53 describes the king's brief rule and his commitment to the worship of Baal. During his two-year reign, Moab revolted against Israelite domination (2 Kings 1:1), and the king himself had a fatal accident (v. 2). God was speaking to him through judgments but the youthful king wasn't listening. When we suffer reverses, the first thing to do is turn to the Lord.

"Lattice" (1:2). Windows, balconies, and even rooftops of wealthy people's homes often boasted latticework. Cooling breezes easily passed through the crossed thin strips of light wood, and still offered individuals privacy. A lattice offered no support; Ahaziah tripped and fell through such a delicate screen.

"Baal-Zebub" (1:2). The original meaning of *Baal-Zebub* is uncertain. The traditional interpretation, "lord of flies," is doubtful. Some take it to mean "Baal prince," while others suggest "lord of fire." If this last is the meaning, Elijah's act in calling down fire from heaven to destroy the soldiers Ahaziah sent to take him is both ironic and symbolically significant.

Why did Ahaziah consult Baal-Zebub? (1:2) No specific reason is given, aside from the note in 1 Kings 22:53 that Ahaziah "served and worshiped Baal and provoked the Lord." We can, however, suggest possible reasons. Perhaps Ahaziah sent to a pagan deity to keep word of the seriousness of his injury from rivals. Perhaps, like his father, he was convinced that the Lord would give him an answer he did not want to hear (cf. v. 8). We can

always find reasons for not doing something we know is right. But we can never avoid the consequences of doing what is wrong.

Why destroy the soldiers? (1:9-14) The question can be answered on three levels. On one level, Ahaziah was judged by God for the arrogance and overt failure to show respect for the Lord implicit in inquiring of another deity. The first and second captains each displayed a similar arrogance, and suffered the same fate as Ahaziah. On a second level, by calling down fire Elijah again demonstrated the superiority of the Lord over the competing deity, Baal-Zebub. But on a third and very personal level, Elijah's response seems33to have been motivated by fear (cf. v. 15). Only when God gave Elijah His personal assurances did the prophet get up, and go to confront the dying king. In this case, the prophet's fear-motivated action did serve the divine purpose. But it is very unwise for us to be ruled by our fears, rather than by trust.

The third captain (1:13-14). We can also look at this story as an illustration of the tension between respect for earthly authorities and for God. The first two captains were arrogant, for they represented the king, and expected God's representative to tremble before them. The third captain had seen the power of God, and he bowed humbly to God's representative. In any conflict between God and the state, the punitive powers of human government are nothing, however great they may seem to be.

Outline
Place
Finder

FAITH-BUILDING
DOWNFALL
DECLINE

Chapter summary. The transition from the confronting ministry of Elijah to the faith-building ministry of Elisha is spectacular. As Elijah and his apprentice Elisha travel toward Jericho, the prophet urges his companion to remain behind (2:1-4). Elisha knows Elijah is about to be taken from him, and refuses to leave (vv. 5-6). Elijah parts the Jordan River and the two cross over on dry land. On the other side, Elisha asks to be Elijah's successor as Israel's premier prophet (vv. 7-9). When Elisha sees a chariot of fire and watches Elijah caught up to heaven in a whirlwind, he knows his request has been granted (vv. 10-12). Elisha returns to the Jordan, and parts the waters himself, confirming his succession (vv. 13-15). Though prophets from Jericho search for the missing Elijah, no sign of him is found (vv. 16-18). Meanwhile Elisha purifies the water supply of a nearby town, symbolizing the healing nature of his ministry (vv. 19-22). Yet when a group of young men publicly ridicule the prophet, his curse brings fierce bears out of the woods to maul them (vv. 23-25). The gentle tone of Elisha's ministry makes him no less a servant of God, and demands no less respect!

Key verse. 2:9: Elisha's desire was to serve.

Personal application. When service is our ambition, there will always be a place for us in God's work.

INSIGHT

Company of prophets (2:3). The revival stimulated by Elijah revitalized the prophetic movement in Israel. We read more about these groups in 1 and 2 Kings than any other O.T. books. Sons of the prophets »p. 237.

"A double portion" (2:9). The reference is to Deut. 21:17, which establishes the right of a father's principal heir to a double share in his estate. Elisha is asking to be the principal representative of God in this age of prophetic revival. Even more is implied: Elisha is expressing his sense of need for special spiritual endowment.

Twice the miracles! As is often pointed out, Elisha has 14 recorded miracles to 7 for Elijah, exactly double that prophet's portion. Elisha's 14 miracles are: (1) separating the Jordan's waters (2:14); (2) healing a spring (v. 21); (3) cursing scoffers (v. 24); (4) filling ditches with water (3:15-26); (5) multiplying a widow's oil (4:1-7); (6) predicting a pregnancy (vv. 14-17); (7) raising a dead son (vv. 32-37); (8) neutralizing poison (vv. 38-41); (9) mutiplying loaves (vv. 42-44); (10) healing Naaman's leprosy (5:1-19); (11) cursing Gehazi with leprosy (vv. 20-27); (12) trapping an Aramean military force (6:8-23); (13) revealing an angel army (vv. 15-16); and (14) predicting a relief for besieged Samaria (6:24–7:20).

Elijah taken up (2:11-12). Many believe Elijah was the second person taken directly to heaven. The other is Enoch, of whom the text says "God took him away" (Gen. 5:24).

"My father!" (2:12) The cry of anguished respect and a deep sense of loss is later repeated for Elisha himself (cf. 13:14).

Where is Yahweh? (2:14) The question does not indicate doubt. Elisha had seen the heavenly chariot and Elijah's ascent, and knew God had confirmed him as Elijah's successor (v. 10). In dividing the waters Elisha answered his question, and demonstrated to the watching prophets that God was with him.

Two miracles (2:19-25). The two miracles set a tone for Elisha's ministry, which first of all involves kindness, and secondly severity. In this Elisha reflects the character of the Lord, who keeps His covenant of love with those who love Him, and repays by destruction those who "hate" Him (cf. Deut. 7:9-10).

Forty-two youths (2:23). These were not boys or children, but young men. They did not so much ridicule Elisha as the notion that God could catch a person up into heaven. Their immediate judgment teaches all Israel that grace is not weakness. The Lord and His prophet must be held in awe.

Chapter summary. Judah joins Joram in a campaign to put down a Moabite revolt against Israel (3:1-7). After seven days the combined forces have exhausted their supply of water, and (at last) appeal to the Lord (vv. 8-11). Elisha replies for the sake of Judah's Jehoshaphat, and God not only supplies water but provides a military victory (vv. 2-27). Back in Israel, Elisha saves a widow and her family by causing an endless supply of olive oil to pour from her single jar (4:1-7). There he also not only promises a son to a childless woman (vv. 8-16), but later brings the child back to life when he suffers sunstroke (vv. 17-37). Elisha also neutralizes poison that has spoiled a company of prophets' stew (vv. 38-41), and prefigures one of Jesus' miracles by multiplying loaves of bread to feed a hungry multitude (vv. 42-44). Each of these miracles symbolizes God's ability to provide for human beings in need: security, sustenance, family, health, food, and life itself.

Outline
Place
Finder

FAITH-BUILDING
DOWNFALL
DECLINE

Key verse. 3:14: Miracles are performed for people.

Personal application. It is God who provides these same blessings for us today, through "natural" means.

INSIGHT

Joram (Jehoram). Kings with this same name ruled in Judah during much of Joram of Israel's reign. Israel's Joram is evaluated in 3:1-5.

Mesha of Moab. The Moabites had been subdued by David. But the Moabites apparently resisted Israelite domination even in Solomon's day, and in open rebellion from the end of Ahab's rule. The Israel/Judah coalition suggests Moab was a common foe and considerable threat. Mesha's name is known from the famous Moabite stone (»p. 232), and he ultimately won his country's independence.

Call a prophet (3:9-11). How like us King Jehoshaphat was. He thinks to seek God's guidance only when his own plans have gone awry. Let's inquire of the Lord first, before we act. »p. 127.

Whose firstborn son? (3:26-27) Scholars have debated the reason why Israel's soldiers returned home after Mesha's sacrifice. Some appeal to ancient texts that seem to record a ritual used in just such a situation, and argue that Israel was terrified that Mesha's sacrifice of his firstborn son would release demonic powers against them. Others speak of a supposed psychological impact of the act, and the horror it aroused. Perhaps a simpler solution is to suppose that Mesha did not sacrifice *his* firstborn son, but the son of the King of Edom! In this case the Edomite allies might have blamed Israel rather than the Moabites, and it would be the Edomite fury that divided the coalition and

forced Israel and Judah to return home.

"Slaves" (4:1-7). A person's family in O.T. times could be seized and sold into temporary slavery to pay a debt owed by the father. Elisha's act demonstrated God's concern for the widow and orphan, who symbolize the poverty-stricken and the powerless in the O.T. Refined olive oil was used in cooking, cosmetics, and burned as fuel in the light always kept burning in even the poorest Heb. home. It could easily be sold by the widow, the debt paid off, and the family's own needs met.

Better to have loved and lost? (4:8-37) Note the agonized Shunammite's cry, "Did I ask you for a son?" In the pain of our loss, it may seem that it would have been better never to have been given what we have lost. God's restoration of the woman's dead son reminds us that no believer's loss is permanent. Health and loved ones will both be restored when we are raised by the Lord, if not before. It is better to have loved and lost, because nothing that God gives us that we truly love can ever be lost.

Famine and food (4:38-44). Desperate need is the background for these two stories in which Elisha provides food for the hungry. God does provide our daily bread. In normal times He does it through normal means: crops grow, we work and earn the money needed to purchase food. We are no less dependent on the Lord in normal times than those Elisha fed in that time of ancient famine.

Outline
Place
Finder

FAITH-BUILDING
DOWNFALL
DECLINE

Chapter summary. The familiar story of the healing of Naaman illustrates God's compassion not only for His chosen people but even for their enemies. Naaman, the commander of Syria's army, has leprosy (5:1). When a captive Jewish girl speaks of a prophet in her homeland who can heal him, Naaman obtains permission to go to Israel (vv. 2-6). The King of Israel sees the Syrian's request for healing as an excuse for renewed war, but Elisha invites the king to send Naaman to him (vv. 7-8). Naaman's resentment at being told to dip seven times in the Jordan River dissolves when he does so, and is healed (vv. 9-14). Convinced now that Yahweh is God, Naaman promises to worship Him only, but obtains a dispensation for occasions when official duties require him to be present at religious ceremonies in his homeland (vv. 15-19). Elisha rejects the rich gifts offered by Naaman, but his servant Gehazi runs after the Syrian and accepts clothing and about 150 pounds of silver, a fortune (vv. 20-23). When Gehazi lies to Elisha, he is cursed with the leprosy of which Naaman was healed (vv. 24-27).

Key verse. 5:26: We are never unobserved.

Personal application. Good deeds and a lack of materialism are still marks of holiness.

Key concepts. Leprosy »p. 83. Anger »pp. 72, 196.

INSIGHT

The young girl (5:2). The Heb. suggests a girl under 12. How fascinating that this captive from Israel's borderlands was more aware than the king of the power God exercised through His prophet (cf. v. 7). The story is a healthy reminder. God can even use a child to spread word of His love.

"The Lord" (5:1). Two things explain the author's assertion that God had given Naaman his victories against Egypt. Heb. thought does not make sharp distinctions between effective, proximate, and other types of causation. Ultimately God is seen as behind all things that happen.

750 pounds of gold (5:4-5). The richness of the gifts Naaman brought to Israel, as well as his description as a "great man" who was "highly regarded" underlines his importance in Aram (Syria). It is striking that he gained that status by military victories won against Israel!

Naaman's anger (5:11). Naaman is angry when God does not behave as Naaman thinks He should! The reaction suggests something of his initial arrogance and pride. How very human to want a God who marches to our tune, rather than be willing to submit. The attitude Naaman reveals undoubtedly cuts more people off from God's grace than open, blatant sin.

Naaman's conversion. Naaman's healing in the Jordan caused a total revolution in his thinking. Naaman acknowledges the Lord as God (v. 15). He commits himself to worship the Lord only (v. 17). And Naaman reveals a transformation of his attitude when the once arrogant general humbly gets down from his chariot to greet a mere servant of God's prophet. True conversion involves all three of these elements: acknowledgment of the Lord as God; commitment to Him only; and an inner transformation of attitude that expresses itself in our actions.

Why did Naaman take home earth from Israel? In O.T. thought, foreign lands were polluted by the existence there of idolatry (cf. Josh. 22:19; Hosea 9:3-5; Amos 7:17). In taking back earth from Israel Naaman acknowledged that the Lord is the God of Israel.

Naaman's request (5:18-19). "Go in peace" means that Elisha did give the exemption.

"Gehazi" (5:20-27). Sometimes those closest to God's exercise of His power take it so for granted that the supernatural seems ordinary. How else could Gehazi have expected to deceive Elisha? Let's be careful that a similar focus on material wealth does not take priority over the spiritual in our lives.

Chapter summary. Elisha causes a lost axhead to float, showing Israel God's compassion for the individual (6:1-7). God also cares for the nation. Elisha continually advises the King of Israel of Syria's military plans (vv. 8-12). The furious King of Syria sends an expedition to capture Elisha. Elisha is granted divine protection (vv. 13-17), and leads the enemy corps into Israel's capital city itself. There the stunned Syrians are fed, and sent home (vv. 18-23). Later hostilities resume, and Samaria is under siege. The population is reduced to eating scraps and even to cannabalism (vv. 24-29). The despairing King of Israel decides to strike out at God by executing Elisha. Elisha pledges that despite the king's lack of faith, the next day the finest of foods will be sold cheaply in the starving city (6:30–7:2). The pledge is kept when the Syrians hear a nonexistent army rushing down on them, panic, and abandon their camp with all its supplies (vv. 3-20). Thus in private and in very public ways, Elisha continues to demonstrate to Israel that the Lord is God, and that faith in Him is not foolishness, but wisdom.

Outline
Place
Finder

FAITH-BUILDING
DOWNFALL
DECLINE

Key verse. 6:33: Why wait for the Lord? He is God.

Personal application. Trust God in good times and in bad.

Key concepts. Angels »pp. 521, 855. Murderer »p. 114.

INSIGHT

Elisha's fame (6:12). Several events clearly show that Elisha's miracles were intended to produce faith beyond as well as within the boundaries of Israel. The healing of Naaman (chap. 5), the reputation won exposing the Syrian plans (6:12), and the release of the army corps that came to capture him (vv. 12-13), all witnessed to God's power. Let's serve Christ's church. But let's never lose sight of those beyond its boundaries.

"Open his eyes" (6:17). The prophet's prayer for his servant is one of the most comforting in all Scripture. However great the dangers that surround us, we too are guarded by the power of our God. His angels, ministering spirits who serve His saints, surround and protect us.

"Blindness" (6:18-20). It isn't that the Syrian soldiers saw nothing. What they thought they saw was an illusion. Only when Elisha prayed that their eyes be opened were they able to see reality, and realize they were inside the walls of Samaria itself. What an image of lost mankind! Unless God opens our eyes, we wander in a world of illusion. Don't be deceived by the scoffers who claim they "know" while believers foolishly rely on "faith." The fact is we see, and they are blind.

Private repentance? (6:30-33) Sackcloth was worn as a sign of repentance and self-humbling. But the king wore it "underneath" his royal robes! Unlike other rulers he did not repent publicly, or call his people to turn to God (cf. Jonah 3:6-10). True repentance involves a change of heart and life that will be seen by others, not disguised. Let's not try to play games with God.

Blaming God (6:31-33). When God did not accept the king's halfhearted "repentance," he became angry with God. He struck out by ordering the murder of Elisha. The Talmud interprets his words "Why should I wait for the Lord any longer?" as a rejection of prayer. He decided God wasn't going to answer, so why pray? Don't let this foolish king's attitude infect you!

Doubting God (7:2). The king's officer went beyond "God won't" to "God can't." As his fate illustrates (vv. 19-20), doubters will discover that God can. But for them it will be too late.

The lepers (7:9). This verse has been the basis for some of history's most powerful sermons on personal evangelism. We who enjoy God's salvation and experience His grace are not "doing right" if we keep the Good News to ourselves.

Chapter summary. Gehazi, once Elisha's servant, is telling the King of Israel about the boy Elisha raised from the dead (chap. 4) when living proof, the woman and the son himself, enter (8:1-6). Clearly, tales of Elisha's miracles have taken root: the content for faith-building is present in Israel. But Israel does not respond and the future is grim. Elisha anoints Hazael, destined to devastate Israel, as the next King of Syria (vv. 7-15). Even Judah suffers a spiritual and consequent national decline under Jehoram (vv. 16-24) and Ahaziah (vv. 25-29). The spectacular works of Elisha have not produced faith in either kingdom.

Key verse. 8:19: Man strays, but God remains faithful.

Personal application. We can provide living proof of the power of God, whether or not others respond.

Key concepts. Anoint »p. 879. Edom »p. 104.

INSIGHT

God's continuing care (8:1-6). The Shunammite woman's "old" husband (4:14) has died and the widow is now head of the household (8:1). The story illustrates God's continuing care of this woman who earlier had cared for His servant. She is sent away to avoid a famine. When she returns God has shaped circumstances so that at the moment she appeals to the king for restoration of her property, Gehazi is telling her story. Never doubt that God keeps on caring for His own.

Foreshadowing (8:1-6). Why is the widow's story here, in a chapter that quickly shifts to focus on international affairs? Possibly because her experience foreshadows that of the nation! As the woman was exiled only to be restored, so Israel, torn from the Promised Land, will be restored in God's time.

"Your son" (8:9). The phrase is typical of the respect shown prophets or rulers. »p. 247

A lie? (8:10-11) Elisha does not tell Hazael a lie. The truth is that Ben-Hadad's illness was not fatal — he was going to be murdered. Hazael was "ashamed" (embarrassed) by Elisha's fixed gaze for Hazael had already planned his master's murder.

Hazael's reaction reminds us that God knows the hidden motives of every person. When our desire is to please Him, we will have no cause for shame.

"Jehoram" (8:16-24). Jehoram's marriage to Athaliah, a daughter of Ahab and Jezebel (1 Kings 16–21) led to his rejection of God and active worship of Baal. His character is further revealed by the murder of his brothers and all other possible claimants to Judah's throne (cf. 2 Chron. 21:4). God did not cut off his line for David's sake, but God did judge him in four

ways: (1) By Edom's successful revolt (2 Kings 8:20-22); (2) By Libnah's revolt (v. 22); (3) By a massive Philistine/Arabian attack that reached Jerusalem (2 Chron. 21:16-17); and (4) By a brief, eight-year reign (2 Kings 8:17). Like so many, Jehoram got what he wanted by wicked means — and watched it all turn to ashes!

"Ahaziah" (8:25-29). Ahaziah failed to learn from his father's disasters.

Illustration. *Israel and Judah both suffered in wars with nearby Syria (Aram), which is often identified by its capital city, Damascus. Moab, subdued in David's time but in rebellion from the days of Ahab, is also mentioned in this chapter.*

Chapter summary. Elisha sends a prophet to anoint Jehu as Israel's next king, and commission him to destroy the house (family) of Ahab (9:1-10). Jehu is acclaimed by his fellow army officers (vv. 11-13), and hurries to Jezreel where Joram of Israel and Ahaziah of Judah are recovering from wounds (vv. 14-20). When the two kings go out to meet Jehu, he kills Joram and mortally wounds Ahaziah (vv. 21-29). Jehu then enters the city, where the aged Jezebel shouts out her defiance from an upstairs window (vv. 30-31). Jehu orders her thrown down to the street below. As Jehu celebrates his successful coup inside, the body of Jezebel is devoured by a pack of dogs (vv. 32-37). Elijah's prediction is thus literally fulfilled (cf. 1 Kings 21:23). Jehu then proceeds to wipe out the rest of the family (2 Kings 10:1-11). He also assembles all officials of the Baal cult, supposedly to worship, but in fact to destroy them (vv. 12-35). The massacre is a political expedient intended to wipe out a religion closely linked with the royal house. Because Jehu fails to turn to the Lord, his rule is marked by a series of military defeats and by the gradual reduction in size of the Northern Kingdom.

Outline
Place
Finder

FAITH-BUILDING
DOWNFALL
DECLINE

Key verse. 9:7: God's instruments are not necessarily godly.

Personal application. Judgment, like blessing, may be delayed. But each will surely come.

Key concepts. Baal »p. 162. Eunuch »p. 715. Idolatry »p. 433.

INSIGHT

Jehu. Jehu's name is recorded on the Black Obelisk of Shalmaneser III of Assyria, as "Jehu, son [successor] of Omri." At that time Assyria called Israel the "land of Omri."

Jehu's commission (9:6-10). Jehu did not do God's will out of piety, but self-interest. If he were to establish himself as king, he would have to wipe out the family of Ahab and also the cult that supported its rule. Jehu is rewarded with a four-generation dynasty (10:s

Justifying assassination (9:25-26). Jehu and other high army officers knew the sentence God pronounced against Ahab. Yet they continued to support the king. Jehu's appeal to Elijah's prophecy at this point is not evidence of faith, but evidence that Jehu intended to use God to justify his assassinations. God's will shall be carried out. But the motive of those who do it is critical.

Jezebel's defiance (9:30-31). Some have found Jezebel's defiance attractive. Certain of her fate, Jezebel calmly applies makeup, and then boldly calls Jehu a traitor (a "Zimri," cf. 1 Kings 16:9-18). It is interesting that Jezebel is the only queen in the Northern Kingdom to hold the high rank of *gebira*, or "queen mother" (2 Kings 10:13). Yet how pitiful her pride

and defiance are. The wicked queen has seen God strike her husband and son, yet is so hardened that she is unable to humble herself before the Lord. There is no glory in pride, no praise in self-destructive behavior. Whatever their title, there is no future for the wicked.

Ahab's offspring (10:1-11). Jehu's subtlety is shown in the story of the 70 princes of Ahab's line. In the ancient world royal princes were often placed in the homes of wealthy and influential friends of the ruling house. Jehu manipulates these guardians into killing their charges. He has rebelled against Ahab, but points out that the kingdom's most influential families have done the same thing! Now they must live, or die, with Jehu!

"Jehonadab" (10:15). The Recabite was the leader of an ascetic group, committed to the Lord and to a life free of materialism (cf. Jer. 35). He was in accord with Jehu as far as wiping out Ahab's family and the Baal cult were concerned. We can support political leaders, whatever their motives, as long as their program accords with godliness. There is no indication that Jehonadab continued to support Jehu when the king failed to follow through with a complete commitment to the Lord.

Outline
Place
Finder

FAITH-BUILDING
DOWNFALL
DECLINE

Chapter summary. In Judah, Athaliah, the daughter of Jezebel and mother of the dead King Ahaziah, determines to seize the throne herself. She murders the entire royal family, but overlooks the infant Joash (11:1-3). Some seven years later the high priest Jehoiada and the commanders of the royal guards resolve to make Joash king. He is crowned, and the evil Athaliah is killed (vv. 4-16). Jehoiada then leads the people in a ceremony of covenant renewal, recommitting themselves to the Lord. In a surge of religious enthusiasm, the temple of Baal is torn down and rampaging crowds smash Baal shrines and kill Mattan, Baal's high priest (vv. 17-19). The boy king, just seven years old, is escorted in triumph to the palace (vv. 20-21).

Key verse. 11:17: Recommitment counts.

Personal application. Evil is never able to establish itself permanently.

Key concepts. Covenant »pp. 32, 62. Revival »p. 233.

INSIGHT

Athaliah. The daughter of Ahab and Jezebel, Athaliah had married Jehoram of Judah, son of the godly King Jehoshaphat. She introduced the virulent form of Baal cult her mother had imported into Israel, and apparently influenced her husband as much as Jezebel had influenced Ahab. Her character is fully revealed in the events portrayed in this chapter. When her 23-year-old son was killed, Athaliah determined to seize the throne for herself. To establish her rule she killed all the members of Judah's royal house—including her own grandchildren! How true it is that what we worship shapes our character.

How could Athaliah overlook her grandson Joash? The genealogy of 11:2 reminds us that kings frequently had many wives and concubines. It is possible Athaliah might not have been aware that Zibiah (12:1) had a child, and so missed him when she carried out her massacre.

"Jehoiada" (11:4). He was high priest of Yahweh in a capital whose queen was then dedicated to the worship of Baal. He was able to put together a coup that involved the Carites (probably mercenaries who formed the royal bodyguard), other palace guards, and the Levites. The Heb. phrase translated "made a covenant with them" (*karot berit le-*) is idiomatic, suggesting that the guards had once supported Athaliah but were now ready to switch sides. This suggests that Athaliah's rule was characterized by the same brutality that marked its beginning, and eroded her support. The wicked person soon alienates friends:

it's dangerous to be too close to evil!

"The crown" (11:12). The word is *nezer*. It was probably an engraved gold plate or headband that was attached to a cloth turban, as was the case for the high priest's *nezer* (Ex. 29:6; 39:30). Pss. 89:4 and 132:18 confirm this was a sign of royalty in ancient Israel.

"The people of the land" (11:18). The meaning of this phrase is debated. Some think it refers to a popular assembly of some sort. Others see it simply as the general populace. Note that the people of the land were enthusiastic—but only became involved after the coup was accomplished. Revival and renewal require leaders who are willing to risk active personal involvement. Don't wait for "the people" to act. Popular support comes after others have taken the lead.

Covenant renewal (11:17). God had remained faithful to His commitments. The ceremonies of covenant renewal mentioned so frequently in the O.T. remind us that it is the people of God who fail. When we fail, let's reconsecrate ourselves to the Lord, and expect Him to revitalize us.

The Baal temple (11:18). There is no indication of when the temple to Baal was erected in Jerusalem, or where it was located. Some think it remained from Solomon's day; others that it was erected by Athaliah. Whatever its source, there is no room in the city of God, or the heart of the believer, for anything that competes with complete allegiance to God. When revival comes to our hearts, whatever symbolizes competition with God must go.

Chapter summary. Guided by the high priest Jehoiada, Joash orders the repair and refurbishing of the temple Solomon erected to the Lord (12:1-5). When the priests were slow to obey, Joash ordered that most revenues be turned directly over to the workmen (vv. 6-16). When the rebuilding project was nearly complete, Hazael of Syria mounted an expedition along the coastal plain. He then turned up into the mountain passes that led to Jerusalem, and Joash used the treasures dedicated to the temple to buy off his forces (vv. 17-21).

Outline
Place
Finder

FAITH-BUILDING
DOWNFALL
DECLINE

Key verse. 12:8: Let those best equipped do the work!

Personal application. Only by involving the laity will we see God's work accomplished.

Key concepts. High places »p. 113. Priest »p. 81. Temple »p. 283.

INSIGHT

Sources of income (12:4). The text indicates five normal sources of income, four of which are identified in this verse. (1) "Sacred offerings" (NIV) is literally "money for the holy things," probably money set aside for sacred utensils and decorative gifts; (2) Census money (Ex. 30:13-14); (3) Money from those who make vows (Lev. 27:1-33); (4) Voluntary offerings; and (5) the regular income of the priests (2 Kings 12:5).

New orders (12:6-8). Despite the king's orders little was done to repair the temple. Apparently the priests were unwilling to divert "their" income to the repair project, and were incapable of doing the work themselves. So Joash had them hand the money over directly to others who would do the work.

What fascinating principles are illustrated here! Those who minister all too often try to hold on to money and power when others are better able to perform certain work. Christian ministers are charged by God with *enabling* the laity to do God's work (Eph. 4:12-13). The more a "professional" ministry guards its prerogatives, the less likely it is that God's work will be done.

When the responsibility and authority of the priests in Joash's time were limited, the work was done quickly, well, and honestly.

Responsibility and authority. Spiritual leaders often hesitate to follow Joash's prescription. Yet the best way to accomplish any task is to give those who will do the work responsibility for it, and the authority needed to carry it out.

The carpenters and builders, the masons and stonecutters. Again we're reminded that there is no lack of persons who have the re-

quired gifts to accomplish God's purposes. When people without those gifts refuse to release or enable those who do, nothing significant can be accomplished.

Not for silver basins (12:13). This is another fascinating comment. Apparently the priests were more interested in decorations and utensils than in secure foundations for the temple where they served. It's easy to focus on organs and new pews and better sound systems for a local church and ignore the more basic needs of human beings in the congregation or community. The priests of Joash's day needed a new set of priorities. And we need to examine our priorities in the light of God's Word.

The priest's money (12:16). There was no "either/or" issue here. The funds were available to support the priests, as O.T. Law provided. But until the work was taken out of the priests' hands, and control of the funds required for rebuilding too, the priests' fears limited what was done. Let's encourage others to give freely to any ministry they may be led to support. God will still supply what is needed for our local church.

Hazael's invasion (12:17-18). Note the irony? The priests had concentrated their efforts on "making silver basins, wick trimmers, sprinkling bowls, trumpets or any other article of gold or silver for the temple" (v. 13). And it was just these objects that Hazael and the Syrians now carried away! How foolish to concentrate on beautifying a building, when material objects are perishable. Let's concentrate our efforts on strengthening the true building of God, the congregation of His people, rather than on making the "silver basins" of today.

Outline
Place
Finder

FAITH-BUILDING
DOWNFALL
DECLINE

Chapter summary. The Northern Kingdom continues its rush toward extinction. Jehoahaz, the son of Jehu, is king of Israel. Late in his reign Syrian domination is lifted when Jehoahaz seeks God's favor (13:1-9). But Jehoash, his son, maintains the evil course set by Israel's kings from the beginning (vv. 10-13). One incident illustrates Jehoash's lack of faith. When a dying Elisha commands him to strike the ground with arrows that symbolize victory over Edom, Jehoash strikes it only three times (vv. 14-19). Elisha dies, and when his body touches a newly dead corpse, the dead man returns to life (vv. 20-21). Again the symbolism is plain. Israel, spiritually dead and destined for exile, will one day be returned to life by God's power. And God's compassion is revealed in the immediate situation. As predicted Jehoash defeats the Syrians three times (vv. 24-25). Meanwhile in Judah Amaziah becomes king, and follows the example set by his father Joash (14:1-4). He is commended for his great restraint and respect for God's Law in punishing rebels (vv. 5-6), but foolishly declares war on Israel (vv. 7-10). Amaziah is defeated. Jerusalem's walls are broken down, and its palace and temple treasures are carried away to the North (vv. 11-22). Jeroboam II, fated to be the most powerful and successful of Israel's rulers, takes the throne (vv. 23-29).

Key verse. 13:19: Obedience should be enthusiastic!

Personal application. Even when the direction of history is most uncertain, we can remain confident God is in control.

INSIGHT

Background: Israel and Syria (13:5). The period shows a sharp reduction of Aramean power. An invasion of northern Syria by Adad-nirari in 805/803 B.C. is background for the panicked withdrawal of Syrian troops from Samaria (chaps. 6–7). Later, in 796 B.C., Ben-Hadad submitted to Assyria. The weakened Syria was then defeated three times by Jehoash (13:18-19, 25). With Assyria occupied by internal troubles, Jeroboam II was able to win control of all Syria and its capital city.

Jehoahaz's army (13:7). Compare his defense force of some 10,000 men and 10 chariots with Assyrian records. Shalmaneser III's campaigns in the west recorded the deaths of 20,900; 25,000; and 20,000 enemy soldiers! During one campaign his army had 120,000 men. Israel was helpless! Only then did Jehoahaz appeal to God.

"The chariots and horsemen of Israel" (13:16). Even the wicked king Jehoash wept at the death of Elisha, but only because he was a national resource; the equivalent of a chariot army! Yet even this cry shows a lack of faith. Elisha died. But God lived. The revival of a corpse that touched the prophet's body showed the vivifying power of God was not limited by the death of the prophet. Let's not make the mistake of trusting in God's ministers, and not in God.

"Jonah" (14:25). Both Jonah and Amos ministered during the reign of Jeroboam II. On the home front Jonah predicted the political and military expansion of Israel. His reluctant mission to Nineveh (the capital of Assyria) was intended to demonstrate to Israel that if God's people would repent they too could avoid judgment. »p. 546.

Jeroboam II (14:23-29). Though hardly mentioned in Scripture, Jeroboam II had the longest reign of any ruler of the Northern Kingdom. He extended Israelite control beyond Damascus in the north, and southward to the Dead Sea, reaching the borders achieved in the days of David and Solomon! The Book of Amos describes the wealth that poured into Israel in this era, but also the social disruption and the increasing gap between the wealthy and the poor. Jeroboam's unconcern with spiritual things, despite the popularity of "religion," is reflected in the injustice described so powerfully in the prophetic Book of Amos. »p. 536.

Outline
Place
Finder

FAITH-BUILDING
DOWNFALL
DECLINE

Chapter summary. In Judah the long reign of Azariah (Uzziah) provides stability (15:1-7). But in Israel the death of Jeroboam II ushers in a period of internal chaos. Pressure from a revitalized and ever-expanding Assyrian Empire grows more intense, and the corrupt faith of the North provides neither a basis for hope nor moral stability. King Zechariah is publicly assassinated by Shallum after a six-month reign (vv. 8-12). Shallum holds the throne only one month before he is killed by Menahem (vv. 13-16). Menahem is able to maintain his hold on the throne through support purchased from Assyria (vv. 17-22). He is succeeded by his son Pekahiah, but two years later Pekahiah is assassinated by Pekah (vv. 23-26). During Pekah's reign the Assyrians take Galilee and deport the Jewish population, a foretaste of the fate soon to befall the whole nation (vv. 27-31). The scene now shifts to the South, to describe Judah's role in the downfall of Israel. There Jotham, who has succeeded Uzziah, is under attack from a coalition formed by Pekah of Israel and Rezin of Syria (vv. 32-38). His successor, Ahaz, one of Judah's most wicked kings, does not rely on the Lord to resist the allies, but sends a "gift" to Tiglath-Pileser and urges the Assyrians to attack his enemies. The Assyrians crush Syria, and place Hoshea on the throne of Israel (16:1-9). Ahaz goes to Damascus to submit to the Assyrian ruler, where he is corrupted (vv. 10-20).

Key verse. 16:7: The right request, the wrong address.

Personal application. We can be calm in the midst of troubles if our hope is fixed in God rather than in modern "Assyrias."

Key concepts. King »p. 130. Assyria »p. 255. Altar »p. 79.

INSIGHT

Azariah/Uzziah (15:1-6). Much more on his long reign is found in 2 Chron. 26.

Thirty-seven tons of silver (15:19). Menahem was maintained on the throne only by this heavy payment for Assyrian support. In the East, the rich and important were generally not taxed. The desperation felt by Menahem is reflected in the note that Menahem "exacted" money from "every wealthy man."

Pekah's reign (15:27-31). Pekah's anti-Assyrian policy led to national disaster. It is likely his and Rezin's pressure on Judah was primarily an attempt to force Jotham and then Ahaz to join them in an anti-Assyrian axis. Verse 29 mentions a policy invented by the Assyrian monarchs: the exchange of populations within the empire. The policy was intended to Assyrianize uprooted ethnic groups and speed up their assimilation.

"Ahaz" (16:1). Perhaps the best-known scene involving Ahaz is recorded in Isaiah 7, where the king is confronted by the prophet. Isaiah urges him not to fear Rezin and Pekah,

and tells him to choose any sign he wishes as proof of Isaiah's words. When the king sullenly refuses, Isaiah not only predicts the imminent downfall of the two kings, but also the virgin birth of the Messiah.

"Sacrificed his son in the fire" (16:3). The reference is to the child sacrifice practiced in the most virulent forms of Baal worship.

"Save me" (16:7). It was the right request, but the address was wrong! Judah's king should have depended on God, not on Assyria. But how could he, since he had so terribly violated God's laws? Let's rely on God, who has our interests at heart. And let's live so that we will always feel free to call on Him.

The Damascus altar (16:10-18). The text tells us that the new altar Ahaz ordered built was used to offer the sacrifices specified in O.T. Law, not pagan sacrifices. But that Law also prescribed the altar on which they were to be made. Halfway obedience is not acceptable to the Lord.

Outline
Place
Finder

FAITH-BUILDING
DOWNFALL
DECLINE

Chapter summary. Israel, now stripped of the fertile lands of Galilee and Gilead, is ruled by Hoshea. Hoshea decides to stop his regular payments of tribute to Assyria, and tries to arrange for help from Egypt (17:1-4). This foolish act brings an Assyrian army down on Israel. Samaria is besieged and finally captured, and the remaining Israelites are deported (vv. 5-6).

At this point the writer incoporates an extensive sermon explaining the fall of Israel in theological terms. The ultimate cause of Israel's downfall is not to be found in world politics, but in Israel's adoption of Canaanite religious practices (vv. 7-18), and in the corruption of the Law introduced by Jeroboam at the founding of the Northern Kingdom and persisted in by Israel ever since (vv. 19-23). As for the Holy Land, the Assyrians resettled it with pagans. These peoples, who simply added Yahweh to their list of deities to be worshiped (vv. 24-41), were the ancestors of the Samaritans, so hated by the Jews of Jesus' day.

Key verse. 17:13: God's patience has limits.

Personal application. Remain true to God, and trust Him to shape the circumstances of your life.

Key concepts. Idolatry »p. 433. Law »pp. 120, 145. Prophet »p. 131.

INSIGHT

Hoshea's revolt (17:1-4). The revolt corresponds with the death of Tiglath-Pileser III in 727 B.C. The death of rulers was typically an opportunity for subject peoples to rebel, as infighting for the throne often followed. Hoshea's envoys were sent to the city of Sais (*So* in Heb.) to meet with the king, who at that time was Tefnekht. When Shalmaneser became Assyria's ruler, Israel's fate was sealed.

"The Israelites" (17:9). In this extended sermon the people of Israel are blamed for destruction of the Northern Kingdom. Yet in the historical review that led up to it, the kings of Israel were held responsible. Some view this as a conflict within the book. Instead it expresses a vital truth. Rulers *are* responsible to set the spiritual and moral tone of a nation. But even if rulers are evil, there is no excuse for citizens following their lead!

The Canaanites' sins (17:16-17). The writer is fully aware that the sins he lists here are the very sins for which God expelled the original Canaanites from the Promised Land (cf. Deut. 18:9-13). The fact that God chose and redeemed the Hebrew people (2 Kings 17:7) makes their sins even more terrible. We who are called by God's name have no excuse when we choose to live as pagans do.

Jeroboam's sins (17:21-23). Jeroboam I was the first ruler of the Northern Kingdom, Israel. He was afraid that if his people went up to worship at Jerusalem, as O.T. Law required, they would soon give political as well as religious allegiance to the competing kingdom, Judah. So Jeroboam set up his own Yahweh cult, with two worship centers, a non-Aaronic priesthood, and a new worship calendar (cf. 1 Kings 12–13). This cult was maintained by every king of Israel.

Samaritans (17:24-41). Assyria's rulers adopted a policy of moving peoples from their homeland and resettling them. Thus when the Jews were deported from Israel, Samaria was quickly resettled. The settlers brought their own gods, but also had Israelite priests imported to teach them to worship the "god of the land." These polyglot people were the ancestors of the Samaritans. Much later, after Judah's Captivity and return to Jerusalem, the Samaritans offered to help rebuild the temple, claiming they too worshiped Yahweh (cf. Ezra 4:2). This offer was decisively rejected: the Samaritans were not descendants of Abraham, Isaac, and Jacob, and had no covenant relationship with the Lord. Hostility between the groups remained in the time of Jesus, with the origin of the Samaritans explaining why "Jews do not associate with Samaritans" (John 4:9).

Assyria

This reconstruction is of a hall in the palace of Sennacherib where many reliefs portray the capture of Lachish, in Judah. It is typical of the war memorials that Assyrian rulers erected to celebrate their triumphs.

The warlike Assyrians dominated the Middle East during what is known as the Neo-Assyrian era, stretching from 911–609 B.C. With an empire centered in what is now northern Iraq, Assyria's aggressive policies had a crushing impact on the two Hebrew kingdoms. Assyria's growing impact on Palestine can be traced from century to century not only through the Scriptures, but through the many documents and war memorials recovered by archeologists. From 911–824 B.C. pressure on the west was resisted. Ahab of Israel was a leading member of the coalition that threw back the Assyrians at Qarqar in 853 B.C. The period 844–744 B.C. saw Assyria crush Syria's military power, but withdraw when rebellions forced its rulers to focus on internal affairs. During this period Israel, under Jeroboam II, and Judah, under Uzziah, were able to greatly expand their territories. The years 744–627 B.C. saw a resurgence of Assyrian power. Its rulers imposed strong central control, and invented the resettlement program designed to break conquered peoples of nationalism and force assimilation into the empire. In 722 B.C. Israel fell, and its people were deported. At the same time Judah was reduced to a vassal state, though it revolted briefly in 704–701 under Hezekiah. The 300-year-old Assyrian Empire crumbled during the years 627–609 B.C., and was supplanted by the even more powerful Babylonians, whose ruler Nebuchadnezzar crushed Judah. While the O.T. prophets predicted God's judgment of Assyria, they also recognized that Assyria was God's instrument, "The rod of My anger, in whose hand is the club of My wrath" (Isa. 10:5).

255

Outline
Place
Finder

FAITH-BUILDING
DOWNFALL
DECLINE

Chapter summary. With the Northern Kingdom crushed, Judah too was vulnerable. But Judah was blessed with a godly king, Hezekiah (18:1-8). When the ring of defensive cities Judah had erected fell to Sennacherib, Hezekiah paid the tribute the Assyrian demanded (vv. 9-16). But Assyria was intent on its policy of population exchange. So Sennacherib sent a delegation to demand Judah's unconditional surrender (vv. 17-19). The delegation openly ridiculed Judah's continuing resistance, including any hope in her God (vv. 20-37). Hezekiah hurried to the temple, to lay the Assyrian demands before the Lord (19:1-4). Isaiah the prophet responded. God would send Sennacherib home, with Jerusalem untouched (vv. 5-9). Hezekiah is threatened again, and again prays (vv. 10-19), and Isaiah's prophecy against Sennnacherib is expanded (vv. 20-34). God strikes the bulk of the Assyrian forces dead. Sennacherib does return home, where he is assassinated by two of his sons (vv. 35-37).

Key verses. 19:18-19: Worship makes a difference.

Personal application. Honor God always, and He will honor you.

Key concepts. High places »p. 113. Covenant »p. 62. Jerusalem »p. 205. Angel of the Lord »p. 37. Prophecy »p. 434.

INSIGHT

Hezekiah's dates. The best way to sort the confusing dates is to assume that he became co-regent in 729/728 B.C., was primary ruler from 720/719 B.C. and ruled independently after Ahaz's death in 716 B.C. The 14 years lie between 715 and 701 B.C., when Sennacherib invaded.

Why is Hezekiah's character mentioned first? (18:1-8) Hezekiah is commended for trust (v. 5), for faithfully following the Lord (v. 6a), and for keeping the Mosaic Law (v. 6b). His close relationship with the Lord was a key to his success (v. 7). Character comes first, for it is the key to the events that follow. To withstand the storms of life, we need to build a relationship with God like Hezekiah's.

Sennacherib's invasion. Assyrian annals trace his brilliant campaign. He subdued the Phoenician cities, then attacked south along the coast. He then turned east, taking Lachish, and isolating the remaining Judean and Philistine cities from any possible Egyptian aid.

Assyrian view of gods (19:32-35). The Assyrians had only contempt for others' gods. Power counted; gods did not. To the Assyrians, Yahweh was of no more account than the idols of the many nations they had defeated. The sly suggestion that the Lord was sending Assyria against Judah suggests some knowledge of the Heb. prophets (18:25). But misunderstanding of Hezekiah's removal of Judah's local shrines (high places) shows the Assyrians

had no real grasp of biblical theology.

"Aramaic" (18:26). The Assyrian envoy's use of Heb. was early "psychological warfare." He wanted all to understand his ridicule and promises, to weaken the will to resist.

Withdrawal (19:9). Sennacherib's initial withdrawal was due to the rumor that an Egyptian army was about to attack. This was not enough to force Sennacherib home, and so Hezekiah lay the later Assyrian demands before the Lord. As promised, not a single arrow flew over the walls of Jerusalem (v. 32).

"My hook in your nose" (19:28). The Assyrians put metal hooks in the noses of their captives to lead them into slavery. God would put His own hook in Sennacherib's nose, and drag him from Judah.

Prosperity in three years (19:29). The poetic image promises restoration of Judah.

Sennacherib's records. The Assyrian account of this campaign claims that Sennacherib took 200,150 Judeans captive, and locked Hezekiah "up within Jerusalem, his royal city, like a bird in a cage." The Assyrian annals also report the heavy tribute paid by Hezekiah, but not unexpectedly omit the deaths in Sennacherib's army. Few monarchs brag about their setbacks! However, Herodotus the Greek historian does report a massive loss—due to field mice who ate the army's weapons and left them exposed to decimation by an enemy!

Chapter summary. The author now includes an incident that took place earlier in Hezekiah's reign, to demonstrate the king's trust in God, and his orientation to prayer. Hezekiah falls ill, and Isaiah announces he is about to die (20:1). The king weeps and prays (vv. 2-3). Isaiah is told to return and tell the king he has been granted an extra 15 years of life (vv. 4-8), and the promise is confirmed by a miraculous sign (vv. 9-11). But Isaiah rebukes Hezekiah when he later welcomes messengers from Babylon without inquiring of the Lord. One day the Babylonians will invade Judah and strip the Jerusalem temple of its treasures (vv. 12-18). But Hezekiah is consoled by the belief that there will be "peace and security" in his own time (vv. 19-21).

Outline
Place
Finder

FAITH-BUILDING
DOWNFALL
DECLINE

Key verse. 20:5: God does hear prayer, and heal.

Personal application. When we walk faithfully with the Lord, and are devoted to Him, we can expect prayers to be answered.

Key concepts. Healing »pp. 412, 610–611, 784. Prayer »pp. 181, 608. Babylon »p. 303. Eunuch »p. 715.

INSIGHT

"In those days" (20:1). The reference is to the reign of Hezekiah, not the time of the Assyrian invasion. Hezekiah died about 698 B.C., so these events took place around 713/712 B.C.

Hezekiah's prayer (20:2-3). No one truly merits an answer to prayer. Yet a righteous life like the one Hezekiah lived gives us a right to appeal for God's grace.

"I will heal you" (20:5). Both Testaments make it clear that God has the power to heal, and that He often does so in answer to prayer. However, we have no automatic "right" to healing or to any of God's blessings. Here God's "I will" reminds us that the Lord is sovereign. Healing depends on God's "I will," not on our "I want." The man or woman of faith recognizes this, and does not presume on God's grace, or suppose that healing depends on the amount of "faith" we can muster.

Why did Hezekiah ask for a sign? (20:8) The O.T. prophet's message was typically confirmed by a miraculous sign, or a prediction that would be shortly fulfilled. Hezekiah did not ask for a sign: he asked what the sign would be. His words were an expression of faith, not doubt. In asking what the sign would be, Hezekiah showed his faith that the prophet's message was from the Lord, and would surely be miraculously confirmed. Compare this with the refusal of Ahaz of Judah to ask for a sign, even though Isaiah told him to do so (Isa. 7:10-11). This incident does not, however, mean that we should expect signs today, any more than we should expect an Isaiah to reveal God's word to us.

The "stairway of Ahaz" (20:11). This is the earliest known "clock" mentioned in Scripture. Apparently a pole was placed so that its shadow traveled down a staircase graduated to show the passage of the hours. To have the shadow reverse itself and move back up the stairs was a clear miracle, and thus served as the confirming sign.

"Merodach-Baladan" (20:12). Cuneiform annals report that Merodach was king of Babylon from 720–709 B.C. During this time he struggled with Sargon II of Babylon. His delegation to Hezekiah was undoubtedly motivated by a desire to encourage an active "second front" against Assyria. Later Merodach was deposed and fled to Elam. He returned briefly in 703 B.C., but when defeated by Sennacherib he once again went into exile. Isaiah's anger at Hezekiah's exposure of Judah's wealth to the Babylonian delegation is probably rooted in Hezekiah's failure to inquire of the Lord.

"Peace and security in my lifetime" (20:19). Hezekiah's reaction to Isaiah's prediction of a Babylonian invasion has often been criticized. Yet it contains wisdom. There is nothing we can do to affect the years that lie beyond our own time. So we should enjoy the blessings that are ours. But there is another, more poignant message. Hezekiah's words are not inspired, and in fact Hezekiah was wrong! Babylon did not invade during his lifetime, but Assyria exerted terrible pressure on Judah. How great a grace that we do not know all the future holds. How vital to know that God is with us, and we are in His hands.

Outline
Place
Finder

FAITH-BUILDING
DOWNFALL
DECLINE

Chapter summary. With the death of Hezekiah his young son, Manasseh, became king. His 55-year rule was the longest in Judah's history. But it was also the most corrupt, for Manasseh reversed his father's policies and actively promoted the old Canaanite religions (21:1-9). The 50-year counter-revival so corrupted Judah that its own future destruction was assured (vv. 10-18). Manasseh was followed by his son Amon, who ruled for only 2 years before he died, to be replaced by a second boy king, Josiah, who was destined to become one of Judah's most godly rulers (vv. 19-26).

Key verse. 21:9: Who we hear depends on who we listen to.

Personal application. The best way to preserve our society from moral and religious corruption is for individuals to listen to God.

INSIGHT

"Twelve years old" (21:1). Second Kings 20 tells us that God announced Hezekiah would die. When the king pleaded for his life, he was given 15 added years. Now we're told that Manasseh, who became Judah's most wicked ruler, was only 12 when he ascended to the throne! If Hezekiah had submitted to God's announced will, Manasseh would never have been born!

What a reminder for us that when God does not answer our prayers, even when what we plead for seems important to us, it is because He really does know what is best.

Manasseh's sins (21:2-9). Manasseh's sins like those of Ahaz (2 Kings 16) duplicate the sins of the Canaanite population that God commanded be exterminated. But Manasseh went further, first in his pollution of the temple with idolatrous symbols, and second in the length of time he influenced Judah's society. His years had a permanent effect on Judah's

population (v. 9), which could not be reversed by Josiah's enthusiastic but brief revival.

Manasseh shed innocent blood (21:16). Tradition says that the Prophet Isaiah was one of those murdered by Manasseh in his persecution of those who worshiped the Lord or opposed his other policies. Typically the phrase "shed innocent blood" is used to describe oppression of the poor and other social injustices.

More on Manasseh. Second Chron. 33 gives us more information on Manasseh. It includes a report of his arrest by the King of Assyria, and of a later return to the throne. Chronicles also tells us that Manasseh turned to the Lord during this time, and tried to turn his people back to God when he was returned to the throne. But by then it was too late. Let's be careful about our choices. The choice of evil may affect us and others so greatly that nothing we do can repair the damage.

Chapter summary. One final revival, led by zealous King Josiah, fails to reverse Judah's slide toward destruction. Josiah becomes king at 8 years of age (22:1-2). At 16 he makes a decisive commitment to the Lord, and at 20 begins a purge of idolatry in Jerusalem (cf. 2 Chron. 34:3). But the key event of his reign is discovery of a lost book of God's Law, probably Deuteronomy, in the Jerusalem temple (2 Kings 22:3-10). Josiah is stunned to discover the terrible punishments his peoples' sins merit. The Prophetess Huldah confirms Scripture's grim vision of Judah's future, but promises the humble Josiah peace in his lifetime (vv. 11-20). Josiah intensifies his efforts to bring about a reformation. He leads his people in a covenant renewal ceremony (23:1-3). He purges the temple of every vestige of pagan worship (v. 4), executes pagan priests, and tears down shrines erected to Baal and Asherah (vv. 5-7). He shuts down local shrines and restores the temple to its central place in worship (vv. 8-9). He continues his purge by desecrating Judah's Topheth, a park where child sacrifices were conducted in his grandfather's time, and where their charred corpses were buried in urns dedicated to pagan deities (v. 10). He smashes every reminder of Judah's preceding half century of enthusiastic idolatry (vv. 11-14). Josiah even leads an expedition into the lost territory of Israel, and fulfills a 300-year-old prophecy by demolishing Israel's worship center at Bethel. Having purged Judah (vv. 15-20), Josiah calls his people together to celebrate Passover (vv. 21-24). Yet Josiah's reforms come too late. The people of Judah, corrupted for generations by idolatry, must face the fierce anger of God (vv. 25-28). Josiah is killed by Pharaoh Neco of Egypt, and Judah is left to face the future without the sheltering faith of her most pious king (vv. 29-37).

Outline
Place
Finder

FAITH-BUILDING
DOWNFALL
DECLINE

Key verses. 22:19-20: There is always hope for the humble.

Personal application. Use whatever influence you have to lead others to God.

Key concepts. Law »p. 120. Passover »p. 59. Covenant »pp. 35, 62. Priest »p. 81. Temple »p. 283. Altar »p. 79. Lord »p. 54. Baal »p. 162. High places »p. 113. Jerusalem »p. 205. Heart and soul »p. 120. Prophet »p. 131.

INSIGHT

Spiritual conditions. Josiah's reforms did not reach the hearts of God's people. Habakkuk, a contemporary, decries the sin and injustice that characterize Judah despite Josiah's earnest efforts (cf. Hab. 1:2-4).

Humbling yourself (22:19). Josiah is commended for being responsive and humbling himself. The Heb. *kana'* suggests public humili-

ation, with undertones of shame and dishonor. But only if one is humbled against his will! A person who humbles himself before God as Josiah did openly confesses himself a sinner, crushed and hopeless. This is our appropriate response when we realize how we fall short of meeting God's standards, and how greatly we stand in need of forgiving grace.

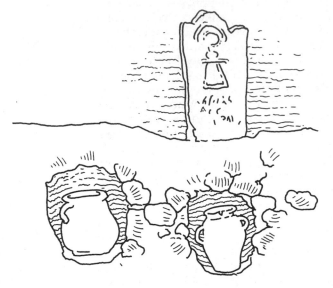

Just outside ancient Carthage lies one of the best known Topheth districts, where young children, newborn to about four or five, were burned as votive gifts to pagan gods by parents begging for some benefits. The fact that such a district existed in Judah is a stunning indication of how firmly God's people were locked in the grip of paganism and sin.

INSIGHT

The international scene. Josiah reigned from 640–609 B.C. These were chaotic years in the Middle East. Ashurbanipal of Assyria died in 626. Within a year Nabopolassar of Babylon won independence. In 612 a coalition of Medes, Babylonians, and Ummanmande (Sycthians?) took the Assyrian capital of Nineveh. Assyria's weakness explains how Josiah was able to enter Israel's territory so easily and purge its pagan religious centers. The allied forces, dominated by the Babylonians, pursued the last Assyrian forces westward. Egypt had earlier forged an alliance with Assyria, and had supplied troops in 616 B.C. In 609 Pharaoh Neco led his army northward, either to aid Assyria or to establish his own claim to Syria/Palestine before the Babylonians could. Josiah led Judah's army out against the Egyptians, and was mortally wounded at Megiddo. For a time Egypt controlled Palestine, demanding tribute and nominating candidates for Judah's throne. Soon, however, the Babylonians swept into the area, and Judah became a vassal of one of history's greatest kings.

Restoring the temple (22:3-7). A sense of who God is, and a desire to worship Him, is a source as well as evidence of personal spiritual renewal.

Spiritual support. Though the writer does not mention them, the Prophets Zephaniah, Habakkuk, and Jeremiah all ministered during Josiah's time. Their active support undoubtedly encouraged the young king. Support would also have come from Shaphan (v. 3), whose influence is seen in his godly sons (Jer. 26:24; 29:3) and a godly grandson, Gedaliah (39:14).

However great an individual is, he or she needs the support of others.

"The Book of the Law" (22:8). Some have argued that Deuteronomy, the most likely candidate for the lost book, was actually written at this time and presented to the gullible young king as an ancient document. But the loss of Scripture is in fact very likely, given the decades dedicated to paganism by Josiah's father and grandfather (2 Kings 21). The king's reaction (22:11-13) and subsequent reforms (23:4-20; cf. 2 Chron. 35:1-19) do suggest that Deuteronomy was in fact the lost book.

Many a sermon has been given on the lost book, reminding believers an unread Bible is a great loss today too.

"Huldah" (22:14). In view of the great male prophets then living, it's significant that Josiah consulted a woman. Let's be as quick to recognize and honor the gifted women of our day.

Desecrating high places (23:8). Shrines which were polluted by burning human bones could not be used later as worship centers. Josiah's desecration of the worship center at Bethel was foretold some 300 years before when that center was established (1 Kings 13).

Horses dedicated to the sun (23:11). White horses were associated with the gods of Assyria and their worship. Assyrian as well as other pagan gods had been worshiped in Judah.

"Jehoiakim" (23:34–24:7). Jeremiah pictures this successor of godly Josiah as a brute who filled Judah with violence and led the people back into apostasy (cf. Jer. 18:18-20; 22:13-17; 26:20-23).

Chapter summary. The Babylonians now invade Syria/Palestine. Jehoiakim, though placed on the throne by Pharaoh Neco of Egypt, is forced to submit, but then rebels (24:1-7). After his death Jehoiachin becomes king, and Nebuchadnezzar himself leads an army to Judah. He takes Jehoiachin to Babylon, and places a puppet, Zedekiah, on Judah's throne (vv. 8-20). But Zedekiah too rebels, and Nebuchadnezzar returns (25:1-2). After a two-year siege, marked by famine inside the walled city, Jerusalem falls (vv. 3-4). Zedekiah's sons are butchered and he is blinded (vv. 5-7). The city walls are broken down, its temple is destroyed, and all the temple treasures are taken to Babylon, along with Judah's citizens (vv. 8-21). Gedaliah is appointed governor, but is assassinated, and the remaining population flees to Egypt (vv. 22-26). Judah too has been torn from the Promised Land and carried into Exile as punishment for her sins. But there, 37 years later, Jehoiachin is released from his imprisonment, foreshadowing the restoration of Judah and Israel to the Promised Land (vv. 27-30).

Outline
Place
Finder

FAITH-BUILDING
DOWNFALL
DECLINE

Key verse. 24:2: All God's promises are kept.

Personal application. Let's not mistake judgment delayed for no judgment at all.

Key concepts. Babylon »p. 302. Manasseh »p. 258.

INSIGHT

International events. In 606 B.C. Nabopolassar defeated Egyptian and Syrian forces, throwing Egypt back to its own borders (cf. 24:7). While this freed Judah from Egyptian domination (23:31-35), the little Jewish state quickly became subject to Babylon. Nebuchadnezzar launched a series of annual invasions of Syria/Palestine in 604/603, deporting Judah's population in stages, and setting up his own puppet rulers. When the last of these, Zedekiah, rebelled, Nebuchadnezzar laid siege to Jerusalem and captured the city on February 16, 597 B.C. At that time he deported most of the land's population. The rest fled after Gedaliah, the governor Nebuchadnezzar appointed, was assassinated.

Jeremiah and Ezekiel. God did not leave His people without guidance during this terrible period in their history. Jeremiah ministered in Judah. Yet his warnings and words from God were rejected, and the prophet himself was persecuted. His sermons give us clear insight into spiritual and social conditions during Judah's last days.

Ezekiel ministered to the exiles in Babylon, where he had been taken with one of the first groups of captives. Ezekiel, especially in chapters 8–11, also reports on spiritual conditions in Judah, and helps us see the utter necessity

of God's purging judgments. The reforms of Josiah had temporarily removed the symbols of idolatry from Judah. But only the severest discipline could expel idolatry from God's people's hearts.

Zedekiah's punishment (25:7). The cruel treatment described is not unusual in the ancient world. Here it is mitigated by the fact that Zedekiah was placed on the throne by Nebuchadnezzar, and was probably bound to the king by formal treaty, which he broke.

"Gedaliah" (25:22). Jer. 40 portrays Gedaliah as an admirable though naive man. He was the grandson of one of Josiah's advisers during that godly king's reformation (cf. 22:3), and his reputation was such that most guerilla bands still roaming Judah laid down their arms and went back to working the land. Interestingly, a clay seal of the era has been found in Lachish that reads, "Belonging to Gedaliah, who is over the house."

Lost years. Jehoiachin was only 18 when he held Judah's throne for a brief three months (24:8). He was taken to Babylon and imprisoned there for 37 years! At last he was released and treated in Babylon as royalty. His experience is symbolic of that of his nation. Doing evil costs many years of anguish that can never be restored.

1 Chronicles

First and 2 Chronicles, a single book in the Hebrew Old Testament, cover events that are also reported in 2 Samuel and 1 and 2 Kings. Yet there is a clear difference in the authors' treatment and purpose. First and 2 Kings trace the response of each ruler of Israel and Judah to God's covenant requirements. The Chronicler focuses on the institutions intended to promote and express faith. He also pays close attention to Judah's godly rulers, and explores how each responded to significant tests of faith. Written for the exiles who returned to Judah from Babylon in 439 B.C., 1–2 Chronicles reminds the struggling Jewish community of the importance of worship, and that God is faithful to those who keep His covenant and maintain trust in Him.

---

1 CHRONICLES AT A GLANCE

KEY PERSON
David *Israel's shepherd king serves as an example of piety and concern with worship. His greatness demonstrates God's faithfulness.*

KEY EVENTS
David becomes king (1 Chron. 11). *His piety and prowess attract supporters.*
David takes the ark to Jerusalem (1 Chron. 13–15). *David emphasizes worship.*
David is promised a perpetual throne (1 Chron. 17). *God's covenant promises to David guarantee a future resurgence of the Jewish state.*
David focuses his attention as king on worship (1 Chron. 22–29). *David gave priority to worship at the temple, setting an example for all time.*

WHERE THE ACTION TAKES PLACE

The action takes place in Palestine, where David welds the 12 tribes of Israel together into a powerful, United Kingdom, and expands its borders tenfold (see map, p. 202).

Date and Authorship. No author is named in the work, and no date of writing is established in the text. Jewish tradition affirms Ezra as the author of 1–2 Chronicles, thus dating the work around the 450s or 440s B.C. Critics once insisted the book must have been written around 165 B.C., but fragments of an actual manuscript of Chronicles found at Qumran makes a date in the Persian period (538–333 B.C.) almost certain. The evident purpose of the book, calling the people of Judah to faith and hope, fits the time of Ezra and Nehemiah well.

THEOLOGICAL OUTLINE OF 1 CHRONICLES

I. GENEALOGY   1–9
II. DAVID   10–29

CONTENT OUTLINE OF 1 CHRONICLES

I. Genealogies (1:1–10:14)
  A. The Patriarchs (1:1-54)
  B. Judah (2:1–4:23)
    1. Hezron's clan (2:1-55)
    2. David's family (3:1-24)
    3. Other clans (4:1-23)
  C. Simeon (4:24-43)
  D. Transjordan Tribes (5:1-26)
  E. Levi (6:1-81)
  F. Other Tribes (7:1-40)
  G. Saul's Line (8:1–10:14)
    1. Benjamin (8:1-40)
    2. Jerusalem's citizens (9:1-44)
    3. Saul's death (10:1-14)
II. David (11:1–29:30)
  A. Acts of David the King (11:1–16:43)
    1. David becomes king (11:1-3)
    2. David takes Jerusalem (11:4-9)
    3. David's war heroes (11:10–12:40)
    4. David and God's ark (13:1–16:43)
      a. The ark sought (13:1-14)
      b. Fellowship restored (14:1-17)
      c. The ark taken to Jerusalem (15:1–16:43)
        (1) Priests and Levites enlisted (15:1-15)
        (2) Joyful worship (15:16–16:6)
        (3) Praise ordained (16:7-43)
  B. Account of David, God's Servant (17:1–29:30)

    1. God's promise to David (17:1-15)
    2. David's response (17:16-27)
    3. Defeat of David's enemies (18:1–20:8)
    4. David numbers his people (21:1-30)
    5. David prepares for the temple (22:1-19)
    6. David organizes for temple worship (23:1–27:34)
      a. He organizes the Levites (23:1-32)
      b. He organizes the priests (24:1-19)
      c. He assigns remaining Levites (24:20-31)
      d. He organizes musicians (25:1-31)
      e. He organizes levitical officials (26:1-32)
      f. He organizes Israel's princes (27:1-34)
    7. David prepares for his successor (28:1–29:20)
      a. He publicly appoints Solomon (28:1-10)
      b. He prepares plans for the temple (28:11-19)
      c. He commissions workmen (28:20–29:9)
      d. He blesses God and his successor (29:10-20)
    8. Solomon is crowned king (29:21-25)
    9. David dies (29:26-30)

Chapter summary. These lists of names seem boring to many a modern reader. Yet they demonstrate the Chronicler's theme. These lists serve as a reminder that God has proven faithful in His commitments to humankind from the beginning. They remind Israel of God's gracious choice of Abraham's family and they move on to affirm that God's purposes will be fulfilled through David's line. Through key names the writer reminds the Jewish people of Creation (1:1-3) and the Genesis Flood (vv. 4-27). The focus then shifts to Abraham, as lists of his descendants by his various wives recall God's promise to make Abraham the father of a multitude (vv. 28-54), including His covenant people (vv. 34-37). The writer then focuses on Judah (2:1-55), the tribe destined to produce the instrument of God's salvation (cf. Gen. 49:10). Within Judah he focuses on David (1 Chron. 3:1-16), whose royal line continues beyond the Exile (vv. 17-24) and from whom the Deliverer promised by the prophets will surely come. Thus simply by listing key names, the Chronicler has provided a bold outline of God's works in history past.

Key verse. 2:1: The choice of Israel remains the pivot of sacred history.

Personal application. Read Christian biographies to gain fresh insight into God's grace and faithfulness.

INSIGHT

Genealogies. Biblical genealogies do not include every ancestor in a family line. In the 18th century, Bishop Usher failed to realize this, and by adding up the years mentioned in the Genesis 4 genealogy, arrived at a date for Creation of 4004 B.C. Thus too the phrase "father of" means simply "ancestor," and may indicate a great great great grandfather, while "was the son of" may indicate a distant or immediate descendant.

Purposes of genealogies in Scripture. At least eight different purposes of O.T. genealogies have been suggested. (1) To show relationships between Israel and neighboring peoples. (2) To show relationships between elements in the story of Israel's origins. (3) To link periods of time not covered by other material. (4) As a means of organizing Israel's men for warfare, by tribe and family. (5) To demonstrate the legitimacy of a person or family's claim to a particular role or rank. (6) To preserve the purity of the chosen people and/or its priesthood. (7) To affirm the continuity of the people of God despite expulsion from the Promised Land. (8) To demonstrate progress toward achieving God's revealed purposes; to show that the Lord is sovereignly shaping history in accord with His own plan. The genealogies of the O.T. play a vital role

in maintaining the integrity, and showing the continuity, of Scripture's story of salvation.

Major genealogies. The following passages contain the major genealogies found in Scripture: Gen. 4–5, 10–11, 16, 21, 25, 29, 35–36, 46; Ex. 6; Num. 1, 3, 36; 2 Sam. 3; Ruth 4; Ezra 2, 8; Neh. 7, 11; Matt. 1; Luke 3. The genealogies of Christ in the N.T. are most closely linked with purposes 5 and 8, above.

Sources. Because genealogies did have several important functions in Heb. culture, careful records were kept. These would include oral tradition, census lists used for military purposes, documentation maintained by priestly families to prove lineage and thus the right to serve as worship leaders (cf. esp. Ezra 2:59-62), even written records for ordinary people, such as the records that proved Joseph and Mary lineal descendants of David a thousand years after his time, and thus required them to go to Bethlehem to be enrolled in a census ordered by the Romans (Luke 2:1-7). While it is hardly conceivable to us today to trace family lines back a thousand years, this was not surprising in biblical times.

God is faithful (3:17-24). What a reminder of God's faithfulness to know, centuries after Judah's crushing defeat and deportation, that God preserved David's line.

Outline
Place
Finder

GENEALOGY
DAVID

Chapter summary. The Chronicler continues his use of genealogies to minister to those who returned from Babylon. How important his lists are to the tiny settlement of some 50,000 Jews resettled in Judea. Despite domination by Gentile world powers, God remains faithful. His purposes will be fulfilled.

The Chronicler gives the genealogy of Judah (4:1-23), of Simeon (vv. 24-43), of the Transjordan tribes (5:1-26), of Levi (6:1-81) and of the remaining families (7:1-40), listing 12 tribes in all. The complement is complete: God's commitment to the descendants of Israel has not failed! The writer then focuses attention on the genealogy of Saul (8:1–9:44), briefly interrupted by genealogies of the inhabitants of Jerusalem (vv. 2-9), with special attention to priests and Levites (vv. 10-34). Why these genealogies? Because they remind Israel that God's faithfulness cuts both ways! Saul is Israel's failed king, whose disobedience led to his rejection by the Lord (1 Sam. 13; 15). God has been faithful to the covenant which guaranteed to discipline covenant-breakers as well as to bless those who are faithful! As for the inhabitants of Jerusalem, they show that man's unfaithfulness cannot frustrate the purposes of God. Survivors have returned to the Promised Land, and God is again worshiped in the city He determined to identify with His name (cf. Deut. 12:5). There is still hope, for God is totally faithful to His Word.

Key verse. 9:2: We can return to God and settle down among His promises.

Personal application. God is faithful to His promises—and us.

INSIGHT

Why are Dan and Zebulun left out? (4:1–7:40) Write down the tribes whose genealogies are listed, and you discover that two tribes are not mentioned. It is not because these tribes disappear from history. Rather the author has included Levi and counted the half-tribe of Manasseh (5:23-24) as a complete clan. So he has reached the number 12 without any mention of Dan and Zebulun. His purpose is to show that God has faithfully preserved the descendants of Abraham, and the number 12 symbolizes the whole people, so there is no need to include genealogies of the other 2 tribes.

Why mention cities and districts? The genealogies in these chapters frequently specify districts and cities within Palestine that were orginally given to families within the tribes. This is an important reminder that God's commitment to Israel was not only spiritual, but temporal as well. God promised His people a land, and though most tribes were dispossessed at the time the Chronicler wrote, they still retain the title deed to the land God originally granted them. It may be hard for us to realize that we too possess blessings we are not currently experiencing. God grants us the title deed, and we rejoice at the certain prospect of what most surely will be ours.

Gibeon vs. Jerusalem (8:1–9:44). The passage is designed to contrast the inhabitants of Gibeon, who are associated with Israel's failed king, Saul, with those who live in Jerusalem, the city of David. While both cities were important centers, God had not chosen Gibeon. But He did choose Jerusalem, not as Israel's political capital but as the location for His temple. It was in Jerusalem, where the ark rested, that God met with His people. It was Jerusalem where the priests offered sacrifices for sin. It was Jerusalem where the Levites led in worship. Thus the repopulation of Jerusalem was evidence that God still poured out salvation and blessing on His people, and a promise that one day the promised Deliverer of Messiah's line would appear. As long as Jerusalem stood ready, and God's people worshiped the Lord there, history would move toward God's appointed and blessed end.

Chapter summary. Now genealogy and story meet. The Chronicler has contrasted Gibeon, the seat of Saul, and Jerusalem, the city of David (8:1–9:44). Now the writer sets the stage for his introduction of David by describing Saul's end. That end is marked by defeat for the nation (10:1-3), and with the towering king crumpled on the ground, pierced by his own sword (vv. 4-7). His body is exposed to shame by Israel's enemies, and even its retrieval is hazardous (vv. 8-12). All this happened to Saul because he was unfaithful to the Lord (vv. 13-14). In contrast the faithful David is chosen by God to "shepherd My people Israel" (11:1-3). He takes Jerusalem and becomes "more and more powerful, because the Lord Almighty was with him" (vv. 4-9). David's loyalty to God is reflected in the loyalty to him of the mighty men God provided to assist in his conquests (vv. 10-47). Again we sense the Chronicler's theme: God can be trusted to punish those who are unfaithful to Him, and to bring success to those committed to the Lord.

Key verse. 10:13: Unfaithfulness assures defeat.

Personal application. Everyone God chooses is, like David, to serve the Lord and shepherd others.

Key concepts. Philistines »p. 185. Jerusalem »p. 205.

INSIGHT

The message of 1 Chron. 10–11. God does punish unfaithfulness. But He does not abandon His people. God raises up David not only to lead his own generation, but to be the focus of a divine commitment to provide an eternal kingdom for God's people (cf. 2 Sam. 7).

Illustration. *The two-page panel below shows Israelites equipped as they would have been in David's day. David's men were foot soldiers, who forwent chariots and horses to rely on the shields, swords, slings, bows and arrows, and short javelins of infantry.*

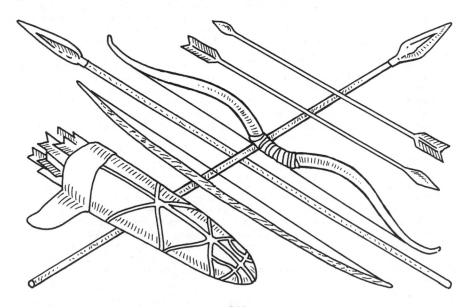

Chapter summary. The author looks back at the time before God kept His promise to make David king. Even though Saul reigned, there was clear evidence of God's faithfulness. During David's outlaw years, while he fled from Saul, fighting men from Saul's own tribe of Benjamin traveled to Ziklag, in Philistine territory, to join the future ruler (12:1-7). Gadites, from the far north, joined David (vv. 8-15). Men of the South, Judah and Benjamin were also among David's early supporters (vv. 16-18). Even chief men of Manasseh, another far northern tribe, joined David before he had become king (vv. 19-21), so that the downfall of Saul was foreshadowed by the growth of David's personal army (v. 22). And when the moment came for David to be acknowledged king of a united Israel, God provided him with a mighty volunteer army, fully supplied; an army of God, ready to follow the lead of David and accomplish God's will (vv. 23-40). The message is clear. When God's time comes to fulfill His promises to the remnant now living in Judah, the Lord will provide the resources needed to keep every one.

Key verse. 12:22: God provides.

Personal application. Expect God to give you the strength to succeed in every task He calls you to perform.

Key concepts. Holy Spirit »p. 73. Warfare »p. 133. David »p. 191.

INSIGHT

Volunteers. God drew volunteers to David, with no indication that he actively recruited supporters. No individual is able to accomplish much alone. God's assembly of a team around us is often an indication of His timing.

God's army. The reported size of David's army, some 339,600 men, has been questioned by critics. But this volunteer army included *all* Israel's fighting men. When every believer gladly commits to serve in God's army, God's work is easily done!

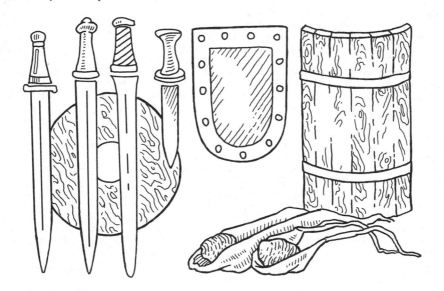

Chapter summary. As king, David calls for bringing the ark of the covenant to Jerusalem. The ark symbolizes the presence of God with His people. It was ignored by Saul, and so David's initiative demonstrates his conviction that trust in God must be the foundation on which a lasting kingdom can be built (13:1-3). But while the escorts are celebrating wildly, God strikes dead a man who reached out his hand and touched the ark (vv. 4-10). David is angry and awed, and leaves the ark at a farm near where the incident happened (vv. 11-14). Meanwhile David is blessed with the friendship of Hiram of Tyre (14:1-2), with a large and growing family (vv. 3-7), and with victories over Israel's traditional enemies, the Philistines (vv. 8-17).

Key verse. 13:3: David determined not to ignore God.

Personal application. God blesses us when we intend to please Him, even though we may fall short.

Key concepts. Ark of the covenant »p. 68. Anger of God »pp. 65, 72. Fear of God »p. 387. Philistines »p. 185.

INSIGHT

Bring back the ark (13:3). The ark was the focus of God's presence with His people (cf. Ex. 25:10-22; 1 Chron. 13:6). Saul's failure to inquire of (seek) God there reveals his general disregard of the significance of the relationship with God. David, however, intended the ark to be in Jerusalem, the political and geographic center of Israel. To David, relationship with God was of central importance, the living heart of the nation. The Chronicles' reminder is both for the postexilic Jews in Judah and for us. He is the focus and center of our lives.

On a cart (13:7). O.T. Law is explicit. The ark is to be carried on poles, borne only by Levites (Num. 4:15). It's good to be eager to be close to God. But we must be careful to approach Him in the way He has ordained.

"Celebrating" (13:8). The text pictures an ecstatic, emotional scene, with God's people joyously shouting out their praise. The celebration was short-lived, as suddenly, unexpectedly, the life of Uzzah was snuffed out as he tried to steady the ark on the jolting cart. The event reminds us that we are to be enthusiastic about God and our faith but emotion is no substitute for knowledge of God's will. If we really love Him, we will show it in the careful study of His Word as well as in raised voices and hands.

Anger and fear (13:11-12). David's reaction is understandable. David had no idea at first why God acted as He did, or what that action meant. We too may feel anger or fear as unexpected tragedy strikes our lives. But we need to learn, as David did, to trust God in all things. And that loss is not a sign His hand of blessing is removed.

How striking that despite David's anger and fear God blessed, not only the home of Obed-Edom where the ark remained, but David and his nation (cf. 14:1-17).

Why strike Uzzah? The ark, a gold-covered wooden chest, was the holiest object in Israel's religion. It represented the point at which God and man met. That holiness required the ark be treated with awe, and be as untouchable as God Himself was in the O.T. era. God struck Uzzah not because his motives were wrong, but because God truly is holy. His people then as now must not only rejoice in Him, but must also hold Him in awe. Only when God is given the respect He deserves will we obey and serve Him only.

God's blessing is on His people (14:1-17). David had shown appropriate concern that God be central in his and his people's life, in seeking to bring the ark to Jerusalem. He had not been careful in every detail of its transport. But God honored David's intentions, and blessed him. The three types of blessings listed here are traditional benefits of a right relationship with God: peace with neighbors, an enlarged family, and victory over enemies.

How good God is to overlook our shortcomings, and to accept our intention to serve Him with our whole heart. As He blessed David, so will God bless us when our hearts are right with Him.

Chapter summary. David's first attempt to bring the ark of God to Jerusalem failed (13:1-14). Now he tries again. This time he observes the rules for its transportation (15:1-15). The grand procession proceeds, and the ark is accompanied by marching bands, choirs, the military, and the elders of Israel, with David himself at the head of the celebrating throng (vv. 16-28). Only Michal, the daughter of Saul, seems to find no joy in the occasion (v. 29). The ark is placed inside a tent David has constructed for it (16:1-3). Levites are assigned to lead in perpetual worship (vv. 4-6) and David contributes an original psalm of thanksgiving in praise of God's greatness (vv. 7-36). At last daily offerings are made and daily worship is conducted in Jerusalem, Israel's capital city and the place God has chosen to be forever identified with His name (vv. 37-43).

Outline
Place
Finder

GENEALOGY
DAVID

Key verse. 16:40: Concern with worship is the key to David's success.

Personal application. There is joy as well as wisdom in putting the worship of God first.

Key concepts. Ark of the covenant »p. 68. Levites »p. 95. Miracle »pp. 57, 679. Love for God »p. 351. Glory »p. 74. Worship »p. 380.

INSIGHT

Why is so much attention given to the ark? The author's purpose is to remind the postexilic community of the vital importance of worship. If the little Jewish community now struggling to survive in part of Judah is to experience the resurgence Israel experienced under David, they will have to be as committed to the Lord as David was. And, as the death of Uzzah shows, the Jews must be careful to observe every regulation having to do with worship! Thus the focus on the ark is a reminder that only a people who worship God in His way can expect blessing.

Joy. The jubilant sense of joy expressed in these two chapters reflects a basic O.T. theme. There "joy" is not as much a private emotion as an experience shared by God's people as they are caught up in worship. Heb. words for joy include: *gil*, joy in God's works or person; *ranan*, shouts of joy uttered at times of sacrifice or remembrance of His saving works; *sus*, enthusiasm excited by God and His Word; and *samah*, a glad or joyful outlook. Joy in the O.T. is a product of divine blessing, which may be material (Deut. 16:15), but also flows directly from personal relationship with the Lord (Ps. 16:11). Thus joy is a distinctive gift from God to believers, and is experienced when He is given first place in our lives. As David's psalm says, "Let the heavens rejoice, let the earth be glad; let them say among the nations, 'The Lord reigns!' " (1 Chron. 16:31) When He reigns in our hearts, we know joy.

"Michal" (15:29). There is a story behind Michal's reaction. »p. 207. Here, however, the author has a simple purpose. Michal, a representative of the house of her father, Saul, does not notice the ark, but sees only David—and she despises him. This is exactly the fault that caused Saul to fall: he just couldn't see the importance of worshiping God. How easily our attention is distracted from the Lord! And how much we need to keep our hearts focused on Him.

Daily worship (16:4-6, 37-42). David's attention to organizing regular, daily worship serves as an example to the postexilic community. And to us.

"Praise" (16:7-36). David teaches us to praise God for His personal qualities (vv. 7-11), His works on our behalf (vv. 12-13), His covenant commitment demonstrated in sacred history (vv. 14-22), and to exult in the glory and strength He will express in the future (vv. 23-36).

269

Chapter summary. David has shown his dedication to God by bringing the ark of the covenant to Jerusalem, and by organizing daily worship (chaps. 13–15). David's desire to build God a temple shows his continuing commitment to worship (17:1-2). Through the Prophet Nathan God tells David not to build a house of worship, but promises His faithful servant that the Lord will give David a house (vv. 3-10a). The play on words does not disguise the awesome nature of the divine promise. God will guarantee David an unbroken line of descendants qualified to take Israel's throne, until One actually establishes an eternal kingdom (vv. 10b-15). David is stunned by this evidence of God's love. He is speechless and can only bless God for His goodness and ask Him to use His power to do what He has promised (vv. 16-27). The report of this event following immediately after the report of David's bringing of the ark to Jerusalem and setting up daily worship, underlines the relationship to worship and blessing. Those who serve God wholeheartedly can expect Him not only to bless, but to send the promised Saviour of David's line. The implication is that the more faithful the worship, the sooner that glad time will come.

Key verse. 17:14: God envisions an eternal kingdom.

Personal application. Doing God's will daily is more important than building temples — unless He calls us to build one.

Key concepts. Temple »p. 283. Davidic Covenant »p. 370. Prayer »p. 181. Messiah »p. 431.

INSIGHT

The importance of 1 Chron. 17. This is one of the pivotal chapters in the O.T. God's promises to David are viewed as a covenant commitment, with the same history-shaping force as His covenant with Abraham (cf. 2 Sam. 23:5; Pss. 89:3, 34; 132:11-12). The covenant has several elments: David will be great, and provide a secure place for God's people, for God will subdue his enemies (1 Chron. 17:8-10); David's line will continue, a perpetual dynasty (vv. 10-11); David's successor will build the temple (v. 11); a Descendant of David will establish an eternal kingdom, and exercise an endless rule (v. 14).

Solomon and the other kings of David's line fell short. But in God's time a Child was born of a virgin, first to win salvation for lost humanity, and ultimately to rule eternally. In God's time Jesus Christ, a Descendant of David, will return to earth and establish the eternal kingdom envisioned in this chapter, and the prophets (cf. Isa. 9:6; 11:1-5; Jer. 17:24-27; Amos 9:11-12; Micah 5:2-4).

Why not David? (17:4) The reason is given in 1 Chron. 22:8; 28:3. David was a fighting man, a "man of blood." God's house, symbolic of the peace and rest that comes through relationship with the Lord, must be built by a man of peace. There is no record of a single war fought during Solmon's 40-year rule!

Not "a" (17:4). The Heb. text says "build Me *the* house." God intended that His temple be built in Jerusalem at a site He would choose.

Promises fulfilled (17:8-10). The next chapters (18–20) describe David's wars, and demonstrate that God was faithful to His promise. Chapter 21 is related to 17:12, and tells how the site for the temple David's son was to build was selected.

Responding to God's promises (17:16-27). David's prayer displays two qualities which are vital to an experience of God's grace. First, David is humble, acknowledging that he deserves nothing that God has given him (cf. v. 16). Second, David has complete confidence that God will keep His promises (vv. 20-27). What an example for the men and women of Judah to follow. As David trusted God, so must the Jewish settlers back in Judah. And so must you and I.

Chapter summary. Chronicles now shows how faithfully God kept the first element of His covenant with David (cf. 17:8-10). The writer details David's victories to demonstrate to those of his own day that God can be trusted to fulfill the other promises made to Israel's shepherd king; promises that mean salvation and greatness for Israel in the future. How faithful was the Lord? David won an unbroken string of victories over the Philistines (18:1-4), the Arameans (Syrians) (vv. 5-11), the Edomites, and others (vv. 12-13). While David did not seek war, he defended the honor of Israel against Ammonite and Aramean alike, and made his people secure (19:1-19). Warfare persisted through David's reign, but David was victorious over every foe (20:1-8).

Key verse. 19:19: Peace sometimes must be fought for.

Personal application. Remembering God's faithfulness in our past is a source of hope for our future.

INSIGHT

"Victory" (18:6, 13). The repetition reminds us that David's concern for relationship with God was the cornerstone of his military success. David was decisive and astute. But it was the Lord who gave him his victories. God expects us to use our abilities, but to credit Him with our successes.

Dedicated to the Lord (18:11). David publicly acknowledged God as the source of his success by dedicating the treasures he took to the Lord.

David's delegation (19:1-19). The story underlines the fact that David's wars were not wars of expansion per se. The enemies in chapter 18 were traditionally hostile to Israel, and had to be fought in order to make God's people secure. Here an unprovoked insult created a fear that led the Ammonites to raise an army against Israel. David's victory enables him to further expand Israel's borders, and put garrisons in nearby lands to ensure peace, and control trade routes. The story implies that the Lord stirred up some of the wars David fought that Israel might occupy much of the land promised centuries before to Abraham.

Why isn't Bathsheba mentioned? (20:1) The war with the Ammonites over Rabbah is described so this is undoubtedly the occasion of David's sin with Bathsheba. Yet the author never mentions that familiar tale. Why? Some have said the omission is evidence that the Chronicler idealized David, and intended to gloss over his weaknesses. That argument is weak, however, as all agree the writer of Chronicles used 1 and 2 Samuel as a source, and that the story of David's failure was well known in Israel. Two much better reasons have been suggested. First, the incident is left out simply because it does not fit the author's theme, which is to demonstrate the importance of worship and the faithfulness of God. The second suggestion is fascinating. The Chronicler looks at history from God's point of view. And from God's point of view, David, who has confessed his sin with Bathsheba, is cleansed and purified. The sin with Bathsheba remains unmentioned simply because the sin has been forgiven—and forgotten by the Lord! How good to know that when God forgives us, He no longer "remembers our sins" (cf. Heb. 8:12).

271

Outline
Place
Finder

GENEALOGY
DAVID

Chapter summary. At some point in David's reign, the king decides to take a military census. The writer says that Satan incites David (21:1), and despite the urging of Joab, David commands that his people be numbered (vv. 2-5). The census is incomplete, as Joab resists, and David realizes he has sinned (vv. 6-8). The Prophet Gad relays God's unusual command: David is to select his own punishment (vv. 9-13). David chooses a plague, and when David prays for mercy, he is instructed to build an altar on a specific site (vv. 14-19). David purchases the field on that site and offers the required sacrifice. David then realizes the Lord has used his sin redemptively, for God has chosen this very site as home for the temple (21:20-30).

Key verse. 21:17: David accepts responsibility.

Personal application. God can transform our sins and failures and bring good out of evil.

Key concepts. Angel of the Lord »p. 37. Confession »p. 892. Altar »p. 79. Sacrifice »p. 78.

INSIGHT

Satan incited David? (21:1) This notation reminds us of the complex causes of the event recorded in this chapter and in 2 Sam. 24:1, where God is said to have been angry with Israel and incited David's act. Later David takes full responsibility himself.

Two points are important. First, while others incited David, and thus were responsible for their acts, David remained fully responsible for his moral decision. We can never honestly say, "The devil made me do it," for ultimately we make our own free choice, and are responsible for what we do. Second, the motives of none of the parties is clear. Satan, the persistent enemy of God's people, may have been motivated by nothing more specific than general hostility. David's motives remain a mystery too. Perhaps we can guess best at God's motives, for 2 Sam. 24:1 says the Lord was angry with "Israel." If this event followed the rebellion of Absalom and Sheba, God's anger may well be a righteous reaction to the people's rejection of David, God's choice for their king.

Numbers in the O.T. (21:5). Most often numbers given in parallel passages in 1–2 Samuel, 1–2 Kings, and 1–2 Chronicles agree. However, there are discrepancies, and in about two thirds of the cases the numbers in Chronicles are higher. The cause is not, as some have suggested, because the Chronicler is giving inflated numbers in an idealization of David's era. Originally Heb. mss. indicated thousands by dots over letters of the alphabet. Only later did scribes decide to write out larger numbers (e.g., to write "two thousand" rather write an "*a*" with two dots above it). Thus numbers in the O.T. were among the most difficult things to preserve accurately.

"Mercy" (21:13). "Mercy" in the O.T. is not only the capacity to be emotionally moved by the distress of others, but also the will to act on their behalf. David's confidence that God is merciful led him to choose the best of the three options. In fact God relented even before David confessed and offered his sacrifice.

Araunah's threshing floor (21:15). Threshing floors were typically located on a rocky height. This particular height had great significance: it was the site of Abraham's symbolic sacrifice of his son, Isaac (2 Chron. 3:1; Gen. 22).

Sacrifice (21:18). David confessed his sin. But it was still necessary to offer an atoning sacrifice. There is no forgiveness without sacrifice.

"The full price" (21:24-25). David paid 50 shekels of silver for the animals that were to be sacrificed (2 Sam. 24:24). It was the land that cost David 15 pounds of gold.

Two kinds of offerings (21:26). The burnt offering was a sacrifice for sin; the fellowship offering symbolized renewed commitment. God showed His acceptance of the offerings by the fire from heaven. This miraculous sign and the appearance of the Angel of the Lord convinced David: Araunah's field was the site God had chosen for His temple.

Why wouldn't David worship at Gibeon? (21:29) David now realized that the Lord had chosen this place as the temple site. Out of respect for that choice, David refused to worship elsewhere.

Chapter summary. God has chosen His site for the building of a temple (1 Chron. 22). Now the rest of 1 Chronicles shows how significant temple worship was to David, and thus teaches how important worship is to be to the postexilic community. David is convinced the temple of the Lord should be of "great magnificence," and dedicates himself to preparing for its construction (vv. 1-5). First, however, he prepares his son, Solomon (vv. 6-13). The heart of the worshiper always has higher priority than the place he or she worships!

But David does not overlook the place. He assembles some 3,750 tons of gold, and 37,500 tons of silver, plus building materials (vv. 14-17). And David urges Israel's leaders to be devoted to God, and support the temple project (vv. 18-19). David also reorganizes the Levites. This tribe was no longer needed to transport the tabernacle, Israel's ancient, portable worship center. When the temple was built they would have important new roles, assisting the priests, maintaining the temple buildings, and leading God's people in praise (23:1-32). God had promised that David's son would build His temple. David believed the promise—and worked toward its fulfillment.

Outline
Place
Finder

GENEALOGY
DAVID

Key verse. 22:19: Devotion is to be expressed in action.

Personal application. Expect God to keep His promises. But don't sit and wait. Work toward their fulfillment.

Key concepts. Temple »p. 283. Peace »p. 427. Levites »p. 95.

INSIGHT

Making preparations. David knew God would keep His promise and that his son would build the Lord's temple. Yet David dedicated the last decade of his life to preparing for its construction. God did keep His promise—and David's work of preparation was a means God used to do so. Let's not sit back and wait for God to keep promises He has made to us. Often God intends our zeal and hard work to be the means He uses to keep His Word!

Magnificence, fame, and splendor (22:5). All our works are to bring praise to God's name.

"A man of peace and rest" (22:9). David, a man of war, lived in intimate relationship with God. But God chose a man of peace to build the temple. Why? As events showed, David was a far more godly person than Solomon. But Solomon's rule, unmarred by a single war, better expressed the symbolism of the temple, which represented God dwelling among His people. When God is present with us, there is peace and rest in our hearts. When God is present with a nation, that nation will know international and social peace as well.

"Discretion and understanding" (22:12). If we are to be successful in performing works

that bring praise to God, we must understand God's will, and be responsive to Him.

Strength, plus (22:14). Certain moral and personal qualities are often associated with obedience in the O.T. These are: *strength*, to resist the pull of inner temptation; *courage*, to choose what is right instead of surrender to the expectations and ridicule of friends; *fearlessness*, to keep on course despite active opposition from hostile others; and *hope*, to overcome discouragement when the fulfillment of God's promise is delayed. If we commit ourselves fully to God, He will equip us with the strength, courage, fearlessness, and hope that will enable us to always choose His will.

David gathered (23:2). The verse is the key to the author's organization of the next chapters. In reverse order he tells us how David involved the leaders (27:1-34), the priests (24:1-19), and the Levites (23:1-32; 24:20–26:32) in preparing for the temple.

"To help" (23:28). Some people think merely "to help" others is insignificant. They want to be the star in the public eye. But 1 Chron. gives more space to the helpers than to the priests!

Outline
Place
Finder

GENEALOGY
DAVID

Chapter summary. These chapters continue the review of David's organization of temple personnel (24:1–26:32). They conclude with a list of David's army commanders (27:1-15) and his secular officials (vv. 16-34). These chapters have little direct application to us today. But they were important to the postexilic community, for they provided a model for that community's organization of worship which could be traced back to David himself. And they underline again the overarching significance of the temple in Jewish life, as four of five chapters dealing with personnel were devoted to the temple, and only one to secular affairs. It is important to be governed well. But it is even more important to pay the closest attention to our relationship with God. The chapters also remind us of the importance of music in the worship and praise of God. See »p. 275.

Key verse. 24:19: Order in all things relating to God.

Personal application. Planned, organized worship as well as spontaneous enthusiasm is appropriate today.

Key concepts. Priests »p. 81. Levites »p. 95. Temple »p. 283.

INSIGHT

23:24. David did not give the Levites their special role in serving God. That choice was God's own, made at the time of the Exodus (cf. Num. 4). David did, however, assign them to new tasks in view of the changes implicit in construction of a permanent temple. We need to be sensitive to new and different ways to serve God and others.

"Drawing lots" (24:5). The use of lots was not resorting to "chance" or gambling. It was instead an expression of surrender to the will of God, who as Sovereign could and would determine how the lots fell. The same principle is seen in the distribution of the land at the time of the Conquest. »p. 152.

The singers (25:1-31). The importance of music in temple worship is illustrated first by the fact that 4,000 of the 38,000 Levites of David's time were assigned to praise God as singers and musicians (cf. 23:3-4). It is also illustrated in the facts that musicians were drawn from each major levitical family, that like the priests they were organized in 24 different shifts (with plenty of time for practice and preparation!), and that the leader of each shift is identified by name.

"Prophesying, accompanied by harps" (25:1). Many commentators take this phrase as the equivalent of "singing praises to God." Quite properly "prophecy" has the sense of forthtelling (proclaiming God's message) as well as foretelling (predicting the future). In their ministry of music, which featured the

singing of psalms, the singers of Israel not only praised God but also taught His people. In this the musicians were as close to God as the prophets and preachers, for they shared the same ministry.

"Gatekeepers" (26:1-19). Though there were also 4,000 gatekeepers, there is less detail given about them and their shifts. It was the duty of the gatekeepers to stand armed guard at 24 key posts. They kept unauthorized persons out of restricted areas, and protected the vast wealth that had been dedicated to the temple treasury. This task too called for "able" and "capable men with the strength to do the work" (vv. 7-8). Every person who serves God in any way must be gifted with the abilities needed to perform his task.

David's army (27:1-24). David's rotation system was typical of his genius. He not only kept his troops in fighting trim, but also maintained close personal contact with each of his generals.

Strikingly, each of these generals is listed among the war heroes ("mighty men") identified in 11:11-47 and 2 Sam. 23:8-39 as a courageous warrior in his own right. Only those who had successfully fought the enemy could lead others in battle.

There's an important principle here, reflected in a question many mission boards ask candidates for service overseas. How active and successful have you been in evangelism with folks next door?

Music In Worship

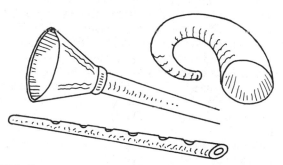

The Old Testament mentions many different instruments used in worship and praise. From top left to right, they include the double pipe (*halil*; 1 Kings 1:40); the trumpet (*hasosherah*; Ps. 150:3); the flute ('*ugab*; Job 30:31); the ram's horn trumpet (*shofar*; Ps. 81:3); the cymbals, which were fitted on the fingers of one hand (*selselim*; 1 Chron. 13:8); the tambourine (*toph*; Ps. 149:3); the lyre (*nebel*; 33:2); and the harp (*kinnor*; 43:4). The *Revell Bible Dictionary* notes that "music permeated Israel's daily life. Instruments were played at family parties (Gen. 31:27; Luke 15:25). Song and dance celebrated the return of war heroes (Jud. 11:34; 1 Sam. 18:6). Kings were enthroned to music (1 Kings 1:39-40; 2 Kings 11:14), and music was played as armies marched off to war. Music provided entertainment at the royal court (2 Sam. 19:35) and at the banquets of the wealthy (Isa. 5:12; 24:8-9). Workmen sang as they performed their tasks, and many occupations apparently used music to pace their work (Isa. 16:10; Jer. 25:30). Even sorrow was expressed in the slow, mournful notes of dirges and laments (2 Sam. 1:17-18; Matt. 9:23)" (1990, F.H. Revell, p. 715). Yet it was in worship that the role of music found its highest expression, such as guilds of professional musicians that lead Israel in worship.

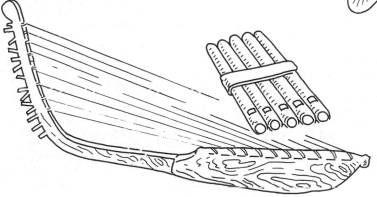

Outline
Place
Finder

GENEALOGY
DAVID

Chapter summary. This Old Testament book concludes with a great outburst of joy and generosity. David calls together all the leading men of Israel (28:1). He reviews the covenant God has made with him (vv. 2-7) and publicly hands over detailed, written plans for the temple to Solomon, whom he identifies as his successor (vv. 8-21). David also challenges the leading men to give generously to the temple project. He sets the example by not only committing the nation's resources, but also by giving all "my personal treasures" (29:1-5). David's officials respond to the challenge. Together they commit some 375 tons of gold to the project (vv. 6-9; cf. p. 224). David expresses his joy and confidence in the Lord in a brief prayer (vv. 10-20). He acknowledges Solomon as king (vv. 21-25) and then, his lifework well and truly done, David dies (vv. 26-30).

Key verse. 29:2: As always David gives everything to the Lord.

Personal application. When we have complete trust in God's ability to meet our needs we too will be free to give generously.

INSIGHT

A third account (28:4-5). This is the third time God's covenant promises to David have been featured in 1 Chronicles (see also 17:1-17; 22:1-19). On each occasion the promises are the foundation on which the following material rests. In each case the author goes on to tell how David acted in view of the promises. What a lesson for us. God's commitments to us are to shape our actions, even as they guarantee our future.

"The kingdom of the Lord over Israel" (28:5). Despite David's fame, he never forgot that the kingdom he ruled belonged to the Lord. Christian leaders must remain servants at heart, remembering that the true ruler of God's kingdom is the Lord.

Motives behind thoughts (28:9). While O.T. Law does describe godly behavior, the O.T. like the N.T. makes it clear that the hidden character of each individual is as much God's concern as his or her overt behavior. True godliness is not found merely in doing right: it is found in wanting to do the right we choose. To God, the motives behind the thoughts that find expression in our actions are at least as important as the actions themselves! The consistent message of Old and New Testaments is that human beings need a change of heart; that only an inner transformation can produce a righteousness God is able to accept.

Inspiration (28:19). David here claims the same kind of inspiration for the detailed design of the temple he handed over to Solomon that Moses claimed for the giving of God's Law. God's hand (His active, personal, guiding presence) was on David as it had been on

Moses (cf. Ex. 25:40; 40:2). The Chronicler thus reminds his readers that appropriate worship of God is as important as appropriate moral and social behavior. The postexilic Jewish community, like many Christians today, downgraded the importance of formal worship. This passage reminds us that our worship is still important to God.

"Be strong and courageous" (28:20). There are a number of parallels between Moses/Joshua and David/Solomon. In each case the former was the source of covenant promises that shaped the future of his successor and the nation. In each case the former received revelations passed down in writing. In each case a successor was commissioned to fulfill the dream of the former. In each case the latter was urged, "Be strong and courageous" (cf. Josh. 1:9). How often the dreams of a great spiritual leader are unfulfilled in his or her own time. But how gracious of God to provide successors, who do fulfill the dream, building on the foundation earlier leaders have provided. If you want to see your dreams fulfilled, build the foundation in your successors' lives. And if you fulfill the dream, be sure to credit those on whose shoulders you stand.

Able to give generously (29:14). David is stunned by the overwhelming amount given by him and his people toward building the temple. He realizes again that God's grace has provided them with such wealth. Again there are lessons for us. We cannot outgive God. We need not hold back but can give generously. Since all we have is from God, He deserves our best.

2 Chronicles

Second Chronicles continues the compelling review of Jewish history begun in 1 Chronicles. While the chronicler covers events reported in 1 and 2 Samuel and in 1 and 2 Kings, he has a different purpose. First and 2 Kings focus on the responses of the rulers of the two Hebrew kingdoms to God, and the impact of those responses on the nation. First and 2 Chronicles emphasize the close attention that Judah's godly rulers paid to temple worship and those institutions through which Israel expressed faith and enjoyed fellowship with the Lord.

These books were written following the return of a small group of Jews to Judah following the fall of the Babylonian Empire. Intent on rebuilding the temple and resettling the Holy Land, the little community soon found itself in a struggle simply to survive. The foundations of the temple were laid; then building stopped for some 18 years. Jerusalem itself was more or less abandoned as the people settled in outlying towns and fought to reclaim Judah's abandoned farmlands. Even when the temple was finished, the city was sparsely populated and its walls a heap of ruins.

It is against this background that the chronicler reviews Jewish history, intent on showing his generation that God is always faithful to those who put Him first. History itself is a call to worship and an invitation to hope. If the struggling community of Jews in Judah will put God first as did godly generations of the past, and show their commitment by a similar zeal for worship, the Lord will surely show His faithfulness to them. The line of David will yet again take Zion's throne and the kingdom of God be established over all the earth.

---

2 CHRONICLES AT A GLANCE

KEY PEOPLE

Solomon *The royal son of David who constructed the first temple and called all Israel to worship the Lord.*

Rehoboam *Solomon's successor, whose harshness led to a division of the kingdom, and arrogance to an Egyptian rape of temple treasures.*

Asa, Jehoshaphat, Joash, Hezekiah, Josiah *The "godly kings" of Judah whose dedication to the Lord brought Judah through especially perilous times, and whose commitment to worship serves as an example to Judah's settlers.*

KEY EVENTS

Solomon dedicates the temple (2 Chron. 6–7). *Solomon's prayer establishes the significance of the temple in Jewish worship.*

Israel rebels against Rehoboam (2 Chron. 10–11). *The Northern Kingdom abandons temple worship and is lost. Subsequent events in the Southern Kingdom show that God is faithful when His people keep covenant with Him.*

Hezekiah's religious reforms preserve Judah when the Assyrians destroy the Northern Kingdom, Israel (2 Chron. 29–32). *Dedication to God is a hedge against future dangers.*

Josiah's response to the rediscovered Book of the Law preserves Judah during his lifetime (2 Chron. 34–35). *Dedication to God guards us against present dangers as well.*

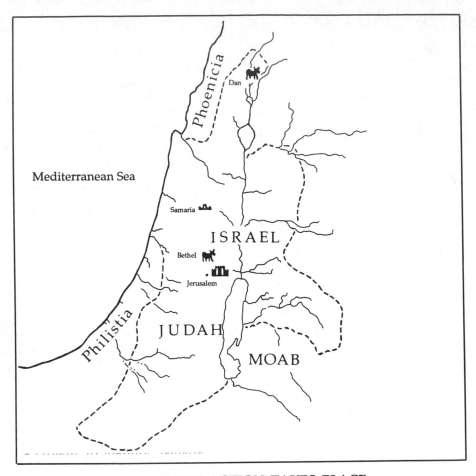

WHERE THE ACTION TAKES PLACE

After the division of Solomon's United Kingdom (above), the chronicler focuses his attention on Judah, in the south. The north, Israel, set up a counterfeit religion with worship centers at Bethel and Dan (cf. 1 Kings 12). The author uses the history of Judah to demonstrate that God blesses His people when they remain faithful and joyfully worship the Lord.

Date and Authorship. The work was certainly written during the Persian era (538–333 B.C.), but no author is identified in the text. Jewish tradition holds that Ezra is the author of 1–2 Chronicles.

Structure. Second Chronicles reveals recurrent cycles seen in Judah's history. Each cycle begins at a high point, with a godly king whose reforms model faithfulness to God. Each cycle ends with a faithless king, who abandons God and brings disasters on Judah. As time progresses each subsequent low becomes deeper, until Judah too is carried away into Captivity. The theological outline (p. 279) gives each cycle the name of the godly king who initiated it.

THEOLOGICAL OUTLINE OF 2 CHRONICLES

CONTENT OUTLINE OF 2 CHRONICLES

I. Solomon's Reign (1:1–9:31)
  A. His Wealth and Wisdom (1:1-17)
  B. His Building of the Temple
     (2:1–5:1)
     1. Preparations (2:1-18)
     2. The structure (3:1-17)
     3. The furnishings (4:1–5:1)
  C. His Dedication of the Temple
     (5:2–7:10)
     1. Placing the ark (5:2-14)
     2. Solomon's blessings and
        prayer (6:1-42)
     3. Solomon's sacrifices (7:1-10)
  D. God's Blessings and Curses
     (7:11-22)
  E. Solomon's Successes (8:1–9:31)
     1. Political successes (8:1-11)
     2. Religious successes (8:12-16)
     3. Economic successes (8:17–9:31)
II. Further History of David's Line
    (10:1–36:23)
  A. Rehoboam (10:1–12:16)
     1. The North rebels (10:1-19)
     2. Rehoboam's defenses
        (11:1-23)
     3. Egypt invades (12:1-16)
  B. Abijah (13:1-22)
  C. Asa (14:1–16:14)
     1. Asa's obedience (14:1-15)
     2. Asa's reforms (15:1-19)
     3. Asa's treaty with Aram
        (16:1-14)
  D. Jehoshaphat (17:1–20:37)
     1. Jehoshaphat's strength
        (17:1-19)
     2. Jehoshaphat's alliance with
        Ahab of Israel (18:1–19:3)
     3. Jehoshaphat's judges (19:4-11)
     4. Jehoshaphat's victory (20:1-30)
     5. Jehoshaphat's last days (20:31-37)

  E. Jehoram (21:1-20)
  F. Ahaziah (22:1-9)
  G. Athaliah (22:10–23:21)
  H. Joash (24:1-27)
     1. Joash restores the temple
        (24:1-16)
     2. Joash turns to wickedness
        (24:17-27)
  I. Amaziah (25:1-28)
  J. Uzziah (26:1-23)
  K. Jotham (27:1-9)
  L. Ahaz (28:1-27)
  M. Hezekiah (29:1–32:33)
     1. Hezekiah cleanses the
        temple (29:1-36)
     2. Hezekiah holds Passover
        (30:1–31:1)
     3. Hezekiah resumes proper
        worship (31:2-21)
     4. Hezekiah's prayer turns
        back Assyria's invasion
        (32:1-23)
     5. Hezekiah's sickness and
        healing (32:24-33)
  N. Manasseh (33:1-20)
  O. Amon (33:21-25)
  P. Josiah (34:1–35:27)
     1. Josiah's revival (34:1-33)
     2. Josiah's Passover (35:1-19)
     3. Josiah's death (35:20-27)
  Q. Jehoahaz (36:1-4)
  R. Jehoiakim (36:5-8)
  S. Jehoiachin (36:9-10)
  T. Zedekiah (36:11-16)
  U. The Babylonian Invasion, and
     Judah's Exile (36:17-21)
  V. Cyrus' Decree Authorizing
     Rebuilding of the Temple
     (36:22-23)

Chapter summary. Solomon is now ruler in the place of his father David. In Chronicles he is notable primarily as the builder of God's temple and a prime example of the blessings that come to a believer when he or she gives God priority.

With his grip on the throne established (1:1) Solomon shows his dedication to God by calling all Israel to a great sacrifice (vv. 2-6). God appears to the king and promises to grant "whatever you want" (v. 7). Solomon asks only for wisdom, to govern God's great people (vv. 8-10). God grants him wisdom and rewards his pious choice by also granting him wealth and honor (vv. 11-13). God keeps His promise, and during Solomon's days silver and gold become "as common in Jerusalem as stones" (vv. 14-17).

Key verses. 1:11-12: Priorities precede blessing.

Personal application. God rewards those who seek to glorify Him by serving others.

Key concepts. King »p. 130. Ark »p. 68. Altar »p. 79.

INSIGHT

Solomon established (1:1). The phrase refers to elimination of early internal threats to his rule (cf. 1 Kings 2:5-46).

Gibeon (1:3). The tent at Gibeon was the original tabernacle constructed in the time of Moses. There too was the original altar on which sacrifices to the Lord were to be burned. Solomon honored the principle of centralized worship, with its teaching that only at one place might legitimate sacrifices of atonement be offered (cf. Ex. 20:24; Lev. 17:3-9; Deut. 12:5).

Tabernacle and temple. There are a number of parallels between construction of the tabernacle and of the temple. These are intended to make clear the importance of worship and the central role of the temple in Israel's faith (»p. 283).

Parallels	Tabernacle	Temple
God provides plans	Ex. 25:8-9	1 Chron. 28:2-3
Materials and builders assembled	Ex. 31:1-6; 35:4-29	1 Chron. 22:13-15; 2 Chron. 2:7-14
Completed according to plan	Ex. 39:42-43	2 Chron. 5:1; 6:10
Dedicated in solemn ceremony	Ex. 40:9-11	2 Chron. 6:12-42
God enters the structure	Ex. 40:34-35	2 Chron. 5:13-14; 2 Chron. 7:1-3
Supernatural fire consumes offering	Lev. 9:24	2 Chron. 7:3

God's promise to David (1:9). That promise states (1 Chron. 17:11-14) that David will be succeeded by a son of his own, who will build the temple. The passage also looks beyond Solomon. It speaks of a Son (descendant) of David whom God will set "over My house and My kingdom forever; His throne will be established forever." Early Jewish and Christian commentators alike saw this as a messianic passage, speaking of an individual from David's line, who would establish God's rule (Messiah »p. 431).

Wisdom (1:10). Wisdom in the O.T. is the skill or ability to apply knowledge. Solomon asked God for knowledge and the skill to apply it so that he might govern God's people.

The O.T. makes it clear that the knowledge a king required was to be found in the written Law of God. Each ruler was to have a personal copy of that Law and was to study it daily (cf. Deut. 17:18-20; 4:5-8). What Solomon sought was insight into Scripture's meaning, so that his heart might be conformed to God's Word, and he would govern wisely.

Our greatest need is for insight into Scripture's practical meaning, that we might find our own way as well as to lead others.

Our heart's desire (1:11-12). God's response to Solomon reminds us that when our priorities are right, God is free to bless us. Wealth and glory are not to be goals that believers set their hearts on. But if, when we set our hearts on the Lord, He also gives us wealth, we can rejoice in His good gifts.

Trade (1:16-17). Most ancient monarchs obtained their wealth by conquest. Solomon, controlling the trade routes that linked Europe, Asia, and Africa, derived his wealth from peaceful trade.

Chapter summary. Solomon responds to the revelation from God by commanding construction of "a temple for the Name of the Lord" and his own palace (2:1-2). He seeks a contract for raw materials and skilled workmen from King Hiram of Tyre (vv. 3-10), who responds enthusiastically (vv. 11-16). Solomon also enrolls descendants of the Canaanite tribes still in Israelite territory to work as forced labor (vv. 17-18). In the fourth year of his reign, building begins on the site chosen by David (3:1-2; 1 Chron. 21). Great care is taken to construct a magnificent building, overlaid and decorated in gold (2 Chron. 3:3-9).

Special care is taken in the temple's inmost room, a curtained section where the ark will be placed, and which the high priest alone will enter, and he only once a year (vv. 10-15; cf. Lev. 16). Just outside the temple Solomon places two pillars, named "established" and "strengthened," quite possibly reminders of the promise of God. He has established Solomon's rule over Israel, and strengthens king and people alike (vv. 16-17).

Outline
Place
Finder

SOLOMON
ASA
JEHOSHAPHAT
JOASH
HEZEKIAH
JOSIAH

Key verse. 2:5: Our best alone can reflect God's greatness.

Personal application. Be outspoken about your intention to honor God, that your actions may bear witness to Him.

Key concepts. David »p. 191. Temple »p. 283. Cherubim »p. 491.

INSIGHT

Temple emphasis (2:1). Six of the nine chapters on Solomon in 2 Chron. are devoted to his construction and dedication of the temple. Solomon's reign was the true golden age of Israel. It was marked by peace, by unmatched prosperity, by unequalled fame, and by great literary accomplishments. Yet God regards building the temple the most significant event of Solomon's reign. Let's give the spiritual similar priority in our lives.

Hiram of Tyre (2:3-10). David had maintained a close relationship with Hiram (1 Kings 5:1). It was natural for Solomon to turn to Tyre, so rich in resources, for raw materials and technical assistance in building the temple. These were, however, bought and paid for, not contributed by Hiram. The privilege of giving to God's work is reserved for believers alone.

Our God is greater (2:5-6). We are often criticized for being narrow-minded and claiming that Christianity is the only "true" religion. Solomon was very bold in making a similar claim in his letter to the pagan king, Hiram. To proclaim that Jesus alone saves is not narrow-minded. It is a simple statement of revealed truth. We must be as honest as Solomon in our witness to the Lord.

Containing God (2:6). The word implies restriction. The universe itself is unable to restrict God to any single location: He is in all places, at all times. We may go to church to meet with the Lord. But we never leave Him there!

A discrepancy? (2:10) The figures here differ from those found in 1 Kings 5. This is not, however, because Chron. "exaggerates . . . wildly." Kings speaks of a luxury brand of oil sent to the royal household. Chronicles of a basic kind sent to Hiram's "servants, the woodsmen." Also Kings speaks of an annual payment; in Chron. the entire amount is in view. Here as in most other cases a careful reading of the text resolves the supposed "error" in Scripture.

Laborers (2:17-18; cf. 2:2). The conscripts were descendants of the Canaanite peoples who had been in the land before the Conquest by Joshua (cf. Josh. 9:1-26; 2 Sam. 21). Again numbers in this passage differ from those in 1 Kings. But here only because 1 Kings groups the foremen and chief officers differently.

"Old standard" cubits (3:3). The standard cubit was about 18" long, the "old standard" about 21. This makes the temple 105 feet by 35 feet, not 90 by 30 as often assumed.

"The cherubim" (3:10-13). The lid of the ark of the covenant featured two of these angels, wings spread over the place where sacrificial blood was splashed each Day of Atonement. Solomon's temple featured cherubim with a combined wingspan of 35 feet! The great gold-plated figures represented angelic beings that Scripture associates with the holiness of God.

Outline
Place
Finder

SOLOMON
ASA
JEHOSHAPHAT
JOASH
HEZEKIAH
JOSIAH

Chapter summary. As the temple was being built, careful attention was paid to furnishing it. A massive bronze altar was constructed in the courtyard, where sacrifices would be burned (4:1). An equally massive metal bowl holding some 17,500 gallons of water stood nearby, with 10 portable tanks holding water to be used by the priests for ritual washings and purifications (vv. 2-6). Gold lampstands and tables, and a profusion of utensils, were created for the temple proper (vv. 7-11). The major pieces that stood outside the temple were cast under the direction of Hiram of Tyre (vv. 12-18), while Solomon is credited with creating the golden furnishings that stood inside God's temple (vv. 19-22). When the work was finished the vast wealth David and Solomon had dedicated to God was placed in the temple (5:1). Then the greatest treasure of all, the ark of the covenant, was carried to the temple by the Levites (vv. 2-6) and set in place in the temple's inner room by the priests (vv. 7-10). As the people and temple musicians praised the Lord the temple was filled with a bright cloud, visible evidence of God's presence in the building dedicated to His name (vv. 11-14).

Key verse. 5:14: God's glory masked the temple.

Personal application. Let's be awed at the thought of God's presence with us, rather than at the beauty of our churches.

INSIGHT

The altar (4:1). The impressive altar, 30 feet square and 15 feet high, was the first object seen as a person entered the temple court. Like the altar of the tabernacle, it witnessed to the fact that none might approach God except through sacrifice (cf. Heb. 8:2-3; 9:12).

The "sea" (4:2-5). The dimensions of this great bowl have been subject to the nit-picking of critics determined to show that the Bible is inaccurate. The argument is that when the circumference of the sea is divided by its diameter, it does not produce the value of pi (3.14159265). Thus, they say, the Bible is clearly "wrong" about the dimensions. But, if the 30 cubits is measured around the *inside rim*, and the diameter is measured *across the top*, to include the "hand-breadth" (3 inch) width of the rim, the outside circumference actually would approximate pi! The Bible is reliable!

"Clay" (4:17). More evidence of the reliability of Scripture can be drawn from this verse. Excavations in the specified location on the "plain east of the Jordan" has revealed thick deposits of clay, such as would be required for casting the massive objects described in this chapter.

What happened to the tabernacle? (5:4-7) These verses suggest that the ancient portable house of worship was brought to Jerusalem, dismantled, and stored in Solomon's temple!

Priests and Levites (5:4-5, 7). Each group had its prerogatives. Levites carried the ark, but only the priests could enter the temple to set it in its place within the temple's inner room. Each believer has his or her own role in ministry. We can rejoice in our privilege, without being jealous of the privileges of others.

"Still there today" (5:9). How can the writer say the poles are "still there today" if he is writing in the Persian period, long after the temple has been destroyed? The answer is found in seeing the Heb. phrase "to this day," which means something like "from then on." Such expressions, found frequently in Chronicles (1 Chron. 4:41, 43; 5:26; 13:11; 17:5; 2 Chron. 8:8; 10:19; 20:26; 21:10; 35:25), can best be understood in this way.

Nothing except the two tablets (5:10). The O.T. and N.T. both indicate that a jar of manna and Aaron's rod were in the ark, a gold-covered wooden chest, along with the Law tablets (cf. Ex. 16:32-34; Num. 17:10-11 with Heb. 9:4). No explanation is offered concerning what happened to these sacred objects.

Praise and a vision of God's glory (5:11-14). It is significant that the joyful praise of the believing community is associated with the visible appearance of God's "glory" when the temple was dedicated. Praise God today too, and you will surely see Him more clearly and be less impressed with the splendor of our church buildings.

Solomon's Temple

The Jerusalem temple was a place where God and human beings might meet. Solomon reflected the Hebrew vision of a transcendent God when he cried out, "The heavens, even the highest heaven, cannot contain You. How much less this temple I have built!" (1 Kings 8:27) The temple might reflect God's glory. But ultimately the Jerusalem temple existed for the sake of God's people, not for God.

The temple served as the place of meeting between God and His covenant people. It was here the Jewish people offered the sacrifices that atoned for their sins; it was here they gathered to praise God during national religious festivals. It was here they humbled themselves in times of national or personal distress; here they sought God's intervention and help. The temple was a visible reminder that God was present with them. As the only authentic place of sacrifice, the temple served as a witness to the great truth that man must approach God as God chooses. All roads do not lead to God, or to heaven! There is one way, and only one, to approach God, the way that God Himself has ordained.

Three temples were erected on the same site, a fourth is predicted by Ezekiel.

Solomon's temple. This first temple stood for nearly 375 years. Then in 586 B.C. it was razed by the Babylonians. Ezekiel 8–11 graphically portrays the idolatrous sins which caused the Lord to withdraw His presence from the temple at that time. During Judah's long history, each period of revival was marked by repair of the temple and restoration of temple worship.

Zerubbabel's temple. A small company of survivors led by Zerubbabel returned to Judah from Babylon in 538 B.C. They built a second temple, less splendid than the first, but a testimony to God's continuing presence with the Jews.

Herod's temple. The second temple was greatly expanded and beautified in a 40-year project undertaken by Herod the Great. Jesus taught in Herod's temple and drove tradesmen from it. This temple, one of the wonders of the ancient world, was destroyed by the Romans in A.D. 70.

Ezekiel's temple. The Prophet Ezekiel predicts that yet another temple will be constructed in the same place when Messiah comes. Today the Mosque of Omar, the second most holy place in Islam, rests on the Temple Mount.

Outline
Place
Finder

SOLOMON
ASA
JEHOSHAPHAT
JOASH
HEZEKIAH
JOSIAH

Chapter summary. The temple is completed, and God's glory, in the form of a cloud, fills it (5:13-14). Solomon blesses the people (6:1-2) and calls on all Israel to praise God for His choice of David and of Jerusalem (vv. 3-6). God has now fulfilled part of His promise to David: Solomon has succeeded him as king and has built the temple David yearned to construct (vv. 7-11). Solomon's confidence in prayer is based in part on this evidence of God's faithfulness.

Solomon then dedicates the temple with prayer. He praises God (vv. 12-15), asks Him to keep His promises to David (vv. 16-17), and goes on to ask the Lord to hear prayers addressed to Him at the temple (vv. 18-39). The temple is to serve as the point of contact with God when an individual or the nation has sinned and finally seeks forgiveness and divine aid. Solomon even asks that God hear the prayers of foreigners who pray "toward this temple" and thus express faith in Israel's God (vv. 32-34). Solomon's great prayer concludes with a poetic summary of his major requests (vv. 40-42).

Key verse. 6:14: God keeps His covenant promises.

Personal application. The basis for our confidence in prayer is not found in how we pray, but in who we pray to.

Key concepts. Covenant »p. 35. Davidic Covenant »p. 370. Model prayers »p. 181. Praise »p. 380. Jerusalem »p. 205. Temple »p. 283. God's choice of individuals »p. 797.

INSIGHT

The glory cloud (6:1). God's visible presence in the O.T. often took the form of a dark cloud (cf. Ex. 19:9; 20:21; Lev. 16:2). But the cloud also symbolized the fact that in O.T. times God was hidden even in His self-revelation. Not until Jesus, when God became human, could the Apostle John write "we have *seen* His glory" (John 1:14, italics added).

To the people (6:3-11). Solomon's first words are spoken for God to all Israel and are delivered facing the people. It features (1) an invitation to praise (v. 4a); (2) a review of the promises to David which God has kept (vv. 4b-6); (3) and a review of Solomon's role in carrying out the revealed will of God (vv. 7-11). We too can pray with confidence when our prayers are in harmony with God's revealed will and we are set on being agents through whom His will is carried out.

To God (6:12-42). These words are spoken facing God and are on behalf of all Israel.

Now, keep the promises (6:16). Praying that God will keep His promises is evidence of faith, not of unbelief. God has promised to meet all our needs, yet Jesus taught His disciples to say, "Give us today our daily bread." Such prayers express dependence on God, and thus honor Him. Just utter such prayers joyfully, for God will surely do for us all He has promised, and more.

"Toward this place . . . from heaven" (6:21). God was not in the temple, though His people were to pray toward it. God was in heaven—beyond the natural universe—and would act "from heaven." Solomon's point is that we pray, because we realize that only supernatural intervention can meet many of our needs.

When we need God's help. Solomon's prayer can be applied to our lives, for we are likely to find ourselves in situations similar to the ones he describes. Let's remember that only God can: (1) declare the innocent not guilty, and repay the guilty (vv. 22-23); (2) forgive us and restore us after our defeats (vv. 24-25); (3) forgive, and transform us so we follow "the right way to live" (vv. 26-27); (4) make us aware of our deepest needs and cause us to fear Him and walk in His ways (vv. 28-31); (5) hear us even in our alienation from Him and graciously answer our prayers (vv. 32-33); (6) uphold us in our struggles (vv. 34-35); and (7) forgive and restore us to fellowship with Him even when we have willfully abandoned His ways (vv. 36-39). We too pray on earth. And God still answers His own and acts for us from heaven.

Sin vs. grace. Most of the troubles Solomon describes in vv. 22-39 are a result of human sin. Rejoice! God's grace is greater than our failures.

Chapter summary. God responds to Solomon's prayer with supernatural fire, which consumes his sacrifices. This event, with the presence of the cloud that fills the temple, symbolizes God's acceptance of the prayer and of the newly dedicated house of worship (7:1-3). Thousands of animals are sacrificed as the dedication of the temple court and furnishings continues, and the people joyfully join in the two-week celebration (vv. 4-10).

Outline
Place
Finder

SOLOMON
ASA
JEHOSHAPHAT
JOASH
HEZEKIAH
JOSIAH

After the festival the Lord appears to Solomon a second time. God has granted Solomon's request and accepts the temple consecrated to Him. The Lord will hear the prayers of those who humble themselves, seek Him, and turn from their wicked ways (vv. 11-16). Solomon himself is both reassured and warned. If he remains faithful, he will continue to experience the blessings of God's covenant promises to David (vv. 17-18). But if Israel forsakes God, the people will surely be torn from their land, and the imposing temple will be a monument marking the disaster rather than a beacon of hope (vv. 19-22). The rest of 2 Chronicles will demonstrate that God kept His promise. When His people were faithful God did hear their prayers.

Key verse. 7:14: Prayer requires right relationship with God.

Personal application. The way we live does have an impact on whether or not our prayers are answered.

Key concepts. Music »p. 274. Prayer »pp. 181, 608.

INSIGHT

Fire from heaven (7:1-3). Other instances in which fire from heaven indicated divine approval are found in Ex. 40:34-38; Jud. 6:20-22; and 1 Kings 18. Another account of this same incident is found in 2 Chron. 5:4-6. The initial sacrifices reported there were followed by the thousands of sacrifices reported in this chapter.

The sacrifices (7:4-7). First Kings 8:63 also reports that thousands of sacrificed animals provided food for the Israelites gathered for what became a two-week festival. God was viewed as the host at such sacrificial meals. Eating of them placed the worshiper under His protection.

The dedication (7:8-10). The feast of the seventh month (5:3) was Tabernacles, at which all adult males were to appear (cf. Lev. 23:33-43). Solomon timed the dedication of the temple for the preceding week, so as many Israelites as possible would be present. Worship is something in which all of God's people are to share.

"All Israel" (7:8). The phrase "all Israel" occurs in 1-2 Chron. some 36 times! God's people are to unite around Him. This does not imply that the distinctives dear to various Christian traditions should be abandoned. But it does remind us that all believers are one in and through personal relationship with Jesus Christ. "All Christians" can become a reality when we focus on those things that are common to us all rather than on our differences.

Prayer conditions (7:14). This prescription for answered prayer is reflected again and again in the Scripture. First the supplicant must be "called by My name." The only other condition is "humble themselves." The words "pray and seek My face and turn from their wicked ways" describe what humbling ourselves means. It means abandoning hope in ourselves to rely completely on God. And it means abandoning our own sinful ways to respond wholeheartedly to God's known will.

In actuality these are not so much conditions that God requires as they are a description of the person who will in fact pray! Only those with a sense of personal relationship ("called by His name") who take relationship with God seriously ("humble themselves") will turn to the Lord for supernatural help.

"My eyes and My heart will always be there" (7:16). This beautiful expression reminds us that God's eyes and His heart are always open to us today. Let us turn to Him joyfully!

Outline
Place
Finder

SOLOMON
ASA
JEHOSHAPHAT
JOASH
HEZEKIAH
JOSIAH

Chapter summary. Two chapters sum up Solomon's greatness and his achievements. Solomon is portrayed as a builder (8:1-6), who enslaved the remnant of the Canaanites in his land (vv. 7-10), and whose piety was consistently displayed (vv. 11-16). He alone of all Israel's rulers engaged in ocean trade (vv. 17-18), and his fame drew rulers from far-off lands, like Sheba, to wonder at his wisdom and his accomplishments (9:1-12). His wealth was legendary (vv. 13-21); "in riches and wisdom" King Solomon was greater "than all the other kings of the earth" (vv. 22-24).

Note that not once do these chapters mention Solomon's weakness for women, which led him into idolatry during his later years. The chronicler is not being deceptive—the story of Solomon's flaws is well known, being fully told in 1 Kings. Perhaps the chronicler is reminding us that God forgives sins, and they are gone. And that God remembers the good we do for Him, forever.

Key verse. 9:22: Greatness follows faithfulness.

Personal application. As the New Testament says, "You know that your labor in the Lord is not in vain" (1 Cor. 15:58).

INSIGHT

"Pharaoh's daughter" (8:11). One of Solomon's major failures is reflected here. He married many foreign wives, the marriages being a normal part of international treaties in those days. But Pharaoh's daughter is not mentioned critically. Instead Solomon is praised for not bringing her into David's palace, where the ark had stood. How gracious of God, to forgive and forget our sins, and to remember our pious acts forever.

"Sheba" (9:1). Most identify "Sheba" as a land lying at the southwestern extremity of the Arabian peninsula, or across the Red Sea in Africa. Sheba was well known for its trade in gold and spices, and it is likely the queen's visit to Solomon was largely for commercial reasons.

Solomon's stables (9:25). Two passages claim Solomon's army could muster 1,400 chariots

Illustration. *Underwater archeologists have recovered remains of the small coastal trading vessels that hugged the coast of the Mediterranean and yet boldly set out on years-long trading journeys. The Israelites were an agricultural people. Only Solomon of all Israel's kings was able to involve God's covenant people in ocean trade, a venture which poured much wealth into the Jewish homeland. Trade goods mentioned in 9:21 include gold, silver, ivory, apes, and baboons.*

(1 Kings 10:26; 2 Chron. 1:14). Two passages also speak of 4,000 stalls for chariot horses (2 Chron. 9:25; 1 Kings 4:26), although some manuscripts list 40,000 stalls. (See NIV margin note for 1 Kings 4:26.) It seems most likely the figure 4,000 was corrupted to 40,000, and that they were manned by some 12,000 charioteers.

Chapter summary. Solomon is dead. But the Solomon style continues with the story of the breakup of the United Kingdom by Solomon's hasty son, Rehoboam. Rehoboam goes to Shechem to be crowned king by the northern tribes (10:1). But the northerners, represented by Jeroboam, demand that Rehoboam pledge to reduce the levy on workmen Solomon had imposed for his many building projects (vv. 2-5). Rehoboam follows foolish advice and actually threatens to make things harder on his people (vv. 6-15). The northern tribes rebel, kill a royal official, and Rehoboam himself barely escapes back to Jerusalem (vv. 16-19). Rehoboam musters his army to force the northern tribes to submit. But a prophet orders Rehoboam and the men of Judah not to fight against their brothers, and the invasion attempt is abandoned (11:1-4). In Israel Jeroboam, now king, sets up a religious system that counterfeits the one established by Moses. Northern priests and Levites, along with all "who set their hearts on seeking the Lord," abandon their homes and move to Judah (vv. 5-8). Strengthened by the influx from the north, Rehoboam devotes the rest of his reign to fortifying Judah against invasion.

Outline
Place
Finder

SOLOMON
ASA
JEHOSHAPHAT
JOASH
HEZEKIAH
JOSIAH

Key verse. 11:16: God is more important than homes and land.

Personal application. Seek advice from many sources, but look to God to guide you to the best choice.

INSIGHT

"**Shechem**" (10:1). Shechem is 30 miles north of Jerusalem. It was a traditional center of the northern tribes and after the kingdom divided was the North's first capital (cf. 1 Kings 12:25). Rehoboam had been crowned in Judah (2 Chron. 9:31), but went to Shechem to be confirmed by the 10 northern tribes (cf. 1 Chron. 11:3).

"**Jeroboam**" (10:2). First Kings 11:26-40 tells us God had anointed Jeroboam to be king of the 10 northern tribes, as a judgment for Solomon's sins. When crowned, his fear that worshiping in Jerusalem would lead to reunification of the kingdom under a descendant of David led him to set up a counterfeit of Mosaic worship in the north (cf. 1 Kings 12).

A king's role (10:7). The advice of the older men reveals a belief that rulers of God's people are to be guardians of their welfare. First Kings 12:7 says it even more clearly: a ruler of God's people is to "be a servant to these people and serve them." Servanthood is basic to all spiritual leadership, whatever one's position (»p. 622).

Do not fight (11:2-4). Force can never produce loyalty. It is foolish to try to coerce allegiance; we must win it. Rehoboam made one mistake in answering the northern tribes harshly. He was wise to listen to God's Word, and not make another mistake. We too are wise if we resist the temptation to "fight against [y]our brothers," and instead serve them.

The fortified cities (11:6-30). When located on a map, the 15 cities listed are seen to lie along Judah's southern and western borders. Apparently Rehoboam saw Egypt as the greatest threat to his smaller and weaker kingdom. He was right!

"**Pasturelands and property**" (11:14-17). Jeroboam's institution of a corruption of biblical religion alienated the godly among the northern tribes. These "voted with their feet," and left "Israel," the Northern Kingdom, to move to Judah. They lost their material possessions—their "pasturelands and property"—but they retained the access to God through the Jerusalem temple that the Lord had promised Solomon He would grant to His people. Sometimes we face a similar decision, with material benefits balanced against the spiritual benefits found in faithfulness to God. We would be foolish indeed not to follow the lead of the ancient Israelites who "set their hearts on seeking the Lord," regardless of the cost. Why exchange material things which no one can keep, for spiritual benefits which cannot be lost?

"**They strengthened the kingdom**" (11:17). Even if Rehoboam had won a civil war, he would at best have obtained reluctant citizens. Those who flooded voluntarily into Judah strengthened the kingdom, because they were committed to it. A few committed volunteers will do far more for God than a church full of reluctant disciples.

Chapter summary. The first cycle in 2 Chronicles begins with Solomon, with an emphasis on his piety. It ends with a report of two flawed rulers, Solomon's son Rehoboam (chaps. 10–12) and his grandson Abijah (chap. 13). After Rehoboam's Judah becomes strong, the king and people "abandon the Law of the Lord" (12:1). God punished their unfaithfulness by permitting Shishak of Egypt to capture Jerusalem and strip the temple of its treasures (vv. 2-11). Rehoboam later repents and humbles himself, but on balance Solomon's son is a king who "did evil" because his heart was not set "on seeking the Lord" (vv. 12-16). He is succeeded by Abijah, who according to 1 Kings 15:3 "committed all the sins his father had done before him" (2 Chron. 13:1-2). But the writer highlights a moment in the king's life when he does rely fully on God—and the Lord enables Judah's army to win a victory over a larger, strategically placed northern force (vv. 3-22). In developing this story, the chronicler underlines his basic point: God hears from heaven and acts for us when we are faithful. And He sees from heaven and acts against us when we transgress our covenant relationship with Him.

Key verse. 13:12: What a comfort to be on God's side!

Personal application. Don't worry whether God is with you. Concentrate on whether or not you're walking with Him!

INSIGHT

"All Israel" (12:1). This phrase generally means "all the people of Judah." Chronicles purposely ignores the history of the North. The chronicler shows that God is faithful to those faithful to Him, and disciplines those who are not.

"Shishak" (12:1-4). This Egyptian Pharaoh ruled from 945–924 B.C. and was the founder of the 22nd dynasty. He reunified Egypt and, when Solomon's powerful kingdom broke up, swept into Judah intent on making it a subject kingdom. Egyptian records list some 150 towns captured in his campaign, but these do not mention Jerusalem. Apparently the attack on Jerusalem (v. 4) was bought off by giving Shishak all the temple's gold.

Abandoned (12:1-2). The chronicler sees the Egyptian invasion not so much as retribution but as instruction. Once Judah had "become strong," Rehoboam and his people apparently felt they no longer needed the Lord and abandoned both worship and obedience. God stood back and permitted the invasion, in part as well-merited punishment, but also as a powerful lesson. Apparently Rehoboam learned! He "humbled himself" (»p. 259), and God preserved Judah and the Davidic line.

The description gives insight into two Heb. words for "abandon." Rehoboam renounced God and His ways. But God merely stood back when permitting invasion. Rehoboam and Judah faced

away from God, but God never turned His back on Judah. Let's remember this when we wonder if God is punishing us. God may intend to teach us a lesson. But He will never turn His back on you or me.

"Abijah" (13:1). The parallel account in 1 Kings makes the negative assessment, "he committed all the sins his father had done before him; his heart was not fully devoted to the Lord" (15:3). Kings also omits the story of Abijah's great act of faith that is reported here. What a reminder for us. Under pressure King Saul refused to trust God (cf. 1 Sam. 13; 15). Now, under similar pressure, Abijah does find the capacity to trust. God may permit us to be tested, not to reveal our moral character to Him, but to reveal our inmost self to us!

"God is with us; He is our leader" (13:10-12). Abijah bases his confidence on the fact that Israel has abandoned temple worship, and thus cannot be in fellowship with the Lord. Judah was then faithful to the ritual requirements of the Law and thus could expect God to help.

It's likely that this theological argument is flawed. Ritual observance was necessary, but not sufficient to win God's favor. The key to God's response in this situation lies in v. 14: "They cried out to the Lord." Complete, utter dependence on the Lord is the key to seeing Him work in our churches, and in our lives.

Chapter summary. The story of Asa, who revitalized Judah's worship, launches 2 Chronicles' second cycle. Asa reverses the trend set by Abijah and purges Judah of foreign altars and local worship centers (14:2-5). As a result Judah "built and prospered" (vv. 6-7). Later, when a superior Egyptian ("Cushite") force invades, Asa appeals to the Lord, and God gives Judah a decisive victory (vv. 8-15). In response to a prophet's encouraging words (15:1-7), Asa renews his efforts to cleanse Judah of idolatry. He repairs the Jerusalem altar (vv. 8-9), and assembles his people for a time of sacrifice and eager recommitment to the Lord (vv. 10-15). The depth of Asa's personal commitment is seen when he ousts the Queen Mother, his grandmother, for idolatry (vv. 16-17), and when Asa dedicates Judah's riches to the Lord (v. 18). In response God gives Judah peace until Asa's 35th year as king.

Outline
Place
Finder

SOLOMON
ASA
JEHOSHAPHAT
JOASH
HEZEKIAH
JOSIAH

Key verse. 15:2: "The Lord is with you when you are with Him."

Personal application. Peace is a product of commitment to the Lord.

Key concepts. War »pp. 133, 554. Peace »pp. 427, 806. Prophet »p. 131. Seeking God »pp. 670, 865.

INSIGHT

"High places" (14:3). God does not share His people with foreign deities. Again and again purging pagan worship centers was the first visible sign of O.T. revival. We are not to worship God first. We are to worship Him alone.

"Seek the Lord" (14:4). The underlying Heb. phrase means "turn to" the Lord. The image is one of looking in God's direction: seeing Him both as the object of worship and source of our help. The theme of seeking God recurs nine times in the three-chapter account of Asa's reign. Clearly renewed concentration on the Lord was the central characteristic of Asa's revival. Looking in God's direction, and seeing Him clearly, can revive us and bring us peace and prosperity!

Asa's army (14:8). When Solomon's kingdom broke up, Rehoboam of Judah could muster only 180,000 men (11:1). Now, just 20 to 25 years later, Asa's army numbers 580,000! The numbers suggest that the exodus of true believers from the northern tribes into Judah (11:16) was truly massive. Usually more people are ready to commit to the Lord in difficult times than we expect!

"Zerah the Cushite" (14:9). Most place the invasion around the 10th to 14th year of Asa, and the 25th to 29th year of Pharaoh Osorkon I. "Zerah," who is never identified as a king, was probably a Nubian general leading Egypt's army.

Relying on God in wartime (14:11-15). The O.T. casts God as the battle leader of Israel's army and credits God when military victories are won (»p. 133). This was part of God's obligation to His people under the Law Covenant:

When Israel was faithful to the Lord, He would fight for them. Asa could rely on the Lord in wartime because he had sought God when there was peace!

Let's concentrate on our relationship with the Lord now, so when troubles come we can have Asa's confidence and find peace by relying on the Lord.

Foundations to build on (15:3). Azariah the prophet's review of history reminds Asa and Judah of the foundations of O.T. faith. Judah must know the true God, have priests who teach, and have the Law of God. The prophet's message is intended to motivate the king and people—and it does.

More idols? (15:8) Some have claimed another discrepancy in Scripture here. Didn't Asa tear down idolatrous worship centers earlier? (14:3) Then how could he do it again less than 15 years later? (cf. 15:10) Actually, the king's second purging of the land demonstrates the persistence of human sin rather than an error in the Bible. Asa's representatives had torn down the symbols of idolatry in every town of Judah—and as soon as they left, some folks had put them up again!

We see this in our own lives. We gain a victory over some temptation or sin, but before we know it we find ourselves tempted again. We have to keep on cleansing ourselves from recurring sins to be fully dedicated to the Lord.

Deposing grandmothers (15:16). Let's not rail against the sin of others, unless we are ready to deal with the sins that are near and dear to us!

Chapter summary. The downturn in the Asa cycle does not take place after his death, but during his own later years. In the 36th year of Asa's reign, Baasha of Israel blocks passes that lead to Judah (16:1). Asa forgets the victory over Egypt of some 20 years earlier, and instead of relying on the Lord, uses the temple treasures to bribe Ben-Hadad of Syria to attack Baasha (vv. 2-4). Syria's attack forces Baasha to abandon work on the forts intended to control the passes, and the people of Judah carry away all the building materials Baasha has stockpiled there (vv. 5-6). Though the strategy has worked, a prophet named Hanani rebukes Asa (vv. 7-9). The king does not repent, but imprisons the prophet and oppresses some of his people (v. 10). Then when afflicted by a serious illness, Asa relies only on his physicians and makes no appeal to the Lord (vv. 11-14). Spiritual decline begins whenever one of God's people neglects seeking God, or fails to rely completely on Him.

Key verse. 16:9: God is watching. Why fear?

Personal application. The only way to guarantee tomorrow is to rely on God in every one of our todays.

INSIGHT

The first "Berlin wall." The fortifications Baasha constructed were intended, like the Berlin Wall, to keep his own people from defecting to Judah (cf. 15:9). They were located along the major north/south trade route between Israel and Judah, five miles north of Jerusalem.

But it worked! (16:2-6) Most folks measure success or failure by whether or not something works. By this measure, Asa's strategy "worked" just fine. Ben-Hadad attacked Israel. Baasha withdrew his troops to fight in the north, and the people of Judah tore down his incomplete forts. But we must measure actions by moral and spiritual criteria. "Was it right?" and "Was it an expression of faith?" are questions we must ask, and be ready to answer. On this basis, Asa's deal with Syria was flawed. By relying on Syria rather than on the Lord, Asa displayed an erosion of faith and subjected Judah to divine judgment.

No repentance (16:7-10). The rebuke of the seer (prophet) Hanani did not bring repentance. Instead Asa imprisoned the prophet and oppressed those who supported him. This is the first report of royal persecution of a prophet, but not the last! (See 18:25-26; 24:20-22; Jer. 26:11, 20-23; Matt. 5:11-12; Mark 6:17-18; John 16:2; Rev. 18:24.)

Asa's illness (16:12). Some see Asa's illness as retribution. It is better viewed as instruction, as an invitation to repent. When something "bad" is intended to move us to seek God, that "bad" thing is intended for good!

While there is no evidence that the Israelites developed a distinct medical science, frequent references in the N.T. suggest physicians were relatively commonplace by the 1st century (cf. Matt.

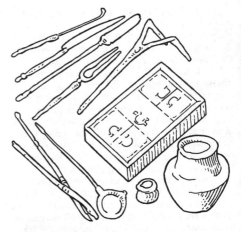

Illustration. *Archeologists have found medical books and recovered physicians' tools from the ancient world (see above). Medicines are referred to only a few times in Scripture. Ointments and healing balms were used to treat wounds (Isa. 1:6; Luke 10:34). A poultice of figs was laid on King Hezekiah's boil (Isa. 38:21). Gall and myrrh mixed with wine served as an anesthetic (Mark 15:23).*

9:12; Luke 4:23; Col. 4:14). While health and healing were blessings that could come only from God, consulting a physician did not seem to indicate a lack of faith. Even Asa is not criticized for seeing doctors, but for seeking help "*only* from physicians" (emphasis mine).

Chapter summary. The third cycle in 2 Chronicles (chaps. 17–23) begins with Jehoshaphat, who is pious during his early years. The cycle ends in the precipitous spiritual decline that marked the reigns of his successors, Jehoram, Ahaziah, and Athaliah.

Jehoshaphat is introduced and his early piety is established (17:1-6). Especially significant is Jehoshaphat's assignment of teaching priests and Levites to circulate throughout Judah and teach God's Law (vv. 7-10). God responds by blessing Judah with prosperity—and Jehoshaphat with power (v. 11). Jehoshaphat fortifies his cities and builds a powerful military machine (vv. 12-19). While there is nothing wrong with this in itself, a powerful army creates two dangers. First, a king may rely on military might rather than the Lord. And second, when a nation has a powerful army, it is all too likely to use it!

Outline
Place
Finder

SOLOMON
ASA
JEHOSHAPHAT
JOASH
HEZEKIAH
JOSIAH

Key verse. 17:9: A knowledge of God preserves a nation.

Personal application. If you want God's blessing, follow the path marked out by the young Jehoshaphat, whose "heart was devoted to the ways of the Lord" (v. 6).

Key concepts. Law »pp. 120, 145. Priest »p. 81. Levites »p. 95.

INSIGHT

Jehoshaphat and Asa. The accounts of the two kings are parallel in several respects, suggesting that basic spiritual principles are involved in their histories. Note:

Parallel	Asa	Jehoshaphat
Reigns begin in reform with building large armies	14:2-8	17:1-19
Battle report	14:9-15	18:1–19:3
Further reforms	15:1-9	19:4-11
Another battle report	16:1-9	20:1-30
The king sins	16:10-14	20:31–21:1

The parallel pattern suggests that early piety leads to success, prosperity, and greatness. But with success comes the temptation to rely on one's own assets rather than on the Lord. It is when we have been most blessed that we're most vulnerable. What we learn from these two kings is that we must remain humble, always aware of our dependence on the Lord, and always ready to respond to His guidance.

"Against Israel" (17:1). Jehoshaphat's early efforts were focused on defense against Ahab of Israel. The defense was spiritual as well as military, as vv. 3-4 make clear. There's always a danger in arming ourselves against an enemy that we become like them.

Removal of the high places (17:6). Though Asa had purged these local shrines twice, the people of Judah again returned to them. Throughout the history of Judah it was necessary over and over again to battle the persistent tendency of God's people to return to idolatry.

Jehoshaphat's third year (17:7). The king ruled for 25 years (872–848 B.C.; 20:31), including a three-year coregency while Asa was incapacitated by his illness (cf. 2 Kings 3:1 with 8:16). It was the third year of his sole reign that Jehoshaphat took the initiative and actively began to promote the teaching of God's Law in Judah.

The teaching team (17:7). The group the king sent throughout Judah to teach God's Law included royal officials, priests, and Levites. There was no separation between church and state; the full weight of the government was placed behind the effort to teach God's Law. Modern nations refrain from commitment to any religion. But commitment to the moral and social principles found in God's Law are critical for national justice and survival.

More and more powerful (17:10-19). Jehoshaphat's active commitment to God was rewarded with international peace and increasing national power. His spiritual reforms were the foundation of Judah's strength. Proverbs 14:34 proved true in Jehoshaphat's time, and it is true in ours. "Righteousness exalts a nation, but sin is a disgrace to any people."

291

Outline
Place
Finder

SOLOMON
ASA
JEHOSHAPHAT
JOASH
HEZEKIAH
JOSIAH

Chapter summary. Jehoshaphat, now secure in his wealth and power, allies himself to Ahab by marriage (18:1). This is a reversal of his earlier attitude toward Israel (cf. 17:1). In time Jehoshaphat agrees to assist Ahab to take Ramoth Gilead from Syria, but urges Ahab to seek God's guidance (18:2-4). The prophets that Ahab produces predict victory. But the uneasy ruler of Judah insists on hearing from a true prophet of Yahweh (vv. 5-6). Reluctantly Ahab produces Micaiah, who announces that Israel's prophets have been deceived by a lying spirit. God intends Ahab to die on the battlefield (vv. 7-27). The allies attack despite this warning. Jehoshaphat, dressed in his royal robes, bears the brunt of the attack but is protected by the Lord. Ahab, who enters the battle in disguise, is struck by an arrow fired at random and killed (vv. 28-34).

Key verse. 18:1: Choices have unexpected consequences.

Personal application. It is never safe to go into partnership with someone who fails to share our faith in God.

Key concepts. Prophet »p. 131. Lying spirit »p. 239.

INSIGHT

Jehoshaphat's marriage (18:1). The woman the king married was Athaliah, a daughter of Ahab and Jezebel. This foolish marriage had tragic consequences for Judah. After the early deaths of her son Jehoram and grandson Ahaziah, Athaliah murdered all but one of her remaining grandchildren and took the throne for herself. Athaliah was committed to Baal worship. She corrupted her son and grandson, and promoted Baal worship when she became queen. Perhaps the most significant choice we make, as far as its impact on future generations is concerned, is whom we choose to marry. Remember Judah's later experience with Athaliah if you're ever tempted to make Jehoshaphat's choice and wed someone not fully committed to the Lord.

"Ramoth Gilead" (18:2). This fertile area had been ceded to Ahab after he agreed to release a defeated Ben-Hadad of Syria (1 Kings 20:34). Ben-Hadad went back on the agreement, and Ahab decided to take the area by force.

"When" can be important (18:3-4). Jehoshaphat demonstrated his usual piety in insisting that the two kings seek God's counsel before going to war with Syria. But Jehoshaphat asked for guidance too late—after he had already promised to fight at Ahab's side.

When we ask God's guidance is vitally important. We're to ask *before* making decisions; not after we have already committed ourselves.

Why didn't Jehoshaphat trust Ahab's prophets? (18:5-6) The prophets of Baal that Ahab and Jezebel had imported had been wiped out prior to this event (cf. 1 Kings 18). Thus these were

prophets associated with the corrupt worship system established in Israel in the time of Jeroboam I (cf. 1 Kings 12). Undoubtedly Jehoshaphat's suspicions were aroused both by this association and by the fact that they spoke in the name of "God" (*el*) rather than in the prescribed "name of the Lord" (*Yahweh*) (cf. Deut. 18:14-22). These "prophets" of Ahab might have been "yes men." Or they might have been sincerely religious. But Jehoshaphat rightly yearned to hear, "thus saith the Lord."

Watch out when the popular view of things is enthusiastically supported by religion. In most cases God's prophets stood alone and stood in judgment on their society. Look for, and consider, the dissenting voice before going along with the crowd.

The "lying spirit" from the Lord (18:16-22). For a discussion, see the parallel passage in 1 Kings 22 where this story is also told (»p. 239).

Who do we hide from? (18:29) Ahab's disguise was an attempt to thwart God's announced intention of ending his life at the battle of Ramoth Gilead. The disguise worked; Ahab was not recognized by the Syrians. But it could not hide him from God, who directed the arrow shot at random to the one vulnerable spot in Ahab's armor.

Let's not deceive ourselves. We can never hide from God, or avoid His just judgment. Our only hope is to run to Him, not from Him. Let's accept His forgiveness and rejoice in our renewal.

Divine protection (18:31). God's protection of Jehoshaphat reminds us that foolishness is not a capital crime. It's a good thing!

Chapter summary. Home after the disastrous campaign with Ahab (2 Chron. 18), Jehoshaphat accepts the rebuke of the prophet Jehu (19:1-3). He remains committed to the Lord and appoints judges to administer the Old Testament's law code throughout Judah (vv. 4-11). When Jehoshaphat is attacked by a coalition of hostile nations, he calls his people together to pray and seek help from the Lord (20:1-4). The king himself leads the assembly in prayer (vv. 5-13), and God answers through another prophet, Jahaziel (v. 14). The prophet promises a victory to be won by the Lord alone, without a battle (vv. 15-17). Jehoshaphat worships, and the next morning Judah's army sets out, its progress marked by hymns of praise (vv. 18-22). As the Jews approach, the invading allies have a falling out. First the Ammonites and Moabites turn on the contingent from Mt. Seir, and when they are wiped out, begin fighting each other (v. 23). When the men of Judah arrive they collect the spoil and return joyfully home (vv. 24-30).

Despite Jehoshaphat's efforts, and despite evidence of God's love and power, his reformation fails. The people as a whole have "still not set their hearts on the God of their fathers" (vv. 31-33). Jehoshaphat allies himself with Israel again, this time for a joint-trading venture, and is rebuked by yet another prophet (vv. 34-36). The venture fails when God brings a storm that sinks the ships (v. 37). Jehoshaphat dies a godly man (21:1-3). His decision to marry into the family of Ahab is about to bring calamity.

Outline
Place
Finder

SOLOMON
ASA
JEHOSHAPHAT
JOASH
HEZEKIAH
JOSIAH

Key verse. 19:2: God emphasizes the good in us.

Personal application. Recognize your weaknesses and guard against them.

Key concepts. Separation »pp. 87, 761. Law »p. 145.

INSIGHT

Loving those who hate the Lord (19:2). The prophet expresses a general principle here. While we are to care for the lost (cf. Matt. 5:44), we are not to "help the wicked" (cf. Rom. 16:17). Time and again Jehoshaphat showed himself unable to learn this basic lesson of relationships. His marriage to Athaliah (18:1), his military support at Ramoth Gilead (18:3), and his later joint trading venture with Ahab's son (20:35-37) reveal that this was one lesson Jehoshaphat never learned. His failure to recognize this weakness and protect himself from it caused later calamities.

Let's examine ourselves for weaknesses. Look for patterns of behavior—and when we find a pattern that reveals a weakness be aware we're vulnerable too!

Judge carefully (19:4-11). Modern politicians like to promise that their "personal convictions" will not determine their acts if elected to office. Thus a governor can say he is against abortion, but also swear not to sign legislation making it illegal! Jehoshaphat took a different, more godly course. He told his judges to hew to the divine standard, and apply God's laws fearlessly. God's Word to timid officeholders may well be, "act with courage, and may the Lord be with those who do well" (v. 11).

"Stand firm and see the deliverance the Lord will give you" (20:17). The prophet's words echo those of Moses at the Red Sea (Ex. 14:13). Usually God provides victory after plunging us into the struggle. Every now and then, however, He reminds us that He alone is the source of every triumph.

Believing the promise (20:18-19). Note the response of Jehoshaphat and the Levites to the prophet Jahaziel's promise. Jehoshaphat believed and his faith overflowed in worship and praise. When we face dangers or difficulties, and find ourselves buoyed up, ready to worship and praise, then we know our faith is real too.

Chapter summary. The spiritual decline at the end of the Jehoshaphat cycle (chaps. 17–22) is pronounced, for the king's successors turn decisively away from the Lord. When Jehoshaphat dies (21:1-3) his oldest son Jehoram becomes king. Jehoram kills his brothers and, influenced by his wife, adopts Baal worship (vv. 4-7). Judgment follows swiftly. States long subject to Judah successfully rebel (vv. 8-11), and a letter from Elijah warns of greater troubles to come (vv. 12-15). As Elijah predicted, Judah is invaded (vv. 16-17), and the king is stricken with an incurable disease (vv. 18-20). Ahaziah succeeds his father, and he too is actively involved in the Baal cult. Ahaziah rules only one year before he is killed by Jehu in his purge of the family of Ahab and Jezebel (22:1-9; cf. 2 Kings 9–10). As God has been quick to bless Judah's faithful kings, so He has been quick to judge the wicked!

Now follows one of the strangest and most dreadful periods in Judah's history. Ahaziah's mother, Athaliah, kills her grandchildren and makes herself Judah's sole ruler! But one-year-old prince Joash is saved, and hidden away (vv. 10-12).

Key verse. 21:14: Retribution walks on the heels of sin.

Personal application. Rewards and punishments both demonstrate the faithfulness of God.

Key concepts. Evil »p. 72. High places »p. 113. Baal »p. 162.

INSIGHT

Retribution. Commentators have noted that the chronicler emphasizes a "theology of retribution." Evil actions have immediate and painful consequences, seen in the swift judgment that struck the wicked Jehoram and Ahaziah. Yet the chronicler actually displays a theology of grace. National and personal disasters are unmistakably connected to wrong acts, just as blessing is unmistakably linked with commitment to the Lord. The punishments imposed warn away from sin and back to godliness.

Parents who intervene to protect their children from the consequences of wrong do them no favor. God, the most loving Parent of all, sets us an example by making sure that suffering follows sin!

"Because" (21:10). The humanist notes only that subject peoples in ancient times typically tried to take advantage of a change of rulers and chose that time to rebel. The chronicler sees the spiritual cause of the successful revolt of Edom and Libnah. Relationship with God is the key, for God controls the circumstances of our lives.

Elijah (21:12). Elijah was God's messenger to the Northern Kingdom, Israel, where he fought Ahab's efforts to promote the cult of Baal (cf. 1 Kings 17–21). His letter identifies Jehoram's sins and the consequences for Judah.

Critics have claimed the letter is an invention

and that Elijah was no longer living. However, 2 Kings 1:16-17 makes it clear Elijah was alive the first few years of Jehoram's reign.

The chronicler's contempt. This is the first time the writer fails to direct the reader to royal annals for further information. "Who would want to know more about *that* man?"

The lives of great men and women are an inspiration to future generations. The lives of the wicked are best ignored and forgotten.

"To no one's regret" (21:20). Live so that your death brings grief, not relief.

Ahaziah (22:1). As Ahaziah's one-year reign fell entirely within the 12th year of Joram (2 Kings 8:25), who was killed at the same time (9:24-27), Ahaziah must have ruled for only a few months. Again retribution was swift.

Athaliah (22:10-12). Athaliah was the only queen to reign in either Heb. kingdom. Her murder of her own grandchildren may have been a religious as well as political act. If all David's male descendants were removed, she could claim the throne—and perhaps make Baalism the official religion of the nation. Why did she survive for six years, when Ahaziah had been dispatched in a few months? Probably because the grandchild who was saved was only a year old. When divine retribution is delayed there is always a good reason.

Chapter summary. The wicked Athaliah has killed her own grandchildren and seized Judah's throne (chap. 22). But one-year-old Joash was overlooked! Now six years later, the high priest Jehoiada, with the army providing security, proclaims Joash king (23:1-11). Athaliah is apprehended and, loudly shouting "Treason," is led away to be executed (vv. 12-15). Jehoiada leads a ceremony in which Judah reaffirms its covenant with the Lord, and cheering mobs tear down the Baal's house (vv. 16-17). Temple worship is reestablished, and the glad people of the land at last enjoy peace (vv. 18-21).

Joash develops into a godly ruler and shows his piety by restoring the temple (24:1-16). But when his mentor, the high priest Jehoiada, dies, Joash turns to idolatry (vv. 17-18). Prophets sent to turn the king back to the Lord are ignored. Joash even kills one prophet, the son of his benefactor, Jehoiada (vv. 19-22). Retribution in the form of a Syrian invasion follows. Joash is wounded in battle and then assassinated by his own officials (vv. 23-27).

Outline
Place
Finder

SOLOMON
ASA
JEHOSHAPHAT
JOASH
HEZEKIAH
JOSIAH

Key verse. 24:17: Weak people are easily influenced.

Personal application. Ask God for strength of character.

Key concepts. Priest »p. 81. Levite »p. 95. Temple »p. 283. Baal »p. 162. Davidic Covenant »p. 370. Taxes »pp. 71, 619.

INSIGHT

Jehoiada's strength (23:1-3). A good measure of the strength of that support—and the unpopularity of the queen—is found in the number of persons involved in the coup. Despite involving thousands of persons, *no one told Athaliah!*

"His weapon in his hand" (23:3-10). Those who joined the coup attempt took a significant risk. There are times when we must stand for our convictions, whatever the danger. It's wise at such times to find others willing to stand with us.

"A copy of the covenant" (23:11). The O.T. states that a Heb. king must have a personal copy of God's Law, and that he must read it and be subject to it (Deut. 17:18-19). Although Joash was only seven, the presentation was more than symbolic. It expressed the commitment of Jehoiada to raise the young king to know and love God's Word.

Today's publishers are making it easier for children to read and understand the Bible. Word's *International Children's Bible* is a simplified translation for children, while Zondervan's *Adventure Bible* contains features that make the NIV come alive for 7–11-year-olds. Choose a Bible your children can and will read.

The priest of Baal (23:17). His killing was not a random mob action, but evidence that the people were truly committed to the Lord (cf. Deut. 13:5-10).

Repair of the temple (24:1-18). Throughout

Illustration. *This scepter featuring an ivory head carved like a pomegranate was probably carried by one of Israel's high priests. The pomegranate, filled with seeds, is thought to represent divine blessing.*

1 and 2 Chron. enthusiastic support of temple worship serves as a symbol of a vital spiritual life. Here it shows the dedication of the king (v. 4), the people (v. 10), and religious officials (v. 13).

Jehoiada chose Joash's wives (24:3). He took no chance that the king might marry another Athaliah!

Joash "listened to them" (24:17). Joash comes across as a man of weak character. As long as Jehoiada lived, he followed the Lord. But with the priest gone, the king was just as easily led into sin. The measure of our children's character is not how they behave while they are at home, but the choices they make after they leave!

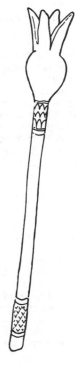

Chapter summary. The Joash cycle continues with the story of his son and grandson. Each imitates the pattern Joash set: Early piety and success is followed by apostasy and disaster. Amaziah does what is right in God's eyes, but not out of personal commitment (25:1-4). He even heeds a prophet's warning and dismisses a brigade of Israelite soldiers he has hired to support his troops in battle (vv. 5-10). Amaziah's obedience is rewarded, and Judah wins the war (vv. 11-13). But the king brings back his enemy's gods and begins to worship them! When Amaziah arrogantly provokes war with Israel, Judah is defeated and Jerusalem's wall is broken down (vv. 14-24). The apostate king also loses support at home and finally is assassinated (vv. 25-28). Amaziah is succeeded by Uzziah. The king has success as long as he seeks the Lord, and Judah becomes the dominant military power in the area (26:1-15). But pride leads to Uzziah's downfall too. He is stricken with leprosy when he intrudes on the priest's office (vv. 16-20). Uzziah is isolated from the people and temple, and control of the nation passes to his son (vv. 21-23).

Key verse. 26:5: Success and godliness are close friends.

Personal application. Doing it "my way" leads to disaster.

Key concepts. Man of God »p. 182. Prophet »p. 131. Parable »p. 166. Arrogance »p. 119. Priesthood »p. 81. Leprosy »p. 83.

INSIGHT

"Wholeheartedly" (25:2). God does not want believers who go through the motions of living a Christian life. It is clear from these two chapters that mere obedience, although necessary, is not sufficient evidence of true commitment. It is especially revealing that neither Amaziah nor Uzziah is portrayed as having a great interest in the temple. They were willing for a time to obey God, but they had no passion for worship! True love for God expresses itself in both worship and obedience.

"God has the power to help or to overthrow" (25:8). God deserves to be worshiped for His own sake. But it's good to be reminded that responding to the Lord is to our benefit as well (cf. 26:5).

"Why?" (25:14-16) In the ancient Near East, victorious people frequently viewed their defeated enemies' deities as abandoning their people to help the enemy. But this makes no sense, as the prophet pointed out to Amaziah. But today the beliefs of many are just as foolish. Astrology, spiritism, new age channeling, and the host of other systems promising help to the hopeless are bankrupt. Perhaps the reaction of Amaziah to the prophet who rebuked him provides a clue. People who reject God simply do not want to know the truth!

Consequences of apostasy. Events of Amaziah's reign set up a contrast between the benefits of faithfulness to the Lord and consequences of unfaithfulness. Compare this chapter with the chronicler's description of the rule of one of Judah's godly kings. There we find building programs, here Jerusalem's walls are torn down. There we see wealth pour into Judah, here the king is plundered. There large royal families, here the king's sons are hostages. There peace, here war. There victories, here defeat. There a loyal population, here conspiracy and assassination.

"Uzziah" (26:1-5). This king, like his grandfather, seems vulnerable to the influence of others (cf. 24:17). Choose close companions wisely. These may be the most important choices you will make!

Power and pride (26:16). Military power and pride seem to go together in the O.T. The real temptation of power, wealth, and success is simple: They tempt us to rely on ourselves rather than the Lord.

Burning incense (26:16-23). In parallel Near East cultures, semidivine kings also served as priests. Perhaps Uzziah's determination to burn incense reflected an arrogant intent to exalt himself.

Chapter summary. The Joash cycle concludes with the story of the steadfast Jotham set against that of Ahaz, the most wicked of Judah's kings to date. Jotham was personally committed to the Lord, but seems to have made no effort to bring revival to his people (27:1-2). Even so, God rewarded his faithfulness (vv. 3-9). On the other hand, Ahaz was personally committed to paganism (28:1-4) and vigorously promoted it in Judah (v. 19), even to the extent of shutting down the temple and constructing pagan worship centers throughout the land (vv. 22-25). The extended story of a prophet's intervention to win the release of some 200,000 Judean captives taken by Israel emphasizes twin themes of this O.T. book. When the nation abandons God, it will surely suffer defeat. Yet even then God will not abandon His chosen people!

Key verse. 28:19: Public policy is still linked with private morality.

Personal application. You may try to witness by deed only, but don't be surprised at the impact of the more vocal wicked on society.

Key concepts. Child sacrifice »p. 453. Prophet »p. 131. Assyria »p. 255.

INSIGHT

Personal piety (27:2). Jotham's personal piety was rewarded by God (v. 6). But personal piety is never enough in a nation's leader. The "corrupt practices" of the people which Jotham's rule left unaffected included sacrificing at high places, idolatry, and immorality (cf. 2 Kings 15:35).

Again we're reminded how little we need office seekers who vow not to permit personal convictions to affect their public acts. Government needs leaders who have convictions and who act boldly on them.

Jotham's 16 years (27:1). Jotham's failure to influence his people may not have been his fault. Comparing figures given in Kings and Chron., it seems Jotham's first 10 years were served as co-regent with his leper father, Uzziah, and his last two or three as co-regent with his son Ahaz. His independent rule may thus have been limited to three or at most four years!

"Ahaz" (28:1-27). Spiritual and political conditions during the reign of this actively wicked king of Judah are reflected in Isa. 1–7.

"God handed him over" (28:5). The theme of divine blessing for devotion and punishment for apostasy is emphasized again. Rezin was king of Aram (Syria) and Pekah of Israel at this time.

"Oded" (28:9-15). The immediate response of the men of Israel to the prophet's demand that their captives be returned is revealing. First, it shows the existence of a sense of kinship that persisted despite over 200 years of division! Second, it shows something of the authority possessed by prophets in O.T. times. Third, the response of the men of Israel to Obed's rebuke is in contrast to Ahaz's response to Isaiah's promise! (Isa. 7) The narrative suggests that Judah is now in worse spiritual condition than apostate Israel!

"Assyria" (28:16). Ahaz' appeal to Assyria for help against Syria and Israel was in direct violation of God's command given through Isaiah (Isa. 7:4-7). Tiglath-Pileser responded, but as the chronicler remarked, "gave him trouble instead of help" (v. 20). The territory Judah lost was not returned, but was organized as Assyrian provinces!

"His time of trouble" (28:22). Troubles that believers experience are most often intended to lead us to rely on the Lord. But if a person is hardened toward God, troubles will often make him or her "even more unfaithful." Ahaz is angry at defeats his own wickedness have caused. But rather than accept responsibility for his actions and repent, he adopts the gods of Syria and actually shuts down God's temple!

His desperate acts demonstrate a basic principle. As long as a person blames others or God for trouble he brings on himself, no healing can take place. The first step toward getting out of trouble is to admit that we're to blame! And the second step is to seek forgiveness.

Chapter summary. Hezekiah became king at a critical time in Judah's history. During his years the Northern Kingdom was defeated and stripped of its Hebrew population by Assyria. Judah's fortified cities were also razed. Jerusalem itself was threatened, and only divine intervention prevented its fall. How can the survival of Judah be explained? The chronicler answers by focusing on the piety of Hezekiah. He devotes three full chapters to describing Hezekiah's religious reforms and the spiritual impact of Hezekiah's reign. First, Hezekiah ritually purifies the temple (29:1-19) and reestablishes regular worship there (vv. 20-36). Then the king calls all his people together to celebrate Passover (30:1-20). The joy of the people is so great that they extend the week long celebration another seven days (vv. 21-27). Once again enthusiastic for Yahweh, the people spread out throughout Judah and smash shrines devoted to pagan gods (31:1). Freewill offerings pour into the temple from all over Judah (vv. 2-15). Genealogical records are consulted, and the descendants of Aaron, supported by the gifts of the people, once again serve the Lord in the temple that represents God's presence in the land (vv. 16-21). Thus it is because Hezekiah sought God, did what was "good and right and faithful," and was devoted to the service of God at His temple that Judah prospered in Hezekiah's day.

Key verse. 31:21: Hezekiah put God first "in everything."

Personal application. Too many Christians miss out on joy because they fail to realize it is a side effect of worshiping God.

Key concepts. Clean/unclean »p. 82. Passover »p. 59. Temple »p. 283. Sacrifice »pp. 78, 84. Priests »p. 81. Genealogy »p. 264.

INSIGHT

Why was the temple closed? (29:3) Hezekiah's father, Ahaz, had locked the temple doors and turned Jerusalem into a center of idolatry (28:24). When he became king Hezekiah put first things first: In the "first month of the first year" of his reign he reopened the temple.

Many things crowd in on us and demand our attention. But the key to well-being is still found in the example of Hezekiah, who first looked after his relationship with God.

Turn their backs (29:6). Often attitudes are expressed in body language. In the Bible, the arrogant are described as "stiff-necked." The humble "bow down." The desperate prostrate themselves. The hostile "rise up against" others. The wicked "lie in wait." In dedicating the temple Solomon had asked God to answer his people's prayer when they looked *toward* the temple.

Our steps to renewal. Hezekiah's step-by-step institution of spiritual renewal in Judah provides an interesting pattern. It involved reconsecration (29:4-14), purification (vv. 15-19),

rededication of the sanctuary (and altar, vv. 20-30), and then encouraging the people to sacrifice too (vv. 31-36). We can follow these same steps: We can consecrate ourselves, purify our lives, dedicate all we have to God—and only then can we urge others to sacrifice to the Lord too.

More conscientious (29:34). Often revival takes root among the lower ranked and the laity before the professional clergy are moved!

Israel's reaction (30:10-11). Hezekiah invited the citizens of Israel, the Northern Heb. Kingdom, to join with Judah in celebrating the Passover. The general reaction was scorn and ridicule, yet "some" responded and came to Judah. We're reminded of another great moment of divine judgment: Sodom, where God saw to it that the one righteous man, Lot, was safely removed before the fire fell. Here Hezekiah's invitation to join Judah in worship comes just before Israel is swept away by Assyria. Most in Israel ridiculed, but some came to Jerusalem and the Lord.

Hezekiah's Jerusalem

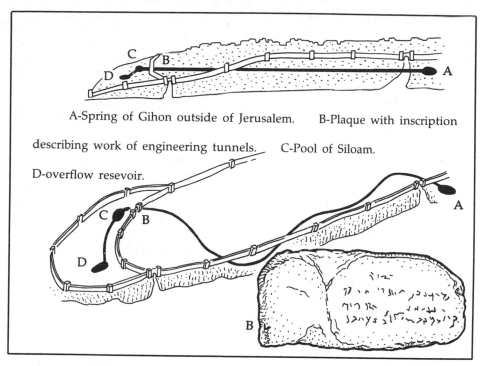

A-Spring of Gihon outside of Jerusalem.   B-Plaque with inscription describing work of engineering tunnels.   C-Pool of Siloam.   D-overflow resevoir.

Faith takes precedence over ritual (30:18-20). A person who took part in any O.T. worship service was to be ritually "clean" (»p. 82; note, however, Num. 9:9-10). Hezekiah's prayer reminds us that while ritual may be a means of expressing faith and honoring God, it never takes precedence over faith. God is not like the strict teacher who flunks a student who hands in his or her paper ten minutes late! He accepts each who "sets his heart on seeking God . . . even if he is not clean according to the rules of the sanctuary."

They destroyed them all (31:1-3). Eradication of competing deities is a vital element in revival (»p. 233). To follow Christ we must rid ourselves of the other things that influence our decisions.

A true return (31:2). The Heb. uses the definite article and says that Hezekiah appointed "the divisions of the priests." The point is that he reinstituted the 24 rotating duty divisions that David had originally set up (cf. 1 Chron. 25). Too often we hear demands for something "new" in our faith that will make it "relevant." What we usually need is a return to basics, a rediscovery of the foundations on which vital spiritual lives have always rested.

Giving (31:5-8). True commitment to God typically results in generous giving to support His work. And giving results in praise to God—and blessing for His people.

Illustration. *The chronicler concentrates on the religious reforms of Hezekiah's 29-year rule. But Hezekiah was also a bold, inventive ruler. One of his most creative projects, designed to supply Jerusalem with water should the city be besieged, was a twisting, 1,750 foot tunnel cut through rock, 150 feet below the surface. The tunnel carried water from the spring of Gihon to the Siloam reservoir (2 Chron. 32:30). According to an inscription cut into the tunnel walls, workmen began tunneling from each end and, despite the tunnel's turns, met in the middle! The inscription, written in script used in Hezekiah's era, reads: "While there were still three cubits to be cut through, [there was heard] the voice of a man calling to his fellow, for there was an overlap in the rock on the right [and on the left]. And when the tunnel was driven through, the quarrymen hewed each toward his fellow, axe against axe; and the water flowed from the spring toward the reservoir for 1,200 cubits, and the height of the rock above the quarrymen was 100 cubits."*

"Genealogical records" (31:16-18). The generosity of the people suddenly made serving God profitable as well as right! The genealogical record had to be searched, possibly because some who were not qualified had "volunteered." We need to be as careful in making sure that those who lean toward "full-time Christian service" are motivated to minister and not just looking for a "job."

Chapter summary. When Sennacherib of Assyria threatens Judah in Hezekiah's day, the king prepares his defenses, and publicly announces his dependence on the Lord (32:1-8). As the Assyrian army batters its way deeper into Judah and threatens the capital, Hezekiah lays the demands of the Assyrians before the Lord, appealing to God to act (vv. 9-20). God does act. The Assyrian army is supernaturally struck down, and Judah is left in an uneasy peace (vv. 21-23). The writer now reports an incident that happened some years before the Assyrian invasion, to show that repentance saved Judah when Hezekiah himself sinned (vv. 24-32).

Despite the lessons of faith taught during Hezekiah's reign, his son Manasseh leads Judah into a depravity so deep that "they did more evil than the [Canaanite] nations the Lord had destroyed" at the time of the conquest (33:1-10). In time Manasseh is taken captive by the Assyrians. He turns to God, humbles himself, and is restored to his throne (vv. 11-14). Although in his remaining years Manasseh purges Jerusalem of idolatry, he is unable to reach the people his own evil ways have influenced (vv. 15-20). And Manasseh is unable to influence his own son Amon who, after a short idolatrous reign, is assassinated (vv. 21-25).

Key verse. 33:17: Some things that God forgives may have consequences that forgiveness does not undo.

Personal application. Better to love God and be a blessing to others, as Hezekiah was, than to reject Him as Manasseh did and bring a curse upon those for whom you care.

Key concepts. Assyria »p. 255. Occult »p. 131. Temple »p. 283. Prayer »p. 181. Healing »pp. 412, 784. Idolatry »p. 433.

INSIGHT

Parallel passages. The story of Jerusalem's deliverance in the time of Hezekiah is found in three passages. For additional notes on Sennacherib's invasion, see 2 Kings 18–19 (p. 256) and Isa. 36–39 (p. 429). For additional notes on Hezekiah's illness, see 2 Kings 20 (p. 257).

New material (32:2-8). Material found in these verses is not in either parallel account. Verses 2-5 make it clear that Hezekiah was determined to resist any Assyrian invasion. The exhortation is typical of the "holy war address" usually made by a priest, to stimulate faith (cf. Deut. 20:2-4).

Challenging God (32:10-19). Undoubtedly the thrust of Hezekiah's exhortation was communicated to the Assyrians. Sennacherib's message is intended to undercut Hezekiah's call to confidence in the Lord. We may well fear when those who are stronger challenge us in our weakness. But we can have great confidence when our enemies challenge God!

The Babylonian visit (32:31). Two different reasons are given for the visit of Babylonian envoys. In 2 Kings 20:12 the envoys come to congratulate Hezekiah on his recovery from a deadly illness. Here the Babylonian envoys inquire "about the miraculous sign." Both reasons are likely, as the sign, the sun's shadow going backward, fits well with the Babylonian preoccupation with astronomy and astrology. It is likely that the envoys also urged Hezekiah to resist Assyria and suggested Babylon might open up a "second front."

Manasseh (33:1-20). Manasseh's personal though belated repentance reminds us that it is never too late for the individual to return to the Lord. Yet the O.T. makes it clear that Manasseh's years mark the point of no return for Judah. Second Kings 23:26 says, "The Lord did not turn from the heat of His fierce anger, which burned against Judah because of all that Manasseh had done to provoke Him to anger" (cf. Jer. 15:4).

Chapter summary. Josiah launches the final cycle in the chronicler's review of Judah's history. Despite the dedication of the young king, his revival is unable to halt Judah's downward slide into idolatry and exile. Yet Josiah's reign did offer Judah one last brief moment of faith and hope.

Outline
Place
Finder

SOLOMON
ASA
JEHOSHAPHAT
JOASH
HEZEKIAH
JOSIAH

Josiah is only 8 when he becomes king (34:1-2). At age 20 he begins to purge the land of idolatry (vv. 3-5). His next great step, taken six years later, is major repair of the temple (vv. 6-13). In the process a lost book of God's Law is found, and the full extent of Judah's apostasy is grasped by the young king (vv. 14-21). God's intent to bring disaster on Judah as punishment is confirmed by the prophetess Huldah, but Josiah is promised that judgment will not fall in his time (vv. 22-28). Josiah responds to this word of grace by redoubling his efforts for the Lord (vv. 29-33). That very year Josiah calls his people to again celebrate Passover, with ceremony unmatched since the time of Samuel (35:1-19). At age 39 Josiah's godly reign ends suddenly. He is killed fighting against Pharaoh Neco, who apparently is rushing to the aid of Assyrian forces about to be crushed by the Babylonians (vv. 20-27).

Key verse. 34:31: The Word condemns, but brings hope.

Personal application. Grace is not intended to make us lax.

Key concepts. High places »p. 113. Temple »p. 283. Levites »p. 95. Women »pp. 163, 394. Prophet »p. 131. Law »pp. 120, 145.

INSIGHT

Parallel passage. For more on the time of Josiah, see 2 Kings 22–23 (p. 259).

Four themes. The chronicler develops four topics: (1) his early reform, (34:1-7); (2) the revival of his 18th year, (34:8-33); (3) his great Passover, (35:1-19); and (4) his early death (35:20-27).

Josiah's kingdom (34:5-6). Inscriptions found in Galilee support the implication that Josiah extended his control into Israel, which was at that time an Assyrian border territory. This was possible because Assyria was weakened by internal troubles.

The lost Book of the Law (24:14). It was 622 B.C. when Josiah read Judah's doom in a long lost book of Moses. The king's immediate response won himself and his nation a last, brief time of peace. Read the words of Moses, and of prophets active in Josiah's day, in the box below.

"If you do not carefully follow all the words of this law, which are written in this book, and do not revere this glorious and awesome name—the Lord your God—the Lord will send fearful plagues on you and your descendants, harsh and prolonged disasters. . . . You who were numerous as the stars in the sky will be left but few in number. . . . Just as it pleased the Lord to make you prosper and increase in number, so it will please Him to ruin and destroy you. You will be uprooted from the land you are entering to possess it. Then the Lord will scatter you among all nations" (Deut. 28:56-64).

"My people have committed two sins: They have forsaken Me, the spring of living water, and have dug their own cisterns, broken cisterns that cannot hold water. Your wickedness will punish you; your backsliding will rebuke you. Consider then and realize how evil and bitter it is for you when you forsake the Lord your God and have no awe of Me" (Jer. 2:13, 19).

"The great day of the Lord is near—near and coming quickly. That day will be a day of wrath, a day of distress and anguish, a day of trouble and ruin. . . . I will bring distress on the people . . . because they have sinned against the Lord" (Zeph. 1:14-17).

Babylon

Illustration. *The city of Babylon [right], beautified by Nebuchadnezzar, was the capital of a vast and powerful empire (above), extending from Mesopotamia to the Mediterranean to Egypt.*

For approximately 100 years, the Babylonian empire was the most powerful state the western world had known. Most importantly, it had a transforming impact on the course of sacred history.

Babylon's history

Babylon may have been the oldest city in the world, founded on the traditional site of Babel (Gen. 11:1-9) by Nimrod (Gen. 10:10). It was capital of a powerful state from circa 2000 to 1595 B.C. During this time it became an educational and literary center, with a famous school for scribes and libraries filled with technical words on astronomy and astrology. The best known product of the era is the law Code of Hammurabi, which dates from 1780 B.C. Although the city was incorporated into the Assyrian empire around 1000 B.C., it persistently resisted outside rule. Babylon city was destroyed in 698 B.C., led by the Chaldean, Nabopolassar. God drew attention to the remarkable progress of the Babylonians when He called out to Judah through Habakkuk, "Look at the nations and watch—and be utterly amazed. For I am going to do something in your days that you would not believe, even if you were told. I am raising up the Babylonians" (Hab. 1:5-6).

Nabopolassar crushed the Assyrian army, took Nineveh, its capital, and completed the extermination of Assyria's remaining forces in 609 B.C. But it was Nabopolassar's son, Nebuchadnezzar II, who ruled 605-562 B.C., who consolidated his father's conquests. A gifted administrator and enthusiastic builder, as well as military genius, it was Nebuchadnezzar who made Baby-

lon truly great. He built some 17 miles of double walls around his city, which lay along the Euphrates River some 50 miles south of modern Baghdad, Iraq. The city featured "hanging gardens," one of the seven wonders of the ancient world, and some 50 temples.

Babylon's impact on sacred history

Nebuchadnezzar made Judah a vassal state in 605 B.C. At that time he took Judah's king, 10,000 leading Jews, and the temple's treasures to Babylon! But Judah proved rebellious, and in 596 B.C. the city of Jerusalem and Solomon's temple were razed, and the majority of the population of Judah was resettled in Babylon. The few Jews remaining in the land fled to Egypt and were lost from view. Humanly speaking the deportation reflected a resettlement policy taken over from the Assyrians.

In fact exile from the Promised Land was a devastating blow. It humbled God's people and at long last purged the Jewish people of their longing for idolatry. In Babylon, the Jews refocused their faith by committed and intense study of the Scriptures. The people began to gather weekly for worship and study of the Word. Thus, it was in Babylon that the synagogue became a basic institution in Jewish life; one which throughout history has provided Judaism with the spiritual strength to survive despite thousands of years of dispersion and persecution.

Chapter summary. The final cycle of the chroniclers' history concludes with the briefest of reviews of Judah's last tragic years. With Josiah dead, Jehoahaz becomes king. In just three months he is deposed by Egypt, which has halted the Babylonian advance (36:1-3). But Babylonian armies soon force the Egyptians back, and Babylon dominates Syria-Palestine. Jehoiakim is attacked and deposed by Nebuchadnezzar in 605 B.C., and is replaced by Jehoiachin (vv. 4-8). The 18-year-old ruler survives only three months (vv. 9-10). Nebuchadnezzar then replaces him with Zedekiah, who rules the last eleven years of Judah's existence (vv. 11-14). The absolute corruption of Judah at the end is well documented in Jeremiah and in Ezekiel 8–11.

The chronicler concludes a last look back. Despite warning delivered by prophet after prophet, the people of Judah despised God and His Word. In the end God handed His people over to Nebuchadnezzar, who carried them away into captivity (vv. 15-21). But God remained faithful to His people! In time, the Babylonian empire was overthrown by the Persians, and in his first year Cyrus of Persia issued a decree permitting the Jews to go home (vv. 22-23).

Key verse. 36:16: God's patience does have an end.

Personal application. However dark present times may be, our gracious God has a bright future for His own.

INSIGHT

Hopes dashed (36:1-13). God's promise to David implied a bright future for the Jewish people, with a kingdom of vast expanse. Yet the last kings of Judah ruled in name only, for the little kingdom was dominated by foreign powers. The chronicler's review makes two points. First, the promise to David was never fulfilled during the existence of Israel and Judah as independent nations. So fulfillment must lie ahead! Surely the fact that God remains committed to His people was revealed in the decree of Cyrus that actually commanded a return home! Second, the promise could not be fulfilled because God's people had refused to respond to His Word. The message to

the little community that has resettled Judah is clear. Respond to God. Worship Him. And the future for the Jewish people remains bright!

The chronicler's sermon (36:14-21). A final sermon makes the message of history even more clear. Mock God and His messengers, and there is no remedy. But God has promised, "If My people, who are called by My name, will humble themselves and pray and seek My face and turn from their wicked ways, then will I hear from heaven and will forgive their sin and will heal their land" (2 Chron. 7:14). There is forgiveness and healing ever available to the people of God.

Ezra

The Book of Ezra continues the history of the Jewish people that was begun in Genesis with the call of Abraham (2100 B.C.). The Old Testament historical books have traced their adventures, through slavery in Egypt (1900-1500 B.C.), through a military conquest of Canaan (1400 B.C.), and through centuries of bare survival during the dark days of the judges (1375-1050 B.C.). The Scriptures have described the chosen people's emergence as a Middle Eastern power under David and Solomon (1010-930 B.C.), and then detailed the division of the land into two competing and often hostile kingdoms (1030 B.C.). Persistently unfaithful to God, first the people of the Northern Kingdom, Israel (722 B.C.), and then of the Southern Kingdom, Judah (586 B.C.), have been torn from the Promised Land and taken captive by a powerful pagan nation. But God has not abandoned the descendants of Abraham. Seventy years of captivity in Babylon have purged the Jewish people of idolatry and focused their attention on the Scriptures. When the Babylonian empire is supplanted by the Persian, the Persian ruler restores the exiles to their homeland. The Book of Ezra, and then of Nehemiah, tells what happens when a small contingent of Jews returns to resettle the Promised Land. Despite opposition from neighboring peoples, discouragement, and even lapses into sin, a Jewish presence is restored in the Holy Land and another temple erected on the site of Solomon's earlier edifice. There, in a tiny district of what was once its own land, the little Jewish community struggles to survive and awaits God's promise of a coming Messiah, God's agent, who will see that all the ancient promises made to Abraham are fulfilled.

EZRA AT A GLANCE

KEY PEOPLE

Cyrus *The Persian ruler who issues the decree permitting the Jews to return home and rebuild the temple.*

Sheshbazzar *Who led the first group of Jews to return.*

Haggai & Zechariah *Prophets, whose ministry encouraged the people to complete the temple after the work had been abandoned for 18 years. Their sermons and visions have been preserved in the Old Testament books that bear their names.*

Ezra *The Bible teacher who led a small group back to Jerusalem some 80 years after the first group returned. His commitment to do, as well as teach, God's Word stimulated a revival.*

KEY EVENTS

Cyrus issues a decree (Ezra 1). *The Jews (and other peoples exiled by the Babylonians) are permitted to return home and encouraged to rebuild the Jerusalem temple.*

A band of some 42,360 Jews return (Ezra 2). *Those who choose to return are moved by enthusiasm for the Lord.*

The temple foundations are laid (Ezra 3). *Worship is reestablished in Jerusalem.*

Opposition halts building (Ezra 4). *Nothing is done for 18 years. Then the preaching of Haggai and Zechariah stimulates completion.*

Ezra returns (Ezra 7-10). *Ezra corrects abuses and urges the Jews to live by God's Law.*

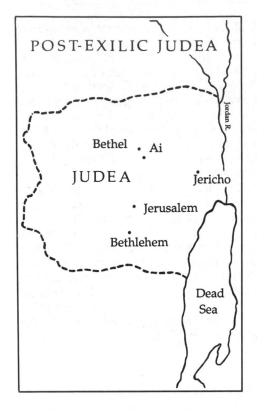

POST-EXILIC JUDEA

Bethel • Ai

JUDEA   Jericho

• Jerusalem

Bethlehem

Dead
Sea

Jordan R.

Chronological Chart:
The Exile and Return

Reign of Nebuchadnezzar	605-562
Ministry of Daniel	600-530?
Reign of Nabonidus	562-539
Belshazzar as Viceroy	?-539
Cyrus the Great	558-529
Fall of Babylon	539
Reign of Cyrus the Great	539-529
Darius the Mede	
Viceroy in Babylon	539/538
Decree of return	539
Temple foundations laid	536
Reign of Chambyses	529-523
Reign of Darius the Great	522-485
Ministry of Haggai	520/519
Ministry of Zechariah	520-475
Temple completed	516
Reign of Xerxes	485-464
Queen Esther	478/477
Reign of Artaxerxes I	464-424
Ezra comes to Jerusalem	457
Nehemiah governor of	
Judah	446
Ministry of Malachi	435
Nehemiah governor again	433-430
Old Testament ends	

WHERE THE ACTION TAKES PLACE

The returning exiles were able to populate only a tiny portion of the land controlled by the Jews in the days of David and Solomon. This district, some 40 miles across, was known as Judea and was part of a larger Persian province.

Date and Authorship. Part of the book is written as a first person report by Ezra. Other parts are third person descriptions of his actions. Many different documents, written in Aramaic, the diplomatic language of the time, are quoted by the author. There are also genealogical lists, which would have been on file in the temple archives. There is no significant reason to doubt that Ezra himself is responsible for the book, which was completed by 430 B.C.

THEOLOGICAL OUTLINE OF EZRA

I. REBUILDING   1–6
II. RENEWAL   7–10

CONTENT OUTLINE OF EZRA

I. The First Return: Rebuilding the
Temple (1:1–6:22)
  A. Background of the Return
  (1:1-11)
    1. The edict of Cyrus (1:1-4)
    2. Return under
    Sheshbazzar (1:5-11)
  B. List of Those Who Returned
  (2:1-70)
    1. Leaders (2:1-2)
    2. Families (2:2-20)
    3. Villagers (2:21-35)
    4. Priests (2:36-39)
    5. Levites (2:40-42)
    6. Temple servants (2:43-58)
    7. Others (2:59-63)
    8. Totals (2:64-67)
    9. Settling in (2:70)
  C. Restoring Temple Worship
  (3:1-13)
    1. The altar rebuilt (3:1-3)
    2. The Festival of Booths (3:4-6)
    3. Rebuilding begun (3:7-13)
  D. Opposition to Rebuilding
  (4:1-24)
    1. During Cyrus' reign (4:1-5)
    2. During Xerxes' reign (4:6)
    3. During Artaxerxes' reign
    (4:7-23)
      a. A letter to the king (4:11-16)
      b. A letter from the king (4:17-23)
    4. The work resumed (4:24)
  E. Completing the Temple
  (5:1–6:22)
    1. Haggai and Zechariah
    exhort rebuilding (5:1-2)
    2. The governor halts work (5:3-5)
    3. A report sent to Darius (5:6-10)

    4. Answer to Darius (5:11-17)
    5. Searching for Cyrus' decree
    (6:1-5)
    6. Darius orders the temple to be
    rebuilt (6:6-12)
    7. The temple completed (6:13-15)
    8. The temple dedicated (6:16-18)
    9. Passover celebrated (6:19-22)
II. Ezra's Return and Spiritual
Reforms (7:1–10:44)
  A. Ezra returns to Israel
  (7:1–8:36)
    1. Preparations (7:1-10)
    2. Authorization by
    Artaxerxes (7:11-26)
    3. Ezra's praise (7:27-28)
    4. Ezra's companions (8:1-14)
    5. Searching for Levites
    (8:15-20)
    6. Prayer and fasting (8:21-23)
    7. Gifts weighed out (8:24-27)
    8. Guarding the gifts (8:28-30)
    9. The journey and arrival
    (8:31-36)
  B. Ezra's Reforms (9:1–10:44)
    1. Mixed marriages found
    (9:1-4)
    2. Ezra's prayer of confession
    (9:5-15)
    3. The people's response
    (10:1-4)
    4. Calling a public assembly
    (10:5-15)
    5. Offenders investigated
    (10:16-17)
    6. A list of the guilty (10:18-43)
    7. The mixed marriages
    dissolved (10:44)

Chapter summary. Cyrus of Persia takes the crumbling Babylonian empire intact. One of his first acts is to reverse the Babylonian policy of deporting conquered people from their homelands. Cyrus issues a decree permitting any Jew who wishes to do so to return to the Promised Land. The decree also permits contributions for rebuilding the Jerusalem temple (1:1-4). God moves many of the captives to return and stimulates all to give generously. Cyrus himself contributes the gold and silver utensils Nebuchadnezzar had taken from the first temple (vv. 5-11). Ezra then provides a detailed list of those who chose to return: some 42,360 Jews, who brought along 7,337 servants and singers (2:1-70). This genealogical honor role later provided the descendants of this first group to return to Judah with a historic claim both to fame and to racial purity.

Key verse. 1:2: Even words spoken by politicians can be true.

Personal application. We can be glad for godly ancestors, but we must make our own personal commitment to the Lord.

Key concepts. Providence »p. 322. Temple »p. 283. Leading »p. 131. Babylon »p. 302. Genealogy »p. 264.

INSIGHT

Jeremiah's prophecy (1:1). Jeremiah 25:1-14 and 29:10 predict that Judah will be held captive in Babylon for 70 years. The first deportation was in 605 B.C. The 70th year was 536 B.C. The proclamation of Cyrus was issued in his first regnal year, 538 B.C. The little company of Jews did return, and the foundations of the temple were laid in 536 B.C.

"Cyrus" (1:1). Two O.T. prophecies name significant individuals hundreds of years before their birth. An unnamed prophet predicted that a descendant of David named Josiah would desecrate an illicit altar dedicated by Jeroboam I. This prediction was made about 930 B.C. and fulfilled in 622 B.C. Isaiah, writing around 700 B.C., identified Cyrus by name: "He is My shepherd and will accomplish all that I please; he will say of Jerusalem, 'Let it be rebuilt,' and of the temple, 'Let its foundations be laid' " (Isa. 44:28).

Did Cyrus believe in the Lord? (1:2) The words of Cyrus' decree have led many to suppose that Cyrus was a true believer. However, archeological finds indicate Cyrus showed similar respect to the deities of all his conquered people, and that the decree of return was an expression of national policy rather than faith-motivated conviction. What is significant for us is not whether Cyrus believed. God shapes history, when men believe—and when they do not.

"Everyone whose heart God had moved" (1:5). Most of those in Babylon chose to stay in the land of their captivity. The exiles had been settled in a district of their own, found employment, and lived generally comfortable lives. Then as now, prosperity dulled the passions of many of the chosen people for a struggle in the Promised Land. Yet let's remember what the text says: Those whose heart God moved did return. The others supported them with gifts (1:4).

And the *Babylonian Talmud*, one of the two most significant corpora of Jewish studies of O.T. law, was developed by the Jewish community of Babylon. God has a place for each person. Let's not be critical of others who may not be called to the same place we have been.

The temple treasures (1:7). The temple treasures had been taken to Babylon not only for their intrinsic value but also as trophies of Babylon's "victory" over Judah's God. Just before Jerusalem's fall, false prophets predicted an immediate return of these items, symbolizing a triumph of *Yahweh* (cf. Jer. 27:16-22; 28:6). Jeremiah promised the utensils would be returned, but much later (27:22). In ordering the treasures returned, Cyrus thus fulfilled another prophet's prediction. What a reminder. God will surely triumph. Don't be disturbed if that triumph is delayed.

"42,350" (2:64). When the numbers given in chap. 2 are added together, they fall about 12,000 short of this total. Some believe the 12,000 were women and/or children. If so, this may account for the many marriages to pagan women which took place (cf. Ezra 8–10).

Chapter summary. When the returnees have settled down in their towns, they reassemble in Jerusalem (3:1). They rebuild the altar of sacrifice (vv. 2-3) and celebrate the Feast of Tabernacles (vv. 4-6). With the daily sacrifices reestablished, they begin work on the foundation of the new temple (vv. 7-9). When the work is complete, all the people come together again for a great celebration (vv. 10-13).

Outline
Place
Finder

REBUILDING
RENEWAL

At first the local peoples, who were settled in Israelite territory by the Assyrians nearly 300 years earlier, offer to help with the temple. Although pagan, they had added Yahweh to their pantheons when they settled in His land. The Jews reject this offer (4:1-3). This arouses the hostility of their neighbors, who write to King Artaxerxes and falsely accuse the Jews of rebuilding the "rebellious city" of Jerusalem (vv. 4-16). The Persian king orders the Jews to stop work on Jerusalem, and the Jews' local enemies force them to stop work on the temple (vv. 17-24). Thus, through lies and intimidation work on the temple of God comes to a halt. The temple will lie unfinished for 18 more years!

Key verse. 3:11: Even beginnings are occasions for joy.

Personal application. Expect opposition, and don't quit!

Key concepts. Altar »p. 79. Temple »p. 283. Festivals »p. 89.

INSIGHT

"**The seventh month**" (3:1-3). *Tishri* corresponds to Sept./Oct. The people had taken about three months to settle in their new homes. This was a sacred month during which the Day of Atonement and the week-long Feast of Tabernacles was celebrated (»p. 89).

"**Despite their fear**" (3:3). The word for fear here is *'emah*, which indicates a terror inspired by men or wild animals. We can measure our faith by what we do when we're afraid, despite our fears!

"**Tabernacles**" (3:4). During the Feast of Tabernacles the Jews lived outdoors in huts or lean-tos. The festival commemorated years of wilderness wandering, when God brought them safely to the Promised Land. What a time to celebrate the Jews' safe return!

"**Cedar logs**" (3:7). Logs from Tyre (modern Lebanon) were also used in the temple built by Solomon (cf. 1 Kings 5:7-12). These giant cedars can grow to 120 feet high, with a circumference of 30 to 40 feet. The wood is fragrant, resists rot, and repels insects.

Look ahead (3:10-13). Laying the foundation was a cause of celebration. The descriptive "great shout of praise" (v. 11) reflects the typically loud expression of both grief and joy in the Middle East. The old remembered the glory of Solomon's temple and were heartbroken that this temple was less than half as large. The young were excit-

ed at the prospect of what lay ahead.

Let's not covet the past. Let's cultivate the attitude of looking ahead expectantly to what God will do next.

Persistent opposition (4:1-23). The author uses various documents to describe a series of attempts to foil the Jews' rebuilding efforts. Verses 1-5 take place during the reign of Cyrus (559–529 B.C.). Verse 6 takes place in the time of Xerxes (485–465 B.C.). Verses 7-23 cover Artaxerxes I (464–424 B.C.). Then v. 24 returns us to the time of Darius I (522–486 B.C.).

Don't expect it will be easy to lead a committed Christian life. We will face persistent opposition too. But we too will overcome if we remain faithful!

Exclusiveness (4:3-4). The returnees had a strong sense of identity as God's covenant people. To permit the half-pagan Samaritans to participate in rebuilding the temple would deny not only this identity but the uniqueness of what God intended to do through the Jewish people.

The claim of the modern believer that Christ alone saves, and our refusal to dilute that message also arouses hostility. But we too must be true to what God is doing through the Gospel and affirm the uniqueness of the Christian message in a world that still believes any road leads to God.

Chapter summary. In 520 B.C. the prophets Haggai and Zechariah urge the Jews to complete the temple, whose foundation had been laid in 536 B.C. Taking on the project is an act of faith, for at this time the struggling community was hardly able to survive (cf. Hag. 1:5-11). When they do begin, the governor of the Persian land-across-the-river district writes to check on the Jews' authority to complete the temple, and for instructions from King Darius (5:1-7). The author quotes the request in the original Aramaic language (vv. 8-17) and also quotes the king's reply. In it Darius confirms the original decree. He orders that all expenses of the temple project be paid from the royal treasury (6:1-12). The Jews' faith has been rewarded, and God has met every need! The temple is completed four years later. It is dedicated with great joy (vv. 13-18), and once again the Jews celebrate Passover before their own temple in their own land (vv. 19-22).

Key verse. 6:8: God meets every need.

Personal application. It is a far greater risk to disobey God than to obey Him!

Key concepts. Temple »p. 283. Taxes »p. 317. Separation »pp. 91, 761. Passover »p. 59.

INSIGHT

"Zerubbabel" (5:2). The name means "seed of Babylon" and reflects his birth there. He is the last of David's line (cf. 1 Chron. 3:19) to be given political power by foreign rulers. In Zech. 3 he serves as a symbol of that line and what the Lord will do through David's descendant, Jesus.

"Tattenai" (5:3-5). Archeologists have found a Persian document dated 5 June 502 B.C. that identifies Tattenai as a *pahat*, a sub-governor who served under the *satrap* overseeing a province which included Syria-Palestine. His questioning of the Jews and letter to Darius is not evidence of hostility. Tattenai was simply a government official carrying out his duties. If anything Tattenai was favorable to the Jews, for he let them keep building after he wrote.

More confirmation. Thousands of tablets discovered at Persepolis in 1933/34 date from the 13th to the 28th year of Darius. They show that the kind of inquiries reported here were sent to the king.

Two local governors? (5:15) Sheshbazzar is identified in this verse as the Jews' local *pekah* (governor). Zerubbabel also has this title (cf. Hag. 1:1; 2:2). Both are credited with laying the temple foundations (Ezra 1:3; 3:2-8; 5:16; Hag. 1:14-15; 2:2-4). The 1st-century Jewish historian, Josephus, identifies them as the same person, with one name Jewish and the other Babylonian, even as Daniel was known by the Babylonian name Belteshazzar (Dan. 1:7). It is also

possible Zerubbabel was an associate governor who took the post when Sheshbazzar died.

Archives stored in the treasury? (6:1) While this may seem a strange place to store records, excavations at Persepolis where records of the reign of Darius were discovered, show that the record storage rooms were in fact associated with the treasury.

"Ecbatana" (6:2). When a search of the Babylonian archives produced no record of Cyrus' decree, a copy was found at Ecbatana. Why Ecbatana? Because the summer palace of Persian kings was there.

Would the government really pay for rebuilding a Jewish temple? (6:4-8) Some have argued that such generosity is beyond belief. In fact the translated decrees of Cambyses and Darius provide instances of just this kind of help for many religions. And bricks stamped with Cyrus' seal at Uruk and Ur prove that temple repairs and constructions were supported by state funds during his reign. These discoveries disprove claims of the "conversion" of Persian rulers, but at the same time demonstrate how accurately the Bible reports historical detail.

Penalties (6:11-12). Such curses were customarily added to decrees and treaties.

"King of Assyria" (6:22). The writings of Herodotus show that many centuries after Nineveh's fall rulers of the Babylonian and Persian empires were sometimes called kings of "Assyria."

Chapter summary. Fifty-eight years elapse between the Passover celebration of 516 B.C. reported in chapter 6 and the events of chapter 7. In the wider empire Darius had proven to be capable, and his aggressive son Xerxes had even burned Athens before being thrown back from Europe by the Greeks. His successor, Artaxerxes, was a weaker ruler, but the massive Persian empire still dominated Syria/Palestine. But now, in little Judah the enthusiasm aroused by the completion of the temple has faded. The teachings of God's Law are increasingly ignored, and temple worship has become routine. At this critical junction, Ezra, a descendant of Aaron and "a teacher well versed in the Law of Moses," arrives in Jerusalem (7:1-10). He comes with donations for the temple—and with a royal commission to appoint judges and to enforce both Old Testament and Persian law in Judah (vv. 11-26). Ezra brings with him a number of leading men from the Jewish community in Babylon (7:27–8:20).

Depending on God alone for protection, the company had set out carrying great wealth. It arrives safely in Judah with all treasures intact (8:21-30). There the new settlers offer sacrifices and deliver the king's orders to the district governor (vv. 31-36).

Key verse. 7:10: "Teach" follows "study" and "observe."

Personal application. When we do God's work we can expect God to enable us (see Ezra 7:9, 28; 8:18, 22, 31).

Key concepts. Law »p. 145. Temple »p. 283. Genealogy »p. 264. Fasting »p. 442. Prayer »p. 181.

INSIGHT

Illustration. *A pious scholar carefully makes a copy of an O.T. scroll. The deep reverence of Ezra for the Law of God was transmitted to his successors. Scribes not only studied the Law but supervised its transmission. To ensure against error, the number of characters on each line as well as in the entire book were counted, and the middle letters of the original line and book had to match or the copy was destroyed. In the Christian era each time a scribe copied the sacred name YHWH he showed his reverence by taking a ritual bath. We can thank the commitment of generations of pious Jewish scribes for giving us a reliable O.T.*

Ezra the scribe. Tradition identifies Ezra as a founder of the scribal movement which had a formative impact on later Judaism. In the days before the Exile, a "scribe" might function as a military officer (Jud. 5:14; 2 Kings 25:19), a royal official (2 Sam. 8:17), or as a professional clerk (Jer. 36:26-32). In postexilic Judaism a scribe was a "teacher well versed in the Law of Moses" (Ezra 7:6).

Modern rabbinic Judaism finds its roots in the scribal movement (Tradition, »p. 617).

Chapter summary. When Ezra has been in Judea for a little over four months he faces the problem of mixed marriages. Deuteronomy 7:1-5 and Exodus 34:11-16 prohibit intermarriage with pagan peoples because, as God's chosen people, the Jews are to be "holy to the Lord." Ezra is appalled to learn that even some of the priests have married Canaanites. He tears his clothes as a mark of public shame and guilt (9:1-5). He then utters one of the Old Testament's most powerful prayers of confession, in which he identifies himself with God's sinning people (vv. 6-15). Ezra's emotional prayer moves others to promise to support Ezra in enforcing the Law (10:1-6). A proclamation orders all the men of Judah to appear in Jerusalem, where Ezra boldly confronts them. The assembly agrees that pagan wives must be divorced and their children sent away (vv. 7-15). Each case is investigated, and the guilty are forced to divorce their foreign wives (vv. 16-17). A list follows (vv. 18-44).

Key verse. 9:6: All are responsible for the sins of society.

Personal application. True shame and sorrow for the sins of others is a key to spiritual renewal.

Key concepts. Shame »p. 354. Sin »p. 34. Confession »p. 892. Separation »p. 761. Holy »p. 86. Prayer »p. 181. Covenant »p. 35.

INSIGHT

Intermarriage (9:1-2). Old Testament laws of racial separation were intended to maintain the distinctiveness of the covenant people. They were also protective, intended to guard against a fall into idolatry. The principle that marriages should be contracted only between believers is also reflected in the N.T. (cf. 1 Cor. 7:39; 2 Cor. 6:14-18).

Ezra's reaction (9:3). Ezra was overcome with grief. Tearing one's clothing is an act expressing extreme distress (cf. Job 1:20; Isa. 36:22; Matt. 26:65). Ezra felt shame and disgrace. As a Jew, he was one with the community and felt a personal responsibility for Judah's unfaithfulness.

It's better to weep over others' actions than to loudly condemn them.

Whose hair do we pull out? (9:3) Ezra tore out some of his hair in his anguish and distress. Later Nehemiah, confronted with the same issue, tore out the hair of the guilty parties (Neh. 13:25). In Neh. 13 the governor is attacking those who went back on their own earlier promise not to marry pagans. The pattern fits a first-century Jewish legal procedure, which called for those first instructed concerning a sin to be dealt with gently. Only those who persisted after being instructed were to be punished.

Moral influence (9:4). Ezra had royal authority in Judah to serve as magistrate. But rather than rely on secular authority, he chose to exert

moral influence. His personal anguish moved those who shared his awe of God to gather around him and swayed the entire community.

We are better off exerting moral influence through teaching and example, than by pressuring for the enactment of "Christian" laws.

Ezra's prayer (9:6-15). While Ezra and Nehemiah may have reacted differently to the remarriage issue, their prayers have much in common (cf. Neh. 9:5-38). Daniel's prayer of confession also bears a striking resemblance to that of Ezra (cf. Dan. 9:4-19). Each contains: a general confession (v. 6), acknowledgment of former sins (v. 7), reminders of God's mercy (vv. 8-9), further confession of the contemporary sin (vv. 10-12), and a final admission of guilt linked with an appeal for mercy (vv. 13-15). This thorough admission of sins can serve as a model for our own prayers of confession today.

"Let it be done" (10:3-4). It's not enough to be sorry for sins. It's necessary to correct them!

No food, no water (10:6). Fasts in O.T. times were partial—during daylight hours only, or refraining from selected foods. Ezra's total fast shows how seriously he viewed the situation.

The guilty (10:18-44). Of the 113 who had married foreign wives, nearly 25 percent were religious leaders! When spiritual decline affects the leadership, there is little prospect for the future.

Nehemiah

The Book of Nehemiah continues the story of the Jews who returned to Judah after the Babylonian Captivity. It takes its name from its central figure, the determined governor Nehemiah. This high official in the Persian court of Artaxerxes asked for the governorship of tiny Judah, that he might rebuild the walls of Jerusalem. He arrived in Judah about 446 B.C., nearly 100 years after the first group of exiles had returned. Nehemiah awakened the enthusiasm of the Jews for the project, firmly resisted the opposition of neighboring peoples, and saw the holy city once again surrounded by the walls. In the ancient world, city walls suggested significance as well as security. With the help of Ezra, Nehemiah also enforced Old Testament laws which the community was again ignoring. After a time, Nehemiah returned to report to the king. The last chapter of the book tells us that Nehemiah returned as governor a second time, probably around 433 B.C., only to find and correct the same abuses that existed before his first term as governor.

Nehemiah has proven one of the favorite Bible books, for it reminds us of the impact a single, committed individual can have on a society. Nehemiah surely is one of the most steadfast and admirable of Old Testament heroes.

NEHEMIAH AT A GLANCE

KEY PEOPLE
Nehemiah *Although he rose to high position in the Persian capital, this wall-builder's heart remained with his people and his God.*
Ezra *The priest/scribe, whose story is told in the book bearing his name, supported Nehemiah's efforts with his teaching.*

KEY EVENTS
Nehemiah returns (Neh. 1–2). *Nehemiah puts the welfare of his people first.*
The walls are rebuilt (Neh. 3–6). *Jerusalem is again a walled city.*
The people correct sins (Neh. 7–10). *Confession and commitment mean revival.*
Nehemiah returns (Neh. 13). *Nehemiah finds the people have broken their promises and enforces obedience.*

WHERE THE ACTION TAKES PLACE

The action takes place in Judea and involves the neighbors of the Jews shown on the map on page 306. For further background, read the introduction to Ezra and see the timeline there, pages 305–306.

THEOLOGICAL OUTLINE OF NEHEMIAH

CONTENT OUTLINE OF NEHEMIAH

Chapter summary. In 446 B.C. Nehemiah is a high official in the Persian court. He is distraught when he hears of conditions in Judea (1:1-4) and prays fervently for his homeland (vv. 5-11). Nehemiah also determines to act. When King Artaxerxes (464–424 B.C.) notices his distress, Nehemiah offers a quick prayer and requests permission to rebuild Jerusalem (2:1-8). The king makes Nehemiah governor of Judea (vv. 9-10).

Nehemiah makes a nighttime survey of Jerusalem, examining its fallen walls (vv. 11-16). Only then does he share his vision of a rebuilt Jerusalem and reveal his royal commission (vv. 17-18). The response of the Jews is enthusiastic, but the pagan officials who rule the larger province ridicule the notion of rebuilding and charge that the act constitutes rebellion (vv. 18-19). Nehemiah answers them bluntly. This is the Jews' city, of which they have no part. With God's help, its walls will rise again (v. 20).

Key verse. 2:8: God opens closed doors.

Personal application. Pray. But then be prepared to work.

Key concepts. Jerusalem »p. 205. Prayer »p. 181. Fasting »p. 442.

Outline
Place
Finder

RESTORATION
REVIVAL
RETURN

INSIGHT

Nehemiah. One of the major values of this book is to be found in biographical study of its main character. Nehemiah was a wealthy official in the Persian capital who sacrificed his own comfort to serve God and his people. His courage in the face of opposition, consistent personal example of commitment to godliness, unwavering trust, and fierce determination that God's people must obey His Law, are displayed over and over again in this short book. Generations of Christian leaders have drawn inspiration from Nehemiah and found principles to apply in their own ministries.

Ruined walls (1:1-4). Unwalled cities in ancient times had no defense against enemies. More significant at this time, unwalled cities were dismissed as insignificant. Thus, for Jerusalem to lack walls was a disgrace to the city God had chosen—and brought dishonor to the Lord!

The Jews had tried earlier to rebuild the walls (Ezra 4:7-23), but had given up. Nehemiah saw this as a continuation of the Jews' historic pattern of sinning against God by lack of dedication to His laws (Neh. 1:5-11).

"Cupbearer" (1:11). The apocryphal book of Tobit (1:22), which also comes from the Persian period, speaks of one cupbearer as "keeper of the signet, administrator and treasurer under Sennacherib." In the ancient world the cupbearer (*masqeh*) was an influential official with direct and constant access to the king.

Instant prayers (2:4-5). Many have observed that Nehemiah's prayer to the "God of heav-

en" took only an instant, between the time Artaxerxes asked his questions and Nehemiah answered. But remember that this instant prayer was preceded by the lengthy petition recorded in 1:5-11.

A relationship with God nurtured by regular times of prayer must be the context for all our "instant prayers."

Nehemiah's enemies (2:10). The two men mentioned here prove to be persistent enemies of the Jews and Nehemiah. Sanballat was the chief political enemy of Nehemiah. He was governor of Samaria at the time (cf. 4:2), a position confirmed by a letter found by archeologists dated to 407 B.C. which names his sons, and calls him *pehah* of Samaria. Tobiah is thought to be a Jew with lands in Gilead. The phrase "Ammonite official" refers to his position as governor of Ammonite lands rather than to his race. Tobiah had many family ties with Jews in Jerusalem (cf. 3:4, 30; 13:4-7).

Testimony time (2:18). Nehemiah's personal testimony that God had brought him to Jerusalem was a key to motivating the Jews to rebuild. Courage to act comes from the conviction that God is with us.

Ridicule (2:19). Ridicule is one of the most effective means there is to discourage us from acting. The superior smirk, the raised eyebrow, the mocking laugh, have kept many a young Christian from living out his or her faith.

Nehemiah kept his eyes on God, and we must too.

Outline
Place
Finder

RESTORATION
REVIVAL
RETURN

Chapter summary. Nehemiah organizes work on the wall, assigning sections to families, neighborhoods, and even guilds of tradesmen (3:1-32). This strategy fixes responsibility for each part of the task. It also creates work teams out of existing groups who have learned to work cooperatively. And it encourages competition, not between individuals but between teams.

But as progress is made on the walls, Sanballat becomes incensed. He and Tobiah step up their rumor and ridicule campaign (4:1-3). Nehemiah simply prays—and keeps the people working (vv. 4-5). When ridicule fails to halt the rebuilding, the enemies plot an armed attack. Then the Jews hear Nehemiah reassure his fearful workers (vv. 6-15). He also organizes a defense: Half his workers are placed on guard while the other half work, and signals are devised to bring reinforcements to any section of the wall under attack (vv. 16-20). Thus prepared, the Jews intensify rather than abandon their building efforts (vv. 21-25).

Key verse. 4:21: To defeat opposition, continue the work.

Personal application. One way to exercise your faith is to plan and organize carefully.

Key concepts. War »p. 133. Enemies »p. 91. Guilt »p. 79.

INSIGHT

"Sheep Gate" (3:1). The gates and various features of the wall surrounding Jerusalem are given names, much as we name our city streets. The list begins at the northeast section of Jerusalem's walls and makes a circuit concluding in v. 32 at the same corner.

Unity of purpose (3:1-32). Some 40 different sections of wall are mentioned in the chapter, each assigned to a different group. To work effectively and quickly, the wall builders displayed a sense of common purpose and commitment.

A common sense of purpose is also important today if Christians are to work together in God's kingdom. That sense of common purpose can unite us, even when we differ in convictions or doctrine.

Close to home. Nehemiah assigned teams to work as close to home as possible. Thus, they had a personal interest in building that section of wall which would defend their own houses or businesses.

We need to encourage rather than discourage personal interest in God's work. For instance, it may be more meaningful to direct giving to a missionary we know and can pray for than to give to a denomination's missionary "program."

Diversity. Nehemiah organized his work groups on several different bases. Some were organized by neighborhood—others by family, social status, and profession.

Don't be afraid of diversity in the church. God gives people different gifts and calls us from different cultures and backgrounds. Yet the church is one, and believers are to work and worship together.

No war of words (4:1-5). Nehemiah has been criticized by some for a meanspirited prayer—asking God to punish the Jews' enemy. But how much better it is to ask God to deal with our enemies than for us to become involved in a war of words—or worse.

"Enemies" (4:11). The term for enemies found here is the Heb. word *sar*, which means to cause harm. Sanballat and his supporters intended to injure the Jerusalem Jews. Nehemiah's prayer was just!

Sneak attack (4:11-13). Like many evil persons, Sanballat was ready to kill the unarmed and unsuspecting. But when the Jews learned, they were armed and ready. Thus, Sanballat was afraid to attack.

Don't be afraid of the threats of bullies. Resist and most will back down.

"Great and awesome" (4:14). Nehemiah's exhortation identifies two bases for courage. Remember that God is far greater than any human enemy. And, be sure that what you are fighting for is right. Defending loved ones provided the Jews with the moral grounds to fight against their attackers, grounds that would not exist if the Jews were the aggressors.

Outline
Place
Finder

RESTORATION
REVIVAL
RETURN

Chapter summary. Internal problems threaten to do what external enemies could not. Nehemiah learns that wealthy Jews have charged their poorer neighbors high interest rates in violation of Old Testament Law. Many are near starvation, and others have been forced to sell children as slaves to pay their debts (5:1-5). Nehemiah confronts the wealthy and gets their commitment to correct the injustice (vv. 6-13). Nehemiah himself sets an example for the rich by paying the costs of administering Judea himself, rather than exercising his right to tax his already burdened people (vv. 14-19). But Sanballat has not given up. He tries to get Nehemiah to meet him, assuming that without Nehemiah's leadership work would cease (6:1-4). When neither invitations nor threats work (vv. 5-9), Sanballat hires a prophet to urge Nehemiah to hide, hoping the act will discredit him. Nehemiah scornfully rejects what he sees as a coward's course (vv. 10-14). And so the wall is rebuilt—in just 52 days (vv. 15-19). With the walls complete, Nehemiah consults the census lists as a first step toward repopulating the holy city (7:1-73).

Key verse. 5:9: Those who do God's work must walk in His ways.

Personal application. Neither enemies nor personal problems can sidetrack us if we remain committed to the task God has set before us.

Key concepts. Poor and oppressed »p. 90. Borrowing »p. 129. Slavery »p. 90. Prophet »p. 131.

INSIGHT

Poverty (5:1-4). Both drought conditions and high taxes placed a great strain on agriculture. But the greed of the wealthy, who loaned desperate families money at high interest and then foreclosed on their property, was the main cause of the dire straits many were in.

Today there are many reasons for poverty. But greed remains the most common cause.

Taxes (5:4). The Persian king collected some 20 million gold *darics* (a Persian coin) annually in taxes. Payment was demanded in gold or silver coin which was then melted down and stored as ingots.

When Alexander the Great took Susa, where Nehemiah had served Artaxerxes, he found some 270 tons of gold and 1,200 tons of silver! The policy stripped the kingdom of coinage, created inflation, and was in part responsible for the serious economic stress in Judea.

"Usury" (5:7). The Heb. word, *massa*, appears only in Nehemiah. It means to impose a burden. The O.T. forbids charging interest on loans to poor neighbors (Ex. 22:25-27; Lev. 25:35-37; Deut. 23:19-20; 24:10-13). These provisions were being violated.

Nehemiah's example (5:14-18). Nehemiah is a pure example of a principle stated in the N.T.

He put his hope in God rather than his riches, and was both "rich in good deeds" and "generous and willing to share" (1 Tim. 6:17-18).

"Remember me" (5:19). Nehemiah frequently appeals to God to "remember" his good works. In biblical idiom "remember" means to repay, either for good or for evil. Nehemiah's appeals were rooted in faith, for he firmly believed "He [God] exists and that He rewards those who diligently seek Him" (Heb. 11:6).

Empty threats (6:5-9). Nehemiah dismissed the accusation of Sanballat and the implied threat, saying Sanballat was "making it up." The Heb. *bada'* appears only here and 1 Kings 12:23. Let's not be afraid when others threaten us with figments of their own imaginations.

Sanballat's plot (6:11-12). The prophet Shemaiah was apparently hired to frighten Nehemiah into taking refuge in the temple, which as a layman Nehemiah could not enter. Nehemiah had only contempt for this attempt to frighten and discredit him.

Repopulation (7:1-73). Walls were necessary, but the fundamental issue was repopulating the city. People, not buildings, remain as the key to the continuation of God's work.

The Persian Era

Illustration. *Gold artifacts and carved reliefs from Susa reflect the power and glory of the Persian empire in Ezra and Nehemiah's day.*

The Persian empire dominated the ancient world between 550 and 330 B.C. In a series of brilliant campaigns Cyrus the Great first united the Medes and Persians. He captured Babylon and simply took over its vast empire. The religion of Persia was Zoroastrianism, a faith which postulated an evil deity opposed by Ahura Mazda, the god of light. The Persian tolerance of other religions is reflected in the support a series of Persian rulers provided the Jews. Darius, the successor to Cyrus, was an effective administrator and developed a network of roads linking his far-flung provinces. Local government was generally left in the hands of native peoples, as the Books of Ezra and Nehemiah reveal.

PERSIAN RULERS IN THE SCRIPTURE

Ruler	Scripture	Description
Cyrus 539–530	2 Chron. 36; Isa. 44; Dan. 10:1; Ezra 1-6	Babylon's conqueror returned exiled peoples to their homelands. In his first year he permitted Jews to return to Judea.
Darius I 522–486	Ezra 4:5; 5:6-7; Neh. 12:22; Hag. 1:1; Zech. 1:1	Cyrus' successor expanded his earlier decree and ordered completion of the Jerusalem temple at government expense.
Xerxes 486–465	Esther	This expansionist ruler twice invaded Europe and twice was thrown back by the Greeks. He is the likely ruler of Esther.
Artaxerxes 465–424	Ezra 7:1, 21-26; Neh. 2:1-8	Nehemiah served this ruler as cupbearer and was granted the governorship of Judea.

Outline
Place
Finder

RESTORATION
REVIVAL
RETURN

Chapter summary. A week after the walls around Jerusalem are completed, the people reassemble in Jerusalem (8:1). Ezra brings out the Book of the Law and reads it aloud to all the people. He interprets the Hebrew text in Aramaic, then spoken by ordinary people (vv. 2-12). The next day the people scatter to gather branches so they can build booths and keep the Festival of Tabernacles (vv. 13-17). Each day of the festival is spent listening to the Scriptures (v. 18). Many have been convicted by the reading of God's Law. They keep on gathering, spending part of the day studying the Law and part in confession and worship (9:1-5). Nehemiah records a typical prayer (vv. 6-37): It expresses the people's renewed awe of God (v. 6), their awareness of Israel's historic rebelliousness (vv. 16-18), God's continuing compassion (vv. 13-31), and a fervent appeal that God would relieve their distress (vv. 32-37). The spiritual revival has a practical impact. The community is ready to make a fresh commitment to the Lord (v. 38).

Key verse. 9:33: God remains faithful in His commitment to us.

Personal application. History teaches us about God and about ourselves and reminds us to keep close to the Lord.

Key concepts. Separation »p. 87. Revival »p. 233. Law »p. 145. Tabernacles »p. 89. Praise »p. 380. Covenant »pp. 32, 62.

INSIGHT

Where does this passage fit? Some scholars suggest that Neh. 8–11 fits better following Ezra's arrival in Judea, or after Ezra 10. But then the naming of Nehemiah would be a later addition.

The sad fact is that history shows God's people are in constant need of revival. It is not surprising that enthusiasm first awakened by Ezra would lag or that a fresh infusion of commitment would be associated with finishing the walls.

"The Book of the Law of Moses" (8:1). The exact writings intended are much debated, but there is no reason to doubt this included the entire Pentateuch (the first five books of the O.T.).

"Giving the meaning" (8:8). Rabbinic tradition understands "making clear" as translating the O.T. Heb. text into the Aramaic language then spoken by the people of Judea.

Conviction and joy (8:9-10). The association of these two may seem strange, but only on the surface. The more we are aware of the extent of our sin, the greater our joy in God's forgiveness.

Tabernacles (8:13-18). This harvesttime festival was typically a time of rejoicing. This particular Feast of Tabernacles, however, was marked with exceptional joy. God had defeated the Jews' enemies. Jerusalem was again a city with walls.

Revival (9:1-3). The revival that followed was marked by: (1) self-humbling, expressed in fasting, sackcloth, and dust on one's head; (2) exclusion of foreigners; (3) confession of

sins; and (4) eager study of God's Word. The pattern fits well with both biblical and modern revivals.

The prayer (9:6-37). This prayer mentions 20 sins of Israel, but 74 facts about God! God's marvelous grace is, as the hymn says, "greater than all our sin."

"In all that has happened . . . You have been just" (9:16-35). This prayer review of history notes the Jew's persistent sins, acknowledges God's judgments, and asserts His mercy. The little community admits that in "all that has happened" in judgment, and in forgiveness, God has been "just."

Both testaments affirm God's justice—His commitment to doing what is right. Both also see two aspects of justice. God is just in punishing the wicked, for as ruler of the universe the Lord is responsible to maintain its moral balance. But God is also just in exercising compassion. It is the right thing for God to punish, and it is also the right thing for Him to forgive.

The N.T. harmonizes these two aspects of justice in the Cross. God did not just overlook His moral obligation and dismiss sin as if it were nothing. In Christ, God took the full punishment sin deserves upon Himself. With sin paid for, God is perfectly free to offer human beings forgiveness and perfectly just to forgive those who respond to the Gospel's good news.

Outline
Place
Finder

RESTORATION
REVIVAL
RETURN

Chapter summary. The revival stimulated by reading God's Word (Neh. 8–9) leads to decisive action. The Jews make a binding, signed commitment, in writing, to observe God's Law (9:36–10:28). The document identifies specific issues in which the community has previously been lax (10:29-39). Now Nehemiah repopulates Jerusalem. He moves one of every 10 families to the city and calls for additional volunteers. This action means that a cross section of the population will reside in the holy city (11:1-24), while the others occupy outlying settlements (vv. 25-36). Nehemiah also registers and organizes the priests and Levites (12:1-26). With this done, a great dedication of the city walls is announced. The celebration is marked by choirs and musicians who lead the population in giving thanks (vv. 27-43). A permanent staff for the temple is appointed and tithes are collected, so that continual services will be held there as the Law commands (vv. 44-47).

Key verse. 10:29: Commitment must be complete—and shared by the entire community of faith.

Personal application. To grow we need to correct our failings.

Key concepts. Covenant »pp. 32, 62. Law »pp. 145, 376. Priests »p 81. Levites »p. 95. Temple »p. 283. Music »p. 274.

INSIGHT

"The binding agreement" (9:38). The word *brit* indicates a contract or covenant. Many generations of God's O.T. people made a formal and personal renewal of their race's commitment to the Lord (cf. Deut. 29; Josh. 24).

Sins to be corrected (10:30-39). The specific issues covered in the "binding agreement" signed by the community leaders and clergy are:

The commitment	The Mosaic command
No intermarriage with pagans (v. 30)	Ex. 34:16; Deut. 7:3-4
Keep the Sabbath holy (v. 31a)	Ex. 20:8-11; 31:14-17
Observe the Sabbatical year (v. 31)	Ex. 23:11; Lev. 25:2-7; Deut. 15:1-3
Contribute the temple head tax (vv. 32-33)	Ex. 30:11-16
Provide required temple offerings (vv. 34-35)	Ex. 23:19; Lev. 6:12-13; Deut. 26:1-3
Offer the firstborn (v. 36)	Num. 18:15-17; Deut. 12:6
Pay all tithes (vv. 37-39)	Lev. 27:30; Num. 18:21-24

The focus of most of these commitments is on worship, as reflected in the last phrase of the document: "We will not neglect the house of our God" (v. 39).

The Levites tithe (10:36). Most giving in the O.T. was intended for the support of those who led the people in worship. Giving was to be a joyous privilege, for the people gave the produce of their land—which God had first given them.

Thus, giving was an expression of joy and thanksgiving. How appropriate then that the Levites, who were supported by the gifts of the people, should give a tithe of their gifts toward the support of the priests. Those who minister must not be robbed of the joy of giving too.

"Lots" (11:1). The casting of lots, small stones or pieces of wood, was viewed by the Jews as a pious way of determining God's will.

Thus Nehemiah left the choice of those who should move to Jerusalem up to God. The practice was used in choosing portions of land to be occupied by the original conquerors of Canaan in Joshua's time.

"Ancestral property" (11:20). The phrase refers to family lands granted at the time of conquest.

Dedication of the walls (12:27-43). The event was a joyous but formal praise service. Similar dedication services were held by Solomon (1 Kings 8) and Ezra (Ezra 6:16). The tone of the service is reflected in the word indicating the second choir, which marched around the walls to meet the first (Neh. 11:38). That "second choir" is literally, "second thanks."

It's good to joyfully acknowledge God as the source of our successes, and to dedicate every accomplishment to Him.

Outline
Place
Finder

RESTORATION
REVIVAL
RETURN

Chapter summary. Nehemiah's governorship of Judea lasts 12 years, after which he returns to Susa. While he is gone, the Jews gradually abandon their "binding agreement" to carefully obey God's Law (10:28-39). When Nehemiah returns for a second term as governor of Judea, he finds that the Jews' old enemy Tobiah has actually been provided guest quarters in the temple compound itself (13:1-9). He also learns that services at the temple have been abandoned. God's tithes have not been paid, and the Levites who served at the temple have been forced to go back to their farms in order to survive (vv. 10-14). The people work on the Sabbath, and at Jerusalem the holy day of rest has been transformed into a market day! (vv. 15-22) Once again some men of Judah, including one of the sons of the high priest, have married foreign wives (vv. 23-31). Nehemiah vigorously corrects each abuse, calling on God to "remember" his faithful service . . . and the priests who defiled their office (vv. 29-30).

Thus the last of the Old Testament's historical books ends on a note of uncertainty. If the people of God so quickly abandoned His Law in the brief absence of Nehemiah, what will happen to them in the centuries that lie ahead? Will they be ready when God's Deliverer, from David's line, comes?

Key verse. 13:22b: God will not forget.

Personal application. It is far more godly to confront sin in other believers than to ignore it.

Key concepts. Temple »p. 283. Sabbath »p. 71. Priests »p. 81.

INSIGHT

"Remember." The Heb. word *zakar* had a range of meaning, indicating not only mental acts but also behavior appropriate to the memory. Thus, to remember the covenant means to be faithful to its laws and rulings.

When one appeals to God to remember there is no implication He can "forget." Instead the phrase is a request that God might respond in an appropriate fashion. When Nehemiah asks God to remember him for the good he has done, he expresses faith that God will reward him.

A parallel. Papyrus records found at Elephantine in Egypt describe a lengthy stay of Arsames, satrap of Egypt, in the court of Darius I between 414 and 410 B.C. As in Nehemiah's case there was a breakdown of order during his absence.

No compromise. The fiery nature of Nehemiah is shown in enforcing his reforms. He throws the household goods of Tobiah out of the temple (v. 8), he rebukes officials (v. 11), confronts violators (vv. 17-18), and even assaults the most guilty (v. 25). His zeal reminds

us of Jesus, who in similar fury overturned the money changers' tables and drove them from the temple with a whip (Matt. 21:12-13).

A pattern for us? When there is sin in the church Ezra's experience reminds us that there is an alternative to Nehemiah's more violent approach. Ezra was "appalled," and his expression of grief led to revival (Ezra 9:3-4). Don't overlook sin in others, but seek God's guidance on how best to respond.

Business as usual. God's O.T. people and those who traded with them were sorely tempted to do business on the Sabbath (cf. Neh. 10:31; Isa. 56:1-8, 58:13; Jer. 17:19-27; Amos 8:5). We too need to be sure we make time for the Lord on our day of worship.

Remembering Nehemiah. We can remember Nehemiah as a leader who accepted responsibility, relied on prayer, showed compassion for the needy, kept his goals always in view, was bold in the face of opposition, motivated others, maintained high standards, and was ever ready to take a stand for what is right. What an example for us today.

Esther

The story of Esther is set in the capital of the Persian empire, early in the reign of Xerxes (486–465 B.C.). It tells of a plot to exterminate the Jewish race, thwarted by the brave and beautiful Esther, who has become Xerxes' queen. That deliverance is still celebrated today in the annual Jewish Feast of Purim.

While the historicity of the Book of Esther has been challenged, it meets every reasonable test. Descriptions of the Persian court and the customs of the times, the provision of precise dates, and the use of Persian names current in the era, as well as the characterization of Xerxes, are completely accurate. Independent confirmation of Mordecai's rise to power comes from a cuneiform tablet found in Borsippa, which identifies Marduka (Mordecai) as an official in the royal court at Susa in the early years of Xerxes' reign!

Esther is one of two books in the Old Testament named for women. It is also one of two that contains no mention of God, the other being the Song of Songs (Solomon). Yet God's supervising presence is felt throughout the book, as events fall together in a pattern that reflects the Lord's ancient commitment to Abraham and his offspring. In fact, the Book of Esther is the Scripture's clearest example of the doctrine of providence. God, although hidden from our view, works through circumstances and human choices to accomplish His own ends. Esther teaches us to see the hidden God revealed in the ebb and flow of personal and world events and to praise Him for His continual care.

ESTHER AT A GLANCE

KEY PEOPLE

Xerxes *The powerful but erratic Persian ruler best known for his failed attempts to invade Europe and defeat by the Greeks.*

Haman *An influential Persian official who is angered by a Jew's failure to grovel before him and who determines to exterminate the race.*

Mordecai *The lesser Jewish official in the Persian court who is hated by Haman. He is the uncle of Esther.*

Esther *The niece of Mordecai, who has recently become Xerxes' queen and who intercedes successfully for the Jewish people.*

KEY EVENTS

A pattern of events fits together showing that despite the attempt of evil men to destroy the Jewish race, God shapes history to preserve His chosen people.

WHERE THE ACTION TAKES PLACE

The setting for the story is Susa, the capital of the Persian empire. During this time a few thousand Jews were resettled in Judea and rebuilt the Jerusalem wall (» p. 317). But several million could be found scattered throughout the empire, with large communities in its principle cities. It's not at all surprising to find Mordecai the Jew in the Persian bureaucracy.

Date and Authorship. The author of the Book of Esther is never identified. As Esther 10:2 implies the death of Xerxes, the book must have been composed sometime after 465 B.C. The period between 450–300 B.C. seems most likely.

A Persian "wise man" casts lots to determine the best date to exterminate the Jews as Haman watches (3:7-15). The act sums up the message of the book. Whatever man may try to do, the hidden God of Scripture providentially controls events and shapes circumstances to serve His own purposes.

THEOLOGICAL OUTLINE OF ESTHER

I. THE SETTING: ESTHER BECOMES QUEEN	1–2
II. THE STORY: HAMAN'S PLOT	3–7
III. SURVIVAL: THE JEWISH PEOPLE ARE DELIVERED	8–10

CONTENT OUTLINE OF ESTHER

I. Esther Becomes Queen of Persia (1:1–2:21)
  A. Xerxes' Great Banquet (1:1-9)
  B. Vashti Dethroned (1:10-22)
    1. Her disobedience (1:10-12)
    2. Her dismissal (1:13-22)
  C. A New Queen Chosen (2:1-23)
    1. The search (2:1-4)
    2. Esther introduced (2:5-11)
    3. The procedure (2:12-14)
    4. Esther chosen (2:15-18)
    5. An assassination attempt thwarted (2:19-23)
II. Haman's Plot Against the Jews (3:1–7:10)
  A. Haman's Hatred (3:1-15)
    1. Hatred aroused (3:1-6)
    2. The day of racial revenge chosen (3:7-15)
  B. Mordecai's Reaction (4:1-17)
    1. Anguish and grief (4:1-3)
    2. An appeal to Esther (4:4-17)
  C. Esther's Banquet (5:1-8)
  D. Haman's Personal Revenge Planned (5:9-14)

  E. Haman's Humiliation (6:1-13)
    1. Mordecai's aid recalled (6:1-5)
    2. Mordecai honored (6:6-11)
    3. Haman's wife foresees failure (6:12-13)
  F. Esther's Second Banquet (6:14–7:10)
    1. Haman invited (6:14)
    2. Haman accused (7:1-7)
    3. Haman executed (7:8-10)
III. Survival and Victory (8:1–10:3)
  A. Mordecai's Vindication (8:1-17)
    1. His elevation (8:1-2)
    2. Haman's decree reversed (8:3-14)
    3. The Jews celebrate (8:15-17)
  B. The Jew's Revenge (9:1-32)
    1. Enemies killed (9:1-10)
    2. Killings in Susa (9:11-15)
    3. Celebration (9:16-19)
    4. Purim instituted (9:20-32)
  C. Mordecai's Greatness (10:1-3)

Outline
Place
Finder

SETTING
STORY
SURVIVAL

Chapter summary. Early in his reign Xerxes throws a great banquet for the officials of his empire (1:1-9). He commands Queen Vashti to appear, but she refuses (vv. 10-12). The experts he consults counsel him to depose her and choose another queen (vv. 13-20). This he does and proclaims throughout his empire that "every man should be ruler over his own household" (vv. 21-22). Shortly after an empire-wide search is launched to find a new queen (2:1-4). One candidate, put forward by her uncle Mordecai, is the lovely Esther, who on her uncle's instruction has not revealed her race (vv. 5-11). Each candidate must spend a night with Xerxes (vv. 12-14), and when Esther's turn comes she pleases him so much that he chooses her to be the new queen (vv. 15-18). One more event serves as background for what is about to take place. Mordecai uncovers a plot to assassinate Xerxes and gets word to the king through Esther. The two assassins are executed, and circumstances are recorded in the annals, a daily diary of palace happenings (vv. 19-23).

Key verse. 1:17: Esther becomes queen.

Personal application. Today's circumstances are preparation for a future known only to God.

INSIGHT

"127 provinces"? (1:1) Some have claimed the book is in error, because there were only 20 satrapies in Darius' empire. But the Heb. word here, *medinah*, was a subdivision of a satrapy. Hebrew has a totally different term for the larger division.

"Xerxes" (1:1). The Heb. is *'ahasweros,* a variant of the Persian *khshayarsha.* The better known name, Xerxes, is the Gk. form of the name. Xerxes' empire did extend from India to the upper Nile, a vast area divided into some 20 satrapies and 127 districts.

Xerxes' banquet (1:4). Some commentators have suggested the 180 day banquet, which assembled administrators from throughout the empire, was something of a working retreat, held to plan the king's subsequent campaign against Greece. The 180 day period culminated in a week long drinking party to which all the men of Susa were invited (1:5-8).

Vivid description (1:6-8). The vivid detail here suggests the writer was an eyewitness who participated in the event. Later, couches of gold and silver, just like those mentioned here, were captured by the Greeks under Alexander. Archeological evidence exists for the luxuries described.

"Vashti" (1:9). The only known queen of Xerxes was named Amestris, who was noted for cruelty and imperiousness. No independent evidence names either Vashti or Esther. Some claim this discredits the Book of Esther, but many similar attacks on Scripture's accuracy have been disproven as new archeological

finds are made. Perhaps Vashti is an alternate name of Amestris. Perhaps one or the other was a subordinate wife. The fact is we simply do not know at this time.

"The seven eunuchs" (1:10). Here the word may simply indicate a palace "official" rather than the castrated males typically placed in charge of Eastern harems (»p. 715).

Vashti's rebellion (1:10-22). Vashti's refusal to obey the command of Xerxes was viewed as setting a precedent for women throughout the empire. Xerxes divorced Vashti and issued a decree that women must obey their husbands.

The decree reflects a principle deeply imbedded even today in the Middle East. The husband rules the home. He alone has the right to initiate or give a divorce. The children of a marriage belong to the father and if a divorce takes place he keeps them. Vashti's defiance of Xerxes thus was a threat to the established social order.

Chronology. The text describes a span of time between the feast in Xerxes' 3rd year and his marriage to Esther in the 7th year. These are the very years Xerxes was absent from Susa on his campaigns against the Greeks.

Mordecai (2:6). It was not Mordecai but his great grandfather who had been taken to Babylon in Nebuchadnezzar's day.

Esther made Queen (2:10-18). No reason is stated for concealing Esther's race. The method of selecting the new queen is typical of the time. The women who failed to be recalled by the king spent the rest of their lives as widows, isolated from all men in his harem.

Outline
Place
Finder

SETTING
STORY
SURVIVAL

Chapter summary. The author now introduces Haman, whose favored status in Xerxes' court has made him arrogant. Haman is angered when Mordecai, a minor royal official, won't bow low before him—perhaps because he reserves this honor for God (3:1-3). Haman learns Mordecai is a Jew and determines not only to kill Mordecai but also to wipe out his people (vv. 4-6). Haman casts lots to choose a propitious day to move against the Jews. Xerxes casually gives Haman permission to commit genocide. Haman creates an edict promulgated throughout the empire identifying the day the Jews are to be destroyed and promising their wealth to their killers (vv. 7-15). Mordecai and his people immediately go into public mourning, an act of self-humbling associated in Scripture with fervent prayer (4:1-5). Mordecai does more. He informs Esther and urges her to intercede with the king (vv. 6-8). Esther is fearful, yet she promises to do what she can. She urges all the Jews of Susa to undertake a total fast on her behalf for three days. Then she will act (vv. 9-11).

Key verse. 4:14: Let God use you . . . or be set aside.

Personal application. Look for opportunities to serve others.

Key concepts. Occult »p. 131. Fasting »p. 442. Covenant »p. 35.

INSIGHT

"**Haman**" **(3:1).** Haman is called an Agagite. Jewish tradition identifies him as a descendant of the Amalekite king, whose people Saul failed to destroy (cf. Ex. 17:8-14; 1 Sam. 15:7-33). Mordecai was of Saul's tribe (cf. Es. 2:5). So rabbinical commentators see this conflict as the historic struggle of the Jewish people with Gentile enemies whose unreasoning hatred persists for thousands of years.

Piety or pride? **(3:2)** Two reasons have been suggested for Mordecai's refusal to bow to Haman. (1) To the pious Jew the act would constitute idolatry. But this seems unlikely: Jews commonly showed such respect to rulers (cf. Gen. 23:7; 2 Sam. 14:4; 1 Kings 1:16). The Targum, an ancient Jewish paraphrase of the O.T. written in Aramaic, sees Mordecai's refusal as an act of pride: (2) He would not perform an act of submission before a hereditary enemy of the Jews. In part, Mordecai was responsible for endangering his people.

Quiet defiance (3:3-5). Mordecai did not flaunt his distaste for Haman. Even Haman did not notice until others brought Mordecai to his attention "to see whether Mordecai's behavior would be tolerated." Verse 5 seems to suggest there was also an anti-Semitic motive.

If conscience calls us to civil disobedience, we needn't make a public issue. But when we act on conscience, someone is likely to make it an issue for us—out of mischief or hostility. Do

what is right. But be ready to pay the price.

Casting lots (3:7). In certain circumstances the Jews had cast lots to determine God's will. Haman also sought guidance, but his use of lots was occult. Many different means were used in the ancient world to seek omens that would give an individual or nation direction (»p. 131). The specific date chosen, perhaps to approach the king but more likely to exterminate the Jews, was controlled by God to provide time to thwart Haman.

The bribe (3:8-9). Haman promised Xerxes 375 tons of silver! The ruler's refusal was probably only a polite way of accepting the bribe. What a measure of Haman's pride! To measure his greed, read the decree. Haman undoubtedly intended to make a profit by appropriating the wealth of the slaughtered Jews.

Stereotyping (3:8-9). Haman did not name the race to be killed, but only characterized them. And Xerxes never asked.

Let's not stereotype groups. Value everyone.

Deliverance will arise (4:14). Esther's reluctance brought an affirmation of faith from Mordecai. Although God remains unnamed, Mordecai is undoubtedly remembering the Lord's promises to Abraham and David, which could not be kept if the race was wiped out.

Fasting (4:16). This is another allusion to God, for prayer is often linked with fasting in the O.T. (Neh. 9:1; Jer. 14:12; Zech. 7:3-5).

Outline
Place
Finder

SETTING
STORY
SURVIVAL

Chapter summary. Esther timorously approaches the king and is welcomed enthusiastically. She invites Xerxes and Haman to a supper in her apartments, but senses the time is not right. So she asks them to return the next evening (5:1-8). Haman throws a party for his friends to boast about his honors. He also celebrates his coming triumph over Mordecai and orders that impressive gallows be built on which to hang him (vv. 9-14). But that night a restless Xerxes is read the court annals and is reminded that Mordecai saved his life (6:1-3). In the morning Xerxes asks an unsuspecting Haman what should be done for a man the king wants to honor—and then commands Haman to so honor Mordecai! (vv. 4-11) Shaken and humiliated, Haman is escorted to the queen's banquet (vv. 12-14). There Esther begs for her life and the lives of her people and points to "this vile Haman" as their enemy (7:1-7). Haman is dragged away and hung on the gallows he had erected for Mordecai (vv. 8-10).

Key verse. 6:1: The Lord is a God of details.

Personal application. Be sensitive not only to what God wants you to do, but also to His timing.

INSIGHT

Why invite Haman? (5:4) Many suggestions have been made. To make Xerxes jealous. To allay any suspicions Haman might have. Perhaps so that Haman's reaction, when Esther accuses him, might reveal his guilt. Perhaps Esther acted in the best traditions of her people, to confront Haman face-to-face rather than speak behind his back.

Tomorrow (5:7). Here again no reason is given for Esther's delay in accusing Haman. While some ascribe her hesitancy to fear, it's probably better to credit her with the spiritual discernment necessary to sense God's timing.

"No satisfaction" (5:13). Personal pride is a burden too heavy for anyone to bear. It makes us so vulnerable to the opinions of others that we can take no pleasure in the good things God provides.

"A gallows" (5:14). The Heb. word is *'es,* which simply means tree. As impaling was a typical means of execution in Persia, it's more likely that the gallows was a high, pointed pole rather than the structure familiar to us. In execution by impaling a person was forced to sit on a pointed stake which penetrated deeper and deeper as he struggled until finally vital organs were reached. It was probably this unbelievably cruel death Haman planned for a man who had done nothing more than to insult him.

The book of chronicles (6:1). The phrase does not refer to the biblical book, but rather the record of daily events during Xerxes' reign. The Heb. says literally, "the book of remembrances, the words/matters of the days."

"What honor and recognition" (6:3). As ancient monarchs were frequently assassinated—and as Xerxes himself would be one day—a failure to reward someone who thwarted the king's murder was politically foolish. The certain expectation of a reward for turning in plotters was cheap life insurance. Somehow the Lord had not only brought awareness of the incident to Xerxes at the right time, He had also caused Xerxes to overlook a reward when the plot was uncovered.

Haman's humiliation (6:6-11). Considering Haman's hatred of Mordecai and plot against him, Xerxes' command that Haman honor his enemy was devastating. Later Haman's wife and friends failed to comfort him—and even predicted his downfall.

The greater our expectations, the more severe our disappointments. The Apostle Paul wisely says that he has learned to be content whatever his situation (Phil. 4:11). Don't fix your hopes as Haman did on the satisfaction of some sinful desire. Settle for the contentment Paul found in knowing the Lord.

Haman's fate (7:9-10). Haman's execution is a pure example of poetic justice. It's also an example of an O.T. law principle found in Deut. 19:19. There it specifies if a witness against (accuser of) another is proven to have lied, "then do to him as he intended to do to his brother." Haman's lies about the Jews were intended to bring about their deaths. It was just that he should die instead.

Chapter summary. Esther is given Haman's personal estate. Mordecai is given authority to undo the harm Haman has done (8:1-8). Because no royal decree can be revoked, Mordecai's new edict grants the Jews both the right of self-defense and to attack their enemies on the day Haman's document had specified their doom (vv. 9-14). Mordecai's edict, sealed with the king's signet ring, brings joy to Jews throughout the empire and even stimulates mass conversions to Judaism (vv. 15-17). When the appointed day arrives, the Jews take bloody vengeance on their enemies (9:1-10). In Susa they are even given permission to extend the massacre an extra day (vv. 11-17). An annual festival, the Feast of Purim, is established to commemorate the Jews' survival and triumph (vv. 18-32). As for Mordecai, he goes on to rank second to Xerxes in the kingdom and do much good for the Jewish people (10:1-3).

Outline
Place
Finder

SETTING
STORY
SURVIVAL

Key verse. 9:19: Deliverance is remembered with joy.

Personal application. In the end, God will right all wrongs and punish those who do His own harm.

INSIGHT

The vengeance of the Jews. Many Jewish, as well as Christian, scholars have been critical of the moral tone of Esther. The queen has been indicted for hiding her Jewish identity, willingness to marry a Gentile, not showing mercy to Haman, and asking the king to permit the slaughter of the Jews' enemies.

Mordecai has been accused of pride, using his cousin for his own advancement, and rejoicing over fallen enemies. The massacre of the Jews' enemies has been termed as wicked as the original plot against them.

Rather than idealize the central characters or defend their actions, we can readily admit that God's O.T. and N.T. people have all too often fallen short of His standards. But the Book of Esther is not intended as an ethical treatise. Instead, it underlines the persecution experienced by the Jews in pagan nations and reminds us that God remains committed to preserving His ancient people.

We're also reminded that we do live in a moral universe. The Hamans of this world will lose everything in the end. God's people, imperfect as we are, will triumph. It may be wrong to seek vengeance, but it is not wrong to rejoice when God brings the wicked low and reveals continuing love for His own.

Moral superiority (9:6-16). Despite the critics, the Jews did show themselves morally superior. Haman's original decree called for extermination of men, women, and children, and permitted plunder. The Jewish defense forces killed only men (vv. 6, 12, 15) and did not take plunder (vv. 10, 15-16). Those killed were known enemies.

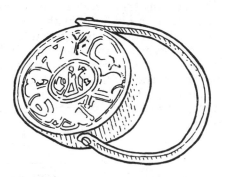

Illustration. *In the ancient world the impression of an individual's signet ring in clay or in a wax seal served as his signature on an official document. The seal shown may have belonged to a king.*

Mass conversions (8:17). The text suggests that the Jews welcomed converts. This was certainly true in the 1st century B.C., during which Jewish missionaries eagerly sought partial and full conversions to Judaism (cf. Matt. 23:15; Acts 15:21).

"Purim" (9:18-32). This is one of two festivals celebrated by the Jews that is not commanded in Scripture. The other is Hannukah, originating in the time of the Maccabees. Purim was a spontaneous expression of joy, and Mordecai's letter simply standardized its date.

Job

The Book of Job probes basic questions that have troubled human beings from the beginning. Why do the righteous suffer? How can the believer remain convinced that God is just when those who worship the Lord so often experience heartrending tragedy? Many literary works of the ancient world gave readers in Mesopotamia, Babylon, and Egypt advice on how to react to suffering. Such works traditionally urged the reader to seek the aid of his or her deity. But none probes the problem of pain with the depth, honesty, and profound insight found in the Book of Job. And none see God with the clear monotheistic vision that marks not only Job but the entire Old Testament.

The story line of Job is simple. Job, a blameless worshiper of God, experiences a series of devastating tragedies. Three friends come to comfort him, but end up arguing that since God is good Job must have done something terrible to deserve his intense suffering. Job refutes them and in the process points to injustices God permits in His world. A young observer suggests that God may have other purposes in suffering than to punish. Then God Himself speaks to Job. The Lord gives no reason for what has happened to Job, but Job realizes he must submit to God rather than question Him. Job is restored and his three pious friends, who have so forcefully defended God, are rebuked by the Lord. Job goes on to live a long and blessed life.

Within this framework the unknown writer of Job, under the inspiration of God's Spirit, provides us with one of Scripture's most penetrating and important works. The book is largely intricate poetry in such diverse forms as lament, wisdom sayings, proverbs, hymns, riddles, curses, and lyrical nature poems. It contains many words and phrases which appear nowhere else in the Old Testament The Hebrew text of Job is the most difficult to translate of any Old Testament book. Yet the book is also one of the most important for believers to explore. Each of us, at times, experiences suffering which we cannot explain. For times like these, a study of Job offers insight and stimulates hope.

JOB AT A GLANCE

KEY PEOPLE

Moses *The deliverer, lawgiver, and leader of the Jews during the Exodus.*

Job *The righteous sufferer tormented by the question, "Why?"*

Eliphaz *A comforter who sees Job as a good man gone astray.*

Bildad *A comforter who argues from traditional wisdom in his effort to prove that Job and his family got only what they deserved.*

Zophar *A comforter who urges Job to repent or die the death that God reserves for the wicked.*

Elihu *A young observer who breaks the cycle of futile reasoning engaged in by Job and his three friends and prepares Job to hear a personal word from God.*

KEY EVENTS

Aside from the sudden tragedies that strike Job, the book uses extended dialogue and monologue to explore the meaning of suffering and God's role in human tragedy.

Job, bowed down by calamities he cannot explain, symbolizes every believer who experiences personal tragedy, suffering, and loss. His cry of "Why?" echoes not only through the book, but in our own hearts as well.

Authorship and Date. The author of the work is unknown. The book, however, contains the authentic words of Job and his friends and seems to be set in the early 2nd millennium B.C. There is no mention in Job of the Law or God's revelation through Moses. Job's long life (140 years), the measurement of his wealth in livestock, his functioning as a priest for his family, all fit the patriarchal period. It is not unreasonable to suppose that Job might have been a contemporary of Abraham, Isaac, or Jacob, whenever the Book of Job was given its final form. This view is perhaps supported by the Genesis 36:4 reference to an Eliphaz who was the first son of Esau and ancestor of the Edomites. The land where Job lived, Uz, is also associated with Edom in Lamentations 4:21.

However, the difficulty in setting the time and place of Job is irrelevant to its timeless and universal message. In the cosmos we human beings live with mystery. It is impossible for us to explain all that happens, to nations or individuals, despite the wonders of God's revelation to us in Scripture and in Jesus Christ. Job reminds us of this reality. And Job affirms the great truth that, despite our lack of knowledge, we can and must have faith.

STRUCTURE OF JOB

The Book of Job is structured in a balanced pattern of threes. After the prologue (chaps. 1–2) and Job's opening lament (chap. 3), there are three cycles of dialogue in which each of Job's three friends speak and are answered by Job (chaps. 4–28). This is followed by three monologues, spoken by Job (chaps. 29–31), Elihu (chaps. 32–37), and by God (chaps. 38–42). The book closes with Job's contrition and an epilogue (chap. 42).

THEOLOGICAL OUTLINE OF JOB

CONTENT OUTLINE OF JOB

Outline
Place
Finder

Chapter summary. Job is introduced as an upright man, who has been blessed with riches and a large family (1:1-5). Then the author draws back the curtain to reveal the invisible world. There God commands all angelic beings to appear before Him (vv. 6-7). He specifically calls Satan's attention to Job, calling him a truly God-fearing man. Sneering, Satan predicts Job will deny God if His blessings are withdrawn. With God's permission, Satan causes calamities that rob Job of everything. Yet rather than curse God, Job worships (vv. 8-22). When God again commands the presence of His angels, God reminds Satan of Job's continuing integrity (2:1-3). Satan again sneers. If Job were made to feel pain, he would openly curse God (vv. 4-5). With God's permission, Satan strikes Job with agonizing boils. Yet despite all Satan can do, Job does not "sin in what he said" (vv. 6-10). We sense something of the intensity of Job's suffering when three comforters are so appalled at Job's condition that they sit silent for three weeks (vv. 11-13).

PROLOGUE
DIALOGUES
MONOLOGUES
EPILOGUE

Key verse. 2:10: We don't have to "know" to remain faithful.

Personal application. Don't let what you fail to understand of God's purposes shake your faith in His constant love.

Key concepts. Angels »p. 521. Satan »p. 501.

INSIGHT

A contest? The Book of Job has often been pictured as a contest between God and Satan, with Job as the pawn. But with the end of chap. 2 Satan retires—defeated—and is not mentioned again in the book. Yet Job's suffering continues! Clearly God has a purpose beyond victory in a supposed "contest" with Satan.

When we suffer let's seek comfort in the knowledge that God has a purpose in mind.

"Blameless and upright" (1:1, 8; 2:3). This description does not imply that Job was sinless, but that he characteristically sought to do what was right out of respect for God.

Sons of God (1:6). The Heb. "sons of God" is rightly translated "angels." The idiomatic phrase as used does not imply family relationship, but the relationship between created beings and Creator. See also the O.T.'s use of "Father" (»p. 141).

"The Lord said to Satan" (1:8). God points Job out to Satan. Satan reacts in character as the adversary of God and His people. Most commentators correctly conclude that God is the real initiator of Job's test. Yet, while Satan uses and discards human beings in a casual and cruel manner, God does not. The reason then for Job's suffering is found in God's character rather than in Satan's.

God the cause? (1:13-22) Job had no awareness of the heavenly scene which the author has drawn for us. Satan clearly organized the timing of the devastating losses experienced by Job to suggest divine intervention.

Let's not blame God for unexpected and awful events. We have no access to the information we need to judge the ultimate purposes of God.

Worship (1:21). The ultimate in worship is to honor God as Sovereign and affirm His freedom to act in our lives. Job's worship must have been especially pleasing to the Lord.

Job's illness (2:7). The brief description suggests boils, ulcers, or other painful skin diseases that cause accute suffering. Other references in Job develop a picture of disfigurement and anguish. Job is subject to sleeplessness (7:4), depression (7:16; 30:15), dimmed eyesight (16:16), putrid breath (19:17), rotting teeth (19:20), emaciation (19:20), and exhausting fevers (30:30). His suffering is so intense and obvious that when his friends see him (2:11-13) they have nothing to say.

"In what he said" (2:10). Satan predicted he would make Job curse to God's face. Despite the anguish caused by his loss of wealth and family, and the agony caused by his illness, Job did not sin "in what he said." Satan, who had set the conditions of the contest, lost.

But what was going on in Job's heart and mind? What thoughts and feelings surged as evidence mounted that the God he served had turned against him? It is this we discover as we move into the body of the book.

Outline
Place
Finder

PROLOGUE
DIALOGUES
MONOLOGUES
EPILOGUE

Chapter summary. At last Job speaks, and all the anguish he has struggled to hold in spills out in a flood of despair. Job curses the day of his birth, wishing fervently that it could be blotted from history. Nonexistence seems preferable to what Job experiences now (3:1-10). Or at least Job might have died stillborn. Then he would lie in the company of the great and insignificant, all of whom have found release from life's turmoil (vv. 11-19). Job cannot understand why God, who gives man life, should then permit that life to be made bitter by misery (vv. 20-24). In a last lament, Job confesses that what he has feared all along has come; in his confusion he is bereft of peace and of quietness (vv. 25-26).

What typically troubles God's saints in their suffering is not the physical pain, but the mental anguish. Job cannot understand the "why" of his experience, which has shaken his most cherished beliefs about God.

Key verse. 3:25: Fear is a sign of uncertainty in any relationship.

Personal application. Expect suffering to cause inner turmoil, but also expect to grow through the experience.

INSIGHT

On being human. One of the great values of Job is that the book teaches us not to try to deny our humanity. Some commentators have been as critical of Job as his three friends for expressing his anguish so strongly. But let's remember God characterized him as a "blameless and upright" man who feared God (»p. 331).

In the O.T. "fearing" God often serves to express both faith and a godly lifestyle (»p. 387). Even the most spiritual of us is subject to human weaknesses. Job's honesty in expressing his feelings reminds us that God understands our feelings and accepts them as we work through our times of suffering to a deeper, more perfect faith. Remember Job, and don't be too hard on yourself if you feel a similar despair.

"May it turn to darkness" (3:4). There is a gentle irony here. God spoke and created day, saying "let there be light" (Gen. 1:3). Now Job wishes he could reverse the process and blot out the day he was born.

If you should ever share Job's feelings, remember that first day of creation. Everything that God creates is intended for, and will bring forth, good. This includes the day you were born, even if you can see no good in it now.

Nonexistence (3:1-10). There is something unique and precious in God's gift of life. It is better to have been born and lived life, even when our enjoyment of it is marred by suffering. Trust God. Remember that while the nonexistent never began, you are a someone who will never end! Whatever this life holds, eternity will be filled with joy.

"Knees to receive me" (3:12). In the Middle East, two midwives walked an expectant mother, giving her support until the baby came. The mother then caught the child between her knees to prevent it from falling to the ground.

The great leveler? (3:11-19) Job is again expressing his emotions in powerful poetic imagery. To Job, both the great men of the world and the insignificant seem to find in death the rest that he yearns for. Job muses he might have died at birth and avoided the turmoil.

Note that despite his despair, Job does not consider suicide. Life is a gift from God. Despite his anguish, Job makes no attempt to end the life he has been given. What a great affirmation of faith for those who contemplate taking their lives. Those who struggle on may very well merit more reward than others who have never plunged into despondency or known the torment of despair.

"Why?" (3:20-25) This is one of the unanswerable questions that makes trust in God an act of faith. Why God gives life and yet permits some who receive that gift to experience misery is answered in part later on in Job. But why God permits you or me to suffer is not answered in this life.

"What I feared" (3:25). This verse may be the key to the reason God permitted Job's suffering. Job fears God and tries to serve Him. Yet he also fears the future. Perhaps through his experience Job will find a deeper faith, one that frees him from terror of the future and permits a deeper love for God.

Chapter summary. Eliphaz is upset by Job's intense emotions. Job has counseled others; he should handle his own troubles better (4:1-6). Eliphaz argues that the wicked are destroyed, not the innocent and upright (vv. 7-21), even though every human being experiences trouble (5:1-7). What Job should do is appeal to God who wounds but also heals and who rescues those who lay their cause before Him (vv. 8-26). To Eliphaz, these generalizations are fixed, universal truths which surely can be applied to Job's case (v. 27).

Job is frustrated that his friends haven't really heard him. Job is in anguish. It is God who has assaulted him and so left him hopeless (6:1-13). Job has asked his friends for nothing but their devotion (vv. 14-23) — and gotten advice that impunes his integrity (vv. 24-30). In the face of a fate that is truly worse than death, Job will not retreat to platitudes, but insists on facing ultimate questions honestly (7:1-11).

Looking now toward heaven, Job cries out to God, "Why have You made me Your target? Why do You not pardon my offenses and forgive my sins?" (vv. 20-21)

Key verse. 7:11: Ask honest questions.

Personal application. Hurting people need comfort, not sermons.

INSIGHT

Do the innocent perish? (4:7) Scripture proves the innocent do perish! Saul's godly son Jonathan died with his wicked father. Bathsheba's husband, Uriah, met an unjust end through the manipulation of King David.

Watch out for those who utter pious platitudes which seem to preserve God's honor, but do so at the expense of truth.

Revelation (4:8-17). Eliphaz claims his views are supported by (1) experience (v. 8) and (2) dreamlike, ghostly revelations (vv. 12-16). Each is a questionable source of truth, something we should remember as we read his future speeches. The doctrine of inspiration does not guarantee Eliphaz's words are true, but only that what he said and thought is accurately recorded.

"Appeal to God" (5:8). How strange to assume that Job hasn't sought God. The advice to "just pray about it" must seem terribly trite to someone who has been pouring out his heart to God in utter anguish.

"God" (5:17). Here, and throughout Job, God is *Shaddai*, the Almighty. The name *Yahweh*, which is the Lord's revelatory and redemptive name, is not used. Job and his friends are limited in their vision of God. They see Him as transcendent, but do not know Him as "the One who is always present" (»Lord, p. 54).

Knowing God's love in Jesus helps to preserve us from the anguish felt by Job.

"We have examined this" (5:27). Eliphaz has

neatly packaged his God as one who must act according to his understanding. After all, if the innocent never perish, and if God hears their appeals, all Job has to do is pray and be healed! Eliphaz never stops to think how presumptuous it is to limit God by his own fallible reasoning. How foolish are the many Eliphaz's among us, whose assurances that "if you only have enough faith you'll be healed" are just as superficial, harmful, and wrong.

God's arrows (6:4). Job sees God behind the events which cause his suffering. How can God be a source of hope? The answer will come much later.

"The devotion of his friends" (6:14). A hand to hold, a loving touch, a person to sit close and be there — these are the gifts of devotion that a despairing person needs from a friend. No advice, however well meant, can match these gifts that comfort and sustain.

My integrity (6:29). Job has nothing left but his inner self. He will not surrender his inner identity, but will speak out in utter honesty.

Why? (6:17-21) In Job's speeches he often shifts from addressing one of his friends to speak directly to God. His anguished cries of "why" express doubts any person might feel in similar circumstances. It's not wrong to question God or His ways. Job's questioning can be an act of faith, for though Job does not understand, he holds fast to the conviction that God is.

333

Chapter summary. Bildad now joins in with a blunt accusation (8:1-22). Surely God does not "pervert justice" (v. 2). The death of Job's children is prima facie proof that they sinned (v. 4). God comes to the aid of a "pure and upright" man (v. 6), and most surely "does not reject a blameless man" (v. 20). One can almost sense Bildad struggling not to blurt out what his argument obviously implies. Job has sinned, or he wouldn't be suffering as he is.

Job agrees with Bildad's premises. God doesn't pervert justice, and He does not reject the blameless. "But how can a mortal be righteous before God?" (9:2) God, the vast, the distant, the unknowable (vv. 3-11), is in fact tormenting Job. And Job has no recourse. God can't be called into court and questioned (vv. 12-20). Job, having abandoned all hope, has nothing to lose. Whether he proclaims his innocence (and thus impunes God's justice) or puts on a pious face and pretends, he is doomed (vv. 21-35). So Job will be completely honest (10:1). Again Job turns to God, and asks "why?" With what sin is he charged? Does God enjoy oppressing him? Why is the Creator destroying His own creation? "Guilty" and "innocent" seem meaningless terms for Job is being crushed (vv. 2-17). How much better if he had never been born (vv. 18-22).

Key verse. 8:3: We can know God is just and still admit that life is often unfair.

Personal application. Pretense does not honor God. Don't change your expression and smile for His sake.

INSIGHT

"Your children sinned" (8:3-4). Bildad's view of God is extremely legalistic. Job's suffering and the death of his children prove that each sinned. There is no room in Bildad's theology for God's mercy or grace. It's all a business transaction. If your balance sheet shows sin, God will get you! Watch out for those who make rigid, simplistic statements about God. A "one-plus-one-equals-two" theology is almost always wrong!

"The former generations" (8:8). Bildad invokes tradition as authority for his views. If a teaching was accepted by the ancients, it must be correct. Our standard must be Scripture itself, not what others have said about it.

Take God to court? (9:24) Bildad's argument has implicitly accused Job of sin. Job now envisions the difficulty of calling God into court so that he can establish his innocence. First, God is beyond human reach, too great and wonderful even to be perceived by man (vv. 1-11). Second, what court could make God answer for His acts? (v. 12) Even an innocent Job would stand no chance facing God in court (vv. 14-20). Finally, the fact is that Job is blameless, but is being destroyed anyway. What use then to speak of justice?

Job's words express despair, but also suggest a fascinating insight which he does not seem to recognize. When life seems unfair the issue is seldom one of guilt or innocence. All pain is not punishment. And all the innocent are not blessed with health and wealth.

"Change my expression" (9:27-28). It's uncomfortable to be around a person who is depressed and in despair. Most of us hurry away, afraid the darkness will swirl around us too. How many hurting people, dreading just that reaction, have put on a smiling mask? Not Job. He knows his friends will not "hold me innocent" (v. 28). Job is going to be totally honest in expressing his thoughts and emotions. In the process he will force his friends to face realities they fear—but which will ultimately lead all four to a truer knowledge of the Lord.

Does it please God? (10:3) Ultimately Job's problem is not with his friends. It is with God. He cannot understand what benefit God receives from oppressing him so.

Later, Job will understand as we must today. God brings even the most difficult experiences into the lives of believers not for His benefit, but for ours. When we are in the shadow of suffering we cannot see the good that will be revealed in us in the end (James 5:11).

Chapter summary. Zophar, Job's third friend, now contributes a lecture (11:1-12) and a sermon (vv. 13-20). He lectures Job for claiming to be right and pure in God's sight (vv. 1-4). If God spoke up, he could produce evidence to show Job hasn't even gotten what his sins deserve! (vv. 5-6) If God punishes, the sufferer must be guilty (vv. 7-12). Then comes Zophar's sermon, a classic example of proclaiming irrelevant truth. The paraphrase: "Be devoted to the Lord. Pray. Stop sinning. Then everything will be fine" (vv. 13-16). What a dagger in the heart of a man who has been devoted to God, but is suffering anyway! And what pain Zophar's description of divine blessing must have caused (vv. 17-20). This is exactly what Job's life was like — and all has been lost, in spite of the fact that Job is not at fault!

Outline
Place
Finder

PROLOGUE
DIALOGUES
MONOLOGUES
EPILOGUE

Job's response is complicated. Job knows what his counselors know, yet why is he suffering rather than the wicked? (12:1-6) Surely, all nature lies in the hand of God. Though God is too vast for man to comprehend, He acts sovereignly and does what He pleases (vv. 7-25). Job knows the truisms his friends have uttered. But they have used those truisms to unjustly smear Job's character and lied to flatter God (13:1-12). If only Job could face God in court, he would be vindicated (vv. 13-19). Job asks only for two things: that God will stop tormenting him and that he have a chance to defend himself (vv. 20-28). Instead, Job is helpless before God (14:1-6). Death is his only hope. His only comfort is the assurance that in time God will remember him and he will be raised, his sins forgiven (vv. 7-17). But until then his hope, and he himself, is gone (vv. 18-22).

Key verse. 13:15: Job is not defiant, but confident.

Personal application. When we hurt it's important to remember that God is not our adversary; He is on our side.

INSIGHT

"I wish God would speak" (11:5). Let's remember that God really is sole judge and arbiter. Paul says, "Let us stop passing judgment on one another" (Rom. 14:13), and James warns against setting ourselves up as judges, even when we have the Law as guide (James 4:11-12).

"Who does not know all these things?" (12:3) This is really Job's problem. He already knows the truisms that his friends have expressed — and discovers that they do not apply in his case!

Job has been forced to realize that the ways of God are mysterious. He is free to act and does act, not limited by finite human understandings. What bothers Job is that God seems to act in ways contrary to what he and his friends have always assumed about Him.

I desire to speak to God (13:3). An old argument states that if God is both good and all powerful then when something bad or unfair happens, we must either doubt the goodness of God or His sovereignty. But Job isn't willing to abandon his belief in God. Instead he wants to challenge God to explain his suffering. Crying out "Why" is far better than saying, "Because I do not understand, I will not believe."

Showing God partiality (13:6-12). Job's friends have no evidence he has committed any sin, yet they call him a sinner! Old Testament Law is clear that only eyewitness testimony can be accepted in court. Therefore Job's friends "speak wickedly" (v. 7) on God's behalf!

Life after death (13:16; 14:7-17). The O.T. does teach resurrection (»p. 522). Here Job notes that the difference between the death of a man and cutting down a tree is that new life springs immediately from the tree. But one day God will call and Job will answer.

Even so Job's speech ends in pathos. In this world he still has no hope and no future.

Outline
Place
Finder

PROLOGUE
DIALOGUES
MONOLOGUES
EPILOGUE

Chapter summary. Eliphaz begins a second round of dialogue. Angry and upset, he accuses Job of undermining piety with irreverent talk (15:1-6). He then launches a series of questions designed to shame Job and accuse him of arrogance (vv. 7-13). Eliphaz's own religious vision has convinced him that man is vile and corrupt (vv. 14-19). He then launches a poetic description of the fate of the wicked, who futilely attack God (vv. 20-26) or ignore Him in favor of wealth and pleasure (vv. 27-35). His speech contains barb after pointed barb, references to what has actually happened to Job (vv. 21, 28, 29, 30, 34). Eliphaz's hostility reflects his view of a God of grim duty, who mechanically and impersonally metes out punishments untempered by compassion or love.

Indignantly Job strikes back. His friends are "miserable comforters" (16:1-5). He has not attacked God, as Eliphaz implied, but God has attacked Job (vv. 6-14). Job has not been corrupt, but pure (vv. 15-21). Yet Job's spirit is broken by his suffering and the conviction that God, the only one who can vindicate him, will not do so during his lifetime. His only hope lies in — and beyond? — the grave (17:1-16).

Key verse. 16:17: Integrity is all Job has to hold on to.

Personal application. Don't expect God to explain.

INSIGHT

"Undermine piety" (15:4). Some today are also shocked that anyone would ask questions about matters of faith. To express doubts or uncertainties, or to struggle with difficult questions, is viewed as an attack on belief in God. But God is great enough to survive our questions and doubts. Anyone who is honest in his or her struggle to understand God is far more likely to come to faith than lose it. The person who truly undermines piety is the one who insists others be satisfied with superficial or pat answers, is unwilling to face difficulties, and is afraid to ask questions. Remember again, it is Job who is the man of faith and the three friends that God condemns at the end of this book.

The whole truth (15:14-35). The witness in court is asked to "tell the truth, the whole truth, and nothing but the truth, so help you God." The problem with the superficial solutions offered by Job's friends is not that what they say is untrue. It is that what they say is not the whole truth. We are to share what we know and believe, but not with the cruel dogmatism of an Eliphaz.

"Miserable comforters" (16:1). A miserable comforter is literally a "comforter of trouble," a person who makes matters worse rather than better. Such phrases as "What could you have done to deserve this?" and "If you had enough faith, you'd be healed" are typical sayings of modern miserable comforters.

Perhaps the most miserable phrase I've heard was addressed to my wife after the loss of a child: "I hope I never do anything to make God punish me like that." The modern sufferer, like Job, needs reassurance that God loves him or her and that even though we cannot understand the "why" of suffering, we care.

True piety (16:12-17). Job has experienced the tragedies that struck him as a violent attack. And his attacker has been God! Yet, as Job describes his reaction (vv. 15-17), we realize that he has not denied God, nor struck back at Him, as Eliphaz implied (15:23-26). Rather than shake his fist at God, Job has humbled himself, wept, and prayed.

What a wonder this is, and how rightly God described Job as a "blameless and upright" man (Job 1:8; 2:3). Despite Job's confusion he has continued to act righteously. When we can do right despite pain, pressure, and agonizing loss, we are truly godly individuals.

Undying trust (17:3-9). Job uses the language of ancient business contracts and asks some "pledge" (down payment) from God as security against the vindication that will surely come. Only God can demonstrate Job's innocence and despite his despair and ambivalence he believes that God will.

Chapter summary. Bildad, as insensitive as ever to Job's feelings, is angry that Job considers the three friends' advice "stupid" (18:1-4). He launches a diatribe in which he pictures the terrifying fate of the wicked (vv. 5-21), trying to bludgeon Job into surrender to Bildad's traditionalism.

Job cries out in the pain of his humiliation (19:1-5). But Job's inner strength remains unmoved. He is sure God has wronged him (vv. 6-12). God's attacks have turned everyone against him (vv. 13-20). Now his three closest friends refuse him pity and join God in trying to tear him apart! (vv. 21-22)

The next verses are stunning in their affirmation of Job's unshakable faith. Rather than change a word he has uttered, he wants each one recorded forever (vv. 23-24). Because the very God who now torments Job is his Redeemer, one future day Job will see the Lord with his own eyes. Then Job will be vindicated. And then at last Job will understand (vv. 25-27). As for his friends, they should be careful what they say. Falsely accusing Job will not go unpunished! (vv. 28-29)

Outline
Place
Finder

PROLOGUE
DIALOGUES
MONOLOGUES
EPILOGUE

Key verses. 19:25-26: God lives, and man will be raised.

Personal application. If we fix our hope in eternity, nothing that happens in our brief lifetime can overcome us.

INSIGHT

Self-centeredness (18:1-4). There are too many people like Bildad in the world. They claim to be sensitive — but are sensitive only to their own feelings, not to others'. Never mind how another may hurt. If they feel insulted they strike out viciously, trying to hurt. They see things only in black and white: either completely right or completely wrong.

If you experience the barbed words of such a person, pity him. The self-centered, insensitive person who is unaware of compassion is miserable indeed.

Externals (18:5-21). Bildad's diatribe focuses on externals: on what happens to a wicked person. His sermon reflects the tragedies that have struck Job, yet misses the mark. What troubles righteous Job is his relationship with God and with his friends. Bildad needs to learn a lesson Jesus phrased succinctly: "A man's life does not consist in the abundance of his possessions" (Luke 12:15). What happens within us is more important than any material consideration.

"I've been wronged" (19:7-20). Job's anguish is rooted in his conviction that God has wronged him. The injustice of it torments him, an injustice that has "stripped me of my honor" (v. 9). Even "little boys [in a culture where children show respect for their elders] scorn me" (v. 18). Job's friends detest him, and his loved ones have turned against him. In the face of these blows to his basic beliefs about the universe and to his sense of self-worth, Bildad's threats seem puny indeed.

Engraved forever (19:23-24). How often we say things we immediately wish we could take back. Now in the strongest terms, Job proclaims the rightness of what he has said. He is willing to have his words engraved in rock. One day what he is saying will be proven true.

"My Redeemer lives" (19:25). Stunningly, Job speaks of the very God who now wrongs him as his *goel*. This Heb. word designates a close relative who is responsible for making sure that justice is done to his kinsman (»p. 90). The position of the pronoun in the sentence is emphatic: "I know that my Redeemer lives." Despite all that has happened to Job and despite his conviction that God has treated him unfairly, Job still believes. God is his Redeemer.

Whatever doubts Job has, and whatever thoughts he expresses, Job is a man of unshakable faith. This is a reality Job's comforters fail to sense, but we must remember.

Resurrection (19:25-27). Job doubts he will be vindicated in this life. But he has no doubt that he will be resurrected and stand before God on the earth in a physical body. How he yearns for that time, when "I myself will see Him with my own eyes" (v. 27). Then Job's torment will end; then he will understand. What a bright promise resurrection holds for us all!

Chapter summary. Zophar is disturbed by Job's view and only in part because it "dishonors" him (20:1-3). Job's view is disturbing because it attacks the shared conviction that God punishes the wicked. This conviction is not only basic to Zophar's view of a moral universe, but is critical to maintain an ordered society. Zophar reaffirms the doctrine that "the joy of the godless lasts but for a moment," and that in the end "distress will overtake" the wicked (vv. 4-29).

Job's response must have been even more disturbing. Job confesses his terror at the thoughts his personal tragedy has awakened (21:1-6). He contradicts Zophar, arguing that in fact many wicked do live an almost idyllic life (vv. 7-16). Even they recognize this—and try to get around it by saying, "Well, their children will be repayed" (vv. 17-21). All man really knows is that death is the great equalizer: The blessed and the bitter lie side by side in the dust (vv. 22-26).

Job's friends have taken his calamities as proof of some hidden wickedness. But that some openly evil are spared Job's pangs shows their position is nonsense (vv. 27-34).

Key verse. 21:17: Reality often challenges popular belief.

Personal application. God does have an answer—though perhaps not the one we expect!

INSIGHT

"Troubled thoughts" (20:1-2). Underlying Zophar's beliefs is the comfortable fact that he is well off. When blessings abound it's natural to assume that we are affluent because we're good. If we're secure it is because we deserve to be.

The poor and oppressed labor under no such delusion. The wicked often take advantage of the righteous poor, and the exploited of this world know the wicked may prosper and the good suffer. Any honest view of reality must take this into account, no matter how "disturbing" it may be.

Job's terror (21:6). All Job's life he has shared the views expressed by his three friends. The disasters that stripped him of everything have forced Job to rethink not just some, but all of his beliefs.

It is frightening to challenge beliefs on which we've based our whole lives. Yet some experiences force us to do so. How important when this happens to be sustained by convictions we need never abandon: "my Redeemer lives" and "in my flesh I will see God" (19:25-26).

Heard, not agreed (21:4-34). Job's reply concludes the second cycle of dialogue. Job's friends have accused him of not listening. Here he quotes or alludes to several of their arguments and refutes them (cf. v. 7 with vv. 11; v. 8 with 18:19; v. 17 with 18:5; v. 19

with 5:4, 20:10; and v. 29 with 20:4). Some people equate hear with agree and assume if we do not agree with them, we haven't listened. Job restates to show he was listening and then goes on to disagree.

The good life? (21:7-16) Job sketches an almost idyllic portrait of the life of the wicked. They live to old age and prosper, yet they consciously reject God. Given that their "prosperity is not in their own hands" (v. 16), Job cannot understand how this can be.

In Hab. 2 God gives us an insight not available to Job. There the Lord shows us that the apparent prosperity of the wicked is fleeting. Within their personalities principles of judgment are actively at work. Without this later revelation, Job cannot understand what God is about. Yet Job faces the facts, despite the challenge they pose to his beliefs.

Be ready to face disturbing facts you cannot understand without abandoning your faith.

Disaster no proof (21:22-33). If the wicked may prosper then there is no one-to-one relationship beween pain and punishment. Thus, what has happened to Job is no proof that he is wicked, and the argument of Job's three friends collapses.

The problems, however, remain. Why has God subjected Job to suffering? Why doesn't God immediately punish sin?

338

Chapter summary. Eliphaz intensifies the pressure on Job, whose arguments seem incomprehensible. How can any man's meaningless life benefit God? (22:1-3) The question implies that God is not personally involved with individuals—that He stands back, impartial, and metes out punishment and reward simply because it's His role as moral judge of humanity. Eliphaz thus can move from general statements about the wicked being punished to accuse Job of society's greatest sins (vv. 4-20) and be totally consistent when he concludes with an impassioned plea to repent. Surely then the impartial, almost mechanical God Eliphaz believes in will deliver (vv. 21-30).

Job moans in deepening despair. If only he could contact God and get an answer (23:1-9). God knows that Job has been righteous (vv. 10-12). What terrifies Job is that God is acting out of the character which Job, as well as Eliphaz, confidently believed was His (vv. 13-17). In fact Job's suffering has forced him to pose a theological problem he and his friends have not only ignored, but denied could even exist. Why is there poverty and oppression? Why are the wicked permitted to prey on the powerless? (24:1-17) Oh, eventually the wicked die. But why does God permit them any "rest in a feeling of security," since "His eyes are on their ways"? (vv. 18-25)

Outline
Place
Finder

PROLOGUE
DIALOGUES
MONOLOGUES
EPILOGUE

Key verse. 24:1: God's judgments are mysterious and delayed.

Personal application. Remain firm in your conviction that God will right every wrong, but in His own time and in His own way.

INSIGHT

Benefiting God (22:1-3). Eliphaz's God is impersonal, uninvolved, self-contained. His God does not need man or take personal pleasure in man's actions. This we know is wrong. In Job 1–2 God expresses His pleasure in Job, as "blameless and upright, a man who fears God and shuns evil" (1:8). And through Satan's defeat Job did glorify God and so benefit the Lord.

When we live for Him the Lord is both pleased and glorified.

Crime and punishment (22:1-20). In the O.T. world guilt was established by witnesses and punishment followed. Here Eliphaz is reasoning backward. Job is being punished, therefore God must have witnessed Job's sinful acts. But how can Eliphaz accuse Job of specific sins, since neither he nor his friends have witnessed Job sinning? Carrying his reverse reasoning a step further, the sins God witnessed must be the worst conceived of in that society—oppression of the weak and contempt for God.

There is one problem with Eliphaz's logic. He was completely wrong! Never accuse or condemn your brothers and sisters on circumstantial evidence. You're almost certain to be as wrong—and cause as much hurt—as Eliphaz.

Job's spiritual progress (23:1-7). Earlier, Job seems to have demanded a trial to show God's injustice. Here he simply yearns to "find out what He would answer me and consider what He would say" (v. 5). In his heart of hearts Job does not believe God is unjust, even though He seems to be acting unjustly.

In this, as in earlier affirmations of his faith, Job is an example to us. We may well cry out "why" as Job does. We may also be honest in facing the apparent inconsistencies between human experience and the nature of God. But we must also be humble enough to believe God does have an answer, even though we do not know what it is. It truly is spiritual progress when we can affirm, "I do not understand how this can be, but I trust God absolutely."

"Times for judgment" (24:1). This verse is the chapter's key. Job does not question God's justice, but only His timing. Eliphaz assumed a knee-jerk God—with sin He reacts immediately. But the N.T. reminds us, "The Lord is not slow in keeping His promise, as some understand slowness. He is patient with you, not wanting anyone to perish, but everyone to come to repentance" (2 Peter 3:9).

Chapter summary. Bildad's brief speech concludes the sayings of Job's friends. Bildad holds that God established order in the material and moral universe. As he shines brighter than any creation material, man in comparison is a moral worm. So all Job's claims of purity are meaningless! (25:1-6)

Job dismisses Bildad with scathing sarcasm (26:1-4). In powerful poetry he affirms God's majesty. Surely we can hardly comprehend even the "outer fringe" of so great a God, much less squeeze Him into the friends' comfortable categories (vv. 5-14). Man is no maggot to God. So Job will maintain the justice of his cause and keep on affirming his integrity (27:1-6). What is more, Job's friends have falsely accused him and they, who speak so learnedly of divine judgment, are themselves in danger (vv. 7-12). Job concludes as his friends have begun. God does, most certainly, punish the wicked (vv. 13-23).

Now the author intrudes with a poem of his own (28:1-28). Job and his friends have struggled to apply their concept of God and His justice to Job's experience with suffering—and have failed completely. And so the author asks, "Where then does wisdom come from? Where does understanding dwell?" (v. 20) The answer is that God understands, and "He alone knows where it dwells" (v. 23). All a man can do is to fear (respect) God and to shun evil (v. 28).

Key verse. 28:23: Back to basics, back to faith.

Personal application. A god no wiser than we are would be a pitiful god indeed.

INSIGHT

Man a maggot? (25:6) For some, it's a theological teeter-totter. If God is to be exalted, man must be degraded. But as Job saw, this is terribly wrong. Yet only in Christ do we realize how wrong Bildad was. Christ chose to become a real human being, "made a little lower than the angels," but raised again to bring "many sons to glory" (Heb. 2:9-10). God's love for us proves man is no maggot. Love marks us out as beings of infinite worth.

"Speaking wickedness" (27:1-6). What a temptation to say what we think others want to hear. The pious platitude often covers up an aching heart or painful doubts. Job has taken a courageous course and will not desert it. However great the pressure, he will be honest with God and honest with others. The fierce honesty that Job chose did not produce any easy or quick answers. But in the end, as we will see, it won commendation from God.

Technology yes, wisdom no (28:1-11). Man had demonstrated amazing technological proficiency, even in Job's time. Metals were mined and smelted, tunnels drilled through the rock, and the sources of rivers and streams explored. The mysteries of the material universe have fallen one by one to the probing genius of humanity.

Today an explosion of technological advances makes us wonder if there is anything in this universe humanity cannot master. The problem is that technological advances are not matched by advances in wisdom—here defined as the capacity to penetrate the moral mysteries of the universe. In the moral realm man is utterly lost and totally inadequate.

God understands (28:28). God is the source of wisdom in the moral universe even as He is the Creator of the material. What we cannot grasp, God knows completely. Far too many people are quick to make moral pronouncements: Gays march for pride; abortion is merely a matter of a woman's personal freedom; sex educators distribute condoms to teens and never mention abstinence. All loudly proclaim their position is "moral," while ignoring God's understanding as expressed in Scripture. The only hope is to abandon human notions of morality and be subject to God.

Chapter summary. Job's dialogue with his friends is complete. Now a lengthy monologue begins a swift movement toward the book's conclusion. Job first describes his former life (29:1-25). He was rich and respected (vv. 1-17), confident and secure (vv. 18-25). Now he is mocked and detested by others (30:1-14) and emotionally shattered (vv. 15-31). He cries out to God, but receives no answer, and as the days of suffering lengthen, "the churning inside me never stops" (v. 27).

Job's final words (31:1-40) constitute what is perhaps Scripture's most powerful picture of the righteous Old Testament saint. If Job had turned aside from the pathway he defines, he would deserve his present suffering. But Job has not sinned. His integrity is intact. And having made this powerful statement, Job falls silent. He has nothing more to say.

Outline
Place
Finder

PROLOGUE
DIALOGUES
MONOLOGUES
EPILOGUE

Key verse. 30:27: Even in surrender to God we can experience emotional turmoil.

Personal application. Whatever our doubts, it is better to suffer despite doing good than to suffer for doing evil.

INSIGHT

Case closed. These chapters are much like a lawyer's final summation of his case. Job contrasts his past blessings and his present suffering and again affirms that he has always acted rightly. The unmistakable conclusion, at least in Job's mind, is that what is happening to him is unfair.

An orderly presentation (29:1-25). The chapter has a distinct pattern:

Blessing (vv. 2-6)
Honor (vv. 7-11)
Job's compassion (vv. 12-17)
Blessing (vv. 18-20)
Honor (vv. 21-25)

Job merited the blessedness of his earlier life and the respect of his friends, for he always showed compassion for the needy and lived a just life.

Unfair (30:1-31). To demonstrate the unfairness of God Job takes each of the themes he introduced in chap. 29 and contrasts his past and present state. Now Job is mocked by young and old (vv. 1-8) and verbally attacked (vv. 9-15). Now there is no blessing from God, but only suffering (vv. 16-17) and affliction (vv. 18-19), however urgently Job pleads (vv. 20-23). Perhaps worst of all, there is no compassion for one who constantly showed his compassion for others (vv. 24-31). No matter how great Job's suffering, there is no relief.

Social justice (31:13-21). The O.T. exhibits a strong sense of social as well as personal morality. These verses isolate a half-dozen characteristics of morality displayed as social justice. These are:

1. Fair treatment of employees (v. 13).
2. Meeting the needs of the poor (v. 16).
3. Strengthening the widow (v. 16).
4. Sharing with the fatherless (v. 17).
5. Seeing the needy are clothed (v. 19).
6. Obtain justice for the poor (v. 21).

Here the Bible teaches that those with resources are responsible for meeting the basic needs of the helpless and protecting them from legal oppression.

There truly is a biblical "social gospel." The Good News means that persons who love God are to demonstrate it by showing active compassion for the needy.

Chapter summary. With the East's characteristic respect for age, Elihu has remained silent while his elders debated. Now they have fallen silent, and Elihu is eager to have his say (32:1-22). In his lengthy discourse Elihu often quotes Job's words and questions specific views Job has expressed (32:11-12; 33:1, 31; 34:5-7, 35-36; 35:16). But Elihu never accuses Job of sin, as the three friends did. What's more, Elihu offers an alternative to the logic which led the three to insist Job must have sinned—and led Job to the agonizing conclusion that somehow God must be acting unjustly. Elihu sees that God may use suffering redemptively.

Pain may awaken a man to spiritual danger and direct his thoughts to God (33:1-33). In this case, suffering is a blessing in disguise. And the believer's conviction that God is good survives despite the suffering of the innocent. This thinking is repeated in Elihu's reprise of Job's argument, but Elihu avoids the fallacy of applying this general principle to Job's case. He points out that God has at least one purpose in suffering other than punishment. The attacks of Job's friends fail, and Job need not torment himself with fears and thoughts that the God he trusts is unjust. In a grand conclusion, Elihu extols the wisdom and awesome majesty of God (37:1-24).

Such a God as ours is not to be doubted, only revered. He will have His own reasons for what has happened to Job. We do not need to know those reasons in order to give Him all our trust.

Key verses. 33:29-30: Suffering can have a redemptive purpose.

Personal application. There will always be an element of mystery in God's dealings with us. We need to accept this and remain unshaken in our trust.

INSIGHT

"I am just like you" (33:6). How refreshing! At last Job hears from someone who does not think of himself as morally superior. Anyone engaged in a ministry of comfort must come with Elihu's attitude. We are all clay. We struggle together. Only the harmless person, who rejects the temptation to condemn or hold others in contempt, can be God's agent of healing.

"You are not right" (33:8-12). Elihu quotes Job's words, not to condemn him, but simply to point out an error in his thinking. There is no attack here, no assumption that Job must have sinned terribly to be suffering now. Elihu simply says, "You are not right" (v. 12).

It's not a sin to be wrong, even when we are wrong about an important issue. Job has claimed that he did not consciously sin, and Elihu will not refute that. But because one didn't sin consciously or willfully doesn't mean he or she is sinless!

Logic, again. Logical reasoning assumes that if A = B and if B is true, then A must also be true. This underlies the argument of Job and his friends. They believe A (that God punishes sin) with B (suffering and loss). Elihu's contribution is to point out that C may also equal B. That is C (God instructs human beings) through B (suffering and loss). Since both A = B and C = B, neither Job nor his friends can hold that B always means A, since B perhaps means C. And, because God's purposes are so complex, perhaps B is also equal to D, E, F, G, H, etc.

In essence, human beings simply cannot reason back from any experience to definitely pinpoint a purpose God may have had in permitting it. Thus the three friends, so secure in their condemnation of Job, were completely out of line. And Job was unnecessarily tormented by the doubt his own rigid theology caused.

What an important book Job is! It encourages us to be gentle with the suffering. It teaches us to avoid dogmatism in the foolish belief that we understand God. And it reminds us that whether we understand or not we can always trust our loving God fully.

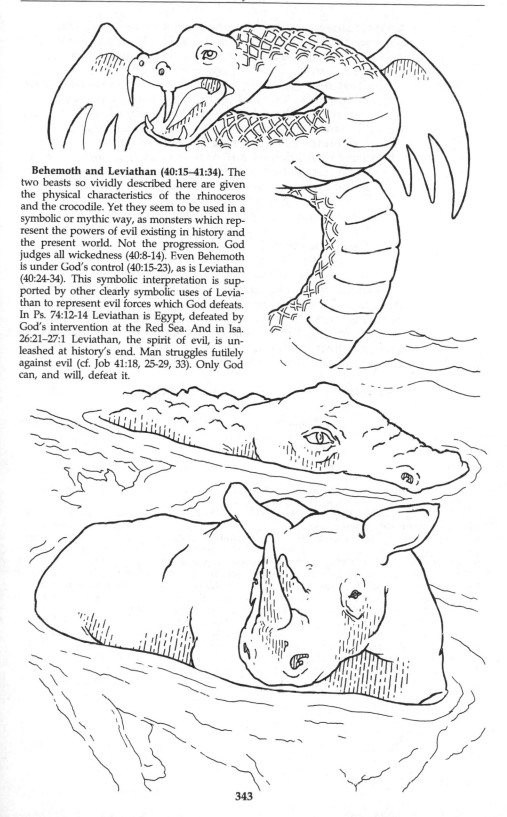

Behemoth and Leviathan (40:15–41:34). The two beasts so vividly described here are given the physical characteristics of the rhinoceros and the crocodile. Yet they seem to be used in a symbolic or mythic way, as monsters which represent the powers of evil existing in history and the present world. Not the progression. God judges all wickedness (40:8-14). Even Behemoth is under God's control (40:15-23), as is Leviathan (40:24-34). This symbolic interpretation is supported by other clearly symbolic uses of Leviathan to represent evil forces which God defeats. In Ps. 74:12-14 Leviathan is Egypt, defeated by God's intervention at the Red Sea. And in Isa. 26:21–27:1 Leviathan, the spirit of evil, is unleashed at history's end. Man struggles futilely against evil (cf. Job 41:18, 25-29, 33). Only God can, and will, defeat it.

Chapter summary. Now the unexpected occurs. God, whom Job has complained is beyond reach, suddenly appears. But God does not come to be questioned by Job. Instead, God poses two series of questions and challenges Job to answer.

The first series (38:1–39:30) disputes Job's knowledge of the physical universe, knowledge which God surely possesses. Job, humbled, realizes how limited his knowledge is (40:1-5). God asks Job, who cannot even master the physical universe, if he will question the Lord's command of the moral universe (vv. 6-14). Surely man's limited authority over evil, as well as nature, must teach human beings not to claim greater competence than God in the moral realm (40:15–41:34).

As we read God's words to Job we recognize the irony of His questions, but must also sense the gentleness in the Lord's voice. God does not explain why Job is suffering. After all, it's really not Job's place to demand that God report to him! Yet the Lord never charges Job with sin. He does not even, as Elihu did, rebuke Job for going too far in questioning the divine justice. The entire monologue by God has one purpose only. The Lord informs Job that He really does know what He is doing, even though Job may not. This, after all, is the essense of relationship with God. The strength to face difficult times is not found in knowing why we must face them, but in the confidence that our great God loves us completely and that He is still in charge.

Key verse. 40:8: We must let God be God.

Personal application. When suffering comes, don't ask to know "why." Just trust in the wisdom and love of God.

INSIGHT

The critic's complaint. Some have angrily rejected these chapters of Job, complaining that God simply paraded His power. They feel God was irresponsible in not giving Job a clear explanation of why he suffered. This God, they cry, is exactly the unfeeling, distant, impersonal God that Job complained about.

They miss the fact that Job's anguish did not have intellectual roots. Job was hurting because he no longer knew who God was nor had a sense of personal relationship with Him. It's not the solution to life's puzzles that evades us, it's the comfort found in the absolute assurance that a God of love is and that He controls the circumstances of our lives.

God accomplished the restoration of Job's confidence through His questions. In this way the Lord brought peace to Job's troubled heart.

Scripture's tone of voice. Often our interpretation of a Bible passage depends on the "tone of voice" we read into it. If we imagine God asked His questions in a harsh tone of voice, we assume He intended to humiliate Job. But if we imagine God asked the same questions in a warm, loving tone of voice, we realize that the Lord intended to instruct and encourage His servant.

Try reading these chapters aloud, speak gently as you would to your own child who's been sobbing after an injury. Then you'll begin to understand that God's questions were intended to comfort Job, by reminding him, "I'm here. It's all right. I'm still here."

Chapter summary. Job responds to God's self-revelation with utter humility. Now that he has seen God, rather than simply heard of Him, Job senses his own limitations—"I despise myself"—and no longer questions or challenges God's justice—"and repent in dust and ashes" (42:1-6).

Outline
Place
Finder

PROLOGUE
DIALOGUES
MONOLOGUES
EPILOGUE

God then rebukes Eliphaz and his two companions. Unlike Job, they "have not spoken of Me what is right." Neither refusal to deal honestly with reality, nor dogmatic claims that equate one's own position with God's, are honoring to the Lord. But God will forgive the three—in response to the prayers of "my servant Job" (vv. 7-9).

What happened to Job afterward? The author takes us years ahead, and reports that all signs of divine blessing were restored. Family and friends returned to comfort him. Job became twice as wealthy as before. He fathered ten more children who all grew to adulthood. And Job, honored by all, lived such a long life that he saw his offspring down to the fourth generation (vv. 10-17).

Key verse. 42:8: Job is vindicated in this life after all!

Personal application. The rewards of faith in God may not come to us in this life, but they will surely come.

INSIGHT

Why? (42:5) In one sense the Book of Job leaves our curiosity unsatisfied. Why did God permit Job to keep on suffering? The prologue, with its explanation of God's contest with Satan, establishes the fact that Job was righteous and remained pious under the most intense pressure. It tells us nothing about God's real reason for letting Job suffer.

Perhaps that reason is suggested in 42:5 and implied earlier in 3:25. In the earlier verse Job speaks of uneasy fears that troubled him despite his many blessings. He confesses that before "my ears had heard of You," a condition he contrasts with "but now my eyes have seen You." Now that Job has seen God and surrendered to Him, he no longer fears. He has no more questions. All his doubts have been relieved by the sudden vision of God in all His greatness.

This may have been the greater good that God always intended to accomplish through Job's pain. And, perhaps, it is the good He accomplishes through ours. Suffering drives many of us to first question God, but later to trust and know Him better. Untold thousands have looked back and seen this as a great and gracious good.

Speak right of God (42:7). It is ironic that the three defenders of orthodoxy are rebuked by God, while Job, who openly expressed his doubts and challenged common convictions, is commended. Yet, as we've seen throughout the book, even Job's accusations were expressed in the context of a deep and abiding faith. On the other hand, the three friends refused to even look at the evidence Job produced, terrified that he was undermining religion. In fact their retreat to tradition and refusal to deal honestly with the truth displayed a lack of faith in God!

Let us believe so deeply in the goodness, love, and power of God that we aren't afraid to face the harshest challenges to our faith. God will stand every test. Only with this confidence can we truly honor the Lord and speak right of God.

Job's blessings (42:10-17). Some critics feel the epilogue spoils the lesson of Job. They want us to leave Uz with Job still crouched on the ground. But James explains why the epilogue is there. It assures us by "what the Lord finally brought about" that "the Lord is full of compassion and mercy" (James 5:11).

We may not see such a happy ending ourselves. Yet looking back at Job we're reminded that the suffering God brings will surely be swallowed up in joy, for the Lord is compassion, and He is mercy. If we don't experience our happy ending now, we will—then.

Then (42:13). Job's wealth in livestock was doubled (cf. 42:12 with 1:3). But the ten children he fathers merely match the first ten. Why? Because in fact his family is doubled, for the first ten are not gone, but await him now in heaven! It really is not now, but then, that we all will experience the full blessing of our God.

Psalms

Every book of the Bible deepens our understanding of our relationship with God. But the Psalms uniquely enrich our experience of that relationship. This book, containing 150 lyric poems, has shaped the liturgy of every Christian tradition and become an integral part of public worship. It has also shaped the prayer and worship of the saints of every age. Individual believers have turned to the psalms for comfort and for inspiration and have found in them models for personal praise and prayer. Every human emotion has its echo in the Book of Psalms. And the wonderful message of Psalms is that God cares—not only about the external circumstances of our lives, but about our every reaction to life's varied experiences.

Psalms is undoubtedly the most subjective of the Bible's books. These poems express the inner reality experienced by those who love God. Their writers openly share doubts and fears, joys and triumphs. They express a deep sense of sin, an overwhelming relief for forgiveness, and the confidence and praise common in human beings who are united by faith to the Lord. John Calvin rightly called Psalms, "An anatomy of all the parts of the soul; for no one will find in himself a single feeling of which the image is not reflected in this mirror."

Understanding Hebrew Poetry

The Psalms are lyric poems, heart songs that touch us deeply. Much of their power derives from a distinctive form of Hebrew poetry, which does not rely on rhyme but on rhythmic patterns of thought. Ideas, emotions, and images are repeated or developed in a variety of ways to create an intuitive response in the reader. While it is not necessary to understand Hebrew poetry to be captivated by the Psalms or to sense their impact, it's important to grasp its principles if we try to interpret them.

Simply put, the key to Hebrew poetry is its parallelism. That is, its tendency to arrange ideas, emotions, and images side by side in a variety of ways. The three simplest forms of parallelism are synonymous, antithetic, and synthetic. In synonymous parallelism a thought is repeated in different words:

> "Our mouths were filled with laughter,
>   our tongues with songs of joy" (Ps. 126:2).

In antithetic parallelism the initial thought, emotion, or image is emphasized by contrasting it with an opposite.

> "A kind man benefits himself,
>   but a cruel man brings himself harm" (Prov. 11:17).

In synthetic parallelism the second line completes the thought of the first:

> "I will lie down and sleep in peace,
>   for You alone, O Lord, make me dwell in safety" (Ps. 4:8).

There are more complex types of parallelism found in Psalms. Yet the basic concept is simple. The power of Hebrew poetry flows from the arrangement and repetition of the emotions, ideas, and images presented by the poet.

Origin of the Psalms

The Psalms are collections of lyric poems, most of which were set to music and used in public worship. There are five different "books" of psalms, represented in our Old Testament by Roman numerals. These are generally agreed to have been collected and added to the "official" hymn book of Israel at different times. Book I (Psalms 1–41) is composed of intimately personal psalms written by David, and probably collected before his death. First Chronicles 25 tells about David's role in originating the temple liturgy, and he is often credited with introducing Israel's "new era of religious poetry." Book II (Psalms 42–72) is also predominantly Davidic, but probably formed as a collection in the time of Solomon. Book III (Psalms 73–89) and Book IV (Psalms 90–106) are thought of as collections from the time of Judah's exile, while Book V (Psalms 107–150) was added after the return from Babylonian Captivity. Undoubtedly many of the psalms were written long before their inclusion in the official collection.

These collected works of Israel's great poets and worship leaders served God's people as hymns sung or chanted at times of worship. They were memorized by individuals and remembered while laboring in the fields or at home. They capture the awareness of Israel that relationship with God is intimate and personal. The Lord of the universe walks beside the believer, and at any moment, with any need, we can turn gratefully to Him.

Special terms in the Psalms

From the beginning, the collection of psalms had a role in public worship. This place is reflected in titles, terms, and phrases found usually in a psalm's superscription. The meaning of some of the terms is unknown, yet together they portray something of the complexity and sophistication of the ancient worship of God.

The word translated "psalm" is *mizmor*. It means a song sung with musical accompaniment and is found in the prefix of 57 psalms. *Maskil* calls for "skill," or "cunning," and is found 13 times. Some 55 psalms indicate "to the chief musician," and Psalms 70–84 are called "psalms of degrees." These may have been sung by pilgrims approaching Jerusalem for one of the major festivals. Or perhaps they refer to the steps of the temple on which the levitical choir stood when praising God. The meaning of *selah*, which is found some 71 times within Psalms, is generally thought to be a musical notation also. Other titles suggest that songs were used on special days, or other occasions, such as a wedding (Ps. 45) or when making a petition (Ps. 38). Actually only 34 of the 150 psalms have no title and thus give no explicit information about author, occasion, or use in Israel's worship.

Literary characteristics

The Psalms are especially rich in imagery and various figures of speech. Metaphor, which implies comparison, is frequently used to enrich the sense of who God is for us. Thus, the Lord is our strong tower, our shield, our sun. Similes also abound: the godly are like a tree, whose deep roots drink in life-giving water. In contrast the wicked are like chaff blown away by the wind. Vivid characterizations also abound.

"The wicked bend their bows;
they set their arrows against the strings
to shoot from the shadows
at the upright in heart" (Ps. 11:2).

Such powerful images flood the psalms, provoking strong emotions and touching the deepest levels of our being.

Another element which makes the psalms so compelling is their involvement of all the senses. Psalm 45:8 celebrates the bride, who may well represent the believing community, by saying:

"All your robes are fragrant with myrrh and
aloes and casia;
from palaces adorned with ivory
the music of the strings makes you glad."

The inner life is just as powerfully portrayed, as in the first of David's great psalms of confession. "When I kept silent," [he remembers] "my bones wasted away through my groaning all day long" (Ps. 32:3). Against such a background even the most insensitive can sense the blessedness of the man "whose transgressions are forgiven, whose sins are covered" (32:1).

Realizing that the Psalms touch on every human experience adds to our understanding of why this book of poetry draws us again and again. And we can appreciate the great gift God has given us, to help us open our hearts to life and to Him.

Authors of the Psalms					
Name	Book I 1–41	Book II 42–72	Book III 73–89	Book IV 90–106	Book V 107–150	Total
David	37	18	1	2	15	73
Asaph		1	11			12
Korah		7	3			10
Moses				1		1
Solomon		1			1	2
Ethan			1			1
Heman			1			1
Anonymous	4	4		14	28	50
	41	31	17	17	44	

The chart shows the dominant influence of David in the Psalms, and thus in shaping the worship life of ancient Israel. While books IV and V show an increase in the number of anonymous contributions, even in them David's works are still prominant. Christians are often tempted to think of first-century Judaism as a rigid, legalistic system which saw God as the bookkeeper who totaled up good deeds and awarded heaven on points. While this may have been the attitude of some, Psalms reminds us that love for God and celebration of His grace, as well as an abiding sense of personal relationship with Him, are essential elements of Old Testament faith as well as that of the New Testament.

Themes of the Psalms

While the psalms are nearly all unremittingly personal, there are recurrent themes. Some of the psalms are *historical*, reviewing God's acts and Israel's responses (Pss. 68, 78, 105, 106). The *penitential* psalms express the writers' sorrow over personal sins and failures, and model confession (Pss. 6, 32, 51). The *imprecatory* psalms cry out against injustice and call on the Lord to overthrow the wicked (Pss. 35, 69, 109, 137). *Liturgical* psalms were used in temple worship at special times of the year or on special occasions (Pss. 30, 92, 120–134). Others may be classified as *praise* psalms; here the focus is on the person or works of God and their intention to exalt Him (Pss. 33, 103, 138). Some are *relational* in that they explore in depth the personal relationship that exists between God and His saints (Pss. 8, 16, 20, 23, 35). A number of psalms are *prophetic*, and these almost universally focus on the person or work of the coming Messiah. Many messianic psalms have been identified by references to them by N.T. writers (Pss. 2, 8, 16, 22, 40, 45, 69, 72, 89, 102, 109, 110, 132). These messianic psalms provide a sharp and clear picture of Jesus, many centuries before His birth. Among other things, *prophetic* psalms proclaim His deity (Ps. 45:6-7; cf. Heb. 1:8), His sonship (Ps. 2:7; cf. Heb. 1:5, and Ps. 110:1; cf. Matt. 22:42-45), His obedience (Ps. 40:6-8; cf. Heb. 10:5-7), His suffering (Ps. 69:9; cf. Rom. 15:3), His death (Ps. 22:1-21), His resurrection (Pss. 2:7; 16:19; cf. Acts 13:33-36), His ascension (Ps. 68:18; cf. Eph. 4:8), and His Second Coming to judge the world (Ps. 46–47; cf. 2 Thes. 1:6-9). In every way the Book of Psalms towers above other ancient and modern works of poetry, capturing not only the genius of men but the complex inventiveness of the God who inspired them.

Psalms' exalted vision

While Psalms touches us at the deepest levels of our personalities and probes every human experience, it also has the capacity to lift our eyes up to see God. Through Psalms' exalted vision of God we are gifted with encouragement, peace, and hope. And we are drawn to worship the One who is rightly the center of our existence and whose praise is our greatest good.

There are several different words for "god" used in the psalms. *Adon* (9 times) and *Adonai* (52 times) indicate Master. *El* (69 times) and *Elohim* (342 times) are the Middle Eastern culture's general words for the deity. But the name that occurs most often in the psalms, some 678 times in the 150 poems, is *Yahweh*, the personal name of God whose meaning was first explained to Moses (Ex. 3). That name, God's covenant name, emphasizes the living presence of God with, and for, His people. It was as *Yahweh* that God released His people from slavery in Egypt. It was as *Yahweh* that He parted the Red Sea, provided Israel with manna as their daily bread, and shattered the power of the Canaanites before Joshua's armies. It was as *Yahweh* that God settled Israel in the Promised Land, gave them a Law to live by, and promised to bless them. It is *Yahweh* the ever-present, ever-faithful, and ever-caring God that we meet in the Psalms. And it is through the Psalms that we sense God is *Yahweh* for us.

He is present with us. He is here, aware of our every emotion, sensitive to our turmoil, powerful to extend His hand in aid. And it is through the Psalms that we realize we are to be there for Him as well. We are to give Him our trust, devotion, obedience, confidence, and praise. Hand in hand with God, we are to live out all our days enriched by His presence and offering Him praise.

PSALM 1: The Way of the Righteous

A righteous person rejects the lifestyle of the wicked (1:1) to find delight in God's Law (v. 2), a choice which yields stability and prosperity (v. 3). The wicked are vulnerable to destruction (vv. 4-6), for God supervises the outcome of man's moral choices.

Key concepts. Blessing »p. 127. Sin »p. 34.

Sinners go from bad to worse (1:1). "Walk" refers to infrequent ungodliness. "Stand" describes the habitual practice of sin. The image "sit in the seat" is of those who instruct others in a community's way of life, so that sitting with scoffers is hardened commitment to sin's ways.

The wicked (1:4). The Heb. root word *ra'ah* means "evil" or "bad." But the emphasis of "wicked" in the O.T. is on the moral deficiencies that find expression in injuring other persons. What characterizes the wicked is pride and viciousness expressed.

Chaff (1:4). The ancient farmer crushed stalks of grain with a weighty, ox-drawn sled and then tossed them in the air. The lighter bits of straw and husks were blown away.

Chaff is a frequent symbol of the wicked. They are insubstantial and worthless, destined to be discarded by God.

PSALM 2: The Coming Messianic King

Human society rebels against God's anointed Messiah (2:1-3), provoking God's scorn and sure judgment (vv. 4-6). God has decreed that His Son will rule the Earth (vv. 7-9). How essential then that we submit now and by taking refuge in the Son find blessing rather than destruction (vv. 10-12).

Key concepts. Messiah »p. 431. Son »p. 897. Father »p. 140.

This prophetic psalm speaks of God's coming Messiah. It is referred to in a number of N.T. passages: vv. 1-2 in Acts 4:25-26; vv. 6-7 in John 1:49; v. 7 in Acts 13:33, Col. 1:18, Heb. 1:5 and 5:6; and vv. 8-9 in Rev. 2:26-27, 12:5, and 19:15.

"You are My Son" (2:7). is the public proclamation that the Son is to inherit the kingdom from His Father. It is a metaphor establishing the Son's right to rule over God's kingdom.

Scepter (2:9). The iron scepter pictures Christ's rule over the rebellious against their will.

PSALM 3: In Flight from Absalom

David describes his feelings of abandonment as the northern tribes proclaim Absalom king and drive him from Jerusalem (3:1-2; cf. 2 Sam. 15). Yet the memory of all God has been to David sustains him (vv. 3-4) and he finds rest (vv. 5-6). David appeals to God for deliverance and finds comfort in remembering how God struck his enemies in the past (vv. 7-8).

No deliverance? (1:2) David had failed morally with Bathsheba before this event, and the sins of his own children led many to conclude that God had deserted him.

David found courage in realizing what God was to and for him (3:3). The phrase "who lifts up my head" is a metaphor for strengthen.

PSALM 4: God as Man's Ultimate Good

The setting is the same as Psalm 3. David pleads for God's help (4:1) and warns his enemies not to wrong him (v. 2) because he is God's own (vv. 3-5). David is able to rejoice despite his desperate circumstances, because all he cares about is God. The Lord, not his lost royal glory, is the source of his joy (vv. 6-7) and the source of his inner peace (v. 8).

Key concepts. Righteous God »p. 120. Call on God »p. 361. »Peace »p. 427.

PSALM 5: An Appeal to God's Character

David prays early and earnestly, confident that God will answer (5:1-3). Since God rejects the arrogant, David, who is reverent and humble, is sure of God's leading (vv. 4-8). David calls on God to declare the wicked guilty (vv. 9-10) and spread His protection over the righteous who take refuge in the Lord (vv. 11-12). David's appeal is rooted in his conviction that God is righteous. God will act in character to preserve him.

God's hatred (5:5-6). The psalm says, "You hate all who do wrong." God's hatred extends to evil acts such as robbery and iniquity (Isa. 61:8) and even to the hypocritical worship of those who violate His moral standards (Isa. 1:13-15; Amos 5:21). While some are shocked by the biblical terminology, it appropriately expresses God's utter rejection of evil and evildoers.

God's "great mercy" (5:7). David immediately balances his reference to God's hatred. Mercy here is *hesed*, a term also translated as "love," "covenant love," and "loving-kindness." *Hesed* reminds us that God is totally committed to humankind. The love we see in Calvary's ultimate sacrifice draws us, as God's mercy drew David, to worship and serve the Lord.

PSALM 6: A Plea for Mercy

Every faithful believer is at times disciplined by God. This penitential psalm expresses the anguish David feels (6:1-3), records his plea (vv. 4-7), and ends with the glad assurance that God has accepted David's prayer (vv. 8-10).

Mercy not justice (6:1-2). He asks God not to consider what he deserves. Appeal is made to God's compassion in the confidence that the Lord does care.

"How long?" (6:3) Here, as elsewhere in the Psalms, the cry expresses frustration.

Surely (6:9). When it hurts too much to wait any longer, meditate on this verse. Surely God blesses the righteous. There can be no doubt that God in His time will bless you.

Psalm 7: A Call for God the Judge to Act

David, innocent of the slanders charged by his enemies (7:1-5), calls on God to vindicate him by punishing the wicked (vv. 6-17).

Key concepts. Anger of God »p. 65. Righteousness of God »p. 120. Judge »p. 874. Punishment »p. 827.

"Arise" (7:6-7). The fervent appeal to God to "arise," "rise up," and "awake" are calls for God to act publicly and so openly vindicate David. At the same time God will establish Himself as a just judge, for David is innocent.

How different this is from Ps. 6's appeal for mercy. There David sensed the fault lay in himself. Here he knows it does not. How confidently we can call on God for help in circumstances in which we are sure of our purity!

"O righteous God" (7:9). God never violates the standards of right and wrong which He established in this sense, the righteousness of God to which David appeals is God's personal commitment to do at all times only what is right.

Both testaments share the conviction that it

is right for God as Judge to "bring to an end the violence of the wicked" (7:9). The Apostle Paul puts it even more strongly; When Jesus returns the wicked will be "punished with everlasting destruction and shut out from the presence of the Lord and from the majesty of His power" (2 Thes. 1:7-9).

God's righteousness has two aspects (7:10-16). He saves the upright in heart and He "expresses His wrath" against evildoers (vv. 10-11). The psalm pictures a relentless pursuit of evil, which even in this world ends for the wicked in disillusionment as the troubles and violence a man relies on "recoils on him" (v. 16).

Thanks for righteousness (7:17). Thank God that in righteousness He saves as well as punishes.

PSALM 8: God's Amazing Concern for Man

In view of God's majesty and the vastness of creation (8:1-3) His concern for human beings and gift of dominion over earth's creatures (vv. 4-9) utterly amazes David.

Key concepts. Mankind »p. 26. Creation »p. 430.

"**Man.**" The Heb. word here is *'enos*, which emphasizes man's mortality and weakness. David is stunned that the all-powerful Creator should exalt such puny beings by caring for us and by giving us dominion over His earth.

Dominion (8:6). The phrase "you made him ruler" reflects the decision of the Godhead to share the divine image with human beings (»p. 26) and give mankind dominion (Gen. 1:26). The biblical doctrine is that humans serve as God's representatives on earth, with responsibility to care for His creation.

PSALM 9: Praise to God for Vindication

God has displayed His righteousness and sovereignty by judging Israel's foreign enemies (9:1-12). Sure that God is known by His justice, David prays confidently for continuing relief from His enemies (vv. 13-20).

Key concepts. Enemy »p. 91. Oppressed »p. 89. Wicked »pp. 29, 350. Praise »p. 380. Hope »p. 465.

Past, present, and future. The psalm weaves together these three elements. David experienced God's vindication in the past. The Lord "rebuked," "destroyed," and "blotted out" His enemies (v. 5). This has given David a present assurance that "the Lord reigns" (v. 7), "will judge" (v. 8), and is "a refuge for the oppressed" (v. 9). So assured, David cries out for future relief from those who now persecute him (v. 13).

PSALM 10: The Cry of the Victim

The psalmist has been victimized by wicked enemies (10:1-11) and cries out, begging God to act quickly (vv. 12-15). Despite the temporary triumph of the wicked, the Lord defends the oppressed (vv. 16-18).

Key concepts. Arrogance »p. 119. Wicked »pp. 29, 350.

PSALM 11: God Our Refuge

When advised to flee from danger (11:1-3), David affirms God's righteousness and His sure judgment of the wicked (vv. 4-7).

Key concepts. Wicked »pp. 29, 350.

"**In His holy temple**" (11:4). The phrase is not associated with worship. It is from His "holy temple" that God dispenses judgment. As long as God exists and as long as God judges, our foundation cannot be shaken, much less destroyed.

Moral foundations (11:4-7). God is (v. 4a); God observes (v. 4b) and examines (v. 4b-5); He hates the wicked (v. 5b); God will rain judgment on the wicked (v. 6); and "upright men will see His face" (v. 7).

PSALM 12. Confidence in God's Promise

David cries out in despair (12:1-3), but his confidence is restored by God's words of promise (vv. 4-8).

PSALM 13: Longing for Deliverance Now

Under pressure, David feels forgotten by God (13:1-2) and cries out for the Lord to act (vv. 3-4). No immediate answer comes, yet David finds peace remembering God's loyal love (vv. 5-6).

PSALM 14: The Corrupt Fool

Because the human race is corrupt and foolish (14:1-3) the godly take refuge in the Lord (vv. 4-6) and long for His kingdom on earth (v. 7).

"The fool" (14:1). The three Heb. words translated "fool" all focus on moral rather than mental deficiencies. *'Iwwelet* pictures the fool as insolent or rebellious, quick-tempered and reckless. *Kesil* pictures him as obstinate and unwilling to learn or do what is right. The word in this verse is *nabal*, which portrays a person closed to God and morality. This fool denies God's existence, and gives himself over to gross and hideous sins.

By nature all human beings are fools, who have "together become corrupt" (v. 3).

"Salvation" (14:7). Ultimately God will set up a righteous kingdom and there will be a "company of the righteous" (v. 5) in it. Who are they? We who have turned from our native foolishness to seek God (v. 2) and call on Him (v. 4).

PSALM 15. A Psalm of Fellowship

David describes the lifestyle of the believer who lives in intimate fellowship with the Lord and so derives strength.

Key concept. Neighbor »p. 661.

"Dwell" (15:1). The image is of one who comes to another's home as a guest.

The blameless believer (15:2-5). Note that the blameless lifestyle is characterized as: *sincere, honest *avoids malicious speech *does nothing to harm or discredit another *avoids vile people *honors and keeps company with those who fear God *keeps promises whatever the cost *lends (to the needy) and charges no interest *can't be influenced against the innocent but champions their cause (cf. Deut. 27:25).

PSALM 16: The Joy of Fellowship with God

Complete personal commitment to the Lord (16:1-4) results in the assurance that God is in control of David's life (vv. 5-6) and guides his steps (vv. 7-8). This assurance brings David a matchless sense of security and joy (vv. 9-11).

Key concepts. Leading »p. 131. Counsel of God »p. 357. Abandon »p. 370. Joy »p. 269.

Release (16:4). The sorrows of those who rely on anything but the Lord "increase," because every other basis of hope is certain to disappoint. Only the Lord is eternal, a sure anchor for our hopes.

Life's boundary lines (16:5-6). The imagery recalls God's gift of Canaan to Israel and its division by lot to each family. David affirms that God has sovereignly assigned him his place in life and finds satisfaction in this gift.

"Always" (16:8). Two Heb. expressions suggest the passage of time: "through all days." Three different expressions indicate continuation. Here the Heb. word is *tamid*, which means "continually." There will never be a time when David looks away from the Lord because his faith and hope will remain unshakable.

God's "Holy One" (16:10). The phrase refers to the Messiah, Jesus.

PSALM 17: A Plea from a Righteous Man

David, confident in his firm commitment to God (17:1-5), remains deeply aware of the dangers faced by a righteous man in living in a sinful world (vv. 6-12). What comfort to know that God will confront the wicked, and the righteous find satisfaction in God's presence (vv. 13-15).

Hearing prayer (17:1). How wonderful to have the assurance when we pray that nothing in our lives is blocking God's response to us.

"The apple of Your eye" (17:8). The reference is to the pupil and to sight. David appeals to God for the Lord's personal attention.

PSALM 18: Gratitude for Deliverance from Saul

David describes God's qualities (18:1-3) and launches into a vivid, image-rich report of divine deliverance (vv. 4-29). David returns to God and praises Him for the many benefits he has received (vv. 30-45). Because of all the Lord has done in showing Himself David's Saviour, the psalmist will praise God forever (vv. 46-50).

Key concepts. Fortress »p. 216. Salvation »p. 426. Warfare »p. 133.

God, for me (18:1-3). David's images of God are personal, relational, and reflect his own role as a warrior. Thus to David God represents his fortress (security), his shield (protection), and the "horn of my salvation" (power to deliver from enemies).

David's integrity (18:19-29). David simply

recognizes the fact that God is committed to those who keep themselves from sin and do not turn away from God.

Credit (18:46-50). This is the nature of praise: to give God credit for who He is and for what He has done.

PSALM 19: Awe at God's Revelation

God has revealed Himself in His creation (19:1-6), but has enriched us most through His revelation in the Scriptures (vv. 7-11). Only by studying and keeping God's Law can we be kept from sin (vv. 12-14).

Key concepts. Glory of God »p. 74. Law »pp. 123, 145. Sins »pp. 34, 362.

Revelation. Revelation is primarily the giving and receiving of information from God. Psalm 19 celebrates two forms of revelation: natural, in which information about God is made known through His Creation; and special, in which information from God is made known directly to human beings.

Universal knowledge of God (19:3). Romans

1:18-20 teaches that God's existence and His power are known through creation.

God's Law (19:7). The Heb. *torah* stands for all written revelation. But here David celebrates the specific "statutes" (v. 7), "precepts" (v. 8), "commands" (v. 8), and "ordinances" (v. 9) that instruct in living a godly life.

PSALM 20: Intercession for the King

God's people pray for their king as he prepares for battle (20:1-5), reassuring the ruler who trusts in the saving power of God (vv. 6-9).

Key concepts. Prayer »pp. 608–609. Chariots »p. 161.

Intercessory prayer (20:1-5). Even the godly David sensed his need for the prayer support of his people. Every wise Christian leader yearns for similar reinforcement from his congregation.

"Trust" (20:7). The issue raised here is reliance. Belief can be intellectual. Trust is a far more personal and challenging concept. Trust in God is resting the full weight of our confidence in Him, counting on Him alone to deliver us.

The psalm suggests seven things in which David and the O.T. congregation trusted God. God can be trusted: *to hear us in time of trouble *to protect us *to send help *to support (strengthen) us *to give us our heart's desire *to make our plans succeed *to answer us with saving power. When God can surely do all this for us, we would be foolish not to trust Him.

PSALM 21: Thanksgiving After Battle

With victory won, the king rejoices in God's strength (21:1-7). In the assurance of future triumphs (vv. 8-12) the king vows to continue to offer God praise.

PSALM 22: Psalm of the Forsaken

The psalmist cries out in deep anguish, feeling himself forsaken by God (22:1-5) and despised by his fellowmen (vv. 6-11). He graphically describes his anguish (vv. 12-18) and begs to be delivered from death (vv. 19-21). With rescue assured, the psalmist praises God and foresees God's blessing of the whole world (vv. 22-31).

Key concepts. Fulfilled prophecy »p. 417. Trust »p. 354. Forsake/Abandon »p. 370.

A messianic vision. Psalms 22, 23, and 24 are viewed as a messianic trio portraying Christ's suffering, intimate relationship with God, and His ultimate triumph.

Psalm 22's first words were uttered by Christ on the cross (cf. Matt. 27:46; Mark 15:34). Other references to Ps. 22 in the N.T. include:

v. 7 with Matt. 27:39-44   vv. 18 with Matt. 27:35
v. 8 with Matt. 27:42-43   v. 22 with Heb. 2:12
v. 16 with Luke 24:39-40   and Heb. 5:7

"Why?" (22:1) David merely felt forsaken by God, but Christ was literally abandoned by Him. In history's most awesome moment God the Father withdrew His presence from the Son; the Holy One isolated Himself from one who at that instant in time became sin for us.

God has listened (22:24). The psalm's anguish ultimately is replaced by a triumphant note of praise. God has heard the prayer of the sufferer for deliverance (cf. vv. 19-21). The victim who is the true subject of this psalm died— and was raised to life again.

Out of that death and through a now endless life Christ, once a victim but now Victor, satisfies the deepest need of all who seek the Lord (v. 26), and will surely cause all nations to bow down to God in an endless kingdom He will rule (vv. 27-31).

PSALM 23: The Shepherd Psalm.

Using the images of a sheep in the care of a shepherd (23:1-4) and of a guest in the home of a generous host (vv. 5-6), David celebrates the security afforded by God's protection.

Sheep. In the ancient Middle East sheep were precious symbols of wealth. Their wool provided yarn for clothing; their bodies were preferred for sacrifice. Yet sheep are dependent creatures who must be guided to food and water and protected from wild animals.

God as Shepherd. Sheep cannot survive alone in the wild, but must always be in the company of a shepherd. The Middle Eastern shepherd loved his sheep, gave each one a name, and cared for each one tenderly. Many a shepherd interposed himself between wild beasts and his sheep, and at night the shepherd lay down and slept in the single doorway to his sheepfold. Any enemy would have to pass him to attack his flock.

How marvelous then for us whom Scripture sees as sheep that God presents Himself as our shepherd. He leads us, protects us, and because He is always with us, we fear no evil.

Guests in God's house (23:5-6). The last two verses picture a guest eating in the home of a generous host. In the Middle East, hospitality was greatly valued. The needs of a guest were gladly supplied, even if the family of the host had to go without as the price of generosity. A person who had taken a meal in one's home was assured of the protection of his host. Even an enemy, once served a meal, was totally secure for as long as his visit should last.

God Himself set a table before David and treated him generously as His guest. Because David is under God's protection, he is sure that "goodness and love will follow me all the days of my life."

Psalm 23 as prophecy. Christ lived His life on Earth as a sheep, then rose to become the Good Shepherd. As prophecy, Ps. 23 reminds us that though Christ walked in the "valley of the shadow of death" and experienced the turmoil described in Ps. 22, He was upheld by God's protective love.

PSALM 24: The Triumph of the King

The psalmist ponders the preparation of those who will accompany the "King of glory" up God's holy hill (24:1-6) and is caught up in a vision of the triumph of a king who is God Himself (vv. 7-10).

PSALM 25: A Prayer for Guidance

David turns to God for guidance and forgiveness (25:1-7) and finds assurance in God's grace to those who fear Him (vv. 8-15). David concludes with an earnest plea for help (vv. 16-22).

Key concepts. Leading »p. 131. Fear of God »p. 387. Covenant »pp. 35, 66. Forgiveness »p. 357.

"My eyes are ever on the Lord" (25:8-15). When you pray, fix your eyes, as David did, on the fact that God is: *good *upright *willing to instruct sinners *loving *faithful *forgiving. What confidence we can have in prayer, not because we pray well, but because of the nature of the God to whom we pray.

PSALM 26: Prayer of a Righteous Man

David describes his blameless life (26:1-8) and appeals to God (vv. 9-12).

Fellowship (26:1-8). Our confidence in prayer rests first on an awareness of who God is. But it also depends on our conviction that we ourselves are living in fellowship with the Lord. We are in fellowship with God if we have: *placed our trust in Him (v. 1b) *remain aware of His love (v. 3) *habitually walk in His truth (v. 3; »p. 892) *refrain from intimate associations with the wicked (vv. 4-5) *maintain our innocence (v. 6) *make open profession of our faith and love for God (v. 7) and *identify ourselves with God's people (v. 8).

PSALM 27: Freedom from Fear

David sets aside his fears (27:1-3), finding release in communion with God (vv. 4-6) and in prayer (vv. 7-14).

Our "stronghold" (27:1-3). Fear is rooted in a sense of our vulnerability and helplessness. David reminds himself that God is his *ma'oz*, a strongly fortified place.

Life's strongest bond (27:10). The bond that God establishes with us in Christ is far stronger than the bond that holds parent and child together.

Psalm 28: A Cry for Mercy

David calls on God (28:1-2), asking Him to show that He distinguishes between the wicked and godly (vv. 3-5). Sure that God has heard this prayer, David is moved to praise (vv. 6-9).

Answered prayer. There are some prayers that we can be sure God will answer, because they are so intimately bound up with who He is, or with His revealed purposes.

When we pray for something that we know is in God's revealed will or purposes, our hearts too should leap for joy.

PSALM 29: God's Power Unveiled in Nature

A thunderstorm towers majestically above the Promised Land arousing David's praise (29:1-2) and sparking the realization that it's the Lord who is enthroned in nature (vv. 3-9). Surely so great a God is able to strengthen and bless His people (vv. 10-11).

PSALM 30: A Psalm of Dedication

David's restoration to spiritual health (30:1-3) moves the psalmist to praise God that His anger is momentary, while His love lasts forever (vv. 4-12).

Key concepts. Healing »p. 412. Anger of God »p. 65.

(30:6-7). Never let yourself feel so secure that you forget everything in this life depends on the favor and blessing of God. Always trust in the Lord.

PSALM 31: Exhortation of the Afflicted

David appeals to God, who is and has been his refuge (31:1-8). He feels his danger intensely (vv. 9-13), but continues to trust in God (vv. 14-18). Having experienced God's goodness, David exhorts "all his saints" to love and trust God (vv. 19-24).

Key concepts. Righteousness of God »p. 120. Idols »p. 433. Truth »p. 892. Hope »p. 465.

"Since you are" (31:3). When we commit ourselves to the Lord, He commits Himself to us.

"Into Your hands I commit my spirit" (31:5). Christ quoted this expression at the moment of His death on Calvary (Luke 23:46). God's honor is not bound up in preserving us from death, but in preserving us through death.

"Put to shame" (31:17). Two Heb. words are translated "shame" in the O.T. *Kalam* indicates the disgrace of a public humiliation and the

crushing blow to the individual's confidence this involves. The most common word, *bos(h)*, also pictures failure of some sort that leads to disgrace.

The psalmist publicly places his hope in God; being "put to shame" would be the result if God failed to deliver him. Because our hope is in God, who does deliver, His name is glorified when He relieves our distress, and at the same time we are vindicated in our faith.

PSALM 32: The Blessings of Forgiveness

David contrasts the blessing of forgiveness experienced with the anguish of refusing to confess sin (32:1-5). Out of the experience he shares advice (vv. 6-7) and conveys the promise that God will guide the forgiven and surround the person who trusts in Him with unfailing love (vv. 8-11).

Key concepts. Confession »p. 892. Guilt »p. 79. Atonement »p. 69. Sacrifice »pp. 78, 862.

Forgiveness (32:1). Hebrew words translated "forgive" include *kapar*, which indicates the removal of sin or ritual defilement by an atoning sacrifice, and *nasa'*. This latter word means to "lift up" or "take away." In forgiveness, God takes away the sin which makes the sinner guilty and releases us from the threat of punishment.

Another word translated forgive is *salah*, which means to pardon. Isaiah urges sinners to turn to God, confident that the Lord will have mercy and will "freely pardon" (Isa. 55:7). Old Testament pardon is closely tied to atoning sacrifices (cf. Lev. 4).

The O.T. makes it clear that we have hope for forgiveness solely because of who God is. There is nothing in human beings that merits pardon, but it's "in accordance with Your great love" that God forgives the sin of His people (Num. 14:19). Yet, despite the clear proclamation of divine forgiveness in the O.T. and the relief expressed by those who experienced it, the O.T.

never explains how a holy God is able to absolve those who believe in Him.

That mystery is resolved in the N.T. where the Gk. word, *aphesis*, is used to indicate remission of sins (cf. Matt. 26:28; Mark 1:4; Luke 1:77; 24:47; Acts 2:38; 5:31; 10:43; 13:38; Eph. 1:7; Col. 1:14; Heb. 9:22; 10:18). The preceding, key N.T. passages link forgiveness with Jesus and His death. Jesus sacrificed Himself taking, as our substitute, the punishment God has decreed for sin. Objectively, then, forgiveness is a loving act by God in which, in view of Christ's sacrifice, He pronounces the guilty innocent and so takes away our sins forever.

Counsel of God (32:8). Objectively, the "counsel" of God is His fixed purpose. Subjectively, God counsels us by leading us to choices which He knows are best for us. How vital to be in fellowship with the Lord, who alone can "instruct you and teach you in the way you should go."

PSALM 33: Praise for God's Faithfulness

The psalmist calls for spontaneous praise to God (33:1-3), the dependable Creator (vv. 4-9) and shaper of history (vv. 10-11). God has shown His loyalty to His people (vv. 12-19), and God's people hope joyfully in Him (vv. 20-22).

Key concepts. Faithfulness »p. 141. Creation »p. 430. God's choice of Israel »p. 124. Hope »p. 465.

Praise is fitting (33:1). Praise is appropriate because: *God's Word is true (trustworthy) *He Himself is faithful in all He does *He loves justice *Earth is filled with expressions of His love *He created all things *He sustains all things *He shapes history to accomplish His purposes *He chose Israel as His inheritance *He watches (pays close attention to) all humanity *He guards those who fear Him *He delivers from death those who hope in Him. How could we not praise such a wonderful God!

Waiting in hope (33:20). In the O.T. "waiting" and "hope" are so intimately connected that one of the Heb. words translated "hope" (*yahal*) is also rendered "wait" at times.

This psalm is an important one for people who are waiting. We have not yet received what we yearn for. But because we know God is dependable, we remain optimistic and are filled with joy. "I will always have hope," Ps. 71:14 affirms.

PSALM 34: A Righteous Man's Praise for Deliverance

David praises God for His continual goodness to him (34:1-7) and calls on the hearer to "taste and see that the Lord is good" (vv. 8-10). Taking the role of a teacher, David urges his people ("children") to do good (vv. 11-14), assuring them that God supervises the results of their choices (vv. 15-16) and responds to the cry of the righteous (vv. 17-22).

Key concepts. Soul »p. 495. Angel of the Lord »p. 37.

Background. This teaching psalm shares lessons David learned when he became discouraged and fled to Philistia. When he was recognized he pretended to be insane and was driven out of his enemy's land. God delivered David despite his lapse of faith, teaching the psalmist that God keeps continual watch on His own.

"This poor man called" (34:6). The key is when we call. David could have called on God while still in his homeland, not after he ventured into the land of Israel's enemies.

"Taste and see" (34:8). Taste is an important figure of speech in the Bible. Everywhere it's used figuratively taste suggests full participation in and/or experience of the thing enjoyed. Here, the invitation to "taste and see that the Lord is good" is a call to rely fully on Him and to experience the benefits of a personal relationship with God.

The blessed man (34:8). The psalm says that man who "takes refuge in" the Lord is blessed. *The Expository Dictionary of Bible Words* (Zondervan, 1985) summarizes the description of the blessed person found in the psalms: one who "does not walk in the counsel of the wicked" (Ps. 1:1), whose "sins are covered" (32:1), and who "takes refuge in Him" (34:8). The blessed one "makes the Lord his trust"

(40:4; 84:12), has regard for the weak (41:1), and possesses the strength of the Lord (84:5). The blessed have learned to acclaim the Lord (89:15), are disciplined by Him (94:12), maintain justice (106:3), and fear the Lord (112:1; 128:1). The ways of the blessed are blameless for they keep the Lord's statutes (119:1-2).

The blessed are those whose help and whose hope is in the Lord (146:5). These are the qualities that bring us the blessings God is so eager to pour out on His own.

"The fear of the Lord" (34:11-16). Here the phrase means "to show respect for" God. How does David suggest we do this? The next verses, quoted in 1 Peter 3:10-12, affirm that God actively observes our actions and so orders the consequences of our moral choices that good is rewarded and evil is punished. Learning to "fear the Lord" means in part to respect God enough that we choose to do what is right and leave the results to Him.

What a contrast this is to "situation ethics." In that system the person looks at supposed results and chooses what he or she hopes will be "good" for the persons affected. But biblical ethics says do the right thing and respect God enough to believe that He will see to the consequences of our choices.

PSALM 35: A Cry for Justice

David calls God to come to his aid (35:1-6) against enemies who have attacked him without just cause (vv. 7-16). David prays God will not be an onlooker but will rescue him as justice requires (vv. 17-25), sure that He will be exalted in David's vindication (vv. 26-28).

Key concepts. Legal justice system »pp. 130, 132.

Treatment of enemies (35:11-16). Jesus taught love your enemies (Matt 5:43-48). While this command is not found in the O.T., David had surely understood and applied this moral im-perative.

"Do not let them gloat over me" (35:24). Don't try to take revenge on enemies. God will balance the moral books. Our role is to follow David's example and do our enemies good.

PSALM 36: A Word about the Wicked

God gives David a word about the wicked (36:1-4). The righteous find relief in God's unfailing love (vv. 5-9). That love protects the upright from hostility of evil men (vv. 10-12).

Key concepts. Wicked »p. 350. Light »p. 685.

Oracle (36:1). Two Heb. words are translated "oracle." *Ne'um* means "an utterance" and affirms divine origin and authority for what is said. *Massa'* is a message of judgment and usually appears where "oracle against" is found in English versions. Each of these words affirms that what is said originates in God and not the person who delivers the oracle.

No fear (36:1). The Heb. word *pahad* is "dread," not the usual term which indicates a reverential awe of God. The wicked persist in

doing evil with no pangs of conscience and no sense of impending divine judgment.

David reminds us that those with no sense of responsibility to God for their actions, or fear of punishment, cease "to be wise and to do good" (v. 3).

God's protective love (36:10-12). Increasing brutal crimes in our society remind us how much we need to experience God's protective love.

PSALM 37: Trust in the Lord and Do Good

David teaches believers how to survive in the land of the wicked. A series of proverbs instructs us (37:1-8), giving way to promises that the wicked will be punished (vv. 9-22). God upholds the just (vv. 23-31), despite the intent of the wicked to harm them (vv. 32-40).

Key concepts. Evil »p. 72. Doing good »p. 849. Trust »p. 354. The wicked »p. 350. Salvation »p. 426.

Response to the wicked (37:1-10). How is the believer to respond to wicked individuals?

Don't	Do
Fret (brood) v. 1	Trust in the Lord v. 3
Be envious v. 1	Do good v. 3
Fret v. 7	Enjoy your blessings v. 3
Be angry v. 8	Delight in the Lord v. 4
Fret v. 8	Commit way to God v. 5
	Trust in Him v. 5
	Be still before God v. 7
	Wait patiently for Him v. 7

Anger (37:8). This anger is what most of us

would call "righteous indignation." It is clearly anger directed at the right thing—wicked wrongdoing. But here anger is linked with the repeated concept of "fret." This is no sudden surge of anger that passes away. This is a smoldering anger, a hostile resentment that we nurture and in time dominates our attitude toward wrongdoers. This is the anger we must release, to replace with a perspective shaped by a quiet trust in God.

"Wait for the Lord and keep His way" (37:34). God doesn't expect us to remain passive while we wait for Him to act. He tells us to be active in doing good.

PSALM 38: Plea of the Overwhelmed

David begs God to stop disciplining him (38:1-2), powerfully describing his emotional turmoil and physical sufferings (vv. 3-12). Yet even when troubled by his sin, David waits for the Lord, confident "my God" will save (vv. 13-22).

Key concepts. Anger of God »pp. 65, 72. Discipline »p. 866. Sickness »pp. 412, 438. Confession »p. 892.

Psalm 39: Putting Pain in Perspective

Silent out of fear of the wicked (39:1-3), David asks God to help him sense the impermanence of life (vv. 4-6). Now, admitting his pain is due to his sins and honoring God for His justice, David's hope is restored (vv. 7-11) and he prays to God for relief.

Key concepts. Guilt »p. 79. Confession »p. 892.

PSALM 40: Lament of a Dedicated Man

Deeply thankful for all God has done, David has fully dedicated himself to the Lord (40:1-10). Yet David cries out for mercy, for even total commitment has not given him an easy life (vv. 11-16). Although "poor and needy," David rejoices in the Lord, "my help and my deliverer" (vv. 17).

PSALM 41: Blessings of the Merciful

This instructional psalm teaches that God will bless the merciful (41:1-3), even taking vengeance on their malicious enemies (vv. 4-9). God remains faithful and merits praise (vv. 10-13).

PSALMS 42–43: A Song of Yearning and Praise

(Note: In many Hebrew manuscripts these two psalms are one [cf. 42:5, 11 with 43:5]). David yearns for God as his enemies taunt him (42:1-5). Although heavily weighed down, he reminds himself to hope in God (vv. 6-11). He cries out to God for vindication, deeply disturbed at his enemies' success (43:1-2). David determines to urgently seek God's presence (vv. 3-4) and finds renewed assurance from God (v. 5).

Key concepts. Hope »p. 465. Praise »p. 380.

"Why?" (43:5) The tone of voice used when we ask "why" tells so much. There's a child's complaining "why." And there's the despairing adult's anguished "why," drawn out by life's unfairness. The repeated refrain, "Why are you downcast, O my soul," of 42:5, 11 is the despairing kind, for David says, "My soul is downcast" (42:5). Yet there is a subtle shift in tone, an excitement, as the question is repeated in 43:5. This is the "why" of freedom rediscovered. Why should I be downcast when my hope is in God?

PSALM 44: The Prayer of a Puzzled People

God is the sole source of Israel's victories over her enemies (44:1-8). Yet the nation experiences defeat (vv. 9-16). Defeat would have been understandable if Israel had denied God, but at this time God's people have been faithful to Him and kept His Law (vv. 17-22). All God's puzzled people can do as they cry out "Why?" is to urge the Lord to act for them soon (vv. 18-26).

Key concepts. Covenant »p. 62. War »p. 133. Law »p. 145.

PSALM 45: Praise at a Royal Wedding

The psalm praises the royal groom (45:1-9), followed by advice for the king's bride (vv. 10-15) and a wedding benediction (vv. 16-17).

PSALM 46: In Praise of Who God Is

The psalmist praises God for the help He gives (46:1-3), His presence now (vv. 4-7), and the future peace He will establish (vv. 8-11).

PSALM 47: Celebrating God's Universal Rule

All peoples are called to praise God (47:1-4). He is acclaimed as He takes the scepter and His throne (vv. 5-9).

PSALM 48: A Song of Zion

God is praised as the ruler and defender of the holy city, Jerusalem (48:1-3), who keeps the city secure (vv. 4-8) and so stimulates the praise of His people (vv. 9-14).

Key concepts. Jerusalem »pp. 205, 451.

"**Zion.**" The hill on which the original Jebusite fortress of Jerusalem stood was Zion (2 Sam. 5:6-9). David brought the ark to this hill.

This psalm's celebratory tone reflects Israel's identification of Jerusalem as God's city, and the joy that the security of His presence provides.

PSALM 49: A Meditation on Wealth and Wickedness

The psalmist announces he is about to solve one of life's perplexing riddles (49:1-4). The wicked who prosper materially are not really blessed, for they trust their wealth and die like the animals, without hope (vv. 5-13). Ultimately the upright will rule, for God will take them to Himself (vv. 14-15). Thus, the believer need not be envious when an ungodly man grows rich, for the doom of such men is sure (vv. 16-20).

Key concepts. Wealth »pp. 129, 836. Wicked »p. 350. Trust »p. 354. Resurrection »p. 522.

Parallel passages. Job 21 argues powerfully that the wicked often do prosper in this world. Psalm 73 relates the feelings of a believer who initially envies the prosperous wicked in view of his own poverty and illness. This psalm reminds us that the "lifestyles of the rich and famous" are deceiving. The wicked wealthy tend to trust their riches rather than God, even though they know that like all living things they face death.

PSALM 50: A Vision of God's Heavenly Court

Asaph describes God's courtroom, where the wicked are indicted. The glorious Judge takes His seat to judge His covenant people (50:1-6). They are examined on two issues: formalism in worship (vv. 7-15) and wickedness in their relationships with others (vv. 16-23). The psalmist's vision is to warn God's people away from those actions which will most surely be judged.

Key concepts. Judge »p. 372. Wicked »p. 350. Covenant »p. 62. Law »p. 145.

Call on God (50:15). The Heb. phrase means to ask God for something and expect Him to act.

God's instruction (50:16). Talking God's Word means nothing; it's living by God's Word that counts.

PSALM 51: Confession of Sin

A year after his sin with Bathsheba David cries out for forgiveness (51:1). He confesses his sin (vv. 2-6) and appeals for a cleansing which will restore his joy (vv. 7-9). When God purifies his heart David again will be able to influence others (vv. 10-14) and, humbled, David will again praise his Lord (vv. 15-17). Then God's people too will prosper (vv. 18-19).

Key concepts. Confess »p. 892. Justification »p. 789. Forgiveness »pp. 357, 863. Holy Spirit »pp. 744, 759.

"Mercy" (51:1). Forgiveness is rooted in God's compassion for the helpless.

"Sin" (51:1-2). These verses use all three basic Heb. words for sin. These are: (1) *hata'*, to sin, miss the mark; (2) *pesa'*, to rebel, transgress; and (3) *'awon*, iniquity, guilt. Each of these words implies an absolute divine standard and defines sin in relation to that standard. We may miss the mark because of our frailties, we may revolt against God's standard, or we may twist it in an attempt to avoid acknowledging guilt. But in fact all people, like David, do sin.

Psalm 51 develops the O.T.'s most complete single statement of a theology of sin. It identifies the nature of man's failure by the key terms used (vv. 1-2). It affirms that sin is against God, who establishes the standard (v. 3). It suggests that the seed of sin is rooted in fallen human nature, so that we not only perform sinful acts but that we ourselves are sinful by nature (v. 5).

"I know my transgressions" (51:3). The story of David's sin with Bathsheba, found in 2 Sam. 11, tells us that he lived with the unconfessed sin bottled up within him for a year, from Bathsheba's conception till the child was born (cf. Ps. 32).

Whenever you or I are aware of transgression, we need to hurry to God to find the forgiveness that brings renewed fellowship with the Lord.

"A sinner from birth" (51:5). The biblical doctrine of depravity is often misunderstood. David says, "I was sinful (*'awon*) at birth, sinful (*hata'*) from the time my mother conceived me." David's very nature was bent out of God's intended shape, so that he fell short of God's design for humankind. It is this flaw in man's nature, which Rom. 5:12-21 traces to Adam's fall, that makes men and women sinners and which generates acts of sin. To say that mankind is depraved means that sin has a firm grip on each human being and that all people perform acts of sin.

How glorious then the hope that rings through this psalm. God can do what we cannot, He can create a clean heart in us. Through God's grace and forgiveness we can be freed from sin's domination.

"Truth" (51:6). The basic concept underlying the Heb. word for "truth" is that of reliability. A thing is true because it accords with reality and can be relied on. *The Expository Dictionary of Bible Words* (Zondervan, 1985) says, " 'Truth in the inward parts' (Ps. 51:6) is probably best interpreted by 1 John 1. It is living honestly with God and self, confessing failures and yet struggling to choose the path God has laid out in revelation."

In short, being real in our relationship with God and ourselves means a total honesty in evaluating all we do.

Create a pure heart (51:10). The Heb. word "create" does not mean to make something from nothing. Instead, it means to originate and is frequently used when an O.T. writer wishes to affirm that God alone is the source of a certain thing. Thus God created the heavens and the earth, an act far beyond human capacity to duplicate. And it is God who, in extending forgiveness, transforms the inner personality of the believer. We are born in sin, but we are reborn with a pure heart.

Taking away the Holy Spirit? (51:11) In the O.T. the Holy Spirit was experienced by believers as an enabling divine presence (»p. 73). But Saul, David's predecessor, had been deprived of the Spirit's presence because of his sin (1 Sam. 16:14). David, then, is expressing concern that his sin might be so great that God would also remove His Spirit from him.

There is a vital difference, however, between the enabling presence of the Spirit we see in the O.T. and the indwelling presence of the Spirit seen in the N.T. God's Spirit is His guarantee of redemption (Eph. 1:13-14).

"Then" (51:13). To reach the lost you and I must live close to God.

What God wants of us (51:17). David calls for a "broken spirit" and a "broken and contrite heart." Don't make the mistake of thinking this means God seeks to crush us, or turn us into weeping nobodies. Each image reflects back on David's willful sin in taking Bathsheba and is an admission of his lack of humility before God. David knew what was right, but did wrong anyway! The broken and contrite heart is ever responsive to God, willing to do His will.

PSALM 52: Reflections on a Treacherous Man

David finds comfort in comparing the certain destruction of the treacherous (52:1-7) with the destiny of the godly (vv. 8-9).

PSALM 53: A Cry for Salvation

Like Psalm 14, this psalm decrys the corruption of the human race (53:1-3) and yearns for the establishment of God's kingdom (vv. 4-6).

Key concepts. Fool »p. 353. Kingdom »pp. 380, 443.

(53:2-3). Human beings measure themselves against one another and deal with grades of good and bad. This psalm reflects God's view that all mankind is depraved. Measured against God rather than against one another, "there is no one who does good" (Ps. 53:1).

David yearns for the time when God will bring his own salvation (53:6). That rescue will be from the sin in our own hearts.

PSALM 54: Praise When in Peril

Although David is being pursued by his enemies, he is buoyed up by the confidence that God is helping him.

PSALM 55: The Anguish of Betrayal

David shares his dismay at betrayal by a close friend (55:1-8). He cries out to God to judge the wicked (vv. 9-11), but still cannot come to grips with the fact that one of his intimates has turned against him (vv. 12-15). Yet despite the terrible experience, David remains confident that the Lord will sustain him and so casts his cares on God (vv. 16-23).

Key concepts. Prayer »pp. 608–609. Wicked »p. 350. Friendship »p. 390. Fulfilled prophecy »p. 417.

PSALM 56: The Antidote to Fear

Fear and trust wage a fierce battle within as David faces enemies who conspire against him (56:1-7). Trust wins out, as David remains confident that God is for him (vv. 8-13).

Superscription. Fear drove David into Philistine territory where he was recognized and had to pretend madness to escape (1 Sam. 21). The experience taught David lessons he shares here.

Fear as an emotion. Fear is anticipation that something terrible may happen to us. Fear is a positive thing when it helps us avoid dangerous situations. It's good to teach a child to be afraid to run out into the street. But fear is negative when it keeps us from doing something we know is right, or moves us to do something that

we know is wrong. Everyone will feel fear. How we handle it is what counts.

The psalm gives us helpful guidance. (1) David felt fear, (2) turned to God to express trust, (3) recalled God's self-revelation in Scripture, and (4) determined not to expect evil, because God was with him.

"When" (56:3-4). It's not a matter of "if" we feel fear, but "when." Yet when fear comes, it need not victimize us. See fear as a fresh opportunity to trust God.

PSALM 57: God's Faithful Love

David triumphantly praises God for deliverance from Saul (cf. 1 Sam. 22–24), thrilled that God "sends His love and His faithfulness" (Ps. 57:1-11).

PSALM 58: Against Unjust Judges

David rebukes judges who pervert justice (58:1-5) and calls on God to judge them (vv. 6-9). The righteous can take comfort in the certainty that ultimately God will reward them while punishing their oppressors (vv. 10-11).

Key concept. Judge »p. 372.

PSALM 59: Unshakable Trust

David cries out as a persecuted innocent (59:1-5). Yet he remains confident that his enemies will not harm him (vv. 6-10), for God will bring them down to demonstrate His royal sovereignty (vv. 11-13). Though his enemies snarl at his heels, David will trust in God's love and praise the Lord (vv. 14-17).

David's vision of God. David is confident because he has a clear vision of God. How does he see the Lord? David's God is: *able to deliver (v. 1); *the historic God of Israel (v. 5); *one who punishes the wicked (v. 5); *David's strength and fortress (v. 9); *his shield (v. 11); *Earth's ruler (v. 13); *and most of all, David's "loving God" (vv. 10, 17).

PSALM 60: A Prayer for Aid in War

God's displeasure assures defeat (60:1-5), while trust in His promise of victory (vv. 6-8) is a solid basis for hope (vv. 9-12).

Key concepts. War »p. 133. Covenant »pp. 32, 62.

PSALM 61: The Cry of the Faint

David confesses his weakness and seeks strength in God (61:1-2). His past experience with God encourages him (vv. 3-7) and he promises to praise God in the future (vv. 8).

PSALM 62: Rest in God

David finds rest in God from the turmoil caused by enemies (62:1-4). He affirms his trust in God and calls us to trust Him too (vv. 5-10). And because of who God is, we can (vv. 11-12).

Key concepts. Rest »p. 857. Trust »p. 354.

"One thing . . . two things" (62:11-12). These are two of the most powerful and wonderful verses in the entire Bible. What a joy to know—and to learn by experience—that God is strong and that He is loving.

PSALM 63: Longing for God

David cries out of his deep longing to experience God's presence (63:1). He suddenly realizes that his soul finds just that satisfaction through praise (vv. 2-8). With the fresh touch of God praise provides him, David has renewed confidence in the Lord and experiences a unique joy (vv. 9-11).

Key concept. Praise »p. 380.

PSALM 64: A Prayer for Protection

David prays for protection from enemies (64:1-2) who plot against the godly (vv. 3-6). When God brings them to ruin all will fear Him, and the godly will rejoice (vv. 7-10).

The perfect crime? (64:6) In fiction, the criminal gets away with the perfect crime. But this really is fiction! A criminal may avoid man's courtroom. But none escape God's justice.

PSALM 65: A Harvest Hymn

The forgiven praise God (65:1-4), deeply aware of the awesome power He has exercised on their behalf (vv. 5-8) and thankful for the agricultural abundance that brings His people prosperity (vv. 9-13).

Key concepts. Forgiveness »p. 357. Wealth »p. 125. Righteousness »p. 120.

PSALM 66: A Psalm of Thanksgiving

The community of faith praises God joyfully (66:1-12). And the psalmist, representing the individual believer, commits himself to praise God and pray to Him (vv. 13-20).

Key concepts. Worship »p. 380. Praise »p. 380. Temple »p. 283. Fear of God »p. 387. Sin »p. 362.

"You . . . tested us" (66:8-12). When we can see God's hand in our pain and praise Him for our suffering, we are becoming mature.
"I will" (66:13). The first 12 verses speak of "we." Here the psalm shifts to "I." When each individual is moved to heartfelt worship the church honors God.

PSALM 67: In Praise of God's Graciousness

The psalmist builds on the famous "priestly blessing" of Numbers 6:24-26 (67:1). He asks that all God's people might continually praise Him (vv. 2-5) and that God might continue to pour out His blessings on them (vv. 6-7).

Key concept. Praise »p. 380.

"Face shine" (67:1). The image symbolizes favor; looking at someone approvingly.
"The peoples" (67:2-5). The "peoples" seems to indicate other nations. Verse 2 explains: The psalmist is eager for the blessings of salvation to be experienced by all.

PSALM 68: A Celebration of Triumph

David celebrates God's power and goodness (68:1-6) before reviewing His historic acts on behalf of Israel (vv. 7-14). These culminate in God's choice of Jerusalem as the site of His sanctuary (vv. 15-18). The result of this triumph is celebrated by God's people (vv. 19-27), who now call on Him to scatter their enemies (vv. 28-31) and praise Him for His majestic rule (vv. 32-35).

Key concepts. Jerusalem »pp. 205, 451. Temple »p. 283.

"Ascended on high" (68:18). The passage foreshadows the return of Jesus to heavenly realms after His resurrection. This event is described in Acts 1:1-11, and its significance is interpreted in John 3:13, 6:62, 20:17, Acts 2:34, and Eph. 4:8-9. (See also Phil. 2:5-11 and 1 Tim. 3:16.) The ascension of Jesus marks His triumph over the powers of sin and death.
"Gifts" (68:18). In Eph. 4:8 the conqueror distributes his spoils to his own people. Jesus, triumphant, distributed spiritual gifts to the church.

PSALM 69: A Prayer for Deliverance

Surrounded by enemies eager to destroy him (69:1-4), David reminds God that though a sinner he is suffering for the Lord's sake (vv. 5-12). David begs God to rescue him (vv. 13-18) and shares his despair (vv. 19-21). He asks the Lord to cause his enemies' downfall (vv. 22-28) and expresses his confidence that God will act (vv. 29-36).

Key concepts. Hope »p. 465. Shame »p. 357. Suffering »p. 877. Prophecy »p. 434.

Prophecy. This psalm grows out of David's personal experience, but also foreshadows the experience of Christ. Passages that the N.T. applies to Jesus are: *the antagonism of his fellows (v. 4 with John 15:23). *his zeal to serve God (v. 9 with John 2:17). *the vinegar offered the sufferer (v. 21 with Matt. 27:48).

PSALM 70: A Petition for Rescue

This brief, urgent prayer appeals to God to respond in view of the psalmist's desperate need.

PSALM 71: The Testimony of the Aged

The psalmist speaks out of mature experience with the Lord. He prays for help (71:1-4), but affirms his confidence in One he has found faithful from his youth up (vv. 5-13). Although in danger, the psalmist will "always have hope" and will always praise God (vv. 14-18). Despite life's troubles, he counts on God to restore him (vv. 19-21) and commits himself to a life of praise (vv. 22-24).

Key concepts. Hope »p. 465. Forsake »pp. 186, 370.

PSALM 72: Honoring the Messianic King

Solomon's prayer to be endowed with wisdom (72:1) prefigures the rule of Messiah, who will judge righteously (vv. 2-7) and rule "from sea to sea" (vv. 8-11). His commitment to rescue the needy (vv. 12-14) wins him an enduring name (vv. 15-17) and brings God unending praise (vv. 18-19).

Key concepts. Messiah »p. 431. Kingdom »pp. 380, 443. Justice »pp. 141, 541. Blessed »pp. 49, 873.

"For" (72:12-14). The little word directs our look back at the prediction, "All kings will bow down to Him" (v. 11). What makes the rule of this king so special? Simply that he is dedicated to save the needy and rescue the oppressed. He has God's own compassion and the power to act on others' behalf. These verses forever change our notion of "rule." The central issue of rule is not the power to use others, but the willingness to serve them.

PSALM 73: Pondering the Prosperity of the Wicked

Asaph confesses envy of the carefree life of the wicked in this world (73:1-12). He became bitter, feeling his own commitment to godliness was all in vain (vv. 13-15). Then, while worshiping, he realized the very prosperity of the wicked was "slippery ground," for they felt no need of God and were vulnerable to judgment (vv. 16-20). Suddenly Asaph felt foolish—and relieved. He had God, now and forever. And having God as his portion far outweighs a carefree life (vv. 21-28).

Key concepts. Wicked »pp. 29, 350. Arrogant »pp. 119, 352. Prosperity/Wealth »p. 125. Envy »p. 864.

Lifestyles of the rich and famous (73:4-12). His initial look describes their material situation (vv. 4-5), but then goes on to sketch its impact on their personality (vv. 6-12). Those who have it all tend to become arrogant. They sense no need for God and no need to be considerate of others.

"Final destiny" (73:17). Everything that happens to us on Earth must be evaluated in terms of its impact on our final destiny.

PSALM 74: A Prayer for Remembrance

Asaph begs God to remember His people in a time of national disaster (74:1-9). He urges God to hurry and restore the honor due His name (vv. 10-17) and to keep His covenant promises to aid His oppressed people (vv. 18-21). The psalm ends with a passionate appeal for God to rise up and to act (vv. 22-23).

Key concepts. Remember »pp. 98, 321. Enemies »p. 91. Covenant »pp. 32, 62. Zion »p. 361. Temple »p. 283.

PSALM 75: Celebrating God's Victory

The psalmist thanks God for appointing a time of judgment (75:1-3). God is judge (vv. 4-8) and is to be praised continually for His certain victory over the wicked (vv. 9-10).

Key concepts. Judge »p. 372. Wicked »pp. 29, 350.

PSALM 76: In Praise of God's Power

God is known in His victories over Israel's enemies (76:1-7). His just judgments teach people to fear Him and bow down (vv. 8-12).

Key concepts. Fear of God »p. 387. Judge »p. 372.

God's anger. Anger makes us draw back from people. But God's anger is different. It's intended to cause us to take Him seriously (to "fear" God) and move us to come to Him (v. 11). Even when directed against us, God's anger never overwhelms His love. Human beings can trust even an angry God to welcome the guilty with open arms.

PSALM 77: Meditating When Distressed

Asaph is unable to find comfort even in prayer (77:1-3). He cannot understand why God seems unwilling to express His covenant love to Israel (vv. 4-9). Yet he finds the answer his troubled heart requires by meditating on God's mighty acts for Israel at the time of the Exodus (vv. 10-20). God who unleashed His power to redeem Israel will surely act for them again.

Key concepts. Reject/Abandon »pp. 186, 370. Miracle »p. 57. Power »p. 430.

PSALM 78: Lessons from History

Asaph's psalm fulfills each generation's obligation to share its knowledge of God with the next (78:1-8). Because one generation forgot God they violated His covenant and suffered defeat (vv. 9-11). So Asaph catalogs the wonderful things God has done in revealing Himself to Israel: He hurled plagues against Egypt (vv. 12-20). He disciplined and fed the wilderness generation (vv. 21-33). He punished and forgave (vv. 34-39). Yet Israel rebelled (vv. 40-55) and turned to idolatry (vv. 56-64). Yet, later God beat back His people's enemies and chose David to shepherd His people (vv. 65-72). How great the sin of man and how much greater the grace of God!

What shall we pass on? **(78:4)** Asaph pinpoints what each generation needs to pass on to the next: "the praiseworthy deeds of the Lord." Let's not hesitate to share what God has done in our lives with our children. They will see and come to know Him through what we impart (v. 7).

"In spite of all this" **(78:32).** It's not enough to be open about who God is and what He's done for us. It's also necessary to be honest about our own frailties and failings. How important for our children to know that He is a loving, forgiving God. He disciplines us when we sin, but never withdraws His love.

PSALM 79: A Prayer for Restoration

Asaph laments over a devastating invasion of Jerusalem (79:1-4) and begs God to deliver His people by judging their hostile neighbors (vv. 5-12). When God acts, His people will praise Him forever (v. 13).

Key concepts. God's wrath »pp. 65, 72. Mercy »p. 880.

PSALM 80: A Prayer for Restoration

The psalmist appeals to God, the "Shepherd of Israel," to save His people (80:1-3). Israel is experiencing God's anger (discipline) (vv. 4-7), for He has withdrawn His protection (vv. 8-16). Again Asaph asks God to restore His people that they may be saved (vv. 17-19).

Key concepts. Shepherd »p. 355. Vine »pp. 414, 692.

PSALM 81: A Tabernacles' Psalm

Tradition identifies this psalm with the Feast of Tabernacles (Lev. 23:33-43; Deut. 16:13-15). Israel is to share the joyful celebration (81:1-2) decreed by God (vv. 3-5) at which His people recall His words to them (vv. 6-16).

Key concept. Tabernacles »p. 89.

PSALM 82: In Praise of Righteous Judgments

God is the universal Judge (82:1) and calls human judges to defend the rights of the helpless (vv. 2-5). Unjust human judges will be judged by God (vv. 6-7).

Key concepts. Judges »p. 372. Justice »pp. 130, 132.

"Gods" **(82:1-6).** The use of *elohim* ("gods") here does not suggest deity, but rather that God in making some men judges shared His prerogatives with them. Jesus referred to verse 6 when defending His claim to be the Son of God (John 10:34). If some of the divine privileges were shared with mere human beings, how could Christ's enemies condemn One whose miracles showed His divine commission from making a somewhat similar, though greater, claim?

PSALM 83: Danger and Deliverance

Surrounding nations actively plot the destruction of Israel (83:1-8). The psalmist calls on God to act and deliver His people (vv. 9-18).

Key concepts. Deliverance »p. 54. Enemies »p. 91. Chaff »p. 350. Shame »p. 357.

PSALM 84: Faith's Pilgrimage

The psalm expresses the yearnings and the prayers of a pilgrim approaching the Jerusalem temple. Each has a place here: longing (84:1-4), pilgrimage (vv. 5-7), and prayer (vv. 8-12).

Key concepts. Blessing »p. 127. Temple »p. 283. Festivals »p. 89. Prayer »pp. 608–609. Trust »p. 354.

PSALM 85: Praise for Forgiveness

The psalmist praises God for forgiving sin (85:1-3) and pleads for restoration and deliverance (vv. 4-7). He listens intently and receives a promise from the Lord (vv. 8-9). Now he is confident that the Lord will soon give what is good (vv. 10-13).

Key concepts. Forgiveness »p. 357. Love »p. 351. Faithfulness »p. 141.

Four foundation stones (85:10). What gives us confidence in future restoration? Four attributes of God: love, which makes Him want to give us what is best; faithfulness, which guarantees He will keep the promises made to us in Christ; righteousness, which assures us He will do right; and peace, which brings all to harmony and balance. Our restoration is assured by who our God is.

PSALM 86: Prayer of the Poor and Needy

David pleads his relationship with the Lord (86:1-4) and God's character (vv. 5-10) when he prays for holiness (vv. 11-13) and protection (vv. 14-17).

Key concepts. Poor »p. 90. Mercy/Compassion »p. 880. Forgiveness »p. 357. Worship »p. 380. Truth »p. 836. Praise »p. 380. Arrogance »pp. 119, 352. Grace »p. 789.

"I" (86:1-4). These verses teach us what's important about the person who prays. He or she is to *come empty, as one who is poor and needy; *come committed, as one who is devoted to God; *come confidently, as one who trusts in God; *come, calling constantly. When this kind of person lifts up his or her soul to the Lord, God hears.

PSALM 87: A Psalm of Ultimate Victory

The psalmist affirms God's love for Jerusalem (87:1-3). One day the nations will honor the Lord (v. 4) and Zion will be praised (vv. 5-7).

PSALM 88: Lament of the Suffering

This psalm captures the grief of the suffering saint of every era. The psalmist shares his anguish (9:1-9a) and records his prayer (vv. 9b-12). Despite his prayers, he has suffered and felt despair all his life (vv. 13-18).

PSALM 89: Psalm of the Davidic Covenant

Psalm 89 honors God's covenant promise to establish King David's line forever (89:1-4). The psalmist praises God's faithfulness (vv. 5-8), His power (vv. 9-13), and His righteousness (vv. 14-18). He records the basic promises made in this divine covenant with the shepherd king (vv. 19-37) and begs God to act on them (vv. 38-52).

Key concepts. Covenant »p. 35. Faithfulness »p. 141. Love »p. 351. David »p. 191. Holiness »p. 879. Anointed »p. 187.

The Davidic Covenant. The basic structure of the O.T. is covenantal. The O.T. echoes and reechoes the conviction that God made specific promises to human beings which not only shape the covenant people's identity but also outline the future of humankind. The core covenant promises given to Abraham set aside his descendants through Isaac and Jacob, the Jews, as a special people. Later covenant promises were given to the Jews through Moses. These were intended to show each generation of Jews the way to experience God's blessing in their lifetime, while awaiting the ultimate fulfillment of God's promises.

Still later, special covenant promises were given to David. These promises revealed the fact that God intends to keep His promises to Abraham through the agency of a Ruler who will be one of David's physical descendants. Until the birth of that King, commonly called the Messiah, or Anointed One, David would always have a descendant on the throne of Israel, or qualified being to sit on that throne. These promises, stated in 2 Sam. 7, are celebrated in this psalm and given fresh expression here. Thus:

89:20-25. The king will be strengthened and sustained by God and his kingdom established.

89:26-27. God will maintain a father-son relationship with the king and appoint him His heir ("firstborn").

89:28-29. God will establish the king's line forever and maintain His covenant forever.

89:30-37. If kings in David's line turn from God they will be disciplined, but the covenant promises will never be withdrawn.

In these promises made to David, that ruler also represents his descendant, Jesus, and so promises of an eternal kingdom and worldwide rule were made to Christ, David's greater son, in the words spoken to David. Ancient rabbi and later Christian theologian alike have understood this psalm to serve not only as David's title to the blessings of God, but as the title deed granted the Messiah as well.

Key words. Several key words and concepts are repeated in this psalm:

Faithfulness (89:1, 2, 5, 8, 33, 49). This is a concept related to the Heb. idea of truth. A person is faithful if her words are true: that is, if her actions match her words. God is a faithful person; that means what He says He will surely do. Thus, God's covenant promises are rock solid: They are fully guaranteed by the very character of God Himself.

Love (89:1, 2, 14, 24, 28, 33, 49). The Heb. word is *hesed*, which means covenant loyalty or steadfast love. Again, the covenant promises given David are guaranteed by the character of God who gave them.

Covenant (89:3, 28, 34, 39). A covenant is a formal, legally binding agreement between two or more parties. Often covenants called for promises to be made by all parties in the agreements. Biblical covenants, however, are commitments by one person, God, to do what He promises a person or group to do. While the word "covenant" is not found in the original 2 Sam. 7 or 1 Chron. 17 accounts of the promises being made to David, this psalm makes it clear Israel saw them as covenant commitments.

"Forsake" (89:30-37). The strong term, *'azab*, used here indicates willful rejection, a conscious choice to reject God. This is typically used when speaking of man abandoning or forsaking God. But it's typically not used of God. He may discipline us, but instead of rejecting us chooses to keep on loving.

"How long?" (89:46) The psalmist at last asks the right question. It's simply a matter of how long. For some of us the answer will be "tomorrow." For others, "not in this life." But whether the blessings we yearn for are to be ours in the next 24 hours or in eternity, God's promises still ring true. He loves us faithfully, and He will keep every commitment made to us in Christ.

For long centuries Israel waited for the promised messianic King to appear. At last, a full 1,000 years after David, He did! Today too we are waiting. In God's own time, Jesus will come again, and the covenant promises granted David will be kept in full.

PSALM 90: A Prayer of Moses

The psalm contrasts the everlasting quality of God (90:1-2) with man's frailty (vv. 3-6), which is a consequence of God's anger against sin (vv. 7-12). Yet God's mighty love can bring joy into the brief lives of His people (vv. 13-16) and make life meaningful and worthwhile (v. 17).

Key concepts. Anger of God »pp. 65, 72. Work »p. 28.

"Everlasting to everlasting" (90:2). Here eternity is not so much in view as "all time," from its beginning to its end. Thus, God is one who continually is.

"Dust" (90:3-6). Human beings, in contrast to God, have only momentary existence on Earth. Other verses in Ps. which emphasize this are 37:2; 102:4; 103:15-16.

PSALM 91: Praise for Security

The psalmist testifies to the benefits of trust in God (91:1-2). God and His angels guard the believer (vv. 3-13), and the Lord Himself promises protection (vv. 14-16).

Key concepts. Trust »p. 354. Faithfulness »p. 141. Angels »pp. 521, 855.

PSALM 92: Joy in God's Works

God's actions stimulate us to praise (92:1-7) and convince us that the wicked will perish and the righteous be rewarded (vv. 8-15).

Key concepts. Praise »p. 380. Joy »p. 269. Wicked »p. 350.

PSALM 93: God Reigns

God is in complete control as ruler of His universe (93:1-2). Creation testifies to His authority (vv. 3-4). And His holy statutes structure the moral universe (v. 5).

PSALM 94: A Prayer for Vengeance

The psalmist appeals to God as the Judge of the Earth to act against the wicked (94:1-7). He cries out, warning those who suppose God cannot see or hear their actions or punish their sins (vv. 8-11). The psalmist then expresses his satisfaction that God will one day take vengeance on those who condemn the innocent (v. 12-23).

Key concepts. Vengeance »p. 428. Judge »p. 372. Widow »p. 126. Fool »p. 353. Punish »p. 827. Wicked »p. 350.

"The ear" (94:9). The ear is more than the organ of hearing. It frequently implies not only reception of the message, but response to it as well. God, who designed the ear that we might hear and respond to Him, also hears and responds to our prayers.

PSALM 95: God, the Great King

The psalmist calls us to acknowledge the Lord as the "great God" above all others (95:1-5) and to worship Him (vv. 6-7). We worship by hearing and responding obediently to His voice (v. 8). Not to respond is to lose our opportunity for rest (vv. 9-11).

Key concepts. Worship »p. 380. Voice/Rest »p. 857.

PSALM 96: Praise from Nature and the Nations

The earth is invited to praise the Lord with a new song (96:1-3). All peoples (vv. 7-11) and creation itself will sing to God the great Creator (vv. 4-6) when He comes to judge the Earth (vv. 12-13).

Key concepts. Praise »p. 380. Glory »p. 74. Holiness »p. 879. Joy »pp. 269, 877.

"Judge" (96:10). God as Creator has the moral right and responsibility to evaluate human actions and to mete out appropriate reward and punishment. Major passages which develop the doctrine of divine judgment include: John 3:19-21, 5:19-30, 8:15-16, 12:47-49; Rom. 2:1-8; 1 Peter 4:5; Heb. 10:30, 12:12, 13:4; Rev. 20:12.

PSALM 97: Honoring the Reign of God

God reigns over creation (97:1). The heavens display His awesome power (vv. 2-6). Idolaters are put to shame (v. 7), but God's people rejoice (vv. 8-9). The response of the godly to the reign of God is to hate evil, rejoice in the Lord, and offer Him praise (vv. 10-12).

Key concepts. Righteousness »p. 120. Shame »p. 357. Evil »pp. 72, 662.

PSALM 98: God's Marvels

The psalmist again proclaims a new song (cf. Ps. 96) (98:1a). The marvels God has worked include salvation (vv. 1b-6), and nature joins the chorus of the saved acclaiming God when He comes to judge the world (vv. 7-9).

Key concepts. Miracles »pp. 57, 679. Salvation »pp. 426, 433. Music »p. 274. Righteousness »p. 433. Judge »Ps. 96, above.

Righteousness in judgment (98:9). Righteousness in the O.T. is rooted in the idea of conformity to a norm. That norm is the revealed will of God, which in turn has its basis in God's character. To say, as Scripture often does, that God is righteous is to affirm both that He is the ultimate standard of what is moral and right and good, and also that He never acts out of harmony with His character.

Scripture also makes it clear how God's righteousness is expressed. Formally, righteousness is expressed in the laws, statutes, and other expressions of God's will found in the Bible. Practically, God's righteousness is expressed in His acts of judgment, as this verse states, and in His gift of salvation, the other major theme of this psalm. Thus, Ps. 98 celebrates a righteousness of God which promises equity to all mankind: salvation to those who believe and judgment to those who persist in sin and unbelief.

PSALM 99: In Praise of God's Holiness and Forgiveness

The psalmist calls all humankind to exalt God because He is holy (99:1-5) and because He forgives those who call upon Him (vv. 6-9).

Key concepts. Justice »pp. 141, 319. Forgiveness »p. 357. Call upon God »p. 361.

God's holiness. "Holy" is a technical religious term. The major emphasis in the concept of holiness is to make a sharp distinction between that which is secular and what is sacred.

PSALM 100: Serving with Gladness

This psalm, affectionately known as "old hundred," thrills with the excitement of worship. We are invited to share the exhilaration and joy of praise (100:1-3) and to gather for worship with thanksgiving and praise (vv. 4-5).

Key concepts. Joy »p. 269. Sheep »p. 355. Thanksgiving »p. 809. Praise »p. 380. Faithfulness »p. 141.

PSALM 101: Commitment of a King

David expresses his commitment to his God of "love and justice" (101:1). David will lead a blameless life (vv. 2-4). He will not permit his people to sin and will advance those whose walk, like his, is blameless (vv. 5-8).

Key concepts. Justice »p. 540. Evil »p. 72.

Politics (101:3b). In politics the popular wisdom says that it's not wise to reject support. David says he will have no association with "men of perverse heart." When such persons try to cling to us we need to take just as firm a stand as David did.

"Every morning" (101:8). David is committed to an active campaign of cleansing his administration. He doesn't wait till a scandal occurs, but makes sure he has "cut off every evildoer from the city of the Lord."

We may not be able to directly apply David's policies in theocratic Israel to modern politics. But the principle of seeking leaders of unimpeachable moral character is valid in every society, in every age.

PSALM 102: A Sufferer's Meditation

The psalmist begs for a speedy relief (102:1-2). His own desperate situation (vv. 3-11) has not shaken his confidence that God will act for His people (vv. 12-22). Though man's life is short and the universe itself is perishable, God is eternal (vv. 23-27) and in the end God's servants will "live in Your presence" (v. 28).

Key concepts. Prayer »pp. 608–609. Suffering »p. 877.

Repeated themes. The lament, a poetic expression of anguish, is seen also in Ps. 22, 69, and 79. The imagery of withering grass, seen here in v. 11, is found in Ps. 37:2; 103:15-16, and also in Isa. 40:6-8. The brevity of life depresses the psalmists, but at the same time it's beneficial, for it leads them to look to God and to eternity for answers.

Our destiny (102:28). Not only will God remain unchanged throughout endless years, but long after the material universe itself has been discarded God's children too will "live in Your presence." Because we have a personal relationship with God our prospects are endless, however short the time we have to spend on earth.

PSALM 103: In Celebration of Deliverance

David praises God for the many mercies (103:1-5) that unveil the compassion of Him (vv. 6-18) and lead all beings everywhere to praise the Lord (vv. 19-22).

Key concepts. Praise »p. 380. Forgiveness »p. 357. Healing »pp. 412, 784. Justice »p. 541. Miracles »p. 57. Anger of God »pp. 65, 72. Compassion »p. 440. Kingdom »p. 380.

God's compassion (103:8-12). Forgiveness is the prime expression of God's compassion for a needy humanity. These verses explain the nature of the forgiveness we enjoy as well as any passage in the O.T. or N.T.

PSALM 104: Praise to God, the Creator

God's greatness is displayed in the Creation He shaped and sustains. This powerful psalm weaves praise for God through its graphic description of majestic elements of creation which show God's power (104:1-9) and the compassionate elements which show His concern for living creatures (vv. 10-23). No wonder the psalmist's heart, and ours, are filled with wonder and praise (vv. 24-35).

Key concepts. Creation »p. 430. Praise »p. 380.

PSALM 105: A History of God's Faithfulness

The psalmist thanks God for His miraculous acts (105:1-5) and traces God's works by relating the history of His faithfulness to Israel (vv. 6-41). God has delivered His people and is to be praised (vv. 42-45).

Key concepts. Miracles »p. 57. Remember »p. 98. Abraham »p. 32. Covenant »p. 35. Moses »p. 55.

PSALM 106: A Confession of National Sin

God's people failed to respond to Him despite His miraculous works for them (Ps. 105). After calling for Israel to praise the Lord (106:1-5) by confessing the nation's historic faults and failures (vv. 6-46), the confessional prayer ends with an appeal for deliverance (vv. 47-48).

Key concepts. Confession »p. 892. Sins »p. 362.

"**We have sinned**" (106:6). The first step toward redemption is to honestly look at our sins and failures and bring them to God. Self-examination is painful, but it's necessary for all.

PSALM 107: Praise of the Redeemed

The psalmist calls the redeemed to praise God (107:1-3). In a series of vivid images he contrasts the lost state with the release that redemption brings (vv. 4-32). Exercising His power over nature, God will remake our barren earth (vv. 33-38) and revitalize our barren lives (vv. 39-43).

Key concept. Redemption »p. 90.

PSALM 108: Praise from the Confident

David praises God and expresses his confidence in God's great love (108:1-5). David prays for God's help in battle (v. 6-9), sure that "with God we will gain the victory" (vv. 10-13).

PSALM 109: A Prayer Against the Unrighteous

The psalmist asks God to act against those who have unjustly attacked him (109:1-5). He expresses his desire that the wicked be found guilty and suffer retribution (vv. 6-15). The psalmist's grim antagonism toward the wicked is seen to be justified as he describes the harm the wicked have done others (vv. 16-20). The psalm ends with an appeal for help against the wicked, who threaten and oppress the psalmist himself (vv. 21-31).

Key concepts. Wicked »p. 350. Guilty »p. 79. Sins »pp. 34, 362. Curse »p. 138.

Help! (109:21-25) One reason God permits injustice is to help us learn from personal experience how devastating such treatment by others really is—we can perhaps sympathize with the hurting.

PSALM 110: A Psalm of the Messiah

The Messiah is exalted as Lord by the Lord (110:1) and His royal victory predicted (vv. 2-3). At the same time He is introduced as a priest, not of Aaron's line but after "the order of Melchizedek" (v. 4). It is to Him, God's King/Priest, that the Lord will give victory (vv. 5-7).

Key concepts. Messiah »p. 427. King »p. 130. Priest »pp. 81, 858.

Psalm 111: Praise for God's Redemptive Works

The psalmist expresses his delight in God's works (111:1-3), and he names many that His saints enjoy (vv. 4-9) and which should lead others to hold Him in reverential awe (v. 10).

Key concepts. Praise »p. 380. Compassion »p. 440. Covenant »pp. 32, 35.

PSALM 112: The Path of Blessing

The psalmist lists not only the blessings won by those who keep God's commands, but the acts that secure them.

Key concepts. Blessing »p. 358. Poor and oppressed »p. 90. Wicked »p. 350.

PSALM 113: The Praise of the Poor

The psalmist calls us to praise (113:1-3) because of God's grace, which reaches out to the poor and needy and lifts them up (vv. 4-9).

Key concepts. Poor and oppressed »p. 90. Grace »p. 789.

PSALM 114: Celebrating the Exodus

The psalmist sees in the miracles of the Exodus God's mastery of all nature.

PSALM 115: A Call to Trust God

The psalmist ridicules Israel's trust in idols (115:1-8) and calls passionately for return to faith in the Lord (vv. 9-11). Recommitment to God will surely bring blessing (vv. 12-18).

Key concepts. Idols »p. 433. Trust »p. 354.

PSALM 116: Praise for Deliverance from Death

The psalmist announces his intent to praise God (116:1-2) and reports his rescue from a life-threatening situation (vv. 3-11). In repayment for God's goodness to him, the psalmist vows to praise God for His compassionate concern for the life and death of His saints (vv. 12-19).

Key concepts. Death »p. 369. Vow »p. 96. Thank offering »p. 78.

PSALM 117: An Invitation to Praise

This brief psalm calls us to praise God for His faithfulness.

"**Praise the Lord.**" Praise need not be long to be meaningful.

PSALM 118: A Praise Psalm for Festival Time

This psalm is sung as a joyful people join the procession at festival time. God is praised for His enduring love (118:1-4), and His help in triumphing over Israel's enemies is recounted (vv. 5-21). These victories foreshadow the messianic triumph to come at history's end (vv. 22-29).

Key concepts. Messiah »p. 427. Future kingdom »p. 443.

"**The capstone**" (118:22). The imagery of the Messiah as the capstone or chief cornerstone is reflected in Isa. 8:14 and 28:16. It is the critical stone in a building, either the stone placed at the corner of a structure on which its weight rested, or the keystone of an arch.

IMAGES OF GOD'S WORD

"A lamp to my feet" (119:105). The flickering light cast by the olive oil lamp of Bible times was only bright enough to show a traveler his next step. Scripture is such a lamp. It gives us just enough light to see where to place our feet so that we can walk safely into our future. The believer does not need a searchlight that casts light on coming weeks and years. All that is in God's hand. We need only enough light to make sure that the next step we take is just and right.

Scripture Gives Trustworthy Light
*It contains God's decrees (v. 1-8)
*It provides a standard by which we are to live (vv. 9-16)
*Its words are our counselors (vv. 17-24)
*It renews our lives (vv. 25-32)
*It gives us understanding of true values (vv. 33-40)
*It is true and trustworthy (vv. 41-48)
*It contains God's promises to us (vv. 49-56)
*It shows how to live close to God (vv. 57-64)
*It keeps us happy despite the hostility of enemies (vv. 65-72)
*Its laws are righteous (vv. 73-80).
*It keeps our hearts blameless (vv. 81-88)

PSALM 119: A Celebration of God's Word

Psalm 119 is an acrostic psalm in praise of the Word of God and its role in the life of the believer. An acrostic follows an alphabetic arrangement. In the original Hebrew each line in each of the 22 sections of this psalm begins with the same Hebrew letter. These letters are shown in the NIV text, and the English spelling of its name is provided.

There are a number of terms that are repeated in the psalm. These are all synonyms referring back to the Word of God. They are:

*Torah (Law), 25 times. Usually the word here indicates the whole body of Scripture's teaching as found in Moses' writings.

*Miswah (Commands), 21 times. This refers to clear, definite directives issued by God.

*Huqqim (decrees), 21 times. The Heb. means "things inscribed" and thus established in law.

*Mispot (judgments), 19 times. The Heb. means a binding judicial decision that establishes a precedent.

*Piqqudim (precepts), 21 times. This word, found only in poetry, is a synonym for edict or precept.

*'edah (statute), 23 times. This is a sober and serious expression of God's standards for human behavior.

*Dabar (word), 20 times. This means a revelation, but also is used specifically of the Ten Commandments God gave Israel through Moses.

*'Imrah (saying), 19 times. Another poetic word, often used instead of dabar.

*Derek (way), 11 times. A metaphor for the way of life believers are to live.

*'Orah (path). Another metaphor of lifestyle. We should not attach too much significance to the narrower meaning of these words.

Throughout the psalm David expresses the joy he finds in Scripture. He calls it "the word of truth" (119:43) and in so doing makes a vitally important statement about its nature. In the Heb. "truth" and "faithfulness" share a common root, 'emet. This root affirms that the statement, thing, or person which is true or faithful is in harmony with reality. That is, that the true can be relied upon because when measured by the actual, it corresponds exactly. To say that Scripture is true means that we can trust it completely, for it pierces all man's illusions and portrays reality as God knows it and as it really is.

Responses of the Believer to God's Word

IMAGES OF GOD'S WORD

"*Walk according* to the Law of the Lord" (v. 1).
"*Keep* His statutes" (v. 2).
"*Obey* [God's] decrees" (v. 8).
"*Living according* to Your Word" (v. 9).
"*Hidden* Your Word in *my heart* (v. 10).
"*Recount* all the laws" (v. 13).
"*Rejoice in following* Your statutes" (v. 14).
"*Meditate* on Your precepts" (v. 15).
"*Delight* in Your decrees" (v. 16).
"*Longing* for Your laws at all times" (v. 20).
"*Let me understand* the teaching of Your precepts" (v. 27).
"I have *chosen* the way of truth" (v. 30).
"I *run in* the path of Your commands" (v. 32).
"*Keep* them to the end" (v. 33).
"I *long* for Your precepts" (v. 40).
"I *trust* in Your Word" (v. 42).
"I will *always obey* Your Law" (v. 44).
"I will *speak of* Your statutes before kings" (v. 46).
"I *delight in* Your commandments because I love them" (v. 47).
"I *do not turn* from Your law" (v. 51).
"I *find comfort* in them" (v. 52).
"I have *promised to obey* Your words" (v. 57).
"I have *considered my ways* and *turned my steps* to Your statutes" (v. 59).
"I *believe in* Your commandments" (v. 66).
"*Put my hope* in Your Word" (v. 74).
"I *do not forget* Your decrees" (v. 83).
"I *have not forsaken* Your precepts (v. 87).
"I have *sought out* Your precepts" (v. 94).
"I will *ponder* Your statutes" (v. 95).
"I *love* Your law" (v. 97).
"I *gain understanding* from Your precepts, therefore I hate every evil way" (v. 104).
"I *love* Your commands more than gold" (v. 127).
"I have *put my hope in* Your Word" (v. 147).
"I *learned* from Your statutes" (v. 152).
"I *have not turned* from Your statutes" (v. 157).
"I *rejoice in* Your promise" (v. 162).
"I *follow* Your commands" (v. 166).
"I *have chosen* Your precepts" (v. 173).

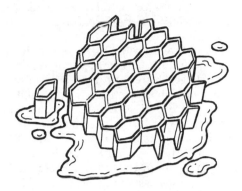

The honeycomb (119:103) was the sweetest substance known in the ancient world. No refined sugar was available, but bees were plentiful in the agricultural highlands of Palestine, and their produce was highly valued by the Israelites. To say that Scripture is sweeter than honey is to say the psalmist values it more than any pleasure.

Scripture is sweet to our taste
  *It renews our life (v. 89-96).
  *It makes us wiser than our enemies (vv. 97-104).
  *It is the joy of our heart (vv. 105-112).
  *It sustains our hope (vv. 113-120).
  *It shapes our values (vv. 121-128).
  *It gives understanding to the simple (vv. 129-136).
  *It provides inner delight (vv. 137-144).
  *It gives us confidence in prayer (vv. 145-152).
  *It is filled with promises (vv. 153-160).
  *It causes us to praise (vv. 161-168).
  *It causes us to overflow with praise (vv. 169-176).

Psalms 120–134 are known as "Songs of Ascent." Tradition says each of these "pilgrim psalms" was to be sung as God's people approached Jerusalem for one of the major worship festivals. Another tradition suggests that the "ascent" was fifteen steps leading up to the temple, and that these psalms were sung by choirs of Levites.

These Psalms reflect the themes found throughout this great book of poetry. **Psalm 120,** is a prayer for deliverance from the wicked that expresses Israel's deep longing for peace. **Psalm 121** is an affirmation of confidence that God will watch over Israel and shelter His people from all harm. **Psalm 122** seeks peace and security for Jerusalem, for it is the site of the house of the Lord and worship is precious to His people. **Psalm 123** looks up to God for mercy, while its companion, **Psalm 124** recalls and acknowledges God's protection in the past. What God has done for us gives us confidence in what He will do for us in the future. **Psalm 125** recounts the blessings of belief, bringing as it does assurance that God will do good to those who are good. **Psalm 126** is both a prayer for captives and a testimony to the conviction that God will bring His people home rejoicing.

Psalm 127 is praise for family. This psalm lies at the midpoint of the "Songs of Ascent" and is filled with a sense of the joy the Israelites took in their children. Children were viewed as gifts of God (cf. Isa. 8:18), and childlessness caused great grief (cf. 1 Sam. 1:3-20; 2 Sam. 12:14-25). Luke 1:24-25 pictures the intimate involvement of mothers and fathers in the nurture of children, reflected in a variety of Old Testament passages (cf. Deut. 4:9-10; Ps. 78:4-6; Prov. 4:3-4).

The rest of these "Songs of Ascent" continue to reflect vital elements in Israel's faith and life. **Psalm 128** is a prayer for the material blessings God promised to those generations of His people who were obedient (cf. Deut. 28:1-6). **Psalm 129** picks up another aspect of God's covenant promises to the godly and calls on Him to take revenge on foreign persecutors (cf. Deut. 28:7).

Psalm 130 is another prayer for mercy. It blends the major elements of mercy as understood in the Bible: The psalmist is in distress (130:1-2). Yet assurance of forgiveness (vv. 3-4) gives him and all God's people strength to wait till He acts in love and redeems (vv. 5-8). **Psalm 131** is a prayer of total trust. The arrogant rely on themselves and refuse to submit to God, but the true believer is as dependent on God as a little child is on his parents. **Psalm 132** is a prayer to be used in public worship. It recalls the joy that marked the day David brought the ark to Jerusalem and celebrates not only God's presence, but His promise that the Messiah will come from David's line. **Psalm 133** praises the unity God's people experience in their identity as brothers, while **Psalm 134** acknowledges that those who serve God are the most blessed of all.

PSALM 135: In Praise of God's Faithfulness and Greatness

The call to praise (135:1-3) concludes with an introduction of its themes: praise of God's choice of Israel (vv. 4, 7-12) and praise of God's sovereign power (vv. 5, 13-18). It concludes with a glad cry urging the house of Israel to praise God together.

Key concepts. Praise »p. 380. God's choice of Israel »p. 124. Idolatry »p. 433.

"Praise the Lord" (135:19-21). Praise in Scripture is most frequently a community activity. What God has done for you and me individually, He has done for all His people. We need to join with others and praise God together as the psalmist exhorts us.

PSALM 136: His Love Endures Forever

Each affirmation of this great worship hymn calls out the response, "His love endures forever." It was most likely used in public worship, with either two choirs or with one choir making the affirmation and the people giving the response.

Key concepts. Love »p. 351. Create »p. 430. Miracles »p. 57.

Creation/Redemption. The twin themes of creation (vv. 1-9) and redemption (vv. 10-26) dominate this psalm. They also dominate the O.T.'s vision of God, who is known through these two mightiest of His acts.

PSALM 137: Grief Untold

Perhaps written during the Babylonian Captivity, this psalm communicates a sense of anguish so deep that it cannot be expressed even in the familiar musical lament. The psalmist tells of the exiles' tears (137:1-4) and of their poignant memories of Jerusalem (vv. 5-6). The psalm ends with an appeal to God to repay those responsible for Zion's fall (vv. 7-9).

Key concepts. Babylon »p. 302. Jerusalem »p. 205. Edom »p. 104. Remember »p. 98.

PSALM 138: Praise for Answered Prayer

David vows to praise God publicly for answering his prayers (138:1-3) and wishes that "all the kings of the earth" might praise God too (vv. 4-5). He is confident, for his sovereign God will fulfill His purpose in David's life (vv. 6-8).

God's answer (138:3). "You made me bold and stouthearted." Don't ask God to do *for* you. Ask Him to make you bold and stouthearted, and then *you* do what needs to be done. David captures a basic biblical truth when he says, "The Lord will fulfill His purpose for me." God has a purpose to be fulfilled in the life of every believer.

PSALM 139: Meditation on God's Greatness

David meditates on the omniscience (139:1-6), omnipresence (vv. 7-12), and omnipotence (vv. 13-18) of God. He then applies these truths to the wicked, whom he calls on God to slay (vv. 19-22), and to himself, whom he calls on God to examine and to lead (vv. 23-24).

PSALM 140: Against the Wicked

David calls on God to thwart the plots of the wicked (140:1-8) and penalize them severely (vv. 9-11), sure that He is committed to the righteous poor (vv. 12-13).

PSALM 141: A Prayer for Protection

David prays at evening (141:1-2) for protection from sin (vv. 3-4) and from sinners (vv. 5-7). He will be safe as long as he keeps his eyes fixed on the Lord (vv. 8-10).

PSALM 142: A Desperate Cry

David cries out for mercy (142:1-2), for he is faint and alone (vv. 3-4). Yet in his desperate need he can cry out to God, sure the Lord will set him free (vv. 5-7).

PSALM 143: A Prayer for Deliverance and Guidance

God's past faithfulness encourages David to call on the Lord to help against present enemies (143:1-6). He prays for God to act quickly, not only to deliver him (vv. 7-9), but also to teach David to do God's will (v. 10). For God to answer will bring honor to His name and be in character with His great love (vv. 11-12).

PSALM 144: Thanks for Future Blessings

David praises God for past victories (144:1-2) and prays for His continued intervention (vv. 3-11). David is sure God will act and the land will overflow with blessings (vv. 12-14).

PSALM 145: A Psalm of Praise

The only psalm with this title in the entire collection, Psalm 145 praises God for His mighty acts (145:1-7), His gracious character (vv. 8-9), and the glory of His coming kingdom (vv. 10-16). Our loving Lord shows His care for His own, who praise Him in return (vv. 17-21).

Praise. *The Expository Dictionary of Bible Words* (Zondervan, 1985) says: "(1) Praise is addressed to God or His 'name.' God Himself, His attributes, or His acts are the content of our thoughts, words, and songs. (2) Praise is linked with the believing community's joy in the person of God. . . . Most praise comes from those who are filled with a sense of joy in who God is and in how deeply He is committed to His people. (3) Praise exalts the Lord. It is in praise that the believer implicitly acknowledges creaturely dependence on God and explicitly acknowledges God's greatness and goodness."

In essence, worship is the expression of respect for Him. Individual worship is first of all an attitude of profound respect for God, demonstrated in a life of obedience.

"Kingdom." God's kingdom is portrayed in two ways in the Bible. First, God's kingdom is universal in that He exercises sovereign control over His creation. Yet, mysteriously, God chose to give human beings the freedom to either submit to Him or temporarily resist His will. Those who surrender to God in faith have been brought, in Paul's words, "into the kingdom of the Son He loves" (Col. 1:13).

The Bible also speaks of God's kingdom in a second, future sense. One day all mankind will acknowledge God's sovereignty and surrender—many unwillingly—to His control. When that happens God's kingdom will be established here on Earth in its fullest sense.

PSALM 146: Lifelong Praise

The psalmist will praise God all his life (145:1-4), first because God is Creator (vv. 5-6) and then because God is so gracious to the needy (vv. 7-9). God reigns (v. 10).

Key concepts. Praise »p. 380. Creation »p. 430.

Trust in princes? (146:3) This psalm was most meaningful to Martin Luther who was forced, because of an emperor's ban, to rely on rulers of German principalities to stand for the Protestant faith. After much soul-searching, he realized that he need not rely on them, or worry, for his "help [was] the God of Jacob" (v. 5).

PSALM 147: Praise to God for Sustaining All

God, who heals the brokenhearted (147:1-3), sustains the universe itself by His power (vv. 4-6). God, who supplies the living on earth (vv. 7-9), takes delight in those who fear Him and grants them peace (vv. 10-15). God, who controls all by His Word (vv. 16-18), has blessed Israel with His commands and decrees (vv. 19-20). Praise the Lord.

Key concepts. Praise »p. 380. Power »p. 430. Peace »p. 427. Music »p. 274.

PSALM 148: O Earth, Praise God!

The psalmist exclaims, "Praise the Lord," and calls on all in the heavens to join Him (148:1-7). Praise also echoes from the earth (vv. 8-14) building to a crescendo as one by one all of Creation joins in the shouts of praise.

Key concepts. Creation »p. 430. Praise »p. 380. Israel »p. 53.

"The people close to His heart" (148:14). It's not favoritism for God to hold Israel close to His heart. It's both divine freedom and divine grace. Freedom, because God chose Israel without reference to Abraham's merits or the merits of his descendants. Grace, because through Israel God planned to make a way of salvation for all humankind.

The wonder is that God cared for our sinful race at all. Today, the wonder is that it is you and me who, despite our flaws, are held close to God's heart.

PSALM 149: Praise for Salvation

The psalmist summons God's people to praise Him wholeheartedly (149:1-3) for the blessings of salvation (vv. 4-5) and for His justice (vv. 6-9).

Key concepts. Praise »p. 380. Music »p. 274. Salvation »p. 426. Saints »p. 724.

Enthusiasm. The early Methodists in England were criticized for their "enthusiasm." Folks were not supposed to get excited about God, as the followers of John and Charles Wesley were becoming. Psalm 149:3 suggests differently. God is worth getting excited about and showing excitement. Perhaps our modern worship needs more of the vitality and ardor that characterizes Israel's worship at its best.

PSALM 150: Praise in God's House

Again the psalmist calls God's people together to offer Him praise (150:1) for His acts of power and surpassing greatness (v. 2). Lest we ignore his first cry, the psalmist calls out again (vv. 3-5) and again (v. 6). "Let everything that has breath praise the Lord."

The importance of praise. How well this 150th psalm sums up the message of the entire collection. Each psalm, probing as it does our deepest emotions, is in fact an invitation to know God better and a summons to praise Him.

What a privilege it is to join the saints of all the ages in a chorus of praise.

Wisdom Literature

The ancient world produced writings in a variety of literary genres. In Egypt and Mesopotamia alike we find treatises on mathematics and astronomy, as well as on magic. We find myths and religious sagas. We also find adventure stories, medical textbooks, love poetry, psalms, and political documents. We find the chronicles of kings and kingdoms as well as the boasts of ancient rulers. We also discover one of the oldest of literary forms, wisdom writings.

The earliest wisdom literature dates from well before 2000 B.C. Wisdom literature is frequently cast as advice given by a father to his son, or an older man to his students. Well-known Egyptian works are ascribed to a father wishing to counsel his son before a long term of imprisonment, to a vizier charged with teaching the royal offspring, and to a sailor motivating his son to study as he enters scribe school. At times wisdom literature is placed in the context of a story, to hold the learner's attention. An Egyptian example is the *Protests of the Eloquent Peasant*, where a man appeals for justice after being wronged by a neighbor. A biblical example is the story of Job.

But what were the widespread concerns that stimulated the writing of so much wisdom literature? Two themes seem to hold the interest of the authors. (1) Some wisdom writings explore philosophical issues. Job and Ecclesiastes fall into this category. Job debates the question of why the godly suffer, and Ecclesiastes struggles with the question of what gives life itself meaning. (2) Some wisdom literature gives advice on how to live a prudent life. Proverbs falls into this category, with its pithy sayings and counsel on the moral and practical decisions every individual must make.

This second kind of biblical wisdom literature does not rely on revelation as its source. The prophets spoke out in the bold confidence that "thus says the Lord." The authors of the proverbs were well aware that they expressed insights gained by observing human experience, as well as from the moral framework provided by Moses' Law. The Law is not referred to for validating proverbial wisdom, although the proverbs in most cultures affirm the necessity of respect for God and moral order. Most sayings captured in our Book of Proverbs are assumed to be self-evident to any right thinking person, yet also important principles for the young and inexperienced to grasp. Within the cultural context of the ancient world, many were self-evident. Similar observations are found both in the biblical Book of Proverbs and in sayings found in Egyptian and Mesopotamian wisdom literature. Note for instance the affinity of proverbs found in the Egyptian *Instruction of Amen-em-ope* to the biblical proverbs.

*Do not carry off the landmark or encroach upon the boundaries of a widow.

*Better is a measure that the god gives thee than five thousand (taken) illegally.

*Better is poverty in the hand of the god than riches in the storehouse.

*Cast not thy heart in pursuit of riches.

*Do not associate to thyself the heated (e.g., angry) man.

Much of wisdom literature, both biblical and extrabiblical, is viewed as sage advice given by the mature to the young. We catch the flavor of most wisdom literature in these lines from Proverbs 3:1-2: "My son, do not forget My teaching, but keep My commands in your heart, for they will prolong your life many years and bring you prosperity."

These and other parallels do not show a dependence of either the Hebrew work on the Egyptian, or the Egyptian on the Hebrew. Instead they reflect the fact that God has given all human beings moral insight. A knowledge of right and wrong, a sense of what marks just and right behavior, is ingrained in human nature itself, and finds expression in at least some of the moral teachings of every human society. The great contribution of revelation is to make us aware that it is not enough to know what is right. We must do what is right. And because all fail to meet not only God's standards but even the standards of their society, revelation teaches us to look to God rather than ourselves for salvation.

Thus wisdom literature, in Scripture or in other ancient societies, has a more narrowly defined function. I describes and urges right action and right thinking. It does not share the prophet's function of creating a sense of sin, or the evangelist's mission of turning man's eyes to God as sole source of salvation.

While the wisdom literature of the ancient world is not revelatory in nature, nor intended primarily to teach religious truths, the wisdom writings of each society do reflect the culture's view of God. In Egypt *Ma'at*, truth or justice, provided an ultimate standard to which the gods themselves were subject. In Babylon, moral laws sprang from the human conscience, and the gods were also governed by moral standards. Even so, the gods defined what was right in any given situation, and their will was to be determined by a study of omens. In Summer, another Mesopotamian society, the gods were natural forces unaffected by moral concerns. In Israel, God was a living, vital presence, who superintended the consequences of human acts, rewarding good and punishing evil. Thus the distilled wisdom expressed in proverbial sayings and advice had unique urgency. By making prudent choices a person expressed his or her fear of God, demonstrating the conviction that God will bless those who do right and punish those who do wrong. The principles of a prudent life may be self-evident in much wisdom literature. But behind the wisdom teachings of the Old Testament lies the conviction that God energetically supports right moral order, and is active in the present experience of human beings.

All the chief literary forms used in wisdom literature are reflected in the Old Testament Books of Proverbs, Job, and Ecclesiastes, and in several wisdom psalms. These are: the sentence saying, or proverb; the short precept followed by a discussion; the rhetorical question; soliloquy; debate; descriptive or contemplative poetry; imaginative tales, and illustrative anecdotes. Through each form the Bible teaches us an important truth. There is no conflict between the prophet's call to righteousness and the sage's invitation to be wise. Righteousness and wisdom are one; for the truly wise man, ever aware of the presence of God, will choose to do what is right.

Proverbs

The Book of Proverbs is a collection of advice and counsel intended to guide the reader's practical and moral choices. The sayings touch on such varied subjects as interpersonal relationships, attitudes toward work and wealth, poverty, and child rearing. While the general principles captured in the proverbs have universal application, their significance in Scripture is defined by the Bible's unique view of God. The God of the Old Testament is a living, active Person, who as the moral Judge of the universe supervises the consequences of human moral choices. Thus the individual who does what is right and good can expect to be blessed, and the individual who does what is wrong or evil can expect disappointment and disaster. An individual who truly fears God, in the sense of holding Him in awe, will make prudent choices and can expect to live a secure and happy life. While specific proverbs and bits of practical wisdom have parallels in other ancient societies, the underlying view of God and of wisdom as a faith-rooted righteousness sets biblical wisdom literature apart.

AMONG THE TOPICS DISCUSSED IN PROVERBS

Child rearing	10:1; 17:21, 25; 19:13, 26; 20:7; 23:24-25
Family life	18:22; 21:9, 19; 27:15-16; 31:30
Friendship	18:24; 22:24-25; 25:17
Laziness	12:27; 20:13; 26:14-15
Poverty and the poor	14:31; 17:5, 16; 18:23; 19:4, 7, 17; 21:13
Social obligations	22:24-25; 23:1-2; 25:6-7, 17; 27:6-10
Wealth	10:22; 11:4; 13:11; 15:16; 16:16; 19:1; 22:1
Work	10:4-5; 12:24; 13:4; 18:9

Date and Authorship. Most of the proverbs are attributed to Solomon (chaps. 10–22), who ruled from 970 to 930 B.C. Some were undoubtedly original; others may have been collected by him. Still other persons added to the basic collection at various times (cf. 22:17). It is likely that the book took its present form in the time of Hezekiah (715–686 B.C.), as suggested by Proverbs 25:1.

Using the Book of Proverbs

You can profitably use the Book of Proverbs as a practical handbook to living wisely in modern times, but keep its nature and characteristics in mind. The sayings found here express general and universal principles which are relevant to all people of all times. These guidelines apply to everyone, not just to believers. The sayings are generalizations, and all general statements have exceptions. Don't mistake a proverb for a promise God is giving to you to claim by faith. If you think on the proverbs and follow their advice, you'll find them a wonderful source of insight into your daily life.

OUTLINING PROVERBS

Because Proverbs is a collection of sayings on many subjects, it is not possible to outline it as we do a typical book of Scripture. The book is typically outlined not by its contents but by its various collections, as reflected in the overview below.

While Proverbs is difficult to outline, it is helpful to note that it contains an extensive moral menu of beneficial and negative traits. That menu, which sums up the thrust of Proverbs' moral stance, is also included below.

OVERVIEW OF PROVERBS

I. IN PRAISE OF WISDOM	1–9
II. SOLOMON'S PROVERBS, I	10:1–22:16
III. COLLECTED SAYINGS	22:17–24:34
IV. SOLOMON'S PROVERBS, II	25–29
V. OTHER'S SAYINGS	30–31

PROVERBS' MORAL MENU

Positive traits		Negative traits	
wisdom	knowledge	folly	laziness
diligence	faithfulness	failure	unfaithfulness
honesty	justice	cheating	injustice
truth	encouragement	lying	dishonor
love	kindness	impurity	strife
joy	generosity	hatred	greed
work	orderliness	anxiety	animosity
self-control	obedience	poverty	drunkenness
integrity	fairness	worry	unteachableness
honor	purity	anger	talkativeness
peace	mercy	wickedness	ignorance
hope	good company	rebellion	deceit
wealth	friendliness	unfairness	criticism
soberness	trust	slander	jealousy
virtue	pleasure	cruelty	bad company
quietness	teachableness	enmity	shame
	contentment	misery	unfriendliness
		envy	pride

Chapter summary. The book immediately states the writer's purpose and theme: he teaches the wisdom so the reader can develop a disciplined life, "doing what is right and just and fair" (1:1-7). Speaking as a father, he warns against those who will try to detour his sons into sin (vv. 8-19) and warns against ignoring his advice (vv. 20-33). He carefully identifies the nature of wisdom (2:1-10) and lists its many benefits (2:11-3:16). Wisdom is foundational to existence, providing perspective on life (vv. 17-35). So wisdom, personified as a lovely woman, is to be desired above all things (4:1-27).

Key verse. 2:4: Respect for God is the source of true wisdom.

Personal application. It is wise as well as right to commit yourself to doing "what is right and just and fair" (1:3).

INSIGHT

Wisdom (1:2-3). The Heb. root that expresses the basic concept of wisdom (*h-k-m*) occurs over 300 times in the O.T. It focuses our attention on a person's basic approach to life, the values and commitments which find expression in his or her lifestyle. In the O.T., wisdom is essentially the choice to be godly. The wise person is sensitive to God, submits to Him, and applies God's guidelines when making daily choices.

The person who is wise will "find the knowledge of God," because God is the source of wisdom (2:5-6). God provides needed perspective, so that we "will understand what is right and just and fair—every good path" (2:9).

"Wisdom literature" in the O.T., which includes Prov., Ecc., Job, and Ps. 19, 37, 104, 107, 147, and 148, describes the way of life to be chosen by the believer. For more on the nature of wisdom in the O.T., »p. 280. For distinctive N.T. insights into wisdom, »pp. 757, 873.

"Fear of the Lord" (1:7). This verse calls the fear of the Lord "the beginning of knowledge." One rabbinic commentary on Proverbs reminds us that fear here is not dread, but "reverence of God expressed in submission to His will." This is in fact the basic sense of "fear of the Lord" throughout the O.T., where it might often be rendered "reverential awe" or even "faith." The commentary rightly observes, "God is the Creator of the universe and of life; it is consequently impossible to obtain an understanding of man's place in the design and purpose of living without a humble approach to Him."

But why is fear of God the "beginning" or starting point? Because the conviction that God is—and is to be honored—the only door that opens to true wisdom. Only when all is oriented to the Lord can true moral knowledge or wisdom be gained.

"Valuable things" (1:13). The foolish sinner is motivated to do wrong by mere things, which he or she sees as having great value. People who value things more than God's approval find ill-gotten gain "takes away the lives of those who get it" (v. 19).

Relationship with God (chap. 3). The basic wisdom issues touched on in Proverbs have to do with personal relationship with God. Only if we know Him and respond to Him will the rest of the counsel in this book produce fruit.

This chapter mentions several basic principles of relationship with God. We are to trust the Lord completely, and acknowledge Him in all we do (vv. 5-6, »trust, p. 354). We are to rely on God's Word rather than our human wisdom (vv. 7-8). We are to honor God by giving generously (vv. 9-10). And we are to remember when hard times come that God loves us still and see our most difficult experiences as the disciplinary love of a Father who cares for us deeply.

"Disciplines" (3:11-12). In the O.T. discipline is typically painful, but it is not primarily punishment. The key Heb. word for discipline is *yasar*, which means to chastise, or to instruct. It does involve correction, but its goal is to make a positive contribution to a person's training in righteousness. As these verses emphasize, *yasar* is exercised in a family setting. The emotion conveyed is not anger or disgust, but love and active concern. A father disciplines his child to help her grow into a praiseworthy adult. Just so God disciplines those who trust Him to help us grow toward moral and spiritual maturity. Bible history and proverbs both demonstrate that at times punishment, a "rod of correction" (Prov. 29:15) is the best way to show love when people will not respond to verbal guidance. The important thing to remember, as these verses emphasize, is that when God disciplines it is because of, and with a continuing attitude of, love.

Outline
Place
Finder

WISDOM
SOLOMON I
SAYINGS
SOLOMON II
OTHERS

Chapter summary. These chapters develop two themes interwoven by a distinctive literary device. The first theme is the dangers of adultery, filled with warnings against the seductive woman. These are developed in 5:1-23 and 6:20–7:27. The second theme is the praise of wisdom, personified as a woman. This is developed in 8:1–9:18. The use of the device is partly explained by the fact that the noun "wisdom" is feminine, but its development reflects the genius of the author who plays off the notion of desirability, contrasting the sensory appeal of the seductress and the total satisfaction to be found in choosing to make one's commitment to wisdom instead. Only 6:1-19 seems to briefly abandon this powerful analogy to introduce brief, typical proverbial bits of counsel and advice.

Key verses. 8:12-14: Wisdom is true power.

Personal application. Beware of moral choices that appeal just to the senses and provide immediate gratification.

INSIGHT

Adultery. Adultery (*na'ap*), according to Heb. law, is intercourse with or by a married or betrothed woman and violates the sixth of the Ten Commandments (Ex. 20:14). The Law commanded Israel to put adulterers and adulteresses to death (Lev. 20:10), although this severe penalty was seldom executed. Prostitution (*zanah*), mentioned in Prov. 6:26, is any intercourse between a man and woman which does not violate the marriage vow. It too is forbidden (Lev. 19:29), but only religious prostitutes, who engaged in sex as part of pagan religious ceremonies, were to be put to death. The N.T. also condemns sexual immorality and calls for discipline by the church of those who practice it (cf. 1 Cor. 5:1-13). However, Jesus' compassionate response to the adulterous woman makes it clear that God's way of dealing with sexual sins, as with other sins, is the way of forgiveness—followed by repudiation of the sinful way of life. The N.T. also makes it clear that sexual immorality is characteristic of a godless lifestyle and that those who practice it will be judged (cf. 1 Tim. 1:10; Heb. 13:4; Rev. 21:8; 22:15).

But here in Prov. the writer is primarily concerned with the consequences of adultery. The foolish person who succumbs finds that in the end adultery brings ruin (5:4, 11, 14). He warns that no one can "walk on hot coals without his feet being scorched" (6:28), that the adulterer will arouse jealousy, earn blows and disgrace, and so destroy himself (6:30-35). While the prostitute "reduces you to a loaf of bread" by treating you as an object rather than a person, the adulteress "preys on your very life" (6:26).

These proverbs also make it clear that, while desire may spring up uninvited, committing adultery involves a choice (6:25). The wise man will turn away from opportunities for sexual adventures, to find joy and satisfaction in the love of his own wife (5:15-20). And, a wise man will remember that his "ways are in full view of the Lord" (5:21).

Characteristics of wisdom. It's helpful to list the characteristics of the wisdom which the writer praises as a divine quality (8:22) and which bring human beings long and blessed lives (9:11-12). Some of the characteristics mentioned in these chapters are: speaks what is right and true (8:6-8); detests wickedness (8:7); is associated with prudence, knowledge, and discretion (8:12); hates pride and arrogance (8:13); walks in the way of righteousness and justice (8:20).

Earlier chapters emphasized the benefits of wisdom. Wisdom protects (2:11-12), prolongs life and brings prosperity (3:1-2), wins favor in the sight of God and man (3:4), leads to riches and honor (3:16), and brings peace (3:17) and blessing (3:18). Wisdom keeps us from stumbling and from fear, so that "when you lie down . . . your sleep will be sweet" (3:24).

"Folly" (9:13). Folly, here "moral rebellion," is also personalized in chapters 6–9 as a woman and set in contrast to wisdom. Wisdom is disciplined, responsive to God, and rewards those who choose her. Folly is undisciplined, sensuous, and brings those who choose her to an early grave.

The contrast between wisdom and folly developed in these first chapters is a fitting introduction to the body of the book, which contains dozens of wisdom sayings.

Chapter summary. These chapters contain proverbs on many different topics. One of the recurrent themes introduced in these chapters contrasts the righteous and the wicked. The righteous are assured of blessing and of God's protection, while the wicked, though they may flourish briefly, are destined for death and destruction. Proverbs in chapters 10–14 that develop the contrast are 10:3, 6-7, 11, 20-21, 24-25, 27-32; 11:3-11, 17-21, 23, 28, 30-31; 12:2-3, 5-7, 10, 12-13, 21, 26, 28; 13:5-6, 9, 21-22, 25; 14:9, 11, 14, 19, 32. This theme is also developed in later chapters, in 15:6, 8-9, 26, 28-29; 16:8, 12-13; 17:13, 15; 18:5; 21:3, 7-8, 10, 12, 18, 26-27; 24:15-16; 25:26; 28:1, 12, 28; 29:2, 6-7, 16, 27.

Outline
Place
Finder

WISDOM
SOLOMON I
SAYINGS
SOLOMON II
OTHERS

Key verse. 10:3: God guarantees justice for all.

Personal application. Wealth, education, appearance—these are not the truly important differences between people. The important difference is whether a person is righteous or not.

INSIGHT

(10:4). The commandment establishing a day of rest says, "Six days you shall labor and do all your work" (Ex. 20:9). Industry is not only commended, it is commanded. It's also common sense, for aside from any moral issue "lazy hands make a man poor."

(10:10). "Winks maliciously" is to spread gossip or to attack by innuendo. The pain caused by vindictive or disparaging remarks stands in contrast to the positive impact of words spoken by the righteous, which are "a fountain of life" (v. 11). See also vv. 21, "The lips of the righteous nourish many."

(10:22). God's blessing on the righteous man brings trouble-free wealth. The thought is that when good fortune is a result of God's blessing, we are free of the anxieties which come when we make our money wrongfully. When riches come bound up in the same bundle with worries and fear, they can never satisfy.

(10:23). What we enjoy as well as what we dislike is a measure of our character. Anyone who finds sin amusing or enjoyable is a fool, not only warped, but also shallow and superficial.

(10:26). "Vinegar to the teeth and smoke to the eyes" are irritations. So is a person who dawdles.

(10:31). The proverb links speech and consequence. The rightous speak wisdom, obey God, and live, while the wicked speak folly, disobey, and die.

(11:1). Leviticus 19:35 36 forbids the use of "dishonest standards," weighted to favor the merchant rather than the seller or buyer. The Jewish Talmud calls for meticulous efforts to keep this command, decreeing that "the shopkeeper must wipe his measures twice a week,

his weights once a week, and his scales after every weighing," to keep any substance from throwing them off. We can't be too careful trying to be fair with others.

(11:10-11). Why should the community rejoice in the prosperity of the righteous? Because both the way a righteous man gains his wealth and the way he uses it benefits society. The righteous businessman employs others, supports schools and government with his taxes and, in the O.T. tradition, shares generously.

(12:1). The Heb. calls the man who hates correction "brutish." The thought is that animals, controlled by instinct, are unable to learn from criticism. The person who gets angry when corrected rather than taking the criticism to heart has as little chance to make moral progress as a dumb animal.

(12:10). Animals are not viewed with contempt because they are less than human. They are viewed with compassion, and we are to accept responsibility to care for them.

(13:8). A rich man may be able to pay ransom, but a poor man is protected from kidnapping in the first place!

(13:24). A parent who fails to discipline his or her children is not showing love. The verb translated here as "hate" is used in a comparative sense. If you really love your children, you don't overlook their faults, but take steps to correct them. The phrase "spare the rod" is euphemistic and does not mandate spanking as a form of punishment, although corporal punishment was certainly practiced in biblical times.

(14:14). The Heb. reads "from upon him a good man" is rewarded. The thought is that we can find a deep satisfaction in doing good, irrespective of material benefits.

Chapter summary. These chapters contain proverbs that instruct on many different topics. One recurrent theme is that of wealth. The proverbs note both the benefits and drawbacks of riches and repeatedly warn that ill-gotten wealth is a curse rather than a blessing. One of the major drawbacks of riches emphasized in Proverbs is summed up in 18:11: "The wealth of the rich is their fortified city; they imagine it an unscalable wall." How foolish this is is seen in the contrast set up by 18:10: "The name of the Lord is a strong tower; the righteous run to it and are safe."

Proverbs that help us put material possessions in perspective include 10:2, 4, 15, 22; 11:4, 28; 13:8, 21, 22; 14:24; 15:27; 16:16; 19:4; 20:21; 22:4; 23:4-6; 28:8, 20, 25.

Key verse. 18:11: Always remember what money can't do.

Personal application. Only the bank of heaven can never fail.

INSIGHT

A "soft answer" has practical value (15:1). But the verse also implies that it sets a standard of conduct. A Talmud comment on this verse commends, "they who are oppressed and oppress not, who listen to insults without retorting, who act lovingly and are happy under trials."

(15:15). Our disposition rather than our circumstances is the key to enjoying life.

(15:27). A person who is free of an eager desire for wealth has the advantage over the driven materialist. The thought here may be that the greedy man troubles his house by ultimately being punished, and his family then experiences hardship. But it is more likely that he troubles his family by inculcating his children with values that bring spiritual disaster.

(16:2). We so easily rationalize and justify our actions. Consciously or unconsciously, we easily fall victim to self-deceit. The Apostle Paul says, "My conscience is clear, but that does not make me innocent" (1 Cor. 4:4). Only God is capable of weighing our secret motives. Let's not be too confident of our innocence, remaining aware of our constant need for God's cleansing grace.

(16:7). Rabbinical commentators observe that it is not God who makes enemies be at peace with the person who walks in His ways. It's the man whose own actions make for peace. The rabbis found profound meaning here, noting that our honesty may not prevent a particular enemy from harming us, but that it makes it easier for others to be honest and helps reduce dishonesty in a community.

Choosing to walk in God's ways is preventative; it keeps others from becoming hostile to us and to God.

(16:9). The rabbis did not see this as a declaration of sovereignty, but a call to purification. If

you choose to live God's way, God will direct your steps to your desired godliness.

(17:14). The imagery is especially clear. We can stop a leak in a dam when it's tiny, but unless we stop it then the hole will enlarge and become a raging torrent. Be quick to forgive and say "I'm sorry," or irreparable harm may be done to important personal relationships.

Friendship (17:17). The most common word for friend in the O.T. is rea'. Its meanings range from "chance acquaintance" to "neighbor" and thus a long term friend. The Leviticus 19:18 command to love one's neighbor uses this term and implies that we are to extend a helping hand to anyone in need with whom we come in contact.

A stronger kind of friendship is implied in some uses of the word 'aheb, "love." Here we have a deep commitment, a bonding like that which existed between David and Jonathan (1 Sam. 18–20). In the same sense, the O.T. says Abraham was a "friend" of God: i.e., loved Him deeply. This proverb uses "friend" and "brother" interchangeably to emphasize that a true friend will stick by us in adversity as well as good times.

Each of us needs to be a friend to the world around us. But we also need close friends who stand by us because a bond of caring has been forged.

(18:24). The phrase "a man of many companions" is characterization. It means a person who indiscriminately multiplies superficial acquaintanceships. He or she is criticized for failing to realize that what really counts is investing time in building deeper, caring relationships with people who will remain faithful no matter what happens. What a reminder for you and me.

Chapter summary. Again the proverbs of Solomon collected in these chapters touch on many themes. One of them, discussed often in the psalms, is the condition of the poor. Proverbs do point out the drawbacks of poverty. But they also offset them with reminders that one's economic condition is not nearly as significant as a personal relationship with God, good marriage, or clear conscience. Specific proverbs that provide a balanced view include: 6:10-11; 10:4, 15; 13:8, 18; 14:20, 31; 17:5; 18:23; 19:1, 4, 7, 17, 22; 22:2, 7, 9, 16, 22-23; 24:3-34; 28:6, 8, 19, 22; 29:7; 30:11-14; 31:8-9.

Outline
Place
Finder

WISDOM
SOLOMON I
SAYINGS
SOLOMON II
OTHERS

Key verse. 22:2: Rich and poor are equal before God.

Personal application. Your reputation is your real wealth.

INSIGHT

(19:1-7). The proverbs are both idealistic and realistic. This section insists that "better a poor man whose walk is blameless" (idealistic, v. 1) and yet is well aware that "a poor man is shunned by all his relatives" and avoided by all his friends (realistic, v. 7). The wonderful thing about the proverbs is that despite their utter realism, they persistently remind us to choose what is right rather than what is expedient. If you face a choice between a blameless walk and wealth, choose the former.

(19:10). It's not fitting because wealth permits the foolish person to indulge himself and thus confirms his folly.

(19:17). The word translated "poor" is one that emphasizes weakness and thus a desperate need for help. When we assist a person in real need, God Himself accepts the obligation to repay us.

(19:18). The rabbis observed that, however perverse a child may be, a father was to keep on correcting, rather than give up and say, "There's nothing more I can do!" We keep on disciplining because in parental discipline there is hope.

There may be even more here. The second part of the proverb suggests some parents become hostile toward unresponsive children and wish to be rid of them. But hope protects us from hostility.

(19:25). A rabbinic saying that sums up this proverb's teaching says, "To the wise man with a hint, to the fool with a fist."

(20:11). Traits shown early in life tend to remain with us throughout our lives.

(20:27). It is better to take the alternate reading in the NIV, "the spirit of man is the Lord's lamp." The rabbis understood this to mean that God's image so shines in the human spirit that man is set apart from the animals. It's this reflection of God which endows us with human abilities and witnesses to His existence

through each of our unique capacities.

(21:13). Again "poor" indicates the weak and needy individual. The verse does not teach that God will not answer, but that if the hard-hearted person should become poor, she can expect no generosity from those she ignored. Today we say it quite simply. "What goes around, comes around."

Training children (22:6). The verse's reference to "in the way he should go" does not refer just to the moral content of nurture, but also to the developmental process. The Heb. suggests that we are to train according to the child's "way," or stage of growth. When we match training in God's way of life to a child's learning style, "when he is old he will not turn from it."

But remember that while this proverb, like the others, states a general principle that has universal application, it will not prove true in every case. If your child should abandon God's ways when mature, don't blame yourself. Human beings are not computers to be programmed. Each of us has the freedom to make moral choices. At times, those given the best of Christian nurture will turn from God despite it.

Foolishness (22:15). One type of "fool" that can be distinguished from the four Heb. words so translated is described by the word 'iwwelet. The word describes a person who is insolent or rebellious, a person who impetuously insists on his or her own way. (See p. 393 for a list of Scripture's kinds of fools.)

Children are headstrong and need to learn self-discipline as well as judgment (v. 6). Despite the objections of some moderns, it is not wrong to use the "rod of correction" (corporal punishment, or spanking) in disciplining such children. At the same time, it's not necessary to use this kind of punishment when a child is responsive and willing to learn.

Outline
Place
Finder

WISDOM
SOLOMON I
SAYINGS
SOLOMON II
OTHERS

Chapter summary. Beginning with 22:17 and continuing through Proverbs 24 is a collection of "sayings of the wise." These too range over a wide variety of topics, touching on basic themes such as wisdom and folly (23:9; 24:3-7), the righteous and the wicked (24:15-16), the family (23:13-16), laziness and hard work (24:30-34), rich and poor (23:4-5), government (23:1-3; 24:21), the fear of the Lord (23:17; 24:21), and many others. This brief special collection reminds us that wisdom literature is primarily concerned with passing on general principles for living a prudent, enlightened, and godly way of life.

Key verses. 23:17-18: The prudent way of life works in the end.

Personal application. The ability to persist in doing right without immediate reward is a sign of spiritual maturity.

INSIGHT

(22:22-23). People tend to exploit those whom they view as helpless and leave the powerful alone. But the O.T. portrays God as the protector of the poor. We oppress the weak at our peril!

(23:9). The thought seems to be, don't bother to explain things to a fool. Even if he understands what you're saying, he won't recognize your insights as wisdom. Plato believed that if a person only knew the good, he would invariably choose it. The Bible knows better. Those who are hardened and unresponsive to God will resist doing good even when they know what it is.

(23:13-14). Some parents overlook a child's faults, pleading that he or she is too young for correction, or that he or she will "grow out of" the wrong behavior. The writers of Prov. took a very different view. A spanking now won't kill your child, but permitting a wayward trait to take root might!

The father's role (23:19-26). The proverb above, as well as 23:19, 22, suggest a major element in the role of the father in O.T. times. In Heb. culture the father was the head of the house and with the wife was to be respected and honored by other members of the family (cf. Ex. 20:12; 21:15, 17). The father was also primarily responsible for the economic well-being of the family (Deut. 1:31). Thus, in the O.T. "the widow and the fatherless" (Ps. 146:9) is an expression that means, simply, powerless and needy.

The primary responsibility of the father was to see to the discipline and spiritual guidance of children. This is reflected in our proverbs (cf. also 10:1; 15:20; 17:21) and also in other such passages (Deut. 6:4-9; 32:7, 45-47; and Isa. 38:19). While each individual is responsible for his or her own choices in life, the father's in-

struction is viewed as invaluable for keeping a child on the path of godliness. So the writer of proverbs says, "listen to your father, who gave you life" and "be wise" (Prov. 23:19, 22).

Perils of drunkenness (23:29-35). A series of proverbs warns against drunkenness by pointing out its drawbacks. The drunken person is quarrelsome, and his senses are so dulled he is likely to get into a fight when no cause exists (v. 29). They waste time drinking and looking for some new drink to try (v. 30). They focus on its sensory appeal rather than evaluate its poisonous impact on their lives and relationships (vv. 31-32). When they are intoxicated they can neither see nor think straight (v. 33) and are completely unstable (v. 34). The drunkard's senses may be so dulled that he doesn't feel blows when he is struck, but when he comes out of his stupor he'll feel the pain—and go right back to the drink which led to it (v. 35).

(24:16). "Seven times" in this verse means "frequently." The righteous may stumble again and again, but he or she will not fail permanently. What a word of comfort this is to fathers who try to guide their children, but are aware of so many faults and failures. Don't be discouraged. You may make many mistakes, but God will enable you to get up, try again—and succeed.

(24:17-18, 29). When we rejoice in an enemy's troubles we display an attitude that is just like his. We join him in wishing another human being harm rather than good. Because God cares intensely that we walk close to Him, the Lord is apt to "turn His wrath away from him" to keep us from our sin—or perhaps to judge us rather than him! A similar wrong attitude is reflected in the common view that we have a right to repay (v. 29).

Chapter summary. These chapters contain a second collection of proverbs attributed to Solomon. Like the other proverbs in this book, they touch on a variety of subjects. At the same time, many of them focus our attention on the fool, who is frequently contrasted to the wise or the righteous person. The Hebrew language distinguishes three kinds of fools, each of which is represented in this book. *'Iwwelet* describes a person who is morally deficient in a way shown by impetuous action and insistence on his or her own way. This root is translated "fool" or "folly" in Proverbs 1:7; 5:23; 7:22; 10:8, 14, 23; 11:29; 12:15-16, 23; 13:16; 14:1, 3, 8-9, 17-18, 24, 29; 15:2, 14, 21; 16:22; 17:12, 28; 18:13; 19:3; 20:3; 22:15; 24:7, 9; 26:4-5, 11; 27:3, 22; 29:9. *Kesil* pictures an obstinate person who consciously rejects fear of the Lord. This fool is often portrayed as sexually immoral. This term is found in Proverbs 1:22, 32; 3:35; 8:5; 10:1, 18, 23; 12:23; 13:16, 19, 20; 14:7, 8, 16, 24; 14:33; 15:2, 7, 14, 20; 17:10, 12, 16, 21, 24, 25; 18:2, 6, 7; 19:1, 10, 13, 29; 21:20; 23:9; 26:1, 3-12; 28:26; 29:11, 20. *Nabal* is a perverse fool, who is closed both to God and morality. His folly is typically shown in gross sins, such as homosexuality and rape. This kind of fool is the subject of Proverbs 17:7, 21 and 30:22.

Key verse. 26:12: What the wise know.

Personal application. It's more dangerous to think you know everything than to be a fool. A fool is more likely to change.

INSIGHT

(25:8-10). The advice in these verses has to do with lawsuits. The counsel Solomon gives is to first be sure you have a sound case (v. 8). Here "put to shame" means simply that the verdict may go against you. The rabbis understood verse 9 as calling for discussion of the matter with one's neighbor. If the matter is settled in your favor, you're not to "betray a confidence" and tell everyone what your neighbor did wrong. Verse 10 shows that anyone who betrays confidences soon loses the trust of others to work out fair and private resolutions in the future.

(25:14). Folks who constantly brag about what they are going to do usually can be counted on not to do it. Only evaluate a gift after you receive it, not before!

(25:28). Self-restraint is our best defense against calamity.

(25:4-5). How do we treat these two, obviously contradictory proverbs? The Talmud suggests that the difference is in the subject on which the fool is making pronouncements. If it's merely a secular matter, ignore him (v. 4). But if a fool makes some pronouncement on a matter of real importance, such as spiritual truths, then he should be answered, lest your silence is taken as agreement and he remains "wise in his own eyes" and thus closed to truth (cf. Prov. 26:12).

(26:20). The best way to silence gossip is not to repeat it.

(26:26). You can conceal your hostility toward an individual, but your talk and actions will make that anger known to the greater community. The rabbis taught that the verse implies some specific hostile act that would lead to court action and punishment.

(27:11). As the worth of a teacher is determined by the accomplishments of the students, so the real value of a godly person's character can often be estimated by qualities exhibited by his or her children.

(28:1). Conscience, like one's shadow, cannot be escaped.

(28:9). A refusal to listen to God's Word disqualifies our prayers, where trying and failing will not.

(28:23). Flattery may win quick acceptance, but honesty wins another's trust.

(29:25). Worry about what others will say or think, and trying to act accordingly, is a moral snare. We can be released only by trusting in God and caring about what He thinks.

Chapter summary. The last two chapters in Proverbs were contributed by two unknowns, Agur and King Lemuel. One late tradition suggests that Lemuel is Solomon and that the lengthy praise of a virtuous woman in Proverbs 31:10-31 was dedicated to his mother, Bathsheba. The real contribution of this passage, however, is to demonstrate that women played an important social and economic role in Old Testament times. The *Expository Dictionary of Bible Words* (Zondervan, 1985) notes that in that agrarian society women actually filled roles that were the same as men. Thus the noble wife of this chapter "supervised a staff of workers (v. 27). She served as buyer for her enterprises (v. 13). She sold what her staff produced (vv. 18-24), and she invested her profits (v. 16). She had the freedom to give to help the needy (v. 20). She was respected for her wisdom and responsibility (vv. 14-15, 26-31)." Each of these is a "business" function, and while the woman's activities were linked to her home and family, the biblical picture of the woman's role is a far cry from the "stay-home-and-care-for-the-kids" concept of many moderns. In Old Testament times women had the opportunity to use their God-given abilities.

Key verse. 31:10: The noble wife is an accomplished person.

Personal application. Watch out for the "biblical view of women" that is merely male chauvinism dressed up in a misapplied text.

Key concepts. Women »p. 723. See also »p. 163, Women in ministry.

INSIGHT

The Bible's portrait of women. The creation story makes it clear that both men and women were created in the image of God and thus are equal as persons (Gen. 1–2). With sin, the biblical ideal for male/female relationships became distorted, as did all other things in life (cf. Gen. 3:16). There is no doubt that in ancient societies, including the Heb., women were subordinate to men. This is reflected in the leadership role Heb. culture arrogated to men for civil responsibility in the household and to male elders as the ones having governmental responsibility for the community.

And, comparatively speaking, males had greater economic value than females, a fact reflected in the monetary values set by age and gender in the O.T.'s laws concerning vows (cf. Lev. 27:1-8). It is also true that women had fewer civil rights under O.T. laws, which does not reflect on the intrinsic worth of women but rather on the biblical law's flexibility in taking cultural patterns into account.

Yet any apparent chauvinism is balanced by a greater appreciation for women in the O.T. than was displayed in other contemporary cultures. It is also balanced by the respect Scripture calls

for toward older women, as well as older men, and toward mothers as well as fathers. The fact that women were not automatically deprived of politically or spiritually sensitive roles by their sex is illustrated by the many significant women the O.T. singles out. Among them are Abigail and Ruth, who functioned within the traditional women's role (1 Sam. 25; Ruth). But there are also women who broke the mold and served as prophets (Ex. 15:20; 2 Kings 22:14; 2 Chron. 34:22) and even one who served as a judge (Jud. 4:4-5).

If we are to see women in adequate perspective we must first of all affirm their absolute unity with men as persons of value and worth. We must also realize that women must be given, within society, opportunities to utilize all the capacities of personhood with which they have been endowed. Women are equal to men in ability, and gifted individuals should be encouraged to use their abilities within, and at times outside of, culturally defined expectations. Like the "noble wife" of Prov. 31, each woman, as well as each man, should be given the opportunity to achieve and be honored for every accomplishment.

Ecclesiastes

The title, Ecclesiastes, means "preacher," as does the Hebrew term *Qoheleth*, by which the writer identifies himself. This teacher is a philosopher, who sets out to explore life's meaning. His cry, repeated in 1:2 and 12:8, sums up his conclusion: " 'Meaningless! Meaningless!' says the Teacher. 'Utterly meaningless! Everything is meaningless!' "

This theme is developed in a number of discourses, the first set demonstrating the meaninglessness of life, and the second drawing ethical deductions from his observations on life.

This pessimistic tone seems out of place in the Bible, a book which is vibrant with hope. But its role in Scripture can be understood when we grasp the nature of *Qoheleth's* study. He limits his search for life's meaning to data gained by the senses within the material universe alone. This is reflected in the phrase "under the sun," which occurs 29 times in the book.

He also relies only on the power of human reason, stating seven times that he "communed with my own heart." In essence, the writer consciously ignored special revelation to find out if life holds any meaning apart from insights provided by God. Given this framework, the book makes an important contribution. It resonates with the emptiness we all feel when alienated from God and demonstrates that apart from a personal relationship with Him, life is meaningless indeed. The Teacher's conclusions also remind us that, while nature does witness to God's existence, and human experience commends a moral lifestyle, only a living Word from God can pierce the darkness in which we live. Reason apart from revelation is powerless to provide mankind with valid spiritual hope.

Interpreting Ecclesiastes

The unique nature of this book also shapes our interpretation. Ecclesiastes is not a word from God, but a word from one of history's wisest men. His conclusions are eminently reasonable, but are frequently wrong! Thus such sayings as "the dead know nothing: they have no further reward," is an appropriate deduction from what man can observe. But it is not true, as other passages of Scripture which are revelation, make clear. If we read this book as an accurate portrayal of the best reasoning of which man is capable, we will sense the emptiness in human beings that God is eager to fill with His love. We will better understand our unsaved neighbors and become more sensitive to their needs.

Date and authorship. The traditional view holds that Solomon is the author of Ecclesiastes. This is suggested by internal evidence, which identifies the author as a descendant of David, who ruled in Jerusalem (1:1), was renowned for his wisdom (v. 16), and possessed unparalleled wealth (2:8) which he used in extensive building projects (v. 4-6).

Some modern scholars have argued that the philosophical cast of the book and its many distinctive words point to a postexilic date. However, the linguistic arguments have all been satisfactorily answered by conservative scholars, and a preexilic date is fully justified. It is likely the book was composed near the end of Solomon's reign, perhaps in his last decade (940–930 B.C.).

THEOLOGICAL OUTLINE OF ECCLESIASTES

I. PROLOGUE	1:1-11
II. THEME PROVEN	1:12–6:12
III. ETHICAL DEDUCTIONS	7:1–12:8
IV. EPILOGUE	12:9-14

CONTENT OUTLINE OF ECCLESIASTES

I. The Theme Stated (1:1-11)
  A. Life Is Meaningless (1:2)
  B. Human Experience Is Cyclical, Meaningless (1:3-11)
II. The Theme Explored (1:12–6:12)
  A. Where Men Seek Meaning (1:12–2:26)
    1. Philosophy (1:12-15)
    2. Pleasure and wealth (2:1-11)
    3. Wisdom (2:12-16)
    4. Accomplishments (2:17-23)
    5. Control (2:24-26)
  B. Human Powerlessness Is Seen in the Laws That Govern Every Person's Life (3:1–5:20)
    1. The seasons (3:1-8)
    2. God alone establishes abiding values (3:9-15)
    3. God brings death (3:16-20)
    4. Man must make the best of his life (3:21-22)
    5. Man cannot escape suffering or cruelty (4:1-3)
    6. Success has drawbacks (4:4-8)
    7. Trials (4:9-12)
    8. Political careers are unstable (4:13-16)
    9. Mere religion is folly (5:1-7)
    10. Retribution strikes wicked and greedy (5:8-17)
    11. One's only hope of contentment is thankfulness for God's gifts (5:18-20)
  C. Where Do We Find Meaning? (6:1-12)
    1. Not wealth or family (6:1-6)
    2. Not wisdom (6:7-9)
    3. No meaning exists—apart from God (6:10-12)
III. What Ethical Guidelines Can Be Found in Life? (7:1–12:8)
  A. Prudence, in View of Sin's Corruption (7:1-29)
    1. Measure values (7:1-4)
    2. Avoid pitfalls (7:5-9)
    3. Choose wisdom (7:10-12)
    4. Acknowledge God (7:13-14)
    5. Avoid self-righteousness/immorality (7:15-18)
    6. Remember sin's impact on wisdom (7:19-20)
    7. Ignore malice (7:21-22)
    8. Wisdom cannot uncover spiritual truth (7:23-25)
    9. Avoid wicked women (7:26)
    10. Remember all are fallen (7:27-29)
  B. Adjust to Life in an Imperfect World (8:1-17)
    1. Respect government (8:1-5)
    2. Acknowledge divine law (8:6-13)
    3. Enjoy life (8:14-17)
  C. Do Your Best Despite Injustices (9:1–12:8)
    1. Shape life in view of coming certain death (9:1-18)
    2. Be prudent (10:1-4)
    3. Expect reversals (10:5-11)
    4. Don't trust fools (10:12-15)
    5. Be responsible (10:16-20)
    6. Be kind to others (11:1-2)
    7. Don't expect to understand God's laws (11:3-5)
    8. Work diligently (11:6-8)
    9. Avoid foolish pleasures (11:9-10)
    10. Honor God while young (12:1-8)
IV. Conclusion (12:9-14)

Chapter summary. The Teacher launches his treatise with a cry: "Meaningless!" (1:1-2) He has examined history and nature and discovered only repeated cycles, with no progress toward any goal (vv. 3-11). The initial pessimistic affirmation is followed by a carefully reasoned presentation of proof. From 1:12 through 6:12 the Teacher explains how he reached his gloomy conclusion. He has looked at those things in which men suppose they find meaning and found each empty and vain. No ultimate value can be found in philosophy (vv. 12-16), in pleasure or wealth (2:1-11), in wisdom (vv. 12-16), or in personal accomplishments (vv. 17-23). In the last analysis, man has no control over his situation in this life (vv. 24-26).

Key verse. 1:2: Apart from God, the Teacher is right.

Personal application. If you look for meaning in the things this world has to offer, you are doomed to disappointment.

INSIGHT

"Meaningless" (1:2). The Heb. word, *hebel*, means brief and insubstantial, empty and futile. The sense of life's emptiness is echoed some 30 times in this brief book. His conviction is that no earthly experience itself, apart from any link with God, can satisfy.

"No remembrance" (1:11). How can life have meaning when the individual not only loses his self-awareness in death, but his existence is not even remembered as Earth evolves on through its endless, weary cycles? We believe that we are unique and important. But how can our lives have meaning if we are not even remembered?

What an answer the rest of Scripture gives. That unique self is not lost, but will exist throughout eternity. We are not forgotten, for each of us is remembered by God. » Eternal life, p. 682.

"Wisdom" (1:13). Here "wisdom" has the meaning of "skillful thought." Man's rational capacities may guide in this life but cannot solve its mysteries.

Ancient existentialism (2:1-11). This recent philosophical school holds that life is meaningless, but that a person can affirm his or her significance by acting. Solomon tried. He tested sensual pleasures; he undertook great building projects; he assembled wealth—and denied himself nothing his heart desired. And all the while he felt as empty as ever. In the darkness of night he thought about his experiences and accomplishments and was filled with a sense of futility: "Everything was meaningless" (v. 11).

Even the wealthiest and most successful men and women of today, in their quiet moments, feel what Solomon felt. There is a void

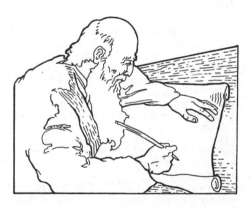

Illustration. *Internal evidence suggests Solomon penned this book in his old age. First Kings 11 tells us that during that time the king abandoned Yahweh to worship the pagan deities of his foreign wives. Ecclesiastes is more than just philosophy. It is the heart cry of a believer who has lost his way and is desperately searching for meaning in a life bereft of God. It is significant that nowhere in this book does the Teacher use the personal name of God revealed to Israel, Yahweh. Rational thought does lead to the author's conclusion that God exists and created the universe, but it cannot lead anyone to saving faith apart from that revelation Solomon chose to reject.*

in every human life that only God can fill.

"God" (2:24-26). Solomon knows there is a Creator and recommends enjoying His gifts.

Chapter summary. The Teacher continues his demonstration of life's meaninglessness. He turns first to observable laws of nature and human experience that render man powerless to significantly affect his fate. Any sense of control that a person achieves is illusory, for the truly significant choices are made for us. The seasons govern our activities (3:1-8). God establishes values (vv. 9-15) and punishes—and decrees death for all (vv. 16-20). A man has only one brief life to live (vv. 21-22). During it he cannot escape suffering (4:1-3). Even success has its drawbacks (vv. 4-8). Trials make it difficult for a person to be independent or face life alone (vv. 9-12). Political careers that appear to lift us above others, are unstable (vv. 13-16). Taken together these facts of life show how limited our human powers are. There is nothing we can do to cross the boundaries that restrict us and remind us of the meaninglessness of life on Earth.

Key verse. 3:11: Our hearts yearn for something that nothing in this life can satisfy.

Personal application. Limitations are intended to remind us of our mortality and point us to God.

INSIGHT

"A time for everything" (3:1-8). This brief and beautiful poem has been celebrated and even set to music in our time. On the one hand, it speaks of order and security: God has created a stable universe marked by reliable patterns. But James Barr rightly points out that the Teacher senses "the frustrating effect of time on human life and labor." The invariable calendar of the seasons and the flow of time imposes its own order on our lives. Time, not man, is the master. Time ridicules our innate sense of importance and shows life to be meaningless.

Man's "burden" (3:10-11). The "burden" the lost carry is awareness that something more exists in this world—and the inability to grasp what it is. Human beings were created with a capacity for eternal things and a realization that this life cannot be all there is. Yet, sin has cut us off from eternity and darkened our understanding and will. What a burden to bear: to yearn for eternity and yet not know God.

"Nothing can be added to it" (3:13-14). This recognition of God has been seen by some as a new factor, marking a transition from pessimism to optimism. Not at all, instead it is an expression of Solomon's continuing frustration. God has already done all that can be done to pattern His universe. Whatever a man may do, he can add nothing lasting to the design of the universe, nor take anything from it. Man is ineffectual, and thus whatever he does is meaningless.

"Man's fate" (3:18-19). This is one of those passages we must understand within the framework the Teacher has established. As far as a person can tell by observation, death is the same for man and animals. The body ceases to breathe and move, the form corrupts. The body of a man, like that of an animal, decays. "Who knows if the spirit of man rises upward and if the spirit of an animal goes down into the earth?" (v. 21) There is no proof. By consciously choosing to ignore revelation, Solomon has condemned himself to live without hope. Reason cannot prove the human personality is eternal. Without divine revelation, life would seem empty and meaningless indeed.

The blessed dead? (4:2-3) Solomon's reasonings have driven him to despair. Self-consciousness is a curse, for the reasonable man realizes that his life is meaningless. Rather than be burdened with that grim knowledge, a person is better off dead, but best off never being born. How terrible depression and despair are.

"Envy of his neighbor" (4:4-8). Here the Teacher argues that man's passion for success and wealth is motivated by a desire to surpass others and thus validate one's own importance. But even a successful quest for wealth and position brings no meaning, and the person at last realizes the futility of toil.

Status too is meaningless (4:13-16). Just wait till the next poll. Your popularity will be down!

Chapter summary. The Teacher has faced man's ultimate insignificance. His reasoning leads to an awareness of God's awesome powers. It is only wise that a vulnerable human being show respect for God, for He holds a life in His hands.

It is folly to merely go through the motions of religion if God is real (5:1-7). It is also folly to love money, which is more likely to harm than help and surely cannot provide life with meaning (vv. 8-17). One may as well enjoy life and avoid reflecting on its meaning as long as possible (vv. 18-20).

The Teacher now sums up his observations. Even the man who has everything leads an empty life (6:1-6). Wise and foolish alike live only a "few and meaningless days," passing "through [life] like a shadow" and leaving nothing behind (vv. 7-12).

Outline
Place
Finder

PROLOGUE
PROOF
ETHICS
EPILOGUE

Key verse. 5:17: A lost man's life is not worth living.

Personal application. Sense the despair that underlies others' lives. Then share the Good News that brings life and peace.

INSIGHT

The sacrifice of fools (5:1-3). This fool goes through the motions of worship, never realizing that he doesn't know God and thus that even as he sacrifices he does wrong. The Teacher stands back, aware that God is a mystery, and so makes no bold theological statements.

Ritual without relationship, like religion without a personal faith, is incapable of giving life meaning.

"Stand in awe of God" (5:4-7). Nature reveals enough about God to cause humans to hold Him in awe. Whatever one promises God had best be performed, for He has the power to punish.

The point is valid, yet it serves to establish Solomon's present estrangement from the Lord. Love, not fear, is the motivating force in the believer's desire to serve God. Knowing only enough about God to fear Him never frees a person from a sense of life's meaninglessness. We must know enough about God to love Him. Then we will see in His love the guarantee of eternal life that gives meaning to our existence, beyond time and throughout eternity.

Meaning and money (5:8-17). Solomon's observations demonstrate the futility of seeking meaning through materialism. The passion for gain creates injustice at every level of society (vv. 8-9). A love for money can never bring satisfaction, for the rich always want more (v. 10). No one can spend all his riches alone—for instance, a person can eat only so much food even if he is a billionaire!

Just look at his money (5:11). Wealth keeps the rich man awake worrying about how to keep it (v. 12) and can be lost by circumstances

beyond the individual's control (v. 13). In the end a man dies, and when he leaves this world he cannot take even one cent with him (vv. 14-17). Solomon rightly concludes that the man who seeks life's meaning in money "eats in darkness, with great frustration, affliction, and anger" (v. 17).

We need to keep this bleak but accurate evaluation in mind. Most of us are vulnerable to the illusion that money could solve all our problems and enrich our lives. Money cannot solve our problems. It cannot give life meaning. And all too often, wealth spoils life rather than enriches it.

He seldom reflects on life (5:18-20). This is a strange paragraph, and not at all the affirmation of simple faith some take it to be. Solomon here recommends that human beings accept the notion that they are limited to the good things this life holds, enjoy them, and seldom reflect on whether life has meaning.

In Ps. 74 Asaph makes an acute observation. The person who prospers and is satisfied with this world's goods is in a slippery place. He never looks beyond this life and never senses any need for relationship with God. Solomon recommends that attitude to dull the pain of life's ultimate emptiness. Asaph decries that attitude, because he believes probing life's emptiness will result in the discovery of God.

"The more the words, the less the meaning" (6:11). The Teacher has tried to find meaning. He has honed the tools of observation, rational thought, and deduction. But rather than making sense out of life, his examination of the reality that man experiences shows that life makes less sense than he assumed.

Chapter summary. Ethics is the study of standards of conduct. *Qoheleth* has concluded that life has no ultimate meaning. But his inquiry has suggested rules he believes can provide some guide to life here on earth. These rules reflect his conclusion that in a sin-cursed society a person must act prudently (7:1-29), and learn to adjust to the imperfections that exist here and now (8:1-17). Further, life must be lived in full awareness of the certainty of death (9:1-18).

The ethical conclusion Ecclesiastes draws is defensive in nature. He urges no zealous pursuit of good, no commitment to unrealistic ideals. And in this too Ecclesiastes differs from the rest of Scripture. Because God is, our labor is never in vain ("empty, meaningless"); we can confidently give ourselves "fully to the work of the Lord" (1 Cor. 15:58).

Key verse. 9:2: On the contrary, righteousness does pay!

Personal application. Commit yourself enthusiastically to God's code of conduct and guarantee an eternal reward.

INSIGHT

Why better? (7:1-4) What assumptions underlie this brief collection of the Teacher's proverbs? Some suggest that sorrow and grief force us to think about the meaning of life and that this is better than living superficially. However, the rest of the book points out that the more eagerly a man searches for life's meaning, the greater his disappointment and frustration. A better reason is seen when we note that this collection launches *Qoheleth's* examination of ethics. What he seems to say is that realism is a better guide. It is best to be aware of life's dark side and live with reality than to deceive yourself and build your life on illusion.

Again the author is right—if his methodology and resources are appropriate. But if we look beyond human experience to revelation, and rely not on reason but on faith, we reach very different conclusions indeed.

The laid-back life (7:7-9). Ecclesiastes takes sides with the stoics. Step back. Don't become too involved. Don't arouse passion or get hope. If we don't care, we can't be hurt too much.

Fight no windmills (7:13-14). Don Quixote is the classic idealist, rushing off to fight windmills in the mistaken assumption they are giants and assuming that a local prostitute is a lady in disguise. The realist may be moved by Quixote's noble delusion, but considers it madness. So does the Teacher. Man can do nothing to make any difference, so he resigns himself to take what comes, enjoy the good, and try to survive the bad.

Just fit in (7:15-18). Moderation is the ethical watchword. It doesn't pay to be wicked. But it doesn't pay to be overly righteous either. If we look for our reward in this life, he's right. If we look for it later, he couldn't be more wrong.

Don't rock the boat (8:5-6). This is a far cry from Rom. 13's exhortation to obey rulers for conscience's sake. It is simple expedience. We have many sayings that express the thought: "You can't fight city hall." "No use swimming upstream." "Go with the flow."

Avoid crime (8:11-13). Even if some get away with crime, it will still "not go well with them." There's always the risk of punishment.

Enjoy your meaningless life while you can (9:9-10). The ethics of the Teacher truly are defensive. Life is ultimately meaningless, but the author's ethical advice is designed to help us hold on to it as long as we can. Life holds no lasting pleasures, so he advises us to enjoy the fleeting pleasures while we can.

Ecclesiastes makes no judgment about a life after death. It shrugs off that issue, saying that "no man knows whether love or hate awaits him" (v. 1). The good and the evil die alike. As far as experience can tell, "the dead know nothing; they have no further reward, and even the memory of them is forgotten" (vv. 5-6).

But when we by faith claim our eternal future in Christ, what a different ethic results. An ethic of love emerges that challenges complacency and is fiercely intent on doing good.

Outline
Place
Finder

PROLOGUE
PROOF
ETHICS
EPILOGUE

Chapter summary. Ecclesiastes continues its exploration of ethics. The writer has called on his readers to shape life in view of the certainty of death (9:1-18). Now he continues to outline his defensive ethics, intended to protect the individual not only from the perils of this life but also from too much speculation on life's meaninglessness. *Qoheleth* calls for prudence (10:1-4), pessimism (vv. 5-11), suspicion (vv. 12-15), responsibility (vv. 16-20), and kindness (11:1-2). One should not try to understand life (vv. 3-5) but work diligently (vv. 6-8) and enjoy life (vv. 9-10).

Solomon's last chapter has been taken as a conversion, a grand return to faith. It is not. It is rather another statement of the fact that man grows old and dies (12:1-5).

Even reason suggests that man's only hope is some attachment to the eternal and the hope that man's spirit "returns to God who gave it" (vv. 6-8). Whatever expectation a man has must lie beyond this world, so man's best hope is to fear God and keep His commandments (vv. 9-14).

Key verse. 12:13: Even reason points us back, at last, to God.

Personal application. Rejoice that you know the Lord and are certain of everlasting blessing.

INSIGHT

Don't expect justice, and you won't be disappointed (10:5-9). The Teacher continues his exposition of defensive ethics. Life may be meaningless, but we still need guidelines to help us make the most of it. Here are some of the things that he advises.

On diligence (10:18). Your accomplishments won't make life meaningful. But if you work hard shingling your roof, at least your bed won't be wet at night.

On wealth (10:19). No, money won't buy happiness, but it will buy most other things. You're much better off with it. After all, you may as well enjoy your misery!

On talk (10:20). What you don't say can't hurt you. What you do say, might. So keep your thoughts to yourself.

On thinking ahead (11:1-2). Be prepared. Spread a little bread around, so when you need help it will be there.

On hesitation (11:4). If you wait for conditions to be ideal, you'll never act. It's just as foolish never to act, as to act rashly.

On overconfidence (11:5). Don't ever think you've got a foolproof plan. You don't understand the processes of nature. What makes you think you can predict how God will act?

On prudence (11:6). Don't put all your eggs in one basket. There's no guarantee what you're counting on will ever work out. Always be working on at least two projects, and at least one of them may pan out.

Cynicism? Viewed as defensive ethics, *Qoheleth's* precepts seem somewhat cynical. They are. He confidently began a search for life's meaning, relying on his own reason and powers of observation. The more he applied himself the more meaningless life seemed to be. Rather than turn then to God, our writer accepted his own conclusions as truth. And then this disappointed man worked out his own system of protective ethics, intended to help him make the best of a meaningless life.

All who reason limiting themselves to the same resources used by Solomon will reach the same conclusion. Rather than experience life as an adventure, they draw back and seek to protect themselves. But the person who knows God and counts on His promises is free. For us life can be vital and exciting, and we can commit ourselves to carry out God's will.

Aging (12:1-5). The verses are literature's classic description of aging, picturing the dimming of sight (v. 2), loss of teeth (v. 3) and hearing (v. 4), loss of strength in the limbs and the waning of sexual desire (v. 5).

God and His commandments (12:13). Here may be the book's first hint that the author knows of God's special revelation in Scripture. But it may refer simply to the moral knowledge God has implanted in human nature.

Song of Songs

The Song of Songs is first of all a love song. It does not mention God, or claim to communicate any message from Him. Instead, it is a drama in poetry, a love story that captures the yearning of bride and bridegroom, set off by a chorus of the bride's friends who rejoice with her. The book, which verse 1 identifies as Solomon's, celebrates the mystery and joy of human love; the gift God gave to mankind when He shaped Eve and Adam for each other.

Jewish and Christian commentators have been uncomfortable with the explicit poetry found here, although sexual references are much more delicate and restrained than in other love poems from the ancient Middle East. Jewish scholars have treated it as an allegory of God's love for Israel, and Christians have seen it as an image of Jesus' love for the church, to be consummated at the Second Coming. But it is better to take this poem for what it seems to be: a celebration of God's gift of married love. It is a refreshing affirmation of the biblical view that in the union of husband and wife there exists a rewarding and total intimacy.

Date and authorship. If Solomon is the author, and there is no significant reason to doubt the tradition preserved in 1:1, the book was written between 970 and 930 B.C. The major objection to Solomonic authorship is that this picture of marital commitment does not seem to fit the record of that king's multiple marriages (cf. 1 Kings 11).

The Story behind Song of Songs

German scholar Franz Delitzsch saw the poem as a drama, telling the story of Solomon's love for a girl from one of Israel's northern villages. The king met and won her love while traveling incognito, returned to the capital, and then came back in splendor to carry her to his palace. Frequent changes in gender let us follow the speeches of the bride and the groom and recognize the chorus of friends. The NIV accurately identifies the words of the Beloved, the Lover, and the Friends in its English text.

If we follow Delitzsch's interpretation, the story behind the poem emerges as follows:

1:1–2:7   The bride longs for her lover. They meet and praise each other.
2:8–3:11 Their love grows, and the beloved praises her lover using images from nature.
4:1–5:1   The lover responds with praise for his beloved.
5:2–6:3   But suddenly the lover disappears, and the beloved cries out in longing for him.
6:4–8:14 The lover returns in splendor. The marriage takes place and is consummated (7:1–8:4), and the triumph of love is joyfully celebrated by all.

Rather than be disturbed by this extremely beautiful love poem, we might well open our hearts to it, and let this most unusual book in Scripture shape our attitude toward married love. It is God who invented sexuality. It is God who made human beings male and female. And it is God who sanctifies the intimacy enjoyed by husband and wife.

INSIGHT

Illustration. *Peoples from Mesopotamia to Egypt cherished enclosed gardens, where they grew flowers, vegetables, and fruit trees. The gardens were a place to relax and to enjoy the shade and delicate scent of growing things. During the summer their owners often built simple shelters where they could spend the night. The Book of Ecclesiastes suggests that Solomon was among those who enjoyed gardens, for he "made gardens and parks and planted all kinds of fruit trees in them" (2:5). It's no wonder then that the lover of Song of Songs speaks of his beloved as "a garden locked up," (4:12) filled with fragrant fruits and herbs. In the world of the ancient Middle East the enclosed garden spoke of sensual pleasures and of peace.*

Images of love. These early chapters are filled with delicate and beautiful images that convey the wonder of developing love. Note these expressions of the Beloved:

"Your name is like perfume poured out" (1:3).

"I delight to sit in his shade" (2:3).

"My lover is like a gazelle" (2:9).

"My lover is mine and I am his" (2:16).

"Let my lover come into his garden and taste its choice fruits" (4:16).

These are matched and surpassed by the images and passionate expressions of her Lover:

"Most beautiful of women" (1:8).

"Oh, how beautiful! Your eyes are doves" (1:15).

"Like a lily among thorns is my darling among the maidens" (2:2).

"All beautiful you are, my darling; there is no flaw in you" (4:7).

"You have stolen my heart, my sister, my bride" (4:9).

"You are a garden fountain, a well of flowing water" (4:15).

Expressions like these, so appropriate to love, help make the nature of this poem very clear, despite efforts of some interpreters to allegorize them, or seek hidden theological truths.

Similes from nature. Moderns would hardly think it romantic to be compared with a flock of goats, a gazelle or henna, nard, and saffron. But the ancient Hebrews were an agricultural people who lived close to nature and sensed the beauty of living, growing things. It's no wonder that nature provides most of the similes and images used to praise one's beloved.

Beloved	Lover	Friends
1:2-4a		1:4b
1:5-7	1:9-11	1:8
1:12-14	1:15	
1:16	1:17	
2:1	2:2	
2:3-13	2:14-15	
2:16–3:11	4:1-15	
4:16	5:1a, b	5:1c
5:2-8		5:9
5:10-16		6:1
6:2-3	6:4-9	6:10
	6:11-12	
	6:13b–7:9a	6:13a
7:9b–8:4		8:5a
8:5b-7		8:8-9
8:10-12	8:13	
8:14		

Chart. *The chart to the right shows the passages that can be attributed to the various speakers in Solomon's dramatic poem. If you do not use an NIV, you may want to jot down the speakers in the margins of your Bible.*

A biblical view of human sexuality. The Song of Songs is the Bible's most explicit and yet delicate exploration of human sexual relationships. Both testaments tend to speak about sex indirectly. The explicit speech of our day, and of other ancient cultures, is foreign to Scripture, which deals with and honors sex as a private and personal matter.

This does not, however, suggest that Scripture has a negative view of sex. Blunt and gutter references to sex tend to trivialize an act which Scripture views as sacred. The Creation story affirms the sexual nature of human beings. But it carefully guards the mystery of sex, lest its special nature be destroyed and its power to bond husband and wife as one be lost.

The Bible does condemn sexual expression outside of marriage. Adultery, premarital promiscuity, prostitution, and such aberrations as homosexuality and beastiality are alike condemned in God's Word. But within marriage, the Scriptures affirm our freedom to enjoy this gift and do not convey any restriction of mutually pleasurable activity.

The Bible identifies three specific functions of sex in human life. One is the procreation of the race, for God told Adam and Eve before the Fall, "Be fruitful and multiply" (Gen. 1:28, KJV).

Another is to satisfy drives that are implicit in human nature. The Apostle Paul, who chose to remain celibate, nevertheless urged those who had a strong sex drive to marry (1 Cor. 7:3-5, 9).

The third function of sexuality is found in the Gen. 1:24 expression, "they will become one flesh." Sex is sacramental: It is a means by which God conveys grace to His people. And the particular grace involved is the bonding of a man and woman together in a union that makes them one in their life on Earth. By preserving sexual expression for the exclusive relationship of marriage, God gave it a unique power to unify. In the intimacy that comes from baring one's total self to another, and to that person alone, a sense of shared mystery is created. As the act of love is repeated again and again, commitment is constantly reaffirmed, trust grows, and two do become one in the deepest level of their personalities.

Song of Songs invites us to briefly lift the veil, and sense the joyful intimacy that sex can help create within marriage. It reminds us that the joy of sex does not depend on technique, but on caring. And it assures us, within the framework of lifelong commitment, every joy that sex can provide is unashamedly ours.

An Introduction to the Prophets

Man's yearning to know the future is reflected in every ancient culture. Cuneiform tablets from Sumer and clay slabs from Mari reveal the involvement of diviners, oracle priests, and ecstatic prophets in every aspect of human life. Astrologers and diviners were important members of the military staff and were consulted before going into battle. In Egypt, priests used magic to forecast the future and relied on the interpretation of dreams. Old Testament prophets also foretold the future and guided military leaders. But the prophets of Israel were not magicians or diviners, astrologers or the purveyors of oracles. The Old Testament prophet was the contemporary voice of God, ringing out boldly, not only to predict future events but to correct sin and to shape a just moral society. For about 700 years of Israel's history, roughly from the time of Samuel to the close of the Old Testament, the prophets served God and their own generation. Their voices often went unheeded then. Yet their legacy of fierce commitment to God and His ways is preserved for us in Scripture. And their grand vision of history's end reminds us today that God has a purpose in the seemingly random international events that shape our time. Through the record preserved in Scripture, the voice of the prophets, in fact the voice of God, is clearly heard today.

Who Were the Prophets?

The prophets were men and women, drawn from every walk of life, who were given a special word from God to announce to their own generations (2 Sam. 24:11; 1 Chron. 17:3; 1 Kings 12:22). Unlike priests and kings, their office was not hereditary. And, while many were called to minister as prophets for life (cf. Isa. 6; Jer. 1), others served briefly, fulfilled a specific commission, and then went back to living an ordinary life (cf. Amos 7:14-15). Each, however, was driven by the conviction that he had been commissioned by God to proclaim a message that was, in sense, "the Word of the Lord" (Amos 7:16).

Prophets frequently are divided between "writing prophets," whose messages are preserved as books of the Old Testament, and "speaking prophets," whose ministry is described but who made no contribution to the canon. The importance of a prophet in history cannot be measured by these categories however. Elijah and Elisha are speaking prophets. Yet these two successfully resisted the vigorous efforts of Ahab and Jezebel to replace Yahweh with Baal as Israel's "official" deity (1 Kings 16; 2 Kings 10).

The works of the writing prophets are divided into two categories. There are the major prophets, whose works are especially long, and the so-called minor prophets, whose works are shorter. The major prophets are Isaiah, Jeremiah-Lamentations, Ezekiel, and Daniel. The minor prophets are Hosea, Joel, Amos, Obadiah, Jonah, Micah, Nahum, Habakkuk, Zephaniah, Haggai, Zechariah, and Malachi. Each of these books is introduced and the contribution of the prophet is explained later in this book, for each must be understood in the context of the writer's time. Yet there are certain similarities common to all prophetic books. And there are certain principles of interpretation that must guide our understanding as we read. So in this introduction to the prophets we need to consider: (1) the prophets as God's contemporary voice, (2) the role of prediction in the prophets' ministry, and (3) interpretation of prophetic writings.

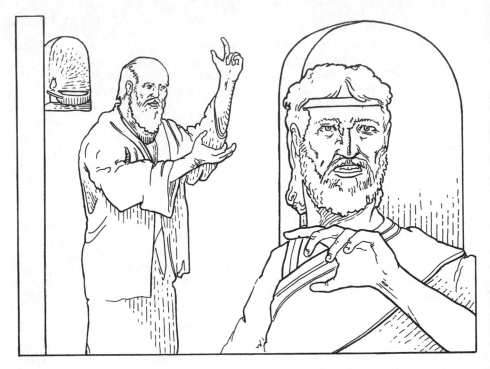

Nathan boldly accuses King David of his sin with Bathsheba and announces God's punishment (2 Sam. 11). No individual or group was able to silence men and women burning with the conviction that God had called them to speak out.

The Prophets As God's Contemporary Voice

A prophet's ministry was often directed to the king. Nathan served David as court prophet, not only confronting him in the case of Bathsheba, but also conveying God's promise to establish David's line on Israel's throne (2 Sam. 7). Other prophets transmitted God's instructions to rulers (cf. 1 Sam. 15), directed military campaigns (cf. 2 Kings 3), and demanded legal reforms (cf. Jer. 34). Yet most of the prophets had a very public ministry, which increasingly focused on religious and social issues. Throughout their era the prophets cried out against idolatry (cf. 1 Kings 18; Isa. 44), and against worship which was mere ritual (Isa. 1:11-15; Amos 5:21-24).

Increasingly, as Israelite society shifted from its agricultural roots to a more urban and commercial society, the prophets also cried out against greed and injustice. God's Law envisioned a peaceful society in which each man rested safely under his own vine and fig tree (1 Kings 4:25; Micah 4:4). Yet when Israel became prosperous, as in the days of Jeroboam II, a wealthy upper class developed. The old values imbedded in the law of mutual aid and sharing were replaced by selfishness and indifference to the poor. Thus Amos, in Jeroboam's day, cried out against oppression of the poor by the rich (2:6-7), against indifference toward the hungry (6:3-6), and against corruption in the courts (2:7; 8:6), as well as against blatant immorality (2:7).

Yet the voice of the prophets was far from harsh. The prophets also spoke of God's undying love for His people. God would surely punish. But His discipline was motivated by love. As Isaiah 54:67 declares, "For a brief moment I abandoned you, but with great compassion I will bring you back." God's voice through the prophets is urgent and demanding, but at the same time warm and caring. Today we can still hear Him speak in the words of His prophets of old.

The Role of Prediction in the Prophets' Ministry

One obvious question arises whenever anyone claims to be God's voice to his or her generation. This question is noted in Deuteronomy 18. The passage has said that a true prophet will be a Jew (v. 17) and will speak in the name of Yahweh (v. 20). It then adds, "You may say to yourselves, 'How can we know when a message has not been spoken by the Lord?' " (v. 21) God's response is, "If what a prophet proclaims in the name of the Lord does not take place or come true, that is a message the Lord has not spoken" (v. 22). On the other hand, when what a prophet proclaims does take place, God has spoken through him. An incident illustrates: Ahab ordered the Prophet Micaiah, who predicted his death in battle, imprisoned "until I return safely" (1 Kings 22:27). Dryly Micaiah answered, " ' If you ever return safely, the Lord has not spoken through me.' Then he added, 'Mark my words, all you people!' " (1 Kings 22:28)

There are essentially two kinds of predictive material in the prophets. There is near-view prediction, of events to happen within the lifetime of the hearer, and far-view prediction, of events to happen beyond the lifespan of the hearers. Near-view predictions, like Micaiah's, served frequently as proof that a person's claim to speak for God was true. They authenticated the spokesman as God's messenger.

Far-view predictions had a different purpose in the prophet's ministry to his contemporaries, although today we can trace the literal fulfillment of many predictions which lay far in the future when they were uttered. Far-view predictions, which describe events to take place beyond the span of the hearers' life, convey Scripture's philosophy of history. Many far-view predictions focus on events to happen at history's end. These describe God's ultimate triumph over evil (»p. 431) and the establishment of righteousness on Earth (»p. 443). They portray a regathering of Israel (»p. 419) and national conversion: a time of unmatched blessing when all the Covenant promises made to Abraham and David, and in Jeremiah's New Covenant, will be kept (»pp. 32, 370, 466). The underlying message of these predictions is that God is in charge of history and that it moves inexorably to His intended end. This message is one of hope and confidence. God has known the end from the beginning. Nothing that happens in history can alter God's plan or weaken His commitment to His chosen people.

Many far-view predictions do describe events that will happen along history's way. The early prophets warned of Assyria's coming devastation of Israel and of Judah's captivity in Babylon. But they also preannounced a return of the Jews to their homeland (cf. Jer. 25, 30). Some of the most important far-view predictions concern the birth, life, ministry, and death of the Messiah. Many more concern events associated with His Second Coming and the climax of the ages. These too enrich our confidence and our hope, for they serve as signposts, reminding us that God's plan remains on track. Because we can look back on predictions which have been fulfilled, we can look ahead with confidence. The details are undoubtedly unclear, but the broad outlines of the future God intends for us are unmistakable. And the message of predictive prophecy remains the same. God is in charge. And God is love indeed.

Interpretation of Prophetic Writings

When studying any Bible passage we need to be sensitive to the message the writer intended to convey to his own generation. This is true for prophetic as well as other kinds of material. We look at the writer's times, at the shape of the moral, religious, and international events of his day. We note the literary forms, the specific meanings of individual words and grammatical constructions. But when interpreting predictive material several very special problems arise.

First we have to ask if a message deals with near- or far-view events. This question is often not easy to answer, in part because a prediction may have an *individual fulfillment*. That is, it may refer both to an immediate situation and also to a distant time, as when a contemporary invasion foreshadows the culminating warfare to take place at history's end. Or the focus may shift within a single prophetic utterance, as in Ezekiel 28, where it seems to switch from speaking of a particular king of Tyre to what many believe is a description of the nature and fate of Satan.

Second, we have to ask if a prediction is conditional or unconditional. In general, predictions of judgment contain an implied condition: if the hearers repent, judgment can be avoided. Jonah's warning, "Forty more days and Nineveh will be overturned" (Jonah 3:4) failed to come true, not because Jonah was a false prophet, but because the people of Nineveh met the implied condition.

Third, we have to ask if a prediction has been fulfilled, or is still to be fulfilled. The prophecies in Isaiah 53 concerning Jesus' death have been fulfilled already. Yet other predictions concerning Christ contain elements which have been fulfilled—alongside other elements which have not. And such elements may occur within the same sentence (cf. Isa. 61:1-2 with Luke 4:18-19).

In any given predictive passage in the prophets the answer to one, or even to all three, of these questions may be unclear. Thus while the general framework of the future sketched in the Old Testament is clear, the details are not. And so we are unwise to speak too confidently about the sequence or minutia of specific future events.

There is one even more basic issue to resolve in our reading of predictive prophecy. Christians are divided as to whether many of the far-view predictions of the Old Testament are to be taken literally or figuratively. Does the promise to the Jews of a national regathering in the land of Israel really concern the physical descendants of Abraham, or does it concern the church as Abraham's spiritual offspring? Does the description of material blessings predict peace and security in a Jewish homeland, or are such prophecies symbolic of the spiritual blessings we enjoy in Christ? There is undoubtedly valid spiritual applications of Old Testament prophecy to contemporary Christian experience. Yet we must note that predictions which have already been fulfilled have consistently been fulfilled in a literal way. Christ's first coming, virgin birth, ministry to the poor, betrayal, crucifixion, and resurrection, even the division of His clothing by lot—all are the subject of prophecy. And in each case they describe events that have taken place in the clearest, most literal way in space and time. If fulfilled prophecy is to be a guide to interpretation of predictions yet unfulfilled, we must treat predictive prophecy as the description of events which will one day be woven into mankind's history.

The study of prophetic books has great value. In them we rediscover the values that God calls His people of every age to live out. And in them we find constant reminders that God is in control of history.

Isaiah

This towering book of prophecy is one of the most beautiful and significant of Old Testament books. Its messages of judgment are balanced by matchless words of comfort and hope. And its vision of the Saviour is the most moving as well as the clearest of all Old Testament portraits. Its 66 chapters make it the third longest literary work in the Bible.

Isaiah's prophetic ministry began the year King Uzziah of Judah died, and spanned the reigns of Jotham, Ahaz, and Hezekiah (about 739–681 B.C.). During this time Assyria crushed Judah's neighbor, Israel, and deported its population. Little Judah was itself invaded by Sennacherib, but survived. It was during these critical and dangerous times that Isaiah recorded his sermons calling for spiritual and moral renewal, and his exalted visions of history's end and the blessings God intends to provide for His own.

One of the book's greatest values is found in its unforgettable images of God. Isaiah's distinctive title for God, "the Holy One of Israel," is used 25 times and captures something of the majestic glory with which He is displayed. He is Creator, King, and Saviour for His people, the "Mighty God" who sends His Servant, the Messiah, to rescue them at a terrible personal cost. Isaiah 53's graphic study of the Servant's suffering is an unmistakably distinct portrait of Calvary, penned some 700 years before Jesus' birth.

ISAIAH AT A GLANCE

KEY PEOPLE

Isaiah   *The prophet, whose personal history is unknown but whose writings are unmatched for energy and beauty.*

Ahaz   *The rebellious king, whose sullen refusal to heed Isaiah led to the prediction of Messiah's virgin birth (Isa. 7).*

Hezekiah   *The godly ruler whose dependence on God won relief from invading Assyrians (Isa. 36–39).*

KEY PASSAGES

Isaiah's call (Isa. 6).   *The prophet is cleansed and commissioned to speak God's Word to a people unwilling to listen.*

A promise of peace (Isa. 11).   *A descendant of David will bring world peace.*

A word of comfort (Isa. 40).   *God, the Sovereign Lord, is our hope.*

God delivers (Isa. 40–48).   *Trust in God brings national deliverance.*

The futility of idolatry (Isa. 44).   *Trust only in the living God.*

The Suffering Servant (Isa. 53).   *Scripture's most vivid picture of the Cross and its meaning, drawn 700 years before Jesus' birth.*

The world to come (Isa. 65:17-25).   *Under God's future rule man and nature at last find blessing and rest.*

Date and Authorship. Critics have argued that chapters 40–66 were not written by Isaiah son of Amoz. Conservatives have argued for the unity of the book. Today this unity is accepted by most scholars who agree that no part of Isaiah ever circulated except as an integral part of our Old Testament book. While many scholars date Isaiah in the 400s rather than 600s B.C., conservatives find no evidence that would compel rejection of the traditional preexilic dating for all the book's contents.

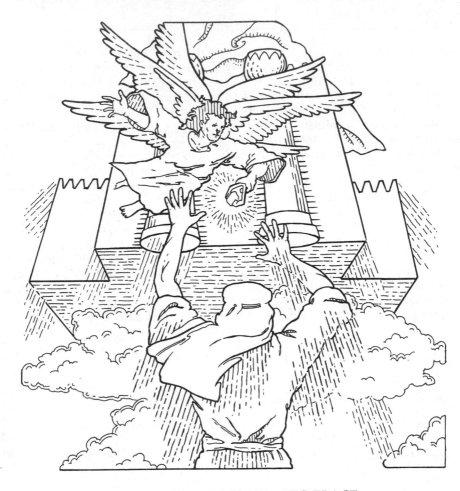

WHERE THE ACTION TAKES PLACE

Isaiah lived and ministered in Judah, then a country reduced in size by military pressure from Assyria. Yet in a real way Isaiah dwells in glory and views all things from heavenly perspective. Isaiah's viewpoint was indelibly impressed on him by a vision described in chapter 6, portrayed in the illustration above. The prophet, then a young man, finds himself in the presence of God. Overcome by God's glory, and deeply aware of his own sinfulness, Isaiah crumbles—only to be cleansed by fire from the temple altar and told his guilt has been taken away and his sin atoned for. When Isaiah hears God ask, "Whom shall I send?" (v. 8) he eagerly volunteers to serve as God's messenger. Isaiah is warned that the people of Judah will not heed him and that in the end their houses will be left empty and their fields will become a wasteland. Yet throughout his long life, Isaiah will never lose sight of God, "seated on a throne, high and exalted" (v. 1). And Isaiah will never forget the echoing cry of the angels around God's throne. "Holy, holy, holy is the Lord Almighty; the whole earth is full of His glory" (v. 3).

Isaiah constantly calls on us to look beyond the present, to remain aware of God, and to be confident in the future that God is shaping.

THEOLOGICAL OUTLINE OF ISAIAH

I. GOD'S WORD TO JUDAH	1–6
II. GOD'S PROMISE OF IMMANUEL	7–12
III. GOD'S WORD OF JUDGMENT	13–35
IV. GOD'S WORD AND HEZEKIAH	36–39
V. GOD'S WORD OF COMFORT	40–66
A. The Promise of Peace	40–48
B. The Prince of Peace	49–57
C. The Pattern of Peace	58–66

CONTENT OUTLINE OF ISAIAH

I. God's Word to Judah (1:1–6:13)
  A. A Call to the Rebels (1:1-31)
  B. Judgment Leads to Glory (2:1–4:6)
  C. Exile Ahead (5:1-30)
  D. Isaiah Commissioning (6:1-13)
II. God's Word about Immanuel (7:1–12:6)
  A. The Sign of Immanuel (7:1-25)
  B. Peace to Be Established by Immanuel (8:1–9:7)
  C. Judgment on Samaria (9:8–10:4)
  D. Messiah's Empire to Supplant Man's (10:5–12:6)
III. God's Word Against the Nations (13:1–23:18)
IV. A Word of General Judgment (24:1–27:13)
  A. God's Punishment of Sin (24:1-23)
  B. Deliverance for Those Who Trust (25:1-12)
  C. Praise of the Redeemed (26:1-21)
  D. Deliverance of the Oppressed (27:1-13)
V. A Word of Specific Judgment on Unbelieving Israel (28:1–33:24)
  A. God's Judgments (28:1–29:24)
  B. A Call for Confidence in God (30:1-33)
  C. Deliverance and Messiah's Triumph (31:1–33:24)
VI. Another Word of General Judgment (34:1–35:10)
VII. God's Word and Hezekiah: Salvation Foreshadowed (36:1–39:8)

VIII. A Word of Comfort: Peace (40:1–48:22)
  A. God as Comforter (40:1-31)
  B. God as Helper (41:1-29)
  C. God's Servant (42:1-25)
  D. God as Saviour (43:1–44:5)
  E. God as Living God (44:6-23)
  F. God as Sovereign (45:1–47:15)
  G. God as Guide (48:1-22)
IX. A Word of Comfort: The Prince of Peace (49:1–57:21)
  A. God's Servant to Restore Israel (49:1-26)
  B. God's Servant to Obey the Lord (50:1-11)
  C. Israel to Awake, Return to God (51:1–52:12)
  D. God's Servant to Suffer and Redeem (52:13–53:12)
  E. God's Future for Israel (54:1-17)
  F. God's Grace for Sinners (55:1-13)
  G. God's Gift of Salvation for Gentiles (56:1-8)
  H. God's Warning of the Wicked (56:9–57:21)
X. God's Word of Comfort: A Program for Peace (58:1–66:24)
  A. Heart Worship (58:1-14)
  B. Confess Sins (59:1-21)
  C. Redemption and Peace Follow (60:1-22)
  D. God's Kingdom Will Come (61:1-11)
  E. Zion Will Be Restored (62:1-12)
  F. God Will Avenge (63:1-6)
  G. God's People Will at Last Understand (63:7–64:12)
  H. All Will Be Renewed (65:1–66:24)

Outline
Place
Finder

JUDAH
IMMANUEL
JUDGMENT
HEZEKIAH
COMFORT

Chapter summary. The powerful opening chapter of Isaiah captures the concerns of all the prophets. Judah has rebelled against the Lord (1:2-3). She persists in sin despite divine discipline (vv. 4-9). Rather than reform, God's people try to bribe Him with a superficial, ritualized religion that the Lord hates with all His being (vv. 10-17). Yet even now God will cleanse the indelible scarlet of Judah's sin if His people will only change their heart attitudes and become "willing and obedient" (vv. 18-20). The chapter closes with a lament over the city which has temporarily become a refuge for murderers rather than a home for righteousness, but which God will surely restore when He judges sinners and rebels (vv. 21-31).

Key verse. 1:4: Relationship remains the key.

Personal application. How foolish to persist in sin.

Key concepts. Rebellion »p. 101. Sin »p. 362. Survivors »p. 427. Sacrifices »p. 555. Prayer conditions »p. 894. Forgiveness »p. 357.

INSIGHT

"**Isaiah**" (1:1). Little is known of the prophet, but his striking literary gifts suggest upper-class birth and education.

"**Children**" (1:3-4). God seeks an intimate personal relationship with His worshipers, the kind children have with a much-loved father. No wonder Judah's rejection of a personal relationship repelled the Lord.

Sickness and sin (1:5-6). Isaiah's image of Judah as a sick nation, debilitated by injury and disease, raises the question of the relationship between sickness and sin. On the one hand, the two are linked by their impact on our lives. Each weakens us. Each makes it impossible for us to enjoy life as God intended. But Isaiah's image also mirrors a fact of O.T. covenant life. God promised to keep an obedient people "free from every disease" (Deut. 7:12, 14-15). And disobedience made His people vulnerable to "severe and lingering illness" (Deut. 28:59). Sickness was one of the rods of discipline God used to warn and correct His people. It would be an oversimplification to assume that all sickness is punishment. But it is certainly true that sins affect us psychologically and make us vulnerable to physical ills. And also, sickness often leads us to reevaluate the quality of our relationship with the Lord.

Healing (1:2-19). Healing is the O.T.'s answer to sickness and to sin. While God is the source of physical healing (Ex. 15:26, »medicine, p. 290), the prophets view the spiritual malady of sin as far more serious. Spiritual sickness (sin) can be healed only by forgiveness and a restored relationship with the Lord

(cf. Isa. 57:18-19; Jer. 33:6).

Imagery (1:8). The verse illustrates Isaiah's powerful use of imagery. The "daughter of Zion" is a personification of the city, Jerusalem, pictured as a child produced by the Temple Mount. The "shelter in a vineyard" is an image of desolation: a rude hut used in late summer by watchmen who kept the birds away from the crops, but abandoned in every other season. And the "city under siege" is an image of desperation and hunger.

"**Trampling of my courts**" (1:12). The image here is of a herd of animals mindlessly muddying God's temple. Religion without righteousness and ritual without commitment remain disgusting to God today.

No answer to prayer (1:15). The psalmist said it, and the prophet echoes his insight. "If I had cherished sin in my heart, the Lord would not have listened" (Ps. 66:18). This generation in Judah loved sin, and God must refuse to heed their prayers.

"**Scarlet**" (1:18). Scarlet and crimson were shades of red drawn from the same source, the crushed body of an insect. Isaiah chose the image not because of the color, but because this was the most securely fixed dye then known. No launderer could remove that color from cloth. Isaiah thus says God can do the impossible and cleanse sinners, even though the stain of sin is fixed as firmly as crimson in the sinner's soul.

"**Afterward**" (1:26). Isaiah's generation may not repent, but one day God will act to punish rebels and restore blessing to the redeemed.

Chapter summary. These chapters alternate between visions of Judah's ideal future and her present reality. Zion (»p. 361) is to be the spiritual capital of the universe (2:1-5). But now the corrupt land (vv. 6-9) faces the devastating judgments of the "day of the Lord" (2:10–4:1). Yet this will not prevent Judah and Jerusalem from fulfilling their destiny. The day that dawns so darkly will clear, and one known as "the Branch" (4:2), the Messiah, will come to cleanse Jerusalem's sins. He will clothe the city with glory and bring her people peace (vv. 2-6).

Key verse. 4:2: No darkness today can dim the bright future God has for His people.

Personal application. Be today what you will be then.

Key concepts. War »pp. 133, 554. Abandon »p. 370. Arrogance »p. 352. Wicked »p. 350. Judge »p. 372. Messiah »p. 432. Poor »p. 90.

INSIGHT

"All nations" (2:2-5). Although Israel was God's chosen people, salvation's blessings are intended for all. This great truth is powerfully affirmed by Isaiah. Here he envisions Jerusalem as capital of the whole Earth, with the nations eager to learn and walk in God's ways. When God reigns from Jerusalem the world will be at peace, and the Lord Himself will settle international disputes.

Those who spiritualize O.T. prophecy have taken this vision to portend the ultimate triumph of the Gospel of Christ and universal conversion. Those who take O.T. prophecy literally believe it pictures the future rule of Jesus after His return.

Judah's sins (2:6-9). This is a total reversal of what God intended. Isa. 1:1-5 shows God intended knowledge of the Lord to flow out from Judah. Instead paganism — with its corrupt values and its idolatry — has flowed into Judah from foreign nations!

What a danger this is for us today. The Christian is to shed light on a dark world, not adopt the world's values and its ways.

The Day of the Lord (2:11-12). This phrase, with its shorter version, "that day," occurs often in the O.T. prophets. It always identifies a critical period of time during which God personally intervenes in history, directly or indirectly, to accomplish a specific purpose which fulfills His announced plan for the ages. Most often the events of "that day" take place at history's end, as in Isa. 7:18-25. Most often, but not always, judgment is described. Thus Zephaniah says, "That day will be a day of wrath, a day of distress and anguish, a day of trouble and ruin, a day of darkness and gloom,

a day of clouds and blackness (1:14-15; cf. Isa. 22; Jer. 30:1-17; Amos 5:18). *The Expository Dictionary of Bible Words* (Zondervan, 1985) notes that "when God intervenes in history, He will also deliver the remnant of Israel, bring about a national conversion, forgive sins, and restore His people to the Promised Land of Abraham" (Isa. 10:27; Jer. 30:19–31:40). The day of the Lord is a day of darkness, but at evening there will be light.

"Boys their officials" (3:4). Again we see Isaiah's gift for powerful imagery. In Hebrew society age was associated with wisdom. To have boys as officials implies headstrong, immature leadership sure to make foolish decisions and lead the nation to disaster.

"The righteous" (3:10). Whatever happens here and now, the righteous can have confidence. We will surely be rewarded for good we choose to do.

"In court" (3:13-14). Frequent courtroom images are found in the prophets; God is viewed pressing formal charges against sinners. Here the accused are the leaders who have exploited rather than cared for the poor, who share God's special concern.

"The Branch" (4:2-6). The metaphorical title indicates a person to "spring up" or "sprout from" David's line. Six O.T. passages use this term of the coming Messiah (Isa. 4:2; 11:1; Jer. 23:5; 33:15; Zech. 3:8; 6:12). In them the Messiah is associated with washing away the sins of God's people "in a single day" (Zech. 3:9) and with the kingdom glory to follow. The Branch, empowered by the Spirit, is to bring justice and righteousness to earth and fulfill the covenant promises given to David (Jer. 33:15-22).

Chapter summary. The chapter opens with what has been called "the Song of the Vineyard" (5:1-7). It is a mournful song indeed, as God laments the necessary abandonment of the "garden of His delight," the people He has cared for so patiently. The image of a well-kept but now abandoned vineyard forcefully drives home the lesson that no generation that produces bloodshed rather than justice can expect to survive. Isaiah then lists a series of woes, formal announcements of impending judgments, on the wicked who monopolize land ownership (vv. 8-10), live profligate lives (vv. 11-17), make evil their life's work (vv. 18-20), distort good and evil (v. 20), are self-important (v. 21), and corrupt justice (vv. 22-25). God's anger burns against such persons, and He will bring foreign armies into Judah to judge them (vv. 26-30).

Key verse. 5:7: The product God seeks is righteousness.

Personal application. The fruit of right relationship with God is still a right relationship with others.

Key concepts. Righteousness of God »pp. 120, 372. Justice »pp. 130, 132. Anger of God »pp. 65, 72.

INSIGHT

Illustration: *Fruitfulness. The fruit of the Middle Eastern grapevine grew close to the ground and was one of the land's three most important products along with olives and grain. Throughout Scripture fruit and fruitfulness serve as metaphors for the visible product of one's inner character (cf. Jesus' teaching in Matt. 7 and Luke 6).*

The clearest expression of the metaphor is found in Gal. 5:22-23, which identifies the fruit God's Spirit produces in the Christian life as "love, joy, peace, patience, kindness, goodness, faithfulness, gentleness, and self-control." The parallel in Isaiah is clear. God looked for His people to produce the fruit of justice and righteousness, but instead the society was marked by injustice and crime.

Vine and vineyard (5:1-5). Israel is frequently spoken of as a vine in the O.T. (cf. Ps. 80:8, 14, 15; Jer. 2:21; Hosea 10:1; Zech. 3:10). God is the keeper of the vineyard who nurtures and protects His people. Yet despite God's loving care, the covenant community continued to produce the bitter fruit of sin rather than the pleasing products of righteousness. Jesus provides perspective when He calls Himself the "true vine" (John 15:1), reminding us that only through an intimate personal relationship with Him can any human being produce the fruit God desires.

"Add house to house" (5:8). God distributed the Holy Land in small parcels so every family would have a homestead. For some to have so much at the expense of others who have less and less is a great and terrible social injustice. The wealthy of our day need to take heed too.

"Wine" (5:11). Wine in Scripture is often associated with joyful occasions (»p. 127). Yet the O.T. bluntly condemns both drunkenness and love of drink (Prov. 20:1; 21:17; 23:20-21), and the N.T. views alcohol abuse as characteristic of a pagan rather than a Christian lifestyle (Eph. 5:18; 1 Peter 4:3).

Evil good (5:20). It's still done. For instance, homosexuality is an "alternate lifestyle" and abortion for convenience is "pro-choice."

Chapter summary. Isaiah now reports his own grand vision of God and his call to prophetic ministry. The focus of the vision is God Himself, "high and exalted," and worshiped as holy by seraphim, a special order of angels (6:1-4). Isaiah is overcome with a sense of his own sinfulness, but is cleansed by a coal from the altar (vv. 5-7). Isaiah responds by eagerly volunteering to serve as God's messenger (v. 8). The offer is accepted, but Isaiah is forewarned. God's people will not respond (vv. 9-10). When Isaiah asks how long this condition will persist he hears a glum reply. Judah will be deaf to God until the land is desolate and empty. Yet enough life will remain in the stump for new life to spring up again (vv. 11-13).

Outline
Place
Finder

JUDAH
IMMANUEL
JUDGMENT
HEZEKIAH
COMFORT

Key verse. 6:8: The only adequate response to forgiveness.

Personal application. Faithfulness is the measure of success.

Key concepts. Angels »p. 521. Holy »p. 372. Unclean »pp. 82, 505. Sin »p. 362. Guilt »p. 79. Forgiveness »p. 357. Calling »p. 757.

INSIGHT

Why chapter 6? The first chapters contain the basic message of judgment and hope Isaiah delivered to Judah. He concludes the section by reporting the experience which authenticates him as God's messenger.

The experience of being in the presence of God and receiving a unique revelation fits a common O.T. pattern. Many others who were commissioned by God shared it, although few were drawn into heaven's throne room. See descriptions of Noah (Gen. 6:11-21), Abraham (Gen. 18:17-21), and Moses (Ex. 32).

The setting. God is seen in a heavenly throne room. The setting emphasizes His majesty, while His attendants' cries emphasize His holiness. The image of His robe filling the temple suggests His utter dominance of the room. As marvelous as the seraphim must be, the Lord Himself is the focus of His servant's gaze. It should be so with us too. Some Christians have marvelous experiences. Some accomplish great deeds. Some may have beatific visions. But our eyes must be so fixed on God that He, not His wonders, claims our full attention.

"Seraphs" (6:2). The Heb. word means "burning ones." These are apparently a distinct order of angelic beings, not to be identified with cherubs or other orders. Their role here is to call to each other, uttering constant reminders that God is "holy, holy, holy" (v. 3).

"Unclean lips" (6:5-6). It is considered polite in the Middle East to speak of oneself in a deprecating way. Even today, no pious Easterner would suggest he is holy or good, but would always speak of himself as an unworthy person or a sinner. Yet Isaiah's cry has no resemblance to mere surface humility. The prophet has seen the Lord and suddenly realizes that he is a man of "unclean lips." The Arabic phrase, *samma sipwatha*, is still used with the meaning of "sinful," as blasphemy and curses are uttered by the lips.

A coal from the altar (6:6). The altar was the place of atonement for sin in Israel's religion, and fire symbolized the burning of a sin offering (»pp. 78, 84). With his sin atoned for, Isaiah can now both worship and serve the Lord.

"Whom shall I send?" (6:8) God knew the answer and had already chosen Isaiah. But the question provided Isaiah with the opportunity to volunteer. God values our service, but more than anything we can do, He values our willingness. Just as God protected Isaiah's freedom of choice by asking rather than commanding, so He protects His own today. As many commentators have observed, the only appropriate response to being forgiven is to eagerly offer our service. But the Lord will not force you to serve Him; we must volunteer.

"How long?" (6:8-13) Isaiah's fellow countrymen will not heed his preaching. When he asks how long they will be unresponsive, Isaiah is told that generation will follow generation "until the cities lie ruined." God's Word always has an impact, whether it is accepted or rejected. Yet Isaiah's mission to Judah would only seem to fail. After the judgment, new life would spring up, as young twigs struggle up out of seemingly dead stumps.

Let's not be discouraged in ministry even when the results are truly discouraging.

Outline
Place
Finder

JUDAH
IMMANUEL
JUDGMENT
HEZEKIAH
COMFORT

Chapter summary. Here begins the "book of Immanuel" (7:1–12:6), which focuses on the Messiah and the Messianic Age. In the late 8th century Judah is threatened by Syria and Israel. These two have tried to force Judah to join an anti-Assyrian coalition (cf. 2 Kings 15–16) and threaten to invade if King Ahaz will not agree. Isaiah meets Ahaz and announces that Judah need not fear (7:1-9). Ahaz shows his disbelief by refusing to ask Isaiah for an authenticating sign (vv. 10-12). Isaiah then launches into a prophecy which combines God's near-view promise to deal with the immediate international situation and the far-view promise that God would fulfill His covenant commitment to David through a virgin-born child (vv. 13-16). And Assyria, which Ahaz has chosen to trust rather than God, will devastate the land of Judah (vv. 17-25).

Key verse. 7:14: The miracle of Jesus' birth is foretold.

Personal application. Count on God's promises.

INSIGHT

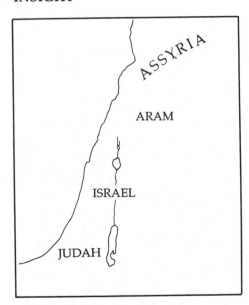

"Ahaz" (7:1). Ahaz, one of Judah's wicked kings, ruled between 735–715 B.C. He appealed to Assyria to aid him against Rezin of Syria (Damascus) and Pekah of Israel (Samaria). Assyria did devastate both Syria and Israel, but also attacked Judah! When making his submission to Tiglath-Pileser in Damascus, Ahaz adopted foreign deities.

Put the Lord to a test? (7:10-12) Ahaz's refusal may sound pious. But Ahaz was commanded to ask for a sign: some clearly supernatural event that would confirm Isaiah's promise. His disobedience was a demonstration of unbelief, not piety.

Immanuel (7:14). The name means "God with us." But the unusual and emphatic position of the words making up the name show it should be understood, "WITH US is God!" Thus, the name Immanuel captures the awe and wonder of the incarnation, and the unimaginable fact that the God of the universe entered the stream of time to become one with us.

Virgin birth (7:14). The Heb. word translated virgin means "young woman of marriageable age." The Heb. ideal of marriage makes its translation as "virgin" likely. However, the intent is absolutely clear in Matt. 1:23 which quotes Isaiah and uses a Gk. word, *parthenos*, which unequivocably means "virgin." In fact, the concept of the virgin birth is a cornerstone of biblical Christianity. Only if Jesus was truly God the Son could He have lived a sinless life and died on the cross as our substitute, a sufficient sacrifice for mankind's sins.

"Before the boy knows enough" (7:16). The boy mentioned here is to serve as a type of the promised son of the virgin and is undoubtedly Isaiah's own son, Maher-Shalal-Hash-Baz (8:1-3). A Jewish boy became bar-mitzvahed, a "son of the commandment," at 12 or 13 years of age. At this time he was considered a moral adult, responsible enough for his own acts to reject wrong and choose the right.

Thus the sign proving Isaiah's words about the salvation to be won by Immanuel would be the destruction of Israel and Syria by Assyria within a dozen years. And this is exactly what happened, for by 722 B.C. just 13 years after Ahaz became king, the two lands he feared lay in waste!

Chapter summary. Ahaz has rejected trust in God to trust in Assyria (see Isa. 7). Isaiah warns that God will now bring this very nation against His people (8:1-10). Even so, the believer is to fear and honor God (vv. 11-18), rather than surrender to the panic that leads others to desperate acts of spiritual rebellion (vv. 19-22). Yet beyond the present gloom the future holds a bright hope. A child will be born, a son given, who will reign as David's royal offspring and bring peace to the world (9:1-7). But first, the Northern Kingdom, Israel, which has turned its back on God, will be totally crushed (vv. 8-21).

Outline
Place
Finder

JUDAH
IMMANUEL
JUDGMENT
HEZEKIAH
COMFORT

Key verse. 9:6-7: The one who comes as a child is God's Son.

Personal application. However troubled the times, do not panic but continue to trust in God.

Key concepts. Assyria »p. 255. Fear of God »p. 387.

INSIGHT

Faithful witnesses (8:1-2). The witnesses were needed to attest to the date and content of Isaiah's prediction that Syria and Israel, which had then invaded Judah, would soon be destroyed (8:4; see Isa. 7) and that Assyria would then "sweep on into Judah" (8:8). Later, their testimony would establish that Isaiah had indeed predicted what would happen before the events took place.

"God is with us" (8:10). These are not words spoken by Israel or Judah, but words Isaiah places in the mouth of the Assyrians! In a stunning reversal, God is not with the armies of His people, but with the army of their most deadly enemy. Yet these words should comfort the faithful in Judah, for they make it clear that God remains in control of history, even when disasters strike.

Fear as a sanctuary (8:10-13). Fear of God is holding Him in awe; it's respecting God as One who is living, all-powerful, acting in our lives. Isaiah speaks to his own disciples (v. 16), tells them to reject the frightened speculation of their fellow countrymen about conspiracies, and remember that God is holy and in control. If we truly fear God, our respect for His power will free us from fear of current dangers. Truly trust God, and you will know peace.

"Signs and symbols" (8:18). In most cases a "sign" in the O.T. is a miraculous event that testifies to God's presence and power and frequently authenticates one of His messengers (»miracle, p. 57). Here the reference is to the symbolic names Isaiah has given his children, which point beyond themselves to the Lord's Word. Isaiah's family was itself a message to his generation. What a reminder that we and our families are also, by our lives if not our names, to be living witnesses to our Lord.

The panic of unbelief (8:19-22). A godly fear of the Lord brings a sense of security. A failure to fear God condemns men to panic when disasters come. Their desperate search for aid will be futile, and they are doomed to "fearful gloom." How ironic that those who reject God typically end up blaming and cursing Him for their fate! (v. 21)

A fulfilled prophecy (9:1-2). Here Isaiah speaks to the most northern of Israel's tribal groups, who were the first to experience the devastation of Assyrian invasion. He promises that these territories, now "walking in darkness," will also be the first to see "a great light." Matthew 4:15-16 sees the ministry of Jesus in Galilee as the fulfillment of Isaiah's prophecy. We often are not able to say just how an O.T. prophecy will be fulfilled. But when it has been fulfilled, we discover that its fulfillment was literal rather than "spiritual" (»p. 408).

A child, a son (9:6). This reference to Jesus the Messiah is also prophetic, illustrating a literal yet unexpected fulfillment of prophecy. The Messiah is a child born, and yet He is also a Son given. Jesus came into our world as an infant even though He existed from eternity as God the Son.

Our choice. Isa. 9:6-7 describes the universal reign of the Messiah. Then the rest of the chapter suddenly shifts to describe the judgment about to be visited on the Northern Kingdom, Israel (vv. 8-21). How are these linked? Jesus' reign is marked by universal allegiance to God. Israel's tragic history was marked from the beginning by rebellion against Him (»p. 230). Those who will not submit to the Lord will surely experience not the blessing of messianic times, but the havoc and ruination that crushed Israel.

Outline
Place
Finder

JUDAH
IMMANUEL
JUDGMENT
HEZEKIAH
COMFORT

Chapter summary. Isaiah 10:1-4 belongs with Isaiah 9 and defines the basis on which Israel's judgment was decreed. God then declares He will judge Assyria, which exceeded its commission by destroying rather than disciplining Israel (vv. 5-19). Even so, a remnant of Israel remains, and God will deliver the survivors (vv. 20-34). The flow of the passage now shows us the primary message of these chapters. A day is coming when the kingdoms of man will be supplanted by the kingdom of God. God's Messiah, guided and empowered by God's Spirit, will judge the Earth, establish righteousness, and even bring peace to nature itself (11:1-9). In that day all the nations of the world will submit to the Lord, and God will bring His chosen people back to their homeland (vv. 10-16). In that day, all Israel will praise God for salvation and make Him known to all the world (12:1-6).

Key verse. 11:10: World peace awaits the return of Jesus.

Personal application. Coming judgment as well as God's love motivate holy living.

Key concepts. Assyria »p. 255. God's Anger »p. 72. War »p. 133. Remnant »p. 427. Day of the Lord »p. 413. Branch »p. 413. Kingdom »p. 380. Holy Spirit »p. 73. Judge »pp. 372, 444. Salvation »p. 426.

INSIGHT

God's rod (10:5). God's Sovereign power enables Him to use even His people's enemies to accomplish His purposes. Isaiah calls Judah to see God's hand in painful experiences.

Assyria's purpose (10:7). While God intends the Assyrian invasion as discipline, Assyria's motive in attacking Israel is rooted in a godless arrogance and pride. Thus God says, "I will punish the king of Assyria" (10:12).

It is *intent* that makes the difference. Let's remember that we may suffer discipline, even though we outwardly conform to Christian standards. God is concerned about motivation as well as actions, and will judge both.

The results of discipline (10:20). Those who survive the Assyrian invasion will "truly rely on the Lord." Suffering purges those who will not believe and deepens the faith of those who do.

"The stump of Jesse" (11:1). Jesse was the father of David. This, with the title, Branch, identifies the person in view here as the Messiah, the descendant of David destined to rule the Earth.

How Messiah judges (11:3-5). The theme of motive introduced in 10:7-11 is amplified here to include the totality of actions and intent. As God, the Messiah knows reality perfectly, so He is able to judge "with righteousness." His decisions, so unlike the decisions of human government that weigh a person's wealth or social standing, will be "for the poor of the earth."

The fact that His judgment will be enforced absolutely is expressed in the image of striking the earth "with the rod of His mouth."

Universal peace (11:6-9). A famous early American painting, "The Peaceable Kingdom," portrays the scene sketched here. Nature itself will be transformed when Christ rules, and those elements in nature which are hostile to man will be transmuted by God's power.

"A banner for the peoples" (11:10). The "banner" mentioned here is a standard, or a flag, raised with the intent of rallying people around it. The term "peoples" is often used in the O.T. of Gentile nations. Thus, the O.T. foresees a messianic age in which all peoples have come to a knowledge of God.

"A second time" (11:11). Many find this phrase significant. Some of the Jews returned to the Holy Land after the Babylonian Captivity, partially fulfilling O.T. predictions of a regathering. Yet in A.D. 70 the Jews were scattered among the nations a second time, as Roman armies battered the Jerusalem of Jesus and expelled all Jews from Judea. This second scattering, which history calls the *diaspora*, was even more severe than the first, and has seen the Jewish people settled in every land but their own. Some take the reference to "a second time" to imply both the dispersion of A.D. 70 and a supernatural regathering to Palestine when Jesus returns (»p. 419).

Chapter summary. With this chapter we enter a section filled with words of judgment and promise, with the darker side of the future emphasized. Isaiah 13–17 contains *massa'*, translated "oracle," which indicates a message of judgment directed against a specific person or peoples with full divine authority. The oracles in these chapters are directed against Babylon (13:1–14:23), Assyria (14:24-27), the Philistines (14:28-32), Moab (15:1–16:14), and against Damascus (17:1-14).

Key verse. 13:11: God will judge the sins of all.

Personal application. Don't judge others blessed by present prosperity. Look to their destiny and your own!

Key concepts. The Day of the Lord »pp. 413, 541. Satan »pp. 501, 655. Babylon »pp. 302, 920. Assyria »p. 255. Edom »p. 104. Philistines »p. 185.

INSIGHT

Eschatological theme: Regathering (14:1-3). Four great eschatological themes dominate the O.T.'s vision of history's end. One focuses on world conflict and divine judgment, a theme reflected in the oracles which compose these chapters of Isaiah (»p. 430). One speaks of a Jewish remnant, survivors of God's acts of judgment (»p. 427). Another theme is that seen here: God's people will be regathered to their own land as the last great moments of history unfold. And the final theme is that of a glorious kingdom, ruled from Jerusalem by the Messiah, which stretches over all the Earth (»p. 445).

The promises of regathering are words of encouragement, intended to be clutched tightly by God's people in their most desperate hours. Here, nestled in a prophecy about Babylon, destined to make Judah captive in a foreign land, is one of those sudden promises (14:1-3). God will have compassion on His people. He will bring the captives home and give them relief from their "suffering and turmoil and cruel bondage."

The following passages speak of a regathering of God's O.T. people at history's end, brought home by the Lord for a final working out of God's purposes: Isa. 11:11-12; 14:1-3; 27:12-13; 43:1-7; 66:20-22; Jer. 16:14-16; 23:3-8; 30:10-11; 31:8, 31-37; Ezek. 11:17-21; 20:33-38; 34:11-16; 39:25-29; Hosea 1:10-11; Joel 3:17-21; Amos 9:11-15; Micah 4:4-7; Zeph. 3:14-20; Zech. 8:4-8.

The promise that "once again He will choose Israel" (Isa. 14:1) reminds us of Paul's strong affirmation in Romans 11. The setting aside of Israel for the Gospel age is temporary, for "God's gifts and call are irrevocable." God still has a place in His purposes for the Jews.

A reference to Satan? (14:12-15) Christians have been fascinated with these verses. Many apply what students of prophecy call the "law of double reference" (»p. 408) and see a shift in focus from proud Babylon to an even more arrogant being, Satan.

Certainly reference to Satan is indirect if present, but Christ in Luke 10:18 applies language used in v. 12 to Satan. It is not at all unusual for the prophets to see in the pride of pagan rulers an arrogance which reflects satanic principles, even as David and certain kings of his line reflect qualities found in Christ.

If the focus does shift now to Satan, we have a unique insight into the essence of his original fall. The five vaunting "I will" statements reveal a twisted passion of the creature to replace the Creator as Lord. But the arrogant effort to rise higher than God leads only to a devastating fall. Isaiah pictures the ruler cast down to the depths, a pitiful creature now and an object of wonder that any might have feared him at all.

There are several lessons for us in this. First, pride does, as the saying goes, "lead to a fall." Put "I" on the throne of life rather than the Lord, and we too are doomed to failure and disappointment. Perhaps this kind of attitude is the ultimate source of evil, first in the universe and surely in our lives. Let's be sure to walk humbly with our God.

Second, it reminds us that Satan is a fallen, and now defeated, foe. He may be mighty now, but God's power is absolute.

Chapter summary. These chapters hold Isaiah's words concerning Egypt, then as throughout the Old Testament era, a world power. Isaiah rejects the efforts of envoys from Cush (the vast area along the upper Nile) to ally with Judah against Assyria (18:1), calling on them to return and watch what God does (vv. 2-6). Then they will acknowledge the Lord's sovereignty by bringing Him gifts (v. 7). Isaiah then predicts devastating judgments on Egypt, along the lower Nile (19:1-15). Yet when the judgments fall a change will come (vv. 16-17). Egypt—and even Assyria—will worship God (vv. 18-25). But the immediate future, acted out by Isaiah, holds nothing but judgment for the two lands (20:1-6).

Key verse. 19:17: Power is fleeting and deceitful.

Personal application. Beware of labeling anyone either all evil or all good.

INSIGHT

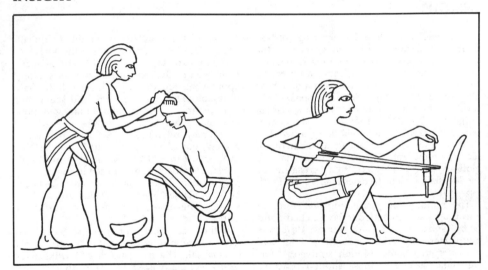

Egypt. More is known of Egypt than any other ancient society. Wall paintings on tombs, like those illustrated above, profusely portray daily life. Documents preserved in the dry climate, along with inscriptions carved in rock, display Egypt's many cultural achievements. These include works on medicine, astronomy, and literature, as well as treatises on magic and religion. In addition, the tombs of Pharaohs have contributed many artifacts which display the wealth and artistic skills of this people.

Scripture acknowledges the accomplishments and even the legendary wisdom of the Egyptians (1 Kings 4:30). Scripture also displays an appreciation for Egypt as a land of refuge. Abraham found food there when famine stalked Canaan (Gen. 12:10). Joseph rose to power in Egypt (Gen. 41–46). There the Jewish population exploded to an estimated 2.5 million persons. Thus, Egypt is viewed with appreciation for its contribution to the shaping of the race.

But Egypt also was the land of bondage, where God's people were persecuted and mistreated. In Egypt, the Children of Israel learned corrupt religious practices: displayed in the Exodus generation's worship of a golden calf (Ex. 32) and nearly 1,000 years later in the corrupt worship described in Ezek. 8–11. Throughout the time of Israel's kingdom Egypt was either an unreliable ally or an open enemy of the Jewish state. And so Scripture's attitude toward Egypt is ambivalent. While its contribution is recognized and honored, Egypt's sins must also be judged.

EGYPT IN PROPHECY

"Cush" (18:1). Cush is rendered "Ethiopia" in many Bible versions. It actually covers much more territory, including all the area in Africa drained by the upper Nile.

Drying up the Nile (19:5-10). The economy of Egypt has always been totally dependent on the Nile River, and Egypt's population still lives in the narrow, vital strip of green that can be irrigated by that stream. God's judgment will totally devastate that land.

Zoan and Memphis (19:11-15). These were the two largest cities in lower Egypt in Isaiah's time and served as important administrative centers.

Reliance on human wisdom, like reliance on pagan deities (19:3), is futile. God's purposes cannot be thwarted. All who presume to try give lunatic ("senseless," v. 11) advice.

Judah to bring terror? (19:17) The warning must seem absurd. Could tiny Judea, only a few hundred square miles in extent, terrorize mighty Egypt? Yet today even without open divine intervention we've seen the forces of "tiny Israel" defeat Egypt and other Arab nations as well.

An altar and monument (19:19). The altar on which the Jews offered sacrifice was constructed differently from altars of other lands (cf. Ex. 20:24-26). The "monument" is a pillar of stones erected to commemorate some event. The fact that both are to serve as witnesses to (reminders of) relationship with God make it clear that the altar is symbolic and not to be used for making sacrifices (cf. Josh. 22).

"A highway" (19:23). The highway symbolizes good will and understanding, free and speedy access. The word, used as an image by Isaiah, indicates the close relationship between once hostile nations forged by a shared commitment to the God of the Jews. When God can say of Egypt and Assyria as well as of Israel, "my people" (19:25), the world will have peace and blessing at last.

While Egypt must suffer God's judgment, the O.T. looks forward to a day when Egypt will be converted to the Lord and worship Him. Isa. 19 describes both Egypt's judgment and that nation's salvation. Concerning judgment: there will be civil strife (v. 2), national defeat (v. 4), and terrible calamities (vv. 5-17). Yet God will send them a Saviour (v. 20). Though God strikes Egypt (v. 22), He will also heal them and hear their prayers (vv. 23-25). When the Egyptians are converted (vv. 18-22), they will openly honor God with an altar and memorial (vv. 19-20). They will pray to God and offer Him sacrifices and gifts (vv. 20-21). Then, with Assyrians and Israelites, the Egyptians too will serve the Lord (vv. 23-25).

Other major predictive passages concerning Egypt are Jer. 46 and Ezek. 29–30. Jeremiah warns of Egypt's imminent defeat by the Babylonians under Nebuchadnezzar, but promises the land will remain habitable. Ezekiel, with Jeremiah, predicts a Babylonian victory. Yet each of these may well stand for the ultimate judgment and subsequent salvation of the Egyptian people, who through God's mighty acts of power once again realize that He truly is the Lord.

Outline
Place
Finder

JUDAH
IMMANUEL
JUDGMENT
HEZEKIAH
COMFORT

Chapter summary. Isaiah continues his predictions of judgments destined to soon strike contemporary nations. The prophet foresees the fall of pagan Babylon, not due to emerge as a dominant world power for yet another 100 years (21:1-10). He also prophesies briefly against Edom and Arabia, who will try futilely to resist Assyria's power (vv. 11-17).

Chapter 22 contains a powerful denunciation of the shallow faith of Jerusalem's people despite deliverance of the city from Assyria in Hezekiah's time (22:1-14). This is followed by a scornful denunciation of two contemporary officials in Jerusalem (vv. 15-25), Shebna for pride, and Eliakim apparently for nepotism.

The oracle of judgment contained in chapter 23 is directed against Tyre, the wealthy Phoenician seaport that lay along the Mediterranean coast just north of Israel. The harbor of this materialistic city would be destroyed and its greatness eclipsed. In the roll call of peoples due to face the divine wrath we realize that every culture of man will surely be judged by God.

Key verse. 22:25: Nothing but God can hold us up.

Personal application. How good to be citizens of heaven!

Key concepts. Babylon »pp. 302, 920. Jerusalem »pp. 205, 451. Edom »p. 104. Judgment »p. 372. Day of the Lord »p. 413.

INSIGHT

"The Desert by the Sea" (21:1). One Greek writer gave this name to the plain on which Babylon stood, as it was divided by lakes and marshy country. All agree the city Babylon or the country Babylonia is intended.

The attack (21:1-5). In Isaiah's day the Babylon of Merodach-Baladan was viewed as a possible rival of Assyria, the power which threatened Judah's existence. Verse 2 echoes the battle cries of Babylon's allies as together they attack Assyria—only to be crushed. The defeat staggers the Jews (v. 3), who had pinned their hopes on a Babylonian victory. Now Judah must prepare to resist Assyria on its own (v. 5).

"The Valley of Vision" (22:1). Commentators agree this refers to Jerusalem. Even though the city sits on mountain ridges, it is surrounded by even higher hills. The point seems to be that Jerusalem has received message after message (i.e., "vision") from God and yet failed to really hear.

Weeping bitterly (22:1-13). The city has been delivered from Assyrian attack in the time of Hezekiah, but Isaiah weeps because he foresees coming judgment (vv. 4-8). This is because when the city was threatened the people hurried to strengthen its defenses (vv. 9-11), but failed to look to God for help, as King Hezekiah did (v. 12). Instead they turned to revelry, determined to enjoy life as long as they could (v. 13).

This overt rejection of God by the people of Jerusalem was a sin that "will not be atoned for" (v. 14).

What a warning to us. Our first resort in time of trouble must be to appeal to God.

"Shebna" (22:15). Pride is the sin of this official, who like the pharaohs of Egypt sought to build himself a lasting monument while his land was in peril. Perhaps we can see a parallel between Shebna and those modern elected officials who put reelection above the good of the nation.

"Eliakim" (22:20). This successor of Shebna is first commended. When he first takes office he will function as a tent peg that gives stability to the kingdom (v. 23). But Eliakim's advancement will corrupt his family, as they seek constant advancement, until their weight breaks another peg—that driven into the wall of a house on which kitchen utensils were held (vv. 24-25).

Let's hang our hopes on the Lord, not even on His servants.

"Cross over" (23:1-16). Tyre and Sidon were twin Phoenician centers, ports planted on the Mediterranean coast just north of Israel. The Phoenicians had colonies throughout the Mediterranean and many commercial ties with Egypt. This roused the suspicions of Assyria and led to a temporary destruction of the ports. The people fled and "crossed over" their colonies or trading partners.

Chapter summary. The focus in Isaiah now shifts again, as the prophet looks beyond the immediate future and the judgment due specific peoples, to speak of divine judgment in a broad, general way. The message of Isaiah is that history moves purposely toward God's intended end. Judgment on all nations will surely come (24:1-23), and *Yahweh* will triumph over all (25:1-12). God will raise the righteous (26:1-19), and in that last, great day the Lord will exalt Israel as He promised from the beginning (26:20–27:1-13).

These chapters define God's relationship as Judge to the whole world and declare that He will punish sin (24:1-23). They then go on to praise God, for His judgment on the nations means the salvation of Israel and the triumph of God over evil (25:1-12).

Outline
Place
Finder

JUDAH
IMMANUEL
JUDGMENT
HEZEKIAH
COMFORT

Key verses. 24:17; 25:9: Judgment saves.

Personal application. Often it's necessary to destroy the illusory works of man to see the reality of God.

Key concepts. "That day" »p. 413. Covenant »p. 35. Music »p. 274. Punish »p. 827. Praise »p. 380. Salvation »p. 426.

INSIGHT

The Isaiah Apocalypse. That's what these chapters of Isaiah have been called. The distinction between prophecy and apocalypse is not at all sharp, but generally prophecy looks at the eschatological future with a historic focus on specific places and nations, while apocalypse is less specific, speaking in broad general terms about events of cosmic significance. In fact Isa. 24–27 cannot be placed squarely in either category, nor can the notion that apocalyptic writings are a later development be used to deny Isaiah's authorship of these chapters.

Universal judgment (24:1-6). The coming judgment affects everyone, whatever their social status (v. 2). Wealth and position are powerless to protect against God's intent to punish sin. The surface of the Earth itself will be twisted and ruined (v. 4), quite possibly by drought (v. 7). It's futile to try to find security in this world, when this world itself is totally vulnerable to the coming judgment of God.

"The everlasting covenant" (24:5). Many see this as a reference to God's covenant with Noah, never again to destroy the Earth by a flood (cf. Gen. 9:11-17). That covenant also implies human moral responsibility, for it makes man responsible to God to account for shed blood (9:4-6). Thus the laws and statutes here are not those of the O.T. law. They are natural moral laws, expressed in human conscience, which God has imbedded in human nature, to which Paul refers in Rom. 2.12-16.

Praise? (24:14-16a) The praise is uttered by those who survive the initial judgments described before. Here Isaiah is like Revelation, in which great hymns of praise are interspersed with awesome visions of terrifying judgments. Who here is giving "Glory to the Righteous One"? The phrase "islands of the sea" (v. 15) suggests they are Gentiles rather than Jews (cf. Isa. 41:5; 42:4).

Punishing the powers (24:21-23). The Heb. term *seba'* is used both of heavenly bodies and angelic armies (cf. 1 Kings 22:19; 2 Chron. 18:18). As punishment is the subject, the reference is most likely to spiritual beings, the fallen angels who are Satan's allies. The whole universe is to be purified by God.

Upside down (25:3-4). When the British army of Cornwallis surrendered to George Washington at Yorktown the band marched out of the fortifications playing a tune called "The World Turned Upside Down." This is what the day of judgment will mean too. The "strong" and "ruthless" (v. 3) will honor the "poor" and "needy" (v. 4). Why? Because the poor, who took refuge in God, will prove to be wiser as well as more righteous than the strong, who rely on their own strength.

Triumph (25:7-10). What will God's final triumph mean for us? The shroud, death, will be destroyed (v. 7). And those who trust in God will praise Him and be glad in His salvation (v. 9). God's judgments are terrible. But the result of judgment is cleansing, release, and joy.

Outline
Place
Finder

JUDAH
IMMANUEL
JUDGMENT
HEZEKIAH
COMFORT

Chapter summary. The "Isaiah Apocalypse" which began at chapter 24 is continued. The prophet has announced God's judgment on all mankind and described the blessings of salvation that follow. Now he records a song of praise, which features the hope of resurrection (26:1-19) and the promise that "in that day" destruction of Israel's oppressors will result in deliverance for God's ancient people (26:20–27:13).

Key verse. 26:19: Shout for joy!

Personal application. Every night of suffering gives way to a dawn of divine blessing, but only for God's own.

Key concepts. Wait »p. 358. Grace »p. 725. Resurrection »p. 522. Guilt »p. 79. Atonement »p. 69. Peace »p. 427.

INSIGHT

"In that day" (26:1). Here, "that day" is the eschatological Day of the Lord, but in its aspect of salvation's bright joy, which follows the darkness of divine judgment. These chapters give us perspective. The punishment that God visits on the Earth purges the world of sin. His triumph is the vindication of His people and their release from oppression.

Inner peace (26:3). This is one of the most beautiful of Scripture's "descriptive promises." It's descriptive in that it portrays the experience of the individual who trusts in God. It's a promise in that each of us today can rely on the Lord and know that trust will bring peace to us as well. Here's a verse all should memorize: "You will keep in perfect peace him whose mind is steadfast, because he trusts in You."

The path of the righteous (26:7). The Heb. word describing God is *yasar*, upright. The path of the righteous is smooth because God Himself is righteous.

In the Yukon of old, one man was often sent ahead to "break trail" for others or a dog sled. This passage reminds us that a righteous God has already broken trail for those who follow Him because they are committed to righteousness too.

Walk while you wait (26:8). To "wait" in the O.T. is to look forward expectantly and with hope. But waiting is never a passive experience for the believer. Waiting for the Lord must be demonstrated by constantly walking in His ways. The way to wait for God is to be actively committed to doing His will.

Irresistible grace? (26:10) Grace is God's kindness compassionately displayed to those who deserve no good at His hands. Everyone lives and breathes only in virtue of God's grace. There is no good thing we experience in life except what comes from His loving hands. But grace is not irresistible, in that many who snatch the gifts refuse to acknowledge the Giver. The appropriate response to grace is not only to accept it, but to acknowledge God and put our trust in Him.

"Your dead will live" (26:19). Some argue this is a figurative application of the idea of resurrection. But there could have been no figure of speech if no belief that "their bodies will rise" existed in ancient Israel.

And what a wonder this is. Storms of judgment may sweep over our earth. Wars may devastate, and disease may ravage. Famines may decimate the land, while starvation stalks our families. There are indeed dread fates that are to be feared. But these are not history's last words! At the end of history—both the history of nations, and the personal history of each individual—the shout of God's promise echoes. "Your dead will live; their bodies will rise!" What a truth to hold fast in troubled times.

"You, O Israelites" (27:12). This chapter's viewpoint narrows as Isaiah looks ahead at the destiny of God's ancient people. God will again tend His vineyard (cf. 27:2-4 with Isa. 5:1-5). As history's final day draws to a close, Jacob's guilt will be atoned for (Isa. 27:9). Here, as often in the prophets, the ancestral name, "Jacob," stands for the Jewish people. And that people "will be gathered up, one by one," and return to Jerusalem and the Promised Land (27:12-13).

Chapter summary. Isaiah's grim predictions of judgment were briefly set aside in the last chapters (Isa. 26–27). But now he returns to his forbidding theme. This time his gaze is focused directly on God's own people, the Jews of Isaiah's time, who represent in both northern and southern Hebrew kingdoms the unbelief of every historic age. In a stunning sermon that has been praised as one of the most powerful of any prophet's preachings, Isaiah decries his people's foolish reliance on a protective "covenant with death" (Isa. 28:15-18). That covenant will be annulled, and death will sweep in, a terrifying scourge (vv. 1-19a). As nature itself follows a seasonal pattern, so history has its pattern. And the planting of sin leads inevitably to a harvest of judgment (vv. 19b-29). Consequently Jerusalem will be besieged and brought low (29:1-4), although God will at last fight against Israel's enemies (vv. 5-9). Until then God's people will be blind to the vision, for their hearts are far from God (vv. 10-16). One day the mockers will be destroyed. Then a shamed Israel will at last stand in awe of God and gain the understanding she now so tragically lacks (vv. 17-24).

Outline
Place
Finder

JUDAH
IMMANUEL
JUDGMENT
HEZEKIAH
COMFORT

Key verse. 28:13: Misread the Word, and there is no hope.

Personal application. Seek God. He will give understanding.

INSIGHT

Decadence (28:1-6). In one of history's most famous studies, Gibbon ascribed the fall of the Roman Empire to drunkenness and decadence. This is the image Isaiah has of Israel's leaders, wearing floral wreaths, staggering drunkenly as the Assyrian forces loomed just over the horizon. The pride of Israel would soon wither. And at history's end God Himself will be the beautiful wreath that crowns His people, and justice will be their strength.

Does our nation seek God as its crowning glory? Do we?

"Do and do" (28:10-13). The repeated phrases are reminiscent of the drunkard's babbling, words said and heard without meaning. But there is more to these verses than this. Isaiah warns that a people who will not hear God's Word will be not only meaningless, but misinterpreted! Rather than a message of salvation (v. 12), the Word will seem little more than a set of rules: "do and do, do and do, rule on rule, rule on rule" (v. 13).

"Covenant with death" (28:15). The phrase simply means that the people of Israel thought they had an agreement worked out by which they could avoid death. But God will soon annul that and strike His people with judgment (28:28).

"A precious cornerstone" (28:16-17). This imagery is picked up in the N.T and applied to Jesus as the Messiah (Rom. 9:33; 10:11; 1 Peter 2:4-6). The stone image is also repeated

in Isa. 8:14, another instance in which contemporary leaders fail. Put the two messianic "stones" in Isaiah together, and we have a fascinating revelation. In human construction, the same stone cannot serve both as the foundation of the building and the capstone, which holds the arch atop it together. But the Messiah is both foundation and capstone in God's building, both the beginning and end. What's more, this stone both is God and is laid by God. Only Jesus, sent by God and yet God the Son, could possibly fulfill this requirement.

Too short a bed (28:20). This is likely a proverbial saying, much like one of our own time: "You've made your bed, Israel. Now lie in it."

Ariel (29:1). The name, applied to Jerusalem, means "altar hearth." It views Jerusalem as the place of sacrifice, an activity in which Judah, oriented to ritual but not heart religion (cf. Isa. 1), was all too deeply involved in. As verse 29:13 complains, "These people come near to Me with their mouth . . . but their hearts are far from Me."

The vision is sealed (29:11-12). Here "vision" refers to the revelation given through Isaiah. Most of those to whom it was delivered could not grasp the words ("read"), and those who knew the words missed the meaning.

"Rules taught by men" (29:13). Jesus quotes this verse and applies it to the externalism that characterized many Pharisees in His day (Matt. 15:9).

Outline
Place
Finder

JUDAH
IMMANUEL
JUDGMENT
HEZEKIAH
COMFORT

Chapter summary. God's obstinate people persist in seeking foreign alliances rather than relying on the Lord (30:1-7). They even pressure God's prophets to say only what they want to hear rather than deliver the Lord's messages (vv. 8-11). This refusal to listen means destruction (vv. 12-13). Yet God longs to be gracious to them. And one day, when at last they cry out to Him for help, God will be gracious to Israel (vv. 14-26) and shatter His peoples' enemies (vv. 27-33). But Isaiah must leave his bright vision of Israel's distant future and return to the situation of his contemporaries. He predicts woe to those who rely on Egypt (31:1-3), and as a token of His ultimate grace God will shield Jerusalem even now (vv. 4-9). This last promise was kept. In the days of Hezekiah Assyria devastated Israel and invaded Judah, but Jerusalem was rescued by an act of divine intervention (cf. Isa. 36–39). As God acted then, He will act in the future to keep His other promises. The present may be dark, but the future is bright for the Jews.

Key verse. 30:15: This is still God's prescription for salvation.

Personal application. See in the present blessings you enjoy God's guarantee of a glorious future.

INSIGHT

Illustration. *In normal times, the bread of the wealthy was prepared from wheat flour and that of the poor from barley. "Bread of adversity" (Isa. 30:20) was prepared when food stores were exhausted and the people were near starvation. It contained a few kernels of grain, pods from trees, and any other seeds that could be gathered and used to make flour. God would soon feed Isaiah's contemporaries on "bread of adversity" because they relied on Egypt's armies rather than on Him for protection. There is no real security in this world apart from the Lord.*

"Egypt's shade" (30:2). The image is more properly Egypt's shadow. It suggests being close to one's protector, in his shadow.

Tell pleasant things? (30:10). It's dangerous for a patient to ask her doctor only for good news. Once a serious illness is diagnosed it can be treated. If that same illness is simply denied, it is likely to kill. It's the same with God's words through the prophets. Their warnings may not be pleasant. But only if we listen and take them to heart is there hope.

"Salvation" (30:15). The Heb. concept of "save" and "salvation" are expressed primarily in the term, *yasa'*. It is typically used of concrete situations in which persons are physically threatened. The N.T. emphasis of salvation from sin and from evil spiritual powers is not common in the O.T. (but see Pss. 45:14; 79:9; Ezek. 37:23). Yet the core concept is applicable in the spiritual as well as material realm. Salvation presupposes (1) a person or nation in danger, suffering some harm, and in need of outside help; (2) a deliverer, or savior, who acts to relieve the distress; and (3) a change in the situation of the sufferer that brings relief.

In this passage "salvation" is relief from national enemies. The only one truly able to deliver is God, and the enemy is Assyria. Only by turning to God and appealing to Him for help will Judah have hope. To rely on Egypt, that is, on any other savior, is to reject God, and all hope.

Images of judgment (30:27-28). Four images suggest the seriousness of the coming judgment. These are fire, flood, "the sieve of destruction," and an animal's jaws.

"Topheth" (30:33). This was the district in the Valley of Hinnom near Jerusalem where apostate Jews burned their young children alive as votive offerings to pagan gods. It would no longer claim the weak and helpless, but the mighty of Israel and Assyria alike.

Men and not God (31:3). Today too the choice exists between relying on the flesh or on the Spirit. Let's choose wisely.

Chapter summary. Isaiah's vision again moves beyond contemporary and future judgment to portray a "king [who] will reign in righteousness" (32:1). This grand messianic vision picks up themes found in other prophecies, portraying first one who does away with life's unfairnesses (vv. 2-8). His judgments will shake the complacent (vv. 9-14), but lead to a pouring out of God's Spirit that brings personal and international peace (vv. 15-20). With the destroyer destroyed (33:1-4), the exalted Lord Himself is to be the foundation for better times (vv. 5-12). That coming will terrify sinners, but seem a refuge to the righteous (vv. 13-16). Jerusalem will become the capital of the kingdom, supplying and satisfying all (vv. 17-24).

Key verse. 32:17: Only God's Spirit can restore.

Personal application. God's best for you lies beyond tomorrow.

INSIGHT

The Messiah and ideal government. Isa. 9 introduced the picture of Messiah as a ruler, announcing that "the government will be on His shoulders" (v. 6). These and other chapters of Isa. give us a vision of ideal government, usually associated with the messianic king. He will correct injustices, judge sinners, and establish righteousness, and "the fruit of righteousness will be peace."

Forever . . . until (32:14-15). There is a vital truth in the saying that Israel's land will become a "wasteland forever" and in the same sentence add, "till the Spirit is poured upon us." Human beings are unable to reverse the effects of sin and its consequences. From our perspective, the devastation truly is forever. Yet God, who created by His Spirit, hovering over the face of the waters, can and will recreate! With man, the darkness is forever.

"Peace" (32:17-18). The Heb. word for peace, *shalom*, expresses a basic and vital biblical concept. The word suggests wholeness and harmony, that which is complete and sound, prosperous, healthy, and fulfilled. The word occurs over 200 times in the O.T. In narrative books it typically is used to describe an absence of hostility or strife. In the psalms and the prophets it goes beyond this, so that in at least 2/3 of the biblical references the word indicates a total fulfillment that comes when persons experience God's presence. Isa. 32:15-16 portrays both the inner peace and material prosperity that will mark the joyful fulfillment of man's hopes under the rule of the Messiah, God's Prince of Peace (Isa. 9:6).

The N.T.'s word for peace, *eirene*, originally meant the ordered life that was possible when a people were not at war. Later, the concept was expanded to include an inner, personal peace. "Peace" is mentioned over 60 times in the N.T., with this later meaning, enriched by the O.T. idea of *shalom*. In Christ our lives are made whole, our relationships are harmonized, and we experience the spiritual and psychological wholeness that God intended for human beings in the original creation (cf. Rom. 5:1; Eph. 2:14-17; Heb. 12:14; Col. 3:12-15).

Righteousness and peace (32:15-17). Peace is possible only where there is righteousness, and righteousness only where God's Spirit transforms humankind. Isa. 57:20-21 says, "The wicked are like the tossing sea, which cannot rest, whose waves cast up mire and mud. 'There is no peace,' says my God, 'for the wicked.' "

Survivors (33:14-16). One of the basic concepts in O.T. prophecy is that the divine judgments foretold will purge sinners, but that the righteous will survive. In fact, the Heb. word *sa'ar* is a technical term, as used by the prophets, where it designates a "remnant" composed of Israelites who are converted and who receive the blessings promised in the O.T. covenants. Thus Isaiah says to the remnant, the Messiah "will be the sure foundation for your times, a rich store of salvation and wisdom and knowledge; the fear of the Lord is the key to this treasure" (33:6). This eschatological remnant is described in Joel 2:32 and Ezek. 6:8-9.

But the concept of a remnant has a present as well as eschatological meaning. However great Israel's apostasy, and however terrible God's judgments, the Lord is committed to preserve a faithful few (cf. 1 Kings 19:18; Mal. 3:16-18). The Apostle Paul applies this doctrine in two ways. First, he shows that salvation has always been by faith and that physical relationship to Abraham was no automatic guarantee of God's favor (Rom. 9:8). And in Rom. 11:26 he declares that God's O.T. promises still stand, for a remnant of the Jews will always be preserved and in a yet future day "all Israel will be saved, as it is written."

Outline
Place
Finder

JUDAH
IMMANUEL
JUDGMENT
HEZEKIAH
COMFORT

Chapter summary. Isaiah continues his description of history's end with his characteristic alternating of images of terrifying judgments and exultant joy. First the prophet addresses the nations, announcing God's anger (34:1-2). Terrible slaughter awaits all their armies, for God has a day of vengeance in store for those who have troubled His people (vv. 3-8). Isaiah focuses on Edom and describes what awaits this hostile people as illustrative of the fate of all nations (vv. 9-16). Yet the final conflict which brings destruction on pagan peoples means the restoration of Israel's hopes (35:1-2). God comes with vengeance, but to save His own (vv. 3-4). In glowing terms Isaiah describes the joy that will soar in the hearts of God's people as His presence works its marvelous transformation of the land and its people. In that day the redeemed, and only the redeemed, will enter Zion singing, filled at last with joy and gladness (vv. 5-10).

Key verse. 35:4: God destroys in order to save.

Personal application. Take no revenge, but expect God to uphold your cause.

INSIGHT

Vengeance. The theme of divine vengeance and retribution dominates these two chapters. While some draw back from this doctrine, concerned with what they assume is an ascription of vindictiveness to God, both O.T. and N.T. boldly affirm the truth that the Lord is a "God who avenges" (Ps. 94:1). Deut. 32:34-35 says, "It is mine to avenge; I will repay. In due time their foot will slip; their day of disaster is near and their doom rushes upon them."

A few times vengeance, *naqam*, is executed through human agencies (cf. Num. 31:2-3; Josh. 10:13). Yet no individual has God's permission to take personal revenge. The reason is that vengeance is a judicial concept. It is reserved for God, as moral and spiritual Judge of His universe, to punish those who persistently reject Him, abandon His ways, and oppress the righteous. Typically vengeance is reserved for history's end (cf. Isa. 63:1-6), and any present time is marked by a divine forebearance that provides individuals and nations with every opportunity to repent and to believe.

In the N.T., the doctrine is expressed in the Gk. *dike* and *dikesis*. This word has the primary meaning of "justice" and emphasizes the fact that vengeance is a judicial function reserved for God alone (Rom. 12:19). In the N.T., vengeance is also typically reserved for the future (Rom. 2:1-11). But its terrors are as graphically described in 2 Thes. 1:5-10 as they are in this and other O.T. prophetic passages.

The real wonder is not that God will certainly punish the unrepentant, but that He chose to vent His anger against sin on Christ rather than on us. Christ's sufferings for us forever disprove the notion that a God of vengeance could not also be a God of love.

World conflict. A second major theme found in the O.T. and seen in these chapters is that of a great world conflict in which the armies of man are drawn up against the Lord and His people. This conflict, destined to take place at history's end and to result in the crushing defeat of man's rebellious forces, is described by many of the O.T. prophets. Among the passages which describe that conflict are Isa. 2:12-21; 30; 34–35; Ezek. 38–39; Dan. 11:40; Joel 2:1-17. The very same vision, of "the kings of the earth and their armies gathered together to make war against the rider on the horse [Christ] and His [heavenly] army" is found in Rev. 19:9.

Recompense (35:3-10). Images of the dread judgment of God are balanced by this portrait of the joy of the redeemed. The Apostle Paul reflects the sense of this passage in Rom. 8:18, where he says, "I consider that our present sufferings are not worth comparing with the glory that will be revealed in us." God's people will suffer while society is corrupted by sin and evil men are bent on oppressing the righteous. But just as God's day of vengeance is just retribution for the wicked, it introduces the divine repayment of the redeemed for past pain.

428

Chapter summary. A historical interlude now intrudes and separates the two halves of Isaiah. The events portray tests, proving the words of Isaiah and demonstrating to Israel that if they would only trust the Lord He could and would deliver them. Thus, these chapters serve as a pivot on which the book turns. Israel has rejected the One who is able to deliver, despite this evidence of His power. Yet, the Lord is by nature the Saviour of His people. The day will come when God will save despite Israel's current unbelief. God is the guarantor of this future, so the faithful Israel can look ahead with undiminished hopes.

Outline
Place
Finder

JUDAH
IMMANUEL
JUDGMENT
HEZEKIAH
COMFORT

The same story is told in similar detail in both 2 Kings 18 and 2 Chronicles 32 (»pp. 256, 300). Sennacherib has devastated the ring of protective fortresses Hezekiah has built along his borders and threatens to advance against Jerusalem. His representative calls on Hezekiah to surrender and shouts his message loudly to demoralize the city's defenders. But he foolishly ridicules God, and Hezekiah prays that God will act to uphold His honor. The Prophet Isaiah responds. God will drive Sennacherib away and not so much as a single arrow will wing its way over the walls of the holy city (Isa. 36–37).

Although the words come true, God's intervention is no guarantee of future protection. In fact Hezekiah's recovery from an earlier illness (Isa. 38) had led to a visit of Babylonian ambassadors. Ostensibly, they came to congratulate the king on his recovery, but most likely also hoped to encourage resistance against the Assyrian colossus that threatened them both. The king welcomed them enthusiastically and showed them everything in his kingdom. He was angrily rebuked by Isaiah, who apparently saw Hezekiah's welcoming of the Babylonian envoys as a failure to rely entirely on God. Isaiah announced that one day, after Hezekiah was dead, the little nation of Judah would be subdued by the Babylonians and the survivors of the Jewish people would be torn from their land and sent into captivity (Isa. 39).

Only those who rely completely on God can experience full deliverance. The people to whom Isaiah ministered had to respond to his message with their whole hearts if there was to be any hope.

Key verse. 37:20: God's glory is of first importance.

Personal application. It is not possible to rely partly on the Lord.

Key concepts. Assyria »p. 255. Blasphemy »p. 64. Cherubim »p. 491. Predictive prophecy »pp. 407, 434. Babylon »p. 302.

INSIGHT

"Aramaic" (36:11). Aramaic was the trade and diplomatic language of the ancient Middle East. While related to Heb., it is a different tongue. Later the Jews who were transported to Babylon adopted Aramaic. When their descendants returned to Judah two generations later that community spoke Aramaic.

Outline
Place
Finder

JUDAH
IMMANUEL
JUDGMENT
HEZEKIAH
COMFORT

Chapter summary. This chapter launches the second half of the Book of Isaiah. Chapters 1–35 emphasized judgment and looked ahead to invasion and the ultimate destruction of Judah. The prophetic standpoint of chapters 40–66 is after these tragic events, and Isaiah looks even further ahead to God's ultimate triumph. While both judgment and comfort are found in each half of Isaiah, the emphasis of the first half is on judgment and that of the second on comfort.

Isaiah's opening cry is, "Comfort, comfort my people" (40:1). He cries out the good news that, despite man's brief, ephemeral life, the "Word of our God stands" (v. 8). Israel's "Sovereign Lord" is coming with power, and He will care for His people as a shepherd cares for his flock (vv. 2-11). The prophet exults in his vision of the greatness of our sovereign Lord: He is Creator and Ruler of all (vv. 12-17); living, enthroned on high (vv. 18-24); incomparable, everlasting, omniscient, and omnipotent (vv. 25-27). This is the God who stoops to give strength to those who put their hope in Him. Comfort? Comfort indeed!

Key verse. 40:9: The key to comfort is to know who God is.

Personal application. Let Isaiah's vision of our glorious God strengthen you.

Key concepts. Shepherd »p. 355. Holy Spirit »pp. 744, 759.

INSIGHT

"**Comfort**" **(40:1).** The Heb. word is *naham*. It's a deeply emotional word, overflowing with feelings of pity and concern. It's a word that often has the meaning of consolation. Isaiah has cried out against the spiritual insensitivity of his generation and warned of devastating divine punishments. But God's love for Israel and Judah has never weakened. So now Isaiah speaks directly to the shaken survivors of the holocaust to come, to comfort and console them. God is God. And God remains committed to His own.

"**Sovereign Lord**" **(40:10).** One key to the second half of Isaiah is found in the prophet's use of various names for God. Here "Sovereign Lord" translates the Heb. *'adonay Yahweh*. The first word is an intensive form of "master" or "lord." It is used only of God in the O.T., emphasizing His greatness and ultimate power and rule. *Yahweh* is the personal name of God, constructed on the root of the verb "to be." It emphasizes God's personal presence with His people (»p. 57). The juxtaposition of these names here is significant, for it links power and love, transcendence, and intimacy. What a wonder that our God, so great that the universe hardly reflects His glory, is so tender and loving toward you and me.

Create (40:26). Isaiah refers to Creation to illustrate God's greatness. God made all things.

He sustains all things. And as other verses in this chapter emphasize, He rules all things (40:21-25). The Heb. word create, *bara'*, is used only of God in the *Qal* stem in which it functions as a technical theological term. Rather than mean "make something out of nothing," *bara'* means to initiate an object or project. The use of the word in this stem in the O.T. emphasizes a great fact.

There are certain things that only God can give being to. He alone could fabricate the material universe and establish nature's processes. He alone could shape male and female in His image and so launch the human race. He alone can transform sinful man's character by creating in us a new heart. He alone could launch history on its course and guide its progress. And God alone will be able to renew this universe, purging it of all evil by initiating a new heaven and earth at history's end. This is the Creator whom Isaiah presents and to whom we give our praise: God. God alone is able to give existence to the world and new life to you and me.

Power, strength, mighty (40:26). These words, used interchangeably in the O.T., emphasize the ultimate power and strength of God. Through personal relationship with Him, His strength flows into and enables you and me.

Chapter summary. The message of comfort found in chapter 40 provides the context for this chapter as well. In that chapter Isaiah spoke of God; here God Himself speaks. While He speaks to the nations, the message is intended to comfort Israel.

God speaks from a courtroom, in which He can take any legal role, for the Lord is the injured party, the prosecutor, and judge (41:1). The Lord goes on to describe the stunning rise of Cyrus of Persia, a historical movement of which the Lord is the author (vv. 2-7), an event that Israel, in captivity in Babylon, is not to fear (vv. 8-10). Israel's enemies will be put to shame (vv. 11-16), and her desperate needs will be met by God (vv. 17-20).

The trial scene resumes, with the gods of the nations in the dock (vv. 21-24). They are proven powerless and false, for only the Lord can predict beforehand what will happen (vv. 25-29). These verses like the first verses of this chapter predict the rise of Cyrus, which lies 150 years in the future as Isaiah writes.

Key verse. 41:10: Tomorrow's wars hold no terrors for those God has chosen as His own.

Personal application. You have trusted God with your eternal soul. Trust Him with your tomorrow as well.

Key concepts. Predictive prophecy »p. 434. Idolatry »p. 433.

Outline
Place
Finder

JUDAH
IMMANUEL
JUDGMENT
HEZEKIAH
COMFORT

INSIGHT

"The place of judgment" (41:1). One of the most frequent images found in the O.T. is that of a trial, or *rib*. Such courtroom scenes are used to present God's case against evildoers and also as a setting for the announcement of divine judgment. Both uses of the setting are seen in this chapter. God preannounces the rise of Cyrus as a judgment to fall on Babylon (cf. Isa. 44:24-28). He also calls the idols of the nation into court to testify (41:21-24).

Calling to God's service (41:2-4). Scholars debate who the person referred to is. It is best to take him as Cyrus the Persian, who overthrew the Babylonian Empire and issued the decree that permitted the Jews to return to their homeland (cf. Ezra). He is called God's servant because he fulfilled God's will in punishing Babylon and in enabling the Jews to return to the Holy Land.

A great truth is emphasized here. God controls the course of history and the rise and fall of nations. Even the pagan serves God's purposes, even though unwittingly. However, you and I have the greatest privilege of all. We can serve God knowingly and gladly.

"My servant" (41:8). In Isa., the term "servant" underlines two things: divine choice and fulfillment of a divinely ordained task. Israel is God's servant, but falls short of completing her mission. As Isaiah will soon reveal, God will send another Servant, His Messiah. He will successfully accomplish the mission God has for Him to do. Yet, even though Israel fell short, that people remained "My servant." God does not discard us when we fail, but remains committed to us in love.

Power, strength (41:10). This is the second time in Isaiah's words of comfort that he has emphasized God's commitment to strengthen and help His people (cf. 41:28-31). The use of these words in the O.T. looks back again and again to God's great acts: Creation, the judgment of the Genesis flood, and particularly the redemption of Israel from Egypt.

What a wonder to realize that the awesome power that God has displayed in history is available to you and me today. We know it is, for God the Creator has said, "I will strengthen you and help you; I will uphold you" (41:10).

"From the beginning" (41:26). The phrase emphasizes the purposive aspects of Creation as these unfold in history. God did not just wind up the world and leave it to run down. From the beginning, He had a plan and purpose to carry out, and history unfolds according to His grand, eternal design. How great God is!

Outline
Place
Finder

JUDAH
IMMANUEL
JUDGMENT
HEZEKIAH
COMFORT

Chapter summary. The chapter begins with the first of several passages known as the "servant songs," because they deal with a "servant of the Lord." The ideal servant introduced here is the Messiah, whom God has empowered and called to establish justice on the Earth (42:1-8). The work of the Servant stimulates God's people to praise (vv. 9-13) and introduces a great wonder. As history's greatest moment draws near, God portrays Himself as a pregnant woman about to give birth (vv. 14-17). Israel, blind and deaf to God's Law, was unable to fulfill the servant's role (vv. 18-25). But now they will come to know God as their Saviour and Redeemer—all because God loves them anyway (43:1-7). Then, and even now, Israel will be able to witness to God's greatness revealed in His saving acts (vv. 8-13). Despite Israel's unfaithfulness, God has remained committed to His people and will continue to meet their needs (vv. 14-21).

Yet how discouraging to God! Despite God's mercy Israel has remained ungrateful, refusing to call on or worship Him and burdening the Lord with their sins. Yet God remains the one "who blots out your transgressions," even while punishing those who persist in their indifference to Him (vv. 22-26).

Key verse. 42:4: The Cross itself did not discourage Christ.

Personal application. If we do not fulfill our mission God will choose another for it, but He will keep on loving us. We are not loved for what we do, but because God is gracious.

INSIGHT

The servant of the Lord (42:1). This phrase has great significance in Isa. It often refers to Israel (cf. 41:8-10; 42:18-19; 44:1-3; 45:4; 48:20). But servant Israel failed to complete her mission for God. As a result, God must send another Servant, the Messiah. He will be empowered by God and be the key that unlocks the captives' chains (42:1-9). He will speak to the nations and display God's splendor (49:1-6).

God will guard Him, although His mission calls for suffering (50:4-10). Although rejected by men, the Servant is destined to be exalted (52:13ff). What follows is a stunning prediction, which graphically portrays the crucifixion of Jesus in detail (53:1-12). Through death, the Servant will achieve God's ends and then will Himself be raised to glory.

These servant songs not only display Christ in His essential beauty, but also serve to model the nature of all servanthood. Anyone who serves God must (a) have a desire to do so, (b) remain humble before others and dependent on the Lord, (c) be committed to winning others' release from sin's grip, (d) accept personal suffering, and (e) rely completely on God for guidance and strength.

Messiah (42:1). The servant songs of Isaiah are clearly about the Messiah, who is destined to be God's agent not only of salvation but also to bring righteousness to this world. While the servant songs emphasize this individual's humility and His sufferings, the term messiah means "anointed one." It was used of those whom God set aside for a special mission and in Israel is linked both with the high priesthood and office of king. It is particularly used to identify the royal descendant of David, who will take His throne at history's end and rule an eternal kingdom (cf. Ps. 2:2; 18:50; 84:9; 89:38, 51; 132:10, 17; Isa. 9:7; 11:1-5). How awesome it is, that the greatest of all deigned to suffer for us. How awesome that He set aside the crown for a cross, so that when He takes up the crown again we might rule with Him.

My Spirit (42:1-3). These opening verses emphasize again the qualities of servanthood. The successful servant is upheld and chosen by God. He is endowed with God's Holy Spirit. He is humble and so sensitive that even those whom society rejects as having no value—mere bruised reeds and bits of carbon-blackened flax—are worth saving to Him. Lord, let us be this kind of servant, of God and of others.

Chapter summary. Israel is God's chosen servant and need not fear (44:1-5). Then a loud voice powerfully affirms God's uniqueness (vv. 6-8) and scorns those who worship idols rather than the living God (vv. 9-20). Israel is called to remember the contrast between the true God and idols and act accordingly (vv. 21-23). Demonstrating His own superiority, the Lord preannounces the appearance of a ruler who will call for the temple to be rebuilt, and names Cyrus, even though his empire lies 150 years in Isaiah's future (vv. 24-28).

Chapter 45 continues this theme, echoing God's promises and defining things Cyrus will do for the Jews (45:1-7). Lest some object to God's use of a pagan ruler, the Lord reminds the listener of His rights as the Father (in the sense of originator or Creator) of Israel and as the potter whose skill shaped earth's clay (vv. 8-14). Following a brief outburst of praise (vv. 15-17), God reminds the listener that He who created the earth formed it to be inhabited. He has revealed Himself, despite man's reliance on dumb idols (vv. 18-21). He cries out, "turn to Me and be saved." His Word will have its impact to the ends of the earth. It will bring shame to those who rage against God, glory to those who believe (vv. 22-25).

Outline
Place
Finder

JUDAH
IMMANUEL
JUDGMENT
HEZEKIAH
COMFORT

Key verse. 44:6: It is utter foolishness to trust in anything but God.

Personal application. A modern man's idols can be CDs and stocks.

INSIGHT

Fear not (44:1-7). Isaiah has shown that Israel has failed as a servant. When you and I are aware of some terrible failure, we too feel fear. But here, as in 43:1-6, God reaffirms His love. God chose, made, formed, and in 43:1, "created" Israel. Those of any age who are God's people are loved despite their deficiencies. How comforting these two passages, filled with unconditional love, can be when we too fail the Lord.

Idolatry (44:6-23). Idolatry dominated the ancient world, not only in O.T. times but in N.T. times as well. Some idol worshipers were superstitious, viewing their figures of wood, stone, or metals as deities themselves. Some idol worshipers were sophisticated, seeing the figures they bowed down to as representations of invisible spiritual beings. But idolatry in any form involved an explicit denial of the Creator.

Paul argues that the basic truth about God is made plain in Creation and that the slide into idolatry is a consequence of rejecting the true God (Rom. 1:18ff). Here in Isa., however, the Lord's scathing contempt for idolatry is expressed in mockery of the "wisdom" of human beings who cut down a tree, burn some of it as fuel, make a few utensils for the home, fashion an idol from the leftovers, and then pray to that idol to deliver them. Only a God who lives, who is capable of action, and who cares, could possibly help anyone—then, or now.

"A detestable thing" (44:19). The Heb. word, siqqus, is a strong word which links idolatry to immoral practices. It is intended to express the fact that religious sins, which involve active rebellion and rejection of God, are extremely wicked.

"Cyrus" (44:24-45:7). Isaiah predicted the fall of Judah to Babylon. Now he predicts the fall of Babylon and the return of the Jews to their homeland. To decisively demonstrate His superiority to idols, the Lord reveals the name of the Persian conquerer who will overthrow Babylon and issues a decree that not only releases the Jews from captivity but authorizes them to rebuild the Jerusalem temple. Some commentators, who deny the possibility of such detailed predictive prophecy, have insisted the mention of Cyrus is evidence of postexilic authorship of the second part of Isa. But in the context the naming of Cyrus is evidence of something far different. It is proof of the power of Israel's living God and a guarantee that history itself moves toward His intended end.

"A righteous God and a Saviour" (45:21). God's "commitment to do right" is revealed in salvation of sinners as well as in His judgment of sin. God has chosen and loved His people. He will be true to His love for us, despite our failures. Here, salvation moves beyond deliverance from present danger to hint of the resurrection at history's end (»p. 426).

Chapter summary. The reference to Cyrus and his victories over Babylon now brings to mind the futile gods of that great civilization, Bel (also called Marduk) and Nebo. Babylon's defeat proves God's superiority (46:1-2). And what a different relationship He has with His people. Pagans carry their gods. The Lord carries His people (vv. 3-4). Israel's incomparable God alone shapes and reveals the future, a future that holds salvation for her (vv. 5-13). Isaiah now leaps forward to describe the fall of Babylon (47:1-4). God permitted Babylon to triumph over His people to discipline them. But Babylon went too far in its inhuman treatment of the captives (vv. 5-7). Babylon's overweening pride and wickedness calls for judgment (vv. 8-11). Disaster will come, and no experimenting with magic spells, no frantic suggestions of stargazers, can save Babylon from the devastation God has ordained (vv. 12-15).

Key verses. 46:9-10: God truly is God.

Personal application. How wonderful to have a God who holds us up, rather than an idol we must lug around on our shoulders.

Key concepts. Babylon »pp. 302, 920. Magic »p. 57. Judgment »p. 372.

INSIGHT

Predictive prophecy. The future is a mystery to man. We can make educated guesses on what the next few years hold, but to accurately predict events that lie 20, 100, or even 1,000 years in the future is beyond our ability. Thus, the stunning accuracy with which God's prophets predicted the future is one of the most convincing evidences of the supernatural origin of God's Word. For a discussion of the role of the predictive in Bible prophecy, see the Introduction to the Prophets, particularly noting p. 407. For a list of fulfilled prophecies concerning Jesus Christ, see p. 439.

Omniscience, omnipotence (46:10). Isaiah ex-

plains God's ability to predict the future. God is God, He is able to "make known the end from the beginning" and "from ancient times" to predict "what is still to come." He established purposes for the universe He created and is powerful enough to guarantee that His purposes will stand.

Theologians describe these attributes of God as omniscience and omnipotence. These Lat. terms affirm that God knows all and that He is all powerful. We shouldn't be surprised that the Bible contains accurate predictions of future events. God, who knows all and controls all, is the source of what truly is the Word of God.

Illustration. *The Neo-Babylonian empire of Nebuchadnezzar was one of the ancient world's most advanced cultures. Its hanging garden was a wonder of the ancient world. Its school for scribes trained scholars who produced technical works in astronomy and astrology, written in cunieform on clay tablets. Yet its medicine relied more on magic than science, and fear of demons accompanied its people as they walked Babylon's broad streets.*

The greatest of man's cultural achievements are meaningless without a true knowledge of God.

Babylon's judgment (47:1-8). Two factors that fix Babylon's fate are defined by Isaiah. One is the arrogant pride described in vv. 7-8. The other is Babylon's treatment of God's people. In showing the Jews "no mercy" the Babylonians unwittingly placed themselves under God's ban. One of God's commitments to Abraham was, "I will bless those who bless you, and whoever curses you I will curse" (Gen. 12:3). In harming God's chosen people the Babylonians determined their own destiny. We need look no further back in history than to Hitler's Germany to see this principle still in operation.

Astrology (47:13). *The New World Dictionary* defines astrology as "a pseudo-science claiming to foretell the future by studying the supposed influence of the relative positions of the moon, sun, and stars on human affairs." Astrology is not new. It was practiced, along with magic and sorcery, in ancient Babylon and in even older cultures. The Heb. phrase translated "astrologers" in the NIV and NASB means "diviners of the heaven." The NIV also trans. *'assap* as astrologer, while other versions render it "conjurer." Our Isa. passage shows how closely astrology was linked with magic—a practice strongly condemned in the Bible.

Chapter summary. The overall mood of comfort is abandoned for a moment, for accusation. Israel has stubbornly resisted God, and pursued idols. This treachery forced God to defend His name by sending Israel into a "furnace of affliction" (48:1-11). Yet all this is a backdrop for grace. God presents Himself anew (vv. 12-16), expresses His yearnings for Israel (vv. 17-19), and dramatically announces the good news of coming redemption (vv. 20-22).

Now the true Servant of the Lord, the Messiah, steps forward. He tells of His mission to Israel and to all humankind (49:1-7). He repeats God's promises to Himself and to Israel (vv. 8-13). Israel may feel God has forsaken her, but the Lord can no more abandon the Jews than a mother can forget the babe at her breast (vv. 14-21). God will restore and exalt His chosen people. He will punish their oppressors, for God is the Saviour and Redeemer of His own (vv. 22-26).

Key verse. 49:9: God has compassion for all mankind.

Personal application. We may feel forsaken, but we can know that we are not.

Key concepts. Servant of the Lord »p. 432. Messiah »p. 432. Redemption »p. 90. Gentiles »p. 798. Restoration of Israel »p. 419.

INSIGHT

Credit (48:5). It was not enough that Israel stubbornly refused to respond to God. They tended to credit His works to other gods (cf. Jer. 44:15-19). Spiritual blindness persists, and today we may credit gracious acts of God in our own lives to luck or to our own genius or hard work. How important to sense God's hand in our lives, to be responsive to Him, and to acknowledge His works for us.

"The Lord's chosen ally" (48:14). The naming of Cyrus as the one to overthrow Babylon and free the Jews (»p. 433) some 150 years before the event made it clear that God alone should receive credit for the return of the future captives.

"What is best for you" (48:17). What a vital insight into divine law and morality. God did not establish moral law to frustrate "natural" human desires. God sets standards to show us "what is best for you." Man can be good and happy. Man cannot be bad and happy. Let's let God direct us in the way we should go, and experience that "peace like a river" (cf. vv. 18, 22).

God's servant. The "law of double reference" may apply in interpreting this prophetic passage, which may point in part to Cyrus, but certainly describes the mission of the Messiah, Jesus Christ. Christ was called to His mission and named long before His birth (49:1). His first efforts were unrewarded (v. 4), but

He is destined to bring Israel back to God (v. 5) and bring salvation to all peoples (v. 6). Although despised, He will ultimately be honored by all (v. 7).

"A light for the Gentiles" (49:6). Paul and Barnabas applied this verse to themselves (Acts 13:47), for their mission was in the spirit of the Servant. Israel had light, rejected it, and needed to be restored. The Gentiles needed light to see the nature of salvation.

There's a lesson here for us. God has provided salvation for all. You and I need to hold up the light of God's Word so others can see what He has done for them.

"Forsaken" (49:14). Anyone who is suffering feels forsaken. It's a natural reaction to pain.

To us, love seems to demand expression in gifts and good things. We have a hard time seeing any painful experience as a love gift, even though a parent who spanks a young child for running blindly into the street hopes the momentary pain will protect the child from a future danger.

Here, when Israel complains, God does not explain again why He has disciplined His people. He simply says, I have not, I will not, forsake you. Let's remember this the next time suffering comes our way. We may hurt. But we are not alone. God's love is like that of a mother for her infant child. He has compassion for us. He really does care.

Chapter summary. Isaiah 50 contrasts two servants. Here we meet the imperfect servant (Israel), who abandoned relationship with God (50:1-3, 11) and the perfect Servant (Christ) (vv. 4-10). This second Servant is sensitive to man's needs and responsive to God (vv. 4-5). He suffers, but He relies on the Lord and remains committed to doing God's will (vv. 6-9). Those who fear the Lord obey this Servant's word (v. 10). Having introduced the Servant, Isaiah speaks urgently to God's people. A series of imperatives emphasizes the need to hear and respond (51:1-16). The sense of urgency is maintained as God warns of coming wrath (vv. 17-23). God's people must awake (52:1-2). God in the past acted to punish (vv. 3-6). He will soon act to save, and the joyous message of salvation will be announced to all (vv. 7-10). The momentous announcement culminates in an even more intense call: Israel is to flee Babylonia and return to a pure and holy life (vv. 11-12). The last verses of the chapter properly belong with Isaiah 53, for they return to the Servant, the agent of God's salvation—but this time to describe His sufferings, through which we will be redeemed.

Key verse. 52:7: The message makes the messenger beautiful.

Personal application. It's always urgent to respond to God's Word.

Key concepts. Righteousness »pp. 120, 372, 433. Justice »p. 141. Jerusalem »pp. 205, 451.

INSIGHT

"You" (51:1-4). God always has good news for "you who pursue righteousness." His news for others isn't quite the same.

The heavens (51:6). The Heb. term, *samayim*, is used in two senses. First, as part of the created universe, the heavens incorporate everything above the earth—the sky and the stars. Second, the heavens are sometimes viewed as the spiritual realm inhabited by God. The imagery is clear. As the natural heavens are far above us, and beyond man's ability to experience directly, so the spiritual realm is "above" and "beyond" natural man's ability to penetrate (cf. Isa. 55:8-9).

The permanent (51:4-6). In this chapter the heavens and earth of the material universe are contrasted with God's salvation and righteousness. The material is impermanent and will "vanish like smoke." God's salvation will remain forever. How vital to anchor our hopes in salvation rather than anything in this passing world.

"Awake" (51:9-11). The prophet's prayer is a cry to God to act and carry out His promises. We need not pray that God will give us the gifts associated with salvation. But it is valid to pray that we will receive those gifts soon.

Don't fear (51:12-16). It's important to understand God's answer to Isaiah's prayer. God says first that He comforts us now. We need not wait till history's end to experience God's presence, and we need not be afraid (vv. 12-13). He also promises that "the cowering prisoners will soon be set free" (v. 14). These words of the God who laid Creation's foundation are our security, whatever troubles may come.

"Awake" (52:1-2). This call to action is addressed to God's people, not to the Lord. They are to "clothe yourself with strength," to "put on your garments of splendor," and to "free yourselves from the chains on your neck." This is no call to self-effort. It is a call to remember who we are as God's beloved and in full faith act as His redeemed.

We are not weak, for God strengthens us. We are not poor, but His grant of holiness makes us splendid. We are not prisoners, but are free to do God's will. Let's stop sitting around as though helpless, and be what we are in Christ.

Beautiful feet (52:7). The herald of good news is always welcome, the thought expressed in the "how beautiful" phrase. The feet are emphasized because he runs to the city with the good news of salvation, to announce that "your God reigns."

Outline
Place
Finder

JUDAH
IMMANUEL
JUDGMENT
HEZEKIAH
COMFORT

Chapter summary. This is the fourth and most compelling of Isaiah's servant songs (52:13–53:13). It contains the O.T.'s clearest description of the sufferings of Christ. Isaiah begins with a sharp contrast: The Servant is valued by God, but rejected by men (52:13-15). Eager for a powerful ruler, God's people see no beauty in the carpenter of Galilee despite His good works (53:1-2). Despised by His own people, Christ was a sufferer, not a conqueror (v. 3). His affliction seems to be evidence of God's displeasure, but His suffering actually is for us, that we might be healed by His wounds (vv. 4-6). He remains humble in life and death. Though innocent, He dies "for the transgression of My people" (vv. 7-9). It was God's intent to crush Him, for Christ is a guilt offering, a substitute paying the price of our sins (v. 10). Yet death is not the end. Beyond the grave "the light of life" awaits the Saviour. He not only rises, but is satisfied that His suffering was not in vain, for by it He "will justify many" (v. 11). Vibrant with new life, Christ is raised to glory. In submitting to God's will, "He bore the sin of many, and made intercession for the transgressors" (v. 12).

Key verse. 53:5: Here is why Christ died.

Personal application. There is no better passage to use in meditating on the death of Christ.

Key concepts. Servant »p. 432. Sin »pp. 34, 362. Sacrifice »pp. 27, 78. Cross »pp. 789, 814. Guilt »p. 739. Justify »p. 789.

INSIGHT

Appearances (52:13-15). Appearances are still deceiving. Let's not look at a man's cash or clothing, but at his commitment and compassion.

"No beauty" (53:1-3). The values that dominate human culture are far from the values held by God. What seems beautiful and majestic to most human beings has no attraction for God. The true beauty of Jesus was His willingness to suffer, and the true majesty was in His humility. Let's concentrate on making ourselves beautiful—to God.

Healing (53:5). Some take this verse to mean that there is physical healing in the Atonement, that the Christian can claim victory over sickness by faith. This interpretation is supported by Matt. 8:17 which applies this verse to the healing ministry of Christ. The problem is that in context, Isa. 53 is clearly speaking about inner healing. And the same word for healing, *rapa'*, is used by Jeremiah of forgiveness and inner renewal (Jer. 17:9, 14; 51:9). Rather than build a theology of healing on a questionable interpretation of this verse, it's better to keep the focus where Isaiah clearly does: on the spiritual health that Jesus died to restore. In Christ, we are truly well again. Our bodies will weaken and die, but we will awake to eternal life. And

then our transformed bodies too will share in our full experience of all Jesus has won for us. See also sickness, »pp. 66, 412, 767.

The meaning of Jesus' death. Theologians in the Post-apostolic Age struggled to explain just why Jesus had to die. This passage in Isaiah gives what is perhaps Scripture's clearest single explanation. Jesus died as a guilt offering; He was a sacrifice who took our sin upon Himself and gave His life to pay for it in full. A clear theology of atonement can be developed from such verses as Isa. 53:5-6, 8, 10-12. See also atonement, »pp. 69, 739.

Servanthood. Christ's suffering for us was a unique event in history. It was unique because He was the Son of God and because His death was a substitutionary sacrifice which won us salvation. At the same time, the Suffering Servant of Isaiah serves as an example to all believers. He reminds us that we too are to seek the welfare of others, even when that causes us personal suffering.

Prophecy. The evidence that Jesus is the servant described in Isa. is compelling, as many details found in this passage can be observed in Christ's life and His death. See also O.T. pictures of Jesus, »p. 439.

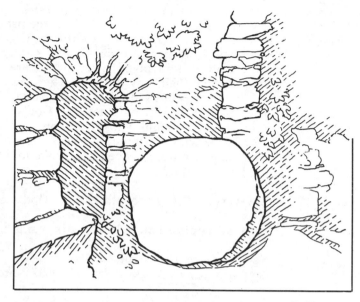

This tomb, cut into the rock of a hillside just outside first-century Jerusalem is identified by some as the tomb of the wealthy Joseph of Arimathea, where Jesus was placed after His death between two thieves. Thus Christ's death and burial spectacularly fulfilled Isaiah 53:9, "He was assigned a grave with the wicked, and with the rich in His death."

OLD TESTAMENT PICTURES OF CHRIST

A partial list of fulfilled prophecies

The Prophecy	O.T.	N.T.
A descendant of David	Isa. 9:6-7; 11:1	Matt. 1:1
Born of a virgin	Isa. 7:14	Matt. 1:23
Born in Bethlehem	Micah 5:2	Matt. 2:1
Lived in Nazareth	Isa. 11:1	Matt. 2:21-23
Rejected by His own	Isa. 6:10; 53:1-3	John 1:11
Enters Jerusalem in triumph	Zech. 9:9	John 12:12-19
Betrayed by a friend	Zech. 11:12-13	Matt. 26:14
Died with criminals	Isa. 53:9	Matt. 27:38
Buried with the rich	Isa. 53:9-12	Matt. 27:57-60
Lots cast for His clothes	Ps. 22:18	Luke 23:24
Offered vinegar to drink	Ps. 69:21	Matt. 27:34
His dying words are given	Ps. 22:1; 31:5	Matt. 27:46; Luke 23:46
No bone is broken	Ps. 34:20	John 19:36
His side to be pierced	Ps. 22:16; Zech. 12:10	John 19:34

Outline
Place
Finder

JUDAH
IMMANUEL
JUDGMENT
HEZEKIAH
COMFORT

Chapter summary. The Servant's suffering, like His mission, is complete (Isa. 53). Isaiah bursts out in a hymn of praise. The future is assured, a new age dawns, and God's covenant of peace is at last in force, forever (Isa. 54:1-10). Benefits of that covenant are described (vv. 11-17). Against this background, a voice cries out to those who are thirsty, urging them to come to God and be satisfied (Isa. 55:1-5). But Isaiah makes it clear that a moral choice is involved. The wicked are welcome, but they must forsake their way (vv. 6-7). The decision to come to God also involves submission. We must abandon the arrogance that leads us to stand in judgment on God's ways and submit to Him whose ways and whose thoughts are higher than ours (vv. 8-9). Those who do submit to that Word of God, which falls as life-giving rain from heaven, will share in a harvest of everlasting joy (vv. 10-13).

Key verse. 54:10: Peace flows from God's unfailing love.

Personal application. Submission remains the path to joy.

Key concepts. Covenant »p. 35. Peace »pp. 427, 806. Anger of God »pp. 65, 72. Wicked »pp. 29, 350. Word »p. 678.

INSIGHT

"O barren woman" (54:1). The barren woman suffered shame as well as a terrible void in her life (cf. 1 Sam. 1). Because of God's Suffering Servant (Isa. 53), we who have been empty without God and have fallen short morally, will know joy.

"Your tent" (54:2-3). Abraham lived a nomadic life, dwelling in tents. This image of expanding the tent calls to mind the Abrahamic covenant. The tiny postexilic community will expand and one day will fill the Promised Land.

"Your husband" (54:6-8). The husband/wife analogy is frequently used to portray God's relationship with Israel. Israel is the unfaithful wife who runs off after pagan lovers (deities) (cf. Hosea). In anger, God is forced to abandon her—but only for a time (cf. Jer. 31:31-34). God is both faithful and compassionate. He will restore His people to their special relationship with Him.

"Compassion" (54:8). The Heb. word here is *raham*, a term that means "to love deeply," and thus "to be compassionate." The verb is used 47 times in the O.T., and 35 of these speak of God's love for human beings. The verses where this powerful word communicates God's special love are: Ex. 33:19; Deut. 13:17; 30:3; 2 Kings 13:23; Ps. 102:13; 103:13; 116:5; Isa. 13:18; 27:11; 30:18; 49:10, 13; 54:7, 10; 60:10; Jer. 12:15; 13:14; 31:20; 33:26; Lam. 3:32; Ezek. 39:25; Hos. 1:6-7; 2:23; 14:3; Micah 7:19; Zech. 10:6.

"Covenant of peace" (54:10). This expression is also found in Ezek. 34:25-31. It is linked with the New Covenant of Jer. 31, for its benefits become possible only after the Messiah forgives the sins of God's people and makes them righteous. Some of the benefits overlap: God will Himself teach His people, and they will be established in righteousness (cf. Jer. 31:31-34). Yet the focus of this covenant is on security. God throws a protective covering over His people so that they will be safe. While this is an eschatological covenant, it has present application to you and me. God's protective covering has been thrown over us as well. God the Holy Spirit is Himself "a deposit guaranteeing our inheritance until the redemption of those who are God's possession" (Eph. 1:14). Because we are God's own we are safe and secure.

"Without cost" (55:1). It costs us nothing. It cost Christ everything.

"Freely pardon" (55:6-7). It is in the free pardon that God offers the wicked that the sharpest difference between God's thoughts and our thoughts are seen. We feel anger and outrage and call for revenge. God feels compassion and love and extends mercy. Thus God's word is gentle and life-giving; in Isaiah's analogy, like the gentle rain that waters the earth and causes life to spring up. What a warm and wonderful view of God (v. 10).

Chapter summary. This new sermon of Isaiah is addressed to Jews still in Canaan, while the messages of Isaiah 40–55 were spoken to those in exile in Babylon. Isaiah urges them to "do what is right" and uses Sabbath-keeping to illustrate obedience to the divine law (56:1-2). Eunuchs were banned from participating in Israel's worship (Deut. 23:1). Isaiah uses them here as a symbol of all those who feel insecure in their relationship with God. If anyone holds fast to God's covenant, he or she will surely be accepted by God and blessed (56:3-8). Yet, Israel acts like beasts of the forest, blind watchmen, and shepherds concerned for their appetites rather than their flock (vv. 9-11). Israel is condemned because the people cannot see God's gracious hand in the death of the righteous (57:1-2), but continue to run eagerly after pagan gods (vv. 3-13). Yet God has a word of comfort for the godly. The Lord is with the "contrite and lowly of spirit." God punishes, but He will heal. But as for the wicked, there is no peace for them (vv. 14-21).

Outline
Place
Finder

JUDAH
IMMANUEL
JUDGMENT
HEZEKIAH
COMFORT

Key verses. 56:4-5: No one with faith is excluded.

Personal application. Be as ready to welcome the social outcast as God has been to welcome you.

Key concepts. Justice »p. 541. Blessed »p. 127. Eunuch »pp. 621, 715. Wicked »pp. 29, 350. Idolatry »p. 433. Peace »p. 427.

INSIGHT

Because (56:1-2). We don't "do justice" to merit salvation. We commit ourselves to do what is right because we believe God's Word that His salvation is close at hand. Such faith changes our lives and results in blessing.

Keeping Sabbath (56:2). The Sabbath was the 6th day of the week (our Saturday). The early Jews kept the Sabbath by resting from ordinary work. During the Babylonian Exile the Jews began to meet for worship and study of the Scripture on this day. The Sabbath served as a symbol of God's work of Creation (cf. Ex. 20:8-11), but also was a symbol of the covenant relationship that existed between Israel and God (cf. Ex. 31:12-17; Jer. 17:19-27; Neh. 13:15-22). In addition, the Sabbath served as a reminder of God's own covenant faithfulness, demonstrated when He delivered His people from slavery in Egypt (Deut. 5:15). It is because the Sabbath was so meaningful in Israel's faith that Isaiah holds up Sabbath-keeping as a symbol of an individual's commitment to keeping God's whole Law.

"To the eunuchs" (56:4). According to O.T. law no eunuch could enter the temple compound to worship (Deut. 23:1-8). The same passage excludes many foreigners from worship. Here, however, God promises that eunuchs will be honored "within My temple and its walls" (v. 5) and that His temple will be "a house of prayer for all nations" (v. 7). This promise to the eunuch and the foreigner are intended to comfort and reassure all who feel themselves unqualified to approach God. None of us merit God's favor. Yet He speaks words of reassurance to us and lets us know in unmistakable terms that we are welcome—and secure.

The death of the righteous (57:1-2). Death is an enemy. But Isaiah foresees a time of national turmoil and suffering that is far worse than death. The passing of the righteous at this time—apparently the death of an unusual number of persons known for their commitment to God—sent a message that was not understood. In view of the coming judgment, death is a gift, for in death the righteous find peace. Death is an enemy. But for us, beyond death lies life and peace.

"Behind your doors" (57:8). The religious Jew attached small tubes containing bits of Scripture to his doorpost. Isaiah complains that while these symbols of piety are present, behind your doors there are pagan symbols.

It's what's inside our homes, and our hearts, that counts.

High and holy (57:15). God, although high and exalted, stoops to be with the lowly. Lowly here is not a social attribute, such as poverty. It is an inner attitude of humility, of simple trust in and responsiveness to God. If this is our attitude, God will stoop to be with us, always.

Outline
Place
Finder

JUDAH
IMMANUEL
JUDGMENT
HEZEKIAH
COMFORT

Chapter summary. As the book nears its close the prophet calls on his listeners to grasp the reality of sin. This provides the backdrop for a revelation of God's purposes in judgment and salvation. He begins by describing a superficial religiousness (58:1-3a) which disguises the hypocrisy of a people whose personal lives (vv. 3b-5) and society (vv. 6-7) are corrupt. Only if Israel experiences a complete spiritual reformation and does away with "the yoke of oppression" will God answer His people's prayers and sustain them (vv. 8-12). Only if God's people honor Him will they discover the joy and blessing to be found in the Lord (vv. 13-14). Sin alienates, and Israel's "iniquities have separated you from your God" (59:1-2). Isaiah follows this announcement with a dread catalog of Israel's sins (vv. 3-15) and the grim announcement that God has "put on righteousness as His breastplate." As a warrior He advances to repay according to what men's actions are due (vv. 16-19). Yet even now there is hope for those who "repent of their sins." God will establish His covenant with them, and with their children (vv. 20-21).

Key verse. 59:2: Sin separates man and God.

Personal application. The only way to find healing is to be honest with yourself and God about your spiritual state.

Key concepts. Hypocrisy »p. 625. Injustice »p. 541. Poor and oppressed »p. 90. Prayer conditions »p. 894. Covenant »p. 35.

INSIGHT

"They seem" (58:2). These folks went to church and consulted their pastors (prophets). They appeared religious. But is Sunday piety a good measure? Not in Israel.

Many would be shocked to learn that one area of southwest Michigan, with the highest percentage of membership in one conservative Protestant denomination, has one of the highest rates of spouse abuse in the U.S.! Don't mistake "religious" for true spirituality.

Fasting (58:3-7). O.T. fasts usually lasted from sunrise to sunset. Fasts were religious in character and undertaken to: (1) express grief (cf. 1 Sam. 31:13), (2) show one's seriousness when appealing to God (cf. Ezra 8:23), (3) indicate repentance (cf. Jonah 3:5-10), and (4) honor the seriousness of the Day of Atonement (cf. Lev. 16:29-31). Later generations added other commemorative days to the religious calendar and remembered them with fasting (cf. Zech. 8:19).

In Christ's time, the zealous Pharisee fasted each Monday and Thursday (Luke 18:12). Jesus condemned the practice of dirtying the face to show others one was fasting, but did not condemn fasting. He fasted 40 days just before beginning His public ministry (Luke 4:1-3). Though there are N.T. examples of fast-ing, the practice is not commanded (cf. Luke 2:37; Acts 13:2; 14:23).

Isaiah's point is that fasting as an expression of piety is of far less concern to God than a righteous lifestyle. Spirituality is shown by the loving quality of our personal relationships (Isa. 58:4) and by our commitment to social justice and to helping the poor and oppressed (Isa. 58:6-7), not by fasting.

Sin's impact (59:2). The Scriptures tell us what sin is (»pp. 362, 798). Isaiah emphasizes the fact that sin separates us from God. While God is ready to forgive, even the believer who habitually practices sin is cut off from fellowship with the Lord (1 John 1:5-10). The N.T. emphasizes the devastating effect of sin on human nature. Sin curses us with spiritual death, a condition that will carry over into eternity unless we receive new life through faith in Christ (Rom. 5:12-21). Sin corrupts human nature; it turns our thoughts to evil acts, arouses wrong desires, and so weakens our wills that we choose the wrong even when we know what is good (cf. Eph. 2:1-3). This reality underlies the grim picture of life in a society of sinners portrayed in Isa. 59:3-15. Sin brings man under the divine wrath (Isa. 59:18). How terrible sin is. But how wonderful that we have a Redeemer.

Chapter summary. The tone now shifts again as Isaiah describes the future glory of Jerusalem. Zion, another name for the Holy City and chosen people, is called to awake (60:1-3). Still drowsy, she is urged to look and see the glory of fulfilled hope (vv. 4-9). Nations that persecuted Israel will honor her (vv. 10-12), and nature herself will overflow (vv. 13-14) as God's presence transforms not only the city but also her people (vv. 15-22). Now Messiah speaks, declaring again His commission to avenge and comfort God's people (61:1-3). The land and its people will be restored (vv. 4-9), as God clothes a personified Zion in garments of salvation (v. 10). Still sustaining a sense of assured joy, the prophet commits himself to pray for Zion until the predicted day of deliverance comes (62:1). For her restoration is assured (vv. 2-7) by the intrinsic power of her God (vv. 8-9). And so Isaiah foresees a great crowd of pilgrims approaching the Holy City (vv. 10-11). And the greatest wonder of all is that these people, the inhabitants of the Zion to come, will be called "the Holy People, for all will be redeemed by the Lord" (v. 12).

Outline
Place
Finder

JUDAH
IMMANUEL
JUDGMENT
HEZEKIAH
COMFORT

Key verses. 61:1-2: The Good News has been preached; the day of vengeance is coming.

Personal application. The present gives no clue to the future.

Key concepts. Holy Spirit »pp. 73, 744. Messiah »p. 432. Justice »p. 541. Jerusalem »pp. 205, 451.

INSIGHT

The future glorious kingdom. One of the most persistent themes of O.T. prophecy holds that at history's end God will set up a kingdom on earth. Its capital will be Jerusalem, and from the Holy City, the Messiah, a descendant of David, will rule over all the peoples of our planet. This theme is seen here, especially in Isa. 60:1–61:6, and in many other prophetic passages. In the O.T.'s bright vision of the future the kingdom comes following God's crushing defeat of evil and the great spiritual conversion which sweeps Israel and extends to the Gentiles. The following passages express the O.T. prophets' vision of this coming glorious kingdom: Isa. 2:1-4; 4:2-6; 9:6-7; 11:1-16; 24:1-13; 32:1-5; 33:17-24; 35:1-10; 52:7-10; 61:1-6; 66:15-23; Jer. 31:1-27; 33:14-34; Dan. 2:31-45; 7:1-28; 9:20-27; Mal. 3:1-5; 4:1-6; Ezek. 20:32-44; 34:20-31; Hosea 3:4-5; Joel 2:28–3:2; 3:9-21; Amos 9:9-15; Obad. 15-21; Micah 4:1-5; Zech. 2:1-13; 14:1-21.

"Look" (60:4). The text says, "lift up your eyes and look." If we simply look around us and see the present distress we may well be discouraged. But if we look up, or if we look ahead, the situation is very different. Everything around us is transformed by the certainty that God is near.

God's presence (60:19-20). The picture here is very like that provided in Rev. 21–22.

"The year of the Lord's favor" (61:1-2). This messianic prophecy was quoted by Christ in the synagogue at Nazareth—but only in part. He closed the scroll after reading the proclamation of the Lord's favor and made no mention of "the day of vengeance of our God" (see Luke 4:17-21). The incident is significant for several reasons. First, it was a public announcement by Jesus of Nazareth that He was the Messiah promised by the prophets. Second, it suggests two comings of Christ, the first to save, the second to judge. And third, it illustrates a difficulty in interpreting O.T. prophecy. Predictive passages typically make no clear reference to times and, as in this verse, may link events separated by thousands of years. See the section on Interpreting prophecy, »p. 408.

"Clothed" (61:10-11). Paul uses the image of salvation's clothing in Rom. 13:14 and Eph. 4:22-24. Christ used it in several parables, as in where the guests were dressed in special garments provided by the host (Matt. 22:11-14). Being dressed in such garments showed the wearer to be an invited guest, with a right to join the celebration.

Only if we are clothed with God's salvation will we enjoy life in the future kingdom of the Lord.

Outline
Place
Finder

JUDAH
IMMANUEL
JUDGMENT
HEZEKIAH
COMFORT

Chapter summary. Now a dramatic dialogue takes place, a watchman cries out to an approaching warrior who is drenched in blood. Is he friend or foe? The answer is that this warrior, the Messiah, has personally defeated the Gentile world powers and now appears to save God's people (63:1-6).

Now we see Isaiah's personal response to the grand revelation. He first breaks out in praise to God for His kindnesses, literally His *hesed*, His covenant faithfulness (vv. 7-10). But Isaiah's vision of the future brings to his mind God's deliverance of Israel in the time of Moses (vv. 11-14). Plaintively, he asks why God has delayed so long in acting for Israel again (vv. 15-19). Isaiah yearns for God to act (64:1-3), but is terribly aware that God's people have continued to sin against Him. How can God act to save a people whose righteous acts are filthy rags in God's sight? (vv. 4-7) Yet God is not only moral governor of His universe. He is also a Father to His people. In His love and grace the Lord will save those who appeal only to His mercy (vv. 8-12).

Key verse. 64:5: We do not deserve what God gives.

Personal application. Don't rely on the good you do, but on the good Father that God has been, is, and will be.

Key concepts. Wrath of God »pp. 65, 72. Mercy »p. 880. Father »pp. 140, 663. Salvation »p. 433. Sin, effects of »p. 442.

INSIGHT

Trampling out the vintage (63:1-6). Isaiah's vision of the Messiah in bloody robes, trampling the nations as a farmer tramples grapes to make wine, is the background for our Civil War's most famous song, "The Battle Hymn of the Republic." Despite the complaints of those who cannot conceive of a God of love taking vengeance, the image of God's Servant, the Messiah, putting down mankind's rebellion to establish justice is fully in keeping with the O.T.'s revelation of the character of God. What should give us pause is not this vision of divine judgment, but our own insensitivity to the injustices God hates.

"Kindnesses" (63:7). The Heb. term is *hesed*, better translated "covenant faithfulness" or "steadfast love." The bloody image of 63:1-6 is balanced by the image of a compassionate shepherd in 63:7-14. God punishes the rebellious, but He is quick as a Saviour to those whom He has chosen, even when they wander from Him.

"You, O Lord, are our Father" (63:16). This affirmation falls short of the deep awareness of God's personal relationship with the individual expressed in the N.T.'s use of "our Father." But it clearly foreshadows it. God is "Father" in the sense of Creator, or source. Yet the creative act of God by which He called Israel to be His own intimately and permanently linked the Jewish people with the Lord, and bound Him to them.

Those who recognized the nature of this relationship found it, as Isaiah did, a source of faith and hope.

We can speculate about God's nature all we wish, but until we know Him as "our Father" He will not be real to us. Nor will we be bound to Him.

Sin's nature (64:5-7). The modern apologist asks, "How can God judge so brutally? How can He trample men like grapes?" But Isaiah asks, "How then can we be saved?" These verses contain a complete though brief description of the impact of sin on human beings. First, sin is habit-forming: We continue to sin against God's ways (v. 5). Second, sin rightly arouses the anger of God and directs it against us (v. 5). Third, sin is defiling, making it impossible for us to approach Him (v. 6). Fourth, sin so corrupts our character that even the best we can do is fouled by base motives (v. 6). Fifth, sin is destructive, shriveling us up from within and creating circumstances that sweep us away (v. 6). Sixth, sin alienates us from God, creating a distaste for the Lord that keeps us from calling on His name (v. 7). Seventh, sin causes God to hide His face from us and to judge us (v. 7). In view of all that sin has done to us, it is no wonder Isaiah cries out, "How then can we be saved?" The answer is in v. 8.

Chapter summary. Here we reach the climax of Isaiah's teaching, in the wondrous promise that God will one day create a new earth and heavens as the home of the righteous. But judgment precedes salvation, as again Israel is pictured as obstinate and sinful (65:1-7). Yet God will preserve a remnant (vv. 8-10) while turning against the rebels among His people and punishing them (vv. 11-16). Then Isaiah introduces the great promise, marked by the cry, "Behold." God will create "new heavens and a new earth" where His people will enjoy long lives in peace and security (vv. 17-25). Thus, men can look forward to the future with fear and with hope. God, the Creator, extends the offer of fellowship to the humble who are responsive to His Word (66:1-6). Zion is told to rejoice, confident that all her troubles are but birth pangs, and soon she will give birth to a glorious future (vv. 7-11). God will bless His land with peace and comfort His children in the day He executes judgment on sin (vv. 12-16).

This book of powerful poetry ends in prose. God pledges that all mankind as well as the Jewish people will find Him at history's end. The new heavens and the new earth He makes will endure. But the bodies of those who rebelled against the Lord will be scattered over old earth's deadened lands (vv. 17-24).

Outline
Place
Finder

JUDAH
IMMANUEL
JUDGMENT
HEZEKIAH
COMFORT

Key verse. 65:17: God will make all things new.

Personal application. What God *will* create should be more real to us than the sorrows we remember, and will soon forget.

Key concepts. Remnant »p. 427. Heaven »p. 926. Creation »p. 430.

INSIGHT

The New Heavens and Earth. Isaiah's vision reaches out beyond time and stretches into eternity. He sees not only a renewal of our earth under the Messiah, but further still He glimpses a totally new creation. O.T. prophecy does not make clear the relationship between a renewal of this earth under the Messiah and the reconstitution of the material universe envisioned by Isaiah. But the N.T. joins the O.T. in looking forward to just such an event. Peter says these "heavens will disappear with a roar; the elements will be destroyed by fire, and the earth and everything in it will be laid bare." Following this "in keeping with His promise" God will create "a new heaven and a new earth, the home of righteousness" (2 Peter 3:10, 13).

And the Apostle John reaffirms the vision reporting, "Then I saw a new heaven and a new earth, for the first heaven and the first earth had passed away" (Rev. 21:1). When the grand drama of sin and redemption has been played out, the curtain will fall. But then a new curtain will rise, a play whose glories we cannot even imagine will open.

Gentile and Jew (65:1-2). Paul refers to these verses in Rom. 10:20-21. The Gentiles were not looking for God, but He was found by them in the Gospel. The Jews to whom God held out His hands in love refused to see Him and turned instead to pagan deities. Yet in the end God's grace will triumph, and both will have a place in the world to come (cf. 65:9, and the O.T. doctrine of the remnant, »p. 427).

Man's future (65:17-25). The description seems to combine elements of the millennial kingdom of the Messiah and the prophesied new heavens and new earth. However students of prophecy sort these elements out, it is clear from Isaiah's warm and comforting description of God that a real transformation of man's state and nature lies ahead. Sin's curse is lifted, lifespan is extended, and peace is brought even to the animal kingdom.

All that is wrong on earth will be set right. When you read prophecies of doom—an atomic holocaust, a greenhouse effect that will melt the ice caps and cause the oceans to overflow our cities, a new Ice Age that will destroy life on earth—do not fear. The real destiny of earth is described by Isaiah here.

Jeremiah

Jeremiah's writings are among the most emotional and intense to be found in the Old Testament They also seem hard for the casual reader to follow. This isn't surprising. The book is actually a collection of sermons the prophet preached over a 20-year span, interspersed with powerful poetic oracles and fervent expressions of his personal reactions to events. Jeremiah was a sensitive person, torn by the rejection of his contemporaries.

Jeremiah's ministry began approximately 627 B.C. and continued past the fall of Jerusalem to Nebuchadnezzar in 586 B.C. A few of his messages are dated during the reign of godly King Josiah (640–609 B.C.), but most date from the times of his successors, Jehoiakim (609–598), Jehoachin (598–597), and Zedekiah (597–586). During the reign of these kings Judah was first threatened and then dominated by Babylon. Jeremiah's unpopular mission was to call Judah to submit to foreign domination as a discipline from the Lord. But the kings and the people of Judah bitterly resented Jeremiah's preachings, even as they rejected God in favor of a host of pagan deities. Ultimately, Judah's refusal to submit brought an overwhelming Babylonian force into the Jewish homeland.

It's against this background that we need to read and understand this magnificent Old Testament book. We can hear again Jeremiah's dramatic sermons calling for a return to God and warning of impending doom. We can wonder at the frequent "prophetic oracles," those brief poetic interludes introduced by "thus says the Lord" and "hear the word of the Lord." We can also meet the writer, as Jeremiah includes more biographical material than any other Old Testament prophet. Perhaps most enriching, we can enter into Jeremiah's spiritual life, for the prophet often shares his innermost feelings in passages that have been called his "personal spiritual diary" (cf. 11:18–12:6; 15:10-21; 17:5-10, 14-18; 18:18-23; 20:7-18). This great Old Testament book, addressed to a rebellious people in a time of national peril, invites us to hear and apply God's Word to our own times. And it helps us appreciate the courage of godly people who often despair, but who continue to wrestle with God in prayer and boldly confront the sins and sinners of their times.

JEREMIAH'S SERMONS

In Josiah's time *Jer. 2:1–3:5; 3:6–6:30; 7:1–10:25; 18:1–20:18.*
In Jehoiakim's time *Jer. 14–17; 22–23; 25–26; 35–36; 45–48.*
In Zedekiah's time *Jer. 21; 24; 27–34; 37–39; 49.*
In Gedaliah's time *Jer. 40–44 (Note: Gedaliah was a governor appointed by the Babylonians after the nation was destroyed.)*
Later messages *Jer. 50–52*

KEY PASSAGES IN JEREMIAH

Jeremiah 2. *The prophet catalogs the sins of Judah.*
Jeremiah 17. *Sin is a heart condition of mankind.*
Jeremiah 23. *False prophets and how to know them.*
Jeremiah 28. *Prophets, the false vs. the true.*
Jeremiah 31. *God promises His people a New Covenant.*
Jeremiah 42–43. *The persistent unbelief of the survivors.*

Illustration. *Jeremiah stands, sunk deep in the muck, at the bottom of one of the giant cisterns intended to hold Jerusalem's emergency water supply. The prophet's imprisonment there, described in Jer. 38, is symbolic of the persecution he experienced because of his desperate efforts to warn the kings and people of Judah of impending judgment. Jeremiah's despair mirrors that of the inhabitants of Jerusalem as the city, besieged by a vast Babylonian army, is about to fall. The Book of Jeremiah gives us startling insights into the spiritual conditions which led to Judah's exile from the Promised Land.*

Date and authorship. Strong internal evidence identifies Jeremiah as the author of the book that bears his name. Much of it was compiled just before Jerusalem's fall in 586 B.C. A few chapters can be dated after the fall.

A THEOLOGICAL OUTLINE OF JEREMIAH

I. JEREMIAH'S MISSION	1–10
II. THE BROKEN COVENANT	11–20
III. JUDGMENT APPROACHES	21–29
IV. THE NEW COVENANT	30–33
V. JERUSALEM'S FALL	34–52

A CONTENT OUTLINE OF JEREMIAH

I. Jeremiah's Mission (1:1–10:25)
  A. Jeremiah's Call (1:1-19)
  B. Warnings of Judgment (2:1–6:30)
    1. God's indictment (2:1-37)
    2. A call to repent (3:1-25)
    3. Invasion is imminent (4:1-31)
    4. Judah's corruption (5:1-31)
    5. Jerusalem's fall predicted (6:1-30)
  C. The Temple Sermon (7:1–10:25)
    1. The Temple no refuge for idolaters (7:1-34)
    2. The penalty for idolatry (8:1-22)
    3. Sin's punishment (9:1-26)
    4. Idolatry is foolishness (10:1-16)
    5. God's people to be exiled (10:17-25)
II. The Broken Covenant (11:1–20:18)
  A. The Covenant Violated (11:1-23)
  B. Punishment of the Ungodly (12:1-17)
  C. The Corrupt Nation (13:1-27)
  D. Drought and Exile (14:1-22)
  E. Judgment Certain (15:1-16)
  F. Jeremiah's Grief (15:17–16:9)
  G. Punishment's Goal (16:10-21)
  H. Man's Sinful Heart (17:1-27)
  I. Parable of the Potter (18:1-23)
  J. Jerusalem to Be Destroyed (19:1-15)
  K. Jeremiah's Lament (20:1-18)
III. Judgment Ahead (21:1–29:32)
  A. Conflict with Zedekiah (21:1-14)
  B. A Call to Justice (22:1-30)
  C. Messiah's Leadership (23:1-8)
  D. False Prophets (23:9-40)
  E. Vision of Figs (24:1-10)
  F. Babylonian Captivity (25:1-38)
  G. Jeremiah Condemned (26:1-15)
  H. Jeremiah Released (26:16-24)
  I. The Babylonian Yoke (27:1-22)
  J. Hananiah (28:1-17)
  K. False Prophets (29:1-19)
  L. False Prophets Denounced (29:20-32)
IV. New Covenant (30:1–33:26)
  A. Freedom to Follow Captivity (30:1-24)

B. God's New Covenant with His People (31:1-40)
  C. Jeremiah Purchases a Field to Show Faith (32:1-44)
  D. Messiah's Coming Rule Described (33:1-26)
V. Jerusalem's Fall (34:1–52:34)
  A. Events Before the Fall (34:1–39:18)
    1. Judah's unfaithfulness to God's Law illustrated (34:1-16)
    2. God's punishment for sin (34:17-22)
    3. The Recabites faithfully keep a forefather's command (35:1-19)
    4. Jehoiakim burns God's written Word (36:1-32)
    5. Jeremiah charged with treason (37:1-21)
    6. Jeremiah imprisoned in a cistern (38:1-13)
    7. Zedekiah seeks a private word with Jeremiah (38:14-28)
    8. The city is captured (39:1-18)
  B. After Jerusalem's Fall (40:1–52:34)
    1. Gedeliah made governor (40:1-16)
    2. Gedaliah assassinated (41:1-15)
    3. The survivors flee to Egypt, despite Jeremiah's word from God to stay (41:16–43:13)
    4. Ishtar worship condemned (44:1-30)
    5. A personal message for Baruch, Jeremiah's secretary (45:1-5)
    6. Jeremiah prophesies against the nations (46:1–51:64)
    7. Jerusalem's fall described (52:1-34)

Chapter summary. Jeremiah identifies the setting for his ministry in Judah (1:1-3). The Southern Hebrew Kingdom has survived the Assyrian invasion which swept away the Northern Kingdom, Israel. But now the little land is threatened by Assyria's successor as the North's great power: Babylon. Some 40 years before Judah's last, crushing defeat God calls Jeremiah to serve Him as a prophet (vv. 4-8) and defines his ministry. Jeremiah will uproot and destroy kingdoms (vv. 9-10).

Two visions underline this grim description of the prophet's mission. He sees an almond tree which, because it blooms late, serves as a prophetic symbol of judgment long delayed but now imminent (vv. 11-12). And Jeremiah sees a pot of boiling liquid, tipping from the North, its contents flooding toward Judah, symbolizing the armies about to crush the Jewish homeland (vv. 13-16). It's Jeremiah's mission to announce God's intention to judge. And the prophet is warned, "They will fight against you" (vv. 17-19).

How strange and wonderful that this most sensitive of men has been sent on a mission that calls for the utmost strength and courage in the face of what will become intense adversity.

Key verse. 1:18: God enables even the sensitive.

Personal application. Don't assume God will not call you to a particular mission because you have no "natural gift" for it.

Outline
Place
Finder

MISSION
BROKEN COV.
JUDGMENT
NEW COV.
FALL

INSIGHT

"The Word of the Lord" (1:2). This and similar phrases are found thousands of times in the O.T. They identify a direct revelation of God to or through a person called to be His messenger to that generation. See Prophet, »p. 131.

"I formed you in the womb" (1:5). The Scriptures here and in other passages view the fetus not only as a human person, but as the specific individual he or she will become when grown to adulthood (cf. Ex. 21:22-23; Ps. 51:5). No support for the purposefully deceptive claim that a fetus is a part of the mother's body is found in either medical science or Scripture.

"I appointed you" (1:5). This verse was not, however, originally intended as ammunition in our time's battle over abortion. It was intended to comfort Jeremiah. The prophet was deeply aware of his own sensitive nature, and felt totally inadequate for the task God assigned (1:6).

God's reminder that "I formed you" and "I appointed you" speak to today. God not only knows us, He made us the way we are! Surely God has equipped us for whatever mission He had in mind.

Jeremiah. Jeremiah was born into a priestly family from Anathoth, about 3 miles northeast of Jerusalem. He was called by God as a *na'ar* (1:6), a youth some 16 to 18 years old. He was then about the age to marry, but God forbade this (16:1-4). Despite the reforms then being instituted by

Josiah, Jeremiah's early preaching took the form of loud denunciations of Judah's paganism. While Jeremiah admired Josiah (22:15-16), he remained appalled at the corruption of Judah's society. For over 20 years the maturing prophet confronted his unheeding people with charges of sin and calls for repentance (25:3).

With the death of Josiah the evils Jeremiah had seen were multiplied. The prophet was about 35 when he began to openly attack Josiah's successor, Jehoiakim (22:13-19). Jeremiah was brought to trial and, although acquitted of capital charges, was nearly killed (26:10-23).

Jeremiah kept on warning Judah against resisting Babylon and charged God's people with abandoning their covenant with the Lord (11:9-17). This led to growing resentment by the people and the leaders of Judah. Citizens of his hometown conspired to take his life (vv. 18-23); even members of his own family were involved (12:6). Everywhere Jeremiah went he heard curses and jeers (15:10-11; 17:15; 20:7). In response, Jeremiah called passionately on God to judge his enemies (11:20; 12:3; 15:15; 17:18; 18:18-23; 20:12). He tried unsuccessfully to give up his ministry (9:2; 15:10-11; 20:9) and experienced despair (20:14-16). But God held him to his task. Grimly, the sensitive prophet kept on preaching his message of impending doom. Jeremiah lived to see Jerusalem destroyed.

Outline
Place
Finder

MISSION
BROKEN COV.
JUDGMENT
NEW COV.
FALL

Chapter summary. This sermon, preached in Jerusalem in the reign of Josiah, scathingly describes Judah's apostasy and pleads with God's people to turn back to Him. God contrasts His people's early devotion (2:2-3) with their shifting drift toward apostasy (vv. 4-8). He indicts the present generation for forsaking Him, the source of "living water," in favor of idols (vv. 9-19). He chooses the metaphor of unbridled lust and rampant immorality (vv. 20-28). Yet despite her sins, Judah has the gall to claim innocence and even bring charges against the Lord for His acts of discipline (vv. 29-37). According to the Law, a divorced woman who had married another man could not return to her first husband. Yet Judah shamelessly pursued idols and then worshiped at the refurbished Jerusalem temple as though nothing had happened (3:1-5). In this Judah is worse than Israel, the Northern Kingdom (vv. 6-10). Even so, God calls Judah to return to Him (vv. 11-14a) and predicts the future blessing of His people (vv. 14b-18). The sermon concludes with an exhortation to disobedient Judah to repent (vv. 19-25).

Key verse. 2:11: There is no explanation for abandoning God.

Personal application. God is willing to forgive. Will we repent?

Key concepts. Idolatry »p. 433. Adultery »p. 85. Repentance »p. 780.

INSIGHT

Changing gods (2:11). Pagans held persistently to their traditional faith, even though their "gods" were unreal. How do we explain the just as persistent tendency of ancient Israel to abandon the true God? There is only one answer: Sin's grip on the unregenerate.

Cracked cisterns (2:13). The invention of plastered, underground cisterns permitted O.T. people to live in highland areas where rainfall was slight. Jeremiah uses the familiar to show the foolishness of Judah's idolatry. It's like leaving a constantly flowing spring to wander off into the desert to dig cracked cisterns unable to hold water—and thus unable to sustain life.

Confrontation (2:17-18). There are times when we must boldly confront others with the consequences of their sins.

Don't confuse me with the facts (2:23-25). The worst deceit of all is self-deceit. Judah loudly insists, "I am not defiled." Yet events prove that God's people passionately chase idols.

The person who knows he or she has sinned has hope. The person who denies sin is beyond redemption, because there is no sense of need.

Useless punishment? (2:30) Successful discipline still depends on the willingness of the person being punished to see his or her faults and take the correction to heart.

Bringing charges against God (2:29-37). It's fascinating that folks who won't even admit God exists are quick to blame Him when troubles come. Even when those troubles are a consequence of their own folly.

"My Father, my friend" (3:1-5). Josiah was a godly king, who in true dedication sought to reform Judah's worship and reestablish her love for God. But the reformation was only superficial. Judah acts like the child who believes that saying "I love you" makes up for repeated disobedience.

God is not as gullible as some parents. Where there is no true repentance, no sense of shame, God sees "the brazen look of a prostitute" and will not hear. Don't talk faith. Live it.

"Return" (3:12-14). The foundation of repentance is acknowledging our sin and recognizing God as merciful.

"In those days" (3:16). God intends to be merciful, and He will be. But will He be merciful to us? This is the challenge of Jeremiah's message to the people of Judah—and perhaps to us. Let's not delay until it is too late for us, but claim His mercy for ourselves now.

Genuine repentance (3:21-28). These last verses of Jeremiah's sermon describe a genuine repentance that is marked by a true sense of sin.

Chapter summary. Jeremiah continues to call for genuine repentance, marked by piety but also truth and justice (4:1-4). The cry is urgent because an enemy army is forming, already on the way (vv. 5-18). Jeremiah preaches but does so in agony, for he is torn by the terrible events he foresees (vv. 19-22). The enemy invasion will be a catastrophe for Judah, leaving the Promised Land a smoking, desolate ruin. The terrors that lie ahead drive Jeremiah up and down the streets of Jerusalem. God's people must listen! They must realize the depth of their sin against the Lord. Jeremiah searches the city but cannot find a single godly person (5:1-2). Surely Judah's punishment is just (vv. 3-9). Judah denies that God has disciplined to judge her (vv. 10-13), thus making certain even more devastating punishment will come (vv. 14-19). Judah is willfully ignorant and rebellious. What is to come is terrible, but Judah's sins are more terrible still (vv. 20-31).

Outline
Place
Finder

MISSION
BROKEN COV.
JUDGMENT
NEW COV.
FALL

Key verse. 4:19: A preacher must care.

Personal application. Don't let your sins deprive you of good.

Key concepts. Idolatry »p. 433. Justice »p. 541. Judgment »p. 372. Adultery »pp. 85, 388.

INSIGHT

Images of repentance (4:3-4). (1) Ground must be plowed before seed is sown. People must tend to their attitude before they will receive God's Word. (2) Circumcision was an outward sign of relationship with God. But it is the heart that must be spiritually receptive. What is inside us comes first. What our lives display follows.

Jerusalem in prophecy. These opening chapters of Jeremiah focus our attention on Jerusalem, the political and religious capital of Judah. The city is also a focal point in prophecy, where it is the site both of a great battle between mankind and God and also the site from which Messiah will rule a lasting, universal kingdom. There are scores of prophecies concerning this city, but here is an overview. Deut. 12:11 foresees God's choice of the city as "the place which the Lord your God will choose." Isa. 29 and 2 Kings 19 promise the city will not fall to Sennacherib, while 2 Kings 22, Isa. 4, Jer. 4–6, Ezek. 8, and many other passages predict the city will fall to Nebuchadnezzar. Dan. 11 describes a future desecration of Jerusalem's temple, and Dan. 9, Luke 13, and Matt. 24 foretell the city's fall to the Romans. Yet the prophets look beyond these disasters and foresee a return of the Jewish people to Palestine and in Joel 3, Isa. 49, and other passages, specifically to Jerusalem. Dan. 9, Jer. 31, and Matt. 24 also foresee the erection of a temple near history's end. Rev. 11 speaks of two supernaturally empowered witnesses destined to preach in Jerusalem in the end times. Joel 3, Isa. 29, and Zech. 14 speak of an assault on Jerusalem by the nations of the world. Yet a bright and endless future is still foreseen for Jerusalem for according to Ezek. 43 and Isa. 62 that city will then host the presence of God. At that time, Isa. 2 and Ps. 102 teach that the nations of the earth will make pilgrimage to Jerusalem to be instructed and blessed by God.

"Oh, my anguish" (4:19). There is always a temptation for those who speak out against others' sins to adopt a self-righteous and condemning attitude. Let's adopt Jeremiah's attitude instead, and weep for those who must suffer the consequences of their sins.

"Go to the leaders" (5:5). Every person is responsible for choices, but those who put themselves forward as leaders are more culpable.

Lying about the Lord (5:12). To say God will not judge sin is a foul lie that reflects on His moral character.

Sins deprive of good (5:25). Oh, what God's people would enjoy if only we remained faithful to Him.

Outline
Place
Finder

MISSION
BROKEN COV.
JUDGMENT
NEW COV.
FALL

Chapter summary. Jeremiah has confronted the people of Judah with their sins and alerted them to the swift approach of divine judgment (chaps. 2–5). Now his sermon reaches its climax as he describes the invasion about to engulf Jerusalem and culminate in God's utter rejection of His people.

Jeremiah describes terror and confusion as the invaders eagerly advance (6:1-5) and then place the capital under siege (vv. 6-8). Most terrible of all, Jeremiah sees the Lord leading the enemy force and using them to pour out His overflowing wrath on His own people (vv. 9-15). As the judgment falls, God grimly repeats again the charge of idolatry that required punishment (vv. 16-21). In a final, desperate effort to awaken the nation and bring about repentance, the Lord graphically portrays the cruelty of the foe (vv. 22-26). Jeremiah uses the image of smelting silver to make his final point. Despite everything God has done to purge the land, there is only wickedness to be found. The crucible must be dumped out; the people must be rejected by the Lord.

Key verse. 6:6: Sometimes it is too late.

Personal application. Repentance is far more attractive than its alternative.

Key concepts. Jerusalem »p. 451. Anger of God »p. 65. Wicked »p. 29.

INSIGHT

"The signal" (6:1). The "signal" (*mas'et*) is a fire, used for military communications. Both trumpet and "signal" were urgent warnings which threw Jerusalem into panic.

What the Lord says (6:6). Jeremiah pictures the Lord urging the enemy on, because "this city must be punished" for her oppression, violence, and wickedness.

It's a mistake to take comfort today in the notion that ours is a "Christian nation" and thus immune to judgment. God used pagan Babylonians to punish evil in Judah. Why should we suppose He would not do something similar in our time?

"The Word of the Lord is offensive" (6:10). It's one thing for a modern society to be pluralistic and permit differences in beliefs and values. It's another thing for a society to become increasingly hostile to Christian beliefs and biblical values. Where the Word of the Lord offends, judgment will surely fall.

"Greedy for gain" (6:13-15). Jeremiah must have felt desperately lonely. He was so out of step with his fellow priests and prophets. While he cried out his urgent warnings, they crooned that everything was all right. They overlooked and ignored the sins and shameful conduct of God's people.

It's so "human" to prefer our comfort and a

secure income to our commitment to God. But in the end, it's far better for us to keep company with the lonely Jeremiah.

"The crossroads" (6:16). Each day brings us to new crossroads. Each day we must choose the good way, and walk in it. There is no peace like the inner peace that comes from knowing we have done what is right.

Incense and offerings (6:20). God scorns the worship of the sinful. This is the repeated message of the O.T. prophets. Religion without righteousness reeks.

"Obstacles" (6:21). The "obstacles" are not stumbling blocks that caused Judah to sin, but rather are the Babylonians God will use to punish Judah's sin. A basic moral law is involved. We are free to choose the path of sin. But if we do we cannot avoid the consequences God has strewn along that path.

"A tester of metals" (6:27-30). In ancient times lead and silver were put in a crucible together and heated. The lead oxidized and carried off the alloys of baser metals, leaving the silver pure. The image of a refiner's fire is found several times in the O.T. and suggests a test for moral quality. Here, however, God's attempt to purify His people is futile. The ore is so impure that no silver can be found, and the whole batch is dumped out.

Chapter summary. This brief sermon, known as the temple address, is one of the most significant of Jeremiah's messages. The people of Judah relied on the fact that Jerusalem was the site of the Lord's temple. Surely God would not permit the city that housed His temple to be threatened (7:1-4). But Jeremiah cried that the city's security depended on the people changing their ways (vv. 5-8). Indifference to righteousness had transformed the temple from God's house to a "den of robbers" (vv. 9-11). God once permitted the Philistines to capture the ark of the covenant when the tabernacle rested at Shiloh (cf. 1 Sam. 4). The temple too will fall into the hands of enemies (vv. 12-15).

But Jeremiah has been forbidden to pray for Judah because they obstinately worship a pagan fertility goddess as the Queen of Heaven (vv. 16-20). What does God care for sacrifices? He wants obedience! (vv. 21-26)

God informs Jeremiah that Judah will refuse to listen to His message (vv. 27-28). The city must figuratively cut off its hair, for it is defiled by idolatry and has degenerated to the extent of offering children as sacrifices at Topheth in the Ben Hinnom Valley (vv. 29-32). So God will utterly crush this sinful generation. The enemy will desecrate the bones of their dead; the survivors will prefer death to life (7:29–8:3).

Outline
Place
Finder

MISSION
BROKEN COV.
JUDGMENT
NEW COV.
FALL

Key verse. 7:4: What does God really care about buildings?

Personal application. No one can sin and yet be secure.

Key concepts. Temple »p. 283. Sacrifice »pp. 78, 82, 555.

INSIGHT

"The Lord's house" (7:1). The temple had become a superstitious fetish to Judah. False prophets assured the people that since God had chosen it for His residence on earth (cf. Ps. 132:13-16), the city was safe. Jeremiah's attack on this popular belief was made in his first public sermon and immediately aroused the hostility of the people.

Moral reform (7:6-7). National security depended on moral reform, not the temple. Note the emphasis on social justice in v. 6. Judah must abandon idolatry, but also (1) abandon oppression, (2) stop taking advantage of the poor ("the fatherless or the widow"), and (3) maintain an honest justice system. Worship of God and morality are the twin pillars on which society must rest.

"A den of robbers" (7:11). The "den" of robbers was the refuge where they hid out in search of their next victim. The analogy is devastating. How could God's people steal, murder, commit adultery and perjury, and worship other gods (v. 9), and then assume "we are safe" because of God's house?

"Shiloh" (7:12). In the days of the judges, Shiloh was the site of the tabernacle, as Jerusalem was the site of the temple in the time of the kings. Yet the Philistines had captured the ark of the covenant, the holiest object in Israel's religion, and destroyed Shiloh. The implied analogy proves Judah's confidence in the temple is misplaced.

"Burnt offerings" (7:21-25). The O.T. Law did call for such offerings, but it called for God's people to obey Him even before it identified the expected sacrifices (cf. Ex. 20; Lev. 1–7). Judah was willing to sacrifice, but not obey.

Cut hair (7:29). The Heb. feminine form tells us that it's Jerusalem who is to cut her hair. The reference is to a person who made a Nazarite vow and was set aside as holy. If defiled, one had to cut off his or her hair to symbolize pollution.

Topheth (7:30-31). A "topheth" was a district set aside for the sacrifice of young children, typically those up to 5 or 6 years old. Such sacrifices were identified by the Heb. letters for m-l-k, mistakenly referred to as sacrifices to Molech in many English versions.

Chapter summary. Jeremiah's temple sermon (7:1–8:3) is followed by a series of poetic oracles containing various messages from the Lord. God reasons with Judah about its obstinacy (8:4-7). He declares the penalty (vv. 8-13) and describes the invading army (vv. 14-17). Responding, Jeremiah expresses his own sorrow in a moving lament (8:18–9:2a). God continues, identifying the blatant sins of the day (9:2b-9) and again threatening judgment (vv. 10-16). What anguish this will cause (vv. 17-22). Yet it will ultimately result in good (vv. 23-24) as evil is purged everywhere (vv. 25-26). The first section of Jeremiah concludes with God's caustic denunciation of idolatry. It is senseless (10:1-5), for God alone is great (vv. 6-16). And it has brought sinning Judah to the point of exile from the Promised Land (vv. 17-22). Jeremiah again responds, this time with prayer. Let God be sensitive to human weakness and correct with justice, not in anger. Let His anger be reserved for the nations that are unwilling to acknowledge God's name and have persecuted His people (vv. 23-25).

Key verse. 9:11: God will judge.

Personal application. It is better to know God than to live in a fortified but sinful city.

Key concepts. Jerusalem »pp. 205, 451. Idolatry »p. 433. Judgment »p. 372.

INSIGHT

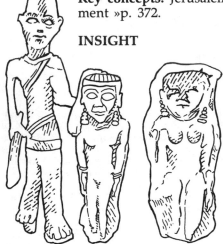

Illustration. *Pagan deities, represented by cast and carved figures like these 7th century B.C. idols, were worshiped in Judah by the same people who presented sacrifices at the Jerusalem temple. The spiritual and moral corruption described by Jeremiah in these chapters led to the Babylonian Captivity, a divine judgment on sin.*

"I am crushed" (8:21). Rather than gloat at the vindication of his ministry, Jeremiah is heartbroken at the suffering of his fellow countrymen.

Love for God and love for others sometimes are in tension. But loving God doesn't mean we must stop caring for others, even when their tragedies are a consequence of their own sins.

What else can God do? (9:7-9) Throughout the era, God's prophets urged repentance. But the people of Judah obstinately persisted in their sins.

If today a person refuses to accept the forgiveness offered in Christ, there is nothing left for God to do but to punish. Don't blame God for the judgments people bring upon themselves (cf. 9:10-16).

Death climbed in through the windows (9:17-22). This brief poem has been called the most brilliant elegy in the O.T. The weeping women are professional mourners hired to wail loudly at funerals. The prophet calls for them to quickly train their daughters, for there will not be enough of such women to put to rest all the slain.

When death, like a robber, climbs in through the windows, every household will be affected. We can lock our doors against disaster. But there is always some window through which calamity can creep unexpectedly. For security, we must rely on the Lord (v. 23).

"The living God, the eternal king" (10:1-16). What a powerful contrast Jeremiah draws between idols and the Lord. We consider them foolish who trusted idols in Jeremiah's day, but humans today who look to material possessions for security and meaning in life are just as simple.

Chapter summary. This chapter launches a new section in Jeremiah and should be read as a unit with chapters 12 and 13. Most place this sermon in the reign of Josiah, after the discovery of a Book of the Law (possibly Deuteronomy) in the temple (2 Kings 22–23). Jeremiah's sermon is an urgent call to return to the Law and obey it. God commands the prophets of Judah to warn His people of the consequences of breaking the Law (11:1-3) revealed to Israel in Moses' time (vv. 4-5). Stubborn refusal to obey the Law has brought curses on God's people (vv. 6-8), yet even now throughout Judah they worship idols (vv. 9-13). No amount of sacrifices can move the Lord to save the wicked people who have done evil and provoked God to anger (vv. 14-17).

Now Jeremiah tells us of the first of many personal crises he faced, and the people of his own hometown plot to kill him because they hate his preaching (vv. 18-20). But God will punish them, and no conspirator in Anathoth will survive the coming invasion (vv. 21-22).

Outline
Place
Finder

MISSION
BROKEN COV.
JUDGMENT
NEW COV.
FALL

Key verse. 11:4: God makes His expectations clear.

Personal application. A life of obedience is pleasant.

Key concept. Covenant »pp. 35, 62. Law »pp. 120, 145. Obey »p. 859.

INSIGHT

Listen (11:1). The imperatives here are in the plural, so God is not addressing Jeremiah alone. Because the command is to deliver a message to the people of Judah, it is best to understand this as an exhortation to all the prophets of Judah. Yet during this era only one or two others joined Jeremiah in complete allegiance to the Lord.

The covenant in a capsule (11:3-5). These verses sum up the commitment God made to Israel when He gave the Jewish people His Law. If they disobeyed He would curse them. If they obeyed He would bless them. It's unfair of authorities to punish a person who is unaware of expectations. But God's people knew from the beginning the conditions under which they would live in relationship with the Lord.

The conspiracy (11:9-14). Josiah instituted religious reforms and even traveled throughout Judah to destroy local worship centers. Jeremiah is referring not to a formal conspiracy, but to Judah's general resistance to Josiah's reform. This attitude was revealed in the people's persistent return to paganism.

"Do not pray for this people" (11:14). Begging God to withhold punishment from those whose unrelenting sins demand it doesn't honor Him.

"Consecrated meat" (11:15). The reference is to sacrifices offered at the temple. It is hypocritical as well as futile to hurry to church after sinning and then return eagerly to your sins.

The plot against Jeremiah (11:18-20). Jeremiah's accusations aroused resentment and hostility. Throughout his four decades of service to God the prophet would know the wrath of kings and courtiers, prophets and priests, and the entire population of Judah. He would be accused of betraying his country. He would be imprisoned and almost killed. But perhaps nothing would hurt as much as this first crisis, when God revealed that the people of his hometown, Anathoth, were plotting to murder him! The conspiracy was even more dreadful because Anathoth was a city settled by priestly families.

Anyone who has taken a stand for his or her moral convictions, or witnessed outspokenly about faith in Christ, will understand the pain of ridicule or rejection. But few have any notion of the hurt Jeremiah experienced when those he had known from childhood wanted to take his life.

God will punish (11:21-23). God did not ask Jeremiah what the prophet wanted Him to do. The Lord simply announced that He would act to punish the conspirators. We know God's verdict of "no survivors" was limited to the conspirators, for Ezra reports that some men of Anathoth returned to that city after the Babylonian Captivity.

Outline
Place
Finder

MISSION
BROKEN COV.
JUDGMENT
NEW COV.
FALL

Chapter summary. Jeremiah warned Judah that God will curse those who violate His Law (Jer. 11). But he wonders about the prosperity presently enjoyed by the wicked (12:1-6). God tells Jeremiah not to be impatient. The Lord will surely abandon the temple and surrender His beloved people to their enemies (vv. 7-13). Later, God will punish the "wicked neighbor" nations who attacked Judah, but later still even they will be blessed, when the Lord returns His own people to their land (vv. 14-17). Jeremiah, and we today, must not draw conclusions from the present situation. We must see prosperity and blessing in the perspective of God's overall plan.

Now in five short segments the Lord reinforces Jeremiah's preaching on sin and punishment. A rotting linen belt serves as a symbol of Judah's corruption by idolatry (13:1-11). A common proverb expressing a wish for prosperity is turned against Judah (vv. 12-14). A warning is uttered against pride (vv. 15-17). Jeremiah is told to warn King Jehoiachin and the Queen Mother, Nehushta, that they will be forced to come down from their thrones (vv. 18-19). They abdicated when they were taken to Babylon by Nebuchadnezzar in 597 B.C. Jeremiah concludes with a description of the captivity and shame awaiting sinning Judah (vv. 20-27).

Key verse. 12:13: God collects His debts in His own time.

Personal application. Don't envy the wicked, however well off they seem to be for the moment. It really is only a moment.

INSIGHT

"The wicked" (12:1-4). Two things trouble Jeremiah about the wicked. First, they seem to prosper while he experiences difficulties (vv. 2-3). Second, when God does punish the wicked, the righteous suffer with them! (v. 4)

We can admit the validity of Jeremiah's complaint, but we cannot conclude that God is unjust. God's purposes are simply more complex and His justice more subtle than we are able to grasp.

Challenge, not comfort (12:5-6). God answers by telling Jeremiah that things will get worse. Even members of his own family have betrayed him and cannot be trusted. Sometimes we need to know how serious things are to find the courage to face them.

"I will" (12:7-13). The wicked whose prosperity so troubles Jeremiah will be punished. When God says "I will" we have to leave that punishment in His hands. Second-guessing God is foolish. We must simply trust Him to do right.

The linen belt (13:1-11). The "belt" was an undergarment, a short skirt worn about the hips. It symbolized both Israel's initial intimate relationship with the Lord and her purity. Some suggest the trip to bury it near the Euphrates is symbolic of the corrupting influence of the pagan religions from the north. The ruin of the belt drove home Jeremiah's message: Idolatry so corrupted God's people that they were no longer of any use to Him.

Arrogance (13:15-17). Pride is a primary sin which hardens a person against God. It stands in contrast to humility, which is an attitude of openness to the Lord and responsiveness to His Word. Jeremiah showed the tenderness of his own heart by weeping for those whose pride made captivity safe.

"The queen mother" (13:18). In the ancient world, mother of the king was an influential and official position. As Jehoiachin was only 18 when he began his three-month reign, the queen mother had even more influence.

The leopard's spots (13:23). Jeremiah quotes the proverb to make an important point. He does not deny belief in man's freedom to choose what is good. But he does insist that when a person becomes "accustomed to doing evil" sin becomes a habit. There is no moment of hesitation, no point at which a person stops and thinks, "Do I really want to do this?" Today many smoke cigarettes even though they know smoking is a cause of cancer and heart disease. Likewise, sin is a habit that once established is hard to break.

Chapter summary. These two autobiographical chapters underline Jeremiah's struggle. A series of droughts causes a famine that exhausts man and beast (14:1-6). It even stimulates Judah to confess sin (vv. 7-9). But God refuses to respond, because Judah has stubbornly refused to remain loyal to the Lord (vv. 10-12). The prophets who mislead Judah are singled out for special punishment (vv. 13-16). Although the hardened nation deserves punishment, Jeremiah is overcome by grief at the prospect of the suffering that lies ahead (vv. 17-18). Again we hear the people plead, unwilling to believe God has really abandoned them (vv. 19-22). But prayer is useless, for God is intent on punishment (15:1-9).

Jeremiah is now close to despair. He has dedicated his life to ministering to the people of Judah, yet all hate him. God tells Jeremiah He has a purpose in the prophet's ministry and will vindicate him in the end (vv. 10-11). And again God predicts the coming exile of Judah (vv. 12-14). Jeremiah is still despondent. He begs the Lord to punish his enemies quickly so he will be vindicated in his own lifetime (vv. 15-18). Now God rebukes His unhappy prophet. Jeremiah must surrender his doubts and fears and trust God completely, despite the animosity of his enemies. God will save. God's prophet—and we—can only trust and obey (vv. 19-21).

Key verse. 15:1: Sometimes it really is too late.

Personal application. Be satisfied with knowing that you do God's will. God will vindicate you in His own time.

Key concepts. Prophets »pp. 131, 462. Fasting »p. 442. Idolatry »p. 433. Confession »p. 892. Punishment »p. 827.

INSIGHT

Despite our sins? (14:7-9) God promised to restore His people when they turned from their sins and turned to Him in confession (1 Kings 8:35-36). But that promise is conditional! That text says when they confess "and turn from their sin."

Even today among Christians the fiction exists that saying "I'm sorry" to God is enough. It's not. True confession involves repentance. Where there is no repentance, confession is a sham (cf. 14:10).

Blaming others (14:13-16). Jeremiah seems willing to offer excuses for the people of Judah. He says it's the prophets' fault. The prophets have misled the ordinary folks. There are two things to note here. First, we are each responsible for our own choices. We can't pass that on to anyone else, even preachers! Second, the prophets were guilty of misleading Judah and would suffer more greatly than others. Don't suppose that "he said it was all right" or "I was obeying orders" relieves us of responsibility.

Empty pleas (14:21). The people of Judah based their hope for relief on an appeal to God

to act for the sake of (1) His name, (2) His temple (e.g., His "glorious throne"), and (3) His covenant. Why was the plea empty? Because Israel's blatant idolatry had already dragged God's name through the mud. His temple was defiled by those who supposed they could sin and still worship. And His covenant had been broken by those who now wanted to claim it.

There comes a time when only judgment can preserve God's honor.

Jeremiah's complaint (15:10-11). How sensitive we all are to the opinion of others. Jeremiah despairs because "the whole land" seems to be against him. When we feel the opposition of others we need to remember the resources God offered His prophet. God has a "good purpose" in Jeremiah's life. He will deliver him. And God will "make your enemies plead with you." This third promise is one of vindication. In the end, those who most resisted Jeremiah's words would be forced to admit he was right all along.

Let's claim these promises, and hold tight to them. If we are doing God's will, whatever others say or think, we are doing right.

Outline
Place
Finder

MISSION
BROKEN COV.
JUDGMENT
NEW COV.
FALL

Chapter summary. God commands Jeremiah not to marry or have any part in the normal social life of his community. He is to form no bonds with a generation doomed to destruction (16:1-9). When people complain that God isn't fair, Jeremiah is to point out their sins (vv. 10-13). In a distant day God will restore Judah (vv. 14-15), but this present generation will surely be punished (vv. 16-18). Jeremiah praises God, confident that one day even pagan nations will realize their idols are no gods at all (vv. 19-20). And God responds with the promise, "I will teach them" (v. 21).

But then the focus shifts back to Judah. Sin is etched so deeply into the national character that devastating judgment is certain (17:1-4). God's people have relied on foreign alliances and listened to false prophets rather than trust in the Lord (vv. 5-8). Their persistent refusal to rely on God reveals the utter depravity of the human heart (vv. 9-13). Faced with delivering this grim message, Jeremiah pleads for help and begs that his persecutors will soon be put to shame (vv. 14-18).

The chapter closes with a call to keep the Sabbath and so put God first (vv. 19-27). Here, as in other passages, Sabbath keeping is symbolic of commitment to the entire Old Testament Law.

Key verses. 17:5, 9: Sin and its source in this one chapter.

Personal application. God's Word is more trustworthy than what our hearts tell us.

Key concepts. Sin »p. 362. Trust »p. 354. Sabbath »p. 71.

INSIGHT

Illustration. *A stone signet ring from the time of Jeremiah. The engraved impressions could not be changed. Pressed in wax or clay, it served as the signature of the owner. Judah's sin was not only engraved on her heart, it was the mark above all others that identified the character of God's straying people (17:1-2).*

Jeremiah, the outsider (16:1-9). God's refusal to permit the prophet to marry or have any part of the normal social life was not a terrible burden, but a great gift. The closer one is to a person the more difficult it is to confront him or her with personal faults.

Then . . . and now (16:14-16). It's good to know that God intends to bless the entire world someday. But it may be little comfort to those who live through a period of present judgment. It's good to know that blessing awaits us in heaven. But it's better to live in such a way that

God can also bless us today.

"Flesh" (17:5). In the O.T., "flesh" (*basar*) focuses attention on human beings as persons who live in and are part of the physical universe. It also emphasizes human frailty. Because we are flesh we are weak and mortal, in contrast to God who is strong and immortal. Because of this inherent difference between man and God, it is foolish as well as morally wrong to have confidence in man—in ourselves, or in others—rather than in God.

Faith's object (17:7). People frequently say, "If only I had more faith." But what makes faith valid is not "how much" we have, but what/whom we have faith in. It's not how strong our faith is, it's how strong the one we believe in is. Jeremiah makes just this point in announcing God's curse on those who trust in man.

"The heart" (17:9). "Heart" (*leb*), in the O.T., frequently stands for the whole inner being of persons. Here Jeremiah explains Judah's illogical passion for idolatry by pointing out that fallen man's personality is "deceitful." Sin has corrupted human nature so that we cannot trust our motives or minds. We have no choice. We must trust God.

Chapter summary. Jeremiah is sent to observe a potter at work in his workshop. When the vessel the potter is making is flawed, the potter squeezes the clay into a lump and begins again (18:1-4). God tells Jeremiah He will work the nation like clay, constantly reforming it through judgment and renewal until Judah takes the good shape that He has in mind (vv. 5-10). Jeremiah shares the message with the people of Judah and urges them to change their ways. But the people insist it is too late and refuse to consider repentance (vv. 11-12).

In another of the poetic oracles that appear frequently in this book, the Lord expresses wonder at the passion of Judah for idolatry and He pronounces judgment (vv. 13-17).

The leaders of Judah are so infuriated by Jeremiah's preaching that they plot to "attack him with our tongues" (slander) and at the same time ignore him (v. 18). Their hostility is even more active: They try to trap Jeremiah, perhaps by accusing him of treason, so as to have him killed. In frustration and fear the prophet calls on God to strike down his enemies when the judgment begins (vv. 19-23).

Outline
Place
Finder

MISSION
BROKEN COV.
JUDGMENT
NEW COV.
FALL

Key verse. 18:5: God can and will do what He chooses.

Personal application. Rightly understood, the image of the potter at work is a picture of God's grace. When we soften our hearts, He can rework us and make us good.

INSIGHT

"Potter" (18:6). The message God intended to communicate through this illustration from ancient life was not, as some have thought, one of divine sovereignty. It was a message of grace. Judah had resisted the divine potter. Yet even now God was willing to begin anew and reshape His people into that good vessel He had had in mind from the beginning. But when Jeremiah preached this good news the people continued to resist the heavenly potter! It was too late to surrender their passion for idolatry and sin. What a tragedy! In the coming invasion the people who were unwilling to change would be crushed by suffering. The few survivors would become workable clay in His hands.

Lebanon's snow (18:14). This puzzling verse makes a simple point. Nature is consistent in following the pattern God designed. Judah abandoned the pattern God provided for His people.

No need (18:18). With priests to instruct them, wise elders to advise them, and (false) prophets to reassure them, who needed Jeremiah? Whenever we feel that we can do without a fresh, contemporary word from God, we are in danger.

Too harsh (18:19-23). Some have questioned this bitter prayer for vengeance. But those Jeremiah inveighs against have not only slandered him, but distorted the truth and so brought judgment upon the entire nation.

Illustration. *The potter's wheel (18:3) was made of a wooden shaft, a thin "throwing head" at the top on which the clay was formed and a heavier wheel below that the potter turned with his feet. As the wheel turns the potter shapes a vessel from slick, moistened clay. Frequently the clay seems to resist the potter's efforts to form it, and he must squeeze it into a lump and begin again.*

Chapter summary. Jeremiah is told to buy a clay jar, take along Judah's leaders, and go to a smouldering garbage dump outside the city (19:1-2). There he proclaimed God's imminent judgment (vv. 3-9) and broke the jar, explaining that this symbolized the destruction God was about to bring upon the city (vv. 10-13). Back in the city, Jeremiah went to the temple and preached the same message to the masses (vv. 14-15). When Pashur, a priest charged with temple security, heard Jeremiah preach he had the prophet beaten and put in stocks (20:1-2). The next day Jeremiah announced that God had given Pashur a new name, one that meant "terror on every side." The priest and his family would be carried captive to Babylon, along with the temple treasures (vv. 3-6).

But when alone, the bold Jeremiah again cries out to God in despair. He is driven to prophesy, but terrified by the hatred and antagonism which his words generate (vv. 7-10). Jeremiah knows the Lord is with him in all his hardships (vv. 11-13), but even the sense of God's presence cannot console him. Why, Jeremiah cries out, was he ever born? (vv. 14-18)

Key verse. 19:11: Judgment is certain.

Personal application. We can be utterly honest in sharing our feelings with God.

INSIGHT

The clay jar (19:1-5). The jar Jeremiah bought was a *baqbuq*. It was a narrow-necked jar about 10 inches high used for pouring water. Because of its shape, once broken the jar could not be repaired. The choice is significant. Once God shattered the nation, that generation could never be restored to the land.

"The Valley of Ben Hinnom" (19:2). The place is as significant as the kind of jar. It not only served the city as a garbage dump, filled with constantly smoldering fires, but was also associated with child sacrifice (Topheth »p. 453). The location served as a reminder of the terrible sins for which Judah was to be judged and as a symbol of the judgment. The sinful kingdom was about to be tossed on history's junk heap.

Smash the jar (19:10-13). Earlier, at the potter's house, Jeremiah had been given a message of hope. God would still "relent and not inflict on it (Judah) the disaster" due if only the people would repent and reform (18:8). The people responded, "It's no use" and refused to try (18:12). Now the smashed jar indicates it is too late.

God says, "This is what I will do." How important it is to respond to God's offer of forgiveness and renewal while there's still time!

"Pashur" (20:1-6). His post as "chief officer" placed Pashur in charge of the temple police, who guarded the treasury and maintained order on the temple grounds. The name was common, and this Pashur cannot be confidently identified with the Pashur of 1 Chron. 9:12.

Jeremiah beaten (20:1-6). This is the first instance of physical violence against God's prophet. The word translated "beaten" in the NIV is *yakkeh*, which means "struck." It's possible that a furious Pashur struck him with his hand (cf. Matt. 26:67). However the "stocks" were clearly intended not just to restrain but to punish. The Heb. word (*mahpeket*) means "causing distortion," and the stocks forced arms, neck, and legs into an extremely painful position. Pashur's unjust treatment of Jeremiah led to a word of divine judgment, which the prophet delivered the next morning.

Insult and reproach (20:7-10). There is little glamour in ministry. Jeremiah experienced the down side of God's calling and shares the anguish he feels. Rather than taking God's Word to heart, his listeners insult and reproach him and even make fun of his pronouncements (v. 10). It hurts deeply when a minister really cares for the people he or she serves, and they do not respond.

"Let me see" (20:11-13). Jeremiah again begs to see his ministry vindicated and his enemies fall. God assures him he will, and he rejoices.

Small consolation (20:14-18). The prophet quickly slips again into despair. There is little consolation in knowing our enemies will pay.

Outline
Place
Finder

MISSION
BROKEN COV.
JUDGMENT
NEW COV.
FALL

Chapter summary. These chapters move us forward in time and relate the ministry of Jeremiah to the last few kings of Judah. First, Jeremiah relates an event that happened when the Babylonians were advancing against Jerusalem in 588 B.C. King Zedekiah sends to ask Jeremiah if there is any hope for God's intervention (21:1-2). Jeremiah announces that God intends to fight for the enemy and that Judah is doomed (vv. 3-7). The prophet then urges the people to flee Jerusalem (vv. 8-10). On the same theme, Jeremiah inserts a message from an earlier time, addressed to the royal house, urging reform of the justice system and predicting judgment (vv. 11-14).

Another message on the theme of royal culpability shows how Jeremiah exhorted the kings to establish justice or expect desolation (22:1-9). He predicts that Shallum (Jehoahaz), taken captive to Babylon after a three-month rule, will never return (vv. 10-12). But his most scathing denunciation is reserved for Jehoiakim. That luxury-loving heretic son of godly King Josiah (vv. 13-17) is destined to die a shameful death and be given a donkey's burial with no mourning at his passing (vv. 18-30).

Key verse. 22:16: All is well when rulers do right.

Personal application. Our lifestyle shows if we know God.

Key concepts. King »p. 130. Justice »p. 541.

INSIGHT

"Zedekiah" (21:1-14). Judah's last king ruled between 597–586 B.C. and was on the throne when Jerusalem fell. The events described here probably took place in the 9th year of his 11-year reign. More on the relationship between Jeremiah and Zedekiah is found in 37:3-10 and 38:14-28. His desperate appeal to God to intervene was rejected. God was on the side of Judah's enemy (21:5) and the city was due to be decimated by plague, famine, and sword.

Surrender (21:8-10). Other passages tell us that Jeremiah's promise that those who abandoned Jerusalem and surrendered to the Babylonians would live was interpreted as treason by the defenders.

"Administer justice" (21:12). This is a repeated theme in words addressed to the king. Holding court was a royal prerogative and set the tone for courts held throughout the land. These messages are filled with denunciations of the practices of the evil kings who took bribes (22:17), extorted funds from subjects (22:17), and defrauded their subjects for personal gain (22:13-14).

Royal responsibility (22:3). The kings of Judah were absolute monarchs, but under God. They were responsible to "shepherd" God's people, which involved maintaining the "just and right" moral order called for in the Law. This is defined in the text as rescuing the oppressed, protecting the resident alien, taking the side of the helpless, and shedding no innocent blood. Any king of Judah who did not fulfill these justice obligations was "wicked" in God's sight. We can take these as the minimum obligations of any government to its citizens.

Knowing God (22:16). The Lord compares godly Josiah to his wicked son Jehoiakim. Josiah did "what was right and just" and protected the poor. "Is that not what it means to know Me?" says the Lord. When the O.T. speaks of "knowing" God it uses *yada'*, which involves gaining knowledge of, developing an understanding of, and responding appropriately to, the Lord.

How does a king show that he "knows" God? Jeremiah says that it is by the way in which he administers justice, fulfilling his responsibility as God's under shepherd.

We can never tell what goes on within another human being. But we can see what comes out of his or her life. Product is a better indicator of relationship with God than profession.

While these verses give a criteria for measuring a king's knowledge of God, Micah 6:8 provides similar criteria by which to measure ordinary people—and ourselves.

Outline
Place
Finder

MISSION
BROKEN COV.
JUDGMENT
NEW COV.
FALL

Chapter summary. The kings, priests, and prophets charged by God with shepherding His people have instead destroyed and scattered them. Jeremiah looks forward to the advent of the Messiah, who will "do what is just and right" (23:1-8). God now gives Jeremiah a word about prophets who "use their power unjustly." This classic denunciation reflects the great tension experienced in Judah near the end, as Jeremiah warned of an imminent downfall, and the false prophets continued to utter false reassurances (vv. 9-12). Most terrible of all, they looked to idols for their messages and promoted wickedness by their own evil lifestyles (vv. 13-15). The predictions of false prophets are lies (vv. 16-22), but God knows the truth about the future and about them (vv. 23-32).

Key verse. 23:19: A lie, like truth, is both heard and seen.

Personal application. Be alert, for false prophets still abound.

Key concepts. Shepherd »pp. 355, 504. Sheep »p. 355. Branch »p. 413. Messiah »p. 432. Prophet »p. 131.

INSIGHT

False prophets. This chapter provides Scripture's classic portrait of the O.T.'s false prophets. They also apply to the N.T.'s false teachers. In each era these are individuals who claim to communicate God's message to human beings. But in neither case are they sent to Israel or the church by the Lord. While it is often hard to identify a false prophet, close examination shows a number of unmistakable signs, which are described on the chart (below).

Omniscience (23:23-24). Many people will do things when out of town that they would not do near home. This is the point the Lord makes when He asks if He is "only a God nearby . . . and not a God far away." The false prophets may assume that God isn't aware of what they're doing, but they couldn't be more wrong! Theologians call the knowledge that God has of all things—past, present, and future—omniscience. God does see us. Everywhere. And always.

False Prophets/False Teachers

	Jeremiah	2 Peter	
Doctrine			
led Israel astray	23:13	2:11	introduce destructive heresies
prophesy by Baal			deny the sovereign Lord
Character and Lifestyle			
use power unjustly	23:10b	2:11	bold, arrogant
are godless	23:11	2:10	despise authority
commit adultery and live a lie	23:14	2:10	follow corrupt desires of sinful nature
		2:15	love profit to be gained
Ministry Characteristics			
they strengthen the hands of evildoers	23:14	2:18	appeals to "lustful desires of human nature"
they fill with false hopes	23:16	2:19	promises "freedom" to the depraved

Chapter summary. Jeremiah relates another event from the reign of Judah's last king, Zedekiah. He has a vision of two baskets of figs presented to God as an offering (24:1-3). The one contained good (acceptable) figs and represented the Jews already carried into captivity by Nebuchadnezzar (vv. 4-7). The other contained bad figs (inedible and thus unacceptable as an offering), representing the Jews still in Judah, who were destined for destruction (vv. 8-10). There is a future for the captive, but doom lies ahead for the "free."

Chapter 25 reports the earlier rejection of Jeremiah's prophetic ministry by the people of Judah (25:1-7). Then God called Nebuchadnezzar, "My servant," and foretold the coming exile (vv. 8-11). Jeremiah then prophesies that after the Jews spend 70 years in captivity, Babylon itself will fall (vv. 12-14). In his vision Jeremiah is then given a cup whose content symbolizes God's wrath, told to pour it out on Judah's enemies (vv. 15-29), and in vivid prophetic imagery he describes God's universal judgment on sin (vv. 30-38).

Outline
Place
Finder

MISSION
BROKEN COV.
JUDGMENT
NEW COV.
FALL

Key verses. 25:11-12: Discipline has limits. Judgment does not.

Personal application. A God who punishes the sins of His own will surely judge those who do not know Him.

Key concepts. Babylon »pp. 302, 920. Exile »p. 138. Prophet »p. 131. Anger of God »pp. 65, 72. Shepherds »p. 504.

INSIGHT

The figs (24:1-10). There is a play on the words "good" and "bad" to describe the baskets of figs. In an initial deportation in 605 B.C., King Nebuchadnezzar took skilled artisans and members of the leading families to Babylon. These were "good" in the sense of "useful" to his great plans for his empire. Comparatively those taken were good/useful, and those left in Judah were bad/useless. We should not suppose that those then in captivity were "good" in a moral or spiritual sense, for the Jews in both settings kept on rejecting prophetic messages. The point of the vision is that those in captivity would be accepted by God—and He chose to bless them. Those in Judah were not acceptable—and would be judged.

Prospects (24:4-7). God promised sweeping blessings to the captives: prosperity, return to the land, permanent establishment in the homeland, and spiritual renewal. This last promise was necessary because God would bless before His people were converted! Look back over your own life, and you too will see God's grace at work providing you with good things before you ever came to Christ.

Persistence (25:3). Jeremiah had preached— and been ignored—for 23 years at this point in his life! And he had almost 20 more years of ministry left, years in which he would be active-

ly persecuted, beaten, ridiculed, and nearly killed.

When we feel like giving up because others fail to respond quickly to what we say, let's remember Jeremiah and imitate his persistence.

"Because" (25:8). Paul speaks of the "Gospel," a word which means "good news," being a fragrance both of life and of death. It is a sweet aroma indeed to those who believe and are saved. It is a deadly odor to those who reject and are lost. This is what the Lord says through Jeremiah here.

"Because you have not listened . . . I will summon . . . Nebuchadnezzar" (25:8-9). Let's always stay on Scripture's good side, by hearing and responding. The other side of God's Word is too dreadful to contemplate.

Seventy years (25:11-12). This prediction of Jeremiah was fulfilled, and the Babylonian Captivity did last for about 70 years, which may serve here as a round number representing a normal lifespan. The specific years suggested by scholars are either 587 B.C. to 520–515 B.C., or between 598 B.C. to 538 B.C.

Escape? (25:28-29) God's principles of moral judgment operate in the entire universe and not just among His own people. Since God has shown He will judge His own people for sin, He surely will judge those who are not His.

Chapter summary. Chapter 26 describes the reaction to Jeremiah's "temple address" (cf. Jer. 7–11). Verses 1-6 summarize the sermon, while vv. 7-11 tell of Jeremiah's arrest and trial. On trial, Jeremiah boldly calls for his accusers to repent (vv. 12-15). Some of the elders and the people resist the demands of the religious leaders that Jeremiah be executed (vv. 16-19). Lest this be seen as a symptom of spiritual responsiveness in Judah, Jeremiah tells us that another prophet, Uriah, was actively pursued and then murdered by royal officials for preaching the same message (vv. 20-24). Divine intervention alone saved Jeremiah.

Chapter 27 describes Jeremiah's ministry during this period and explains the hostility of the prophets and priests who wanted him dead. Jeremiah sends a wooden yoke as a warning to envoys from nearby nations who have gathered to discuss the Babylonian threat. The prophet urgently counsels surrender (27:1-11). He gives the same message to Zedekiah, warning him not to listen to lying prophets who predict independence from Babylon (vv. 12-15). And Jeremiah bluntly tells the priests and people that all the temple articles will soon be taken to Babylon (vv. 16-22).

Key verses. 26:4-6: There's always an "if" in God's warnings.

Personal application. We may not like what God says at times, but we are always wisest to listen.

Key concepts. Prophet »p. 131. False prophet »p. 462. Temple »p. 283. Babylon »p. 302. Yoke »p. 722.

INSIGHT

Like Shiloh (26:1-6). The priests and false prophets argued that because God's temple was in Jerusalem, He was bound to preserve it. Thus there could be no danger to Jerusalem from Babylon. Jeremiah reminds them that in Samuel's time the Philistines captured the ark of God and destroyed the tabernacle, which then stood at Shiloh (1 Sam. 4). A worship center was no protection to a sinning people.

Priests, prophets, and people (26:7-9). The priests and prophets didn't like Jeremiah's message because it contradicted their theology. The people simply didn't want to have their illusions destroyed. Let's hold our doctrines humbly. Persecuting others in God's name has been a curse in the church as well as in ancient Israel.

Jeremiah's defense (26:12-15). The prophet does not plead for his life. He knows that humanly speaking his enemies have the power to kill him. But he knows too that his life is in God's hands. Instead he simply states, "The Lord sent me," using the occasion to plead with the people to repent. What a noble moment for Jeremiah. And what an example for you and me.

Precedent (26:17-19). Some elders suggest a legal precedent that saves Jeremiah's life. Prophecy against the temple wasn't considered a capital offense in Hezekiah's day, almost 100 years earlier. They also are fearful. It isn't safe to kill someone who speaks in God's name.

"Uriah" (26:20-23). The killing of a contemporary of Jeremiah's proves that no real change of heart is indicated by the decision to spare Jeremiah.

"Any nation" (27:1-11). When envoys from nations along Babylon's southern borders gathered to plot how to regain their freedom, Jeremiah wore a wooden yoke and warned them to submit to Nebuchadnezzar. God showed His grace to pagan nations as well as His own people in O.T. times.

Prophesying lies (27:12-16). The religious establishment in Jeremiah's day was lined up against him, encouraging Zedekiah to rebel against Babylon by predicting victory.

How often God's spokesmen are outshouted by the greater numbers lined up on the other side. If we are willing to do God's will, we'll recognize His voice today.

Chapter summary. Jeremiah's conflict with false prophets continues. A pseudo-prophet named Hananiah breaks the wooden yoke Jeremiah is wearing to symbolize submission to Babylon and announces that God will even send Judah's captives home within two years (28:1-11). God tells Jeremiah to forge a yoke of iron to symbolize His unalterable intention to judge Judah—and to announce that Hananiah will die within the year. And he does! (vv. 12-17) Jeremiah then sends a letter to the elders among the exiles in Babylon, telling them to settle down and prepare for a lengthy stay (29:1-19). Another prophetic word of judgment is directed against false prophets in the captive Jewish community (vv. 20-23). A special word of condemnation is directed against Shemaiah, who had written from Babylon urging the Jerusalem authorities to silence Jeremiah (vv. 24-32). The false prophets may outnumber Jeremiah and may outshout him as well. But God has not sent them, He will surely judge them as well as the people who are so eager to be deceived.

Outline
Place
Finder

MISSION
BROKEN COV.
JUDGMENT
NEW COV.
FALL

Key verses. 29:8-9: No one has to be deceived.

Personal application. Read 29:11-14, and remember that no time of discipline is devoid of hope.

Key concepts. Babylon »p. 302. Prophet »p. 131. False prophet »p. 462. Captivity »p. 138.

INSIGHT

"The seventh month" (28:17). Hananiah's confrontation of Jeremiah took place in the fifth month (28:1). God didn't wait the whole year to bring about Hananiah's death, but did so in less than two months. There was no way the people and priests of Judah, who witnessed the confrontation that took place (28:1), could avoid linking Jeremiah's prediction with Hananiah's demise. God shouts out His warnings.

Only holding our hands tightly over our ears and squeezing our eyes shut permits us to miss what He has to say.

Hope (29:11-14). These are undoubtedly among the most comforting verses in Scripture. The exiles in Babylon are to settle down and wait, for God knows the plans He has for them, plans to give them a hope and a future. In the O.T. "hope," either *miqweh/tiqwah* or *yahal* invites us to look ahead in confident expectation. Each assumes a time of waiting. But the latter especially reminds us that our future is guaranteed by our personal relationship with God. Because He is our God, He has plans for us. And those plans are good—both beautiful and beneficial. Like the exiles, we may have to wait for God's plans for us to bear fruit. But we can wait confidently, because our hope is in Him.

Illustration. *The yoke Jeremiah wore was made of a wooden bar or bars, tied by leather thongs to the neck of an ox or other work animal. It symbolized submission and servitude and underlined the prophet's urgent call to Judah and the surrounding nations to submit to Babylon. The false prophet Hananiah broke the wooden yoke and announced that Hananiah would die within the year. His subsequent death both judged the false prophet and authenticated Jeremiah as God's messenger. Yet even with this proof, the leaders and people of Judah refused to respond.*

465

Chapter summary. Chapters 30–33 constitute one of the most critical prophetic sections in the entire Old Testament. This cluster of prophecies was given during the last 18 months of the siege of Jerusalem (32:1). In it Jeremiah reveals a stunning vision of God's plans for His people's future. First, God will bring "Israel and Judah back from captivity and restore them to the land" (30:1-3). After a time of terrible trouble (vv. 4-7), God's people will be freed from every oppressor and ruled by the Messiah (vv. 8-11). Israel's spiritual wounds will be healed (vv. 12-17), and Jerusalem will be rebuilt (vv. 18-22).

In keeping with other Old Testament portraits of history's end, fierce judgment (vv. 23-24) will give way to blessing (31:1-6). Familiar themes are repeated: God will restore Israel's joy (vv. 7-14), so despite present sufferings God's people are to look forward expectantly (vv. 15-22). The future is bright with hope (vv. 23-26), and under the Messiah the nation will be exalted higher than ever (vv. 27-30). And now Jeremiah leaves the familiar themes, to introduce a stunning new revelation: God intends to make a New Covenant with Israel that stands in contrast with the Law Covenant. That New Covenant will work the inner transformation that will make Israel's ultimate blessing possible at last (vv. 31-34).

Key verses. 31:33-34: New Covenant promises.

Personal application. God's Law belongs in the heart.

Key concepts. Covenant »p. 35. Law covenant »p. 62. Eschatological themes »pp. 419, 427, 428, 443. Messiah »p. 432.

INSIGHT

The New Covenant. Biblical covenants spell out what God will do. A covenant is God's pronouncement: "I will." But the fulfillment of covenant promises often lies far ahead in time. One covenant is different, because it defines how God related to O.T. believers while awaiting history's end. This covenant was the Law Covenant. Jeremiah tells us that the New Covenant makes the Mosaic Covenant irrelevant. That covenant told Israel how to behave and specified blessings for Israelites who obeyed God's Law and punishments for those who disobeyed.

In contrast, under the New Covenant God will "put My law in their minds and write it on their hearts" (31:33). That is, under the New Covenant God promises believers inner transformation. In a New Covenant relationship the believer will know God in a personal way, his sins will be forgiven, and he will respond to God's inner promptings from the heart.

Jeremiah says this New Covenant is to be made with "the house of Israel," i.e., the Jews (31:31). The covenant itself looks forward to a time when Messiah appears and a national conversion takes place. Then all the benefits described by Jeremiah will be made available to that people, who at last recognize and acknowledge their Redeemer.

Jeremiah predicted a New Covenant would be made and described what would happen when the covenant promises were fulfilled. Jesus identified His death on the cross as the institution of the New Covenant (Matt. 26:28; 1 Cor. 11:25). And the fulfillment of the New Covenant promises made when Jesus sacrificed Himself awaits history's end.

But there is another unique feature to this covenant. Its benefits are experienced today by those who put their trust in Christ, the promised O.T. Messiah. It's as though someone put 1 billion dollars in the bank for you, to be yours in 25 years. The 1 billion is untouchable before the specified time arrives—but the depositor did say you could receive the interest now! Just so, Heb. 10:16-17 applies the central promises of the New Covenant to believers today. God forgives the sins of those who believe in Jesus now, and He begins His transforming work in every believer's heart. Through faith in Christ we enjoy a New Covenant relationship with God.

Chapter summary. The Babylonian army is besieging Jerusalem and Jeremiah is under guard when the Lord tells him to purchase a field in territory occupied by the Babylonians (32:1-7). Jeremiah pays for the field and has the transaction witnessed, and then tells the witnesses that although the land will be occupied for a "long time," in the future "houses, fields, and vineyards will again be bought in this land" (vv. 8-15). Jeremiah has obeyed, but remains puzzled so prays asking God for illumination. Why buy a field in a land soon to be overrun by the Babylonians? (vv. 16-25) God responds that He is about to hand Judah over to Babylon as a punishment due them for their sins (vv. 26-35). But a remnant of God's people will be restored to their land and blessed with great prosperity (vv. 36-44). Jeremiah's purchase symbolized God's intention to restore His people to the Promised Land.

Key verse. 32:25: Ask why after obeying.

Personal application. Faith sees things not as they are, but as they will be.

Key concepts. Babylon »p. 302. Captivity »p. 142. Prayer »p. 181.

INSIGHT

Obedience precedes illumination. Jeremiah bought the field offered by his uncle, even though the land in question was occupied by the enemy. After he did what God wanted (32:8-9), he then asked the Lord to explain (vv. 16-25).

What a lesson for us who tend to insist on knowing "why" before we do what we sense God wants us to do. Let's obey first, and seek understanding later!

"Baruch" (32:12). Baruch served as Jeremiah's secretary (scribe) during his later years. We learn more about Baruch in the following chapters.

Jeremiah's prayer (32:16-25). Commentators observe five things about Jeremiah's prayer. (1) Jeremiah first confesses who God is: vv. 17-18. (2) Jeremiah is deeply conscious of God's grace: vv. 19-22. (3) Jeremiah is sensitive to the justice of God's judgment on Judah: vv. 23-24. (4) Jeremiah recognizes God's good hand even in the present suffering (see "to this day"): v. 20. (5) Jeremiah ponders how to reconcile God's faithfulness in judgment to His command to Jeremiah to buy the field: v. 25. Honest prayer will often express our puzzlement. Despite all we, like Jeremiah, know about God, we will be unable to explain completely what He asks us to do.

"I am the Lord" (32:26). We need not explain supposed conflicts between what is now and what God promises. God reminds Jeremiah and us that He is God. Because the Lord is who He is the future for Israel was bright, even though Jeremiah's time was one of unrelenting darkness. Remember that God is God in your life too. However dark your today, tomorrow's prospects are unspeakably bright.

Illustration. *The earliest copies of the O.T. were found preserved in clay jars like the one in which Jeremiah preserved a copy of the deed to his uncle's field. The wrapped deed was circled by string and the string "tied" with a blob of clay which bore the imprint of the owner's seal. This was placed in a sealed jar, to keep the document from deteriorating over the years.*

Outline
Place
Finder

MISSION
BROKEN COV.
JUDGMENT
NEW COV.
FALL

Chapter summary. This chapter concludes the section called "The Book of Consolation," which introduced the New Covenant. God exhorts Jeremiah to call on Him for even greater revelations (33:1-3). Jerusalem will fall (vv. 4-5), but God will heal the land, restore Judah and Israel to it, and "let them enjoy abundant peace and security" (vv. 6-13). When that promise is fulfilled, the promised Messiah from David's line will rule (vv. 14-22). The peoples murmur that God has rejected His chosen people, but the Lord reaffirms His commitment to the Jews in the strongest of terms (vv. 23-26). Centuries later, the Apostle Paul would write of a similar rejection of Israel in favor of the Gentiles who respond to the Gospel message. He too would echo the assurances God gave Jeremiah, and flatly say "God's gifts and His call are irrevocable" (Rom. 11:29).

Key verses. 33:20-21: Has God really rejected Israel?

Personal application. God will keep every promise, whether made to Israel or to you and me.

Key concepts. Captivity »p. 138. Branch »p. 413. Messiah »p. 432. Covenant »p. 35. Davidic Covenant »p. 370.

INSIGHT

"**Unsearchable things**" (33:3). The Heb. word (*basur*) means "inaccessible." There is no way any human being could gain this knowledge apart from divine revelation. Apart from revelation we human beings can have no real knowledge of origins or of destiny. How important then not only to ask God, but to accept His answers!

"**I will heal**" (33:6). It took no revelation from God to predict the downfall of Jerusalem. The city was even then under siege by an overwhelming force, its inhabitants decimated by plague and starvation. What was "inaccessible" was the picture of a bright future drawn for the prophet by the Lord.

"**Joy and gladness**" (33:10-11). These verses contain the closing benediction used in modern Jewish wedding ceremonies.

King, priests, and Levites (33:17-18). In the final restoration envisioned here both the Heb. monarchy and worship will be restored. These promises have never been fulfilled in a literal sense. This is understandable, as they hinge upon the appearance of the Branch (Messiah) to rule over restored Israel. The only way in which these promises could be fulfilled in any literal way would be at the return of Jesus.

Note that the promise in these verses is not that monarchy and priesthood would continue forever, but that David's royal house would continue to exist, as would the priestly line. When the Branch rules, as "do what is just and right" indicates, then Israel will be restored and be whole.

Has God rejected Israel? (33:23-25) One of the persistent views held today by many Christians is that God has rejected the Jews as a people. The O.T. prophecies and promises are thought to be fulfilled "spiritually" in the church. There can be no national, earthly future kingdom such as is described by Jeremiah and the other O.T. seers. The problem with this view is that the promises of a messianic kingdom and a specific future for a Jewish people regathered to the land promised Abraham, Isaac, and Jacob are reaffirmed in the O.T. at just such historical junctures as this! God rejected Jeremiah's generation. But at the same time, God through the prophet stated that He would regather the people of both Israel and Judah to the Jewish homeland and fulfill the promise given to David of a dominant Hebrew kingdom to be ruled by a descendant of David. God's words to Jeremiah seem decisive: "If I have not established My covenant with day and night and the fixed laws of heaven and earth, then I will reject the descendants of Jacob and David my servant and will not choose one of his sons to rule. . . . For, "I will restore their fortunes and have compassion on them.""

Chapter summary. As the nation is about to fall to the Babylonians, Jeremiah is given a message for Zedekiah, Judah's last king. The king will be captured, but God promises he will die in peace, mourned by his people (34:1-7). This is a reward for Zedekiah's initiative in winning his people's agreement to free their Hebrew slaves, who according to Moses' Law should be kept in servitude for only seven years. But the people soon go back on the solemn oath they swore before God and take back their slaves—dooming themselves to death at the hands of the Babylonians (vv. 8-22). To underline the wickedness of Judah, Jeremiah tempts members of the Recabite family with bowls of wine. They refuse to drink, because generations before the family patriarch had commanded his descendants to drink no wine (35:1-11). The family which showed such respect for its forefather was praised and rewarded—and Judah, which showed no respect for God but persistently disobeyed Him—was promised punishment (vv. 12-19).

Outline
Place
Finder

MISSION
BROKEN COV.
JUDGMENT
NEW COV.
FALL

Key verse. 35:17: God does call.

Personal application. No one is ever "free" from the consequences of his or her choices.

Key concepts. Babylon »p. 302. Prophet »p. 131. Slavery »p. 90. Covenant »p. 35. Vine »p. 414.

INSIGHT

"Zedekiah" (34:2). Zedekiah was a weak and vacillating ruler. In one interview with Jeremiah he confessed his fears and even begged the prophet not to tell his officials about their conversation (38:14-28). Yet he apparently did take the lead in getting his people to agree to release Heb. slaves kept over the legal 7-year period. God rewarded him for this act of piety, whatever its motivation.

How great is the grace of God to reward even the evil for doing good and thus encouraging them to do even more good. And how great the flaw in human nature that accepts blessings from God, yet refuses to submit to His will.

Slavery. This institution in Israel was unlike that of other ancient societies. A fellow Heb. might be purchased, but only for a period of seven years. At the end of that time, his master was to free him and to generously supply him with funds to start a new life. In essence, slavery in the Mosaic Law was a social mechanism designed to protect the poor and enable them to reach self-supporting status. But in Judah slavery had been corrupted, and wealthy individuals enslaved their fellow-Jews for life.

What had been intended as a gracious provision for the poor became an institution of oppression.

"Walked between the pieces of the calf" (34:19). In O.T. times a covenant was a legally binding agreement. The most solemn of ancient covenants was the "covenant of blood," in which the parties walked between pieces of a sacrificial animal. It was this most binding of covenants, concluded "before the Lord" (with God as witness), that the people of Judah repudiated when they recaptured their slaves. God rightly sees this as symptomatic of the Jews' persistent repudiation of their covenant with Him. The broken promise is a decisive revelation of the moral and spiritual condition of the people God will surely judge.

"Freedom" (34:17). Human beings foolishly assume that "freedom" is the right to do whatever they please, without restraint or restriction. The sarcastic comment here underlines a great reality. People can do whatever they please, but they cannot choose to avoid the consequences of their actions. True freedom is found in obeying God, who directs us to that path which brings reward rather than punishment, blessing rather than curse, joy rather than grief.

Respect. We can sense the pain in God's words to Judah as Jeremiah contrasts the obedience of the Recabites to their forefather's command with the disobedience of Judah to God's commands.

The best way we can show our respect for God today is to pay attention and listen to (obey) Him.

469

Outline
Place
Finder

MISSION
BROKEN COV.
JUDGMENT
NEW COV.
FALL

Chapter summary. Much of the Book of Jeremiah was written long after the prophet delivered his sermons. This chapter gives the circumstances. Jeremiah has been forbidden to enter the temple area (36:5), so he dictates the messages he has given to a skilled scribe named Baruch. Baruch then goes to the temple compound during a religious festival and reads the scroll aloud from an upstairs window (36:1-10). This is reported to the king's officials, who politely ask Baruch to read his material to them. They realize at once that it has been dictated by Jeremiah (vv. 11-19). After urging Baruch and Jeremiah to hide, the officials take the scroll to King Jehoiakim. The king listens as the document is read, but shows his utter contempt for God's Word by cutting up the scroll and burning it (vv. 20-23). Rather than repent, the king orders the arrest of Jeremiah and Baruch (vv. 24-26). Jeremiah dictates another copy of his book and sends a message to the king. Because of Jehoiakim's contempt for God's Word he will die, and none of his descendants will succeed him on David's throne (vv. 27-31).

Key verse. 36:24: Repentance shows respect.

Personal application. Read Scripture with a proper sense of awe, realizing it is God's own Word to you and others.

Key concept. Scripture »p. 843.

INSIGHT

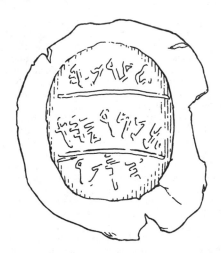

Illustration. *A bulla is a blob of clay used to seal documents which have been impressed with a seal to show authorship. One of the most exciting finds, among a group of bullae from the royal archives in Jerusalem, dates to the 7th century B.C., the time of Jeremiah. It reads: "Belonging to Berechiah son of Neriah the scribe." Scholars believe it is likely the impression of the seal of the Baruch, son of Neriah, who served as Jeremiah's secretary and who boldly read the prophet's scroll in the Jerusalem temple!*

Scroll. In Jeremiah's time documents were recorded on papyrus or parchment, fastened to a wooden roller at one or both ends, and rolled up.

"Restricted" (36:5). Most believe the authorities had forbidden Jeremiah access to the temple due to his earlier sermons there denouncing the religious and political leadership (cf. Jer. 7–10).

The day of fasting (36:6). The events described date from December, 605 B.C. No biblical religious holiday was held during this month. It's likely the fast was occasioned by some national misfortune, such as a plague or impending invasion.

Lesser officials (36:11-19). These officials showed concern for Jeremiah's life as well as respect for Baruch. Their warning to Baruch to take Jeremiah and hide showed that they were well acquainted with the king's character, accurately predicting his reaction!

How hard it is to be "in the middle." We need wisdom to show respect for God and His ways, and at the same time be responsible to those in authority over us.

Jehoiakim's rejection (36:27-31). Do right. Let God judge those who do wrong.

Chapter summary. A powerful position is no guarantee of strength of character. This is evident in these two chapters that trace the relationship between Jeremiah and King Zedekiah during the siege of Jerusalem by the Babylonians. Zedekiah begs Jeremiah to pray for the city (37:1-5), but the prophet can only promise impending defeat (vv. 6-10). When the siege is temporarily lifted, Jeremiah tries to leave the city but is accused of treason and arrested (vv. 11-15). This begins his imprisonment, first in a dungeon and later in an official's courtyard (vv. 16-21). While there Jeremiah urges the people to go over to the Babylonians and save their lives, arousing the fury of Jerusalem's "hawks" (38:1-4). The prophet is thrown into a cistern to die (vv. 5-6) and then rescued (vv. 7-13). King Zedekiah, terrified of both the Babylonians and his own officials, secretly asks Jeremiah what to do. But he is afraid to follow the prophet's advice (vv. 14-23), even terrified lest someone discover he had asked (vv. 24-28). Through it all the prisoner shows courage and strength of character, the king utter weakness.

Outline
Place
Finder

MISSION
BROKEN COV.
JUDGMENT
NEW COV.
FALL

Key verse. 38:5: There is always something a person can do.

Personal application. You don't have to be "somebody" to be courageous.

INSIGHT

"Zedekiah" (37:1). Jeremiah 36:30 reports God's judgment on Jehoiakim. That judgment has come true. Jehoiakim was not succeeded by his son, but by his brother Zedekiah. As the chapter opens, it is 18 years after the scroll burning incident reported in chap. 36.

Why ask? (37:3) Why did Zedekiah send messengers to Jeremiah? Earlier the prophet had announced the city's doom (34:2-7). Perhaps when the Babylonians temporarily lifted their siege (37:5) Zedekiah thought God had relented. But the prophet continued his blunt and bold assertion that the Babylonians would surely attack and burn the city (37:8). In fact it was only a short time later that the Egyptian column hurried back home, and the Babylonians returned to Judah.

What a plethora of lessons for us! Don't suppose that a temporary withholding of judgment means the danger is past. Don't expect God to change His mind on moral issues. And don't be afraid to speak God's Word boldly, even when circumstances seem to contradict what the Lord says must surely come.

Why did Jeremiah leave Jerusalem? (37:11-15) Some expositors have agreed with Jeremiah's enemies, that he had taken his own prophecies seriously and was about to go over to the enemy. But Jeremiah was committed to stay and warn his own people as long as there was hope of saving even one! His own explanation makes sense. Jeremiah intended to go home—

Anathoth was just three miles from Jerusalem—and put his affairs in order before the Babylonians returned.

Don't expect your enemies to believe your explanation of your actions, even when you're telling the truth.

Where are your prophets? (37:19) The "prophets," who were Jeremiah's enemies, had insisted that the Jews already captive in Babylon would be released and that Jerusalem would never be attacked. Jeremiah's question points up their failure to predict accurately, proving they are false prophets (cf. Deut. 18:22). By then the king knew that Jeremiah truly was God's spokesman. His continuing failure to heed Jeremiah's words and his fear of his officials reveals the utter weakness of this last of Judah's kings. Real power is not rooted in position. Real power is rooted in character. The proof? See 38:5.

God and country? (38:4) We make a mistake when we assume that the priorities of God and country are always the same. The officials who complained that Jeremiah was weakening the people's morale were undoubtedly correct. But did this make him a traitor? Jeremiah put God's Word and values first and believed that if his country did the same, all would be well.

We need to follow Jeremiah's example. God must be put first, country a distant second. And when the two are in conflict, we must make Jeremiah's choice, and be faithful to God.

Chapter summary. For 40 years Jeremiah has urgently warned Judah that God will demand an accounting for their constant disobedience and incessant sins. Now his life work is vindicated, as the city of Jerusalem falls to the Babylonians whom he has predicted will destroy it.

And so Jerusalem falls after a 2 1/2 year siege, in July of 586 B.C. (39:1-3). Zedekiah flees, but is captured near Jericho. His sons, and the nobles who were Jeremiah's most vicious enemies, are killed. The king is blinded and taken to Babylon (vv. 4-8). In contrast, Jeremiah is released from prison and allowed to choose his own future. He decides to stay with the scattering of poor people to whom Nebuchadnezzar has given lands and allowed to stay in Judah (vv. 9-14).

Key verse. 39:5: He hesitated, until it was too late.

Personal application. Never doubt that God's Word will be fulfilled.

Key concepts. Babylon »pp. 302, 435. Jerusalem »pp. 205, 451. Captivity »p. 138.

INSIGHT

Illustration. *Babylonian war memorials show Jewish prisoners being led into captivity after the fall of Jerusalem in July of 586 B.C.*

Predictions fulfilled (39:3). Jeremiah 1:15 contains the prediction, "kings will come and set up their thrones in the entrance of the gates of Jerusalem." The event described in 39:3 is specific fulfillment of the prediction. The gate mentioned separated the upper and lower city, and the officials probably met to plan mopping-up operations. By the way, Nergal-Sharezer was Nebuchadnezzar's son-in-law; he took the name Neriglissar when he succeeded him on Babylon's throne.

Zedekiah's fate (39:6-8). The brutal treatment of the king was not unusual in ancient times, especially considering the trouble caused Babylon by Judah's chronic rebelliousness. The blinding shows how two seemingly contradictory prophecies were fulfilled. Jeremiah told Zedekiah he would see the king of Babylon and be taken there (32:3-4), and Ezekiel predicted Zedekiah would die in Babylon without seeing it (Ezek. 12:13).

"Jeremiah" (39:11-14). Nebuchadnezzar undoubtedly heard reports from Jewish deserters of Jeremiah's urgings that the Jews surrender. He was most likely viewed as a Babylonian sympathizer and treated accordingly.

"Ebed-Melech" (39:15-18). Earlier this Jewish official had rescued Jeremiah from sure death in one of the city cisterns (38:1-13). His act was motivated by faith (39:18) and was rewarded as God spared his life, while other officials died.

Outline
Place
Finder

MISSION
BROKEN COV.
JUDGMENT
NEW COV.
FALL

Chapter summary. Jeremiah 40–45 describe events and prophecies after the fall of Jerusalem. The first chapters deal with events in Judah. There Jeremiah is released, and Gedaliah is appointed governor of the few Jews who remain in the land (40:1-6). Gedaliah provides land for the survivors and works hard to reestablish their confidence (vv. 7-12). He is warned of a plot to kill him, but the honest governor refuses to believe evil of one he views as a friend (vv. 13-16). Gedaliah is assassinated (41:1-3), and his killer launches a reign of terror (vv. 4-10). The killer then escapes (vv. 11-15), and the remaining Jews are terrified that the Babylonians will exact vengeance for the murder of governor Gedaliah (vv. 16-18). The remaining Jews plead with Jeremiah for guidance and promise to obey God's word to them, whether they like it or not (42:1-6). After 10 days the Lord speaks and tells the remainder not to fear Nebuchadnezzar. God will protect them in Judah. But the prophet warns the leaders not to go to Egypt (vv. 7-17). God, through Jeremiah, underlines His warning. The remnant must not go to Egypt (vv. 18-22). The remnant is now confronted with the same choice the nation had earlier faced. Will they obey God and live? Or disobey and die?

Key verse. 42:3: Knowing God's will is only of value if we are willing to do it.

Personal application. We can either learn from mistakes — or make them all over again.

INSIGHT

Faith? (40:2-3) The Babylonian official showed respect for Jeremiah's faith and teachings. This need not imply he believed in the prophet's God. Even so, he showed more respect for Jeremiah than did the prophet's own people!

"Gedaliah" (40:9-10). The man appointed governor worked hard for his people and won their trust by promising to represent their interests to the Babylonians. His assassination was a tragedy for the remaining Jews.

Ishmael (40:14). Ishmael was a member of the royal family and had been a court official (41:1). Perhaps he was jealous of Gedaliah. At any rate, he let himself be used by the king of the Ammonites, who may have wanted Gedaliah assassinated and the last Jews driven from their land so he could occupy part of it.

Sacred ruins (41:4). The pilgrims brought gifts to the "house of the Lord." The temple

had been destroyed. But just as today's "wailing wall" in Jerusalem is considered holy, apparently the temple ruins were considered holy by the remnant.

Flee to Egypt? (41:16-18) The assassination of Gedaliah and the small Babylonian garrison terrified the remaining Jews, whose first impulse was to escape to Egypt.

It's dangerous for any of us to act on impulse. We need to stop, think, and especially ask God for guidance.

"We will obey" (42:1-21). The 10-day delay must have intensified the stress felt by the little company of Jews. But when the answer came, it was unmistakable. God would care for the Jews if they remained in Judah. If they disobeyed and fled to Egypt, they would die. Based on the proven reliability of Jeremiah's predictions, only one choice made sense. But would God's stubborn people obey?

Outline
Place
Finder

MISSION
BROKEN COV.
JUDGMENT
NEW COV.
FALL

Chapter summary. Following the assassination of Gedaliah, the Judean governor appointed by Nebuchadnezzar, the remaining Jews plan a flight to Egypt. But first they ask Jeremiah for a word from God. God's answer is: Stay in Judah (Jer. 40–42). The answer doesn't please the frightened survivors who accuse Jeremiah of lying (43:1-3). Johanan rallies the support of the people and leads them to Egypt in defiance of God's command (vv. 4-7). In Egypt, Jeremiah predicts a successful invasion of that land by Nebuchadnezzar (vv. 8-13). There is no safety in Egypt for the retreating Jews.

Now comes Jeremiah's last prophecy, probably dated about 580 B.C. The Jews are destroying themselves by their refusal to obey God's Word (44:1-10). The few who have fled to Egypt will perish there, pursued by famine, plague, and the sword (vv. 11-14). Even now the fugitives refuse to respond. Defiantly, they pledge to keep on worshiping their pagan deities (vv. 15-19). All Jeremiah can do now is to confirm God's judgment on this stubborn remnant of His people (vv. 20-30).

Key verse. 44:7: It is foolish to disobey.

Personal application. Don't let yourself become so hardened by sin that repentance is impossible.

Key concepts. Arrogance »p. 352. Prophet »p. 131. Idolatry »p. 433.

INSIGHT

"Arrogant men" (43:1-3). The leaders had promised to heed God's word through Jeremiah. Now they looked for a way out. They found it by accusing Jeremiah of lying and of being so weak-minded that he was under the influence of his secretary Baruch.

Arrogance is insistence on getting our own way. One sign of arrogance is finding some way to blame others for our own wrong or guilty choices.

"Johanan" (43:2). Earlier he had warned Gedaliah that Ishmael intended to assassinate him and had volunteered to murder Ishmael (40:15). With Gedaliah gone, Johanan rallied the people around himself—and led them to reject Jeremiah's divinely sponsored advice.

Arrogance in a leader is especially dangerous. To be a true leader a person must first submit to God and determine to do what is right, whatever the consequences. Johanan seems to have been a leader who maintained his position by leading people where they wanted to go rather than where they should.

Nebuchadnezzar's invasion (43:8-13). The Babylonian monarch did not conquer Egypt, but he did invade it in 568/567 B.C. The expedition was intended to punish the Egyptians. It did, and after that peace was maintained.

Learn from past sins? (44:1-10) Sin hardens

human beings. Even God's unmistakable judgments on Israel's sins failed to lead the fleeing Jews to repentance. The longer an individual or a people remain involved in sinful practices, the less likely they are to be willing to change. The German philosopher Hegel wrote, "What experience and history teach is this—that people and governments never have learned anything from history, or acted on principles deduced from it."

"They will all perish in Egypt" (44:11-14). God does not leave us to learn from experience. He makes His will very clear. And He spells out the consequences of disobedience.

Twisted reasoning (44:15-19). A person can always find an excuse for doing what he or she knows is wrong. The rebellious remnant subbornly insisted on practicing idolatry—and justified their choice by saying that when they had followed these practices before the Babylonian invasion all was well with them. When a person insists on taking poison for their health, they are truly beyond help.

"But . . . "(44:26). "You can't make me" is a true statement, whether uttered by a contemporary of Jeremiah or someone in our day. Yet there is always a "but." A person can "go ahead," but he or she cannot escape the consequences of any act.

Outline
Place
Finder

MISSION
BROKEN COV.
JUDGMENT
NEW COV.
FALL

Chapter summary. Jeremiah now appends a number of divinely inspired messages. The first is addressed to his secretary, Baruch, and is a word both of rebuke and comfort. Baruch came from a socially prominent family and had advanced education. He had expected to gain an important position and was deeply grieved that his association with Jeremiah had ruined his prospects. God rebuked his ambition in this time of national disaster, promising him the greatest gift of all: his life (45:1-5).

What follows is a series of messages about 10 foreign nations (Jer. 46–51). The first message concerns Egypt. It describes the defeat of that nation at Carchemish (46:1-6) and taunts the humbled land (vv. 7-12). It also predicts a future invasion of Egypt by Nebuchadnezzar (vv. 13-19) and describes the doom of that great nation (vv. 20-26). As for scattered Israel (Jacob), God's people will once again know peace (vv. 27-28).

The second message concerns the Philistines and predicts doom for this ancient but weakened enemy of the Jews (47:1-7).

Key verse. 46:18: God is the Master of world events.

Personal application. How marvelous that in times of national upheaval God continues to care for His own.

Key concepts. Egypt »p. 420. Philistines »p. 185. Prophecy »p. 434.

INSIGHT

Ambition (45:1-5). Baruch came from a family of achievers. His grandfather was governor of Jerusalem in Josiah's time (2 Chron. 34:8) and his brother the staff officer in Zedekiah's court (Jer. 51:59). He had expected to receive some high office, but found himself the secretary of the most hated man in Judah!

God told Baruch what He tells us. Be the best you can be, but don't expect to be more than you are (v. 5). Self-seeking ambition was hardly appropriate when the nation was facing divine judgment—or at any other time.

Judgment on foreign nations. Each major O.T. prophet makes predictions about foreign nations. Typically these oracles focus on a nation's sins. Jeremiah does not identify their sins, but does detail their judgment. The O.T.'s prophetic condemnation of the pagan states that opposed and often oppressed God's people rests on certain basic convictions about God. The God of the O.T. is the God of the universe, not just the nation. His authority over world events is complete.

God is also holy, and events on earth are rooted in His moral nature. Thus, the greatest of national disasters must be seen as vindicating the Lord's righteousness rather than as malicious or vengeful acts.

Lastly, while God must and will judge wickedness wherever it occurs, the Lord delights most in salvation. He warns before He judges.

Well equipped (46:2-6). Jeremiah describes a superbly equipped army. But rather than winning a victory, this superior force is gripped by terror and flees. God, not force of arms, determines the outcome of man's battles.

No remedies? (46:10-11) Egypt was famous worldwide for her physicians and medical achievements. The prophet uses irony here. The defeated nation has no medicine to heal her wounded pride.

"Only a loud noise" (46:16-17). Big talk is empty without action. The prophet is quoting the view of demoralized mercenary soldiers hired by Egypt. They have no confidence in Pharaoh and talk about deserting him.

"Punishment on Amon" (46:25). Amon was the chief god in the Egyptian pantheon. His residence was at Thebes, the capital of Upper Egypt. The defeat of the nation would reveal the powerlessness of the gods the Egyptians relied on to give them victory.

Look beyond captivity (46:27-28). The people of Judah, languishing in captivity in Babylon, might take little comfort from the defeat of Egypt. But God gives them a special word of promise. God will save, and their descendants will be rescued from the land of their exile.

Chapter summary. Jeremiah continues his series of messages concerning foreign nations. As his eyes sweep from the west to the east, he describes the judgments due to fall on state after state. The cities of Moab, which invaded Judah in Jehoiakim's reign, will be ruined and lie desolate (48:1-10). Her pride will be broken by a sudden, great blow (vv. 11-19), and her downfall will be complete (vv. 20-28). While the arrogant weep, joy and gladness depart the shattered land (vv. 29-39) and are replaced by terror of Moab's invader (vv. 40-47). Similar destruction awaits Ammon (49:1-6), Edom (vv. 7-22), Damascus (vv. 23-27), the Arabian tribes of Kedar and Hazor (vv. 28-33), as well as the distant kingdom of Elam (vv. 34-39). God had delivered all these peoples into the hands of the Babylonians. And what God decreed would surely come to pass.

Key verse. 48:30: No nation can withstand God.

Personal application. Live a godly life daily, and trust God to take care of world events.

Key concepts. Judge »p. 372. Edom »p. 104. Sovereignty »p. 430.

INSIGHT

"Moab" (48:1-47). The Moabites lived east of the Dead Sea and frequently came in conflict with Israel. The Moabites were descendants of Lot (Gen. 19:30-38) who chose to fight rather than permit the Exodus generation to pass through their lands on the way to Canaan. The Moabites earned Israel's unending hostility by following the advice of the seer Balaam and attempting to corrupt Israel's faith and morals (Num. 22–24). A resurgent Moab was subdued in the time of David, but rebelled a few decades later (2 Kings 3). A number of O.T. prophecies are directed against this hostile people (Deut. 23:3; Ps. 60:8; 83:6-7; 108:9; Isa. 15–16; 25:10-12; Jer. 9:26; 25:21; 27:3; Ezek. 25:8-11; Amos 2:1-3; Zeph. 2:8-11). The Moabites were crushed by Nebuchadnezzar and vanished as a nation.

Exiling Chemosh? (48:7) Chemosh was the god of the Moabites. The verse refers to the practice of pagan peoples of taking their idols with them when they went into exile (Jer. 43:12; Isa. 46:1-2).

"Wine left on its dregs" (48:11). The image was clear to Jeremiah's first readers. Wine was poured gently from the storage jar to serving jars so as not to disturb the dregs, impurities which had settled to the bottom. Similarly God had treated Moab gently. But now the nation's experience will be like that of jars violently shaken and smashed.

Pride (49:29). Moab's pride is mentioned in strong terms, 6 times in this one verse. Pride is destructive, in large part because it keeps a person or nation from listening to others and from responding to God.

Weeping for Moab (49:31-32). Judgment is a necessity, but never a pleasure.

Isaiah and Jeremiah on Moab. The two major prophets share a common vision of Moab's future, as is seen by comparing the following verses.

Isaiah	Jeremiah	Isaiah	Jeremiah
15:2	48:1	15:7	48:36
15:2-3	48:37	16:2	48:20
15:3	48:38	16:6	48:29
15:4	48:34	16:8-9	48:32
15:5-6	48:5, 34	16:10	48:33
15:5	48:3	16:11	48:36
16:7	48:31	16:12	48:35

"No sons"? (49:1) The Ammonites had occupied territory given to the tribe of Dan. God asks a rhetorical question. It introduces the promise that although this northern tribe was carried captive into Assyria 150 years earlier, their descendants will yet regain their inheritance.

Unique accuracy (49:7-12). Details of this prophecy show how accurately it fits the culture and the times. Teman was known for its wisdom (Ezek. 25:13); but did not foresee disaster. Dedan was known for commerce (Ezek. 25:13) and is warned to recall its traders.

Chapter summary. Jeremiah's final prophecy concerning foreign nations is directed against Babylon. It's the longest of the 10 and maintains a dual emphasis. Babylon will fall. And the Jewish exiles will return to their homes. Jeremiah begins with an announcement of Babylon's coming doom (50:1-10). The mighty empire's sins must be judged (vv. 11-16), even as Israel must be returned to her land (vv. 17-20). God will take vengeance on Babylon (vv. 21-28) for her arrogant self-exaltation (vv. 29-32). God will come forward as Israel's Kinsman-Redeemer and strike Babylon down (vv. 33-40) forever (vv. 41-46). Jeremiah then describes the vengeance God will take on Babylon (51:1-14), demonstrating both his omnipotence and the worthlessness of Babylon's idols (vv. 15-26). In the day God summons all nations against Babylon (vv. 27-33) that city's defenses will prove useless (vv. 34-44). The prophecy closes with a warning to the Jews to flee Babylon before the disaster takes place (vv. 45-48) and affirms "Babylon must fall" (vv. 49-53). When the final collapse comes the great city will be deserted, her walls leveled, never again to rise (vv. 54-58).

Outline
Place
Finder

MISSION
BROKEN COV.
JUDGMENT
NEW COV.
FALL

Key verse. 51:49: God keeps His promise to curse those who curse the descendants of Abraham (Gen. 12:3).

Personal application. Deal gently with others, that God might have no reason to deal harshly with you.

Key concepts. Abrahamic Covenant »p. 32. Babylon »pp. 302, 920. Regathering of Israel »p. 419. Divine vengeance »pp. 428, 748.

INSIGHT

Contradictions? In other passages Jeremiah predicts the rise of Babylon and urges his people to submit to Nebuchadnezzar. He even urges the captives to pray for the prosperity of that city (29:7). Now Jeremiah calls for the Jews to flee and announces God's verdict against those who the Lord earlier claimed as His instrument. Others point out that these chapters describe the violent overthrow of Babylon, while its fall to Cyrus was in fact peaceful. But these are not inconsistencies. The fact that any group or person is used by God to fulfill His purposes cannot excuse their sins. Thus Babylon had to be, and would be, judged; Jeremiah simply fulfilled his mission as God's prophet in predicting the empire's ultimate doom. As for the violent overthrow of the city, that did take place later. Nowhere does Jeremiah say Cyrus would be the agent of the city's destruction.

Retribution (50:10). "Do to her as she has done to others" is a basic principle of divine judgment that operates in personal as well as international relationships.

Keeping covenant (50:17-18). Another basic principle of God's working in history is stated in

these verses which reflect His original covenant promise with Abraham. God still blesses those who favor His people and curses those who are hostile to them.

Israel's redeemer (50:33-40). O.T. Law gave the right to a willing relation to rescue a near relative, repurchase his lost lands, and avenge injury or death. What Babylon and other enemies fail to realize is that God is Israel's kinsman and has chosen to act on their behalf.

"The Medes" (51:11). This was a general term for the people of northwest Iran. The Medes had joined Babylon in destroying Nineveh, the capital of Assyria, in 612 B.C. In 539 B.C. they were allied with the Persians who overthrew the Babylonian empire.

"The wall of Babylon" (51:44). The Gk. historian Herodotus admired Babylon's great wall, which was wide enough at the top for chariots to race. Today only a heap of rubble remains.

Babylon. In the N.T., the city is symbolic of sinful human society and man's accomplishments. Like the proud city of old, man's pride will be brought low and sinful human accomplishments turned to rubble.

Outline
Place
Finder

MISSION
BROKEN COV.
JUDGMENT
NEW COV.
FALL

Chapter summary. Chapter 52 is a historical note appended to Jeremiah's book. It describes the fall of Jerusalem and vindicates the prophet's life work. All his predictions of judgment to come, all his conflicts with false prophets and rebellious monarchs, have come true. And so Jeremiah leaves us with a reminder that the Word of God through His prophets is trustworthy indeed. The fact that this is the fourth account of the city's fall is also significant (cf. 2 Kings 25; 2 Chron. 36:11-21; Jer. 39:1-14). Jerusalem's fall decisively demonstrates God's firm commitment to judge sin, even when the sinners are His own dearly beloved.

Jeremiah's account begins with a brief summary of Zedekiah's reign (52:1-3) and a description of the fall of the city (vv. 4-11). Jeremiah then details the destruction of the temple, whose presence the Jewish people had expected to protect them despite their many sins (vv. 12-23). Jeremiah also reports the execution of the religious leaders who had opposed his teachings (vv. 24-27). Jeremiah records how many men (the number does not include women or children) that Nebuchadnezzar took away to Babylon (vv. 28-30). The last paragraph of the Book of Jeremiah tells of the later release of Jehoiachin of Judah from prison and the leading position he was given among captive rulers in Babylon (vv. 31-34).

Key verse. 52:3: God did what He said He would.

Personal application. Count on God's reliable Word.

INSIGHT

Temple furnishings (52:17-23). The victors carefully packed the temple utensils used in worship for transportation to Babylon. Little did they know that those same vessels of gold and silver would come back to the Holy Land, released from their exile by the decree of Cyrus, the conqueror of mighty Babylon (Ezra 1:7-11).

The captives (52:27-30). The passage has two problems. First, the dates do not match with the indication that captives were taken to Babylon in Nebuchadnezzar's first year (cf. Dan. 1:1-3). The answer is that there were actually four deportations. The last was after the assassination of Gedaliah, about 582 B.C., so it is not counted as one of the three deportations that took place during the reign of Judah's last kings, in 605 B.C, in 587 B.C., and in 586 B.C. Second, the numbers given here do not match the number of captives reported in 2 Kings 24. This may be due to Jeremiah's inclusion of only adult males, or perhaps because Jeremiah

only listed those taken from Judah itself.

Jehoiachin's restoration (52:31-34). Cuneiform tablets excavated in Babylon confirm the Bible's account of the later favor shown Jehoiachin. An old Jewish story tells of Evil-Merodach being imprisoned by his father and being befriended by Jehoiachin. The story suggests that later when Evil-Merodach succeeded his father on Babylon's throne he remembered the Jewish king's friendship and gave him a place of honor.

More significantly, the Babylonian king's act reminded the Jewish people that the Lord had not forgotten David's line, even though their lawful ruler was blind and imprisoned.

The fall of Jerusalem and the exile of the Jews was not the end of Scripture's story of redemption. God had judged sin. But God would also return His people to the land. When the days of discipline have passed, the age of salvation will surely begin.

Lamentations

The Book of Lamentations preserves the anguish felt by the Jews of the Babylonian Captivity as they contemplated their irrecoverable past. Jerusalem had been destroyed. That destruction was so complete that no trace of the original temple of Solomon, or the royal city's mighty walls, have been found by modern archeologists. Only a barren hill marked the site as it was last seen by those dragged off in chains to a strange land. The five acrostic dirge poems that make up this brief Old Testament book reveal a deep sense of remorse. The people realize that their homeland has been lost because of Judah's sins. The anguish is compounded by the fact that as yet the captives have been unable to recover the lost vision of a bright future for their race.

The book is composed of five poems, each written as an acrostic. Each line or group of lines begins with a consecutive number of the 22-letter Hebrew alphabet. The sophisticated style as well as uniform emotional and theological perspective indicate a single author.

Lamentations does maintain a consistent theological outlook: Judah's loss can be traced to God's sovereignty, His justice, and His commitment to a morality which His people abandoned. Yet Lamentations is primarily a book that plumbs the depths of human sorrow, not from an individual's perspective, but from the perspective of an entire people. Reading the book we experience something of the overwhelming sense of despair that can grip communities and even whole nations. Even the prayers recorded in Lamentations are desperate prayers; cries of anguish rather than affirmations of hope. It is terrible as well as wonderful to be human. It is terrible indeed if we surrender to our human bent to sin. The day must come when we will look back on our lost opportunities, and realize that the misery we endure now is a consequence of our own chronic craving for sin. If nothing else, reading the Book of Lamentations reminds us the pleasures of sin are at best momentary, the painful consequences lasting and deep.

Date and Authorship. The poems in this book are best dated early in the Babylonian Captivity, probably between Jerusalem's fall in 586 B.C. and the release of King Jehoiachin of Judah from prison in 562 B.C. (cf. 2 Kings 25:27-30). The captives are still overwhelmed by grief, and have not yet laid hold of the promise of a return after 70 years given through the Prophet Jeremiah (cf. Jer. 25).

The text specifies no author, though a Jewish tradition suggests that the aged Prophet Jeremiah made his way to Babylon after leaving the last Jewish fugitives in Egypt, and that he himself wrote these poems.

AN OUTLINE OF LAMENTATIONS

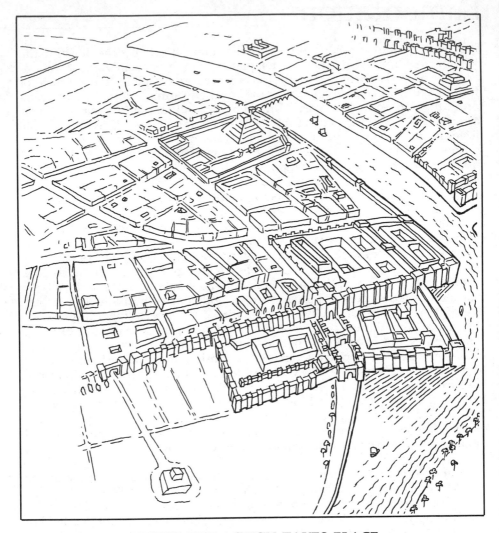

WHERE THE ACTION TAKES PLACE

The Jews were settled in a suburb of the great city of Babylon along the "Kebar River." This was one of the many irrigation canals dug across the fertile plains surrounding the city that served as hub of the far-flung Babylonian Empire. Despite the anguish we sense in Lamentations, the exiles' living conditions were comfortable. The typical Jew may have owned his own home, and maintained a vegetable garden (cf. Jer. 29:4-7; Ezek. 8:1; 12:1-7). Recovered Babylonian records show Jewish names on records of business transactions, and at least one prosperous trading house was owned and operated by Jews. We also know from Jeremiah and Ezekiel that the Jewish community was permitted at least limited self-government, and had its own elders, priests, and prophets. But the Book of Lamentations drives home a great truth. The anguish expressed in this brief poetic book reminds us that material comforts can never fill that void in the human heart which cries out for fellowship with the Living God.

Chapter summary. The first dirge (1:1-22) focuses on the city of Jerusalem. The poet sees the city as a grieving widow, bereft of her children, dirty, poverty-stricken, and despised, bitterly remembering happier times (vv. 1-11b). The tearful city cries out to God. She describes the utter contempt others have for her, hoping desperately to awaken God's compassion (vv. 11c-16). The poet cries out too (v. 17), and then records Jerusalem's confession. It is Zion's own sin that caused God to judge her with the present distress (vv. 18-22).

The second dirge (2:1-22) emphasizes the destruction God caused in unleashing His anger on the Holy City. Without pity, a grimly determined God has laid Zion waste, rejecting His city and its temple (vv. 1-9). In utter agony, Zion's proud inhabitants have crumpled to the ground. They are terrified, tormented, and stunned; shattered by the events which have at last revealed the futility of false prophets' reassurances. God has done as He promised and planned (vv. 10-17). The writer calls his people to prayer (vv. 18-19), and they cry out, describing their condition in pitiful terms, and acknowledging God as the cause of their pain (vv. 20-22).

The third dirge (3:1-66) details either the personal complaint of the poet, or perhaps represents the experience of "every man." The poet shares his deepest feelings of anguish (vv. 1-20), but then reaffirms a hope that is anchored in the goodness and grace of God (vv. 21-39). The exiles must engage in self-examination and must return to God (vv. 40-51). In calling on God the poet sensed God come near and say, "Do not fear" (vv. 52-57). Though calmed, he cannot contain a last cry to God to judge those enemies whose brutality has brought him and his people such pain (vv. 58-66).

Key verses. 1:18; 3:22: Both justice and grace are revealed in every disciplinary act of God.

Personal application. God is willing to make us suffer if this is what is required to turn our hearts back to Him.

Key concepts. Jerusalem »p. 205. Zion »p. 361. Captivity »p. 138. Judge »p. 372. Babylon »p. 302.

INSIGHT

Dirge. Somber, funereal poems had a place in the literature of most ancient Middle Eastern cultures. These five dark reflections on the fall of Jerusalem were traditionally read by the Hebrew people in mid-July, on a date set to commemorate the fall of Jerusalem.

God's doing (1:5). These poems acknowledge the fact that the Exile is God's doing, a judgment brought about by Judah's "many sins." Deut. 28:36, 44, 63-68 foresees the Captivity and explains its causes.

A turning point (1:18-22). Jerusalem confesses "the Lord is righteous" and "I rebelled." This is a place to which every person or people experiencing divine discipline must come if there is to be any hope of restoration. But don't expect that confession to result in an immediate change of circumstances. Acknowledging God's righteousness and admitting our fault is a turning point, a first step that must be followed by a long hike back along the path of righteousness.

Personal pain (3:1-20). In the third dirge the poet speaks for himself. There is no personification here, no observation of another's suffering. However sensitive we may be to others, our experience of personal suffering is bound to be more intense. Here Jeremiah (?) shares how the invasion of his homeland and the loss of all he holds dear has affected *him*.

Chapter summary. The fourth dirge (4:1-22) reflects a time shortly after the second. The captive Jewish community has begun to realize the full significance of the city's loss. The poet begins with a series of images that contrast Jerusalem's past prosperity with the present devastation (vv. 1-11). He then describes the sins of the priests and prophets, who "shed the blood of the righteous" by condoning injustice (vv. 12-16). The Jews had foolishly believed that being ruled by one of David's dynastic line would protect them, and so had sinned insolently (vv. 17-20). That hope now dashed, Zion faces the grim reality of divine judgment. Judah is being punished for her sins. Surely the nations that oppressed her will be punished as well (vv. 21-22).

The final dirge (5:1-22) is a cry for relief. This poem is not an acrostic, and the use of some 45 Hebrew words ending in *u* bolsters the sense of lament. The poet cries out to God to act in view of the dread condition of His people (vv. 1-18). This final poem of the collection closes with an appeal to God, who reigns forever, to restore and renew the exiles, "that we may return" — to God, and to the Promised Land (vv. 19-22).

Key verses. 5:21-22: Hoping against hope.

Personal application. God judges His own, but never utterly rejects us.

Key concepts. Anger of God »pp. 65, 72. Abandon »pp. 186, 370. Remember »p. 98.

INSIGHT

"Gold" (4:1). Even gold and gems are worthless when people flee a total disaster. In panic people run on, leaving them dulled in the dust. There is nothing like a threat to one's life to provide perspective on man's "valuables"!

People (4:2). The stunned people of Judah realize that *they themselves*, as well as their treasures, no longer appear of any value. The terrible suffering caused by the Babylonian invasion has stripped the proud people of Judah of all their arrogance, and forced them to reevaluate their view of their treasures, themselves, and their relationship with God.

Sin (4:10-11). The extreme suffering of the people of Jerusalem during that city's siege led some of its "compassionate women" to cannibalize their own children! How dreadfully the capacity of every human being to sin was revealed in that city's last days.

Bloodguilt (4:13-16). The guilt of prophets and priests was incurred in a variety of ways. They incited the leadership to resist Babylon and so brought disaster on the city. They also

were responsible for the death of at least one prophet whose message was like that of Jeremiah (Jer. 26:20-23). Finally, Ezek. 22:1-12 shows that the concept of "bloodguilt" was quite broad, and included acts which threatened the well-being and thus shortened the lifespan of another. The active hostility of the religious leadership to Jeremiah and their indifference to the needs of common men, as well as their destructive meddling in politics, all contributed to the corruption of Jewish society and made judgment inevitable.

"Unless" (5:21-22). Lamentations closes on an uncertain note. The poet expresses the captives' appeal to God for restoration. But they have been forced at last to consider the possibility that God might be so angry with His sinning people that He has "utterly rejected" them.

God did not utterly reject His O.T. people. In time He brought a remnant back to the Jewish homeland. He pruned, but did not purge. God remains committed always to His own.

Ezekiel

In 609 B.C. the Babylonians crushed combined Assyrian and Egyptian forces at Carchemish, on the Euphrates River. Unchallenged, Babylonian armies under Nebuchadnezzar then swept southward, invading Syria-Palestine in 605 B.C. Nebuchadnezzar made Judah a vassal state, and took a number of young nobles to Babylon, including the future prophet, Daniel. Later, when Jehoiakim of Judah rebelled, Nebuchadnezzar returned with another army. He sacked Jerusalem early in 597 B.C. and took Jehoiachin, the 18-year-old successor of Jehoiakim, to Babylon. Nebuchadnezzar made Jehoichin's uncle Zedekiah Judah's ruler, and at that time deported a larger group of Judah's upper and middle class to Babylon. This group, which included a young priest named Fzekiel, was settled in the region of Tel Aviv, along a wide canal linking two branches of the Euphrates known as the "Kebar River." The settlers were treated as colonists rather than slaves, and enjoyed many privileges. But, encouraged by false prophets in Judah, they looked for the early downfall of Nebuchadnezzar and a quick return to their homeland. Back in Judah, Jeremiah continued to shout his strident warnings to submit to Babylon. And then, among the captives, a new prophetic voice joined in. In June/July of 593 B.C., Ezekiel was called by God and delivered his first message to the captives. Between 593 B.C. and the final destruction of Jerusalem in 586 B.C., Ezekiel uttered a number of carefully dated prophetic messages predicting the judgment of Judah. After the fall of that city the prophet fell silent for a dozen years, and then resumed his ministry with a new and different message. God intended to restore Judah, and Ezekiel spoke glowingly of the glories of a future messianic kingdom.

Ezekiel remains one of the most fascinating of prophetic books, in part because of the varied means used to communicate its message. Visions, symbols, allegories, and parables all are found in the prophet's vital ministry. Ezekiel casts himself as a watchman, responsible to warn his community of impending doom. His book reminds Christians that we too are watchmen, called to urge others to turn to the Lord while there is still time.

EZEKIEL AT A GLANCE

KEY PEOPLE

Ezekiel *A young priest in the Jewish community in Babylon, who is called by God to serve as His prophet.*

KEY EVENTS

God's glory (Ezek. 1). *Ezekiel sees visions of God's glory that emphasize His transcendence and majesty.*

Judah's sin (Ezek. 8–10). *Ezekiel sees the hidden sins of Judah's leaders and people who cause God's presence to desert the Jerusalem temple.*

Personal responsibility (Ezek. 18). *Ezekiel emphasizes the responsibility of each individual for his or her own choices, and teaches that each will be judged for his or her own actions.*

The watchman (Ezek. 33). *Ezekiel defines the clear but limited responsibility that the believer has for others who do not trust in God.*

Israel's restoration (Ezek. 37). *Ezekiel foresees the regathering and restoration of the nation Israel.*

Final battle (Ezek. 38–39). *Ezekiel describes God's intervention in man's final attack against the chosen people.*

Glory ahead (Ezek. 40–48). *Ezekiel describes a new temple to be built in Messiah's time.*

WHERE THE ACTION TAKES PLACE

Ezekiel ministered to the Jewish community in Tel Aviv, Babylon. But his messages concerned the fate of those who still lived in Judah. Here Ezekiel is shown acting out the destiny of those in his homeland. Head covered in shame, he carries his few possessions away from his shattered house, acting out departure to captivity.

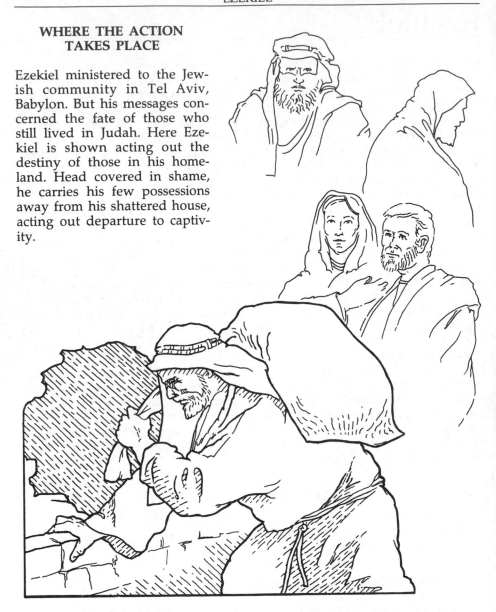

Date and Authorship. Few question the statements of the biblical text, that the author of this book is Ezekiel, a young priest taken to Babylon with the second group of captives in 597 B.C. His book is distinctive in that a number of his messages are carefully dated, and provide a clear chronology of his ministry. The dated messages are: Ezekiel 1 (June/July 593); 8 (Aug./Sept. 592); 20 (July/Aug. 591); 24 (Dec./Jan. 589/588); 26 (March/April 587); 29 (Dec./Jan. 588/ 587); 29 (March/April 571); 30 (March/April 587); 31 (May/June 587); 32:1 (March 585); 32:17 (April 585); 33:21-33 (Dec./Jan. 586/585); 40 (March/April 573). These years are identified in Ezekiel as X number of years "of the exile of King Jehoiachin." Since we know that Jehoiachin was taken in 593 B.C., the dates prophetic messages were given are easy to calculate.

THEOLOGICAL OUTLINE OF EZEKIEL

CONTENT OUTLINE OF EZEKIEL

Outline
Place
Finder

JUDAH
NATIONS
RESTORATION
TEMPLE

Chapter summary. Ezekiel launches his book with a precise description of the setting for a spectacular vision (1:1-3). He then goes on to report an indescribable vision, struggling to find analogies that will help us sense something of the reality he experienced. The first part of the vision features four "living creatures," whose aspects have symbolic meaning (vv. 4-14). These creatures are oriented to a crystalline structure replete with gigantic wheels, representing freedom of motion and mobility (vv. 15-21). The structure seems to dissolve into an icy, endless, vast expanse. And there, high above, Ezekiel sees a sapphire throne, and a bright figure surrounded by brilliant light (vv. 22-28). While no language has the capacity to express what Ezekiel saw, the overall impression is intense and clear. Ezekiel saw a vision of God as glorious Lord of the universe, unlimited in His sovereign power, awesome in His essential holiness. Throughout his years of ministry the Lord continued to appear to Ezekiel in this form, encouraging him, and reminding him of the nature of the One we all serve (cf. 3:12, 23-24; 8:2-4; 9:3; 10:1-20; 11:22-23; 43:2-4).

Key verse. 1:28: A sight of God's glory stimulates worship.

Personal application. Don't focus on the details of Ezekiel's vision, but on the overall impression it conveys.

INSIGHT

"The thirtieth year" (1:1). Most agree that Ezekiel means his own thirtieth year. This vision constituted his call to prophetic ministry, and according to O.T. Law priests began their ministry at age 30 (cf. Num. 4:3, 23, 30, 39, 43; 1 Chron. 23:3).

Ezekiel's priesthood (1:3). The fact that Ezekiel was a priest is significant. The temple is one of his major concerns (cf. chaps. 8–11), and he would have been familiar with the laws governing worship. His priestly descent also qualified him to describe the great temple to be built in the time of Messiah's restoration of Israel and Judah to the homeland.

The indescribable vision. We know that Ezekiel struggled to find analogies that would let him communicate his vision. We know he felt that he struggled, for Heb. words such as "resembling" (*ke*), "looked like" (*demut*), "like" (*kemar'eh*), and "appearance" (*mar'eh*) recur again and again in this chapter. Some people have become bogged down seeking to explain the details of Ezekiel's vision, and artists have even toiled to portray them. But the best way to sense the reality Ezekiel portrays is to read the chapter quickly, opening ourselves to receive an impression of the awe-inspiring majesty of our God.

Symbolism? (1:1-21) The figures which Ezekiel says looked like living creatures are also seen in Rev. 4, and are generally taken to be of that order of angels called cherubim (»p. 491). The four "faces" are generally taken to be symbolic of the orders of animal creation: human, birds, wild animals, and domesticated animals.

The wheels and the rapid movement of the entire structure under the direction of the Spirit of God (vv. 20-21) suggest the universality and freedom of God. Most deities in ancient times were supposed to be associated with a particular land. Now Judah was bowed under a Babylonian yoke and was soon to be destroyed. Yet Judah's God was not limited to that land. He moves freely in Babylon, and indeed through the heavens. What a message for those who feared that by being cut off from the Promised Land they had been cut off from God.

The fiery figure of God (1:22-28). Brightness is associated with God's glory and holiness throughout Scripture. A burning figure surrounded by fires so pure they glow with primary colors as the rainbow is also in Dan. 10:6 and Rev. 4:3, 5.

"Facedown" (1:28). Ezekiel is overwhelmed and falls down. His awed response is appropriate. Ezekiel is about to be called to ministry, and those who minister must serve God in awe of His holiness as well as in appreciation of His love.

Chapter summary. God now commissions Ezekiel. The prophet is to carry God's word to rebellious Israel, whether they respect or reject his message (2:1-7). That message will be a discouraging one, of lament, mourning, and woe (vv. 8-9). The prophet "eats" the scroll on which God's word is written, symbolically assimilating the message and making it his own. Despite the initial sweetness of his call, the message with which God was sending him burned bitter in his stomach (3:1-11). It is sweet to be called by God, but the cost of discipleship can be high! When the vision ends Ezekiel sits mute among his fellow exiles for seven days (vv. 12-15).

Again God's word comes to Ezekiel, and explains that he is to serve as a "watchman for the house of Israel." He is one who sees impending danger, and warns the wicked to turn from his ways. And Ezekiel will be held accountable for speaking out! His words of warning may make the difference between life and death (vv. 16-21).

Outline
Place
Finder

JUDAH
NATIONS
RESTORATION
TEMPLE

Key verse. 2:7: Faithfulness, not success, is important.

Personal application. We are responsible to warn others, but not for the choices they make afterward.

Key concepts. Son of man »p. 645. Fear »p. 363. Holy Spirit »p. 759.

INSIGHT

"Son of man" (2:1). Ezekiel is identified by this name over 90 times. In this book it suggests the prophet's human frailty. The name is found elsewhere in the O.T. only in Dan., where it has a different, eschatological significance. In the Gospels the name "Son of man" is given to Christ, where it most often emphasizes His humanity and His dependence on God's Holy Spirit.

Response to God's message is no measure (2:5). This is so hard for us to realize. It is so easy to become discouraged when others do not respond to our sharing of God's Word. Yet the Lord told Ezekiel, and through him us, not to measure the importance of our ministry by how others respond. God's people are called to faithfully communicate God's Word. It is faithfulness, not success, that is the measure of our worth as His servants.

Don't fear (2:6-8). How others respond is only one issue. The other is, how will we respond to opposition? God's word here is, don't be afraid. And don't stop. We dare not be infected with the rebelliousness of others, and stop speaking God's words.

Eat the scroll (3:1). God's message to His people was written on a rolled-up length of papyrus which Ezekiel is told to eat. The act is symbolic of taking in and assimilating the message. Only when the prophet had made God's

Word a part of his very being would he be able to share it with others. When God's Word becomes a part of us, we are able as well to share the message.

Sweet taste, bitter ministry (3:3-11). The bitterness Ezekiel feels comes after God tells him that his efforts will apparently be unrewarded. It is both discouraging and bitter to try again and again and yet fail to reach others. Yet there is an eternal sweetness to the Word of God, which sustains us in the most difficult of times.

Hard as flint (3:9). The prophet was to be more stubborn in doing God's will than the Jewish community was in resisting it. Ezekiel's name means "God is strong." If we draw strength from the Lord we will be able to keep on doing good, whatever the difficulties.

"A watchman" (3:16-21). The role of the watchman in ancient times was to remain at his post, on guard for any danger that might threaten his city or homeland. Then the watchman gave the alarm, so defenses could be prepared. The watchman had an important, but limited duty. He must give the alarm. But he could not be responsible for the reaction of those he warned. If he failed to warn his community the watchman bore bloodguilt. But if he did his duty, whatever happened then was not his fault. So it is with us and the Gospel.

Chapter summary. Ezekiel begins his confrontation with his stubborn community by "playing toy soldier." He uses a clay tablet to represent Jerusalem, and builds a ramp and siege works against it (4:1-3). For 390 days he lies before the toy city on his right side, and for 40 more on his left side, representing the punishment due Israel and Judah (vv. 4-8). During this period he eats only enough to barely keep him alive, representing the famine due to strike Jerusalem (vv. 9-17).

Continuing his symbolic acts Ezekiel takes a sharp sword and cuts off his hair and beard, dividing it into thirds, and treating each third in a representative way (5:1-4). The prophet's strange behavior must have drawn every member of the Tel Aviv community to watch and to wonder. And then, when the time was right, Ezekiel spoke. God will surely punish and scatter His sinning people, and be avenged for their constant sins. Jerusalem and Judah are destined to become a ruin, and her people will be destroyed by war, famine, and plague (vv. 5-17).

Key verse. 4:4: Curiosity compels attention.

Personal application. Preaching isn't the only way to win a hearing for what you have to share.

Key concepts. Jerusalem »pp. 205, 451. Idolatry »p. 433. »Anger of God »pp. 65, 72. Law »pp. 120, 145. Judgment »p. 372. Unclean »p. 82.

INSIGHT

"Ramp" (4:2). When ancient armies besieged walled cities one mode of attack was to construct wide, earthen ramps that topped the city fortifications.

The 390 and 40 days (4:5-8). The days are said to represent years during which Israel and Judah suffer divine punishment. The specific years these days represent is uncertain, and much debated by scholars. One possibility is that the 390 years are calculated from the time Jeroboam I set Israel up as a separate kingdom, and initiated a false worship system (»p. 230). If so, divine punishment is equated with loss of contact with God, whom the people of the Northern Kingdom no longer worshiped in Jerusalem. Judah's 40 years might relate to the undated withdrawal of God's glory from the Jerusalem temple, which Ezekiel describes in chap. 8–11. The terrors of war, plague, and starvation are not as awful to contemplate as a loss of personal relationship with the Lord.

Wheat, barley, etc. (4:9). When food was scarce, beans, lentils, and typically discarded seeds were mixed with the sparse supply of wheat and barley and ground together to make flour for bread. These "fillers" represent famine.

Shaving head and beard (5:1-4). This symbolic act has many aspects. It represents defilement, for a shaved priest could not minister at the temple (Lev. 21:5). Shaving all hair was also a forbidden pagan rite in honor of the dead (cf. Isa. 22:12; Amos 8:10)—in this case, the death of the sinful nation. The hair itself symbolized the inhabitants of Jerusalem, and the way in which Jeremiah disposed of it represented their fates.

Explanation (5:5-17). Ezekiel's dramatic and strange actions had been the talk of the community. But the prophet had to explain their meaning. There is a school of Christian thought which assumes that if a believer lives a good life, his acts are sufficient witness to the world. Without words any act of witness is liable to be misunderstood.

Accusation, and verdict (5:6-17). Verses 6 and 7 contain God's accusation. His people have rebelled against God's laws and decrees, and conformed to the standards of pagan nations. This was no unwitting failure, but a sin against revelation and knowledge.

The verdict follows. God will judge the city without pity. All those who have defiled it and the temple will perish, and the few who remain will be scattered. Famine and wild beasts, not peace, await those who reject God.

Outline
Place
Finder

JUDAH
NATIONS
RESTORATION
TEMPLE

Chapter summary. Ezekiel now launches the first of the major oracles of impending judgment that mark his book. Canaanite religion, marked by idolatry and immorality, was practiced at shrines located on hilltops. Thus God's word through His prophet is addressed to the "mountains of Israel," and announces their coming destruction. The words, however, foretell the eradication of idolatry from the entire Promised Land (6:1-14). Four poetic oracles describe the judgment about to fall on Judah. (1) The entire land is to be purged (7:1-4). (2) Judah will be surprised and horrified as the terror strikes the land (vv. 5-9). (3) The judgment will fall immediately, for the day of doom is here (vv. 10-11). (4) Death is the sentence that has been passed on all (vv. 12-13). Though trumpets will blow calling the people of Judah to resist Babylon's invading armies, the wicked city of Jerusalem will be so weakened it will be unable to resist. Following calamity after calamity, pagan nations will take possession of the land promised to Abraham's seed (vv. 14-27).

Key verse. 7:2: Judgment may be delayed, but it is sure.

Personal application. Divine retribution is certain.

Key concepts. Idolatry »p. 433. Adultery »p. 85. Anger of God »pp. 65, 72. Judge »p. 372. Day of the Lord »pp. 413, 541.

INSIGHT

The whole land polluted (6:2-3). The four geographical features mentioned — mountains, hills, ravines, and valleys — symbolize the entire land. All has been polluted by pagan altars and the immorality associated with Canaanite religion.

Scattering bones (6:5). This act desecrated the shrine site, and made it unsuitable for future worship. It is the bones of the worshipers themselves God will scatter in Judah, thus also underlining the inability of pagan deities to save those who honor them.

Dance for joy (6:11). God directs Ezekiel to "strike your hands together and stamp your feet and cry out." In that culture these actions expressed joy. The command is intended to express God's joy not at the suffering of His people but at the downfall of idolatry. The "Alas" Ezekiel is to shout is a mocking cry of derision, mimicking those who see the nation's destruction from a human rather than divine point of view. In fact there could be nothing better for Judah than to be purged of sin, despite the terrible cost.

"The end has come" (7:1-13). While the prophecy is directed against seventh century B.C. Judah, these verses foreshadow a similar time of awesome judgment which the prophets foresee at history's end.

The budded rod (7:10). The rod here is the rod of divine judgment. Its budding symbolizes the imminence of a judgment about to burst into full flower.

Buyer and seller (7:12-13). The reference is to the O.T. Law of the Year of Jubilee. A person could sell the right to farm the land his family had received in Joshua's allotment of property in the days of the Conquest, but could not transfer it permanently. Each 50th year, at Jubilee, rights to a property were to revert to the family of the original owners. The buyer of land or the seller might rejoice, depending on how far away or near the Jubilee year was. But Ezekiel warns that such considerations are now irrelevant. Neither will possess land in Judah, for it will be occupied by foreign conquerers.

Helpless and humiliated (7:14-18). The vivid images of moral and material weakness remind us of the deceptive impact of sin. The corrupt are arrogant as long as all is going well. But when Judgment Day arrives, "every hand will go limp, and every knee will become as weak as water." Don't be troubled by the proud sinner. The person who lives a humble life in dependence on the Lord has chosen the one way that provides security and ultimate joy.

Chapter summary. This chapter introduces a single vision which Ezekiel was given in Aug./Sept. of 592 B.C. It came as he lay on his side before a toy Jerusalem under ·siege (cf. chap. 4) and fully explains to the leaders of the exiled Jewish community why there is no hope for their homeland. Chapter 8 is background for the phenomenon described in chapters 9–11: the withdrawal of the presence of the Lord from the Jerusalem temple.

Ezekiel is taken in his vision to Jerusalem, where he witnesses the idolatry practiced in the Holy City. He sees an idol, perhaps an Asherah pole (cf. 2 Kings 21:7), erected within the temple compound (Ezek. 8:1-6). Going further Ezekiel is shown the leading men of Judah secretly worshiping images in private rooms inside the temple's inner court (vv. 7-13).

Ezekiel is then shown women outside the temple compound's north gate worshiping Tammuz, a primeval fertility goddess whose rites involved mourning the dearth of water that marked the hot, dry Middle Eastern lands (vv. 14-15). Finally Ezekiel was shown 25 men at the very entrance to the temple, turning away from it to worship the sun (vv. 16-18). Each of these pagan rites were being practiced in the very shadow of God's temple, fully illustrating abandonment of the Lord and the loss of holiness.

Key verse. 8:18: Abandoning God has consequences.

Personal application. Remain sensitive to God's presence.

Key concepts. Temple »p. 283. Idolatry »p. 433. Priest »p. 81.

INSIGHT

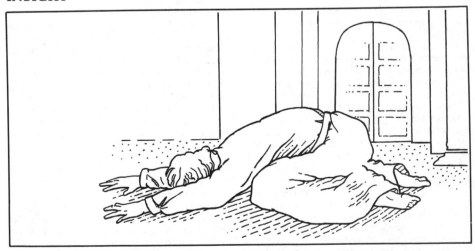

Illustration. *Commentators suggest the 25 men worshiping the sun in Ezek. 8:16 were priests. They are in a court only priests were allowed to enter (2 Chron. 4:9). The 25 represent the 24 shifts who served the temple plus the high priest.*
This is the ultimate sin: those commissioned to serve God turn from Him to worship a nature deity.

Chapter summary. As Ezekiel's vision continues, executioners appear, and an angelic scribe is dispatched to mark those in Jerusalem who remain faithful to God (9:1-11). At the same time God's "glory," that bright expression of the divine presence, moves from the temple's holy of holies to its entrance. There coals of fire representing God's wrath are given the angelic scribe (10:1-7). The image of God attended by cherubim in a great, mobile structure is the same that Ezekiel saw in his first vision (Ezek. 1). Now the "glory" leaves the temple entirely, and takes its place on the throne (10:8-22). God is withdrawing His protection from His sinning people! The cooking pot which metaphorically protects the meat within it (11:3) will not save the wicked, who will be cast out to be killed (vv. 1-7). Those who have not known God in His gracious aspects will recognize Him when He comes in judgment! (vv. 8-15) The message is dark and terrifying. Yet Ezekiel concludes with a word of hope. One day God will bring His people home and give them a heart responsive to Him (vv. 16-21). With this last word God's glory leaves the city. As Ezekiel is carried back to Babylon, he sees the divine presence, hanging over the eastern mountains, waiting (vv. 22-25).

Outline
Place
Finder

JUDAH
NATIONS
RESTORATION
TEMPLE

Key verse. 9:10: Our acts pass judgment on us.

Personal application. Count on God's grace, but don't discount His holiness.

Key concepts. Glory »p. 74. Temple »p. 283. Angel »p. 521. Judge »p. 372. Captivity »p. 138. New Covenant »p. 466. Regathering »p. 419.

INSIGHT

"Mark" (9:4). The command to mark those who still have a heart for God is a happy reminder of two truths. Even when outnumbered, true believers are never alone. And, God does note our faithfulness!

"Forsaken"? (9:9) The people of Judah had mistaken their national peril as evidence that God had forsaken them, or did not see them. Nothing could have been further from the truth! Their peril was in fact proof that God did see, and was actively involved in their society! Judgment too is evidence of God's presence.

Cherubim. This special order of angelic being is mentioned infrequently in the O.T. Genesis 3:24 depicts them as guardians of the way to Eden. Most passages, however, associate them directly with the throne and/or presence of God, perhaps as guardians of His glory. Key verses that mention cherubim are Ex. 25:18-20; 1 Sam. 4:4; 2 Sam. 6:2; 2 Kings 19:15; 1 Chron. 13:6; 28:18; Pss. 18:10; 99:1.

"Meat" (11:3). The diet of the ordinary O.T. citizen seldom included meat. Thus it was a precious commodity, protected in the cooking pot. The saying that "we are the meat" and the city

the cooking pot thus reflected the view that the Jews were precious to God, and the walled city in which they lived, featuring as it did God's temple, guaranteed their safety. God later turns this saying against them, saying the wicked generation will not be "meat" to Him, nor will the city save them.

Pelatiah's death (11:13). Ezekiel's report in Babylon of Pelatiah's death in Judah, long before the word could reach the exiles, served to authenticate his message. There was no hope that Jerusalem or the Jewish state would survive.

"Heart of flesh" (11:19). "Flesh" in the O.T. usually represents mortality, or man's life on earth. Here the "heart of flesh" contrasts with a heart of stone. It represents responsiveness to God in contrast to a stubborn rebelliousness. God will bring His chosen people back to their homeland. But He must first cleanse and transform them from within. This teaching is in clear parallel to Jeremiah's promise that God intends to make a New Covenant with His people to replace the old, ineffective Law (Jer. 31–33).

Outline
Place
Finder

JUDAH
NATIONS
RESTORATION
TEMPLE

Chapter summary. A new series of messages to rebellious Israel, running from Ezekiel 12–19, is launched with the phrase, "The word of the Lord came to me" (12:1-2). Despite the recent national setbacks, the Jewish captives were still optimistic about an early return home. In these messages Ezekiel systematically destroys the foundations of their false hopes. In this chapter, Ezekiel rejects the view that if judgment does lie ahead, it will not come in his listener's lifetime. He begins with a dramatic portrayal of deportation, symbolizing the fact that soon the exiled community would be joined by the survivors of the latest Babylonian invasion (vv. 3-7). As the curious flocked to watch, Ezekiel announced that soon God would scatter all His people among the nations (vv. 8-16). Shaking, he acted out the terror soon to be experienced in Jerusalem (vv. 17-20). Despite the skeptics' arguments that the warnings of earlier prophets had not yet come true, they would soon experience their dread reality (vv. 21-28).

Key verse. 12:27: "Not yet" doesn't mean "never."

Personal application. Don't mistake judgment deferred for no judgment at all.

Key concepts. Exile »p. 138. Rebellion »p. 101. Oracle »p. 359. Babylon »p. 302. Remnant »p. 427. Judge »p. 372.

INSIGHT

Rebellious (12:2). Grasping spiritual truth is a matter of attitude rather than intelligence. Eyes to see and ears to hear speak of man's natural capacity to process information. Don't be surprised when the "wise" of this world ridicule biblical faith. The failure to truly see or hear is rooted in mankind's attitude toward God. Only a heart open to the Lord will grasp and respond to His truth.

The drama (12:3-7). The exiles for whom Ezekiel performed had all been taken captive themselves, in 605 B.C. or in 597 B.C. They would all recognize what Ezekiel was acting out.

So you that cannot see (12:6, 12). Ezekiel was acting out the fate of Zedekiah, Judah's king. When the Babylonian armies broke into the city, he tried to escape in disguise, but was caught and blinded by Nebuchadnezzar (2 Kings 25:4-7).

"They will know . . . when" (12:15). The thought is repeated three times (cf. vv. 16, 20). The Jews of Jerusalem and the exiles will know God is Lord after judgment has fallen. Ultimately every human being will acknowledge that God is the Lord — willingly, or unwillingly. How vital the "when." We can acknowledge Him now, in salvation. Or later, in judgment. When it is too late.

Vision (12:21). Most of the Heb. words trans-

lated "vision" come from the root *hazah*. Each indicates a revelation from God; a special, mystical means through which God communicated His message to O.T. prophets.

The proverb (12:22). The "proverb" is a saying that sums up common wisdom, or a people's point of view. The belief the proverb expresses is, simply, that the message of judgment delivered by Ezekiel and earlier prophets like Isaiah simply was not true. The argument underlying it is basically, "It hasn't happened yet — so it can't happen!" That notion is foolish, whether it's held by a Californian living in an earthquake zone, or a non-Christian hearing about Christ's Second Coming! God's patience in delaying judgment is evidence of grace, not evidence no judgment lies ahead!

"Many years from now" (12:26-28). Even those who did believe Ezekiel, did not believe that his words would affect *them*. Maybe someday. But not now. Maybe someone. But not us. God's response through Ezekiel was, "Not someone . . . you!" And, "Not someday . . . soon!"

The attitude of the people of Ezekiel's day is still pervasive in the church. Only if we truly believed judgment was coming to *us* and *soon* would we break the bondage of our materialism, and live completely for the Lord.

Chapter summary. Ezekiel was a lone voice of doom shouting out against a chorus of prophets and prophetesses who gave a bright, optimistic picture of the future. Why believe him rather than them? God's answer is that "their visions are false and their divinations are a lie" (13:1-7). God Himself is against the false prophets who offer Judah a barren hope, and they will be consumed in the holocaust they deny is coming (vv. 8-16). God is also against the "prophetesses" who rely on witchcraft, and they too will be punished (vv. 17-23).

The leaders of the exiles sit down with Ezekiel. But they have already "set up idols in their hearts." They are determined to go to the false prophets and actually encourage them to predict what they want to hear! Both people and prophets thus will surely come under the judgment of God (14:1-11). God would not listen even if the most righteous of men prayed for this people. Their righteousness would save them, but no one else (vv. 12-20). Sword, famine, and plague will strike the Holy Land, and only a few will survive (vv. 21-23).

Outline
Place
Finder

JUDAH
NATIONS
RESTORATION
TEMPLE

Key verse. 14:11: Punishment saves.

Personal application. We are responsible for the leaders we choose to follow.

Key concepts. Prophet »p. 131. False prophet »p. 462. Occult »p. 131. Idolatry »p. 433. Repentance »p. 780. Remnant »p. 427.

INSIGHT

"Foolish prophets" (13:3). The Heb. is *nabal*, a spiritual rather than intellectual trait. It is used of the arrogant and irreligious. The false prophets were not simply wrong, but willfully so.

"Whitewash" (13:10). A true prophet should point out cracks in the moral and spiritual wall which is any people's only reliable protection (v. 5). The false prophets, however, were busy slapping whitewash, covering up the flaws that portended disaster. People still try to make pretty the outside to disguise inner flaws and corruption. But when the storm of judgment comes and the walls collapse, no one cares about whitewash! Never mind how spiritual you appear to others. Care only about the reality of your relationship with the Lord.

Cloth bands and veils (13:17-23). Archeologists have found Mesopotamian texts on magic and sorcery that describe practices mentioned here. For instance, barley bread (v. 19) was used by Hittite and Syrian sorcerers in divination, and as elements in pagan sacrificial rituals. The intrinsic evil of occult practices is seen in its impact: these women disheartened the righteous, and encouraged the wicked to keep on doing evil.

Idols in the heart (14:3). The Heb. reads literally "have brought up their idols upon their hearts." Moses' Law commanded that God's words and laws "are to be upon your hearts" (Deut. 6:6). The phrase in Ezekiel means simply that the elders of the Exile were committed to idolatry.

And then goes to inquire of Me (14:7). God's answer to any who are committed to their idols and yet dare to seek His guidance is a powerful, personal word—of judgment. Never expect good from God unless committed to Him.

Righteous men (14:12-20). The allusion is to Abraham's intercession for Sodom (Gen. 18). God promised to spare the wicked cities of the plain if only 10 righteous men could be found within them (v. 32). The story generated the belief that God would not judge if a few righteous men could be found to pray for the rest. But the presence of three of history's most righteous men could not save Judah.

Two interesting notes. Daniel was already a legend in his own time and is listed as one of the three! This supports the traditional view that the Book of Daniel was written in the time of the Exile, not the second century B.C. as critics claim. Also, the paragraph contains a theme developed in Ezek. 18. In the coming disaster God will spare righteous individuals, but not the wicked.

Outline
Place
Finder

JUDAH
NATIONS
RESTORATION
TEMPLE

Chapter summary. Another source of Judah's confidence was rooted in the conviction that the Jews were God's chosen people. But, the prophet points out, they were chosen to be a righteous people. Instead they have become like a vine that produces no grapes, which men burn because it is useless (15:1-8). As for God's choice, history reveals it was a product of pure grace. The first ancestors of God's people were utter pagans (16:1-5). Like a newborn child they were cast out to die, but God rescued and nurtured them (vv. 6-7). Later God chose to "marry" this orphaned child and enriched her beyond measure (vv. 8-14). In return the "chosen people" became a spiritual and moral prostitute, abandoning God in unbridled passion for idolatry and immorality (vv. 15-34). Being a "chosen people" thus makes the judgment of Judah more certain! Like any who commit adultery and shed blood, she is sentenced to death (vv. 35-43). Indeed, Judah is more perverted than others in history who have suffered divine judgment (vv. 44-58). Yet despite all this, after "I deal with you as you deserve," God will recall His people and make a new, unbreakable covenant with them (vv. 59-63). And, lest Ezekiel's generation objects that they are being punished for the sins of their ancestors, Ezekiel sets forth an allegory (17:1-10). Judah's present king, Zedekiah, ignored God's word to submit to Babylon (the first eagle), rebelled, and reached out toward Egypt (the second eagle) (vv. 11-21). Thus this generation too sinned, so God's judgment was fair. Yet ultimately God Himself will replant His people in the Promised Land (vv. 22-24).

Key verse. 16:47: The chosen can be worse than the rejected!

Personal application. High privilege brings responsibility.

Key concepts. Covenant »pp. 32, 35, 62. Prostitution »p. 135.

INSIGHT

The useless vine (15:1-8). The most important thing about being chosen by God is to realize what we have been *chosen for*.

"Live!" (16:6) In ancient times girl children were frequently unwanted, and were "exposed." That is, they were simply thrown out on the rubbish heap to die. Being "chosen" was not to be a source of pride for Judah, but rather a reminder of how gracious God is. He takes the worthless and the unwanted, and not only calls out, "Live!" but makes the unlovely beautiful.

"Prostitution" (16:15-19). Against the background of God's grace, the persistent unfaithfulness of Judah is inexplicable, and terrible. Unlike the normal prostitute who collects a fee for her adulteries, Judah actually pays the pagan partners of her spiritual prostitution (vv. 32-33). The prophet's point is powerfully driven home. The Jews *were* God's chosen people. But this only makes her actions more reprehensible and

judgment more certain (vv. 35-43).

Three sisters (16:44-58). Ezekiel likens three cities to three sisters who have chosen a lifestyle of prostitution. Sodom was destroyed by fire from heaven (Gen. 18–19). Samaria, the capital of the northern Heb. kingdom, Israel, was destroyed by the Assyrians and her people taken captive. How could Jerusalem, which is worse than the others, hope to escape?

Not on the basis of My covenant (16:59-63). God was committed by covenant to the Jewish people, so the restoration of Jerusalem is assured. But God will go beyond this, and make an atonement so effective it will reclaim foreign nations as well! The shame to be experienced by God's covenant people is rooted in the magnitude of the grace they rejected.

Eagles (17:1-8). The eagle frequently symbolizes divine power, but especially God's power exercised in judgment (cf. Deut. 28:49).

Chapter summary. Ezekiel answers another objection of the obstinate exiles. If God did punish Judah, it would be for the forefathers' sin. So there was nothing they could do (18:1-4). In response God underlines a basic biblical truth. Each person is responsible for his or her own actions, as demonstrated in three illustrations (vv. 5-9, 10-13, 14-18). A stunning application follows. In the coming invasion, the "soul that sins" (i.e., the person who sins) is the one who will die. Conversely, the person who is righteous and does righteousness will live! This ruling is carefully explained (vv. 19-24), and then the Jews' charge that "the way of the Lord is not just" is confronted directly. Righteousness and unrighteousness are not inherited, but each is an individual choice. It is Israel that is unfair in applying the concept to moral issues (vv. 25-29). A final plea is addressed to individuals: "Repent, and live" (vv. 30-32).

Outline
Place
Finder

JUDAH
NATIONS
RESTORATION
TEMPLE

Key verse. 18:20: Each man is judged for his own acts.

Personal application. Accept responsibility for your own acts, for you and I are responsible.

Key concepts. Wickedness »pp. 29, 350. Righteousness »p. 413. Sin »pp. 34, 362. Guilt »p. 79. Death »p. 741.

INSIGHT

The proverb (18:2). The saying takes a fatalistic point of view, implying the "crooked teeth" of children result from their parents' actions. Thus if something bad happens to their generation, it will be a result of others' choices and there is nothing they can do about it! The saying misapplies Ex. 20:5, which teaches that children tend to follow the example set by parents. There is no implication in that O.T. saying about "punishing the children for the sins of the fathers to the third and fourth generation" that the children's own acts are not the basis of the punishment!

"Soul" (18:4). The saying "the soul that sins is the one who will die" has been frequently misunderstood. The Heb. word "soul" (*nephesh*) is frequently used as a reflexive pronoun, standing for "the person himself." And "death" here is physical, not a euphemism for eternal punishment. What Ezekiel is saying is that in the coming invasion God will so order things that wicked persons will be killed, while He will preserve the life of the righteous. Thus Ezekiel answers the complaint, "It makes no difference what we do," by affirming, "It makes a life or death difference!"

Three examples (18:5-18). The illustration of a righteous father, wicked son, and righteous grandson has historic roots. Godly King Hezekiah had a wicked son, Manasseh, who fathered the righteous King Josiah.

The principle explained (18:19-24). Ezekiel makes several points. (1) When anyone lived by Moses' Law, he would survive (v. 19). (2) The unrighteous sinner would die physically (v. 20a). (3) No father or son will be punished for the other's sins (v. 20b). (4) Each lived or died by his own choices (v. 20c). (5) The wicked has hope, if he turns to God and does righteousness (vv. 21-22). (6) God takes pleasure in the wicked man's repentance, not in his punishment (v. 23).

Accountability. Most O.T. passages on accountability focus, as does Ezek. 18, on the concept that God sees mankind's actions or orders appropriate consequences, either through natural or supernatural means (cf. 2 Chron. 24:20-26; Ps. 10:15; Ezek. 23:35). In general these consequences are to be expected in this life, with an eternal balancing of accounts implied but not explained. The N.T., however, shifts the focus to the future, relocating the point at which man will be held accountable.

All will give an account at "the day of judgment" (Matt. 12:36; Rom. 14:12; etc.). Choices we make now have eternal, not just temporal, results.

God's pleasure (18:30-32). Some have assumed that since God had ordained judgment, He must be cruel and vindictive. Not so. God takes pleasure in repentance. He judges those who will not repent, because He must.

Outline
Place
Finder

JUDAH
NATIONS
RESTORATION
TEMPLE

Chapter summary. The exile's last hope was that Zedekiah could be trusted to throw off the Babylonian yoke. Ezekiel now demolishes that in a funeral dirge chanted over Judah's leaders. The cubs of the lioness who represents David's royal line have proven ineffective. Jehoahaz was taken bound to Egypt and died there (19:1-4). Jehoiachin was caged by Nebuchadnezzar and taken captive to Babylon (vv. 5-9). Shifting images, the vine Zedekiah is destined to be uprooted and burned (vv. 10-14). The leaders of God's people are *not* reliable, for the nation's history is marked by rebellion. They rebelled in Egypt (20:1-9), in the wilderness (vv. 10-26), following the Conquest (vv. 27-29), and persist in Judah of Ezekiel's day. One day God's grace will prove irresistible, and then His people will be ashamed (vv. 30-44). But now a forest fire of judgment will roar down on Jerusalem (20:45–21:7). The leaders have despised God's acts of discipline and now will be slaughtered (vv. 8-17). When the Babylonians hesitate between attacking Judah and Ammonite territory, God will see to it the omens they consult bring them to Jerusalem (vv. 18-27). Judgment on Ammon can wait. But judgment on Judah can tarry no more (vv. 28-32).

Key verse. 21:13: It's dangerous not to learn from discipline.

Personal application. Deliberate disobedience assures discipline.

Key concepts. Law »pp. 120, 145. Rebellion »p. 101. Babylon »p. 302. Judge »p. 372.

INSIGHT

Why? (20:2-7) Why wouldn't the Lord even let the elders of the exiles ask Him a question through the prophet? The time of judgment for the "detestable practices" that marked Israel's history had arrived. We can look back at our choices and see the direction in which they tend. If the tendency has been and still is toward evil, we have reason to fear. If the tendency has been and still is toward good, we can have hope.

"Confront" (20:4). It is important to know why judgment falls. If we listen, we can avoid it. If we do not, we can at least later admit that God was just and right.

Why 400 years? (20:8-9) Here (and only here) the O.T. indicates that the great length of time the Hebrew people spent in Egypt as slaves was due to their adoption of the gods of Egypt as idols.

A pattern. The chapter repeats a pattern in Israel's relationship with God. God blessed, His people rebelled, and God judged them in order to cause a return. We can establish a better pattern in our relationship with God today. God blesses. We can respond with thanks

and obedience. And keep on being blessed.

"Never happen" (20:32-38). Judgment isn't a sign God has abandoned. It is evidence that He keeps on being committed to us. Israel *wanted* to desert God and serve pagan deities (v. 32). God says "Never." His love is greater than all our sin. We can stray, but God will bring us back to Him.

"Afterward" (20:39). The emphasis seen earlier in Ezek. 12 is repeated here. After God has judged, then His people will recognize their sin and His grace and be ashamed. How tragic that some insist on waiting till "afterward" to confess sins and accept the forgiving grace of our God.

The parable (20:45-49). Ezekiel's parable of a forest fire sweeping southward is dismissed as "just a story." The prophet provides God's blunt commentary. Not a "story," but reality, for Jerusalem lies south of Babylon and the exiles.

"O profane and wicked prince" (21:25). There is no hope for the Jews in Zedekiah, last in a line of wicked leaders. Judah and he must prepare for judgment.

Chapter summary. Ezekiel now concludes his stern messages concerning the certainty of Judah's imminent judgment. Jerusalem (22:1-5) and Judah's rulers (vv. 6-12) have deliberately violated God's commands (vv. 13-16). The city is destined to become a refiner's furnace, heated white-hot to purify its people (vv. 17-22). Religious authorities are unjust and greedy; priests disregard God's instructions for holy living; the political leaders ("officials," Heb. *sarim*) misuse their power for personal gain; and the people have followed their lead (vv. 23-31). In an extended allegory Ezekiel accuses Israel's leaders of leading God's people into political as well as spiritual adultery, in seeking security through alliances with pagan world powers rather than in the Lord (23:1-4). The charge was true of the Northern Kingdom, represented by her capital, Samaria (vv. 5-10), and it is true of the South, represented by Jerusalem (vv. 11-35). God will surely judge the twin nations for their prostitution and commitment to violence rather than to good (vv. 36-49).

Outline
Place
Finder

JUDAH
NATIONS
RESTORATION
TEMPLE

Key verses. 23:48-49: Stop, or be stopped!

Personal application. Imitate the godly among your leaders, not the wicked.

Key concepts. Violence »p. 29. Justice »p. 541. Exile »p. 138. Poor »p. 90. Adultery »p. 85. Assyria »p. 255. God's anger »p. 65.

INSIGHT

Three themes (22:1-31). Three themes are developed in this chapter. The first is that Judah's behavior proves Jerusalem's people have violated the Mosaic code (vv. 1-16). The second is that judgment displays the people's impurity (vv. 17-22). The third is that Judah's moral flaw runs through every strata of her society (vv. 23-31). The second is perhaps the most interesting.

Just as the hot fires of the smelter's furnace cause the dross to come to the surface and reveal the purified silver, so in times of divine judgment human beings are driven to act according to their character. The selfish become more cruel and self-centered; the godly more compassionate and caring. Remember this when troubles come to you, and let the fires of God's judgment on society bring out the best in you!

Society's collapse (22:7-12). Whenever the attitudes detailed here appear in a society, it is near collapse. What are the signs? The undermining of parental authority (v. 7a). Injustices that take advantage of the poor and helpless (v. 7b). Indifference of leaders to the best interests of those they rule, as well as indifference to the things of God (v. 8). A legal reign of terror, including murders (v. 9a). Leaders

engaging in sex sins (vv. 9b-11) and seeking illicit personal profit (v. 12).

When any society forgets God and strays from its spiritual foundations, its leadership will become corrupt and the nation will ultimately fall. Where is our society today? Apply Ezekiel's criteria and decide for yourself.

"I looked for a man" (22:30). Never underestimate the power of an individual to affect the future of his or her nation.

Two sisters (23:1-49). The Northern Kingdom is called *Oholah*, which means "her tent," a possible reference to the illicit worship centers set up at Dan and Bethel. The Southern Kingdom is called *Oholibah*, "My tent is in her," probably a reference to the fact that God's temple was in Jerusalem, the capital of the South. Both sisters were spiritual and political prostitutes, and both were destined to be judged.

God's judgment (23:48-49). God has four purposes in judging His sinning people. To end wickedness in the land; to instruct other nations of the consequences of unrighteousness; to punish the two wicked cities; to bring Israel and Judah to a saving knowledge of the Lord.

Chapter summary. On the very day that Nebuchadnezzar began his siege of Jerusalem, in Dec./Jan. 589/588 B.C., Ezekiel is told to speak a final word to the Jewish exiles in Babylon (24:1-2). He speaks a poetic parable about a cooking pot (vv. 3-5), which represents Jerusalem. Its inhabitants are due to be "boiled" in the fires of the Babylonian siege (vv. 6-8). The intense heat will sear the meat off the bones and char them, and the empty pot will be heated red-hot till it is cleansed of impurities (vv. 9-14).

Then God warns Ezekiel of a crushing personal blow. His beloved wife is to die, and Ezekiel is permitted only silent groans. This is totally contrary to Old Testament funeral practices, which featured loud wailings and passionate expressions of grief (vv. 15-17). His wife does die, and the heartbroken Ezekiel responds to his loss as God commanded (v. 18). Ezekiel explains that he is a sign. Soon the delight of the exiles' eyes—the Jerusalem temple, and their relatives there—will be destroyed too. They will groan within, for it will then be clear the city fell because of their own sins (vv. 19-24). Ezekiel is struck dumb then (cf. 3:24-27), to remain silent until word comes from Judah that his predictions have been fulfilled. Thus God's people will know that all that has happened is from the Lord (24:25-27).

Key verse. 24:16: When God judges, all suffer.

Personal application. Don't suppose the believer is immune to pain when God judges a sinful society.

INSIGHT

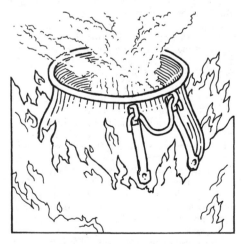

Illustration. *The cauldron of Ezekiel's parable (24:1-14) is a sir, usually a pottery cooking pot. Verse 11 tells us this pot is copper: it will be heated till its metal glows without cracking, and all the meat within will be seared till even the bones are charred. The image is one of the total destruction of Jerusalem's inhabitants and the purification by fire of the Holy City's site.*

Ezekiel's wife (24:15-17). Ezekiel's grim words to the exiles convey the image of a stern, strong, unyielding and almost insensitive person. Ezekiel utters none of Jeremiah's cries of deep personal anguish. With set face he stoically carries out God's commands. And then one brief phrase reveals a very different inner man. His wife is the one in whom his eyes delight. With her his deepest human feelings are expressed. And now she is to be taken away. We learn three lessons here. Don't be misled by a stern visage about the sensitivity of the inner man. Don't ever suppose that the believer is immune from suffering. And don't imagine that pain excuses a person from obeying the Lord. Ezekiel hurt. But he obeyed.

A sign (24:20-24). What was the meaning of Ezekiel's strange reaction to his wife's death? As a "sign" he modeled the experience of the citizens of Jerusalem. The disaster would be so great, the dead so many, that the people would be stunned with grief, unable even to honor the dead with the appropriate rites.

The prophet's silence will end (24:25-27). It took about three months to travel from Jerusalem to Babylon. Thus about three months after the city's fall, a messenger would arrive, and then Ezekiel would speak again. As we will see, the messages of his later days were filled with hope!

Chapter summary. This chapter begins a different collection of the Prophet Ezekiel's messages, addressed against foreign nations. The collection extends from chapters 25–33. The messages were given at different times, and are unified here by their common theme rather than by chronology. The first, brief oracles (messages announcing judgment) are spoken against Judah's near neighbors, Ammon (Ezek. 25:1-7), Moab (vv. 8-11), Edom (vv. 12-14), and Philistia (vv. 15-17). Then Ezekiel launches an extended judgment oracle against Tyre (26:1-6), to be carried out by Nebuchadnezzar of Babylon (vv. 7-14). Tyre's allies will tremble at this dominant city's fall (vv. 15-18). The city will "die," never to "live" again, as its site is left forever a barren rock (vv. 19-21).

Outline
Place
Finder

JUDAH
NATIONS
RESTORATION
TEMPLE

Key verse. 25:3: Treat God's people right!

Personal application. God's moral governance extends to pagan nations as well as His own people.

Key concepts. Judge »p. 372. Covenant »p. 32. War »p. 133. Moabites »p. 476. Edomites »p. 104. Philistines »p. 185. Babylon »p. 302.

INSIGHT

Judgment oracles (25:1-17). Each follows the same pattern. There is an introduction, an indictment, and a verdict. The basis of the judgment on nearby nations is found in Gen. 12:3, which warns that those who curse Abraham's descendants will be cursed by God.

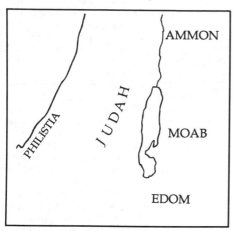

"Ammon" (25:1-7). In O.T. thought rejoicing over the misfortune of another is the same as having a part in causing it (cf. Prov. 17:5). Ammon is thus guilty and God's verdict is passed against them. Josephus says that Ammon and Moab both fell to Babylon five years after the fall of Jerusalem.

Tyre. The extensive oracle against Tyre extends from chaps. 26–28. Chapter 26 predicts Tyre's destruction. In Ezekiel's time Tyre was a master trader, whose ships traveled the Mediterranean and whose colonies dotted its shores. The city, part on an island protected by her fleet and part on the mainland, was fabulously wealthy. Yet the people of Tyre were enthusiastic about the fall of Jerusalem, seeing it as an opportunity to further increase its own wealth. This was not only because Tyre expected to gain commissions from the sale of much of the Holy City's spoil, but also because Judah had controlled the important land trade routes in the area. Tyre, just 35 miles from the Sea of Galilee and 100 miles from Jerusalem, expected that more of the land routes' income would swell her own coffers.

Tyre's destruction (26:7-14). Ezekiel predicts that Nebuchadnezzar will begin a process that will result in the utter devastation of Tyre. Verses 7-11, using the pronoun "he," describe the Babylonian assault. The pronoun shift to "they" in v. 12 speaks of later assaults against the proud city.

Over 150 years after Ezekiel uttered his prophecy against Tyre, Alexander the Great literally demolished the mainland city and threw "your stones, timber and rubble into the sea," making a causeway out to the island fortress! And so Tyre fell, and its site has remained barren rock to this day.

Chapter summary. Ezekiel's prediction of the endless death of Tyre (26:1-21) is followed by messages about the doomed city. First comes a funeral dirge, picturing the great commercial center as a merchant ship. The prophet describes her construction (27:1-11) and then lists her trading partners (vv. 12-24). This passage gives the clearest of all antiquity's portraits of the geography, sea trade routes, and trade goods of the era. The prophet completes his metaphor with a vivid description of the sinking of richly laden Tyre (vv. 25-36). Ezekiel then relates God's word concerning the "ruler" of Tyre (28:1-10), which he follows with a funeral dirge celebrating the fate of a "king" of Tyre (vv. 11-19). Many take the shift from "ruler" to "king" to indicate a shift of prophetic focus from a literal ruler to a being he typifies, Satan. This interpretation, though uncertain, is popular with some commentators. God's words concerning Tyre conclude with a message directed against Sidon (vv. 20-24) and a typical promise that Israel will be restored to her land (vv. 25-26).

Key verse. 27:27: Prosperity does not last.

Personal application. Any success that breeds arrogance is sure to be followed by a fall.

Key concepts. Wealth »pp. 124–125. Interpretation of prophecy »pp. 406–408. Regathering »p. 419.

INSIGHT

The ship's song (27:1-36). The extended metaphor in this poetic description of Tyre and her fall is one of the most powerful to be found in ancient or modern literature. The funeral dirge sums up the world's preoccupation with material wealth and prosperity and the pride success breeds. The sudden sinking of the ship not only portrays the demise of Tyre, but the vulnerability of all material possessions to destruction. The last two verses particularly display the anguish of those who pin their hopes on things—only to see them suddenly, irretrievably gone.

Real wisdom? (28:1-10) The ruler of Tyre had "great skill in trading" and so amassed great wealth. But success produced an arrogance that demands divine judgment. Real wisdom acknowledges God as the source of every blessing and values relationship with Him above material gain.

Does "king of Tyre" refer to Satan? (28:11-29) It seems most natural to take this poem as a repetition, for emphasis, of Ezekiel's critique of the fall of earthly Tyre and its human rulers. Yet many see the passage as addressed indirectly to Satan. Why? (1) The description "model of perfection," and "blameless . . . from the day I created you" seems an inappropriate description of any human ruler. (2) "Eden, the garden of God"

is described as the gem-filled center of earthly rule, and is taken as the province of Satan before Adam's creation. (3) "A guardian cherub" again is hardly an appropriate description of a pagan king. But it would fit Satan's prefall role as an important angelic being. (4) "Till wickedness was found in you" does not fit the doctrine of human depravity, but seems to indicate a specific act of sin which corrupted the being described. (5) "I expelled you . . . I threw you to earth" seems to fit Christ's words about Satan's expulsion from heaven, as recorded in Luke 10:18. While these same verses admit metaphorical and poetic interpretation references to the human rulers of Tyre, those who see Satan in this passage believe they are more appropriately rooted to him.

In opposition, one commentator states that "each characteristic given about [the king] in these verses can be explained in light of the cultural and religious context of that day."

"Sidon" (28:20-23). This coastal city was a sister to Tyre and also a commercial center.

Israel's return (28:25-26). The brief message reminds the exiles that God, who has punished Judah for her sins, will restore His people at history's end, when He completes judgment on pagan nations.

Satan

The Bible presents Satan as a powerful being who is the active enemy of God. The Hebrew word *satan* means "adversary," as does the Greek *satanas*. This creature's fierce hostility toward human beings is seen first in Genesis, where he is seen as the agent influencing Eve to disobey God's command. Thus he was an instrument in that sin which unleashed sin's corrupting power on our race. Christ calls Satan "the evil one" (Matt. 13:19, 38) and graphically portrays his character (John 8:44; 1 John 3:8). His hostility toward human beings is shown in causing physical suffering (Job 1:11-22; Luke 13:16; 2 Cor. 12:7), in blinding men to the Gospel (Matt. 13:19; 2 Cor. 4:3-4), and in opposing God's saints (Eph. 6:11-18; 1 Peter 5:8; 1 Thes. 2:18).

Jesus described him as the leader of rebel angels who joined in a primeval revolt against God, for which he was banished from heaven. Though many are unwilling to apply Ezekiel 28:12-15 and Isaiah 14:12-14 to Satan, the hints in these passages of a once-perfect and powerful being, who fell through pride, is in harmony with John 8:44's indication that Satan is a fallen angel.

The New Testament portrays confrontations between Jesus and Satan or his minions (Matt. 4:1-11; Luke 11:14-22; 13:10-11). It describes the Cross as a decisive defeat for the devil (Col. 2:15): God's final victory is guaranteed. At history's end Satan will rouse mankind to a final, futile effort to defeat God (2 Thes. 2:9; Rev. 12:7-12). He will be defeated and doomed forever (Matt. 25:41; Rev. 20:1-3).

Outline
Place
Finder

JUDAH
NATIONS
RESTORATION
TEMPLE

Chapter summary. Ezekiel moves on to an extensive series of oracles (announcements of judgment) directed against Egypt. Egypt had urged Judah to rebel against Babylon, but had failed to support her. Pharaoh will fall (29:1-6), the Egyptians will be scattered by the Babylonians (vv. 7-16), and Nebuchadnezzar will loot the land (vv. 17-21). Nebuchadnezzar's successful invasion of Egypt (30:1-19) will break Pharaoh's power (vv. 20-26), even as the Babylonian's crushed Assyria (31:1-18). The series concludes with a funeral dirge for Egypt (32:1-16) and a final lament (vv. 17-32).

Key verses. 29:6-7: Egypt's judgment is explained.

Personal application. Pride causes even nations to fall.

Key concepts. Egypt »p. 420. Babylon »p. 302. War »p. 133. Day of the Lord »p. 413.

INSIGHT

Background. Egypt and Tyre were allies in this era. Egyptian support of Tyre lengthened the siege of that city to some 13 years. During this time Tyre exported her wealth by sea, so when the city fell in 573 B.C. there was no way for Nebuchadnezzar to recover his military expenses. As God had condemned Tyre (cf. chaps. 26–28), the Lord through Ezekiel promises Egypt to the Babylonians. The wealth of Egypt would be forfeited to Nebuchadnezzar. One partial text from Nebuchadnezzar's archives indicates Babylon invaded Egypt in 568/567 B.C., though no complete records of such an expedition have been translated as yet.

A crocodile (29:2-5). This image of Pharaoh, who as her ruler represents Egypt, is appropriate. The animal dominated the Nile, and the crocodile god, Sebek, was considered Egypt's protector.

"Captivity" (29:8-16). If Egypt fell in 568 B.C. (see above), any captives would have been released in the Persian period, as were Judah's.

Head rubbed bare and shoulder made raw (29:18). The reference is to injuries caused by carrying heavy loads and symbolizes the burden borne by the Babylonians of an unrewarded 13-year siege.

A horn for Israel (29:21). In the O.T. a "horn" represents strength, or leadership, and frequently the Messiah. Here it represents the strengthening of Judah's rekindled hope, as the people see God's faithfulness in carrying out Ezekiel's prediction against Egypt, and listen to his fresh prophecies of the Jews own restoration to their homeland.

"People of the covenant land" (30:5). Jews are among those to fall with Egypt before Babylon. How can this be? Second Kings 25:23-26 describes how the last Jews left in Judea after the destruction of Jerusalem fled to Egypt when their governor, Gedaliah, was assassinated.

Broken arms (30:20-26). The message is directed against Pharaoh Hophra, who in 588 B.C. had halfheartedly tried to draw Babylonian forces away from the siege of Jerusalem (cf. Jer. 34:1; 37:5). Egyptian monuments show a flexed arm was a symbol of Pharaoh's strength, and one of Hophra's formal titles was "strong-armed." With both arms broken, Pharaoh would be totally unable to resist.

The cedar (31:1-9). The magnificent tree represents Assyria, the most powerful empire of history until recent times. Proud Egypt, like Assyria (v. 2), was destined to fall. The point is that God, who brought down Assyria, is certainly able to fell Egypt.

The funeral dirge (32:1-16). The exiles in Babylon had recently learned of Jerusalem's fall when Ezekiel chanted this dirge in March of 585 B.C. Egypt had witnessed the fall of Judah and may have felt proud of her own survival. Ezekiel, however, pictures that great southern land as already dead. God has condemned her, and none of her many gods will be able to help.

The message against Egypt recapitulated (32:17-32). This final prophecy, uttered in April of 585 B.C., sums up God's word concerning contemporary Egypt and concludes Ezekiel's messages concerning foreign nations.

Chapter summary. Ezekiel has fulfilled his commission as a watchman. He has warned the people of Judah (chaps. 4–24). The judgment that struck them was no fault of the watchman, but their own fault for failing to listen. Now Ezekiel has another warning. Each exile must turn from evil, for God "will judge each of you according to his own ways" (33:1-20).

Outline
Place
Finder

JUDAH
NATIONS
RESTORATION
TEMPLE

The disaster Ezekiel predicted has happened, and Jerusalem is fallen. The prophet has also delivered his oracles condemning foreign nations. Now his book turns to the issue of Israel's restoration to the Promised Land. The theme of God's covenant promise of Canaan to Abraham is introduced with a word to the scattered Jews left in the land after Jerusalem's devastation. They think that promise means they are secure, despite their own sinful lifestyles (vv. 21-26). But God intends to make the land a desolate waste because of them, and they will die (vv. 27-29). When the exiles see the homeland devastated and empty, they will realize "that a prophet has been among them" (vv. 30-33). God's promises cannot be claimed by the wicked.

Key verse. 33:20: It's an individual choice.

Personal application. Be a faithful witness. Why be responsible for the condemnation of others?

Key concepts. Wicked »p. 350. Covenant »pp. 32, 35. Prophet »p. 131.

INSIGHT

Accountability for others (33:1-9). Ezekiel 18 emphasizes that each individual is responsible for his or her own moral/spiritual choices. Here the faithful Ezekiel, who has been a faithful watchman in warning his fellow-countrymen, is reminded that he must still stand his lonely vigil. It is up to him to warn others of the danger of wickedness, and to urge reform. How an individual responds is up to him. This principle establishes our limited responsibility for others. Their choices are expressions of their own free will, not determined by heredity or environment. But those who know the truth are responsible to share it, so the choices others make can be informed rather than blind.

Save yourself? (33:9) Ezekiel's warnings here and in chap. 18 threatened physical death for those who persisted in disobeying God. If the prophet had failed to fulfill his commission, he would have become one of the disobedient, and thus subject to physical death himself.

Repentance (33:14-16). Ezekiel's warnings are invitations. So it is with every threat of divine punishment. God does not want us to fear, but to repent. The past will be wiped out, and we can look ahead to a fresh, new life.

"Not just" (33:20). The image is of a set of balancing scales used to weigh grain. The Heb. verb trans. "not just" means "out of adjustment." But God's scales are just: each individual's acts will be carefully and accurately weighed by God.

"The land" (33:23-29). God promised Canaan to Abraham, so those of his descendants left after Jerusalem's destruction now rely on their supposed claim to the covenant promises (Gen. 12). But that promise is to be fulfilled at history's end. Only by bonding to God in faith and obedience can any generation expect God's blessing in its own time. So God scornfully points out their sins (Ezek. 33:25-26) and announces He intends to purge them from the land and leave it desolate (vv. 27-29). Never assume that you can claim God's promises while you make a habit of sin.

"A beautiful voice" (33:30-32). The exiles of Ezekiel's day were "churchgoers." They made it a regular practice to come to the prophet, sit down, and listen to his words. But to them the prophet's eloquent speech was only entertainment! They did not come to hear, and then put into practice, the word of their God. What a reminder for us today. Do we go to church to see friends, listen to the choir, and enjoy the preacher's jokes? Or do we go to hear God's Word and take it to heart?

Chapter summary. While each individual is responsible for his or her moral/spiritual choices, the leaders who set the tone of a society are accountable as well. In this powerful chapter Ezekiel presents God's indictment of his people's "shepherds" — their political and spiritual leadership (34:1-6). As is typical in legal cases, the accusation is repeated (vv. 7-8) just before the divine verdict is announced. God will remove the leaders and hold them accountable (vv. 9-10). Then, to encourage His people, the Lord looks ahead and promises a day in which He Himself will shepherd His flock. He will regather Israel, restore them to pastures in their own land, and will heal the weak (vv. 11-16b). The Lord will establish justice and "David," the promised Messiah to come from his line, will tend them (vv. 16c-24). When God executes His covenant of peace, Israel will rest secure in its own land, and be fully restored to personal relationship with Him (vv. 25-31).

Key verse. 34:10: Leadership is an awesome responsibility.

Personal application. Leadership involves putting others first.

Key concepts. Sheep »p. 355. Shepherd »p. 355. Regathering »p. 419. Messiah »p. 432. Interpreting prophecy »pp. 407–408.

INSIGHT

Human "shepherds" (34:1-6). The shepherd metaphor for leaders was common in the ancient East. This passage helps us understand the role of the leaders of God's people. Each accusation found here implies a positive trait which we should look for in those who function as leaders in the church. The condemned traits in these verses are: *taking care of themselves rather than the sheep *profiting from those being led, without taking care of them *actually harming those being led *failing to strengthen the weak *failing to seek the lost *ruling harshly and brutally. Each trait is in total contrast with the model of ideal spiritual leadership we have in Christ, the "Good Shepherd" (John 10). It is His character and His commitment to others we have a right to expect in human spiritual leaders (1 Peter 5:1-4).

Interpreting Ezekiel (33:1–39:29). These chapters look forward to a restoration of God's people to the Promised Land. The unresolved question is, what restoration is in view? Some see these chapters as allegories, that point to the spiritual blessings that are ours in this, the Church Age. Some think all Ezekiel was speaking of is the return that took place under the Persians, which is described in Ezra and Neh. "David" is Zerubbabel, who was of the royal line and served as civil governor of the little community. Others believe Ezekiel is speaking of a yet future return of Israel asso-

ciated with the second coming of Jesus the Messiah. Any reading of these passages which respects the plain sense of the text leads to the conclusion that Ezekiel's prophecies are as yet unfulfilled.

"My servant David" (34:24). This phrase is used regularly by the prophets to indicate the promised Messiah (cf. Jer. 23:5-6; 30:9; Ezek. 37:24-25; Hosea 3:5). Thus the ultimate restoration of Israel to her land and the age of peace and justice is clearly linked with Messiah's appearance. As these predictions were not fulfilled during Jesus' life on earth, they are usually related to His second coming.

Trinity in the O.T.? The passage promises that God Himself will shepherd His people (34:11-16), and also that Messiah will be their "one Shepherd" (v. 23). By implication both the Lord who speaks and the coming Descendant of David are God.

The covenant of peace (34:25). This covenant is mentioned here and in 37:26-28; 39:25-29. It is not the same as the New Covenant, but will be initiated after the New is fulfilled. Under it God will remove foreign nations, shower blessings on Israel and her land, and guarantee complete security. At that time God's people will realize He is the Lord, and the people will be totally dedicated to His ways.

Outline
Place
Finder

JUDAH
NATIONS
RESTORATION
TEMPLE

Chapter summary. Ezekiel continues his vision of the future. When God institutes His covenant of peace (34:25), He will remove the foreign oppressors, represented by Edom (35:1-15). The chapter follows a familiar pattern. God announces that He will judge Edom. He specifies the charge which justifies His verdict in verse 5, and expands it in verses 10-15. God continues with good news for the mountains of Israel. They have been trampled by foreign armies, and polluted with pagan shrines. Now the peoples who plundered them will suffer (36:1-7). And the land will again feel the footsteps of God's own people and know the bite of their plows (vv. 8-12). The empty land will be filled again—forever (vv. 13-15). God's people had been scattered because of their uncleanness and God's concern for His own holy name (vv. 16-21). Their return will further display God's holiness and greatness, for God will give the people He gathers "a new heart and a new spirit." Then they will keep His laws and live in the land. Only then will they be God's people and will the Lord be His people's God (vv. 22-32). And what consequences the cleansing and restoration of Israel will have! The land will become a paradise, the people increase, and knowledge of God will spread throughout the earth (vv. 33-38).

Key verse. 36:8: There is a sure future for Israel.

Personal application. Blessing follows discipline.

Key concepts. Edom »p. 104. Prophecy »p. 434. Regathering »p. 419. Future kingdom »p. 443.

INSIGHT

Edom (35:1-15). Edom was noted for long-term hostility toward Israel and Judah, a fact often noted by other prophets (Isa. 11:11-16; Dan. 11:41; Amos 2:1; Mal. 1:2-5). Here "Edom" stands for all nations who have acted like her. The specific accusations against foreign nations which call for divine judgment are: (1) hostility toward Israel (Ezek. 35:5), (2) a desire to possess the land (v. 10), (3) disrespect for God who gave His people the land (v. 10), and (4) refusal to submit to the Lord (v. 13).

A word to the land (36:1-12). This prophecy is addressed to the land rather than the exiles. Why? Ezekiel's intent is to encourage the exiles and assure them that God has not abandoned His people. None of the exiles would live to see these prophecies fulfilled, yet the land remains. And so God speaks to the land.

Israel's future according to Ezek. 36. After occupying nations are crushed, God promises: *He will prepare the land for Israel's return by making it fruitful (vv. 8-9). *He will bring back all Israel and create a populous, prosperous community (vv. 10-11). *He will keep His promise to Abraham complete, though that promise's

full expression has not been kept before (v. 12). *He will guarantee their permanent possession of the land, and never again will they be dispossessed.

Clean, unclean (36:16-23). In the Mosaic Law a person who was ritually unclean (»p. 82) was unable to participate in worship. Thus the concept of "clean" and "unclean" implied a state or condition which had a significant impact on relationship with God. The Law also extended the ritual concept of clean and unclean to moral acts (Lev. 16:30-31). Later the moral dimension was emphasized, as in Ps. 106:39. The prophets particularly saw in the idea of ritual uncleanness a powerful image of the inner defilement caused by sin. The people must be cleansed, for they were polluted by idolatry and wickedness (Jer. 2:23; Ezek. 20:7, 18, 30-31). This then is the background for God's word to the mountains of Israel. God's holiness required that His people be expelled from His land. But God's word to the land continues. God will cleanse His people, and when He does they will be restored to the Promised Land, and to their relationship with Him.

Outline
Place
Finder

JUDAH
NATIONS
RESTORATION
TEMPLE

Chapter summary. Ezekiel's predictions concerning the restoration of the Jewish exiles to the Promised Land continue. He is given a vision that pictures a staged process of return—a strange vision of dry bones scattered in a desolate valley (37:1-10)—which is then carefully explained (vv. 11-14). The prophet then goes on to describe the reunification of the people and nation under the messianic King (vv. 15-28). Then come a few brief verses that sum up the Old Testament's vision of the future of the Jewish people and of their ancient land. God says, "I will establish them and increase their numbers, and I will put My sanctuary among them forever. My dwelling place will be with them; I will be their God, and they will be My people. Then the nations will know that I the Lord make Israel holy, when My sanctuary is among them forever" (vv. 26-28).

Key verse. 37:23: There is one condition to be God's own.

Personal application. God unites people who share a common allegiance to the Saviour.

Key concepts. Regathering »p. 419. Holy Spirit »p. 759. King »p. 130. Messiah »p. 432. Davidic Covenant »p. 370. Temple »p. 283.

INSIGHT

The vision explained (37:11-14). The bones are identified as all Israel, dry and thus "dead" for a great period of time, and without hope of seeing God's covenant promises fulfilled. This is followed by a physical restoration which symbolizes national restoration, and a return to life which symbolizes spiritual restoration. The rest of the chapter is clearly a vision of history's end and the establishment of Messiah's kingdom.

The vision applied? This vision has fascinated Christians because of its obvious parallels with the recent history of the state of Israel. Prior to 1948 the Jewish people had no national homeland, but were scattered among most of the nations of the world. Despite the rise of Zionism early in this century, there seemed no hope that the Jews would ever again have a national identity, much less within the Promised Land. The holocaust intensified the conviction of many that only organization as a nation could offer security to any Jew. After a long struggle a tiny state was organized in a fraction of the territory once occupied by the mighty kingdom of David and Solomon. The little Jewish state fought for its very existence in those early years, and later in other wars with surrounding Arab states. Through those wars its land holding has gradually been expanded, though even today the nation remains small.

But Israel was organized as a secular rather than a religious state. Even though religious courts and parties are influenced, the nation is far from the theocracy envisioned in Scripture. To many, recent historic events in the Middle East seem to suggest a stunning fulfillment of Ezekiel's prediction that God's ancient people would be regathered to the land and live there as a nation without spiritual life.

Those who apply Ezek. 37 to recent events see the existence of Israel as an exciting indicator that the second coming of Jesus is drawing near. If this passage does speak of the present Jewish state, then the coming of the Messiah and the conversion of the nation must be drawing near!

When He does come, the rest of the prediction will find its fulfillment in a great turning to Christ as the Messiah for whom God's people have hoped through the ages. And then, at last, God's promises of restoration and blessing can be completely fulfilled.

One kingdom, one king (37:15-23). The promise refers to the unification of the Jewish people in a single nation. It reflects the division that isolated the North (Israel) from the South (Judah) for centuries in O.T. times.

Chapter summary. Ezekiel's last bold prophecy describes a foreign invasion of the Holy Land, thrown back only when God intervenes. This is the sixth and last of a series of messages delivered the night before the exiles received news of Jerusalem's fall. God's people have been restored to their land and live in peace (38:7) when armies attack from the north (vv. 1-16). The prophet's predictions of an aroused God who crushes Israel's enemies in a final, decisive battle at history's end, now come true, as the Lord uses the elemental forces of nature to crush the invaders (vv. 17-23). The destruction of the enemy is further developed in chapter 39. God, Israel's Holy One, defeats the enemy and so displays His commitment to Israel (39:1-8). The defeat is so great that it takes Israel years to dispose of the abandoned weaponry (vv. 9-10), and months of effort by the entire population to bury the dead and cleanse the land (vv. 11-16), even though scavenger animals and birds feast on the dead (vv. 17-20). The nations will recognize God's hand in the defeat (v. 21). Israel at last will know God, and that He who scattered them for their sins has now regathered them for His glory (vv. 22-29).

Outline
Place
Finder

JUDAH
NATIONS
RESTORATION
TEMPLE

Key verse. 38:8: Wars lie ahead till the very end.

Personal application. Whoever the final enemy is, our present help is God.

Key concepts. Prophecies of history's end »pp. 427–428, 443.

INSIGHT

Who are Gog, Magog, and the others? (38:1-3) This question has been studied and discussed extensively. No satisfying conclusion has been reached, and the most popular solutions are questionable at best. For instance, the Heb. word ro's (ro'sh) has often been taken as a proper name, indicating Russia. But the word is not used in a geographical sense elsewhere, but always means "head." The NIV rightly links it with nesi', and translates the two as a single phrase, "chief prince." All one can say is that the territorial references seem to suggest eastern Turkey and parts of Russia and Iran.

Gog's allies (38:5-6). These verses picture the enemy force being joined in their attack on Israel by peoples from other directions. Those that can be identified are Persia (Iran), Cush (Ethiopia, Africa), and Put (probably Libya).

God to drag out the enemy army? (38:1-6) God does not cause the hostility to Israel. But He does create conditions which lead them to express that hostility.

"Plunder and loot" (38:12). The more obvious motive for the attack is not theological but material. Peaceful Israel has wealth the enemy desires.

The destruction of God's enemies (38:17-23). While Gog is not referred to by name in other O.T. passages, there are many indications of a final battle in which Israel's enemies are destroyed by God. Among them are Deut. 30:7; Isa. 26:20-21; and Jer. 30:18-24. The direct intervention by God in a clearly supernatural way both vindicates His role as Judge of the universe, and His faithfulness to the ancient covenant promises given Abraham.

Does this passage describe a modern war? Many assume so and interpret the seven years it takes to "burn" the enemy weapons as the time it takes to dismantle and reclaim the metal in modern tanks and guns. Many also look for trends in international relationships that seem to them to portend increased hostility toward Israel on the part of Soviet Russia and the Arab nations. But it is always questionable to interpret current events with the fulfillment of Bible prophecy until *after* that fulfillment takes place. When what Ezekiel describes comes to pass, we will all be sure just what it is these chapters actually describe.

Outline
Place
Finder

JUDAH
NATIONS
RESTORATION
TEMPLE

Chapter summary. Thirteen years after Ezekiel uttered his promises of restoration (chaps. 33–39), he is given a culminating vision. He sees restored Israel, a holy nation ruled by God, whose glory will be resident in a magnificent new temple. This vision is reported in Ezekiel 40–48. The prophet gives the date and setting (40:1-4), and launches an extensive description of the restoration temple (40:5–42:20). In great detail he describes its outer (40:5-27) and inner courts (vv. 28-47), and the magnificent house of God that stands within them (40:48–41:26). He describes the priests' rooms in buildings just outside the inner court (42:1-14) and carefully establishes the measurements of the temple area (vv. 15-20). Then in his vision the prophet sees the glory of God return to take up residence in the temple (43:1-12). It is here that the first portion of his vision ends, for this is the entire point of the restoration temple. God's intent is to renew His Old Testament people, to make them holy, and to dwell among them. The temple is nothing more or less than an earthly focus for the essential presence of God.

Key verse. 43:7: God intends to be with His people.

Personal application. Nothing is more important to God than our personal relationship with Him.

Key concepts. Restoration »p. 419. Temple »p. 283. Glory »p. 74.

INSIGHT

Ezekiel's temple (40:1–48:35). The intent of these chapters is much debated. Some argue the vision relates to a smaller temple constructed by the returned exiles, or to Herod's grand construction. But nothing in history past matches the structure, liturgy, or topographic features emphasized in Ezekiel's vision. Others take the whole section as a grand allegory symbolizing the Church Age, while still others assume the passage is intended to portray the heavenly realities which every earthly temple mimicked. It is best, however, to understand it as the culmination of Ezekiel's earlier teaching concerning a restoration of Israel. That teaching is that God's O.T. people will be restored to the land. They will be spiritually renewed there and will be governed by God Himself. How appropriate then for Ezekiel to conclude his great prophetic work with a description of the residence of the God who has committed Himself to dwell among His people, and of the worship of God by a people who have at last been made holy and taken final possession of the Promised Land.

A literal approach? While some object to such a literal approach in interpreting this and other prophetic passages, there are abundant clues in the chapters themselves that this is intended. For instance, Ezekiel is told to write down details of the temple plan and worship regulations, to "inform the house of Israel," "so that they may be faithful to its design and follow all its regulations" (cf. 40:4; 43:10-11; 44:5). This same attention to detail was commanded for construction of the tabernacle (Ex. 25:9) and Solomon's temple (1 Chron. 28:19). Whatever the interpreters may say, it is clear that Ezekiel himself understood his vision and his instructions in a literal rather than allegorical way.

The return of God's glory (43:1-8). In chaps. 8–11 Ezekiel described the departure of God's "glory," that visible expression of His presence, from the temple Solomon had constructed. The withdrawal at that time symbolized God's temporary abandonment of His protection from the city and the Jewish people. Now Ezekiel sees that same "glory" coming back to Jerusalem and resting in the rebuilt temple. At last God has fully restored His relationship with the Jewish people, and the covenant promises given Abraham are truly fulfilled.

"That they may be ashamed" (43:10-12). Even prophecies which have a distant fulfillment are to have a contemporary impact. God intends the exiles to see His grace in the promise of restoration, and repent of their sins.

Chapter summary. Ezekiel's vision of the restoration temple continues with a description of its regulations and of the distribution of the Holy Land. Ezekiel describes a surprising feature of the future temple: it will have an altar of sacrifice (43:13-27). The east gate, through which God's glory entered, is to remain shut (44:1-3). In the temple a restored and holy priesthood (vv. 17-31), with Levites, will minister before the Lord (vv. 4-16). A special district will be set apart for the priests and the sanctuary (45:1-12), and sacrifices commemorating atonement will be made there (vv. 13-20). The leaders and people will gather to celebrate the great religious festivals established in the Old Testament's worship calendar (45:21–46:15), and none of God's people will be separated from his property (vv. 16-18). Ezekiel even describes the great kitchens where the priests' share of the holy offerings will be prepared for them (vv. 19-24).

Now Ezekiel describes the land itself and notes great topographical changes. A crystal river will flow from the temple and revitalize the land (47:1-12). The boundaries of the land are fixed (vv. 13-23), and each Hebrew tribe is allotted a portion (48:1-7, 23-29), with the center portion dedicated to the Lord (vv. 8-22). And there, in the Lord's portion, in the center of the Promised Land, is the restored Jerusalem, the city of the people and of the temple of God (vv. 30-35).

Key verse. 48:35: The city's name sums up its significance.

Personal application. It is always appropriate to celebrate what God has done for us.

Key concepts. Jerusalem »pp. 205, 451. Temple »p. 283. Sacrifice »pp. 28, 78, 84. Atonement »pp. 69, 739. Levites »p. 95.

INSIGHT

Why sacrifice? This is one of the strongest arguments against the view that Ezek. 40–48 describes a yet-future restoration of Israel under Jesus the Messiah. The problem is theologically based. Since Christ's one sacrifice won our salvation, what need would there be for further animal sacrifices? Even more, wouldn't such future sacrifices deny the salvation won for us by Jesus? Most of the worship practices seen here in Ezek. are similar to those in the Mosaic system, but certain offerings and sacrifices are omitted or modified. Perhaps most important, however, is the fact that O.T. sacrifices never cleansed from sin, but rather prefigured the sacrifice of Jesus.

It is not unlikely that the future sacrifices described here (and incidentally mentioned by other O.T. prophets, as Isa. 56:5-7; 60:7; 66:20-23; Jer. 33:15-22; Zech. 14:16-21) would serve to commemorate Jesus' finished work. Christ's death on the cross is the reality which underlies all sacrifice. If animal sacrifices in O.T. times looked forward to it, there seems to be no compelling reason why such sacrifices after Israel is restored to her land might not look back.

Outline
Place
Finder

JUDAH
NATIONS
RESTORATION
TEMPLE

Daniel

Daniel is a favorite book both of children and of students of biblical prophecy. As a young teen, Daniel was taken to Babylon from Judah by Nebuchadnezzar's forces, among the nobles exiled there in 605 B.C. The first half of the book relates events from Daniel's long life in Babylon, from his early training as a teen, through his years of prominence in the administration of both the Babylonian and Persian Empires. The winsome stories of Daniel's courage and his commitment have been told and retold to children. And Daniel's adjustments to life at the center of a great pagan world empire have been studied by Christian adults, for we too are challenged to live godly lives in often hostile human societies.

But it is the second half of the Book of Daniel, filled with reports of his visions, that has attracted students of prophecy. Several of the visions of Daniel focus on the history of the world from his time to the arrival of the Messiah. But in his book Daniel also shares a great apocalyptic vision of history's end; visions which Christ referred to when speaking of His own second coming.

However one understands the prophetic portion of Daniel, there are many rich lessons for living taught in this brief Old Testament book. Daniel rightly wins a place as one of history's most admirable men, and Daniel's experiences are without parallel in providing modern Christians with insight into principles of practical Christian living. Whether the focus of our interest is the mundane or the magnificent, a study of the Book of Daniel is both a satisfying and an enriching experience.

DANIEL AT A GLANCE

KEY PEOPLE
Daniel   *The author, whose adventures as a teen and an 80-year-old still have power to inspire us.*
Nebuchadnezzar   *The ruler of the great Babylonian Empire, whose contact with Daniel led him to come to know the true God.*

KEY EVENTS
Daniel interprets Nebuchadnezzar's dream (Dan. 2).   *God's revelation of the great king's dream brings Daniel to prominence in Babylon's administration.*
The fiery furnace (Dan. 3).   *Three of Daniel's fellow captives refuse to worship the king's idol and are miraculously rescued by the Lord.*
Nebuchadnezzar's madness (Dan. 4).   *Pride leads to a divine humbling of the great king and to his acknowledgment of the Lord as God.*
Daniel in the lions' den (Dan. 6).   *The 80-year-old Daniel is faithful to God, and the Lord preserves his life.*

KEY PROPHECIES
Visions of the years to come (Dan. 7–8).   *Vivid dreams outline history from Daniel's day to the time of Christ.*
Revelation of the seventy sevens (Dan. 9).   *An angel reveals a specific schedule for the appearance of Israel's long-awaited Messiah!*
Images of history's end (Dan. 11–12). *An angel describes terrible events to take place at the end of time, when all prophecy is destined to be fulfilled.*

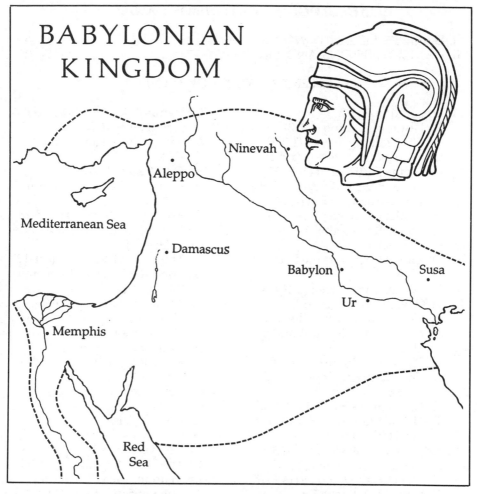

WHERE THE ACTION TAKES PLACE

Daniel was taken from Judah when he was a young teen, and enrolled in the school for future civil servants in Babylon. He lived the rest of his life in the capital of that empire, taking a leading role in its administration and serving as an adviser of one of history's greatest rulers, Nebuchadnezzar (shown above). Daniel also served the great king's successors, including the Persian Cyrus, who conquered Babylon.

Date and Authorship. Daniel's descriptions of the Persian and Macedonian Empires that followed Babylon are so specific that some, who doubt the possibility of predictive prophecy, have advanced a number of arguments against Daniel's date and authorship. Conservative scholars have answered every objection, and have also shown that the book's intimate knowledge of court details provides compelling evidence that it could not have been written centuries after Daniel's time. There is no compelling reason to question either Daniel's authorship, or the book's composition shortly after Cyrus' conquest of Babylon in 439/438 B.C.

THEOLOGICAL OUTLINE OF DANIEL

I. DANIEL'S LIFE AND WORK   1–6
II. DANIEL'S VISIONS AND PROPHECY   7–12

CONTENT OUTLINE OF DANIEL

I. Preparation (1:1-21)
  A. Historical Setting (1:1-2)
  B. The Training School (1:3-7)
  C. Faith's Commitment (1:8-16)
  D. Divine Equipment (1:17-21)
II. Nebuchadnezzar's Dream (2:1-49)
  A. The Astrologers Fail (2:1-13)
  B. Daniel Intercedes (2:14-23)
  C. Daniel Relates the Dream (2:24-35)
  D. Daniel Interprets the Dream (2:36-47)
  E. Daniel Is Promoted (2:48-49)
III. The Fiery Furnace (3:1-30)
  A. Nebuchadnezzar's Idol (3:1-3)
  B. All Commanded to Worship (3:4-7)
  C. Three Jews Refuse (3:8-18)
  D. The Three Are Condemned (3:19-23)
  E. God Delivers His Own (3:24-27)
  F. Nebuchadnezzar Honors the Lord (3:28-30)
IV. Nebuchadnezzar Humbled (4:1-37)
  A. The Second Dream (4:1-7)
  B. The Dream Described (4:8-18)
  C. Daniel Warns the King (4:19-27)
  D. The King Is Punished (4:28-33)
  E. The King Repents (4:34-37)
V. Belshazzar's Feast (5:1-31)
  A. Temple Vessels Used (5:1-4)
  B. A Hand Writes on the Wall (5:5-9)
  C. Daniel Is Called (5:10-16)
  D. Daniel Interprets the Writing (5:17-28)
  E. Daniel Is Honored (5:29-31)
VI. Daniel in the Lions' Den (6:1-28)
  A. The Conspiracy (6:1-9)
  B. Daniel Is Sentenced (6:10-17)
  C. Daniel Is Delivered (6:18-24)

  D. Darius Acknowledges God's Sovereignty (6:25-28)
VII. A Vision of Four Kingdoms (7:1-28)
  A. Four Beasts (7:1-8)
  B. A Vision of God's Triumph (7:9-14)
  C. An Angel Interprets (7:15-28)
VIII. A Vision of Ram, Goat, and Little Horn (8:1-27)
  A. The Vision Described (8:1-12)
  B. The Angel Gabriel Interprets the Vision (8:13-27)
IX. Revelation of Seventy Weeks (9:1-27)
  A. Daniel Prays (9:1-19)
  B. God Grants Daniel Knowledge of the Messiah's Time (9:20-27)
X. Daniel's Persistent Prayers (10:1-21)
  A. Daniel's Vision (10:1-3)
  B. God's Angel Messenger Delayed (10:4-14)
  C. The Delay Explained (10:15-21)
XI. Tribulation Ahead (11:1-45)
  A. The Persian Empire (11:1-4)
  B. Wars That Follow (11:5-20)
  C. Persecution of the Jews (11:21-35)
  D. A Later-Day Great Persecution (11:36-39)
  E. Rise and Fall of the Antichrist (11:40-45)
XII. Tribulation and Triumph (12:1-13)
  A. The Great Tribulation (12:1)
  B. Resurrection and Judgment (12:2-3)
  C. Sealed Prophecies (12:4)
  D. Specification of a 3½-year Period (12:5-7)
  E. Daniel's Final Commission (12:8-13)

Chapter summary. Young Daniel is taken to Babylon in 605 B.C., and enrolled with three other young men drawn from Judah's nobility in a school Nebuchadnezzar established to train future administrators for his empire (1:3-8). There Daniel resolves to remain faithful to God, and not break any of the strict Jewish dietary laws. He approaches the school's "chief official" respectfully, and proposes a 10-day test when the official expresses concern that the diet will harm the young Jews' health (vv. 9-14). Daniel and his friends not only remain healthy, but when tested by Nebuchadnezzar himself at the end of their training, surpass all the others already in his service (vv. 15-21). Thus the introductory story sets the tone for the personal section of this fascinating book. Daniel is a model for all who would remain faithful to God and yet must live successfully in the secular world.

Key verse. 1:8: "Resolve" is the key.

Personal application. Never abandon your commitment to God in order to "get along" in the world.

Key concepts. Babylon »pp. 302, 435. Unclean »p. 82.

INSIGHT

No discrepancy (1:1). Jeremiah 25:1 says Jehoiakim was taken captive in his fourth year as king, while Dan. 1:1 says it was his third. An error in the Bible? No. Archeologists have learned that the two cultures used different systems to count years of reign. Both systems fix the deportation of the king, and Daniel, in 605 B.C.

The royal academy (1:3-5). Nebuchadnezzar's intent to find the best men in his far-flung empire to administer it, rather than reserve such posts for ethnic Babylonians, is only one example of his shrewd and enlightened government.

Vegetarians (1:12). Daniel's appeal to be given nothing but vegetables and water is not evidence of a vegetarian commitment. Moses' dietary laws forbade Jews to eat the meat of "unclean" animals (Lev. 11; Deut. 14). The only way the young men could be sure of having a truly kosher diet was to avoid all meat. Some have also noted that most meat in pagan societies came from animals which had first been dedicated to some deity. The decision to avoid meat may also have reflected the young Jews' rejection of idolatry.

Set priorities (1:8). Compromise always seems easy. No one would be harmed if Daniel and his friends decided to "fit in" at the royal school. Why make an issue of something as morally neutral as diet? What kind of witness would it be to make a fuss about something pagans might think of as foolish? Besides, couldn't they do more for God if they went along and won a high position in government? Take a stand now, and they might never get another opportunity!

Such thoughts probably crossed Daniel's mind. But Daniel did the wise and right thing. He made *doing what God said* his first priority. No rationalization can justify disobedience. This is the first thing any Christian who wishes to live a godly life in a secular society must realize.

Decent pagans? (1:9-10) Some believers can be totally obnoxious when "taking a stand" for their faith. Daniel, however, was respectful, and sensitive. He did not demand, but "asked permission." He recognized the validity of the official's concern that allowing Daniel to change his diet might put the official himself in jeopardy. We can "put God first" and still show due respect for and sensitivity to those around us. Let's not assume that all non-Christians are enemies. There really are "good pagans" around us. When we show respect, God may very well cause our officials "to show favor and sympathy to" us too.

"All kinds of literature and learning" (1:17-20). Archeology has revealed what the four young Jews must have studied. This would include spoken Chaldean; cuneiform writing in Chaldean and Akkadian; spoken and written Aramaic; and a great mass of Sumerian religious, magical, astrological, and scientific writings. When commitment to God is strong, a pagan education in a pagan society need not corrupt us.

Chapter summary. Nebuchadnezzar stuns his "wise men" by demanding that they interpret a disturbing dream, and prove their explanations are valid by telling him what the dream was (2:1-9). His distraught "astrologers" frantically argue that this is impossible. Furious, Nebuchadnezzar orders "all the wise men of Babylon" executed (vv. 10-12). Daniel and his friends, now numbered among the wise men, are arrested. But Daniel asks Nebuchadnezzar for time, urges his friends to pray, and waits on the Lord (vv. 13-18). That night God reveals the dream and its meaning (vv. 19-23). Daniel tells the king his dream (vv. 24-36) and explains its meaning (vv. 37-45). Convinced, Nebuchadnezzar honors Daniel's God and gives Daniel and his friends high positions in his administration (vv. 46-49).

Key verse. 2:28: There is no limit to what God can do.

Personal application. When in danger don't panic. Turn to God.

Key concepts. Dreams »p. 99. Occult »p. 131. Heaven »p. 609. Kingdom »p. 443. Prophecy »p. 434.

INSIGHT

"The second year"? (2:1) Using the Babylonian mode of reckoning regnal years, 602 would be Daniel's third year in the royal academy.

Wise men (2:2). The text mentions four classes of "wise men," each of which has some relationship to the occult. It may be that the king summoned these four classes because their "expertise" was in the realm of the supernatural. The fact that Daniel and his friends were not called suggests that, while they would have studied the culturally significant texts on these subjects, they had no direct involvement in practices forbidden by the O.T. (cf. Deut. 18:9-13).

Prove it (2:5-9). Nebuchadnezzar must have already harbored doubts about the supposed powers of the practitioners of the occult. His anger may well be rooted, not in the frustration of a petulant autocrat, but in the suspicion that he had been deceived for years by their claims of access to the supernatural. Against this background, his threat to brutally execute the wise men if they failed does not seem so unreasonable. Anyone today who has been deceived for years by "New Age" thinking, or some cult, might well be angry too.

"Mystery" (2:18). The Heb. word *raz* occurs only in Daniel, where it indicates a revelation whose meaning was hidden until interpreted by or to Daniel. In the N.T. *mysterion* occurs 27 times, where it identifies the revelation of some truth not divulged in the O.T.

"He urged them to plead" (2:18). Faith is expressed both in knowing that God can help, and in asking Him to help.

Knowing God (2:20-23). Daniel was able to meet the crisis calmly because he knew God well. These verses are well worth memorizing. They remind us of who God is and so encourage us to trust.

Crediting God (2:27-28). Some are tempted to take credit for their special gifts or abilities. Not Daniel. He took great care to explain that interpreting dreams was beyond his natural capacity. God was the source of the revelation he had received. Let's adopt Daniel's attitude today. The Apostle Paul reminded those tempted to brag of their own and others' spiritual accomplishments, "Who makes you different from anyone else? What do you have that you did not receive? And if you did receive it, why do you boast as though you did not?" (1 Cor. 4:7) All we have and are is from God.

The king's dream explained (2:36-45). The image represents successive kingdoms to dominate the Middle East, including Judah, until the Messiah comes to set up God's eternal kingdom. The basic prediction is repeated in visions reported in Dan. 7-8 (see chart, p. 519). For an explanation of why God's kingdom has not yet been established, despite the passing of these ancient kingdoms long ago, see Daniel's prophecy of the 70 weeks (p. 520) and the calculations on associated chart (p. 521).

Promotion (2:48-49). Honor God by putting Him first, and promotion will surely follow if this is His will for you.

Chapter summary. Nebuchadnezzar calls Babylon's officials to share in his dedication of a towering idol, perhaps representing the figure in the dream reported in chapter 2 (3:1-3). At a given signal everyone bows down before the idol—except Daniel's three Hebrew companions (vv. 4-12). Enraged at this "disrespect" Nebuchadnezzar still gives the three Jews another chance to comply (vv. 13-15). Quietly expressing their commitment to God, the three refuse (vv. 16-18). Nebuchadnezzar has them tied and hurled into a blazing furnace, but the king is utterly stunned when he observes four, not three, figures, unharmed, "walking around in the fire" (vv. 19-25). The king calls to the three, and when they walk out of the furnace there is no odor of smoke on their unscorched clothing (vv. 26-27). Once again Nebuchadnezzar has been given evidence of the power of God and has been forced to acknowledge Him. This time the king issues a decree that no one "say anything against the God of Shadrach, Meshach, and Abednego" (vv. 29-30).

Key verses. 3:17-18: Serve God no matter what.

Personal application. Anyone who serves God in the hope of obtaining some benefit is not serving God.

Key concepts. Idolatry »p. 433. Rescue/save »pp. 426, 433. Trust »p. 354.

INSIGHT

Where was Daniel? The best explanation is the simplest. He was not present, perhaps because he was away on business, perhaps because he was ill (cf. 8:27), or perhaps because Nebuchadnezzar knew Daniel would not worship his idol and so exempted him. If the story had been made up later, as some say, the hero of this book would hardly have been left out!

A late invention? Critics have pointed to the Gk. names of two of the instruments mentioned in 3:7 as evidence that Daniel was written in the Hellenistic period, some 250 years before Christ. But renowned archeologist William F. Albright pointed out that Gk. culture was known in Egypt from the seventh century B.C. on, and that Gk. mercenaries served in the armies of Nebuchadnezzar. Far more significant is the fact that the 2nd century Jewish translators of the O.T. into Gk. (the Septuagint) were unable to render the titles of the officials mentioned in 3:3 correctly. If Daniel were a 2nd century invention, how could the author have accurately used words whose meaning had been lost in that age?

The gold image (3:1). In the measurement of that era the image was 6 by 60 cubits, reflecting the numerical system based on sixes rather than on tens, as ours is today. "Gold" implies an overlay, not a solid image. Given the 10 to 1 dimensions, the image probably was raised on a high pedestal. It seems likely that the image was based on the king's dream, and expressed his great pride. How easy it is to distort divine revelation to serve our own self-centered ends!

One world religion? (3:7) There is a parallel here with Revelation 13:11-18, which depicts a ruler of symbolic "Babylon" demanding all the world worship him, and imposing death on all who do not conform.

Jealousy (3:8-12). The Heb. has a word untranslated in the NIV that describes the accusers of the three: *gubrim*. They are members of the master race, and the term adds a tone of contempt to their identification of the three as "some Jews" Nebuchadnezzar had (foolishly?) appointed to high position. Anti-Semitism is hardly new! Nor is racial prejudice.

God is able (3:17-18). Faith clings to the conviction that God is able to save from any danger. But faith also affirms that whether or not God does save is a matter for *Him* to decide. Whether or not God chooses to act we, like the three Hebrews facing a fiery death, must continue to trust in Him.

The fourth figure in the fire (3:25). Many commentators assume the figure is Christ. One thing is sure. In our time of trial Jesus most surely walks with us today.

Chapter summary. The fourth chapter shows God continuing to deal with the proud Nebuchadnezzar. This time the story is told in the king's own words. He begins with an affirmation of praise (4:1-3) and then tells of yet another dream that no one could interpret (vv. 4-8). The king calls Daniel, relates his vision, and asks for an interpretation (vv. 9-18). Daniel is clearly alarmed, for the dream portends disaster. Nebuchadnezzar will become mad and be driven away from human society. Only when he acknowledges God's sovereignty will he be restored (vv. 19-26). Daniel urges the king to renounce his sins, and do what is right by showing kindness to the oppressed (vv. 27-28). But a year later Nebuchadnezzar is bursting with pride as he looks out over the city he has built, and the dread dream becomes reality (vv. 29-33). Yet at the end of seven "times" the king's sanity is restored, and he humbly and gratefully "praised the Most High" (vv. 34-35). His throne was restored as well, and the king concludes by affirming that "now I, Nebuchadnezzar, praise and exalt and glorify the King of heaven" (vv. 36-37).

Key verse. 4:37: Some lessons are learned the hard way.

Personal application. The severest trials can bring the greatest blessings.

Key concepts. Dream »p. 99. Angels »p. 521. Prophecy »p. 408.

INSIGHT

Nebuchadnezzar. Chapters 2–4 all describe God's dealing with Babylon's pagan ruler. Why would God remain so patient? Perhaps to demonstrate the persistence of His grace. Perhaps to encourage you and me when we, like Daniel, must work with someone who forgets so outrageously every spiritual lesson taught. How could the king have turned God's revelation through his first dream into an idol? How could the king have returned to his pride after being thwarted at the fiery furnace? We humans do have a unique capacity for perverseness! But God has an unmatched commitment to grace. Let's remember Nebuchadnezzar and not give up on others.

Historical setting (4:4). The story is set in a time of relative peace after Nebuchadnezzar's major conquests and massive building projects. It best fits after the fall of Jerusalem, during the lengthy siege of Tyre when Babylon launched no other major military operation. Not unexpectedly no record of a lengthy madness has been found in the royal archives, but it could have occurred any time between 582 and 573 B.C.

Nebuchadnezzar's dream (4:9-17). The great tree that provided shelter to the world was the ruler himself (cf. v. 15). His judgment was intended to demonstrate to all that "the Most

High is sovereign over the kingdoms of men." It was easy not only for Nebuchadnezzar but also all his officials to suppose the ruler was the ultimate authority. How hard it is to remember that God is sovereign. And how painful His reminders when we forget.

Pride (4:17-18). Trees symbolize pride. Isaiah warns, "The Lord Almighty has a day in store for all the proud and lofty, for all that is exalted (and they will be humbled), for all the cedars of Lebanon, tall and lofty, and all the oaks of Bashan . . . the arrogance of man will be brought low and the pride of men humbled; the Lord alone will be exalted in that day" (Isa. 2:12-13, 17).

"Seven times" (4:25). In Daniel each "time" (*'iddanin*) represents a year.

Madness and restoration (4:33-37). The demented king sank to the level of a beast, living outdoors in an area where temperatures ranged from 120 in the summer to below freezing in the winter.

Restored, the king at last responded appropriately to the Lord. Nebuchadnezzar (1) glorified God, (2) honored Him as sovereign Ruler of the universe, (3) expressed his own total dependence on God's will, and (4) acknowledged Him to be right in everything He does. "And those who walk in pride He is able to humble."

Chapter summary. Nebuchadnezzar died in 563 B.C. The events in this chapter take place decades later, in 539 B.C. Belshazzar, son of the current ruler Nabonidus, throws a banquet despite the presence of a besieging Persian force outside Babylon's mighty walls (5:1). Drunk, he ridicules the God that Nebuchadnezzar's decrees had exalted by using bowls dedicated to God at the Jerusalem temple as wine cups, and to make offerings to pagan deities (vv. 2-4). When a hand miraculously appears and writes on the wall, the terrified ruler demands an interpretation, and the now aged Daniel is called for (vv. 5-12). Daniel interprets the message and announces that since Belshazzar has not followed Nebuchadnezzar's example of honoring God, the kingdom is about to be torn from his hands (vv. 13-28). The king keeps his promise to reward Daniel, but that very night the Persians enter the city and Belshazzar is killed (vv. 29-30).

Outline
Place
Finder

LIFE
VISIONS

Key verse. 5:22: Knowing isn't doing.

Personal application. God measures us not by how much of His truth we know, but by how committed we are to act on it.

INSIGHT

"Belshazzar" (5:1). For many years the reference to Belshazzar was pointed to as proof that the Book of Daniel lacked historical accuracy, and was of a late date. Then archeologists discovered evidence not only of his existence, but of his role as regent for his father Nabonidus! Thus Belshazzar's promise to make Daniel "third highest" ruler was explained. Belshazzar himself was only second highest! What had been presented as proof of Daniel's late date became evidence that it was written hundreds of years earlier than supposed, before the historical records of the era had been lost.

"Your father" (5:11, 18). Nebuchadnezzar was not the literal father of Belshazzar, despite these references. Belshazzar was the son of Nabonidus, who assassinated Labashi-Marduk, himself the son of Neriglissar, Nebuchadnezzar's son-in-law, who himself had assassinated the great king's son, Evil-Merodach! "Son of" and "father of" were commonly used in the ancient world to indicate successors and predecessors of rulers, whether or not there was an actual relationship.

"The inscription" (5:25). No vowels are recorded in the written form of the family of languages to which both Hebrew and Aramaic belong. The handwriting might well have been read as "mina," "shekel," and "peres" (half-shekel). This represented a descending order of weights with monetary value. While it might represent a progressive devaluing of the kingdom once headed by Nebuchadnez-

zar, its interpretation remained a mystery. Daniel added different vowels so that it read "numbered, numbered, weighed, divided." Even this had no meaning till it was explained by Daniel. Belshazzar's acts had been carefully numbered and weighed and found wanting. His kingdom was about to be divided and taken from him.

God numbers and weighs the acts of all men and women. May we not be found wanting.

False security. The rulers feasted because they supposed themselves safe behind massive walls. They did not know the Persian force had altered the flow of the river that passed through the city. When the water level fell, the enemy simply walked along the riverbed under the river gates' protective grills, and surprised the Babylonians within. Some 80 years later the Greek historian Herodotus wrote, "Had the Babylonians been apprised of what Cyrus was about . . . they would have made fast all the street-gates which gave upon the river, and mounting upon the walls along both sides of the stream, would have so caught the enemy as it were in a trap. . . . Owing to the vast size of the place, the inhabitants of the central parts, long after the outer portions of the town were taken, knew nothing of what had chanced, but as they were engaged in a festival, continued dancing and revelling until they learnt the capture but too certainly."

What an image of so many moderns, who feel secure behind walls of wealth or position, never realizing that doom is near until it is too late.

Chapter summary. Daniel, now in his 80s, is given a key place in the administration of the Persian Empire, which has now supplanted the Babylonian (6:1-3). The fiercely honest Daniel arouses the hostility of his corrupt coworkers, who determine to get rid of him (vv. 4-5). They appeal to the pride of the Persian ruler, and get him to decree that no one can make a request of man or god other than himself for 30 days. When Daniel goes to pray as usual, the whole group accuses him of violating that law (vv. 6-12). The distraught ruler is unable to save Daniel, for custom demands that no decree once issued by a Persian ruler can be changed. As Daniel is thrown to the lions the king's last hope is that somehow Daniel's God will be able to save him (vv. 13-16). After a sleepless night, the king rushes to the den, only to discover Daniel, alive and well (vv. 17-23). The plotters are then thrown to the lions, and the king decrees that throughout his realm all men must honor Daniel's God (vv. 24-28).

Key verse. 6:16: Events can turn hope to faith.

Personal application. Keep on doing what is right, and rely on God to guard you.

INSIGHT

"Darius" (6:1). The identity of "Darius the Mede" in Daniel has caused confusion. Since 9:1 says he was "made ruler" (*homlak*), which implies appointment by a higher authority, most believe "Darius" here is a title rather than a personal name, in the same way that "Caesar" served as a title in the later Roman Empire. Persian records suggest that Gubaru, one of Cyrus' generals, served as the ruler of Babylon and regions west of the Euphrates even after the great conqueror's death. Very likely Gubaru is the "Darius" of the Book of Daniel.

Promotion (6:1-3). The prospect of Daniel's promotion aroused intense jealousy. Part may have been racial antagonism. Part was the natural jealousy of those who see better qualified persons raised above them. Let's follow Daniel's example: be honest, work hard, do a good job. But if promotion comes, don't expect others to be happy for you. Some will be jealous, even to the extent of starting rumors or plotting against you. If that happens, keep on doing right and trust your cause to God.

No grounds (6:3-4). Happy is the believer who gives no grounds for others to accuse him or her, aside from commitment to the Lord.

"The decree" (6:6-9). This not only flattered Darius, but seemed a wise political move. It would emphasize the new Persian control of the old Babylonian lands. And the 30-day limit would reassure the population that their traditions were not threatened by the new rulers. Darius had no idea it was intended as an attack on Daniel.

"Windows opened toward Jerusalem" (6:10). Daniel prayed where he always had, in his own home, in an upstairs room. He did not directly challenge Darius' law, but neither would he retreat from his open commitment to God. There's a balance here that is difficult for us to maintain.

"It cannot be altered" (6:8). Negative critics have ridiculed this law as "improbable," despite the statement here and in Es. 8:8. Yet Didorus Siculus, a 2nd-century historian, reports that in a fit of rage Darius III (335–331 B.C.) condemned a man named Charidemus. Later he "blamed himself" for making "the greatest mistake," but "it was not possible for what was done by the royal authority to be undone." Again Scripture is shown to be historically accurate.

Budding faith (6:16). Not knowing, but still hoping, may be evidence of budding faith.

"My God" (6:22). It is the personal relationship expressed in "my," and the assurance of innocence, that makes us confident when dangers threaten.

Daniel's accusers (6:24). O.T. Law says of any who maliciously bear false witness, "then do to him as he intended to do to his brother" (Deut. 19:19). The principle seems to work out often in human experience. Another biblical illustration is the case of Haman, who was hung on the gallows he erected for Mordecai (see Es. 7). Be sure to deal honestly with others. The only person anyone really cheats is himself!

Chapter summary. Daniel first sees four beasts who kill and supplant each other (7:1-8), with God appearing to put an end to the last beast (vv. 9-14). An angel explains that the beasts represent successive kingdoms. A ruler will arise from the last kingdom to oppose God and the saints, after which God will appear to establish His eternal kingdom (vv. 15-28). In his second vision Daniel sees a ram and he-goat struggling (8:1-12). The Angel Gabriel explains this vision, which gives a general summary of the rise of Medo-Persia and Greece and the four-part division of the empire after the death of Alexander the Great (vv. 13-27). Verses 23-25 seem to describe Anthiochus Epiphanes, who persecuted the Jews in the 160s B.C., but who here serves as a type of the Antichrist destined to appear at history's end.

Key verses. 7:13-14: Today is uncertain, tomorrow is sure.

Personal application. What counts is where we're going.

Key concepts. Prophecy »p. 434. Tribulation »p. 626. Kingdom »p. 443. Antichrist »p. 522. Messiah »p. 432. Angels »p. 521.

INSIGHT

Chart. The visions of this chapter and of Dan. 2 unquestionably portray the kingdoms of Babylon, Medo-Persia, Greece, and Rome.

"Son of man" (7:13). This is the only O.T. passage in which this term is used of the Messiah.

	Babylon (605–538 B.C.)	Medo-Persia (538–331 B.C.)	Greece (331–146 B.C.)	Rome (146 B.C.–A.D. 476)
Daniel 2:31-45 Dream image (603 B.C.)	Head of gold (2:32, 37-38)	Breast, arms of silver (2:32, 39)	Belly, thighs of brass (2:32, 39)	Legs of iron Feet of iron and clay (2:33, 40-41)
Daniel 7 First vision: Four beasts (553 B.C.)	Lion (7:4)	Bear (7:5)	Leopard (7:6)	Strong Beast (7:7, 11, 19, 23)
Daniel 8 Second vision: Ram and goat (551 B.C.)		Ram (8:3-4, 20)	Goat with one horn 8:5-8, 21) Four horns (8:8, 22) Little horn (8:9-14)	

Chapter summary. Daniel's vision of the "70 weeks" is pivotal for those who interpret prophecy in any literal way. Daniel learns from Scripture that God intends to restore His people (9:1-3) and goes to prayer to beg God to keep His promise of restoration soon (vv. 4-19). God sends Gabriel, who explains that God has decreed "seventy sevens" for the Jews and the Holy City (vv. 20-23). At the end of that time He will complete His plan for the world (v. 24). Gabriel goes on to explain when to begin counting, and how the time period is divided, focusing on events in the 70th week, which is separated from the other 69 by the "cutting off" of the Messiah (vv. 25-27).

Key verse. 9:24: God knows where history is going.

Personal application. Christ will return, "when" is up to God.

INSIGHT

Seventy seven's. The "sevens" in the text are years, indicating a period of 490 years was to pass from a specified date until history's end.

Purpose: Destiny

- to finish transgression
- to make an end of sin
- to make atonement for iniquity
- to bring in everlasting righteousness
- to seal up vision and prophecy (i.e., to fulfill it)
- to anoint the most holy place

Chronology

69 SEVENS OF YEARS	70TH WEEK
(360 days each = 173,880 days)	

445 B.C.	A.D. 32	A.D. ?
Decree to rebuild	Messiah	Period of
Jerusalem	cut off	prophetic
(Neh. 1–2; Dan. 9:25)	(Dan. 9:26)	culmination

Support for the Time Gap
1. It is characteristic of Old Testament prophecy in general (e.g., Isa. 61; Luke 4).
2. The language of Daniel 9:26—"After the sixty-two 'sevens,' the Anointed One will be cut off."
3. History: "The people of the ruler who will come" (not the enemy prince himself) "will destroy the city and the sanctuary" (Dan. 9:26). This happened in A.D. 70 when a Roman army under Titus destroyed Jerusalem.
4. The New Testament (Matt. 24) expects that the events of the seventieth week are yet future.

Chapter summary. Daniel is so disturbed by his vision that he fasts, mourns, and prays for three weeks (10:1-3). An angel appears and, after explaining the delay (vv. 4-14), strengthens Daniel before giving God's answer to Daniel's prayer (vv. 15-21). This chapter is one of the most important in Scripture for angelology, and suggests that an invisible war is constantly fought in the spiritual world which has great impact on the course of nations and the experience of individuals.

Key verse. 10:12: God hears every prayer.

Personal application. Don't be discouraged when your prayers are not answered immediately. God hasn't forgotten you.

Key concepts. Prayer »pp. 181, 608. Angel »p. 855. Demon »p. 659.

INSIGHT

Angels. The Heb. word (*mal'ak*) means "messenger." Angels are "heavenly beings" (Ps. 89:6) who are direct creations of God (Job 1:6). They are of different orders and type (cf. Gen. 3:24; Ps. 18:10; Ezek. 1:5-14). One powerful angel, Gabriel, is named four times (Dan. 8:16; 9:21; Luke 1:19, 26). Among the missions given angels in O.T. times were guarding God's people (2 Kings 6:17; Ex. 23:20; Dan. 3:28). Angels also serve as agents executing divine judgment (Gen. 19:1; 2 Sam. 24:17; Isa. 37:36). The O.T. and N.T. teach that many angels joined Satan in his rebellion, and these may be the demons of the Gospels (cf. Matt. 25:41; Jude 6; 2 Peter 2:4). Daniel 10 suggests that angels were created with varying powers, or ranks. God's angelic forces are in a struggle with Satan's, and depending on the rank of the dark angel, one of Satan's forces may hold up the ministry of an angel dispatched to our aid by the Lord. The identification of angels as the "prince of" Persia and other secular powers indicates that the spiritual war focuses on controlling human societies and shaping political events for evil or for good.

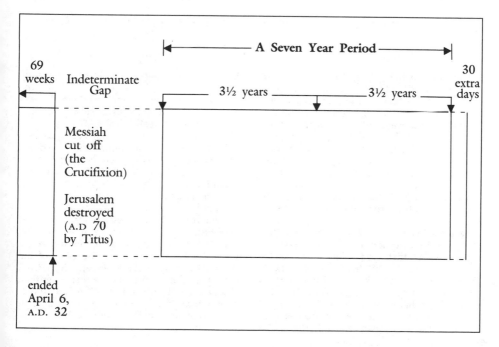

69 weeks

Indeterminate Gap

A Seven Year Period

3½ years — 3½ years

30 extra days

Messiah cut off (the Crucifixion)

Jerusalem destroyed (A.D 70 by Titus)

ended April 6, A.D. 32

Chapter summary. This difficult passage is a complicated expansion of earlier revelations of events near history's end. Interpreted literally rather than allegorically, the passage begins with a description of the Persian Empire to the death of Alexander the Great, whose empire was divided up between four of his generals (11:1-4). It goes on to describe wars between the Ptolemies in Egypt (the South) and the Seleucids of Babylon/Syria (the North) (vv. 5-20). In time the Seleucids dominate Palestine and one of them, Antiochus Epiphanes, institutes a great persecution of the Jews (vv. 21-35). Many of Antiochus' characteristics serve as a type of the Antichrist, his latter-day counterpart, who is then introduced (vv. 36-39). Though the Antichrist initially succeeds, he soon falls (vv. 40-45), although the Jews experience great tribulation before his defeat (12:1). At that time the dead will be raised and judged (vv. 2-3), and the prophecy is "sealed" to indicate it is an official and binding statement of God's intent.

The chapter ends with the prediction of a 3 1/2 year period, focusing these events in the last half of Daniel's earlier prophecy (»p. 520) of the 70th week (vv. 5-7). Yet another time period is mentioned, focusing on a period of 45 days (1,335 days minus 1,290 days), whose significance is uncertain, except for the promise that those who survive the terrors of the end time will know the blessing of God.

Key verse. 12:2: Eternity lies beyond time.

Personal application. Whatever earth's future holds, our destiny is in heaven.

Key concept. Prophecy of the future »pp. 419, 427–428, 443.

INSIGHT

The Antichrist (11:36-39). In Gk. *anti* means "in place of" first, then "against." The name occurs only five times, all in John's N.T. writings. Antichrists (plural) reject God and His Son and are motivated by the passion that will move "the" Antichrist to attempt to supplant Him at history's end. Both Dan. 11 and Rev. 13 picture a specific individual as the Antichrist, and though not named it is clear that he is referred to in 2 Thes. 2:1-12 as well. Called "the beast" in Rev., he will be defeated and condemned at the return of Christ (Rev. 19:11-21).

Resurrection (12:2-3). This is the definitive passage on resurrection in the O.T. Other passages suggest that God's intent to deliver reaches beyond this life (Job 14:14; Pss. 17:15; 73:23-26), and some make it clear that death is not the end for human beings (cf. Isa. 26:8, 19). Yet it is here that we are told all the dead will arise, that they will then face judgment, and that one of two destiny's awaits. Certainly the

doctrine of a resurrection is taught clearly enough in the O.T. for Jesus to rebuke the Sadducees, who denied the possibility, by saying, "You are in error because you do not know the Scriptures" (Matt. 22:29).

The resurrection of Jesus, however, establishes the doctrine without a doubt, and served as a keystone of apostolic preaching (Acts 2:24-26; 3:15-26; 10:40; 13:34, 37; 17:18-32). Though we do not know everything that will be involved in our own resurrection, the raising of Christ is God's guarantee that we too will rise (cf. 1 Cor. 15; 1 John 3:1). First Thessalonians 4 describes the return of Jesus and our resurrection: "The Lord Himself will come down from heaven, with a loud command, with the voice of the archangel and with the trumpet call of God, and the dead in Christ will rise first. After that, we who are still alive and are left will be caught up with them in the clouds to meet the Lord in the air. And so we will be with the Lord forever" (vv. 16-17).

Hosea

Hosea, whose name means "salvation," has been called the "gentlest" of the Old Testament prophets. He was called to one of sacred history's most difficult missions. Hosea married a wife, Gomer, who abandoned him for a series of lovers, breaking the marriage covenant which bound them together. Yet Hosea's love for his wife was so great that he could not give her up. When her profligate ways led to slavery, Hosea bought her and brought her back home, to lead a holy life. In this the prophet shared God's own experience with His people, Israel. Though bound to the Lord in a covenant relationship, Israel turned away from Him to pursue idols and the adulterous lifestyle associated with paganism. That idolatry would ultimately lead the nation to enslavement too. Yet God could not stop loving, anymore than Hosea could. God too will one day bring His humbled people home, and they will again commit themselves to Him.

The Book of Hosea is deeply moving. As we sense the prophet's pain, we also enter into the pain God feels when His beloved people are unfaithful to Him. God's love truly is a love that will not let us go.

HOSEA AT A GLANCE

KEY PEOPLE
Hosea *The gentle prophet whose persistent love ultimately wins the prize.*
Gomer *The unfaithful wife, whose choices lead to ever deeper degradation until, helpless, she is rescued by her abandoned husband.*

KEY PASSAGES
Consequences (Hosea 8–9). *Breaking covenant with God leads to disaster.*
Endless love (Hosea 11). *God's love will not permit Him to give His people up.*
Blessing ahead (Hosea 14). *Ultimately repentance will bring blessing.*

Date and Authorship. Little is known of Hosea or his wife Gomer, though geographic references in the book place him in the Northern Kingdom, Israel. Internal evidence and Hosea 1:1 suggest he ministered between 750–730 B.C. During this period both Hebrew kingdoms experienced great prosperity. Yet this was also an era marked by a growing chasm between wealthy and poor and by a total disregard for social justice. The people were "religious," but the North followed a counterfeit system of worship devised by Israel's first king, Jeroboam I (»p. 230). The general disregard for God's Law made it clear that the people had strayed from the Lord, as did the open worship of Canaanite deities in many villages. Only devastating judgment, which fell on Israel in 722 B.C. and on Judah in 586 B.C., would bring Israel to the place of repentance, a place Gomer's descent into slavery finally brought her as well.

WHERE THE ACTION TAKES PLACE

The Northern Kingdom, Israel, is the site of Hosea's ministry. Yet the real focus of the action of this book is the human heart. It is the heart of Gomer, who cannot remain faithful, and the heart of Hosea, who cannot abandon his commitment. And the site is your heart, mine—and especially the heart of God.

THEOLOGICAL OUTLINE OF HOSEA

CONTENT OUTLINE OF HOSEA

Chapter summary. Hosea is directed by God to marry Gomer, an "adulterous wife" (1:1-3). Each of his three children is given a symbolic name which foreshadows the bitter future awaiting God's people and Hosea's own anguish (1:4–2:1). Hosea's personal story is interrupted with a beautiful poem in which God portrays His people Israel as a wayward wife. Though the Lord withdraws His love for a time so Israel may experience the consequences of her sins, He continues to yearn for the day when, cleansed, His covenant people will return to Him (vv. 2-23). Hosea draws strength from the example of God's faithfulness to His sinning people. He buys his prostitute wife Gomer, who has been reduced to slavery, and brings her home again (3:1-3). One day Israel's heart will again turn to God. Hosea too is willing to bear the pain until his wife's heart turns to him again (vv. 4-5).

Key verse. 3:1: Model God.

Personal application. "What would God do?" is still a better guide than "What does the Law permit?"

Key concepts. Adultery »pp. 64, 85. Prostitution »pp. 45, 135. Divorce »p. 136. Judgment »p. 372. Restoration »p. 419.

INSIGHT

Hosea's marriage. Four major views of Hosea's marriage to Gomer have been proposed. (1) The story is not literal. (2) Gomer was already a prostitute with children when Hosea married her. (3) Gomer's "prostitution" is spiritual rather than moral. She began to worship idols. (4) Gomer was a chaste woman when they married. The words "adulterous wife" describe her tendency and character and were prophetic when uttered by God. This last interpretation is preferred, for it most clearly parallels God's experience with Israel.

Grounds for divorce? Few Christians question that adultery, to say nothing of prostitution, constitutes valid grounds for divorce. But the experience of Hosea reminds us of a greater truth. Adultery, or any sin, is first of all grounds for forgiveness! Considering the example of our loving and faithful God we may be led, as Hosea was, to suffer the pain and seek a reconciliation.

"Your mother" (2:2, 4). The mother here is Israel, the children individual Israelites. Both the historic nation and contemporary individuals are guilty of spiritual adultery in forsaking God.

"I was the one" (2:8). This is one of Scriptures' most touching verses. God keeps on supplying us with good things, even when we do not acknowledge Him. Even when we use His good gifts to finance our wickeness. How amazing God's grace and patience!

Consequences (2:9-13). When patience does not bear fruit, God has other methods. One is to withdraw the blessing and let us experience the consequences of our sins.

"I am now going to allure her" (2:14). The Heb. word (*patah*) suggests persuade by showing benefits. Relationship with God often looks more attractive from the depths of discipline than the pinnacle of prosperity!

God doesn't give up (2:19-23). God acts in love, compassion, faithfulness, righteousness, and justice—all to win His people to Himself. Our part is to respond to His initiatives, and acknowledge Him.

When we do acknowlege Him, God responds to us and showers us with blessings. And the greatest blessing of all? "I will say to those people . . . 'You are My people'; and they will say, 'You are my God' " (v. 23).

Hosea and Gomer (3:1-3). How difficult it was for Hosea and Gomer to feel comfortable with one another again. The emotional distance is suggested in the word translated "wife" (*issah*, "woman," without the possessive "your"). It is also suggested in the paltry price (some believe this was a gift to Gomer herself!) paid by Hosea. Yet where there is commitment (v. 3) love can grow again, and intimacy ultimately can be restored.

Chapter summary. The Book of Hosea now records the preaching of this prophet whose personal pain reflects so brightly the pain experienced by the Lord. Hosea begins with an indictment identifying Israel's sins (4:1-4). He then focuses on the sins of the priests (vv. 5-11a) before specifying sins that have become commonplace in the nation as a whole (vv. 11b-19). The indictment leads to a warning addressed to priests, people, and king (5:1-7). The trumpet sounding the alarm will soon be heard in the north, as Assyrian armies advance to tear the nation to pieces. God will not help, "Until they admit their guilt. And they will seek My face; in their misery they will earnestly seek Me" (vv. 8-15).

Key verse. 5:4: Check the heart.

Personal application. Chase sin and catch judgment.

Key concepts. Law »pp. 120, 145. Priest »p. 81. Idolatry »p. 433. Prostitution »pp. 45, 135. Adultery »p. 85. Assyria »p. 255.

INSIGHT

Sinful society (4:1). Three things characterize corrupt cultures of any age. They care nothing for faithfulness (*'emet*, »p. 141), they are void of loving commitment to others (*hesed*), and they possess no true knowledge (*da'at*) of God. Without these qualities a society deteriorates until "there is only cursing, lying and murder, stealing and adultery; they break all bounds, and bloodshed follows bloodshed" (v. 2). By this standard, where is our society today?

Not my priests (4:5-11a). The "priests" of the Northern Kingdom, Israel, were not drawn from the family of Aaron, but from "all sorts of people" (cf. 1 Kings 12:31; 13:33). These religious leaders who had not been called or sanctified by God not surprisingly "ignored the law of your God" (v. 6). Spiritual leadership is not to be sought lightly. Leaders must be called and ordained by God.

Feeding on sins (4:8). The priests enjoyed benefits because people sinned. Some take this to refer to bribes. It may simply refer to the fact that the priests received a portion of every sin offering. The more the Israelites' sinned, the more offerings they brought, and the better the priests ate! Godly priests stand against sin and mourn when others pursue it. The grief modern spiritual leaders feel over the sins of their people is still a test of their hearts.

"Prostitution" (4:11-14). The prostitution referred to here is ritual prostitution linked with the idolatry of the Canaanites. Sex acts were supposed to stimulate the gods, and the fertility of the land was supposed to result from their intercourse.

Note God's unwillingness to punish "your daughters" and "daughters-in-law" because the men were consorting with cult prostitutes as well. There was no double standard in O.T. times! Women would not be punished while God held back from punishing the men. Both would be punished together.

"Ephraim" (5:3). At times this leading northern tribe stands for all Israel. Here, however, the tribal area is in view. It is here that the worship center of Dan is centered, where the true faith in *Yahweh* has been corrupted and all God's people have been led astray.

"Unfaithful" (5:7). Given Hosea's experience with Gomer this must have been one of the most dreadful accusations the prophet could make against God's people. The "illegitimate" children are literally "strange" (*zar*). Their parents' sins have twisted them as well.

Never suppose that our sins have no impact on our children. They do!

"Benjamin" (5:8). The area of this southern tribe lay tight against the territory of Judah. Thus Benjamin faced a dual challenge: to resist the corrupting spiritual influence of the North, and to prepare to resist the Assyrians who would soon invade Israel.

"I will go back" (5:15). God knows He must not restore those He punishes until the suffering has had its intended effect. Don't be so sorry that you have disciplined your children that you give them hugs before they have admitted guilt and come to you for forgiveness.

Chapter summary. Repentance will be expressed by a faith that turns back to the very God who has punished (6:1-3). But now a frustrated God must deal with a fickle, wicked people (vv. 4-11). Despite God's desire to restore Israel's fortunes, people and ruler continue their love affair with sin at home (7:1-7) and for security rely on treaties with pagan nations rather than on the Lord (vv. 8-16). Thus Hosea warns of the sure approach of judgment. Israel has broken His covenant and rebelled against His law and must now reap the punishment her deeds have sown (8:1-10). No multitude of sacrifice can cause God to relent: He will remember their wickedness and punish their sins (vv. 11-14).

Key verse. 8:7: Play now, pay later.

Personal application. Sin's pleasures still aren't worth the consequences.

Key concepts. Repentance »p. 780. Prophets »p. 131. Sin »p. 362. Covenant »pp. 35, 62. Altar »p. 79. Punishment »p. 827.

INSIGHT

Repentance (6:1-3). No discipline can have its desired impact until the culprit is ready to repent. What is involved in repentance? A change of heart about ourselves that involves admission of guilt (cf. 5:15). And a change of heart about God, which trusts that He will restore us even though He has punished us till now (6:1-3). When we can say both, "I deserved it," and "I trust God to heal and restore me," then we have come to true repentance.

"What can I do with you?" (6:4) Many a parent has echoed God's frustration. The answer is, keep on disciplining. Keep on loving. Like ancient Israel children have freedom of choice. Let's be constant so they can have an anchor for the inner change they need to make.

Warnings (7:1-2). Sometimes we try to reason with our unresponsive children. God reasoned with Israel too, by sending them prophets to utter warnings. But by acting against the prophets' advice Israel simply revealed the depth of her sin. Sometimes words won't help us with our children either, and all our warnings seem to do is to make our offsprings' rebellion more obvious. It usually takes more than words to reach the rebellious.

"Flocking together" (7:12). Israel's "peer group" was foreign nations, who arrogantly determined to band together and go their own way rather than depend on the Lord. Getting in with the wrong crowd is just as big a mistake today as in the past. God has a net big enough to throw over the whole flock and will "punish their sins."

Illustration (8:7). The "whirlwind" of this verse is a tornado. It is a symbol of destruction and chaos as well as judgment. Only devastation of all hopes can shatter the wall of arrogance and pride some construct around themselves. Sin's terrible consequences are intended to break down our defenses against God. When that happens the superficial in our relationship with God (cf. vv. 11-13) will be shattered. Then man's only hope is that repentance described at the beginning of chapter 6.

Why wait till the whirlwind strikes to find your way back to God?

Chapter summary. Now, clearly and specifically, the prophet describes the punishment about to befall Israel. God's unfaithful people are doomed to captivity, this time in Assyria (9:1-9). The glories of Israel's past, when like a child God's people enjoyed all the pleasures of its father's house, will be stripped away. God will "reject them because they have not obeyed Him; they will be wanderers among the nations" (vv. 10-17). The once blessed and prosperous land must bear its guilt and become a desolate wilderness (10:1-8). Sin has made punishment certain (vv. 9-11). God's advice, to show righteousness and reap the fruit of love, has been rejected (vv. 12-13a). Soon the roar of battle will drown out Israel's cries for help, and the nation will be completely destroyed (vv. 13b-15).

Key verse. 10:13: There's always a reason.

Personal application. Sow righteousness. Let the crop of wickedness mature into punishment in someone else's field.

INSIGHT

"Ephraim" (9:3). Here the tribe stands for the entire Northern Kingdom, which it leads. This time "Egypt," the ancient symbol of slavery, lies to the north in Assyria.

"The bread of mourners" (9:4). In the East relatives bake bread and kill animals to feed the mourners who come to the house to lament and share in the family's grief. The mourners eat with tears in their eyes, weeping and lamenting. The image is of the death of Israel's hopes as a nation. God's people will gather in foreign lands, there to weep and mourn over the glories that are past.

A fertility curse (9:11-12). The O.T. views children as a divine blessing, granted to the faithful (Deut. 28:4, 11). Here God warns that judgment includes a curse that casts the pall of death over the whole process of procreation. And announced that any who may survive will not live a normal lifespan. Sin mortgages the future of untold generations.

"Gilgal" (9:15). Gilgal is doubly associated with Israel's sins. Though originally the camp from which the Conquest of Canaan was launched in Joshua's time (Josh. 4:19–5:12), it was corrupted by Israel's kings and became a cult center for a counterfeit worship of Yahweh (cf. Amos 4:4; 5:5; Hosea 4:15; 12:11). It also served as a resort area for the wealthy who oppressed the poor in Israel. As a center noted for its false religion and social oppression "Gilgal" probably serves here as a metaphor for the nation.

"They will be wanderers among the na-

tions" (9:17). This is the ultimate punishment specified in Deut. 28 for rejecting the Lord. From the Assyrian Captivity in 722 B.C. till now, the great majority of the Jewish people have been "wanderers among the nations." Even in the time of Christ, when it has been estimated that 1 person in 10 in the Roman Empire was Jewish, only a small percentage of them lived in the Holy Land.

Deceitful hearts (10:4). The moral corruption of the society is shown by "promises," "false oaths," and "agreements." The whole legal structure is required because of a basic dishonesty that infects the land, a fact attested by the lawsuits that "spring up like poisonous weeds." A litigious society will not exist if men are honest with one another.

Unrealized potential (10:11-14a). Israel, like a trained heifer, was called to a task by God—to work His land and enjoy its produce. There was the potential of sowing righteousness and reaping unfailing love. But Israel not only failed to realize her potential, she abused her position as God's servant. As a result the people now face punishment.

God calls all of His people to service. If we are committed to Him—if we commit ourselves to the tasks to which He calls us—we will fulfill our potential, and will reap the fruit of His love.

"Depended on your own strength" (10:13). Don't look in the mirror and admire your spiritual muscles. Look to God, and admire His.

Outline
Place
Finder

WIFE
PEOPLE

Chapter summary. Judgment has been decreed. Yet God's heart is torn by that love for Israel which shaped His relationship with this people from the beginning (11:1-4). Despite Israel's determined refusal to repent (vv. 5-7), God cannot bring Himself to give His people up. Compassion overrules, and God will resettle Israel in their homes after their days of discipline are past (vv. 8-11). Yet God's sinful people must and will be punished (11:12–12:2). In the beginning Jacob, the father of the 12 tribes, showed a passionate desire for God, to which his descendants must return (vv. 3-6). Israel's current passion is for dishonesty and worldly wealth (vv. 7-8). God has sent messenger after messenger to Israel (vv. 9-10), but hardened Ephraim (Israel) has "bitterly provoked [God] to anger." The people must be repaid for their sin (vv. 11-14).

Key verse. 11:8: God's love has no end.

Personal application. Respond to God's love with enthusiasm, not with indifference.

Key concepts. Baal »p. 162. God's anger »pp. 65, 72. Egypt »p. 420.

INSIGHT

Love. The general word for "love" in the O.T. is 'aheb, the word used here of the controlling element in God's relationship with Israel. The intensity of "love" varies with the subject and object. One can "love" good food (as Gen. 27:4) or wealth (Ecc. 5:10). Yet "love" also describes the relationship between a father and his son (Gen. 22:2), as well as the relationship that is to exist between a person and his or her neighbor (Lev. 19:18).

The most significant use of 'aheb, however, is to explain God's acts in history and to express His attitude toward His people. Love was God's motive for choosing Abraham and Isaac and Jacob (Deut. 4:37). Love moved God to deliver Israel from slavery in Egypt and bless them (v. 38; 7:13-15). Looking back, the prophets see God's love stamped on every event in His people's history (Hosea 11:1; Mal. 1:2-3). Even discipline is an indication of a parent's loving concern for his offspring (cf. Prov. 3:12). Here in Hosea 11 we have perhaps the strongest of all O.T. affirmations of God's love for His people. That love is a compassion which persists despite rebellion and unfaithfulness. It is a commitment which, while it has room for discipline, leaves no room for abandonment. In the end God's love will triumph and even defiant Israel will repent and receive the rich blessing God yearns to pour out.

What a comfort and a challenge for us today. It is a comfort, for it reminds us that when we fall short, and are tempted to shrink back from God in fear and shame, He keeps on loving us and invites us to return. And it is a challenge for, like Hosea himself, we are called to love others as God loves us.

A child (11:3-4). The imagery is of a toddler learning to walk, encouraged by a stooping adult who shows infinite patience and concern. When you stumble and fall, picture God, bending down to lift you up, saying "That's all right. Let's try again. Walk for Daddy."

"God, and not man" (11:9). Human beings lose patience. "That's the fifth time you've been late! One more time, and you're out!" We also tend to have legalistic relationships. "You did that! Then it's all right for me to do that to you too." God is different. His love is patient. His love cannot be weighed on balance scales. He is God, not man.

Feeding on wind (12:1). The image is one of futility. The multiplied "lies and violence" are involved in making futile treaties with Assyria and Egypt. While negotiating a treaty with Assyria, Israel might be sending gifts to Egypt to gain support against Assyria (2 Kings 17:4).

"In the womb" (12:3). The reference is to Jacob's lifelong competition with Esau (Gen. 25; 27), in which only Jacob cared about inheriting the covenant promise God had given Abraham.

"But" (12:14). God's love and patience have no end. But this does not mean that He will permit His chosen people to sin impudently. The time will come when the "guilt of . . . bloodshed" will bring punishment. The wonder is that afterward, those who will follow the Lord will be restored.

Chapter summary. Ephraim, the most respected of the northern tribes, has led Israel into Baal worship (13:1-3). Yet the Lord is God, who cared for His people so tenderly (vv. 4-6), but who is about to turn on Israel and destroy the rebellious nation (vv. 7-9). The North insisted on its own king and kingdom and in doing so rejected God (vv. 10-13; cf. 1 Kings 12). God, who redeems from death (Hosea 13:13), will bring death and destruction to the Northern Kingdom (vv. 14-16).

Despite this grim portrait of Israel's immediate future, the Book of Hosea concludes with one of the most comforting of the Old Testament's visions of Israel's destiny. God invites Israel to return, bringing only an appeal for forgiveness and an affirmation of renewed faith (14:1-3). In response God will heal His people and restore their lost splendor (vv. 4-8). In both judgment and in grace God displays the rightness of His ways and defines the path in which the godly are to walk (v. 9).

Key verse. 14:2: All we can offer God is ourselves.

Personal application. Judgment on the left and grace on the right keep us in the center of God's will.

Key concepts. Baal »p. 162. Guilt »p. 79. Idolatry »p. 433. Compassion »p. 440. Salvation »p. 426. Confession »p. 892.

INSIGHT

"Ephraim" (13:1). The tribe which proudly asserted its primacy in the North (cf. Jud. 8:1-3; 1 Kings 12:26-33) was the site of a worship center at Bethel which was corrupted by Baal worship (Hosea 13:1-3). This brought spiritual death to the nation and would soon bring physical death as well (»p. 741).

"But I am the Lord" (13:4-8). God revealed Himself in grace, and the only result was that God's people became proud and forgot Him. For believers prosperity always holds more spiritual perils than suffering. One of the greatest perils is that when God's people become proud and unresponsive, He must act to punish them.

Guilt stored up (13:12). The Heb. is *sarar*, tied up in a bundle for safekeeping. God is quick to forgive confessed sin. He graciously delays punishment to give us many chances to change. But those who reject every gracious overture, and assume God does not care what they do, will be surprised. No sin is forgotten, but preserved for the day of reckoning.

Rebirth (13:13). Israel like a "child without wisdom" fights passing through the birth canal to experience spiritual rebirth.

Death's power limited (13:14). Death has no power over God's redeemed. This great affirmation has many applications. In context, it is an encouragement to turn to God and live. In

the N.T. it is a reminder of God's final victory over physical death, won through Christ's resurrection, to be experienced by us at our own resurrection (1 Cor. 15:55).

"Take words" (14:2). God does not ask us to bring gifts or sacrifices. Rather He asks us to bring words when we come to Him. Three kinds of words are identified: words of confession ("forgive all our sins"), words of praise ("the fruit of our lips"), and words of commitment ("we will"). When you and I come to God today, these three kinds of words are still the most important things we can bring to the Lord.

Love freely (14:4). When God heals and receives sinners He chooses to love us "freely." The thought is "unconditionally." God doesn't hold our past against us. He simply showers love on us.

Fruitfulness (14:5-8). God's love has a vital, transforming impact on His people. The O.T. often uses figures of speech that involve trees and flowers when indicating divine blessing. Much of Palestine is semiarid, and verdant growth suggests abundant rains and prosperity. Thus spiritual as well as material prosperity are represented by the blossoming of a lily, the young shoots of a cedar, and the fragrance of a cedar.

Joel

Natural disasters are often called "acts of God." In modern terms this simply means that no human being had any control over a particular event. But in Old Testament times many a "natural disaster" was literally an act of God: a sovereign shaping of events to teach a spiritual lesson. Nowhere is this displayed more unforgettably than in the Book of Joel, which describes a terrible infestation of locusts. The insect horde stripped the land of vegetation, facing God's people with starvation, and leading the prophet to call all Israel to prayer and fasting (1:13-14). But even more, the locust invasion stimulated a grand vision of a yet-future "Day of the Lord." In that day God will bring foreign armies against Palestine, to work an even more terrible devastation. This vision of future judgment is the background for God's own urgent call to His people: They must "return to Me with all your heart" (2:12). The Book of Joel concludes with one of the most towering of Old Testament promises. Whatever the immediate future may hold, a time is coming when God will pour out His Spirit on all peoples. He will judge pagan nations, and bless His ancient land.

Joel's powerful images and his urgent calls for reform remind us that personal relationship with God has priority over the affairs of this life. When we are too preoccupied with worldly activities, we are too preoccupied! Yet Joel's promises of future blessing foreshadow not only the glory days at history's end, but also our present age. For the Spirit Joel predicts will be poured out has come on Christ's church, and the wonder of God's living presence within us is realized for all those who trust in Christ.

Date and Authorship. Little is known of the author, whose name means "Yahweh is God." He lived and prophesied in Judah sometime prior to the destruction of the temple in 586 B.C. Several dates have been suggested, ranging from the ninth century B.C. to the seventh century. Most commentators, however, tend to support an eighth-century setting, based on his failure to mention Assyria or Babylon, while naming six other nations who were significant in Israel's eighth-century experience. The apparent wealth before the locust plague struck, and the formalism of Judah's worship, suggest possible placement in the prosperous time of Uzziah. Joel's message rings true in every time of prosperity, when God's people are tempted to give superficial allegiance to the Lord rather than the total commitment His majesty requires.

WHERE THE ACTION TAKES PLACE

The ministry of Joel is set in Judah, the southernmost of the two Hebrew kingdoms. Joel mentions a number of locations in the South, showing he was intimately familiar with his homeland and its people.

JOEL AT A GLANCE

KEY THEMES
Repentance *Two powerful hortatory passages vividly describe what is involved in true repentance (1:13-20; 2:12-17).*
Revival *True revival is only possible when God's Spirit acts in the hearts of His people, as He will at history's end (2:28-32).*

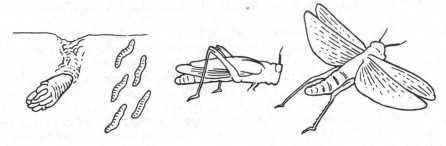

Illustration. *The devastation caused by locust swarms in the ancient world was not only due to the depradations of the mature, but also to the eggs they laid. Just as new growth returned, the locust larvae emerged from eggs to feed. Then the crawling young covered the ground. Joel 1:4 uses four different Hebrew words for locusts, which many believe represent the stages in their life cycle shown above.*

THEOLOGICAL OUTLINE OF JOEL

I. THE LOCUST PLAGUE   1:1–2:27
II. THE DAY OF THE LORD   2:28–3:21

CONTENT OUTLINE OF JOEL

I. The Locust Plague (1:1–2:27)
  A. The Locusts (1:1-4)
  B. Joel's Interpretation and His
    Warnings (1:5-20)
    1. Awaken to danger (1:5-7)
    2. Mourn (1:8-10)
    3. Despair (1:11-12)
    4. Repent (1:13-18)
    5. Call on God (1:19-20)
  C. A Near "Day of the Lord"
    (2:1-27)
    1. An invading army
      described (2:1-11)
    2. A plea for heart
      repentance (2:12-17)
      a. Seek God's mercy
        (2:12-14)

      b. Seek God's grace
        (2:15-17)
    3. God's reply to Judah's
      plea (2:18-27)
II. God's Commitment to Judah's
  Future (2:28–3:21)
  A. God Will Pour Out His Spirit
    (2:28-31)
  B. God Will Save All Who Call on
    Him (2:32)
  C. God Will Execute Judgment
    (3:1-16)
  D. God Will Bless His People
    (3:17-21)

Chapter summary. A terrible locust plague devastates the land of Judah (1:1-4). Joel alone seems to sense the spiritual significance of this act of God. Using a series of active verbs Joel urges his generation to wake up, to mourn, even to despair (vv. 5-12). He calls on the priests who minister before God to declare a national fast (vv. 13-14), for Joel realizes that the locust plague is an indication of divine displeasure; a forerunner of even more devastating judgment (vv. 15-18). Joel himself calls urgently to the Lord, setting an example for his generation (vv. 19-20).

Outline
Place
Finder

LOCUSTS
DAY OF
THE LORD

Key verse. 1:14: An appropriate response.

Personal application. Seek to sense God's purpose in what happens to you, and to our nation.

Key concepts. Drunkenness »p. 824. Repentance »p. 780. Day of the Lord »pp. 413, 541. Fasting »p. 442.

INSIGHT

All responsible (1:2). Joel addresses his words not only to leaders but also to "all who live in the land." We can't shift responsibility for the tone of our nation only to leaders.

Signs of the times (1:2). Great locust swarms were not uncommon in the ancient world. Amos speaks of a swarm that infested Israel, the Northern Kingdom (4:9). But the swarm in Joel's day wrought such unusual destruction that it was clearly an act of God. Joel is stunned others in his society fail to see God's hand in what has happened, or realize its meaning. Let's be aware that God is sovereign and be sensitive to what He may be saying to us through events.

"Wake up" (1:5-7). The exhortation is directed to "drunkards." While some take this as an expression of Joel's concern that his society is filled with pleasure seekers, it is more likely the usage is symbolic. A drunkard falls into a drugged sleep, insensitive to all around him. What concerns Joel is the insensitivity of God's people to the spiritual implications of the locust disaster.

"Mourn" (1:8-10). The serious economic impact of the locust plague should have caused grief and concern. An appropriate response would have been deep mourning. Yet the people could not seem to see beyond today, or realize the serious problems God's judgment created for tomorrow. Judah reacted much as modern citizens do to deficit spending by the U.S. government. With indifference.

"Despair" (1:11-12). The fruit of the vine and fig tree frequently symbolize God's blessing on the Holy Land. The destruction of these significant resources should have caused despair and symbolized God's displeasure. Yet not even the farmers, who were most immediately affected by the locust swarm, seem to be aware of the seriousness of the situation.

A plea to those who minister (1:13). In Israel the priests were to be most sensitive to God and were charged with distinguishing between the "clean and unclean" in the land. Joel urges these spiritual leaders to actually lead: to "spend the night in sackcloth" and "declare a holy fast."

Sackcloth was rough, scratchy clothing. Wearing it, like fasting, showed that an individual felt deeply the grief, or the fear, that he was bringing before the Lord. The priests should have been moved. The devastation of the land meant the grain and drink offerings that fed *them* would no longer be brought to the temple! Yet these spiritual leaders too were so spiritually insensitive that they, like the people, missed the meaning of the locust invasion. They too failed to hear God's voice in the judgment He directed against them.

"I call" (1:19-20). Unable to move any in Judah by his urgent words, Joel sets a personal example. Others will not call on the Lord, but Joel does.

What should you and I do if the leadership of our churches seems insensitive to God? How should we react if no one listens to our urgent warnings? Just as Joel did! We don't despair. We don't strike out angrily at others. We turn to God, and in so doing model the response that the Lord wants all of His people to make to Him.

Outline
Place
Finder

LOCUSTS
DAY OF
THE LORD

Chapter summary. The vision of the locust horde dissolves into a vision of an invading foreign army (2:1-2). There are many parallels. They find the land a garden and leave it a waste. They swarm, unstoppable, over the whole land. And, as God caused the insect infestation, so He Himself leads the foreign hosts against His own people (vv. 3-11). The vision of the dark disaster that lies ahead is lightened by an invitation. Even now God's people can turn to Him with all their hearts. God is gracious, and the possibility exists that He may relent (vv. 12-17). When God does relent, He will reply to His people's pleas with a promise of prosperity (vv. 18-19). He will drive the foreign armies back (vv. 20-21). He will give Israel prosperity and a "teacher for righteousness" (vv. 22-24) and will repay fully the years the locusts have eaten (vv. 25-27). On this note the theme of this chapter ends, though our English text contains a few verses that are better placed with chapter 3.

Key verse. 2:12: It's still not too late.

Personal application. Repentance must be from the heart.

Key concepts. Day of the Lord »pp. 413, 541. War »p. 133. Repentance »p. 780. Grace »p. 725. Future war »p. 428.

INSIGHT

"The Day of the Lord" (2:1-2). The phrase indicates any time in which God personally and actively intervenes to judge or to bless. It is particularly associated with the end of time, but expressions of the "Day of the Lord" may take place at any point in history. Commentators debate whether the invading army described here is that of Assyria or Babylon, or the armies other prophets predict will invade Israel as history draws to a close. What we must remember is that God is not limited, but can act for or against us at any time.

Assyria (2:3-11). The prophet's vivid description of the invaders, and his analogy with the locust swarm, do fit the Assyrian military machine that crushed the North and punished Judah not long after Joel's time. War, for all its terrors, is but a pale reflection of divine judgment that awaits those who refuse to respond to Him.

"Even now" (2:12). One of the great truths affirmed by Joel is that it is not too late to appeal to God until it is too late. Joel appeals to his people, as we appeal today. Judgment is coming. But "even now" turn to the Lord.

True repentance (2:13). Repentance isn't saying, "I'm sorry." It is a matter of the heart rather than of words, or even of actions. If our heart truly is broken by our sins, and we yearn to return to the Lord, then a change of life will follow. But it must begin in our hearts.

"A holy fast" (2:15-17). When enough individuals "rend their hearts," the whole congregation will be moved.

God's jealousy (2:18). The Heb. word, *qana'*, expresses a very strong, passionate emotion, and is often translated "envy." When used to describe God's feeling for His people, it indicates a fierce commitment. God cares so much for His people that He is moved to action, not only to punish when sin interrupts His fellowship with His beloved, but also to bless when His people are responsive to Him. The biblical concept that God is a jealous God protects us from the view of some that God is distant, detached, unmoved by either our sins or our troubles. God does care, intensely, about us. And about how we live our lives.

"The northern army" (2:20). This passage seems to parallel Ezek. 38–39. It may suggest that now Joel is speaking of the invader prophesied to attack Israel in history's final battle.

Instruction in righteousness (2:23-24). Outward blessing mirrors the inner transformation experienced by a people who now live holy lives.

Repayed (2:28). God owes us no repayment for the years we waste in sin, or the suffering we experience while under judgment. But God does repay, so richly that we feel nothing has been lost. What a great and gracious God!

Chapter summary. Joel's prophecy concludes with a description of God's eschatological program. First God will provide for individuals by pouring out His Spirit on all people (2:28-31), in response to their cry to Him for salvation (v. 32). As for the people whom God considers His inheritance, Israel, the Lord will restore their fortunes, and judge the nations who have oppressed them (3:1-8). He will arouse the latent hostility of the nations toward the Jews and cause them to advance against His people (vv. 9-12). Then, as the enemy armies deploy against the Holy Land, God will miraculously intervene on their behalf (vv. 13-17). After that day of God's judgment of pagan nations, Judah and Jerusalem, the sins of her peoples pardoned, will enter an era of lasting prosperity.

Outline
Place
Finder

LOCUSTS
**DAY OF
THE LORD**

Key verse. 2:28: God's Spirit is poured out on all.

Personal application. Don't forget that daughters as well as sons are intended to prophesy.

Key concepts. Holy Spirit »p. 776. Women »pp. 163, 394, 723. Salvation »p. 433. History's end »pp. 428, 443.

INSIGHT

Pouring out the Spirit (2:28-32). The Apostle Peter quoted this passage to explain manifestations of the Holy Spirit's coming on the early Christians on the first Day of Pentecost after Christ's resurrection (cf. Acts 2). Only elements of the passage applied: the pouring out of the Spirit (Joel 2:28), and the promise of salvation to all who call on the Lord (v. 32). It is not unusual for an O.T. prophecy to have partial expression at some point in time prior to the moment of complete fulfillment that is its primary focus (»pp. 405–408).

"Sons and daughters" (2:28). In the age initiated by the pouring out of God's Spirit women as well as men have a role in ministry.

"Wonders" (2:30-31). The specification of changes in the physical universe signify that the ultimate fulfillment of this prediction is set at history's end. Joel's promise that the Spirit would be poured out on all was used by Peter to *explain* what happened on Pentecost and show that it had roots in the older revelation. His use of the passage then does not imply that the prophecy itself was fulfilled.

"Everyone who calls" (2:32). In much of the O.T. the "everyone" addressed falls within the community of Israel. Yet O.T. prophecy looks forward to a time when Gentiles too will share the blessings of redemption (»p. 798). The stunning aspect of this prophecy is seen only in its partial fulfillment in the church. Today "everyone" truly is every one, without regard to race or tradition. The last phrase underlines the fact that this open invitation is God's will. It is He who has decided to call to all.

Final war (3:9-12). The picture of a great final struggle is found in many prophets (cf. Isa. 17:12; 24:21-23; Micah 4:11-13; Zech. 12:2-3) as well as in Rev. 16:14-16; 19:17-19. Man's last hostile attack against God's people is put down by God, and ushers in an era of universal peace.

"The valley of decision" (3:14). This is not a valley where mankind makes a decision for or against God. It is the valley where God renders His judicial decision against rebellious humankind.

Millennial blessing (3:18-21). After the final battle Judah is destined to know perpetual blessing. The geographic change noted here, with a fountain flowing out of the Lord's house, has a counterpart in Ezekiel's much later description of a temple rebuilt as God's house among His redeemed people (cf. Ezek. 40–48).

Amos

It was the most prosperous of times. The Northern Hebrew Kingdom, Israel, was led by the dynamic Jeroboam II. He had waged successful war against Israel's hostile neighbors, and won control of trade routes that poured wealth into Samaria. The land was fertile, the rains fell, and bumper crops were harvested. It was a golden age: proud public buildings were erected, and the wealthy built spacious residences near the popular worship centers at Bethel and Dan, where they could enjoy the splendid rituals that satisfied their delight in ostentation and pomp. But beneath the glittering surface of society dark tragedies were hidden. The rich, in total disregard for God's Law and for their fellow Jews, dispossessed farmers from their hereditary plots of land to build great personal estates. The poor were further oppressed by merchants who used unjust weights when buying and selling grain, and who mixed husks with the barley kernels. More and more people were forced to sell themselves and their children into slavery. Justice was for sale to the highest bidder. The wives of the rich demanded more and more luxuries. And no one gave a thought to the anguish of those who were defrauded to satisfy their desires.

It is against the background of this society that we read the words of Amos, a farmer from nearby Judah, who was unexpectedly called by God to go to Israel and condemn that nation's injustice and apostasy. In blunt, bold language the prophet exposes every sin, and in so doing stands in judgment of injustice wherever it occurs. Amos remains one of the most relevant books of the Old Testament. The words of that prophet speak to the well-to-do of every age, warning any society which ignores the poor and oppressed.

AMOS AT A GLANCE

KEY PEOPLE

Amos *God's angry man, who denounces injustice in Israel, and expresses God's concern for the poor and oppressed of every age.*

Amaziah *The high priest of Bethel who rejects Amos' message and tries to drive him out of Israel.*

KEY THEMES

The plight of the poor. *God is deeply concerned about the economic oppression that characterizes Israel's society (1:6, 9; 3:9-10; 4:1; 5:12; 8:4-6).*

Judicial corruption. *Judgments favored the rich (2:6-8; 3:10) and ignored dishonesty and fraud (5:7-24; 8:5-6).*

Idolatry. *The worship at Bethel and Dan is in violation of O.T. Law (cf. Deut. 12:1-19) and thus idolatrous (Amos 5:26; 8:14). However, enthusiastic worship marked by idolatry, and offered by a personally and socially immoral people, is never acceptable to God.*

Amos the Man

Amos was a layman, a "herdsman" from Tekoa, about 10 miles south of Jerusalem. He is identified as a sheep rancher (1:1; 7:14) and cultivator of the sycamore-fig (v. 14). The first identifies him with the rich, for he was not a simple shepherd. But the second identifies him with the poor, for the sycamore-fig was their food. How appropriate that God chose this man to speak to the wealthy of Israel about the poor and oppressed of that land.

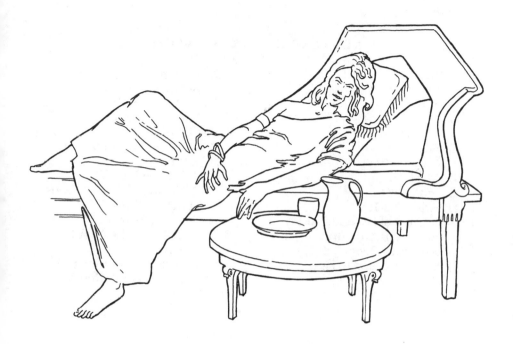

WHERE THE ACTION TAKES PLACE

The Northern Hebrew Kingdom, Israel, is the scene of Amos' ministry. But its setting is more appropriately in the streets outside the luxury homes of the rich and famous, whose lifestyles Amos condemns. Inside women reclined on ivory inlaid couches, feasting on meats and drinking bowls of exotic wines while listening to the latest popular music group (4:1; 6:4-6). They competed to be fashionable, contemptuous of the fact that the price they paid for a pair of sandals might have saved a needy man forced by the courts to sell himself into slavery to pay a usurious debt to some wealthy creditor (2:6). In a very real sense, the "action" in Amos takes place in the hearts of each hearer: hearts that are either hardened by selfishness and greed, or hearts that are touched by the needs of the poor and oppressed and who seek to remedy the injustices that condemn many to poverty.

THEOLOGICAL OUTLINE OF AMOS

CONTENT OUTLINE OF AMOS

Chapter summary. Amos briefly introduces himself and notes the historical setting of his ministry (1:1-2). He then records a series of brief announcements of divine judgments against eight nations (1:3–2:16). Each is introduced with a formula which emphasizes the certainty of the judgment God has determined. The oracles have a special order. Amos begins with the most distant nation, and then, in a wide swing, moves to lands circling Israel. One can almost hear the delighted "Yes! Yes!" of his listeners as they hear the prophet denounce one enemy after another. But then, unexpectedly, the prophet pounces. The severest condemnation of all is reserved for Israel itself. How his listeners' hearts must have sunk as Amos' finger at last pointed directly at them! God's judgment is impartial. Sin is condemned, wherever it is found.

Outline
Place
Finder

JUDGMENTS
INDICTMENT
VISIONS

Key verses. 2:6-8: Sin provokes God's wrath.

Personal application. Sin is sin wherever it is found, in others — or in us.

Key concepts. Judgment »p. 372. Sin »pp. 34, 362. Law »pp. 120, 145. Idolatry »p. 433. Justice »p. 541. Poor »p. 90. Nazarite »p. 96.

INSIGHT

"Amos" (1:1). See "Amos the Man," »p. 536.

The earthquake (1:2). Amos carefully specifies that his ministry was launched "two years before the earthquake." Why? The prophet's message of doom was scoffed at in prosperous Israel. Things hadn't been so good for generations! Then, as Amos' words still echoed, a tremendous earthquake struck the land, a divine reminder that all in this world is transitory and vulnerable. Only in God and in His ways can a man find true security.

The pagan nations (1:3–2:3). The basis of their judgment is their hostility toward and mistreatment of God's people. For background, see: Philistines »p. 185. Tyre »p. 499. Edom »p. 104. Moab »p. 476.

"For three sins . . . even for four" (1:3). This repeated refrain is found in wisdom literature (cf. Prov. 6:16) and other prophets (cf. Micah 5:5-6). It typically denotes an indefinite number. Here it underlines the existence of serious sins which God must and will judge.

Judah's sins (2:4-5). Judah's sins are identified in a general way only: the people of the South have rejected God's laws and followed false gods. Amos will be much more specific in naming the sins of the Israelites. How eager we are to learn the details of others' faults and failures! But the only sins whose specifics we need to know are our own.

Selling the righteous (2:6). The phrase means only that those who are sold are in the right, not that they are blameless. "They" here are the oppressing classes in Israel. People with power and influence cared so little for the rights of the needy that they would take so paltry a bribe as a pair of sandals to decide against them.

Denying justice (2:7a). The wealthy were so indifferent to the poor that they walked all over their rights, as disinterested as if they were walking along a road. Where no one cares about the needy the legal system itself will become corrupt and the poor will be denied access however just their cause.

A modern example is a N.Y. court's decision that a minister is not allowed to speak for the unborn even from his pulpit. Not only is there no legal interest in the rights of unborn children, but basic constitutional guarantees of freedom of speech and the separation of church and state are callously set aside. Each society must ask: Who speaks for the helpless? And each must answer for its indifference and unconcern.

Using the same girl (2:7b). The phrase likely refers to slave girls, who by tradition might be given as a secondary wife to a son of the household. But to simply use such a person as a sexual plaything for the men of the household violated the letter and spirit of O.T. Law concerning slaves, and showed the utter moral corruption of the land (cf. Ex. 21:7-11).

Outline
Place
Finder

JUDGMENTS
INDICTMENT
VISIONS

Chapter summary. The indictment of Israel is based on the fact that the Hebrew people were chosen by God. Therefore their punishment is utterly certain, for they have violated a special, intimate relationship not enjoyed by others (3:1-2). Amos then pairs several effects with their causes (vv. 3-6), culminating in the observation that when disaster comes, God must be the cause. God has revealed to His prophet the effect that Israel's sin must bring: an enemy will overrun the land (vv. 7-12). God will punish Israel for her sins and destroy the lavish homes of the rich with the altars of her worship centers (vv. 13-15). The pampered women of Israel will be led away in rags (4:1-3). The very worship of the rich is sin in God's sight (vv. 4-5). And this in spite of ample warnings God provided in the form of hunger (v. 6), drought (vv. 7-8), failed crops (v. 9), and plagues (vv. 10-11). Because Israel has ignored the Lord's messengers, they must now prepare to meet God Himself, who comes in judgment (vv. 12-13).

Key verse. 3:2: Privileges imply responsibility.

Personal application. God gives us ample warnings before He judges. So pay close heed.

Key concepts. Choice of Israel »p. 124. Prophet »p. 131.

INSIGHT

"**Chosen**" **(3:2).** The Heb. word is *yada'*, "known." It speaks of intimacy and close personal relationship.

Cause and effect (3:3-6). The point of Amos' illustrations is that each effect must have a cause. Two walk together because they've agreed to do so. A bird is found in a snare only because the snare had been set. It follows that disaster is an effect of some action, in this case action by the Lord. This section is foundational to the impact of the list of disasters provided in 4:6-11. It should have been clear to Israel that their sufferings were God's messengers, warning them against their sins.

We are not to take every personal disaster as a warning of judgment or judgment itself. But we are to examine ourselves to discover if anything in our lives might have moved God to act.

Disaster (3:6). Older versions have "evil." The Heb. word here (*ra'ah*) means "evil" in both an ethical sense and an experiential sense. God does not do anything that is morally wrong, but His judgments on sin undoubtedly are experienced as "bad news" by human beings!

God's voice (3:7-8). God's voice sounds through His prophets like the warning roar of the lion. God does not keep His intention to judge sin secret, but clearly reveals His plans. There is no excuse for not heeding God's words.

Knowing how to do right (3:10). The fortresses of Israel are pictured not as centers for the defense of the land and its people, but as strongholds in which riches taken *from* the people are preserved for the wealthy! The rich have plundered their own land, and in the process their moral sense has become so warped that they no longer can separate right from wrong.

"**The lion's mouth**" **(3:12).** The remains of a sheep eaten by a wild animal was saved to prove that the shepherd had not stolen it (Ex. 22:13). When the enemy invades the land of Israel only a few torn remnants of the people will be snatched from the invaders.

Altars and summer homes (3:14-15). Together the two symbolize the flaws in Israel's society: false religion, and a passionate materialism that produced a wealthy class at the expense of the poor. The summer and winter houses are most likely two residences maintained by the rich, while the dispossessed poor lived in the streets.

"**Cows of Bashan**" **(4:1).** The rich upland area was known for its fat cattle. Amos likens the rich women to cattle, intent only on being well fed, totally indifferent to the poor. See illustration »p. 538.

Warnings ignored (4:6-11). Psalm 32:9 urges believers not to "be like the horse or the mule, which have no understanding but must be controlled by bit and bridle." Israel was even worse: God's people were unwilling to be controlled even though God used the rod.

Chapter summary. Amos is so certain of the coming judgment that he utters a "lament" over Israel, a mournful poem expressing grief at the death of a near relative (5:1-3). Even so, the prophet shares God's urgent call to reform. That call contains a list of indictments that helps us see clearly the oppression which marked the Northern Kingdom's social order. It ends with a prediction that reflects God's awareness that, whatever He may say, Israel will not respond (vv. 4-17). Thus when God acts next, it will be a dark day for His people (vv. 18-20). For God actually hates the sterile and empty worship of this people who love ritual, but ignore justice and morality (vv. 21-27).

The luxury of the complacent testifies against them (6:1-7), but their pride will be crushed by an enemy God will stir up against them (vv. 8-14). The oppressors will be oppressed, and there will be no refuge for them in God.

Outline
Place
Finder

JUDGMENTS
INDICTMENT
VISIONS

Key verse. 5:24: There is no substitute for justice.

Personal application. Don't bother to worship God if you oppress your fellowmen.

Key concepts. Exile »p. 138. Poor »p. 90. Good »p. 849.

INSIGHT

Blessing reversed (5:3). God promised Abraham to multiply his offspring. But that blessing could be experienced only by obedient generations. Sin has reversed the blessing: rather than increase tenfold, this generation will *decrease* tenfold!

Doing justice. Underlying the O.T. concept of "justice" is the conviction that human beings have both rights and obligations. God is the source of the moral and ethical norms that define these rights and obligations. What's more, God revealed His norms to Israel in the Law. One who lives with others the way the Law describes "does" justice.

We can hardly overemphasize the importance the O.T. places on "doing justice." Prophet after prophet reminds Israel that one can only live in fellowship with God by doing justice in his or her relationships with others (cf. Isa. 58:2-10; Jer. 22:15-17). As these passages and others point out, doing justice means more than refraining from harming another. It requires an individual and the nation to take active initiative to "do away with the yoke of oppression" and to "satisfy the needs of the oppressed." When God asks us if we were committed to doing justice, it will not be enough to reply, "Lord, I did not wrong another person." We must be able to say we "defended the cause of the poor and needy."

Where to look for God (5:4-5). Israel is told not to seek God at its splendid houses of worship. The word translated "seek" (*daras*) means to turn to God in trust and confidence. If Israel really wants to respond to God, the place to find Him is among the poor and oppressed, and the way to express faith is to stand against oppression.

Legal justice (5:7-11). In these verses "justice" (*mispat*) means fair and unbiased court decisions.

"Good, not evil" (5:14). Every life has a basic moral direction, shaped and maintained by daily choices. Our calling is to love good and to let good shape the course of our life.

"The Day of the Lord" (5:18-20). This phrase often serves as a technical theological term marking the setting of described events and placing them at history's end (»p. 413). The prophet's vision of history's end has a glorious aspect: Israel is redeemed and given a premier place among the world's nations under the Messiah. This delighted the people of Amos' day, who were eager for God to act. But Amos warns them that the Day of the Lord is also a day of judgment. And it is the dark and bitter aspect of God's visitation this generation will experience. The lesson for us is clear. Look eagerly for Christ's return—but not if you're living a life of sin.

Wealth (6:3-7). Riches are not intrinsically evil. But too often wealth promotes self-indulgence and makes us indifferent to others. It's the misuse of wealth that Amos condemns.

Chapter summary. Israel has been charged and found guilty. Now in a series of visions Amos is shown the nation's future. Judgment by locusts (7:1-3) and fire (vv. 4-6) are turned aside. But then the prophet sees God, measuring His people with a plumb line, determining that He must spare Israel no longer (vv. 7-9). Then a personal experience drives home the necessity of judgment to the prophet. Amaziah, the high priest at Bethel, where Amos has been preaching, accuses Amos of conspiracy and demands he stop preaching. God's word has been rejected by both the spiritual and secular authorities who represent the nation! Now God pronounces judgment on Amaziah and reaffirms the doom of Israel. Amaziah's wife will sell herself in Bethel, the priest's sons and daughters will be killed, and Israel will surely go into exile (vv. 10-17).

Key verse. 7:13: God is greater than any king.

Personal application. No one successfully resists God.

Key concepts. Prophet »p. 131. Exile »p. 138.

INSIGHT

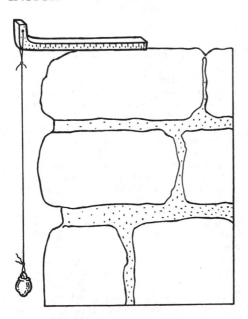

Illustration (7:7-9). *The plumb line is a simple but basic builder's tool. A weight attached to a line was held against a wall to measure its vertical trueness. In eighth-century Israel skilled builders constructed walls like that shown in the illustration. But when God measured the morality of Israel's society, it was shown to be so far from true that the whole construction had to be torn down.*

"The king's share" (7:1). The first crop was commandeered by Jeroboam, who maintained a large army. A locust plague at that time would leave the people without food until the next year, and cause starvation.

This, and a second proposed judgment, were held back in answer to Amos' prayer. But punishment can be delayed only so long, however righteous the one who prays for sinners.

"Seer" (7:12). The word *(hozeh)* was an ancient term equivalent to "prophet." Amaziah, in using it, recognizes Amos' office, but still refused to listen to his message.

"The king's sanctuary" (7:13). The words are revealing. The chief priest's allegiance was not to God, but to the king! It's easy to be confused about allegiance. In the Christian community too we feel loyalty to human leaders. The danger always exists that in seeking to please or protect men we may forget that our ultimate loyalty is to God.

"The Lord took me" (7:15-16). God still calls unlikely people to important ministries (»p. 536).

Accountability (7:16-17). People are free to make any choice they wish, as Amaziah did in choosing loyalty to king over loyalty to God. But we remain accountable to God for such choices.

Chapter summary. Amos is given another vision, this time of a basket of ripe fruit (8:1-2) which signifies the time is ripe for the judgment of Israel: a judgment which God goes on to describe in grim detail (vv. 3-14). Yet another vision reveals God standing by the altar, which in Old Testament faith symbolizes both sacrifice and judgment on sin (9:1). From this significant location God commands the temple to collapse and destroy the nation. The temple stands for the corrupt religion of Israel, a nation riddled with injustice, which will surely destroy its complacent and sinful adherents (vv. 2-7).

Despite the immediate prospect of a divinely directed disaster, the Book of Amos concludes on a note of hope. God will destroy "the sinful kingdom." Yet some will survive, to be scattered among the nations. One day God will rebuild the nation under a Descendant of David (vv. 8-12). In that day there will be blessing and peace (vv. 13-15).

Outline
Place
Finder

JUDGMENTS
INDICTMENT
VISIONS

Key verse. 9:10: God will permit His own to live in sin.

Personal application. Hope of God's future grace sustains us in times of suffering.

Key concepts. Altar »p. 79. Messiah »p. 432. Future kingdom »p. 443.

INSIGHT

Songs and suffering (8:3-4). There is a terrible irony in this picture of worshipers enjoying special music in a cathedral while just outside the needy beg in utter desperation. The image calls every congregation of believers to honest self-examination.

Profiting from poverty (8:6). Because the poor are socially powerless it is easier to defraud them than others. Typically prices for food in poor sections of our own cities are much higher than in more affluent suburbs, and rental is high for poorly maintained living space. Not every building owner is a slumlord, nor every market intent on fraud. But there clearly is too much "skimping the measure, boosting the price and cheating with dishonest scales."

No sun at noon (8:8-10). The words are metaphorical, and describe such a shattering of what Israel has assumed is the "natural order" of things that the people will be thrown into utter panic and despair.

"The shame of Samaria" (8:14). The word ('asmah) also means guilt, a guilt incurred by putting their trust in the idolatrous worship conducted at Dan and Beersheba.

No escape (9:1-4). The prophet describes the frantic efforts of the people of Israel to get away from God. The effort is futile, and reminds us that "man is destined to die once, and after that to face judgment" (Heb. 9:27).

Cush, Israel, Philistia, and Aram (9:7). These words were devastating to the Israelites, who counted on God's choice of Abraham to guarantee their present security. God supervised the history of these nations even as He supervised the history of Israel. God's choice of Israel was no basis to presume He would continue to bless whatever His people did. We too are a chosen people, recipients of God's grace. But election conveys no license on us to sin. Or to suppose that God has no concern for others.

The city of God (9:8-10). Human beings often confuse what St. Augustine called the "city of man" with the "city of God." We identify what God is doing with a particular society or nation. God was about to literally end Israel's existence as a nation and scatter the few survivors in pagan lands. Did this mean the end of what God had been building throughout history? Not at all. God's plans did not depend on the continued existence of the eighth-century B.C. nation at all!

What a lesson for us to learn. We have taken comfort in supposing that ours is a "Christian nation," important in God's plans. But at best we are a city of man, temporary recipients of God's grace, and privileged to serve Him. If our nation should crumble as ancient Israel did, let's take comfort in the fact that we are first of all citizens of the unshakable city of God.

Obadiah

Jacob and Esau were twin sons of Isaac, the son of Abraham. While Esau was indifferent to spiritual values, Jacob passionately desired to inherit the covenant promises of God. Now, centuries later, the descendants of these twin brothers form two nations: Judah, holding Jerusalem and the hills and valleys to the south of the Promised Land, and Edom, occupying the area south and east of the Dead Sea. Each has held its territory from the 13th century B.C. Yet, from the time of David, a deep hostility has existed between them. The occasion of this one-chapter book of prophecy directed against Edom is the participation of the Edomites, in some way, in a successful attack against Jerusalem. Given the similarities between Jeremiah 49:9, 14-16 and Obadiah 1-5, many commentators believe the attack in view is that by Nebuchadnezzar's army in 586 B.C. The impressive predictions of destruction were fulfilled shortly afterward, when Edom was destroyed by Nabonidus, the last of the Babylonian rulers. Though no certain date can be fixed for this prophecy, most place it shortly after the destruction of Jerusalem by the Babylonians.

The book's message, underlined in other prophets as well, is that while God judges His people, He remains committed to them.

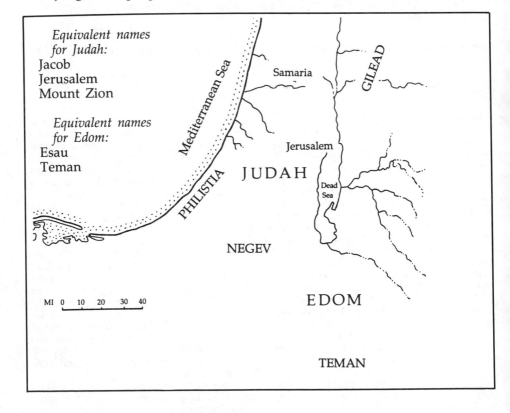

Equivalent names
for Judah:
Jacob
Jerusalem
Mount Zion

Equivalent names
for Edom:
Esau
Teman

Mediterranean Sea

Samaria

GILEAD

PHILISTIA

JUDAH

Jerusalem

Dead
Sea

NEGEV

MI 0 10 20 30 40

EDOM

TEMAN

Chapter summary. The brief book explores the relationship between Judah and Edom. The prophet first looks forward to a Day of the Lord in which the nations will cut Edom down in battle (vv. 1-9), even as in the past Edom collaborated with foreign powers to cut down Judah (vv. 10-14). In a yet-future Day of the Lord the house of Jacob, the Jewish people, will occupy the Promised Land, while Edom like the other nations hostile to God's people will be consumed (vv. 15-21).

Key verses. 10-11: Judgment always has a basis.

Personal application. Choose your sides carefully.

Key concepts. Covenant »p. 32. Pride »p. 352. Edom »p. 104. Day of the Lord »pp. 413, 541. Gentiles »p. 798. Kingdom »p. 443.

INSIGHT

"Pride" (vv. 3-4). The unusual word used here (*zadon*) is used of food or water that boils up. Edom's pride is rooted in the fact that its frontiers were defended on one side by a ridge of high cliffs and on the other by a series of forts guarding against attack from the desert. It is easy to become proud when we feel invulnerable, whether because of wealth or position or military might. Yet when any person or society scornfully asks, "Who can bring me down?" there is always one reply. The Lord.

Nothing to be left. Both thieves and grape pickers overlook at least something. But when God judges Edom nothing will remain.

Throughout the O.T. the prophets promise Israel and Judah that when God judges, there will be survivors, from whom He will rebuild the nation. There is no such gracious promise made to those who are not His covenant people.

"That day" (vv. 8-9). In this book as in other O.T. prophets it is important to understand the range of meanings of "that day," or "the Day of the Lord." It is *always* a time when God acts in human affairs to judge or bless. It may refer *either* to a relatively near historic event, or a distant event located at history's end. Or it may refer *both* to a near event and to culminating events at history's end. Edom's "Day-of-the-Lord" destruction is to take place in the near future. But Judah's "Day-of-the-Lord" blessing is to be placed at history's end.

"Because" (v. 10). The basis of Edom's judgment is violence against "your brother Jacob." The relationship of the two peoples makes Edom's hostile acts more heinous, though it has been displayed throughout history (Ex. 15:15; Num. 20:14-21; Deut. 2:4; Jud. 11:17-18). The word for violence, *hamas*, indicates actions which are both morally wrong and unnecessarily brutal.

"The day" (vv. 11-14). A specific attack on Jerusalem in which Edom delighted and thus participated is the proximate cause of Edom's judgment. Edom did not necessarily actually loot the fallen city. God knows the attitudes of our heart, and we are as responsible for them as for overt acts of sin.

Which invasion? There were six invasions of Judah which might fit the book, though the last fits best. These are: By (1) Shishak of Egypt (1 Kings 14:25-28); (2) Arabs and Philistines (2 Chron. 21:16-17); (3) Syrians (2 Chron. 24:23-24); (4) Edom (2 Kings 14:7-14); (5) Several enemies during the time of Ahaz (2 Chron. 29:8-9), and Assyria in the reign of Hezekiah (2 Kings 18–19); (6) The Babylonians, who destroyed the city and its temple (2 Chron. 36:15-22).

"For all nations" (vv. 15-18). As God dealt with Edom so God will deal with all nations hostile to God and His chosen people. This is the core of the prophecy, the central principle which governs the destiny of nations who have dealings with God's own. The principle of judgment is restated here: "As you have done, it will be done to you."

"Deliverers" (v. 21). The word is from the root *ys'*, the same root from which "Joshua" and "Jesus" are constructed. Salvation and peace will spread from Mt. Zion when the Lord restores Israel and establishes His kingdom on earth.

Jonah

Jonah might well be called the Old Testament's "patriotic prophet." A resident of Israel, his was the happy task of predicting the military successes won by Jeroboam II, and the almost unprecedented prosperity of his era (2 Kings 14:25). But when God called Jonah to go predict the downfall of Nineveh, the capital of an Assyrian Empire destined to destroy Jonah's homeland, the prophet fled in the opposite direction! Jonah himself explained: He feared that the people of Nineveh might repent and that God would relent (Jonah 4:2). When the reluctant prophet finally did preach in Nineveh, his fears were realized.

Despite the simplicity of the familiar story, it is one of the richest of Old Testament books in terms of teaching pointed spiritual lessons. God is shown to be deeply concerned with the welfare of people of every nation, not just of Israel. God is also shown to be gracious in dealing with His prophet. Even though Jonah was knowingly, willfully disobedient, God gave this patriotic prophet a second chance. Perhaps one of the most fascinating lessons is seen in the timing of Jonah's experience, during the reign of Jeroboam II. It was during this same reign that Amos' brief, fiery ministry took place. That prophet confronted the rich of Israel and condemned the social injustices that developed with prosperity. Amos too announced judgment and called on the people of God to repent. The significance of Jonah is that God's grace toward Nineveh served as a vivid object lesson for Israel, His own people. If Israel would repent she too could be saved. Unknown to Jonah, his mission to Nineveh was in fact a mission to Israel as well.

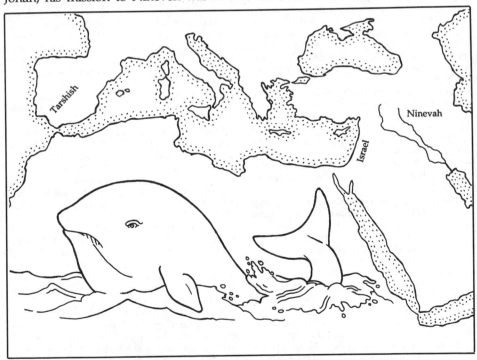

WHERE THE ACTION TAKES PLACE

Called to go to Nineveh, the Prophet Jonah took a ship bound for Tarshish, in Spain. Disobedience could hardly have been more willful or direct.

Date and Authorship. The book's author is identified as Jonah the son of Amittai, who is also mentioned in 1 Kings 14. This enables us to set a date for Jonah in the mid-eighth century B.C., perhaps around 760 B.C. The date and authorship of this book, the only one of the "later prophets" that adopts a completely narrative style, remained unchallenged until the 19th century. At that time critics who were unwilling to accept the supernatural elements in the story as historical suggested the book was actually a parable written much later in the Persian period. There is, however, no indication that the book was ever viewed by Jewish rabbis as anything but a true historical account of actual events.

THEOLOGICAL OUTLINE OF JONAH

I. DISOBEDIENCE 1
II. SUBMISSION 2
III. MISSION 3
IV. MOTIVES 4

CONTENT OUTLINE OF JONAH

I. Mission Refused (1:1–2:10)
  A. Jonah Disobeys (1:1-3)
  B. God Sends a Storm (1:4-5)
  C. Jonah Confesses (1:6-10)
  D. Jonah Thrown Overboard (1:11-16)
  E. Jonah Swallowed by a Great Fish (1:17)
  F. Jonah Prays and Submits to God (2:1-9)
  G. Jonah Is Vomited onto Dry Land (2:10)

II. Mission Accomplished (3:1–4:11)
  A. Jonah Preaches in Nineveh (3:1-4)
  B. The Ninevites Believe and Repent (3:5-9)
  C. God Relents (3:10)
  D. Jonah Is Angry (4:1-4)
  E. Jonah Waits and Watches (4:5-8)
  F. Jonah Is Rebuked for Lack of Compassion (4:9-11)

Outline
Place
Finder

DISOBEDIENCE
SUBMISSION
MISSION
MOTIVES

Chapter summary. Jonah disobeys God's command to preach in Nineveh, and boards a ship for Tarshish (1:1-4). When the ship is threatened by a terrible storm Jonah admits he is the cause and insists the terrified sailors throw him overboard (vv. 5-16). There Jonah is swallowed by a great fish (*not* a whale!) that God has specially prepared (v. 17). From inside the belly of the fish Jonah prays a significant prayer of submission (2:1-9) and is vomited on dry land (2:10).

Key verse. 2:4: Look again to God.

Personal application. God gives us many a second chance too!

Key concepts. Wickedness »p. 29. Assyria »p. 255. Lots »p. 325. Fear God »p. 387. Prayer »p. 181. Temple »p. 283. Vow »p. 96.

INSIGHT

"Jonah ran away" (1:3). Believers do not say "no" to God in words, but by actions. It is not what we say but what we do that counts. Note that at this point in the story there is no mention of Jonah's motives. Why? Because when God says "go" there is never any valid reason to refuse.

"Tarshish" (1:3). The name means "to smelt," and thus the city was associated with metal trade. The furthest known metal producing port in the 8th century B.C. was Tartessus, in Spain. Most believe this port was Jonah's destination. The identification is not vital, however. What is key is that metal producing areas along the Mediterranean were in the opposite direction from Nineveh.

Jonah and the sailors (1:6-16). Even out of fellowship with God, Jonah had an evangelistic impact on the sailors. His admission that he was the reason why God brought the great storm; his demand the sailors throw him overboard; the sudden stilling of the storm as soon as Jonah left the ship; all these witnessed to God's greatness and led the crew to greatly fear "the Lord" and to make "vows to Him."

It's a mistake to assume just because God is using someone in others' lives that that person must be godly. The Lord uses imperfect agents and even some who are actively disobeying Him at the very time they serve as channels of grace. And do not hold His servants in awe, as though what God does is a testimony to some human being's holiness.

At the same time, note this. Out of fellowship, Jonah was God's agent to bring knowledge of God to a boatload of sinners. Later we'll see that, back in fellowship, Jonah was God's agent of deliverance for a great city! Let's live in fellowship with God, and be clear channels through which His grace can flow, unimpeded.

God's sovereignty. There are several "miracles" in the passage, not just one. God's control of the sea, bringing a great storm, shows He controls nature. When lots were cast to determine who had offended God and brought the unusual storm, Jonah was chosen. When Jonah was thrown overboard, the storm stopped. Why then be surprised when the text tells us God "provided" a "great fish" to swallow Jonah, or that he was preserved alive in its belly? Either God is fully capable of controlling all events in this world, or He is not. It is not the miracles of Scripture that are questionable, but the critics' limited view of who God is.

"The grave" (2:2). The Heb. says "sheol," a poetic name for death or the grave often found in Heb. poetry. The next verses graphically portray the prophet's experience as ocean currents tumble him over and over and tendrils of swaying seaweed wrap themselves around his shoulders. Jonah's experience reminds us that even when humanly speaking it is too late, God can and does answer our cries for help.

"I remembered You" (2:7). In the O.T. to "remember" typically means to act on a thing remembered rather than simply call it to mind. In jeopardy Jonah recalled who God is and cried out in prayer. We too can recall God's grace and act on knowledge of His character by praying to Him.

"I will" (2:9). Jonah's obedience is a response of gratitude to God. God has acted to save him. Note too that the pagan sailors made vows to God after they were saved, rather than before. We commit ourselves to serve God not as a bribe to win His favor, but because we have been recipients of His grace.

Chapter summary. Given a second chance, Jonah now travels to Nineveh. Trudging through its suburbs he begins to announce that the city is to be destroyed (3:1-4). Amazingly, the people of Nineveh believe the foreign prophet's message, and the king decrees both a ritual fast and moral repentance (vv. 5-9). God then relents, and withholds the predicted destruction (v. 10). But Jonah is angry and frustrated. The patriotic prophet had feared that Nineveh might repent, for Jonah had *wanted* Nineveh destroyed (4:1-4). Eaten up with bitterness Jonah waits outside the city, still hoping to witness its destruction. There, to "ease his discomfort," the Lord causes a vine to grow and provide shade (vv. 5-6). But the next day the Lord sends a worm that destroys the vine, making his despondent prophet upset enough to want to die (vv. 7-8). The lesson is lost on Jonah. Yet he who is upset when God withdraws compassion from him should hardly be angry if God displays even greater compassion in dealing with others (vv. 9-11).

Outline
Place
Finder

DISOBEDIENCE
SUBMISSION
**MISSION
MOTIVES**

Key verse. 4:2: Knowing God doesn't guarantee doing right.

Personal application. We are not called to believe God is compassionate but to be compassionate because He is.

Key concepts. Repentance »p. 780. Fasting »p. 442. Compassion »p. 440. Anger »pp. 72, 196, 359.

INSIGHT

"**A second time**" (3:1). Jonah is often called the "gospel of the second chance." God is gracious and will not let us run away from obedience—even if He has to place storms and a great fish in our pathway.

Was Jonah a false prophet? If the test of a true prophet is that his words come true (Deut. 18:22), how do we explain the failure of Jonah's message of judgment? The answer is that nearly every message of judgment is conditional, a truth that Jonah clearly understood (Jonah 4:2). The principle is illustrated in 2 Sam. 12:14-23; 1 Kings 21:27-29; and 2 Kings 20:1-6.

"**Nineveh**" (3:3). At the time Nineveh was a great city, with at least four times the population of Samaria, the capital of Israel (120,000 to the 30,000 estimated by archeologists). The Heb. calls it "a distance of three days," referring to its suburbs as well as the walled central city.

Why would Nineveh respond? Events had prepared the people of Nineveh for the prophet's message. Assyria was led by weak rulers between 782 B.C. and 745 B.C., and was threatened by mountain tribes from the north who had driven their frontiers within a hundred miles of the capital. The danger of destruction was very real in Nineveh in this period.

"**God**" (3:8, 10). The name *Elohim* is used in this passage, not the personal, revelatory name of God, *Yahweh*. We should not conclude that the people of Nineveh experienced genuine conversion. God has compassion on those who do not know Him but do what is right, even as He has on His own people.

God's character (4:1-3). Jonah had experienced God's grace when he had been rescued and given a second chance to obey. But he objected to God's acting in character in withholding judgment when Nineveh repented.

We who are undeserving ourselves of God's mercy can hardly object when God showers His mercy on others who may be undeserving too.

The 120,000 people (4:11). The number either refers to the entire population, or to young children. Since the maximum estimated population at that era was about 175,000, the former is the better interpretation. The saying "not tell their right hand from their left" refers to a lack of moral knowledge, stemming from the fact that Assyria had not been granted special revelation from God.

Micah

Micah, a contemporary of Isaiah and Amos, prophesied during a period of unparalleled prosperity in both the Northern Hebrew Kingdom, Israel, and in the Southern, Judah (ca. 785–745 B.C.). Like his fellow prophets, Micah was not deceived by the ostensible power and affluence of his time. Moral and spiritual decay were widespread, eroding the foundations of society. God neither could nor would overlook the idolatry and the injustice which increasingly characterized the lifestyle of a people who had been called to live in a covenant relationship with Him.

While Israel and Judah lived out their fantasy, God was at work forging Assyria into a world power. Tiglath-pileser III (745–727 B.C.) gained control in that northern land, and engineered a remarkable resurgence. Soon the divided Jewish homeland would experience the ravages of Assyrian armies, and the North would cease to exist as a nation.

But first God sent prophets to both kingdoms, prophets who pinpointed the sins of the twin nations and who urged repentance. Each not only condemned the sins of Israel and Judah, but each shared a grand vision of the way of discipline that would both honor God and guarantee the nation's preservation.

Little is known of Micah, whose words were addressed to both Israel and Judah. But it is his message that was important, in his own day and in ours. Micah shows us a God who is committed both to the judgment of sin and to His covenant obligations. God will judge the sinful society. Yet from the purified remnant God will construct a kingdom that will endure, a kingdom made righteous and completely committed to the Lord.

MICAH AT A GLANCE

KEY THEMES

Social sins (Micah 2:2; 3:1-3, 9-12; 6:8). *God cannot tolerate corruption in society or in individuals.*

The promised Ruler (Micah 5:1-5). *A King to be born in Bethlehem will rule Israel's future kingdom.*

God's moral requirements (Micah 6:8). *Perhaps the Old Testament's simplest, clearest statement of God's expectations of the believer.*

Israel's ultimate restoration (Micah 7:8-20). *A fresh vision of the coming day when God will personally shepherd His people and exalt them.*

Date and Authorship. Micah was a resident of Moresheth, a town in Judah near the home of Isaiah, whose sensitivity to social problems Micah shares. The reference to a coming destruction of Samaria (1:6) indicates he began his ministry prior to that city's capture in 722 B.C., perhaps in the 740s, the last decade of Jotham's reign. His ministry, which spilled over into the reign of Hezekiah (715–686 B.C.), is referred to in Jeremiah 26:18-19. There Micah is remembered for his bold announcement that the city of Jerusalem, like Samaria, will be destroyed. Today Micah is remembered more for his stunning prediction of Jesus' birth, and his warm and positive description of a life lived in fellowship with God.

Illustration. *Over 500 years after Micah's prophecy, scholars consulted by Herod turned to Micah 5:2 and told him that God's promised Messiah would be born in Bethlehem. Just so, God shaped events, using even the decree of a Roman emperor who had probably never heard His name, to bring Mary and Joseph to the little town destined to be the birthplace of our Saviour.*

THEOLOGICAL OUTLINE OF MICAH

I. JUDGMENT	1–2
II. PURIFICATION	3–5
III. VICTORY	6–7

CONTENT OUTLINE OF MICAH

I. Judgment and Restoration (1:1–2:13)
  A. Judgment Approaches (1:1-7)
  B. Micah's Warning (1:8-16)
  C. Indictment of Oppressors (2:1-5)
  D. True vs. False Prophets (2:6-11)
  E. Promise of Hope (2:12-13)
II. Israel's Leaders Indicted (3:1–5:15)
  A. Rulers Indicted (3:1-4)
  B. Religious Leaders Indicted (3:5-8)
  C. Impact of Corrupt Leaders (3:9-12)
  D. Zion to Be Exalted (4:1-8)
  E. Zion to Be Powerful (4:9-13)
  F. Zion's King to Come from Bethlehem (5:1-4)
  G. Zion to Know Peace (5:5-6)
  H. Zion to Be Vindicated (5:7-9)
  I. Zion to Be Purified (5:10-15)
III. God's Kingdom to Triumph (6:1–7:20)
  A. The Present Kingdom's Corruption (6:1-8)
  B. The Present Kingdom's Doom (6:9-16)
  C. The Prophet's Lament (7:1-6)
  D. The Godly Man's Attitude (7:7-10)
  E. The Ultimate Triumph of God's Kingdom Is Assured (7:11-20)

Outline
Place
Finder

JUDGMENT
PURIFICATION
VICTORY

Chapter summary. After identifying himself, Micah immediately launches a description of the judgment bearing down on Samaria, the capital of Israel (1:2-7). His vision is so terrible that Micah himself is stricken with grief (vv. 8-9a). In a brief poem the prophet describes the plight of those who will experience the coming defeat and be driven into exile (1:9a-16). Yet this judgment, as all God's acts of judgment, is just. It is a necessary response to the behavior of His people. For there is a wealthy class in Israel which is driven by materialism and oppresses the poor for financial gain. God's judgment is a response to the corruption that riddles Israel's society (2:1-5).

Micah's ministry draws the rebuke of false prophets, who are embarrassed by the negative tone of Micah's message and fear he will give them a "bad name" among the rich, whose gifts they passionately desire (vv. 6-11). But Micah's message is not negative. It is a word of hope! After the cleansing judgment, God will gather Israel's survivors and personally lead them to an era of rest (vv. 12-13).

Key verses. 2:1-2: God is just.

Personal application. Rather than reject unpleasant truths, welcome them. Respond, and avoid judgment.

Key concepts. Sin »pp. 362, 442. Prostitution »pp. 45, 135. Prophet »p. 131. False prophet »p. 462. Justice »p. 541. Remnant »p. 427.

INSIGHT

Watch, and learn (1:2). Micah's description of the devastating judgment about to strike Israel is not addressed to God's people at all! Instead the prophet summons the peoples (e.g., nations) of the earth, and "all who are in it." They are to observe what God does to His people. Why? Because the terrible punishment they witness serves as a warning that God is holy and simply will not permit iniquity to go unpunished. This is one of the major values of O.T. history to us. We watch, and learn. And, hopefully, we reject the sins that bring judgment.

Who? (1:5) The Heb. says "who" is Jacob's transgression rather than "what." The answer is Samaria and Jerusalem, the two capital cities of the kingdoms. The cities are personified as prostitutes (v. 7), for at the very heart of national life both idolatry and injustice reign.

Micah's concern? (1:8-9a) These verses may describe the prophet acting out the destiny of those who will be taken captive. Or it may picture his own distress for his people. It is appropriate to grieve—even for those who deserve the consequences their sinful acts bring.

Painful puns (2:9b-16). The brief poem names a number of towns clustered in a district due to bear the brunt of Assyria's attack. The poem uses wordplay based on the name of each city,

contrasting it with what is to come. Citizens of Shaphir ("beautiful") are to be naked and ashamed. Those in Zaanan ("come out") will not come out, and so on. The very names that gave cities their identity will mock the people of Israel who live there, as every good fortune is transformed to disaster.

Oppression (2:1-5). The social injustice emphasized here is that of the wealthy who defrauded the poor of their ancestral lands to build great estates. In most of Israel's history agriculture was the basis of prosperity. When families were driven from their land a poverty class was created. The exploitation of these newly poor by the rich characterized the mid-eighth century.

The comfortable few (2:6-11). Even those who were supposed to be prophets rebuked Micah and urged him not to preach. This despite the fact that the greedy rich treated passersby as enemies to be stripped of loot, and even drove widows from their homes. Why would the prophets rebuke a man who so clearly was doing God's work? Because they wanted to share in the financial prosperity of the wicked who paid their salaries. We have to be careful not to mimic these false prophets. We must speak God's truth boldly, not considering possible personal financial loss.

Chapter summary. Micah contrasts Israel's present state and the ideal to which God is committed to bring His people. Governmental (3:1-4) and religious leaders (vv. 5-8) ignore justice and proclaim, "Peace!" Yet Israel and Judah are both corrupt, unjust societies, doomed to experience disaster (vv. 9-12). Still, in the last days God's vision of pagan nations approaching Jerusalem to come to know God and His ways will surely be fulfilled (4:1-8). "Now" the people are about to cry out in agony as judgment strikes them down. But then God will make the survivors of His people a world power (vv. 9-13). This will be accomplished through a King, to be born in Bethlehem (5:1-4), whose authority will extend over the land whose people will soon invade Israel (vv. 5-6). God's Word will be vindicated in that day of His triumph (vv. 7-9), after His people have been purified by judgment (vv. 10-15).

Outline
Place
Finder

JUDGMENT
PURIFICATION
VICTORY

Key verse. 4:2: Past and future hinge on the coming King.

Personal application. Vindicate God's love for you by living a holy life, lest He be forced to vindicate Himself by judging you.

INSIGHT

"Justice" (3:1). In context "justice" is honest government, fair to rich and poor alike. The image of tearing flesh from the poor graphically communicates the prophet's point: corrupt and evil government officials use their position for personal gain rather than to serve the people.

"Peace" (3:5). The Heb. word means more than the absence of war. It means health, wholeness, and security. While the other prophets lied to Israel about its spiritual condition, Micah spoke out powerfully for justice and "declared to Jacob [Israel] his sins." Today when religious leaders turn a blind eye to corruption and evil in society, they too become partly responsible for it. The motives and lies of the religious leaders of the prophet's day are described in vv. 9-12.

God's vision of the future (4:1-8). Prophecy tells us what the world *should* be like, as well as what it will be like. We are each to evaluate present realities against what God's prophets say should be.

A world without war (4:3-4). One major element of the world foreseen by the prophets is its utter peacefulness. Disputes will be resolved by appeal to God's Word, not war. But peace is an ideal that can only be realized when God sets up His kingdom on earth. Until then man's passions will generate wars and rumors of wars. Peace will be the dream of all, but every dreamer will awaken to the reality of strife.

The fact of war in our present world, and the vision of a world without war, drive home the fact that humanity is lost in sin. The world

as well as the individual desperately needs a Saviour.

"Horns of iron" (4:13). In the O.T. horns generally symbolize power, and iron horns, dominant power. The people whose sin makes them easy prey for the nations will one day be exalted above them—after they have been redeemed (v. 10).

Fulfilled prophecy (5:2). This well-known prediction of the birthplace of the Messiah who is destined to be Israel's King illustrates how prophecy is fulfilled: literally and accurately. When King Herod was told by the visiting wise men that the destined "King of the Jews" had been born, he asked the scribes where. They turned to this passage in Micah, and told Herod the Christ would be born in Bethlehem. The Jews too expected prophecy to be fulfilled literally, just as it was (see also »pp. 405–408).

Israel abandoned (5:3-4). The promised Ruler will end Israel's alienation from God and her homeland. He will also lead "the rest of His brothers" back to God and grant them universal peace. The birth of the King in Bethlehem is the pivotal event of history, for the Jews and for all.

"I will destroy" (5:10-15). God systematically destroys everything His straying people might rely on: their military (v. 10), their walled cities (v. 11), and especially their idols. This is both punishment and preparation. How often God must destroy the empty things we rely on before we will trust fully in Him.

Outline
Place
Finder

JUDGMENT
PURIFICATION
VICTORY

Chapter summary. This chapter is in the familiar form of a lawsuit which God brings against Israel. In chapters 3–5 the prophet condemns Israel's leaders and shows the contrast between the corrupt society they had shaped and the glorious and peaceful kingdom to be formed by the coming Messiah/King. Now God calls earth itself as a witness to hear God's charge against His people (6:1-2). As for them, they will not listen, complaining that serving God is too great an emotional and financial burden. Yet all the time the response God has yearned for is simply to do good and walk humbly with the Lord (vv. 3-8). In view of the violence and wickedness of the people God will not acquit them but will surely punish (vv. 9-16).

No society which is marked by violence, lying, and deceit will stand—especially when it is called by God's name.

Key verse. 6:8: Here is "what is good."

Personal application. The good life is simpler than we think.

Key concepts. Moses »p. 55. Offerings »p. 78. Mercy »p. 858. Justice »p. 541.

INSIGHT

"Burdened"? (6:3) The Heb. root expresses weariness. Does relationship with God place a load on the believer? Do we carry *Him*? God's answer is to remind Israel of all He did to carry *them* (vv. 4-5). In fact, relationship with God lifts our burdens as He frees, guides, protects, and teaches us.

If you or I become weary of trying to live for God, think what life would be like without His everpresent grace! This is just what Micah asks his contemporaries to do.

"With what shall I come?" (6:6-7) Israel's first implied response to God's case against them was, "It's too hard to serve God." Their second is, "What does God want, anyway?" If we take this as a sarcastic reaction we might paraphrase, "Does God want to ruin us? Would 10,000 sacrifices be enough? Does He want our children too?"

This is a conscious distortion of known truth, for their question is answered in Deut. 12:10. What God asks is that His people respect Him, walk in His ways, and love Him completely.

An unforgettable verse (6:8). This is one of the great, pure statements of the O.T., which in simple and beautiful terms sums up the heart of our walk with the Lord. This ethical injunction is not intended as a way of salvation, but as the way the saved are to walk. When we commit it to memory, and practice it daily, we will please both God and our fellowman.

What is "good"? (6:8) "Good" here is practical and moral, not speculative or philosophical. God's version of good has three basic elements. (1) "Act justly," which in the O.T. is a response to God which finds expression in a commitment to fairness in interpersonal relationships and in our social institutions. (2) "Love mercy," which goes beyond fairness, to a heart response to the needs of others which compels a person to help when this is possible. (3) "Walk humbly" with God, which here means to remain responsive to God, submitting gladly to His will. The prescription sets boundaries within which we are to live. We cannot let sympathy push us to do that which is unfair or violates God's known will. We cannot be so rigidly "fair" that we have no room for compassion or caring.

Shall I forget? (6:9-11) God is the one who established the standards of justice and caring which Israel has violated. The question He raises is something we need to ask ourselves. Should God's people expect Him to abandon not only His own standards but His compassion for the needy, to spare those whose sins deserve punishment? The sins of Israel, laid out again in vv. 9-16, literally demand punishment.

"Save nothing" (6:14). When God judges the land, its productivity will be destroyed. What irony. The very thing that motivated the rich to do evil—wealth and plenty—will be lost because in their pursuit of it they oppressed others. The end never justifies the means. Evil means will actually keep a person from gaining his ends.

Outline
Place
Finder

JUDGMENT
PURIFICATION
VICTORY

Chapter summary. In Micah 3–5 visions of God's future kingdom were cast against and underlined the corruption in eighth-century Hebrew society. Now the apparent defeat of God's purposes in the generation portrayed so tragically in Micah 6 is set against the prophet's vision of the Lord's ultimate triumph. Spiritual setbacks may discourage us. But we must remember that God is not defeated! Victory will be His in the end.

Micah feels the misery of Israel's spiritual defeat and expresses his pain and disappointment in the moral and spiritual contamination of his society (7:1-7). While at such times the godly sit in darkness, Micah hopes in the Lord, sure that God will vindicate the believer in His time (vv. 8-10). The day is coming when Israel's society will be reestablished (vv. 11-13). At that time God will shepherd His people, and the nations will turn to the Lord (vv. 14-17). Micah concludes with a hymn of praise to God. The Lord is forgiving and compassionate. He will rid His people of their sins. He will prove true to His promises to Abraham and triumph in the end (vv. 18-20).

Key verse. 7:19: Forgiveness first. Then transformation.

Personal application. Remain faithful, and God will vindicate you whatever others may say today.

Key concepts. Justice »p. 141. Hope »p. 465. Forgiveness »p. 357.

INSIGHT

Loneliness (7:1-2). Micah imagines himself going out in an orchard at harvesttime and finding no fruit. He is hungry for fellowship, but feels totally isolated. He knows no one else who honestly seeks to serve God. Elijah experienced similar feelings (1 Kings 19:14).

What do we do when our coworkers or acquaintances seem as hostile as the men and women of Micah's day were to him? First of all we do feel lonely and isolated. But Micah has positive suggestions to make later on.

"Watch in hope" (7:7). Micah's solution is practical. Put your hope in God, not in changing your situation. Look to what God will do, not to what others are doing around you. The word "hope" is a key one in the O.T., indicating both a willingness to wait and a settled confidence that what God has for us in the future is good.

Bearing God's wrath (7:9). The godly suffer when an unjust society is shattered. This is not unfair because even when we do not participate in wickedness we bear a certain responsibility for events which happen around us. Micah accepts this as justice. And he remains confident that God the judge will also be his lawyer and plead his cause. Micah's sins are not willful. He will not only be pardoned, but his enemies will ultimately confess his righteousness.

"The day for building" (7:11). Micah lives in a day of tearing down. The corrupt society of Israel is about to be utterly destroyed and the surviving population taken captive to Assyria. When everything seems to be tumbling down around us, it's hard to believe that a day for building up will follow. But Micah knows that God is faithful. There remains a glorious destiny for the people He has chosen, for He will call them back to their land.

"Your staff" (7:14). The shepherd's staff was used to drive off wild animals and protect the sheep. Micah prays for the arrival of that day when God acts to restore His people and defeat their enemies (vv. 14-17).

They will turn to the Lord (7:17). God's intervention will humble the nations, but will also heal them! At last they will have an appropriate awe (fear) of God, and so will turn to Him. It is important to remember that the hurts that humble you and me are also meant to heal us and turn our hearts back to God.

Who is like our God? (7:18-20) What sets our God apart? His willingness to pardon sinners and to forgive our transgressions. Even when we fail Him, He remains faithful to us. In faithfulness He will cleanse and transform us and keep every promise He has made.

Nahum

The Book of Nahum has been criticized by some as an "orgy of hatred." Nahum is a single focus book. It describes and reflects on the imminent destruction of Nineveh, the capital city of the mighty Assyrian Empire. What bothers many is that the book's vivid portrait of God's judgment of Nineveh lacks the sense of grace and compassion that balance the most grim warnings in the other prophets. But Nahum's message was not addressed to the citizens of Nineveh.

He spoke to the oppressed people of Israel and Judah, who for over a century had suffered the brutal depravations of Assyrian armies. These people had seen their homes destroyed, their crops burned, their wives and daughters raped, their children dashed against stone walls. That oppression took final form in 722 B.C. when the Assyrians totally destroyed Samaria and carried the people of Israel into captivity. This history of the relationship between Assyria and Israel/Judah puts the book in perspective. Rather than an orgy of hatred, Nahum is a celebration of just retribution. It is a cry of praise, affirming the justice of a God who has judged His own people harshly for their heinous sins and now shows Himself to be fair by meting out evenhanded judgment to their oppressors.

Nahum has frequently been ignored by believers because there seems to be little here that applies directly to Christian life or experience. Yet there are basic theological values expressed in this little book. God is sovereign and God is moral judge, not only of His people but of the whole world. He is able to judge sin wherever it is found, and He accepts this responsibility. As Nahum says, "The Lord is a jealous and avenging God . . . slow to anger and great in power; the Lord will not leave the guilty unpunished" (1:2-3).

The name "Nahum" means comfort. It must have been a comfort to the Jews who had suffered under the Assyrians to know that God would soon act in retribution. It was also a comfort to realize that one day, the power of hostile nations destroyed, the people of God will live and worship in peace, unthreatened by external enemies.

Date and Authorship. Little is known of the Prophet Nahum, or of his home. Most believe it was located in Galilee, which experienced the brunt of the initial Assyrian invasions. We can place his writing with some accuracy: He wrote before the collapse of the Assyrian Empire in 612 B.C. and after the destruction of Thebes, which took place in 663 B.C. (cf. 3:8). It is not unreasonable to assume that the book was written shortly after the overthrow of the Northern Kingdom and the exile of its population.

NAHUM AT A GLANCE

KEY THEMES
Causes of the fall of Nineveh. *Opposition to God (2:2-3, 8-9, 11, 13, 15); decadence (3:12-13, 15-18); cruelty (3:1, 4, 19).*
Descriptions of the fall of Nineveh. *Disaster (1:10; 2:9, 10; 3:11, 13). Flood (1:8; 2:6, 8). Dispersal (1:8; 2:1, 7-8; 3:7, 10-11, 16-18). Fire (1:5, 10; 2:3-4, 13; 3:3, 13, 15).*

Illustration. *Nineveh fell when floodgates controlling the flow of water from the great reservoir system constructed by the Assyrians were thrown open. The resultant flooding apparently caused a collapse of the palace and city's defenses (2:6). The empire's well-equipped soldiers were unable to withstand the assault.*

THEOLOGICAL OUTLINE OF NAHUM

I. THE LORD   1

II. THE CITY   2–3

CONTENT OUTLINE OF NAHUM

I. The God of Israel (1:1-15)
  A. God's Greatness (1:1-6)
  B. God's Actions (1:7-11)
  C. God's Intent (1:12-15)
II. Nineveh's Fall (2:1–3:19)
  A. A Warning (2:1)
  B. A Promise to Israel (2:2)

C. Its Destruction (2:3–3:19)
  1. Destruction described (2:3-13)
  2. Destruction reviewed (3:1-6)
  3. Destruction celebrated (3:7-11)
  4. Nineveh ridiculed (3:12-19)

Chapter summary. Nahum's first chapter focuses not on Nineveh but on God. He describes Israel's "jealous and avenging God" (1:2-3), and then pictures Him as a warrior striding over the land, terrorizing His enemies but bringing relief to those who trust Him (vv. 4-8). Only now does Nahum introduce the Assyrians, portraying them as plotting evil against the Lord (vv. 9-11). God will destroy this nation which has afflicted His people (vv. 12-14); a destruction which will be celebrated in Judah as a harbinger of peace (v. 15).

Key verse. 1:2: God does take vengeance.

Personal application. God will act against those who are the enemies of His people.

Key concepts. Jealousy »p. 534. Anger of God »pp. 65, 72. Evil »p. 72. Vengeance »p. 428. Guilt »p. 79. Peace »p. 427.

INSIGHT

"Jealous" (1:2). Jealousy in God is a positive emotion; a deep, emotional concern for the well-being of those for whom He cares. It is this passion for His own people who have been injured by Assyria which has filled Him with the anger about to be expressed in the judgment of Nineveh.

"Vengeance" (1:2). God's vengeance is retribution, an appropriate response to man's sin. While we human beings are often carried away by our anger, as the text points out, God is carried away by His grace. He is "slow to anger." Only when the guilty *must* be punished does He act to take vengeance.

The dust of his feet (1:4-6). Nahum has made statements about God. Now he resorts to imagery to bring home the impact of what he has said. The image in these verses is that of an armed soldier on the march, stirring up the dust as he treads across the ground. This soldier is so powerful that nature itself draws back in awe, and the earth "trembles at His presence." One helpful way to study the Bible is to follow Nahum's lead. He stated a truth about God. Then he found an image which powerfully communicates the reality that truth expresses.

"The Lord is good" (1:7). Nahum is a difficult book because the writer frequently shifts, to speak in one verse to Nineveh, in the next to Israel and Judah. Here he reminds us that, however terrible God may be to His enemies, we who trust God experience Him as good. He is good to us. His judgment falls on those who are His foes, because they do us harm. This is proof of the depth of His love for and goodness to His own.

Plotting evil against the Lord (1:9, 11). Two thoughts are expressed: evil, which is not simply wrong action but the intent to harm, and wickedness, which is a lawless disregard for what is right. Not only have the Assyrians affirmed their independence from the moral constraints imposed by God on all mankind, but they have determined to harm God by harming His people.

God does not distinguish between us and Him in this. When we are harmed, He is harmed. Evil done to us is evil done to the Lord.

"Like dry stubble" (1:10). In the hot season in Israel farmers burned the thorns and stubble in their fields. These were so dry that they seemed to explode when touched by the flames, disappearing in an instant. This is to be Nineveh's fate: a sudden, explosive destruction that leaves nothing behind (cf. v. 12).

"I will break their yoke" (1:12-13). Again God addresses His own people. The domination of Assyria will end. God's vengeance not only punishes the guilty, it brings freedom to God's own.

"You, Nineveh" (1:14). The speaker shifts again and addresses Nineveh. The command for its destruction has been given. "I will prepare your grave" reminds us that what God says is certain and sure.

Celebration (1:15). The thought that we have seen before is given clear expression here. Israel and Judah literally, joyfully, triumphantly, celebrate the destruction of Nineveh. Fear is gone, and the prospect of peace opens out before God's people at last.

Chapter summary. Nahum begins this second section of his book with a warning to Nineveh (2:1) and a promise to God's people (v. 2). He then takes four consecutive looks at the destruction of the great enemy stronghold (2:3-13; 3:1-6; 3:7-11; 3:12-19). Each describes the successful attack on the city, mocks the city's crumbling defenses, and interprets the fall as divine judgment. The repeated poetic description of Nineveh's defeat underlines its certainty. But it also emphasizes the growing exultation of an oppressed people who can hardly believe their ancient enemy is gone, and so must savor the defeat again, and again, and again.

Key verse. 3:14: No one weeps when the cruel die.

Personal application. We too will know relief from oppression, for God will act in His time.

INSIGHT

A mocking call to arms (2:1). Nineveh's armory, of over 40 acres, contained all the weaponry that had made the Assyrian Empire great: bows, arrows, swords, spears, armor, chariots. Yet the prophet's call to arms is mocking. Whatever the Assyrians may do will be futile, for God has determined that the city will fall.

Restored (2:2). Israel and Judah needed to be restored, because both Heb. kingdoms were devastated by massive Assyrian armies.

The river (2:6, 8). The extensive system of reservoirs and canals that supplied the city and its surrounding farmlands with water was used to bring down the city. Exactly how it was used, however, remains in some doubt. Most believe the opened floodgates poured water *into* the city, flooding its lower regions and undermining its fortifications. This seems implied in the reference to the collapse of the palace (v. 6). However, it is possible that the opening of the river gates drained water *away* from the city, making it vulnerable through the riverbeds, or leaving its population without drinking water, as v. 8 may suggest.

Archeologists have been unable to determine which use of the rivers was made by the attackers.

Four analogies. The prophet uses four images to drive home the guilt of Nineveh. The city is a lion who terrorized the neighborhood and is finally killed in the den where he took human prey to feed his cubs (2:11-12). Nineveh is a prostitute, who enslaved others by witchcraft (3:4). Nineveh is like the Egyptian city of Thebes, which dominated all the lands around her but was destroyed by Assyria itself (vv. 8-10). Nineveh's forces are as numerous as the locusts who ravage the countryside, yet these swarms will disappear under the enemy assault (vv. 15-17).

God is against Nineveh (2:13; 3:5). God is against every oppressor. As Nineveh fell, so will every defense of the wicked when at last God acts to judge.

Clap your hands (3:19). The cruel are seldom mourned. Their demise is such a relief that those they have harmed cannot help but feel a surge of joy.

Habakkuk

The Prophet Habakkuk lived in Judah and ministered there, probably during the reign of Josiah (639–609 B.C.). Josiah, a godly king, called for revival. But despite a superficial veneer of religion, that society was marred by injustice.

Many earlier prophets had seen injustice in Judah's society and sternly condemned it. But under Manasseh, Josiah's grandfather, Hebrew society became committed to idolatry and associated social evils. Josiah, who came to the throne as an eight-year-old, called his nation back to God. After finding a lost book of God's Law, he rooted out idolatry, reestablished temple worship, and attempted to administer God's ancient Law. But he could not root out the corruption now deeply rooted in the people and institutions of his nation.

When Habakkuk begged God for an explanation of why he permitted the wicked to sin and the innocent to suffer, the prophet was given an answer. God, even then, was shaping the Babylonians into a world power. The Lord would use these pagan armies to punish His own people. Habakkuk understood, for the use of enemy nations to discipline Israel and Judah was a well-established precedent. But there was still a moral issue that troubled the prophet. How could God use a less righteous people to discipline the more righteous? How could God permit the Babylonians to succeed?

This problem has troubled believers in one form or another from the beginning. Why does God permit the wicked to succeed in this world? Why doesn't He act, so that the good rather than the wicked prosper? The answers we find in Habakkuk show us that the wicked do not succeed—and that no one, good or bad, can avoid the disciplining hand of God.

There are moral and theological questions raised by sin's presence, in our own lives and in the ways of the wicked. Perhaps the best and most satisfying answers to be found in Scripture are revealed here in this small, but vital, Old Testament book.

Date and Authorship. Habakkuk, who calls himself "the prophet," may also have been a Levite who eagerly participated in Josiah's reforms, but was troubled by the moral laxity that he continued to observe. While his work is not dated, his reference to the unexpected emergence of Babylon as a great power even then taking place (1:5-6) persuasively suggests he ministered during Josiah's reign.

HABAKKUK AT A GLANCE

HABAKKUK'S QUESTIONS
Why does God permit injustice? *Does God tolerate wrong among His own? (1:2-4)*
Why is God silent when the wicked win? *How does God judge nations? (1:12-17)*

GOD'S ANSWERS
God judges His own when they sin. *God does not permit injustice (1:5-11).*
God judges the pagan as they sin. *The wicked do not win (2:2-20).*

GOD'S ANSWER TO AN UNANSWERED QUESTION
What are the godly to do when the Lord judges their society? *Trust (3:3-19).*

Illustration. *Habakkuk retreated to one of the mountaintop stations from which guards watched for the approach of enemy armies. But Habakkuk looked back over his own nation's countryside, determined to explore the reasons why God permitted the injustice that was rife in Judah's society. We too need to take time out to meditate and to struggle with life's important issues.*

THEOLOGICAL OUTLINE OF HABAKKUK

I. PROBLEMS   1–2
II. PRAYER   3

CONTENT OUTLINE OF HABAKKUK

I. The First Problem (1:1-11)
  A. Why Does God Permit Sin in the Covenant Community? (1:1-4)
  B. God Will Judge; He Is Bringing the Babylonians (1:5-11)
II. The Second Problem (1:12–2:20)
  A. Why Does God Permit the Wicked to Triumph? (1:12–2:3)
  B. God Does Not: He Is Judging the Wicked Even Now (2:4-20)
III. Habakkuk's Prayer (3:1-19)
  A. Prayer (3:1-2)
  B. A Revelation of Divine Judgment to Come (3:3-15)
  C. Habakkuk's Fear, and His Trust (3:16-19)

Chapter summary. Habakkuk is deeply disturbed at the violence and injustice he sees in Judah's society. He appeals to God, asking how the Lord can permit such conditions to exist among His people (1:1-4). God explains that He does not tolerate wrong, but even now is preparing the Babylonians, a nation which will serve as His rod of discipline (vv. 5-11). Habakkuk, familiar from the Law and from history with national disaster as divine punishment, accepts this (v. 12). But now Habakkuk senses an even more perplexing question. How can God remain silent when the more wicked (in this case, the Babylonians) triumph over the less wicked (Israel)? Won't the triumph of the wicked make him more arrogant and turn him even further from submission to the Lord? (vv. 13-17)

Key verse. 1:12: Not death, but purification is in mind.

Personal application. God's Word has answers to life's most troubling questions.

Key concepts. Violence »p. 29. Justice »p. 541. Holy »p. 372. Judgment »pp. 372, 724.

INSIGHT

"Listen" (1:2). The Heb. concept of "listen" means more than simply hear. There "to listen" implies "to respond." Habakkuk knows that God hears his complaint. What he cannot understand is why God does not act in response to his plea.

In this case God explains to the prophet—for our instruction. You and I typically will not know just why when there seems to be no answer to our prayers. But we can be sure that God does hear and has reasons for any apparent delay.

Violence, injustice, and wrong (1:3). When these terms are used in the O.T. without reference to some specific foreign enemy, they typically characterize conditions among God's people. Despite Josiah's religious reforms, there had been no moral and social transformation. Habakkuk has been driven to a conclusion that we should remember: Conversion with transformation is imitation.

"Law is paralyzed" (1:4). God's Law was locally administered by elders, who heard civil as well as criminal cases. To work, this system required honest judges and witnesses who would not lie. What Habakkuk says is that there are so many more wicked than righteous persons that justice "never prevails" in the courts (»pp. 130, 132).

Be amazed (1:5). The subject is the sudden rise of the Babylonians, who in mere decades supplanted the great Assyrian Empire. Several phrases—"watch," "I am going to do . . . in your days," and "I am raising up" all suggest

the revelations Habakkuk received came early in Josiah's reign, perhaps the 620s B.C.

"The Babylonians" (1:6-11). These verses graphically described the military strategies adopted by the Babylonian forces, featuring swift, slashing cavalry attacks (vv. 8-9) and sieges featuring construction of great earthen ramps that over-topped the highest walls and permitted an assault on a city's forces.

"To execute judgment" (1:12). Deuteronomy 28 specifies a number of punishing disasters God would use to discipline Israel if they abandoned Him and His ways. Habakkuk knows that defeat in war is among the disciplines God has warned about (28:25-29), and thus unhesitatingly accepts the Lord's announcement. "We will not die" means that Habakkuk knows the coming invasion will not totally wipe out the Heb. people. Somehow the nation will live, for this is discipline, and not destruction. For more on war, see »p. 133.

Tolerating the treacherous? (1:13-17) This is the deeper problem Habakkuk raises. If the wicked *succeed* they will exalt their power as their god. Even worse, it will seem to all that mankind is like fish in the sea, with no moral governor supervising human affairs. How can God permit the wicked to prosper and thus raise questions, not only about His moral governance of the universe, but about His very existence?

How many times you and I have wondered how God can let the wicked prosper. How good that chap. 2 has an answer!

Chapter summary. Habakkuk determines to wait until God answers his second complaint (2:1; cf. 1:13-17). And answer God does! (2:2-3) The Lord shows Habakkuk that He does *not* tolerate the treacherous. Even as the wicked appear to triumph, God is in fact at work judging them! Their success is superficial, for the wicked are never satisfied (vv. 4-5). Their mistreatment of others creates enemies (vv. 6-8). They are driven to build "secure" retreats which will never protect them (vv. 9-11), for they have no future (vv. 12-14). Coming disgrace is certain (vv. 15-17), for they have no place to turn for guidance or help (vv. 18-20). When we understand what is going on within the heart of the wicked, and when we understand that forces their wicked acts set in motion will surely destroy them, we realize that God does *not* tolerate them. At the height of their success He is in the process of judging them. Severely.

Key verse. 2:4: Riches without satisfaction are meaningless.

Personal application. Don't be deceived by appearances. The wicked, however rich or powerful, are not to be envied.

Key concepts. Revelation »p. 354. Arrogant »p. 119. Idolatry »p. 433.

INSIGHT

"My watch" (2:1). The Heb. noun (*mismeret*) indicates a place where a person's duty of keeping watch is fulfilled. This may have been atop a city's walls, or the "rampart" (*masor*) may have been constructed on a mountain height looking toward the northwest, from which enemy forces approached Judah. The prophet is committed to watch and wait until God answers his complaint.

"Make it plain" (2:2). We might paraphrase the meaning here by saying "Write it on a billboard, so large a running man might read it." What God is about to reveal to the prophet is important, and everyone needs to understand the Lord's response.

"The righteous will live by his faith" (2:4). This phrase, which contrasts the victorious wicked and the righteous, is quoted by Paul in Rom. 1. There it served as the key which led to Martin Luther's conversion and unlocked Luther's rediscovery of the biblical doctrine of justification by faith.

In this context, however, the phrase means that the righteous person, whose trust is in God, will be faithful to Him, and thus will live.

Never at rest, never satisfied (2:4-5). This is the first revelation. However "successful" the wicked are, nothing they gain can give them rest or satisfaction. As feeding fuel to a furnace simply makes it burn hotter, so the apparent success of the wicked only makes their desires burn hotter! What a terrible judgment this is. To have everything you want — except satisfaction.

Debtors arise (2:6-8). Those who make themselves wealthy by extortion and violence create enemies. In time, these "debtors" will arise and pay the wicked person back! The hostility that wickedness creates is additional evidence of the present judgment of God on sinful women and men.

Fear (2:9-11). The uneasiness and underlying insecurity felt by the wicked person is expressed in his drive to "set his nest on high" and so "escape the clutches of ruin." The money in numbered Swiss accounts, the bodyguards, and electronic warning systems all testify to the fears that stalk the wicked and drive them.

Living with anxiety, and being driven by fears, is hardly a blessed state. God *is* judging the wicked, even while they seem to be most prosperous.

No future (2:12-14). God intends to fill the earth with knowledge of the Lord, not with monuments to murderers. Whatever the wicked accomplish will crumble, and the wicked person himself will be forgotten.

Certain disgrace (2:15-17). This is similar to vv. 6-8, but emphasizes the shame the arrogant will experience when the fall comes. Instead of being admired, the wicked will be ridiculed and objects of contempt. How *that* hurts the "beautiful people" of any society!

No escape (2:18-20). No idol of man's creation can protect the wicked against the judgment that is and will befall them. No one "gets away" with sin. God is judging the wicked even when they seem to others to be most successful.

Chapter summary. Habakkuk understands and accepts God's explanation and, in faith, asks God to hurry. Act, he says, "in our time" (3:1-2). But Habakkuk does not really understand what he asks. And suddenly, in an overwhelming vision, the Lord reveals something of what judgment means (vv. 3-15). The Lord shows Habakkuk the elemental power expressed and yet hidden in historic moments of judgment: on the plains of Midian in the time of the Exodus (vv. 3-7; cf. Num. 13); in the cataclysmic judgment of the Genesis flood (3:8-10; cf. Gen. 6); and again in the crushing of Egypt in Exodus days (3:11-15).

Habakkuk reacts with stunned horror, for suddenly he sees the awfulness of the coming judgment on Judah (v. 16a). How foolish to casually invite God to visit judgment on anyone.

Yet Habakkuk, now fully aware of the anguish he as well as the people of Judah must experience, struggles back to faith. When everything men count on to provide happiness is stripped away (v. 17), Habakkuk will "be joyful in God, my Saviour" (v. 18). Like the deer or mountain goat that travels safely on dangerous, rocky heights, God will guide the prophet—and all the godly—despite the hazards of the coming day (v. 19).

Key verse. 3:19: God protects in times of national disaster.

Personal application. God guides His own through troubled times.

Key concepts. Judgment »p. 372. Trust »p. 354.

INSIGHT

Pray wisely (3:1-2). One of the most important things we can learn in the spiritual life is to pray wisely. Habakkuk's request for speedy judgment seemed wise to the prophet. After all, he knew that in wrath God would remember mercy. Yet the prophet had no real conception of what divine judgment would mean to his people, or to himself. It's wisest for us to ask God to do what is best and to be gracious. Otherwise the Lord may give us what we ask for—and later we'll discover that is not what we wanted!

"The Holy One" (3:3). The name is associated with both forgiveness and judgment. Here judgment is in view, and Habakkuk is given visions of God acting in judgment. It was best for Judah that God judge that straying nation soon. These visions, however, were to prepare the prophet and the reader for what was to come. We too must be emotionally prepared and committed to holding tightly to God when troubles come.

Visions of judgment (3:3-15). These poetic descriptions are intended to pull away the veil of space and time and look beyond the material universe to sense God's elemental power unleashed in judgment. While the specific incidents in which God's anger flared are only hinted at, the place references and the descriptions suggest three historic incidents. The first picture is of God marching from Sinai along the path His people traveled after receiving the Law, to punish them for the sins committed along the way and the idolatry at Midian. Other word pictures suggest the Genesis flood, and the destruction of the Egyptian army after Israel's Exodus from Egypt.

What we are to realize is that the historic events, as terrible as they are, are pale when compared to the burning anger of God which the material universe currently conceals. How awful it will be for those who one day experience that anger face-to-face.

The pinnacle of faith (3:19). Faith is that wonderful capacity to trust God and find comfort in Him when all in this world seems to crumble around us. Habakkuk has sensed the disaster which will soon strike Judah and discovered that despite everything he can still rejoice in the Lord. As for the dangerous times ahead, the prophet is sure that God will guide his feet, as He guides the feet of a deer or goat that walks daily on dangerous mountain heights.

Zephaniah

Zephaniah, like young Jeremiah, Habakkuk, and Micah, ministered during the reign of Josiah of Judah. The emergence of so many powerful prophets during this king's reign suggests how significant the moment was. As Josiah, who became king at age eight, matured, Assyrian power was at a low ebb. The nation enjoyed a brief period of relief from foreign intervention, and attention was focused on internal affairs. The primary concern of the young king, which was increasingly evident, was the moral and spiritual reform of his people. We can divide Josiah's reign into three stages: a pre-reformation time, from 640 to 628 B.C., a period of intense reform, from about 629–622 B.C., and a post-reform period from 622 to Josiah's death in 609 B.C.

Commentators debate which of these periods Zephaniah's messages belong to. Yet it is clear from history and from the other prophets that despite Josiah's personal commitments, the people remained indifferent to *Yahweh* and involved in pagan religious practices. So at this critical time Zephaniah, whose name means "*Yahweh* protects" or perhaps "Precious to *Yahweh*," boldly announced his grim message of imminent judgment. Yet the same God who announces through Zephaniah that "I will sweep away everything" has a promise for His people. In a coming Day of the Lord, God's judgment will extend to all people. Then, with Judah's evil purged, the Lord at last "will gather you; at that time I will bring you home."

ZEPHANIAH AT A GLANCE

MAJOR THEMES OF ZEPHANIAH

Pride. *Arrogance is mankind's major sin (2:10; 3:11), and produces rebellion against God (3:1-4), idolatry (1:4-6, 8-9) and injustice (1:7-13; 3:3-5).*

Judgment. *God will respond to mankind's pride by a judgment expressed in the "Day of the Lord," which is to have an immediate impact on Judah (1:14-17), a future impact on all nations (2:4-15).*

Purification. *God's judgment will have a purifying effect on the survivors of Judah (2:7; 3:9-20) and thus is intended to correct as well as punish. A humbled and believing Israel will be returned to the Promised Land (3:14-20).*

Authorship. While little is known of Zephaniah aside from his name, several things can be deduced from his book. We do know from the lineage reported in 1:1 that Zephaniah was an aristocrat, one of the royal family. Yet rather than enjoy the rights of his privileged position, the young prophet took a passionate stand against religious and moral depravity in his society. Although burdened with a message of judgment, Zephaniah was also confidently optimistic. He continued to hope, proclaiming that in the end God would usher in an era of peace. His lineage and the fact that he ministered in Jerusalem (cf. 1:4, 8, 12) suggest it was his home and that he was intimately acquainted with the capital, its people, and its ways. Bold and brave, Zephaniah serves as an example of a man of commitment and faith.

THEOLOGICAL OUTLINE OF ZEPHANIAH

I. JUDGMENT   1–2
II. JERUSALEM   3

CONTENT OUTLINE OF ZEPHANIAH

I. Introduction (1:1)
II. Judgment Day (1:2–2:15)
  A. Against Judah (1:2–2:3)
    1. Warning (1:2-3)
    2. Judgment ahead
       (1:4-13)
    3. Judgment described
       (1:14–2:3)

  B. Against the Nations (2:4-15)
    1. Philistia (2:4-7)
    2. Moab, Ammon (2:8-11)
    3. Cush (2:12)
    4. Assyria (2:13-15)
III. Jerusalem's Future (3:1-20)
  A. Judgment Soon (3:1-8)
  B. Peace at Last (3:9-20)

Chapter summary. Zephaniah, a young nobleman (1:1), is given a word of warning from the Lord. The world is to be swept by destruction (vv. 2-3), and Judah is to be the first to feel the punishing blows from the Lord's hand (vv. 4-9). None will be spared (vv. 10-13)—and that great, dark, terrible Day of the Lord is quickly approaching (vv. 14-18). The only hope for Judah, a "shameful nation," is to seek the Lord humbly before the dread moment arrives, in hopes the righteous will be sheltered from God's anger (2:1-3). For there will be no shelter found in surrounding nations: when the day of judgment comes Philistia (vv. 4-7), Moab and Ammon (vv. 8-11), Cush (Egypt) (v. 12), and Assyria (vv. 13-15) will all be swept away as well. Truly God will "sweep away everything from the face of the earth" (1:2).

Outline
Place
Finder

JUDGMENT
JERUSALEM

Key verse. 2:3: Seek God!

Personal application. There is no hope for the world. But there is hope for the individual who turns to the Lord.

Key concepts. Judgment »p. 372. Baal »p. 162. Anger of God »pp. 65, 72. Day of the Lord »pp. 413, 541. Jealousy »p. 534.

INSIGHT

Fire and brimstone preaching? Some folks look down their noses at what used to be called fire and brimstone preaching. "Hell" isn't heard too often in our churches. Yet Zephaniah reminds us that God is going to judge sin and sinners. Zephaniah's vivid descriptions of a day of judgment sweeping down on Judah, and the terrible urgency with which he speaks, serves as an important reminder for us. The Gospel message is a message of love. But it is a love that snatches sinners from eternal fires! Warnings of the judgment to come is an integral and essential part of our Good News.

Judge of all (1:2-3). This general statement reminds us that God is judge of all mankind.

Judge of Judah (1:4–2:3). Despite the general statement, the prophet immediately focuses our attention on Judah. Why? Because God is especially the judge of His own people. We who are called by His name are rightly held to higher standards of behavior than others. As 1 Peter 4:17 reminds us, judgment begins "with the family of God; and if it begins with us, what will the outcome be for those who do not obey the Gospel of God?"

Judgment described. The text looks at judgment from three perspectives: (1) Its cause, for Judah has been unfaithful to the Lord (1:4-9). (2) Its universality, for every social class will be judged (vv. 10-13). (3) Its terrors, for it will be marked by horrors too awful to comprehend (vv. 14-18).

"The great Day of the Lord" (1:14-18). This familiar prophetic image of a "Day of the Lord" refers primarily to what God has prepared to take place at history's end. But it also is used to identify events or periods of time in the flow of history when something *similar* takes place. Here the description of the dark and bitter judgment to fall on all mankind at history's end is appropriate in Zephaniah's warning to Judah, for when the Babylonians invade the land what they experience will be very similar to the terrors of the judgment that will strike all in the end times.

There is also a brighter aspect to the Day of the Lord. After judgment purifies God's people, survivors will be welcomed into His glorious and peaceful kingdom. This promise is conveyed later, in chap. 3. But it also forms the background for the invitation God extends in 2:1-3.

"Seek the Lord" (2:3). What characterizes a person who truly seeks the Lord? The prophet mentions humility, expressed in a willingness to submit to God and "do what He commands." He mentions righteousness, which is a commitment to doing what is right and also to establishing what is right within one's society.

"Seek" is perhaps the most important word here. We are not to approach our faith casually, but with an eager commitment. Seeking God and seeking righteousness are both to be the major concerns of our lives.

Chapter summary. Jerusalem is critical in Old Testament history and prophecy. The city was not only the political but also the religious center of ancient Israel. In prophetic vision it is to be the capital of the Messiah, the Ruler from David's line that God promised will bring the Jewish people both prominence and peace.

The prophet's first remarks are addressed to contemporary Jerusalem as representative of God's people in Zephaniah's day. The holy site has become a "city of oppressors," and God has decided to assemble the nations to consume it (3:1-8). But the judgment is intended for purification. Though the population will be scattered, they will be brought back (vv. 9-10), and the sinners will turn to the Lord (vv. 11-13). In that wonderful day a renewed people, who have at last experienced salvation, will rejoice in the Lord (vv. 14-20).

Key verses. 3:11-12: Everyman's choice.

Personal application. Salvation is intended to change us—and to change our future.

Key concepts. Jerusalem »pp. 205, 451. Fear of God »p. 387. Salvation »pp. 426, 433. Trust »p. 354. Regathering »p. 419. Future kingdom »p. 443.

INSIGHT

Oppressors, rebellious, defiled (3:1). The description is tragic in view of God's intention that His people of every age should reflect His character and so represent Him to the world. But let's not be too scornful of ancient Israel. Instead let's ask how well *we* represent the Lord today. As an individual am I caring, sensitive, honest, fair, responsive to other's needs? As churches do we stand for both justice and mercy, demonstrating God's compassion for all? Are we serious about influencing our society toward what is godly and righteous?

God's people of every age are to live by the highest possible standards. Representing God in our world calls for more than not doing wrong. It calls for us to actively do good and right.

"The Lord within her" (3:5). The Lord is among His people even when they fall terribly short. But then God is among them as the standard against which their shortcomings can be measured—by themselves, and by all. How many times have non-Christians remarked to a believer, "I didn't expect that from *you*"? Because of the standard God sets by His presence, all rightly expect the best from God's own.

"Accept correction" (3:7). Those who do not accept correction invite more severe punishments.

"Then" (3:9). Even the most severe judgment imaginable, which God has just announced in v. 8, will not prevent Him from doing His people good in the end. But first God must remove those who "rejoice in their pride" (v. 11).

Pride vs. humility (3:11-12). The two attitudes are utterly basic and reflect our orientation to the Lord. Pride is arrogant, self-centered, insolent toward authorities, presumptuous, and unwilling to submit to God, but passionately intent on getting its own way. Humility is responsive, trusting, unassuming, eager to submit to God, and primarily concerned with pleasing God rather than self. One of these two attitudes is dominant in every individual, though displayed more clearly in some than in others. The first question we need to ask ourselves is not, "What do I believe about God?" but "What is my attitude toward Him?"

"I will give" (3:20). Through Zephaniah God tells his O.T. people that, despite the failure of that generation, the future for the chosen people is bright. He says the same thing to us today. Yes, God disciplines us when we sin. Yet in the future we too will be purified, transformed, and blessed. The words, "I will give" remind us that all we will have is ultimately a gift. Our transformation and our happy future are expressions of God's grace, not rewards earned by our own merits. Only because God is committed to give can Zephaniah look ahead with confidence. Only because God is gracious today can we say with confidence, "Heaven is mine!"

Haggai

Haggai is the first of three postexilic prophets who ministered in Judah to the tiny community established after the Jews were permitted to return to their homeland. Haggai, whose name means "festal," or "festival," appears briefly in Judah to accomplish a specific mission. His carefully dated sermons focus our attention on a four-month period in 520 B.C., when Haggai called God's people to complete rebuilding of God's temple, begun 18 years before (see The Postexilic Prophets, p. 572).

Haggai's message has nothing in common with the prophets who cried out in Israel before the Assyrians crushed the Northern Kingdom in 722 B.C. and before the Babylonians invaded and destroyed Judah. He says nothing of idolatry, nothing of injustice or violence. Instead Haggai simply urges the people of Judah to put God first and to demonstrate their commitment by finishing construction of the temple.

There is another important difference. The words of the former prophets were largely ignored by God's people and led to national disaster and captivity. But Haggai's words were heard, and the whole community rallied to the task. A new, though much smaller temple rose on the site of Solomon's magnificent building. God was to be put first, and His worship was to be celebrated again in a house dedicated to His name.

Date and Authorship. Haggai is mentioned by Ezra (5:1; 6:14) and Zechariah (8:9). But little is known of him as a person. The date of Haggai's ministry is easily established, for the day each sermon was given is precisely identified. With adjustments made for the lunar calendar used in Old Testament times, scholars suggest the sermons can be dated 21 September, 17 October, and 18 December of 520 B.C. Given the book's single theme and brief extent, it is best to use the four sermons themselves as a structure for the outline of Haggai.

OUTLINE OF HAGGAI

21 September 520 B.C.

I. Challenge to Rebuild (1:1-15)
A. Haggai's Call (1:1-11)
B. The People's Response
(1:12-15)

17 October 520 B.C.

II. An Encouraging Word (2:1-9)

18 December 520 B.C.

III. Blessing and Defilement (2:10-19)
IV. A Word to "Zerubbabel" (2:20-23)

Chapter summary. The precise references to dates in the reign of King Darius, well known from secular history, allow us to date Haggai's ministry in 520 B.C. (1:1). The prophet briefly sketches the struggle of the little Jewish community to exist during the 18 years since their return from Captivity and yet criticizes them for self-centeredness. They build their own houses, but let the temple, the house of God, remain a ruin (vv. 2-6). God's word is clear and simple. The economic difficulties they have experienced are a message from God, a warning to put God first in their lives (vv. 7-11).

The response of the governor and high priest and of all the people is immediate. They obey and within three weeks the whole community is hard at work, intent on completing the temple of the Lord (vv. 12-15).

Key verse. 1:2: Time for everything—but God.

Personal application. Put God first and everything else in your life will fall into place.

Key concepts. Temple »p. 283. Discipline »p. 387. Priest »p. 81.

INSIGHT

Zerubbabel and Joshua (1:1). Ezra 2:2 identifies Zerubbabel as the individual who led the exiles back to Judah. He was a member of the royal family of David, which indicates something of the generous character of Cyrus, who appointed him governor (*pehah*) of the little district of Judea.

Joshua the high priest is mentioned in both Ezra 3:2, 8 and Neh. 12:1, 8. He held the highest priestly rank.

It is significant that the two most influential leaders in Judah responded so quickly to the prophet's message. When leaders respond quickly to God it is much easier for the believing community to follow.

Not time (1:2). How modern an objection! Sorry, there just isn't time right now for prayer. I'd like to read my Bible, but I have to get up so early for my work. And at night I'm too tired to do anything but collapse and read the news.

The people of Judea were also busy: too busy with their own affairs to have time or money to invest in rebuilding the temple of God. As a result *they* lost out!

"A purse with holes" (1:5-6). What a series of images in these two verses. Their point is so clear. The harder the people of Judea worked, the further behind they got! Compare also vv. 10-11.

There's a lesson here for us. God is the one who makes any effort bear fruit. We need to put Him first. When we do, the Lord will bless.

"Honored" (1:8). The temple in ancient Israel was a focal point not so much of faith as of worship. It was the visible symbol of God's presence among His people, so that in O.T. times the people of God, wherever they might be, turned toward the temple to pray. When the Jews first returned to their homeland they had immediately set up an altar of sacrifice and laid the foundations of the temple. But that had been 18 years before! Since then the bare stones of the foundation were mute testimony to the failure of the community to put God first. Thus the empty foundations were a clear indication that God was not truly honored or held in sufficient awe in the community.

"I am with you" (1:13). What a message from the Lord! Despite the fact that you've ignored Me, I'm on your side. Don't misunderstand the troubles you've had, I'm on your side.

God so often must overlook our failures. And on our part, we must learn to interpret our disappointments as corrective or guiding events. We must never forget that God *is* on our side.

In Haggai's day, that meant trusting God enough to leave each individual's personal pursuits to rebuild the temple. In our day, that means you and I trust God enough to give His Word, and His work, daily priority.

Chapter summary. The chapter contains three encouraging messages Haggai gave the returned exiles during the months of work on the new temple. The first message was a promise that, despite its smaller size and less expensive decoration, the glory of the new temple would surpass that of Solomon's (2:1-9). This prediction surely came true, for Jesus Himself walked and taught in this "second temple," enlarged by Herod.

The second message is in the form of a lived parable. Haggai asks the priests a technical question about the Law. The question and its answer drive home the fact that the mere presence of a holy place among the people does not make *them* holy. In fact they are defiled by sin and indifference. Yet now that they have put God first, the Lord will bless (vv. 10-19).

The final message is addressed to Zerubbabel, who represents David's royal line. When God shakes the nations at history's end, the One whom Zerubbabel stands for, the Christ, will exercise God's authority on the earth (vv. 20-23).

Key verse. 2:9: Not gold, but God is the true glory.

Personal application. God blesses because we respond to Him, not as a response to our good works.

Key concepts. Blessing »p. 127. Glory »p. 74. Law »pp. 120, 145. Messiah »p. 432. Clean/Unclean »p. 82. Coming kingdom »p. 443.

INSIGHT

"Covenanted" (2:4-5). The covenant God refers to is His firm commitment to His chosen people. We have received just this kind of commitment from God in Jesus Christ. Whenever a task seems too great for us, we can remember God's words to that responsive generation that completed the second temple: "My Spirit remains among you. Do not fear."

Shake the heavens and earth (2:6). This is the only verse in Hag. quoted in the N.T. Hebrews 12:26 relates it to the end of the world, when God will introduce a cosmic earthquake that destroys every human society and calls all mankind to judgment.

"The Desired of the nations" (2:7). Ancient Jewish and early Christian commentators interpreted this as a reference to the Messiah. There are other interpretations. Some take "the desired" (*hemdat*) to mean precious "things," which in the Messianic Age will be offered to God at the rebuilt temple.

A dual warning (2:10-14). The two questions posed here underline a basic element in O.T. ritual law. Holiness is not "catching," but defilement is. That is, if a person is touched by a holy thing he will not be made holy, but a holy thing will be defiled if touched by something unclean.

What lessons did these lived parables teach? First, they warned the revived community that disobedience and spiritual indifference are catching. A few malcontents in the community of faith can corrupt the whole. How important then to encourage everyone to maintain an attitude of enthusiastic trust in the Lord.

Second, and most important, the preexilic Jewish community had felt safe because their city held God's temple. Haggai warns them that rather than being considered holy because they are in contact with the new temple, this generation must remember that their sins will defile the Lord's house! They must live committed lives, or God will cause this temple to be destroyed even as Solomon's temple was dismantled by the Babylonians!

Blessing ahead (2:15-19). God will now bless His people. But it will be because they have put Him first, not because once again there is a temple in Jerusalem.

Signet ring (2:20-23). The signet ring was the "signature" of a person, a symbol of his authority. Here Zerubbabel stands for the Messiah to come from the same (Davidic) family line. The meaning of the image is that one day the Messiah will exercise God's authority on earth, shattering the power of foreign kingdoms and establishing the chosen people of God.

The Postexilic Prophets

The little kingdom of Judah was ultimately crushed by the great Babylonian Empire in 586 B.C. and its remaining population taken captive. This was in accord with a long-standing policy, intended to root out nationalism and integrate defeated peoples into the empire.

Babylon reached its height under Nebuchadnezzar. Subsequent Babylonian rulers were weak, and in 539 B.C. Cyrus the Persian captured the capital city and took over the empire.

Cyrus reversed Babylonian policy and permitted ethnic groups to return to their homelands. He also urged them to reestablish their traditional religions and pray to their gods on his behalf. In accord with this policy the Jews in Babylon were not only invited to return to the Promised Land, but were also provided with the gold and silver objects used in temple worship.

Only a few of the Jews in Babylon responded to the invitation. Those who did, some 50,000 in all, found their homeland in ruin, fields overrun with weeds, homes fallen down. And they also learned that the neighboring peoples were hostile to their efforts to rebuild. Two Old Testament books give a brief history of that time. Ezra gives us insight into the early years and then describes conditions some 80 years after the return. And Nehemiah takes up the story a few years later, giving us the perspective of a dedicated believer who left a powerful post in the empire's capital to serve God and His people as Judah's governor.

Three different prophets whose works are found in the Old Testament ministered in Judah after the return. Haggai and Zechariah were contemporaries. Each ministered in 520 B.C., and Haggai's known activities are limited to a few brief months in that year. Each of these two was instrumental in moving the people to a brief recommitment to God, which resulted in finishing the temple after a lapse of some 18 years. Zechariah's expanded ministry also warned the little community that centuries would pass before the promised Messiah would appear and encouraged them to wait faithfully. His positive ministry has led to a distinctive nickname given him later by commentators: He is "the prophet of hope."

The third postexilic prophet is Malachi. But this prophet paints a far darker picture of the community than either Haggai or Zechariah. Ezra and Nehemiah both were deeply concerned because they found the same indifference to the Lord and violation of His laws that earlier prophets had cried out against. Each of these two strong leaders led a short-lived revival movement, marked by repentance and recommitment. Yet Malachi, writing after both of them sometime in the 450s B.C. shows us that once again the people have slipped into a sharp spiritual decline.

The three postexilic prophets, taken together, lead us to the heart of biblical faith. Faith calls for an eager commitment to God that is expressed in service (Haggai), even though the believing community must wait for generations for the fulfillment of its hopes (Zechariah). When that commmitment wanes, the community slips quickly into sin (Malachi). Whatever we do, we must keep the Lord as the focus of our lives and encourage one another to follow Him.

Zechariah

Zechariah is frequently called the "prophet of hope." As a young man he reinforced the urgings of Haggai that led exiles who returned from Babylon in 539/538 B.C. to finish rebuilding the fallen temple of the Lord in 520 B.C. (»p. 569). His book contains a series of fascinating visions conveying vital spiritual truths (1:7–8:23) and an extended portrait of events leading up to God's final victory at history's end (9:1–14:21). How these last chapters must have encouraged the little Jewish community, struggling economically and surrounded by hostile enemies. And how it can encourage us today, to meditate on the coming, certain triumph of God over evil.

Two themes emphasized in Zechariah are of special interest to Christians. First, this little book is filled with references to Christ. Messianic references include mentions of Christ's lowliness and humanity (6:12). They describe His betrayal by Judas (11:12-13), His deity (3:4; 13:7), His priesthood (6:13), and His kingship (6:13; 9:9; 14:9, 16). Zechariah also speaks of the Messiah's being struck down by the Lord (13:7), His second coming (14:4), His glorious reign (9:10; 14), and His establishment of world peace (9:9-10; cf. 3:10). In few Old Testament books do we find such constant attention given to the coming Saviour.

The other theme which interests modern Christians is eschatology, the study of end times. The last section of Zechariah describes a culminating siege of Jerusalem (12:1-3; 14:1-2). The enemy is temporarily successful (v. 2), but the city is defended by the Lord (vv. 3-4). He personally intervenes to destroy the invaders (12:9; 14:3). God's intervention causes great changes in the very structure of the Holy Land (vv. 4-5), and initiates a Messianic Age (vv. 16-19) in which Jerusalem and God's people at last become truly holy (vv. 20-24).

THE PLAN OF ZECHARIAH 9–14

Judgment/Salvation 9:1-8			Judgment/Salvation 14:16-21
King Arrives 9:9-10	Shepherd Rejected 11:4-17	War/Victory 12:1-9	War/Victory 14:1-15
War/Victory 9:11-10:2	War/Victory 10:3b-11:3	Messiah Pierced 12:1–13:1	Shepherd Struck 13:7-9
	Idols Present 10:2, 3a		Idols Suppressed 13:2-6

Critics once argued that Zechariah was a composite, constructed from the work of several different contributors. Recently the view that the book is a "disorganized collection" has been shown false. Instead the last section of Zechariah is written in a sophisticated literary form called *chiasmas*, diagramed above. This undated section of the book was undoubtedly written later than earlier, dated messages which range from October of 520 B.C. (1:1-6) to dates in 519 B.C. (1:7–6:16) and 518 B.C. (7–8). But there is no reason to suppose it was written by anyone other than Zechariah.

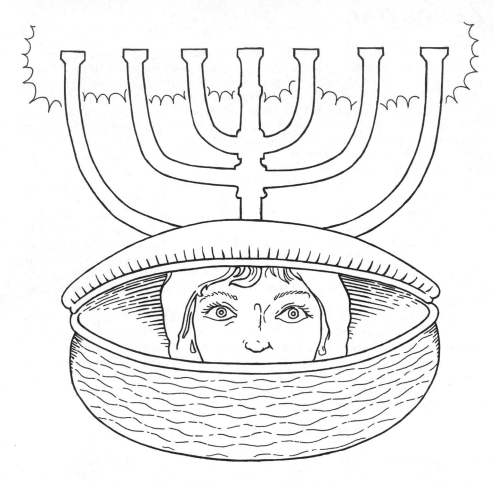

Illustration. *Strange objects fill the visions given Zechariah. Here a woman representing evil peers from a "measuring basket" that represents wickedness (5:5-11). Behind the basket a golden lampstand taken from a different vision (4:1-14) represents light shed by the Spirit of God, who empowers His people to do what is right and good. As we study Zechariah we discover that, as unusual as these visions may be, each communicates important truth about faith and life.*

Date and Authorship. Zechariah was a "young man" (2:4) when called to prophetic ministry in 520 B.C. Genealogies found in Scripture indicate that he was a member of a prominent family of priests. As a child Zechariah came back to the Jewish homeland with the first group of returning exiles. As an older adult the prophet succeeded his grandfather Iddo as head of the family (cf. Neh. 12:16).

Nothing else is known about his personal qualities, but the concern for faith and holiness that shine through his writings suggest he was a man whose hope was firmly anchored in the Lord and in the prospect of redemption ahead. The dates given within the book permit us to date many of his writings and visions, although most believe chapters 9–14 were written later than the others.

THEOLOGICAL OUTLINE OF ZECHARIAH

I.	NIGHT VISIONS	1–6
II.	FASTING	7–8
III.	MESSIAH'S REJECTION	9–11
IV.	MESSIAH'S TRIUMPH	12–14

CONTENT OUTLINE OF ZECHARIAH

PART I (1–8)
  I. Introduction (1:1-6)
  II. Eight Night Visions (1:7–6:8)
    A. A Horseman (1:7-17)
    B. Four Horns (1:18-21)
    C. A Surveyor (2:1-13)
    D. The High Priest's Filthy Clothes (3:1-10)
    E. A Gold Lampstand and Two Olive Trees (4:1-14)
    F. A Flying Scroll (5:1-4)
    G. A Woman in a Measuring Basket (5:5-11)
    H. Four Chariots (6:1-8)
  III. Crowning the High Priest (6:9-15)
  IV. Questions about Fasting (7:1–8:23)
    A. The Questions (7:1-3)
    B. God's Rebuke (7:4-7)
    C. Call to Repent (7:8-14)
    D. Restoration of Israel (8:1-17)
    E. Kingdom Joy Ahead (8:18-23)

PART II (9–14)
  V. Messiah's Advent and Rejection (9:1–11:17)
    A. God's Triumph (9:1-8)
    B. The King's Coming (9:9-10)
    C. Prosperity (9:11–10:1)
    D. Rebuke of Deceitful Leaders (10:2-3a)
    E. Joy and Restoration (10:3b–11:3)
    F. Fate of the Good Shepherd (11:4-17)
  VI. Messiah's Suffering and Acceptance (12:1–14:21)
    A. Joy in Jerusalem (12:1-9)
    B. Sorrow for the One Pierced (12:10–13:1)
    C. Deceitful Leaders Rejected (13:2-6)
    D. The Shepherd Killed (13:7-9)
    E. Final Victory (14:1-15)
    F. The Lord King of All at Last (14:16-21)

Chapter summary. The book is launched with a call to repentance (1:1-6): "Return to Me, and I will return to you." The message fits the time specified in 1:1. Zechariah spoke to support Haggai's exhortation to the postexilic community to put God first and rebuild His temple (»p. 569).

This simple message is followed by a series of eight "night visions," three of which are reported in these two chapters. These visions all concern the future of Jerusalem, during the passage of the centuries, or at history's end. The first vision is of horsemen who patrol the earth and report that at present the nations which have oppressed Judah are at peace. There will be no immediate judgment, and no immediate relief for the Jews (vv. 7-17). The second vision is of horns and of wreckers who destroy each horn as it emerges. This parallels Daniel's vision of four world kingdoms, which must rise and fall before Messiah comes (vv. 18-21). The third vision is of a builder with a measuring line, who is laying out the New Jerusalem which God is committed to construct at history's end (2:1-13). Whatever history holds, at history's end God's people and the Holy City will be exalted above all the nations of the earth.

Key verse. 2:12: Tomorrow is uncertain, forever is sure.

Personal application. Don't let temporary setbacks destroy your faith.

Key concepts. Word of the Lord »p. 449. Repentance »p. 780. Jerusalem »pp. 205, 451. Angel »p. 521. Anger »pp. 65, 72.

INSIGHT

Not like dad (1:4). Just because the older generation was unfaithful to God is no reason for their sons and grandsons to be unfaithful. What an encouraging word! Our choices are not determined by the example or training we have received. We are free to choose for ourselves. So let's choose God and good.

Silence is not evidence (1:12). Zechariah is upset that the whole world is at peace. He knows that to reestablish Israel God must "shake the heavens" (Hag. 2:6). The Lord reassures the prophet, explaining that He is jealous of (passionately concerned for the welfare of) Jerusalem and angry with the nations that oppress her.

There's a reminder here for us. God's failure to act against evil is not evidence of unconcern. God will act, but on His schedule rather than ours.

"I will" (1:16-17). In O.T. times as today, faith is based not on what we see, but on what God says He will do.

Four horns (1:18-21). Here as in other O.T. prophecy a horn represents power and authority. It's significant that as pagan world powers arise, so do "craftsmen" that tear them

down. The dynamics of their destruction are explained in Hab. 2 (see »p. 563).

"A city without walls" (2:4). In the biblical world, cities were walled in order to provide some security from invading armies. To be without walls meant that a community was helpless. Here, though, God introduces something new. Future Jerusalem will be without walls because its population is so great no one will dare attack it! And God Himself "will be a wall of fire around it" (v. 5).

"Scattered" (2:6). At the time Zechariah ministered, far more Jews lived in the cosmopolitan cities of the Persian Empire than lived in Jerusalem. The same scattered condition of God's O.T. people existed in the time of Christ, and today.

"The apple of His eye" (2:8). The "apple" of the eye is the pupil, the most sensitive part. God is extremely sensitive about how individuals and nations relate to His chosen people, the Jews.

"Become My people" (2:11). God's love is not exclusive. It is wide and deep enough to envelop all peoples. The Good News of salvation for all who believe is not limited to the N.T. Here Zechariah looks forward to the faith response of the nations to Israel's Messiah.

Chapter summary. The night visions that God gives Zechariah concerning the present and future of Jerusalem continue. The prophet is shown a vision of the high priest dressed in filthy clothing which represents sin, standing before the Angel of the Lord (3:1-3). He is assured of forgiveness and given clean clothing to wear. Then the high priest and his associates, the people of Judea, are promised that at the future coming of the Branch (the Messiah) all Israel's sin will be removed (vv. 4-10).

This vision is followed by another, in which Zechariah sees a lampstand ("candlestick") and two olive trees. In the complex vision the pipe overflowing with oil for the lamps represents the abundant power of the Holy Spirit. The trees represent the priestly and royal functions in Israel, and the two branches the current high priest (Joshua) and governor (Zerubbabel). The imagery also suggests the future union of the royal and priestly powers in the person of God's Messiah (4:1-14).

These visions both comforted and challenged God's people. The Lord purifies a people that they might glorify Him. God Himself supplies abundant power—for completion of the temple, and so that a purified and holy people might reflect His own character in this present, fallen world.

Outline
Place
Finder

VISIONS
FASTING
REJECTION
TRIUMPH

Key verse. 4:6: God supplies.

Personal application. Draw on the Spirit's overflowing power.

Key concepts. Angel of the Lord »p. 37. Priest »p. 81. Sin »pp. 362, 442. Forgiveness »p. 357. Holy Spirit »p. 776.

INSIGHT

"Joshua" (3:1). The high priest represents the entire nation, which according to Ex. 19:6 is to be a "kingdom of priests." The nation's sins, which have given Satan a basis on which to accuse her, are represented by filthy clothing. The Heb. word (so'im) is the strongest word for filth and loathsomeness the language offers.

Salvation (3:3-7). What a clear metaphor. Sin is removed, a new character is given, and the believer is called to walk in God's ways.

"Symbolic of things to come" (3:8-10). The vision of Joshua's cleansing and the call of his companions foreshadows the day the "Branch" (a familiar term for the Messiah) will remove the sins of all the people "in a single day."

"Seven eyes" (3:9; 4:10). In Scripture seven is symbolic of perfection, and eyes represent God's omniscience. The future the visions predict has been designed by an all-wise, all-knowing God. That future, the key to which is God's intent to forgive man's sin, is "written in stone," engraved and absolutely certain.

Symbols in the fifth vision (4:1-14). This complex vision contains many symbols. Their likely meanings in context are: *The lampstand—* the abundance of God's power through the Holy Spirit. *The two olive trees—* the priestly and royal offices. *The two branches—* Joshua/ Israel, and Zerubbabel. *The two golden pipes that pour out golden oil—* the Spirit's abundant power flowing to God's servants. God promises the leaders in Zechariah's day, so lacking in human resources of wealth and manpower, to supply them through His Spirit with all the strength they need to succeed. Just as God will do for those who serve Him today.

"By My Spirit" (4:6). The verse remains one of the most challenging, and encouraging, in Scripture. We rely not on our own strength or ability, but on the Spirit of God.

"The day of small things" (4:10). It's easy to become discouraged when we see how little we can do and how little we have to do it with. This was the case in Judea, where a relatively insignificant temple was being built to replace Solomon's magnificent edifice. But days of small things are *beginnings*, not endings! When we step out faithfully to do the small things God calls us to, the Lord has a way of making them—and us—great!

Outline
Place
Finder

VISIONS
FASTING
REJECTION
TRIUMPH

Chapter summary. Zechariah's night visions continue. The prophet is shown a massive, 30 by 15 foot flying scroll. The scroll represents God's curse on sin; its ability to fly shows the impossibility of escaping divine judgment (5:1-4). This is followed by a vision of an enlarged measuring basket that contains a woman who symbolizes wickedness. In his vision Zechariah sees the basket and its content lifted up and taken to Babylon. The removal of wickedness from the Holy Land, and its concentration in Babylon, sets the stage for history's final conflict between good and evil (vv. 5-11).

The third vision features four war chariots. These emerge from between bronze mountains and are charged with going "throughout the earth." The imagery suggests the coming judgment which God will visit on the pagan world (6:1-8).

In the last of the eight night visions the prophet sees a crown being forged for Joshua the high priest. On the day Messiah triumphs, the two offices of priest and king will be united in Him. Then the Messiah will "build the temple of the Lord" and so focus the hearts of all the people on the worship of God (vv. 9-15).

Key verse. 6:13: Christ sums up all things in Himself.

Personal application. What's fitting for the people of God is worship, not wickedness.

Key concepts. Law »pp. 120, 145. Curse »p. 138. Wickedness »p. 350. Branch »p. 413. Messiah »p. 432. Priest »p. 81. King »p. 130.

INSIGHT

The unrolled scroll (5:1-4). Documents were written on rolled parchment or paper in Zechariah's time. This scroll represents God's Law and its condemnation of sin. It is unrolled so it can be read and large so that its words are plain. God has not hidden either His standards of righteousness or His condemnation of those who violate the Law. The specific curses mentioned here are drawn from each tablet of the Ten Commandments: the one represents sins against God, the other sins against one's fellowman. The fact that the scroll flys suggests that the Law searches them out wherever they may be.

Why is wickedness a woman? (5:7-8) The reason is that the Heb. word translated "wickedness" is a feminine noun. There is no suggestion here that women are more sinful than or inferior to men.

What happens to wickedness? (5:7-11) The basket and its symbolic rider is removed to Babylon. The mention of a "house" prepared for the basket there may refer to pagan worship. The symbolism reminds us that wickedness (the Heb. word covers moral, social, and religious evils) is rightly associated with pagan worship and should have no place in a community that worships the Lord.

The four chariots (6:1-8). In chap. 1 the prophet saw horsemen at rest. Now he sees four angelic spirits represented by war chariots. They emerge from between mountains of bronze, a metal used in forming Israel's altar of sacrifice and representing judgment. Commentators link the colors of the horses with imagery found in Rev. 6. Commentators suggest that the colors are also significant, perhaps representing war and bloodshed (red), plagues and other judgments (dappled). The worldwide judgment symbolized here at last sets God's Spirit at rest, for His righteous wrath has finally been expressed.

Building God's temple (6:9-15). With the world judged, the Messiah, represented here by the high priest Joshua, is crowned. As the actual Joshua built the second temple in Zechariah's day, so the One he symbolizes will construct God's true temple and call all humankind to worship the Lord. In the Messiah, the function of priest and king will be united at last, and God will reign not only in our hearts, but in the world of men.

Outline
Place
Finder

VISIONS
FASTING
REJECTION
TRIUMPH

Chapter summary. In December of 518 B.C. a delegation came from Bethel to ask whether the people should continue to fast and mourn on dates set aside during the exile to commemorate the fall and destruction of Jerusalem and Solomon's temple (7:1-3). God's response is a rebuke. Were the people sorry about the sins of the past, or only sorry about the disaster? (vv. 4-7) Ritual had no meaning to God before the Exile, nor does it have meaning after. The issue was and is whether faith is real and is expressed as compassion and maintaining justice in the land (vv. 8-14). The rebuke is tempered by the prophet's revelation that the Babylonian Captivity was an expression of God's jealousy (passionate concern) for His people. The same passion which in the past was expressed in judgment will, in the future, produce a righteous society that is abundantly blessed by the Lord (8:1-17). When God brings in the age of blessing, mourning will be turned to joy. The Jews present weak and oppressed condition will be reversed, and powerful nations will journey to Jerusalem to seek the Lord (vv. 18-23).

Key verse. 7:5: Motive counts.

Personal application. We are called to be now what we will be when Jesus comes.

Key concepts. Justice »p. 141. Temple »p. 283. Remnant »p. 427. Jerusalem »pp. 205, 451. Future kingdom »p. 443.

INSIGHT

Fasting. Fasting is abstaining from food, and in O.T. times usually lasted from sunrise to sunset. Four motives for fasting are mentioned in the O.T.: (1) To express grief, mourning, as 1 Sam. 31:13. (2) To express the urgency of appeals to God in times of personal or national danger, as 2 Sam. 12:16 and Jer. 36:1-10. (3) To express the sincerity of repentance, as 1 Kings 21:27. (4) To honor the solemn character of the Day of Atonement, the only day on which fasting was commanded by God, as Lev. 16:29, 31. The ritual fasts mentioned in Zech. 7–8 were *not* commanded by the Lord.

In N.T. times religious Jews fasted Mondays and Thursdays as an expression of religious devotion. Jesus did not condemn this practice, but did condemn those whose motives were to *appear* spiritual to others (Matt. 6:16-18). While illustrations of fasting in relationship to worship appear in the N.T. (Luke 2:37; Acts 13:2; 14:23), the practice is neither taught nor encouraged in the N.T. epistles.

Christ's own 40-day fast had special significance all its own (Matt. 4 »p. 605).

For Me, or yourselves? (7:5-6) The Jews of Babylon, where the practice of fasting on these dates was originated, were expressing grief at their situation, not sorrow that they had sinned so terribly against God. Whatever we do we must ask ourselves, is this "for Me" (that is, am I looking at it from God's perspective, identifying with His purposes, desires, and concerns) or am I looking at it from a selfish standpoint.

God's concern (7:8-10). This is one of the clearest of Scripture's many expressions of God's heart. It's not in ritual but in relationships that we honor the Lord. It is not in religion but compassion that His love is sensed by others.

A challenge (7:11-14). When the forefathers refused to listen to God He judged them. Will we learn from history and repent? Or will history repeat itself and we be judged?

"Marvelous"? (8:1-17) Can the weak and insignificant faith community in Judah believe God will reverse their fortunes and again make Jerusalem great? More important, since God promises to make them holy, will they choose to live righteous lives now? (vv. 15-17) In view of what *is* it may seem impossible, but it is not impossible (marvelous) to God. It is the same with us. God can take us, weak and sinful as we are, and by His Spirit make us strong and good. Let's trust Him, and commit ourselves, now, to His ways.

Outline
Place
Finder

VISIONS
FASTING
REJECTION
TRIUMPH

Chapter summary. Chapters 9–11 adopt a unique literary form called *chiasmus*. The sequence of seemingly unrelated topics actually is linked, but in a complex pattern not discussed here. To see the linkage, see the diagram »p. 573.

Zechariah 9–11 provides vignettes of the Messiah's advent and rejection. The prophet begins with a promise: God will defend Jerusalem and destroy attacking nations (9:1-8). The city's people are called to rejoice. The messianic King will enter Jerusalem bearing salvation, and He will be riding on a donkey's colt (vv. 9-10, cf. Matt. 21:1-9). In His day God will save His people by conquering their enemies (Zech. 9:11–10:1). God will judge the unreliable human leaders of the nation and will care for the house of Judah, the family from which the Messiah will come to completely restore His people (vv. 2-12). Then, stunningly, the prophet predicts Judah's rejection of the promised Messiah, God's appointed Shepherd-King! The theme is introduced with a brief poem lamenting the judgment on the Promised Land that this rejection will provoke (11:1-3). Zechariah describes Israel's rejection of God's Good Shepherd, and their valuing Him at a mere 30 pieces of silver, the price set in the Old Testament for a slave. It is this rejection that will cause God to break the two staffs, "Favor" and "Union" which represent God's grace and the reunion of the long-divided people under the Messiah (vv. 4-14). With God's Messiah rejected and removed, the Lord permits His people to become victim to worthless shepherds who will feed on rather than protect them (vv. 15-17). What a reminder. No one can reject God's Shepherd, Jesus the Messiah, and expect to be blessed.

Key verse. 9:9: The King has come, and will return!

Personal application. Reject the Saviour, reject salvation.

Key concepts. Prophecy »pp. 417, 438. Messiah »p. 432. Covenant »pp. 35, 370, 466. Cornerstone »p. 375. Shepherd »p. 355.

INSIGHT

First coming emphasis. Although the passages speak of the Messiah as One who will deliver God's people, specific prophecies focus on Christ's first coming. Among them are: (1) His appearance in Jerusalem riding a donkey's foal (9:9). This passage and the Triumphal Entry (cf. Mark 11:1-10) emphasize both peace and humility, two unlikely qualities of a conqueror! (2) His rejection by His people and His betrayal (by Judas) are predicted, with the specific price (30 pieces of silver) His enemies payed the betrayer. A striking detail is the description of the money, thrown down in the house of the Lord, and because it was blood money, used by the priests to buy a potter's field rather than returned to the temple treasury (Zech. 11:12-13). Not every detail of predictive prophecy is un-

derstood before it is fulfilled. But when prophecy is fulfilled, it is done so literally.

"From Judah" (10:4). Judah is the tribe of both King David and the Messiah. In this prediction Christ is identified as "cornerstone" (the most important stone in any construction, either of the foundation or of an arch); as "tent peg" (the support on which the state is hung); as "battle bow" (the warrior/protector of the state). In rejecting the conqueror who violates their expectations by appearing in humble, peaceable guise, the people of Israel forfeit every chance to reestablish their nation. For all hinges on Him.

How good that God is faithful, and that Jesus, the Messiah, will come again!

Christ's Second Coming

Old Testament portraits of the Messiah were both dramatic and puzzling. The promised Saviour/King is pictured as a powerful Ruler who subdues Israel's enemies, enforces world peace, and brings God's ancient people back to the Lord, restoring Israel to prominence. Yet the Messiah is also portrayed as a sufferer, rejected by His own people, a seeming victim of God's judgment. The people of Jesus' time did not reconcile these two visions of the Messiah, and thus they rejected the humble Teacher who entered Jerusalem riding on a colt, in accord with Zechariah 9:9. Today, looking back, we realize the Old Testament is speaking of *two* appearances of the Messiah. In the first coming Jesus the Messiah suffered and died to redeem those who believe. In His second coming He will appear as a warrior and put an end to all God's enemies (2 Thes. 1; Rev. 19–20).

Yet it is significant that Old Testament prophecy actually makes it clear that two comings *must* be in view. Isaiah 53, a passage considered messianic long before Christ's birth, gives details of His sufferings and says plainly that this person who was "pierced for our transgressions" (v. 5) was "cut off from the land of the living" (v. 8). Yet after His death (v. 9) He "will see the light of life" and be given a "portion among the great" (vv. 11-12). Daniel 9 uses the same language to predict that the Anointed One (the Messiah) will be "cut off and have nothing" (9:26). Putting these passages together with the prediction in Zechariah 12:10, "They will look on Me, the One they have pierced," and with other similar passages, we learn an important truth. Two comings of the Messiah *are* taught in the Old Testament. And one coming clearly takes place after the Deliverer promised by God has been rejected, put to death, and raised to life again!

There is, however, another important implication of the concept of two comings of the Messiah. The first coming was not a "point" in time, but a line. His birth, teaching, and healing, His suffering, death, and resurrection took place over an extended period of time. Some wrongly assume that the Second Coming takes place in a moment of time. Yet it is important to realize that the events the Old and New Testaments associate with Christ's return also involve a time line. In fact, Daniel 9 indicates that *at least* seven years are consumed in the fulfillment of predicted events associated with the Second Coming! What we can be sure of is that whatever time it takes, whatever the sequence of events, all that the Scriptures announce will be fulfilled. Jesus will come again. And the words of the prophets will take clear shape as history draws to its intended end.

Outline
Place
Finder

VISIONS
FASTING
REJECTION
TRIUMPH

Chapter summary. This final section of Zechariah focuses on a single period of time. The whole people of Israel are the subject, the name *Yahweh* is mentioned again and again, and the peoples of the earth have a major role (12:1). What will happen during this future period of time?

God will deliver Israel from attacking nations (vv. 2-9) and effect the spiritual conversion of His own people. They will be delivered from sin and purified when they at last "look on Me, the One they have pierced" (12:10–13:9). When the city of Jerusalem is under siege by a great coalition of nations (14:1-2) the Lord will appear, with a host of angels ("holy ones"), and a great earthquake will split the Mount of Olives (vv. 3-8).

Then the Lord will establish the kingdom of the Messiah over the whole earth (vv. 9-11). Israel's enemies will be chastised (vv. 12-15), but the survivors of all nations will be reconciled to the Lord and come up yearly to worship Him at Jerusalem (vv. 16-19). From that time on Israel and Jerusalem and all her people will be "holy to the Lord" (vv. 20-21).

Key verse. 12:10: Christ must be acknowledged.

Personal application. It's not whether Jesus will rule our world in the future, but whether He rules in our hearts today.

Key concepts. Jerusalem »p. 451. Davidic Covenant »p. 370. World conflict »p. 428. Day of the Lord »pp. 413, 541.

INSIGHT

"The Lord" (12:1). The unique personal name of God, *Yahweh,* occurs again and again throughout these chapters. That name, which means "the One who is Always Present," emphasizes God's redemptive involvement with His people (»p. 54). Here at history's end God's active commitment to Israel is fully displayed.

Supernatural enablement (12:8). Every ability will be enhanced, so the least individual will be like the undefeated warrior, David, and the royal line like the Angel of the Lord (»p. 37). While the hyperbole is intended to emphasize God's enablement, it may have prophetic significance, for Christ, David's Descendant, is also the Lord.

Spiritual renewal (12:10). The Spirit is the One who gives grace and who moves the recipients to respond with supplication.

"The pierced One" (12:10). The Heb. preposition means look "to" rather than look "on." The people of Israel do not suddenly see the returning Christ, but suddenly realize that Jesus is the Messiah and look to Him in faith. The fact that Christ came as a humble Teacher, and permitted Himself to be crucified, will no longer be a stumbling block to Jewish faith. "Grieve bitterly" emphasizes the genuineness of the conversion.

Prophets ashamed (13:4-5). The national conversion leads to a rejection of all idolatrous religious practices—including purging the land of false prophets. These are false prophets here, who try to explain away self-inflicted wounds intended to attract the attention of pagan gods who love the smell of blood (cf. 1 Kings 18:25-28).

Their explanation? Just an accident while wrestling for fun at a friend's house!

"The Mount of Olives" (14:4). The topographical changes described here are also portrayed in Ezek. 47 and Rev. 21. The passage provides the background for Jesus' reference to faith removing "this mountain" (Mark 11:23) and to the angel's promise that when Christ returns His feet will stand on the Mt. of Olives (Acts 1:11).

"The Lord will be King" (14:9). These chapters provide one of the clearest summaries in the O.T. of the events associated with Christ's second coming. Yet this picture is reflected again and again in the O.T. prophets. The details are not defined, but the broad outline is clear. There is war on the earth, with its nations gathered against Israel.

God's Spirit moves and the realization sweeps Israel that Jesus, the One they have pierced, truly is their Messiah. The foreign forces are crushed when Christ appears with angelic forces and sets up His rule over the entire earth.

Malachi

Malachi has always been placed last in the Old Testament canon. Though no date is stated in the book, the Jewish Talmud classifies this book with Haggai and Zechariah as postexilic. Given this, the content suggests the prophet wrote during the interval between Nehemiah's two terms as governor (cf. Neh. 5:14; 13:6), about 430 B.C., or after Nehemiah's second term, nearer to 400 B.C. It's important to establish the time that Malachi wrote, for the historical context adds poignance to the message of the book.

The Babylonian Captivity of 586 B.C. was a divine judgment on the persistent sins of idolatry and injustice that corrupted preexilic Hebrew society. During the Captivity the Jewish people decisively rejected idolatry and turned to intense study of the Scriptures. When the Babylonian Empire fell, Cyrus the Persian issued a decree permitting the Jews and other captive peoples to return to their homeland. At that time those captives who were spiritually motivated responded. Some 50,000 enthusiastic Jews returned to the homeland, laid foundations for a new temple, and began the struggle to make their long-abandoned farms productive again.

When enthusiasm waned, God sent the Prophets Haggai and Zechariah, who stimulated a revival that led to completion of the temple some 18 years after its beginning. About 50 years later Ezra, a dedicated student and teacher of God's Law, came to Jerusalem. Spiritual motivation had again waned, and Ezra observed a variety of practices contrary to Old Testament Law. His grief stimulated another brief revival. Yet a few years later when Nehemiah, a Jew who was also a high official in the Persian court, came to Jerusalem to rebuild its walls, those same biblical laws were again being ignored. Nehemiah corrected the abuses. But as soon as he returned for an unspecified period to the Persian capital, the people strayed again! Somehow each new spiritual beginning quickly lost momentum, and the people became disinterested and disobedient.

It is this pattern that forms the background to the little Book of Malachi, the last book of the Old Testament. The prophet's charges against the sins of his day are responded to with sarcastic questions and denial. Somehow the nation has again failed to keep God first despite experiences of His forgiving grace. Malachi thus reminds us that, until the Christ comes, we can expect to see no just society established on earth. But we can expect those who love the Lord to talk together about Him, and by their lives to continue to display the distinction that exists between the righteous and the wicked in this present, evil world (3:16-18).

MALACHI AT A GLANCE

QUESTIONS MALACHI ANSWERS

How have You loved us? (Mal. 1:2) *God's choice of Israel proves His love.*

How have we despised Your name? (Mal. 1:6) *Failure to honor God is disrespect.*

How have we defiled You? (Mal. 1:7) *Failing to give God our best cheapens Him.*

Why shouldn't God hear our prayers? (Mal. 2:14) *You break faith with your wife.*

How have we wearied God? (Mal. 2:17) *By calling the evil person good.*

What do you mean, "return" to God? (Mal. 3:6) *If you violate God's Laws, you've left Him and thus must return.*

How do we rob You? (Mal. 3:8) *By failing to pay required tithes.*

What have we said against You? (Mal. 3:13) *Saying it is futile to serve God is to deny Him.*

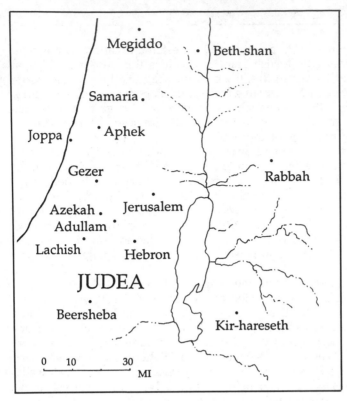

Megiddo

Beth-shan

Samaria

Joppa

Aphek

Gezer

Rabbah

Azekah
Adullam

Jerusalem

Lachish

Hebron

JUDEA

Beersheba

Kir-hareseth

0   10   30
MI

*The tiny district of
Judea and its capital,
Jerusalem. Though far
more Jews lived
scattered in foreign
nations, the homeland,
which is the center of
Jewish faith and hope, is
the one place in which
the pure Old Testament
religion could still be
practiced. The failure of
this community to
wholly follow the Lord
reflects once again the
desperate need for the
appearance of the
prophesied Messiah.*

VALUES OF MALACHI

The Book of Malachi reminds us of "games believers play" and calls us to reexamine our own relationship with the Lord. No halfhearted commitment will do, for truly the Lord is "a great King" (1:14).

CONTENT OUTLINE OF MALACHI

I. Introduction (1:1)
II. Dispute about God's Love (1:2-5)
III. Dispute about Respect to Be
Shown to God (1:6–2:9)
   A. The Priests' Failure to Render
Respectful Service (1:6-7)
   B. The Priests' Offering of
Unacceptable Sacrifices (1:8-9)
   C. The Priests' Attitude of
Boredom with Worship (1:10-14)
   D. God's Rebuke (2:1-9)
IV. Dispute about Unfaithfulness in
Covenant Relationships (2:10-16)
V. Dispute about God's Justice
(2:17–3:5)
   A. Confusion of Evil with Good
(2:17)

   B. Warning of Coming
Judgment (3:1-5)
VI. Dispute about Repentance (3:6-12)
   A. Neglect of the Tithe (3:6-9)
   B. Blessing to Follow after
Repentance (3:10-12)
VII. Dispute about Speaking Against
God (3:13-18)
   A. The Faithless Warned (3:13-15)
   B. The Faithful Encouraged (3:16-18)
VIII. The Day of the Lord (4:1-6)
   A. It Is Coming (4:1-3)
   B. Reminder to Observe the Law
(4:4)
   C. Prediction That "Elijah" Will
Come First (4:5-6)

Chapter summary. Malachi, whose name means "My messenger," has a word from God to the Jewish community in Judea. Yet when God announces His love His people scornfully respond, "How have You loved us?" (1:1-5) When the Lord complains that He is not being honored by His people, they bluntly deny His charge despite clear evidence that the priests are indifferent and worse than careless in performing their ministry (vv. 6-14). God sternly rebukes His priests, whose apathy and distorted teaching have corrupted the nation (2:1-9). But God has a dispute with the people too. Their marriages to foreign wives and their quickie divorces, motivated by passion, reflect their disloyal character (vv. 10-16). It's because they are a people who break faith, with one another and with God, that the Lord no longer hears or answers their prayers.

Key verse. 1:2: God loves and chooses.

Personal application. Indifference invariably leads to sin.

Key concepts. Priest »p. 81. Sacrifices »p. 78. Divorce »p. 136.

INSIGHT

"Esau" (1:2-5). The reference is to Edom, a nation whose people descended from Esau, the brother of Jacob (Israel), the ancestor of the Jewish people. "Hated" here is used as a legal term, meaning the decisive rejection of a claim.

The nation Edom was historically hostile to the Jews. God judged them, and they were removed from their homeland. But after the Babylonian Captivity the Jews were brought back to their homeland. Thus history itself demonstrates God's choice of and love for the Jews (Edom »p. 104).

Honor superiors (1:6). This is the point made in v. 6. A person who is subordinate shows respect for his superior. But the priests, who were the servants of God, offered Him crippled and lame animals as sacrifices. Such actions by priests and people revealed contempt for God, whom they should have honored as the great King He is (v. 14).

If God is first in our hearts our choices will reflect love for Him, and our every action will honor Him.

A simple test (1:8). We can apply Malachi's test today. If we would be embarrassed to offer what we intend to give to God or do for Him to a person that we respect, our offering is unworthy of the Lord.

What a burden (1:10-12). Remember that the prophet is speaking of priests who find serving God boring and burdensome! It's bad enough when we wake up on Sunday morning and think, "Oh, no, church again." It's perhaps worse if the preacher thinks it! The prob-lem of course is that some people go to church as a duty or simply to hear a favorite preacher. Others go to be seen in fine clothes or to fill an important position. What we are really to go to church for is to worship the Lord. When we attend for any other reason, in time going to church—like serving in the temple—loses meaning. It is God Himself who keeps faith vital and alive.

Covenant with Levi (2:3-6). Priests in Israel were drawn from the family of Levi and were charged with teaching God's Law. Their fail-ure to reverence God has corrupted them and distorted their teaching, with the result that they have led many ordinary people into sin.

Accurate interpretation of the Scripture does not depend so much on education as it does on personal dedication to and love for the Lord.

Unanswered prayer (2:13-14). It is often our own unfaithfulness to God, not His failure to hear us, that keeps us from receiving answers to prayer.

Divorce (2:14). The cause of the divorce that God hates is an all too common practice. An older man, moved by passion, gets rid of his first wife in favor of a younger, more physical-ly attractive woman. Whatever valid cause there may be for a divorce, mere sexual desire is *not* one!

God's people are called to live in a covenant (committed) relationship with Him and with one another. Any departure of covenantal liv-ing indicates a breakdown of one's love for, and commitment to, God.

Chapter summary. God warns Israel that He intends to send a messenger to prepare His way. The ministry of preparation involves confrontation and warning, for when Messiah comes He will judge sinners and impose righteousness (3:1-5). According to New Testament references John the Baptist, the cousin of Jesus, fulfilled this prophecy in his preaching just before Christ began His public ministry (Matt. 11:10; Mark 1:2; Luke 7:27).

Malachi then returns to those things in Judea's lifestyle that God must condemn, including departure from God's Law (Mal. 3:5) and actually robbing God by withholding tithes (vv. 6-12). In addition, the people have "spoken against" God by claiming there is no value in serving Him because they see no immediate financial profit in it! (vv. 13-15) Yet within the straying nation there are still individuals who love the Lord and talk about Him. God takes note of them and will treat them as His special treasure (vv. 16-18).

The book ends with a warning. God will yet judge the nations. So the community must be careful to keep His Law. God will send the Prophet Elijah to His people before that Day of the Lord—lest God strike the land with a curse (4:1-6).

Key verse. 4:6: The Old Testament ends with a warning.

Personal application. Stay close to others who love the Lord. They will nurture your own faith and commitment.

Key concepts. Covenant »pp. 35, 62. Judgment »p. 372. Occult »p. 131. Tithes »p. 103. Day of the Lord »p. 413. Law »p. 145.

INSIGHT

Fire and lye (3:2). The Second Coming, in view in this verse, focuses first on purification. The refiner's fire removed impurities, just as the strong lye used by refiners cleansed the gummy material from newly made cloth.

Come near for judgment (3:5). If we want God near us, we had better be sure our ways are just. God's presence is a blessing for His obedient children, but a danger to those who are impure.

Personal and social sins (3:5). The sins that Malachi identifies are typical of those condemned by earlier prophets—and by N.T. writers.

"Return" (3:6-7). The reaction of the people should be understood as feigned shock: "What do You mean, return? Who left?" This despite the evidence of the sins v. 5 identifies, and the fact that little attention is given to the responsibility of paying tithes to support those who lead in worship at the temple.

While the N.T. does not teach a tithe, our commitment to the Lord can still be measured in part by our willingness to give (»2 Cor. 8–9).

"Test Me" (3:10-12). If the Jews would trust God enough to pay the tithes required by the temple, God would bless them. Don't be taken in by media ministries that misapply this verse to promote fund-raising. But don't forget at the same time that no one can outgive God. Don't hesitate to respond to the Spirit's promptings as to your giving. God is still able to "pour out" blessings.

Does it pay? (3:13-15) God doesn't reward His followers with material rewards that "moth and rust corrupt." He has better treasures for us.

Fellowship counts (3:16-18). Those who are faithful to the Lord do need each other for encouragement and support. Seek fellowship with others who put God first. Shared commitments can keep you faithful even in a hostile society.

Elijah's ministry (4:4-6). We reconcile people to one another by first reconciling them to God. Elijah's ministry was partially fulfilled by John the Baptist. Many believe Elijah himself is in view in Rev. 11:1-14.

The Land Jesus Knew

As the first century dawned, the little homeland of the Jews was better known as the kingdom of Herod the Great. It extended along the Mediterranean coast, from a wadi known as the "river of Egypt" some 30 miles below Raphia, northward to Caesarea, a spectacular port city created by Herod. Along its southernmost border Herod's kingdom extended some 70 miles inland to the southern tip of the Dead Sea. Above the Dead Sea the kingdom ranged over the Jordan River, but nowhere extended more than 80 miles from the coast. Then, above Caesarea, the king's lands cut sharply away from the coast, encompassing the Sea of Galilee and reaching beyond it to the east to incorporate Gentile-occupied territories. All together the kingdom of Herod stretched no more than 80 miles across and only 160 miles from south to north.

While Herod was a personal friend of the Caesars, and an arrogant, driven sponsor of spectacular building projects, the land he ruled was in fact an insignificant and backward district. It was a buffer kingdom that was in effect a part of the Roman Empire and, shortly after Herod's death, was incorporated into it. Herod's lands were valuable, for they exported wheat and other agricultural products needed by the Empire. But the notion that anything really significant might happen there would never have crossed the mind of the Romans, whose administrators and legions ruled the world.

Still, the land where Jesus was born was viewed differently by different people. In the first century about 1/10th of the population of the Roman Empire was Jewish, though only about 500,000 or 600,000 Jews lived in their ancient homeland. Most major cities of the empire had relatively large Jewish populations. These men and women looked to Jerusalem for spiritual and legal guidance. Pairs of sages, the scribes, and "teachers of the law" mentioned in the Gospels, went out from Jerusalem with official word about the dates of Jewish holy days and to settle disputes within the Jewish communities by applying the ancient Mosaic Code. To the empire's Jews, Judea and especially Jerusalem was far from insignificant: it was the Holy City, the focus of their faith, and gifts poured into the temple treasury from Jews around the world.

Jerusalem had a reputation even among pagans. The Jerusalem temple had been expanded and beautified by Herod the Great. By the end of his 40-year reconstruction project, it ranked as one of the wonders of the ancient world. Many a wealthy Gentile traveler made a pilgrimage to Jerusalem to see the temple, even though he or she was unable to enter its inner confines. The port city of Caesarea also gained a worldwide reputation. Herod's engineers had created an artificial harbor using giant cut blocks of stone and then built a magnificent city on a barren coastal plain. The city boasted administrative centers, an open-air theater, a hippodrome for chariot races and the games so popular among the Romans, and temples dedicated to traditional Roman deities.

Talk to the Jewish citizens of Herod's kingdom and you'd find other perspectives on what all Jews held to be the "Holy Land." The priestly elite, wealthy and comfortable in their position, were satisfied with the status quo. The Pharisees, also a well-to-do class, concentrated their attention on observing every detail of God's Law, and looked forward to the resurrection of the just. Still, among the common people of Judea and especially of Galilee, the history and future of the little land was more important than the present.

In the present the average person struggled to make a living, working in the city as an artisan, serving on one of the large estates of the king or the wealthy as a hired laborer, or struggling with his own small plot of land. Taxes were staggeringly high: the temple took a tenth, the landlord and the king far more, and one could not even go to a city with produce to sell without paying additional duties along the road and at the city gates. Within the city, bakers, glass makers, metalsmiths, potters, and perfumers plied their trades and paid their taxes. And waited. They waited, looking expectantly for God to act.

Throughout the little land the Jewish population remained convinced that God had spoken to Abraham and promised that the whole land would belong to his descendants. God had spoken to Moses and confirmed the chosen position of the Jews by giving them a Law to live by. God had exalted His people in the time of David, making Israel one of the most powerful nations of the Middle East. And God had promised that one day a Descendant of David would appear to lead His people back to greatness. In that day Herod and his Roman overlords would be cast out. The promised One, the Messiah, would rule not only the Promised Land but would dominate all foreign nations as well. While some of the people, called Zealots, urged armed rebellion now, and another minority, the Essenes, demanded the religious separate themselves from an impure society, the majority of the people simply waited. They lived normal daily lives. They watched their children grow up and educated them in the Scriptures. They celebrated weddings and grieved at funerals. They knew the tragedies and joys that all human beings are heir to. And all the while they waited, expectant, sure that God would keep His promises and that deliverance would come. Perhaps even in their own time!

One Extraordinary Life

It was nearly 30 years after the death of Herod the Great in 4 B.C. that a young Man, the oldest Son in the family of a now deceased carpenter, began to preach and teach in Galilee. He taught with unusual authority and also performed spectacular authenticating miracles. Many assumed He was the Messiah the Scriptures foretold. As the Jesus movement grew, the religious leaders of Jerusalem sent delegations to hear Him preach. He offended some and disappointed others. Yet when He came to Jerusalem the enthusiasm of the crowds was so great that the leaders feared He might actually stimulate an uprising and that the Romans would come and take away not only the nation but, more importantly, *their* privileged place! But as the months passed Jesus assembled no army and issued the Romans no ultimatum. Popular enthusiasm waned.

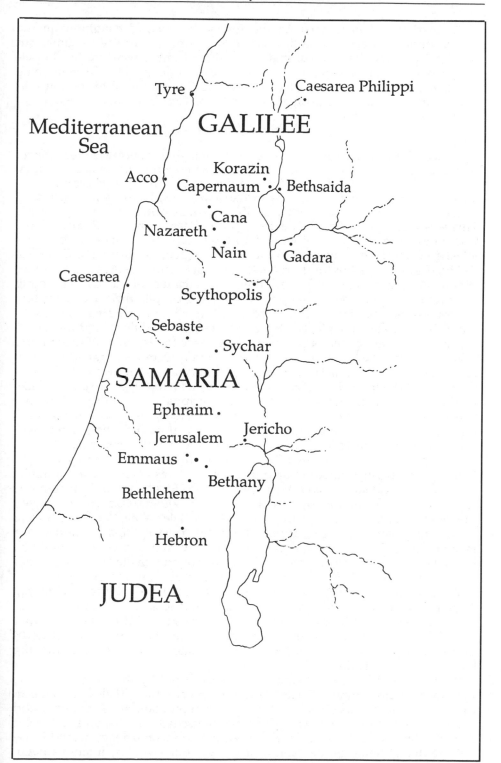

Tyre

Caesarea Philippi

Mediterranean
Sea

GALILEE

Acco

Korazin
Capernaum

Bethsaida

Cana

Nazareth

Nain

Gadara

Caesarea

Scythopolis

Sebaste

Sychar

SAMARIA

Ephraim

Jericho

Jerusalem

Emmaus

Bethany

Bethlehem

Hebron

JUDEA

It's hard for us to understand the forces that shaped conditions in the Jewish homeland and in the lifestyle of the population in Jesus' time. But some grasp of the dynamics of that time is important as we read the Gospels and explore in greater depth Jesus' own extraordinary life. To gain some sense of those times we need to look at Palestine's political history, at religious parties, and at the geographical flow of Gospel events.

Political History

In 63 B.C. the Roman Pompey, in reorganizing the eastern Mediterranean world, confirmed a priest named Hiercanus as governor of Galilee, Samaria, Judea, and Perea. The vizier (chief administrative officer) of Hiercanus was an Idumaean named Antipater, who had two sons, Herod and Phasael. These two succeeded their father in 43 B.C. when Antipater was murdered. This was just a year after the death of Julius Caesar, and the Roman world was plunged into 15 years of war. Herod, who escaped Galilee when it was attacked from the east, went to Rome where he became a friend of Octavian, destined to become the future ruler that history knows as Augustus Caesar. When Rome confirmed Herod as king of Hiercanus' old lands, the young ruler returned and won the support of the Jews, despite their hatred for him as a pro-Roman foreigner. He poured vast funds into expanding and beautifying the Jerusalem temple, created a local Gentile "nobility," and through a mixture of sensitivity and brutality brought peace to his corner of the empire.

When Herod died in 4 B.C., the lands of Herod were distributed to several of his descendants. Archelaus, an incompetent tyrant, governed in Judea and brutally put down Jewish uprisings against him. Herod Antipas ruled Galilee, holding power there until A.D. 39. Herod Agrippa I, a grandson of Herod, was ruler of Judea between A.D. 37–44. His son, Herod Agrippa II, maintained some power in his great grandfather's territories until the whole nation was razed in a rebellion that led to the destruction of Jerusalem in A.D. 70.

Yet there were other levels of government in the land ruled by Herod's family. The Jewish Sanhedrin, or ruling council, was charged with administering the biblical law which was in effect in the Holy Land. And procurators, Roman officials supported by a military force of some 3,000 men, supervised the Herodian rulers as well as the people as a whole. While the Romans were willing to govern through puppets, they did insist on final authority. For instance, only the Roman governor had the right to pass a sentence of death in the land. These various levels of authority not only made life complex, but the demands of each for financial support placed a burden on the people.

The situation was even more complicated by the Jews' intense nationalism. They resented the Herods and the Romans, and tensions remained great at most moments during these decades. A successful rebellion against other foreign rulers in 167 B.C. under the Maccabees, and the conviction that God's promised Messiah would soon free the nation once again, made for anything but a docile population!

When Jesus lived, this situation was exacerbated by the character of the Roman governor, Pontius Pilate. This fifth procurator of Palestine came to the Holy Land in A.D. 26 and established a reputation as an arrogant and stubborn man. While in Judea, of course, he issued his infamous judgment against Jesus, fearful that another accusation of incompetency would cause him trouble at home. So the land of Jesus was one swept by intense antagonisms toward the government, and by desperate hopes and dreams.

Herod's insensitivity and cowardice are both illustrated by an incident in which he ordered Legion standards, considered idols by the Jews, brought into Jerusalem by night. When confronted by a Jewish delegation protesting this desecration of the Holy City, Pilate stamped and yelled and threatened the envoys with death. In the end, Pilate backed down and ordered the standards withdrawn—even as later he gave in to the shouts of crowds who insisted he crucify Jesus, a man Pilate knew was innocent of the charges against Him.

Religious Parties

The Pharisees. These "separated ones" were a small but extremely influential group of laymen committed to strict observance of the Law and rules of ritual purity. Although Josephus reports that there were only about 6,000 of them in the Holy Land in Jesus' day, they were highly thought of by the people.

The Revell Bible Dictionary (1990) sums up their theology. "Doctrinally, the Pharisees were orthodox. They were supernaturalists who believed in the existence of angels. They believed in immortality and expected the righteous dead to be resurrected and rewarded. They believed the testimony of the Scriptures that God would one day send a Messiah to restore freedom in Israel . . . The Pharisees believed that the Old Testament Scriptures were the Word of God, but also that Moses had communicated an oral law of equal standing, and that this oral law was found in their traditions."

It was this that first brought the Pharisees into conflict with Jesus. When delegations of Pharisees traveled to Galilee to hear the popular new teacher and observe His way of life, they noted that He was far less rigid than they. And Jesus specifically rejected their claim of religious superiority. God required a

Illustration. *A Roman centurion in full uniform, holds a legion standard.*

righteousness greater than theirs (Matt. 5:20). And their beloved traditions hindered rather than aided efforts to love and serve God (Matt. 15:2; Mark 7:3-5). Later, as it became clear that Jesus claimed to be God's unique Son, the hostility they already felt toward Christ's teachings hardened into determined and open opposition.

The Sadducees. This group, whose name means "righteous ones," are mentioned by name only about a dozen times in the New Testament. Most extrabiblical information that we have about them comes from hostile sources. Yet it's clear that this was the aristocratic party of Jesus' day, made up of the well-to-do and dominated by the hierarchy of upper-level priests who supervised temple worship. This was also a party which led the movement to introduce Greek culture in Judea and thus would be considered the political "liberals" of that time. With the Pharisees, this group dominated the Sanhedrin and took the lead in the plot to dispose of Jesus.

The Revell Bible Dictionary (1990) summarizes what is known of their theology. "The Sadducees denied the possibility of life after death and scoffed at the common belief in resurrection (Mark 12:18). They also rejected the existence of angels or spirits (Acts 23:8). The Sadducees believed in the total freedom of the human will, uninfluenced by fate or God's providence. The Sadducees held that only the five books of Moses were authoritative and rejected the traditional interpretations of the Law so dear to the Pharisees."

A third group of persons mentioned in Scripture is composed of "lawyers," "teachers of the law," or "scribes," depending on the translation one uses. This class is made up of men who had dedicated their lives to a study of Old Testament Law and traditional interpretations of it. These were the sages, the rabbis, whose years of study under an acknowledged master had won them coveted recognition as an "expert in the Law." Both the Sadducees and Pharisees had members who were "teachers of the law," but membership in either of these two dominant religious groups did not automatically convey the coveted "expert" rank.

Other groups existed in the land of Jesus. There were the Zealots, eager for armed overthrow of the Romans, and the Essenes, who withdrew to desert communities or lived separated lives among the general population and called one another "brother." Despite the attempts of some to demonstrate Jesus' dependence on such groups for His teachings, they are not mentioned in the Gospels nor did they shape Jesus' thinking. In fact it was the revolutionary nature of Jesus' teaching—about the law, about God as Father, about the forgiveness of sin, and particularly about faith in Himself as the Son of God, that deeply divided the nation and aroused the hostility of the two leading factions in first-century Judea's religious and social life. Soon the issue polarized the nation. Although the multitude held back, uncertain, it became more and more clear that one must be for Jesus, or against Him.

The Geographical Flow of the Gospels

Students of the New Testament have long noted that descriptions of Jesus' ministry are concentrated in different geographical areas of the Holy Land. There is an introductory report of Christ's birth, preparation for public ministry, and initial acts. Then Jesus' ministry was concentrated in Galilee. In time it shifted to Judea and Perea and then, after a brief report of events while Christ traveled toward Jerusalem, the Gospels highlight His significant last week in the capital, where He died and was raised to life again.

Jesus' birth is described, but His childhood is mentioned only briefly in the New Testament. The critical moment described in three of the four Gospels is the young adult Christ's baptism by John the Baptist. This act was not a confession by Jesus of any need to repent, but rather a bold identification with John's preaching. Immediately following the baptism, Jesus was led by God's Spirit into the wilderness. After fasting for forty days He was confronted and tempted by Satan. Christ's victory over temptation demonstrated His personal qualifications as Victor over sin. With this established, Christ began His ministry.

HARMONY OF THE GOSPELS

	Matthew	Mark	Luke	John
I. BIRTH AND CHILDHOOD (4/5 B.C.)				
Genealogy of Jesus	1:1-17		3:23-38	
Birth of John the Baptist			1:5-25, 57-80	
Jesus' Birth Foretold (Mary)			1:26-38	
Jesus' Birth Foretold (Joseph)	1:18-25			
The Birth of Jesus	2:1		2:1-7	
Angels Announce the Birth			2:8-20	
Jesus Presented at the Temple			2:21-39	
The Wise Men Come	2:1-12			
The Family Flees to Egypt	2:13-23			
Childhood, and Visit to Temple			2:40-50	
Growth to Manhood			2:51-52	
II. MINISTRY PREPARATION (A.D. 29)				
John the Baptist's Preaching	3:1-12	1:1-8	3:1-20	
Jesus Is Baptized	3:13-17	1:9-11	3:21-22	
Jesus Tempted in the Wilderness	4:1-11	1:12-13	4:1-13	
III. BEGINNING OF JESUS' MINISTRY				
John Points Out Jesus				1:19-34
The First Disciples Attracted				1:35-51
The First Miracle: Water to Wine				2:1-12
Jesus Cleanses the Temple				2:13-25
Jesus Explains "Born Again"				3:1-21
John Testifies about Jesus				3:22-36
John Imprisoned			3:19-20	
Jesus Travels in Samaria				4:1-42

	Matthew	Mark	Luke	John
IV. GREAT GALILEAN MINISTRY				
Jesus Arrives	4:12-17	1:14	4:14	4:43-45
Heals Nobleman's Son				4:46-54
Calls First Disciples	4:18-22	1:16-20		
Jesus Heals the Sick	8:14-17	1:21-34	4:31-41	
Jesus Travels and Preaches		1:35-39	4:42-44	
Jesus Performs Many Miracles	8:1-4; 9:1-35	1:30–3:12	5:1–6:19	
Jesus Confronts Pharisees	12:1-21			
The Twelve Appointed		3:13-19	6:12-16	
The Sermon on the Mount	5–7		6:20-49	
Jesus Heals a Soldier's Servant	8:5-13		7:1-10	
Jesus Raises a Widow's Son			7:11-17	
John the Baptist Doubts	11:2-19		7:18-35	
Jesus Anointed by a Prostitute			7:36-50	
Jesus Makes Another Tour			8:1-3	
Jesus' Family Protests	12:46-50	3:31-35	8:19-21	
Jesus Speaks in Parables	13:1-53	4:1-34	8:4-18	
Jesus Performs a Series of Miracles	8:14-17; 9:18-34	4:35–5:43	8:22-56	
Jesus Rejected at Nazareth	13:54-58	6:1-6		
Disciples Sent Out to Preach	9:36–11:1	6:7-13	9:1-6	
John the Baptist Executed	14:1-12	6:14-29	9:7-9	
The Twelve Return		6:30-32	9:10	
Jesus Feeds 5,000	14:13-21	6:33-44	9:11-17	6:1-14
Jesus Walks on the Sea	14:22-33	6:45-53		6:15-21
Jesus Teaches on "Uncleanness"	15:1-20	7:1-23		
Jesus Near Tyre and Sidon	15:21-28	7:24-30		
Jesus Heals Near Decapolis	15:29-31	7:31-37		
Jesus Feeds 4,000	15:32-39	8:1-10		
Jesus Warns against Pharisees	16:1-12	8:14-21		
Jesus Heals a Blind Man		8:22-26		
Jesus Affirmed as the Christ and Son of God	16:13-26	8:27-37	9:18-27	6:68-69
Jesus Transformed	17:1-13	8:38–9:13	9:28-36	
Jesus Heals Epileptic Boy	17:14-21	9:14-29	9:37-43	
Jesus Predicts His Death and His Resurrection	17:22-23	9:30-32	9:43-45	
Jesus' Last Galilean Ministry	17:24–18:34	9:33-50	9:46-50	7:1-9

Jesus' ministry was both aggressive and itinerant. Christ first chose twelve disciples. He then went out and traveled the land with them. He did not wait for people to come to Him, although soon crowds gathered to hear Him and to witness His miracles. No, Jesus traveled the rocky hillside paths that crisscrossed Galilee. He preached beside the sea, on hilltops, sitting in a home in Capernaum, and in the synagogue of His hometown, Nazareth. Christ lived by His famous saying, "The Son of Man came to seek and to save what was lost" (Luke 19:10). It was seeking that marked His early ministry. Every man and woman in the Jews' ancient homeland needed to hear about—and to hear—Jesus.

In His travels Jesus healed the sick, showing both the authority He had from God and the love God had for human beings. In His travels He taught using parables to deepen His listeners' awareness of His Father's love and all that means to a people who lived such precarious lives. But His message was also challenging. The believer must "seek first His kingdom and His righteousness" (Matt. 6:33). God is not only to be trusted. He must have absolute priority in our lives.

Illustration. *A 1st-century traveler in Galilee or Judea, equipped as were Christ and His disciples.*

As the Gospels complete their tracing of the Galilean ministry of Jesus, the focus shifts to His confrontations in Judea with the leaders of the land. That ministry culminates in a decision by the leaders to kill Jesus, as quickly as they possibly could.

The ordinary person traveled on foot, carrying a wooden staff. He was shod in open sandals and carried a "purse" in which food—typically bread and dried raisins or figs—were placed. Any money was normally wrapped in the folded cloth belt worn around his waist. His clothing consisted of a rough outer cloak that fell to mid-calf and at night served as his blanket. This was worn over a shorter tunic. A rectangle of cloth might be worn on his head as shelter from the sun, tied there by another strip of cloth.

Matthew 10 tells how Jesus sent His followers out to preach where He did not have time to go, dependent as Christ Himself was on whatever food or shelter might be offered in the towns they visited.

Illustration. *The rift between Jesus and the Pharisees and other religious leaders deepened as His ministry shifted to Judea. Christ's compassion for sinners, His contempt for a religion of ritual devoid of mercy, and His ever more clear claims to be one with Israel's God hardened opposition to Him.*

The bulk of every Gospel's account of Jesus' life is concerned with events that took place in Jerusalem during the week before Christ's death. We can distinguish what took place each day of that week and sense not only the growing tension, but the anguish and then the triumph of its culminating events: the crucifixion, and then the resurrection, of Jesus Christ.

	Matthew	Mark	Luke	John
VII. JESUS' LAST WEEK, PASSOVER A.D. 33				
Sunday				
The Triumphal Entry	21:1-9	11:1-10	19:29-40	12:12-19
Jesus Views the City	21:10-11	11:11	19:41-44	
Monday				
Jesus Curses a Fig Tree	21:18-19	11:12-14		
Jesus Cleanses the Temple	21:12-13	11:15-19	19:45-48	
Healings in the Temple	21:14-17			
Tuesday				
The Fig Tree Is Withered	21:19-22	11:20-25		
Jesus Challenged by the Elders	21:23–22:46	11:27–12:37	20:1-44	
Pharisees Condemned by Jesus	23	12:38-40	20:45-47	
The Widow Gives Her Mite		12:41-44	21:1-4	
Greeks Try to See Jesus				21:20-36
Jews Reject Jesus' Claims				12:37-50
Jesus Teaches on History's End	24–25	13:1-37	21:5-38	
Jesus Predicts Crucifixion	26:1-5	14:1-2		
Jesus Anointed by Mary	26:6-13	14:3-9		12:2-8
Judas Agrees to Betray Jesus	26:14-16	14:10-11	22:3-6	
Wednesday				
Thursday				
The Passover Meal Held	26:17-29	14:12-25	22:7-22	13:1-38
The Last Supper Teaching				14–16
Jesus' High Priestly Prayer				17
Prayer at Gethsemane	26:36-46	14:32-42	22:39-46	18:1
Jesus Arrested	26:47-56	14:43-52	22:47-53	18:2-12
On Trial before Annas				18:12-14, 19-23
On Trial before Caiaphas	26:57-68	14:53-65	22:54	18:24
Peter Denies the Lord	26:69-75	14:66-72	22:54-62	18:15-18, 25-27
On Trial before the Sanhedrin	27:1	15:1	22:66-71	
Suicide of Judas	27:3-10			
Friday				
On Trial before Pilate	27:11-14	15:2-5	23:1-5	18:28-38
Taken to Herod			23:6-12	
Returned to Pilate	27:15-26	15:6-15	23:13-25	18:39– 19:16
Mocked by Soldiers	27:27-30	15:16-19	22:63-65	
Led to Calvary	27:31-34	15:20-23	23:26-32	19:16-17
Jesus' Crucifixion	27:35-56	15:24-41	23:33-49	19:18-37
Jesus' Body Buried	27:57-60	15:42-46	23:50-54	19:38-42
Saturday				
Women Visit the Tomb	27:61	15:47	23:55-57	
A Guard Set over the Tomb	27:62-66			
Sunday				
The Women Return	28:1-8	16:1-8	24:1-12	20:1-10

	Matthew	Mark	Luke	John
VIII. RESURRECTION APPEARANCES OF JESUS CHRIST				
To Mary Magdalene		16:9-11		20:11-18
To the Other Women	28:9-10			
Report by the Guards	28:11-15			
Two Unnamed Disciples		16:12-13	24:13-32	
Peter			24:33-35	
The 10 Apostles		16:14	24:36-43	20:19-25
The 11 Apostles				20:26-31
By the Sea of Galilee				21:1-14
Questioning of Peter				21:15-25
The Disciples, in Galilee	28:16-20	16:15-18		
The 11 at Olivet			24:44-49	
At the Ascension	28:18-20	16:19-20	24:50-53	

The life and teaching of Jesus can only be understood in the context of first-century Judaism as it was practiced in Galilee and especially in Judea. Yet the significance of Jesus can only be understood in the context of God's plan for all humankind. The Hebrew people were chosen to be the avenue of divine revelation, the womb within which the promise of a Saviour could be nurtured. With the birth of God's Son that promise was kept: He appeared to be the Saviour of all who believe. Yet while Christ's birth, death, and resurrection form the fulcrum on which all history turns, His ministry was as much promise as fulfillment. Christ died for our sins to provide us forgiveness and sent His Holy Spirit to supply the dynamic power we need to live holy lives.

In the Gospels we meet Jesus the Man and see His ministry in the context of a land and people that He knew. Yet the meaning of Jesus explodes out of that land and culture, with a Good News that promises transformation to human beings of every age and every society. The Man and His message, the Man and His meaning, are for every person of every time.

Matthew

During the first three centuries of the Christian era Matthew's Gospel was the most admired and quoted of the New Testament's portraits of Jesus. This, of course, is exactly what a Gospel is: a portrait of the Person who is Himself the Good News of God's forgiving love.

Matthew's Gospel is the one most rooted in the Old Testament and most concerned with issues that were important to the Jewish people. It contains the most quotes from the Old Testament and the most references to fulfillment of prophecy. It also has the most to say about Old Testament Law, showing its distortion by the traditions so loved by the Pharisees and refocusing attention on the heart rather than behavior.

Perhaps the most distinctive theological contribution of Matthew has to do with the kingdom. The Old Testament prophets were convinced that God intended to set up an earthly kingdom under the Messiah, a descendant of David, who would lift Israel to glory and establish God's righteous rule worldwide. The death of Jesus on the cross raised a critical question. If Jesus is the Messiah, what has happened to the kingdom? Matthew tells us.

First, in the Sermon on the Mount he shows us that God's kingdom has present expression in the gathered and individual lives of believers. Second, in portraying the reaction of the Jewish people to Jesus, he shows us that the promised kingdom was offered to them, but rejected when they refused to acknowledge Christ as Messiah. Third, in reporting the prophetic words of Jesus recorded in chapters 24–26, he explains that the kingdom is coming, but delayed. It will be established when the King returns.

While the theme of the kingdom provides the framework around which this Gospel is constructed, its greatest value to us is still found in the images of Jesus it conveys. We share His contemporaries' awe as we witness His miracles. We are humbled as His teachings strip away our excuses. We are thrilled as we hear Him describe the new and vital life we are invited to live as citizens of the present kingdom of our God. Every chapter helps us grow in our appreciation for who Jesus is. And every paragraph of this matchless Gospel invites us to trust and love Jesus more.

MATTHEW AT A GLANCE

KEY PEOPLE

Jesus of Nazareth *The carpenter who became an itinerant preacher is shown to be the Son of God, our Saviour and Lord.*

Simon Peter *This "prince of the apostles" typically represents the Twelve. He is their vocal and impulsive leader.*

The Pharisees *These zealous legalists as a class represent religious opposition to Jesus and serve as a foil against which His revolutionary teachings are most clearly seen.*

KEY EVENTS

Jesus' birth (Matt. 1–2) *Christ is born of a virgin in fulfillment of prophecy.*
Sermon on the Mount (Matt. 5–7) *Jesus explains life in God's present kingdom.*
Jesus is rejected (Matt. 16) *Only the disciples acknowledge Jesus as Son of God.*
Jesus is crucified (Matt. 26–27) *Jesus goes to the cross—for us.*
Jesus is raised again (Matt. 28) *The Son of God conquers death itself.*

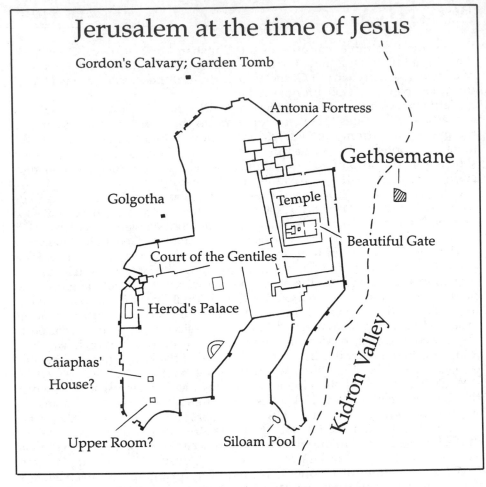

Jerusalem at the time of Jesus

Gordon's Calvary; Garden Tomb

Antonia Fortress

Gethsemane

Golgotha

Temple

Beautiful Gate

Court of the Gentiles

Herod's Palace

Kidron Valley

Caiaphas' House?

Upper Room?

Siloam Pool

WHERE THE ACTION TAKES PLACE

Most of Jesus' teaching ministry took place in the fields and small towns of Galilee and Judea. Yet the focus of the last third of each Gospel is on Jerusalem, the Holy City. There Christ drove the money changers from the temple, challenged priest and Pharisee, and was illegally tried and condemned. And just outside this city Jesus was crucified, buried, and raised again.

Date and authorship. It's not possible to establish the date this Gospel was written. Despite the theories of some scholars who argue for late first century composition, it seems most likely the book was completed and began to circulate between A.D. 40 and A.D. 60.

The author of the Gospel is not identified in the text, but from the very beginning it has been known as the Gospel of Matthew. There is no reason to doubt that the book was in fact written by Matthew, the onetime despised tax collector, who later became one of Jesus' twelve disciples (cf. Mark 2:14-17; Luke 5:27-32). Few people would have better understood the transforming power of divine forgiveness.

THEOLOGICAL OUTLINE OF MATTHEW

I. PREPARATION	1–4
II. PREACHING	5–7
III. PROOF	8–17
IV. PRACTICE	18–20
V. PURPOSE	21–28

CONTENT OUTLINE OF MATTHEW

I. Preparation of the King (1:1–4:25)
 A. Jesus' Genealogy (1:1-17)
 B. Jesus' Birth (1:18–2:23)
 C. Jesus' Baptism (3:1-17)
 D. Jesus' Temptation (4:1-11)
 E. Jesus Calls His Disciples (4:12-25)

II. Preaching of the King (5:1–7:29)
 A. Kingdom Principles (5:1-12)
 B. Kingdom Priorities (5:13-48)
 C. Kingdom Practices (6:1-18)
 D. Kingdom Perspectives
  (6:19–7:29)

III. Proof of the King (8:1–17:27)
 A. Jesus' Miracles (8:1–9:34)
  1. Power over sickness (8:1-22)
  2. Power over nature (8:23-27)
  3. Power over demons (8:28-34)
  4. Power over sin (9:1-17)
  5. Power over death (9:18-34)
  6. Power for the harvest
   (9:35-38)
 B. Jesus' Authority (10:1–12:50)
  1. Authority delegated (10:1-42)
  2. Authority explained (11:1-30)
  3. Authority affirmed (12:1-50)
 C. Jesus' Parables (13:1-53)
 D. Jesus' Glory (13:54–17:27)
  1. Rejection at home
   (13:54–14:12)
  2. Jesus' power displayed
   (14:13-36)
  3. Rejection by religious
   leaders (15:1-20)
  4. Jesus' power displayed
   again (15:21-39)
  5. Rejection by people and
   religious leaders (16:1-12)
  6. Confession of faith by the
   disciples (16:13-28)
  7. Jesus' glory displayed in
   transfiguration (17:1-27)

IV. Practice Promoted by the King
  (18:1–20:34)
 A. Greatness in Relationships
  (18:1-35)
 B. Grace in Relationships
  (19:1–20:16)
 C. Servanthood in Leadership
  (20:17-34)

V. Purpose of the King (21:1–28:20)
 A. Presentation as King
  (21:1–23:39)
  1. The triumphal entry (21:1-11)
  2. Challenged by the religious leaders (21:12–22:46)
  3. Condemnation of the religious leaders (23:1-39)
 B. Preview of the King's Return
  (24:1–25:46)
  1. The years between (24:1-28)
  2. The King's coming (24:29-41)
  3. The King's command to
   watch while waiting
   (24:42–25:46)
 C. Passion of the King
  (26:1–27:66)
  1. The plot to kill Jesus (26:1-5)
  2. Jesus anointed (26:6-13)
  3. Judas betrays Jesus (26:14-16)
  4. The Last Supper (26:17-35)
  5. Gethsemane (26:36-46)
  6. Arrest and trials
   (26:47–27:31)
  7. The crucifixion (27:32-56)
  8. The burial (27:57-66)
 D. The Resurrection of the King
  (28:1-20)
  1. The empty tomb (28:1-7)
  2. The risen Christ revealed
   (28:8-17)
  3. The King issues His Great
   Commission (28:18-20)

Outline
Place
Finder

PREPARATION
PREACHING
PROOF
PRACTICE
PURPOSE

Chapter summary. Matthew launches his Gospel with a genealogy, intended to serve as a "record of origins" of the one he will show is the promised Messiah of Israel (1:1-17). In summary fashion Matthew identifies key ancestors in the line of Jesus, with particular emphasis on His descent from King David. This is vital, for the Old Testament stresses the fact that the Messiah must come from David's line (vv. 6-17). At the same time Matthew wants us to understand that this descendant of David is more than a mere man. He is also the Son of God, conceived by a unique work of the Holy Spirit, in fulfillment of one of the most unusual of all Old Testament prophecies: A virgin will have a child to be given a name which means "God with us!" (vv. 18-25)

Thus at the very beginning of his book Matthew states the basic truths which shape every person's perception of Jesus Christ.

Key verses. 1:22-23: The key to faith.

Personal application. Faith isn't measured by its strength, but by its object.

Key concepts. Genealogy »p. 264. Davidic Covenant »p. 370. Messiah »p. 432. Immanuel »p. 416. Holy Spirit »p. 73.

INSIGHT

A record of origins (1:1). This is the meaning of the Gk. phrase translated "a record of the genealogy" in the NIV and "generations" in older versions. Matthew's report of Christ's origins is not limited to the first 17 vv. of chap. 1, which contains a genealogical list. The record of origins actually extends to 2:23 and includes the author's detailed account of Jesus' early childhood. Matthew especially wants his Jewish readers to know exactly where Jesus came from. He leaves no gap in his report, so there will be no question about Jesus' heritage.

Sacred history? Some liberal theologians have tried to isolate "sacred" history from "real" history. Their contention is that something did not have to really happen to be "true" in a religious sense. Jesus didn't really have to have been born of a virgin: This is just faith's way of saying Jesus was special. Matthew does not share this view. The Jesus he presents is the Jesus of history, and Matthew takes great pains to make sure his readers know the key details of Christ's birth and earliest years.

The Jesus we trust really was born of a virgin, and really is God's Son.

"Father of." The phrase is frequently used in the O.T. in the sense of "ancestor." "Father" may mean grandfather, or a distant relative.

"Fourteen generations"? (1:17) Hebrew genealogies typically skip generations, and they often are arranged in groups for ease of memorization. Here groups of 14 may be symbolic. The numeric value of "David" in Heb., where letters also serve as numbers, is 14. To list Jesus as the last of two series of fourteens would seem significant to the Jewish reader and be another indicator that He is the fulfillment of the promises given David.

Pledged to marry (1:18). The Jewish "engagement" indicated here by *mnesteuo* was more binding than ours; it was a formal stage in contracting a marriage. The breaking of the marriage contract, even at this stage, was considered a divorce and would imply adultery.

Joseph's character. Joseph must have felt betrayed when Mary was discovered to be pregnant. Even so he was willing to protect her by arranging a private divorce (before just two witnesses, cf. Num. 5:11-31). The comment, "a righteous man" (v. 19), reminds us that righteousness is not stern insistence on the letter of the law, but is well flavored with mercy and compassion.

"From the Holy Spirit" (1:20, 23). Scholars argue that the Heb. word in Isa. 7:14 does not necessarily mean "virgin." But there is no question that the Gk. word in 1:23 does and must mean "virgin." No human being was the agent of Jesus' conception. That agent was the Holy Spirit, and the child born was truly human, yet was also God the Son. He was Immanuel: a name meaning "with us is God."

"Jesus" (1:21). The name reminds us of the purpose of Christ's birth. It means "Saviour," and Christ came to "save His people from their sins."

Chapter summary. Jesus' birth in Bethlehem, which fulfilled Old Testament prophecy (Micah 5:2), is noted by Persian astronomers/astrologers who saw "His star" and journeyed to Judea to worship the promised messianic King (2:1-2). When Herod asks where the new King is, his advisers consult the Scriptures and identify Bethlehem as the predicted birthplace (vv. 3-6). Matthew contrasts magi, so eager to honor the King, with brutal Herod, who was intent in his desire to have this rival killed. When the visitors, warned by God in a dream, leave for home without reporting back to Herod (vv. 7-12), the king orders the execution of all boy children in the district up to two years old. Joseph again shows his pious character as he responds immediately and flees to Egypt when warned by God in another dream (vv. 13-18). Later, again in response to divine guidance, Joseph leads his little family back to Israel to settle in Nazareth, a town in Galilee (vv. 19-23).

Outline
Place
Finder

PREPARATION
PREACHING
PROOF
PRACTICE
PURPOSE

Key verse. 2:11: Responding with worship and gifts.

Personal application. God will guide us too—if we are as ready to respond as Joseph was.

Key concepts. Prophecy »p. 434. Dreams »p. 99. Angel »p. 521.

INSIGHT

"Bethlehem" (2:1). Throughout the passage Matthew points to prophecies which Jesus' birth and early life fulfilled (cf. vv. 6, 15, 17-18, 23) to prove to Jewish readers that Jesus is the promised Messiah.

King Herod. Herod the Great was near death at the time the magi visited. Yet this paranoid man, who executed several of his own sons on suspicion that they planned to overthrow him, was so jealous of his power that he determined to murder an infant who surely could never come to the throne till long after Herod's own death.

Sin corrupts sinners, and holds them in its grasp.

The magi (2:1). Originally the term *magoi* was applied to a class of scholars, wise men, and magicians who served as advisers to Persian rulers. It's not clear just what the term meant in the 1st century, although it is applied both to these authentic wise men and the charlatans described in Acts 8:9 and 13:6, 8.

The star (2:2). It is uncertain whether the star was a supernova, a comet, a conjunction of planets, or a totally supernatural apparition, as may be implied in 2:9. It is clear the magi and Matthew recognize it as the fulfillment of Num. 24:17. The large Jewish community in "the east" developed a major body of O.T. interpretation.

Joseph. Matthew 1 and 2 present Joseph as an admirable man. He was compassionate and concerned, even with the thought Mary had

Illustration (2:11). *Frankincense was an expensive incense, usually contained in a sealed alabaster jar, like the one shown above. The gifts have been seen as symbolic of the magi's recognition of Jesus' deity, although this is not necessarily implied. What the gifts did do was finance the flight to Egypt (v. 13). God still provides.*

betrayed her commitment to him. We also see him obedient, even when marriage to Mary might impune his character, for it would imply he was the father of her child.

He was also consistently responsive to God's guidance, following God's lead immediately whenever guidance was given. We know little about Joseph beyond what we see here. But clearly he was a godly man, whose character reflected God's own.

Herod's murder of the innocents (2:16-18). Jesus was probably between 6 and 20 months old at the time. Bethlehem was some 5 miles from Jerusalem. Its population at the time suggests at most some 10 or 12 children were killed in the brutal act so characteristic of the evil Herod.

"Rachel weeping" (2:18). How does this quote express the anguish experienced by the Jews at the time of the Exile, "fulfilled" in the slaughter of the innocents? Jeremiah's context is one of hope. The tears mark the climax of the suffering. Here too there is joy in the pain. The innocents die, but the Saviour lives.

Outline
Place
Finder

PREPARATION
PREACHING
PROOF
PRACTICE
PURPOSE

Chapter summary. Matthew skips over Jesus' childhood and picks up the story with John the Baptist. This prophet is sent to prepare the people for the imminent appearance of Christ. John's message is one of repentance, recommitment, and warning. God is about to act, and His people must be ready to respond (3:1-10). John called those who responded to his message to demonstrate their repentance by submitting to water baptism (vv. 11-12). The text tells us that Jesus made a special trip from Galilee to be baptized by John, although John saw no need for Christ to submit to a rite that implied a need for repentance (vv. 13-14). Jesus insisted, saying that it was right to identify Himself with John's message (v. 15). After the baptism, the Holy Spirit in the form of a dove descended on Jesus, and the Father's voice from heaven identified Jesus as "My Son."

Key verse. 3:11: Christ's baptism counts.

Personal application. Take a stand with those who do right.

Key concepts. Kingdom of heaven »p. 380, 620. Pharisees »p. 625. Repentance »p. 780. Holy Spirit »p. 73. Righteousness »p. 124. Son of God »p. 896. Baptism »p. 742.

INSIGHT

"John the Baptist" (3:1). John was the cousin of Jesus. His stern appearance and warnings were in the tradition of the O.T. prophets. His practice of baptizing those willing to repent was new.

Baptism. John's baptism was not linked with the ritual cleansing baths practiced by the Jews, but was an innovation. The Gk. word, *baptizo*, means to immerse, and is used in both literal and figurative senses in the N.T. John's water baptism was the means by which individuals publicly: (1) identified with John's message, (2) confessed a need for a personal change of heart, (3) committed themselves to live by O.T. standards of righteousness, and (4) expressed eagerness to welcome the Messiah whom John said was near. John's baptism is not the same in nature or intent as Christian baptism, which symbolizes union with Christ in His death and resurrection (cf. Rom. 6).

"Repent" (3:2). John's call for repentance assumes that despite the verbal respect shown the Law, God's people had departed from total covenant commitment and needed a radical change of both attitude and behavior.

"Is near" (1:3). God's kingdom is that realm in which He exercises His power and His will is obeyed. Jesus is about to be introduced, not only as Messiah/King but as one totally subject to God and one through whom God's miraculous power is to be displayed.

"Pharisees and Sadducees" (3:7). These religious leaders did not come in response to John's message but came to judge its acceptability. We are not to judge God's Word, but to respond to it.

"Produce fruit" (3:8-9). Physical descent from Abraham qualified a person for membership within the covenant community. It guaranteed opportunity, but not salvation. Only a heart response to God which results in a life in harmony with His will will do—then or now.

Baptize with the Holy Spirit and with fire (3:11). Christ will baptize (immerse) believers with the Holy Spirit and unbelievers with fire. Those who respond are to be immersed in the Spirit and empowered to live a godly life. Fire in both Testaments is associated with judgment when the unsaved are in view (cf. Isa. 9:19; Jer. 4:4; Amos 1:4, 7) and with purification when believers are in view (Isa. 6:6-7; 1 Peter 1:7).

"Fulfill all righteousness" (3:15). Jesus' baptism was no implicit admission of sin, but rather an act by which He identified Himself with John and his message.

When we see a person take a stand for what is right, let's stand with him or her.

"A voice from heaven" (3:17). God had been silent for over 400 years, since the close of the O.T. God's voice from heaven identifying Jesus as His Son is the public announcement that He is about to act and the Messianic Age is about to dawn.

Chapter summary. Matthew continues his account of Jesus' preparation for ministry. The Spirit leads Christ into the desert where He fasts 40 days. Even in His weakened condition He defeats Satan (4:1-11). In overcoming temptation Jesus shows us how to overcome also, by acting on principles found in God's Word. Only when Christ has demonstrated His personal commitment to God, a necessity for anyone who ministers, does He begin to preach. His initial preaching ministry is focused in Galilee, and His message at this point is the same as John's: "Repent, for the kingdom of heaven is near" (vv. 12-17). John's Gospel tells us that Christ had met several of His disciples earlier. Matthew simply tells us that Christ called them in Galilee, telling them, "Come, follow Me" (vv. 18-22). Matthew also introduces a major element in Jesus' ministry. As He preaches, He also heals "every disease and sickness" (vv. 23-24). Word of the miracle-working teacher spreads quickly and great crowds gather from every Jewish-occupied district (v. 25).

Outline
Place
Finder

PREPARATION
PREACHING
PROOF
PRACTICE
PURPOSE

Key verse. 4:4. Jesus met and overcame temptation as a man.

Personal application. We defeat temptation by understanding and acting on the Word of God.

Key concepts. Fasting »pp. 442, 655. Satan »p. 501. Temptation »pp. 27, 655, 871. Disciple »p. 657. Healing »p. 611.

INSIGHT

"If You are the Son of God" (4:3). The "if" here means "since." Satan acknowledges Jesus is God's Son.

"Man" (4:4). Jesus will meet temptation using only the resources available to human beings.

"Bread" (4:4). Throughout the O.T. and N.T. bread is viewed as the basic food which sustains physical life. This underlies all metaphorical uses of bread in the Bible, such as Christ's claim to be the "Bread of Life" (John 6:48).

Not bread alone (4:4). Satan's first attempt was intended to lead Him to disobey God out of a sense of physical need. Jesus' firm commitment reminds us that we are spiritual as well as physical beings and that we are not to permit the physical to override our commitment to do God's will.

If again (4:5-7). In the Gk. this "if" is one of uncertainty. Satan is saying, "If You are really God's Son and He loves You, how could He let You suffer like this? You'd better do something to quiet Your inner fears and prove God's love." Jesus again quoted the O.T., this time a passage which forbids testing God. The believer must live by faith, not sight.

How vulnerable we are to doubts and fears when things go wrong for us. How much we need to remember that God does love us and that we are to live by faith.

"The kingdoms of the world" (4:7-10). God intends Jesus to rule all the world's kingdoms. But first Christ was to go to the cross. Jesus' commitment to worship God and serve only Him reminds us that we are to consciously subject ourselves to the known will of God.

It is written. In each case Jesus recalled a principle found in God's Word and acted on it. We need to study and know Scripture. But most of all, we need to practice its principles.

John's imprisonment (4:12). This event meant John's ministry was complete, and it was time for Jesus, the one he spoke of, to begin in earnest. It's significant this beginning was in Galilee. At that time the population was mixed, with many Jews but also many Gentiles present. The great light dawning in this area (vv. 15-17) may foreshadow the fact that the salvation Jesus brings is for all.

"Follow Me" (4:19). What makes a disciple is his or her willingness to follow Jesus. Following Him produces people who share Christ's concern for drawing others to God.

News spread (4:23-25). This is still the best way to communicate the Gospel. Not through sermons. But through the reports of ordinary people who are excited about Jesus.

Chapter summary. Matthew summarizes the preaching of Jesus in a passage famous as the "Sermon on the Mount" (chaps. 5–7). Jesus begins with a series of statements known as the "Beatitudes" (5:1-12). These surprising statements of blessing underline the difference between human values and God's and call us to view life and success God's way. As salt and light, believers must savor and illuminate God's ways, which alone can preserve and guide humanity (vv. 13-16). Christ rejects the charge of critics that His teaching is intended to abolish the Law and the Prophets. Instead Christ has come to explain the real meaning of ("fulfill") the Law (v. 17). His explanation of Law reveals the defects in the Pharisees' claim to righteousness (vv. 18-20). In a series of examples Jesus shows that God demands righteous intent as well as lawful acts. Righteousness is a matter of the heart and not only behavior (vv. 21-42). In calling for "perfection" Jesus reminds us that true righteousness is actually found only in being like God (vv. 43-47).

Key verse. 5:20: Legal righteousness is not enough for God.

Personal application. If our heart is right, we will do right.

Key concepts. Blessing »p. 49. Light »p. 685. Law »pp. 145, 376. Adultery »p. 388. Divorce »p. 136. Father »p. 663.

INSIGHT

"Blessed are" (5:3). The text doesn't say those Jesus discusses will be blessed, but that they are. It is better to be poor in spirit, to mourn, and to be meek, than to adopt the attitudes of the world. The poor in spirit recognize their spiritual destitution and depend on God. Those who mourn are sensitive to their spiritual faults and seek God's help and comfort. The meek are malable, open, and responsive to God. Those who hunger and thirst for righteousness are the only ones who seek it.

The merciful both forgive and have compassion for others and are thus sensitive to God's forgiveness that frees them from guilt and comforts them. The pure are purified by their devotion to God and so are spiritually able to sense His presence. The qualities so far named equip us to bring peace to others, although they also make us vulnerable to persecution. Our reward is to be called "sons of God" now and to experience His present kingdom rule in our lives.

Fulfilling the Law (5:17). As a theological term current in the 1st century, every rabbi's ambition was to "fulfill" the Law, in the sense of explaining its true meaning.

"Until everything is accomplished" (5:18-20). Jesus' teaching does not challenge the authority of O.T. Law.

Righteousness (5:21-48). Each example contrasts what "was said" (in the Law) with Jesus'

explanation of what God intends human beings to understand. In saying "do not murder" God was speaking not only against the act, but against the hostility toward and contempt for others which leads to murder. In saying "do not commit adultery" He was teaching that we must not see others as objects to be used.

Law, thus, is not simply rules to live by, but God's statement that He judges the heart and not merely our acts. True righteousness requires the harmony of our heart with the character and motives of God.

"Divorce" (5:31-32). This example also calls us to examine motives in marriage and our level of commitments in relationships. It is not Jesus' statement of a new and higher law, any more than the other examples state new laws. If "no divorce" were a new law, then an angry word or lustful look must also be new laws and call, as do murder and adultery, for execution.

An eye for an eye (5:38-42). This legal principle was intended to keep victims from taking revenge. He could require equivalent payment for an injury, but could not use an injury to an eye, for example, to blind and cripple or to kill the person who caused it. Here Jesus explains that what God really wants is for us, as He Himself does, not to seek revenge but to treat others with grace. It is God's way to do good to those who injure Him. This is to be our way too.

Jesus on the Law

Jesus expresses His total allegiance to the Old Testament Law in Matthew 5:17-18. At the same time He points out the inadequacy of the views held by the teachers of His day. The many illustrations Jesus then develops make His point. Law identifies behaviors which are wrong. But it also reveals attitudes, values, and motives which must be transformed if human beings are to be truly in harmony with God (5:19-48). Only transformation of the inner man, via a redeemed and sensitive heart, can make a human being truly righteous in God's sight.

The same point is made in other passages which record Christ's sayings about the Law. Matthew 7:12 and 22:36-40 give Jesus' summation of the Law. When asked by an "expert in the law" about the greatest commandment, Jesus said, "Love the Lord your God with all your heart and with all your soul and with all your mind. This is the first and greatest commandment. And the second is like it: Love your neighbor as yourself. All the Law and the Prophets hang on these two commandments." Here too Jesus shifts attention from compliance with the detailed instructions contained in the Old Testament to heart attitude.

John 1:17, Matthew 11:13, and Luke 16:16-17 contain Jesus' teachings that a day is coming in which Mosaic Law will be superseded. Jesus said, "The Law and the Prophets were proclaimed until John. Since that time the good news of the kingdom of God is being preached." The Old Testament economy was not rejected, but all that it implied is fulfilled with and in Jesus. He is the Prophet which the first Testament said would come and whose revelations supersede the Mosaic code. That same Old Testament envisions a time when the Law is unnecessary, because God has written it not on stone tablets but in the hearts of believers (cf. Jer. 31).

Another passage that bears on the Law is Matthew 19:3-9. Here the Pharisees ask for an interpretation of the Law on divorce, found in Deuteronomy 24. Jesus responds by pointing to God's intention as revealed in the Creation. When pressed, Jesus says that God permitted divorce because human hearts were hard. That is, God knew that sin would so warp some marriages that divorce was necessary to dissolve a relationship which otherwise would be destructive. The point here is that the ruling in Deuteronomy 24 proves that Law is a lowered standard! It's not a way for man to climb closer to God. It's proof that God in grace required less of Israel than strict righteousness would demand!

Rightly understood, Law reveals the failure of human beings to be truly godly and leads them to cry out to God for grace. No wonder the "poor in spirit" are blessed. Only they realize their spiritual bankruptcy. Those who rely on a righteousness measured by the do's and don'ts of law never realize that they must appeal to God, to be forgiven and transformed within.

Outline
Place
Finder

PREPARATION
PREACHING
PROOF
PRACTICE
PURPOSE

Chapter summary. Relationship with God is a personal, not a public kind of thing. Thus our acts of righteousness (6:1), our gifts of loving concern (vv. 2-4), and our prayers of devotion (vv. 5-8) are to be done "in secret" to please Him rather than to win a reputation for piety with our fellowmen. The disciple's prayers are also personal, approaching God as "our Father" and expressing our delight in His will and our dependence on Him (vv. 9-13). The "in secret" relationship we have with God will transform our attitude toward others (vv. 14-15). We will put aside all hypocrisy, and our expressions of commitment will be directed to God rather than to others (vv. 16-18). An "in secret" relationship with God will free us to value heavenly rather than earthly treasures, thus transforming our values (vv. 17-24). Knowing God in the intimate, private, and personal relationship a child has with a father will free us from anxiety, for we will realize that our Father will meet our needs as we concentrate on doing those things that please Him (vv. 25-34).

Key verse. 6:6: Faith's inner life is the key.

Personal application. Strive to please God, not to look good to others.

Key concepts. Father »pp. 140, 663. Hypocrite »p. 625. Prayer »p. 894. Satan »p. 501. Fasting »p. 442. Temptation »pp. 27, 655. Forgiveness »pp. 634, 863. Anxiety »p. 636. Kingdom »p. 606.

INSIGHT

Prayer (6:9-13). The foundation of prayer is personal relationship with God as our Father. This model prayer teaches us how to relate to Him. Recognition of Him as "in heaven" and "hallowed" (set apart and holy) puts us in the proper frame of mind as we come to Him. It reminds us that we are to be holy because of who He is. "Your kingdom come" is more than an eschatological hope. It is an expression of our willingness to submit to His will, now, that He might rule in our lives. The request for "daily bread" expresses both dependence on Him and confidence in Him. We trust God so much that we ask only for "daily" bread—not great wealth. "Forgive us" expresses our awareness that we fall short in all things and must rely on a constant flow of God's grace—and the last phrase expresses willingness to relate to others as God relates to us. The final request not to be led into testing is another recognition of intrinsic helplessness. But this is balanced by the joyful recognition that our Father is able to deliver us when testing does come, for He is greater than the evil one (Satan).

This Lord's Prayer is not so much a formula to be repeated as it is a revelation of the attitude with which we approach God as Father: an attitude of awe, submission, dependence, and com-

plete confidence in His "Father-love."

If you do not forgive (6:14-15). This is not a threat, but a warning. Forgiveness is like a coin: It is a single unit with two sides. The attitude which enables us to accept forgiveness is the same attitude which compels us to extend it. If we are unable to forgive others, our hardness will prevent us from accepting God's forgiveness.

"Fasting" (6:16-18). The very pious Jew in Jesus' time refrained from eating or drinking during daylight hours two days a week, even though this is nowhere commanded in the O.T. Jesus does not condemn the practice, but does condemn those who paraded their supposed piety by putting ashes on their face and looking mournful.

Bad eyes (6:22-23). The eye enables us to see our way. A bad eye tries to focus on God and worldly possessions and thus confuses the person so he cannot see his way through life. We must have a single eye, giving God our sole attention and letting His will guide us through life.

Run after God (6:31-32). Don't let anxiety about earthly things lead you to "run after" them. We can be sure that if we run after God our Heavenly Father will meet our material needs.

Chapter summary. Jesus has established that relationship with God is an "in secret" kind of thing (chap. 6). The theme continues as Christ reminds us to judge ourselves, not others (7:1-6). In a series of brief sayings Christ encourages us to depend actively on God. We are not to wait passively, as if we might expect only the crumbs God casually drops for us, but are to confidently ask, seek, and knock (vv. 7-12). How important that we focus on living for God—in His way (vv. 13-14). While we are not to judge others, we are to distinguish between the true and false prophet. The way we do this is by observing the fruit of their lives, those words and actions which spring from and reveal their innermost motivations (vv. 15-20). It is not verbal commitment to the Lord that counts. Only doing His will is an adequate expression of relationship with Him (vv. 21-23).

Jesus' lengthy Sermon on the Mount concludes with a powerful illustration. We build on a solid foundation by putting Jesus' words into practice. Only then will we be able to withstand the storms of life (vv. 24-28).

Outline
Place
Finder

PREPARATION
PREACHING
PROOF
PRACTICE
PURPOSE

Key verse. 7:24: Jesus' teachings are rock solid.

Personal application. Don't just listen to what Jesus teaches. Put it into practice.

Key concepts. Judging »p. 874. Eye »p. 608. Hypocrite »p. 625. Prayer »p. 894. Fruit »p. 614. Lord »p. 750.

INSIGHT

Measure for measure (7:1-2). Jesus is speaking words of hope, not warning. His point is that people tend to treat us as we treat them. If we are judgmental, they will respond the same way. Why is this a word of hope? Because if we break the pattern and relate to others in nonjudgmental ways, we can expect to be treated the same.

Hypocritical? (7:3-5) It is hypocritical to judge others, for to be a judge one must not be guilty himself. We can only judge others on appearances: on what we see.

Pearls to pigs (7:6). Pigs in Palestine were wild and vicious, as well as "unclean." Most see the metaphor as a reminder that some will reject the Gospel and the disciple's way of life with contempt and scorn (cf. Prov. 9:8). The principle of measure for measure (above) is generally—but not universally—true.

Prayer power (7:7-11). The imperatives ask, seek, and knock remind us that we are to pray actively and persistently. How much better to pray for others and not to judge them. How much better to pray God will remove our own faults and flaws than to hide them. How much better to pray God will change the hearts of the "dogs" and "pigs" who are hardened to the Gospel. All these things should remind us of our dependence on God and of His willingness to shower us with good gifts.

"In heaven" (7:11). The metaphorical use of "heaven" as the realm of God doesn't imply, as some have said, a "primitive" view of the universe. Instead it shows a deep awareness that God exists in a realm which no human being can penetrate, any more than a human being can walk among and directly experience the starry heavens. Isaiah 55:9 sums up, "As the heavens are higher than the earth, so are My ways higher than your ways and My thoughts than your thoughts."

Four warnings (7:13-27). Jesus concludes His sermon with four warnings, each featured by paired contrasts: two ways (vv. 13-14), two trees (vv. 15-20), two claims (vv. 21-23), and two builders (vv. 24-27). Let's be sure we choose between each wisely.

"As one who had authority" (7:28-29). The rabbis and teachers of the Law of Jesus' day cited the opinion of earlier teachers as authority for their views. Jesus spoke as the Son of God and stunned His listeners with His assumption that His word was enough. It was. And it still is.

Outline
Place
Finder

PREPARATION
PREACHING
PROOF
PRACTICE
PURPOSE

Chapter summary. Jesus taught with authority. Matthew now launches a report of a series of miracles which authenticates His right to speak for God. Jesus is able to heal with a touch (8:1-4) or with a word that cannot be limited by distance (vv. 5-13). He heals those who trust Him and those who are in the grip of demons (vv. 14-17). Christ did not use His powers to win an easy life for Himself or for His disciples (vv. 18-22). He committed Himself to serve, even though His powers enabled Him to exercise control over nature's most awesome forces (vv. 23-27), and even though the supernatural world too was forced to submit to His will (vv. 28-34). The incidents Matthew records show that Jesus did speak with divine authority—and that He lived by His teachings of servanthood and love.

Key verse. 8:27: The evidence leaves no question.

Personal application. Who better might we trust than a person whose power and love know no limits?

Key concepts. Miracle »pp. 61, 979. Leprosy »p. 83. Healing »p. 611. Centurion »p. 658. Demons »p. 659. Prophecy »p. 434. Faith »p. 35.

INSIGHT

Willing and able (8:1-4). The leper questioned Jesus' willingness, because as one who was an outcast and ritually "unclean," he felt worthless. Never feel you have no value in the eyes of the Lord. Jesus is both willing and able to heal.

"Under authority" (8:9). "Authority" is *exousia*, and means "freedom of action." The greater authority a person has, the less others can limit his freedom of action. The centurion's remark that he was a "man under authority" conveyed the fact that he derived his authority to command his soldiers from a source, Caesar, whose freedom to command those in the empire was unlimited. His affirmation was a statement of faith: his belief that Jesus acted under and with the full authority of God, and thus that distance from his suffering servant could not limit His power to heal. It was this total confidence in Jesus that Christ commends (v. 10)—in centurions, and in you and me.

Peter's mother-in-law (8:14). The centurion represents healing in response to faith. Peter's mother-in-law represents service as a response to healing. When Christ touches our lives, we too are to "get up and begin to wait on (serve)" Jesus.

"To fulfill" (8:17). Prophecy knows both multiple and partial fulfillments. Multiple fulfillment means that a particular event does not exhaust the meaning of the prophecy, while partial fulfillment means that something is implied in the prophecy, but does not sum up its entire meaning.

The Isa. passage Matthew quotes is ultimately and completely fulfilled in our purification from sin and in a resurrection that frees us from every human frailty. Christ's healings when on earth exemplify both multiple and partial fulfillment of prophecy. More, they demonstrate His ability to provide all that Isa. 53 promises will be ours through the atonement.

Following Jesus (8:18-20). Jesus didn't use His power to make it easier for Himself, but to meet the deepest needs of others. Why should we expect following Jesus to provide a life of ease, rather than a life of self-sacrifice and service?

"Lord" (8:21). Lord was also used in N.T. times in polite address, as we might use sir.

Burying father (8:21-22). Christ's reply was not heartless, for the man's father was still living. The phrase means "let me wait till my father dies, and I fulfill my obligation to him."

Christ's answer reminds us that our first obligation is to the Lord. Don't volunteer for discipleship unless you intend to put God first.

Fear (8:23-27). If Christ is with us, fear is unnecessary. Our security isn't rooted in our circumstances, but on our relationship with God.

Leave the region (8:28-34). It's not surprising the demons tormented the two men, for they're hostile to both man and God. What is surprising is the reaction of the residents. Human beings are to value the health and well-being of others more than material possessions. But they could not sense the wonder of Jesus' works, nor their intent.

Chapter summary. The evidence that Jesus speaks and acts with divine authority mounts. Christ demonstrates His right to forgive sins by healing a paralytic (9:1-8). He then shows the transforming power of forgiveness by calling a tax collector, despised for the practice of extorting more money than was due, as a disciple (vv. 9-13). Even John's disciples miss the point of Jesus and wonder why Christ's disciples do not fast, an act which suggests mourning (v. 14). But Christ's presence calls for celebration, not mourning. A new age is dawning, in which old practices and ways of looking at faith will not fit (vv. 15-17). Christ then performs unique miracles, healing a chronic disease and raising a dead girl to life, which futher illustrate His power to bring newness and vitality to all (vv. 18-26). The chapter closes as Jesus opens blind eyes and frees stopped mouths, but is unable to reach the religious leaders who choose to remain blind to the meaning of His miracles. Instead they ascribe His wonders to Satan (vv. 27-34). How poignant is Jesus' call for workers to spread His good news of healing and new life (vv. 35-38).

Outline
Place
Finder

PREPARATION
PREACHING
PROOF
PRACTICE
PURPOSE

Key verse. 9:6: Forgiveness does transform.

Personal application. Nothing in your past can hold you back when you open your life to Christ's transforming power.

Key concepts. Forgiveness »pp. 357, 634. Sins »pp. 34, 442. Pharisees »pp. 625, 658. Mercy »p. 858.

INSIGHT

"Which is easier"? (9:5) It is easier to say "your sins are forgiven," because this is an inner, unseen work. In saying "get up and walk" Jesus gave visible evidence that He spoke with divine authority and so could forgive sins too.

Healing and faith (9:6-8). The stories of healings in this section have a fascinating aspect. Some are definitely linked with the faith the disabled person had in Jesus (8:1-2, 5-10; 9:20-22, 27-29). In others faith plays no direct role (8:14-15, 28-33; 9:1-7, 32-33). Especially significant is 8:16: "He healed all the sick."

Christ does respond to our faith. But He also performs His wonders freely and spontaneously. God can heal despite our doubts, and even strong faith does not guarantee healing.

Tax collectors (9:9). Wealthy men bid for the right to collect taxes. They then recovered their investment by extorting more than was due. In N.T. times these men were considered both collaboraters with the foreign enemy and dishonest oppressors of the poor. The fact that Matthew's house was large enough for "many" to eat there suggests he was a major rather than minor tax collector. His response demonstrated the power of forgiveness.

"Desire" (9:13). When God says He desires mercy, He means that He has made a choice of mercy. Some will criticize you if you associate with sinners. But if we seek the lost out of compassion we, like Jesus, will need to spend time with them.

New and old (9:16-17). These two illustrations from ordinary life suggest the impossibility of fitting the message Jesus brought into 1st-century Judaism. Jesus called for a new perspective on sin, forgiveness, and transformation.

The noisy crowd (9:23). Jewish funeral custom called for mournful music and loud wailing, as well as for burial the day of death.

"Son of David" (1:27). The phrase is a title more than a name. The blind men recognized Jesus as David's descendant, that is, the Messiah. Because they knew who He was, they were able to believe when challenged by Christ to trust Him. And their trust led to complete healing.

The Pharisees' reaction (9:34). The evidence of Christ's works was overwhelming. Only those who were willfully and determinedly blind to the meaning of Jesus' works could fail to realize who He was. The flaw is not in the evidence, but in the hearts of men who will not accept it.

Outline
Place
Finder

PREPARATION
PREACHING
PROOF
PRACTICE
PURPOSE

Chapter summary. Jesus sends His twelve disciples out to teach and preach. He equips them for this ministry with power over demons and diseases (10:1-5). Their powers, however, were not to be used for selfish purposes. Like Christ, they were to travel in poverty, dependent on the willingness of those to whom they ministered to meet their basic needs for food and lodging (vv. 6-15). Jesus warns them to expect hostility as well as welcome—something believers throughout the ages have known. Their goal, as ours, is not to be successful or popular, but to live humbly as Jesus did, taking His trust in the Father as our example, and refusing to fear man (vv. 16-31). The message the disciples carry is the most critical in the world. It's not a message intended to bring earthly peace, for it will stir up opposition. Yet its acceptance or rejection determines each person's eternal destiny (vv. 32-42).

Key verse. 10:24: We are to live as Jesus lived.

Personal application. Seek servanthood, not success.

Key concepts. Disciple »p. 657. Miracle »p. 57. Peace »pp. 427, 815. Acknowledge »p. 120. The believer's cross »p. 618.

INSIGHT

Illustration: "Take no bag" (10:10). *The "bag," called a "purse" in older versions, held food for a journey. Coins were wrapped in the folds of the belt travelers wore around their waist.*

"The Twelve" (10:2-4). Whenever the Twelve are listed (Mark 3:16-19; Luke 6:13-16; Acts 1:13), or even when a few are mentioned, Peter heads the list. There is no doubt Peter was the premier apostle, marked both by weakness and by great strength of character (»p. 711).

Only to Israel? (10:6) Why did Jesus tell the Twelve to go only to Jews? The answer is in 10:7. At that time they were to preach that the kingdom God promised to David was "at hand." Later, when Jesus, the King, had been rejected by Israel the message changed to the word of the Cross, and this Gospel is for everyone!

Hospitality (10:11). In biblical times travelers depended on the hospitality of others for a place to stay. Thus hospitality was greatly valued in that society, and many were glad to welcome travelers. If the disciples were not welcomed, it would be because the householder rejected the One they represented.

There's a lesson for us here. Whatever special gifts or abilities we may have, we need to remain continually dependent on the Lord. And we must forgo using our gifts to benefit ourselves rather than to serve others.

Shrewd and innocent (10:16). The two quali-

ties are both vital for disciples, but must be in balance. Shrewdness without innocence is cunning, and innocence without shrewdness is ignorance. When the two are in balance Jesus' followers demonstrate both foresight and courageous trust in God.

Be prepared (10:20). What prepares a believer to meet a crisis successfully is not speech-writing but commitment. In the 1st century persons called to confront a governing council invariably hired a professional orator to speak for them. The Christian is to rely on the Holy Spirit and face persecutors with confidence.

Stand firm (10:22). The Gk. verb *hypomeno* means to endure patiently rather than to fight back. "To the end" does not specify a particular time, but rather means "endure without breaking down." Some believers have endured, even to the point of losing their lives. The martyrs' examples remind us that we need not give in to pressure, but can find strength in the Lord to endure.

"Hairs of your head" (10:30). God knows everything about us. He counts, because we are important in His eyes!

Disowning God (10:33). When "disown" stands in contrast with "acknowledge," it means to reject the claims of Jesus presented in the Gospel.

"A man against his father" (10:34). Jesus' words emphasize the necessity of full commitment to the Lord, even if this means going against one's family's wishes.

Chapter summary. Now the text introduces the theme of disbelief, despite Jesus' miraculous proofs. John the Baptist has been imprisoned by Herod. Even he is puzzled that Jesus has not acted to establish the kingdom predicted in the Old Testament, and so he sends disciples to ask if Christ really is the Messiah (11:1-3). Jesus points to His miracles of healing (vv. 4-6) and then goes on to praise John as greatest of the prophets, great enough to be the "Elijah" the Old Testament predicts will come before the Messiah (vv. 7-15). Christ then accuses the people of the day. They like neither the stern John nor the merciful Jesus (vv. 16-19). Those who fail to respond to God's messengers and Jesus' miraculous proofs face a judgment more stern than Sodom's. But those who do respond to Christ as little children will find rest in Him (vv. 20-30).

Outline
Place
Finder

PREPARATION
PREACHING
PROOF
PRACTICE
PURPOSE

Key verse. 11:27: Faith is a gift.

Personal application. Rest is found in being yoked to Jesus.

Key concepts. Messiah »p. 432. Prophet »p. 131. Elijah »p. 234. Miracle »p. 679. Kingdom »pp. 443, 605. Sodom »p. 37.

INSIGHT

Evidence (11:4-6). John, in prison, may well have been discouraged and doubted. Even persons with great faith do. Jesus' response is an allusion to Isa. 35:5-6, 61:1, and possibly also to 26:19 and 29:18-19. All four Isa. passages mention judgment as well as beneficial miracles. Jesus thus subtly affirmed that He is the Christ of history's end as well as of the historical moment. John, because he was a man of faith, would understand and believe.

"Greater than John"? (11:11) How can the "least" of contemporary believers be greater than John, greatest of the O.T. prophets? There are a number of theories, ranging from the N.T. believer's full possession of the Spirit, to our greater knowledge of Christ. Perhaps the best interpretation focuses on John's role as the O.T. prophet who most perfectly pointed to Christ. We are "greater" because we can witness to Him more perfectly, now that Christ's revelation of Himself is complete.

"Forcefully advancing" (11:12-15). Jesus' point is that in the incarnation God has broken into history to vigorously advance His kingdom, and that action has stimulated the resistance of "forceful" (*biastes*, "violent") men. God's actions are welcomed by believers and resisted by unbelievers.

"Elijah" (11:14). John has the same kind of preparatory ministry that will be performed by another "Elijah" to appear before Christ's coming in power. If Israel had accepted Christ as Messiah in the 1st century, John's ministry was enough like Elijah's that he could have been considered the fulfillment of the prophecy.

"Like children" (11:17). Jesus describes two games commonly played by children in the streets: wedding and funeral. He speaks ironically. No matter how God invites His people to respond, they pout and mutter, "I don't wanna' play." They didn't like John — he was too strict — and they didn't like Jesus — He's too friendly with sinners. How foolish to ignore a message from God — and then blame the messenger!

Ignoring the evidence (11:20-24). What a statement! If Christ had appeared in Sodom and performed His miracles and given His teaching, those openly wicked people would have responded! Isn't it interesting that religious and good people are often harder to reach than the wicked?

"Little children" (11:25-26). The "wise and learned" insist on standing in judgment on all they hear. But little children simply respond to an adult's word. We need to approach Scripture like little ones, ready to hear and obey.

"Rest" (11:28). The Gk. word here (*anapouo*) means to calm, comfort, and refresh. It reflects the O.T. concept of rest as release from the pressures and tensions of life and of the peace that follows.

"Yoke" (11:29). A yoke was a wooden frame that fit over the shoulders of draft animals, harnessing them to each other and to the plow they pulled together. Being yoked to Christ means to rely on Him, to give Him our burdens, and to accept the necessity of walking with Him, side by side.

Outline
Place
Finder

PREPARATION
PREACHING
PROOF
PRACTICE
PURPOSE

Chapter summary. Despite the miracles which supported Jesus' claims, opposition of the religious elite stiffens. They accuse His disciples of "doing what is unlawful on the Sabbath" (12:1-8), and when Jesus heals on the Sabbath they attack Christ Himself. Christ's actions expose the indifference of the Pharisees to human need—and they respond by plotting to kill Him! (vv. 9-14)

Rather than engage in angry debate Jesus withdraws to continue His healing ministry (vv. 15-21). But when Jesus heals a demon possessed man, and the crowd speculates that He might be the promised Messiah (vv. 22-23), the desperate Pharisees accuse Him of getting His powers from Satan. Christ ridicules the notion, but warns them that they have committed an "unforgivable sin" (vv. 24-32). Their words have revealed the evil in their hearts (vv. 33-37). When the Pharisees demand a miraculous sign, Jesus promises only the "sign of the Prophet Jonah," speaking of His coming resurrection (vv. 38-45). Later, Jesus claims that all those who do the will of God are His brothers and sisters (vv. 46-49).

Key verse. 12:34: Words and acts reveal heart attitude.

Personal application. God values mercy and compassion.

Key concepts. Sabbath »pp. 71, 664. Messiah »p. 432. Pharisee »p. 625.

INSIGHT

Breaking the law? (12:2-9) Neither Jesus nor the disciples broke biblical Sabbath law. What they did violate was rabbinical interpretations of the O.T. command that no "work" be done on the Sabbath. To the rabbis this was "reaping," one of 39 classes of "work" they forbade on the Sabbath.

Lawful (12:3-8). Jesus' point is that the rigid interpretation is not in accord with Scripture. He then adds that the Pharisees miss a key interpretive principle: the clear statement that God desires mercy.

The point is driven home as Jesus heals on the Sabbath, establishing the basic principle that there is no conflict between law and doing good (vv. 9-13).

"Jesus withdrew" (12:15-21). Quarreling is unproductive. Let's avoid it and get on with the ministry of caring for others.

Do miracles produce faith? (12:24) The reaction of the Pharisees reminds us that miracles do not produce faith. Those who do not believe will struggle to find some other explanation for the supernatural. On the other hand, miracles can strengthen the faith of those who already believe.

"Blasphemy against the Spirit" (12:30-32). The specific act which generated this response was ascribing miracles that Jesus performed in the power of the Spirit to Satan. This specific "unforgivable sin" could only be committed when Jesus was on earth.

Anyone who worries if they have committed the unforgivable sin could not have, for their very concern shows that they are not hardened against the Lord.

"The Son of Man" (12:32). Jesus frequently uses this phrase as a personal pronoun, meaning me or I. When used in this way it emphasizes Christ's complete humanity as one of us.

Fruitfulness (12:33-37). In Scripture this image is consistently used of acts which flow from and reveal character. See John 15 and Gal. 5:22-23.

Careless words (12:34). These are words spoken when a person is not trying to look pious: spontaneous expressions which reveal what is in a person's heart.

The greater the revelation, the greater the judgment (12:39-42). Even pagans responded to lesser revelations of God through Jonah and Solomon. Now God's chosen people refuse to respond to His Son.

The unoccupied house (12:43-45). Jesus has driven out demons. But that miraculous work is meaningless without subsequent commitment to Christ. The person without faith in the Messiah is defenseless against evil powers. How dangerous to have experienced the touch of God, yet hesitate to commit to Him.

Chapter summary. As resistance hardens, Jesus begins to speak in parables. The parables summarize contrasts between the form of God's kingdom the Jews expect and the form of the kingdom Jesus is about to institute.

Outline
Place
Finder

PREPARATION
PREACHING
PROOF
PRACTICE
PURPOSE

The Parable	Kingdom Expectations	Unexpected Form
The sower 13:3-9, 18-23	Messiah rules all *nations.*	*Individuals* respond to God's invitation.
Wheat/tares 13:24-30, 37-43	Citizens *rule* the world with Christ.	Citizens live *among* people of the world.
Mustard seed 13:31-32	Kingdom begins in majestic *glory.*	Kingdom begins in *insignificance.*
Leaven 13:33	The kingdom *includes* only the righteous.	Citizens *become* increasingly righteous.
Hidden treasure 13:44	The kingdom is *public,* for all.	The kingdom is *hidden* and for individual "purchase."
Priceless pearl 13:45-46	Kingdom *brings valued things.*	The kingdom requires *abandoning* earthly values.
Dragnet 13:47-50	Kingdom *begins* with separation of unrighteous.	Kingdom *ends* with separation of the unrighteous.

Key verse. 13:11: Faith enables understanding.

Personal application. Man builds great buildings. God builds godly men and women.

INSIGHT

Parables. The Gk. word means "to set alongside." Most parables in Scripture are incidents, objects, or persons: concrete situations that illuminate some abstract concept. In most cases parables are intended to make something more clear, as do the stories of the Good Samaritan and Prodigal Son. Parables are also found in the O.T., as Isaiah's illustration of a vineyard to explain the judgment about to befall Judah. Here, however, seven parables set alongside the kingdom over which Jesus rules in this present age concealed rather than illustrated Jesus' meaning. They were meant to be understood only after the present kingdom form, in which Christ rules in the hearts of believers, was fully established.

Mystery (13:11). In the N.T. mystery (*mysterion*) is a technical theological term applied to a new revelation of some aspect of Christian life or experience which was not (fully) revealed in the O.T.

"Hear" (13:15). The O.T. concept of "hear" is clearly defined in this verse. To "hear" is not simply to listen, but extends to understanding and acting on what has been said.

What tragic irony. Christ who came to reveal the Father has only caused Israel to cover her eyes and press her hands against her ears. Since they will not hear, they will surely lose what little capacity for spiritual sight and hearing they had possessed.

Jesus in Nazareth (13:53-58). The final incident reported in this chapter illustrates its thrust. Israel rejects Christ because He does not act to institute the glorious kingdom the people so passionately desire. In Nazareth the people are offended because Jesus, despite His miraculous powers, has lived among them as an ordinary man.

How foolish to demand that God act according to our expectations, rather than to freely express His own sovereign will.

Outline
Place
Finder

PREPARATION
PREACHING
PROOF
PRACTICE
PURPOSE

Chapter summary. Everyone in the little Jewish homeland seems to have a theory about Jesus' miraculous powers. Herod's notion is that Christ must be John the Baptist, whom he has executed, risen from the dead (14:1-12). Jesus simply continues to minister. He heals and even feeds a hungry crowd that follows Him into a wilderness area (vv. 13-21). Matthew then reports an incident that reveals the budding faith of Jesus' disciples. Christ walks on storm-tossed waters to join His disciples in their boat. This first stuns them, but then stimulates both worship and faith (vv. 22-36). Unbelievers like Herod misinterpret miracles. The disciples, who believe, understand the evidence and realize who Jesus is.

Key verse. 14:33: Those with Him understand.

Personal application. Don't expect others to recognize the miracles you see God perform for you.

Key concepts. Disciple »p. 657. Miracle »p. 679. Bread »pp. 605, 683.

INSIGHT

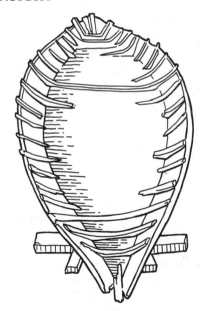

Illustration. *In 1989 the level of the Sea of Galilee fell and remains of a boat dating from Jesus' time was discovered buried in the mud. The broad beamed, 27-foot boat shows us the kind of craft Jesus' disciples were in when the incident reported in this chapter happened.*

Some motive! (14:9) Herod held John in some awe, convinced he was a prophet. But he was more worried that his guests would criticize him for breaking a foolish promise

than concerned with doing what was right. Acting on fear of what others might think rather than on personal conviction is always foolish. And always wrong.

Only a little (14:13-20). The disciples can be commended for their concern for the crowds that followed Jesus (v. 15). Caring is a necessary first step in ministry. But it's necessary to take a second step also. We need to be willing to act, even though we're terribly aware of how little we have to offer. Christ can multiply our "loaves and fishes" as He did those of the disciples so long ago. If we care, and reach out to help, Jesus will provide.

Peter's example (14:22-31). Peter has been criticized for looking away from Jesus. Actually, we need to applaud his readiness to step out on the sea. After all, the other disciples stayed in the boat! It's true that if we step out in faith we risk failure. But only by stepping out will we personally experience Christ's power.

Little faith (14:31). Peter had enough faith to get out of the boat. But in the waters his attention was distracted. He looked at conditions rather than at Christ. Even a little faith, when focused on Jesus, quiets our doubts.

"Why did you doubt?" (14:31) The question is one we need to ask ourselves when we falter. If we do, we'll realize how foolish our fears are in view of who Christ is.

They worshiped Him (14:33). This is the culmination. The miracle the disciples witness is correctly explained. Jesus is the Son of God. Awed and thankful, the disciples confess and worship Jesus as Lord.

Chapter summary. Jesus' miracles stimulate worship from His disciples (14:33). But they generate only hostile antagonism from His people's religious leaders, who again challenge Christ on the basis of traditional interpretations of Old Testament Law (15:1-2).

Jesus in turn challenges tradition, showing that the rabbis' approach to Scripture has actually distorted and nullified God's Word (vv. 3-9). "Cleanness" is no matter of ritual observance, but a matter of one's heart (vv. 10-20). Again Matthew uses contrast. He tells the story of a pagan woman whose faith is rewarded and thus reveals the futility of the Pharisees' legalistic approach to religion (vv. 21-28). The chapter ends with another story of contrast. While the Pharisees argue about the Law's minutia, Jesus expresses God's concern for human need by feeding thousands (vv. 29-39).

Outline
Place
Finder

PREPARATION
PREACHING
PROOF
PRACTICE
PURPOSE

Key verse. 15:18: Spiritual purity is inside out.

Personal application. Guard your heart, and your life will be pure.

Key concepts. Clean »pp. 82, 505. Parable »pp. 166, 615. Evil »p. 662. Faith »pp. 35, 872. Bread »p. 683.

INSIGHT

"Tradition" (15:1-2). In the centuries before Christ, Jewish sages (rabbis, teachers of the Law) had concentrated on applying O.T. Law to every aspect of Jewish life. Their goal was to "build a hedge" around the Law, explaining each command's implications so thoroughly that no one would break it being unaware. This intent, motivated by deep respect for the Scriptures, seems commendable. But in fact it represented a dangerous approach to Scripture and created a legalistic attitude which in fact distorted the Law's intent.

Jesus draws attention to two flaws in the approach, which had been enthusiastically endorsed by the Pharisee party. First, tradition had taken on the authority of Scripture itself, so that in fact the "commandments of men" were often substituted for—and even contradicted—God's commands. Second, in focusing on what man must do to keep the Law rather than on what God graciously does for man, the hearts of the legalists became cold. Religion became a matter of externals rather than of personal relationship. Jesus' focus on people and on servanthood threatened the structure that tradition erected and so aroused the active hostility of the religious elite.

Honoring parents (15:3-7). Possessions might be "devoted to God" but used by the owner as long as he or she lived. The "gift" was thus a legal fiction, that gave a person an excuse not to use his possessions to help a parent or other relative in need. In effect this interpretation of the O.T.'s teaching on vows allowed a person to "legally" subvert God's intent when he called for His people to honor (respect, support, care for) parents.

"Unclean" (15:10). The O.T. calls for believers to be ritually clean in order to approach God. Later the prophets applied the imagery to one's moral as well as ritual condition. Here Jesus focuses on the moral, but shifts emphasis. It is not immoral acts that make a person unclean. It is an unclean heart that expresses itself in wicked and immoral acts. We don't need to clean up our lives. We need to let God cleanse our heart. Then our lives will be clean.

Only to Israel? (15:21-28) In the O.T. vision of the prophets the kingdom Messiah was to set up was Israel's kingdom. Jesus, the King, was "sent only to the lost sheep of Israel" in that Israel must be given the first opportunity to respond to Him.

This persistent Canaanite woman, a Gentile, appealed to Jesus for help and acknowledged Him as Lord. Her healing illustrated the great truth that Israel had missed. Relationship with God is a matter of faith. No natural birth into a chosen nation can provide what can come only through a supernatural rebirth through faith.

Jesus has compassion (15:29-39). Let's not approach God bragging about our spiritual accomplishments and demanding His favor. Let's come as needy sinners, dependent on His grace. Jesus has compassion, and we do stand in need.

Outline
Place
Finder

PREPARATION
PREACHING
PROOF
PRACTICE
PURPOSE

Chapter summary. The Pharisees again demand, and are refused, a miraculous sign (16:1-4). Christ warns His disciples against the Pharisees' "yeast," that legalistic attitude which underlies and finds expression in their teaching (vv. 5-12). Jesus sends His disciples to circulate among the crowds and find out who they say He is. The Twelve report that the crowds view Jesus as a great prophet only (vv. 13-14). In contrast Peter confesses Jesus as the promised Messiah ("Christ") and as "Son of the living God" (vv. 15-16). On this reality Christ's church will be built and triumph (vv. 17-20).

This chapter describes the turning point in Christ's ministry. Before He spoke of the kingdom. Now His message is one of the Cross (vv. 21-23). Before He spoke to the crowds, now His ministry is primarily to the disciples (vv. 24-28). From now on Christ's path will lead Him straight to Calvary.

Key verse. 16:21: The turning point.

Personal application. Following Christ may mean the death of our old self. But it also means life to our new.

Key concepts. Miracle »p. 679. Prophet »p. 131. Resurrection »p. 737.

INSIGHT

Interpreting the signs (16:1-4). The two groups mentioned here represent the Sanhedrin, the ruling religious council. They have shown they cannot interpret spiritual signs, for Jesus has performed many authenticating miracles. Signs will not convince a person who is determined not to believe.

Who is Jesus? (16:13-14.) It is still an insult to call Jesus just a good man, or even a great man. Anything less than acknowledging Jesus as God the Son defames and denies Him.

"The Christ" (16:16). "Christ" is the Gk. translation of "Messiah," meaning the Anointed One. Peter was saying that Jesus is the deliverer promised by the O.T. prophets.

"This rock" (16:18). Three different interpretations have arisen in church history of Jesus' statement, "You are Peter, and upon this rock I will build My church." (1) Some take Peter as the rock and use the text to justify the belief that Peter was the "first pope." But though "Peter" in Gk. means "little stone," rock (*petra*) indicates a massive rock formation. (2) Some take Peter's confession of Christ as the rock and see the church as built on those who likewise confess Christ as the Son of God. (3) It seems best to take the truth Peter recognized, that Jesus is God's Son, as the reality which serves as the foundation for His church. Because Jesus is the Son of God, Satan can never prevail against those who are His own.

"The gates of Hades" (16:18). "Gates" focuses attention on the fortifications that surrounded ancient cities and suggests perhaps a metaphor for Satan's armies. Others note that "hades" represents death in Scripture and see a promise that death cannot conquer Jesus' own.

"Keys of the kingdom of heaven" (16:19). This is another metaphor. As keys were symbolic in O.T. times of a chief steward's position, Jesus clearly is speaking of some significant role in the Church Age to come. That role is made more clear by how the keys are used, to "bind and loose."

Binding and loosing (16:19). The Gk. syntax offers no clear indications of meanings. It is best to see the role Christ assigns in relation to His statement concerning foundations. Christ is the foundation. Peter has confessed Christ. Peter and the disciples were then commissioned to confess Christ before others. That confession, and how men respond to it, is truly the key to heaven. A response of faith opens the door to new life in Christ. A rejection closes the door on life and confirms ultimate judgment.

Our cross (16:24-26). The cross here does not symbolize suffering, but rather the decision to do the will of God whatever the cost. When we deny our "old man's" drives and desire to choose God's will for our lives, we take up our cross. By that choice we lose our old self, and we begin to become the new self that God will enable us to be. By losing our (old) life, we find our (new) life in Jesus Christ.

Chapter summary. This chapter contains Matthew's last related miracles of Jesus. It is the final proof of who He is, offered not to the crowds but to the disciples. The first and most wonderful proof is witnessed only by Peter, James, and John, who see Jesus "transfigured," as the brightness of His essential deity radiates from Him (17:1-13). Returning to the crowds Jesus heals an epileptic His disciples had been unable to help (vv. 14-21). Despite His evident powers, Christ speaks again of being killed, and then raised again (vv. 22-23).

Outline
Place
Finder

PREPARATION
PREACHING
PROOF
PRACTICE
PURPOSE

The chapter concludes with an incident that illustrates a point Israel's response to Jesus has made clear. Peter unthinkingly commits Jesus to pay a temple tax. Jesus then points out that earthly kings do not collect taxes from their children.

The very fact that God imposed a temple tax shows that birth into the Old Testament covenant community does not automatically convey personal relationship with God! (vv. 24-27) To become a child of God, we must have faith in His Son.

Key verse. 17:2: Jesus, as He really is.

Personal application. Maintain balance in thinking about Christ between the compassionate Jesus and the glorious Son of God.

Key concepts. Healings »p. 784. Faith »pp. 35, 458, 740.

INSIGHT

The Transfiguration (17:1-2). This unique display of Jesus' glory was restricted to those who already recognized Him as God's Son. As we trust Christ we can expect more and greater revelations of His presence and power.

"Moses and Elijah" (17:3). Why these two? Many reasons have been suggested. Perhaps the best is that Moses is the model prophet, a type of the Christ to come and introduce God's new covenant revelation. And Elijah is the forerunner, destined to reappear just before Christ returns to institute God's kingdom on earth.

Building tabernacles (17:9). Our calling is not to build a settlement enclosing Jesus, but to carry the message of the resurrected Christ to the world.

John the Baptist as Elijah. See p. 613.

"Terrified" (17:6-8). The terror is not of Jesus, but is caused by the disciples' total unfamiliarity with such a display. "Transfigured" here is *metamorphao*, to change in form. They had sensed the hidden glory of Jesus, but were unready for even this muted manifestation of His essential glory.

Let's not become so "familiar" with the Jesus of the Gospels that we fail to sustain a sense of awe in our own relationship with the Lord.

Little faith (17:20). It is more likely the word indicates poverty of faith than extent. A poor

Illustration (17:24). *The temple tax was a two drachma coin to be contributed by every Jewish adult male. The priests insisted that drachmas cast in Tyre, valued the same as a Roman denarius at about a day's wage for a laborer, be used. A duodrachma and tetradrachma coin of the era are shown here.*

faith is easily distracted from Jesus and forgetting who He is, accomplishes little.

Exempt (17:24-27). Today there is no temple tax, for believers in Christ are now God's sons and daughters.

Outline
Place
Finder

PREPARATION
PREACHING
PROOF
PRACTICE
PURPOSE

Chapter summary. In a sequence of teachings and experiences Jesus shows His disciples the way to greatness in God's kingdom (chaps. 18–20). The underlying principle is seen in a little child's responsiveness to Jesus' call (18:1-5), a quality the disciples are urged to maintain (vv. 6-9). We do this by remembering that we human beings are sheep, who are likely to go astray and must be brought back not with recrimination but with joy (vv. 10-14). We are brothers and sisters who are sure to sin against each other, but who are to be confronted and then granted unlimited forgiveness (vv. 15-22). And if it seems too hard to forgive multiplied offenses, we are to remember the overwhelming debt that God, our Heavenly Father, has forgiven us (vv. 23-35).

Key verse. 18:3: A change for the better.

Personal application. Respond to God's Word, don't assess it.

Key concepts. Kingdom »pp. 380, 606. Sin »p. 362. Heaven »p. 437. Sheep »p. 355. Forgiveness »pp. 357, 634. Wicked »p. 350.

INSIGHT

Kingdom lifestyle (18:1). This entire three-chapter section is about the pathway to greatness for Christ's disciples. Teaching and events are interwoven to teach us how to live as citizens of the present kingdom of Jesus. Most important to a kingdom lifestyle is responsiveness to Christ's word, especially to His word about preserving one another's commitment to the Lord. Ultimately, the key to living as citizens of God's kingdom is to respond to His call to commit ourselves to servanthood, as Christ served for the Father's sake.

"Like little children" (18:2-5). Christ taught and performed miracles for three years in the little Jewish homeland—and the adults of His time either overtly rejected His claims, or held back, uncertain. Now He calls a little child and "had him stand among" the disciples. The child responded to Jesus' call when adults had not.

To be followers of Jesus, much less great in God's kingdom, we must be like a little child in our response to Christ's word.

Causing little ones to sin (18:6-9). Jesus uses hyperbole to emphasize the importance of maintaining "little oneness" in the community of faith.

We must do nothing that will discourage others from responding as a child to Christ's word.

"Look down on" (18:10-11). Caring, not contempt, is our calling.

"Sheep" (18:12-14). Sheep were greatly valued in Palestine. But their weaknesses were well known. Sheep were helpless, unable to defend themselves. And they were foolish, prone to go astray. Jesus reminds us that we human beings share this last characteristic. As believers we and others will stray. But when this happens, we are to be brought back into the company of God's sheep with rejoicing, not recriminations. Welcoming back those who have strayed is one way we preserve "little oneness" in the community of faith.

Brothers (18:15). Believers are family as well as flock. In any family, brothers do sin against and hurt one another. Here Jesus emphasizes the necessity of reconciliation. The one who is hurt is to confront the other in an effort to win reconciliation. If the offender will not acknowledge his fault others are brought in because there can be no reconciliation without confession by the one at fault and forgiveness by the one offended. In going to another person we show our readiness to forgive. To preserve "little oneness" in the church we must insist the offender face his or her fault.

"How many times"? (18:21-22) "Seventy times seven" means we are to extend unlimited forgiveness to others. God's transformation of sinners takes time and can only take place in a community commited to love and forgiveness.

The unpayable debt (18:23-35). In modern terms the first servant owed some $12 million—a truly unpayable debt. It is hard to forgive, but let's remember how much God has forgiven us!

Wicked (18:35). God's compassion is not won by forgiving. But it is unthinkable that those who are forgiven fail to forgive. Only the wicked who will not receive forgiveness act this way.

620

Chapter summary. Jesus has taught that the way of greatness for citizens of God's kingdom is to live in the community of faith so as to preserve each believer's responsiveness to Christ. Now, in incident and teaching, Matthew explores futile pathways to greatness that religious people sometimes take. The Pharisees and their questions represent the way of legalism and self-righteousness (19:1-14). And a rich young man represents the way of a self-serving philanthropy (vv. 15-30). It's so easy for religious people to feel that discipleship is practiced by rigid adherence to do's and don'ts, or by an enthusiastic commitment to doing good—and so to miss the simple pathway of love Jesus describes in Matthew 18.

Outline
Place
Finder

PREPARATION
PREACHING
PROOF
PRACTICE
PURPOSE

Key verse. 19:14: Come as children.

Personal application. God loves us because we are His, not because of what we do for Him.

Key concepts. Pharisees »p. 625. Divorce »p. 136. Law »pp. 120, 145, 376, 607. Wealth »pp. 125, 838. Disciples »p. 657.

INSIGHT

"Is it lawful"? (19:3) The question is characteristic of the Pharisees, who boasted about their superior commitment to keeping each detail of the Law. It was, however, the wrong question. The right question: "Is there any way to restore a crumbling marriage?" The answer is, "Yes." Jesus has already shown how, in Matt. 18. We remember we are like sheep and seek restoration; we confront and forgive; and we keep on forgiving.

"At the beginning" (19:4-6). Jesus did not answer this question but restated God's creation ideal of a lifelong, monagamous marriage.

Why then does God's Law permit divorce? The Pharisees, who saw Law as the highest possible expression of God's will, blurted out this question. Jesus' reference to the "hardness of your hearts" is often misunderstood. What He means is that God, knowing how sinful human beings are, was aware that some would not accept a Matt. 18 lifestyle. So some marriages would be marred by sin, and destructive. So God permitted divorce even though this was not His ideal will.

Legalism's futility. Jesus' words to the Pharisees struck down their claim to superiority, based on self-righteousness won by keeping God's Law. Jesus showed that Moses' Law was not the highest standard, but in fact showed God's grace, for He was willing to stoop to meet human beings where we are rather than requiring us to live up to an ideal. Grace, not a self-righteousness won by performance, is key to relationship with God.

Divorces and marries (19:9). The nature of "marital unfaithfulness" (*porneia*) has been much debated and is uncertain. The force of the saying makes it clear that divorce is never to be undertaken lightly or for selfish purposes (to marry a younger, more attractive spouse). It is not, however, a "new law" that abrogates the O.T. permission or its rationale, for human beings still are cursed by hardness of heart.

"Little children" (19:13-15). Even the Pharisees didn't view "little children" as subject to Moses' Law.

Let's relate to God as little children, responsive to Him rather than self-righteously trying to keep a law. If both parties do, marital as well as other relationship problems can be solved.

In search of eternal life (19:16). The young man's question reveals his motivation. He does good to others "to get eternal life." God's children are to do good to others because we value and care for them as God does. This rich young man's benevolence was self-serving. As such he is as far from the kingdom as the self-righteous Pharisee.

Sell all (19:21). The command is not for all Jesus' followers. It was spoken to the rich young man for a specific purpose. When he rejected the command of Christ, he broke the "first and great" commandment of the Law: to love and serve God with his whole heart. Christ's command revealed to the young man and to us that his money rather than his God came first.

Leaving all to follow Jesus (19:28-30). God doesn't command us to give everything away. But we are to abandon all. There is to be nothing in our life that is so precious it keeps us from doing God's will.

Outline
Place
Finder

PREPARATION
PREACHING
PROOF
PRACTICE
PURPOSE

Chapter summary. Jesus tells a parable about a third futile path which the religious take. His story of workers in a vineyard teaches that every relationship with God rests on His grace and generosity. We wrongly assume that the harder we work, the greater our reward. It is not self-effort, but responsiveness to Christ's words that count (20:1-16).

Jesus again predicts His death (vv. 17-19), but the disciples are too focused on visions of power when Christ becomes king to hear what He says (vv. 20-23). Jesus uses emotion stimulated by the politicking of James and John to drive home a major truth. Greatness in Christ's kingdom is found in serving, not in power or position (vv. 24-28). He then demonstrates the attitude that must underlie our practice as, despite concern over His coming crucifixion, He stops to heal two blind men who cry out for His aid (vv. 29-34).

Key verse. 20:25: Greatness is for servants.

Personal application. In stooping to serve others we become great in God's kingdom.

Key concepts. Kingdom »p. 380. Cup »p. 646. Slave »p. 90.

INSIGHT

"Denarius" (20:2). A silver coin minted by the Romans. It had approximately the same value as other silver coins, the drachma, dariac, and the shekel. A denarius was the standard wage for a day's work in N.T. times.

Unfair (20:3-18). We can understand the feelings of those who worked hard all day and saw those who had done less receive equal pay. But the parable drives home a great truth. Each workman had done exactly what the owner of the vineyard had asked of him. And the reward given was based on the owner's generosity, not by measuring how much each worker accomplished.

Similarly God calls us to different tasks in His kingdom and rewards not on the basis of how much we do, but on how faithfully we respond to His will. And when He does reward us, what He gives us is not so much something we have earned, but a gift that demonstrates His generosity and His grace. After all, we do owe Him everything.

On the way (20:17-19). The events in this chapter take place while Jesus and His disciples are "going up to Jerusalem." He goes willingly, responsive to the Father's will, even though He knows the suffering that awaits.

Right and left hand (20:20-21). The phrase indicates the highest and most powerful of political positions, next to the ruler.

"The two brothers" (20:24). The other disciples were angry with James and John, realizing that they had put their mother up to making the request.

"Rulers of the Gentiles" (20:25). Jesus contrasts the world's greatness with kingdom greatness. The world's way is represented by power and authority. The ruler is over others. He demands that others serve him. He uses coercive power to force compliance. The ruler magnifies himself at the expense of others.

Among you, servanthood (20:26-28). The contrast Jesus now draws is one of Scripture's clearest expositions of servanthood. The servant abandons power and authority in order to serve God and others. He is among, not over, others. He chooses to minister to others. The servant does not coerce, but by the power of his example and love motivates others to make their own personal commitment to God and to good. In carrying out this ministry the servant does not magnify his own importance, but emphasizes the importance of others.

The world rejects servanthood as a model of leadership. The Christian must affirm servanthood, for Jesus Himself "did not come to be served, but to serve, and to give His life as a ransom for many."

"Two blind men" (21:29-34). The crowd hushed the two blind men, considering them beneath the interest of the Teacher. But Jesus stopped, despite His own burden, to ask "What do you want Me to do?" This is servanthood: to value others, despite their unimportance to the world, and to set aside our own concerns to meet the outcast's needs.

Chapter summary. Matthew now begins his account of Jesus' last week on earth. In his account of events leading up to the Cross we discover the ultimate purpose for which Christ came.

As Jesus enters Jerusalem He is acclaimed by the crowds as "Son of David," a messianic title (21:1-11). He drives the merchants from the temple courts, again to the enthusiastic plaudits of the crowd (vv. 12-17). The next morning as Jesus approaches the city He sees and curses a fruitless fig tree, which represents an Israel which appears spiritually vital but has failed to produce fruit (vv. 18-22). When the religious leaders challenge Jesus, He asks a simple question that shows up their claims to authority (vv. 23-27). He tells two stories that charge them with failure to respond to God (vv. 28-32) and also reveal their motives for hating Jesus (vv. 33-46).

Outline
Place
Finder

PREPARATION
PREACHING
PROOF
PRACTICE
PURPOSE

Key verse. 21:43: It is dangerous not to respond to God.

Personal application. We must either love Jesus, or fear Him.

Key concepts. Prophecy »pp. 417, 434. Davidic Covenant »p. 370. Temple »p. 283. Parable »p. 166. Kingdom of God »p. 380.

INSIGHT

Fulfilled prophecy again (21:4). Most references to fulfilled prophecy in Matt. are found in the account of Christ's birth and in the account of His last week and crucifixion. God's entry into our world, and His death on the cross for us, are the heart of the Gospel.

Riding a donkey (21:5). In the ancient world when a king rode a horse, it symbolized war. When he rode a donkey, it symbolized peace. The people missed the symbolism. They expected Him to lead a rebellion against Rome, and when He did not, the shouts of "Hosanna" quickly became the cry of "Crucify Him."

Unlike the people of Christ's day we must be willing to set aside our preconceived notions and let our perspective be reshaped by God's Word.

Buying and selling (21:12-13). The verse does not mean nothing should be bought or sold in modern churches. It refers to the fact that the priests insisted temple fees be paid in a particular coinage, and money changers overcharged.

Jewish writings report that the high-priestly family that dominated in the 1st century was despised by the people for dishonesty and greed.

No wonder Jesus was angry that the temple dedicated to worship of the Lord had become a "den of robbers."

"Do not doubt" (21:21-22). The verse does not teach, as some have suggested, that faith is a condition of answered prayer. Rather it reminds us that God often communicates His will to us in such a way that we are able to pray confidently. When His Spirit removes the uncertainty that is rightly present in most of our prayers, "you will receive whatever you ask for in prayer."

Chief priests and elders (21:23-27). These men claimed the right to be the final arbiters of Scripture and of God's will. Jesus raised a question they were afraid to answer — and showed up their hypocrisy. If they had any real authority they would speak boldly — as Christ had throughout His ministry.

Their weak "we don't know" showed them for what they were: mere men, without any real spiritual authority at all.

"Two sons" (21:28-32). The gloves are off now. Jesus bluntly accuses the religious leaders of being persons who say they will obey God, but then fail to do so. The prostitutes and sinners these religious men despise are better than they. They said "no" to God, but in the end they obeyed.

When you saw this (21:32). The evidence of God's work is His transformation of sinners.

"The tenants" (21:33-39). Jesus' parable reveals the motives of His enemies. They hate Him because He owns the vineyard which they have taken possession of. They do not want to submit to God. They want to be God. We too must be careful not to prefer our will to God's.

"Taken away" (21:40-46). We cannot be part of the kingdom of God apart from allegiance to the King. All the religious leaders of Jesus' time controlled was the outward, now empty shell of religion. The reality is found only by faith in Jesus Christ.

Outline
Place
Finder

PREPARATION
PREACHING
PROOF
PRACTICE
PURPOSE

Chapter summary. Jesus tells a parable to show the significance of His rejection. The Jews are like guests invited to a wedding banquet, a common figure for Messiah's kingdom. But they make all sorts of excuses not to come. So the king invites "anyone" and fills his hall (22:1-14). The invitation of God will be extended to all, and "whosoever wills" may come!

The religious leaders again try to trap Jesus. The Pharisees pose a trick question about taxes to be paid to Rome (vv. 15-22), and the Sadducees attempt to trip Him up with a common puzzler concerning resurrection (vv. 23-33). Jesus answers a final question (vv. 24-40), and then Christ poses a question which His antagonists cannot answer, silencing them at last (vv. 41-46). This is the last attempt of the leaders to defeat Jesus with words. Soon their hatred will lead them to drag Him to the cross.

Key verses. 22:37-40: Love sums up law.

Personal application. Augustine said it. Love God—and do what you please. If you love, what He wants will please you.

Key concepts. Kingdom »p. 380. Pharisees »p. 625. Resurrection »p. 522. Law »pp. 145, 607. Messiah (Christ) »p. 432.

INSIGHT

Call of God. The word translated "invitation" means "call." In the epistles this becomes a technical theological term (»p. 828). In the Gospels God's "call" is an invitation, but more. It's a command and requires a decision. The invited in Jesus' parable had the freedom to refuse to come.

But all who do refuse Christ's invitation will be excluded from redemption's final celebration.

Invited again and again (22:4-5). The king not only invites his guests again and again, but carefully describes the celebration to make it as inviting as possible. Only when the invitation is rejected and the king's messengers (Here, the prophets?) rejected, does the king act against those who reject him.

"Wedding clothes" (22:11). Evidence suggests that kings on certain occasions provided their guests with special garments. Many commentators see here a reminder that no one will be welcomed by God unless clothed in a righteousness He alone can provide.

"Chosen" (22:14). God invites all, but His purposes are not thwarted by those who refuse to respond. Those who come were chosen all the time.

Taxes to Caesar (22:15). The specific tax in view was a poll tax, imposed by the Roman emperor, to be paid by all adults. This tax, a hated symbol of subservience to Rome, actually stimulated the bloody revolt of A.D. 6 led by Judas of Galilee. The Pharisees' intent was to force Jesus to one of two positions: to support the tax and thus lose much popular support, or to reject the tax and thus be vulnerable to a charge of treason. Jesus' classic answer was more than clever avoidance of a trap. It is a guiding principle for us to apply. When there is no conflict between the claims of human government and God, we obey the secular power.

Levirate marriage (22:23-33). The Sadducees' question reflects a practice regulated, but not initiated, by Moses (cf. Gen. 38:8). The question is hypothetical, as younger brothers also had the right to refuse marrying a childless older brother's widow (cf. Deut. 25:5-7).

"Resurrection" (22:24-33). Jesus' exegesis of the O.T. is proof that the resurrection rests on the text of a verb: "is." What a clear affirmation of the unique authority of every word from God.

"The greatest commandment" (22:34-40). Some 1st-century rabbis were actively involved in trying to establish a hierarchy of biblical laws, while others insisted all commandments were of equal importance. Jesus says all laws "hang on" love for God and neighbor, meaning Law and the Prophets can be understood and lived only by one who loves both God and others.

The Messiah is God (22:41-46). Psalm 110 was recognized in the 1st century as messianic. Jesus demonstrates that David's decendant is superior to David because He is the Son of God.

Chapter summary. Following a series of controversies, Jesus bluntly warns against the Pharisees and leaders who have rejected His claims (23:1-12). In the strongest possible terms Christ characterizes them as fools, hypocrites, and even "sons of hell," and announces a series of seven woes—denunciations that imply both anguish and divine judgment (vv. 13-14, 15, 16-22, 23-24, 25-26, 27-28, 29-32). Jesus identifies this generation's leaders with those of the past who killed the prophets. Yet He weeps over the city, expressing God's amazing yearning to gather His own to Himself despite their sins (vv. 33-38). One day He will. But not until God's ancient people acknowledge Jesus as their Christ (v. 39).

Outline
Place
Finder

PREPARATION
PREACHING
PROOF
PRACTICE
PURPOSE

Key verse. 23:15: Even religious power corrupts.

Personal application. Strive to be a servant, not a "leader."

INSIGHT

"Moses' seat" (23:2). The reference is to a stone seat in the front of 1st-century synagogues where a "teacher of the law" sat when making authoritative statements in settling a dispute or giving instruction.

Pharisee (23:2). The Pharisees were a relatively small group of dedicated laymen, committed to the most rigorous interpretation and keeping of Mosaic and oral Law (»p. 591). The Pharisees had no right to give authoritative teaching, yet the theological position they represented was expressed through many who were "teachers of the law."

This initial reference is intended to define a theological position.

Irony (23:2-4). Jesus is *not* supporting His opponents' claim to teaching authority, but using irony, in which the intended meaning is the opposite of the usual sense of the words. His "non-ironical" advice is don't do what they do, for their teaching binds rather than frees.

Servants among (23:8-12). Jesus warns against hierarchy in the Christian community. Only if we live together as brothers, honoring Jesus rather than a mere human being as "Teacher," can we avoid the pride that condemned the Pharisees. Christian leaders are to be servants, not masters. Christian leaders are to be among, not over, their brothers and sisters in the family of faith. Let's make a conscious commitment to live a life of servanthood.

"Hypocrites" (23:13, 15, 23, 25, 27, 29). The Gk. word, found 16 of 26 times in Matthew's Gospel, is used of someone acting in a play. Actors in Gk. plays wore exaggerated, painted masks intended to represent the characters they played. *The Expository Dictionary of Bible Words* (Zondervan, 1985) points out that the Gospels portray religious hypocrites as persons who act with calculation intended to impress observers (Matt. 6:1-3), focus on exter-

Illustration: Phylacteries and tassels (23:5). *The long tassels on prayer shawls and exaggerated bands on the small boxes containing Bible verses that the Pharisees wore when praying in public were intended to impress men, not appeal to God.*

The more interested we are in the opinions of others the less we will be sensitive to the desires of the Lord.

nal trappings of religion and ignore the central, heart issues of love for God and others (Matt. 15:1-21), and who use spiritual talk to hide base and corrupt meanings (Matt. 22:18-22). This chapter is a blunt warning to hypocrites of every era.

Oath (23:16). An oath is a sworn commitment or vow. God has bound Himself with an oath to keep His promises, an act intended to emphasize the certainty of those things we hope for in Christ (cf. Heb. 6:17). But Jesus stands against oaths (cf. Matt. 5:36-37), because in His time oaths actually were used to conceal intentions. This conclusion is drawn from the distinctions the rabbis drew between valid and invalid oaths.

How revealing! If we are trustworthy persons, our word will be enough to bind us, and oaths will be irrelevant.

"Zechariah" (23:35). This martyred messenger is hard to identify, but may have been the son of Jehoiada mentioned in 2 Chron. 24:20-22.

Lament over Jerusalem (23:37-39). God is rightly angry with those who kill His messengers and reject His words. Yet He is also filled with compassion for them. The fact that Jesus is the "I" who has "longed to gather your children together" is a clear claim to be God. Only when Jesus is acknowledged as "He who comes in the name of the Lord," the Messiah, will Jerusalem's people know peace.

Outline
Place
Finder

PREPARATION
PREACHING
PROOF
PRACTICE
PURPOSE

Chapter summary. Jesus stimulates three questions concerning the end of the age by announcing that the second temple will be destroyed (24:1-3). The disciples' questions are answered in reverse order: When will this happen? is answered in verse 36. What will be the sign of Your coming? is answered in verses 30-35. What will be the sign of the end of the age? is answered in verses 4-29. But more important than questions about the future is Jesus' word of advice to the disciples and to us: "Watch, because you do not know on what day your Lord will come" (v. 42). Our challenge is not to solve the mysteries of prophecy, but to be faithful in our service to our Lord until He comes (vv. 36-51).

Key verse. 24:42: Concentrate on the "now."

Personal application. Serving Jesus now is more important that debating the shape of the future Scripture describes.

INSIGHT

Interpretations abound. Scholars vigorously debate how the prophecies of this chapter are to be interpreted. Certain things, however, seem clear. Jesus will come at history's end. Until Jesus returns we can expect to experience the consequences of sin in society (wars) and in nature (earthquakes, famines). While we wait, we are to concentrate on carrying out our absent Lord's instructions. Whatever our understanding of this complex and difficult passage, it is faithfulness that will count.

Matthew 24 and O.T. prophecy. In answering the disciples Jesus links His teaching with specific prophecies of Daniel. It seems clear that any interpretation of the passage thus must "fit" with the vision of the future expressed in the O.T. prophets. If we accept this, the following understanding of Matt. 24 emerges.

"The age" (24:3). Daniel specified a period of 70 "weeks" (sevens) of years till Messiah came and fulfilled all prophecy. But the last seven years was set off from the others by the "cutting off" (death) of the Messiah. As the disciples' question is asked with a view to their own O.T. vision of the future, it is best to take "the age" Jesus is speaking of as the final seven years of Daniel. Thus the answer does not deal directly with the centuries between the death of Jesus and the beginning of the last seven of Daniel's years. Many Christians believe that beginning is to be marked by the rapture of the church (cf. 1 Thes. 4:13-17).

The abomination of desolation (24:15). The event is the erection of a statue of the anti-Christ in a Jerusalem temple (cf. 2 Thes. 2:4). A historic corollary was Antiochus Epiphane's sacrifice of a pig on the Jerusalem temple's altar in the 160s B.C.

"Great distress" (24:21). The Gk. word (*thlipsis*) means tribulation and is used of terrible sufferings, slaughter, and disease. All the O.T. prophets predict such a period prior to God's great redemptive intervention on behalf of His people at history's end. Jesus' reference to this distress as "unequaled" in the history of the world fits the O.T. prophetic vision.

"Son of Man" (24:30). Frequently this phrase is used by Jesus as the personal pronoun, "I," in such a way as to emphasize His humanity. Here it draws on Daniel's use of that phrase to emphasize Christ's deity (cf. Dan. 7:13-14).

The sign of the Son of Man in the sky (24:30). *Semeion* (sign) here probably means "standard" or "banner." Jesus' return will be visible, announced by trumpets (cf. Isa. 11:12; 18:3; Jer. 4:21; 51:27) and Christ's unfurled banner in the heavens.

"This generation" (24:34). The generation in view is that which is alive when the terrible events described in Matt. 24 take place. No one then living will know when Jesus will return triumphant. But they can know it will happen within the years that mark a normal lifespan.

No one knows the day or hour (24:36). How foolish we are to worry about dates, when Christ Himself is unconcerned about the specific time! Our calling is to trust in God's goodness and to concentrate on obeying the desires He has revealed so clearly in the Word.

"The days of Noah" (24:37-51). Jesus' point is that life will seem to be going on normally when Second Coming events take place. How foolish to say, "I'll wait till just before I die," or "Till just before Christ comes" to trust and serve Him.

God doesn't give warnings. He calls us to choose, now. And to serve Him faithfully.

Chapter summary. Jesus continues instructing His disciples concerning His second coming. His return may seem delayed to those eager to participate in the wedding feast, but those who are wise will be ready however long the wait (25:1-13). While the Master is gone, servants must actively use whatever they have been entrusted with in His interest (vv. 14-30). When Christ does come, there will be a final judgment in which He separates the righteous and unrighteous, the blessed and the cursed, and assigns each to his or her eternal state (vv. 31-46).

Outline
Place
Finder

PREPARATION
PREACHING
PROOF
PRACTICE
PURPOSE

Key verse. 25:13: Heed repeated warnings!

Personal application. God needs alert and watchful Christians.

Key concepts. Kingdom »p. 380. Servant/slave »p. 90. Angel »p. 521. Sheep »p. 355. Righteous »p. 120. Bless »p. 127. Curse »p. 138. Hell »p. 924.

INSIGHT

Wedding customs (25:1-13). Marriage customs of the time called for the groom and close friends to go to the bride's home. After various ceremonies the bride was escorted to her home, after dark. All members of the bridal party were to carry torches, those without were gate crashers, not invited to the several days of festivities that marked a wedding feast.

The point of the parable. It strains the context to search for hidden meanings, to find significance in the missing oil, or to draw attention to the note that they all fell asleep. Like most stories, this makes a single, vital point. Despite the awareness of all that the bridegroom was coming, only five of the young women in Christ's story prepared. We will either be prepared for Christ's return, or we will fail to take the Gospel message seriously.

The fact is that the rejected virgins in this story were never prepared for the coming of the bridegroom, or emergence of the kingdom of God.

The parable of the talents (25:14-30). "Talent" is a unit of weight. It became a monetary term as that unit of weight used of the metals that served as money—gold, silver, or copper. A talent of silver represented some 20 years wages for a day laborer and thus was worth far more than the $1,000 suggested in the NIV notes.

The point of the parable is that good servants felt responsible and immediately set about using the funds entrusted to them in their master's behalf. What's more, they worked faithfully at serving him. The poor servant was not faithful in carrying out this responsibility.

Lessons from this parable. Till Christ returns we are to use every resource He has given us in His service. How exciting to realize that whatever those resources may be, our reward is based on faithfulness, not the size of our achievements (cf. 25:21, 23).

Rejection of the servant (25:22-30). To make this parable suggest that a believer can lose salvation if he or she fails to serve Christ is to distort its theme. The parable futher defines the general theme of "watching" while Christ is away. Watching does not mean settling down to inactivity. It means wholehearted commitment to Christ's purposes in this present world. While God will commend those who are faithful in this mission, He will surely judge the "worthless" servant who fails to make every effort to serve Him.

Sheep, goats, and Jesus' brothers (25:31-46). There are various interpretations. It may be best to view Christ's "brothers" as active believers of any era, who face hunger, thirst, and suffering for His sake. Those who are welcomed by God for "inviting them in" do so not simply from a humanistic concern, but because they choose to take a stand with the outcasts who represent Christ. Their support of Christ's brothers indicates they have chosen to take a stand for rather than against Christ's kingdom.

"Eternal fire" (25:41). How significant that the eternal fire was "prepared for the devil and his angels." Christ has done everything He can to keep every human being from this dread fate. Only a man's decision against Christ can condemn him.

Outline
Place
Finder

PREPARATION
PREACHING
PROOF
PRACTICE
PURPOSE

Chapter summary. Events now rush to a close, as Matthew describes the final two days of Christ's life. The chart below integrates reports of the four Gospels concerning Christ's trials and crucifixion.

Religious trials	
Before Annas	John 18:12-14
Before Caiaphas	Matt. 26:57-68
Before the Sanhedrin	Matt. 27:1-2

Civil trials	
Before Pilate	John 18:28-38
Before Herod	Luke 23:6-12
Before Pilate	John 18:39–19:16

Sequence of events at Calvary	
Jesus offered drugged drink	Matt. 27:34
Jesus crucified	Matt. 27:35
Jesus cries, "Father, forgive them"	Luke 23:34
Soldiers gamble for Christ's clothing	Matt. 27:35
Jesus mocked by observers	Matt. 27:39-44; Mark 15:29
Jesus ridiculed by two thieves	Matt. 27:44
One thief believes	Luke 23:39-43
Jesus promises,	Luke 23:43
"Today you will be with Me"	
Jesus tells Mary, "Behold your son"	John 19:26-27
Darkness blots out the scene	Matt. 27:45; Mark 15:33; Luke 23:44
Jesus cried, "My God, My God"	Matt. 27:46-47; Mark 15:34
Jesus cries, "I thirst"	John 19:28
Jesus cries, "It is finished"	John 19:30
Jesus cries, "Father, into Your hands"	Luke 23:46
Jesus releases His spirit	Matt. 27:50; Mark 15:37

Key verse. 26:64: Jesus is who He claimed.

Personal application. Meditate on the Cross, and remember what your salvation cost Christ.

Key concepts. Passover »p. 59. Crucifixion »p. 814. Lord's Supper »p. 767. Denial »p. 673. Priest »pp. 81, 858.

INSIGHT

Illustration. *Biblical words for briers, brambles, spiny plants, and thistles overlap. So it is impossible to identify the exact thorns woven into a crown and pressed down on Jesus' brow. Yet thorns are appropriate. They are first mentioned as a consequence of sin (Gen. 3:18), and continue to serve as symbols of evil (Prov. 22:5; Matt. 7:16; 13:22). Symbolically Jesus wore our sins.*

Abandon (27:46). The Gk. word (*enkataleipo*) is intensive, with strong moral and emotional overtones. Christ was not abandoned to the grave (Acts 2:27). Yet at the moment of death an awesome rent was torn in the very fabric of the Godhead. It was this separation from God, the ultimate meaning of "death" in Scripture, that was the price Christ paid for our sins.

Chapter summary. Death could not hold Jesus, but energized by the power of the Spirit He burst forth from the grave. The following charts the resurrection events and the post-resurrection appearances of Jesus.

Outline
Place
Finder

PREPARATION
PREACHING
PROOF
PRACTICE
PURPOSE

Resurrection events

Three women start for the tomb	Luke 23:55–24:1
They find the stone rolled away	Luke 24:2-9
Mary Magdalene hurries to tell the disciples	John 20:1-2
Mary, James' mother, sees the angels	Matt. 28:1-2
Peter and John arrive, look in tomb	John 20:3-10
Mary Magalene returns, sees angels, then Jesus	John 20:11-18
Mary, James' mother, returns with others	Luke 24:1-4
These women see the angels	Luke 24:5; Mark 16:5
Leaving, they too meet Jesus	Matt. 28:9-10

Other post-resurrection appearances of Jesus

To Peter, the same day	Luke 24:34; 1 Cor. 15:5
To disciples on the Emmaus road	Luke 24:13-31
To the apostles (minus Thomas)	Luke 24:36-45; John 20:19-25
To the apostles (including Thomas)	John 20:24-29
To seven by the Lake of Tiberias	John 21:1-23
To about 500 in Galilee	1 Cor. 15:6
To James in Jerusalem and Bethany	1 Cor. 15:7
To many at the Ascension	Acts 1:3-11
To Paul near Damascus	Acts 9:3-6; 1 Cor. 15:8
To Stephen when he is stoned	Acts 7:55
To Paul in the temple	Acts 22:17-19; 23:11
To John on Patmos	Rev. 1:10-19

Key verses. 28:18-20. A last command to obey.

Personal application. Christ is with us when we witness.

Key concepts. Resurrection »pp. 737, 808. Crucifixion »p. 814.

INSIGHT

Sunday (28:1). The Sabbath (Saturday) is sacred to the Jews, and commemorates God's work of Creation. Christians from the beginning have celebrated the "first day of the week," commemorating the resurrection of Jesus Christ (cf. Acts 20:7; 1 Cor. 16:2).

Authority of Jesus (28:18). When Jesus claimed "all authority in heaven and on earth," He meant that there is no one or thing with power to limit His freedom of action (cf.

»p. 610). It is significant that this affirmation is linked with the command that we "go" and make disciples of all nations.

How often Christians hesitate to witness to others. How much we need to remember that nothing—no hardness of others, no ridicule, no hostility of government or ruling power—can limit the power of the Gospel or prevail against those who obey Christ's command.

Mark

Mark is the briefest, and in some ways the most attractive, of the four Gospels. Its sparse, unpretentious prose provides uniquely vivid images of Jesus as a Man of action. Mark's narratives are marked by the frequent use of *euthys*, "immediately," which carry us along from scene to scene up to the culminating act of Jesus' courage in boldly facing the cross. His use of the present tense draws us into the scenes he sketches and helps us see events as the writer does, as an eyewitness.

Many believe this Gospel was written to appeal to the Roman mind, shaped to emphasize Christ's strenuous life and manly characteristics. Mark's vigorous but blunt Greek reflects the language of the common man, and his practice of transliterating Latin words in Greek, and using Latin constructions or expressions, supports the notion that he directed his writing to the Roman elements in the population of the first-century empire.

Yet most believe that Mark was not himself an eyewitness of most of the scenes he describes. Rather early tradition tells us that Mark is the "interpreter" of Peter, whose accounts are actually summaries of Peter's preaching about Jesus. A report by the church historian Eusebius in his *Ecclesiastical History* (3.39.15) quotes a lost document written by Papias (about A.D. 140), who in turn cites the Apostle John as authority for the following information about this Gospel. "Mark, who became Peter's interpreter, wrote accurately, though not in order, all that he remembers of the things said or done by the Lord. For he had neither heard the Lord nor been one of His followers, but afterwards, as I said, he had followed Peter, who used to compose his discourses with a view to the needs of his hearers, but not as though he were drawing up a connected account of the Lord's sayings. So Mark made no mistake thus recording some things just as he remembered them. For he was careful of this one thing, to omit none of the things he had heard [from Peter] and to make no untrue statements therein."

Like the other Gospels, Mark thus organizes his material not by strict historical sequence, but by the logic of the image he wishes to communicate about Jesus. Drawing on the stories he heard over and over again as Peter preached about his Lord, Mark provides us with a special vision of Jesus. He reminds us over and over again that "gentle Jesus" was no weakling, but a man of courage, commitment, and complete, active dedication to carrying out His mission here on Earth.

Meet John Mark

Mark is a fascinating character in his own right. We know that Peter stayed in Mark's mother's house in Jerusalem after he was released from prison (Acts 12:12). Later the youthful Mark accompanied Paul and Barnabas on their first missionary journey (Acts 12:25; 13:5). Paul was disgusted when Mark abandoned the team at Pamphylia (v. 13). When Barnabas wanted to give Mark another chance, he and Paul quarreled so bitterly the two friends went their separate ways. Paul enlisted Silas as his partner for the next mission, and Barnabas took Mark and set out on a missionary journey of his own (Acts 15:36-41). It turned out that Barnabas was right to give young Mark a second chance. Mark developed into an effective missionary and later became a valued companion of the Apostle Paul himself (Col. 4:10; Phil. 24; 2 Tim. 4:11). And Peter speaks of Mark as a dearly loved son (1 Peter 5:13).

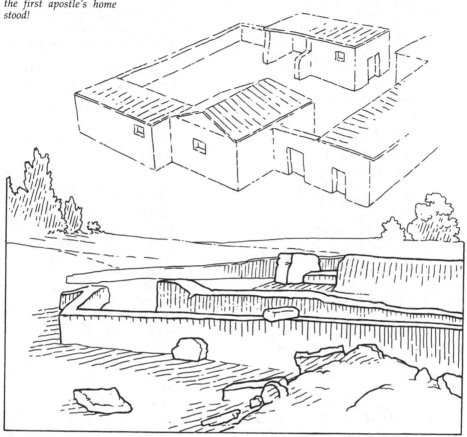

Illustration. *First-century ruins long identified as "Peter's House" may actually stand where the first apostle's home stood!*

WHERE THE ACTION TAKES PLACE

Mark's Gospel traces Jesus' ministry in Galilee and leads us to its climax in Judea. The Bible tells us Peter's fishing business was in Galilee, along the shore of its famous sea. One of the most fascinating of recent archeological explorations indicates that a structure in Capernaum long identified as "Peter's House" is actually erected on the ruins of a large home that was possibly occupied by the fisherman disciple!

THEOLOGICAL OUTLINE OF MARK

CONTENT OUTLINE OF MARK

I. Prologue (1:1-13)
  A. John's Ministry (1:1-8)
  B. Jesus' Baptism (1:9-11)
  C. Jesus' Temptation (1:12-13)
II. Ministry in Galilee (1:14–8:38)
  A. Calling Disciples (1:14-20)
  B. Driving Out an Evil Spirit (1:21-28)
  C. Healing Peter's Mother-in-law (1:29-31)
  D. Healing Others (1:32-39)
  E. Healing a Leper (1:40-45)
  F. Conflict with Religious Leaders (2:1–3:6)
    1. Jesus heals (2:1-12)
    2. Jesus eats with sinners (2:13-17)
    3. Jesus asked about fasting (2:18-22)
    4. Jesus Lord of the Sabbath (2:23–3:6)
  G. Selecting the Twelve (3:7-19)
  H. Jesus Challenged (3:20-35)
  I. Parables of the Kingdom (4:1-34)
  J. Triumphs of Jesus (4:35–5:43)
    1. Over a storm (4:35-41)
    2. Over demons (5:1-20)
    3. Over sickness and death (5:21-43)
  K. Rejection in Nazareth (6:1-6a)
  L. Sending Out the Twelve (6:6b-13)
  M. Views of Jesus' Identity (6:14-16)
  N. Death of John (6:17-29)
  O. Jesus Feeds 5,000 (6:30-44)
  P. Jesus Walks on Water, Heals (6:45-56)
  Q. Dispute with Pharisees (7:1-23)
  R. Faith and Healing (7:24-37)
  S. Jesus Feeds 4,000 (8:1-10)
  T. Jesus and Pharisees (8:11-21)
  U. A Blind Man and Spiritually Blind Men (8:22-30)
  V. First Mention of the Passion (8:31-38)
III. Journeying to Jerusalem (9:1–10:52)
  A. Jesus' Transfiguration (9:1-8)
  B. Jesus on Elijah (9:9-13)
  C. Jesus Heals Child with Evil Spirit (9:14-29)

  D. Jesus Again Predicts His Death (9:30-32)
  E. Jesus Questioned about Greatness (9:33-37)
  F. The Challenge of Discipleship (9:38-50)
  G. Jesus on Divorce (10:1-12)
  H. Jesus Blesses Children (10:13-16)
  I. Jesus on Riches (10:17-31)
  J. Jesus Again Predicts His Death (10:32-34)
  K. Jesus Teaches Servanthood (10:35-45)
  L. Jesus Restores Blind Bartimaeus (10:46-52)
IV. Jerusalem Ministry (11:1–13:37)
  A. Triumphal Entry (11:1-11)
  B. Fruitless Fig Tree (11:12-14)
  C. Cleansing the Temple (11:15-19)
  D. Jesus on Prayer (11:20-26)
  E. Jesus' Authority (11:27-33)
  F. Parable of Tenants (12:1-12)
  G. Taxes to Caesar? (12:13-17)
  H. Jesus on Resurrection (12:18-27)
  I. Jesus on the Great Commandment (12:28-34)
  J. Jesus on the Messiah (12:35-37)
  K. Jesus Warns Against Teachers of the Law (12:38-40)
  L. The Widow's Gift (12:41-44)
  M. Jesus on the Future (13:1-37)
V. The Passion of Christ (14:1–16:20)
  A. The Plot Against Jesus (14:1-2)
  B. Jesus Anointed (14:3-9)
  C. Jesus Betrayed (14:10-11)
  D. The Lord's Supper (14:12-26)
  E. Peter's Denial Predicted (14:27-31)
  F. Jesus in Gethsemane (14:32-42)
  G. Jesus Arrested (14:43-52)
  H. Jesus on Trial (14:53-65)
  I. Peter Denies Jesus (14:66-72)
  J. Jesus Before Pilate (15:1-15)
  K. Jesus Mocked (15:16-20)
  L. Jesus Crucified (15:21-32)
  M. Jesus Dies (15:33-41)
  N. Jesus Buried (15:42-47)
  O. Jesus Raised Again! (16:1-8)
  P. The Disputed Ending (16:9-20)

Chapter summary. Mark's preamble is brief. Jesus is God's Son (1:1). He was presented by John (vv. 2-8), certified by a voice from heaven (vv. 9-11), and met the active hostility of Satan (vv. 12-13). Disciples who followed Him from the beginning (1:14-20) saw Him drive out demons (vv. 21-28) and heal the sick (vv. 29-34). He was dedicated to actively doing God's work by preaching the Good News (vv. 35-39). He not only demonstrated God's power by performing miracles, but He also expressed God's love by His compassion for the helpless (vv. 40-45). This is the Jesus Mark wants his first-century readers, and us, to know. Jesus, the Son of God, yet a powerful, vigorous, and totally admirable Man among men.

Outline
Place
Finder

GALILEE
TO JERUSALEM
JERUSALEM
PASSION

Key verse. 1:1: Jesus Himself is the Good News!

Personal application. We are to admire Jesus as well as love Him.

Key concepts. Gospel »p. 737. Prophecy »pp. 417, 434. Baptism »p. 604. Satan »p. 501. Kingdom »p. 380. Disciples »p. 657. Evil spirits »p. 239. Authority »p. 610. Prayer »p. 694. Leprosy »p. 83.

INSIGHT

"The Son of God" (1:1). Mark's goal is twofold. He intends to show us in Jesus the ideal man, committed, active, and vigorous. And he intends to show that Jesus was the Son of God: God here in the flesh. This key theme is emphasized over and over in Mark's brief Gospel (cf. 1:11; 3:11; 5:7; 9:7; 12:6; 13:32; 14:36, 61; 15:39).

And so (1:2-3). The quote here is a weaving together of O.T. texts: Mal. 3:1, which the rabbis linked to Ex. 23:20, and Isa. 40:3. The O.T. Scriptures identify John as one who prepares the way for the Lord. Thus the O.T. points to Jesus as God the Son. The testimony of Scripture, of John, of the voice from heaven (Mark 1:9-11), and the victory Jesus won over Satan in the wilderness, all serve to demonstrate Mark's christological theme. The only way to understand this Man Mark writes about is to see Him as the Son of God.

It's the same today. Some think of Jesus as a great teacher, others as a good man. One stream of modern Jewish scholarship insists we understand Jesus as a rabbi in a long established tradition. Mark says that to understand Jesus we must begin with His deity. There is no other way to know Him.

Conflict with Satan (1:13). In Matt. and Luke the temptation accounts emphasize Jesus' triumph over Satan. Mark fails to mention this. Mark's purpose is to affirm Jesus' deity, and he does this by showing here and throughout the book how Christ is in constant conflict with Satan.

A man is known by his enemies as well as his friends!

Jesus' authority over evil spirits (1:21-27). "Authority" in Scripture is rooted in the idea of "freedom of action" (»p. 610). Human freedom of action is very limited. We can't take off and fly. We are limited by the law of gravity. We can't shrug off sin. We are limited by the warping impact of wrong acts on our personalities. We can't make our own moral laws. God is the standard and the judge of morality. We can't heal our own diseases. The best we can do is cooperate with medical treatments. No wonder those who watched Jesus work His miracles were stunned by Jesus' "authority." He acted freely in ways that no mere human being could act. "He even gives orders to evil spirits and they obey Him" (v. 27).

There really was no excuse for Jesus' generation to reject Him. Or for us to. He has proved He is the Son of God. Only God has the freedom to act as Jesus did. This is the message of His miracles.

"Compassion" (1:40-46). There is another message in His miracles, seen in His reaching out to touch the leper. The act is significant because this disease rendered anyone who even touched a leper religiously "unclean." How this man must have yearned but to know the loving touch of another human being! So Jesus, "filled with compassion," touched Him. The Gk. word, *splanchnizomai*, indicates a pity so great that one is moved to meet another's need. Jesus' entire life on earth shows that He is God. And that God cares.

Outline
Place
Finder

GALILEE
TO JERUSALEM
JERUSALEM
PASSION

Chapter summary. Mark continues his vivid description of Jesus' ministry. Jesus scandalizes the religious leaders by forgiving a paralytic's sin, even though He proves His freedom to do so by healing him (2:1-12). He later demonstrates His power over sin by calling—and transforming—a tax collector. Even this arouses the criticism of the religious (vv. 13-17), who have never realized that God is more concerned with human need than with ritual (vv. 18-20). The old ways of viewing faith are worn out, unable to contain the new revelation Jesus brings (vv. 21-22). A dispute over the Sabbath brings out an important point (vv. 23-28). This new revelation Jesus brings is in harmony with the real meaning of Old Testament faith, for Christ is Lord.

Key verse. 2:22: No one can squeeze Jesus into their mold.

Personal application. We must let Jesus define our beliefs, rather than trying to make Him fit them.

Key concepts. Sin »pp. 34, 362. Pharisee »p. 625. Sabbath »p. 664.

INSIGHT

Seeing their faith (2:4). Persistent faith moves us to overcome every obstacle and come to Jesus. After that everything is up to Him.

Forgiveness of sin (2:5). The N.T. has two distinct words translated "forgive." One means "be gracious to" and expresses all that one human being can do for another. The word here, *aphiemi*, means "to send away." God does not overlook our sins. He actually wipes out the sins themselves! It was the use of this word that shocked Christ's onlookers. Who can wipe out sins but God? No one.

How clear the message. Jesus is God!

Healing and forgiveness (2:1-7). Modern medicine sees a vital connection between health and mental well-being. The Bible links all sickness and suffering to our separation from God. Sickness is a symptom and a result of sin. Thus man's deepest need is not for physical healing, but for spiritual wholeness. Jesus cared enough to meet the paralytic's deepest need, even as He meets ours.

With this need met in our lives, healing of the body often follows (cf. »p. 412, »p. 290, »p. 611, »p. 784).

Divine prerogatives (2:2-5). Those who argue that Jesus never claimed to be God ignore this passage. The religious experts of His day did not. Jesus claimed a divine prerogative and thus laid claim to be God. Forgiving and healing are equally impossible for man, equally easy for God.

"Levi" (2:13-16). We know Levi as Matthew, the writer of the first Gospel.

Eating with sinners (2:16). Only those who are so in touch with God that they do not fear contamination are free to associate with sinners.

Those who are uncertain of their own commitment to the Lord (wisely) avoid them. The problem is that they also (unwisely) criticize others who (like Jesus) spend time with sinners. Let's remember that God loved and called us when we were sinners too!

"The Pharisees were fasting" (2:18-20). How easy to focus on people's practices. Both John's disciples and the Pharisees fasted, though there was a vast difference in their spiritual commitments. Jesus' disciples did not fast, but in spirit were close to John's disciples and far from the Pharisees.

Let's not focus so much upon the practices of other Christians. Let's focus on the real issue: heart relationship to Christ.

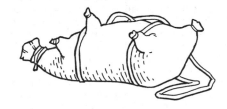

Illustration (2:21-22). *The tightly sown skins of goats were often used to hold wine. The fresh skin stretched as the grape juice in it fermented. But old skins could no longer stretch, so new wine would cause them to burst. The debate over Sabbath practices that follows (vv. 23-27) illustrates that contemporary Jewish faith was so brittle that it had no room to "stretch" to meet human need. See Luke 5's telling of these parables for their full, fascinating significance (»p. 656).*

Chapter summary. Jesus again is confronted by opponents who are eager to find some basis to accuse Him. Christ ignores their challenge and heals the man's shriveled hand, announcing by His act that, rightly understood, no law given by God prevents doing good to a person in need (3:1-6). After this fifth conflict Jesus leaves the area where He has been teaching, but is followed by those eager for healing (vv. 7-12). After Jesus officially appoints the Twelve as His disciples (vv. 13-19), a delegation of experts in the biblical law appear and argue that Christ's powers come from Satan (v. 22). Jesus ridicules their argument (vv. 23-27) but announces that their blasphemy against the Holy Spirit reveals a fixed attitude which condemns them absolutely (vv. 28-30). When His anxious and upset family (vv. 20-21) arrives, Jesus stuns His listeners by identifying Himself with a new family God is creating from those who do the will of God (vv. 31-35).

Outline
Place
Finder

GALILEE
TO JERUSALEM
JERUSALEM
PASSION

Key verse. 3:35: God's children are our real family.

Personal application. Choose to resist or submit to God's will.

Key concepts. Sabbath »pp. 71, 664. Evil Spirit »p. 239. Demon »pp. 659, 895.

INSIGHT

Would, not could! (3:2) How significant that Jesus' enemies knew He could heal if He wished to. Faith in Jesus isn't just a matter of knowing about Him. It is a matter of submitting to Him.

Doing good on the Sabbath (3:4). There are three traditional interpretations of Jesus' meaning. (1) Man must be concerned with relieving the distress of others. (2) God's will is best served by healing rather than plotting to kill, as the Pharisees were doing, v. 6. (3) Jesus is committed to destroying Satan's disfiguring works every day.

Rightly understood, no command of God prevents us from doing good to others by meeting crying needs.

Anger and distress (3:5). Jesus' opponents cared neither about worship or the crippled man. They were in the synagogue to find a new way to attack Jesus (v. 3). Jesus felt anger and deep distress.

But what insight the tenses of the Gk. verbs provide! "Anger" is aorist, viewing this emotion as a point of time, or moment. "Distress" is present, viewing this emotion as a continuing, pervasive thing. We may be momentarily angry at those who reject Christ and choose sin over righteousness. Yet our dominant emotion must be distress over the impact of their choice on them!

Testimony to Jesus (3:11-12). Only a saved sinner can really know who Jesus is—or tell others what Christ can do for them.

Apostle (3:14). The Gk. word means "one sent on a mission as an envoy." The word serves as a technical term identifying the twelve men Jesus chose to follow Him during the years of His earthly ministry and to lead the church after His resurrection. This special use is extended to include Paul in Acts and the epistles.

But "apostle" also is used in an extended way in Acts and the epistles, where it seems to be used of those who had an itinerant evangelistic ministry (i.e., missionaries) (cf. Acts 14:14; Rom. 16:7; 1 Cor. 12:28; 2 Cor. 11:13).

"Take charge" (3:21). The Gk. word (keatesai) means arrest when used elsewhere by Mark. How fascinating. Yet at times we too want to restrain God when we don't understand His current workings! At least His family's intention was motivated by concern for Jesus Himself.

The unforgivable sin (3:28-30). See »p. 614.

Clear implications (3:22-27). Jesus' stories make points that His acts should already have drawn inescapably. Jesus can't be in league with Satan, for He is destroying Satan's work. And Jesus must be more powerful than Satan. The refusal to see the clear implications of Jesus' miracles reveals that hardened, willful attitude which prevents anyone from receiving forgiveness.

Doing God's will. Here obeying is accepting Jesus' abundantly proven claims.

Outline
Place
Finder

GALILEE
TO JERUSALEM
JERUSALEM
PASSION

Chapter summary. Opposition to Jesus has developed despite His miracles of healing. So Christ turns to parables that reveal truth in a form that requires faith to accept and understand (4:1-2). The parable of the farmer sowing seed tells us that God's Word is sown in all the world. But only in those who truly accept it will it produce fruit (vv. 3-20). Three brief illustrations have a distinctive meaning here in Mark. Christ, the lamp, will not always be hidden (vv. 21-23). Till then, the more a person appropriates what Jesus says the more one will understand about Jesus (v. 24), while failure to respond to Jesus now will mean the loss of all spiritual insight (v. 25).

The next parable is unique to Mark: the image of growing seed is Jesus' promise that the "underground" growth of His kingdom will result in a glorious harvest at history's end (vv. 26-29). A last parable, concerning a mustard seed, affirms that despite seemingly insignificant inauguration, Christ's kingdom will ultimately prove glorious and great (vv. 30-34). As Christ calms a storm at sea it is abundantly clear that it is wise to trust Him, however little we may understand (vv. 35-41).

Key verse. 4:11: Faith grasps what unbelief cannot see.

Personal application. Think deeply about what Jesus says.

Key concepts. Parable »p. 615. Kingdom »p. 380. Miracle »p. 679.

INSIGHT

Ears to hear (4:9). One Gk. scholar paraphrased this saying, "Think this one out for yourself, if you can."

Secrets of the kingdom (4:11). The Gk. word *mysterion* indicates something now revealed that has been hidden. Their truths are hidden in the open; those hardened in unbelief will never grasp their implications.

Parables (4:11). One possible meaning of the Gk. word and its Heb. antecedent is "riddle." This is a good way to translate "parable" here.

"So that" (4:12). Why would Jesus conceal truths about His kingdom? The best answer is one that emphasizes grace. The determined unbeliever would not understand what Jesus was saying and thus could not be held responsible for rejecting it.

Sovereignty and human responsibility (4:14-20). We cannot excuse our failures to respond to God by claiming that a sovereign God should have made us respond. God gives us freedom. He expects us to use it to respond when He speaks today.

Anxiety, "the worries of this life" (4:19). The Gk. word originally meant "to care," or "to be concerned about." Its usage in Scripture makes it clear that anxiety is often legitimate, as commendable concern (cf. 1 Cor. 7:33; 12:25-26). Here in Mark Christ is simply stating a fact of life. In this world there are necessary concerns

we must attend to. Still, a focus on even legitimate concerns can be carried too far. This is the point of Jesus' teaching in Matt. 6:25-34 and Luke 12:22-34. Ultimately we must commit ourselves to God and put Him first, trusting Him to meet our needs.

Context determines (4:21-25). Each of the three brief sayings in these verses is found in other Gospels—with different applications. Such proverbs were undoubtedly used frequently by Jesus to make differing points, depending on the context in which they were used. Here the context is riddles focused on the nature of His kingdom.

"The" lamp (4:21). In Gk. the word for lamp has a definite article, "the" with it, suggesting that the lamp represents Jesus. His essential nature is currently "hidden," but is "meant to be disclosed." One day His glory will be seen by all.

The mustard seed (4:31). Some have attacked Jesus' credibility here, saying that if Christ were God He would know a mustard seed is not the smallest of seeds. But Jesus simply uses the smallest seeds with which His listeners are familiar. Don't despise the day of small things. Something great is on the way!

Jesus' power (4:35-41). Isn't it wise to trust the Man who can still the raging storm?

Chapter summary. Evidence of Christ's mastery over nature (4:35-41) is followed by an incident which demonstrates His mastery over supernatural forces. In the non-Jewish district of Gerasa Christ expels demons from a wild man and sends them into a herd of pigs (5:1-13). Fearful of such power, the people beg Him to leave (vv. 14-20). Back in Jewish territory Christ is called by a desperate father to heal a dying teenage girl. On the way He is touched by a woman crippled by chronic menstrual flow — and she is healed! (vv. 21-33) This miracle performed for a woman who had a deep faith in Jesus (v. 34) may have strengthened the faith of the father. When a messenger comes to tell him his daughter has died, Jesus encourages him to "just believe." He then goes and raises the girl from the dead (vv. 35-43).

Outline
Place
Finder

GALILEE
TO JERUSALEM
JERUSALEM
PASSION

Mark's swift sequence of miracle upon miracle, each underlining another aspect of Christ's authority, demonstrates unmistakably that Jesus is the Son of God.

Key verse. 5:34: Mark emphasizes the role of faith.

Personal application. Faith enables us to experience God's power.

Key concepts. Demons »pp. 659, 895. Healing »pp. 412, 611, 784.

INSIGHT

"**Gerasenes**" **(5:1).** This region on the eastern side of the lake was mostly populated by Gentiles. The district extended some 30 miles from the city of Gerasa to the shore.

"**Fell on his knees**" **(5:6).** This was no act of worship, contra the KJV, but a forced recognition by the evil spirits in the man of Jesus' superiority. Paul reminds us that when Jesus returns, every knee will bow and every tongue confess that Jesus Christ is Lord (Phil. 2:10-11). Human beings can bow in faith and worship now. Or, like the evil spirit in this story, be forced to their knees when Jesus returns.

"**Legion**" **(5:9).** A Roman legion had 6,000 men.

Send us among the pigs (5:12-13). What is the significance of sending the demons into the pigs? Perhaps to demonstrate that the man had truly been demon-possessed and that the demons who tormented him were gone. Perhaps too to make it very clear that traffic with demons is dangerous, for these evil supernatural beings are bent on destruction.

Fear (5:14-15). How strange! Human beings often fear the power of God that is able to deliver, but not the power of the evil that enslaves us.

Materialism (5:16-17). It seems the financial loss involved in the destruction of the herd of pigs weighed more heavily in the Gerasenes' balances than the deliverance of the demon-possessed man. No one who puts possessions before people will ever be comfortable around Jesus.

Go . . . and tell (5:18-20). It would be wonderful to be with Jesus. But we have a mission here.

Synagogue ruler (5:22). This was an important lay position, involving maintenance of the building and overseeing worship.

Suffered a great deal under many doctors (5:26). It's perhaps humorous that Luke, a physician himself, leaves out these details (Luke 8:43).

Your faith has healed you (5:34). Here, as in other passages, Mark emphasizes the role of faith in benefiting from Jesus' wonder-working powers.

This does not mean that faith guarantees healing or that healing cannot take place apart from faith. Note that there is no mention of faith in the story of the deliverance of the demon-possessed man, just above. What faith does do is cause us to appeal to Jesus and to rely on Him. It's faith that brings us to Jesus. It's Jesus who works wonders in our lives.

They laughed at Him (5:37-43). Jesus refused to treat the death of the girl as final. The "laugh" here is ridicule, for in everyone's mind death was final. What a lesson for us. With Jesus there is always hope. "Too late" is not to be a part of the Christian's vocabulary, for God is able to redeem even our hopeless situations.

Outline
Place
Finder

GALILEE
TO JERUSALEM
JERUSALEM
PASSION

Chapter summary. When Jesus comes home to Nazareth, now as a visiting Rabbi, His neighbors show bitter resentment. Who does Jesus think He is, anyway? Their unbelief is a barrier that keeps Him from performing miracles there (6:1-6). But Jesus must reach as many in Israel as possible and so commissions the Twelve to go preach and heal (vv. 7-13). Word about Jesus permeated the little land, leading to widespread speculation about who He is (vv. 14-16). Mention of Herod's theory that Jesus is John the Baptist raised from the dead leads to a digression, as Mark relates the story of John's execution (vv. 17-29). This story told, Mark returns to his theme and tells of Jesus' miracles of feeding the 5,000 (vv. 30-44), of walking on the stormy sea of Galilee (vv. 45-53), and continued healings of many (vv. 54-56). The citizen of Nazareth, like many today, could not see the obvious. Jesus is the Son of God.

Key verse. 6:34: If we really care, we teach.

Personal application. Use what you have and let Jesus multiply it.

Key concepts. Prophet »p. 131. Apostle »p. 635. Miracles »p. 57.

INSIGHT

Illustration: *Carpenter's tools of the 1st century. Well-worn tools of Jesus' earthly trade like these probably hung in His old home in Nazareth.*
How hard it is even today to see the spirituality of "ordinary" people.

"Mary's Son"? (6:3) Persons were identified by their father even after his death. This may be a reference to Jesus' birth before Mary and Joseph's marriage was complete.
Brothers (6:3). These are children of Mary and Joseph. James became a leader in the Jerusalem church (Acts 12:17; 15:13; Gal. 2:9, 12) and wrote the N.T. book bearing his name.
By twos (6:7). Official representatives of the Sanhedrin traveled by twos, to corroborate each other's testimony in accord with Deuteronomy 17:6.
"Herod" (6:14). The person mentioned here is Antipas, Herod the Great's son. He was tetrarch, so the title "king" here is a courtesy title. His theory about Jesus reflects the guilt and fear he

rightly felt over ordering John's execution.
"Up to half my kingdom" (6:23). The phrase is not to be taken literally, but was intended to express an intent to be generous.
Feeding the 5,000 (6:30-42). The importance of this story is shown in its careful introduction and in the fact that twice Jesus refers back to it (6:52; 8:17-21). Why so important? It illustrates the compassion of Jesus for the hungry. It drives home the responsibility of Jesus' disciples not only to care, but also to act (cf. v. 37). And it encourages us to realize that however limited our resources, Christ can multiply them if we commit what we have to His service and that of others.
Jesus walks on the waters (6:45-51). The details are many. It happened in midlake, during the fourth watch—by Roman reckoning, 3-6 A.M. And it further confirmed the disciples' faith. How precious are the private miracles we experience.

Chapter summary. Mark now deals with the religious leaders who evaluated Christ's teaching and miracles—and rejected His claims. The religious focus on tradition and ritual (7:1-8) and in doing so "nullify the Word of God" (vv. 9-13). Jesus points out the hypocrisy of their external approach to religion, when the real issue is the state of one's heart (vv. 14-23). Traveling beyond Jewish territory, Jesus heals the daughter of a Gentile woman who appeals to Him. The juxtaposition of incidents underlines the hardness of the leaders of God's people. The men who lead Israel are blind, but even a pagan woman realizes who Jesus is (vv. 24-30). Finally, Jesus heals a deaf and dumb man in the same area. The Pharisees choose not to hear or acknowledge Jesus, but Christ will open the ears of Gentiles, and they will glorify God (vv. 31-37).

Outline
Place
Finder

GALILEE
TO JERUSALEM
JERUSALEM
PASSION

Key verse. 7:13: Appearing religious isn't being religious.

Personal application. Don't confuse ritual with true religion.

Key concepts. Clean, unclean »pp. 82, 617. Pharisees »pp. 625, 657. Hypocrite »p. 625. Tradition »p. 617. Heart »p. 737.

INSIGHT

From Jerusalem (7:1). These leaders came not to listen to Jesus, but to investigate Him!

Ceremonial washing (7:4). The various washings prescribed by tradition in 1st-century Judaism were not for sanitary but religious purposes. They involved symbolic cleansing from contamination by any association with not only a Gentile but with a possibly defiled coreligionist. The stress placed on such ceremonial washings is reflected in the fact that a major section of the Jewish Mishna, *Tohoroth*, ("cleanness"), is dedicated to it. Jesus viewed the preoccupation of Pharisees and teachers of the Law with such matters as a hypocritical concentration on externals.

Worship in vain (7:7). The Gk. word *maten* is used only here and in the parallel passage in Matt. 15:9. Its essential meaning is "purposeless."

There is no use at all in trying to worship a God who is concerned with the human heart by fiddling with externals.

"Corban" (7:10-11). Jesus mentions this concept to illustrate how traditional interpretations of Mosaic Law can in fact distort its intent. To declare something "corban" was to legally dedicate something as a gift to God, and so legally exclude one's parents from any assistance derived from it. Of special note is that the one who declared something "corban" did not even have to actually give it to the temple! It was a legal fiction. Thus an interpretation of law was used to avoid the clear intent of God expressed in Scripture (cf. Ex. 20:12; 21:15).

"Nullify" (7:13). The Gk. word here, *akyroo*, means to make void or legally cancel. However we may interpret Scripture, we cannot do so in any way that it makes void any clearly expressed intent of God.

To the crowd (7:14). How often in church history have spiritual leaders been out of touch with God and revival been a lay movement! Here the leaders will not listen, so Jesus speaks to the crowd.

Evil from within (7:17-23). How foolish to make religion a matter of any externals, when the problem lies in the human heart. To be acceptable to God, we must be cleansed from within.

"Lord" (7:28). This is the only time in Mark's Gospel that Jesus is called "Lord." And this by a Gentile woman!

"Dogs"? (7:24-30) The story troubles many. Why is this woman compared to puppies (*kynarioi*) under the family table? Jesus' point is that anyone's first concern is to feed his family—and the Jews have been God's chosen people, His special family. The woman is not offended, but delighted. If she is this close to God, then she has a right to the crumbs! How different her attitude is from that of the Pharisees, who are unwilling to say "Lord," or sit down at the table of truth Jesus spreads!

Deaf and dumb (7:31-37). This miracle too is performed in Gentile territory. The Jewish leaders refuse to hear what Jesus says. He will open the ears of strangers, and their loosened tongues will sing His praise.

Outline
Place
Finder

GALILEE
TO JERUSALEM
JERUSALEM
PASSION

Chapter summary. Still in Galilee, Jesus provides food for a crowd of 4,000. Strikingly, the disciples fail to remember His earlier miracle and wonder where they will ever find the food (8:1-10). But their lapse of memory is less serious than the settled skepticism of the Pharisees (vv. 11-13). Jesus warns His disciples against the yeast (teaching) of the Pharisees, but His disciples still fail to understand (vv. 14-21). There follows an unusual miracle of healing that is neither instantaneous nor accomplished by a spoken word (vv. 22-26). Yet whatever method Jesus chooses to use, His works are miraculous. But faith has been created only in the hearts of His disciples (vv. 27-30), and even they question Jesus' announcement that He must soon die (vv. 31-33). To follow Jesus we must surrender our own wills and willingly submit to God's will. Only in this way will those who believe find the new life Christ comes to bring (vv. 34-38).

Key verse. 8:21: Ponder the meanings of Jesus' works.

Personal application. Let's not live on the surface of faith.

Key concepts. Pharisee »p. 625. Disciple »p. 657. Healing »p. 611. Christ »p. 646. Satan »pp. 501, 655. Our cross »p. 618.

INSIGHT

Insight, or not? (8:4) Some have suggested this was an insightful statement on the part of the disciples, who did not expect Jesus to meet every need by performing a miracle. Certainly we should have this kind of insight ourselves. In context it is more likely that the disciples spoke out of doubt, failing to remember and apply their earlier experience of Christ's power (cf. 6:30-44). After all, even mature believers all too often fail to remember what the Lord has done in their lives.

"Satisfied" (8:8). Jesus always provides enough to meet our needs—with plenty left over.

Even more abundant provision (8:8). It may seem that after this miracle there was less bread left over than after the first. Not at all! In Mark 6 the word for basket is *kophinos*, a wicker container in which travelers usually carried food. Here, though, the basket is a *spyris*, a storage basket large enough so that Paul could sit in it when being let down over the wall of Damascus (Acts 9:25).

"A sign" (8:11). Jesus' miracles are called *dynameis*, works of power. The Pharisees were not satisfied with evidence of Jesus' power, although it was unmistakable. They asked for a *semeion*, a sign, from heaven. They were not sincere but asked only to test and trouble Him. When a sign was at last given, in the Resurrection, they still did not believe. Faith doesn't rest on miracles. Faith rests on recognizing God's Word, and God's Son.

"This generation" (8:12). The Pharisees asked for a sign. But this phrase includes the whole Jewish community of Christ's day. The evidence already given was conclusive. Greater proofs would serve no purpose.

An unusual miracle (8:22-26). A slow-working miracle using mud as an agency rather than just the spoken word? Why? John Calvin suggested that it underlines Jesus' freedom—and reminds us not to suppose that the Lord must act and in ways that we expect, or have experienced Him to work before.

"You are the Christ" (8:29). Every true believer will join Peter in this confession.

Peter rebuked Him (8:31-32). How contradictory. We cannot affirm Jesus as Christ and then challenge His choices! He is either God, and we submit to Him, or He is not, and we may go our own way.

"Deny" (8:34). The Gk. words are *arneomai* and *aparneomai*. In a situation where a person makes a decision, "deny" means "reject." But when a person has a strong personal faith in Jesus, it means unfaithfulness to or abandoning the relationship.

What does it mean here to "deny yourself"? It means to decisively reject the motives and desires that well up from our sin nature, and choose instead to follow Jesus completely. When we take daily steps of obedience we gradually become the new person that Christ died for us to become.

Chapter summary. Jesus has announced His coming death (8:31-38). Now He makes another prediction. Some standing with Him will see God's kingdom "come with power" (9:1). Just six days later three of His disciples witness a transformation of Christ, a stunning display of His glory (vv. 2-13). Back in the valley, Jesus drives an evil spirit from a boy His disciples had been unable to help (vv. 14-29) and again predicts His death (vv. 30-32). His disciples seem totally unaware of the pain Jesus feels and fall into a dispute about which of them is "greatest" (vv. 33-37). Mark then reports a series of single-theme enigmatic statements made by Jesus, as the company travels toward Jerusalem and His crucifixion. The theme is that of relationship to Jesus' followers. Those who act in Christ's name are "for us" (vv. 38-40). Those who are hospitable to Jesus' followers will be rewarded (v. 41). Those who cause Christ's followers (His "little ones") to sin face terrible judgment (vv. 42-48). For Jesus' disciples must always maintain that uniqueness which offers hope to the world (vv. 49-50).

Outline
Place
Finder

GALILEE
TO JERUSALEM
JERUSALEM
PASSION

Key verse. 9:2: Jesus Himself is the kingdom's power.

Personal application. To reach the world Christians must live as family.

Key concepts. Kingdom »pp. 380, 443. Evil spirit »p. 239. Prayer »p. 609. Belief »p. 35. Sin »p. 362.

INSIGHT

"Some" (9:1-4). Three of the Twelve saw the kingdom "come with power"—in the transformed Jesus, accompanied by Elijah and Moses who represented resurrected O.T. saints.

"Rabbi" (9:5). This title of respect was used in N.T. times by ordinary folk when addressing someone who was a recognized religious authority, an expert in O.T. Law.

"Risen from the dead" (9:9). Jesus' death and resurrection now becomes a prominent theme (cf. 8:31-32; 9:12-13, 31-32; 10:32-34). Mark emphasizes the disciples' total confusion and failure to understand what Jesus was saying. Like so much biblical prophecy, its meaning could be fully understood only after it was fulfilled.

Elijah comes first (9:12-13). »p. 613.

"O unbelieving generation" (9:19). Most agree Jesus is referring to His disciples and is both disappointed and disturbed about their lack of both faith and understanding. Yet how patient Jesus was with them! As He is patient with us, even in our own sluggish faith.

"Help me overcome my unbelief" (9:24). Faith has two aspects: objective and subjective. Objectively our faith is in Jesus, and He is unshakable. Subjectively our faith is often mixed with hesitancy and doubt. The way to overcome uncertainty is to remember that what makes faith valid is not its subjective strength, but the trustworthiness of its object. We can confidently affirm this truth: "I can't, but Jesus can."

"Only by prayer" (9:29). We can never take for granted any authority God has given us (cf. 6:67). Any ministry must be performed in total reliance on the Lord.

"Afraid to ask" (9:32). We too may be ashamed at times of our lack of understanding. But we never need be afraid to ask God for insight.

Greatness (9:34). Greatness in Christ's kingdom is a matter of sacrifice, not superiority.

Welcoming a little child (9:36). Greatness involves caring about people who can do nothing to repay you. It's hardly praiseworthy to help your boss because you want a raise, or a relative from whom you hope to inherit. Instead, welcome little children, who have nothing to give but gratitude.

If your eye offends (9:42-48). The thrust of this saying is clear. Entering life is so important that even the most radical means should be taken to avoid whatever would keep a person out.

The images of mutilation should be understood to symbolize spiritual surgery. For instance, in Scripture the "eye" stands for "sight," that is spiritual perception (cf. Matt. 6:22-23; Eph. 1:18).

Outline
Place
Finder

GALILEE
TO JERUSALEM
JERUSALEM
PASSION

Chapter summary. As Jesus travels toward Jerusalem and His crucifixion He is met by a delegation of Pharisees intent on tripping Christ up on a point of law. He answers the divorce question they pose (10:1-12), but again emphasizes the fact that His kingdom must be approached in a childlike, rather than legalistic, way (vv. 13-16). Christ is then approached by an honest seeker, a young man intent on winning eternal life. But when challenged to give up his wealth, the man refuses, showing clearly that riches, not Christ, exercise lordship in his life (vv. 17-31). Jesus again predicts His death (vv. 32-34), but the disciples remain insensitive. James and John actually lobby for the two chief places in Christ's coming kingdom, still unaware that greatness in Christ's kingdom is expressed in service to others (vv. 35-45). Jesus illustrates the pathway of service when He stops on His way to the cross to heal a man who is blind (vv. 46-52).

Key verse. 10:45: Let Jesus be your example.

Personal application. Be sensitive to the needs of others.

Key concepts. Pharisee »p. 625. Law »pp. 123, 606. Adultery »p. 64. Wealth »p. 125. Rewards »p. 759. Servanthood »p. 622. Healing »p. 611.

INSIGHT

Hardness of heart (10:5-9). Divorce is lawful, but is an accomodation to human weakness. God permitted divorce because sin would so distort some marriages that it was better for the relationship to be dissolved. This did not, of course, reflect God's intent in establishing marriage, so in one sense criticism of Herod misses the point. Any divorce is evidence of falling short of God's idea and thus involves sin.

Male adultery (10:10-12). The rabbis held a man could not commit adultery against his wife. Jesus contradicts this view and thus raises the status of women. A man is as obligated to be faithful to his wife as she is to him.

Children unimportant? (10:13-16) When Jesus' disciples "rebuked" parents who tried to bring their little children to Jesus, Christ was "indignant." Note that the Pharisees had had easy access to Jesus! How foolish when we place our emphasis on the important persons of this world and ignore the little ones who are much more important to the Lord!

The rich young man (10:17). He clearly took a works/righteousness approach to salvation, wanting to earn his way to heaven by "doing." How strange seeing "inherit" and "do" in the same sentence.

All one can do to "inherit" is be born—again.

"Good" (10:18). Greek has two words for "good," both of which are used in the N.T. One (*agathos*) sees the good as useful or beneficial and is a moral term. The other (*kalos*) tends to stress the aesthetically pleasing aspect and thus suggests "beautiful." In an ultimate sense, only God is truly good. This underlies the question Jesus posed. Is the young man acknowledging Jesus as God, or only suggesting he is "good" in a comparative sense?

His face fell (10:22). There is nothing in riches themselves to give anyone joy.

Amazement (10:24-26). Popular theology twisted the O.T.'s teaching that God would bless the obedient with wealth and assumed that the mere possession of wealth was evidence of closeness to God. Besides, a man with wealth could give alms and gifts to the temple, offer multiplied sacrifices, and thus commend himself to God. Jesus' disciples were confused when Christ warned that the rich, who tend to rely on their riches, have great difficulty entering God's kingdom. The poor, who abandon reliance on their own efforts to throw themselves on God's mercy, are much better off.

We who have left everything (10:28-31). We cannot out give God. Whatever we give up for His sake, we will receive back multiplied. Even what we surrender is family, the relationships we build in God's new community will be better.

Chapter summary. Three themes dominate in chapters 11–13. There is Christ's initial entry into the city, His conflict with the religious leaders, and instruction given His disciples. It all begins with Christ's triumphal entry into the city at the time of the Passover festival (11:1-11). Returning the next day He curses a fruitless fig tree (vv. 12-14) and then drives merchants from the courts of a temple where equally fruitless worship is conducted (vv. 15-19). The next day the fig tree has withered away (vv. 20-21), giving Jesus an occasion to make several important comments on faith and prayer (vv. 22-25).

Arriving at the temple, Jesus is confronted by a delegation of religious authorities who challenge His right to have driven out the money changers. When Jesus poses His own question, these men who claim to speak for God are afraid to answer (vv. 26-32). Disdainful, Jesus dismisses them and turns away (v. 33).

Outline
Place
Finder

GALILEE
TO JERUSALEM
JERUSALEM
PASSION

Key verse. 11:9: Don't just recognize Him. Commit to Him.

Personal application. Real relationship with God produces fruit.

Key concept. Jerusalem »p. 205. Temple »p. 283. Faith »pp. 35, 458.

INSIGHT

Who did they welcome? (11:1-11) The very cries of praise contain an element of denial. The crowds were excited at the prospect of the "coming kingdom of our father David." They expected a Messiah who would reestablish the earthly glory known during David's reign 1,000 years before (cf. Messiah »p. 432; Future kingdom »p. 443). It's always a mistake to welcome Jesus because we think He is going to do something we want. We must welcome Jesus as Lord and gladly submit to what He wants.

"Buying and selling" (11:12-17). One modern Jewish scholar sees Jesus' attack as a repudiation of the O.T. sacrificial system, as animals are what was being bought and sold. But the text's emphasis is on "den of robbers." Others see it as an attack on sharp practices by which the merchants, in collusion with the priests, robbed pilgrims coming to the temple to worship. But perhaps the linkage of quotes from Isa. 56:7 and Jer. 7:11 indicates the distortion of O.T. faith that the trade in sacrificial animals represented. This had in effect robbed Gentiles of their privilege of approaching God in the outer court, now cluttered with hawksters and tradesmen.

Let's do nothing to hinder others from coming to the Lord.

"I tell you the truth" (11:23). This phrase is often used by Jesus to emphasize the importance of what He is about to say.

Faith, prayer, and forgiveness (11:24-25). The three are linked, for only the firm conviction

Illustration (11:12-14, 20-25). *Fig trees near Jerusalem were fully leafed out by March or April, but had no fruit till June. Why did Jesus curse this tree? He was acting out a parable. The tree represented Israel, in full leaf but fruitless (cf. Hosea 9:10; Nahum 3:12; Zech. 10:2). The cursing of the tree represents the withering away of the nation which rejected its Messiah.*

that God can remove all obstacles moves us to prayer, while a spirit of forgiveness—accepted, and extended to others—assures us of our welcome before God's throne. Faith works miracles, not because it gives us confidence in ourselves, but because it moves us to trust all to God.

"We don't know" (11:27-33). Never claim to be a leader unless you are willing to make a decision and take a stand.

Outline
Place
Finder

GALILEE
TO JERUSALEM
JERUSALEM
PASSION

Chapter summary. Jesus' confrontation with the religious authorities continues. He tells a story that is clearly directed against them but, unable to arrest Him, they skulk away (12:1-17). Then the Sadducees, members of a religious party that denies the supernatural, try to ridicule Christ's affirmation of the resurrection (vv. 18-23). They fail utterly, as Jesus shows, to understand the Scriptures they supposedly honor (vv. 24-27). One teacher of the Law, with more insight and openness than the others, asks Jesus about the most important of the commandments. Jesus' answer, and the man's response, reminds us that not all teachers of Scripture in first-century Judaism were like the authorities who hated the Lord (vv. 28-34). Jesus shows up these so-called "teachers of the Law" and warns the common people against them. They mask their greed in piety and defraud the very widows whose commitment the Lord honors (vv. 35-44). What a stunning turnaround for Jesus to call us to honor the poor and scorn the rich!

Key verse. 12:12: Exposure always brings some reaction.

Personal application. The godly person when confronted with his or her sins acknowledges them—and is forgiven.

Key concepts. Parable »p. 166. Taxes »p. 624. Resurrection »p. 522. Law »pp. 120, 145, 606. Love »p. 126. Messiah ("Christ") »p. 432.

INSIGHT

"Them" (12:1). The ones Jesus spoke to surely included His adversaries, for v. 12 describes their reaction. Confrontation always arouses some response. Our goal in confrontation should be to provoke repentance. But even if the other chooses not to repent, it is still important to confront.

What then will the owner do? (12:9) No one who rejects the Son is safe from retribution. For all who reject are like the religious leaders of Christ's day, unwilling to step down and acknowledge Jesus' lordship.

"He will come and kill those tenants" (12:9). This warning was literally fulfilled in A.D. 70 when the Romans destroyed Jerusalem and decimated her population. Prophets warned the early Christian community, which moved en masse from the city before disaster struck.

Jesus, our foundation (12:10-11). The significance of this quote is shown by allusions to it in Acts 4:11 and 1 Peter 2:7, as well as Ps. 118:22.

Jesus, the rejected stone, is the key to the entire structure God has been building throughout history. Ignore or displace Jesus, and no religious faith will stand.

Kill with words (12:13-17). The test question was intended to at least discredit Jesus and at most to provide a basis on which He might be accused of treason to the Roman government. Jesus' classic answer establishes a basic princi-

ple of Christian experience. We are to live according to civil law as long as that law does not directly conflict with divine law. There is another principle too. We are not to look for conflict between human law and divine unless conflict is obvious.

"The book of Moses" (12:18-27). The Sadducees denied the authority not only of oral tradition, but also of every O.T. writing other than the five books of Moses. It is significant then that Christ quotes from Ex. 3:6, a book they held was authoritative, to prove that the believing dead actually live—and will be raised again.

We learn three lessons from this incident. (1) Jesus confirms the full inspiration and authority of the O.T. Scriptures, even to the tense of a verb. (2) Death is not the end for human beings. And (3) it profits us nothing to say we believe the Bible if we are ignorant of its teachings.

On the "greatest commandment" (12:29-31), see the parallel passage in Matt. 22 »p. 624.

Widows and wealth (12:38-44). Jesus contrasts the greed of the wealthy, who give amounts that are meaningless to them, with the generosity of a widow who gives all she has. There is even more implied. The wealthy care nothing for people, but only for what they can extract from them. God puts people first and values even the poor.

Chapter summary. Jesus' disciples are impressed by the magnificent temple enhanced in Herod the Great's 40-year building program. Jesus looks ahead and sees the temple mount scoured and empty (13:1-2). The prediction stimulates common questions: When? And, how will we know? (vv. 3-4) Christ's answer emphasizes the turmoil the world will know before He comes (vv. 5-8) and the dangers to be faced by His followers (vv. 9-13). As to the beginning of the end, that is to be marked by an act of the Antichrist, setting up an abomination on the temple mount. The period this act introduces is the "great tribulation" foretold by the Old Testament's prophets, and at the end the Son of Man will return visibly to gather the elect and punish the reprobate (vv. 14-27). The generation then 'iving will survive to see God act and Christ return (vv. 28-31). Jesus' final words are the ones we should study most carefully. He tells us to be constantly alert to serve Him while we are waiting, for He may return at any time and yearns to find us ready to greet Him (vv. 32-37).

Outline
Place
Finder

GALILEE
TO JERUSALEM
JERUSALEM
PASSION

Key verse. 13:33: Hidden revelations.

Personal application. We need not be concerned about when Christ returns, but about how to live until then.

Key concepts. Temple »p. 283. Tribulation »p. 626. Judgment »p. 372. Second Coming »p. 581.

INSIGHT

Jesus is Lord. What does Christ's lordship mean in a practical way? It means on one hand that He has the right to guide and direct us and to claim our full allegiance. But here Mark shows us a Jesus who is Lord of history. He speaks as confidently about the future as He does the past. Tomorrow is as real to Him as today. Nothing lies ahead of us that will surprise our Lord—or that He has not already prepared for.

The temple. The temple Herod beautified and expanded covered approximately one sixth of the entire city of Jerusalem! No wonder the disciples were impressed. Yet no material structure can outlast the passage of time. Only human beings, whose conscious existence persists after physical death, are eternal and thus of infinite value.

Don't worry beforehand (13:11). Pagans did worry—and hired orators to defend them when government officials put them on trial. What a difference from the attitude Jesus commends. God will give His followers what they need to say, when the need arises.

"The abomination that causes desolation" (13:14). This act is described in Dan. 9:27, 11:31, and 12:11. A Satan-empowered ruler will emerge and desecrate the temple site with an idolatrous image of himself. Liberal commentators identify the sacrifice of a pig on the temple altar by Antiochus Epiphanes in 167 B.C. as the fulfillment of Daniel's prophecy. But Christ speaks of it as yet ahead. It is perhaps best to apply the rule of multiple fulfillment and see that act as a partial fulfillment of an event which lies ahead. We can be confident of one thing. Prophecies that have not yet been fulfilled most surely will be!

"The Son of Man" (13:26). In most usages this phrase identifies Jesus as a true human being. When Christ uses it of Himself He is emphasizing His solidarity with us. But here, in the context of prophecy, the phrase takes on the meaning given it in Dan. 7:13-14. Jesus is the human being whom Daniel saw. And Jesus will fulfill all of Daniel's prophecies about history's end when He returns.

Unknown (13:32-37). If all Christians spent as much time concentrating on how to live for Jesus until He returns as some do drawing charts and speculating on how each revealed detail of the future fits together, the church would be a much more loving and serving institution.

Outline
Place
Finder

GALILEE
TO JERUSALEM
JERUSALEM
PASSION

Chapter summary. Mark sketches two scenes. In Jerusalem the religious leaders plot to kill Jesus (14:1-2), while in Bethany a woman pours her life savings, invested in expensive perfume, over His head (vv. 3-9). We must give Jesus all or be His enemy. It is at this point Judas makes his fateful decision to betray the Lord (vv. 10-11). A few days later Jesus eats the Passover supper with His disciples (vv. 12-16). He announces that one of the Twelve will betray Him (vv. 17-21). Other Gospels report that Judas slips away before Christ shares bread and wine, instituting what we celebrate as the Lord's Supper (vv. 22-26). As the supper ends Jesus predicts a self-confident Peter will deny Him (vv. 27-31) and leads the eleven to Gethsemane where He prays (vv. 32-42) before being arrested (vv. 43-52). Jesus is taken to the house of the high priest, where He states that He is "the Christ, the Son of the Blessed One," and is charged with blasphemy (vv. 53-65). Outside, a fearful Peter does deny his Lord, and realizing what he has done breaks down and weeps bitterly (vv. 66-72).

Key verse. 14:24: This death has meaning.

Personal application. Mark demands that we take sides.

Key concepts. Passover »p. 59. Disciple »p. 657. New Covenant »p. 466. Lord's Supper »p. 767. Deny »p. 612.

INSIGHT

"Expensive perfume" (14:3). Life savings were often invested in jars of such ointments that maintained or grew in value.

Mary's act (14:3-9). John 12:3 identifies the woman as Mary. Mark emphasizes the disciple's rebuke (*embrimaomai*, expression of violent displeasure). Jesus praised Mary's sensitivity. She alone was aware of the sense of doom that weighed Jesus down, and her act was prophetic. May we be as sensitive to Christ as Mary was.

"Money" (14:10-11). John describes Judas as most indignant at the "waste" of perfume — because he stole from the band's treasury and thought of his lost profits. How Mary and Judas differed. One was concerned with Jesus, one with money. No one can serve both Christ and a passion for personal gain.

One who dips the bread (14:20). In the Middle East eating together established a symbolic bond of mutual trust and commitment.

"Just as it is written" (14:21). History's greatest miscarriage of justice was part of God's plan. Judas' betrayal was perhaps history's greatest sin. The good God worked through it illustrates that He is able to redeem every situation, bringing His good out of the worst that men do.

Peter's promise (14:27-31). We commend Peter's commitment to Jesus. It was very real, and his promise not to "fall away" was utterly sincere. But Peter's subsequent failure reminds us how vulnerable and weak we all are. Only moment by moment reliance on Christ can protect us. If we begin to think we can stand, we will surely fall.

"Keep watch" (14:34). Jesus did not want the disciples to be on guard against the coming crowd, but to be there for Him in His moments of overwhelming sorrow.

"This cup" (14:36). In O.T. and N.T. the word "cup" when used figuratively focuses on an experience someone is to undergo. Thus the "cup of God's wrath" is an image of judgment to be experienced by the wicked (Rev. 14:10). What was Jesus' cup? It was the experience of suffering that the Father Himself poured out for the Son. Although dreadful, it led directly to resurrection and joy — for Him, and for us as well.

"A young man" (14:51). Commentators agree that Mark is speaking of himself in this verse.

Jesus on trial (14:53-65). For the order of Jesus' trials, see »p. 627.

"The Christ" (14:61-62). The Gk. word "Christ" is a translation of the Heb. "Messiah." Both mean "anointed" and are titles of the deliverer God promises Israel through the O.T. prophets. In the 1st century the Jews understood "son of God" in a messianic sense, not in the N.T. sense of affirmation of Jesus' essential deity.

Chapter summary. Events now move swiftly. Jesus is taken to Pilate, who gives in to the pressure applied by Jewish leaders and orders Christ's crucifixion (15:1-15). Jesus is beaten and mocked (vv. 16-20). He falls on the way to Golgotha and a pilgrim is forced to carry Jesus' cross (v. 21). At Golgotha He is crucified and ridiculed by His enemies (vv. 22-32). With the cross shrouded in a supernatural darkness, Jesus utters His last cry and dies (vv. 33-41). Jesus is buried quickly in a nearby tomb, which is then closed (vv. 42-47). It seemed to all, friend and foe alike, that Jesus' death was the end.

Outline
Place
Finder

GALILEE
TO JERUSALEM
JERUSALEM
PASSION

Key verse. 15:34: Forsaken, for us.

Personal application. He died for us; we live for Him.

INSIGHT

Illustration. *The Romans reserved crucifixion for criminals and slaves. The cross (stauros) was usually a pole fixed in the ground with a detached crossbar. Here Jesus is shown carrying the crossbar to the execution ground, and nailed to the assembled t-shaped instrument.*

Pilate's motives. See John 18 »p. 695.
Jesus is mocked (15:16-20). The sadistic ridicule of Jesus was preceded by a flogging (John 19:1-3). This entailed severe loss of blood. The brutal treatment meted out to Jesus was no more than a pastime for the soldiers, auxiliaries recruited from non-Jews across the empire. Their heartlessness illustrates how low human beings can sink—and the utter necessity of Christ's death to rescue humanity from the morass of sin.
Forced to carry the cross (15:21). Simon had to be forced, because touching the cross, an instrument of death, would make him ceremonially unclean and unable to participate in the

important religious festival for which he came "in from the country." Romans 16:13 may suggest he and his sons later became Christians. How differently he must have felt about bearing something of Jesus' awful burden then!
Crucifixion (15:24). Crucifixion caused the victim extreme pain. Cicero, the Roman senator and philosopher, called it "the cruelest and most hideous punishment possible."
"Two robbers" (15:27). These *lestas* were rebels against Roman rule, terrorists in modern terms. What a contrast between Jesus, the Man of peace, and the men of violence on either side.
The temple veil (15:38). The veil separated all from the holiest place in the temple, where God's presence dwelt. Its tearing from top to bottom symbolized the free access to God that Christ's death won for believers (cf. Heb. 10:19-22).
"The Son of God" (15:39). Mark's story of Jesus' life is enclosed by this affirmation as by bold quotation marks (cf. 1:1).

Outline
Place
Finder

GALILEE
TO JERUSALEM
JERUSALEM
PASSION

Chapter summary. Mark picks up the story three days later. The Sabbath past, women intending to wrap Jesus' body in spices arrive at the tomb only to find an angel — and Jesus gone (16:1-8). In many ancient Greek manuscripts, Mark's Gospel ends here. But other manuscripts add 11 more verses. These disputed verses tell of the disciples' continuing doubt (vv. 9-13), which is resolved only when Jesus appears personally to the eleven and rebukes their lack of faith (v. 14). This version ends with Christ's confirmation of the eleven as His envoys and His promise of special powers (vv. 15-18). After Jesus is taken up into heaven, the disciples do go out and preach everywhere, and God continues to work His wonders through them (vv. 19-20).

Key verse. 16:6: The tomb is empty. Christ is risen.

Personal application. Jesus lives to empower us too.

Key concepts. Resurrection »pp. 629, 737, 771. Baptize »p. 604.

INSIGHT

Resurrection. The resurrection of Jesus is the climax of each of the four Gospel accounts. The literal, bodily Resurrection of Jesus confirms His claim to deity and makes the meaning of Christ's death clear. Without the Resurrection, the story of Jesus is one of history's greatest tragedies.

With it, the story is one of triumph and the foundation of all our hopes.

Anointing the body (16:1). Jewish practice called for burial of a body on the day of death. No embalming was attempted. The oils used in anointing the dead, and the spices placed in the strips of cloth wrapped around the body, were intended to express devotion and to reduce the stench of decay. Because Jesus had died late on a day preceding the Sabbath, when no one could work or touch a dead body, this care of the corpse had been delayed.

Rolling away the stone (16:3). The women apparently knew nothing of the guard placed at the tomb. They worried about moving the heavy, circular stone, set in a slanted track so it could be rolled down to seal the tomb. They could only open it by rolling the stone up the slant with great difficulty.

"A young man" (16:4-5). Matthew 28:2 identifies this individual as an angel.

"He has risen" (16:6). There is only one adequate explanation for the empty tomb: that is that Jesus actually did rise from the dead. We have the testimony of prophecy that it would happen. We have the testimony of many witnesses that it did happen. We have the stunning transformation of the devastated and goalless disciples into a band of bold, confi-

dent evangelists, carrying the message of the Resurrection throughout the known world. And we have the experience of uncounted millions of Christians across the ages who have experienced Jesus' transforming touch in their lives.

"Trembling and bewildered" (16:8). The story of the Resurrection was no invention of calculating followers of a dead and disproven Messiah. No one was more surprised than Jesus' closest friends. The Resurrection remains a mystery, as this sudden ending of Mark's Gospel in most manuscripts emphasizes. But this mystery is the central reality of Christian faith!

Mark's extended ending (16:9-20). Greek manuscripts known to early church fathers didn't contain these verses. Even so, most of the Gk. manuscript's traditions do have the longer ending. In tracing these texts back, scholars believe the longer ending appeared in the first half of the 2nd century. A marked difference in vocabulary between the longer ending and the rest of Mark also suggests it was not part of the original work.

Some 73 of the 167 words in this ending are not used elsewhere in Mark. The style of writing also has been compared with Mark's style and found distinctly different. Finally, both the rebuke of the disciples by Jesus (16:14) and the emphasis on miraculous signs (16:17-18) has no parallel in Mark or in other accounts of Christ's post-resurrection dealings with His followers. Evidence from every line of research seems to suggest that these 11 verses were not part of Mark's original text.

Luke

Luke's writings are the most literary of the New Testament books, distinctive in the original for their fluid style and beauty. Luke is the only Gospel writer who wrote a sequel—Acts—which tells the story of the early church and its spread. Unlike the other Gospels, whose content can be traced back to eye-witness accounts of Jesus' life shared by His disciples Matthew, John, and Peter (the source of Mark's Gospel), Luke's account is developed through what we today call "investigative reporting." Luke tells us in his introduction (1:1-4) that his work is the result of careful research, that he has written an "orderly account," and that his purpose was to enable the reader "to know the certainty of the things you have been taught." It's most likely that Luke did the bulk of this research during the years Paul was held in Ceasarea awaiting trial (cf. Acts 23-27).

Like the other Gospel writers Luke has an audience in mind and shapes his material to stress themes of special interest to him and his readers. Most agree Luke is writing for the Hellenist—the person whose roots are in Greek culture, and whose ideal is *arete*, "excellence." Luke, ever mindful of Jesus' deity, still holds Him up as the ideal human being, who redefines excellence.

In Jesus, "excellence" is seen not as a personal superiority that devalues others, but a personal superiority expressed in concern for others. And the others Jesus values are those lightly dismissed by human societies: women, the poor, and the powerless. Jesus' reliance on prayer and on the Holy Spirit reveals mankind in its true relationship with the universe, dependent on a God who exists beyond us and yet loves us so much that He chooses to be fully involved in our human lives. All this makes Luke perhaps the warmest and most sensitive of the four Gospels and provides the most attractive of their portraits of Jesus Christ.

SPECIAL THEMES IN LUKE'S GOSPEL

Salvation for all. *Each Gospel is salvation history. Yet Luke takes pains to show us that salvation is for all, not just Israel. Luke speaks of Samaritans (9:51-54; 10:30-37; 17:16), Syrians (4:25-27), and Romans (7:2-10) who experienced the grace of God, and the Great Commission to preach the Gospel to all nations (24:47).*

Women are important. *Women, children, the poor, and the disreputable were lumped together in first-century society and viewed as unimportant. Yet Luke emphasizes the role of Mary, Elizabeth, and Anna in the birth stories. He tells of Mary and Martha (10:38-40), Mary Magdalene (8:2ff.). He shows Jesus' compassion for the widow of Nain (7:11ff.), a bent woman (13:11), the widow who gave all (21:1-4). And women are often featured in parables, like that of the lost coin (15:8ff.) and unjust judge (18:1ff.).*

The poor count. *Jesus came to preach the Gospel to the poor (4:18; 7:22). The blessing He has for them (6:20) stands in contrast with the woe He pronounces on the rich (6:24). Jesus was born poor (2:24) and lived among them most of His life. Luke's interest in this class is seen over and over, in verses like 1:53; 6:30; 14:11-14, 21-23; 16:19, and many others.*

WHERE THE ACTION TAKES PLACE

Physically, the story of Jesus is limited to the little land of Palestine. But Luke places Jesus' ministry in a distinctive social context. Luke shows us a Jesus who brings Good News to the despised of society, the victims of prejudice (the Samaritan), the discredited (Zaccheus, the tax collector), and the discriminated against (the woman, seen here searching for a coin lost from the dowry that protected her independence and sense of self-worth).

Date and Authorship. Well-established early tradition identifies Luke, the dear friend and physician who accompanied Paul on many missions, as author of both Luke and Acts. Both works were probably finished before the end of Paul's first Roman imprisonment, in A.D. 63. It seems likely that Paul's years in Caesarea awaiting trial (Acts 23–27) gave Luke the opportunity he needed to travel in Judea and Galilee and interview those whose personal stories and eyewitness accounts he relies on for his information about Jesus' life.

THEOLOGICAL OUTLINE OF LUKE

CONTENT OUTLINE OF LUKE

Introduction (1:1-4)
I. Jesus' Birth (1:5–2:52)
   A. Two Births Foretold (1:5-80)
   B. Jesus' Birth (2:1-7)
   C. The Shepherds (2:8-20)
   D. Temple Presentation (2:21-40)
   E. Jesus the Boy (2:41-52)
II. Preparation (3:1–4:13)
   A. John's Ministry (3:1-20)
   B. Jesus' Baptism (3:21 – 22)
   C. Jesus' Genealogy (3:23-38)
   D. Jesus' Temptation (4:1-13)
III. Ministry in Galilee (4:14–9:62)
   A. The Nazareth Sermon (4:14-30)
   B. Healings (4:31-44)
   C. Three Miracles (5:1-26)
   D. Calling Levi (5:27-32)
   E. Fasting (5:33-39)
   F. The Sabbath (6:1-11)
   G. Choosing the Twelve (6:12-16)
   H. Sermon on the Plain (6:17-49)
   I. Healing a Slave (7:1-10)
   J. Raising a Widow's Dead Son (7:11-17)
   K. The Baptist Asks Jesus Questions (7:18-35)
   L. Women Jesus Helped and Depended on (7:36–8:3)
   M. Parables (8:4-18)
   N. Jesus' Family (8:19-21)
   O. Power over Nature (8:22-25)
   P. Power over Demons (8:26-39)
   Q. Power over Death (8:40-56)
   R. Sending the Twelve (9:1-6)
   S. Herod the Tetrarch (9:7-9)
   T. Feeding 5,000 (9:10-17)
   U. Discipleship (9:18-27)
   V. Transfiguration (9:28-36)
   W. The Disciples' Flaws (9:37-62)
IV. Galilee to Jerusalem (10:1–19:27)
   A. The 70 Sent out (10:1-24)
   B. The Good Samaritan (10:25-37)
   C. Jesus on Prayer (10:38–11:13)
   D. Jesus and Demons (11:14-26)
   E. Jesus' Teachings (11:27–13:17)
   F. Jesus on God's Kingdom (13:18-30)
   G. Jesus' Warnings (13:31-35)
   H. Jesus Dines with a Pharisee (14:1-24)
   I. Discipleship and the Lost (14:25–15:32)
   J. Jesus on Money (16:1-31)
   K. Jesus on Service (17:1-19)
   L. Jesus' Coming (17:20-37)
   M. More on Prayer (18:1-14)
   N. Jesus on Trust (18:15–19:27)
V. Jesus in Jerusalem (19:28–21:38)
   A. His Triumphal Entry (19:28-44)
   B. Temple Teachings (19:45–20:8)
   C. Traps Avoided (20:9-47)
   D. His Vision of the Future (21:1-38)
VI. Jesus' Passion (22:1–24:53)
   A. The Betrayal (22:1-6)
   B. Upper Room Events (22:7-38)
   C. Arrest and Trial (22:39–23:25)
   D. The Crucifixon (23:26-56)
   E. The Resurrection (24:1-53)

Outline
Place
Finder

BIRTH
PREPARATION
GALILEE
TRAVELING
JERUSALEM
PASSION

Chapter summary. After a brief introduction (1:1-4) Luke relates angelic announcements of the coming births of John the Baptist (vv. 5-25) and of Jesus (vv. 26-38). Luke reports the joy of the two kinswomen, Elizabeth and Mary (vv. 39-45) and includes a copy of Mary's magnificent praise poem, commonly known as "the Magnificat" (vv. 46-56). He relates the unusual circumstances of John's birth and the sense of expectation that it created in the countryside (vv. 57-66). Luke finally includes a prophetic utterance of Zechariah, the father of John, that identifies the mission John will perform as forerunner of the Messiah (vv. 67-80). In drawing together this material, much of which is unique to his Gospel, Luke focuses our attention on the atmosphere of expectation that God began to create among His people in preparation for the appearance of the Saviour. But he also focuses our attention on the beautiful characters of Mary and Elizabeth, women of faith and commitment.

Key verses. 1:32-33: Jesus' destiny.

Personal application. Praise God when He acts in your life.

Key concepts. Angel »p. 521. Virgin birth »p. 416. Prophecy »p. 434.

INSIGHT

"Priestly division" (1:5). Priests were organized in 24 teams, which rotated for temple service. Members of the duty team drew lots to see who had the privilege of burning incense inside the temple (vv. 8-10).

"The spirit and power of Elijah" (1:17). The reference is to Mal. 3:1 and 4:5-6 and clearly identifies John's mission as a forerunner of the Messiah, sent to prepare the Jewish people for their Redeemer.

"Gabriel" (1:19). Gabriel is one of two angels named in Scripture (cf. Dan. 8:16; 9:21). The other is Michael (Dan. 10:13, 21; Jude 9; Rev. 12:7).

Telling Good News (1:19). The Good News is always, in some way, about Jesus. Luke emphasizes telling God's Good News. He uses the Gk. verb 10 of the 11 times it is found in the Gospels (2:10; 3:18; 4:18, 43; 7:22; 8:1; 9:6; 16:16; 20:1). This, of course, is what the Good News of Jesus is for: Telling!

My disgrace (1:25). Children were so highly valued in Jewish society that a childless woman felt intense shame (cf. 1 Sam. 1).

Jesus, as the angel describes Him (1:26-38). The angel who told Mary of Jesus' coming birth emphasizes the role of God's grace (1:29-30, 34-35, 38) and of God's Spirit (1:35), and describes Jesus Himself as God's Son (1:32, 35) and announces that He will rule David's kingdom (1:32-33).

Elizabeth and Mary. One was too old to have children, the other, just entering her teens and betrothed but not wed, was too

young. God often does the impossible and the unlikely, to remind us His power is not restricted by our limitations.

Zechariah and Mary. Zechariah, the priest, asks the angel for a sign (1:18). Mary, the young maiden of Galilee, submits in simple faith to the Lord. It is wrong to worship Mary. But it is more than right that we admire and emulate her.

Mary's marital status (1:27). The Gk. specifically states Mary was a *parthenos*, a virgin. She was bound by a legally binding marriage contract to wed Joseph when she came of age. While sexual intercourse was not permitted in this relationship, Mary was still "wed" to Joseph.

The Magnificat (1:46-56). Some question whether a young, uneducated country girl could have composed this magnificent prophetic poem. Yet Mary might have been well acquainted with the O.T. passages alluded to from worship in the synagogue and talk in her home. Mary undoubtedly thought deeply on the angel's visit and may have composed her psalm over a period of weeks, guided by the Spirit who spoke through her.

Her praise poem has four distinct parts: (1) personal adoration and thanks (vv. 46-48); (2) celebration of God's attributes (vv. 49-50); (3) acclaim for correcting injustice (vv. 51-53); and (4) praise for the mercy shown Israel (vv. 54-56).

The Benedictus (1:67-80). Zechariah's prophetic poem praises God for the Messiah (vv. 68-75) and the role of his son, John (vv. 76-79).

Chapter summary. Luke's clear, straightforward telling of the story of Jesus' birth anchors the events in history and links them to prophecy. God uses an emperor's decree to guide a Galilean couple to Bcthlehem (2:1-5), so the Messiah might be born in David's hometown, the locale of His predicted birth (vv. 6-7; cf. Micah 5:2). Ecstatic choirs of angels share the news of His birth with local shepherds (vv. 8-15), who find and worship the Christ Child (vv. 16-20). Jesus is circumcised (v. 21), and when He is brought to the temple some 40 days later His identity is revealed to a man named Simon (vv. 22-35) and a prophetess named Anna (vv. 36-40). Luke skips over Jesus' early childhood, but does tell of a visit to the temple when Jesus was twelve, at which He stunned teachers of the Law with His insights (vv. 41-50). Still, Jesus lived a normal childhood in a typical Jewish home, respecting His parents and winning the respect of all (vv. 51-52).

Outline
Place
Finder

BIRTH
PREPARATION
GALILEE
TRAVELING
JERUSALEM
PASSION

Key verse. 2:10: Christmas' greatest gift.

Personal application. Christmas joy is to be ours daily.

Key concepts. Davidic Covenant »p. 370. Salvation »p. 426. Angels »p. 521. Temple »p. 283. Holy Spirit »p. 759.

INSIGHT

The date of Jesus' birth (2:1-3). The census was an enrollment of citizens required as a basis for calculating taxes. Quirinius was imperial legate for Syria in A.D. 6, but this may have been his second time in office. Besides, Luke speaks of the census that brought Joseph and Mary to Bethlehem as a *prote* (which probably means "earlier" here rather than "first"). So the year of Christ's birth continues to be debated.

Why shepherds? (2:8-20) Shepherds in the 1st century were of very low social status. How appropriate to announce the Good News first to ordinary folks, rather than the rich and famous.

Childbirth law (2:21-24). Leviticus 12:1-5 calls for a mother to offer a sacrifice for ritual purification after the birth of a child. It was fulfilling this requirement of O.T. Law that brought the family to the temple. (See also Lev. 12:6-8.)

Witnesses in Judaism (2:25-36). Simon and Anna represent the best in O.T. Judaism, a truly righteous man and a dedicated woman who worships and prophesies. Each received a revelation from God concerning Jesus and witnessed to His identity as the Messiah. The Pharisees and others who opposed Christ so vigorously in no way represented the many true believers in the first-century's community of faith.

"My Father's house" (2:41-52). This saying has often been cited to show that Jesus very early understood His unique relationship with God. The passage is perhaps more amazing in its emphasis on Jesus' humanity. Even knowing who He was, the child Jesus chose to live in submission to Mary and Joseph and grew up as a typical Jewish youth.

Humanity of Jesus. Theologians have puzzled over the exact relationship between Jesus' humanity and deity. All we can say with confidence is that Jesus is both God and man. As a human being, He descended from Adam, was born, and lived a normal human life. He felt hunger and physical exhaustion. He knew rejection and pain. He enjoyed wedding celebrations and parties. He felt pity for the helpless, frustration at the dullness of His followers, and anger at the heartless indifference of the religious leaders to human suffering. He was truly human, in the best and the ideal sense of that word. As a human being He is our example.

Submission (2:51-52). Jesus' responsive obedience to His parents as a child gives perspective to the troubling issue of submission in other human relationships. The Gk. words *hypotasso* and *hypotage* imply that a person subordinates himself or herself to another. The N.T. emphasis is on voluntary submission to existing social structures. First century Christian slaves chose to submit to their masters, citizens to the government, and wives to husbands. When we see Jesus choose to submit to parents we realize a vital and basic truth. Submission is not an act of an inferior, or an admission of inferiority!

Chapter summary. Luke now carefully identifies just when John the Baptist began to utter his prophetic call to repentance (3:1-3). His message is urgent for the Messiah is about to appear, and so the people must turn to God now, before it is too late (vv. 4-14). John's ministry excited the people and aroused speculation that he himself might be the Messiah—especially when he dared rebuke Herod Antipas, ruler of Galilee (vv. 15-20). But John spoke of Jesus, whom God identified as His own Son at Christ's baptism (vv. 21-22), even though His human ancestry could be traced back to Adam (vv. 23-38). John was the forerunner. Jesus, Son of God and Child of humanity, is the Messiah of whom the prophets speak.

Key verse. 3:23. Jesus' ministry would reveal His origins.

Personal application. Honor those today who point you to Jesus, not to themselves.

Key concepts. Repentance »p. 780. Ritual Washing »p. 639. Genealogy »p. 264.

INSIGHT

Illustration. *John's image of an ax put to the roots of a tree is symbolic (3:8-9). The Jews relied on their descent from Abraham to establish relationship with God. John's message is that God is not concerned with the root, but with the moral fruit in each person's life. As far as the root is concerned, an ax is about to be put to that, and then relationship with God will be a matter of faith entirely—a faith that produces the fruit of righteousness.*

Luke's dating (3:1-3). If Luke used the Roman system of calculating rulers' dates, the 15th year of Tiberius would fall between August A.D. 28 and August A.D. 29. The Syrian dating would place it from autumn A.D. 27 to autumn A.D. 28.

Showing repentance (3:10-14). The change of mind and heart represented by "repentance" has to be reflected in a change in behavior. Ordinary people must share gladly, tax collectors must stop defrauding, and soldiers stop extorting bribes.

Look at your own life before and after Christ. There surely will be changes you have made. Or should make now!

"About thirty" (3:23). Thirty is a rounded off number here and may even have indicated the mid-thirties. At the same time, it is significant that according to the O.T., priests must reach 30 before they could serve (Num. 4:47).

The two genealogies of Jesus (3:23-37). The genealogy here and that given in Matthew differ, especially in the identification of the immediate ancestors of Joseph. There are other differences: Matthew's group is symmetrical, Luke's simply a list. Matthew begins with Abraham and focuses attention on David; Luke traces Christ's line back to Adam. The differences have generally been explained by assuming (1) Matthew gives Joseph's line, and Luke reports Mary's. Both are in the Davidic line. Or, (2) Matthew traces the legal line, Luke, Christ's actual descent. There are other alternatives, but two things are clear. The two genealogies are not in conflict, as several reasonable explanations for differences exist. And, Luke does intend to remind us that not only is Jesus a true human being, but is the model of what humanity was intended to be—and will become through His saving work.

Chapter summary. Jesus' first challenge is clearly coordinated by the Holy Spirit, who leads Him to a desolate area to fast and then permits the weakened Saviour to be tested by Satan. Christ's victory demonstrates Luke's theme: Jesus is an ideal human being, unlike the fallen Adam and Eve (4:1-13). But rather than being welcomed by His people, even those in His hometown angrily reject Him (vv. 14-30). Luke then reports two incidents that underline Jesus' uniqueness: He not only teaches with authority by exercising it over demons (vv. 31-37), this man uses His authority to help and heal His fellow human beings (vv. 38-44).

Outline
Place
Finder

BIRTH
PREPARATION
GALILEE
TRAVELING
JERUSALEM
PASSION

Key verse. 4:36: Jesus fulfills man's destiny.

Personal application. Care for others in Jesus' name and power.

Key concepts. Authority »p. 610. Miracle »p. 679. Demons »p. 895.

INSIGHT

"**Devil**" (4:2). The devil (»p. 505) is an evil angelic being, hostile to human beings, who exercises great power in this world to shape society to appeal to man's sin nature (Eph. 2:2). He is described as snaring man (1 Tim. 3:7), oppressing people (Acts 10:38), as man's adversary (1 Peter 5:8), and as putting evil intent into the hearts of sin-bent persons (John 13:2). But the devil is far from all-powerful. Believers can use the resources God supplies to stand against his "schemes" (*methodeia*, "craftiness") (Eph. 6:11). When we resist the devil as Christ did at His temptation, Satan will flee from us (James 4:7).

Temptation (4:2). The Gk. words *peirazo* and *peirasmos* are translated both "test" and "trial" as well as "tempt" and "temptation." What they have in common is a situation which places us under great pressure. James 1 is especially good in helping us deal with these situations, it reminds us that God never tempts people, in the sense of luring them to do evil (James 1:13). God does however test, as He permitted Satan to test Jesus, to demonstrate to us and to all that we can overcome in His strength. Adam and Eve failed the test. Through Christ you and I can overcome.

Fasting (4:2). Medicine tells us 30 to 40 days of total fasting depletes the body's resources and causes intense hunger and near exhaustion. Even in this weakened state Jesus remained true to His commitment. He trusted and acted on God's Word.

The power of the Spirit (4:14). Jesus' conception (1:35), baptism (3:21-22), temptation (4), and now His ministry are all linked to the working of God's Spirit. If Jesus depended on empowerment by the Spirit, how much more must we.

Jesus' mission (4:18-19). This quote from Isa. 61:1-2 focuses on the nature of Jesus' ministry. He brings Good News to the oppressed and healing for those who hurt. Jesus purposely omitted the final phrase of 61:2: "the day of vengeance of our God." Jesus introduces a day of grace, with forgiveness extended to all. Judgment is delayed till His return (cf. 2 Thes. 1:5-10).

"**All spoke well of Him**" (4:22). It was Jesus' "gracious words" (His "message of grace") that won immediate approval. What changed the crowd's attitude was His stories of O.T. prophets whom God sent to Gentiles. Jesus' view that God's grace must extend to all outraged those who claimed a right to His special favors. Let's guard against this attitude. If we live because of God's grace, let's not be upset if He displays grace to someone we find less "deserving."

"**Amazed at His teaching**" (4:32). The rabbis of Jesus' day based their instruction on a great body of historic interpretation of Scripture going back hundreds of years. What stunned Jesus' listeners was the fact that He spoke as if He had authority and did not need to rely on tradition. What amazed them even more was Jesus' power, demonstrated in casting out a demon. Jewish and pagan exorcists of the era used lengthy incantations and supposedly magical liturgies. But Jesus simply commanded, and the demon was forced to obey.

"**Sickness**" (4:40-41). Don't suppose that people of biblical times ascribed all disease to demons. Luke, a physician, distinguishes between the two here and elsewhere. Jesus has power over both man's natural and supernatural ills.

Chapter summary. Luke now reports Jesus' selection of His best-known disciples, Peter, James, and John. Their call by Jesus was to totally change the direction of their lives (5:1-11). Now accompanied by some of His disciples, Jesus heals a leper (vv. 12-16) and arouses the hostility of the religious leaders by announcing the forgiveness of a paralytic's sins (vv. 17-21). Jesus then demonstrates His power to forgive by performing another "impossible" act: He heals the paralytic (vv. 22-26). The Gospel writers each link this event with the call of Levi. Jesus' power to forgive is shown, even today, in the transformation He works in the lives of sinners (vv. 27-32).

When Jesus is questioned about fasting He dismisses the traditional practice. His teaching is so new and vital it cannot be contained in the form of first-century Judaism (vv. 33-39).

Key verse. 5:10b: Jesus changes our destiny too.

Personal application. Let Jesus' teaching reshape you too.

Key concepts. Disciple »p. 657. Peter »p. 711. Leprosy »p. 83. Forgiveness »pp. 357, 863. Healing »p. 611. Fasting »p. 442.

INSIGHT

The disciples. This is not the first time Jesus had met the disciples. John 1:35–2:11 tells us that several first met Jesus when John the Baptist was preaching. They went with Him to a wedding in Cana, He spent time in their homes in Capernaum, and they also watched the first time Jesus drove money changers from the temple.

What a model for evangelism. It's not necessary to press for a decision on a first meeting. It takes most of us time to get to know Christ. But there always is and must be a moment of decision, when Christ calls, and we make an informed decision to follow Him.

"Worked hard all night" (5:5). Fishing was a demanding trade. The men fished at night and sold or salted their catch and dried or mended nets during the day.

"Go away" (5:8). Peter's reaction is not at all surprising. He had just seen Jesus more clearly, as seen in the shift of address from Master, a term that acknowledges superiority, to Lord, which here suggests the first glimmering recognition of who Jesus really is.

The trouble is, when we see Jesus more clearly we also see ourselves more clearly. His beauty exposes our flaws; His perfection reveals our sinfulness. Man's first reaction to such a revelation is often, "go away." But only by coming to Jesus can we find forgiveness for our sins and inner personal renewal.

"Don't be afraid" (5:10). Some are afraid to trust Jesus because they're afraid He will change their lifestyles. He will. But for the better.

On healing the paralytic. See Mark 2 »p. 634.

Why eat with tax collectors and sinners? (5:30) Many Christians have been criticized for the very thing Jesus was attacked for: associating with the "wrong kind of people." The problem is that while we are to separate from evil, we are also to call sinners to repentance. And Jesus' way of doing this was not to shout at sinners from a distance, but spend time with them. Because we can't tell another's motives, we must not criticize fellow believers just for associating. But because we are to examine our own motives, we must ask ourselves the Pharisee's question. "Why do you eat and drink with tax collectors and 'sinners'?"

New wine (5:37-39). *The Expository Dictionary of Bible Words* (Zondervan, 1985, p. 458) says: "This parable looks at the human reaction to old and new covenants. A fresh squeezing of wine must be put into wineskins that are superior because they are new, able to stretch and respond as the wine matures.

"But what of the final statement showing how people evaluate the two wines? First, it shows a hasty decision, for the new wine has not had time to mature when it is rejected. Second, it shows a foolish decision. Wine is used up, even as the pattern of faith and life expressed in the Mosaic Code is now exhausted. The old skins are empty!

"Jesus must be accepted on His own terms. As we let the Gospel message infuse our lives it gives us a fresh, new shape, chosen by God's Spirit, in which the new wine of God's work within us matures toward beauty and holiness."

Chapter summary. Opposition to Jesus centers around the rigid ideas of keeping the Sabbath held by the Pharisees and rejected by Jesus, the "Lord of the Sabbath" (6:1-11). Jesus now designates the 12 Apostles (vv. 12-16). They are with Him when He repeats elements of His basic teaching, called the "Sermon on the Mount" in Matthew's Gospel. Here His Beatitudes (vv. 17-26), His call to love enemies (vv. 27-36), and His warnings against judging (vv. 37-42) are expounded on a flat plain (v. 17). The sermon concludes with the familiar reminder that a good man's heart produces good things (vv. 43-45) and that a wise man will put Jesus' words into practice, making them the foundation on which he builds his life (vv. 46-49).

Key verse. 6:40: What counts isn't knowing but being like Jesus.

Personal application. No one really knows God's Word till he or she puts it into practice.

Key concepts. Sabbath »p. 664. Pharisees »p. 625. Apostles »p. 635. Blessing »pp. 49, 358. Love »pp. 661, 680. Enemies »pp. 91, 607. Judging »p. 874. Fruit »pp. 614, 792.

INSIGHT

Sabbath controversy (6:1-11). Here as in the other Gospels conflict with the religious leaders over Sabbath-keeping is accentuated. The dispute is over what is permitted on that holy day. Jesus, claiming divine authority as Lord of the Sabbath (» Son of Man, p. 615), makes it clear that human need has precedence. The rabbinic emphasis on ceremonial observance has distorted God's intent in giving man the Sabbath as a day of rest.

To destroy life? (6:9) The question seems puzzling on two counts. The man was not in danger of dying. And failing to heal doesn't seem the same as destroying life. But the point is that Jesus is showing the radical heart of O.T. commands. Anything that impairs the quality of human life as God intended it to be *does* destroy life. And a failure to set the destructive right is killing.

For discussion of the Beatitudes, see »p. 605.

On the plain (6:17-49). Those who point to "discrepancies" between this passage and Matt. 5–7 ignore the obvious. We think nothing of our politicians repeating the same themes speech after speech. Why should anyone expect Jesus, traveling and teaching about the kingdom He intends to inaugurate, never to repeat Himself? Luke places this sermon of Jesus "on a level place" so we will not mistake it for Matthew's account of a sermon "on a mountainside" (Matt. 5:1) which, while it touched on the same subjects, was an entirely different talk.

Love as God loves (6:27-36). People love those who love and reward them in return. There is very little reward here for loving ene-

mies. Some will change. But many will be even more hostile because you are gracious. Remember two things. God rewards those who love their enemies, and His rewards are better than any ordinary folks can offer. And, in loving enemies, you will become more like Jesus, who actually gave His life for those who rejected and hated Him (cf. Rom. 5:7-8).

Some will respond (6:37-38). If we live love some will respond and use with us the measure we used with them.

Disciple (6:40). The word translated "student" here is *mathetes*, "disciple." In N.T. times learners attached themselves to a teacher. They lived and traveled with him, listened to his teachings, asked him questions, and were asked questions in turn. Their goal, however, was not simply to learn what their teacher knew. Their goal was to be like their teacher in every way. Jesus used this mode of teaching to train His twelve disciples for future leadership in the church.

"Fully trained" (6:40). The Gk. word, *katerismenos*, means "put into proper condition," or "made complete." Our greatest need is not for skills, but for spiritual maturity. As we become more like Christ, God will use us.

That speck in our brother's eye (6:41-42). If we all looked after ourselves, there'd be no need to peer critically at others.

Floods come (6:46-49). Floods rushed down slopes in rocky Palestine, sweeping everything in their path away. Life too has its disasters. If not firmly anchored in obedience, we will be swept away.

Outline
Place
Finder

BIRTH
PREPARATION
GALILEE
TRAVELING
JERUSALEM
PASSION

Chapter summary. Two incidents heighten our awareness of what Jesus is doing in Galilee. He is exercising His unique authority by healing (7:1-10), and He is demonstrating His power, even power to raise the dead (vv. 11-17). Even so, John the Baptist himself is troubled by doubts. Jesus does not seem to be doing what John thinks He should do—reestablish David's kingdom (v. 18). Jesus has John's disciples observe His healings and sends them away (vv. 19-23). Then Christ commends John as a great prophet, amazed that the leaders could not even see the significance of sinners repenting, but instead criticized both Himself and John (vv. 24-35). The lesson is driven home when Jesus visits a Pharisee's home. The Pharisee haughtily judges Jesus when a woman "who had led a sinful life" weeps and washes His feet. The Pharisee has no sense of the power of forgiveness, or what the mission of Jesus to earth really is (vv. 36-50).

Key verse. 7:47: Forgiveness comes first.

Personal application. Sense what Jesus is doing. Don't try to dictate what He should do.

Key concepts. Pharisee »p. 625. Forgiveness »p. 357. Love »p. 778.

INSIGHT

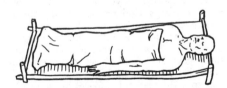

Illustration: Restoration to earthly life (7:11-15). *The "coffin" was a bier, a flat pallet or bed frame. A body was not embalmed, but was buried the day of death. What Jesus did for the widow in raising her son was not resurrection.*

Jesus restored him to earthly life, as He did a young girl (8:40ff.) and Lazarus (John 11). Each died again, later. Resurrection is the transformation of the earthy body, the replacement of the mortal with immortality. Jesus was the first person in history to experience resurrection. But not the last! (cf. »pp. 737, 823)

Centurions (7:1-10). These officers in the Roman army were highly motivated, competent, and generally decent persons. It is perhaps surprising that the N.T. universally portrays centurions in a good light (cf. Mark 15:39; Acts 10; 22; 26).

Here the centurion models "great faith" and illustrates one of Luke's key themes. Faith in Jesus is for Gentiles as well as for Jews. Those Gentiles who do believe will surely be blessed.

"Are You the one"? (7:19) John's question is comforting. If a man of such great commitment and faith can have doubts, we need not be overwhelmed at our own uncertainties. But John's question is also a warning. John made the mistake of expecting Jesus to act as John supposed He must. Let's never suppose that God must limit Himself to act as we think He should. We must adjust to what God is doing.

"Greater than He" (7:28). John announced the kingdom. We participate in it. Our privilege is greater. And so is our responsiblity.

Acknowledging God's way is right (7:29-35). This was not lip service, but a change in the moral direction of one's life. It is stunning that the religious of Jesus' time could not see that such a response was proof God was at work.

Forgiveness received awakens love for God (7:36-50). In announcing the woman's sins were forgiven Jesus simply stated what was already true. The woman's love proved she had been forgiven. Love does not come first: It is a response to God's working in our lives.

The incident summarizes themes developed in this chapter. Christ is compassionate and powerful. He heals bodies and souls. Those who have faith in Him experience His power in both physical and spiritual realms. None of this the Pharisee, representing the leaders of 1st-century Judaism, could see or understand. Unlike John, whose questioning came *from* faith, their doubts were a blunt denial of the clear evidence of who Jesus was and is.

Chapter summary. Luke now reports yet another preaching tour of Galilee (8:1-3). Luke recounts now familiar parables, using a farmer sowing seed to describe reactions to the Word Jesus is sowing (vv. 4-15). This is followed by sayings intended to stress the importance of how Jesus' listeners themselves hear (vv. 16-18). For relationship with Jesus is not based on earthly bonds, but on the response of faith to God's Word (vv. 19-21). Again Luke emphasizes the authority of the One speaking these words. Jesus is authenticated by miracles that reveal His power over nature (vv. 22-25), demons (vv. 26-39), and physical death in its progressive and its ultimate stages (vv. 40-56).

Outline
Place
Finder

BIRTH
PREPARATION
GALILEE
TRAVELING
JERUSALEM
PASSION

Key verse. 8:18: Listen wisely.

Personal application. No word from God helps us if we fail to respond to it.

Key concepts. Parable »p. 615. Healing »p. 611. Death »pp. 369, 741.

INSIGHT

"Women" (8:2-3). Luke is the only one who mentions that there were women in Jesus' traveling party and that women provided money that helped fund His mission. The fact is not surprising, however, as parallels exist in early Judaism of women giving generously to support a favorite rabbi. Note that the women mentioned, like many others, had "their own means." Women in the biblical world were far more "liberated" than one might suspect.

The soils explained (8:11-15). In each telling of this parable in the Gospels the stress lies on the differing soils (hearts) and how they respond to the sown Word. The point is that God's Word does not uniformly evoke faith, not because the Word is defective, but because human beings are free to respond as they choose.

The reasons given? (1) Satan deliberately snatches the Word from man's consciousness (v. 12). (2) Human beings respond emotionally and superficially and when "it doesn't work," or persecution comes, abandon the Word without ever really having received it (v. 13). (3) People become so involved in the depressing (or exciting!) events of their daily life that they are distracted and gradually forget God's salvation message (v. 14).

Lest we become discouraged and stop sowing, Jesus also notes that some soil is "good." And the Word sown on that soil produces an abundant crop. Those who do respond make it all worthwhile!

The lamp on a stand (8:16-18). In Palestine a lamp was kept burning all night in even the poorest of homes. Entering the darkened home a person could see the dim olive-oil-fueled lamp, but little else. This is why in the illustration the person sees the light—but not the contents of the room. But this is the point. One must see Jesus first and only. When we have fixed our eyes on Jesus, we can be sure that the hidden things of our life will gradually be revealed to us. He is the key to our understanding of all things and possession of all spiritual insights. Seeing Him we will be given more. Not seeing Him, even the little spiritual insight we have will be taken away.

"Demons" (8:26-39). The belief in demons was common in ancient cultures, but seldom mentioned in the O.T. (only Deut. 32:17, Psalm 106:36, 37). However, demons are spoken of often in the N.T., and the Gospels are filled with references to these evil spirits. It may well be that Jesus' presence stimulated an unusual outburst of demonic activity, as Satan marshaled his forces to resist the Lord.

In the Gospels the hostile intent of demons, who most likely are the fallen angels mentioned in both Testaments (» Angels, p. 521; Satan, p. 505). Their antagonism toward human beings is shown in their oppressing or possessing persons (Matt. 8:16, 28, 33; 9:32; 12:22-28; Mark 1:32; 5:16-17; Luke 4:33-35; 9:42; etc.). Thus the N.T. portrays demons as living, malignant, conscious individual beings, subordinate to Satan and active in their allegiance to his kingdom. They will also share the fate of Satan, which is an eternity in what the Bible calls the "lake of fire" (Rev. 20:14; cf. Matt. 25:41).

Sickness and death (8:40-56). The process of death is at work in us even when we are most healthy. How gladly we affirm Jesus' power over death in all its forms.

Chapter summary. We now near the end of Jesus' time in Galilee, and there are yet many places needing His ministry. So Jesus commissions His twelve disciples, empowers them to preach and to heal, and sends them out (9:1-6). As they travel they hear much speculation about who Jesus really is (vv. 7-9). Later, after Jesus had fed thousands with just a few loaves of bread and fishes (vv. 10-17), the disciples reported the people's gossip and Peter, speaking for them all, acknowledged Jesus as the Christ (vv. 18-22). The disciples were correct—but following Jesus would not be easy, for it meant surrendering one's will to God and so "losing" the old life in exchange for one that is different and new (vv. 23-27). Jesus' transfiguration, just a few days later, prefigured what Christ's own self-surrender would mean: after the cross there would be a return to glory. The implication is clear. Glory awaits us when we too surrender fully to the Lord (vv. 28-36). When we do we will learn a new way to greatness (vv. 37-56). But to choose that way we must pay the price and put God above all human values (vv. 57-62).

Key verse. 9:62: Choose once for always.

Personal application. What we gain in following Jesus is far more than we lose.

Key concepts. Christ »p. 646. Cross »p. 618. Evil spirit »p. 239. Samaritan »p. 254.

INSIGHT

"All demons" (9:1). Jesus gave the disciples miracle-working power (*dynamis*) and authority (*exousia*). Their powers were further demonstration that God's kingdom was breaking in on man's world.

"Shake the dust off your feet" (9:5). Jewish travelers returning to their homeland typically shook the "unclean" dust of their journey through pagan lands off their feet. By rejecting Jesus' disciples, a town placed itself outside the community of faith.

Who is this? (9:7-9). At the end of Jesus' ministry in Galilee the people had all the evidence necessary to answer this central query. The failure of the crowds to realize Jesus was the Christ was in fact rejection (John 1:10).

"You give them" (9:13). Each Gospel records this miracle and this command of Jesus. It's not enough for us to see the needs of others. Being aware makes us responsible.

Peter's confession (9:18-36). On Peter's confession, the meaning of "losing yourself," and the Transfiguration, see pages 618, 640.

"The greatness of God" (9:43). Matthew and Mark in telling this story draw attention to the role of prayer. Luke, who speaks of prayer more than either of the others, chooses to focus here on the greatness of God. His emphasis is a necessary balance. All too often we

speak as if effective prayer depended on us. In fact, it is God who answers prayer and so displays His greatness. Be wary of those who boast of the power of their prayers, rather than wonder at the grace and greatness of our God.

Competition (9:46-50). Jealousy and rivalry between the disciples draw attention away from Jesus. Then the disciples are upset about someone acting in Jesus' name who "is not one of us."

What a terrible impact the spirit of competition has in the church, for whether we are upset and jealous of someone in our group or someone outside it, our rivalries in fact draw everyone's attention away from Jesus.

"Heading for Jerusalem" (9:53). Intense religious hostility existed between the Samaritans and Jews. Jesus' party was refused shelter because He was headed toward Jerusalem. How do we react to hostility? Graciously. For Jesus rebuked the disciples' suggestion that they act militantly in return.

Discipleship's demands (9:57-62). Following Jesus calls for personal sacrifice (vv. 57-58), and even repudiation of normal family responsibilities (vv. 59-60), to concentrate completely on serving God (vv. 61-62).

Chapter summary. Jesus has left Galilee and His itinerant ministry will now focus in Judea. He sends 72 followers ahead to warn that God's kingdom is near (10:1-12) and laments over those cities where He has preached and been rejected (vv. 13-16). The messengers return, excited at their new power over evil spirits. But Jesus is joy-filled at the salvation of those who have chosen to believe in and follow Him (vv. 17-24).

Questioned by an expert in Old Testament Law, Jesus tells the story of the Good Samaritan to show the full extent of the Law's demands on the believer. For love for God and neighbor require unlimited commitment to meeting needs (vv. 25-37). Later, at Mary and Martha's home in Bethany, Jesus gently rebukes the harried Martha for her anger at Mary, who expresses her love for God by listening intently to Jesus (vv. 38-42).

Outline
Place
Finder

BIRTH
PREPARATION
GALILEE
TRAVELING
JERUSALEM
PASSION

Key verse. 10:27: Love comes first.

Personal application. We love God by responding to Him, others by reaching out to them.

Key concepts. Kingdom »p. 380. Satan »p. 501. Samaritan »p. 254. Love »pp. 126, 351, 529, 680, 690-691, 778, 814.

INSIGHT

Vulnerability (10:3). The instruction is intended to strip Jesus' representatives of everything on which they might normally depend: extra money or clothing. Only when we realize we are defenseless are we likely to truly depend on God.

"Stay in that house" (10:6-7). In N.T. times travelers were dependent on the hospitality of others. Those unwilling to welcome the disciples would be those who did not want to be identified with Jesus. People have always been known by the company they keep—or invite to visit them.

Korazin and Bethsaida (10:13-16). These cities lay near Capernaum at the north end of the Sea of Galilee. Most of Jesus' early ministry was concentrated in this area. This privilege carried with it a heavy responsibility.

Those who hear God's Word most clearly are most responsible to respond.

Sources of joy (10:17-21). These verses compare superficial and significant sources of joy. The 72 were excited at their power over demons. Jesus directed their attention to a much greater reason to rejoice: their names were written in heaven. Whatever happens to you or me in this world, no one can take this ultimate source of joy from us. Because of Jesus, our names are written in glory.

Jesus Himself was filled with Spirit-generated joy over those to whom God revealed Himself. Let's rejoice at the salvation of others.

"He wanted to justify himself" (10:29). The expert in O.T. Law had a clear grasp of the Law's central requirements. But he was also aware that he fell short of fulfilling them. There are only three ways a person can react when that awareness dawns: (1) We can acknowledge we are sinners and appeal to God for mercy. (2) We can concentrate on the things we do well and pretend we do not fail in others. (3) We can cut the Law's requirements down by reinterpreting them, so we can live up to what are essentially lower standards. It's this third approach the expert in Law took. He wanted to define "neighbor" in such a way he could claim he had kept the commandment.

"Neighbor" (10:25-37). Jesus' story defines "neighbor" in the most rigorous of ways. Any person in need is your "neighbor," even if he is a member of a race that is a traditional enemy!

"Only one thing is needed" (10:36-42). The Samaritan story illustrates love for neighbor. The Mary and Martha story illustrates love for God. Martha was busy preparing a large meal for Jesus and His disciples. Mary ignored her sister and sat at Jesus' feet, the traditional place of a disciple.

Jesus' rebuke might be paraphrased, "Just a casserole, Martha, not a smorgasbord." Love for God is expressed best in listening and responding to Jesus' words, not in busily doing "for" Him.

Outline
Place
Finder

BIRTH
PREPARATION
GALILEE
TRAVELING
JERUSALEM
PASSION

Chapter summary. Jesus teaches His disciples that prayer grows out of personal relationship (11:1-4) and though it calls for persistence (vv. 5-8), can be offered in complete confidence in God's love (vv. 9-13). When Jesus is accused of performing His works by satanic enablement rather than by the Spirit He ridicules the rumor (vv. 14-22) and warns that any cleansing from evil spirits not followed by a filling with the Spirit must ultimately fail (vv. 23-28). Jesus again warns of judgment because "this generation" has not repented despite His preaching (vv. 29-32). He uses the familiar image of a lamp to point out that only when a person receives light from God's Word will one's life be light rather than darkness (vv. 33-36). Jesus' blunt confrontation with truth continues as He announces a series of woes on the Pharisees and teachers of the Law for their flaws and failures (vv. 37-54).

Key verse. 11:9: Prayer power!

Personal application. Through prayer we tap the greatest power of all.

Key concepts. Prayer »pp. 608, 609. Father »pp. 140, 663. Demons »p. 659. Evil spirit »p. 239. Darkness »p. 824. Pharisee »p. 625.

INSIGHT

The Lord's Prayer. See »p. 608.

Friend, or father (11:5-8). The point of Jesus' story is that even a friend would get up and get the food for one who knocks persistently. Even if his motive was just to get rid of a nuisance. How much more will God, who is a Father, and who deeply loves us, quickly respond to our prayers!

"Though you are evil" (11:13). The Gk. word for evil here is *poneros*, the stronger of two roots so translated. *Poneros* is used to portray active rebellion against God and good, a treachery deeply embedded in the human heart. This key concept in the biblical vision of sinful human nature indicates that the energy generated within the human personality is channeled toward the wicked. Yet Jesus' illustration notes that even the lost at times reflect the beauty God designed into humanity at the Creation. Even a fallen man knows how to give good gifts to his own child.

Again Jesus is emphasizing by contrast. If a sinful human being gives good gifts to his children, how much more will God, a totally good being, give good gifts to we who through faith have become children in His family? Oh, what utter confidence we can have when we pray!

"I will return" (11:24-26). Jesus compares the work of Jewish exorcists and His own. Those exorcists might expel demons, but Jesus alone brought about an inner renewal that filled the life of the once-possessed person with transforming power.

Whatever demons a person may be freed from—drugs, drink, gluttony, passion, or lust for power—unless God takes up residence in that person's life he or she will fall again.

Another sign (11:29). The miracles of healing and exorcism were not enough, and people demanded yet another sign. The "sign of Jonah," a return from the grave, was to be given. But as Jesus knew, not even this would generate faith.

If we will not believe the Word of God, we will be judged. Not even miracles can convince a person who will not believe.

The lit lamp and good eyes (11:33-36). The familiar image has a different application here. The lit lamp is Jesus, whom God has put on a stand through the confirming wonders Christ has performed. The "good eye" lets in the light, so that the whole person is enlightened. On the other hand, bad eyes will not admit light, thus keeping the whole person in darkness. The only way a person can have light, and see truth as it really is, is to let Jesus' words in and accept them.

The foolish Pharisees (11:40). The word translated "foolish" is *aphron*, which indicates willful ignorance. This group, characterized here and in Matt. 23 (»p. 625), is not in error because they cannot see, but because they will not see the light shining in Jesus.

Chapter summary. Jesus has openly confronted the Pharisees (11:37-53). Now He warns against the Pharisees' orientation — hypocrisy. Only by fearing God and not man can a person be free of it (12:1-12). The story of the rich fool warns against another orientation — materialism (vv. 13-21). But it is not only the rich who are trapped into thinking life in this world is the be all and end all. The average person can become so anxious about needed food and clothing that he or she forgets to trust God — and forgets the ultimate value of the treasures that can be ours in heaven (vv. 22-34). A series of examples reminds the disciples that the believer's calling is to do God's will now, as a faithful servant (vv. 35-48).

What will happen if we take this teaching of Jesus seriously and commit ourselves fully to Him? It will not lead to peace now and may bring suffering (vv. 49-53). But how important in this critical time of crisis to read the signs right and make our commitment to Jesus before judgment day arrives (vv. 54-59).

Outline
Place
Finder

BIRTH
PREPARATION
GALILEE
TRAVELING
JERUSALEM
PASSION

Key verse. 12:56: Make peace before judgment day arrives.

Personal application. Look beyond today when making choices.

Key concepts. Pharisees »p. 625. Wealth »p. 125. Anxiety »p. 636. Fear »p. 363. Peace »pp. 427, 815. Judgment »p. 372.

INSIGHT

"Hypocrisy" (12:1-5). The word means play-acting. Here Jesus pinpoints the cause. The playactor is fearful of what other people think and desperate to look good to them. If you really care about what God thinks of you, you won't be caught in the trap of pretending to live up to others' expectations.

"Teacher, tell my brother" (12:13-14). Rabbis ("teachers") were expected to render judgments in case of disputes by applying rabbinical law. Jesus refused to become involved, but presents principles that get to the underlying issues. A legal judgment will not resolve the greed or the anger in the brothers' relationship.

The rich fool (12:16-21). Again the word is *aphron*. The wealthy man willfully ignores God's principles for living life.

The brother "without" was motivated by greed. So is the wealthy man "with." Abundance of material possessions has no contribution to make to life's real meaning.

"Do not worry" (12:22-31). Jesus now extends His teachings from abundant possessions (wealth) to necessities. We are physical beings in a material universe and must have food, drink, and shelter to survive. Jesus chal-lenges us not to be anxious even about necessities and gives us two vital insights. We need not be anxious because we have a Heavenly Father who cares for us. And, we must not be anxious because that would shift the focus of our attention from God to the things of this world.

"Your Father" (12:30). God acts as our Father. He rewards us (Matt. 6:1); disciplines us (John 15:2); listens to our prayers (Matt. 6:6); knows and meets our needs (Luke 12:30); gives us good gifts (Matt. 7:11); is merciful to us (Luke 6:36); and dearly loves us (John 16:27). O.T. saints knew that God was "like a Father" to Israel. Jesus brings the awesome God of the O.T. into fresh, intimate perspective. He is "our Father."

"Treasure" (12:32-34). Treasure is that to which we give priority in our lives. Material treasures are fleeting and unreliable. But putting God's kingdom first stores up treasures that outlast eternity.

"Be ready" (12:35-59). A series of illustrations reminds us that the world is rushing toward judgment day. To be ready, believers must serve God actively — and unbelievers must make peace with God before it's too late.

Chapter summary. Israel has failed to produce the fruit of faith and righteousness God demands and must repent or face imminent judgment (13:1-9). Yet another Sabbath controversy illustrates the insensitivity to human need of the religious leaders, who are more concerned with custom than caring (vv. 10-17). Jesus then warns His listeners not to misunderstand God's kingdom. Rather than coming in glory, it enters humbly and will become glorious (vv. 18-21). Salvation will not come to the nation as a whole, but to individuals who make personal, often difficult, decisions (vv. 22-30). Looking over the milling crowds Jesus expresses His deep anguish for the doomed city, whose people utterly refuse to turn to the Lord (vv. 31-35).

Key verse. 13:7: God waits . . . but only so long.

Personal application. God has planted us to produce fruit.

Key concepts. Repentance »p. 780. Fruit »pp. 414, 792. Hypocrite »p. 625. Kingdom »p. 380.

INSIGHT

Repent or perish (13:1-5). First-century Jews viewed disasters as direct divine retribution for personal sins. Like Job's friends, they assumed that since God is just, suffering proved guilt a priori. Jesus rejects this view. All are sinners. Unless a person repents, he or she is in peril of eternal judgment, not just physical death.

One more year (13:6-9). God is patient. But judgment will not wait forever.

The Sabbath (13:10). The O.T. established the seventh day of the week as a day of rest. Over the years experts in O.T. Law had debated the nature of "work" and had developed numerous rules that restricted Sabbath activity. It was all right to spit on a rock, but not on loose earth, for that would be plowing. One could travel only a certain distance from home on the Sabbath—but if a person left a personal possession at the limit of a Sabbath day's journey, that place became "home" to him and he could travel an equal distance further. This multitude of rules governing Sabbath activity was held to be binding on good Jews.

Each of the Gospels portrays conflict between Pharisees and Jesus over the Sabbath. This is a typical case. Jesus heals on the Sabbath. The scandalized synagogue ruler tells the people not to come for healing on the Sabbath. There are six days for that. Christ labels this hypocrisy, for well-established rabbinical rulings authorized helping one's trapped animal on the Sabbath. Are human beings of less value to God than a person? When understanding of a biblical concept rules out compassion, then we have distorted or misunderstood what the Word says.

"Humiliated" (13:17). Apparently Jesus' words and actions drove home the truth so sharply that even His opponents had to recognize He was right. But there is a vast difference between realizing one is wrong and repenting.

The Gospel "writ" small (13:18-21). God's work has always seemed insignificant to human beings. But it has dynamic power and exhibits vital, transforming growth in lost people and corrupt societies.

Not how many, but who (13:22). One person in the crowd shouted out his question about how many would be saved? Jesus ignored that question and made a vital point. The issue is: Who will be saved? And the answer is: those who choose personally to enter through the "narrow door." People must pass through that door one by one.

Inside and outside (13:28-30). Most Jews of Jesus' day counted on their privileged position as descendants of Abraham to gain them entrance to God's kingdom. Jesus teaches that salvation is a matter of personal faith, not of being born into a nation, a family, or even a church. How stunned those who missed the narrow gate will be, to see even Gentiles celebrating with Abraham, and themselves locked out.

Pharisees warning Jesus? (13:31) When folks who hate you seem to be watching out for your interests, beware!

"I must" (13:33). The Gk. word (dei) conveys a strong sense of necessity. Jesus is required by His commitment to God and His love for us to go to Jerusalem and the Cross.

Chapter summary. The Sabbath issue is raised again when a Pharisee invites Jesus to dinner—and places an obviously ill person at the table "in front of Him." Jesus heals him and gives some dry advice to His host (14:1-14). Jesus then tells a parable about a great banquet, representative of God's kingdom, and guests who are too preoccupied with their own affairs to respond to His invitation (vv. 15-24). Yet choosing to follow Jesus is not a choice to be made lightly. Along with the reward, one must be aware of the cost. When that choice has been made it is final and involves the surrender of all (vv. 25-35).

Outline
Place
Finder

BIRTH
PREPARATION
GALILEE
TRAVELING
JERUSALEM
PASSION

Key verse. 14:23: Heaven will be filled.

Personal application. Count the cost of following Jesus in pennies, the reward in millions.

Key concepts. Sabbath »p. 664. Pharisee »p. 625. Disciple »p. 683.

INSIGHT

Illustration. *The events of this chapter are tied together by the setting. Banquets were very special social occasions in the 1st century. In rabbinical literature banquets frequently symbolized the kingdom of God.*

Exalting yourself (14:11). Places of honor at banquets were those closest to the host. The spiritual principle is clear. Don't push for glory. Let God honor you.

One application (14:12-14). Jesus applies the principle above in a fascinating way. If His host really cares about honor from God, he should invite the poor and powerless, who can never repay him in this life. How is this an application? Simply in that God is concerned for the poor. He will exalt the person who

cares for the helpless, rather than the powerful who can reward here and now.

Compel them to come in? (14:23) The Gk. word translated "compel" in older versions and "make them" in the NIV is *anankazo*. It does involve compulsion, but not necessarily external, physical force. The greatest compulsion of all comes from inside as a positive response to a morally powerful command or invitation. The invitation so lightly dismissed by Israel will prove compelling when extended to the Gentiles—the outcasts of Jesus' illustration.

Hate (14:26). Again, "hate" is used in the sense of decisive rejection of competing claims to one's allegiance. Count the cost. But choose to follow Jesus to the end.

Outline
Place
Finder

BIRTH
PREPARATION
GALILEE
TRAVELING
JERUSALEM
PASSION

Chapter summary. Three parables are clustered here, each told in response to critical mutterings of the Pharisees who attack Jesus for associating with "tax collectors and 'sinners'" (15:1-2). The Parable of the Lost Sheep emphasizes heaven's joy over the repentance of a single sinner (vv. 3-7).

The same theme is seen in the Parable of the Lost Coin (vv. 8-10). Jesus then tells perhaps the most famous of His parables: the Parable of the Prodigal Son (vv. 11-32). The story of the straying son focuses attention on three persons. The younger son, representing "sinners," who repents after "wild living" leads to despair and disaster. The father, who represents God, whose unchanged love impels him to eagerly welcome his sinning child home. And the elder brother, who represents the critical Pharisees, who have no love for their fellowman and thus are unable to celebrate repentance in others.

Key verse. 15:20: God is waiting eagerly.

Personal application. Don't let sins keep you from a God who is eager to welcome you back home.

Key concepts. Parable »p. 166. Sheep »p. 620. Father »pp. 141, 663.

INSIGHT

"Tax collectors" (15:1). This occupation was considered immoral or dishonest. Taxes charged by the Herods and Rome placed an extremely heavy burden on the poor, and those Jews who collected them were heartily resented. Most of those involved extorted extra for their own enrichment.

"Sinners" (15:1). Luke uses this term to show the contempt of the Pharisees for ordinary people, who were not as strict in observing the minutia of traditional interpretations of the Law.

"Welcomes" (15:1). Luke pictures Jesus' attitude toward these social outcasts who habitually come to see and hear Him. "Eat with" shows an intimate association, a table fellowship the Pharisees would never permit lest they be contaminated.

We too ought to be so loving that we attract the "wrong kind of people." The stories Jesus tells in this chapter remind us why we should welcome them.

Searching (15:3-7). The shepherd is a frequent O.T. image of God, as sheep are a frequent image of Israel. The story of the lost sheep pictures God actively searching for the individual who strays.

Jesus' story draws attention to the joy the shepherd feels as he finds the lost sheep and swings it up on his shoulder to bring it home again. In this story the "joy in heaven" over the repentant sinner is God's joy.

Sharing (15:8-10). The woman's lost coin was likely part of her dowry and thus especially precious to her. Women in the 1st century often wore dowry coins as a headdress or necklace, strung together on a cord. In this story, again, the thoroughness of the woman's search for the lost is emphasized. But here the joy is shared with all her friends and neighbors. Jesus' point is that the repentance of a lost sinner is a cause of celebration throughout heaven. How is it that on earth the Pharisees are sourly critical? How can they be so out of touch with God?

An eager welcome (15:11-27). Human beings are not passive in salvation. Where the first stories focused on God's active search for the lost, the story of the prodigal reminds us that sinners must make a choice to turn to God from their empty lives. The image of the eager father, whose eyes seldom stray from the road along which the lost son must return, is one of Scripture's most appealing pictures of God the Father. There is no need to hesitate over repentance. We need never fear that we will be rejected by our God of "Father-love."

"The older brother" (15:25-32). The story now turns against the Pharisees, who like the older brother have no grasp of grace. Instead of rejoicing at the restoration of a brother, they're filled with resentment. They neither appreciate what they have, nor do they want anyone else to share it!

How we need to guard against this attitude in our own relationship with God and with others. Grace must make us gracious.

Chapter summary. Jesus tells two parables directed against the Pharisees' love for money. The first, traditionally known as the Parable of the Unjust Steward, makes a simple point. Money has no value in itself, but is to be used in this world to make preparation for the next (16:1-12). Each person must make a choice between commitment to materialistic values and commitment to God (vv. 13-15) and covenant values (vv. 16-18).

Jesus' second parable draws back the veil and shows the sneering Pharisees how serious this issue is. In the hereafter, the roles the rich man and beggar play in this life mean nothing. Blessing is a matter of repentance and faith, and only those who respond to God's Word through Moses and the prophets will be blessed (vv. 19-31). Even a resurrection miracle cannot convince those who will not believe God's Word.

Outline
Place
Finder

BIRTH
PREPARATION
GALILEE
TRAVELING
JERUSALEM
PASSION

Key verse. 16:13: Each much choose.

Personal application. Let God be your treasure always.

Key concepts. Pharisees »p. 625. Wealth »pp. 124–125, 838.

INSIGHT

"Manager" (16:1). The *oikonomos* was a person who managed funds or property for another person. In N.T. times he might be a slave or an employee.

The reductions (16:6-8). The cash value of each reduction, adjusted for the cost of each product, is about 500 denarii, or 16 months wages for a day laborer.

Commend the shrewd manager? (16:8) Some suggest that the amount the estate manager took off the creditor's bill was graft he had dishonestly charged on top of what was due his master. Even if this were the case, it's irrelevant to Jesus' point. The manager is not commended for his dishonesty, but for realizing that he can use money to prepare for his future.

"Use worldly wealth" (16:9). The Bible views wealth like other special gifts, as a resource to be used in serving God and others. The whole parable reminds us that nothing we possess is truly "ours," but belongs to God. He has entrusted it to us, and we are his *oikonomos*, commissioned to use what we have in His service. Because of this basic biblical perspective on material possessions, the story of the unjust steward is particularly apt and applicable.

"Two masters" (16:13). The statement is psychologically true. The idea of commitment to serving God and money is self-contradictory, because the two motivate us to make very different choices.

For instance, a person who owns housing occupied by the poor might experience conflict between a desire to make a profit from the property and to maintain it in decent condition.

These motives are so contradictory that he must choose (love) one and reject (hate) the other! We can't serve God and money simply because we have to choose between the vastly different courses each calls for.

Missing commitment (16:16-18). In their drive to force their way into God's kingdom by a rigorous legalism, the Pharisees missed the basic message of covenant commitment to God and others. For divorce, see »pp. 140, 621.

"Lazarus" (16:20). Because Jesus did not use personal names in His parables, many commentators suggest this story relates actual events.

Begging (16:20). The N.T. mentions several people forced by illness or disability to beg to maintain their lives (Luke 16:20; John 9:8; Acts 3:2-11). In the 1st century, and in rabbinical Judaism, giving to the destitute was considered a great good deed, meritorious in God's eyes (cf. Matt. 6:1-4).

"In hell" (16:23). The Gk. word is *hades*, a general term for the place inhabited by the dead.

Life after death (16:23). Not "life," but "alive." The rich dead man is pictured as self-conscious, aware, able to see, feel, and remember. There is no biblical basis for the notion that death is an unconscious state. The human personality, fully conscious and aware, does outlast physical death!

Listen to God's Word, now (16:31). Jesus' sad observation that the rich man's brothers would not listen (i.e., respond, act on what they heard) even if one rose from the dead was quickly proven true.

Jesus was raised. But His enemies, determined not to believe, continued to reject Him.

Chapter summary. Jesus now gives private instruction to His disciples. They are linked by concern for attitudes which must be nurtured within the believing community. Things that cause others to sin must be guarded against (17:1-2). Sins in the community must be confronted, confessed, and forgiven (vv. 3-10). Later, the healing of ten lepers underscores the principle of praise and thankfulness (vv. 11-19). And a question raised by the Pharisees about the coming kingdom of God stimulates Christ's instruction to the disciples to wait steadfastly for His return (vv. 20-37). The lessons taught are certainly for us too, for we must guard in our churches against causes of sin, must encourage confession, forgiveness, thankfulness, and a steadfast commitment to serving God while we await the return of our Lord.

Key verse. 17:10: The servant's role.

Personal application. Obeying Jesus is the least we can do.

Key concepts. Repentance »p. 780. Faith »p. 35. Obedience »p. 807. Pharisees »p. 625. Kingdom »pp. 380, 443.

INSIGHT

What causes people to sin? (17:1) Very possibly Jesus is referring to the cynical and worldly attitude of the Pharisees, illustrated in Luke's report of Christ's parables on wealth found in chap. 16. The material Luke provides now may well be just the antidote we need.

Confronting sin? (17:3) It is not "spiritual" to let yourself be victimized by other Christians. It is popular—and sounds spiritual—to promote a passive forgiveness. But Jesus puts forgiveness in a very different perspective. He says: (1) confront by rebuking the person who has sinned against you; (2) he is then to own up to his sin and repent; (3) only then if he repents, are we to forgive. Why the if? Because to bring reconciliation forgiveness must be received as well as extended. If another person is unwilling to acknowledge his fault, he will not receive our forgiveness.

We must always be willing to forgive (17:4). But we cannot say "I've forgiven him or her" until we have rebuked the sin and the person who sinned against us has repented.

The apostle's reaction (17:5-10). The disciples saw how hard it would be to accept responsibility for rebuking, obtaining repentance, and extending unlimited forgiveness. So they asked for more faith. Jesus' response can be paraphrased, "Faith is fine for moving mountains, but I told you to confront and forgive."

The story of the servant drives this last theme home. A servant's task is to obey his master. If Jesus is Lord, we are responsbile to do what He tells us. And Jesus tells His followers to confront, repent, and forgive as a way

of life in the faith community.

How often we cry out for more faith, when all that is really necessary is obedience to the commands of our Lord.

One returned (17:11-19). Faith healed not only the one leper who returned, but also the nine who appealed to Jesus for pity—and then took off!

What will move us to stay close to Jesus? What will move us to that obedience Jesus has just said is so critical? A spirit of praise and thankfulness, that keeps us ever mindful of all Jesus has done to heal us from the deadly disease of sin.

Not visibly (17:20). The Pharisees, as Jesus' stories reported in Luke 16, were materialists. The only "kingdom" they cared about was the kingdom to be established in this world at history's end.

But during this present age you and I are to experience a hidden, spiritual kingdom of God. We are not to seek after those pseudo-kingdoms human beings dream of, saying, "There He is," as if Christ can be found in their utopias. When Christ returns, His presence will be visible and unmistakable. Till then we must focus on the hidden, inner kingdom Christ establishes in the hearts of believers.

Christ's return as revelation (17:30). The Gk. word is *apokalupsis*. It is used here of a visible unveiling of reality at history's end, to be seen by all. Christ will break into the material world. But when He does, it will be first to judge and only then to establish a visible kingdom here.

Chapter summary. Luke now strings together a number of brief incidents concerning parables and people. His story of the persistent widow teaches perseverance and patience in prayer (18:1-8). His story of the Pharisee and tax collector illustrates the basic truth that only those who acknowledge they are sinners will rely on God's mercy and thus experience forgiveness (vv. 9-14). The necessity of an attitude of complete reliance on God is emphasized in Jesus' response to little children (vv. 15-17)—and in the response of the rich young ruler to Jesus (vv. 18-30). But the most powerful message of reliance is expressed by Jesus Himself. He shares with His disciples about His coming death (vv. 31-34) and yet gives freely to a blind beggar who cries out for mercy (vv. 35-43). When we truly rely on God, we are freed enough from our own burdens to express God's kind of caring for others.

Outline
Place
Finder

BIRTH
PREPARATION
GALILEE
TRAVELING
JERUSALEM
PASSION

Key verse. 18:14: The way up is still down.

Personal application. How freeing it is to rely fully on Jesus.

Key concepts. Prayer »p. 608. Pharisee »p. 625. Wealth »p. 125. Son of Man »p. 614. Davidic Covenant »p. 370. Healing »p. 611.

INSIGHT

Delay in answers to prayer (18:1-8). The Psalms are filled with cries of suffering believers to God. We too often face difficult times when we pray desperately, and yet heaven seems shut up and God indifferent. This story teaches that while we may charge human beings with utter indifference to others' suffering, we cannot so charge God. God does care about His "chosen ones." We can keep on praying with confidence during the waiting period, sure that God will see we "get justice, and quickly."

"Quickly" (18:8). We're often stunned at how fast our children grow up. And often frustrated at how slowly time passes as we wait for a long-planned vacation. Days pass at a constant, measured rate, but how we feel about the passage of time changes. God knows that it often hurts us to wait. This story encourages us to realize that deliverance is closer than it seems. In fact God is already acting, quickly, to bring us the blessing He yearns for us to know.

I'm not like others (18:9-14). If we compare ourselves with others, we can always find someone who is "worse." But we are to compare ourselves with God. In view of His perfection, we all fall short and stand in desperate need of mercy.

"Me, a sinner" (18:13). The one qualification for salvation is to be a sinner—and know it. The person who thinks himself righteous never gets in line before the gate of "mercy."

"Little children" (18:15-17). Emphasize the "little." As children get older even they develop a slight contempt for adults and begin to think they can get along on their own. Only an attitude of total dependence on God enables us to experience His present kingdom.

Sell all you have (18:18-25). The ruler relied on the good his wealth enabled him to do, not on God. Thus he was unwilling to be stripped of his wealth, despite Jesus' command. There is no clearer evidence of reliance on God than to obey the commands of Jesus. And no clearer evidence that we do not rely on the Lord than to disobey. For more, see »p. 621.

"Very sad" (18:23). The deep emotion expressed by *perilypos* tells us that the rich ruler really did want to follow Jesus. This was not an easy choice for him. He was not like Esau, who quickly traded his birthright for a bowl of stew (Gen. 25:29-34).

Yet never mistake spiritual yearnings for true spirituality. Our spirituality is seen not in what we want to do, but in what we choose to do!

Hard for the rich (18:24-36). The theme is again one of dependence. When we have nothing, it is much easier to rely on God. When we have all, we may not sense our need for God. Even more difficult is the thought of giving up everything we rely on to rely wholly on the Lord. Yet this is what Jesus calls for: complete surrender of all to Him. It may help us to surrender if we remember that, whatever we give, we cannot outgive God.

Outline
Place
Finder

BIRTH
PREPARATION
GALILEE
TRAVELING
JERUSALEM
PASSION

Chapter summary. This chapter brings us to the end of Jesus' journey and His entrance into Jerusalem. Contact with Jesus transforms a tax collector of Jericho (19:1-10) and leads to Luke's clear statement of the purpose of Christ's mission to Planet Earth (v. 10). The parable about funds entrusted to a man's servants while he was away sums up our mission on Planet Earth as we await Christ's return (vv. 11-27).

Luke now describes Jesus' Triumphal Entry into Jerusalem and His acclamation as the Messiah, the prophesied "King who comes in the name of the Lord" (vv. 28-40). But the shouts do not reflect a true understanding of who Jesus is and that failure to recognize Him will lead to disaster for the nation (vv. 41-44). Here symbolizing the utter necessity of a heart return to God, Jesus again cleanses the temple of its merchants (vv. 45-46). The act arouses the fury of the religious leaders, who are even more determined to kill Him (vv. 47-48).

Key verse. 19:10: Jesus' purpose.

Personal application. Make serving Jesus and others the purpose of your life.

Key concepts. Taxes »p. 611. Parable »p. 166. Davidic Covenant »p. 370.

INSIGHT

"**Chief tax collector**" **(19:2).** Zacchaeus held a relatively high position in the Roman tax system. These positions were obtained by making high bids for the privilege, the cost of which was recovered by charging ordinary people exorbitant rates.

"**I must stay at your house**" **(19:5).** We reach people by spending significant time with them — in settings where they feel comfortable. Don't be surprised when people don't accept an invitation to come to church. If you really want to reach them, go where they spend time.

All the people muttered (19:7). Eating in a person's home was a significant act in biblical times, signifying fellowship and acceptance of the other by both guest and host.

Jesus' motive was not considered by the crowds. But His love for the lost must move you and me.

"**Four times the amount**" **(19:8).** O.T. Law demanded less restitution in cases of theft (Lev. 5:16; Num. 5:7) than Zacchaeus promised. The proof of salvation is not that we do what we must to make things right, but that we gladly do more.

Background of Jesus' Parable of the Ten Minas (19:11-27). Archelaus, a son of Herod the Great, had hurried to Rome to beg permission to rule as a client king of Rome. His request was opposed by his own Jewish sub-

jects, who disputed his right to reign. Herod was given power and did return. One can imagine what he then did to those who had taken a stand against him! With these events fresh in the awareness of His listeners, Jesus pictured Himself as a rejected ruler who will surely return to claim His kingdom.

The parable corrected the notion that God's glorious kingdom was to appear on earth "at once" (v. 11). It explains His own rejection by His people and why He must go appeal to God the Father. The parable explains what Christ expects of His followers while He is gone — e.g., the use of the resources granted to each in His Master's service (vv. 12-19). And the parable, building on the anger of Archelaus, underlines the seriousness of the call to serve productively until Christ does come back again (vv. 20-24).

The Triumphal Entry. See p. 623.

Jerusalem doomed (19:41-44). Jesus' prediction came true in A.D. 70 when the Roman army, under future emperor Titus, destroyed the city. For decades no Jew was allowed to approach its site, or even to visit the holy hill on which the temple once stood.

A den of robbers (19:45-48). When our churches lose their character as houses of prayer and centers of teaching about God, they too are likely to be taken from us.

Chapter summary. In Jerusalem the right of Jesus to cleanse the temple (19:45-48) and teach is challenged. Jesus asks a question that shows the hollowness of the "authorities' " claim to power and refuses to answer them (20:1-8). Instead He tells a parable that exposes the motives of their plot to kill Him: They do not want God to rule. They want to rule God's people and exploit them for themselves! (vv. 9-19) Unable to act openly, the religious leaders try desperately to trap Jesus into some statement that can be used against Him. Their delegations not only fail (vv. 20-26 and 27-40), but Jesus asks a question that silences them (vv. 41-44). Jesus then warns the onlookers against the teachers of the Law, whose piety conceals their inhumanity and whose punishment will be severe (vv. 45-47).

Key verse. 20:14: Motives revealed.

Personal application. Let Christ be Lord, because He is!

Key concepts. Parable »p. 166. Taxes »pp. 611, 624. Pharisees »p. 625. Resurrection »p. 522. Davidic Covenant »p. 370.

INSIGHT

"Authority" (20:1-6). A person who truly exercises authority granted by God will not fear mere human beings, nor avoid taking a stand on controversial issues. The religious leaders claimed to have authority, but their actions showed the hollowness of that claim. What a contrast between the hesitance of the "leaders" and the bold affirmations of our Lord.

"The inheritance will be ours" (20:14). True spiritual leaders are marked by their sacrifices for others, not the profits made from them.

Caesar's to Caesar (20:20-25). What Caesar claims is irrelevant unless it interferes with our duty to God. And very little in the material world that is the concern of history's Caesars can interfere with the spiritual duty we owe the Lord.

The dead live (20:27-40). As Jesus' story reported in Luke 16:19-31, Christ's response to the hypothetical case posed by the Sadducees emphasizes the fact that physical death does not terminate the self-conscious existence of the individual. God is the God of the long dead Abraham, Isaac, and Jacob. For this to be true, the dead must exist now. What a comfort as we think of our own loved ones who have passed away.

No marriage in heaven (20:34). In the resurrection there is no marriage. But this does not mean husbands and wives are separated. It simply means that the intimacy we experience here on earth is a symbol of a reality we will experience in glory. The joy a married couple finds in their union will not be taken away, but

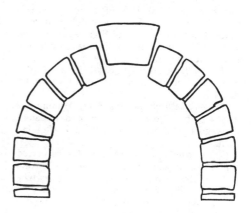

Illustration: Christ the Cornerstone (20:17-18). *The "cornerstone" was either the key stone in the foundation, on which a structure rests, or the key stone in an arch, which binds the structure together. Each image beautifully reflects the role of Christ in God's plan of salvation. Everything rests on Him, and He holds all things together. Those who launch themselves against this stone will be crushed, along with all their hopes.*

will be multiplied, as we experience a closeness with others that is beyond us here and now.

Chapter summary. A widow's gift underlines the attitude that God can commend and contrasts starkly with that displayed by the religious elite of Jesus' day (21:1-4). Jesus then shares a vision of the future with His disciples. His lecture covers five major topics. (1) Believers must not be deceived by disasters and assume the end of the world has come (vv. 5-11). (2) Believers must expect and not be disheartened by the persecution which will surely come (vv. 12-19). (3) Jerusalem will fall to the Gentiles and be under their domination until the coming era ends (vv. 20-24). (4) As the end approaches the laws which maintain a stable universe will themselves be shaken (vv. 25-28). (5) Until the end comes, God's people are to watch and pray (vv. 29-38).

Key verse. 21:13: A purpose in persecution.

Personal application. Jesus controls the future; we control our choices today.

Key concepts. Future »pp. 419, 427–428, 443. Persecution »p. 760.

INSIGHT

Give out of poverty (21:1-4). The measure of a gift is not how much is given, but how much there was to give.

The do's and don'ts of looking toward history's end (21:5-38). This might be a good title for Luke's report of Jesus' eschatological (end-times) teaching. Not all of them apply to you and me. But the ones in italics have direct relevance to our outlook on life.

(1) Don't be deceived (v. 8). Jesus' return won't be a secret. There's no need for us to set dates.

(2) Don't be frightened (vv. 9-11). Human history will be filled with wars and disasters. How good to know God will look after His own.

(3) Don't worry about yourself when persecuted, but witness to your persecutors (vv. 12-16). After all, the folks in real trouble are the ones who oppress God's saints! Let the Spirit fill your mouth with words about Jesus and your hearts with love for your enemies.

(4) Don't give up, even when everyone seems to turn against you (vv. 17-19). Stand firm on the foundation of your faith in Jesus. Others can hate you. But they can't do you any lasting harm.

(5) Do flee Jerusalem when it is besieged (vv. 20-24). This advice applied both to the Jews then living and to the lost who will dwell in the city as history's end draws near.

(6) Do take heart when the universe itself shows massive destabilization (vv. 25-31). This is a sign that Christ is soon to appear and is a cause for believers to rejoice rather than fear.

(7) Do exult in the certainty that God's Word is trustworthy, however uncertain life may be (vv. 32-33). This reminder is for the last generation, but we can certainly take heart from it in our own hard times today.

(8) Do be watchful, pray, and persevere and so earn the approval of the Son of Man (vv. 34-36). Life here has its pressures, and many of them are intense. But let's keep our eyes on Jesus, and let nothing distract us from serving Him.

This generation (21:32). Many commentators take "generation" here to refer to the Jewish race. In parallel passages the saying may point to the generation living when the signs begin.

Above: **Peter's "sword" (22:49).** The word translated sword means a cutting instrument and was used of knives as well as of weapons of war. Mark identifies Peter as the one who pulled out his knife to defend Christ—and was gently rebuked by the Lord, who said, "No more of this."

Chapter summary. Luke's report of last-day events follows the pattern so familiar from Matthew and Mark, but is also filled with unfamiliar details. Judas agrees to betray Jesus, delighting his enemies (22:1-6). At a Last Supper with His disciples Jesus institutes Communion (vv. 7-23) and deals with a running dispute between them over which will be greatest (vv. 24-30). Jesus also warns an incredulous Peter that he will soon deny the Lord (vv. 31-38) and then leads the little company to the Mount of Olives and Gethsemane (vv. 39-46). When Jesus is arrested the disciples first try to resist, but then flee (vv. 47-53). Peter follows when Jesus is taken to the high priest's house, and there, outside in the courtyard, Peter does deny the Lord (vv. 54-62). Now events rush toward their conclusion. Jesus is accused by the leaders of His people, condemned by Pilate, and rejected by the crowds who prefer the release of a terrorist to that of Jesus (22:63–23:25). He is crucified as friends, enemies, and bored soldiers look on, but even on the cross He awakens faith in a criminal condemned to die with Him (vv. 26-43). Jesus dies (vv. 44-49), and His body is hurriedly placed in a borrowed tomb (vv. 50-56). The story of Jesus seems, but only seems, to be at an end.

Outline
Place
Finder

BIRTH
PREPARATION
GALILEE
TRAVELING
JERUSALEM
PASSION

Key verse. 23:43: Death isn't the end.

Personal application. History truly is His story.

INSIGHT

"**The Feast**" (22:1). Passover was followed by this seven-day celebration (cf. Ex. 12:15-20). By Jesus' time "Passover" was applied to the whole period.

"**Chief priests and teachers of the Law**" (22:2). Jesus' early opponents were the Pharisees, an influential law fellowship. Here the people intent on getting rid of Jesus are the religious and political leaders, in essense, the governing body of both the Jewish faith and the nation.

"**In remembrance**" (22:17-19). These words in Jesus' institution of the Lord's Supper harken back to the O.T. concept of *zikkaron*. The word, translated "memorial," or "remembrance," indicated a festival or practice or object intended as a link for future generations with a distinctive act of God. Through the *zikkaron* God's people sensed their personal participation, along with the original generation, in the act God performed for them.

Thus, the Lord's Supper is a unique institution or sacrament. In observing it we are drawn back into history and realize that we truly were there at the Cross. What Jesus did then echoes throughout history, as real today as in the 1st century, for we appropriate by faith all that Jesus accomplished in giving His body and blood for our sakes.

"**Decreed**" (22:22). The word (*horismenon*) reminds us. From a time-bound perspective Jesus death was a miscarriage of justice. But from God's point of view it was the keystone of His plan not only to provide salvation, but to set all things right.

"**When you have turned back**" (22:31). Peter's denial shook the fisherman as nothing else had. In no other situation do we see bold, brash Peter reduced to tears (cf. 22:62). Yet the denial was a temporary failure. And undoubtedly it served always to remind Peter that he must rely on the Lord rather than on his own best intentions.

Failures do hurt. But remember, however great the failure, you *can* "turn back" and learn from your mistake(s).

Curiosity only (23:8). Herod serves as an example of the superficial man. He'd heard about Jesus. He was interested. All he really wanted to do was to be entertained. But Jesus was silent. He does not reveal Himself to the curious. But He is always there for the honest searcher.

The conversion of the criminal (23:38-43). Only Luke records the conversion of one of the two criminals, a mugger who used violence when taking what was not his. Let's remember as we read the passion account that Jesus didn't die just for the nice people of this world. Jesus paid the price for all humankind's sins, that all who believe might be with Him in paradise.

Chapter summary. Luke's account of the Resurrection is more than an account of events. It interprets those events in the light of Old Testament teachings about the Messiah (24:6-7, 19-27), and in view of Christ's own statement of His mission (vv. 45-47). Luke's account closes not with the Resurrection but the Ascension and reminds us that the risen Christ is to be worshiped (vv. 50-53). The Resurrection is in fact God's seal on the promise of salvation.

So Luke tells us about women who visited the tomb (vv. 1-11) and the curiosity that brought Peter to peer into the empty crypt (v. 12). Luke tells us about two disciples Jesus walked with along the road to Emmaus, explaining the Scriptures that spoke of the Messiah (vv. 13-29). Luke reports their excitement when they finally recognized Jesus and rushed back to tell Jesus' followers in Jerusalem (vv. 30-35). Finally, Luke tells of His appearance to His still confused disciples and of opening their minds so at last they understood the meaning of His life and death (vv. 36-49). And Luke concludes with a reminder of who Jesus is: exalted in heaven, God, worthy ever of our worship, the source of our joy (vv. 50-52).

Key verses. 24:46-47: Written, and now accomplished.

Personal application. Don't be slow of heart to trust or to worship the risen Saviour.

Key concepts. Angels »p. 521. Resurrection »pp. 629, 737, 823. Death of Christ »p. 813. Messiah »p. 431.

INSIGHT

He told you (24:9). The angels reminded the women of something each Gospel writer emphasizes. Jesus told His disciples ahead of time that He would die and come to life again (cf. Luke 9:22, 44-45; 18:31-34). It's not surprising they did not grasp the significance of what Christ was saying.

Now they remember. But still do not understand.

Wondering what had happened (24:12). Luke's description of the puzzlement and despair (cf. 24:21) that crushed Jesus' disciples makes utterly clear the foolishness of the rumor started by the Jewish leaders, that the disciples had stolen the corpse. The death of Jesus meant an end to all their hopes. They were in no mad state of mind to honor their dead leader by pretending He had been raised.

"Foolish" (24:25). The word Jesus used of the two on the Emmaus road is *anoetos.* In five of its six N.T. occurrences it is used of believers. Unlike the "fool" of the O.T., whose problem is moral, this word describes an individual who sees things from a distorted perspective. He or she has not adopted the divine viewpoint.

Jesus then proceeded to display the divine viewpoint on His own death by going back to the O.T. Scriptures, to demonstrate that the Messiah "had to" suffer such things and only then enter His glory.

It's not enough to have correct information. We must be able to intepret it correctly. The N.T. writers' use of the O.T. is rooted in the post-resurrection instruction Jesus gave concerning the real meaning of O.T. texts (cf. 24:44).

"It is true" (24:34). Belief in a literal, physical resurrection of Jesus is supported by three lines of evidence. There is the evidence of fulfilled prophecy. There is the evidence of eyewitness testimony. And there is the evidence of millions of lives transformed by faith in Him over the span of some two millenia.

Like Him (24:36ff.). First John 3:2 tells us that when Jesus returns we will be "like Him."

This Lucan passage tells us much about the resurrection body. It is real, made of flesh and bones (v. 39). It resembles the ordinary body, as Jesus' form still bore the scars of the cross (v. 39). It is capable of eating (v. 41). It is not limited by space: Jesus suddenly appeared among them in what another Gospel says was a closed and locked room (v. 36). We do not know the wonders that await us. But there are wonders indeed.

John

John's portrait of Jesus is the most theological of the four Gospels. He launches his work by presenting a Jesus who existed with God and as God before the creation of the universe. He entered His creation as a human being, lived among His creatures, and His every act and teaching calls us to believe in Him as Saviour and Lord. John's unique style features contrasting concepts that confront us with the necessity of belief. Christ is the focus of a cosmic struggle between life and death, light and darkness, truth and falsehood, love and hate. No wonder John is consumed with concern that we, his readers, respond to Jesus by placing our complete trust in Him—and live out that trust daily. In fact John's key word, *belief,* occurs 98 times in the Greek text of his 21 chapters!

This feature of John helps us sense the Gospel's value to you and me. Study of John's unique portrait of Jesus can enrich our faith in Christ and enable us to walk trustingly hand in hand with our Lord.

THEOLOGICAL THEMES IN JOHN'S GOSPEL

Jesus' deity   *John wants us to realize that Jesus Christ truly is one with the Father (1:1, 14), who in His own Person reveals the Father (1:18), and is Himself the only avenue through whom God can be approached (14:6). Jesus' claim of deity is clearly seen in John 5:18, 9:35-37, 17:5, and other passages.*

Atonement   *John understands Jesus' death as a sacrifice made to pay for mankind's sins. As the Lamb of God, He takes away the sins of the world (1:29), is lifted up on the Cross that those who believe might have eternal life (3:14-15), and gives His life for the world (6:51; 10:10).*

Eternal life   *John sees life as more than mere earthly existence, but as a fulfillment of human destiny that extends on through eternity. As Creator Jesus is the source of all life (1:4). As Saviour Jesus gives the gift of eternal life to all believers (3:15-16; 10:10; 20:31).*

Belief/Faith   *Faith is our response to Jesus, a response marked by trust in Him and by trusting ourselves to Him. Because of who Jesus is, all who trust Him are secure.*

Date and authorship. Most believe John's is the last of the Gospel accounts to be written. It was penned some time between A.D. 45 and A.D. 100 , with the later date much more likely. Very early testimony that "John, the disciple of the Lord, who also had leaned upon his breast, had himself published a Gospel during his residence in Ephesus in Asia" (Irenaeus, A.D. 180). Internal evidence makes it clear that the author was an eyewitness to most events he describes.

Illustration (John 13:1-17). *Jesus stoops to wash Peter's foot, which rests in a basin used in the first century for footwashing. Jesus' act scandalized His disciples. But it made an unforgettable impression on them, and on us. If we are to follow Jesus we must adopt His attitude toward servanthood and live as He died—for others.*

WHERE THE ACTION TAKES PLACE

Most of the action in John's Gospel takes place in Judea and Jerusalem. Yet there is another distinctive about the setting. John describes Jesus' public ministry (1:19–12:20). But then unlike the other Gospel writers he invites us into the Upper Room to share the very private ministry Jesus had with His disciples that fateful night (13:1–17:26). John's images of both the public and private ministries of Jesus drive home the great truths that His Gospel has been written to emphasize. Jesus, the Son of God, has accomplished our redemption. All we can do is respond to Him with total trust.

One distinctive feature of John's Gospel is its extended account of the "private teaching" Christ gave His disciples at the Last Supper.

THEOLOGICAL OUTLINE OF JOHN

I. Prologue	1:1-18
II. Public Ministry	1:19–12:50
III. Private Ministry	13:1–17:26
IV. Passion	18:1–20:31
V. Epilogue	21:1-25

CONTENT OUTLINE OF JOHN

I. Prologue (1:1-18)
  A. The Eternal Word (1:1-5)
  B. His Announcement (1:6-8)
  C. His Reception (1:9-13)
  D. His Incarnation (1:14-18)
II. Public Ministry (1:19–12:50)
  A. Early Ministry (1:19–4:54)
    1. John's witness (1:19-34)
    2. Followers attracted (1:35-51)
    3. The first miracle (2:1-11)
    4. Cleansing the temple (2:12-25)
    5. Nicodemus' interview (3:1-21)
    6. John's witness again (3:22-36)
    7. Woman at the well (4:1-42)
    8. Healing an official's son (4:43-54)
  B. Controversy and Conflict (5:1–8:59)
    1. A paralytic healed (5:1-15)
    2. Monologue on life (5:16-47)
    3. Five thousand fed (6:1-24)
    4. Monologue on Bread of Life (6:25-71)
    5. Jesus teaches in Jerusalem as opposition hardens (7:1-52)
    6. Jesus releases an adulteress (8:1-11)
    7. Jesus claims deity (8:12-59)
  C. Opposition Intensifies (9:1–12:50)
    1. Jesus restores sight (9:1-12)
    2. The Pharisees reject the evidence (9:13-41)
    3. Jesus' monologue on the Good Shepherd (10:1-21)
    4. The leaders charge Jesus with blasphemy (10:22-42)
    5. Jesus raises Lazarus (11:1-44)
    6. The leaders plot to kill Jesus (11:45-57)
    7. Jesus is anointed for burial (12:1-11)
    8. Jesus is acclaimed in Jerusalem (12:12-19)
    9. Jesus predicts death (12:20-36)
    10. The leaders still refuse to believe (12:37-50)
III. Private Ministry (13:1–17:26)
  A. The Last Supper (13:1-30)
  B. The New Commandment (13:31-38)
  C. The Way to God (14:1-14)
  D. The Gift of the Spirit (14:15-31)
  E. The Vine and Branches (15:1-17)
  F. The World and Jesus' Disciples (15:18–16:4)
  G. The World and the Holy Spirit (16:5-15)
  H. The Promise of Joy (16:16-33)
  I. Jesus' Priestly Prayer (17:1-26)
IV. Jesus' Passion (18:1–20:31)
  A. Arrest and Trials (18:1–19:16)
  B. Crucifixion (19:17-37)
  C. Burial (19:38-42)
  D. Resurrection (20:1-29)
  E. John's Purpose (20:30-31)
V. Epilogue (21:1-25)
  A. Jesus by the Sea (21:1-14)
  B. Peter Reinstated (21:15-23)
  C. Conclusion (21:24-25)

Outline
Place
Finder

PROLOGUE
PUBLIC
PRIVATE
PASSION
EPILOGUE

Chapter summary. John takes us back, beyond Creation, to show that Jesus has been God the Son from eternity past. He existed before His birth, coequal with God the Father, the source of light and of life itself (1:1-5).

Before He began His ministry on earth the presence of Jesus, the preexistent Word, was announced and pointed out by John (vv. 6-9). Yet, though He made the world itself, and came to a people He as God had called out long ago, He was neither recognized nor received by His own (vv. 10-11). Here John introduces a central theme of his Gospel. Those who do receive Him, by believing on His name, become the children of God (vv. 12-13). The awesome truth is that in Jesus God Himself did become flesh and live among us (v. 14). Jesus is the turning point of sacred history, the source of a grace that surpasses law, the visible expression of the unseen God (vv. 15-18).

Key verse. 1:14: God has been among us.

Personal application. See the glory of God in Jesus.

Key concepts. Creation »p. 430. Light »p. 685. Belief »p. 740. Flesh »p. 26. World »p. 893. Law »p. 145. Grace »p. 789. Son of God »p. 790.

INSIGHT

"The Word" (1:1). The Gk. word is *logos*, which usually emphasizes the message of a spoken word. John's point is that a key role of the Second Person of the Trinity has always been communication. The Son is the Spoken Word, the living expression of all that God has ever sought to communicate about Himself.

With God, and was God (1:1). John's point is that Jesus is both identical with the God of the O.T. and yet is distinct from Him. The concept, so familiar although mysterious to us, was stunning in the world of the 1st century. The Jews emphasized the uniqueness and unity of the O.T.'s one God. The pagans imagined a class of beings they called "gods." But John affirms that God is one, yet exists in distinct, separate personalities.

The concept is difficult, but the teaching is clear. The Word (Jesus) existed eternally with God as one God.

Jesus as Creator (1:3). John credits the Word with Creation. Psalm 19 exalted the created universe for speaking so plainly of God without language, so that its message can be "heard" in every language. Additional testimony is found in Col., which calls Jesus the "image of the invisible God" and says "all things were created by Him" (Col. 1:15-17).

Here in John the tense of "were made" (*egeneto*) implies a creative act, not a process. Jesus spoke, and the universe sprang into existence.

Life (1:4). The word *zoe* is used 36 times by John. This distinctive term for "life" draws attention to the vitalizing principle which makes physical life possible and even more often to eternal life. The saying that life was "the light of men" means that as the source of all life, Jesus is the focus of all our hopes.

Light and dark (1:5). These are frequently contrasted by John, representing not only the forces of good and evil, but also reality and illusion. The powers of darkness are ranged against the light revealed in Jesus, but have proven unable to "overcome" (*katelaben* is best taken this way, rather than as "understand").

"The world" (1:10). Here *kosmos* suggests the society as a whole. Christ made humankind and created the biosphere in which we live. But when He came to join us, humanity had no awareness of who He was or the significance of His presence.

All who receive him (1:12-14). But Jesus was recognized as God incarnate by some! These "received" Him. This image, receive, is the first John uses to define "believe."

If you do not see a gift held out to you, or if you see it but do not accept it as real, you won't stretch out your hand to take it. Believing in Jesus involves seeing Him presented as God's Son, accepting that description as real, and simply stretching out your hand to accept God's gift of eternal life. You then become what you were not: a child of God.

Chapter summary. John the Baptist's ministry stirs the Jew's ancient hope of Messiah's appearance, and John himself is mistaken for the coming King (1:19-28). Then God shows John that his cousin, Jesus, is actually the Son of God when Jesus is baptized (vv. 29-34). The first contact of Jesus with men who later become His disciples is made when John points Christ out as the Lamb of God, and two men curiously trail after Jesus (vv. 35-42). On that same occasion Jesus calls two others to follow Him and is confessed as Son of God by Nathanael (vv. 43-51).

Jesus now leads His informal little company back to Galilee, where they see Him turn water into wine at a wedding (2:1-10). The miracle stimulates their belief (v. 11), and Jesus spends more time with them in Capernaum, where the men lived (v. 12). But the disciples see a different Jesus when they travel together to Jerusalem for the Passover festival. In Jerusalem He explodes with anger and clears the temple of traders and money changers. There too He bluntly confronts the religious leaders and performs many additional miracles (vv. 13-25).

Outline
Place
Finder

PROLOGUE
PUBLIC
PRIVATE
PASSION
EPILOGUE

Key verse. 2:11: Miracles encourage faith.

Personal application. Based on the evidence it is foolish not to believe in Jesus.

Key concepts. Prophet »p. 131. Disciple »p. 657. Miracle »p. 57.

INSIGHT

"Elijah" (1:21). Malachi 4:5 predicts an "Elijah" is to appear before the Messiah comes in power. Jesus said that had He been accepted by His own, John's ministry could have been considered to fulfill this prediction.

John's role (1:23). Every Christian can model John. We too point others to Jesus.

"The Lamb of God" (1:29). The name given Jesus here reflects the atonement theme in this Gospel. Lambs were sacrificed on O.T. altars as sin offerings. But the true Lamb of God which all O.T. sacrifices symbolized is Jesus who "takes away the sin of the world."

"I did not know Him" (1:31). Know is used here in the sense of "recognize." John knew his cousin so well, other Gospel writers tell us, he refused at first to baptize Jesus (Matt. 3:14). John's baptism was for sinners, and John knew Jesus did not need to repent! When the Spirit descended on Jesus God revealed to him who Jesus really was: "the Son of God" (1:34).

Come and see (1:39). Today we spend time with Jesus in the Word and by associating with His people. Anyone willing to spend the time in honest searching for the truth about Jesus will find Him.

"The first thing" (1:41). We know conversion is real when "the first thing" one wants to do is share Jesus with loved ones.

Under the fig tree (1:48). The interplay of Jesus' deity and humanity is a fascinating study. At times the Gospels describe His human limitations: He is tired, discouraged, lonely, in anguish, and near despair in Gethsemane. And then His essential deity shines through, as here, when Jesus is aware of something not available through the senses. Nathanael, a "true Israelite" in his spiritual insight as well as character, realized at once that Jesus must be the Son of God.

Why involve me? (2:4) According to custom, hosts at a wedding feast treated the company with wine, and the guest's name was mentioned when the wine was poured. The phrase, "My time has not yet come," may mean nothing more than, "it is not my turn to treat." Even so Jesus did act, and the water He called for was miraculously transformed into the best wine of all.

Miracles and their impact (2:11). Jesus' miracles caused onlookers great amazement. His opponents tried to explain them away, by charging that Jesus was in league with Satan. His disciples found their faith strengthened. And some were stimulated to a superficial kind of "belief" about Jesus that fell short of trusting themselves to Him (2:23-24).

Outline
Place
Finder

PROLOGUE
PUBLIC
PRIVATE
PASSION
EPILOGUE

Chapter summary. The fact that Jesus did perform miracles was beyond dispute. This brought a Pharisee named Nicodemus to question Jesus (3:1-2). Jesus stunned Nicodemus by saying that before any spiritual questions can be dealt with a man must be "born again" (v. 3). Even though the concept of a spiritual rebirth has roots in the Old Testament, Nicodemus was totally confused (vv. 4-9). Jesus challenges Nicodemus to accept Christ's testimony (vv. 10-15) and goes on to explain the awesome cost to God of making eternal life available to humankind (vv. 16-17). Salvation now becomes an issue of belief or unbelief: only by trust in the Son of God can those who are "condemned already" pass from death to life (vv. 18-21).

At this point John introduces another witness to the truth Jesus has presented: John the Baptist. By divine revelation John confirms what Christ has said and Christ's miracles have attested. Whoever believes the Son has eternal life. Whoever rejects the Son remains under the wrath of God (vv. 22-36).

Key verse. 3:16: A beacon inviting faith.

Personal application. The life Jesus gives us is eternal.

Key concepts. Pharisee »p. 635. Kingdom »p. 380. Life »p. 682.

INSIGHT

"Nicodemus" (3:1). He was a member of the "ruling counsel" (the Sanhedrin, the governing body of religion and state under Rome). He was a Pharisee, zealous in his dedication to God's Law. He was "Israel's teacher." The Gk. text says "the teacher of Israel," so he held high religious office that involved interpreting Scripture authoritatively. He did come to Jesus with an open mind, ready to listen to this Man whose miracles suggested God intended to give a new revelation through Him. Later Nicodemus became a disciple (cf. 7:45-52; 19:38-42).

"Born again" (3:6). The phrase is distinctively Johannine (cf. 1 John 2:29; 3:9; 4:7; 5:1, 4, 18). But its meaning is clear. God acts supernaturally to make us His children (John 1:12-13). The spiritual life He infuses leads to moral transformation (1 John 2:29) and enables us to love God and others (1 John 4:7; 5:1-2). As natural birth begins our life on this earth, so spiritual birth brings us into the spiritual world and makes us God's "born ones."

"Born of water and the Spirit"? (3:5) There are many views. Is this hendiadys, in which two words refer to the same thing? Is the water baptism, or perhaps the fluid gushing out at childbirth? It may be best to see "water" as a reference to John's ministry, representing repentance.

You do not understand (3:10). The O.T. foresaw a coming day in which God would change the heart—the inner personality—of His people (cf. Ezek. 11:19). Nicodemus was Israel's teacher, but did not understand the principle underlying new birth.

"Lifted up" (3:14). When God's sinning people in the wilderness were devastated by deadly serpents, Moses put a snake, the symbol of their judgment, on a pole. All who looked at that symbol were promised life.

All people are helpless before the deadly curse of sin. In lifting Christ up on the cross, also a symbol of judgment, God makes Him the object of faith.

"God so loved" (3:16). In the 1st century one word for "love," *agape*, was quite weak, expressing only fondness. The N.T. writers picked up this word and infused it with new and stunning meaning. That meaning is defined in God's giving of His beloved Son, for us. First John 4:9 says, "This is how God showed His love . . . He sent His one and only Son into the world that we might live through Him." God chose to love sinners. God expressed His love in self-sacrifice. Christ incarnate and crucified forever gives meaning to the phrase, "God is love" and fills us with awe as we realize, "God loves me."

"Condemned" (3:18). Lost sinners stand condemned already. People aren't lost because they don't believe in Jesus. They simply remain lost unless they put their trust in Him.

Chapter summary. When Jesus is traveling through Samaria He engages a woman at a well in conversation (4:1-8). When Jesus speaks of the "water" He can provide that will quench her deepest thirst, and shows that He knows her sins, she turns the conversation to theological controversy (vv. 9-26). Convinced that Jesus is the Messiah, the woman hurries to call her fellow villagers out to see Him (vv. 27-30). The salvation of the woman at the well is deeply satisfying to Jesus (vv. 31-38). And when the Samaritans come to see Jesus for themselves, He stays two more days and many more believe (vv. 39-42). Arriving back in Galilee, Jesus is approached by a royal official desperate over the illness of his son. Jesus promises the boy will live, and the official takes Jesus at His word. His trust is vindicated when the child is found well, his recovery dating from the moment Jesus had made His promise (vv. 43-54).

Outline
Place
Finder

PROLOGUE
PUBLIC
PRIVATE
PASSION
EPILOGUE

Key verse. 4:23: What God is still looking for.

Personal application. Cut through all the theology and one issue remains: Do we take Jesus at His word?

Key concepts. Samaritan »p. 254. Water »p. 684. Messiah »p. 432.

INSIGHT

"**Living water**" (4:10). The phrase indicates a spring of flowing waters in contrast to water in a well or cistern. Jesus is speaking metaphorically; the woman is thinking concretely. Jesus is speaking of humanity's greatest thirst, for right relationship with God. The woman is thinking only of physical thirst.

"**The gift of God**" (4:10). When people know what God is willing to do for them, all as a free gift (*doron*), then and only then are they able to face their sins and seek the Lord.

"**Call your husband**" (4:16). The challenge immediately shifted the woman's focus to the moral realm and to her true need. Yet the request was not improper. In that culture a married woman was not to talk with a strange man without her husband present.

Her blunt reply was not yet a confession. It meant, "I don't need to. I'm not married."

The man you have (4:17-19). Jesus stripped away the facade. Sin shows that our need for God, and our even unrecognized thirst, is real!

You Jews say (4:20). How quickly folks want to shift the subject from sin to theology. Jesus did answer her question. But He was not sidetracked.

God seeks worshipers (4:23-26). Sin is not threatening when the sinner realizes punishment is not an issue. God is seeking worshipers. He isn't looking for new ways to judge us. When the woman linked this message of hope to the Messiah, and Jesus announced He was

Illustration. *Drawing water from the town well was an important social event for women in the ancient Middle East. The fact that the Samaritan woman came alone suggests, as does Jesus' reference to five "husbands," that she was rejected by the other women of the community. How amazing that God does not reject sinners, but seeks them.*

the Promised One, then she was ready to surrender all.

Many believed (4:39). The Gospel is to set off chain reactions. One won can lead to many, many more.

Outline
Place
Finder

PROLOGUE
PUBLIC
PRIVATE
PASSION
EPILOGUE

Chapter summary. Back in Jerusalem, Jesus heals an invalid at the pool of Bethesda (5:1-9). The incident stimulates a controversy, as Jesus had told him to pick up his bedding and walk— and it was the Sabbath (vv. 10-14). When the man reports Jesus is the one who healed him and told him to carry his bedding, the Jews (John's term for the religious leaders in distinction to the common people) persecute Him (vv. 15-16).

Jesus then publicly identifies Himself with God the Father (vv. 17-18) and not only goes on at length to prove His claim is valid, but also insists that He is the source of eternal life (vv. 19-30). This claim is validated not only by Jesus' miracles, but by the Scriptures themselves. Any who reject Him stand accused by the very book they claim to believe is God's Holy Word! (vv. 31-47)

Key verse. 5:24: Belief brings life.

Personal application. Eternal life isn't something we will have in the future. It's something we possess now.

Key concepts. Healing »pp. 412, 611, 784. Deity of Jesus »pp. 678, 687. Father »pp. 140, 663. Truth »p. 892.

INSIGHT

An angel stirs the water? (5:4) This verse is omitted from the NIV because no manuscripts of John from earlier than the 4th century contain it. Most believe this was a superstition, added to the text long after John wrote.

"Do you want to get well?" (5:6) The question is psychologically and spiritually acute. Many do not want to see their situation change, no matter how grim it is. The paralyzed man undoubtedly made his living begging. He would be responsible to make his own living.

Physical, psychological, and spiritual healing all have this in common: One who is healed must change and take responsibility for his or her own self. All too many people resist the Gospel because they do not want to "get well!"

He told me (5:11). How much wiser to obey the Healer than those who tell you what to do, but neither care about you nor have ability to help!

He told the Jews (5:15). The healed man has been criticized for a lack of gratitude and even for "blaming" Jesus when he was caught carrying his bedding. But Christ never told the man not to report who had healed him.

It's unwise for us to invent motives and then criticize anyone, especially this man, who obeyed Jesus by carrying his bedding even though he knew it was the Sabbath.

I work (5:17). Jesus pointed out that God does not take the Sabbath off, but keeps the universe running. So of course Jesus works also. This identification of Himself with the creative works of God was tantamount to a claim of deity.

Equal with God (5:18). Some even today say that Jesus never claimed to be God. Such people simply do not read the N.T. carefully. Jesus' enemies knew very well exactly what He was claiming. They refused to believe and determined to kill Him.

Cross from death to life (5:24). Sin condemns and kills. All have sinned, so all are both condemned and spiritually dead. Belief in Christ removes condemnation and brings eternal life.

"Eternal life" (5:24). Eternal life is more than endless. It has a unique quality and character all its own. Eternal life is God's own life, infused with His vitality and moral character, given to us through spiritual birth. Those with this life can have fellowship with God and with other believers, for we are linked to Him and one another by eternal bonds.

John 5 is one of the N.T.'s basic passages on eternal life. Other key passages link eternal life with faith (John 3:15-36) and with Christ's shepherd work (10:10-18, 25-30). Possession of eternal life will show itself in obedience and love (1 John 2–3). The bondage that is our heritage with death is broken by Jesus' life-giving cross (Rom. 5:12-21), and the Holy Spirit's power flows through us, enabling us to express our new nature in righteous living here and now (Rom. 6:1-11). It is this, a wonderful new and eternal life, which we possess immediately when we believe in the Son (1 John 5:10-12).

Chapter summary. Jesus feeds a great crowd that followed Him, intrigued by His miracles (6:1-14). Enthusiastic over Jesus' ability to feed them, the crowd intends to make Him king "by force" (v. 15). That evening the disciples see Jesus walking on the water (vv. 16-21), and the next day the crowds set out, intent to find Jesus wherever He may have gone (vv. 22-24).

When Jesus is found He challenges their motives for seeking Him, and when the crowds still insist He provides bread (vv. 25-31), presenting Himself as the true Bread from heaven. Believing in Jesus means "eating" His flesh as bread and "drinking" His blood. Only by fully participating through faith in all Jesus is and has done will men and women find salvation (vv. 32-59).

This difficult teaching offends many who had called themselves Jesus' "disciples" and many leave (vv. 60-66). The 12 disciples stay, convinced there is no place else to go. Jesus has the words of eternal life. He is the Holy One of God (vv. 67-71).

Outline
Place
Finder

PROLOGUE
PUBLIC
PRIVATE
PASSION
EPILOGUE

Key verse. 6:33: Bread sustains life.

Personal application. We don't need to understand everything; Jesus says to trust Him fully.

Key concepts. Bread »p. 605. Miracle »p. 61. Prophet »p. 131.

INSIGHT

"How far will they go"? (6:9) This is the only miracle reported in all four Gospels. It reminds us that Jesus is able to stretch any resources we may have to meet our needs—and others'.

"Make Him king" (6:15). Kings rule, they are not ruled by their people. The very intent of the crowds to force Jesus to become king shows how weak their allegiance was to Him.

Don't come to Jesus intending to use faith for your own purposes. Come to Jesus as a subject, willing to let Him rule in your heart.

"Rabbi, when did you get here?" (6:25) Jesus' most significant miracles are performed to nurture existing faith. Walking on the water (vv. 16-24) was shared with the disciples, but never mentioned to the crowds.

Some things God does for you and me need to be held close to our hearts, and not shared with outsiders.

Bread from heaven (6:26-59). Bread was the basic food of the ancients. It is symbolic of all that sustains life here on earth. As "bread from heaven" Jesus is affirming that He is essential to provide and sustain spiritual life.

The concept of "eating" Christ's flesh is symbolic too (vv. 53-54). Material bread must be eaten and digested—it must become part of us.

In the same way all that Christ is must become a part of us. We must appropriate Him by faith, take Him in completely that He might become a part of us and sustain us.

"What miraculous sign"? (6:30-31) The people haven't forgotten the feeding of the 5,000. Not at all! They ask for proof—and then define the proof they'll accept! In Moses' time God provided manna, a bread from heaven that sustained that generation for nearly 40 years. This question is pure manipulation. We'll believe, if you feed us for years too! But manna was not the true bread from heaven. God has something better for us—Jesus Himself.

Came down from heaven (6:33). This claim is repeated six times in this chapter! Only one from heaven could do all Jesus promised.

"I am the Living Bread" (6:51). Jesus alone is able to meet man's need for eternal life.

"The Jews" (6:52). Here as elsewhere John uses this phrase to distinguish the religious leaders from the rest of the Jewish population.

Flesh and blood (6:55). These are analogous to bread and water. As the one satisfies physical needs, the other satisfies spiritual needs.

Disciples turning back (6:66). The word "disciple" is used in both a technical and ordinary sense in the N.T. The technical use refers to apprentices in training under an established teacher. The Twelve were Jesus' disciples in this sense. But "disciple" also meant an adherent, someone who went along with a movement without a deep commitment to its principles or leader. It was this kind of "disciple" who "turned back."

Outline
Place
Finder

PROLOGUE
PUBLIC
PRIVATE
PASSION
EPILOGUE

Chapter summary. Jesus delays going up to Jerusalem for one of Judaism's three required religious festivals. Then He travels incognito (7:1-13). Halfway through the eight-day festival Jesus begins teaching publicly in the temple courtyard. Jesus attributes His teaching directly to God, rather than rabbinical "seminary training," and insists anyone who chooses to do God's will will recognize it. When challenged, He bluntly states that the judgment of the religious leaders is flawed and that they do not keep the Law they claim to honor (vv. 14-24).

Widespread speculation that Jesus is the Christ angers the leaders even as His sayings puzzle them (vv. 25-36). But the crowds also hesitate when, on the last day of the festival, Jesus calls on His listeners to believe in Him (vv. 37-44). The religious leaders' fury is intensified when their own guards refuse to arrest Jesus, and Nicodemus, one of their number, hesitantly defends Him. It's clear that the leaders absolutely refuse to believe Jesus could be the Christ (vv. 45-52).

Key verse. 7:17: Commitment produces certainty.

Personal application. Don't ask to know God's will until you are ready to do it.

Key concepts. Feasts »p. 89. Demons »p. 659. Law »p. 606. Pharisee »p. 625. Christ (Messiah) »p. 432.

INSIGHT

Jesus' brothers (7:1-9). There is both jealousy and unbelief in the brothers' barb about "wanting" to become a "public figure." Later at least two of Jesus' brothers, James and Jude, did believe and became leaders in the young church.

Don't write off those who don't respond at once to the Gospel. Often it takes time.

Intimidation (7:12). John uses the phrase "the Jews" of Judaism's religious hierarchy. Their power to cut any Jewish person off from Israel's religious and social life kept those who did think Jesus was the Messiah from speaking out.

Not studied (7:15). All advanced theological training was given by recognized rabbis to groups of disciples. The leaders acknowledged that Jesus had an advanced grasp of their religion, but could not imagine how this was possible, as He had never been apprenticed to one of them.

Choose to do God's will (7:17). This is a vital and basic principle. To know Jesus and develop spiritual understanding a person must make a conscious, determined choice to do God's will. If we make that choice, God will show us what His will is, and we can live it, step by step.

Circumcise on the Sabbath (7:23). Boy infants were circumcised the 8th day after birth, even if this fell on the Sabbath. Jesus showed up the flawed reasoning of His opponents. They permit a rite symbolic of purification affecting one member of the body on the Sabbath. How can they complain of Jesus who cleanses and heals the *whole* body?

We know where this man is from (7:27). The Jews *assumed* Jesus was born in Galilee, because He lived in Nazareth. Yet if they had checked the records, that given the Jewish concern with genealogies surely existed, they would have learned He was born in Bethlehem, of David's family line (vv. 41-42).

How tempting it is to use Scripture against others—without checking the facts, or our interpretation. Let's be more honest than Jesus' enemies in our use of the Bible.

There is of course a double meaning in Jesus words. He actually "came from" God—and His enemies "knew" He was just a human being. They were wrong on all counts!

"Water" (7:37-39). In the O.T. water is associated with ritual cleansing from defilement and with blessing. Isaiah 44:3 speaks of a future outpouring of God's Spirit as pouring "water on the thirsty land." This is surely the image Jesus alludes to here as He promises to pour out the Holy Spirit as the source of "living (e.g., running, fresh water; a spring or stream) water" for those who believe in Him.

Chapter summary. Jesus is teaching again in the temple courts when the religious leaders drag in a woman caught in the act of adultery and challenge Him to sentence her. He avoids their trap by calling on "any one of you" who is without sin to cast the first stone—and one by one they leave (8:1-11). When Jesus next preaches He calls Himself the "Light of the world." When the Pharisees demand proof, Jesus points out that God, His Father, has already testified—through the miracles He has performed (vv. 12-18). The confused Pharisees press the point, and Jesus bluntly warns them they will "die in their sins" unless they believe in Him (vv. 19-30). It is foolish to rely on physical descent from Abraham, when spiritual kinship to the great patriarch is the real issue (vv. 31-41). Antagonism to Jesus shows that they are in the spiritual line of Satan, not of Abraham, and are unrelated to God (vv. 42-47). The furious leaders charge that Jesus is demon-possessed, but He calmly identifies Himself with the "I Am" (*Yahweh*) of the Old Testament (vv. 48-58). His enemies realize that Jesus is claiming to be God and pick up stones, intent on stoning Him to death (v. 59).

Outline
Place
Finder

PROLOGUE
PUBLIC
PRIVATE
PASSION
EPILOGUE

Key verse. 8:58: Jesus is and always was.

Personal application. Not to accept Jesus on His own terms is to reject Him.

INSIGHT

The trap (8:1-11). Old Testament Law called for the death sentence for adultery. This penalty, however, was almost never imposed in Israel. If Jesus said, "Stone her," He would appear harsh. If He did not, He could be accused of not upholding the Law.

This story may not have been in the original text. But it is clearly consistent with the character both of Jesus and of the Pharisees.

"The Light of the world" (8:12). In John "light" is closely linked with distinguishing between the true and the false, between reality and illusion. As the "Light of the world" Jesus becomes the one and only source of illumination of spiritual reality. Believe in Him and we see all as it really is. Refuse to believe in Him, and we are left with only "human standards"—and darkness.

Below and above (8:23-24). A person on a hill can see more than one in a valley. But there is more to Jesus' saying than this. God, in heaven, sees all accurately. Man, corrupted by sin, has distorted vision.

"Truth" (8:31-32). In John "truth" is that which is in full correspondence with reality. We can't know this kind of truth in theory, but must experience the reality Jesus' words portray by putting them into practice. If you and I want to "know the truth" about anything, we must be disciples, holding firmly to Jesus' teaching

and putting His words into practice.

Spiritual slavery (8:34). Slavery here is being lost in the world of illusion. Because the person who sins is not obeying Jesus' words, that person has no contact with spiritual reality. Like the Pharisees, he or she may think all is well. But in fact that person is lost, separated from God, and doomed unless he or she turns to Christ for salvation. The person who chooses sin is bound by invisible chains.

Freedom (8:32). Freedom is the experience of life—of relationship with God, with one's self, with others, and with the material world—as God intends it to be for human beings. This freedom is discovered by us only when we listen to Jesus' words and put them into practice.

Freedom is not unrestrained indulgence in anything we may want to do when we want it. Freedom is being who we really are, creatures shaped by God for fellowship with Him, creatures who find joy and fulfillment only in loving and serving Him. Freedom is freedom to be who we are intended to be. And the way to freedom is marked out by the words of Jesus Christ.

"I Am" (8:57-58). *Yahweh*, God's personal name in the O.T., can be translated "I Am." In saying He saw Abraham and in affirming the eternity of His being, Jesus laid clear claim to being the God of the O.T. And was so understood by the Jews.

Outline
Place
Finder

PROLOGUE
PUBLIC
PRIVATE
PASSION
EPILOGUE

Chapter summary. Opposition to Jesus continues to intensify. When Jesus heals a man born blind (9:1-12), the Pharisees badger the healed man. They cannot deny the miracle, but will not admit He is God's messenger (vv. 13-16). The blind man finally cuts through to the heart of the issue: "If this man were not from God, He could do nothing" (vv. 17-33). The blind man is thrown out by the religious leaders, but is found by Jesus, and believes in Him (vv. 34-38). Jesus' concluding remark sums up the spiritual state of the Pharisees. The blind see, and those who claim to see are blind. Only if they could not see would they be guiltless. But because they could see if only they would, the guilt of the leaders remained (vv. 39-41).

Key verse. 9:33: The obvious is true.

Personal application. We can see spiritual truth if we are willing to accept it.

Key concepts. Sin »p. 34. Pharisee »p. 625. Sabbath »pp. 71, 441, 664.

INSIGHT

Sickness and sin (9:1). Popular theology held that sickness was a punishment for sin. In the case of a person born blind, this posed a theological riddle. Was the blind man punished for sins he would commit? Or were sins of the parents being punished in the son? (cf. Ex. 34:7) Jesus' answer is important. "Neither . . . sinned." God had another purpose in the man's disability (v. 3).

In Scripture sickness and sin are related, in that Adam's fall introduced both into the universe. An individual's sickness is thus not necessarily a punishment for his sins, though it is a witness to humanity's sinful condition.

We should not wail, "Why is God punishing me?" when we or our loved ones suffer.

There is, however, an even more positive message. God did intend to redeem the blind man's suffering by using it for His glory. Christ's healing of this blind man reminds us that, in often unexpected ways, our suffering can be used by God for good.

Mere curiosity (9:2). The disciples weren't moved by compassion, but by theological curiosity. Our first concern should be, like Christ's own, for the sufferer. Let's meet people's needs and wrestle with the theological questions afterward.

"As long as it is day" (9:4). Use each opportunity to help. In saying "we" Jesus included us in defining this ministry principle.

Go wash (9:7). Jesus usually healed simply by speaking the word. Here He told the blind man to "go" and did not even promise healing. The blind man however did set out to do as Jesus said. And in obeying he gained his sight.

The incident is an illustration of the truth Christ expressed to His disciples in John 8:31-32. We come to know the truth by putting Jesus' words into practice. We who are blind and cannot see spiritual reality not only come to see reality, but we experience it as well.

"He put mud on my eyes" (9:15). Witness is telling what you know by experience. We may not know much about Jesus, but anyone can tell what Jesus has done for him or her.

They were divided (9:16). The Pharisees were not divided over whether to believe in Jesus. They were divided as to how to explain His miracle away.

"Do you want to become His disciples too?" (9:27) This remark drips with sarcasm and reflects the blind man's frustration with the constant nagging of the Pharisees.

"We know that God does not listen to sinners" (9:30-33). The blind man is bolder than his parents, who refuse to take any position on their son's healing because of the known hostility of the religious leaders to Jesus (cf. vv. 20-23). The once blind man openly expressed the obvious fact that the leaders were intent on trying to hide. The blessing of sight restored was so great that nothing the leaders could do would intimidate him.

Let's remember this and freely share our own faith in Christ. There is nothing we might possibly lose that compares with what we have gained.

Not ignorance (9:39-41). There was no way that the Pharisees could claim ignorance. Their rejection of Jesus was deliberate, so they were guilty of the most terrible of all sins.

Chapter summary. Jesus speaks of familiar things as He describes Himself as the Good Shepherd, willing to give His life for the sheep (10:1 18). The leaders again express frustration: How can they explain Jesus and His words away? (vv. 19-21) When they insist Jesus tell them plainly if He is the Christ (vv. 22-24), Jesus tells them, "I did tell you!" Jesus again restates His claims. Rather than believe, the furious leaders intend to stone Him for blasphemy! (10:25-33) In view of the leaders' utter hostility, Jesus goes back across the Jordan, and many follow to hear His teaching (vv. 34-42).

Outline
Place
Finder

PROLOGUE
PUBLIC
PRIVATE
PASSION
EPILOGUE

Key verses. 10:30-33: Jesus' greatest claim.

Personal application. Jesus shepherds us today.

Key concepts. Sheep »pp. 355, 620. Shepherds »pp. 355, 504.

INSIGHT

Thieves and robbers (10:1). The *kleptes* takes by stealth, the *lestes* by force. God's sheep were exploited by their own leaders and by the Romans. Neither had any concern for the welfare of the people.

Entering by the gate (10:2). Jesus came as Israel's rightful Messiah and came openly and honestly.

All who came before Me (10:8). Jesus is referring to the many false messiahs, who aroused national passions and claimed to be sent by God to deliver the people from foreign enemies. They, however, came to exploit the people rather than serve them—to gain, rather than give.

Hired hands (10:12-13). These are the religious leaders, who are concerned only with their own safety and ease and not with the sheep. Jesus is the Good Shepherd because the sheep are His and are precious to Him. He cares about them so much that He willingly gives His life for them. This self-sacrifice is completely voluntary, the true measure of God's love for lost humankind.

"Because you are not My sheep" (10:26-28). How do we recognize God's people? What are the marks of faith? They believe in Jesus. They listen to Jesus' voice. They follow Him. Confession, obedience, and allegiance are the marks of the true believer.

"I and the Father are one" (10:30). Jesus is God. This is another clear claim by Jesus of deity. His hearers understood exactly what He meant—and thus were ready to stone Him for blasphemy.

"Blasphemy" (10:33). The Heb. term means to spurn, or to treat with contempt. The Gk. word means to slander, to speak abusively of, or to "speak lightly of the sacred." It's far more serious than the casual curse or misuse of God's name common in our time. Jesus was charged

Illustration: The Good Shepherd at the gate. *At night sheep were kept in an enclosure with a single opening, the gate. The shepherd slept in the doorway so that no wild beast could attack, except over his own body. Jesus as the "Gate for the sheep" interposes His own body between us and sin and Satan. He actually gave His life that we might have life. He truly is the Good Shepherd.*

with blasphemy because He claimed the right and authority that belonged to God alone (cf. also Matt. 26:65; Mark 2:7; 14:64; Luke 5:21).

This fact reminds us that no one can dismiss Jesus as a "good man." He was either an impious deceiver, a madman, or exactly who He said He was: God the Son, God with us in human flesh.

"You are gods" (10:34). See Ps. 82:6 »p. 369.

Outline
Place
Finder

PROLOGUE
PUBLIC
PRIVATE
PASSION
EPILOGUE

Chapter summary. Jesus was close to a little family living in Bethany, near Jerusalem. When Lazarus became sick, his sisters sent an urgent message to Jesus (11:1-3). Inexplicably, Jesus did not respond till days later (vv. 4-16). When He arrived Lazarus was dead. Jesus spoke to the sisters of Himself as "the Resurrection and the Life," a reality they acknowledged. But even these firm believers limited Jesus' power to "the last day" (vv. 17-27). Jesus, deeply moved at the pain of the two sisters, called for Lazarus' tomb to be opened (vv. 28-40). When this was done He called to Lazarus—and the dead man, restored to life, came out of his grave (vv. 41-44). This even more notable miracle stunned the religious leaders and hardened them in their determination to kill Jesus (vv. 45-57).

This familiar story is one of the most moving of Gospel tales about Jesus, for it shows the depth of affection and trust that existed between Him and His friends.

Key verses. 11:25-26: Life is assured in Jesus.

Personal application. Don't limit Jesus' power to act in your present.

Key concepts. Death »p. 369. Life »p. 682. Resurrection »p. 658.

INSIGHT

"The one you love" (11:3). It's easy to pray when we or a loved one first becomes sick. We believe firmly that Jesus does love us. The problem comes when there seems to be no response from God. The events reported in this chapter not only display Christ's power, but also help us deal with those painful delays in answers to prayer that trouble God's saints so often.

"Jesus loved Martha and her sister and Lazarus" (11:3-6). This seems to us in such conflict with the fact that, after hearing of their need, Jesus "stayed where He was two more days."

Don't let God's inactivity cause you to question His love.

"For your sake" (11:12-15). Restoring Lazarus would create more joy, and do more to strengthen faith, than any ordinary healing could. God's delays are intended to bless!

"That we may die with Him" (11:16). Thomas' reaction reminds us that Jesus' life was threatened by the leaders of His people. Thomas and the others may have wrongly supposed Jesus did not hurry to Bethany out of fear. Yet it shows the depth of the disciples' commitment to Jesus that they felt they would rather die with Jesus than live without Him.

"He will rise . . . at the last day" (11:23-24). Martha had total faith in Jesus. But even so she unconsciously limited His power to act in her present. Jesus would raise her brother—in the future. But Jesus intended to raise him now.

Never make the mistake of limiting Jesus' power to act in your present. Neither time, space, nor apparent impossiblity can restrict our Lord's ability to meet our deepest needs.

"I am the resurrection and the life" (11:25). Jesus is Lord of both physical and spiritual life. Belief in Jesus infuses a spiritual life in us that persists even though the physical body dies.

The greatest miracle of Jesus was not raising Lazarus to physical life again, for Martha's brother would again die. The greatest miracle was and is in Jesus' power to give endless spiritual life to us who believe in Him.

"Jesus wept" (11:35). Often pointed to as the shortest verse in the Bible, it is also one of the most important. If Jesus delays His answers to our prayers it's not because He's unconcerned. He shares our suffering. He weeps both with and for us.

Restored faith (11:45). Early popular excitement over Jesus disappeared after His teaching on the bread of life (6:66). Later miracles now convince many who hesitated, while hardening opponents.

Take away our place (11:47-50). The political and religious leaders of Judaism totally misunderstood Jesus' motives and feared an uprising that would strip them of their power when the Romans intervened. Evil men will always ascribe evil to others' motives, however pure those may be.

Chapter summary. As the Passover week approaches Jesus stays with Mary, Martha, and Lazarus in Bethany. One night a woman slips in and pours expensive perfume on His feet. Judas objects, angry that the gift wasn't sold and the funds turned over to the group's treasurer—Judas himself (12:1-8). Still things seem to be looking up: many hearing of the Lazarus miracle are openly expressing allegiance to Jesus (vv. 9-11). When Jesus is gladly acclaimed by Jerusalem's crowds, His enemies are near despair (vv. 12-19). But Jesus is not deceived. He tells His disciples (vv. 20-28a) and then the crowds that He is about to be killed (vv. 28b-36). Through it all the leaders refuse to believe and the prominent few who refuse to acknowledge Him do so because they fear being ostracized (vv. 37-43). But Jesus is still the One God has set forward as the object of our faith. Everyone must hear His words and display faith by keeping those words, or fall short of finding eternal life (vv. 44-50).

Outline
Place
Finder

PROLOGUE
PUBLIC
PRIVATE
PASSION
EPILOGUE

Key verse. 12:44: Faith in God is faith in Jesus.

Personal application. Let nothing keep you from confessing faith in Christ.

Key concepts. King »p. 130. Christ »p. 646. Son of Man »p. 615.

INSIGHT

Mary's gift (12:3). The gift likely represented Mary's life savings, as 500 denarii (Gk.) was a very large sum to ordinary people. It represents a simple yet profound motive. Mary wanted to give Jesus her best.

"Judas" (12:4-6). Even Christ's betrayer tried to sound spiritual, expressing a concern for the poor that he surely did not feel. Watch out for those who criticize your or others' best instincts by using religion against you. Piety often cloaks hidden motives.

"Hosanna" (12:13). The word means "save now!" The crowd's excitement reflected their belief that Jesus was about to set up an earthly kingdom and expel the Romans.

A crisis (12:9-19). The stir created by raising Lazarus brought fresh crowds to Jesus. His renewed popularity created a panic among His enemies and convinced them that a crisis existed. How significant. The gift of life given to Lazarus moved Jesus' enemies to act against Him and to take Jesus' life! The eternal life Jesus gives also comes at the cost of His own.

"Greeks" (12:20). These were Gentiles, not Greek-speaking Jews. Jesus does not explain His refusal to see them, except to say that the "time has come."

"Kernel of wheat" (12:24). The image is poignant. In surrendering its identity the seed multiplies itself. Jesus' death was not loss but gain.

He who loves life will lose it (12:25). The saying here is different from a similar saying in Matt. 16. Here Jesus uses two words for "life." By losing one's self (*psyche*) through exchanging worldly drives and motives for submission to Christ's will, a person gains spiritual life (*zoe*), which is experienced here and in eternity.

For this reason (12:27). Jesus was determined to fulfill the purpose for which He had been born. Let's not ask for release from the suffering which all too often gives our life unique meaning.

"When I am lifted up" (12:30-33). The phrase "lifted up" speaks first of the Cross, but also of the Resurrection. It is the Resurrection which infuses the Cross with meaning, even as Christ's glorification puts His suffering in perspective.

"All men" (12:32). Jesus does not suggest all will be saved, but that all humanity is invited to look to the Cross and live. Perhaps this is His answer to the Greeks who approached Philip. The Cross was His message to them, as it is to all.

"They loved praise from men" (12:42-43). Did the silent minority of leaders who "believed in" Jesus truly believe? Probably so. And many may have taken an open stand for Jesus after His resurrection. Yet their silence was in itself a kind of betrayal.

It is hard to see how we can believe wholeheartedly in Jesus and still worry about the opinion His enemies may have of us!

Outline
Place
Finder

PROLOGUE
PUBLIC
PRIVATE
PASSION
EPILOGUE

Chapter summary. The Last Supper took place on Thursday night and its theme was of love (13:1). Jesus demonstrates that theme by personally washing His disciples' feet, a courtesy usually performed by a menial servant (vv. 2-5). Peter objects, but Jesus insists. The act is symbolic of spiritual cleansing as well as a model of the attitude believers are to adopt toward one another (vv. 6-17). Then, weighed down by the knowledge, Jesus identifies Judas Iscariot as His betrayer, and that man slips away to make final arrangements (vv. 18-30). Yet history's greatest tragedy will glorify God, in a way the disciples will understand only later (vv. 31-33). Then Jesus gives His disciples what He calls a "new command." His followers are to love one another as Jesus loved them — self-sacrificially, totally, and with a mutual commitment that will amaze the world and mark them as Christ's own (vv. 34-35). Peter, missing the significance of the command, fastens on an earlier remark and rashly pledges to lay down his life rather than leave Jesus. Little does he know that soon he will disown his Lord (vv. 36-38).

Key verses. 13:34-35: The new commandment.

Personal application. Christ's last living command is love!

Key concepts. Passover »p. 59. Clean »pp. 82, 505. Love »p. 351.

INSIGHT

Love's full extent (13:1). The Gk., *eis telos*, indicates love without limits. Jesus gave everything and keeps on giving.

Footwashing (13:4-5). The courtesy was appreciated in the Middle East, where sandal-shod feet became dirty walking dusty streets. Usually feet were washed by a servant. The disciples were uncomfortable that Jesus, the Lord, would take this role and wash their feet.

Bath and footwashing (13:8-10). Jesus was speaking symbolically. The bath represents the cleansing of the whole person by the inner transformation faith in Jesus accomplishes. Most conservative commentators see a symbolic link between footwashing and the believer's need for continual cleansing from sins committed as she walks through life. To them, the bath represents conversion and footwashing daily confession of known sins.

An example (13:14-15). Jesus makes one implication of His act absolutely clear. He is both Teacher and Lord. Yet He humbled Himself to give us an example of the attitude we need to adopt toward others in the Christian community. Our only competition should be to see who can better serve others.

Fulfilling the Scripture (13:18). The allusion is to Ps. 41:9, in which David laments his betrayal by a trusted friend. Jesus identifies the historic incident as prophetic: It foreshad-

ows the parallel event of Christ's own betrayal by Judas.

What happened to David now happens to David's greater Son.

Satan entered (13:27). Judas had already made his bargain with the religious leaders to betray Jesus. Christ's statement let Judas know that Jesus knew and gave him a last chance to repent.

Satan can tighten his grip only on those who make a hardened, final decision to reject Jesus.

Love, the new commandment (13:34-35). The call to love is not new, but is embedded in the O.T. as well as the N.T. Yet the command here is "new" (*kainen*: "fresh," vibrantly new, rather than "recent") in three ways. (1) There is a new focus. We are still to love our neighbor, but now a more intense love is to be directed toward "one another." (2) There is a new standard. We are no longer to love others "as you love yourself," but "as I [Jesus] have loved you." Christ's own committed, self-sacrificial and limitless love is the yardstick by which we are to measure our love for our Christian brothers and sisters. And (3) there is a new outcome. As the Christian community is infused by Christlike love, the world of lost humankind realizes that Jesus is real — and that we are His.

Chapter summary. Jesus continues to share with His disciples at the Last Supper the evening before His crucifixion. He encourages, urging them to keep on believing that He has revealed the Father to them (14:1-14). And He promises that when He is gone, the Father will send the Holy Spirit to them, to continually reveal Jesus to those who love and obey Him (vv. 15-24). Jesus also encourages the disciples to be glad for His sake and their own. Christ's restoration to the Father will bring Him joy as well as benefit Jesus' followers (vv. 25-31).

Outline
Place
Finder

PROLOGUE
PUBLIC
PRIVATE
PASSION
EPILOGUE

Key verse. 14:6: Jesus is central.

Personal application. The Holy Spirit is our living link with Jesus today.

Key concepts. Trust »p. 354. Believe »pp. 35, 458. Father »pp. 140, 663. Holy Spirit »pp. 73, 744. Love »pp. 126, 351. Glory »pp. 74, 694.

INSIGHT

Antidote for troubled hearts (14:1). Trust in God and Jesus sets our hearts at ease.

"My Father's house" (14:2). The "house" is modeled on 1st-century villas, which had many rooms constructed around an open garden area. The 1st-century home held the extended family; adult children and their spouses lived as members of the father's household. God doesn't offer us "mansions" on some distant acres, as the KJV suggests. He provides us with an apartment in His own home, where we can be close to Him.

The Way, Truth, and Life (14:6). The thought of Jesus leaving threw Thomas into despair. If Jesus left, how could he ever learn the way to Him? Christ's answer was that *He* is the Way, the Truth, and the Life.

In a personal relationship with Jesus we discover the way to God, the truth that puts our existence in perspective, and an eternal life that is to be lived here and now.

God's self-revelation (14:9-11). Philip's request that Jesus show the disciples the Father misses a vital point. God is a Person. He could be adequately revealed only *in* a Person. Jesus thus responds by pointing out that He is so intimately linked with the Father that His words and acts *are* in fact the Father's words and acts.

God is perfectly revealed in Jesus, so one who has seen Jesus has seen the Father.

"Greater things than these" (14:12). Some think Jesus is referring to the worldwide spreading of faith by the Spirit-empowered disciples. Perhaps the works are greater in nature rather than extent. It's not surprising God expressed Himself through the sinless Jesus. But for the Spirit to take sinful human beings, and use us as agents of God in this world, is a greater wonder indeed.

Ask in My name (14:13). *The Expository Dictionary of the Bible* (Zondervan, 1985, p. 454) notes that to "pray in Jesus' name" means: "(1) to identify the content and motivations of prayers with all that Jesus is and (2) to pray with full confidence in Him as He has revealed Himself." This is because a "name" in the biblical world represented the character and quality of the person or thing named.

Love and obedience (14:15, 21, 23, 24). Obedience is pictured in Scripture as a love response. True obedience is not unwilling or dutiful conformity to an external standard, but rather is a joy-filled reaction to the initiative God has taken in showing us His love in Jesus. Love and obedience are so intimately bound together that one who does not love God will not truly obey. They are so bound together that obedience is an indication of the reality of our love for the Lord.

"Show Myself to Him" (14:21). Our own sense of Jesus' presence and reality in our lives depends on obedience. When we respond to God's love with obedience, we are close to Him. When we do not, we stray, and He seems unreal to us.

The Holy Spirit, the Counselor (14:15, 26). The name is *parakletos*, one who comes alongside and helps. The Holy Spirit's ministry to the believer is beautifully portrayed in the name, and in this passage. He is "with" and "in" the believer, an ever-present resource (v. 16). He teaches us all we need to know to respond to Jesus daily, and He gives us an inner peace that is independent of our circumstances (vv. 26-27). The Spirit's presence makes it possible for us to choose not to be troubled or fearful. He is the unbreakable link of our living relationship with the Lord.

Chapter summary. Jesus continues His last-night teaching. He compares His future relationship with the disciples to that of a vine to its branches. He is the source of spiritual vitality and fruitfulness. His disciples must thus remain "in" Him, intimately connected by responsive obedience to Jesus' commands (15:1-17). The world of lost mankind will hate Christ's disciples even as it hated Jesus. Yet the Spirit, resident in the believer, will testify about Him to the world, even as the disciples themselves must testify (vv. 18-27).

Key verse. 15:4: We must "remain in" Jesus.

Personal application. Without Jesus we can do nothing, with Him all things.

Key concepts. Fruit »pp. 414, 792. Love »pp. 126, 690–691. World »p. 893.

INSIGHT

Three relationships. This chapter identifies and defines three relationships that are part of every believer's experience: relationship with Jesus (vv. 1-11), relationship with other believers (vv. 12-17), and relationship with the indifferent and hostile world of nonbelievers (vv. 18-27).

Experiencing our union with Christ. The image of the Vine and branches focuses on the experiential aspect of a theological reality. We are united with Jesus (Rom. 6:1-14). To produce spiritual fruit, we must "abide in" the relationship that faith has established. This passage is not dealing with salvation but with fruitfulness.

The Vine. In the O.T. the vine is a metaphor of Israel, fruit a metaphor of a righteous life and society. Here Jesus extends the vine metaphor to include all believers. In the N.T. the fruit metaphor continues to suggest righteousness (»p. 792).

"The Gardener" (15:1). In calling the Father the "Gardener" Jesus offers us real hope. Who could have greater skill in nurturing our growth?

Pruning (15:2, 6). The pruning of a vine involves cutting back live wood to improve its fruitfulness and the removal of dead wood that might spread decay. Pruning does not threaten the salvation of any believer. The Gk. of v. 6 says, "like the [not a] branch that is thrown away." The emphasis is on the metaphor, not the believer. The branch of the grapevine has no use but bearing fruit. The stringy wood cannot be carved or used in building. It can only be thrown out and burned. Jesus is saying that the person who does not abide in Him is as *useless* as the branch that is thrown away. We are called to bear fruit. And God prunes true believers so that we will.

Prayer (15:7). We "remain in" Jesus experientially by responding obediently to Him (v. 10). This places us where we are sensitive to His leading and praying in His will. Such prayers God answers!

Glorifying God (15:8). We glorify God by doing that which brings Him praise. Here Jesus says that this means bearing fruit. Living a good life glorifies God because we could never do it without an intimate, dependent relationship with Jesus (v. 4).

"Love each other" (15:12-17). The key to an abiding relationship with Christ is "obedience." The key to relationship with other believers is "love." As we will see, the key to relationship with the world is "testify" (v. 27).

Chosen (15:16). The initiative in salvation always belongs to God. He loved us before we knew Him. He sent Christ to redeem us while we were in our sins. He reached out with the Good News, and His Spirit wooed us before we expressed any inclination to respond to Him. What a marvel, that chain of choices that brought us to Jesus and bonded us eternally to Him.

The world's hate (15:18). Here, as in other passages, the "world" (*kosmos*) to John is the whole of human society as it exists without God. This world was hostile to Jesus, and we can expect it will be hostile to Jesus' followers.

The world's hostility is rooted in a failure to know God (v. 21), but more specifically in a fierce anger that flared when Jesus did reveal God to them (v. 24).

How are we to respond? As Jesus did, by testifying about God (v. 26). Never mind others' hate. God is still choosing believers out of the world wherever the Gospel message is heard!

Chapter summary. Jesus now concludes His Last Supper night teaching with insights into the future His followers can expect. They can expect to be rejected by the leaders of their own people (16:1-4). They can expect to be supported in the world by the active, convicting ministry of the Holy Spirit (vv. 5-15). They can expect that Jesus will come again (vv. 16-24). Finally, they can expect to find peace in the certain knowledge that Christ and God the Father are one (vv. 25-33).

Key verse. 16:7: God's Spirit is essential to us.

Personal application. Never forget that God the Holy Spirit is present with you.

Key concepts. Holy Spirit »pp. 73, 744, 759. Glory »p. 694.

INSIGHT

"Synagogue" (16:1-2). Jesus describes the hostility of the disciples' own culture to His message. Whatever our world, we will not really "fit in" as long as we are openly committed to Christ. This warning is not intended to frighten us, but to prepare us.

Good for you (16:7). God was present in Jesus' incarnation in one place on earth. But the Holy Spirit is present in all places, in and available to every believer. This is one reason why it was to every disciple's advantage that Jesus returned to heaven. The unique work of the Holy Spirit in believers today could only begin after Christ had won us salvation by His death and given us the power to live a new life through His resurrection.

The Spirit's ministry (16:8-15). Christ described the Holy Spirit's ministry to the world as one of conviction. To the believer the Spirit's ministry is one of guidance and revelation of truth. There is also a ministry to Jesus, of displaying Him through we who represent Christ here on earth.

"Convict the world" (16:8-11). The word "convict" (elencho) is a legal term for bringing in a verdict of guilty. The Holy Spirit's ministry to non-Christians is to convey a sense of doom, an awareness that they stand condemned. The sense of guilt is developed in three areas: (1) "In regard to sin, because men do not believe in me" (v. 9). The issue is not the sins men commit, but the single condemning sin of unbelief. The Spirit convinces the non-Christian it is wrong not to believe in Jesus.

(2) "In regard to righteousness, because I am going to the Father" (v. 10). Jesus' return to God established a new standard of righteousness. No longer could righteousness be viewed as a matter of do's and don'ts. It's not a matter of living as perfect a life as Jesus. Many might say, "I kept that commandment." But none would claim, "I lived as perfect a life as Jesus Christ."

(3) "In regard to judgment, because the prince of this world now stands condemned" (v. 11). No one can ever again say, "God doesn't punish evil, so I can do whatever I want." God showed His commitment to judge by placing His own innocent Son on a cross. Surely He will judge guilty sinners.

"Guide you into all truth" (16:12-13). Jesus' disciples often heard His words, but could not grasp their meaning. The Holy Spirit's inner ministry is focused on helping them—and us—grasp the reality of Christ's words and then experiencing that reality by obeying His words.

This verse has sometimes been misapplied, and some have taught that Christians must agree on every point of doctrine. The Holy Spirit's ministry, however, was focused on serving the disciples as a guide as they struggled later to understand and express in the Epistles what Jesus had taught. Today, the Spirit guides us as we strive to apply Jesus' teachings to our own experience.

Asking Jesus (17:23). This "ask" (erotao) suggests asking a question rather than making a request. Christ's point may be that after the Resurrection His authority will be so well established He will no longer be cross-examined, as the disciples were doing then.

Asking again (17:26). Asking in Christ's name (See comments on 14:13, p. 691.) does indicate a request. Sure of who Jesus is, the disciples and we confidently approach the Father, sure of our welcome because Christ champions us before God's throne.

"Joy" (16:22-24). Joy is ours because its source is not in this world of change and decay. No one can take away a joy that is rooted in Jesus and experienced as answers to prayer.

Trouble and peace (16:33). The wonder is not that God permits us to have troubles, but that He gives us peace in our troubles.

Chapter summary. The private portion of John's Gospel concludes with an intimate look at Jesus at prayer. In what has been dubbed Christ's "high priestly prayer," our Lord prays for Himself (17:1-5), for His disciples (vv. 6-19), and then for all believers (vv. 20-26).

Key verse. 17:4: Bring God glory.

Personal application. Our lives like Jesus' are to be lived to glorify God.

Key concepts. Prayer »pp. 608–609, 894. Name »pp. 59, 691. Sanctify »p. 824. World »p. 893. Righteous »pp. 120, 433.

INSIGHT

Glorify God (17:4). The Gk. word, *doxa*, indicates the high opinion of a person by others. In the N.T., however, this Gk. word takes on the quality of the O.T. *kabod*, which emphasizes the majesty of God seen in His self-revelation. When Christ speaks of His actions bringing God glory He means that the beauty and majesty of God's nature has been revealed in what He has done. When the Father exalts Jesus in the Resurrection, that act will display the majesty and beauty of Jesus.

The amazing reality we see in Christ's prayer is that we too can glorify God. When we do God's will, He expresses Himself through us. Even we can display the beauty of our God.

"You gave me" (17:6). The disciples were God's gifts to Jesus, snatched "out of" the world. This is God, active in salvation. But human beings are active too: we "accept" Jesus' words, "believe" that God sent Him, and "know with certainty" that Christ is from God. It is irrelevant to pit sovereignty against free will in debating how salvation is appropriated. God gives. And we believe.

Keep them safe (17:12). It's just as irrelevant to debate whether a person once saved can be lost. God's own power protects and keeps Christ's own. And they persist in faith to the end.

"Protect them" (17:15). God does not remove us from danger but protects us in the midst. We are on a mission in this world in which we live as aliens. Therefore we cannot be taken out of it.

"Sanctify them" (17:17). God's way is not to take us out of the world, but to take the world out of us. The Gk. *hagiazo* means to set a person apart. Through God's Word He sets us apart from sin and from evil, that we might glorify Him.

"For those who will believe" (17:20). Christ's prayer was for us as well as the Twelve.

"One as We are one" (17:22-23). This verse has been misused to promote the idea that

Illustration. *Christ is usually portrayed in Gethsemane bowed down in prayer. Here He is best portrayed standing, His commitment made. Triumphant, He looks beyond the Cross to the glory that is to be His when He returns to the Father. Jesus also prays for His disciples and for us.*

Christ prayed for the organizational union of modern Christian denominations. Instead, Jesus prays that you and I might experience oneness with Him, even as He lived in a oneness relationship with the Father. How is this possible? While He was here on earth Jesus lived in oneness with the Father by being always responsive to the Father's will (John 5:19-20; 6:38; 8:28-29; 14:9-11). By being responsive to Christ's will, we live in oneness with Him. It's this uniquely personal relationship that Christ prays we will experience with Him.

Chapter summary. John, like the other Gospel writers, covers the events leading up to Jesus' crucifixion thoroughly and also adds fresh details. He reports the jolt that went through the mob come to arrest Jesus when He tells them "I Am" and identifies Peter as the disciple who drew a sword to defend Him (18:1-11). John reports Jesus' examination before both Annas (vv. 12-14) and the high priest (vv. 19-24) and gives colorful specifics about Peter's denial of the Lord (vv. 15-18, 25-27). John's most significant contribution, however, is his detailed description of the trial before Pilate and the frustrated attempts of that weak governor to release a person he knew very well was innocent (18:28–19:16). John also adds a graphic account of Christ on the cross and His undying concern for Mary (vv. 17-27). John just as vividly describes Jesus' death (vv. 28-37) and then, in Joseph of Arimathea's borrowed tomb, His burial (vv. 38-42). Decades had passed before John wrote down his account, but these events clearly were indelibly impressed on his memory. It was a night and day no one since has been able to forget.

Outline
Place
Finder

PROLOGUE
PUBLIC
PRIVATE
PASSION
EPILOGUE

Key verse. 19:30: Jesus' life was given, not taken.

Personal application. As you read John's account, remember you were there. He died for you.

Key concepts. Resurrection events »p. 629. Crucifixion »p. 647. Cross »pp. 789, 814. Death of Jesus »p. 813.

INSIGHT

The arrest (18:3). The other Gospels describe a mob (*ochlos*) rather than a military detachment. It's probable a small team of Roman soldiers and temple guards set out to take Jesus and quickly gathered a crowd of the curious.

They fell (18:6). There's no natural explanation for the arresting officers "fall to the ground." There may, however, be a supernatural one. Jesus' words, "I am He" incorporates the "I Am" claim He made earlier in asserting His deity (cf. 8:24, 28, 58). Even the veiled reference to His essential nature momentarily stuns His enemies.

"Malchus" (18:10-11). The Gk. identifies him as "the servant" of the high priest. This indicates a high position in the religious heirarchy. Malchus was likely the leader of the group come to arrest Jesus. John's observation that Peter struck the "right ear" and his naming of Malchus are just the kind of detail that abounds in John's eyewitness account.

"Peter" (18:11, 15-18, 25-27). Peter is shown to be a very human and complex person. He is brave and at one moment ready to fight against overwhelming odds for his Lord. Yet at the next moment, his courage collapses when he is questioned by serving maids out-side the high priest's house.

How like us Peter was. Christians have faced martyrdom bravely. Yet many still hesitate to witness for the Lord when threatened only by ridicule or indifference.

"Annas" (18:12-14, 19-24). This individual had been high priest from A.D. 6 to 15. Although he was deposed by the Romans, he was able to control the post through four of his sons who succeeded him, and through his son-in-law, Caiaphas. Caiaphas was actually high priest from A.D. 18 to A.D. 36, when Christ's public ministry took place. Annas' influence is shown in references to him as high priest (cf. Luke 3:2) and in the control he exercised over Jesus' movements that last night.

Peter's denial (18:15-18, 25-27). It is likely that John was the "other disciple" who, with Peter, trailed Jesus to Annas' home. John says he was "known to" the high priest's household and so was able to observe Jesus' trial from inside the house.

But what a contrast between Peter and Judas. Peter wept bitterly and turned back to Christ. Judas despaired rather than repented. God can forgive our failures if only we turn back to Him.

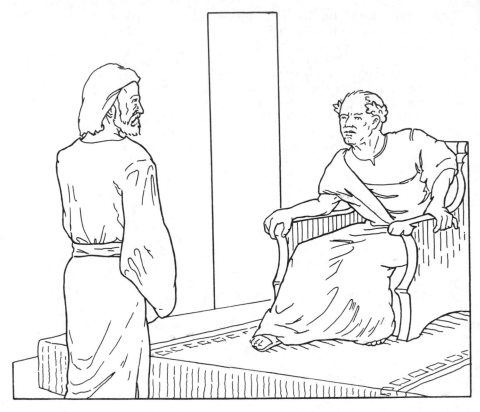

Illustration. *Secular historians portray Pilate as a brutal, greedy man, who was still such an effective administrator that he served in Judea as prefect or procurator for 10 years. Yet he was also a protege of a powerful Roman, Sejanus, who had just been executed in Rome. Pilate was thus very vulnerable to any accusation that he was "no friend of Caesar" just at the time Jesus came before him. Pilate might not have freed Jesus to soothe the Jews, but would have to preserve his own skin.*

"No right to execute" (18:31). The motive was not so much to observe the legalities, as the later stoning of Stephen shows (Acts 7:54-60). Anyone hanged on a tree was under God's curse (cf. Deut. 21:22-23). Crucifixion would "prove" to the people that Jesus could not have been the Messiah, and their rejection of His claims would be vindicated. How little they knew. Jesus took God's curse on Himself for all mankind (Gal. 3:13).

On the side of truth (18:37). Jesus admitted to being a king, but totally confused Pilate by asserting His kingdom had neither land nor troops. Even here Jesus seems to reach out to touch Pilate rather than defend Himself. If only Pilate will listen to (hear and respond correctly) to what Jesus says he will learn (by experience) the truth (reality) Jesus is describ-

ing. Pilate shrugs off the appeal with a scornful, "What is truth?" (v. 38) Clearly Jesus is harmless, and Pilate is willing to let Him go.

Power to crucify (19:10). Pilate's statement is absurd in view of the way he is being manipulated to execute Jesus against his own desire. There is nothing more pitiful than a person with great power—and no character.

"Guilty of a greater sin" (19:11). The reference is to the high priest and hierarchy of the Jews. Pilate was weak and easily manipulated. The religious leaders willfully rejected overwhelming evidence that Jesus was sent from God.

The crucifixion. For the order of events, »p. 629.

Mary (19:26-27). The writer of this Gospel, John, took Jesus' mother into his home.

"Blood and water" (19:34). Apparently the heavier red corpuscles had separated from the blood serum.

No bone broken (19:36). No bone of the Passover lamb was to be broken (Ex. 12:46), a link which defines Jesus' sacrifice to protect us from death.

Joseph and Nicodemus (19:38). At least two of the religious elite did believe in Jesus.

No shroud of Turin? (19:40) Jesus' body was buried "wrapped," with spices, "in strips of linen." There's no suggestion here of a shroud.

Chapter summary. Several different followers went to Jesus' grave and discovered the empty tomb on the first day of the new week (20:1-3; see also Resurrection Events chart, p. 629). Again John adds eyewitness details: He tells of seeing the empty strips of linen in which Jesus' body had been wrapped (vv. 4-9). And he shares the story of other witnesses. Mary Magdalene is the first to see Jesus alive again (vv. 10-18). Jesus appears inside a locked room to speak to all His disciples but Thomas (vv. 19-23). Later Jesus returns when Thomas is present, and the disciple who earlier earned the nickname "Doubting" immediately fell to his knees in adoration and worship (vv. 24-29).

Then, stepping back, John shares the focus and purpose of his book. He has recorded a true account of Jesus' miracles and His teachings, His death and rising to life again, "that you may believe that Jesus is the Christ, the Son of God, and that by believing you may have life through His name" (vv. 30-31).

Key verse. 20:31: The evidence is in.

Personal application. Join the disciple in witnessing to a living Christ.

Key concepts. Resurrection »pp. 522, 712, 737, 808. Disciples »p. 657. Believe »pp. 35, 458, 740, 790.

INSIGHT

"**The first day**" **(20:1).** From the very beginning the church has set aside Sunday, the first day of the week, and commemorated the resurrection of Jesus (cf. Acts 20:7).

The graveclothes (20:5-7). Jesus had passed through the linen strips. They probably still held their shape, because of the sticky myrrh and aloes wrapped with them.

John believed (20:8-9). John entered after Peter's discovery, looked, and believed. Only later did any of the disciples understand the Scripture. Today too faith precedes understanding.

Mary Magdalene (20:10-16). Her first reaction, "Who took His body?" continues to show the psychological state of Jesus' followers. None of them expected a resurrection, despite what Jesus had earlier said. Two words for "see" are found in v. 14. Mary "observed" a figure near the tomb, then she "perceived" it was Jesus.

Today many see the Jesus of history, but too few recognize Him.

Don't hold on (20:17). Jesus didn't refuse to let Mary touch Him. He told her not to detain Him.

Your Father (20:17). Before Jesus always spoke of "My" Father. This post-resurrection appearance is the first time He adds "and your Father." Only by His death and resurrection could Jesus bring those who believed in Him into God's family.

"**He breathed on them**" **(20:22).** This is possibly an Aramaic idiom meaning "he gave them courage." That encouragement was in the form of a promise of the Holy Spirit.

Do we forgive? (20:23) The Gk. construction is literally, "If you forgive anyone his sins, his sins have been forgiven." It is in the Gospel we proclaim forgiveness. Sharing the Gospel places us in the role of forgiving or not forgiving sins, depending on the response of the hearer.

Doubting Thomas (20:24). The story of Thomas serves as a climax to the theme of John's Gospel. He struggled with unbelief and doubt and insisted on the most unmistakable proofs. His phrase "I will not believe it" (v. 25) rightly shifts the issue of belief and unbelief from the intellect to the will. Yet when confronted by Jesus he recognized Him, fell on his knees and believed.

It's not wrong for non-Christians to demand evidence for faith. But don't expect proofs alone — whether from prophecy, miracles, testimony, or arguments showing the Bible to be the supernatural Word of God — to convince them. Believing is a matter of the will. All we can do is present Jesus to others as clearly as possible. When they recognize Him they will either choose to believe, or choose not to.

Chapter summary. John's Gospel has reached its climax. But John cannot help reminiscing about Jesus' post-resurrection times with His disciples. He tells of a fishing trip to the Sea of Galilee (also called Tiberias) sponsored by Peter. Jesus appears on shore, tells His disciples to cast out their nets one more time, and fills them with a great haul of fish (21:1-14). That morning Jesus gently confronted Peter, and asked, "Do you love Me?" three times—once for each of Peter's earlier denials. That same morning Jesus restores and recommissions Peter, charging him to "feed My sheep" (vv. 15-19). On that same occasion Jesus rebuked Peter for asking about John's call. It's enough, even for leaders, to follow Jesus themselves and let others be responsible for their own responses to the Lord (vv. 20-23).

John closes on a note of regret. There's so much more he could share about Jesus! But surely there are not enough books published in the whole world to record His first-century words and works, to say nothing of the work He has carried on in believers for the millenia since then (vv. 24-25).

Key verse. 21:15: Love, expressed in caring.

Personal application. Concentrate on following Jesus and don't concern yourself with how He is leading other disciples.

INSIGHT

Peter goes fishing (21:3). The "we'll go with you" reminds us that Peter really is the leader of the disciples. But we have no insight into why Peter decided to go back to his old trade. It may have been restlessness. Or a feeling he needed to support his family. Whatever the reason, the expedition was an exercise in futility. They caught no fish!

Actually no one who follows Jesus can go back to his or her old way of life. Jesus calls us to something fresh and new. It's not that we must change jobs. He changes us, and we find no real satisfaction except in doing His will.

Peter's example. Peter must have felt as we do when we fail the Lord: eager for acceptance, yet uncertain and ashamed. At such times let's follow Peter's example. Peter was so eager to see Jesus again he jumped out of the boat and swam to shore (v. 7). There he rushed to bring fish when Jesus asked for them (v. 11).

Don't let sins drive you from the Lord. Hurry back to Him and show your love by ready obedience.

"Do you love Me?" (21:15-17) The "more than these" is uncertain. Does Jesus ask if Peter loves Christ more than the other disciples do? Or more than he loves the others? Or perhaps more than he loves his boats and nets, and his old life as a fisherman? Whatever

the intent, the significance is clear. We are to love Jesus most of all.

"Love" (21:15-17). Different Gk. words for "love" are used in the repeated questions and answers. Many a sermon has been based on the fact that Christ's first two questions were, "Do you *agapao* Me?" and "Do you *phileo* Me?" in the third, while each of Peter's replies proclaimed a *phileo* love for the Lord. *Agapao* here may indicate that Jesus asks for a more committed, deeper love than Peter—once burned!—feels able to affirm. But Jesus accepts the love Peter *is* able to give and calls him to serve.

Pasture and shepherd (21:15-17). Christ called Peter to serve and nurture others.

Peter's death (21:18-19). Tradition tells us that Peter was crucified in Rome, but at his request upside down, for he did not feel worthy to die as his Lord had.

What about John? (21:20-22) There's an important principle here. We're to concentrate on following where Jesus leads us. And we're to let others follow where Jesus leads them.

The church is not a hierarchy, with overseers telling others what God's will is for them. The church is an organism, and each believer is directly connected with Jesus Christ, the church's living head. We each are to love and follow Him—and let others follow where they are led.

Regions Beyond

After Jesus' death and resurrection, the Gospel exploded out of little Palestine and swept the known world like a quickly spreading flame. The Book of Acts relates the beginnings of the church, describing a short period of consolation in the Jewish homeland, a gradual spread to nearby lands, and then a sudden explosion of missionary activity spearheaded by the Apostle Paul. In a few brief decades, between the A.D. 30s and 60s, churches were established in most of the major population centers of the Roman Empire, including Rome itself. It was during this period that most of the books of the New Testament were written. And here the New Testament historical account in Acts ends. But secular histories and the writings of church fathers enable us to pick up the story.

At first the new religious movement was ignored by the authorities, who saw it as a harmless branch of Judaism. But as more and more people became Christians rumors about the new faith spread. Christians refused to worship the emperor, an act which pagans in those days saw primarily as an affirmation of loyalty to the government. Christian soldiers in the Roman legions refused to offer homage to legion Eagles, the standards they followed into battle. And many Christian soldiers, committed to following Christ as Peace-Giver, refused to fight even when they faced execution for this stand. For some 200 years Christians experienced official and unofficial persecution, and it was not until the conversion of the Emperor Constantine in the A.D. 300s that Christianity gained official acceptance and support.

Somehow a faith born in a backwater on the fringes of a mighty empire had proved so dynamic and vital that it swept the world, despite the rumors, despite official persecution, and despite the fact that its teachings were in essential opposition to beliefs deeply embedded in the first-century world.

One World: Its Culture

To understand the story told in Acts, and the society reflected in the New Testament epistles, we need to step back in time, to meet a young visionary who was also a decisive man of action. His name was Alexander, king of Macedon from 336 to 323 B.C., whose conquest of Persia and the East earned him the title, "The Great." Alexander was only 20 in 334 B.C. when he led a force of 40,000 Greek soldiers across the Hellespont, the narrow straits that separate Europe and Asia. His outnumbered force won victory after victory, finally defeating the Persian ruler, Darius, in 333 B.C. Alexander continued south and swept along the sea coast. He took Tyre using a tactic prophesied centuries earlier in Ezekiel 26 and added Egypt to his spoils. After this Alexander returned to Persia, once again forging a chain of victories that brought him to the very heart of that ancient empire. When the defeated Darius was assassinated by a subordinate, Alexander proclaimed himself Darius' heir and began to rule.

But Alexander had been driven by more than a young man's passion for power and glory. Alexander was driven by a vision of the future: a vision of *oikumene*, of the whole inhabited earth united by a single language and culture. To Alexander that language must be Greek, the culture Hellenic.

The young ruler set about establishing Greek-style cities throughout his empire—and then turned his attention to yet more conquests. In 327 B.C. Alexander conquered what we now call Afghanistan and crossed into India. Only when his armies refused to follow him farther did Alexander turn back to Babylon. There, at age 33, Alexander contracted a fever and died.

Alexander's dream of one world, of *oikumene,* did take shape. His successors followed his policy of Hellenization, and gradually Greek language, culture, and ideals took root. Peoples of the East might retain their own languages, customs, and laws. They might worship the gods and goddesses of their ancestors. But among the educated classes, gradually seeping down to permeate the thinking of all, Greek language and thought were established. The *Revell Bible Dictionary* (pp. 43–44) sums up Alexander's influence:

> Through his conquests, Alexander spread and firmly rooted Greek culture and language throughout the eastern world. The Hellenized cities attracted large Jewish communities. In time, there came to be about a million Jews in Egypt, with another two or three million in Greek speaking regions such as Syria, Asia Minor, Libya, Greece, and Rome. Jewish members of these communities were affected by Greek thought and values, and many lost their ability to speak the Aramaic of their homeland. Their need of a Greek version of the Old Testament led Ptolemy II of Philadelphius (285–246 B.C.) to sponsor the translation known as the Septuagint. This made the Old Testament available not only to Jews but also to the general population. A number of Jewish Hellenists (Jews who adopted aspects of Greek culture) even attempted to show that the nobler visions of Greek philosophers had their source in the Jewish Scriptures.
>
> The availability of the Old Testament in Greek and the efforts of Jewish apologists had an impact. One Jewish Hellenist, Philo (20 B.C.–40 A.D.), rejoiced because the laws of Moses "attract and win the attention of all, of barbarians, of Greeks, of dwellers on the mainland, of nations of the East and West, of Europe and Asia, and of the whole inhabited world from end to end." How striking this is, in view of the fact that the Book of Acts reveals that most churches founded by Paul had a core not of Jewish believers, but of Gentiles who had already been attracted to the synagogue and the purity of Old Testament faith.
>
> In two ways, then, Alexander's Hellenization of the eastern world prepared for the Christian message: (1) it provided a common tongue, Greek, in which the Gospel could be preached and spread abroad, and (2) through the activities of Hellenistic Jews, Gentiles were attracted to the Old Testament's vision of God, and were thus readied to become the believing core of local churches everywhere.

One World: Its Government

Although the bonds forged by a common culture may well have exceeded his dreams, Alexander had not been able to unite the *oikumene* politically. Yet when Jesus was born in Bethlehem, and as the church rushed out to share the Gospel with all, the world was one, held together by complex bands fashioned of Roman legions, Roman administrators, Roman roads, and Roman law.

The Roman Empire was amazingly complex. In the first century it included some 54 million people, of whom about 5 million were Jews. The empire included many different ethnic groups. While Roman law was supreme, each people was allowed to follow its own customs and maintain its own court systems. Under this policy the Jewish Sanhedrin, for example, administered the Law of the Old Testament not only in Judea, but also served as a supreme court for all Jews, frequently sending out pairs of sages to settle cases in Jewish communities anywhere in the empire. Roman taxes were relatively light and in return peoples throughout the empire received many benefits.

Perhaps the greatest of these benefits was peace. Roman power was supreme, so the peoples in it were not torn by wars with their neighbors. Another benefit, linked to prosperity, was the great mobility that the empire promoted. There were no national borders to cross, no foreign languages for traders to learn. A network of roads, constructed so that Roman legions could be moved quickly, permitted rapid transit of people, goods, and information. And large merchant ships carried cargoes swiftly throughout the Mediterranean basin and even to the British Isles.

The *Revell Bible Dictionary* comments (p. 870), "The Empire, which gave the varied peoples of Europe and the Mediterranean a common language and permitted free movement of persons and ideas, was essential to the spread of Christianity. Christians preached and wrote in Greek, the language understood by nearly everyone. Missionaries freely crossed borders that in later nationalistic ages would have blocked their passage. Everywhere Christians found a spiritual hunger unsatisfied by the existing philosophies, religions, superstitions, and belief in magic. The gradual expansion of Roman power, culminating in the establishment of a unified empire by Augustus, is evidence that God was at work, preparing the world for the birth of His Son and the spread of the Gospel."

Illustration. *Roman highways were constructed to last. First a foundation of large stones was laid, followed by a layer of smaller stones. This was cemented together with lime. Then a third layer of small stones was spread above this, and the whole was capped with flat blocks of flint paving stones. The roads were arched, and gutters ran along their sides to carry off rain water. Several of the two- to three-foot-thick roads constructed in the 1st century still exist today.*

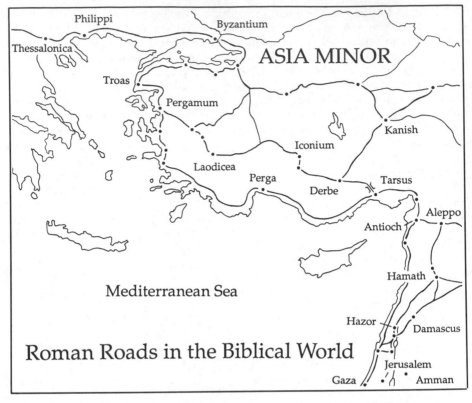

Illustration. *The map shows the extent of the Roman Empire as it existed in the 1st century. The lines indicate the Roman roads that linked major population centers and made it so easy for Christian missionaries to spread the Gospel.*

The story of how God prepared the first century political world for Christ's birth is a fascinating one and involves another very special person. He was born Caesar Octavian in 63 B.C. After the murder of his uncle Julius Caesar in 44 B.C., Octavian embarked on a ten-year civil struggle that saw him emerge as the sole ruler of the Roman Empire. He began his rule in 31 B.C. and was voted the title *Augustus* ("revered," or "sacred") in 27 B.C. It was at his initiative that the pirates and brigands who infested the empire were put down. It was his wise policy of minimum interference in local affairs that reduced nationalism and created a favorable climate for the prosperity which marked his era. A birthday inscription A.D. 7 honored Augustus by summing up the attitude of the empire's grateful population. "Everything was deteriorating and changing into misfortune, but he set it right and gave the whole world another appearance."

God was working through this energetic and insightful ruler, as he had worked in Alexander, to prepare the first-century world for His Son's birth.

One World: Its Religions and Beliefs

The world of the first century was one politically and culturally. But it apparently was not united in its faiths. The austere religion of the state honored the ancient Roman deities, and revered the emperor. The cities and the

Illustration. *Large cargo vessels hugged the shores of the Mediterranean. Passengers camped on deck, supplying their own food, mattresses and cookware. Some 276 persons had room on the decks of one ship Paul took (cf. Acts 27:37).*

population honored state deities and the emperor on public occasions. But many also worshiped the gods and goddesses of their nations, or took part in one of the mystery religions which promised present and future blessings through initiation into secret rites.

In the Golden Age of Greece, creative philosophers had set out to discover the secrets of the universe by the application of man's intellect. Several hundreds of years had passed, and although itinerant philosophers still taught in the streets of every city, the optimism that had marked philosophy's early days had long faded. Epicureans preaching pleasure vied for disciples with Stoics counseling emotional restraint and Cynics who decried materialism. Many an educated person was drawn to the monotheistic teaching and moral commitments of Judaism, but drew back from converting to a religion whose ritual laws and restraints seemed unreasonable to the Hellenist. Conscience, consistently portrayed in Greek literature as a dark accuser, continued to accuse. Impersonal Fates wove the patterns that controlled all events and held even the gods hostage. The individual was helpless, burdened with a sense of guilt, aware that this world could not satisfy and yet fearful of the next.

A sense of desperation can be sensed not so much in the literature of the age but in the way ordinary persons turned to magic. Charms were worn to ward off evils. Ritual formulas were chanted and secret ingredients were carefully mixed in hopes of winning love, curing diseases, harming enemies, and gaining wealth. In Ephesus, the center of the world-renowned religion honoring Artemis, books of magic worth 50,000 drachmas [equivalent to nearly 170 *years* of wages] were burned by converts to Christianity! The faiths of the ancient world could not comfort a population whose material situation had improved, but whose spiritual hungers were unsatisfied.

It was into *oikumene,* a world that was unified by language, culture, politics and by its spiritual hungers, that Christian missionaries ventured with the message of Jesus Christ. And the first-century world responded!

What was it that brought thousands and ultimately millions to faith in Christ? It was more than the power of a better idea, or a superior theology. As we read Acts and the New Testament epistles we realize that at least two major factors attracted first-century men and women. First, the Christian message was vibrant with hope. God in Christ broke into man's world, demonstrated his love and power, and in the Resurrection revealed an endless, triumphant life which Christ offers to every man. The God and Father of Jesus is not bound by fate, but is in firm control of the natural and supernatural world. The Christian need not feel helpless, but can turn to this God in prayer, and because prayers are offered in Jesus' name, be sure every request is heard. There is no need to turn to magical manipulation in a desperate effort to influence powers who have no concern for human beings. The Christian has a personal relationship with the Ruler of the universe Himself, and this once hidden Being has shown in Jesus that He truly cares.

There was a second major influence as well. Christianity created communities of love. The first century, like our own age, was an age of isolation and loneliness. Even though neighbors formed clubs that met regularly and helped pay for the burial of members who died, few had experienced the total acceptance and affirmation that could be found in the Christian community. Jesus had given His disciples a new commandment: Love as I have loved you. The early church became not simply a people committed to Jesus, but also a people committed to one another. Leaders served rather than dominated. Social class became less important, as believers ministered to each other with the spiritual gifts granted each one by God. It was neither easy nor automatic, but gradually Christians created a unique society of saints within the larger context of the pagan culture—a society in which others were accepted, loved, cared for, supported, encouraged, rebuked, and honored.

And how attractive this new community was to the lonely men and women of the first century, who lived as we live today, fractured, isolated lives. To know Christ, and to experience His love through others, was more than millions could resist. And so the Gospel was shared, in word and in deed. And so the world of the first century was won.

As we read Acts and the Epistles we need to remember that in many ways that world was like our own—filled with empty, spiritually hungry people, whose material advantages could not satisfy their deepest longings. Today too the only way to reach the world is to share the same, powerful Gospel of Jesus Christ—in word, and in deed.

Acts

The world of the first century was alive with myths and fables, saturated with hucksters promoting mystery religions and magical powers. So Luke, a physician who accompanied Paul on several of his missionary ventures, set out to deliberately and accurately record the beginnings of Christianity. He wrote not as an evangelist, but as a historian. And he wrote not for the unsaved, but for believers. His clear intent was to demonstrate, in his Gospel and in Acts, the second volume of his work, that Christian faith is rooted in no myth. Christianity has its roots in history—real space and time—in the birth of a Saviour in Palestine who was both God and Man, whose Gospel was spread by eyewitnesses. Luke wants us to understand the story of Jesus, from its roots in Old Testament prophecy, through its authentication in miracle, to its spread by eyewitnesses of His resurrection.

Luke's history of the spread of the Gospel is never dry. Instead it is alive with stories of people and events, vibrant with high drama. For example, Luke shows us the stunned surprise created when Peter suddenly appears at a prayer meeting where Christians have gathered to beg for his release from prison, and he vividly pictures the sullen Paul exulting at the stoning of Stephen. Scene after scene comes alive as Luke, in the most literary Greek of the New Testament, invites us into the world of the first century and convinces us without arguments that God has been at work in space and time. He shows that the Gospel of Christ, Good News for all humankind, is not only true but promises hope and transformation for us all. The story of the spread of the Gospel in Acts is our story—and history.

ACTS AT A GLANCE

KEY PEOPLE

Peter   *Blunt, impetuous Peter is still the leader of Jesus' disciples, preaching the first evangelistic sermon to Jews (Acts 2) and to Gentiles (Acts 10). Peter is the leading figure in Acts 1–11.*

Paul   *Zealous and antagonistic Saul is transformed into a committed Christian when Christ actually speaks to him on the road to Damascus (Acts 9). Paul is the leading figure in Acts 12–28, which tell of his missionary adventures.*

Stephen   *Bold leader, first martyr of the early church (Acts 7).*

Barnabas   *Gentle and strong, Barnabas played a vital role in helping Paul find his place in the early Christian community and traveled with him as a missionary.*

KEY EVENTS

The Holy Spirit comes   *God's Spirit baptizes believers on Pentecost (Acts 2)*

Peter preaches   *The first evangelistic sermons are recorded (Acts 2–3)*

Paul converted   *A rigorous Pharisee discovers grace (Acts 9)*

Gentiles won   *A Roman centurion and his household become the first Gentile converts to Christianity (Acts 10–11)*

The Gentile mission   *Paul sets out on his first missionary journey and wins enthusiastic response among the Gentiles (Acts 12–13)*

The first council   *Leaders discuss how to include Gentiles (Acts 15)*

Paul arrested   *Paul detained, goes to Rome for trial (Acts 20ff.)*

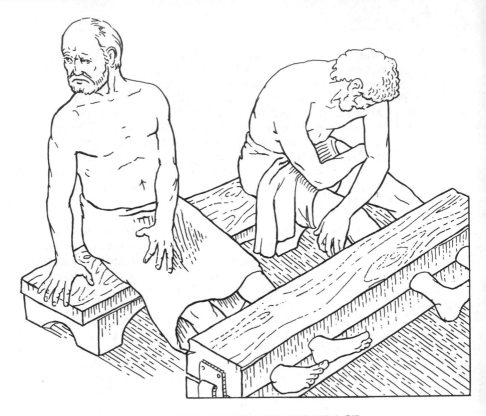

WHERE THE ACTION TAKES PLACE

Acts leads us from Jerusalem and to many of the important cities of the Roman Empire in Asia Minor and in Europe. In dramatic sketches Luke shows us the trials and triumphs of missionary life. Above, Paul and Silas are imprisoned after being beaten in Philippi (Acts 16). There they praise God, are released by an earthquake, and lead their jailer and his household to Christ. We see that God is with the missionary team as it travels throughout the known world sharing the Gospel and the planting church.

Date and Authorship. The author is Luke, who also wrote the Gospel that carries his name. His history tells the story of the early church from Christ's resurrection in A.D. 33 to Paul's first imprisonment in Rome about A.D. 63. The three decades spanned by Acts saw the Christian message carried by missionaries like Paul throughout the Roman Empire and vigorous churches started in every major population center.

THEOLOGICAL OUTLINE OF ACTS

CONTENT OUTLINE OF ACTS

I. Introduction (1:1–2:47)
  A. Dedication (1:1-5)
  B. Instructions of Christ (1:6-8)
  C. Ascension of Christ (1:9-11)
  D. Waiting in Jerusalem (1:12-26)
  E. Coming of the Spirit (2:1-47)
    1. His descent (2:1-13)
    2. Peter's sermon (2:14-41)
    3. The early church (2:42-47)
II. Mission to Israel (3:1–9:43)
  A. Apostolic Witness in Word (3:1–4:31)
    1. A healing (3:1-10)
    2. A Gospel sermon (3:11-26)
    3. Arrest (4:1-7)
    4. Witness to the Sanhedrin (4:8-31)
  B. Apostolic Witness in Works (4:32–5:11)
    1. Christians share (4:32-35)
    2. Barnabas an example (4:36-37)
    3. Ananias and Sapphira lie and die (5:1-11)
  C. Apostolic Witness in Wonder (5:12-42)
  D. Church Witness in Caring (6:1-7)
  E. Individual Witness in Stephen's Martyrdom (6:8–8:3)
  F. Effective Witness in Philip's Evangelism (8:4-40)
    1. In Samaria (8:4-25)
    2. Of an Ethiopian (8:26-40)
  G. Supernatural Witness (9:1-43)
    1. Paul's conversion (9:1-31)
    2. Peter's healing ministry (9:32-43)
III. Mission to Gentiles (10:1–15:35)
  A. The Conversion of Cornelius (10:1–11:18)
    1. Cornelius' vision (10:1-8)
    2. Peter's vision (10:9-16)
    3. Peter's sermon (10:17-43)
    4. Gentiles given the Spirit (10:44-48)
    5. The church's response (11:1-18)
  B. The Church in Antioch (11:19-30)

1. The first Gentile congregation (11:19-26)
2. Famine relief sent to Jerusalem (11:27-30)
  C. Interlude: Peter's Imprisonment and Release (12:1-24)
  D. The First Missionary Journey to Gentile Lands (12:25–14:28)
    1. Missionaries appointed (12:25–13:3)
    2. Cyprus (13:4-13)
    3. Antioch (13:14-52)
    4. Iconium, Lystra, Derbe and return home (14:1-28)
  E. The Jerusalem Council Debate on Basis for Accepting Gentiles (15:1-35)
IV. Further Missionary Journeys (15:36–19:20)
  A. Paul and Barnabas Split (15:36-41)
  B. Paul Forms a New Team (16:1-5)
  C. Two Missionary Journeys (16:6–19:20)
    1. God's guidance (16:6-10)
    2. Philippi (16:11-40)
    3. Thessalonica (17:1-9)
    4. Berea (17:10-15)
    5. Athens (17:16-34)
    6. Corinth (18:1-17)
    7. Return to Syria/Palestine (18:18-23)
    8. Apollos visits Ephesus/Corinth (18:24-28)
    9. Ephesus (19:1-19)
    10. Summary (19:20)
V. Paul's Imprisonment (19:21–28:31)
  A. Paul Journeys to Jerusalem (19:21–21:16)
  B. Paul Arrested (21:17-36)
  C. Paul Defends Himself (21:37–23:22)
  D. Paul Witnesses to Romans at Caesarea (23:23–26:32)
  E. Paul Sent to Rome (27:1–28:16)
  F. Paul Imprisoned in Rome for Two Years (28:17-31)

Outline
Place
Finder

JERUSALEM
SAMARIA
GENTILES
WORLD
IMPRISONMENT

Chapter summary. Luke picks up the story of Jesus from where he left off in his Gospel (1:1-3). He focuses attention on Jesus' postresurrection promise of the Holy Spirit, a central theme in this book (vv. 4-5). The disciples are still concerned with God's coming kingdom. Jesus tells them to focus on witness and promises them power when the Holy Spirit comes "in a few days" (vv. 6-8). After this, Jesus rises visibly into the heavens (vv. 9-11), and the little company of believers returns to Jerusalem to wait (vv. 12-13). There they meet "constantly" for prayer (v. 14), and there too they choose a man to replace Judas as one of the Twelve who will take the lead in witnessing to the risen Christ (vv. 15-26).

Key verse. 1:8: Power and purpose.

Personal application. Jesus empowers us and calls us to witness.

Key concepts. Resurrection »p. 737. Kingdom »pp. 380, 443. Holy Spirit »p. 744. Disciple »p. 657. Lots »p. 325.

INSIGHT

"Holy Spirit" (1:2). Luke's Gospel emphasizes the ministry of the Holy Spirit in the life of Christ. In Acts Luke emphasizes the role of the Holy Spirit in the growth and development of the young Christian church. Acts has often been dubbed "the Acts of the Holy Spirit through the Apostles" rather than "the Acts of the Apostles." The Holy Spirit is mentioned in Acts 1–2, 4–11, 13, 15–16, 19–21, and 28.

Baptized with the Spirit (1:5). This event, to take place "in a few days," is described in Acts 2. But it is not defined there. First Cor. 12:13 defines Spirit baptism as that work of the Holy Spirit by which He unites believers with Jesus and so forms the living body of Christ. Because of this, Pentecost, when the Holy Spirit first came upon Christ's disciples, is often called the "birthday of the church."

Description, not doctrine. Confusion over "baptism of the Spirit" has been generated by drawing doctrine from events in Acts rather than from the teaching of the epistles.

Restoring the kingdom (1:6). The disciples expected Jesus to immediately set up the earthly kingdom predicted by the prophets (»p. 439). Christ did not deny the prophets' vision, but rather redirected their attention. God will keep His O.T. promises—in His own time. The disciples were to concentrate on bringing Christ to the world.

"Power" (1:8). Communicating Christ effectively requires as much spiritual power as performing miracles. How encouraging to realize the Spirit is with us and that it is He who

works when we share the Lord with others.

Pattern (1:8). The verse contains a rough outline of the book, which tells of the Gospel's spread in Jerusalem, Samaria, and the world.

Witnesses (1:9). A witness is a person who "gives evidence" (*martureo*), basing his or her testimony concerning actual events on direct, personal knowledge. The apostles gave this kind of evidence concerning Christ's life and resurrection. You and I can give this kind of evidence concerning God's work in our lives.

Ascension and return (1:10-11). The visible return of Jesus to heaven is evidence for His future return from heaven. As He was able to do one, so He is fully able to do the other.

Joined in constant prayer (1:12-14). The disciples were told to wait, not to be inactive. Where there is nothing else we can do, we can always pray.

"Women" (1:14). Luke was careful in his Gospel to show the active involvement of women among Christ's followers. In Acts he continues to be sensitive to women and their role in the spread of the Gospel (cf. especially Acts 18).

Judas' fate (1:18). This does not conflict with Matthew's account. Judas hanged himself, but the rope broke and his body burst in the fall.

Prayer and lots (1:23-26). The apostles found two candidates who were qualified to join them, but did not know which God chose. This is the last report of determining God's will by casting lots. After the Spirit came, there was no need.

708

Chapter summary. On the symbolically significant Day of Pentecost the Holy Spirit falls visibly on the gathered disciples, and they begin to speak in "other tongues" (2:1-4). Stunned crowds gather, each hearing the believers praise God in "his own native tongue" (vv. 5-13). Peter then quiets the crowd. He explains the phenomenon by referring to Joel's Old Testament prophecy concerning a day when God will "pour out His Spirit" (vv. 14-21). Peter then proclaims Christ as God's Messiah and Saviour in a sermon that contains the basic elements of apostolic preaching (vv. 22-37). Some 3,000 heed his urgent call to "repent and be baptized," to accept forgiveness of sins through Jesus, and receive the gift of the Holy Spirit (vv. 38-41). With great enthusiasm the new converts commit themselves to live in the new Christian community (vv. 42-47).

Outline
Place
Finder

JERUSALEM
SAMARIA
GENTILES
WORLD
IMPRISONMENT

Key verse. 2:38: The invitation still stands.

Personal application. Salvation is the first step, commitment to Christian community the second.

Key concepts. Prophecy »p. 434. Repentance »p. 780. Baptism »p. 742.

INSIGHT

"Pentecost" (2:1). The day fell 50 days after Passover and was originally a harvest festival (Lev. 23:15-16). In N.T. times it also commemorated Moses' giving of the Law on Sinai.

Visible signs (2:2-3). Three phenomena occurred together that made the coming of the Holy Spirit on Pentecost an unmistakable and unique event: (1) the rushing wind, (2) the visible flames resting on each believer present, and (3) speaking in "other tongues." There is no record of these three being present together at any other time.

Filling with the Spirit (2:4). The image is common in the O.T. where it emphasizes the Holy Spirit's empowering of the individual for service (cf. Jud. 6:34; 14:19). In the N.T., the Gk. verbs meaning "to fill" are always in the passive voice when filling with the Spirit is described. We "are filled," we do not fill ourselves.

The Spirit dwells in every believer (1 Cor. 6:19), and as we live in fellowship with God He will fill us. When He does we are enabled both to serve and to grow (cf. Gal. 5:19-23).

"Tongues" (2:3). There is great debate over the nature and significance of the "gift of tongues." Here, however, the text gives definite clues. These "tongues" were recognized as the "native languages" of visitors who had come to Jerusalem for the festival (v. 8).

The prophecy (2:15-21). Peter explains what has happened by quoting a prophecy which is being partially fulfilled. The fact that the ulti-

mate fulfillment of O.T. prophecies was often foreshadowed by partial fulfillment was understood by Peter's listeners. The elements of the prophecy he emphasizes are (1) the pouring out of the Spirit, which takes place "before" (no time specified!) the Day of the Lord comes, and (2) during which "everyone who calls on the name of the Lord will be saved" (v. 21).

Apostolic preaching (2:22-41). Peter's sermon here and other sermons recorded in Acts contain critical elements in common. These are:

Jesus is a historic person	2:22	
Jesus crucified and risen	2:23-24	3:13-15
All this was prophesied	2:25-35	3:18
Jesus is God's Messiah	2:36	3:20
All who turn and believe will be forgiven and given the Holy Spirit	2:37-38	3:19, 21-26

These themes remain basic elements of the proclamation of the Gospel in our day.

A promise for all (2:39). The invitation to respond to the Gospel remains unlimited. But acceptance of the Gospel carries with it a very special obligation: to share it with "all."

The Christian community (2:42-47). This paragraph is often taken as a description of the ideal Christian community. It is united around the apostles' teaching, fellowship, prayer, sharing, and praise.

"Breaking of bread" (2:42). This phrase refers to the Communion service.

Chapter summary. As Peter and John approach the temple to pray, a beggar cries out for alms. Instead Peter stops and in Jesus' name heals him completely (3:1-10). The miracle draws a crowd, and Peter seizes the occasion to preach Christ, repeating again the key themes found in all Gospel preaching (vv. 11-26): Jesus, crucified and risen again (vv. 11-15); Jesus, living and powerful through faith in His name (v. 16); Jesus, the Christ of Scripture and prophecy (vv. 17-25); Jesus, sent to bless and to turn each person from his or her wicked ways (v. 26). Even as apostolic preaching centered on Jesus Christ, so does our faith and witness today.

Key verse. 3:19: God wipes out sins.

Personal application. Find refreshment in repentance.

Key concepts. Begging »p. 667. Healing »p. 611. Miracles »p. 679. Repentance »p. 780. Forgiveness »pp. 633, 863.

INSIGHT

"To the temple" (3:1). The early Christians worshiped regularly at the temple (cf. 2:46). Jesus was Israel's Messiah; they saw no need to make a break with Judaism or O.T. forms of worship. For these early chapters of Acts even the Sanhedrin looked on Jesus' followers as a sect of their historic faith.

"The time of prayer" (3:1). Regular times of prayer were early morning, the ninth hour (3 P.M.), and the late evening. The fact that the cripple was being carried to the temple then suggests he regularly went to beg when the crowds were thickest.

"In the name of Jesus" (3:6). In Heb. thought the name does not identify a person as much as express his character or being. In a real sense the power of the person was sensed as being present in his or her name. Thus, what Peter was saying was, "*In the power* of Jesus Christ of Nazareth, walk!"

That power did flow. The cripple's feet and ankles were strengthened, and the man walked and leaped, living proof of the power of Jesus.

"Recognized" (3:10). The man, a "cripple from birth," begged regularly in the temple and was thus well-known. There could be no question of deceit; a real miracle had occurred. Onlookers may also have recognized fulfillment of a prophecy related to the coming of the messianic age: "Then will the lame leap like a deer" (Isa. 35:6).

Street preaching (3:11-26). Peter gave no polished sermon after healing the cripple. The themes are the same as are found in his sermon on Pentecost. But this is street-corner preaching, blunt, unpolished, straightforward.

It makes no difference in what context the Gospel is preached. The message is always essentially the same: Jesus, crucified, risen, coming again, the source of salvation and blessing for all who believe.

Names of Jesus (3:12-16). Here Jesus is identified as "God's Servant," a clear reference to the messianic title established in Isa. 42–53. Jesus is also called the "Holy and Righteous One" and the "Author of Life." All this explains why the name of Jesus is so powerful. He is the One foretold by the O.T. and identified there as God Himself.

"Repent . . . that your sins may be wiped out" (3:19). Faith in Christ is the only condition for salvation. How does it happen that repentance is mentioned so often in Peter's early sermons? According to the *Expository Dictionary of Bible Words* (Zondervan, 1985, p. 522), "repent" (*metanoia*) indicates "a decision that changes the total direction of one's life." As Peter reminds his listeners, they "disowned" Jesus and "killed" him. Now Peter calls on them to believe in Him as Messiah and Saviour, a choice which is repentance—in that to believe now would involve a decision that reversed the direction of their past lives.

"In ignorance" (3:17). Peter doesn't want to make his listeners feel guilty about what they have done. He wants them to turn to Jesus. There's no need for us today to hammer away at others' sins. What they need is not to feel more guilty, but to hear the good news that God forgives.

The Apostle Peter

Illustration. *Peter strains at the nets in one of his fishing boats. Financial success enabled him to move from Bethsaida to Capernaum (John 1:44; Mark 1:21), where land was dear, and construct a large house for his family.*

Jesus took this rugged, successful commercial fisherman and commissioned him as a disciple. In fact Peter is the leading disciple. He is mentioned first on each list of the Twelve. Along with James and John, he is one of an inner circle of three. The Gospels constantly portray him as taking the lead: he asks questions, gives unsolicited advice, leaps from a boat to join Jesus walking on the sea, expresses his conviction that Jesus is the Christ, fervently affirms his loyalty, draws a sword at Gethsemane, and strikes out at those who came to take Christ prisoner. In Acts he is again the unquestioned leader. He preaches the church's first great evangelistic sermon (Acts 2), boldly confronts the Sanhedrin (Acts 4), and first shares the Gospel with a Gentile at the house of Cornelius (Acts 10).

Christians have been divided over the meaning of Christ's statement, "You are Peter, and on this rock I will build My church . . . . I will give you the keys of the kingdom of heaven" (Matt. 16:17-19). Roman Catholics interpret this as Peter's commission to be the church's first pope. Most Protestants, and many early church fathers, take the "rock" to be the truth expressed in Peter's affirmation, "You [Jesus] are the Christ, the Son of the Living God" (16:16). And the "keys" are the Gospel, which Peter was the first to proclaim to mankind's two great classes, Jew and Gentile.

Yet for all his prominence and enthusiasm, Peter was a flawed human being. Peter could call Christ "Lord" in one breath and in the next dare to correct Him (Matt. 16:20ff.). Peter could fervently affirm his loyalty and a few hours later deny the Lord (Mark 14). And Peter could even hypocritically deal with the Gentiles and earn Paul's rebuke (Gal. 2:11-21). How like us Peter was in his weaknesses. How we might yearn to be like him in his strengths.

Outline
Place
Finder

JERUSALEM
SAMARIA
GENTILES
WORLD
IMPRISONMENT

Chapter summary. Temple officials rush to investigate the crowds that gather after a cripple is healed (Acts 3) and detain Peter and John for questioning (4:1-4). When the Sanhedrin meets to investigate (vv. 5-7), Peter boldly asserts that the miracle has been performed in the name and power of Jesus, "whom you crucified" (vv. 8-12). Peter's courageous speech stuns the leaders. Yet all know Peter and John have performed an "outstanding miracle." The best thing seems to be to frighten these "ordinary men" and "stop this thing from spreading any further" (vv. 13-17). But Peter and John are unimpressed (vv. 18-22). When released, they gather the church for a prayer which serves us well as a model today. It is filled with praise and expressions of confidence in God, which leads to a request which, when fulfilled, will truly glorify God (vv. 23-30). That prayer is answered (v. 31), and the church, united in faith in love, continues to witness powerfully to God's grace (vv. 32-37).

Key verse. 4:12: Why we must preach.

Personal application. Opposition is a cue to pray, not quit.

Key concepts. Name »p. 691. Salvation »pp. 742, 744, 849. Prayer »pp. 181, 608. Fill with Spirit »p. 709. Giving »p. 781.

INSIGHT

"The Sadducees" (4:1-2). This party took the lead here not only because the apostles were "teaching," but because they were in effect attempting to prove resurrection by reference to the case of Jesus. This Jewish party denied resurrection.

Peter's explanation (4:5-12). Peter's defense was a bold attack. The miracle was performed in the "name" (e.g., the power) of Jesus. The miracle in effect proved that Jesus, who was unjustly crucified (by "you") is in fact Israel's Messiah and the only source of salvation.

"No other name" (4:12). Here too "name" is used in the sense of the "power" or "authority" of Jesus Himself. Jesus is the only source of salvation, the only one able to forgive sins and provide new spiritual life.

"Unschooled, ordinary men" (4:13). Jewish law in the 1st century forbade punishing an "unschooled" person for a first offense, assuming he acted in ignorance. Instead he was instructed and then punished if a second offense occurred. This policy was followed here. Peter and John were warned and threatened. When they persisted in preaching Jesus, they were arrested again—and flogged (Acts 5:40).

We can't help it (4:18-20). What a model for us. When we "cannot help" doing what is right, we have made real spiritual progress.

The believer's prayer (4:23-30). The prayer is a model in several respects. (1) It recognizes

God as sovereign, vv. 24, 28. He is in charge. (2) It affirms God's Word as relevant, vv. 25-27. It applies Ps. 2 to the present situation. (3) It asks for enablement, not relief, v. 29. Christians can expect to share Christ's sufferings as they carry on His mission. (4) It asks for God to act, v. 30. God is able to work in our world, through miracles hidden as well as visible.

God's will (4:28). God's will has several different meanings in the N.T. It may refer to God's revealed standards of moral behavior. It may refer to His guidance of an individual to perform a specific act, or His shaping of an individual life. But God's will may also refer to God's fixed and unalterable purpose: that which God has determined must happen, and shall happen. God's will is used in this last sense here. Other passages using God's will in the same sense include John 6:38-40, Gal. 1:4, and Eph. 1:5-11.

"They shared everything" (4:32-37). This passage has been used to support "Christian communism." Instead it is a clear example of the concept of giving taught in the N.T. No one lost control of his or her own possessions (communism). But each Christian cared more about other persons than material possessions (Christianity).

May the values displayed in the early Jerusalem church shape all our attitudes toward wealth and others.

Chapter summary. A couple, jealous of the respect won by the generosity of persons like Barnabas, also sell property to make a contribution to the poor. But they conspire to pretend to give all, while keeping part back. The deceit brings each sudden death—and fills the church and city with awe (5:1-11). In these early days the apostles perfom many miracles, and great crowds fill the city to hear them preach and see healings (vv. 12-16). Their popularity infuriates the high priest and Sadducees. They arrest the apostles—but the Lord opens the prison doors. The next morning the officials are stunned to hear the apostles are back in the temple preaching (vv. 17-26). The apostles are re-arrested, but again Peter boldly proclaims Jesus "whom you had killed" (vv. 27-32). After a heated debate the Sanhedrin decides simply to flog the apostles and order them not to speak of Jesus anymore (vv. 33-40). But the apostles rejoice in the privilege of suffering for Jesus and never stop "proclaiming the good news that Jesus is the Christ" (vv. 41-42).

Key verse. 5:41: An unusual privilege?

Personal application. Be bold, let God worry about the future.

Key concepts. Holy Spirit »pp. 73, 744. Fear »p. 363. Healings »p. 611. Miracle »pp. 57, 679. Sadducee »p. 592. Pharisee »p. 591.

INSIGHT

It belonged to you (5:4). Ananias and Sapphira were not condemned because they failed to give all. They had full rights over their property. They were condemned because their deceit was a reintroduction of the hypocrisy which had corrupted so many of the religious in Judaism.

Believers today who mask their real motives by public piety should take warning from Ananias and Sapphira. God's decisive response to their deceit may not be repeated today. But God's attitude toward hypocrisy in the church has been clearly revealed!

"No one else dared join them" (5:13). "Join" here is *kollao*, to closely associate with. Many Christians have been admired for their courage. But only conversion to Christ gives an onlooker courage to stand beside the believer when such association means persecution.

Open doors (5:19-21a). Acts reports three occasions when God opened prison doors (cf. also 12:6ff.; 16:26ff.).

"This new life" (5:20). In the N.T. new "life" and "salvation" are used interchangeably. The essence of God's saving work is not seen in the forgiveness of sins, though this is vital, but in the infusion of His own life, which makes a human being a child of God spiritually.

Making them guilty (5:27-28). The apostles were guilty of disobeying an order of the San-

hedrin. But they hardly made the leaders "guilty of this man's blood." Not long before, this very crowd made themselves responsible, shouting, "Let His blood be on us and on our children" (Matt. 27:25).

"Forgiveness of sins" (5:31). Forgiveness is *aphiemi*, a verb used to describe the canceling of debts and the pardoning of crimes, as well as the forgiveness of sins. In forgiveness God sends away or removes our sins, making guilt irrelevant.

"A Pharisee" (5:34). Acts suggests a shift in attitude of the Pharisees, who were the initial opponents of Jesus. Now the Sadducees are those most hostile to the early church (cf. also Paul's defense before the Sanhedrin in Acts 23). In part, this is because we meet different Pharisees than the hostile hypocrites of the Gospels—for many 1st-century Pharisees were truly dedicated to God. In part, this may be because belief in resurrection was a main tenet of the Pharisees' faith and had been ridiculed by the Sadducees. The resurrection of Christ would give them support in their long conflict with Judaism's other major party and may have moderated their attitude toward the apostles and the church.

Worthy to suffer disgrace (5:41-42). Suffering for Jesus is suffering with Jesus and has been a source of unusual joy through the ages.

713

Outline
Place
Finder

JERUSALEM
SAMARIA
GENTILES
WORLD
IMPRISONMENT

Chapter summary. When an ethnic dispute over the fair distribution of food strains harmony in the young Christian community, the apostles guide the church to select deacons, who take on that responsibility (6:1-7). One of these deacons, Stephen, is especially effective in debating those who attack the faith (vv. 8-10). Frustrated by Stephen's skill, his opponents falsely accuse him and he is called before the Sanhedrin, the governing council and supreme court of Judaism (vv. 11-15). There Stephen makes an inspired defense, drawing on sacred history to demonstrate the persistent rejection by God's people of the agents of salvation sent by Him. Then Stephen applies his history lesson. Israel's resistance has culminated in the council's murder of God's Righteous One, the Messiah! (7:1-53)

This bold accusation infuriates the council. When Stephen claims to see Jesus at God's right hand, the place of power, the council members lose control. Stephen is hurried out into the streets and stoned to death (vv. 54-60).

Key verse. 7:52: A proud heritage?

Personal application. How we face our faults reveals our character.

INSIGHT

Ethnic strife (6:1). There's nothing new about racial hostility. The Jews of Palestine were more than a little suspicious of coreligionists from outside the homeland, who spoke Gk. primarily and might not even know Aramaic. The purity of their faith was questioned by both Pharisee and Essene. It seems both the label "Hellenist" and the attitude were carried over when members of both groups converted to Christ. Mistrust and perhaps real discrimination led the Hellenic Jews to complain to the apostles.

Every church will have dissension. Not its existence, but how we deal with it, is the measure of our spirituality.

The apostles (6:2). The Twelve did not impose a solution, but suggested the process by which the church would resolve its own difficulties. Leaders should not dictate, but guide and direct.

The first deacons (6:1-6). The term comes from the Gk. word *diakonos* ("servant," "minister"). The word group is used of an office in the early church (Rom. 16:1; 1 Tim. 3:8-13). But the N.T. emphasis is on acts of service, especially acts which respond to human need by loving service extended for Jesus' sake. The *Expository Dictionary of Bible Words* (Zondervan, 1985, p. 443) surveys passages using the word group and notes that such ministry includes: "caring for those in prison (Matt. 25:44), serving tables (meeting physical needs,

Acts 6:2), teaching the Word of God (Acts 6:4), giving money to meet others' needs (2 Cor. 9:1), and all service offered by Christians to others to build them up in faith (1 Cor. 12:5; Eph. 4:12)."

Although there was an office of deacon in the early church, their service kind of ministry was open to all.

Greek names (6:5). It is significant that each of the deacons selected by the church had Gk. rather than Heb. names. What an expression of trust—to put one's own fate in the hands of members of the complaining minority!

We can learn much from the early church. Don't blame. Deal with the problem openly. Make it a matter of prayer. Challenge the church to work out its own solution. Focus on selecting godly people who are known and trusted by the community to take responsibility.

Converted priests (6:7). It is unlikely that these were members of the hierarchy. But there were thousands of ordinary priests in Jerusalem from whom the "number" of converts came.

Martyrdom (6–7). Stephen was the church's first martyr. The word comes from the Gk. term for "witness." It was applied to those who testified to the reality and significance of their faith by suffering death rather than deny Jesus.

"Saul was there" (8:1). Later the young Saul will experience conversion and become Paul, the hero of Luke's history of the early church.

Chapter summary. After Stephen's stoning intense persecution scattered the Jerusalem believers (8:1-3). But those who fled the holy city shared Christ wherever they went (v. 4). Philip, one of the seven deacons (cf. Acts 6:1-7), not only preached in Samaria but also healed there (8:5-8), astonishing not only ordinary people but even a charlatan named Simon who had made his living impressing others with his supposedly supernatural powers (vv. 9-13). This revival in Samaria brought Peter and John to check on what was happening (v. 14); and the apostles, discerning the conversions were authentic, prayed that the Samaritans too might be given the Holy Spirit (vv. 15-25). Meanwhile Philip himself was directed away from the cities and towns to wait by a desert road. There he shared the Gospel with a single traveler, an Ethiopian official, who believed and immediately was baptized by Philip. Then Philip returned to his preaching to the crowds (vv. 26-40).

Outline
Place
Finder

JERUSALEM
SAMARIA
GENTILES
WORLD
IMPRISONMENT

Key verse. 8:4: A topic for gossip.

Personal application. We can talk about Jesus wherever we are.

Key concepts. Samaritans »p. 250. Miracles »pp. 57, 679. Baptism »pp. 604, 708. Repent »p. 780. Angel »pp. 521, 855.

INSIGHT

"Persecution" (8:1-4). This first persecution had positive results, as persecutions often have throughout church history. The scattered believers preached ("gossiped") Christ, and the Gospel message spread (»p. 760). As the church father, Tertullian, said, "The blood of the martyrs is the seed of the church."

Miracles (8:6-7). The miracles that marked the ministry of Jesus continued in the early days of the church as signs authenticating those who bore the Gospel message as God's spokesmen. As Acts progresses, the role of the miraculous diminishes, and the epistles nowhere suggest that Christian leaders or missionaries continued to perform them.

The Holy Spirit's coming (8:14-17). Some have seen in this report evidence that believers do not receive the Holy Spirit at conversion, so that His coming upon Christians is a separate and distinct work of God. But this is one of those passages that reminds us not to build doctrine on experiences reported in Acts. God withheld the Spirit in this one case for a purpose. A centuries-long religious hostility existed between the Jews and Samaritans. By giving the Holy Spirit through the apostles, God indicated (1) the unity of the Samaritan and the Jewish believers as members of one church, and (2) the primacy of the apostles as leaders of that one church. The N.T. teaches every believer has the Spirit of God (1 Cor. 12:7, 13).

"Philip" (8:5). Philip is the second of the seven deacons listed in Acts 6:1-7.

Simon the Sorcerer (8:9-24). Apparently Simon's "belief" was superficial, like the belief of those described in John 2:23-25, who were excited by Jesus' miracles but were not committed to Him. Many early church fathers identify this Simon with a heretic who later opposed the apostles and corrupted Christians in Rome.

Clearly after his public baptism and supposed conversion, Simon was still "full of bitterness and captive to sin" (8:23) and far more interested in profit than in godliness.

Accept the word (8:14). This phrase is used in the N.T. to mean "believe in Christ."

"Eunuch" (8:27). The term usually indicates a man who has been castrated early in life. Many ancient Middle Eastern rulers preferred their high officials be eunuchs, believing that without families their loyalty to the ruler would be undivided. The title "eunuch" was sometimes granted to high officials without that person suffering castration.

For one man (8:26-40). Perhaps the most striking element in the story is that God led Philip away from an effective evangelistic campaign that was reaching hundreds to witness to a single individual. Let's never forget that every individual is important to God. Our witnessing to a single person is as important as the mass evangelist's outreach to thousands.

Chapter summary. Saul has already been introduced as an individual intent on destroying the young Christian movement (8:1-3). Saul sets out for Damascus with authority to arrest any Christians found in the Jewish community there (9:1-2). On the way Jesus appears to him, and Saul falls, stunned and blinded, to the ground (vv. 3-9). A Damascus believer called Ananias is sent by God to restore Paul's sight and tell him that he has been selected by God to carry Christ to the Gentiles (vv. 10-19). Paul's conversion is real. He begins at once to preach Christ in Damascus. There he is so effective some Jews conspire to kill him. Saul escapes and returns to Jerusalem, where only Barnabas is willing to take a chance on this one-time persecutor of the church. But in Jerusalem too Paul's zeal stirs up persecution, and the brothers escort the fiery evangelist to Caesarea and "send him off" to his home in Tarsus (vv. 20-31). Meanwhile Peter continues to minister in the Jewish homeland, performing notable miracles, even raising one much loved female believer from the dead (vv. 32-43).

Key verse. 9:15: God often chooses the unlikely.

Personal application. The person least likely to convert often makes the most committed Christian.

Key concepts. Gentile »p. 798. Resurrection »p. 658.

INSIGHT

"Letters" (9:1-2). In the first century, ethnic communities in the Roman Empire were governed by their own national laws. Thus the Jewish community in Damascus was under the authority of the ruling council in Jerusalem. Saul's letters of authority from Jerusalem granted him power of arrest in the Syrian city.

"The Way" (9:2). Early Christianity was considered a sect of Judaism. Christians called themselves adherents of "the Way" (Acts 19:9, 23; 22:4; 24:14, 22). Their critics identified them as "the sect of the Nazarenes" (24:5, 14; 28:22).

"A light from heaven" (9:3-9). Saul/Paul's conversion experience is described here and in Acts 22 and 26. The repetition underlines the significance of Saul's unique conversion by a direct revelation of Jesus.

The experience must have convinced Paul that Jesus was alive, that opposing Christianity was in effect persecuting God, and that such a vital link existed between Jesus and His own that attacking believers was in effect attacking Jesus Himself. Everything that Paul had believed now underwent radical revision. Out of this transformation came an understanding of the O.T. and God's plan which redirected the Christian movement and shaped the church's theology forever.

Saints, brothers (9:13, 17). These two terms were used within the church to identify believers. "Saint" is literally "holy one," indicating both that believers have been set apart by God and that true believers choose to live a holy life. In the N.T. "brother" is used in the sense of "fellow believer," affirming the intimate relationship between saints established by a common faith in Jesus and common relationship with God the Father.

Saul's destiny (9:15-16). This key verse sums up the story of Paul's life reflected later in Acts and Paul's own 13 N.T. letters. Through Paul the church became primarily Gentile rather than Jewish.

"They tried to kill him" (9:23, 29). Saul was a zealous, abrasive individual as a Jewish persecutor of Christians. He was just as zealous after his conversion—and possibly just as abrasive. His bold, blunt evangelism consistently aroused such intense hostility that his opponents were determined to kill him. It may well be significant that the Jerusalem Christians "took him" to Caesarea and "sent him off" to Tarsus. Once Saul was gone, Luke tells us the church "enjoyed a time of peace" and that it "grew in numbers" (9:31).

Zeal is commendable. But later, a more mature Paul wrote young Timothy that "the Lord's servant must not quarrel; instead he must be kind to everyone. . . . [and] "those who oppose him he must gently instruct" (2 Tim. 2:24-25).

The Apostle Paul

Illustration. *A second-century document describes Paul as "a man of small stature, with bald head and crooked legs . . . with eyebrows meeting and nose somewhat hooked." Yet this man, who was "unimpressive" in person (2 Cor. 10:10), was a bold defender and preacher of the Gospel and at the same time a tender, loving friend to new converts (cf. 1 Thes. 2:11-13).*

The Apostle Paul emerges as the most significant figure in the early church. First a persecutor, he became an aggressive promoter of the Gospel. Paul spearheaded the explosion of the early church beyond Judaism into Gentile society. Some years after his conversion Paul was invited by Barnabas to share leadership of a predominantly Gentile congregation formed in Antioch. After a time, the two led a team of missionaries which set out to share Christ with all in the Mediterranean world. Paul's success in winning converts among Gentiles raised troubling questions about the relationship of Christianity to Judaism and the relationship of Gentile to Jewish Christians.

Paul contended for full acceptance of Gentile Christians without requiring them to follow Jewish customs. He also worked out the full meaning of the Christian Gospel as it relates to Old Testament revelation. His letters, particularly Romans and Galatians, show that the critical element in both Testaments is a grace gift of righteousness, given freely by God and claimed only by faith, apart from works.

Paul's letters also develop the basis for a Christian lifestyle that looks to the Holy Spirit, whose living presence enables believers to live a life of love that more than fulfills the requirements the Old Testament expresses in the Mosaic Law. Christianity rests not on the Old Covenant God made with Abraham's offspring, but on a vital New Covenant, predicted in the Old Testament, that God in Christ makes with all humankind. Transformation, not reformation, and new birth, not physical birth, mark Christianity. And this understanding of our faith has been shaped by the great apostle whom God chose, and has used, to set the course Christians have followed for nearly 2,000 years.

Chapter summary. These chapters constitute a dramatic turning point in church history. For the first time Gentiles hear and respond to the Gospel. It happens when an angel tells a Roman army officer, Cornelius, to send for Peter (10:1-8). Meanwhile Peter has a vision which reveals that God is able to declare "clean" in this new age that which was "unclean" in Old Testament times (vv. 9-16). Peter understands the message (vv. 17-23) and goes to the house of Cornelius. There Gentiles believe—and the Holy Spirit makes His presence known by enabling the new Christians to speak in tongues (vv. 24-46). The evidence is unmistakable, and Peter signals acceptance of Gentiles into the church by baptizing them with water (vv. 47-48). When Peter returns to Jerusalem he is criticized for going into Cornelius' house. But when he tells what happened there the Jewish Christians offer praise. "God has even granted the Gentiles" faith (11:1-18).

When a predominantly Gentile church is established in Antioch, Saul/Paul is recruited by Barnabas to serve as one of its leaders (vv. 19-30).

Key verse. 11:18: Praise God for the unexpected.

Personal application. Be open to let God change even long-held beliefs and prejudices.

Key concepts. Angel »p. 521. Clean/unclean »pp. 82, 505, 617. Holy Spirit »pp. 73, 744. Baptism »pp. 604, 708. Tongues »p. 709.

INSIGHT

Gentile converts. First-century Jews actively sought Gentile converts. But such converts had to accept all the obligations laid on Jews by O.T. Law. The idea that a Gentile could have a direct relationship to God, without in fact first becoming a Jew, was not only foreign in 1st-century Judaism but was also repugnant. This is why the direct conversion of Cornelius to Christianity was such a shock and stimulated criticism of Peter in the Jerusalem church, which was and which saw itself as Jewish.

"Unclean" (10:9-23). In 1st-century Judaism Gentiles were themselves considered "unclean." Thus a pious Jew could not enter a Gentile house or eat with Gentiles without defiling himself and becoming ceremonially "unclean." The vision granted Peter taught him that God was about to declare "clean" a whole class of persons.

Peter's sermon (10:34-43). This brief summary of Peter's sermon is in full harmony with the earlier evangelistic sermons recorded in Acts. The heart of the Gospel is the historic Christ, crucified and risen again, in accord with the teachings of O.T. Scriptures.

"Tongues" (10:44-46; 11:15-17). These verses explain the appearance of tongues in this situation. The fact that Gentiles were given this gift, just as the apostles had been on Pentecost (cf. Acts 2), was proof of God's acceptance of Gentiles into the church. Peter's phrase "at the beginning" (v. 15) suggests that this event was not only unusual because it involved Gentiles, but also because speaking in tongues was not a common phenomenon in the early church.

Luke's concern. Luke introduces this story after telling of Paul's conversion to make an important point. While Paul led the evangelistic effort in Gentile lands, it was not his idea to evangelize Gentiles directly. That took place on God's initiative, and the person who opened the door to Gentile converts was Peter, not Paul. It's popular for some to say that Paul, whose letters do establish the shape of Christian faith, "corrupted" an earlier, simpler Gospel. Not so. Paul was simply God's instrument to explain what the Lord had already established as priorities.

"Barnabas" (11:25). This delightful man, whose name means "Encourager," had risked introducing the persecutor Saul into the church after his conversion (9:27). Now he searches out Saul to share in ministry in Antioch's Gentile church. How we need people like Barnabas today.

Chapter summary. Back in Jerusalem John's brother, James, one of the original 12 disciples, is executed and Peter is arrested (12:1-7). But God intervenes. As the church prays, an angel releases Peter and leads him outside his prison (vv. 8-19a). Then Herod who has ordered the persecution (Agrippa I) is stricken with a terminal disease and dies (vv. 19b-24).

The church has nearly reached the limits of its expansion within Judaism. Now Luke's history moves away from Jerusalem and Judea. Barnabas and Saul, who had brought relief funds to support Christians through a devastating famine in Jerusalem, return to Antioch (v. 25; 11:27-29). They are about to set out on Christianity's first great missionary venture.

Key verse. 12:16: God answers despite doubts.

Personal application. Expect God to do more than you expect!

Key concepts. Persecution »p. 760. Prayer »pp. 609, 894.

INSIGHT

Here the door has a different significance. The believers' prayers have been answered, but locked behind their closed door they simply can't believe that Peter stands outside.

When we pray, let's throw open the doors of our lives and eagerly look for God's answer to appear.

The miracle. God's act of intervention on behalf of Peter reminds us that the Lord did not desert the original Jewish church when Luke's focus shifts to Gentile evangelism. Just because we're not on the front pages of our newspapers doesn't mean God is not actively involved in our lives.

Herod Agrippa. This grandson of Herod the Great grew up in Rome and was a close friend of the emperor Caligula as well as of his successor Claudius. His influence in Rome enabled him to regain the entire kingdom governed by his grandfather. His persecution of the apostles was undoubtedly political, intended to gain the support of his Jewish subjects (cf. 12:3).

Luke's mention of worms matches an infection of intestinal roundworms. Such worms grow from 10 to 16 inches long. They can clog the intestines, causing extreme pain and even vomiting of the worms and death.

Executing the guards (12:18-19). Roman law decreed that guards who permitted their prisoner to escape should suffer whatever penalty was intended for him. Of course, neither the law nor Herod made any concession to miracles! This second event again underlines God's intervention for the Jerusalem church.

Paul and Barnabas' mission (12:25). Acts 11:27-30 tells of the Antioch church's concern

Illustration. *The home where the believers were gathered to pray for Peter probably featured just such an ornamental door. Several biblical figures of speech speak of doors: an open door is an opportunity (1 Cor. 16:9); Jesus calls Himself "the Door" by which we are saved (John 10:9, NASB); Jesus knocks at "the door" (to our hearts) and waits for us to invite Him in (Rev. 3:20).*

for their Jewish brothers in Jerusalem. Luke emphasizes Gentile concern for Jews to remind us that the Christian movement truly was one.

Chapter summary. Following the leading of the Holy Spirit, the church at Antioch commissions Barnabas and Paul as history's first official Christian missionaries (13:1-3). Their first adventure takes place on the Island of Cyprus, where Paul curses a sorcerer with blindness and witnesses the conversion of the Roman proconsul (vv. 4-12). In Pisidian Antioch Paul preaches first in the Jewish synagogue, stimulating great interest in his message about Jesus (vv. 13-43). But when great numbers of Gentiles turn out the next Sabbath to hear him, the Jewish elders are jealous and hostile. Paul then declares his intention to go directly to the Gentile community with his message of salvation, and a great revival sweeps the countryside (vv. 44-49). The Jews, however, incite persecution of the missionaries. Paul and Barnabas are forced to leave. But they leave behind a vital, joy-filled young church (vv. 50-52).

Key verse. 13:46: Paul's missionary strategy.

Personal application. Concentrate your efforts on those who seem ready to respond.

Key concepts. Synagogue »p. 612. Occult »p. 131. Gentiles »p. 798.

INSIGHT

Holy Spirit guides (13:2). God is committed to guide any believer who honestly seeks and will do His will. In O.T. times general guidance was found in the moral and ritual laws provided in the five books of Moses. In national or personal situations not covered — such as who should lead an attack in battle — God guided through Urim and Thummim (»p. 70) or prophets (»p. 131). In the N.T. era the means of divining shifts, with general principles guiding choices being found in the letters of the apostles. Situational guidance — such as when missionaries should be sent out and who should go — is now provided directly by the Holy Spirit, who dwells within believers (cf. also Acts 20:22; Rom. 8:14).

When we have a difficult choice to make we need to be sensitive to the Spirit, and expect Him to give us a sense of peace when we are moving in God's chosen way.

"Sergius Paulus" (13:7). The Roman proconsul undoubtedly "wanted to hear" the missionary's message in his official capacity. He was checking out rumors and charges of disruption in the Jewish community. Paul's display of power in blinding the evil sorcerer, Elymas, helped convince the "intelligent" Roman, who "believed" (cf. 14:1; 17:34; 19:17).

"Paul" (13:9). From this point on Luke identifies Saul (cf. 13:2) as Paul (cf. 13:13) and Paul also emerges as the leader of the missionary team. Earlier it was "Barnabas and Saul"; now it becomes "Paul and his companions."

"Antioch" (13:14). An earlier emperor, in the 280s B.C., had given some 16 cities the name of his father and his son, "Antiochus." This Antioch is far from the one where the missionaries began.

Paul's address (13:16-41). An address by a member of the synagogue or visitor was a part of typical 1st-century Sabbath observance. It would not be unusual for Paul, probably dressed as a Pharisee, to be invited to speak.

Paul's sermon is similar to Peter's early messages. He identifies Jesus as a historic person, a descendant of David, who is thus qualified by birth to be the Saviour (vv. 16-23). He shows how prophecies were fulfilled in Jesus' announcement, His death, and His resurrection (vv. 24-37). He promises forgiveness to those who believe in Jesus (vv. 38-39) and warns that a choice now must be made (vv. 40-41).

The sermons of Acts remind us how clear the simple Gospel is. Let's not confuse it by being drawn into arguments with the unconverted about peripheral issues, whether about the Bible, abortion, creationism, etc.

Jealousy (13:45). How tragic to be so upset over another's popularity that we ignore the truly vital issues of life.

"God-fearing women" (13:50). The description "God fearer" was given to persons who were adherents of Judaism's moral and theological vision without becoming converts and adopting a Jewish lifestyle, which involved a commitment to keep the ritual as well as moral elements of Jewish law.

Chapter summary. The missionaries continue on their swing through Asia Minor. They visit Iconium, where the Gospel message again creates such dissension that Paul and Barnabas are forced to flee (14:1-7). In Lystra and Derbe the two missionaries are mistaken for pagan gods. They barely succeed in keeping an enthusiastic crowd from offering sacrifices to them. But some Jews, who have followed them from Antioch and Iconium just to hinder their work, succeed in turning the crowd against them. Paul is stoned and left for dead, but revives and continues preaching (vv. 8-20). Despite the hazards, the missionaries win a "large number of disciples." Finally they return to their home church and report how God has opened the door of salvation to the Gentiles (vv. 21-28).

Outline
Place
Finder

JERUSALEM
SAMARIA
GENTILES
WORLD
IMPRISONMENT

Key verse. 14:20: Perseverance.

Personal application. Focus on your successes, not on the opposition.

INSIGHT

Iconium. This was a prosperous cosmopolitan center patterned on the Gk. city-state. Paul followed his normal pattern by going first to the Jewish synagogue to launch his ministry. This strategy was dictated first by Paul's continuing concern for his own people (cf. 13:46; Rom. 9:2-5), and second by his awareness that Gentile adherents of Judaism, who attended synagogue services, were those most likely to respond to the Gospel. In fact most 1st-century churches had a core of Gentile believers who already had some familiarity with the O.T.

"Apostles" (14:4, 14). The term is used in both a restrictive and general sense. In the first sense the Twelve and Paul are Apostles, with a capital "A." In the second sense persons like Barnabas, who undertook itinerant evangelistic missions, are apostles, lower case "a." Today we would probably call these apostles "missionaries."

Lystra. This was an ancient, native city whose inhabitants spoke their own language. Paul's healing of a cripple there evoked a superstitious response. Inscriptions discovered near Lystra, dating some two centuries before Paul's visit, suggest Zeus and Hermes had long been worshiped in this part of the province of Galatia. Also an ancient legend reported by Ovid just 50 years earlier reported that the two gods had once before visited the area disguised as humans—and had severely punished the area for not welcoming them! It's likely the people's quick response was motivated by fear rather than enthusiasm for their deities!

Appointing elders (14:23). The apostles did

Illustration. *Greek statues of Zeus, like the one shown here, portray him as a large, powerful figure. This may suggest something of how Barnabas, Paul's companion and one of the most attractive of N.T. people, may have looked.*

not appoint elders on their first visit because it took time for congregations to recognize who among them would mature spiritually. "Appoint" here is *cheiriotonesantes*, "to elect by a show of hands." The apostles confirmed those that the young churches had already discerned were spiritually qualified to lead (cf. 1 Tim. 3).

Chapter summary. Mass Gentile conversions created serious stress in the early church. Jewish Christians accepted the conversion of Cornelius, but did not consider implications. Now some believers from Jerusalem travel to Gentile churches teaching it is necessary to become a Jew in order to be a true Christian and be saved (15:1). Paul and Barnabas dispute this teaching and soon head a delegation to Jerusalem to "see the apostles and elders about this question" (vv. 2-5). There the church holds its first general council. After much discussion and prayer, a consensus is reached and is stated by James (vv. 6-13). Scripture foretells a day when Gentiles as Jews will bear God's name (vv. 14-18). They should be free then to turn to God as Gentiles, without unnecessary hindrances (vv. 19-21). This conclusion is made official in a letter circulated to Gentile churches, where it is received with joy (vv. 22-35).

The church has resolved a major theological dispute harmoniously. Yet Paul and Barnabas find themselves entangled in a bitter personal dispute—which they do not resolve (vv. 36-41).

Key verse. 15:19: No hindrances.

Personal application. When you witness make the Gospel the only issue.

Key concepts. Circumcision »p. 36. Brothers »p. 716. Pharisees »p. 591. Elder »p. 835. Gentile »p. 798. John Mark »p. 630.

INSIGHT

Circumcison (15:1). This rite was the physical sign that a person was included among God's O.T. people. In effect these self-appointed teachers from Jerusalem argued one must convert to Judaism to become a real Christian.

"Pharisees" (15:5). Believers who had belonged to this religious party still practiced rigorous observance of the Law as Christians. Their zeal for the Law led them to suppose that all true believers must adopt their pious but legalistic lifestyle.

It's so easy to impose our convictions on others. And so wrong!

"No distinction" (15:9). God purified Jew and Gentile by faith as Jew and Gentile. Thus faith in Christ is the issue, not those other characteristics on which human societies focus. To introduce other considerations than faith would distort the Gospel of God's grace (v. 11).

Law a yoke (15:10). "Yoke" here is used in a figurative sense common in the O.T.: as a symbol of bondage and oppression (Ex. 6:6-7; Isa. 10:27; Jer. 27:11). While no clear theology of the Law had yet been developed by the church to reflect changes brought by Christ (»p. 790), Peter already was sensitive to the fact that the Law was a burden rather than an

aid to believers—an awareness not at all shared by Jewish rabbis of the time.

"James" (15:13). This James is the brother of Jesus, the author of the N.T. Book of James. He was noted for his personal piety, commitment to prayer, and adherence to O.T. Law!

All involved (15:22). Apostles, elders, and "the whole church" were involved in the process that resolved the church's first great challenge. The pattern seen here involves: clear statement of the issue, arguments by both sides, evidence from experience and Scripture, good communication with the whole church, and a resulting sense of unity.

Requirements (15:22). Their exact character is debated. They probably involve issues that had an impact on Jewish sensibilities and thus fellowship between Jewish and Gentile believers. If so, they should be understood as: eating food from temple meat markets (cf. 1 Cor. 8), marriages to relatives, eating strangled animals still containing the blood. The moral standards of the O.T. are known (v. 21), so only distinctive convictions are noted.

Paul and Barnabas dispute (15:36-39). Watch out for personal conflicts which are harder to deal with than doctrinal differences!

Chapter summary. The issue of the basis of Gentile inclusion in the church officially settled, Paul sets out with Silas on another missionary journey. Timothy is added to Paul's party at Lystra (16:1-4). Through a vision Paul is led to leave Asia Minor and cross into Europe (vv. 5-10). There his first convert is a woman of Philippi, named Lydia, whose home becomes Paul's base (vv. 11-15). When the apostle expels a demon from a slave girl he is accused by her owners, who stir up the crowds to attack Paul and Silas. The city magistrates summarily order the pair beaten and thrown into prison (vv. 16-24). That night an earthquake shatters the prison doors, and the jailer and his household come to Christ (vv. 25-34). When the magistrates try to release Paul the next day, he informs them he is a Roman citizen, whom they have beaten illegally. The terrified officials hurry to the prison and politely beg Paul and Silas to leave (vv. 35-40).

Outline
Place
Finder

JERUSALEM
SAMARIA
GENTILES
WORLD
IMPRISONMENT

Key verse. 16:31: The promise still stands.

Personal application. Be faithful and even disasters will turn out to the glory of God.

Key concepts. Demon »p. 659. Believe »p. 740. Saved »p. 841.

INSIGHT

Timothy circumcised (16:3). This Timothy is the young apprentice of Paul to whom two N.T. letters are addressed. Paul has been criticized for his compromise in having Timothy circumcised. But in Jewish law a child is of the faith of its mother, and Timothy's mother was Jewish (cf. 2 Tim. 1:5). Paul's purpose was to remove a barrier that would have kept Timothy from ministering effectively to Jews, not because circumcision had to do with salvation.

"Macedonia" (16:9). This ancient Gk. kingdom was a province of the Roman Empire.

Lydia: women in the church (16:13-15). As the first European convert to Christianity, Lydia takes her place with other prominent, ministering N.T. women. These include Priscilla (Acts 18), who Paul calls a fellow worker in Christ (Rom. 16:3), and Phoebe, whom he calls a "deacon" of the church in Cenchrea (Rom. 16:1). In harmony with Acts 2:17, "Your sons and *daughters* will prophesy" (emphasis mine), women were given a more prominent place in the early church than they are allowed in many of our modern congregations.

Unlawful customs (16:21). The charge was that Paul was teaching a *religio illicita*, an illicit (unprotected by law) faith, and thus corrupting society. Coupled with the scornful "these men are Jews," the charge aroused the passions of the mob. The magistrates, rather than investigate, had the two flogged and jailed for disturbing the peace.

Suicide (16:27). The jailer expected to be executed if the prisoners had escaped. Suicide seemed easier to him.

"What must I do to be saved?" (16:31) The jailer's question reflects some knowledge of Paul and his preaching, not at all unlikely in a city the size of Philippi. Paul's response remains one of the simplest, clearest answers to this vital question to be found anywhere: "Believe in the Lord Jesus, and you will be saved."

And your house? (16:31) This verse has been mistakenly taken to teach that the children of believers are guaranteed salvation. Why mistaken? First, because "household" in N.T. times included family members, servants, and freemen who were obligated in some way to the head of the family. Second, because the promise is not that the household will be saved by the jailer's faith, but that the offer of salvation by faith is made to the household as well as the jailer. In fact, it often happened that when the head of a family did believe, "household" members were influenced by his faith to convert as well (cf. 11:14; 16:15; 18:8; 1 Cor. 16:15).

Roman citizens (16:37). Relatively few persons living in the Roman Empire were citizens. Only a citizen could hold office. Citizens had the right of free travel and a guarantee of protection. Citizens were not subject to local courts, but had access to Roman courts wherever they traveled. As a citizen Paul frequently claimed his rights.

Chapter summary. Paul's party continues to Thessalonica, where again an enthusiastic response from Gentiles arouses the fierce jealousy of the Jews. These create so much disturbance that the apostle is urged to leave the city (17:1-9). But in nearby Berea the Jewish population is enthusiastic and responsive to the Gospel. Then hostile Jews from Thessalonica arrive and again stir up a riot (vv. 10-15). Paul is the focus of the hostility, so while the others stay on in Berea the apostle travels to Athens. There Paul cannot keep silent and soon finds himself preaching a unique sermon on that city's Mars Hill. This carefully crafted evangelistic sermon does not quote an Old Testament unfamiliar to pagan Greeks, but uses a philosopher's approach to lead hearers to the central truth of Paul's message: the resurrection of Jesus (vv. 16-31). The idea of resurrection, totally foreign to his audience, brings ridicule. But, as always, some believe (vv. 32-33).

Key verse. 17:31: Bad news can be good news.

Personal application. Suit your approach to your audience. But don't change the Gospel to make it more "respectable."

Key concepts. Creation »p. 430. Resurrection »pp. 522, 737, 823.

INSIGHT

Thessalonica. This city of some 200,000 lay about 100 miles from Philippi along a major Roman highway. It had a large Jewish population, and Paul went first to the synagogue, as he always did (»Acts 13, p. 720).

Jewish evangelism (17:1-3). Paul's preaching strategy in the synagogue context is defined here: He told about Jesus, showed that His death and resurrection were in harmony with O.T. prophecy, and urged belief in Him as the promised Christ.

"Greeks" (17:4). The "God-fearing" Greeks and prominent women were Gentiles who had been attracted to Judaism. When they responded to Paul's message, Jewish jealousy was intense. First-century Jews took great pride in winning converts and in influencing non-Jews.

"Another king" (17:7). Paul's preaching of Christ did involve mention of "the kingdom of God" (cf. 14:22; 19:8; 20:25; 28:23, 31). His enemies distorted this and brought a patently false accusation of treason against him.

Don't expect people who are hostile to you and the Gospel to be fair.

"More noble character" (17:11). The Berean Jews were "more noble" because they valued truth and so daily tested Paul's teaching against their standard of truth, the O.T. The Thessalonian Jews had been more concerned with the number of Greeks who showed respect for Judaism! than with truth.

You and I are "more noble" when we too set aside personal considerations in order to discern, and do, God's will.

Gentile evangelism (17:22-31). Paul's address was before Athens' "Council of Ares," the government of this Gk. city-state. His strategy was: (1) seek a point of contact, which here was an altar dedicated to an "unknown god," vv. 22-23; (2) discuss the nature of God and His relationship to the creation, showing that even Gk. poets and philosophers have glimpsed the truths Paul now presents, vv. 24-28; and (3) affirm that God, who calls on all to reject idolatry and repent, has not only appointed a day of judgment but has proven His intervention in human affairs by the resurrection of Jesus, vv. 29-31.

While the form of Paul's sermon is philosophical and ideally suited for its context, the content remains totally biblical. We can change approach to suit an audience. We can never change the message itself.

Judgment day (17:31). One basic element in the Christian message is that God, though more intent on repentance than punishment, will judge human beings (cf. 1 Peter 4:5; Heb. 10:30). As Rom. 2:8 says, "For those who are self-seeking and who reject the truth and follow evil, there will be wrath and anger." The fact is that as sinners every human being is already condemned, already under the wrath of God. Only trust in Christ can provide forgiveness and acquittal on judgment day.

Chapter summary. Paul's next mission is to Corinth, a vital commercial center on a narrow isthmus of land, with ports on two seas. There too the Jews turn against him, although many of the more prominent Jews become Christians (18:1-11). When Paul is brought before Gallio, whom secular sources identify as a prominent Roman known empire-wide for his wisdom and wit, that proconsul dismisses charges. Gallio's decision that the Jewish/Christian debate involves "your own law" is in effect a legal determination that Christianity is a licit (legal) religion—a sect of Judaism (vv. 12-17). Some time later Paul moves on (vv. 18-23). But two of Paul's converts, Priscilla and Aquila, are able to instruct a gifted Jewish preacher named Apollos, who becomes a Christian and is soon a great help to the church at Corinth (vv. 24-28).

Outline
Place
Finder

JERUSALEM
SAMARIA
GENTILES
WORLD
IMPRISONMENT

Key verse. 18:26: A sensitive approach.

Personal application. Don't correct ignorance publicly, but instruct privately.

Key concepts. Women »p. 723. Synagogue »p. 612. Disciples »p. 613.

INSIGHT

The edict of Claudius (18:2). This expulsion order was issued in A.D. 49. According to the historian Suetonius it was because "the Jews were indulging in constant riots at the instigation of Chrestus." The Gospel had reached Rome, and the dispute in the Jewish community between those who believed Jesus was the Messiah and those who did not was intense.

Aquila and Priscilla (18:1). This couple are later commended by Paul as "fellow workers in Christ Jesus" to whom "all the churches of the Gentiles" are grateful (Rom. 16:3-4). Apparently Priscilla was the more gifted of the two: After this first mention, her name always occurs first when they're discussed.

Titus Justus and Crispus (18:7-8). The name of the first identifies him as a Roman citizen, and his large house suggests wealth. Crispus is identified in the text as the *archisynagogos*, and leadership of the synagogue also suggests wealth. Thus, leaders of both the Gentile and Jewish community were converted. While Paul's letters to Corinth show the church had many problems, there was no direct rift along Gentile/Jewish lines.

The church truly is one, and we can live together despite differences.

Eighteen months (18:11). It's unclear whether Paul stayed another 18 months, or whether the total time he spent in Corinth was 18 months.

"Gallio" (18:12). This official's father (Marcus Annaeus Seneca) and his brother (Lucius Annaeus Seneca) were both famous. His brother wrote of Gallio, "No mortal is so pleasant to any person as Gallio is to everyone." Luke emphasizes the decision of the prominent Roman administrator and jurist because it established a precedent. His purpose is to show that Christianity should be treated as a legal faith, and so persecution of Christians would be a violation of Roman law.

Paul's vow. Despite his passionate involvement in Gentile evangelism, and his insistence that O.T. Law was not binding on Gentile believers, Paul did not reject his cultural heritage. He was a Jewish Christian, not a Jew who had abandoned Judaism to become a Gentile. Thus, there is no compromise in Paul's decision to undertake a Nazarite vow, or to go to Jerusalem where such a vow had to be completed and his hair presented to the Lord (cf. Num. 6:1-21).

Apollos and John's baptism (18:25). John the Baptist had called for repentance in view of the fact that the Messiah would appear soon. Apollos knew of and accepted this teaching. He simply had not yet heard of Jesus.

Inviting Apollos home (18:26). The gracious way Priscilla and Aquila dealt with Apollos is an example to us all. They might have stood up and corrected him publicly—making him embarrassed or defensive. Instead they remained quiet in public. They invited him to their home. They "explained . . . more adequately." Rather than stress where Apollos was wrong, they affirmed what was right and went on from there. What a guide to correcting error without losing the person!

Chapter summary. Paul moves on to Ephesus, site of a spectacular temple and center of the cult of the goddess Artemis in Asia. There Paul meets others who know only John's baptism but who quickly believe (19:1-7). At first Paul teaches in the synagogue, but when the Jews refuse to believe he continues his mission in a public lecture hall (vv. 8-10). Paul's teaching is supported by miracles of healing and exorcism, and because of them many turn from occult practices to adopt Christianity (vv. 11-22). The revival is so great that it threatens the livelihood of silversmiths, who make and sell religious trinkets to tourists. Their leader, Demetrius, plays on both financial and religious motivations to stir up a riot against Paul (vv. 23-34). But the city officials, fearing they will have to answer to Rome for any rioting, succeed in quieting the crowd and disbursing it (vv. 35-41).

Key verse. 19:19: Expensive, but worthless.

Personal application. Neither religion nor superstition satisfies. Only Jesus.

Key concepts. Holy Spirit »p. 73. Baptism »pp. 604, 708. Tongues »p. 709, 770. Miracles »p. 679. Evil spirits »p. 239. Magic »p. 57.

INSIGHT

Illustration. *The medal in the margin shows the goddess Artemis (Diana) as she was portrayed in Ephesus. The multiple breasts suggest the fertility and sexual theme of much Oriental religion and may well identify this goddess with the nature deities of the East rather than the chaste huntress of Gk. mythology.*

Ephesus. This important city drew wealth from trade but primarily from the magnificent temple of Artemis, regarded as one of the Seven Wonders of the ancient world. In Paul's day pilgrims and sightseers were the primary support of the city's economy.

"When you believed" (19:2). As Paul became acquainted with the "disciples" at Ephesus it became clear something was lacking. His question about receiving the Holy Spirit shows that Paul expected any true believer to have received the Spirit on conversion. His discovery that they knew only John's baptism explained everything. Like Apollos, they knew the Messiah was coming. They just didn't know He had arrived!

Tongues and prophecy (19:6). There is no reason suggested why this extraordinary sign was given here. But the text does indicate that Ephesus was a center of occult practices (cf. 19:13-20). It may be that the gift of tongues was given here as a witness to others of God's supernatural presence in a city where Satan was so obviously active.

"Extraordinary miracles" (19:11-12). In the ancient world "Ephesian writings" was a common term for books on magic and spells. The dark domination of people's minds by the occult may explain why God demonstrated His powers by working miracles through Paul.

Exorcism (19:13-19). Exorcism in ancient times drew on the belief that names had special powers, for they expressed the essence of the one named. Jewish exorcists were highly regarded in ancient times because pagans believed they had access to unique names of a powerful deity.

The use by the "seven sons of Sceva" of Jesus' name suggests that Paul had succeeded in convincing the population that Christ's name should be held in awe—but had not penetrated the darkness of many who saw no difference between the Gospel and magic.

The victory of the demon over the seven sons increased the pagan population's awe of Paul and his message. The fact that many did truly believe is shown in public burning of thousands of dollars worth of books on magic.

The riot (19:23-41). Other passages suggest this riot threatened the apostle's life (cf. Rom. 16:4; 1 Cor. 15:32; 2 Cor. 1:8-11). Luke wants us to see that Paul had a good relationship with leaders of the provincial government (v. 31) and that city officials rebuked the crowd and not Paul (vv. 35-40) for the "commotion."

Chapter summary. Now Paul turns toward Jerusalem where he will face further dangers and imprisonment. On the way he revisits churches in Macedonia (20:1-6). In Troas Paul speaks all night—putting a young listener to sleep. When the young man, Eutychus, falls from a window and is killed Paul revives him (vv. 7-12). But tensions build as Paul meets with elders of the Ephesian church and reveals that he is driven to go to Jerusalem, despite constant warnings by the Holy Spirit that "prison and hardships" face him there (vv. 13-24). The whole gathering is near tears as Paul tells them that they will not likely see him again and warns the leaders of the coming dangers against which they must guard the church (vv. 25-31). After they pray together, Paul bids his dear friends a last, tearful good-bye (vv. 32-38).

Outline
Place
Finder

JERUSALEM
SAMARIA
GENTILES
WORLD
IMPRISONMENT

Key verse. 20:24: More important than life.

Personal application. If we are not committed to something more important than our own lives, then they are meaningless.

Key concepts. Resurrection »p. 658. Repentance »p. 780. Faith pp. 35, 740. Sanctified »p. 824. Holy Spirit »pp. 73, 744.

INSIGHT

"The first day of the week" (20:7). This is the first certain reference in Acts to the use of Sunday as a Christian day of worship. See also John 20:19, 26; 1 Cor. 16:2; and Rev. 1:10.

"To break bread" (20:7). This is not sharing a meal but celebrating the Lord's Supper.

"Compelled by the Spirit" (20:22). Compulsion is Paul's description of his response to a strong, inner direction to return to Jerusalem. Some, in view of the warnings given by the Holy Spirit that prison and hardships await (v. 23), have thought Paul traveled to Jerusalem against God's will. However, there is nothing incompatible with God both leading a believer into danger and warning him or her of it. Jesus surely knew what awaited Him as He traveled toward Jerusalem and the Cross. Paul knew too—and like the Saviour, determined to follow God's leading whatever the cost.

"The Gospel of God's grace" (20:24, 32). Grace is one of the most significant concepts in Scripture. Grace can be defined as "God's free actions—based on Jesus' death and motivated by love—to redeem all who believe and to make them righteous" (*Expository Dictionary of Bible Words*, Zondervan, 1985, p. 319).

The Gk. word, *charis*, indicates kindness or favor. It is transformed in the N.T. into a technical theological term describing God's attitude toward and saving acts performed for sinful humankind. Grace is seen in the O.T. in the psalmists' expressions of helplessness that move them to plead with God for mercy and their confidence that He will respond. But in the N.T. grace becomes a key that gives human beings a totally new perspective on personal relationship with God. In Rom. 3 Paul shows that all people are sinners, without any righteousness of their own. So God has acted in Christ to unveil a righteousness that has no relationship to law or to human works, but one which is freely bestowed by God in response to faith in Jesus.

Even more stunning is the revelation of that great act of grace. Only by God becoming a human being, taking our sins on Himself, and paying the full penalty they deserve could He declare us righteous in His sight.

We will never plumb the depths of what the N.T. calls God's grace. Key passages on grace that help us glimpse its meaning include Rom. 3 (above); Rom. 4, which shows that grace is not incompatible with O.T. teaching on salvation; Rom. 11, which probes sacred history to show the grace in God's past acts; and Eph. 2, which sums up lost humanity's dread condition and affirms that "because of His great love for us, God, who is rich in mercy, made us alive with Christ even when we were dead in transgressions—it is by grace you have been saved" (vv. 4-5).

Outline
Place
Finder

JERUSALEM
SAMARIA
GENTILES
WORLD
IMPRISONMENT

Chapter summary. As Paul nears Jerusalem he is again warned, this time by a prophet named Agabus. Paul will be bound there and handed over to the Roman government (21:1-11). Paul will not be dissuaded (vv. 12-16). The party arrives safely in Jerusalem, where Paul reports to a receptive church on his mission among the Gentiles (vv. 17-26). But when Paul goes to the temple he is recognized by some Jews from Asia and accused of desecrating the holy place (vv. 27-29). Before Paul can be killed he is rescued from an angry mob by a cordon of Roman soldiers (vv. 30-36). Paul receives permission to speak to the crowd (vv. 37-40), and when they hear him speak in Aramaic, the crowd quiets and listens to him (22:1-2). Paul states his credentials as a pious Jew (vv. 3-5) and then tells the story of his conversion on the road to Damascus (vv. 6-21). But when Paul reports that God sent him to preach to the Gentiles (v. 22), the crowd shouts him down and Paul is taken inside the military barracks (vv. 23-24). Before Paul can be examined by flogging he identifies himself as a Roman citizen and is quickly unchained (vv. 25-29). The next day the Roman commander, hoping to sort out the situation, brings Paul before the Jewish governing council (v. 30).

Key verse. 21:13: Commitment.

Personal application. God often transforms our disasters.

Key concepts. Prophet »p. 131. Gentiles »p. 789. Law »pp. 120, 145, 376, 606. Citizenship »p. 723.

INSIGHT

"**Through the Spirit**" **(21:4).** The Spirit's message caused the believers concern. Luke is not saying that the believers were instructed to try to dissuade the apostle.

Ready to die (21:12). Luke clearly draws a parallel between Paul's commitment and that of Jesus. In both cases the Jews were hostile; the victim was to be handed over to the Gentiles and was to suffer. Like Christ, Paul remained committed to do God's will. While this comparison highlights Paul's heroism, it reminds us that we too are called upon to follow Jesus' example.

The Nazarite vow (21:20-25). Paul had been slandered by his Jewish opponents as a person who rejected Jewish customs and the O.T. Law. To correct this false belief the leaders of the Jerusalem church suggested Paul complete his own Nazarite vow with four others and thus publicly identify himself as a person who kept Jewish customs. Once he had shown he was no enemy of the O.T. Law, Paul, as well as the gifts he brought from Gentile churches, could be openly welcomed. Paul's teaching

that Gentile converts were not responsible to keep the Law was no issue. The Jerusalem church itself (Acts 15) had affirmed that.

Greeks in the temple (21:28). Paul didn't bring Gentiles into the temple, an act which even the Roman govenment conceded deserving of the death penalty. But riots are easily begun, whether or not the charge is correct.

Aren't you the Egyptian? (21:38) The Roman commander's assumption that Paul was an insurrectionist is fascinating. Despite it he had led his soldiers into a mob to rescue a person he thought a criminal. Roman commitment to "law and order" was a very real and commendable aspect of Roman character and rule.

Jew vs. Gentile (22:21). Paul's defense was in harmony with O.T. teaching and Jewish thought—until he said God sent him to the despised Gentiles, thus implying an equality of the races. The crowd's reaction suggests the intensity of Jewish feelings about their own privileged spiritual position and that of the lower-class Gentiles.

728

Chapter summary. Paul is brought before the Jewish governing council by the Roman commander, who is determined to find the cause of the intense hostility Paul seems to arouse (23:1). After a rocky start (vv. 2-5), Paul identifies himself as a Pharisee and affirms the resurrection of the dead. This starts another round of a long-standing dispute between Pharisee and Sadducee. The argument becomes so violent that the Roman commander, fearful for Paul's life, orders him returned to the military barracks (vv. 6-11). When a plot to kill Paul is reported (vv. 12-22), Paul is sent with a guard of soldiers to Caesarea, the seacoast city that is the hub of Roman government (vv. 23-35).

Outline
Place
Finder

JERUSALEM
SAMARIA
GENTILES
WORLD
IMPRISONMENT

Key verse. 23:11: God rules.

Personal application. God uses the hostility of our enemies.

Key concepts. Pharisee »p. 591. Sadducee »p. 592.

INSIGHT

"Good conscience" (23:1). Paul's claim itself seems to have enraged the high priest. Why? The 1st-century Jewish historian Josephus reports that this Ananias, high priest from A.D. 48–59, was known for his greed and dishonesty. Even the Talmud ridicules Ananias for his avarice and brutality.

Don't be surprised any time the evil hate and strike out at the good.

Paul's apology (23:5). Ananias was in the wrong in violating due process. But in reacting Paul had unwittingly violated Ex. 22:28. The fact others wrong us does not give us license to do wrong to them. Paul understood and was willing to live by this principle.

"The Resurrection" (23:6-9). Paul's ploy in introducing the Resurrection may have been intended to divide the Sanhedrin. But ultimately it was not intended to confuse the issue. The issue, in fact, was the Resurrection, the critical proof that Jesus is who Paul claimed Him to be—the Messiah and Son of God.

Members of the Pharisee and Sadducee parties became so intensely involved arguing this issue which had traditionally divided them that they in essence forgot about Paul, except as a symbol of their long-standing resurrection dispute.

"Violent" (23:10). Arguments can quickly become loud and impassioned in the Middle East even today. The Roman garrison commander might easily have believed Paul was in serious danger as the leading men of 1st-century Judaism shouted, gestured, and even shoved one another.

"Take courage" (23:11). The angelic encouragement must have meant much to Paul during the next two years as he was forced to wait, the charges against him unresolved, in Caesarea.

God may not send an angel to encourage us in our times of waiting. But this report of the angel sent to Paul reminds us that God has a purpose and direction for our lives too—even when it seems He has set us aside.

Did the Jews, who bound themselves with an oath not to eat or drink until they killed Paul, actually starve? (23:12-15) No. The rabbis permitted four kinds of vows to be set aside without penalty: vows of incitement, vows of exaggeration, vows made in error, and vows that cannot be fulfilled by reason of constraint. In effect, a person could make any vow and if things didn't work out, could find some excuse to set the vow aside! How contradictory to the spirit and the letter of Num. 30:2 which says, "When a man makes a vow . . . or takes an oath to obligate himself by a pledge, he must not break his word but must do everything he said."

Paul's nephew (23:16). Nothing is known about this sister or her family. However, the very failure to mention her suggests Paul was disowned by his family when he converted (cf. also Phil. 3:8).

Paul transferred under guard (23:23-35). One of the strongest commitments of the Roman Empire was to protect its citizens. Since Paul was a Roman citizen (»p. 723) the commander of the Jerusalem garrison could not risk an assassination and quickly moved to get Paul to the provincial capital, Caesarea. The significant number of troops assigned to escort Paul suggests how serious the commander judged the threat to his prisoner—and to himself—if anything should happen to the apostle.

Chapter summary. In Caesarea, the Jewish leaders charge Paul with crimes against their religion (24:1-9), charges which Paul disputes (vv. 10-21). The astute governor, Felix, delays judgment. He keeps Paul in jail, in part to please the Jews, in part hoping for a bribe, yet also curious about Paul's teaching (vv. 22-26). For two years Paul is kept in Caesarea under house arrest (v. 27).

Then a new governor, Festus, arrives. The Jewish leaders see this as a good time to press for Paul's conviction (25:1-8). Festus, willing to do the people he will govern a favor and so set a positive tone for his administration, asks Paul to go back to Jerusalem for a religious trial (v. 9). Paul refuses and claims the right of every Roman citizen to be tried in Rome itself, in Caesar's court. Festus, his problem of what to do with Paul resolved, quickly agrees (vv. 10-12).

A few days later when King Agrippa makes a courtesy call on the new Roman governor, he asks to hear Paul (vv. 13-27). Paul's defense is in the form of his personal testimony and a challenge to Festus to believe (26:1-29). Although unpersuaded, the governor and king agree that Paul is innocent (vv. 30-32).

Key verse. 25:11: A simple stand.

Personal application. It's not wrong to claim your rights.

INSIGHT

Paul's first defense (24:1-27). Nearly equal space is given to the Jewish charges (vv. 1-9), Paul's reply (vv. 10-21), and Felix's relationship with the apostle (vv. 22-27). It's clear that Paul created no political crimes and that hostility toward him and the Christian movement is rooted in religious differences. This is important to Luke, whose book is partly intended as a defense of the Christian movement.

"Tertullus" (24:2). It was common practice to employ a professional orator to present one's case before any 1st-century court. Form often carried more weight in these presentations than fact—something suggested in Tertullus' complementary opening remarks (vv. 2-3). These are stunning, in view of the fact that contemporaries describe Felix's time in office as marked by great cruelty, total disregard of his subjects' rights, and greed.

The charges (24:5-8). Paul is accused as (1) a troublemaker who stirs up riots, (2) a ringleader of the Nazarene sect, and (3) a desecrator of the Jerusalem temple. The first charge alone, if proven, would merit death. Felix had already crucified numerous leaders of local uprisings for breaking the *Pax Romana* (Roman peace).

Paul's answer (24:10-13). Paul answers point by point: (1) I couldn't stir up a revolt in just 12 days, (2) I didn't speak publicly anywhere, and (3) all these charges are unsubstantiated.

The real cause (24:14-16). Paul is hated because of his commitment to Jesus, even though his faith is in total agreement with the teachings of the O.T. which both groups honor in common.

If you're going to be persecuted, make sure you are persecuted for your commitment to Jesus rather than for doing wrong. A clear conscience is a basis for confidence when you are under attack.

"Well acquainted with the Way" (24:22). "The Way" was the name then given the Christian movement. Felix had been governor in Palestine for some 10 years. As such he would have carefully tracked all movements among the people he governed. Luke's statement does not at all suggest that Felix believed, or even that he was an inquirer.

Drusilla and Felix (2:25). Drusilla was the young daughter of Herod Agrippa I, who deserted one husband to marry the more powerful Felix. Both listened to Paul's talk of "righteousness, self-control, and judgment to come" and the need for faith in Christ. The conscience of Felix at least was troubled enough for him to "be afraid," but not afraid enough to repent and believe.

When the Holy Spirit convicts it is dangerous to delay. There is no more "convenient" time to believe than "now."

Mixed motives (24:25-26). Felix obviously was more concerned with this world than the next. What a tragic mistake.

Illustration. *The city of Caesarea was one of Herod the Great's most spectacular building projects. His engineers created an artificial harbor from massive blocks of stone. The city served as the Roman capital of the province, and Paul was imprisoned there for some two years.*

"Festus" (25:1). Festus was an honest ruler who died in A.D. 62 during his term in office.

Hostility (25:3). The intense hostility of the ruling Jews is shown in that they made accusing Paul one of their first orders of business with the new governor. They were even willing to risk alienating him, which assassination of a Roman citizen in the governor's custody would surely have done!

The appeal to Caesar (25:10). In the 1st century a citizen living in the provinces could appeal to Caesar when a possibility of capital punishment existed. Festus was no doubt pleased to have the case out of his jurisdiction.

If guilty (25:11). Paul's stance is consistent with his teaching in Rom. 13. The believer is to be subject to secular government. If a believer breaks the law, he can still affirm the rule of law by not attempting to avoid just punishment.

"Agrippa and Bernice" (25:13). Agrippa was the great-grandson of Herod the Great, who at the time ruled a nearby kingdom. In the A.D. 70s Agrippa tried unsuccessfully to influence the Jews against rebelling against Rome, whose side he took. Bernice was his sister. Persistent rumors in Palestine and Rome suggested the two had an incestuous relationship. Bernice later became the mistress of Titus, the Roman commander who sacked Jerusalem.

Festus' reaction (26:24). Ever the pragmatic Roman, Festus was amazed at the idea of a resurrection. He believed Paul had become so engrossed in Jewish studies that he had lost his grip on reality. How like modern "scientific" thinkers who cannot imagine a spiritual reality beyond the material universe.

Agrippa's reaction (26:25-27). Paul's direct appeal to Agrippa embarrassed the king. Whatever he might believe in secret, he was surely not going to admit sympathies with beliefs Festus openly thought to be madness.

Yet we too often make as difficult a choice: to go with the skeptical crowd or take an open stand for Jesus.

Could have been (26:32). Festus is equivocating. He had the right to acquit Paul even after his appeal, but was too politically wise to do so.

Outline
Place
Finder

JERUSALEM
SAMARIA
GENTILES
WORLD
IMPRISONMENT

Chapter summary. Paul, with Luke and other friends, sets sail for Rome under guard, in company with other prisoners (27:1-2). It is late in the year and progress is slow. Paul warns of danger if the centurion in charge of the party insists on pushing on (vv. 3-12). They set sail anyway. Just as Paul warned, they are caught in a terrible storm and driven for days (vv. 13-20). On the fourteenth day Paul is given a vision. God will keep the whole ship's company safe. The awed centurion orders all to stay with the ship, and the next day the ship runs aground on the Island of Malta (vv. 21-44). As Paul had promised, everyone reaches shore safely. On Malta Paul escapes death by snakebite (28:1-6) and heals a leading man of the island (vv. 7-10). After wintering on the island, they continue to Rome where the Christian community welcomes Paul (vv. 11-16), and Paul arranges to share Christ with leaders of the Jewish community (vv. 17-29). Paul's two years under house arrest give him an unmatched opportunity to witness to many in the capital of the empire (vv. 30-31).

Key verse. 27:25: Faith.

Personal application. Faith gives us courage.

INSIGHT

Historical accuracy. Studies of ocean travel on the Mediterranean have impressed scholars with the accuracy of Luke's description of ports, weather conditions, and types of vessels. Even the critics agree these chapters must be based on the journal of an actual 1st-century traveler. Of course, this is hardly a surprise to those who believe in the reliability of God's Word.

"Julius" (27:3). Again Luke portrays a centurion in a good light. He is a member of the "Imperial Regiment." What was he doing in Caesarea? We do not know, but we do know that centurions were trusted officers, the backbone of the Roman army, who were often sent as couriers and on detached-duty special missions. Apparently Julius, on his way back to Rome, was given command of soldiers guarding a party of prisoners.

Myra (27:5-6). This was a prosperous city near the port of Andriaca. Julius left the smaller coastal vessel there and arranged for transport on one of the great grain ships traveling to Rome.

Dangerous waters (27:9-10). Typically no one traveled these waters after the 11th of November. Reference to Yom Kippur, which fell at the end of September/early October, suggests this November date was dangerously near.

Passing ropes (27:17). The nautical phrase is uncertain. Rope may have been strung from end to end to keep the ship from breaking apart in the middle when slammed down in a trough created by giant waves. This is easier to envision than passing ropes under the ship during such a storm.

We gave up hope (27:20). The missionary party as well as the sailors and other travelers had given up hope of survival.

Paul's affirmation (27:23-25). Three things characterize Paul's assurance: (1) Paul knows that he belongs to God. (2) Paul serves God. (3) Paul has faith that God will keep His word.

If these three things characterize our relationship with God we too can "keep up" our courage, however dark the situation may appear.

Saved (27:30). The word saved is used in an ordinary as well as theological sense in both Testaments. Typically it means deliverance from some life-threatening or debilitating danger. As this story shows, even this salvation is from God.

"The soldiers cut the ropes" (27:31-32). Paul now has so much credibility that he is in effect in charge of the ship. Authority does not rest on position alone. Authority comes with integrity and with demonstrated competence. Paul had been proven right before, and now was the ship's company's only hope.

Kill the prisoners (27:42). The rule that any who allow prisoners to escape must suffer their penalty had its drawbacks. For the prisoners!

Illustration. *The above shipwreck suggests something of the size and construction of the typical Roman vessel of the era. The 1st-century Jewish historian Josephus tells of traveling on a ship that carried 600 passengers and crew and being shipwrecked. In that shipwreck, however, only 80 passengers survived!*

Malta. The island is small, about 18 miles long and 8 wide, lying between Sicily and the African coast. The probable site of "St. Paul's Bay" has been identified. In Paul's day Augustus had settled retired army veterans there, and its population spoke Gk. as well as its original Phoenician.

"Justice" (28:4). The word capitalized in the NIV as Justice (*Dike*) refers to a goddess worshiped in Malta. The snakebite was at first assumed as proof Paul was a criminal. When he survived, it was thought to be proof he was a god.

How foolish it is to jump to conclusions from observation of an incident or two. Let's be more wise in withholding judgment on others, whether that judgment condemns or exalts.

Rome (28:15). The site where Paul was met by enthusiastic representatives of the church of Rome is well known. The Three Taverns Inn lies just 33 miles from the city property, along one of the most famous of ancient Roman roads.

Meeting with Jewish leaders (28:17-28). Apparently no accusations had been forwarded from Jerusalem to the Jewish community in Rome. Paul meets them out of his deep concern for his own people and his conviction that the Jews have the right to hear the Gospel first (cf. Rom. 1:16). His presentation wins little response, and Paul feels released to concentrate on ministry to Gentiles.

Church history tells us Paul was acquitted and continued to minister for a time. But in the end he was rearrested and executed in Rome.

Romans

The Book of Romans is the theological cornerstone of the New Testament, the greatest of Paul's epistles. A church noted for its faith (Rom. 1:8) had been planted in Rome by early Christian converts rather than by any apostle. Paul's letter, focusing as it does on relationships between Jew and Gentile, seems to suggest that tensions existed in this church. Paul deals with them by showing that Jewish and Gentile Christians alike require a righteousness that can be obtained only as a gift of God—a righteousness that then can and must be lived out in personal and corporate Christian life. Paul's first readers surely recognized themselves in his letter.

Yet at the same time, Paul's letter answers the most difficult questions posed by Jesus' appearance, crucifixion, and resurrection. Where is the unity between the Old and New Testaments? Aren't law and faith contradictory principles? Doesn't the new revelation deny the old? Isn't God being inconsistent? These very issues lay at the heart of the hostility of first-century Jews to Christianity. In resolving tensions within the Roman church, the Apostle Paul's letter also answers the most profound of our theological questions about the harmony of God's whole Word.

The key to Paul's reconciliation of the Old and New Testament revelations is found in his concept of "righteousness." In first-century Judaism "righteousness" was conformity to the written or oral Law. Following Jesus, Paul insists that righteousness requires actually being like God in motive and act. Only God can transform a sinful human being, to make him or her truly like the Lord.

RIGHTEOUSNESS IN ROMANS

Gospel Righteousness (Rom. 1). *The Gospel is about a righteousness which comes from God "by faith from first to last."*

Need for Righteousness (Rom. 2–3). *The Jew with the Law and the Gentile without it both have sinned and desperately need a righteousness neither possesses.*

Righteousness and Faith (Rom. 3–4). *God has always accepted faith in place of the righteousness human beings do not possess. Jesus' sacrifice of Himself makes this possible and is the basis for the forgiveness freely offered both Old and New Testament saints.*

Righteousness realized (Rom. 6–8). *Faith unites the believer with Jesus in His life as well as His death. The Holy Spirit within gives us the power to live righteously here and now, if we but live by faith.*

Righteousness in history (Rom. 9–11). *God has consistently operated on principles imbedded in the Gospel in Old Testament as well as New Testament eras.*

Righteousness in the faith community (Rom. 12–16). *Believers are to live out God's righteousness in relationships within the Christian community. Paul gives a beautiful description of righteousness as God's character finds expression in the way Christians live together in the Lord.*

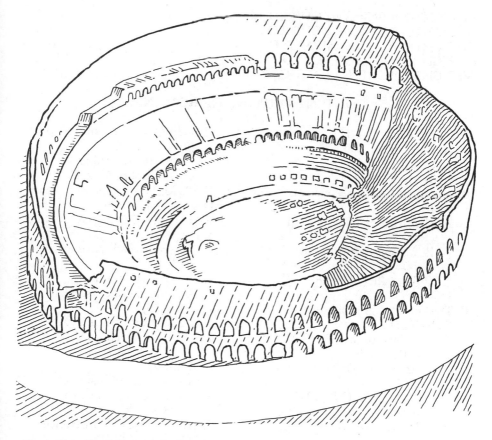

Illustration. *The Colosseum of Rome was built in A.D. 75–80, about a quarter century after Paul's letter was sent to that city. Hundreds of Christians suffered death there to entertain the populace. What a testimony the shouting mob remains to man's desperate need for righteousness. And what a testimony the brave death of the martyrs is to the transforming power of faith.*

Date and Authorship. The early church and even modern critics agree with the letter's opening verses: This is the Apostle Paul's letter to the Romans. Most commentators believe Paul wrote this letter in A.D. 56 or 57, while the apostle was in Corinth. Phoebe, from nearby Cenchrea, carried the letter (Rom. 16:1-2), and Gaius (16:23) was the most prominent of Paul's Corinthian converts (1 Cor. 1:14). Thus Paul's letter reached Rome several years before he came to the city as a prisoner to be tried by Caesar's court (Acts 28).

THEOLOGICAL OUTLINE OF ROMANS

CONTENT OUTLINE OF ROMANS

Chapter summary. Paul identifies himself as an apostle, set apart to spread a Gospel which brings grace and peace from God (1:1-7). Paul shares his desire to visit Rome and defines the theme on which he is writing: a Gospel which brings salvation and righteousness to everyone who believes (vv. 8-17).

Salvation is desperately needed by a race which rightly lies under divine wrath (v. 18). For humanity has reacted against God, rejecting the knowledge all men have of Him (vv. 19-20), preferring to create their own gods and follow a pathway which leads inexorably to ever greater depravities (vv. 21-32).

Cast against the dark background of lost man's corrupt society, what "good news" the Gospel is! Humanity has not chosen to know God. But God has chosen to reveal His love and grace to man anew.

Outline
Place
Finder

REQUIRED
PROVIDED
IMPARTED
PROVED
PRACTICED

Key verse. 1:17: Faith is the beginning and the end.

Personal application. Without Christ, this could be you!

Key concepts. Apostle »p. 635. Holy Spirit »pp. 73, 744. Peace »p. 806. Faith »pp. 35, 740. Righteousness »p. 734. Wrath »pp. 65, 72. Idolatry »p. 433. Homosexuality »p. 37.

INSIGHT

Self-identity (1:1). Paul sees himself as a servant of Christ on a mission. What a positive way for us to see ourselves too.

Jesus' nature (1:3-4). These verses clearly affirm both the humanity and deity of Jesus. As a descendant of David, His human nature qualifies Him to be Israel's Messiah (Isa. 11:1).

Jesus' resurrection (1:4). The literal, physical resurrection of Jesus didn't make Him God's Son, but demonstrated conclusively that He is the Son of God. Recognizing this reality, Paul gives Jesus His appropriate title as deity: Jesus (personal name) Christ (O.T. identity as Israel's promised Messiah) our Lord (identification with *Yahweh*, the personal name of God in the O.T., »p. 54).

Paul's attitude (1:12). Servants live among God's people as one of them. They do not use their position to lift themselves above others.

"The Gospel" (1:16). The word means "good news." The Christian Gospel is about Jesus (its content) and reveals God's gift of righteousness (its significance). It brings salvation (its outcome) to all who believe (its invitation).

"Faith from first to last" (1:17). Salvation has past (forgiveness), present (power to live a godly life), and future (resurrection transformation) aspects. Faith in Christ is the key to experience every aspect of salvation—from first to last.

The wrath of God revealed from heaven (1:18). The sin and injustice that mar society and make life so painful is a divine judgment on humanity for rejecting Him and choosing immorality. Crime and injustice both express man's sinful nature and constitute a present divine judgment on sin.

"Suppress the truth" (1:18). It's not that people cannot know the truth about God. The problem is that they actually stifle the truth they do know.

Creation's witness (1:19-20). Creation is God's "radio station," sending the message that God exists to all. Paul implies more. Human beings are created with an internal radio receiver. People see this truth and understand it—but suppress rather than respond to God's self-revelation.

"Although they knew God" (1:21). Man's sinfulness is not seen just in wicked acts but in the way people respond to God. A couple on a date hold hands because they feel close and want to become closer. But when men "knew God," rather than worship Him they quickly jerked their hands away—to worship creatures rather than the Creator.

The consequences of rejecting God (1:26-32). Paul lists as consequences the ultimate depravities: in morals, homosexuality (vv. 26-27); in character, wickedness and greed (vv. 28-29); in relationships, envy, murder, deceit, and malice (vv. 30-31); in polity, publicly approving those things they know God condemns (v. 32).

Outline
Place
Finder

REQUIRED
PROVIDED
IMPARTED
PROVED
PRACTICED

Chapter summary. Most of Paul's Jewish readers would with delight "pass judgment" on the Gentiles the apostle describes in 1:26-32. But Paul quickly silences them. God does not judge by what men approve, but by what they do (2:1-2). Anyone who ignores his own sinfulness, Jew or Gentile, shows contempt for God's kindness (vv. 3-4) and stores up wrath against the day God will judge each person's acts (vv. 5-11). As for Gentiles, God has implanted the capacity to make moral judgments—and they will be judged for failing to live up to the demands of their own conscience (vv. 12-16). Yes, the Jews have God's Law and are proud of their "superiority." But they in fact break the Law (vv. 17-24), and so their membership in the Old Testament covenant community is meaningless to God (vv. 25-27). The real mark of relationship with God is inward, a "circumcision" performed by the Holy Spirit that sets a person, heart and soul, apart to the Lord (vv. 28-29).

Key verse. 2:14: Man's moral nature testifies to God.

Personal application. Acts are the real measure of morality.

Key concepts. Judge »pp. 372, 874. Judgment Day »p. 724. God's righteousness »pp. 372, 433. Gentile »p. 798. Law »pp. 120, 145, 606. Circumcision »pp. 36, 126.

INSIGHT

Illustration: A circumcision knife. *Each Jewish boy was circumcised the 8th day after birth, and so united to the O.T. covenant community, to whom God had given His Law. But possessing the Law was meaningless, unless a person kept the Law. Soon Paul will show that no one has ever lived up to the demands of his or her own conscience, to say nothing of the higher demands of God's Law.*

Dialogue (2:1-11). When reading this passage, imagine Paul dialoguing with a Jew who enthusiastically endorses his condemnation of the Gentiles. Paul's stunning charge is that the Jews are self-righteous, doing the same thing they condemn the Gentiles for doing—ignoring the fact that God will judge their sins.

Saved by good works (2:7). Paul will soon show that no one truly does good (3:9-18). Here his purpose is not to describe a way of salvation, but the fruit of salvation. When God judges our works, those who possess eternal life will persist in doing good, not to win salvation, but because they care about "glory, honor, and immortality," and not the things of this world.

Conscience (2:12-16). The Gk. world viewed conscience as a dread accuser, constantly to mind the faults and failures of the past. Here Paul teaches that this faculty, shared by all men, shows that God has planted a moral sense in human nature which stands in judgment on those same issues of personal and social relationships with which God's Law deals. God will not judge the pagan who does not know the standards revealed in Scripture by biblical Law. He does not have to!

God will judge human beings by their own sense of what is right and wrong—and the day of judgment will reveal that *every human being* has failed to live by his own standards, much less by God's!

Inconsistency (2:17-24). Paul ironically reviews the basis for Jewish claims of spiritual superiority. But Jews break the Law, just as Gentiles violate their conscience—so the claim of superiority is an expression of raw pride. And the effect of that pride is that the Gentiles ridicule not only the hypocrisy of the Jews, but also God!

"Circumcision" (2:25-29). Circumcision is an outward, physical sign of membership in the covenant community. But relationship with God requires an inner, spiritual circumcision of the heart. Apart from an inner transformation all the Jew relies on for salvation is an empty sham.

Chapter summary. The great advantage the Jews have is possession of the Word of God. Whether or not they believe it is irrelevant. Lack of faith cannot nullify God's faithfulness (3:1-4), and God will judge sinners whatever complaint they register (vv. 5-8). The fact is Scripture charges everyone with sin (vv. 9-18). That legal determination brings dread silence as humankind stands before the dread bar of divine judgment (v. 19). It also causes a great shift in our understanding of the function of divine Law. God's Law is not intended to save, but to make us aware of our sin! (v. 20)

Then suddenly the bad news is transformed into good! God has revealed a righteousness that has nothing to do with the Law. Since all have sinned, all need to be justified by a grace gift given those who have faith in Jesus (vv. 21-23). Why by Jesus? Because He is the propitiating sacrifice, the basis on which God can be righteous in forgiving our sins (vv. 24-26). Doesn't this make Law meaningless? Not at all. It establishes Law in the role God always intended it to have—as a mirror showing us our sin and pointing us toward faith (vv. 27-31).

Outline
Place
Finder

REQUIRED
PROVIDED
IMPARTED
PROVED
PRACTICED

Key verse. 3:25: God is free to forgive.

Personal application. Plead nothing to God but Jesus' blood.

Key concepts. Faithfulness »p. 141. Justice »p. 145. Sin »p. 34. Law »p. 790. Righteousness »p. 120. Faith »p. 740. Justification »p. 789. Grace »p. 789. Propitiation »p. 895. Sacrifice »p. 862.

INSIGHT

Bringing out God's righteousness (3:5-8). Here is the argument. In punishing sin God shows Himself righteous, therefore sinners contribute to God's glory. So should they be penalized for doing something that actually benefits God? Paul rejects this, saying *me genito!* God forbid!

Total depravity (3:9-18). This much misunderstood Christian doctrine doesn't mean that any person is as evil as he or she might be. It does mean that "all have sinned." That is, that *every* human act is tainted by man's sin nature and thus less than perfect and so unacceptable to God. It's in this sense that "there is no one who does good, not even one" (v. 12).

Guilty (3:19). The Law serves as a standard of righteousness. Measured against it, every individual falls short and thus subject to punishment. It's not that we will be judged by God. We have been. And God has pronounced us guilty.

"A righteousness from God" (3:21). Any righteousness found in Law must come from human acts. Any righteousness God provides must come from His acts.

"Through faith" (3:22-23). The means by which the righteousness that comes from God is claimed, whether one is a Jew or a Gentile. Paul makes the stunning statement—and will go on to prove—that this truth is taught in the Law and Prophets (the O.T.) themselves! It is not simply a N.T. truth.

A propitiating sacrifice (3:25). The NIV use of the word "atonement" here is weak. The Gk. word *hilasterion* draws on both Gk. culture, in which "propitiation" implied averting terrible punishments and moving the gods to act favorably, and Heb. culture, in which "atonement" implies the sacrificial death of a substitute who takes the punishment an offerer deserves. Jesus surrendered Himself up to death, represented here in the shedding of His blood. As a substitute He took the awesome penalty our sins deserved and thus saved us from the punishment that we deserve.

Upholding the Law (3:31). The Jew believed passionately that Paul's teachings of grace and salvation by faith undermined Law and thus denied God's O.T. revelation. Paul says that instead the Gospel upholds Law, but gives it the place God always intended it to have.

Outline
Place
Finder

REQUIRED
PROVIDED
IMPARTED
PROVED
PRACTICED

Chapter summary. Paul demonstrates from sacred history that salvation always has been a gift of God received by faith. Righteousness was "credited to" Abraham because he "believed God" (4:1-3). "David says the same thing" in speaking of the blessedness of forgiven sins (vv. 4-8). Abraham was credited with righteousness *before* his circumcision, that unique sign that marked a person off as a Jew in Old Testament times. Thus Gentiles can look to Abraham's experience as a precedent! (vv. 9-12) And, since the promises given Abraham and transmitted to his offspring, Israel, are rooted in faith, not in law, the Jew too must rely on faith rather than works! (vv. 13-17)

What then is the nature of that faith Abraham exercised? It was simply confidence that God was able to do what He promised and that He would surely keep His word. When we believe God's promise of salvation in Jesus, we too are credited with a righteousness we did not—and could never—earn on our own (vv. 18-25).

Key verses. 4:23-24: A timeless truth.

Personal application. What a trustworthy God we have!

Key concepts. Justification »p. 789. Works »p. 872. Righteousness »p. 734. Wicked »p. 29. Forgiveness »pp. 357, 863. Sins »p. 362. Circumcision »p. 36. Law »pp. 145, 606. Hope »p. 465.

INSIGHT

"Abraham" (4:1). Abraham is the towering figure to whom the Jews traced their origins and special place as God's chosen people. By quoting Gen. 15:6 Paul proves the roots of O.T. faith are also anchored in an imputed rather than earned righteousness.

"Wages" (4:4). The idea is the same in all cultures: "Wage" implies a transaction involving an exchange of services for money or something of value. Paul insists that God does not relate to us as an employer, "paying" us with salvation in exchange for some service we render by doing what is right and good. Since we have all sinned, the only wage we have "earned" is death! (Rom. 6:23) Instead, God relates to us through promise and freely gives us righteousness (salvation) if we have faith in Him. Since "wages" and "gift" are contradictory concepts, "law" and "promise" can never be mixed in relating to God. We must choose to relate to either by faith, or by works. We can't have it both ways.

Forgiveness (4:5-8). David's psalms show that God forgives the sins of the person who believes. Faith solves both mankind's basic relationship problems. The man who believes is credited with righteousness and his sins are forgiven.

"Credited" (4:4-5, 10, 22-23). The Gk.

logizomai was a common accountant's term in N.T. times. It meant "to make an entry in an account book." Paul's meaning was clear to his 1st-century readers. God would make an entry in His account book next to the name of the person who believes in Jesus, saying in effect, "This person is righteous in My sight."

Guaranteed (4:13-15). If salvation depended in any way on us, we would surely be lost. But since our salvation depends on God keeping His promise to those who believe, we have the most certain of any possible guarantees.

Jesus as object of faith (4:24-25). Paul makes two vital points in Rom. 3 and 4. In 3:24-26 Paul shows that the offering of Jesus as an atoning sacrifice is the *basis* on which God forgives the sins of both O.T. and N.T. saints. But Jesus has *not* always been the *object* of saving faith. For instance, Abraham did not know or believe that Christ would appear and die for him. What Abraham believed was God's promise that he and Sarah would have a child, despite their advanced age. So in history past God's promise, whatever that promise might be, was the object of a believer's faith. Today, however, the *basis* of salvation and the *object of faith* are one: Jesus Christ. All God's promises are focused in and through Him. It is faith in Jesus, and faith in Him alone, that saves today.

Chapter summary. The believer now stands in a unique relationship with God which provides a new perspective on all of life (5:1-5). That perspective is rooted in the conviction that a God who was willing to give up His Son to bring us to Himself will surely, now that we are His, keep on working in us (vv. 6-11).

What difference does Christ make in our situation? Paul summarizes in one of the New Testament's key theological passages (vv. 12-21). Adam introduced death and sin into every person's experience, bringing us under condemnation and releasing those dark forces that make human life short and miserable. In contrast, Christ as a second Adam created a new race of human beings, righteous rather than sinful, upheld by grace rather than weighed down by failure, alive rather than dead to the bright hope of life lived in the light of God's holiness and love. In Jesus Christ all things truly have become new!

Outline
Place
Finder

REQUIRED
PROVIDED
IMPARTED
PROVED
PRACTICED

Key verse. 5:8: History's clearest "I love you!"

Personal application. Let the certainty of God's love give you a new perspective on all of life.

Key concepts. Justification »p. 789. Peace »p. 806. Glory »p. 74. Suffering »p. 877. Holy Spirit »pp. 744, 759. Love of God »pp. 351, 529, 680. Reconciliation »p. 778. Salvation »pp. 742, 849.

INSIGHT

"Therefore" (5:1). All we enjoy as Christians, and all that Paul is about to explain, depends on the sacrifice of Christ for us and our faith in Him.

A litany of blessings (5:1-5). Note specifically: (1) peace with God, (2) access to God and to grace, (3) joy in our future prospects, (4) a new perspective on suffering, (5) a confident hope in God that pays present dividends in a continuing sense of His love for us.

Never dismiss true Christianity as "pie in the sky bye and bye." Relationship with Jesus is a banquet table piled high with a feast we can enjoy here and now.

Perspective on suffering (5:3-4). The new perspective is that suffering has a positive purpose. Suffering shapes us for good.

"Poured out" (5:5). God's inexhaustible supply of love is poured out generously by the Holy Spirit who lives within us. Whatever happens to us, we are surrounded by love.

Objective proof (5:6-8). The believer's experience of God's love is subjective. But there is objective evidence as well. Christ's willingness to die for us when we were sinners is unmistakable proof of God's amazing love.

Enemy to friend (5:9-11). How foolish to suppose that God who showed such love for us when we were enemies would ever desert us now we are His own.

Two Adams (5:11-21). Theologians delight in this passage and debate just how "death came to all men" through Adam's sin. But Paul's point is practical. Our racial heritage from Adam is one of sin and death and alienation. But now we belong to Christ, the founder of a new race, and our heritage in Him is righteousess and life.

"Death" (5:11-12). "Death" is a complex term in both Testaments. Here it is not so much biological as a description of man's spiritual condition, powerless in the grasp of an inner moral corruption that alienates human beings from God and makes final judgment a dread certainty. Adam's sin insinuated both biological and spiritual death into our race, making both our present and future dark and grim. In contrast, Jesus interjects life, the opposite of death, making us alive to God and guaranteeing a bright eternal future.

"Sin" (5:11-21). "Sin" may refer to specific acts that violate standards established by God, but also may focus attention on corrupt human nature. In this latter sense "sin" is a principle that "lives" (dwells, Rom. 7:17ff.) in the human personality. It is a distortion of that which God created—a warping of our natural desires, understandings, and wills—so that we want and choose that which is wrong.

Outline
Place
Finder

REQUIRED
PROVIDED
IMPARTED
PROVED
PRACTICED

Chapter summary. We who were joined to ("baptized into") Christ were so truly united with Him that His death was our death—a death that frees us from the power of sin in our lives (6:1-7). More, His resurrection is our resurrection. Sharing that life, we now are able to live to God (vv. 8-10). We can experience this spiritual reality—by faith. We count ourselves dead to sin on the basis of God's Word, we choose not to let sin rule, and we offer every part of ourselves to God as His instruments to be used for righteousness (vv. 11-14).

Now Paul digresses briefly: What we experience depends on what we choose. If we choose to sin, we will be slaves of sin. If we choose to obey God, we will serve the ends of righteousness (vv. 15-18). And what a difference the choice makes! The outcome of obedience is a holiness which pays eternal dividends. But the only wages sin pays is death (vv. 19-23).

Key verse. 6:4: New life is the goal.

Personal application. Choose life. You can.

Key concepts. Sin »pp. 741, 798. Death of Christ »p. 813. Grace »p. 789. Law »p. 790. Righteousness »p. 808. Holiness »p. 879. Death »p. 741.

INSIGHT

The contribution of Rom. 6. Paul has said God "credits" righteousness to the one who believes in Christ (Rom. 4). He has shown that Christ also gives life to the one who believes (Rom. 5). Now he shows us that life is Christ-life: a resurrection life that frees us to be righteous as well as to be credited with righteousness.

Baptized into Christ (6:3). This is not water baptism, but rather that work of the Holy Spirit by which the believer is organically united to Jesus (cf. 1 Cor. 12:13; Eph. 4:5; Col. 2:12; Gal. 3:27). This act of God joins us to Jesus so completely that His death and resurrection become our own. The closest analogy may be seen in laws governing marriage in some states. When husband and wife are united, the possessions of each become the joint property of the other. The husband may have earned whatever wealth he has. But through the marital union the wife shares in it. Similarly through our union with Christ we share in all He has, including power to live a new life.

Present tense salvation. The salvation God gives us is complex and complete. Romans 6 is about "present tense" salvation. We are *being saved* by Christ as He releases us from the grip of sin and enables us to live a righteous life now.

Rendered powerless (6:6). The tendency toward sin remains imbedded in the human personality even after conversion, and we feel its pull. But we do not have to choose sin. Our sin nature no longer has the capacity to dominate us, even though we retain freedom of choice and can choose to sin if we wish. Never say, "I couldn't help it" when you do wrong. The Gospel's good news is you can help it. Christ saves us from the power of sin.

The role of faith. Romans 6:1-10 presents basic truths that serve as the foundation for living the Christian life. Romans 6:11-14 shows us what we are to do, based on these truths. Here, as in past tense salvation, the key is a truly biblical faith. And that kind of faith "counts on" the reality of our death with Christ so that the choice we make is to reject sin and choose to do righteousness.

Counting on our union with Christ does not create that unity. It already exists. Counting on our union with Christ enables us to experience that union in our daily lives.

Choose your master (6:16-23). Life is made up of daily choices. But there are also basic, life-shaping choices each of us makes. Paul asks us to consider and make one of those life-shaping choices now. We can follow our sinful human desires and live a life marked by the deadness that characterizes the unsaved. Or we can choose to commit ourselves to God, determining that we will reject sin and make His will our goal in life.

Chapter summary. Paul has argued that law and faith are contradictory principles. In Romans 7 he shows how a believer can be legally free from obligation to the Law, and then explores why release from that obligation is essential.

Christ's death frees the Christian from obligation to the Law (7:1-3). This is essential because law stimulates man's sinful nature (vv. 4-7). Paul values the Law because it makes him aware of sin's existence within his personality and because it stands as a witness to all that is holy, righteous, and good (vv. 8-12). But rather than help Paul be good, the Law has made him aware of the power of his sinful nature, aroused desires that he does not want to feel, and energized evil actions he hates as well (vv. 13-18). Paul has thus become aware of a terrible inner struggle, between an "I" who takes pleasure in sin and an "I" that wants to do good (vv. 19-20). He struggles against indwelling sin, but the harder Paul tries to keep the Law the more he finds himself a prisoner of his sinful nature (vv. 21-24). He finds rescue in Christ (v. 25).

Outline Place Finder

REQUIRED
PROVIDED
IMPARTED
PROVED
PRACTICED

Key verse. 7:4: Our link to God.

Personal application. Look to please Jesus, not keep the Law.

Key concepts. Commandment »p. 749. Sin »p. 741. Good »pp. 27, 648.

INSIGHT

Law. The fact that Paul uses *nomos* here with various meanings may cause confusion. God's Law in this passage is the O.T. revelation of moral standards of righteous behavior. But the "law" Paul finds operating in his personality is the "universal principle" of sin and death that grips fallen human beings. In this chapter Paul explores the relationship between God's Law and the law (principle) of sin. He expresses the sense of hopelessness he felt as he tried to respond to God's Law, but found sin within preventing him. In 8:2 Paul introduces another "law" (universal principle) which solves his problem—and ours!

Released (7:1-3). A spouse is no longer bound by the law of marriage to a partner who has died. Death freed him or her from that law. Similarly the death of Christ, which we shared in our union with Him, frees us from all legal obligations to God's Law.

Free to be righteous (7:4-8). Some folks are terrified at the idea the Christian has no obligation to keep God's Law. Paul shows that we must be freed from such obligations. Why? The Law spoke to our sinful nature and cried, "Don't." The result was not a quenching of the desire to sin, but an arousal of our "sinful passions." And we did sin, bearing "fruit for death." God now calls us to relate directly to Him through the Spirit. The Spirit will speak to our new nature, stimulating us to serve and so "bear fruit to God." Freedom from law does not promote sin, but righteousness!

Covet (7:7). Coveting is not just wanting what we do not have, but wanting something we could only have at another's expense. Somehow law is like the mother's instruction to her little boy: "Don't eat the cookies. They're for church." Her "don't" seems to make the cookies more appealing!

The law weak (7:7-11). Paul views law here as a system. That system includes revealed standards, but also includes you and me. Paul says that what is wrong with the system isn't a flaw in the divine standards. They are holy, just, and good. What's wrong is that we are flawed and so respond sinfully when God speaks. The law (system) is weak through "sinful flesh!"

"The body of death" (7:18, 24). Here the NIV accurately translates "flesh" by "sinful nature," appropriate when Paul uses the term theologically. Human nature itself is corrupted by sin to the extent that it cannot respond to God.

The agony of defeat (7:21-25). Paul's experience as a believer parallels that of many Christians today. They struggle to do right, but seem to fail again and again. The only hope is to stop struggling—and seek another route to righteousness!

Outline
Place
Finder

REQUIRED
PROVIDED
IMPARTED
PROVED
PRACTICED

Chapter summary. How does the Christian live a righteous life without a constant struggle to keep God's Law? Paul introduced another universal principle: the law of life lived in the power of the Spirit (8:1-2). Old Testament Law failed to produce righteousness. So in Christ God condemned "sin in sinful man" and provided His Spirit, who enables believers to fully meet the Law's requirements without "trying" (vv. 3-4). We focus on responding to God's Spirit rather than on trying to keep laws (vv. 5-8). If we're controlled by the Spirit who brought life to Christ's dead body, He will bring life to us who are spiritually dead (vv. 9-12). Our obligation is not to the Law, but to respond to the Spirit's promptings (vv. 13-16).

Paul now looks ahead. One day creation itself will be renewed, even as we are being renewed (vv. 17-25). Meanwhile the Spirit helps us in our weakness, praying with and for us (vv. 26-27). It's our relationship with God that brings us victory, for He has chosen us not to muddle on in the pit of sin but to be transformed into the image of His Son (vv. 28-30). On the way God will never forsake us, nor even permit us to be charged with sin (vv. 31-34). We are God's loved ones. Nothing can separate us from the love of God in Christ our Lord (vv. 35-39).

Key verse. 8:11: Resurrection life is ours.

Personal application. God truly will make you like Jesus.

Key concepts. Law »p. 743. Holy Spirit »p. 759.

INSIGHT

The concept. The goal of a baseball player is to get on base. But he does it by watching the ball, not peering intently at the base when the pitcher winds up. This is Paul's point. Our goal is to be righteous, and it is true that the Law describes righteousness. But we get there by keeping our eyes fixed on Jesus and our hearts responsive to the Spirit, not by trying to keep the Law. Augustine said, "Love God, and do what you please." What you "please" then will be good.

"Mind" (8:6). The word here is *phronema*, which means "way of thinking." We must re-orient our whole approach to life so that we seek to be responsive to God the Spirit and rely on Him, rather than seek to keep God's Law and rely on our own strength.

Holy Spirit (8:11). This verse affirms one of the most exciting of the Spirit's ministries. He vitalizes us here and now, even though we are sinful human beings, infusing us with that same power which raised Jesus from the dead, enabling us to live holy lives. Every one of our spiritual failures shouts out, "We can't." And every spiritual victory affirms, "But He can!"

Witness of the Spirit (8:14-16). How do we know that what Paul is speaking about is real?

The Spirit's presence in us is unmistakable! We sense His promptings and respond. We find a new freedom in our relationship with God. Deep down, our changed lives and sense of closeness to God make it absolutely clear—we are God's children. If you do not feel it, believe it. If you believe it, and act on it, you will surely feel it.

Salvation future tense (8:18-25). The Spirit's work within us is present tense salvation: We are being saved from the power of sin and becoming righteous. When Jesus returns we will be saved completely, liberated from the last vestiges of sin which cling so persistently to us.

Predestined to bear Christ's image (8:28-30). God had this purpose in mind when He saved us. No one and no thing can keep Him from His goal—or us from our destiny in Jesus.

"In all things God works for the good" (8:28-29). The text does not say that everything that happens to us is good, in the sense of pleasurable. God doesn't even promise pleasure. He does promise that all things will contribute to our good, in the sense of being for our benefit. And even that benefit is described. God will use our every experience to make us more like our Lord.

Outline
Place
Finder

REQUIRED
PROVIDED
IMPARTED
PROVED
PRACTICED

Chapter summary. Paul now takes up another issue. God counts as righteous human beings who have faith and actually makes righteous believers who live by faith. But is God righteous in His treatment of Israel, seemingly setting aside His ancient people in favor of the Gentiles? In three sweeping chapters Paul proves that God is righteous in all His ways.

Paul expresses his personal anguish over Israel's rejection of their Messiah (9:1-5). But history shows that God's initial choice of Israel was sovereign and free, not dependent on the works of any of the patriarchs (vv. 6-13). The Old Testament consistently portrays God as a sovereign being. In fact He has exercised His sovereign choice to save rather than destroy His people despite their sins (vv. 14-29). God's choice of the Gentiles to obtain a righteousness they never sought is simply another expression of that sovereign grace that has always marked His actions (v. 30). As for Israel, that people stumbled through no fault of God, but because they pursued righteousness as if it could be obtained by works rather than faith (vv. 31-33). In everything God has been consistent and totally fair.

Key verse. 9:15: God is free—to be good.

Personal application. God elects to be merciful.

Key concepts. Covenant »p. 35. Election/Choice »pp. 124, 797. Mercy »p. 858. Harden »p. 56. Wrath »pp. 65, 72. Righteousness »p. 734. Faith »p. 35. Works »p. 872.

INSIGHT

Israel. In this section Paul speaks of "Israel," not of the Jews, to emphasize the roots of that people's identity as God's chosen people. Yet Paul, in speaking of Israel, makes a distinction between "descendant of Abraham" and "member of the covenant community." The true covenant community has always been composed not of the natural children of Abraham but his spiritual children, who have Abraham's kind of faith.

In making this argument Paul is laying a foundation that enables him to argue strongly that today's "Israel," the chosen covenant community of God, is composed of Gentiles as well as of Jews who believe God's promises about Jesus, His Son.

God's freedom to choose (9:6-13). God made promises to Abraham. He then chose who should inherit them. Isaac, not Abraham's son Ishmael, was chosen. If someone argues that Ishmael was not the son of Sarah, Paul presents the case of the twin sons of Rebekah and Isaac. They shared both parents. Yet God chose the younger, Jacob, rather than the older, Esau—and this before the twins were born! Clearly God has always chosen, sovereignly and freely, those He includes within the line of promise. Consequently God's decision to include the Gentiles is fully consistent with His character and grace. For unless God chose to be merciful, no one would be saved!

"Esau I hated" (9:13). The verse does not mean God condemned Esau before his birth. In its O.T. context it means that God decisively rejected Esau's claim to the covenant promises which would be his as older son.

"The potter" (9:21). The potter quickly squeezes unresponsive clay into a lump. God does not do this, even to those who resist His will. Rather He "bears with great patience" those who are objects of His wrath.

Paul's point is that God is not like a potter, who treats His material with contempt. Humans are not clay. God is not responsible for their sinful condition. Those who are "prepared for destruction" have chosen to do evil. Despite the fact that their evil cries out for judgment, God remains patient.

Sovereignty. We need not hesitate to affirm God's sovereign power. He is the only one who can be trusted to use such power wisely. And He has proved in Christ that He uses it to choose the course of love and grace.

Outline
Place
Finder

REQUIRED
PROVIDED
IMPARTED
PROVED
PRACTICED

Chapter summary. Paul has shown righteousness has always been a gracious gift, sovereignly bestowed by God on those who have faith (Rom. 9). Now he argues that God has not rejected His covenant people. They have rejected Him.

Paul cares passionately for his own race. He admits their religious zeal (10:1-2). But he knows their problem well: they "disregarded" God's righteousness and tried to establish their own, even though the two are totally different in nature (vv. 3-11). Whether Jew or Gentile, one must be saved by faith (vv. 12-13).

But now we sense another objection. How can the Jewish race believe, not having heard this stunning message? (vv. 14-15a) But, Paul says, the Good News was preached. Israel simply did not believe. "Hearing," which in biblical thought implies responding appropriately, requires first a message, but then requires understanding and acceptance by those to whom the message is given. Even in Old Testament times Israel did not understand and refused to accept what God cried out to them through Moses and the prophets (vv. 15b-21). The message of salvation by faith has echoed throughout history—and been ignored.

Key verse. 10:10: Inside, and out.

Personal application. Let your mouth express what is in your heart.

Key concepts. Saved »pp. 426, 742, 744, 849. Righteousness »p. 734. Law »pp. 145, 606, 743, 790. Faith »pp. 35, 740. Justified »p. 789. Heart »p. 120. Name »p. 691.

INSIGHT

"Brothers" (10:1). Here Paul is addressing his natural brothers, the Jews, not his brothers in Christ. While faith in Christ creates a unique family relationship between believers, you and I like Paul retain close ties with the yet unconverted. Let's follow Paul's example, and continue to identify with and care deeply for them. For other similar uses by Paul of "brother" see 9:2, Acts 2:29, 3:16-17, 22:1, 28:17.

The end of the law (10:4). The Gk. word *teleos* indicates (1) the achievement of an intended goal, and (2) the completing of a process, such as the process of growing toward maturity. The *Expository Dictionary of Bible Words* (Zondervan, 1985) notes that this verse may mean that law has come to an end because it has been superceded by Christ. Or it may mean that Christ is the logical end of the Law, implying that law unveiled sin in such a way that human beings were forced to turn to Jesus to obtain righteousness.

"Heart" (10:6-10). The word is used in its O.T. broad sense, to indicate the whole person, the conscious self with every spiritual, intellectual, rational, and volitional capacity. A heart belief, or a heart response to the Gospel,

is a whole person response. It is not just intellectual belief about Jesus, but total commitment to Him.

Mouth and heart (10:10). The heart represents man's inner nature, the mouth is the expression of that inner nature in this world. "Secret believer" is something of a contradiction in terms. If we are truly committed to Jesus our lives will express that commitment in no uncertain terms.

"No difference" (10:12-13). Everyone has equal standing with God. We're all sinners. And we're all invited to believe and be saved.

"Good news" (10:14-15). The Gospel imperative is imbedded deeply in these verses. People do need to hear if they are to believe. That means they need a messenger. The bare fact of that need, coupled with the fact that we have God's Good News, constitutes a divine commission. We do not need a special call to "full-time service" to be sent by God. We are sent to our neighbors and friends, compelled simply by knowing the open secret than can transform their lives and their eternity.

All day long (10:21). God's invitation is still open. He continues to offer salvation to the lost.

Chapter summary. Paul continues his defense of the righteous-ness of God's dealings with Israel. In sovereign grace God has chosen those who show faith, not those who "qualify" by mere physical descent from the patriarchs (Rom. 9). Israel's present rejection has come because they sought righteousness by works, not by faith, despite God's constant proclamation of His Good News (Rom. 9). And there is more! Now, as in the past, God has reserved for Himself Israelites who do believe (11:1-4). These too have been chosen by grace, not on the basis of their works, and those who rely on works have been hardened in their self-chosen path (vv. 5-10).

It is true that the present mass conversion of Gentiles is a "mys-tery"—an event not revealed in the Old Testament. But the Gen-tiles have been, as it were, grafted into an essentially Jewish tree. When God's time comes He will restore the natural branches (vv. 11-24). Paul continues his stunning revelation of God's once hid-den plan. When the "full number" of Gentiles has been saved God will keep the promises made through Old Testament proph-ets and then "all Israel will be saved" (vv. 25-32). Paul concludes with a doxology. How wonderful the complex purposes and plan of our awesome, Almighty God (vv. 33-36).

Outline
Place
Finder

REQUIRED
PROVIDED
IMPARTED
PROVED
PRACTICED

Key verse. 11:29: God won't go back on His promises.

Personal application. How good to know God is trustworthy.

Key concepts. Baal »p. 162. Election »pp. 124, 797.

INSIGHT

"A remnant" (11:1-6). This is an important concept rooted in the O.T. No matter how ter-ribly the Israelites sinned, God always pre-served a core of godly survivors with whom He could begin again. Paul points out that many Jews in his day had become Christians. These are the modern remnant. Their conver-sion shows that God remains faithful to His O.T. people.

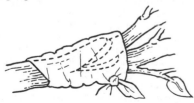

"Hardened" (11:7-10). The Gk. porosis is a strong term. God stiffened the already existing attitude and character of His rebellious people and brought about the growth of a calcified layer of thinking about religion that cemented Israel into a permanent insensibility. Never

suppose that rejecting God's grace carries no consequences. It does. This hardening is a di-vine judgment.

Gentile and Jew (11:11-21). Jewish rejection of God's "by-faith righteousness" made room for vast numbers of Gentiles to be "grafted in" the "tree" rooted in God's ancient covenant with Abraham. This should not be a matter of Gentile pride, but a warning. Never abandon the principle of salvation by grace through faith.

"Mystery" (11:25). This is a technical theologi-cal term in the N.T. used to indicate an aspect of God's eternal plan not revealed in the O.T., but which has now been unveiled. Here the mys-tery is the unexpected salvation of Gentiles as a consequence of Israel's *rejection* of God's Good News, rather than as a consequence of Israel's *conversion*, as is indicated in the O.T. prophets.

"All Israel will be saved" (11:25-26). Paul looks back here to promises made Israel by Isa-iah (59:20; cf. Jer. 31). The present massive Gen-tile conversions to Christ do not mean that God has repudiated the words of the O.T. prophets. When the "full number" of Gentiles has been converted, history's focus will return to Israel (11:29).

Outline
Place
Finder

REQUIRED
PROVIDED
IMPARTED
PROVED
PRACTICED

Chapter summary. God has acted to provide (Rom. 3–5) and impart (Rom. 6–8) righteousness. Now Paul moves to practical issues that are deeply rooted in the theology of this treatise on righteousness. "By-faith righteousness" has a distinctive, beautiful shape all its own!

On the basis of all God has done Paul urges believers to open themselves up to transformation rather than conform to this world's ways (Rom. 12:1-2). He shows that the practice of righteousness requires intimate ties to the new faith community. God has created a new thing: a living body. He has given each member gifts that enable him or her to contribute to the welfare of the whole (vv. 3-8). And to function as a body, believers must practice love and serve one another. They must strengthen those interpersonal bonds that enable them to minister (vv. 9-21).

Key verses. 12:1-2: Try it. You'll like it.

Personal application. Find a local church and become involved.

Key concepts. Mercy »p. 858. Body »p. 768. Love »pp. 661, 690. Spiritual gifts »p. 768. Good »p. 644. Evil »pp. 72, 662.

INSIGHT

"Living sacrifices" (12:1). God does not want us to die for Him, but to live for Him daily.

"Conform" (12:2). J.B. Phillips catches the meaning of this exhortation in a powerful paraphrase: "Don't let the world around you squeeze you into its own mold" (PH). The world exerts all sorts of pressures to force us to adopt its ways of thinking. But believers are not Jell-O. We don't have to conform. We can be transformed from within by God.

"Mind" (12:2). The Gk. word is *nous* which views mind as "capacity to perceive." We're no longer to look at life's issues as mere human beings, but let our perceptions be reshaped by God's own revelation of reality in the Scriptures.

Test and approve God's will (12:2). To truly perceive life from God's perspective we must live it in His way. Paul assures us that this is not the great risk some fear it to be. The word *dokimazo* indicates a test intended to display the genuineness of that which is tried. Paul is saying, "Trust God's will to be good, test your confidence by doing God's will, and you will discover God's way truly is good, pleasing, and perfect."

"Sober judgment" (12:3). When we look at ourselves honestly, we realize we need others in the body of Christ and others need us. Christians are interdependent persons. Like members of a human body, we need to be in place to be effective and to function as God intends. Don't isolate yourselves from other Christians. Find a local church where you can be significantly involved in sharing faith and life with others.

"Love" (12:9). Each N.T. description of the church as the body of Christ emphasizes the importance of love. Why? To function at all any body must have all its members united to each other. No one could live if an arm were in one room, a leg in another. The N.T. reminds us that it is love that binds the body of Christ together, uniting believers in a "one" relationship which enables Christ's body to be responsive to Him, its Head.

The shape of love (12:9-18). Love is not an abstract concept in Scripture. It is a way of life. This passage describes many ways that you and I can express God's love to others. Let's not complain if our local church isn't characterized by the way of life described here. Let's begin to live love ourselves among its members. Love is not only wonderful. It's catching.

Vengeance (12:19). In the Bible "vengeance" is a judicial function. It is justice, not revenge: It is punishment of sin. But don't suppose vengeance is ours to mete out. It is God's prerogative alone. And don't suppose He will draw back from this moral responsibility (2 Thes. 1:5-10).

"Burning coals" (12:20). Most suggest kindness induces a stinging sense of remorse in those whose actions merit punishment. It may be that remorse will only be felt on judgment day and unrequited kindness shown to the wicked and rejected will be the cause of even more severe judgment.

Chapter summary. Living out God's "by-faith righteousness" affects our relationships with other believers (Rom. 12). It also affects our relationship with the secular state and all our fellow human beings (Rom. 13). Christians must submit to governing authorities by obeying their rulers, paying taxes, and following established laws (13:1-5). Authorities are in fact God's (often unwitting!) servants, and our submission is a mark of respect for God (vv. 6-7). Christians must also show love to their fellow human beings (v. 8). In fact all the commandments are rooted in love: each calls us to avoid that which might harm a neighbor and so living love will in practice fulfill God's Law (vv. 9-10). This obligation is urgent, for history rushes toward its end and we must clothe ourselves with Christ rather than gratify the desires of our sinful nature (vv. 11-14).

Outline
Place
Finder

REQUIRED
PROVIDED
IMPARTED
PROVED
PRACTICED

Key verse. 13:5: Why submit to government?

Personal application. Do what is right because it is right, not because you have to.

Key concepts. Submission »pp. 867, 880. Love »pp. 126, 661, 690. Law »pp. 120, 145, 606. Sin »p. 741.

INSIGHT

Governing authorities (13:1-6). Secular government is God's servant not in any conscious sense, but in that it serves His purposes. Any human government must enforce a minimum level of justice or that government would collapse. For instance, if criminal behavior were not punished society would collapse. Christians, out of respect for an institution God uses for good even when rulers do not consciously serve Him, are to support the government by showing due respect for rulers, by paying taxes due, and by obeying secular laws.

God or Caesar? Christians have held from the earliest years that when a secular law violates a clear commandment of God, the believer is to obey God. We are fortunate that in our society God's Law and our nation's laws so seldom come in direct, open conflict.

"Because of conscience" (13:5). Governments have coercive power that enables them to make citizens conform to their laws. Paul tells us to be law-abiding not because we have to, but because it is the right thing to do. Motives matter to God.

A debt (13:8). "Debt" is used in its normal sense. We have an obligation to fulfill: to love others. Paul makes a key point here. Under the Law, God's covenant people were obligated to show love. There that obligation is broken down into specific commands that show how to love one's neighbor. In this era, God simply says "love," knowing that as we are moved by a real love for others we will do everything the Law requires!

We might compare this to a father's insistence that his daughter's suitor spell out just how he will treat her. Paul in the father's role would simply ask, "Do you love her?" confident that if the suitor truly loves his daughter he will treat her right.

Commandments today (13:9-10). The commandments of the O.T. are still instructive today, for they help us understand both righteousness and love. We may well measure our actions against them, to make sure that we understand the love we are to live.

But the commandments themselves neither help us be righteous or show love. Paul says that as we live by faith—relying on the Spirit to guide and empower us and on God's Word to shape our perspective on life—love will lead us to acts which are in full harmony with His commandments.

"The night is nearly over" (13:12). History may roll on for centuries. But it is still true that "the night is nearly over." In Christ a great light dawns, showing us truth and righteousness and calling us to a faith that transforms us into righteous men and women. How impossible then that we should let ourselves sink back into a darkness corrupted by sinful acts. How overjoyed we should be to clothe ourselves with Christ and live His kind of life in our lost world.

Chapter summary. Paul now returns to focus his thoughts on the practice of faith-based righteousness in relationships within the Christian community. Believers are to accept one another without condemnation for personal convictions (14:1-2). We have no right to judge others on such issues, for they are matters of conscience, to be settled between the individual and the Lord. Believers must then "stop passing judgment on one another" (vv. 3-12). Instead each person needs to be sensitive to how his or her choices affect others (vv. 13-18) and choose to do those things which "lead to peace and to mutual edification" (vv. 19-21). In this way we protect each person's conscience and the quality of his or her personal relationship with the Lord (vv. 22-23).

Key verse. 14:9: One Lord.

Personal application. Be responsible to Jesus for your conscience, and don't try to make others responsible to you.

Key concepts. Judging »pp. 372, 874. Unclean »pp. 82–83, 617. Kingdom »pp. 380, 606, 620.

INSIGHT

"Disputable matters" (14:1). A matter is "disputable" when it involves choices which God has not spoken clearly of in His Word. Adultery and theft, for instance, are not disputable matters. Many of the convictions which Christians hold dearly—do's and don'ts some passionately believe are God's will even though Scripture is silent—fall into this category.

"Accept" (14:1). The Gk. *paralambano* is a powerful relational term. It means to welcome, as with open heart and arms, eager and ready to share all of life. This is the kind of love we owe one another in Christ.

"Passing judgment" (14:1). Passing judgment means determining, on the basis of our own beliefs and convictions, that another person is sinning. When a person engages in an act which the Bible calls sin we are not "passing judgment" to call that act sin, but rather are agreeing with God. It's important to have this distinction clearly in mind.

The church is to discipline believers who sin. But neither individual nor congregation has any right to pass judgment.

Strong and weak (14:2). Surprising to many, it is the "weak" (*aetheneia*: frail, incapacitated) faith that has problems with the freedoms that others with a stronger faith enjoy! Strong faith realizes that spirituality is not a matter of do's and don'ts, but of loving and serving God while enjoying His good gifts.

"Look down on" (14:3). The problem with judging others is that it distorts relationships and keeps us from extending and receiving ministry from one another. It is our relationships, not whether we eat meat or only vegetables, that God cares about.

Christ as Lord/accountability (14:5-9). This vital passage affirms the essential truth that we are all personally responsible to Jesus Christ for the choices we make. We are accountable to Him for He is Lord.

Too many Christians—leaders and laypeople—act as if fellow believers were accountable to them rather than to Jesus. When we pass judgment on others, we usurp Jesus' role as Lord and deny Him the place that is rightfully His in our fellow believer's life. What a terrible sin this is.

"Instead" (14:13-18). How are we to approach "disputable matters"? Not by looking at how others pass judgment, but instead by examining what we do! And the question we need to ask is not, "Do we have the freedom to do this?" but rather, "Will my exercise of freedom cause harm to a brother/sister?"

"Destroy" (14:15). The word is *apollymi*, used here in the sense of causing ruin or downfall. The next verses help us to understand Paul's meaning. A misuse of freedom may "tear down," *katalyo*, God's work in a fellow believer (14:20) rather than "build up," *oikodome*, that person (14:19). Let's not flaunt our freedoms in front of others of weak conscience, who may be torn down by our actions rather than being built up spiritually.

How can you tell when to give up a freedom? There are no rules. But Jesus is Lord and He lives. Ask Him!

Chapter summary. Paul continues the topic developed in Romans 14. Practicing righteousness requires us to live love with one another. This means we must stop judging others and instead evaluate how the exercise of our freedoms affect them! We strong ones must "bear with" the weak, in the interest of building them up (15:1-4). Our goal is the experience of a God-given spirit of unity enabling us to glorify Him together (vv. 5-6). And Paul says it again. Accept (welcome) one another in the same way Jesus welcomed us—unconditionally—just as we were (vv. 7-8). Our unity will glorify God. We in turn will be filled with joy and peace and overflow with hope (vv. 9-13).

Paul now begins a lengthy conclusion. He has written not because he doubts the Roman church, but because he has such confidence in it (vv. 14-16). He has not visited Rome yet, in part because he is driven to preach to those who have not yet heard of Jesus (vv. 17-22). Yet Paul plans to visit, perhaps on the way to Spain. Meanwhile, he asks them simply to pray for him in his struggles to serve God (vv. 23-33).

Outline
Place
Finder

REQUIRED
PROVIDED
IMPARTED
PROVED
PRACTICED

Key verse. 15:7: A pathway to praise.

Personal application. Christ's welcome of us establishes the pattern for the welcome we must give to others.

Key concepts. Glorify God »p. 694. Gentiles »p. 798. Priest »p. 81. Sanctify »p. 824. Holy Spirit »pp. 73, 744. Prayer »pp. 181, 609.

INSIGHT

The problem. Paul's exposition on disputable things in Rom. 14 seems to leave us in a sad state of being captive to the weakest Christian's conscience! If we are really to surrender our own convictions to the convictions of the immature, Christianity seems doomed to sink into a joyless, captive legalism. Can this really be what Paul intends?

The solution: unity (15:1-7). Paul unhesitatingly identifies himself with the "strong," who know that convictions which burden the Christian with lists of do's and don'ts are held in error. But he gives a three-step solution to the situation in which strong and weak are bound together in a single congregation.

First, the strong are obligated to take the initiative. They do this by considering what is most helpful and upbuilding for the weak, rather than insisting on their own rights that they might please themselves. This attitude adopted by the strong is the first key to a solution.

Second, by showing love and concern and actively reaching out to embrace the weak, they build that "spirit of unity among your-

selves" which enables the congregation to (1) follow Christ Jesus and (2) praise God together. A unified, committed, and worshiping community creates a context in which the weaker as well as the stronger brethren can grow!

Third, in that context of community strong and weak learn to "accept (welcome, cf. 15:7) one another. Paul's statement of the basis of acceptance here is significant. In the earlier debate over "disputable matters" a person was accepted or condemned on the basis of his or her agreement with an individual's convictions. Now at last the church has learned to accept one another on the same basis that Christ accepts us: as we are—fully, completely, because we are loved and valued for ourselves.

As our congregations reach this level of spiritual maturity the "weak" will become "strong," and the issue of "disputable matters" will no longer exist.

Join in my struggles (15:30-33). Even the great apostle felt a need for prayer support. How much greater our need must be!

Outline
Place
Finder

REQUIRED
PROVIDED
IMPARTED
PROVED
PRACTICED

Chapter summary. As Paul closes this great letter to the Romans he gives much space to personal greetings. We might well wonder why. Why would God choose to include a lengthy list of names?

The answer may be simply that in these names we sense more clearly what it means to practice a "by-faith righteousness" in Christian community. Paul did not write theory. He shared what he himself practiced. And the proof is that he knows and loves such a diverse group of persons so well. There are women and men, both of whom are viewed as "fellow workers in Christ." There are Greek names and Jewish names. There are simple folk and city officials, the likely poor and the undoubtedly rich. All these, together, are united in Paul's heart and mind. All these are brothers and sisters, bound to the apostle by ties of God-inspired love. In these last chapters of Romans he urges us to have the same love for those who in our day are, in Christ, brothers and sisters of our own.

Key verses. 16:25-27: He is able.

Personal application. Build your own community of love.

Key concepts. Saint »p. 716. Church »p. 799. Brothers »p. 716.

INSIGHT

"**Phoebe**" (16:1). The word describing her as a "servant" is *diakonia*, "deacon." Except for the feminine ending, it is the same word all English versions render "deacon" in the pastoral epistles and take to indicate a leadership office in the church. Apparently Paul was not as negative to women in leadership as many moderns are.

"**Priscilla and Aquila**" (16:3). This couple, introduced in Acts 18, was very close to the Apostle Paul and deeply involved in ministry. It is significant that, except for the verse in which the two are introduced, the name of the wife always precedes that of the husband. Apparently her gifts were greater than his, and Scripture gives mute testimony to the respect with which she was held in the early church.

The house church (16:5). For nearly three centuries Christianity was a "small group" phenomenon. Early Christians built no large churches or cathedrals. Instead they met in homes for worship and sharing. Based on the size of homes in 1st-century cities, meetings must have accommodated a very limited number of people. Yet as Paul's letters show, there was a sense of identity with the greater body of all believers who lived in the city, and beyond that with believers throughout the world. The way of loving one another learned in the "small group" N.T. church carried over into the way

Christians related to one another at every level.

Divisions and obstacles (16:17). Paul's way is still the best for dealing with people who try to split a church: "Keep away from them."

"**Erastus**" (16:23). This Corinthian city official is also mentioned in Acts 19:22 and 2 Tim. 4:20. An inscription found in the ruins of 1st-century Corinth identifies an Erastus who held the high office of *aedile*; he is most likely the Christian Erastus who, when Paul wrote Romans, held the lesser office of "director of public works."

Since holding any office in a 1st-century city required both that an individual be a Roman citizen and that he have enough wealth to spend his own funds on public projects, we can see that the church included the high as well as the low. And yet, the church Paul wrote to and of was, and could be, one.

He is able (16:25-27). How is it possible to take sinful human beings, motivated by selfish and sinful passions, separated by racial prejudice and vast social differences, and create a community bonded together by selfless love? Only God could do it in the world of the 1st century. And only God can do it today.

The message of Romans is that through a righteousness imputed to us by faith and made real by continuing trust in our living Lord *He will* do it.

1 Corinthians

In the first century, Corinth was the finest city in Greece. A dynamic, cosmopolitan city of some 250,000 in Paul's day, Corinth lay on a narrow isthmus of land and boasted ports on both the Aegean Sea and the Gulf of Corinth. Cargoes and even small vessels were transported over the five mile wide strip of land, enabling seamen to avoid a long and dangerous sea route around the Peloponnesian Peninsula.

Paul spent a year and a half in Corinth and founded a church there (Acts 18). In this first letter to that church, written about five years later, the apostle deals with a variety of disputes and problems. In fact problems give this letter its structure, and Paul deals with one flaw after another in the congregation's life together.

Paul's first letter to the Corinthians is one of the most helpful of the New Testament epistles for moderns. On the one hand, it reminds us not to idealize the early church. Living together as Christ's people has always been a challenge, and even the most committed of God's people have found it a difficult, continuing struggle. No church will be ideal, yet we are called to work toward the ideal of a people living and growing together in harmony. In fact it is because we all struggle that this letter is so valuable. In it Paul gives the Corinthians, and us, problem-solving principles that apply in any age, and in any congregation.

PROBLEMS IN CORINTH

A problem with unity (1–4)   *How do Christians preserve the unity of the church in spite of divisive issues and party spirit?*

A problem with sin (5–6)   *How do Christians preserve the purity of the church when members choose to sin? How do we relate to sinning brothers and sisters? How do we relate to non-Christians whose lives are characterized by habitual sin?*

A problem with divorce (7)   *Is it more spiritual to divorce than remain married? What if one's spouse deserts him or her?*

A problem with disputes over doctrine (8–10)   *How do we deal with doctrinal differences in the church? Is there a way to resolve them? Can we live in harmony with people who differ from us doctrinally?*

Problems with women and worship (11)   *What is the place of women in church meetings? What is the significance of the Lord's Supper?*

Problems with spirituality (12–14)   *What is true spirituality? How does spirituality relate to spiritual gifts? What is the role of the gift of tongues in church meetings?*

Problems with resurrection (15)   *How important is resurrection in Christianity? What will our resurrection be like?*

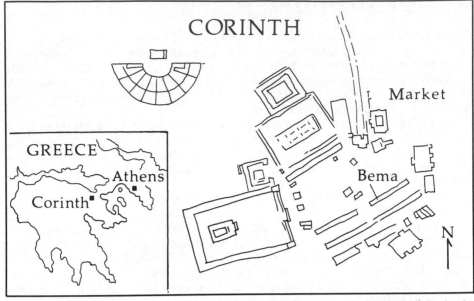

CORINTH

Market

GREECE

Athens

Corinth

Bema

N

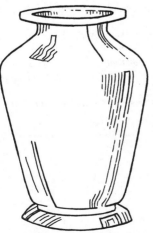

Archeologists have worked in Corinth for decades and uncovered many finds that fascinate the student of Scripture. In excavating the city center (above) an inscription was found mentioning a city official, Erastus, who is mentioned in Rom. 16:23 and other N.T. passages!

Left. An inscription referring to the makellon, or meat market, over which such controversy developed in 1st-century Corinth. The meat sold there was from animals that had been offered to pagan idols. Some believers were horrified at the association with idolatry; others argued that idols had no real existence, so there was nothing wrong with trading at meat markets.

Lower left. Large empty brass vases were placed at the back of the stage in the theater at Corinth. These, the "sounding brass" of 1 Cor. 13:1 (KJV), not as the NIV has it, a "clanging cymbal." Paul's point is that one who ministers without love may reach others—but his or her own life will be empty: "I gain nothing."

Date and Authorship. The Apostle Paul wrote this letter, probably about A.D. 57. He wrote from Ephesus in response to the report of problems among the Corinthian brothers and sisters that were tearing the church apart.

Distinctive Contribution of 1 Corinthians

First Corinthians 15 contains the New Testament's clearest exposition on the resurrection of Christ and of believers. It makes unmistakably clear the Bible's promise of a literal, bodily resurrection for every Christian.

Yet the greatest contribution of this book is interpersonal. Paul tells us that the Corinthian congregation enjoyed a full complement of spiritual gifts, and yet this is the only church the apostle calls "worldly—mere infants in Christ" (3:1). A study of this great New Testament letter helps us see the way "mere men" approach divisive issues and then shows us the way that adopting God's perspective can restore harmony and unity to a local body.

THEOLOGICAL OUTLINE OF 1 CORINTHIANS

CONTENT OUTLINE OF 1 CORINTHIANS

Chapter summary. Paul's greeting reminds the Corinthians of their call to be holy (1:1-3) and expresses his thanks for the strengths they exhibit (vv. 4-9). But the apostle quickly turns to the first of a series of serious problems that keeps the church from reaching its spiritual potential.

The Corinthian fellowship is torn by factions, each arguing the superiority of one Christian leader over another (vv. 10-12). Deeply upset, Paul cries out, "Is Christ divided?" (1:13-17) Paul then begins to lay a foundation for dealing with factionalism and indeed with any dispute. The Gospel itself is by any human standards "foolishness." But human standards themselves are "foolishness" in view of a divine wisdom which turns man's values upside down. We believers must hold to the central reality of our faith, Christ, for He is the source of all our righteousness, holiness, and redemption (vv. 18-30). Believers can hardly boast about the supposed superiority of any human leader. The only one worth boasting about is Christ (v. 31).

Key verse. 1:25: Adopt God's perspective.

Personal application. Appreciate gifted leaders, but give your allegiance only to Jesus.

Key concepts. Apostle »p. 635. Church »p. 794. Spiritual gifts »p. 768. Righteousness »p. 734. Holiness »p. 879. Redemption »p. 790.

INSIGHT

"Called" (1:1-3). Paul immediately names himself an apostle of Jesus Christ who has authority as His representative through divine appointment (call). Paul's letter is thus authoritative teaching and must be accepted as such.

Strengths (1:4-9). Paul bluntly confronts the church's flaws. But he also affirms their strengths. No congregation's situation is so bad there are not some positives to emphasize, some source of encouragment and hope.

"Strong to the end" (1:8). "End" is *teleos*, the achievement of an intended goal. Despite our faults, God preserves His own and keeps on working in us to present us blameless when Jesus returns.

"Divisions" (1:10). The Gk. word, *schismata*, means tears or cracks. The debate over Christian leaders has destroyed the unity of the local congregation and led to antagonisms. As Paul will point out in 1 Cor. 12, unity of the body is essential for spiritual growth and the exercise of spiritual gifts.

Some have taken this passage as an argument against the existence of different denominations. It is not—unless we argue that our group is "best" or "right" and so separate ourselves from others who are equally members of Christ's body.

The basis of unity (1:13). We are united in Christ, the focus of all true Christian faith. Our salvation depends on His crucifixion. Our life as Christians flows from that union with Jesus effected by the baptism of the Holy Spirit, the "baptism into the name" of Jesus (cf. 1 Cor. 12:13). Because we have Christ in common, there is no room for antagonistic divisions and factions.

"Foolishness" (1:18ff.). The word here is *moros*, the most common and strongest of the N.T. words translated "fool" or "foolish." The word indicates those who look at reality with a distorted perspective, typically because they fail to take God into account. Paul illustrates human foolishness by noting that both Jew and Greek despise the Cross. Yet the Cross puts the greatest moral issues in the universe in perspective. Through the Cross we discover the justice, grace, and forgiveness of God. Paul's point is that in the matter of factions, the Corinthians have neglected to look at the church from God's perspective and so fall into the "foolish" ways of the non-Christian.

God's wisdom (1:18ff.). Paul argues that human wisdom, here the ability to see and understand reality, is shown to be foolishness by the Cross. Christians must abandon human philosophy's appeal to rationalism and rely on revelation if we are to resolve our differences and maintain our essential unity in Christ.

Chapter summary. Paul abandoned the approach taken by itinerant philosophers and teachers when he came to Corinth, to rely totally on God's Spirit in his presentation of the Gospel (2:1-5). Paul's present appeal does display "wisdom," but a secret wisdom which is beyond the comprehension of mankind (vv. 6-10a). That wisdom has been revealed in words by the Spirit of God who, being God, knows the thoughts of God. And the spiritual truths contained in those Spirit-shaped words are interpreted by the Spirit to those who through faith in Christ possess the Spirit (vv. 10b-15). Because the Spirit both reveals God's Word and illuminates its meaning for us, we can know and do the mind of Christ.

Key verse. 2:11: God's Spirit knows the unknowable.

Personal application. God teaches His people His ways.

Key concepts. Holy Spirit »pp. 73, 744. Revelation »pp. 354, 691, 799. Wisdom »pp. 280, 387, 757. Spiritual »p. 793.

INSIGHT

Christ alone, and enough (2:1-5). The cities of the empire were filled with itinerant teachers who attracted disciples by *hyperochen logou* (impressive oratory) and *sophia* (here, philosophical argument). Paul determined not to rely on either to win hearers to Christ. Realizing his frailty, he simply proclaimed a crucified Saviour and left it up to the Spirit to win converts.

What a freeing thing this is. Our effectiveness in sharing the Gospel with others does not depend on our skills, training, or knowledge. The Spirit works powerfully through the message itself. We can share despite our frailties, for our confidence is in the power of God.

Man's blindness (2:6-9). Paul quotes a pagan poet to illustrate limitations of human wisdom. The quote is from Empedocles (5th century B.C.): "Weak and narrow are the powers implanted in the limbs of man; many the woes that fall on them and blunt the edges of thought; short is the measure of the life in death through which they toil. Then are they borne away; like smoke that vanishes into the air; and what they dream they know is but the little that each hath stumbled upon in wandering about the world. Yet boast they all that they have learned the whole. Vain fools! For what that is, no eye hath seen, no ear hath heard, nor can it be conceived by the mind of man." Human beings have no capacity to grasp or understand reality.

Revelation and God's Spirit (2:10b-11). Here Paul focuses attention on one of the distinctive works of the Holy Spirit. As God He is privy to the very thoughts of God. He is the One who spoke through the prophets (cf.

1 Peter 1:12) and apostles (Rom. 16:26; 1 Cor. 2:10; 14:6; Gal. 1:12; 3:23; Eph. 3:3, 5). This passage makes the central point that humans are limited; they are unable to grasp the origins, ends, or meaning of life through information grasped by the senses or attained by flights of imagination. In the N.T. "revelation" refers primarily to this communication of information from God, although the Gk. word is also used in other senses as well.

Illumination (2:13-16). This is the special work of the Holy Spirit by which He enlightens believers to the meaning of Scripture's objective revelation. This does not mean that a non-Christian is unable to understand what the Bible teaches intellectually. It does mean that the person without the Spirit will not accept Scripture's testimony as an accurate portrayal of reality and will be unable to apply revealed truth appropriately as a guide to personal decision-making.

Carnal (2:14). The NIV "man without the Spirit" is *psychikos*, typically rendered in older versions as "the carnal man." The word is best translated "soulish" and means persons limited to natural rather than supernatural capacities. In contrast, possession of the Spirit makes a believer *pneumatikos*, "spiritual," with the supplied capacities needed to understand revealed truths and apply them in personal moral decisions.

The mind of Christ (2:16). Natural man may ridicule the claims of the believer in discerning reality. But because the Spirit links us with Jesus we know Him and can discern His will.

Chapter summary. The Corinthians, in becoming distracted from Christ in their arguments over the merits of mere human leaders, act like the unsaved. Their jealousy and bickering prove they are "worldly" (*psychikos*, "soulish") using mere human capacities and not the spiritual insight provided to believers by the Spirit (3:1-4).

Paul explains. Human leaders are servants of God: It is God who is the source of all growth (v. 5). God's priority is the congregation, not the leaders. Leaders are workers in God's field: The church is the field (vv. 6-9). Leaders are builders.

Christ is the foundation. The church is God's temple (vv. 10-17). The work of leaders, like that of all believers, will be evaluated by God in time (vv. 10-15). But boasting about mere human leaders, and so exalting one's party over brothers who adhere to a different leader, is utter foolishness (vv. 18-22). Believers have Jesus Christ and in Him possess God (v. 23).

Outline
Place
Finder

UNITY
DISCIPLINE
DIVORCE
DOCTRINE
WORSHIP
TONGUES
RESURRECTION
ENCOURAGE

Key verse. 3:23: What more do we need?

Personal application. See yourself as a servant, and serve.

Key concepts. Worldly/Carnal »p. 758. Servant »pp. 90, 432, 622. Works »p. 872. Temple »p. 283.

INSIGHT

"Brothers" (3:1). This affectionate term takes some of the bite out of Paul's criticism of the Corinthians. We must really care about any whom we rebuke, and make that love apparent if the rebuke is to be accepted.

"Jealousy and quarreling" (3:3). James 3:15-16 is much more blunt than Paul. Such "wisdom" is "earthly, unspiritual, of the devil. For where you have envy and selfish ambition, there you find disorder and every evil practice."

The church (3:5-10, 16). The N.T. consistently speaks of the church as the people of God. At times "church" is the universal organism made up of all believers of all times. At times "church" encompasses all believers in a geographical area, such as Corinth or Asia. At other times "church" is the little gathering of Christians who meet in someone's house for worship and prayer.

The N.T. also uses several symbols to help us better understand the nature of the people God has called out to be His own. The symbol of a living body (Rom. 12; 1 Cor. 12; Eph. 4) stresses the interdependence of a people whose growth depends on an intimate fellowship in which spiritual gifts are freely exercised. The image of a holy temple (1 Cor. 3:16; 1 Peter 2:4-5) emphasizes the commitment of God's people to holiness and worship. The image of a family (John 13:33-34; Eph. 3) emphasizes the importance of loving, close, personal relationships. The image of a field, here, emphasizes the growth toward maturity God seeks to stimulate in the people called by His name.

"Only servants" (3:5). How foolish to ignore the Master and argue over which servant is most important!

Christ the foundation (3:10). Don't let your faith rest on any human leader. Count on Christ.

Rewards (3:12-15). The "day" in view here is that of Christ's return. Let's not waste time evaluating the service others render to God. Jesus will do that Himself.

Note that what is tested by fire here is not the believer. It is the works of service performed by the believer. The Christian is in no danger of hellfire. The worst that can happen is that the service we render Christ will be flawed, of such materials as pride or ambition, rather than works of love and commitment. How gracious of God to promise us rewards for those things we do out of love for Him (cf. 1 Cor. 13).

"God's Spirit lives in you" (3:16). The indwelling Holy Spirit is the source of power for the Christian life. Only through His enablement can we serve God acceptably or live the holy and good lives God calls all His people to. Because the Holy Spirit does live in us, we are God's holy temple and we can be holy. Paul's warning is directed to believers. If anyone "brings ruin on" (*phtheiro*) God's temple, God will bring ruin on him.

759

Chapter summary. Paul sums up his argument against faction-alism. Leaders are servants of God; their qualities are to be evaluated by the Lord and not by mere human beings (4:1-5). If the Corinthians remember this, they won't make the mistake of comparing one leader with another and will recognize differ-ences as a matter of divine gift (vv. 6-7). With mild but stinging irony, Paul suggests the Corinthians who stand in judgment on their spiritual leaders see themselves as kings—wise, strong, and proud—looking down on the apostles, except the one their faction honors, as foolish, weak, and dishonored (vv. 8-13). Then, taking the sting from his remarks, Paul affirms his love. But he also shows an iron determination. The arrogant among the Corinthians disrupt the kingdom of God. Unless they re-pent they will be disciplined (vv. 14-21).

Key verse. 4:7: No basis for pride.

Personal application. Don't criticize your leaders. Pray for them.

Key concepts. Judge »p. 874. Conscience »p. 738. Arrogance »p. 119.

INSIGHT

Entrusted with God's secret things (4:1). The Gk. *oikonomous,* "entrusted," indicates a "house steward." Paul is saying that he has been appointed to manage God's message of salvation, not as one in control of it but one who is responsible to the Master. Since Paul is responsible to God, he cares "very little" if he is judged by others.

What a freeing thing it is to care nothing for what others say and give yourself completely to be faithful to the Lord.

"I do not even judge myself" (4:3). There is little value in introspective self-examination. Our calling is not to be judges but servants. All God asks is that we do not choose sin (and so keep a clear conscience) and serve Him as faithfully as we can.

The solution to pride (4:7). Some are proud because they have fine voices. Some are proud of their ability to teach or preach. Others are proud of their honesty or kindness. We can and should rejoice in the special abilities each of us has. But we are not to be proud of them, as though our ability makes us better than others. Paul sums up the reason in one verse: "What do you have that you did not receive? And if you did receive it, why do you boast as though you did not?" Praise God for any gift that makes you special, but don't be proud. After all, it is a gift!

Irony (4:8-13). Paul uses this subtly sarcastic literary device, in which the intended mean-ing of words is the direct opposite of their usual sense. How clear it is that the "worldly"

(3:1-3) folk of Corinth who acted as if they were so superior to the apostles were in fact spiritually inferior.

Real superiority (4:11-13). True spiritual su-periority is described here!

Persecution (4:12). The usual word for per-secution is *dioko,* to run after with the intent of doing harm. Jesus tells us to expect persecu-tion because the world we live in is hostile to Him (John 15:20). The *Expository Dictionary of Bible Words* (Zondervan, 1985, p. 484) sums up how to respond to persecution. "We remem-ber that suffering persecution is part of what it means—in certain situations at least—to live as a Christian (1 Thes. 3:4; 2 Tim. 3:12). Like Paul, 'when we are persecuted we endure it' (1 Cor. 4:12). We respond by loving and bless-ing our persecutors and praying for them (Matt. 5:44; Rom. 12:14). And through it all we remember that no 'hardship or persecution' will be able to separate us from the love of God (Rom. 8:35-36)."

"Faithful" (4:17, cf. v. 2). Here Paul commends Timothy, his young companion in ministry, as "faithful." The word, *pistos,* means loyal, reliable, and trustworthy. It is frequently used in the N.T. to commend believers for car-rying out their assignments (Matt. 24:45; 25:21-23), and for steadfast endurance (Eph. 6:21; Col. 1:7; 4:7).

"Power" (4:19-20). Paul refers here as in 2 Cor. 13 to the ability of God to deal supernaturally with those who are citizens of His kingdom. The Corinthians talk big, but wield no power.

Chapter summary. Paul turns to another problem in Corinth. There is open sexual immorality, and the church has ignored it! Paul tells the believers to "put [the guilty person] out of your fellowship" (5:1-5). Using the figure of yeast that works through the whole lump of dough, Paul warns that a Christian congregation dare not permit sin to go undisciplined, lest the congregation become corrupt (vv. 6-8). Paul then adds a word of correction. He does not mean believers are forbidden to associate with unsaved people who are immoral. The principle of separation he has just laid down applies to those who claim to be Christians (vv. 9-11). Judging outsiders is God's business, not that of the church (vv. 12-13).

Key verse. 5:3: Take a stand against sin.

Personal application. Church discipline is a biblical imperative.

Key concept. Sex »pp. 402, 836.

INSIGHT

Passing judgment (5:3). In 4:5 Paul said "judge nothing before the appointed time." Isn't he being inconsistent now in passing judgment on the guilty believer in Corinth? The answer is no. The believer is not to judge the quality of service, motives, or commitment of others. But what God has revealed are sins is different. In this case, Paul and the Corinthian church are supposed to judge. In judging they will simply agree with God that the behavior in question is sin and follow His rules for dealing with sin.

Church discipline. The intent of church discipline is to preserve the moral purity of a congregation. Church discipline is *not* to be applied in cases of doctrinal difference or interpersonal conflict. Church discipline is to be applied in cases of *persistent, open sin* by a member of the congregation.

Church discipline involves cutting off the sinning believer from fellowship. As Paul says, do not "associate with" (5:9) the believer under discipline, not even to eat with him or her (5:11).

Matthew 18:15-17 suggests a process that most believe should be applied to issues of discipline. The person who does wrong is approached privately and given an opportunity to repent. If there is no response, a group of church leaders speaks with him or her. If there is still no repentance, even after the whole church has been informed, "treat him as you would a pagan" (v. 17).

There is an important rationale behind this discipline process. Persistent sin interrupts fellowship with God. The church on earth is to act out, and so make unmistakably real to the sinning brother, the fact that he is alienated from the Lord.

There is also an important goal. The process of church discipline is not intended to punish a fellow believer, but to bring him or her to repentance. This is exactly what happened in Corinth, and in his second letter Paul commands to "forgive and comfort" the man since he has repented and abandoned his sin.

Purity (5:6-8). In O.T. times leaven (yeast) was carefully removed from every household before the annual Passover festival. Paul sees this as an analogy for the necessity of holiness in the church. Every bit of yeast (sin) must be carefully removed from the community whose Passover lamb is Christ and whose celebration is endless because of Him.

Separation (5:10). The Christian is to be separate from sin and worldly practices. But the Christian is not to be isolated from the people of the world.

Some cannot understand why the church is not to "judge those outside the church." But the reason is simple. God will judge sinners Himself. Our ministry is to carry the Good News of forgiveness to all. Rather than condemn sinners, we show love to them. Rather than turn from them, we hold up the Gospel for them to see and believe.

Chapter summary. Paul now writes about lawsuits between Christians, which the Corinthians were bringing to secular courts instead of to the church (6:1-3). His argument that the Christian community should settle its own disputes rests on an empire-wide right to various nationalities to settle cases by applying their own laws rather than Roman law. Certainly believers are better suited to settle moral issues involved in noncriminal cases than pagans (vv. 4-6). Paul then condemns not the victims but the "wicked" who are using the courts to defraud others. No wickedness has any place in a church whose members are washed, sanctified, and justified in the name of Jesus (vv. 7-11).

Paul then returns to the question of sexual morality. Sex is not just a "natural function" like eating (vv. 12-13a). The human body, redeemed by God and indwelt by the Spirit, is holy and must not be given over to sexual sins (vv. 13b-20).

Key verse. 6:8: Not use, but misuse of the law.

Personal application. Settle disputes within the church—if you can.

Key concepts. Kingdom »pp. 380, 606, 620. Angels »p. 521. Wicked »pp. 29, 350. Union with Christ »p. 692. Temple »p. 283. Holy Spirit »pp. 73, 744, 759.

INSIGHT

Disputes (6:1). The cases are lawsuits, not criminal actions, which are in the province of secular courts (Rom. 13:3-4).

"Before the saints" (6:1). Well established empire practice permitted ethnic communities to settle disputes themselves, based on their own national laws. This was true even when the community was a small district within any city of the empire as well as in the homeland. Paul urges Christians to follow this principle and settle their own disputes.

Typically in Judaism a panel of three judges handled such cases. Paul tells the church to set up a similar panel of judges. Certainly it is better to handle disputes based on biblical principles rather than pagan law!

"Lawsuits" (6:7). The word is *pragma echon* and indicates various types of property cases.

"Why not rather be wronged"? (6:7-8) This verse has been twisted by many moderns and applied in such a way that *victims* are left with no redress. This is not Paul's point. The existence of the lawsuits shows a malicious spirit: It is those who "do wrong" rather than those who are wronged who bring the lawsuits.

The O.T. made every individual who knew of wrongdoing responsible to bring it before the elders of the community. The O.T. community of faith was to be committed to righteousness. A Christian who victimizes another

and then quotes these verses to claim that the victim is unspiritual in seeking legal redress completely misses Paul's point.

Paul's point is that such issues must be dealt with within the church family. If a congregation fails to establish appropriate mechanisms for judging disputes, a believer who is concerned about the purity of the body must go to secular court. As Matt. 18:17 says, a brother who will not respond to the discipline of the church is to be treated as a pagan.

A warning (6:9-10). Those who wickedly seek to cheat others must remember that such persons have no place in the kingdom of God.

Christian freedom (6:12-13). Freedom is not license. Before engaging in any action Paul says we must consider whether it is beneficial—that is, if it contributes to personal and corporate spiritual growth. We must also consider whether it has the potential of overpowering and dominating us, and so threatening the lordship of Christ in our lives. Paul flatly condemns sexual immorality—and those who argue that it is like eating, merely a natural function and therefore nonmoral.

A biblical perspective on the body (6:15, 19-20). Through our union with Christ our bodies have become His, temples in which the Holy Spirit dwells. Whatever we do in the body must honor Christ, for He is present in us.

Chapter summary. The Corinthians were confused about Paul's teaching on marriage. Some had taken his recommendation of celibacy as an apostolic ruling and refrained from sex or even divorced their mates. Paul here deals with a number of complex issues. First, he teaches that sex within marriage is not only good, but essential (7:1-6). He thinks it better if the unmarried remain unmarried, but tells those with strong sexual drives marriage is best for them (vv. 7-8). The married are to stay married (vv. 9-11), but if a nonbelieving spouse refuses to live with a believer, the believer is "not bound" (vv. 12-16). A general principle in the Christian life is to "retain the place in life" God has assigned. The principle applies to one's married state as well (vv. 17-28). There are advantages in remaining unmarried (vv. 29-35), but it is not wrong to marry if a person feels he or she ought to, whether one be a virgin or widow (7:36-40).

Key verse. 7:7: Be yourself.

Personal application. Commit yourself, whether to your marriage or to singleness.

Key concepts. Marriage »pp. 26, 801. Divorce »p. 136.

INSIGHT

Good not to marry (7:1). The rabbis considered marriage a man's duty. Paul here quotes a view current in Corinth, with which he only partially agrees. It is good not to marry now, because of a present crisis (7:26, 29, 35).

Sex in marriage (7:2-5). Marriage is intended not only to meet man's need for procreation and companionship, but also to meet sexual needs.

Some in Corinth apparently believed they should have a "spiritual," sexless marriage. The Gk. construction implies "Stop depriving one another, as you are doing." Paul commands husbands and wives not to cease normal sexual relationships except by mutual agreement for a brief time. Sex is not wrong, it is a gift (»p. 836).

"Must not separate" (7:10-14). Paul's clear teaching is that Christians are not to initiate separations or divorces. He says this in the context of the Corinthian's general confusion about sexuality and the practice of some who divorced in order to live more "spiritual" lives.

This instruction has been misunderstood as a blanket condemnation of divorce under any circumstances. However it does not negate Jesus' words about why God permitted divorce (Matt. 19:8). Old Testament Law permitted divorce because "your hearts were hard." That is, sin would so distort some marriages that divorce was permitted. To tell a woman who is abused by her husband she must not leave him on the basis of this verse is a tragic misunderstanding of the text, and of God.

No divorce (7:10-11). Again Paul is writing to deal with a specific problem. The believer may say he or she divorces a spouse because "it is good for a man not to marry" (v. 1). Any believer in Corinth who has done this has two options. She can remain in the unmarried state, or she can be reconciled with her husband. This kind of divorce frees no one from marital bonds!

Marriage to unbelievers (7:12-14). Many in Corinth were converted while their spouses were not. This passage contains a unique use of the idea of sanctification, or being set apart to God. In a mixed marriage the children are in a special way set apart to God through the ministry and influence of the believing parent. This is unusual because it reverses the O.T. principle that when something "unclean" touched something "clean" the "clean" item or person was made unclean. Because of the dynamic power of the Spirit of God living within the believer, cleansing power now flows out of our lives and affects all in contact with us.

"Not bound" (7:15). If the unbeliever takes the initiative and leaves the believer, the Christian is "not bound." In both Rom. 7:2 and 1 Cor. 7:39 "bound" (*deo*) is used in the sense free to marry. It seems clear that a Christian divorced by anyone unwilling to live with him or her is in fact unmarried and free to marry again.

Chapter summary. Paul moves now to a heated Corinthian dispute over an issue of doctrine. Should Christians eat meat from animals that have been offered first to pagan deities, and can they take part in a dinner party the host dedicates to a god or goddess?

Paul begins by teaching that such disputes must be approached not on the basis of "knowledge" but of "love" (8:1-3). Those who argue that pagan idols are "nothing at all" and only God is real have a point (vv. 4-6). But not everyone has this "knowledge" and those who indulge "defile" the weaker conscience of those who do not realize the eating or not eating is irrelevant to true spirituality (vv. 7-8). By failing to be sensitive to the harm the exercise of their freedom does to the "weak," the "strong" Christian sins against love, which is far worse than being "wrong" about a point of doctrine (vv. 9-13).

Key verse. 8:1: Love is the key.

Personal application. Differ in doctrine, but continue to love.

Key concepts. Idols »p. 433. Sacrifice »p. 27. Freedom »pp. 469, 685. Conscience »p. 738. Sin »pp. 34, 362.

INSIGHT

Background. In 1st-century cities animals offered to pagan deities were divided into three portions: one was burned, one was given to the priest, and the third to the offerer. Typically priests sold unused portions of meat. The knotty doctrinal problem resulted. Was this meat contaminated or not? Some insisted it was not, because the gods of the pagans were unreal. Others were troubled by the association with idolatry.

"Knowledge" (8:1-3). Such disputes typically feature deductions drawn from what an individual knows. The problem is all have "knowledge" from which they draw conclusions. But none of us know enough to be sure. The other problem is that a claim to superior knowledge "puffs up" individuals. Such arrogance divides us rather than helps us work through our differences productively.

"Love" (8:1-3). Paul says that love is a better way to approach differences. Why? J.B. Phillips paraphrases, "While this 'knowing' may make a man look big, it is only love that can make him grow to his full stature" (PH). The person who loves opens himself up to God and to others, grows spiritually, and comes to understand the issue more clearly!

"We know" (8:4-6). Paul here summarizes not his own teaching but the argument of one of the factions in Corinth. Paul does agree in principle with this point of view. It is true that God, the Father, is the Creator of the entire

universe, and that Jesus is Lord of both its material and spiritual dimensions. The question is, does this "knowledge" mean that the person who sees this truth is free to visit temple meat markets.

Let's always remember that we can be "right" if judged on the basis of knowledge and totally "wrong" when our actions are evaluated on the basis of love.

The conscience is weak (8:7-8). A "weak" conscience here is one which is frail or faulty. It condemns a person for doing something that is not intrinsically wrong. Paul reminds the "strong" in Corinth that some (perhaps new Christians?) have been so immersed in paganism that any contact with it seems corrupting. Paul wants the Corinthians to stop arguing about who is "right" and see what the insistence of the strong's point of view is doing to other believers.

Defiled (8:7). The word *moluno* here indicates a sense of guilt.

Food is irrelevant (8:8-13). In arguing that food is irrelevant to one's relationship with God the "strong" have in fact convicted themselves. What we eat is irrelevant—but how our actions affect others in the body is not irrelevant.

If the food we eat is so unimportant, the Corinthians should be glad to give up their right to eat food until the conscience of their weaker brothers has become strong.

Chapter summary. Paul has called on the "strong" brothers in Corinth to give up their rights to eat meat sacrificed to idols for the sake of their weaker brothers (1 Cor. 8). Now he reminds his readers that he himself has rights (9:1-12a), which he has consistently given up (vv. 12b-18). Paul has chosen this way of life in order to share Christ with all (vv. 19-23) and because he is committed to pleasing God (vv. 24-27).

Key verse. 9:19: Others first.

Personal application. Never insist on your rights at the possible expense of others.

INSIGHT

Illustration (9:24-27). *Paul sets his sights on his goals, not on his rights. As an athlete gladly surrendered pleasures while in training to win a crown woven of leaves, Paul sets aside his rights in order to achieve spiritual goals.*

The seal of Paul's apostleship (9:2). Paul established the church of Corinth and won its first converts. The very existence of the church testifies to Paul's commission as Jesus' apostle.

"A believing wife" (9:5). This is Scripture's only reference to the other apostles' practice of taking wives with them. It specifically mentions Peter's wife, another proof he was married.

Financial support of those in ministry (9:6-14). Paul argues from an O.T. precedent that those who give full time to meeting the spiritual needs of people deserve to receive financial support from them. Most pastors in our churches actually deserve considerably more financial support than they are given!

Paul's choice (9:15-18). Paul has chosen not to accept financial support. In preaching "without charge" Paul not only wins reward

but also proves that his motives in ministry are genuine. In another epistle Paul tells the Thessalonians that he supported himself to give them an example of the importance of work (2 Thes. 3:7-10).

Why surrender rights? (9:19-23) Paul does what he encourages the Corinthians to do. He gives up things that are not important to relate better to those who need his ministry. This is not "compromise," rather evidence of a deep love for others that puts their well-being first. He follows Jewish customs when with Jews and Gentile customs when with Gentiles, knowing the customs of each group have no real significance. And when he is with the "weak" he does nothing to violate the conscience of them.

It is truly difficult to live a selfless life. But that is what Paul lived, and that is what God calls us to live as well.

"Disqualified" (9:27). The rules of the Christian "game" are strict and call for consistent self-discipline. We cannot lose our salvation. But we can lose the prizes our dedication to the Lord might otherwise win.

Chapter summary. Paul now deals with a separate issue raised by the Corinthians, which also involved eating and idolatry. First he reminds these Christians that activities associated with idolatry led ancient Israel into gross sin (10:1-10). The reports of idolatry's dangers were written down as a warning to Christians (v. 11). The self-confidence of the "strong" in Corinth places them in danger, for human nature remains subject to the same temptations that caused Israel to fail (vv. 12-13a). When temptations come we are to look for the "way out" God provides, not expose ourselves to them (v. 13b).

Isn't it common sense, Paul says, that those who gather around the Lord's table and participate in the blood of Christ have no place at a meal dedicated to demons? (vv. 14-22) Paul then returns to the principle laid down in 6:12. Never mind "permissible." The question is, is an act constructive. Does it contribute to our own and others' spiritual growth?

Paul then sums up the impact of his teaching by giving specific instructions on the issues in question (vv. 23-30). And he leaves the Corinthians, and us, with another principle to apply. "Do all to the glory of God." Not because you have rights. Not because you have freedom. But act to glorify our Lord (10:31–11:1).

Key verse. 10:13: All human beings are vulnerable.

Personal application. Don't expose yourself to temptation and then blame God for not rescuing you. You always had a way out.

Key concepts. Temptation »pp. 27, 655, 871. Idolatry »p. 433. Demons »pp. 659, 895.

INSIGHT

Spiritual privileges (10:1-5). Paul uses the analogy of cloud and rock to point out that the Israelites were bound to God by redemption and were sustained by God's grace. But the participation of Israel in these spiritual privileges did not make them immune to temptations to idolatry and the immorality associated with it.

A way out when tempted (10:11-13). Human nature is always vulnerable to temptations. But God is faithful in that with temptation He provides a "way out." God will help us deal with the temptation so we don't succumb. But never forget that we're not to place ourselves in situations where appeals to sinful human nature are strong!

"Faithful" (10:13). God remains committed to us. This, not the "knowledge" the Corinthians relied on, is the source of our security.

Background (10:14ff.). Dinner parties were the major way in which 1st-century people socialized. Typically a dinner party was dedicated to a pagan god or goddess. The Corinthian Christians debated whether it was right to

attend such a dinner party. The trouble was that participation in the feast symbolized eating at the pagan deities' table and thus implied coming under his or her protection. This issue is slightly different, though similar, to the question of whether one can eat meat purchased at a temple meat market.

Participation in the blood of Christ (10:14-22). The blood of Christ symbolizes His saving work, in which Christians participate through faith. Paul is blunt on this issue. A Christian cannot "participate" both in the idolatry of a pagan feast and the Christian community.

Resultant rulings (10:23-30). Paul sums up. (1) Don't take part in social events specifically dedicated to a pagan god or goddess. (2) Feel free to eat meat sold in the meat market, without making it an issue. (3) If you're at an unsaved friend's for dinner, don't ask where he got the meat. But if he makes an issue of it, refrain from meat for the sake of his conscience. This may assume the questioner is a believer. Or it may suggest an unsaved person is testing, or ridiculing, a person's commitment to Christ.

Chapter summary. Paul now turns to public worship. Some women in Corinth were so excited about participating in church meetings that they abandoned wearing their veils as a symbol of their new equality with men in Christ (11:2-16). Paul instructs them to "pray or prophesy" in church with heads covered, not uncovered as men do (vv. 2-10). Men and women are interdependent. No woman has to be like a man to have worth and value (vv. 11-16).

Also, some upper class Corinthians had turned celebration of the Lord's Supper into a dinner party and embarrassed their lower class brothers by serving them inferior or no food, or even not permitting them to come till supper was over. This despised the essential nature of the "church of God" (vv. 17-22). The Lord's Supper is a chaste, unadorned service of remembrance, proclaiming the Lord's death (vv. 23-26). Shifting the focus of this service from the body and blood of Christ is a terrible sin and led to God's judgment of many in Corinth by illness and even physical death (vv. 27-32). The Lord's Supper is holy, not an occasion to party! (vv. 33-34)

Key verse. 11:5: Women do pray and prophesy.

Personal application. Our worship services are to reflect spiritual realities, not our prejudices.

Key concepts. Image »p. 25. Church »pp. 794, 799. Sickness »pp. 412, 438.

INSIGHT

"**Head**" (11:3). The word's use does not imply superiority/inferiority, as Jesus is not inferior to the Father. Paul's point is that this is a divine order in creation which is right and good.

Head covering (11:5). There is great debate about the nature of the "veil" or "head covering." Information currently available doesn't make clear what head covering implied in 1st-century society. But in not covering their heads, women were asserting their equality with men by symbolically adopting a culturally defined male prerogative.

Image and glory (11:7-9). God's creation of Adam was "very good," for the first man was made in the image of God, to reflect glory on the Lord. The fact that God is head of the man exalts man rather than demeans him! Similarly Eve was created to be the glory of Adam. This creation relationship does not make women inferior, but exalts women. Women are not only fully human, having come from (*ex*) man, but also for man in the sense that Adam was created for God. To glorify God there is nothing more a man or woman can do than to be what he and she were created to be.

A sign of authority (11:10). The covered head is not a sign of a man's authority over women, but of the authority of a woman to "prophesy and pray" in church as a woman. You don't have to be male to participate fully in the life of Christ's church.

The Lord's Supper (11:23-26). The simple, solemn service is conducted "in remembrance" of Jesus' death. The phrase reflects the vital O.T. concept of *zikkaron*, "memorial." This might be a memorial festival, a place, or an object intended to remind Israel of God's acts for them in the past. By contact with the *zikkaron* the living sensed their participation with past generations in God's historic acts. Thus the Lord's Supper is a unique, holy occasion for the gathered church to sense the participation of every member with Jesus in His death. In the Lord's Supper we are present at the Cross and testify to it.

Sickness and sin. Some Corinthians totally missed the significance of the Lord's Supper. Rather than making it a time of shared participation in the holy, they made it an occasion for dinner parties, like those dedicated to the pagan deities with which they were familiar. Lest God judge us, let us approach the Lord's Supper with awe and proper self-examination.

Chapter summary. Paul turns to another problem. The Corinthians misunderstood spirituality. They associated it with the more spectacular spiritual gifts (12:1-3). In this chapter Paul gives a basic explanation of spiritual gifts (vv. 4-11) and emphasizes that they are to be exercised in the context of the church as a single, living organism (vv. 12-13).

In the body every gift is essential (vv. 14-24). Division in the body based on the supposed superiority of one gift over another—like any divisive issue—affects the whole body's growth and health (vv. 25-27). Though all have different gifts, each believer is equally a gifted member of the body of Christ (vv. 28-31).

Key verse. 12:7: Each is gifted.

Personal application. Our gifts are to enable us to serve others, not feel superior.

Key concepts. Church »pp. 768, 794. Spirituality »p. 792.

INSIGHT

Background (12:1-3). In the ancient world ecstatic utterance was viewed as a sign of possession by the gods. Epilepsy was a "divine disease" and the mutterings of drugged priestesses at such Oracles as that of Delphi were assumed to convey messages from the gods. Paul refers to this in noting that when pagans and ignorant, "you were influenced and led astray by dumb idols."

The problem was that this attitude toward the ecstatic was carried over by converts to Christianity. As a result ecstatic utterances, such as tongues, was viewed by many in Corinth as evidence of intimate contact with God. Those with this gift were "more spiritual." And even when their utterances contradicted basic Christian truth, some were awed enough to believe them. It is against this cultural background that Paul develops teaching on true spirituality, spiritual gifts, and the proper exercise of the gift of tongues.

Now concerning (12:1). The Gk. text does not contain "gifts." It is better to read the verse without it and see these chapters as an exposition on "the spiritual."

Spiritual gifts (12:4-7). These verses contain key teaching on spiritual gifts. (1) There are different kinds. (2) Each comes from the Holy Spirit. (3) No gift indicates a person has "more of" the Spirit than another, for "the same God works all of them in all men." (4) Each person has a spiritual gift. (5) These are distributed sovereignly by the Spirit (cf. v. 11). (6) They function within the church for the "common good" of the body.

Lists of gifts (12:7-10). These verses and

Rom. 12:6-8 list spiritual gifts. Typically N.T. lists begin with the more important and move to the less important. In view of the purpose of gifts—to benefit the body—it is easy to see why messages of wisdom and of knowledge (listed first) are more important than tongues and interpretations of tongues (listed last).

It is likely that these lists of spiritual gifts are representative rather than exhaustive. Any way in which God enables us to contribute to the spiritual life and growth of other believers requires the exercise of a spiritual gift. To understand your gift, serve others and see how God uses you in their lives.

"All baptized by one Spirit" (12:13). This key verse defines biblically "baptism of the Spirit." It is not a post-salvation coming of the Spirit on believers to enable them to speak in tongues. It is that work of the Spirit by which He unites all Christians to the living body of Christ. The word "all" here is key, for if there is no believer who is not so baptized this work of the Spirit must take place at conversion.

The body of Christ (12:12ff.). This is one of three major images used to define what the church is. The church is a living organism, in which each member makes a necessary contribution to the health of the whole. The context of "body" in this passage emphasizes the necessity of close, loving interpersonal relationships as a necessary condition for spiritual gifts to function and the church to be what it is, the body of Christ.

Desire the greater gifts (12:31). The encouragement is directed to the church, not individuals, to stop emphasizing less significant gifts.

Chapter summary. Paul now shifts his focus from gifts to the "most excellent way" (12:31b) to measure and express spirituality. That way is love, a quality so vital that without it not even the most significant of spiritual gifts can enrich the one who possesses them (13:1-3). And "love" is no abstract, philosophical notion. It is practical, observable, expressing itself in everyday actions and attitudes (vv. 4-7). Even the most signficant of spiritual gifts remain limited, their exercise distorted by our own limitations and imperfections (vv. 8-12). Despite this, we can count on faith, hope, and love. But the greatest of the qualities which are foundational in Christian experience is love (v. 13).

It is love that is the measure of a person. It is love that is the measure of true spirituality, of true closeness in one's relationship with the Lord.

Key verse. 13:2: Love is essential.

Personal application. Don't be overly concerned about what your gift is. Concentrate on how you can love others.

Key concepts. Tongues »pp. 709, 770. Prophecy »p. 131. Faith »pp. 35, 872. Love »pp. 126, 661, 690. Hope »p. 465.

INSIGHT

"I am nothing . . . I gain nothing" (13:1-3). Even the "greater gifts" Paul mentions in chap. 12 are no indication of a person's spirituality. One may have outstanding gifts and spiritually be "nothing."

The thought is made dramatically clear in the image of "sounding brass" (KJV, not "resounding gong," v. 1). Large, empty brass vessels were used in the theater at Corinth to amplify the voices of actors. Sound came from them, but they themselves were empty. Without love, however great our gifts, we are spiritually empty and void. We are "nothing" indeed! How foolish we Christians are, then, to confuse giftedness with true spirituality.

"Love" (13:4-7). Paul here gives us a "behavioral definition" of love. He tells us how love behaves in relationships with others. This enables us not only to understand the nature of love, but also gives us criteria by which we can evaluate the spirituality of others. It's important not to misunderstand. Paul doesn't invite us to judge others. He wants to make sure that we realize who among us are the truly spiritual. If we understand this, we will know who to model and who in the fellowship is truly qualified for leadership.

How important this instruction was for the "worldly" Corinthians. How important it is for us, for our generation tends to exalt the gifted and elect the successful, ignoring whether or not their love indicates true spirituality.

Illustration. *First-century mirrors had polished metal surfaces. The best of them distorted the image of the person looking into them, offering only a "poor reflection" of reality. Similarly the gifts of prophecy, tongues, and knowledge, as vital as they may be, can offer only an imperfect image of the spiritual realities they represent. Let's appreciate spiritual gifts and their contributions. But remember that our religion is anchored in faith, hope, and love. And that "the greatest of these is love" (1 Cor. 13:13).*

Prophecy, tongues to cease? Many argue on the basis of the grammar of v. 9 that these spiritual gifts were no longer to be exercised after the end of the apostolic era. What is important is that even then, v. 13, love was of greater significance!

Chapter summary. Paul returns to gifts and points out the limitations of tongues. Gifts like prophecy which edify (spiritually build up) the church are more important than tongues (14:1-12), as intelligible speech is more meaningful than unintelligible (vv. 13-19). Unbelievers may be impressed by ecstatic speech. But if they attend a church meeting where everyone speaks in tongues they will conclude "that you are out of your mind." But if they hear God's Word in normal speech, they will be convicted and converted (vv. 20-25).

Paul now describes an "ideal" first-century house church meeting. Everyone has something to contribute. No one speaks in a tongue unless someone with the gift of interpretation is present. Two or three "preach" and their message is carefully weighed (vv. 26-32). In weighing the prophet's message, women remain silent (vv. 33-35). Paul sums up. Tongues must not be forbidden. But exercise of this gift is to be regulated, as the whole service is to be (vv. 36-40).

Key verse. 14:36: All exercise their gifts in church.

Personal application. Don't condemn or misuse any spiritual gift.

INSIGHT

"Prophecy" (14:1). Some hold that "prophecy" here is "foretelling," the equivalent of modern preaching. Yet the N.T. speaks of prophets who gave revelations, not simply interpreted Scripture (cf. Acts 11:27-30; 13:1-3; 21:10-11). Later epistles warn of false prophets (2 Peter 2:1; 1 John 4:1) and indicate each prophetic message must be carefully evaluated. While much debated, the prophet of 1 Cor. 14 may be either a foreteller or may bring a special and unique message from God.

Tongues (14:2). Some make a distinction between "tongues" in this epistle and "tongues" reported in Acts. There the hearers understood what was said, here the listener cannot understand without an interpreter (cf. 14:9). But because 1 Cor. is the *only* epistle where tongues are mentioned, no firm conclusion can be drawn.

Tongues for unbelievers? (14:22-25) The intent of these verses is widely debated. If we paraphrase, "Unbelievers see tongues as a sign, but believers are not to," the confusion is resolved.

This also clears up Paul's instruction. Even though unbelievers may see tongues as a sign, they need to hear the Gospel in ordinary speech to be convicted of sin and acknowledge God's presence with His own.

"When you come together" (14:26-30). This is the only real description of what happened during the meeting of a local body of believers in the 1st century. Everyone seems free to participate and make his or her own contribution.

Tongues are spoken when an interpreter is present. Those with the gift of prophecy used it to instruct and encourage. This picture of a church meeting is notable for its difference from our church assemblies, where only a few minister and the majority remain silent observers. If we take Paul's teaching on spiritual gifts seriously, we will meet in smaller groups at some time during the week where we can each minister and grow.

Women remain silent (14:33b-36). The *Expository Dictionary of Bible Words* (Zondervan, 1985) says, "This blunt instruction has been interpreted: (1) To decisively rule out female participation. (2) To be added by someone other than Paul. (3) To be an example of Paul's inconsistency and antifeminine view. (4) To contradict Paul's statement in 1 Cor. 11. (5) To deal with some specific problem in Corinth."

In 1 Cor. 14:26-40 Paul is dealing not only with disorderly meetings but also with the question of prophetic revelation (v. 30). Paul has indicated "two or three prophets should speak and the others weigh carefully what is said" (v. 29). The verb rendered "weigh" is *diakrino* ("judge, discern"). Thus it is best to take this instruction to indicate women are to remain silent during this process. This is in harmony with 1 Tim. 2, which implies "authoritative teaching" is the role of male church elders.

The spirits of the prophets (14:32). God doesn't override human control and "make" a person jump up and interrupt.

Chapter summary. The last problem Paul deals with is the confusion of the Corinthians over the doctrine of resurrection. This was particularly confusing to the pagan, for resurrection was a concept totally foreign to Greek thought (cf. Acts 17:16ff.). First Paul establishes the resurrection of Jesus as a historic fact (15:1-11). He then stresses the centrality of resurrection in Christian faith (vv. 12-18), linking it to the culmination of God's plan to establish God's rule through Christ over all things (vv. 19-29). If there were no resurrection there would be no reason for believers to make choices that lead to suffering here and now! (vv. 30-34)

Outline
Place
Finder

UNITY
DISCIPLINE
DIVORCE
DOCTRINE
WORSHIP
TONGUES
RESURRECTION
ENCOURAGE

As to how the dead are raised, there are at best analogies. As a seed bursts into new and transformed life, so will we, trading our natural, sinful bodies for imperishable bodies that shine with the beauty of God Himself (vv. 35-49). Every believer will be transformed, and then, death and sin left far behind, we will experience the victory won for us by our Lord Jesus Christ (vv. 50-58).

Key verse. 15:54: We know what lies ahead!

Personal application. Strive now for a better resurrection.

Key concepts. Resurrection »pp. 522, 737, 808. Death »p. 741. Law »pp. 120, 145, 606, 743. Sin »pp. 34, 741.

INSIGHT

Resurrection. Paul deals with several issues and establishes several key truths. First, the resurrection of Jesus was a historic, not "spiritual" or "mythic" event. Second, resurrection is a critical element in God's eternal plan to establish His kingdom rule. Third, our resurrection involves a transformation from mortality to immortality, from sinner to sinless, from Adamlikeness to Christlikeness. Fourth, the hope of resurrection gives our life on earth new focus and meaning. We dedicate ourselves to live for God, confident that our "labor in the Lord is not in vain" (15:58).

Believe in vain? (15:2) "Vain" is *eike*, and focuses on result or outcome. Thus to believe "in vain" means Christian faith apart from resurrection means to believe without prospect of any reward.

Death to be destroyed (15:26). The word is *katargeo*, used in theologically significant passages with the meaning of "abolish" or "nullify." Paul's point is that death, which has exercised such power over the human race, will become totally irrelevant. Our destiny is life and immortality in our Lord.

"Baptized for the dead" (15:29). Paul does not endorse the practice. He simply points out that it is inconsistent for the Corinthians to undergo baptism as a surrogate for someone who is dead if they really do not believe in resurrection.

Ignorant of God (15:34). The behavior of the Corinthians as well as their confusion about basic Christian truths shows a lack of knowledge, not a lack of salvation.

Let's not judge others on what they do not yet understand. Faith in Christ is what counts. But faith is supposed to be a foundation for growth, not an excuse to remain ignorant.

Death, sin, and the law (15:56). This is a key passage to help us understand the relationship between these critical biblical concepts. The law is the "power of sin" in the sense taught in Rom. 7:1-13: God's Word as law energizes man's sin nature to produce acts of sin. And sin is "the sting of death" in that man's sin nature is dead to God, but threatens us with eternal separation from God. What Christ brings us in His resurrection, and promises will be fully ours when our own resurrection comes, is not death, sin, and law, but life, righteousness, and the Spirit of God.

"Give yourselves fully" (15:58). We stand firm by committing ourselves to actively serve God. How wonderful to know that no labor performed in His strength and for His glory will ever be in vain.

Chapter summary. Paul concludes his first letter to the Corinthians with words of encouragement. Paul encourages the Corinthians to regularly set aside money for the contribution they intend to make to the struggling Galatian churches (16:1-4). He expresses his earnest desire to visit them and his confidence in his representative, Timothy (vv. 5-11). He mentions Apollos and commends other faithful Christians by name (vv. 12-18). Finally he sends on the "warm greetings" of Priscilla and Aquila, ending his letter with "my love to all of you in Christ Jesus" (vv. 19-24).

Key verse. 16:24: Yes, confrontation is love!

Personal application. There is no excuse for abandoning love when it's necessary to correct or rebuke others.

Key concepts. Giving »p. 73, 103, 781. Accept »p. 750. Submission »pp. 867, 880. House church »p. 752.

INSIGHT

The collection (16:1-4). This is a key paragraph on N.T. giving: (1) The collection was "for God's people." Giving typically was to relieve believers in parts of the empire that were suffering from famine or some other natural disaster. (2) A collection was taken the first day of every week (Sunday), when Christians met. Justin Martyr, in the 2nd century, reports this practice was followed in the churches. (3) Giving was "in keeping with income." Those with more could give more, but all were to share in the grace of giving. (4) The exhortation reflects an early importance placed on organized and regular giving.

"Timothy" (16:10). This younger protégé of Paul was often sent on special missions. This practice is reflected in Paul's "pastoral letters" to Timothy and Titus, which give these younger leaders instructions on how to carry out such ministries.

"Apollos" (16:12). Apollos was not a convert of Paul's, but of Priscilla and Aquila while the two were living in Corinth (cf. Acts 18:18-28). A gifted orator, Apollos made a great impression on the Corinthians and one of the factions in that church claimed him as mentor (1 Cor. 1-4). Paul's reference to Apollos suggests they were friends. Apollos was not a subordinate of Paul's, but made his own decisions about where he was called to minister. Paul respected this freedom of his coworker to be responsible to God rather than to the apostle.

"Submit to such" (16:15-16). How strange that many Christians still show great awe of those who exploit them and little respect for those dedicated to serve them. Paul urges the Corinthians to be responsive to servant leadership, rather than to the arrogant and proud.

2 Corinthians

Paul's first letter to the Corinthians was blunt and, to some, may have seemed harsh. It's clear from the document we call 2 Corinthians that, while Paul's command that the church discipline the immoral brother was obeyed, a core of hostility to the founding apostle exists. From Paul's description of his antagonists in chapters 10–13, it appears that "false apostles" from outside have exploited the existing hostility and led a serious anti-Paul rebellion.

Scholars actively debate just what contacts Paul had with Corinth between his first and this "second" epistle. Most suppose Paul visited the church after his first letter and later wrote a "severe letter" carried to Corinth by Titus (2 Cor. 2:3-4, 9; 7:8, 12). Titus reported the church's positive response (2 Cor. 7:5-16). But later Paul heard of new, even more serious problems and so wrote this letter, 2 Corinthians, before he finally visited the church (cf. Acts 20:2-3).

Second Corinthians contains a movingly personal defense by Paul of his apostleship and ministry (1–7), instructions that define the New Testament theology of giving (8–9), and a powerful affirmation of his apostolic authority (10–13). The letter is valuable not only for its insight into Paul's heart, but also as a guide to anyone who seeks to serve others in a godly, loving way.

THEOLOGICAL OUTLINE OF 2 CORINTHIANS

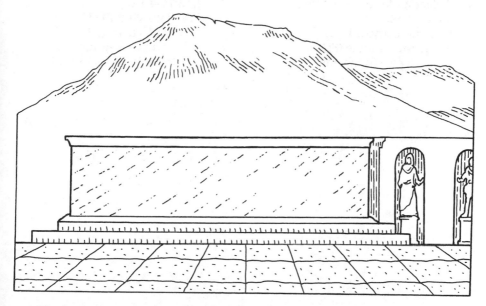

The "Judgment Seat" in Corinth. *The raised platform was used for public proclamation, announcing winners of athletic games, commendations, and judicial sentences. Christians will appear before the "judgment seat" (bema) of Christ (2 Cor. 5:10).*

CONTENT OUTLINE OF 2 CORINTHIANS

Outline
Place
Finder

MINISTRY
GIVING
AUTHORITY

Chapter summary. Paul's vulnerability and openness are stunning, especially in view of the fact that he writes to a church where many openly oppose him. After a brief salutation (1:1-2), Paul praises God for providing comfort (vv. 3-7). The great apostle freely shares moments when he has felt desperate and depressed (1:8-11). Paul also carefully explains the reasons for a delay in making a planned visit to Corinth (1:12–2:4). One very positive consequence of Paul's first letter to the church is the repentance of the brother there who was engaging in immorality (1 Cor. 5:1-8). The Corinthians had followed Paul's instructions and put the sinner out of the fellowship. Now Paul urges them to show compassion and welcome him back (2:5-11). With continuing humility Paul expresses again his own sense of personal inadequacy, for he is the agent of a Gospel with life and death impact (vv. 12-16). How could Paul trivialize such a Gospel by peddling God's Word for profit, or failing to be utterly honest and sincere? (v. 17)

Key verse. 1:4: Why be vulnerable?

Personal application. What really qualifies us to help others is hurting ourselves and being comforted by God.

Key concepts. Apostle »p. 635. Salvation »p. 732. Forgive »p. 863.

INSIGHT

Comfort (1:3). Nine of 17 N.T. occurrences of *parakaleo/paraklesis* are found in 2 Cor. 1:3-7, where they have the meaning of comfort and encouragement. Paul's point is that our own sufferings enable us to identify with those who suffer—and enable them to identify with us. Then they will sense the reality of the comfort we have received from God and find their own comfort in Him.

The principle is important. Ministry requires vulnerability. Our human frailties, which make us susceptible to suffering, at the same time enable us to display God's comforting love. Only when we show our weaknesses can we also reveal the strength of our Lord.

Despair (1:8-11). It's only human when attacked to defend by pointing to our strengths. Instead, Paul freely shares his weaknesses! It is amazing to see the apostle speak of being under pressure "beyond our ability to endure." Why does Paul take this tack? Paul knows that he cannot force others to respond to his authority. He must rely on God to cause a change of heart.

Ministry which leads to a change of heart requires us to be open and utterly honest and rely wholly on God to do His transforming work.

"Your prayers" (1:11). The "only human" response when others resist our authority is to try to prove we are so important that the others need us. Paul continues to model God's approach to ministry by letting the Corinthians know that they are so important that he has a need for their prayers. How different spiritual leadership is from "only human" ways!

Untrustworthy (1:12–2:4). Paul had changed his plans for a trip which would have brought him to Corinth. His enemies seized on this change to charge that Paul couldn't be trusted—and added that Paul was just a tyrant, who cared nothing for those he ruled so autocratically.

This charge deeply wounded the apostle. How could a person committed to serve God, one of whose essential qualities is faithfulness, act out of mere fickleness? (1:17-22) Paul changed his plans because a visit at that time would have been painful to both the intransigent Corinthians and to him.

How foolish it is for us to ascribe the worst of reasons to the actions of others. And how important for us to communicate our motives and reasons for the actions we ourselves take.

The Gospel's aroma (2:14-17). The *Expository Dictionary of Bible Words* (Zondervan, 1985) says, "Just as O.T. sacrifices for sin made on O.T. altars sent out an aroma . . . so Paul's ministry and life . . . wafts the unique fragrance of the knowledge of God among mankind. The odor attracts some and repels others. One's response makes the difference between life and death."

Chapter summary. Paul now introduces the concept which is foundational to his whole concept of ministry: the "New Covenant." Paul needs no letters of recommendation to demonstrate his apostolic call. The transformation God has worked within the Corinthians themselves makes them living letters, proof of the new covenant quality of Paul's service (3:1-6). Paul then contrasts new and old covenant ministry (vv. 7-18). The old covenant administered by Moses offered no inner transformation. This is illustrated by Moses himself, for after leaving God's presence he put a veil over his face so the people would not see the splendor, which God's presence had imparted, fade away. In contrast, because God's Spirit now lives within the believer a process of transformation is taking place. That transformation, marked by increasingly clear reflection through the believer's life of the splendor of Christ Himself, is the mark of New Covenant ministry.

Key verse. 3:18: The process is taking place.

Personal application. Be open and let others see what God is doing to transform you.

Key concepts. New Covenant »pp. 35, 466.

INSIGHT

Letters of recommendation (3:1-3). Traveling teachers in the early church typically carried letters introducing them (cf. Acts 18:27). Paul's opponents apparently attacked Paul's credibility by asking, "Where are his letters?"

Letters from Christ (3:3). Every true believer is an "open letter" from Christ, because his or her life will show God's work within his or her personality. Since Paul won many of the Corinthians to Christ, they themselves are "letters" that attest his ministry, competence, and call.

Old vs. New Covenant (7–11). Paul knows there is no way O.T. Law can bring righteousness. But the Gospel, fulfilling God's promise through Jeremiah of a New Covenant, can bring righteousness (3:9).

Because Law came from God it was glorious, even though Law was temporary as well as inadequate. But the New Covenant is far more splendid!

Our hope (3:12). Our hope is that we will experience a progressive transformation as the New Covenant does "bring righteousness" into our lives. This makes us "very bold." We no longer have to pretend we're perfect. We can be honest with others. They will see our flaws and failures, but because God is at work in us, they will also see the face of Jesus as He works His changes within. It is the hope, the certain expectation, that God is changing us from within, that frees us to be real.

"Their minds were made dull" (3:12-15). The veil Moses wore to hide the radiance which

shone from his face, after private moments with God (Ex. 34:29-35), worked both ways. It hid Moses' face. But it also concealed vital truths about relationship with God.

The danger of concealing ourselves from others is that in the process we will keep them ignorant about the God who is at work in us. Symbolically, Paul says, that veil still lies over the O.T., concealing its real meaning from those who follow Moses.

Transformation (3:18). God is committed to make those who believe in Jesus like Jesus. This is taught often in the N.T. (cf. Rom. 8:29; 1 Cor. 15:49-54; Col. 3:10; 1 John 3:2). The ultimate fulfillment of this commitment awaits our resurrection. But as this verse points out, the Holy Spirit even now is at work within us, energizing a gradual process directed toward making our moral characters more like the Lord. Through this gradual but real change in us others today see Jesus' face.

The Holy Spirit (3:17, 19). The Holy Spirit has a variety of ministries to believers. Some are named: baptism, sealing, filling, distributing spiritual gifts. He leads believers, He empowers them for holy living, and here we see that He works a progressive moral transformation as we are obedient and responsive to the Lord. That transformation is displayed in character and personality, producing the fruit of love, joy, peace, patience, kindness, goodness, faithfulness, gentleness, and self-control (Gal. 5:22-23).

Chapter summary. God's New Covenant infuses the Gospel with dynamic, transforming power (2 Cor. 3). Therefore, Paul neither loses heart nor relies on anything other than light shed by the Gospel message itself (4:1-6). Although he feels himself little more than a clay vessel, weak and vulnerable, that vessel bears God's greatest treasure (vv. 7-12). Whatever the difficulties, whatever the setbacks, whatever the troubles experienced in ministry, Paul believes. Knowing God in Christ, he is confident in not only his own eternal destiny but also the destiny of the Corinthian believers (vv. 13-15). With his eyes fixed on eternal truths which can be experienced but not seen, rather than on the temporary setbacks and momentary troubles that mark life on earth, Paul simply does not—he *will not*—lose heart (vv. 16-18).

Outline
Place
Finder

MINISTRY
GIVING
AUTHORITY

Key verse. 4:7: His, not ours.

Personal application. Circumstances change. God does not.

Key concepts. Gospel »p. 737. Satan »pp. 500–501, 655. Light »p. 685. Eternal »p. 799. Death »p. 741.

INSIGHT

"Setting forth the truth plainly" (4:1-2). Don't hesitate to speak out if you're not as skilled or as clever or as knowledgeable as others. It is the message, not the messenger, that's the key.

The Gospel veiled (4:3-4). Don't blame yourself if others reject a "plain" presentation of the Gospel. Satan has "blinded the minds" of unbelievers. We're not told how. But the title "god of this age" implies that the citizens of this age willingly submit to and follow Satan's ways.

"This age" (4:4). This temporal phrase has several different forms (e.g., "this present age" Titus 2:12, "the present evil age" Gal. 1:4). This age is far from perfect; evil spiritual forces are arrayed against the Gospel. But even in the present darkness, God's Gospel light shines.

Subject to death (4:7-12). The life of one ministering in the present evil age isn't easy. A majority are blind to the Gospel, believers are immature and antagonistic, and the ministering life is one of pain, pressure, and suffering.

Eyes fixed on the eternal (4:16). What enables Paul to minister so optimistically is his settled conviction that "what is seen" is "temporary." Is the Corinthian church shattered by disputes? Do some there seem to delight in making Paul's life miserable? Do they continue to approach issues without any spiritual insight? Yes. But this is temporary. Paul looks beyond this to the faithfulness of God and remains confident that God's Spirit *will* transform the immature and glorify Himself in even this carnal company.

Illustration: *Clay cooking vessels like those found in every 1st-century household kitchen. Clay vessels were the least valued by the woman of the house. They were easily broken and cheap to replace. In contrast, metal and glass vessels were expensive and most likely to be on display. Paul sees himself as a clay vessel. What is important is the ministry he has been given and the message he bears to the world. Paul doesn't want to be put on display, as if he or any other servant of God were what is important. Today too the Spirit within us and the Gospel we share deserve priority.*

Chapter summary. Life itself is among those "temporary" things which man can see (4:18). But the Gospel promises that beyond this life, eternal life awaits. The Spirit, whose transforming work we experience (3:18), is the down payment who guarantees our eventual deliverance (5:1-5). This gives Paul such confidence that he concentrates completely on pleasing God, sure that the quality of each person's work will be recognized at Christ's "judgment seat" (vv. 6-10; see illustration, p. 774).

Paul, sure that the unseen is real, relies on the love for Christ that God plants in the believer's heart on conversion. He does not become discouraged by others' slow spiritual progress, convinced that Christ died to so change believers that they will live for Him rather than for themselves (vv. 11-15). Paul thus will not measure anyone by his or her behavior, as the world evaluates. He will count on the unseen work of God that makes believers new creations. And Paul, as God's ambassador, will continue to do his own reconciling work as our Lord did His: by appealing, not by counting the Corinthians many sins and not by holding those sins against them (vv. 16-20). God dealt with our sins in Christ in order to make us righteous. Christ's sacrifice was not in vain, and God's work will not fail! (v. 21)

Key verse. 5:17: We are not what we seem.

Personal application. Follow Paul's example. Don't be discouraged. Just love the immature to spiritual maturity.

Key concepts. Love »pp. 126, 691. Righteousness »p. 808.

INSIGHT

"A building from God" (5:1, 4). Some take this to indicate believers will have a temporary body until we receive our resurrection bodies.

"Persuade" (5:11). Paul rejects the use of force or manipulation in favor of persuasion. Paul's goal is to encourage a free, spontaneous commitment to the Lord by the resisting Corinthians. Many means can be used to force others to conform to our wishes. But only seeking to persuade rather than coerce will we help them choose to follow Jesus.

"Take pride in what is seen" (5:12). Paul's competitors were concerned about appearances. Paul isn't. He cares about what is in the heart. In consequence, the approach he takes to ministry seems crazy to his critics. It isn't. And he wants the Corinthians, and us, to under-stand.

"Christ's love compels" (5:14). Only love for the Lord will move anyone to truly follow Him.

"He died for all" (5:15). Christ's work is finished, and it was not futile. Paul is convinced God's purpose of transforming the Corinthians will be accomplished, despite all the present evidence of their spiritual immaturity.

Christ, from a worldly point of view (5:16).

Looked at in this way, Christ was an utter failure: a rejected religious reformer, who suffered a criminal's death. Yet the eyes of faith see Him in resurrection glory and worship Him as God. Since our way of looking at Christ is so radical, Paul says we need to see Christians as new creations. They may appear utter failures, contentious and rebellious, from a worldly viewpoint. Paul looks beyond this. He sees God's work within, is convinced that they *will* change, and so is filled with hope.

Reconciliation (5:16-20). *Katalasso* means to restore to harmony. God has done everything needed in Christ to bring us into harmony with Him (positionally). But individual believers must choose to bring daily life and attitude into harmony (experientially). Paul's mission is to persuade believers to make that choice for themselves. Paul does this by not counting their sins and not holding their sins against them. Paul does it by continuing to forgive and love, by continuing to express confidence, and by continuing to remind the Corinthians that in Christ every believer is called to "become the righteousness of God."

Chapter summary. Verses 1 and 2 belong with chapter 5. God's grace has made believers new creations, with the potential to live truly righteous lives. That wonderful day when human beings can at last experience such a salvation is now. How tragic if the Corinthians' hardness made such grace of no practical, transforming value to them at all (6:1-2).

Paul has done all he could, as God's servant, to help them along (vv. 3-4). They should trust him, for he has suffered physical (vv. 5-6) and emotional abuse (vv. 7-8) and constant misunderstanding (vv. 9-10). Yet Paul has openly shared the love in his heart with the Corinthians—and how he yearns for them to respond with similar love to him (vv. 11-13).

He then warns about being yoked with unbelievers (6:14–7:1).

Outline
Place
Finder

MINISTRY
GIVING
AUTHORITY

Key verses. 6:12-13: Love must be given.

Personal application. Keep on loving even when love is not returned.

INSIGHT

Unequally yoked (6:14–7:1). Old Testament Law forbade yoking a donkey and an ox as a work team (Deut. 22:10). This image is behind Paul's urgent appeal not to be "unequally yoked" with unbelievers.

Commentators agree these verses lie outside the flow of Paul's argument. Yet they do bear directly on present righteousness, a theme that dominates chap. 5. The Corinthians are not to avoid all contact with the unsaved (1 Cor. 5:9-10). But they are to avoid "partnerships," which involve compromise of Christian standards, practices, or goals. Christianity and secular/pagan values are not compatible. Paul quotes Isa. 52:11 and Ezek. 20:34, 41 as guidelines. Don't get tangled up with pagans. Separate from them and their ways, and seek the approval of God.

Receive God's grace (6:1). When we receive Christ we receive His transforming grace. That grace surrounds us and wells up within us. Paul reminds us that God's grace has been given to us for a transforming purpose. But as the Corinthians' experience shows, believers can resist grace. Unless we respond to God in willing obedience we will experience no present transformation. God doesn't work in us against our will.

"Now is the time" (6:2). Isaiah 49:7 is addressed to God's Suffering Servant, promising to vindicate this One whom men rejected and despised. Jesus is the Servant. We show that His sacrifice had a redeeming purpose by responding to God's grace and living holy lives today.

Contrasting perspectives (6:8-10). In chap. 5 Paul called on us to stop looking at things from a "worldly point of view." Here he sets up a series of contrasts. The carnal (worldly) Chris-

tian and Paul's opponents may see him as an imposter, whom they have unmasked. They may dismiss him as poor, sorrowful, broke, and useless. But from God's viewpoint Paul, who has proven his servanthood by his willingness to suffer hardship, is genuine, vitally alive, full of joy, with access to the spiritual resources that make others rich, and thus "possessing everything."

How important to avoid superficial judgments about others. And about what is truly valuable in life.

"A fair exchange" (6:11-13). When you love, you deserve to be loved in return. But Paul shows us that sometimes we have to keep on loving a long time before others reciprocate.

Outline
Place
Finder

MINISTRY
GIVING
AUTHORITY

Chapter summary. Paul again expresses his love for the Corinthians and his confidence in them. Such "great confidence in you" may seem strange in view of the conflicts that erupted so often in Corinth. But it is based on Paul's conviction that God will surely perform His transforming work in the believers there (7:2-4; cf. 5:14-17).

Now comes word of what seems to be a breakthrough, perhaps delivered even as Paul is writing this letter. Titus returns from a visit to Corinth to report that many there did care and were responding to the apostle's appeals (vv. 5-7). Paul mentions a letter which "caused you sorrow." This missive, known to scholars as Paul's "severe letter," has not been preserved. But it clearly had an impact on many in the busy trade center of Corinth (vv. 8-13). Paul was also delighted at the report by Titus of his warm reception. So at this point in his letter Paul seems relieved, and all in Corinth seems on the mend (vv. 14-16).

Key verse. 7:9: Good grief!

Personal application. Don't hesitate to correct someone you love just because it's unpleasant for you—or for him/her.

Key concept. Joy »p. 803.

INSIGHT

Background. This conclusion to the first part of 2 Cor. and Paul's emphasis on his authority as an apostle in chapters 10–13 has led some to believe that after Titus' report, others from Corinth told Paul of renewed resistance, stimulated by "false apostles" who vigorously attacked Paul's authority. This may or may not be the case, as there were always some in Corinth who were active supporters of the apostle. The positive response may have come from them, while other splinter groups continued to attack Paul's credibility.

"Great pride" (7:4). Here pride is a positive emotion, an almost parentlike joy in the accomplishment of a much loved offspring. If we're going to be proud, let's follow Paul's example and be proud of others' spiritual progress.

"Sorrow" (7:7). The Gk. word used here is *lypeo*, which indicates an experience of great stress, which brings physical and/or emotional pain. Paul suggests in vv. 8-11 that we can react in one of two ways to sorrow. We can let it produce a change of heart and make us more sensitive spiritually. Or we can respond with resentment and self-pity. In the latter case, sorrow is turned inward and hardens us to the Lord. What makes our sorrow godly or worldly is what we do with it!

"My letter" (7:8). Most believe Paul is referring to a lost epistle, sent to Corinth after the book we know as 1 Cor. was written. However, it is possible, despite the gentleness we sense in 1 Cor., that it seemed harsh to the Corinthians and that it is the letter Paul mentions here.

"Repentance" (7:10). In the O.T. the Heb. word that parallels the N.T. meaning is *sub*. In 164 of its over 1,000 appearances it is used of man's covenant relationship with God and indicates a distinct turning, either from evil to God, or from God to idols. Similarly the N.T. *metanoeo* indicates a change of commitments that is expressed as a change both of mind and attitude that issues in an appropriate change of behavior. As John the Baptist insisted, one must "produce fruit in keeping with repentance" (Matt. 3:8).

In some passages "repentance" is the functional equivalence of conversion and initial turning to God. Here "repent" is a change of mind about the sins and worldly ways which Paul has confronted concerning the church of Corinth. And a change of heart toward the apostle himself.

Proved yourself innocent (7:11). The Gk. word used here is curious, for *hagnos'* basic meaning is "to be free of ceremonial defilement." The most likely meaning is that those who had responded so positively to Titus had now put themselves right and were purified of any previous guilt.

Outline
Place
Finder

MINISTRY
GIVING
AUTHORITY

Chapter summary. Paul now gives instructions concerning a collection being taken up for Jerusalem Christians. In doing so he lays out a total philosophy of New Testament giving which replaces the Old Testament principle of the tithe.

Paul urges believers to respond to the needs of others and give generously, but not because they have to give (8:1-8). In giving we follow Jesus, who gave everything for us. So it is appropriate to give what we can (vv. 9-12). Paul says that giving is sharing: It is meeting desperate needs so that our brothers and sisters can live and function as believers. And it is reciprocal, for we will receive when we are in need (vv. 13-15).

After a few organizational and procedural remarks (8:16–9:5) Paul returns to basic principles. Generous giving means a rich return, for no one can outgive God (vv. 6-9). We need not fear to give. God can and will supply what we need (vv. 10-12). And our giving brings God glory through prayers of thanks that will also bring the giver's name before the Lord (vv. 13-15).

Key verse. 9:7: Give with your heart.

Personal application. Let God guide you into the joy of giving.

Key concepts. Tithe »pp. 73, 103. Wealth »pp. 124–125, 838.

INSIGHT

Background. Three things help us understand N.T. teaching on giving. (1) Giving was primarily to meet the needs of Christians who were vulnerable because of famine or other life-threatening situations. (2) The word for giving Paul uses is *koinonia,* "fellowship," or "sharing." (3) Paul's vision of the church as the body of Christ shapes his teaching on giving.

The blood system carries the elements each cell needs to survive and function throughout the body. Money is nothing more or less than life-bringing blood. Giving is sharing it with those in such need they could not survive or function as the church without it. With these foundational concepts in mind, we can see a number of principles in these chapters intended to guide our giving as Christians.

Why no mention of a tithe? The O.T. tithe was a tax paid to God, the owner of the Promised Land, and was paid in crops produced by the land. It was used to support the nation's priests and worship system and also to help provide for the poor. The N.T. assumes a stewardship based on God's ownership of *all* we have and are. There is no "rent" to pay, no temple or priesthood to support. As Christians become aware of needs — whether globally or locally — they are to give out of love.

Principles of N.T. giving found in 2 Cor. 8–9. *Give yourself.* God wants us, not our money. When we have surrendered ourselves to the

Lord, our giving will fall into line (8:5).

Remember Christ's example. He gave everything to enrich our lives. The riches we have in Him are the true riches, not material wealth (8:9).

Give as you are able. Giving is not intended to impoverish the giver. It is not the size of the gift but willingness, measured against how much we have, that pleases God (8:10-12).

Give to meet needs. Giving is intended to provide for the basic needs of other Christians who are destitute. This principle reflects the vulnerability of the 1st-century world to famines and of the church to persecutions which often meant believers lost their means of livelihood. The principle, however, remains that giving was a response to needs and that our major concern still must be with human need rather than with "brick and mortar" issues. For the church of Jesus is people.

Giving is like sowing. Giving is an investment in our eternal future. The bigger the investment the greater the return (9:6).

Giving is personal. How much a person gives is between him or her and the Lord. God isn't interested in money given grudgingly (9:7).

Giving is an expression of trust. God is able to meet our needs and to provide much more, so we can give joyfully and without fear (9:8-11).

Giving stimulates prayer. The recipient praises God and prays for the giver (9:12-15).

Chapter summary. Paul returns to a defense of his ministry, this time against attacks made by "super-apostles" (11:5) who are also "false apostles" (11:13).

Paul tells those in Corinth who are still antagonistic that they are "looking only on the surface of things." His authority as an apostle is both spiritual in nature—and overwhelmingly powerful (10:1-11). Paul then indirectly ridicules the false apostles who have come to Corinth and boast of the superiority of their teaching and wisdom over that of others. Paul will speak only of his own ministry and work with no concern for that done "in another man's territory" (vv. 12-16). In fact, however, all boasting is illegitimate. God is the one who does the work (v. 17), and He is the source of the only commendation that counts (v. 18).

Key verse. 10:4: Count on God.

Personal application. We can do better than the other person, and still fall far short of what God wants. So don't compare.

Key concepts. World »p. 893. Obedience »p. 807.

INSIGHT

Christlike (10:1). "You can't win" is often all too true. Paul has been accused of being both "timid" and "bold," both too soft and too harsh. So he couches his appeal "by the meekness and gentleness of Christ." Meekness is not weakness, in Jesus, Paul, or a minister. And it is much preferred to the harsh "boldness" Paul will be forced to adopt unless "some people" in Corinth respond to his godly approach!

Gentle (10:1). The Gk. word is *erieikia*, a word that means thoughtful and considerate. It is used of a person who looks for a way to make peace in a calm, decent way.

Spiritual warfare (10:3-5). We can wage successful spiritual warfare only by abandoning worldly ways and attitudes. The Christian's approach is to introduce truth which the Spirit can use to reshape the other person's way of thinking and perceiving. The ways the worldly person "fights" is of no value in achieving this goal.

Captive thoughts (10:5). Some understand this as thwarting the plans (thoughts) of the enemy and so winning allegiance to Christ. Others take it to indicate the Christian's struggle to bring every purpose into harmony with Christ's will and ways, so that He might be victorious through us.

Punish disobedience (10:6). We can gain an insight into Paul's understanding of punishment and power in chaps. 12–13 of this book.

"Authority" (10:8). The last four chapters of this book provide significant insights into the nature of spiritual authority. Here, as in other passages, "authority" is *exousia*, freedom of action. What Paul is saying is that the spiritual leader's authority is given for a purpose: "building you up rather than pulling you down." This purpose also *limits* the leader's authority. Rather than a right to control behavior, the leader has only the right to influence response. Like his giving, the Christian's obedience must be "not reluctant or under compulsion" (cf. 9:7).

Classifying and comparing (10:12). Human beings often seek to establish their authority over others by arguing for their superiority over those with some claim to authority. How foolish! All real spiritual authority comes from God. You can't get it by measuring yourself by yourself or by others! You may fool some people. But you will still have no real authority at all.

Proper limits (10:13-15). Paul's enemies in Corinth were trying to establish their authority by comparing their "strengths" against Paul's "weaknesses." These false apostles had invaded his territory and disrupted the Corinthian church which Paul founded. But Paul shows up their folly by pointing out that anything significant that is accomplished is done by God. All boasting is to be in what God has done.

Chapter summary. Paul's deep concern for the Corinthians now moves him to do what he has just shown to be "foolish" — boast and present his own credentials (11:1-6). Unlike the "super-apostles" who boast in Corinth, Paul hasn't taken money from the Corinthians. Those who try to undermine his ministry for their own benefit are "false apostles," simply masquerading as "angels of light" (vv. 7-15).

Paul then turns back to himself and his own "boasting" (vv. 16-21a). Paul's credentials are impeccable. He, like the false apostles, is a Hebrew. He has proven his commitment as a servant of Christ by his sufferings and privations (vv. 21b-27) and by his own emotional burden for all the churches (vv. 28-29). Indeed, it is such "weaknesses" that Paul is most comfortable boasting about — for reasons he will explain in chapter 12 (vv. 30-33).

Key verse. 11:13: Looks good?

Personal application. Don't judge another by appearances, but by his or her faithful service over a span of years.

Key concepts. Apostle »p. 635. False Prophet »p. 462. Righteousness »p. 739.

Outline
Place
Finder

MINISTRY
GIVING
AUTHORITY

INSIGHT

Why trust Paul? The Corinthians had grounds to think paying attention to Paul was wise. First, his "godly jealousy," that proved his love (v. 2). Second, the propensity the Corinthians have shown to be led astray and listen to others who preach a different Jesus than Paul preaches (vv. 3-4). Third, the fact that Paul is "in the least inferior" to the "super-apostles" who are weaning the church away from its founding father (v. 5). These three remain a good test when someone calls on us to change allegiance.

Lowering one's self (11:7). One strange argument mounted against Paul was apparently that he didn't take money from the Corinthians. Certainly if he were an apostle, he would have a right to support. Since he didn't accept it, he must not be an apostle. Paul responds with irony. What a sin it must have been for Paul to lower himself to pursue manual labor, just so he could eat while he spent himself to lift the Corinthians beyond idolatry!

Masquerade (11:13-14). Satan came to Eve pretending he wanted to help. He didn't, but if he had been open about his intent to lead the first pair into sin, Eve would have rejected him out of hand. Of course Satan's minions try to look and sound righteous. What true believer would ever be led astray by them if they were open about their own wicked intent?

An apostle would accept prison, beatings,

Illustration: leather-working tools (11:7-10). *While Paul was in Corinth he supported himself by laboring as a leather-worker* (skenopoios; Acts 18:3). *The work is difficult, demanding, and had low status in class-conscious Corinth. Thus Paul did "lower himself" in the eyes of many and provided fuel to the charge of his critics who might ask scornfully, "Would an apostle do that?"*

shipwreck, danger, and starvation to minister to others. And as an apostle he would suffer deeply every setback experienced by those he loved in the churches he founded.

Again we're reminded how the little things human beings set such store in reflect what is truly important in life. How vital that we Christians not be drawn away by such illusions.

Outline
Place
Finder

MINISTRY
GIVING
AUTHORITY

Chapter summary. Paul explains that "weaknesses" are a source of boasting. After the apostle received a stunning revelation, being carried to heaven itself (12:1-6), Satan struck him with a "thorn in the flesh." Most think this was a serious and disfiguring illness. Paul prayed earnestly for its removal, but was told "no." Through this experience Paul learned "weakness" was a special call to rely on the Lord, who delights in showing His strength in weak people (vv. 7-9a). Now Paul gladly exposes his weaknesses, so his successes might be clearly seen to be achieved in Christ's power (vv. 9b-10).

Despite his so-called "weaknesses" Paul hardly needs to take a backseat to the "super-apostles" the Corinthians are enamoured with (vv. 11-13). Paul loves the church more (vv. 14-18). Even this humiliating "defense" is motivated only by fear that when Paul visits he will find them still hardened and immature (vv. 19-21).

Paul then concludes with a warning. Apostolic authority is real. Christ is speaking through Paul. If they do not respond to Christ, the Lord, who is "powerful among you," will Himself discipline them (13:1-4). The believers must examine themselves now. If not, when Paul comes, punishment will surely follow (vv. 5-10). His appeal uttered, the apostle says a very brief "good-bye" (vv. 11-14).

Key verse. 12:9: Real strength.

Personal application. Don't be afraid to be, or appear, weak.

Key concepts. Authority »p. 782. Apostle »p. 635.

INSIGHT

"Weaknesses" (12:5). In context, Paul is speaking primarily of anything that makes him appear weak in the eyes of those to whom he ministers. What Paul has learned is that when he appears weak in others' eyes he is actually strongest, for then God works through him most effectively.

What a message for us. Spiritual effectiveness doesn't depend on our abilities—or even on how others view us! It depends solely on our willingness to rely entirely on Christ for results.

Paul's thorn (12:7). There is much debate over just what chronic illness Paul had. One suggestion is that it was a most unattractive eye disease. The argument is supported by a reference at the end of Galatians to Paul adding a postscript to that epistle in "large letters."

Christians and good health (12:8-9). Some say healing is provided believers in Christ's crucifixion. But Paul was not healed. Some say God will answer any prayer if we only believe hard enough. Paul did not lack faith, but he was not healed. This and other N.T. passages such as Phil. 2:25-27 remind us that Christians can suffer poor health and other difficulties without the cause being either sin or a lack of faith. God had a purpose in permitting Paul's suffering.

How good to be confident of two things. When we suffer, God does have a good purpose in view. When we are weak we can expect God to show His power in and through us.

Authority exercised (13:1-4). Chapter 11 shows that spiritual authority lacks coercive powers. How then can Paul warn and punish? The answer is Paul does not. What happens is that Paul, as an apostle and spiritual leader, is in a special way Christ's spokesman. Christ is speaking through him. Refusal to respond to Paul is a refusal to respond to Jesus.

While Paul lacks power to punish, Jesus does not. He is "powerful among you." In his first letter Paul even noted that many of the Corinthians were ill and some had even died because they corrupted the Lord's Supper (1 Cor. 11:30). So Paul does not need any coercive power at all. He speaks for Jesus. Jesus will do the disciplining if Christians fail to respond.

What a relief for those in spiritual leadership. Like Paul, we can love and give and let God punish those who do not respond to His Word.

"Examine yourselves" (13:5-6). If those in the church chronically reject God's words and ways, checking to see if they're saved isn't just wise. It's essential!

Galatians

The little Book of Galatians has been called the "Magna Charta of Christian liberty." In bold, clear strokes the Apostle Paul reveals how grace frees the Christian from law, not that we might sin, but that we might discover a new power for righteous living through faith and the Holy Spirit.

This book was written to meet a great need in the early church. Wherever Paul went and established churches he was trailed by "Judaizers." These were Jews—sometimes Jewish believers—who came to the newly founded churches and taught that to be a real Christian one must submit to Old Testament Law and in effect convert to Judaism. This did have a certain logic. Jesus was a Jew, and the roots of Christianity were undoubtedly Jewish. So many new Christians followed the teachings of the Judaizers. Paul vehemently rejected their "faith/works" Gospel and writes urgently to explain why mixing works with faith robs the Gospel of its power in the believer's life.

Few New Testament books had more influence in shaping the Reformation's rediscovery of salvation by faith alone. Martin Luther so loved the book he called it by his wife's name because, he said, "I am wedded to it." As important as this book has been historically, it is perhaps even more important to us as individuals. It is here we learn the futility of struggling in our own strength to do what is right. It is here we discover the freedom of being renewed from within and so enabled by God to become persons who are right: right with God and right with our neighbor through good and loving acts that express the reality of Christ alive within us. Along with Paul's letter to the Romans, this book constitutes a complete theology of the Christian life and a guide to the source of power that we need to live that life daily.

GREAT VERSES IN GALATIANS

"I have been crucified with Christ and I no longer live, but Christ lives in me" (2:20).

Jesus living in us is the source of our freedom and our power for holy living.

"Christ redeemed us from the curse of the law" (3:13).

The penalty for our failure to keep God's Law has been paid, and we are free.

"You are all sons of God through faith in Christ" (3:26).

God has adopted us and taken us all into His family. We are "sons" now (see p. 791).

"God has sent the Spirit of His Son into our hearts" (4:6).

With sonship comes the gift of God's Spirit, to be our ever present companion.

"If you let yourselves be circumcised, Christ will be of no value to you at all" (5:2).

Jesus is present to live His life through us. But if you take a legalistic approach to life, His presence will not help you.

"Keep in step with the Spirit" (5:25).

The Holy Spirit transforms us from within, guides us and gives us power. Rely on Him and find freedom to be truly good.

Illustration. *In Roman law a special ceremony marked an individual's recognition as a "son." Whether a family member by birth or adoption, only when recognized as a "son" did an individual achieve full rights of that relationship, with all the privileges and responsibilities of family membership. Paul tells us in Gal. 4:5 that we Christians achieve this status in God's family through our faith in Jesus Christ.*

Date and Authorship. The Apostle Paul wrote this letter to churches he had founded in the district of Galatia. While debated, most scholars believe the churches lie in South rather than North Galatia. These would be churches in Derbe, Lystra, Iconium, and Pisidian Antioch founded early in Paul's ministry (cf. Acts 13–14). Scholars also debate whether this letter was written before or just after the decision of the Jerusalem Council (Acts 15) that released Gentile converts to Christ from any responsibility to keep Jewish law. If early, this letter may have been written and begun to circulate by A.D. 49 or 50.

THEOLOGICAL OUTLINE OF GALATIANS

CONTENT OUTLINE OF GALATIANS

Chapter summary. Paul identifies himself as an apostle sent by Jesus and God as he begins this critical letter (1:1-2). After wishing the churches grace and peace (vv. 3-5), Paul expresses amazement that they have turned so quickly to a "different gospel"—one which is a perversion of the truth Paul teaches (vv. 6-9).

Because the strategy of those carrying this "different gospel" features a personal attack on Paul, the great missionary feels compelled to defend his apostleship. This defense is begun here and carried on through chapter 2. Paul has been accused of making the Gospel "easy" to please men: Does his condemnation of those bringing the "other" gospel sound wishy-washy? (v. 10) Paul has been accused of distorting the true Gospel. But he received his Gospel directly from Jesus rather than from men! (v. 11) After Paul's conversion he did not even consult with the other apostles, but went off on his own to study (vv. 12-17). It was years before he even saw Peter and James and then they praised God for Paul's ministry to the Gentiles (vv. 18-24). The inescapable conclusion is that the innuendos and attacks on Paul's credibility are simply not true!

Key verse. 1:8: Other gospels?

Personal application. There is only one Gospel. Hold to it.

Key concepts. Apostle »p. 635. Grace »p. 792. Peace »p. 806. Gospel »p. 737.

INSIGHT

"Sent" (1:1). The significance of a messenger depended not on his own status, but on the status of the one who sent him. Paul claims the highest status of all, for he was sent "by Jesus Christ and God the Father." Two prepositions further emphasize Paul's position. His apostleship is neither from (*apo*) or through (*dia*) men. Not "from men" sets Paul apart from the false apostles, who were never commissioned by God at all. Not "through men" sets him with the Twelve, directly commissioned by Jesus.

"Grace and peace" (1:3). The familiar greeting wishes for the churches were a constant experience of God's favor (grace) and total well-being (peace) that are ours in Jesus Christ. What an important reminder at the very beginning of this letter. Every spiritual blessing we have is found in Jesus—not in the corrupt "gospel" of the Judaizers.

"A different Gospel" (1:6). Greek has two different words for "another." One, *allos*, is another of the same or similar kind. The other, *heteros*, is another of a radically different kind. Any gospel which mixes works with faith, and law with grace, is an utter distortion of the Good News about the salvation we have in Jesus Christ.

Wishy-washy Paul (1:8-10). Those bringing the "different" gospel claimed that Paul had shaved the truth. He was afraid that if he'd called for a full commitment to the Law that he would not "win the approval of" the men he preached to. Paul notes that his heated reaction in bluntly labeling the "different gospel" a heresy worthy of eternal condemnation is hardly in keeping with the weak portrait of his character offered by his critics.

Paul's familiarity with Judaism (1:13-17). No one could claim Paul was in error about the Gospel because he did not understand Judaism.

"Reveal His Son in me" (1:13-16). Paul's conversion involved a radical transformation. He had been a persecutor of the church, a zealous and hostile promoter of Judaism, until God "called me by His grace." The experience of grace so changed Paul that he was transformed. Rather than persecute Christians, he committed his life to love and serve others. It's true that God revealed His Son through the great apostle's teaching. But it is as significant that God revealed His Son in the new life lived by the apostle and the transformation of his character. What an important reminder. God still intends to reveal Jesus—in us.

Chapter summary. Paul's defense of his apostleship continues from chapter 1 with a survey of his relationship with the 12 Apostles. This picks up a theme introduced in 1:1. Paul was commissioned directly by God, not "through" men. Thus, he has always met and dealt with the Twelve as equals rather than as a subordinate!

Outline
Place
Finder

APOSTLESHIP
FAITH
FREEDOM

When Paul went up to Jerusalem to participate in the Acts 15 council, which discussed whether Gentile Christians should be commanded to keep Old Testament Law, Paul stood up for the "truth of the Gospel" of grace (2:1-5). And his position was affirmed by the church's Jewish "pillars"! They accepted Paul fully and praised his ministry to the Gentiles without modifying his message in any way (vv. 6-10). Later, when Peter himself hesitated to identify himself fully with Gentile converts because he feared the opinion of some Jewish believers, Paul openly rebuked him. Peter's withdrawal from the Gentiles was inconsistent with the Gospel's basic principles of justification by faith rather than law. It was not enough for Peter to teach the Gospel. He must practice it (vv. 11-16). Nothing must be allowed to confuse the wonderful truth that the Christian life is Christ alive in us, the true and only source of righteousness (vv. 17-21).

Key verse. 2:20: Christ in us.

Personal application. The Christian life is not a matter of trying, but of relying.

Key concepts. Circumcision »pp. 36, 126. Freedom »pp. 469, 685. Gentiles »p. 898. Hypocrisy »p. 625. Law »pp. 120, 145, 606, 743.

INSIGHT

The Jerusalem Council (2:1-10). Read about this critical event in early church history in Acts 15 (cf. »p. 722).

Eating with Gentiles (2:11-13). In the 1st century Gentiles were considered a contaminated and contaminating race. No truly pious Jew would eat with a Gentile. But the Gospel message changed all this, linking Jew and Gentile in a single fellowship. Each, through faith in Christ, had salvation and common access to God as their own Father. When Peter refused to eat with Gentiles for fear of Christians who continued the strict practice of Judaism, his act denied something essential to the Gospel message.

Justified (2:18). This judicial term means to be declared righteous, or innocent. It refers to God's pronouncement, as Judge of the universe, that the person who believes in Jesus is righteous in His sight. Paul shows us in this epistle and in Romans that justification is not only legal but experiential. God works through the Holy Spirit to actually make those who believe righteous men and women. »Righteous, pp. 607, 734, 808.

Crucified with Christ (2:20). The theme is found in both Rom. (6:6) and Gal. (here; 5:24; 6:14). It is rooted in the concept of identification with or union with Jesus. In God's sight the believer is so linked with Jesus that His death is considered ours. Even more, we are united with Jesus in His resurrection, and so have access to God's own power for holy living.

The (transforming) grace of God (2:21). "Grace" is a word filled with unique meaning, a word that expresses a complex set of understandings about our relationship with God. Grace views God's attitude toward us as one of love and acceptance. Grace is an admission that unaided, we are trapped by sin and incapable of winning God's favor. Grace is the triumphant announcement that God will come to the aid of all those who trust Him and give salvation as a free gift. Grace is a way of life, an attitude that rejects dependence on our own strengths or abilities and yet affirms that through Jesus we are able to live good and righteous lives. Grace is choosing to be and do good, relying on Christ for enablement.

Outline
Place
Finder

APOSTLESHIP
FAITH
FREEDOM

Chapter summary. These chapters contain one of Paul's clearest explanations of why faith must, and has always been intended to, replace Law. Paul begins by scornfully asking why the Galatians, who have begun their Christian life in faith, abandon the faith principle to turn to Law (3:1-5). His carefully reasoned argument, from 3:1–5:12, is traced in the box on the facing page (791).

Three keys help us understand Paul's argument in this section. He shows that spiritual life and vitality have always come as a gift, through God's promise. Then he shows that Law is a late-comer, with a limited and temporary function. And he shows that Law brings bondage rather than freedom.

What then does faith in God's promise bring us? Paul shows that through faith we become "sons" of God (see illustration, p. 786). Through faith we are released from bondage and given a unique "freedom" which enables us to be and do what is truly good.

Key verse. 3:29: Be who you are.

Personal application. Let grace rather than Law guide.

Key concepts. Law »pp. 120, 145, 376, 606, 743. Gospel »p. 737. Righteousness »pp. 607, 734, 808. Justify »p. 789. Curse »p. 138. Promise (Covenant) »p. 35. Holy Spirit »pp. 73, 776.

INSIGHT

"Foolish Galatians" (3:1). The word is *anoetos*, which challenges their powers of perception. They have missed the very essence of the Gospel.

Law, or believing? (3:2) The direction the Galatian churches have taken violates their initial experience with God. Paul's question helps us gain perspective too. Were we saved by faith or works of the law? If faith is so potent that it can provide eternal salvation, why not see what faith can do in our daily lives?

Abraham's example (3:6-9). Abraham is the person to whom Jew and Gentile look as the prototype of personal relationship with God. That relationship was rooted in faith. Faith must then have the critical role in the relationship of Gentiles with God, for God promised to bless them "along with" Abraham.

"Christ" (3:10-14). Christ crucified is the object of the believer's faith. "Believing" as a subjective experience is meaningless. What counts is relying on the Person of the Saviour, expecting God to do through Him what God has promised. This kind of faith is the key to living the victorious Christian life, as well as the key to salvation.

"Under a curse" (3:10). Paul's point is that faith and Law are mutually exclusive principles. Anyone who relies on observing the Law becomes responsible to keep it perfectly ("do

everything"). Since no one can do this, any who approach relationship with God through Law are already cursed.

Christ became a curse for us (3:13). By dying for us Christ took the "curse" of God upon Himself and exhausted it. The O.T. verse quoted is Deut. 21:23. By being crucified Christ became cursed and technically became guilty of "all" (cf. v. 11). Because faith unites us to Jesus, His death is considered ours and in Him our sins have been punished, so that we are set free.

"Christ redeemed" (3:13; cf. 4:5). The Gk. word, *exagorazo*, means to "purchase out of slavery" by the payment of a price. This is one of the N.T.'s basic images to explain the meaning of Christ's death. His death was the purchase price that had to be paid. Because the price has been paid, believers have been taken off the slave market. We were purchased by God to be released from our slavery to sin and the Law, never to be back in bondage again.

Law in perspective (3:15-22). Paul writes now for those who are enthusiastic about the Law as "the" way to achieve righteousness. Such people overlook the fact that Law appeared long after the promise to Abraham and functions alongside rather than instead of it. They overlook the fact that Law is temporary, intended to function only until Jesus appeared. And they overlook the fact that Law

The Argument of Galatians 3:1–5:12

I. Law is opposed to life. This is shown by:	3:1-18
A. Experience: The Galatians received life through faith, not Law (3:1-5)	
B. Example: Abraham received spiritual life through faith before Law existed (3:6-9)	
C. Scripture: It testifies that the just will live by faith (3:10-18)	
II. Law has a very limited role. It is limited:	3:19–4:7
A. In duration: It is temporary (3:19-20)	
B. In ability: It cannot give life (3:21-22)	
C. In function: It is merely a servant who guides a young child (3:23-24)	
D. In relevance: It is nullified today, since believers are now "sons" of God (3:25–4:7)	
III. Law is inferior. It brings the believer:	4:8–5:12
A. Discontent: It robs us of joy (4:8-19)	
B. Bondage: It robs us of freedom (4:20–5:1)	
C. Powerlessness: It drains us of faith by turning our attention to useless self-effort (5:2-12)	

INSIGHT

identifies sins, instead of making a person righteous. Rather than imparting life, Law convicts so that people might turn to Christ — the source of life given freely to those who believe.

Sons of God (3:23-25). Paul pictures Law as a *paedagogus*, a household slave charged with supervising underage children. Faith frees us from our spiritual childhood, so we no longer need Law.

Social distinctions irrelevant (3:26-28). The position of "son" in the Roman world was special. An individual was an adult member of the family, accountable directly to the *pater familias* (the father), with privileges of access to him and his resources. In saying that believers are now "sons" in the family of God, Paul makes all other relationships insignificant. There is now no advantage in being a Jew rather than a Gentile, a man rather than a woman, a free man rather than a slave. All share the highest social position possible, full adult membership in the family of the universe's greatest power.

Because we are sons (4:1-7). Sonship has made a radical change in the situation of the believer. Under O.T. Law Israel was held prisoner, "locked up" to keep them out of trouble until Jesus came (3:23). Now sons, God has given believers His Spirit. The cry "Abba, Father," implies a clear distinction between slave and family member. Only a child has the privilege of such warm and direct address. Only a child has such immediate access to a parent. Paul's point is that "sons" have no need to be locked up and no need of a guardian. As sons we have direct access to God and also a matchless resource that enables us to be holy — the Holy Spirit Himself.

Adoption (4:6). The word translated "full rights as sons" is *huiosthesia*, "adoption." This significant legal act in Roman law severed an individual's old relationships and canceled all his old debts and obligations. The father became owner of the adoptee's possessions, and the new son became his new father's heir. The father had the right to discipline the son and became liable for the new son or daughter's actions. In adoption each party became committed to support and care for the other. What a change this means in our position! We owe all now to God. And for His part, God commits Himself fully to guide us and discipline us, that we might bring credit to Him as members of His household.

Outline
Place
Finder

APOSTLESHIP
FAITH
FREEDOM

Chapter summary. Paul has shown that Christ has set us free from the Law and from slavery. We are now sons of God (Gal. 4:1-7) in the "free" line of Isaac and not the "slave" line of Ishmael (4:21-31). And God has set us free to experience freedom! (5:1) This freedom can only be experienced if we in faith rely on grace. If we turn back to Law we cut ourselves off from all Christ's resources (vv. 2-6). Paul emotionally expresses his anguish. How could these converts ever have become so confused? (vv. 7-12) The fact is that the Christian's "freedom" is from domination by one's sinful nature, allowing opportunity to love and serve others (vv. 13-15). Only living "by the Spirit" can release us from the domination of the sin nature—and this has nothing to do with Law (vv. 16-18). The works of the sinful nature are so obvious (vv. 19-21) and so diametrically opposed to the fruit produced in the human personality by God's Spirit (vv. 22-26) that Law is obviously irrelevant. What need is there of laws against evil if the Spirit in us produces only good?

Key verses. 2:22-23: His work is obvious too.

Personal application. Responding to the Spirit is exercising your freedom to do what you know is right.

Key concepts. Freedom »pp. 469, 685. Justified »p. 789. Law »pp. 120, 145, 606, 743, 790. Love »p. 690. Sin »pp. 741, 798.

INSIGHT

"For freedom" (5:1). Many consider this verse the key to the entire epistle. Looking back, it proclaims the believer's freedom from Law. Looking ahead, it proclaims the believer's freedom to be righteous. Many fear freedom, anxious that people will take the removal of restraints as a license to sin. That was a real concern as long as man was like a wild animal. But in Christ God changed the believer's "animal" nature and gave us His own Spirit. We're free from the Law not because God no longer cares about righteousness, but because we have been changed into righteous persons.

Fallen from grace (5:2-4). These verses which have troubled many do *not* deal with salvation. They describe the present experience of the person who attempts to earn God's approval ("be justified") by being circumcised and adopting the Jewish law/lifestyle promoted by the Judaizers—who so viciously attacked Paul. The word "alienate" (*katargeo*) here simply means "to be disconnected." Fall from grace here is slipping away from fellowship with Jesus, that fellowship which is essential if we are to experience the grace which alone enables us to live godly lives. As Jesus reminded His disciples, "Apart from Me, you can do nothing" (John 15:5).

"Emasculate themselves" (5:12). The original

has a pun, a play on the word circumcision. Paul is saying, "Those guys are so eager to cut you—I hope the knife slips and they cut their own off!"

"The desires of the sinful nature" (5:16). "Desire" (*epithymia*) speaks of those drives and passions which have their root in man's sinful nature and which, like an engine, drive sinful man's actions. As Paul says, the acts of the sin nature are obvious.

"They are in conflict" (5:17; cf. vv. 22-23). The Spirit is also like an engine. He provides energy for the new nature, which drives the converted in the opposite direction from the sin nature. His works too are obvious, for the Spirit produces the fruit of the Spirit in the believer's personality.

"Keep in step with the Spirit" (5:25). Several similar phrases are found in this chapter: "live by the Spirit" (v. 16), "led by the Spirit" (v. 18), and again "live by the Spirit" (v. 25). These images make the same point. In our Christian life we are to live by faith, responsive to God's Spirit as He guides our choices, showing our reliance on Him by confidently doing what we know is right. And we can tell if we're in step with Him by noting whether our lives are marked by sinful acts—or by the Spirit's fruit.

Chapter summary. Paul's letter concludes with a series of exhortations and reminders. The believers have a responsibility to and for each other (6:1-5) and to those who serve full time among them (v. 6). Paul also reminds his readers that the choice they make, to please the passions of their sin nature or to please the Spirit, will have a definite impact on their present and on their eternity (vv. 7-10).

Paul's last word, written in his own hand rather than by a secretary (v. 11), urges his Galatian friends to keep their focus on Jesus. Neither circumcision nor uncircumcision are relevant to the Christian life. It is all Christ and the new creation believers become in Him (vv. 12-18).

Outline
Place
Finder

APOSTLESHIP
FAITH
FREEDOM

Key verse. 6:2: Reach out.

Personal application. Don't get tired of doing good.

Key concepts. Circumcision »pp. 36, 126. Law »p. 790.

INSIGHT

"You who are spiritual" (6:1). Only those who are truly responsive to the Holy Spirit will have the insight and tenderness needed to restore a sinning brother or sister. Note that the restoration is to be done "gently" — and that gentleness is one of the fruit of the Spirit.

"Restore" (6:1). The Gk. word is *katarizo*. It is a medical term, used of setting a broken bone. We're to help the broken mend, not to expose them to shame or to ignore the damage sin does to their lives.

Each other's, or your own (6:2). There's no real conflict between these verses. The "burdens" we're to help others bear are a heavy load, too big for a person, and typically carried by a pack animal. But the "load" we are to carry ourselves is the *phortion*, the "pack" normally carried by soldiers on duty.

Reaping, sowing. Paul's point is that there are natural laws in the spiritual as well as the material realms. Sow seeds in the ground and in time they produce a crop. In the same way the moral acts a person sows produce a crop as well.

There's a story of a farmer who ridiculed his churchgoing neighbors, worked every Sunday, and had a bumper crop. He sent a letter to the local paper deriding their faith. His profit proved God didn't care — or couldn't act. Paul said God is not mocked: Our acts are seeds, growing slowly, but sure to produce a crop in keeping with our planting. The paper's editor understood the principle, and after the farmer's letter printed this observation. "God hasn't harvested His crops yet."

"Do good to all" (6:10). The old obligation to love one's neighbor (Lev. 19:18) still exists. But a new and even more important obligation has been created by our membership in the family of faith. We now have brothers and sisters, and they must be our first concern when it comes to doing good.

Paul's primary reference may be to giving to those in need (cf. v. 6). In case our resources are limited, our first concern should be to others in the family of faith.

Ephesians

Ephesus was the queen city of Asia. Though its port facilities were silting up in the first century, Ephesus remained the Asian center of the cult of Artemis. Its temple was one of the wonders of the ancient world, drawing many thousands of visitors to the city annually. Its priesthood used their wealth to become the bankers of the East, accepting deposits and paying interest, and making vast loans to individuals and even nations. First-century Ephesus represented the materially "successful" religion of that era. Yet Ephesus also displayed the spiritual void that existed in the first century. Ephesus was a center of occult practice, as its citizens turned to magic, witchcraft, and sorcery to manipulate hostile spiritual powers to their advantage.

Against this background of religion and superstition, Paul writes of the church created and sustained by God. The Father is the architect of this temple, Jesus its builder, and the Holy Spirit the divine presence that dwells in it. God's temple is not constructed of stone but of living flesh. Its treasury is void of gold and silver, but stocked with spiritual blessings in heavenly places. God's church is vitally alive, its every member recreated for good works. God's church is not directed by a priesthood but by Christ, its living Head. God's church is not at the mercy of hostile spiritual forces but guarded by One whose power is supreme above every rule and authority. God's church is no heap of cold marble, but rather a vital, loving family, enriched and sustained by caring relationships. God's temple is not some ancient, weathering edifice but a growing, nurturing fellowship, which keeps on building itself up in love. How appropriate this epistle was written to the Ephesians, where pagan religion ruled but left life empty and unfulfilled.

KEY VERSES DESCRIBING THE CHURCH IN EPHESIANS

"We were also chosen" (1:11).

God selected His building material with care.

"God . . . appointed Him to be head over everything for the church" (1:22).

Jesus is the living, active Head of His church and He guides and directs His people today.

"In Him the whole building is joined together" (2:21).

Jesus binds us together as one. Social and cultural differences are irrelevant in Him.

"That you may be filled to the measure of all the fullness of God" (3:19).

Living together as a loving family we experience God's love and grow in godliness.

"Keep the unity of the Spirit through the bond of peace" (4:3).

We are one in Christ's church, and we are to live with others so that we experience that unity.

"The whole building . . . grows and builds itself up in love, as each part does its work" (4:16).

Each member in the body is called to serve others. What we each contribute is essential for the church as a people to grow and mature.

"Put on the new self created to be like God in true righteousness and holiness" (4:24).

God gives us new life, and places us in a church which is His living body and the context in which we are to be transformed.

Illustration. *The magnificent temple of Artemis (Diana) stood just outside the city in a lush valley. It was 342 feet long, 164 feet wide, and featured 100 outside columns each over 55 feet high. The temple's roof was a white marble tile. A monthlong festival to Artemis drew a half million pilgrims annually from all over the Mediterranean world. In contrast, how humble meetings of Christians, who gathered a few at a time in houses, must have seemed. And yet the temple was empty of both meaning and hope. And the fragile church of Christ, formed of living persons rather than cold stone, brought and still brings vitality, transformation, joy, and eternal life to humankind.*

Date and Authorship. The letter was written by the Apostle Paul, who had spent over three years (A.D. 54–57?) in Ephesus. This stay, as reported in Acts 19, had a tremendous impact on the city and the 230 other communities in the Roman province of Asia. Not only were thousands of dollars worth of books on magic publicly burned by those who became Christians, but the economic health of those who depended on pilgrims coming to the Temple of Artemis was threatened.

The Ephesian letter was written from Rome, where Paul was imprisoned and awaiting trial. Two other letters, Colossians and Philippians, were also written from Rome, probably A.D. 59–61.

THEOLOGICAL OUTLINE OF EPHESIANS

I. THE CHURCH AS PEOPLE	1–2
II. THE CHURCH AS BODY AND FAMILY	3–4
III. THE CHURCH AS CHRIST INCARNATE	4–6

CONTENT OUTLINE OF EPHESIANS

Greeting (1:1-2)
I. The Church As People (1:3–2:22)
  A. A Chosen People (1:3-14)
  B. An Empowered People (1:15-23)
  C. A Recreated People (2:1-10)
  D. A United People (2:11-22)
II. The Church As Body and Family (3:1–4:16)
  A. Heirs Together in One Body (3:1-13)
  B. Growing Together As One Loving Family (3:14-21)
  C. Bound Together by One Lord (4:1-6)
  D. Built Up Together by What Each Supplies (4:7-16)
III. The Church As Christ Incarnate (4:17–6:20)
  A. Like Christ in Attitude (4:17-24)
  B. Like Christ in Relationships (4:25-32)
  C. Like Christ in Holy Living (5:1-20)
  D. Christlikeness Defined (5:21–6:9)
    1. In husband/wife relationships (5:21-33)
    2. In child/parent relationships (6:1-4)
    3. In slave/master relationships (6:5-9)
  E. Spiritual Resources Enabling Christlikeness: the Armor of God (6:10-18)
Farewells (6:19-24)

Chapter summary. After brief greetings (1:1-2), Paul launches into a powerful expression of praise for what each Person of the Godhead has done in crafting, accomplishing, and effecting our salvation (vv. 3-14). The special role of each Person defined here is one of the clearest proofs in the New Testament of the Trinity. Paul then moves on to report the content of his continual prayer for the Ephesians (vv. 15-22). His deep desire for these Christians, and God's desire for us today, is that we know Him better, grasp and experience His "incomparably great power for us who believe," and find fullness in Jesus, whom God has exalted over all things as head of the church.

Outline
Place
Finder

PEOPLE
BODY & FAMILY
INCARNATION

Key verse. 1:4: Chosen for a purpose.

Personal application. Take hold of all God gives us in Jesus.

Key concepts. Praise »p. 380. Blessing »pp. 49, 127. Adoption »p. 791. Grace »p. 789. Redemption »p. 790. Forgiveness »p. 634. Wisdom »pp. 280, 757. Mystery »p. 747. Will »p. 712. Holy Spirit »p. 73. Hope »p. 465. Power »p. 430. Head »p. 802. Church »p. 794.

INSIGHT

Trinity (1:3-14). This doctrine holds that Scripture's one God exists in three coequal Persons. The word "trinity" is not found in the Bible. But the N.T. clearly teaches what the O.T. intimates: Jesus is God the Son, who from eternity was God with the Father (cf. John 1:1-14; Phil. 2:5-11), and that the Holy Spirit is a Person of the same kind (cf. John 14:16).

Divine roles in salvation's grand design (1:3-14). God the Father is pictured as the One who devised the plan of salvation (vv. 3-6). God the Son carried out the plan, shedding His blood to win us redemption and forgiveness (vv. 7-13). And God the Holy Spirit "included us in Christ" when we believed and remains in us as the guarantee of our complete redemption (vv. 14-15).

Spiritual blessings (1:3). A "blessing" is the granting of good. In the O.T. blessings were primarily material; now they are primarily spiritual and thus more significant. Material goods are temporary, spiritual are eternal. What are the blessings? Adoption as sons (v. 5) and redemption and forgiveness of sins (v. 7) are mentioned in the text.

God's choice of individuals (1:4, 11). The verb *ekelegomi* implies a free choice in which some are selected from many. Three things should be kept in mind. First, Scripture affirms a sovereign God who is free to choose apart from any consideration of human actions (cf. Rom. 9). God chose to provide salvation despite His rejection by sinful man. Second, God is said to have chosen us, the church, "to be holy and blameless" through "adoption as sons." Some note that

this does not say God chose those to be saved. Third, whatever the role of God in choosing us "before the foundation of the world" His choice in no way forces any individual to believe, or keeps any individual from believing in Jesus. The Gospel invitation is real, and we do freely choose to believe or reject the Gospel.

"Predestined" (1:5). The Gk. word *proorizo* means to "mark out ahead of time." It is found 6 times in the N.T.: Acts 4:28, Rom. 8:29-30; 1 Cor. 2:7; Eph. 1:5, 11. See "God's Choice," above. And note that predestination is "in love" (v. 5).

"A deposit" (1:14). *Arrabon* is a word from the world of trade that means a down payment, guaranteeing the seller will ultimately receive the full price of goods contracted for. The Spirit is our guarantee of resurrection.

Paul's prayer (1:15-23). This and other prayers of Paul in Ephesians and Colossians can serve as a good guide when we are praying for others. Paul's concern is that believers understand and use the spiritual resources that are ours in Christ.

Raised to sovereign authority (1:19-21). The power God exercises "for us" is more than resurrection power. It is a power that catapulted Jesus to the place of supreme authority in the universe.

Don't let feelings of powerlessness sap your commitment to what is right. We are not powerless but draw freely on the greatest power of all.

"Head over everything" (1:22-23). Jesus hasn't retired! Our concern must be to seek and do His will, for He is head of the church.

Chapter summary. God determined to form the church of flawed material because of His great love for sinners (2:1-4). He took those who were dead in sin and made us alive in Christ, literally recreating us to make us suitable for the good works which He also prepared for us to do (vv. 5-10). This process of recreation in Christ also closed the gap between the Jew, who had enjoyed a covenant relationship with God, and the Gentile, who was locked out of that relationship (vv. 11-13). By bringing both Jew and Gentile to God through the Cross Jesus settled the long-standing hostility between the races, removing its cause (vv. 14-18). As a result Jew and Gentile are now "fellow citizens," members of God's great household and together parts of a holy temple God's Spirit is building even now (2:19-22).

Key verse. 2:10: Our new identity.

Personal application. Seek every day to be what you are, not what you once were.

Key concepts. Sin »pp. 34, 442, 741. Love »pp. 351, 529, 680. Mercy »p. 880. Dead »p. 741. Grace »p. 789. Works »pp. 849, 872. Covenant »p. 32. Peace »pp. 806, 815. Alien »p. 66. Citizen »p. 723. Temple »p. 283.

INSIGHT

Conversion (1:2-10). Conversion is often treated as an emotional experience of psychological change. Paul treats it as a stunning spiritual transformation: the passage from a state of spiritual death to a state of spiritual life. This passage does have psychological implications. Before conversion, a person "used to follow the ways of the world" and be driven by the "sinful nature's desires and thoughts." After conversion, a person's life is reoriented toward God and doing good. The reality of the inward change must in time be reflected in a true change of life, or the conversion is unreal.

Human nature corrupted (2:1-3). Man was created in God's image. But that was distorted in the fall. Both fallen human nature and our terrible condition apart from salvation are described here.

"The gift of God" (2:8). Only here is *doron*, found 19 times in the N.T., used of a gift given by God to man. Salvation is something that we appropriate by faith. But it is a gift and cannot be earned by anything a person might do.

"This not from yourselves" (2:8). Theologians have argued whether the faith or salvation is given by God. The grammar of the Gk. sentence does not make this clear. It seems best, however, since the theme is salvation by grace (v. 8a) to understand Paul to mean that God acted graciously to give salvation to those who believe (see Faith »pp. 35, 740).

"Good works" (2:10). Good works cannot contribute in any way to our salvation, but are an expected product of salvation. Paul makes it clear that God created us in Christ Jesus—that is, gave us our new life in—order that we would be able to, and would do, good works. What are "good works"? Any activity which is beneficial to God or our fellowman, and whose beauty reflects honor and glory to the Lord.

"Gentiles" (2:11-12). This term is used in the N.T. of all persons other than Jews. In the 1st-century Roman Empire Jews made up about 1/10th of the population. What made the Jews special was their unique relationship with God, through covenant promises given their forefather Abraham and the Law given by Moses. These deep-seated differences created a sense of superiority on the part of the Jews and of hostility on the part of many Gentiles. Anti-Semitism is not new, and in the two centuries before Christ many cities in Asia and Europe had anti-Jewish riots.

"One new man" (2:14-22). Jesus' death "put to death" the basis of hostility between Jew and Gentile by providing access to God to both groups through His sacrifice. Not only can the two live in peace now, but they are to live as one.

Let's take this great truth to heart and seek oneness with our fellow-Christians whatever their race or background, that we might be one temple displaying God's holiness to all.

Chapter summary. Paul's unique role has been to serve as Christ's apostle to the Gentiles. It has been given to him to explain previously unrevealed truth: the fact that God intended to bond Jew and Gentile together as one believing community, one body of Christ (3:1-7). Paul does not deserve his commission, but exults in it and the untold wonder of God's complex, eternal plan (vv. 8-13). It's with a deep sense of his privilege as a minister of this eternal Good News that Paul prays for the Ephesians. Specifically, he prays that, now the family of one Father, the believers in Ephesus might discover in their growing love for one another the incomprehensible love of Christ. And that this will enable them to be filled to the measure of the fullness of God (vv. 14-19). Deeply moved by this exalted vision, Paul pens one of the Bible's most beautiful, and important, doxologies (vv. 20-21).

Outline
Place
Finder

PEOPLE
BODY & FAMILY
INCARNATION

Key verses. 3:17-18: Love is the way.

Personal application. Draw close to those God has drawn close to Him.

Key concepts. Grace »p. 789. Mystery »p. 747. Apostle »p. 635. Love »pp. 126, 690. Prophet »p. 131. Gospel »p. 737. Gentiles »p. 798. Power »p. 430.

INSIGHT

The prisoner of Jesus (3:1). Paul is in chains in Rome, but he is not a prisoner of the empire, or restrained for any crime. The chains that count bind him to Jesus, and he is tied to Him for the sake of the Gentiles to whom he brings the Gospel.

The administration of God's grace (3:2). Here and in Eph. 1:9 oikonomia is used in the sense of one charged with implementing a strategy. Paul is the one God has chosen to open the door of equality in salvation to all people.

"Holy" (3:5). Holy is used in the sense of being set apart, not as an implication of moral superiority. The apostles and prophets were set apart by God to convey the Spirit's new revelation.

"Heirs together" (3:6). As early as Gen. 12:3 it was clear that God intended to save Gentiles as well as Jews. This theme is also repeated in the prophets (cf. Acts 15:1-21). What is stunningly new—the "mystery" Paul speaks of—is that the Gentiles should be accepted by God on the same basis as the Jews and that racial distinctions should be lost as the two are bonded together in a single body.

"Manifold wisdom" (3:10). The Gk. polypoikilos means "much varied." God's eternal plan is more complex and multifaceted than O.T. saints had imagined.

Let's not make the mistake of trying to squeeze His complex and "much varied" purposes into our own theological pigeonholes.

"Eternal" (3:11). The eternal exists outside of and is unaffected by time. Paul is saying that the church is not an afterthought.

The church as family (3:14-15). Paul says the family "derives its name" from God the Father. In biblical thought "name" sums up "essential identity." According to Paul, the fact that God is Father gives believers their essential identity, which is "family." This is one of three dominant images of the community of faith in the N.T. and draws attention to the necessity of close, intimate family—and thus loving—relationships.

Trinity again (3:14-17). The Father gives us our identity, the Spirit strengthens and empowers, and Christ "dwells in our hearts through faith" as the wellspring of transforming love.

"Rooted and established in love" (3:17-18). The love Paul speaks of here is the family love which is the theme of this prayer. God's love is real, yet "surpasses knowledge." How can we come to experience such a love and be filled with its presence? Paul's answer is that God has made us a family so that His love might be practically expressed in Christian interpersonal relationships. In giving and receiving love within the fellowship of faith we experience and thus come to know a love that is beyond our ability to conceptualize. In loving and being loved we learn God's love is real and are filled with Him.

Chapter summary. Paul now urges attitudes which express love and maintain unity (4:1-3). He reminds the Ephesians of all that binds Christians together (vv. 4-5). This unity is essential, for God has provided His church with gifted persons (vv. 6-10) who are to equip God's people for those "works of service" which enable the body to mature and to build itself up in love. Such growth demands that each part does its own work and so contribute to the whole (vv. 11-16).

Here Paul's letter takes a new tack. The church is the body of Christ. As such it is His representative in the world. We are to reject all that corrupts and "be like God in true righteousness and holiness" (vv. 17-24). To accomplish this we must maintain intimate relationships within the church fellowship (vv. 25-28). We must rid ourselves of hostility, in favor of treating one another as God treats us in Christ (vv. 29-32).

Key verse. 4:24: Our goal.

Personal application. Growth takes place in fellowship.

Key concepts. Body »p. 768. Baptism »p. 742. Satan »pp. 501, 655. Mature »p. 859. Transformation »p. 776. Truth »pp. 836, 685. Righteousness »pp. 734, 808. Redemption »p. 790.

INSIGHT

"**Worthy**" (4:1). The Gk. *axios* means literally to balance the scales. Our doctrine is to be balanced by our way of life.

Four qualities (4:2). These distinctly Christian virtues are essential if we are to "keep the unity of the Spirit."

"**One baptism**" (4:5). Here "baptism" more likely refers to the work of the Holy Spirit (1 Cor. 12:13) than the water baptism rite of initiation.

He gave gifts to men (4:7-8). Paul, under inspiration, modifies the original psalm. What Christ captured from the enemy through His death, resurrection, and ascension has been distributed to the church. While our booty includes "spiritual blessings" (cf. Eph. 1:3), it also includes spiritual gift given to "each one" (4:7; cf. Rom. 12:6-7, Cor. 12:1-13).

In this passage Paul calls on us to see leaders as Christ's gifts to the church, charged with equipping believers to develop and employ their own spiritual giftedness (vv. 9-16).

"**He ascended**" (4:9-10). Paul reminds us that the Christ who lived a humble life among men was exalted after His resurrection to become the supreme power in the material and spiritual universe (cf. Eph. 1:20-22). Jesus rose to be Lord of all.

Body building (4:14-16). Paul spells out one implication of the body analogy. An arm can do the rest of the body no good if it is severed.

The church like a body needs "every supporting ligament." It is love that holds the body together. It is each person doing his or her part—exercising his or her gift within the body—that produces spiritual growth.

"**Your old self**" (4:22). Paul refers to the sin nature which is set on a course of corruption. Don't try to reform. You won't succeed. Any person's only hope is a new self "created" by God. As Eph. 2:1-10 reminds us, this new creation takes place when we believe in Jesus. Now it is up to us to decide whether we will follow the pull of old, sinful desires or respond to the new self's pull toward righteousness. God won't force you to be godly. But if you choose righteousness, He will enable you.

"**Anger**" (4:26). Anger is an emotion. Sin is a choice. You may feel anger, but you can choose not to sin. »Anger pp. 72, 196, 359.

"**Work**" (4:28). Work is more than a means of self-support or even self-fulfillment. Work is a way to earn money we can share with those in need.

"**Grieve the Holy Spirit**" (4:30). The thought is that disobedience to any of these commands causes the Holy Spirit, who is in us, great and terrible sorrow and distress. The closest parallel may be that of a parent who suffers when a child commits a crime. How it hurts God when we are hostile to one another.

Chapter summary. As Christ's body on earth, we are to imitate God, for Christ incarnates Himself in us (5:1-2). To represent God here on earth we must decisively reject every kind of immorality and impurity (vv. 3-7). It is our transformation from darkness to light that reveals God and so we must be very careful to live in the light (vv. 8-20).

Outline
Place
Finder

PEOPLE
BODY & FAMILY
INCARNATION

Paul then explores three sets of relationships and defines how to live as children of light in each. First, he establishes an overarching principle: We are all to submit to one another out of reverence for Christ (v. 21). In marriage this means that husbands take the role of Christ and put their wives first, thus freeing the wife to submit to a husband she knows she can trust (vv. 22-33). In the family this means children are urged to obey parents, but parents are not to "exasperate" children by harsh, unfair treatment (6:1-4). In households with slaves, slaves are to give sincere obedience to their masters, while masters treat their slaves with consideration and respect (vv. 5-9).

Paul concludes with a creative summary of the teaching of Ephesians. He pictures our spiritual resources as elements of the panoply of a heavily armed Roman foot soldier. Equipped with all God has provided, we are well able to win the spiritual battles we must fight (vv. 10-18). Paul concludes with a request for prayer and well wishes (vv. 19-24).

Key verse. 5:21: How we imitate God.

Personal application. Christ reveals Himself in the way we live and the way we relate to others.

Key concepts. Love »pp. 126, 529, 680, 690, 778. Sex »pp. 402, 836. Adultery »p. 388. Light »p. 685. Submission »p. 867.

INSIGHT

"A fragrant offering" (5:1-2). The phrase means an offering that pleased God. We please God by imitating Jesus' love for others, a love that often calls us to make personal sacrifices.

Moral contrast (5:3-7). There is to be a dramatic, visible difference between the lifestyle of Christians and the people of this world. When we so compromise with this world's ways and values that a clear moral distinction is lost, we are unable to represent Jesus accurately.

"Light" (5:3-13). This extended passage gives the clearest N.T. definition of the contrasting moral differences between light and darkness. In most other passages, and particularly in John's writings, "light" has a different emphasis.

"Filled with the Spirit" (5:18). We might paraphrase, don't live under the influence of alcohol but under the influence of the Spirit. How important that we drink deep of Him, and let Him give direction to our lives.

The supportive impact of worship (5:19-20). It has been said, "You can't be Christian alone." It's hard enough to live as God's lighthouse in a dark world without feeling isolated and alone. Paul urges the Ephesians to draw together for shared worship. When we all keep God as the focus of our lives, we shine brightly with His light.

"Submit to one another" (5:21). "Submit" is a complex concept which needs to be defined by the context in which it is used. Here there is no question of power or of position, as we find in Rom. 13. Here Paul calls for all believers to develop an attitude of submission, a willingness to be responsive and to yield to one another out of love. It is wrong to read hierarchy into this verse or into the passage which follows. Rather, we see the development of a sensitivity to others that frees us from pride and enables us to act at all times in loving, caring ways. For more on Eph. 5–6, see p. 802.

"Head" (5:23). In the O.T. "head" may mean a literal head, the first in a series, the beginning or source, and often indicates the top of a mountain or chief of a clan. These same meanings are carried over into the N.T. with two additional theologically significant uses. (1) Christ is head of the church, a living organism. Passages in which this image occurs emphasize His role as sustainer, protector, source, and director of the body (cf. Eph. 1:22; 4:15; 5:23; Col. 1:18; 2:10, 19). (2) Head in 1 Cor. 11 is used in the sense of source or creation order. It is a mistake to read "head" in the sense of superior/inferior.

Headship of the husband (5:22-23). To make sure that we do not misunderstand headship in marriage as the right of a husband to dominate his wife, Paul specifies in which way the husband's headship is to be expressed. Specifically the husband is head, "as Christ loved the church and gave Himself for her, to make her holy" (vv. 25-26). In marriage headship emphasizes the husband's Christlike role of sustaining and protecting his wife and encouraging her personal and spiritual growth.

"Wives, submit" (5:22). Each partner in a marriage has a privilege. The husband's privilege is to put his wife first, as Christ put us first when He died for us. The wife's privilege is to set the tone of submission by being responsive and caring. Neither is "over" the other; each ministers to the other in his or her special way.

Who decides? The frequent argument that this passage does not convey on the husband the right of final decision misses an important point. The believer's task is not to decide, but rather to discern the decision that Christ as head over everything has already made! When the husband loves as Christ, and the wife responds as the church (v. 22), then together they will discern God's will.

Honor parents (6:2). This involves more than obedience, which may be only compliance with the demands of a stronger person. Honor involves respect and appreciation.

"First commandment, with a promise" (6:2). This is not the first of the Ten Commandments with which a promise is associated. We need a comma to see what Paul is saying. This is the first (*protos*) commandment, in that it is the first parents may use to introduce the child to God and His ways. If children respect parents they will respond to their nurture, come to know God, and so "enjoy long life on the earth."

Slavery (6:5-9). Slavery was entrenched in the 1st-century Roman empire. Often slaves were better off than freedmen, who might enjoy less food and poorer living conditions. But slaves were property, without freedom and without personal rights. The N.T. does not attack the institution, but faith in Christ did undermine it. Paul's teaching about the church as one body and one family, in which social distinctions were of no real significance, weakened the atti-

Illustration. *The heavily armored Roman foot soldier was the core of the army. Paul shows that Christ has equipped us just as well for our spiritual battles.*

tudes which supported slavery. This gives slaves new motives for serving their masters and masters a new perspective on their slaves, as persons and as family.

The armor. Each image picks up a theme from this book. "The belt of truth" (6:14) is openness and honesty that create a climate of trust and unity (cf. 4:25). "The breastplate of righteousness" (6:14) is moral purity (5:3). "Feet fitted with the readiness that comes from the Gospel of peace" (6:15) is the full acceptance of others, despite race or social class, that enables us to experience the peace Christ made between us through the Cross (2:11-22). "The shield of faith" (6:16) is confidence in the supreme power of Christ our living head (2:20; 3:20). "The helmet of salvation" (6:17) is realization of our new identity in Christ as God's new creations (2:1-10). Only "the sword of the Spirit" (6:17) is defined in the armor passage, and this is because Paul has not mentioned the Word of God earlier in his letter.

Philippians

Paul's letter to the Philippians is warm and personal. The church had sent an emissary to Paul, who was in prison in Rome. This man, Epaphroditus, carried funds for the apostle's support. In Rome, Epaphroditus became ill and nearly died. One reason for Paul's letter is to explain why he is sending Epaphroditus back to Philippi and to ask them to welcome Paul's young coworker, Timothy. Paul also intends to encourage those who are upset about his imprisonment. Rather than despair, they should feel the joy that wells up in Paul himself, for Paul's jailing has resulted in even more active promotion of the Gospel by others.

As all have noted, the key word in this brief letter is "joy" or "rejoice." Despite his chains, the apostle experiences an inner delight and no hardships can rob him of his joy. What a reminder this letter is of the vast difference between mere happiness, which depends on circumstances, and joy, which is rooted in spiritual realities. As we read Paul's words we find ourselves directed, through his experience, to those things which can bring us joy as well.

Philippians is also notable for verses in chapter 2 which many believe are a hymn or a creed used in the early church. These verses exalt Christ as One who, though by very nature God, chose to become a human being, suffer death on the cross, and was subsequently exalted by God "to the highest place."

SOURCES OF JOY SEEN IN PHILIPPIANS

"Joy, because of your partnership in the Gospel" (1:5).

The Gospel brings us into fellowship with other believers, with whom we share so much. Our fellow-Christians are a real source of joy.

"Christ is preached. And because of this I rejoice" (1:18).

Preaching Christ in a lost world is to be a first priority of believers. We can find joy not just in our own sharing of the Lord, but in the ministries of others.

"Make my joy complete by being likeminded, having the same love, being one in spirit and purpose" (2:2).

We also find joy in the unity and harmony of the body of Christ, a unity which we can achieve when our attitude mirrors the humility of Christ.

"Rejoice in the Lord" (3:1).

The Christian's ultimate source of joy is our Lord Himself. Because we are permanently united to Him, nothing can threaten the wellspring of our joy.

Illustration. *The first convert in Asia was a woman, Lydia, a "seller of purple" (Acts 16). The illustration shows the tops of vats set into the floor. Thread was soaked and drawn through the top opening. The ridge around the top caught any drops of liquid and directed them back into the vat. Purple clothing was very expensive and Lydia, who invited Paul's missionary team to stay at her home, was undoubtedly well-to-do.*

THEOLOGICAL OUTLINE OF PHILIPPIANS

CONTENT OUTLINE OF PHILIPPIANS

WHERE THE ACTION TAKES PLACE

Philippi lay in Macedonia, some 10 miles from the Aegean Sea. After The battle of Actium in 31 B.C. the city was made a Roman military colony and a number of soldiers were retired there. This status gave the city the right of self-government, immunity from taxes, and the citizens were treated as if they lived in Italy. Astride a major trade route, and the only "colony" in Macedonia, the people of this leading (*prote*) city were proud of their community.

Acts 16 reports the experiences of Paul in Philippi. This is the city where he cast a demon out of a slave girl and ended up in prison, only to be freed by an earthquake and lead the Philippian jailer to Christ.

Outline
Place
Finder

GOSPEL
UNITY
COMMITMENT
THE LORD

Chapter summary. Paul is under house arrest in Rome when he writes this letter to the Philippians. After a brief greeting (1:1-2), Paul expresses the joy he finds in thinking of the Philippians and all they mutually share in Christ (vv. 3-8). His prayer is that their lives will overflow with love and righteousness (vv. 9-11). Apparently the Philippians viewed Paul's imprisonment as a setback to the Gospel. Paul now shares his own evaluation: his chains have in fact served to advance the Gospel by stimulating many others to greater boldness (vv. 12-19). Paul has no personal anxiety about dying and in fact is convinced he will be released (vv. 20-26). But whatever happens, he urges the Philippians to always behave in a "manner worthy of the Gospel of Christ" (vv. 27-30).

Key verse. 1:18: Paul's priority.

Personal application. Share the Gospel. Gain a brother and a rich source of joy.

Key concepts. Gospel »p. 737. Righteousness »p. 734.

INSIGHT

"Overseers and deacons" (1:1). These are the two classes of local leaders in N.T. church. "Overseer" is "bishop" in older English versions, the equivalent of the "elder" of Timothy and Titus.

Peace from God (1:1). Paul typically mentions grace and peace in the introduction to his letters. Grace is God's favor. Peace in these greetings refers to the inner serenity experienced by those who maintain confidence in the Lord. At the same time our inner peace is rooted in the peace that Jesus makes between sinners and God. Through Jesus we no longer fear, but rejoice in God's love and forgiveness.

"Partnership in the Gospel" (1:5). The Gk. word, koinonia, means "sharing" or "participation." It is possible Paul refers to the wholehearted welcome he experienced there (Acts 16:15) and to the continuing prayer and financial support provided by this church (cf. Phil. 4:16; 2 Cor. 11:9).

Confidence (1:6). God worked a wonderful transformation in the Philippians when He first saved them. Paul has no concern that the God who has begun to work in them will desert them now. How good to know that God is totally committed to you and to me. He will continue His transforming work until it is gloriously completed when Jesus comes.

Paul's prayer (1:9-11). Paul's prayer is for a discerning love, which will be expressed in pure and blameless ways and produce individuals and a church marked by righteousness.

All too often people use love as an excuse. But never forget, the truly loving thing to do is also the right thing to do.

Preaching out of envy and rivalry (1:15). We may well emulate Paul's attitude. Even if someone's motive for doing good is to embarrass us or show us up, let's rejoice in the good that is done. God will judge the motives.

"To live is Christ and to die is gain" (1:21). Paul has made serving Christ the central, driving purpose of his life. After such a life, death can only mean gain, for rich rewards await.

You and I do not need to serve Christ in the same way Paul did, as an itinerant missionary and church planter. But we do need to make serving the Lord in our daily life our own central purpose.

"I will remain" (1:25). Many a Christian has come to realize that heaven is home and that no real satisfaction can be found in this life. Why then doesn't God take us home when we are converted? Paul has been shown that he will "remain"—to further help and nurture the Philippians.

"A manner worthy" (1:27). Here Paul uses a Gk. verb, politeuesthe, which means "live as a citizen." The Christian is to fulfill all his or her obligations as a member of a community of those who have responded to the Gospel. And the key responsibility is to stand firm in one spirit. To be worthy of the Gospel we must function harmoniously within a local community of faith.

"A sign" (1:28). The Christian's refusal to be intimidated by external foes was evidence that the salvation believers experienced was real—and that their enemies were doomed. Steadfastness is a compelling witness to the Gospel's trustworthiness.

Chapter summary. Paul's joy in his fellowship with the Philippians will be even greater if they exhibit the unity to which every church is called. Achieving unity calls for an attitude of humility (2:1-4) that mimic's that of Jesus (v. 5).

Now Paul inserts a powerful hymn or creed in celebration of the incarnation, humiliation, and obedience of Jesus—a course which not only led Christ to the cross but ultimately exalted Him to the "highest place" (vv. 6-11). By following Jesus' example the church will be able to work out solutions to its own problems (vv. 12-13), but must do so together—without murmuring or complaining (vv. 14-18). Paul then inserts a personal note, a special recommendation of Timothy (vv. 19-24) and Epaphroditus (vv. 25-30) who will carry his letter.

Outline
Place
Finder

GOSPEL
UNITY
COMMITMENT
THE LORD

Key verse. 2:5: Christ our example.

Personal application. Attitude is the key to unity.

Key concepts. Joy »p. 803. Humility »p. 259. Healing »p. 784.

INSIGHT

Paul's exhortation (2:1). External threats (1:27-30) to the church have always proven less dangerous than internal. Shared union with Christ, love for one another, and mutual participation in the Spirit should encourage all Christians to draw together in a supportive fellowship.

Attitude the key (2:2-4). This is perhaps Scripture's clearest portrait of the "humility" called for in the Gospel. It is not a weak man's surrender, but a strong man's rejection of selfishness and determination to be actively concerned with the needs and interests of others.

An early hymn? (2:4-11) The poetic form of these verses have led some to argue it is an early church hymn. Whatever its origin, this account of Christ's incarnation serves as a supreme illustration of humility, as God the Son willingly surrendered the prerogatives of deity to die as a human being for our sins.

The hymn also makes another important point. The way up for us too is down. We must follow Jesus along the way of humility.

Incarnation (2:6-8). This is the Christian doctrine that in Christ God became a true human being, while at the same time remaining deity. This hymn is one of several powerful affirmations of this basic doctrine. Others are found in John 1:1-14, Gal. 4:4-5, Col. 1:15-19, and Heb. 1.

"Appearance" (2:8). The Gk. word is *skemati*. The word speaks of outward appearance, so the phrase may be paraphrased, "and looking as though He were merely human." Jesus was a true human being. Paul's point is that He was much more: one who "in very nature" was God and equal with Him.

"Work out your own salvation" (2:12-13).

This verse does not even hint that one must work for his eternal salvation. Some take "salvation" here in a theological sense, not that once salvation is in us it must be worked out or expressed. It is most likely, however, that "salvation" is used in a non-theological sense, with the meaning, "work out solutions to your own daily problems."

How good to know as we face problems that God "works in us," showing us His will and enabling us to act according to His good purpose.

"Generation" (2:15). The word is used here in the broadest sense, to depict lost mankind. Against the background of general human depravity God expects us to "shine like stars."

If we expect to be effective in holding out "the word of life" (v. 16), we need to shine. It is the brightness of the Christian's life that sheds light on the Gospel message we hold out for others to see.

A fine recommendation (2:19-24). Note these qualifications: A genuine interest in other's welfare. A concern for Christ's interests. A record of faithful service. Set these as your goals and you too will go far.

"Ill, and almost died" (2:25-30). Paul's note raises a question. Why didn't the apostle, who had healed many and performed notable miracles, simply heal his friend? Perhaps the best answer is that Paul did not possess healing or miracle-working power, but that he was the channel through which God exercised that power when it suited God's purposes. All human beings are vulnerable to sickness and death. Even Christians have no "right" to miraculous healings.

Chapter summary. The unity of the church at Philippi was also threatened by Judaizers—men masquerading as believers who insisted that Christians were obligated to keep the Mosaic Law and, in effect, become Jews. Paul is very blunt about these "men who do evil" (3:1-3). As far as Jewish credentials were concerned, Paul's were more impressive (vv. 4-7). But in coming to Christ, Paul abandoned all such things. They were rubbish compared to knowing Christ and experiencing a life infused with His resurrection power (vv. 8-11). But such a life requires complete commitment to a goal that always lies beyond us, yet whose pursuit offers a heavenly prize (vv. 12-14). Paul urges his readers to develop just this kind of mature attitude and to follow his example (vv. 15-17). As for those whose lives show another pattern, particularly a pattern revealing desires and goals that focus on this world, they should be noted and ignored (vv. 18-19). A real Christian's citizenship is in heaven and his/her heart is fixed on home (vv. 20-21).

Key verse. 3:10: A heavenly desire.

Personal application. A concern for heaven enables us to live a truly righteous life on earth.

Key concepts. Circumcision »p. 36. Flesh »p. 743. Righteousness »pp. 607, 734. Resurrection »p. 737. Maturity »p. 859. Example »p. 867. Cross »pp. 618, 789. Second Coming »p. 827.

INSIGHT

Faultless legalistic righteousness (3:6). Paul is drawing an important distinction. A person may so live by laws and rules that no one can charge him or her with breaking them. But this is only an external righteousness and not the inner complete moral harmony with God that the Lord requires. Paul had taken pride in conformity to the Mosaic Law until he realized that it neither commended him to God, nor made him a truly righteous man.

The power of Christ's resurrection (3:10-11). Some have been troubled by Paul's apparent uncertainty: that he will "somehow" be able to "attain to the resurrection from the dead." But Paul is writing here of a present life lived in that same resurrection power which raised Jesus from the dead. The *Expository Dictionary of Bible Words* (Zondervan, 1985, p. 529) asks, "What is resurrection power? This is one of the most exciting of N.T. themes. Paul writes that 'If the Spirit of Him who raised Jesus from the dead is living in you, He who raised Christ from the dead will also give life to your mortal bodies, through His Spirit, who lives in you' (Rom. 8:11). The point Paul makes is that the Holy Spirit, the agent of Jesus' resurrection, lives within the believer. This means that resurrection power is available to us even in our mortality." It is this present resurrection—a rising

above mere human limitations to live a truly righteous life—that Paul is speaking of here in Philippians.

"Forgetting what is behind" (3:13-14). The word Paul uses means "overlooking." Our past is irrelevant and those things we once relied on now must be discarded, that all our energy might be given to following Christ.

The goal (3:14). The goal is complete, present, experiential knowledge of Christ. And in a real way, this is also the prize. We press on, because Christ is too vast to know perfectly. Yet the more we learn of Him, the greater our joy and reward.

Citizenship in heaven (3:20-21). In the 1st century citizenship conveyed the right to hold office, the privilege of appeal to Roman courts, and protection anywhere in the empire. A citizen was not even responsible to local laws or courts without his consent. Paul reminds us that we are citizens of heaven. We live under God's protection. We can appeal directly to Him with any need. We do not give our consent to live by the values or ways of this world, but by the laws of heaven. We have a Ruler to whom we look, whose power "enables Him to bring everything under His control" and who will ultimately transform our bodies as well as our hearts and minds.

Chapter summary. The first verses look back. Paul urges those he loves to stand firm in the Lord (4:1). He has written of unity. Now he pleads for harmony between two women, each of whom is committed to the cause of the Gospel (vv. 2-3). Then Paul looks ahead. His dear friends will find the Lord their surest source of joy. Because of Him they need not be anxious. Because of Him, prayer brings the blessed gift of peace (vv. 4-7). And in response to Him, the Philippians are to focus on the beautiful and praiseworthy and to practice the same (vv. 8-9).

On a personal note Paul now turns to their financial support. He has great joy in it as an evidence of their concern, though he is as content when destitute as when well off. What thrills Paul is that in sharing with him the Philippians are giving to God, who will meet their needs and reward them (vv. 10-20). The letter concludes with the briefest of greetings (vv. 21-23).

Outline
Place
Finder

GOSPEL
UNITY
COMMITMENT
THE LORD

Key verse. 4:6: Real joy.

Personal application. All else may fail, but Jesus never.

Key concepts. Gospel »p. 737. Prayer »p. 609. Giving »p. 781.

INSIGHT

Agree in the Lord (4:2). This is not intellectual agreement, but interpersonal harmony. How tragic when believers with similar commitments and goals of serving God can't get along because of personality clashes.

"Prayer" (4:6). This is one of the most memorized verses of Scripture. We can commit all our concerns to the Lord. We will still care deeply about those things we pray for. But because we know God hears and cares too, we can care without being anxious.

"With thanksgiving" (4:6). Thanksgiving is to accompany requests, not be triggered only by answers to our prayers. We thank God because we know that God has not only heard our request, but will send what is good. Because our prayers have been answered even as we pray, thanks are appropriate.

"The peace of God" (4:7). This is the inner peace or sustaining confidence that God gives us when we pray with thanksgiving. That last phrase, "with thanksgiving," is important. Thanksgiving is an expression of assurance, and a reminder, that God has heard and will answer our prayer.

Think on these things (4:8). The Gk. word here is *logizomai*, which implies concentrated, focused effort. The verb form reminds us that we are to keep on stressing those things which share the qualities Paul lists: the true, which is the reliable and honest; the noble, or

worthy of respect; the right, which conforms to God's standards and merits approval; the pure, which is moral and chaste; the lovely, which is pleasing and agreeable; the admirable, which is worthy of praise.

A pattern for teaching (4:9). God's truth is to be communicated as concepts — learned, received, and heard. But to be perceived as reality rather than philosophy, truth must also be "seen in" the teacher. When truth is communicated in words by those who model the lived meaning of those words, then and only then are they likely to be "put into practice." And only when we put God's truth into practice will we sense the God of peace with us.

"Content" (4:12). What is Paul's secret of contentment "in every and any situation," whether destitute or well supplied with funds? He has just shared it. It is to present his requests to God with thanksgiving — and then stop worrying about his circumstances.

"Receiving" (4:14-19). It is often more difficult to receive graciously than to give graciously. Paul wants his friends to know he is truly grateful for their financial contribution, without making them feel obligated to send more. He does this by expressing the greatest joy he derives from their generosity. Their offering will be an "acceptable sacrifice," which pleases the Lord. And they will experience God at work to meet their own needs.

Colossians

All agree that Paul wrote his letter to the Colossians to combat a heresy. There's little agreement about the exact shape of that heresy. Yet it clearly contained both pagan and Jewish elements and, though masquerading as a form of Christianity, it denied Christ His central place and distorted the Christian lifestyle reflected in all the New Testament writings. In attempting to reconstruct the heresy from the truths Paul puts forward most strongly, many scholars have concluded it was an early form of Gnosticism.

Gnosticism takes its name from the claim of its proponents to have access to a superior, hidden knowledge, or *gnosis*. The Gnostics made a sharp distinction between matter and spirit. The material was essentially evil; God and good were essentially spiritual. It followed that God could not have created the world, that Christ could not be God incarnate, and that what Christ did on the cross in a material body could not really accomplish salvation. Salvation could only be achieved when the divine spark held captive in the material body was released. What a person did in the body mattered little, so some adopted the most profligate lifestyles, while others turned to asceticism to loosen the cords which held the inner man to the body.

There is great value in the Book of Colossians for Christians today. In warning those being influenced by an early heresy the Apostle Paul has sketched for us a bright, clear vision of Jesus Christ and His central role not only in God's plan, but in our lives. As we read this great book prayerfully we cannot help but be brought closer to our Lord.

THE COLOSSIAN HERESY AND PAUL'S RESPONSE

The material world is evil; God is spiritual. God can have nothing to do with the material universe.

"For by Him [Jesus] all things were created; things in heaven and on earth, visible and invisible" (1:16).

If Jesus created the world, He could not be God.

"God was pleased to have all His fullness dwell in Him" (1:19).

Well, nothing that happens in the material world can really make a difference spiritually.

"You . . . were [God's] enemies in your minds because of your evil behavior. But now He has reconciled you by Christ's physical body through death" (1:21-22).

But we don't need to be reconciled. Our bodies are evil because they are material. Our minds aren't material and so we are good.

"You were dead in your sins and in the uncircumcision of your sinful nature. [Then] God made you alive with Christ. He forgave us all our sins" (2:13).

Well, real spirituality is still a matter of one's inner life. We approach God mentally and what we do here is irrelevant to Him.

"As God's chosen people, holy and dearly loved, clothe yourselves with compassion, kindness, humility . . . do it all in the name of the Lord Jesus" (2:12, 17).

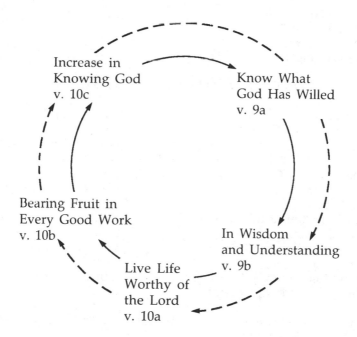

Chart: Colossians 1:9-11. *Paul's prayer outlines the way in which believers can experience true spiritual growth. Spiritual growth begins with a knowledge of objective truth revealed in Scripture: "what God has willed." But we treat that truth with "wisdom and insight," seeking to understand its practical implications for our daily life. We then apply God's truth, making choices which please Him in every way and are "worthy of the Lord." As we do live a worthy life, we "bear fruit in every good work" and we come to know God in a personal intimate way, not just intellectually but experientially as well. There is no end to this wonderful process that offers us so much. We can keep on studying His work, keep on letting God's Word shape our choices and our character. As we do we will not only find our lives are fruitful, but also that we grow closer to the Lord.*

Date and Authorship. This letter was written by Paul during his first Roman imprisonment, most likely between A.D. 59 and 61. It is one of the most important of the New Testament letters in its clear affirmation of the centrality of Jesus Christ and explanation of how Jesus relates to our every experience.

Colossae

The city of Colossae lay in the Lycus River valley in what is now Turkey. Its population was a mixture of Greek, Jewish, and native Phrygians, along with Roman army veterans. The heresy Paul deals with in his letter seems to be a mixture of Jewish, pagan, and pseudo-Christian concepts. The letter was later circulated to other congregations (cf. 4:16) to guard them against similar errors.

THEOLOGICAL OUTLINE OF COLOSSIANS

CONTENT OUTLINE OF COLOSSIANS

Chapter summary. Paul's greeting (1:1-2) is followed by heartfelt thanksgiving for the impact of the Gospel (vv. 3-8) and a prayer which outlines the way to spiritual fruitfulness (vv. 9-11) in Christ's kingdom (vv. 12-14). Paul then quickly draws the Colossians' attention to Christ. The Jesus Paul describes is the real Christ: the One in whom we find redemption and forgiveness. This Christ is the visible manifestation of the invisible God, the heir of all creation (v. 15). This Christ is the creative source of the visible and invisible universe, who not only made all things but whose power holds all things together (vv. 16-17). He is supreme over everything and though God in His fullness, His blood shed on the cross is the source of reconciliation for all humankind (vv. 18-20). Paul says it again: God in Christ took on a physical body and in that body He died to make us holy (vv. 21-23).

As for Paul, he gladly accepts any personal sufferings in order to share the great mystery of the Gospel: that this glorious Christ now takes up residence in the believer and is Himself the hope of all the glorious things that await you and me here, and in eternity (vv. 24-29).

Key verse. 1:19: The real Jesus.

Personal application. Christianity must be Christ-centered.

Key concepts. Faith »p. 740. Love »p. 690. Hope »p. 465. Inheritance »p. 745. Redemption »p. 791. Forgiveness »p. 634. Firstborn »p. 855. Church »pp. 768, 794. Reconcile »p. 778. Gospel »p. 737.

Outline
Place
Finder

TRUTH
WAY
LIFE
NOTES

INSIGHT

"Saints" (1:4). The word, meaning holy ones or set apart ones, is frequently used with the simple meaning, "believers" or "Christians."

Producing fruit and growing (1:6). It's good to remember when folks come crying for something better, that the Gospel has proven its vitality and life-changing power the world over, in every age.

Knowing God (1:9-12). Scripture makes a distinction between knowing *about* God, knowing Him in a saving way through faith, and knowing God, in the sense of experiencing His presence. Paul's prayer reminds us that to know God in this way we need to grasp the implications of Scripture for living and put God's Word into practice (»p. 811).

Knowing God's will (1:9). Here the phrase is to *thelematos autou,* "that which God has willed." We know what God has willed through His objective revelation as found in the Scriptures. Knowing God personally and experientially starts with the objective revelation given us in God's Word.

"The image of the invisible God" (1:15). *Eikon* here means "manifestation." God is perfectly expressed and revealed in Jesus (cf. John 1:18).

Christ as Creator (1:16-17). Three prepositions are used: Creation is in (*en*) Him, in that His person and power enfolded it. Creation is through (*dia*) Him, in that He was its agent. Creation is for (*eis*) Him, in that He is the goal toward which all this moves. Creation thus from the beginning depends on Christ and is intended to redound to His glory.

"Alienated from God" (1:21). The word here is *apallotrioo,* found only here and in Eph. 2:12 and 4:18. It indicates a desperate state of utter separation and isolation, which in lost humanity's relationship with God is also marked by hostility. It is our own evil which makes us hostile to, and which alienates us from, God.

Christ's death (1:21-22). The Gnostics downgraded the role of Christ, assuming that if He took on a material body He must have been very distant from God. But not only was God fully present in Christ, the death of Jesus was the means God used to bring man and the universe back into harmony with Him. The actual, literal death of Jesus is the means God used to save us and make us holy.

Outline
Place
Finder

TRUTH
WAY
LIFE
NOTES

Chapter summary. Paul prays constantly that the believers in Colossae and Laodicea may really understand what they have in Christ, who is the storehouse where God has placed all the "treasures of wisdom and knowledge" (2:1-5). Gnostics claim access to a superior knowledge, but the secret of the Christian's life is to remain rooted in the Lord (vv. 6-7). Paul then lists a series of warnings. Spiritual reality is not to be found in "deceptive philosophy," but in union with a Christ in whom all the fullness of the Deity lives in bodily form (vv. 8-15). Spiritual reality is not found in legalism (vv. 16-17), in the worship of angels (vv. 18-19), or in an asceticism which makes a person look good, but has no value in restraining expressions of one's sin nature (vv. 20-23).

Key verses. 2:2-3: Where to look.

Personal application. Deepening our relationship with Jesus is the one way to a vital spiritual life.

Key concepts. Mystery »p. 747. Circumcision »pp. 36, 126. Sin »p. 741. Union with Christ »p. 692. Cross »p. 789. Angels »p. 521.

INSIGHT

Prayer (2:1). It's good to pray for those we know and love. But our vision needs to reach beyond this little circle to other brothers and sisters whom we may not have met, but whose needs we have come to know.

Treasures in Christ (2:2-3). The Gnostics claimed a superior, hidden knowledge that was superior to the revelation provided in the Christian Gospel. In fact, the treasures of wisdom and knowledge are "hidden" in Christ. Here "hidden" does not mean concealed, but stored up, to be accessible to us.

Life in Christ (2:6-7). Four participles describe how we relate to Christ to draw on His riches: (1) Rooted (*errizomenoi*). The tense looks back to that saving faith that initially united us to Jesus. The tense always comes first. (2) Built up (*epoikodomoumenoi*). Here the tense emphasizes a continual process of growth. (3) Strengthened (*bebaioumenoi*). The present tense shows a continual process of deepening faith, described in 1:9-11. (4) Overflowing with thankfulness (*perisseuontes*). Again a continual experience, abounding through the meaningfulness of our experience with Jesus.

"Philosophy" (2:8). Hollow and deceptive philosophy depends on human tradition. The whole system presented by the false teachers in Colossians was mere "basic principles of this world"—an ignorant child's play with ABC's—not the advanced truth they claimed.

"Fullness" (2:9). Earlier too Paul spoke of Christ possessing the fullness (*pleroma*) of God. In this chapter Paul means simply that all God

can be and is for us is summed up in Jesus. We don't need a "better way" because relationship with Jesus provides us with all of God.

Real circumcision (2:9-15). Jewish elements in the "deceptive philosophy" of the false teachers emphasized circumcision—an external rite. But faith unites us with Jesus, and this baptism accomplishes a circumcision which "puts off" the sinful nature. This is the "fullness" we have been given in Christ and find only in Him.

"The Cross" (2:14). The phrase is frequently used in the N.T. as a term for the Gospel.

"Canceled the written code" (2:14). Because we could not meet the Law's demands it was "against us." But it is no longer. The Gk. word means to "wipe out" or "wipe away." The blood of Jesus washed all that was written against us off the bill of indictment, and we are free.

"Powers and authorities" (2:15). The reference is to hostile angelic or supernatural powers.

"Worship of angels" (2:18-19). Developed Gnosticism supposed that a long row of angels stood between the material universe and the immaterial God. The most powerful angels were the furthest from the material. Many worshiped and sought to contact these angels.

Asceticism (2:20-23). Paul says do's and don'ts are of no "value in restraining sensual indulgence." People who "don't" get proud, and condemn folks who "do." And these sins are as much an expression of the flesh, or sin nature, as the action the person is proud of refusing!

Outline
Place
Finder

TRUTH
WAY
LIFE
NOTES

Chapter summary. The Gnostics argued that the body was hostile to the spirit, for the material was essentially evil. Some turned to asceticism to weaken the body. Some gave in to licentiousness, dismissing what the "evil" body did as morally irrelevant. But Paul has shown that God entered the material world and in a real human body won us salvation. Now he shows that the way we live in our body does make a difference. In fact, true spirituality is living a human life, here on earth in union with God.

Since we have been raised with Christ (3:1-4), we "put to death" the sins that belong to our earthly, sin nature (vv. 5-8). We have put on a new "self," renewed in God's image (vv. 9-11). Thus, as God's people we live with others the kind of life Jesus lived here on earth, so that all we do can be said to be done "in the name of the Lord Jesus" (vv. 12-17). Here too Paul reminds us that we are each to live this way in the framework of the role we have been assigned — as spouse, parent or child, slave or free. In whatever setting we find ourselves we can live in a way that expresses, and pleases, God (3:18–4:1).

Key verse. 3:17: What we do in the body does concern God.

Personal application. Everything we say and do reflects on the God we claim to know and love.

Key concepts. Holy »p. 86. Wrath »p. 72. Name »p. 691. Submission »p. 867. Headship in marriage »p. 802.

INSIGHT

"Right hand" (3:1). This is the traditional symbol of royal power. In being raised with Christ we have been given vast power for godly living.

"Things above" (3:2). A heavenly orientation is the believer's ultimate concern in his or her relationship with Christ. As Paul will soon go on to show, our focus on things above is to make a significant difference on our life below.

"You died" (3:3). Since we died and were raised with Christ, anything foreign to Jesus should be foreign to us.

"Put to death" (3:5). As those who have been raised with Christ we must let our old life wither away and die. Everything evil is under God's wrath, and everything evil in us was punished in Christ's death for us. We're to let it die.

"The new self" (3:9-10). The image of a new creation is common in Paul. We died with Christ and were given new life by Him. We are still our conscious self, the same person. But at the same time we are new persons. The old in us died, now something new and holy is planted deep within.

The Creator's image (3:10). Paul saw God's image "is being renewed." A constant process of reshaping us is going on. And as our

"knowledge" — perspective, understanding, attitudes, and outlook — grows the effect is to become more and more like our Creator.

Clothed with compassion (3:12-14). How does God's life in us express itself in practice? In the way that Christians relate to each other, showing the compassion, kindness, humility, and readiness to forgive that Jesus demonstrated when He was here on earth, revealing God in His own way of life. In a real sense, the church as the body of Christ is a continuing incarnation of the Lord, to whom we are all intimately linked.

Let peace rule (3:15-17). A beautiful calm and harmony emerge as Christians focus on living as God's new people. As God's people assemble and worship Christ together both unity and peace will result. Unified and confident, God's people will focus on what is really important in the Christian life — doing whatever we do in Jesus' name and giving God thanks through Him.

"Admonish" (3:16). The Gk. word means to "warn or advise." It reemphasizes the practical dimension of Christian teaching. The series of instructions Paul gives in 3:18–4:1 are examples of admonitions.

Outline
Place
Finder

TRUTH
WAY
LIFE
NOTES

Chapter summary. Paul concludes his lifestyle instructions with a word about prayer and witnessing (4:2-6). He then introduces Tychicus, who will carry this letter (vv. 7-9), and sends greetings from several mutual friends who are currently with him in Rome (vv. 10-15). Finally Paul instructs the Colossians to send the letter on to others when it has been read and studied in Colossae (vv. 16-18).

Key verse. 4:4: Everyone needs prayer.

Personal application. How easy it is for people to accept our instruction when they know we care about them.

Key concept. Prayer »p. 608.

INSIGHT

Devoted to prayer (4:2). The Gk. word, *kartereite*, suggests strength and persistence. Prayer is a Christian's continual duty, one calling for an active watchfulness rather than lethargy.

"For us" (4:3). One of Paul's strengths was his awareness of his need for prayer. When we feel we are capable of going it on our own, we are in serious spiritual danger.

"Every opportunity" (4:5). Opportunities come for Christians to witness when they relate to others with tact and sensitivity. Don't antagonize non-Christians and then blame them for failing to accept the Gospel.

Conversation full of grace (4:6). Here as in several other passages "grace" (*charis*) is used in the sense of attractive, pleasant, or winsome. Some have noted that "salt" in Hellenistic culture symbolized wit. Christians aren't to be dull folks, or overweening and boring. Everything about the believer should be as attractive as possible and so open up opportunities to answer questions about Christian faith.

"Tychicus" (4:7-8). This associate of Paul is mentioned several times in the N.T., but little more is known about him than is found in this passage.

"Onesimus" (4:9). This runaway slave, whose story is told in the letter to Philemon, is much better known than his companion Tychicus.

See that it is read in Laodicea (4:16). The letters that make up our N.T. were all quickly copied and circulated among the 1st-century churches. Lists of the letters accepted by all the churches from the early 2nd century show how quickly the N.T. letters were recognized as Scripture by the church throughout the Roman world.

1 Thessalonians

This letter to the Thessalonians may be the earliest of his epistles. Thessalonica was the largest commercial center in southeastern Europe in Paul's day. It lay on the Aegean Sea and the major road called the Via Egnatia. The city had a large Jewish population and an active synagogue where Paul could speak and reach his fellow Jews and a large number of Gentiles, called "God-fearers," who accepted Scripture's religious and moral vision without converting to Judaism. The city had supported Augustus in the civil war that saw this emperor come to power and had been rewarded with the status of a free city, permitting its officers to govern internal affairs.

Paul came to Thessalonica early on his second missionary journey (Acts 17). The brief account in this book seems to suggest that soon after preaching on three Sabbaths in the local synagogue, the Jewish population, jealous over the responsiveness of leading Gentiles to Paul's message, staged a riot. Paul may have been in the city longer. However, as he mentions, working there at his trade (1 Thes. 2:9; 2 Thes. 3:8) he was able to establish a strong and thriving church (1 Thes. 1:9) and before leaving received two gifts from Philippi, five days' journey away (Phil. 4:16). He was also there long enough to firmly ground the church in basic Christian teachings, many of which he alludes to in this letter. Still, considerable confusion did seem to exist over one vital theme—the return of Christ. And so, in the two letters of Paul to the Thessalonians, we have the New Testament's clearest picture of what will happen at the time of Jesus' return.

As we read the Thessalonian letters it's important to remember that, just as Jesus' first coming involved a span of years, from His birth to His death and resurrection, what we call the Second Coming also involves events which are spread over a span of years. The Thessalonian letters, like the Old Testament prophets, speak of a time of great tribulation. They speak of the appearance of a "man of lawlessness," the Antichrist. They describe Jesus' personal return to catch His church up to meet Him in the air and a terrible appearance with armies of angels to "take vengeance" in "flaming fire" on all those who do not know God. Paul gives us no charts showing how all these events fit together. But he does remind us these things are coming. Perhaps very soon!

KEY DOCTRINES MENTIONED IN 1 AND 2 THESSALONIANS

Inspiration and authority of Scripture	1 Thes. 2:13; 2 Thes. 2:15; 3:6, 17
One God existing in three Persons	1 Thes. 1:1, 5-6; 4:8; 5:19; 2 Thes. 2:13
Jesus is God	1 Thes. 3:11-12; 2 Thes. 2:16-17
Salvation based on Christ's death	1 Thes. 4:14; 5:9; 2 Thes. 2:13-14
The believer's union with Christ	1 Thes. 1:1; 5:5; 2 Thes. 1:1
Sanctification expressed in way of life	1 Thes. 4:3-12; 5:12-18
The importance of prayer	1 Thes. 3:11-13; 5:23-24; 2 Thes. 1:11-12; 2:16-17; 3:5, 16
Jesus' return for His church	1 Thes. 4:13-18; 2 Thes. 2:1
Appearance and activity of a "lawless one"	2 Thes. 2:1-11
Terrible judgments on sinners	1 Thes. 1:10; 2:16; 2 Thes. 1:6-10
Peace and glory for believers	1 Thes. 1:10; 5:9; 2 Thes. 1:7, 10, 12; 2:13-14
Christian responsibility to work till then	1 Thes. 4:11-12; 5:14; 2 Thes. 3:6-15

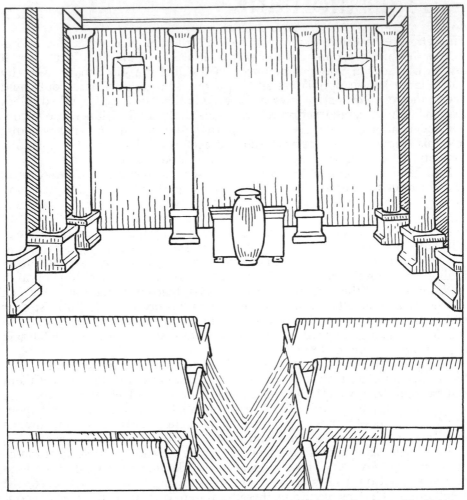

A 1st-century synagogue. *At the front of the building was the "ark of the covenant," a highly decorated container for the scrolls of sacred Scripture. Chairs facing the congregation were reserved for the leading men of the religious community. The service featured a number of set prayers and psalms, the reading of Scripture, and also exhortation and teaching. Qualified visitors were often invited to address the congregation. Paul's missionary strategy was to go first to the local synagogue and preach there. This was motivated by Paul's love for his own people, but also by the realization that Gentiles who attended synagogue services were the most likely to respond to the Gospel. The core of most of the churches Paul founded was formed of believers won at the city synagogue.*

Date and Authorship. First Thessalonians was written by Paul to the church he founded in Thessalonica. Paul was in the city in the summer of A.D. 49, but quickly forced out by riots stimulated by a hostile Jewish population. He wrote from Corinth, perhaps as early as the spring of A.D. 50.

THEOLOGICAL OUTLINE OF 1 THESSALONIANS

CONTENT OUTLINE OF 1 THESSALONIANS

Chapter summary. Paul begins his letter with thanksgiving for the way the Thessalonians have responded to the Gospel. After a brief greeting (1:1) Paul expresses his thanks for a trio of evidences that the conversion of these believers is real (vv. 2-3). Paul goes on to further explain his confidence. The way these people have responded to God's Word demonstrates the reality of His work in them. The Gospel came to them (vv. 4-5), they welcomed that Word (v. 6), and their lives showed its impact: They became agents who spread the Word in their city and the region it dominated (vv. 7-8) and word of their sincerity in turning to God from idols has spread everywhere (vv. 9-10).

Key verse. 1:5: The Word's impact.

Personal application. The best evidence the Word has been heard is that it then is shared with others.

Key concepts. Church »p. 794. Works »p. 872. Love »pp. 126, 691. Hope »p. 465. God's choice of individuals »p. 797 Gospel »p. 737. Holy Spirit »pp. 744, 759.

INSIGHT

Remembering (1:3). All too many of us have unpleasant memories of our upbringing, a church experience, or even of our children. Paul's memories are pleasant and stimulate him to prayers of thanksgiving. Three positive traits seem important to God: work, labor, endurance. These are important because they are the product of three Christian virtues which only the Holy Spirit can produce in a person's life: faith, love, and hope.

We have no control over the memories with which others leave us. But we do have control over the memories we leave our loved ones! Let's let the Spirit work in us, so that when we are remembered it will be with a joy stimulated by the practical expression of our own faith, love, and hope.

"He has chosen" (1:4). Both God's activity in saving an individual and the individual's inner response to the Lord are hidden, taking place in eternity past and within the heart. But the reality of a person's salvation soon becomes evident in the life of the believer. The true Christian becomes an "imitator" of the Lord. A changed life reveals God's choice and our faith.

"Power" (1:5). The Gk. word *dynamei* refers to the Spirit's power operating in and through the person who shares the Gospel. When we witness we're not alone. Let's consciously rely on the Holy Spirit.

"Deep conviction" (1:5). This is the conviction of the speaker, the utter certainty that the Gospel message is God's own Word.

The effect of the Gospel (1:6-7). Five things trace the impact the Gospel had in Thessalonica and is to have wherever it is preached. (1) The Gospel is welcomed, that is, listeners are converted. (2) The converts adhere to Christ, "in spite of severe suffering." (3) The converts experience joy despite their difficulties. (4) The converts quickly imitate or pattern their lives on that of their teacher and the Lord. (5) The converts become evangelists, who go on to share the Gospel they have heard with others.

Yes, "only believe" is the way to be saved. But after salvation each of us is called to a new, challenging, and disciplined way of life.

"Severe suffering" (1:6). The Gk. word *thlipsis* means hardship or tribulation. It's found frequently in the Thessalonian letters, evidence that the antagonism Paul aroused in the Jewish community persisted and was directed against the new church.

To God from evil (1:9). Reformation alone doesn't work. A person can give up drink, drugs, or crime. But unless he or she turns from evil to God, no real change can be maintained. Reform, no. Complete renewal through the power of the Gospel, yes.

Outline
Place
Finder

HEARD
SHARED
LIVED

Chapter summary. Paul now describes his ministry in Thessalonica. His pictures of the relationship he developed with the Thessalonians are warm and intimate, close and caring. They help us realize the relational context in which the Gospel message is to be shared. Few are won by preaching to vast audiences; most are won to Christ by family or friends.

Paul has been so close to the Thessalonians that he is sure they know his motives and total honesty (2:1-6). They remember a love that was like a mother's for an infant: a giving, sharing love that moved the apostle to pour himself out as well as share the Gospel (vv. 7-8). It was a love that moved him to work to support himself rather than burden anyone (v. 9). It was a love that led him to deal with each individual believer as a concerned father guides and corrects his adolescent children (vv. 10-12). That same love moves Paul to pray for them constantly now that they are separated (vv. 13-16) and tears Paul apart emotionally with longing to see them again (vv. 17-20).

Key verse. 2:8: Effective evangelism.

Personal application. A word spoken in love is the most likely to be heard.

Key concepts. Church as family »p. 799. Gospel »p. 737. Gentle »p. 782. Righteous »p. 734. Satan »p. 501.

INSIGHT

Opposition to the Gospel (2:2-3). Some people in every age dislike the Gospel and oppose it. The things they say haven't changed from the 1st century to today. The Gospel is "error," *planes*, which means self-delusion or deceit. The motives of preachers are impure (cf. v. 5). Preachers try to trick the unwary into a foolish commitment.

It's tragic when impure motives or trickery mark those who claim they promote the Gospel. Paul goes on to show us how to set such attacks to rest!

"Praise from men" (2:5-6). What might corrupt a person who preaches the Gospel and so expose the Gospel itself to criticism? We've seen all too much of such things in our own time: greed with a desire to "build an empire" and so look big in the eyes of the world. How vital that we care only how God evaluates our service for Him.

Motives in ministry (2:7-9). Paul describes what motivates him and how his motives find expression in ministry. He is motivated by a love that is like a mother's love for a helpless infant. That deep love expressed itself in Thessalonica by: (1) gentleness, marked by tenderness rather than authoritarian brusqueness. (2) Sharing, not only the Gospel but "our lives as well." The phrase means the missionary team encouraged complete openness and revealed their inmost thoughts and motives. (3) Toil

and hardship, working in order not to burden anyone with their support.

When our leaders demonstrate love in these ways we can trust them and follow them gladly.

More on relationships (2:10-12). Paul's description of the relationship he developed with the Thessalonicans continues, with a shift in image. Paul now is a father, with adolescent sons who need guidance. What's significant here is that Paul claims to have given this guidance to "each one of you." Ministry is individual, not just public! Paul somehow found time to know each individual so well that he knew who needed "encouraging" (exhortation), who needed "comforting" (warm support), and who needed "urging" (an authoritative command).

The Gospel is communicated most effectively in a context of relationships in which you share yourself and come to know others intimately.

Hope, joy, and crown of rejoicing (2:17-20). There are personal benefits for the evangelist in his ministry. What will thrill Paul most is the fact that when Christ returns, he will be able to present the believers to the Lord as his gift.

Joy (2:19-20). Joy is produced by the Holy Spirit (Rom. 14:17; Gal. 5:22). But it is most often linked in Scripture with God's work in fellow believers whom we love (cf. Rom. 16:19; 2 Cor. 1:24; 7:7; Phil. 1:4; 2:2; 4:1; 2 Tim. 1:4; etc.).

Outline
Place
Finder

HEARD
SHARED
LIVED

Chapter summary. Paul continues the description of his deep affection for the Thessalonians. That affection motivated his sharing of the Gospel with them and was expressed in the relationship he developed with church and individuals (chap. 2). That love continues to motivate Paul and in fact stimulated him to send Timothy to check on their progress (3:1-5). What's more, Timothy's report gave, and continues to give, Paul a thrill of joy (vv. 6-9). It also stimulated him to pray for them even more earnestly (v. 10) and to wish for them that overflowing love and inner strength which will keep the church blameless and holy till Jesus comes (vv. 11-13).

Key verse. 3:6: Sometimes we feel we have to know.

Personal application. Keep in touch with those you love.

Key concepts. Trials »p. 871. Persecution »p. 760. Love »pp. 661, 690, 691, 778. Holy »p. 81.

INSIGHT

Weakness (3:1). Paul isn't ashamed to confess a weakness for those he loves. He couldn't hold out against his anxious concern for the Thessalonians' spiritual well-being. He just had to know.

"Timothy" (3:2). Timothy accompanied Paul on many of his missionary journeys. Paul frequently sent him as a messenger and troubleshooter to visit churches for him. Two of Paul's N.T. letters contain his mission instructions for Timothy. Here Timothy's mission was to "strengthen and encourage you in your faith."

Destined for trials (3:3-4). The word here is *thlipisis* which indicates severe difficulties and a serious test of faith. Paul knows that such experiences are unavoidable and an integral part of Christian experience.

To find out about your faith (3:5). While trials are certain, how we respond to them is not! Paul knows that we have the freedom to respond wrongly as well as wisely. What a relief it is to find out that those we care about have made right rather than wrong choices.

Two kinds of good news (3:6-8). Paul was relieved to find out that he was remembered with warmth and affection. How painful unreturned love would have been! And Paul was delighted to hear that the faith of the Thessalonians remained firm.

Prayer in return for joy (3:9-10). Paul senses the bond that exists between him and the Thessalonians is stronger than ever and is filled with joy. This in turn motivates him to even more persistent, more earnest prayer. The best thing we can do for those whose love gives us joy is pray for them.

"Love increase and overflow" (3:12). Love for other believers in the local body is shown throughout the N.T. to be the key to spiritual growth, unity, and increasing experience of God's presence.

"Blameless and holy" (3:13). Love will strengthen us in our mutual commitment to live holy lives. When Jesus comes He will bring His "holy ones" (angels) and yearns to find holy believers here awaiting Him.

822

Chapter summary. Paul now instructs the Thessalonians further on living to please God (4:1-2). Paul reminds his converts that God calls believers to live holy lives, separate from sexual immorality and lusts (vv. 3-8). He urges them to love each other and all the brothers even more than they do now (vv. 9-10) and reminds them of the importance of honest work (vv. 11-12). Finally, he clears up a misunderstanding about Christ's return. When Jesus comes for His church the dead in Christ won't "miss out," as some thought they might. When Jesus comes in the cloud to gather His church, the dead will rise and then they, with the living, will rise up together to meet the Lord in the air (vv. 13-17). What a source of comfort and encouragement for those who have lost loved ones. Reunion awaits, in the presence of Christ (v. 18).

Outline
Place
Finder

HEARD
SHARED
LIVED

Key verse. 4:1: Worth working at.

Personal application. When the Word doesn't find expression in the daily life of the believer, it has not really been heard.

Key concepts. Immorality »pp. 45, 60, 135, 388. Love »pp. 661, 690. Work »p. 28. Second Coming »pp. 581, 827.

INSIGHT

"More and more" (4:1). Never be satisfied even with significant spiritual achievement. The Christian life is one of open-ended growth. There is always more for us to attain to. And what a joy this is. Life for us remains challenging; the vista of our future features bright new visions lying just over the top of the next hill.

Sexual purity (4:3-8). The Gk. *porneias* here encompasses all sex sins which holiness demands the Christian reject. Like other temptations, sexual temptations have a positive side. When we resist them, they enable us to develop self-control (v. 4). The pagan who ridicules the believer for his "hang-ups" is himself the captive of his own "passionate lusts." The person who masters his body has the real freedom. The person who is driven by her glands acts like an animal rather than a human being, and so loses touch with her real self by indulging in sex sins.

Work (4:11-12). Paul mentions two values of work here: (1) it gains respect and (2) it keeps us from being dependent on others. In 2 Thes. 3:6-15 work is also basic to self-respect and taking personal responsibility. And Eph. 4:28 points out that if we work we not only care for ourselves, but gain something to share with others in need. So the value of work is not found in the wealth it produces but in the

personal responsibility work reflects, the respect it earns, and in the opportunities its earnings give us to do good.

The rapture (4:13-18). In the premillennial understanding, this is the name usually given to the event described here. Its relationship to other aspects of the Second Coming is debated. But the reassurance these verses provide that we will be united with loved ones who have passed away has been experienced by all.

"Fall asleep" (4:13). The image is a frequent euphemism for death. The parallels are obvious: neither the sleeping nor the dead are aware of or respond to what is happening around them. Yet the sleep of death, which seems so permanent to the pagan, is shown here to be more like sleep than one could imagine. For just as a drowsing person awakens with the dawn, so the "sleeping" believer will awaken at Christ's return, to endless and glorious life.

The resurrection of believers (4:16). This passage pictures the raising of the dead "in Christ," a technical theological term for Christians. This is not the restoration to life of the unconverted, which is described in Rev. What happens to us in our resurrection is described in 1 Cor. 15.

Outline
Place
Finder

HEARD
SHARED
LIVED

Chapter summary. Paul reminds the Thessalonians that no one knows the time of the Lord's coming (5:1-3), so they must remain "awake" and alert, focusing together on living God's Word (vv. 4-11). He concludes his letter with a series of brief reminders of just what this means (vv. 12-22) and a benediction promising that our faithful God will "sanctify them through and through" till Jesus returns (vv. 23-28).

Key verse. 5:6: Expect His coming.

Personal application. The promise of Christ's return tomorrow is intended to purify the church today.

Key concepts. Second Coming »pp. 581, 823, 827. Light »p. 685. Salvation »pp. 742, 744, 849. Holy Spirit »pp. 73, 744, 759.

INSIGHT

Know well (5:2). The Gk. word *akribos* means accurate, precise knowledge. Paul made it very clear that the time of Christ's return for His church was unknown, but that it would be unexpected. That is, no precise signs would indicate it was about to happen and so warn believers to get ready.

Theologians speak of the "imminence" of Jesus' return, simply meaning it could happen at any moment.

"Darkness" (5:4-7). Darkness here and frequently in Scripture is the opposite of "light." Darkness is spiritual—without insight into reality as God knows and has revealed it. Darkness is moral—the realm in which sin is practiced. Those who live in darkness lie under the wrath of God.

Sons of light (5:4-11). Here "light" is both a moral and perspectival term. The believers do not stumble around in darkness, but are aware that Christ's return is imminent. As a result they are alert and self-controlled, a quality related in 4:4 to moral purity. Paul's point is that knowing Christ may return at any moment motivates us to live morally pure lives and so be ready for Him. Those who do not share this perspective lack the motivation to live morally and so live in a state of moral as well as mental darkness.

Drunkenness (5:7). Both Testaments speak of drunkenness. While neither O.T. nor N.T. condemn the use of alcohol itself, each condemns drunkenness. The *Expository Dictionary of Bible Words* (Zondervan, 1985, p. 238) sums up: "The images associated with drunkenness in the O.T.—such as reeling and staggering (Ps. 107:27; Isa. 19:14), wild spending and poverty (Deut. 21:20; Prov. 23:21)—suggest a loss of physical control and a loss of judgment." In the N.T. "drunkenness is associated with evil

practices (1 Thes. 5:7) and mention of it is found in lists of sinful practices that believers are not to engage in (1 Cor. 5:11; 6:10; Rom. 13:13; Gal. 5:21; 1 Peter 4:3). Paul's best known statement on drunkenness is 'Do not get drunk on wine, which leads to debauchery. Instead, be filled with the Spirit' (Eph. 5:18). Christians are to surrender control and judgment, not to alcohol, but to the Holy Spirit, who will teach us how to glorify God."

"He died for us" (5:10). His death was so sufficient in winning salvation for us that whether we are awake or asleep we will live together with Him. This assurance is no basis for lax living. It is the opposite. In appreciation for all Jesus has done we encourage each other and build each other up in actively living our faith.

"The Spirit's fire" (5:19). The Gk. indicates stopping something actually being practiced. It suggests that some were repressing the exercise of certain spiritual gifts—in context, prophecy.

Prophecy (5:20). In the N.T. church this involved prediction and instructions concerning local matters, a distinct spiritual gift (»p. 770).

Sanctify you through and through (5:23). Like save, "sanctify" has various meanings. It can stand for the finished work of Christ applied to the individual at salvation, through which we are pure in the sight of God (cf. Rom. 15:16; 1 Cor. 1:2). It can also indicate the gradual moral transformation toward actual holiness worked as the believer responds to the Word of God and the Spirit (cf. John 17:17; 1 Thes. 5:23; Heb. 10:29). The Christian has a holy standing through the work of Christ. As we respond to the Spirit of God He makes us more and more holy in our present state.

2 Thessalonians

Paul's second letter to the Thessalonians was also written from Corinth, the last location Paul, Silas, and Timothy were known to have been together. It was probably written shortly after the first letter, in response to new developments in Thessalonica. There persecution had intensified, and many of the victims were struggling with despair. The only way out seemed to lie in the return of Christ, and rumors had started that Paul himself was saying the time of the end had arrived! One practical impact of this on the church was that many simply stopped work and lived off others. Why worry if Jesus is coming back tomorrow?

In this letter Paul deals with each of these three issues. The Christian is suffering now, but God will repay the persecutors—and reward the faithful (1:1-12). As for Christ's return to earth, that takes place after the "Day of the Lord" described in Old Testament prophecy—after the Antichrist appears (2:1-17). As a result, there's no basis for the idleness of some. Paul's simple solution to that problem is don't feed idle people. If they're able-bodied and still won't work, they won't eat!

Paul's letter has many a helpful reminder for us. Christians do experience persecution, and redress is not always experienced in this world. But Christ will surely balance the books when He comes. In the meantime, we live as citizens of God's kingdom, always aware that the sinful human society is doomed.

Descriptions of Judgment

"They will be punished with everlasting destruction and shut out from the presence of the Lord and from the majesty of His power" (2 Thes. 1:9).

"For if God did not spare angels when they sinned, but sent them to hell, putting them into gloomy dungeons to be held for judgment; if He did not spare the ancient world when He brought the flood on its ungodly people . . . if He condemned the cities of Sodom and Gomorrah by burning them to ashes, and made them an example of what is going to happen to the ungodly . . . then the Lord knows how to rescue godly men from trials and to hold the unrighteous for the day of judgment. This is especially true of those who follow the corrupt desire of the sinful nature and despise authority" (2 Peter 2:4-10).

"The day of the Lord will come like a thief. The heavens will disappear with a roar; the elements will be destroyed by fire, and the earth and everything in it will be laid bare" (2 Peter 3:10).

"Then the kings of the earth, the princes and generals, the rich, the mighty, and every slave and every free man hid in caves and among the rocks of the mountains. They called to the mountains and the rocks, 'Fall on us and hide us from the face of Him who sits on the throne and from the wrath of the Lamb! For the great day of their wrath has come, and who can stand?' " (Rev. 6:15-17)

"The rest of mankind that were not killed by these plagues still did not repent of the work of their hands; . . . nor did they repent of their murders, their magic arts, their sexual immorality or their thefts" (Rev. 9:20-21).

"The sea gave up the dead that were in it, and death and Hades gave up the dead that were in them. . . . Then death and Hades were thrown into the lake of fire. . . . If anyone's name was not found written in the Book of Life, he was thrown into the lake of fire" (Rev. 20:13-15).

THEOLOGICAL OUTLINE OF 2 THESSALONIANS

CONTENT OUTLINE OF 2 THESSALONIANS

Chapter summary. As is his practice, Paul wishes the recipients of this letter grace and peace (1:1-2). He also expresses his thanks for the growing love for one another evidenced in the Thessalonian church and particularly for their perseverance in the face of growing persecution (vv. 3-4). Rather than meeting persecution with fear or doubts Paul reminds them that the active hostility of the unsaved is evidence that God's judgment is correct: People are sinners and desperately need the salvation they have experienced! (v. 5)

When Jesus returns, the persecutors will be punished terribly and they, who are victims now, will be revealed as Jesus' own holy people (1:6-10). Paul is not praying that the Thessalonians find immediate relief from their trials, but that they may be worthy of God's calling and fulfill His purposes in them (vv. 11-12). It is important to God and for us that we meet challenges well, not that we be released from them.

Outline
Place
Finder

JUDGMENT
ANTICHRIST
IDLENESS

Key verse. 1:9: Judgment is sure.

Personal application. Difficult times are a special invitation to us to grow.

Key concepts. Churches »p. 794. Persecution »p. 760. Trials »p. 871. Perseverance »p. 864. Justice »pp. 141, 372. Angels »p. 521. Name »p. 691. Glorify »p. 694. Calling of God »p. 828.

INSIGHT

"Faith" (1:4). Here *pistis*, linked as it is with perseverance, is better understood as "faithfulness." Perseverance itself is the capacity to endure the persistent trials forced on the believers by their adversaries.

"Evidence" (1:5). This verse goes with vv. 3-4. The hostility of the unconverted and the perseverance of the saints despite tribulations shows God's "judgment" is right. Two thoughts may be expressed here. The victimization of innocent Christians now is evidence that will be cited for the rightness of divine judgment then. It is also true that God's declarative judgment, the Christian being righteous in His sight, is also proven now by the godly, patient way in which believers respond to tribulation.

The Second Coming (1:7-10). The Second Coming involves a series of events, ranging from Christ's return "in the air" to catch up resurrected believers (1 Thes. 4), to the terrible "flaming fire" judgment described here, to the destruction of the material universe itself portrayed in 2 Peter 3. Some students of prophecy argue, based on Daniel's prophecy of 70 weeks (»p. 520), that the O.T. and N.T. predictions require at least a seven-year period to be fulfilled.

The books balanced (1:6-7). Many complain that God is not fair. The wicked prosper, and the good suffer. Paul insists that God is not simply fair. He is just. And justice requires that He "pay back trouble to those who trouble you" and "give relief, to those who are troubled." God is fair. But He does not balance the books every weekend.

Punishment (1:8-9). Gk. words translated "punish" include *dike*, which indicates a just or righteous response to those who do evil; *kolazo*, which indicates the painfulness of the experience for those who are being punished; *timoria* and *epitimia*, which indicate a rebuke administered as punishment; and *paideuo* which means to guide or direct, sometimes by punishment. In these verses the root is *dik-*, a righteous response to those who do evil. God's punishments are not vindictive, but they are harsh when wickedness must be redressed.

Prayer for the suffering (1:11-12). Paul knows that difficulty and tribulation in the Christian's life, even when caused by active persecution, are permitted for God's own positive purposes. So Paul prays that the believers may respond in a worthy way and fulfill the purposes He has in mind for them. When troubles persist, let's also ask God for such strength, not just for relief.

Outline
Place
Finder

JUDGMENT
ANTICHRIST
IDLENESS

Chapter summary. Rumors had been sweeping the Thessalonian church that Paul identified the present tribulation as the onset of the "Day of the Lord." This Old Testament phrase is used in prophecy to indicate the culminating events associated with history's end (2:1-2). Paul points out that this could not possibly be: The "man of lawlessness" (the Antichrist) has not yet appeared (vv. 3-5). The evil principle that will find full expression in the Antichrist is at work in present history, but its full expression is currently held back by the Holy Spirit (vv. 6-7a). When the Spirit's dampening presence is removed the Antichrist will be unveiled, identified by demonically energized miracles that delude the unconverted (vv. 7b-12).

As believers called to live in troubled times, the Thessalonians must rejoice in their salvation and in the awareness that when Jesus comes they will share His glory (vv. 13-15). So Paul, raising his hands in benediction, blesses them with encouragement, hope, and strength for every good deed (vv. 16-17).

Key verse. 2:13: It's what's ahead that counts.

Personal application. Usually the way out is to tough it.

Key concepts. Day of the Lord »pp. 413, 541. Temple »p. 283. Satan »p. 501. Sanctification »p. 824. Glory »p. 74. Gospel »p. 737.

INSIGHT

"The rebellion" (2:3). The Gk. *apostasia* is the deliberate abandonment of a professed position. Not a mass defection of professing Christians, this may be a mass abandonment of moral standards affirmed by society.

Lawlessness (2:2). The Gk. *anomia* is not lack of law, but active violation of moral principles.

Antichrist (2:3). The word itself occurs only in John's writings, in a general way to indicate those who are hostile to Christ (1 John 2:18, 22) and also of a personal, specific individual who is "the" Antichrist (2:18). The Gospels refer to this same person as a "false Christ" (Matt. 24:24; Mark 13:22). Our understanding of this person and his role is drawn from Dan. 11–12, Matt. 24 and Mark 13, and Rev. 11, 13. These passages portray an individual energized by Satan, who leads humanity in a last, futile rebellion against God.

In this passage Paul describes his motivation—"He will oppose and will exalt himself over everything that is called God"—and also a specific act—he even "sets himself up in God's temple, proclaiming himself to be God." This act is described in Dan. 11 and referred to by Jesus in Matt. 24:15 as the "abomination that causes desolation."

Paul's point in reviewing these teachings is clear. If the rebellion has not occurred, and the Antichrist has not appeared, it can't be that

prophecy's "Day of the Lord" has arrived.

"In God's temple" (2:4). References to the Antichrist's desecration of God's temple has led many to believe that the Jerusalem temple will be rebuilt before Jesus returns to carry out the vengeance described in 2 Thes. 1.

The final rebellion. A brief discussion of the world conflict to come at history's end, as described by the O.T. prophets, is found on p. 428.

Counterfeit miracles (2:9). Revelation 13 gives a further description of supernatural powers exercised at history's end by the Antichrist and his chief supporter. It is fascinating that while the miracles Christ performed failed to produce faith in Israel, lost humanity will be completely deceived by the Antichrist's miracles and link hands with Satan. There is no defense against delusion except for faith in Jesus Christ and reliance on His revealed Word.

Called through the Gospel (2:14). A "call" is issued by a person of higher rank to those of lower rank. It is an invitation, but also more than an invitation. It is a command that requires the person called to respond.

In the epistles, Paul frequently uses "call" and "called" in a distinctive theological sense. The "called" have *heard* and *responded.* In consequence these are folks who have been saved through the Gospel and are already involved in life's greatest adventure.

Chapter summary. Paul is well aware that everyone in the present difficult times needs prayer — himself included. God will answer prayer and not only strengthen His people but deliver them from the evil one (3:1-5).

Outline
Place
Finder

JUDGMENT
ANTICHRIST
IDLENESS

Paul then deals rather bluntly with believers who have used the rumors about history's imminent end to quit work and live off their more industrious brothers and sisters. Don't feed them. Let them go to work and take care of themselves (vv. 6-10). And Paul adds an interesting reason why most folks really need to work: They not only sponge off others, but also go around gossiping and stirring up trouble. We're to keep busy, but keep busy "doing what is right" (vv. 11-13). These instructions of Paul concerning work are to be strictly obeyed and anyone who fails to obey is to be disciplined by the church (vv. 14-15). The letter closes with a brief personal note (vv. 16-18).

Key verse. 3:9: The best way.

Personal application. Live by the rules you give others.

Key concepts. Wicked »p. 29. Evil »pp. 72, 662. Satan »p. 501. Work »pp. 28, 823. Example »p. 867.

INSIGHT

Paul's prayer (3:1-3). The issue of eschatology has been handled. God is not about to pull His people from the fires of their present trouble by Jesus' visible return. What God will do is protect His own from wicked and evil persons — and from Satan. Suffering is never easy. But it's good to know that we'll not be forced by it to surrender.

Do and continue to do (3:4-5). Our best response to difficulty is to keep on doing what we know is right, sure of God's love and His own long-term commitment to us.

"We were not idle" (3:7-9). One of Paul's reasons for going to work in the cities where he paused for any length of time was to give his converts a model to follow. Leaders must always be sensitive to the implications of their actions and the way their choices may affect others.

Give rules (3:10). Superiors have a right to give rules. But they had better follow those rules themselves if they expect others to obey them.

Busybodies (3:11). The Gk. word, *periergos,* means a meddler! Folks who force themselves into everyone else's business make no contribution to anyone. If you've got nothing to do, get to work "doing what is right" (v. 13).

Do not associate (3:14-15). Paul views a refusal to support oneself and going around making trouble as matters for church discipline. The command not to associate is not intended as permanent ostracism, but as a means to change the reluctant individual's attitude and behavior.

When we discipline, it's always to be without any feeling of punishing an enemy, but with the realization we're trying to help a brother. See church discipline, »p. 761.

"My own hand" (3:17). It was common for persons to dictate letters to a scribe or personal secretary. Paul followed this practice in writing at least some of his letters. He says here, however, that a final greeting "in my own hand" is well-known as a sign of any letter's authenticity.

1 Timothy

Paul's two letters to Timothy, along with Titus and Philemon, are unique in the New Testament. They were written to individuals rather than to churches. The first three of these letters are commonly called the "pastoral letters." This is because 1 and 2 Timothy and Titus were written to instruct young leaders about how to carry out their itinerant ministries. Even so, about 10 percent of the material in these letters has to do with church organization or program. Paul concentrates most of his advice in two areas: These young leaders are to urge the churches to maintain purity of doctrine and lifestyle.

Paul's first letter to Timothy was apparently written during that imprisonment in Rome with which the Book of Acts concludes. Most believe that Paul was released from this imprisonment, went off on another preaching mission, and was subsequently arrested and taken to Rome again. Paul's second letter to Timothy was written during this second imprisonment, which the apostle did not survive. Eusebius, an early church historian, reports that "Paul is said, after having defended himself, to have set forth again upon the ministry of preaching, and to have entered the city [Rome] a second time, and to have ended his life by martyrdom. While then a prisoner, he wrote the second epistle to Timothy, in which he both mentions his first defense, and his impending death."

It is clear from several references within these letters, as well as testimony of history, that the pastoral epistles date from near the end of the Apostolic Age. Only the letters of John may be later in origin. Thus the pastorals reflect the growing hostility of many in the Roman world to the church and the dangers a developed faith continues to face today.

"Church" Organization

Scripture traces a fascinating evolution of church organization. In Jerusalem, the church was led by the apostles and by elders. When a crisis arrived, the apostles led the church to elect "deacons," who worked out and supervised a plan to meet the specific need (Acts 6). As the church exploded out of Judea new forms of government emerged. The first Gentile church, located in Antioch, was led by a team which included prophets and teachers (Acts 13). These undoubtedly supervised the life of all the believers who met in the city in small house churches. Paul's missionary journeys pushed the boundaries of the church even further and created fresh organizational needs. Guidance was provided by teams of local elders, chosen for their spiritual maturity by the Christian community and confirmed by the apostles on subsequent visits (Acts 14:23). Also itinerant teachers such as Apollos traveled through the empire, sharing their particular teaching within the cities they visited. Some of these teachers were false teachers, and local prophets and elders were charged with examining their teaching and discerning errors. When Paul wrote the pastorals each city seems to have had its own bishops/elders, plus deacons, who provided special services to the Christian community. Some individuals were fully supported by the church so they could give full time to ministry. At this stage, leadership teams still supervised the entire community rather than local house churches. Yet by A.D. 115, letters of Ignatius reveal that each local congregation had one bishop, several elders, and several deacons. The church had become more and more highly structured, but perhaps somewhat less dynamic than before.

Timothy. Timothy was a dearly loved companion of the Apostle Paul, who looked on him as a son as well as fellow soldier (1 Tim. 1:2, 18; 2 Tim. 1:2). Timothy was the son of a Jewish mother and Greek father (2 Tim. 1:5). He traveled with Paul on both the second and third missionary journeys and was sent on a number of special missions by the apostle (1 Cor. 4:17; 16:10; Acts 19:22; 2 Cor. 1:1, 19). He was not always successful on his missions. The sense of a somewhat ineffectual leader is strengthened by Paul's encouragement that Timothy not permit people to "look down on you because you are young" (1 Tim. 4:12). The hesitant Timothy is also exhorted to be strong and given rather thorough instructions on how to complete his task.

At the same time Timothy is one of the more admirable of the New Testament's "next generation" of Christian leaders. Paul commends him to the Philippians, saying, "I have no one else like him, who takes a genuine interest in your welfare. For everyone looks out for his own interests, not those of Jesus Christ. But you know that Timothy has proved himself, because as a son with his father he has served with me in the work of the Gospel" (Phil. 2:20-22).

THEOLOGICAL OUTLINE OF TIMOTHY

CONTENT OUTLINE OF 1 TIMOTHY

Chapter summary. Paul addresses this letter to Timothy, a young coworker he has sent on a troubleshooting mission to Ephesus (1:1-3a). Timothy's mission: to silence false teaching so that the Gospel's truth might produce its fruit of love (vv. 3b-5). Too many would-be teachers of the law prattle on without knowing what they're talking about. They fail to realize that laws are passed against sins—and thus are irrelevant to the good men who would not break them anyway! (vv. 6-11)

As for Paul, he is eternally thankful that God saves sinners and transforms them into His servants (vv. 12-15). In fact, Paul sees himself as history's clearest example that God's mercy reaches the worst of sinners, a source of hope for others wanting to believe and receive eternal life (v. 16). No wonder Paul breaks out in a doxology of praise! (v. 17)

As for Timothy, he must hold on to faith and a good conscience and so fulfill his promise (vv. 18-20).

Outline
Place
Finder

TASK
INSTRUCTIONS
ADVICE

Key verse. 1:5: Sound doctrine's goal.

Personal application. You can test the purity of your doctrine by the love it produces in your heart.

Key concepts. Love »pp. 126, 661, 690, 691. Heart »p. 120. Conscience »p. 738. Law »pp. 123, 145, 606, 743, 790. Sin »p. 798.

INSIGHT

"My true son" (1:2). The Gk. word *gnesios* means "genuine." Timothy had faithfully served with Paul and proved himself (cf. Phil. 2:22).

"Myths and endless genealogies" (1:4). These are most likely the "Jewish myths" mentioned in Titus 1:14. Religious literature of the period shows many treated the O.T. genealogies as a source of symbolic truth having to do with the apocalypse. This approach stimulated endless arguments and drew the speculators further and further from the true meaning and intent of Scripture.

Why sound doctrine? (1:5) Paul's command to stop false teachers is intended to restore an emphasis on Gospel truths. Commitment to truth purifies the heart, cleanses the conscience, and produces unhypocritical faith—and this results in love for God and others. Don't brag about your doctrine. Unless that doctrine has changed you from within, you've missed its meaning.

Not for good men (1:8-11). Paul's point is hard to miss. Law says "You shall not. . . ." Yet we only say "Don't" when a person is already doing something wrong. If no one committed adultery, for instance, why pass a law against it? So law is directed *against sinful people* and has no relevance to the truly good who never do such things anyway.

Paul's point is that the Gospel works an inner transformation, and its "sound doctrine" directs us into a lifestyle of holiness and love. Why then become involved in those endless discussions about the Law that marked 1st-century rabbinical Judaism and characterized the false teachers who sought to distract believers from a healthy focus on Christ?

Proper use of law (1:8). Paul defines the proper use of law in Rom. 3:1-20; law is to convict sinners and demonstrate their guilt.

Violent (1:13). In Phil. Paul notes that he was "faultless" as far as keeping Moses' Law was concerned (3:6). Yet here he admits that he was also a violent (*hybristes*) person. Perhaps Paul is remembering how he "consented" to Stephen's death. We don't have to actually strike another person to be hostile, hating, and thus violent. Even though his persecution of the church let him express his violence in a "lawful" way, Paul now sees within himself all the corruption that marks society's lawbreakers. Clearly in his own case the Law was no help in making him good. It only helped him conceal his sinfulness from himself.

"Faith and a good conscience" (1:19). If we keep on trusting and keep on doing what is good, we like Timothy will realize our potential.

Outline
Place
Finder

TASK
INSTRUCTIONS
ADVICE

Chapter summary. How is Timothy to carry out his mission of keeping the focus of the Ephesian church on sound doctrine and thus help them grow in love? First, he is to urge that the church pray for rulers—that the Christian might live peacefully in society and spread the Gospel (2:1-7). Within the church men are to maintain holiness and unity (v. 8), while women dress and behave in ways appropriate to those who worship God (vv. 9-10). In a much-debated passage, Paul also seems to restrict women from the role of those who give authoritative teaching in the church. And Paul bases his instruction on a theological rather than cultural argument (vv. 11-15).

Key verse. 2:5: He still brings us together.

Personal application. When Christians honestly disagree over the interpretation of a passage, study both sides, and then do what you believe is most pleasing to God.

Key concepts. Holy »pp. 86, 879. Women »p. 723. Submission »p. 867.

INSIGHT

Prayer comes first (2:1). "First of all" indicates the primacy of prayer in church meetings. Four of the N.T.'s seven words for prayer are used in this verse: *deeseis,* an expression of desire or need; *proseuche,* a general term for public and private prayers; *enteuxis,* which suggests bold but conversational prayer, confident of access to God; and *eucharistia,* which means giving thanks.

Prayer for leaders (2:2). Hostile leaders curtail the rights of the church to meet, study, and evangelize. Paul urges prayer for all in authority, that the government might permit free expression of Christian faith.

God's desire (2:4). There's a difference between God's desires and what will happen. Christ's death provided a basis for the salvation of all men (v. 6). Yet not all will believe.

Let's remember when we pray for unconverted loved ones that God wants them to be saved—so we are surely praying in His will. Let's remember too to use the freedom we have under our government to share the Gospel freely.

"One mediator" (2:5-6). The basic meaning of mediator (*mesites*) is a person who intervenes between two parties to restore or make peace. In giving Himself as a "ransom for all men" Jesus became qualified for the role of mediator between God and man. He alone can bring us together.

A ransom (2:6). *Antilytron* is found only here in the N.T. and means the "price of a person's redemption."

Clean and committed (2:8). We are to pray with "holy" or devout hands. Commitment is expressed in the act of prayer, moral purity in the unity of the praying community.

Women's dress (2:9-10). Paul's admonition doesn't restrict women from dressing attractively, just from dressing to attract attention! The best way for any person, male or female, to express his or her individuality is through good deeds that express a godly character.

Society then as now seems to have pressured women to dress as sex objects, as though their value or worth were determined by the ability to stimulate males sexually. This was as demeaning to women then as it is now.

"Quietness and full submission" (2:11). The Gk. *hesychia* is translated "quiet" here and "silent" in v. 12. It means a receptive, restful attitude that promotes learning. Nothing here suggests surrender of any intellectual or spiritual capability.

Teach or have authority (2:12). The two should be linked: to teach with authority. Many believe authoritative teaching is a role reserved for church elders, an office which no N.T. reference indicates was held by women. Paul then goes on to make the point that in the Fall Eve was deceived and seems to draw the conclusion that thus an authoritative teaching role is inappropriate.

Kept safe through childbirth (2:15). "Save" is used in the N.T. of both physical and spiritual deliverance. Vine's creative interpretation suggests that the role of bearing children will keep Christian women safe from pressures urging them to take inappropriate social roles.

Chapter summary. Paul now moves to discuss elders, who do have the role of issuing authoritative teaching in the local church. Eldering is a noble task (3:1) which requires the elder to have a developed Christian character (vv. 2-7). Deacons also are to be "worthy of respect" and demonstrate maturity in the faith (vv. 8-13). The church of God is such a special fellowship, the very household of the Lord, that people must conduct themselves in it correctly (vv. 14-15). Surrendering to the wonder of it, Paul introduces another brief poem which may be one of the earliest creedal statements of the church (v. 16).

Outline
Place
Finder

TASK
INSTRUCTIONS
ADVICE

Key verse. 3:16: More wonderful than we think.

Personal application. Don't tiptoe in a cathedral, but do walk carefully in the church of God.

Key concepts. Leadership »pp. 610, 867, 883. Deacons »p. 714. Church »pp. 768, 794, 799.

INSIGHT

"Overseer" (3:1). The word is *episkopos*, which is frequently translated in older versions as "bishop." A study of N.T. texts suggests that it is used as a synonym of *presbuteros*, elder. Thus "bishop" and "elder" refer to the same person, the same office.

The husband of one wife (3:2). The phrase has been interpreted to rule out the possibility of a divorced person holding this office but, interestingly, not to rule out a widower who has been remarried. Most commentators agree, however, that it simply means monogamous: a one-woman kind of man who is totally faithful to his wife.

Fifteen qualifications (3:2-7). These verses list 15 qualities to consider when selecting elders. Note that the qualifications do *not* mention seminary training or possession of any particular spiritual gifts. Instead they are *character* qualifications. Spiritual leaders are to be the kind of person that Christian teaching is intended to produce. Let's show great care in choosing godly persons as our spiritual leaders and not be influenced by the wealth or social status that attract men of the world.

Elder character traits in brief (3:2-7).
Above reproach: Totally faithful to his wife.
A one-woman man: Totally faithful to his wife.
Temperate: Sober, careful, and deliberate.
Self-controlled: Disciplined, reasonable.
Respectable: Modest, honorable, well-behaved.
Hospitable: One who welcomes visitors.
Able to teach: Able to explain and apply.
Not given to drunkenness: No tendency toward wine.
Not violent: Not hostile, antagonistic.
Gentle: Kindly, reasonable, forebearing.

Not quarrelsome: Not combative or contentious.
Not a money lover: Cares for people, not things.
Good manager of his family: Directs family life.
No recent convert: Mature and humble.
Of good reputation: Admired by outsiders.

"Worthy of respect" (3:8, 11). The Gk. word *semnos* is found only four times in the N.T., three of them in the pastoral epistles. It describes a person who is decent and whose approach to life is essentially moral and ethical.

"Deacons" (3:8-13). This office whose function is best illustrated in Acts 6 also must be filled with individuals who are evaluated first of all on spiritual and character qualifications.

"Their wives" (3:11). In Gk. *gyne* can mean both "woman" and "wife." Thus it is possible here that Paul is speaking of deaconesses rather than the wives of deacons. Certainly Phoebe, mentioned in Rom. 16:1, did hold this office. In context, however, this particular verse seems most likely to be speaking of the wives of deacons, for vv. 8-10 and 12-13 clearly do refer to male deacons.

God's household (3:15). The 1st-century household incorporated all members of the head of the house's family and all those slaves and freemen who were obligated to him or under his protection. It is the unique relationship of the church with God, as a household made up entirely of sons, that makes it the support and mainstay of the truth. If we have such a significant role, we must surely choose leaders who display the beauty of God's truth in their lives and will lead us along the same path.

"The mystery of godliness" (3:16). Jesus Himself is the sole message as well as object of the church's faith.

Outline
Place
Finder

TASK
INSTRUCTIONS
ADVICE

Chapter summary. Paul has given brief instructions concerning worship (chap. 2) and leadership (chap. 3). Now he gives instructions concerning false teachers and teachings which can sap the vitality of Christ's church. The source is demonic, the teachers are morally corrupt, and the teachings deprive us of things God has given in order to bless us (4:1-5). Timothy is to have nothing to do with such blathering, but rather to concentrate on growth in righteousness (vv. 6-8), keeping his hope fixed on the living God (vv. 9-10).

Timothy is also to command and teach a similar commitment. Despite his youth, Timothy will be effective if he sets an example by his life (vv. 11-12) and devotes himself to the preaching and teaching of Scripture (vv. 13-14). And so Paul sums up: Watch life and doctrine. Persevere in them and everything will be all right (vv. 15-16).

Key verse. 4:12: Sound advice.

Personal application: Don't ignore either your lifestyle or your doctrine.

Key concepts. Demons »pp. 659, 895. Example »p. 867. Scripture »p. 843.

INSIGHT

Seared consciences (4:2). The conscience is man's moral sense. It convicts when we choose to do that which we know to be wrong. Paul suggests here that scar tissue will form over a conscience which is persistently violated. Such a person may no longer *feel* guilty, but surely will *be* guilty.

Forbid marriage (4:3). The Bible maintains a positive attitude toward marriage and sex within marriage. God is the one who created male and female with the capacity for sensual delight. But He also designed a context—marriage—where those delights could not only be experienced but could contribute to the growth of intimacy desirable for two people who are expected to share their earthly life together. The ascetic who forbids marriage—and free sexual expression within marriage—perverts God's good gift just as does the promiscuous individual who seeks sex outside marital bonds.

Everything good (4:4-5). Paul here echoes God's own words as recorded in Gen. 1. Thanksgiving and consecration by Scripture and prayer reminds us that our *use* of everything is good as well—as long as we use what God has provided within the context He intends.

"Truths of the faith" (4:6). Timothy was "brought up in" the truths of the faith. Paul's pointed advice makes it clear that "truth" is not simply something to be believed, but to be lived. Thus Paul emphasizes the importance in any ministry of not only commanding and teaching truths, but also of setting an example by living them. We have not really grasped Scripture's truths until they begin to find expression in our lifestyle.

Your youth (4:12). We all can find some reason to hang back, uncertain and tentative. If it's not youth, it's lack of knowledge, training, or something else. Paul's words to Timothy are a fine reminder to us. If we concentrate on setting an example in speech, life, love, faith, and purity, others will respect and respond to us, whatever our other shortcomings may be.

"Your gift" (4:14). Paul here clearly refers to an unusual equipping, publicly announced by a prophetic utterance when Timothy was set apart to serve with Paul in spreading the Gospel.

Laying on of hands (4:14). The N.T. frequently mentions a laying on of hands associated with setting individuals aside for special tasks or offices (cf. Acts 6:6; 13:3; 1 Tim. 4:14; 2 Tim. 1:6). These were, however, performed by different persons: the apostles, a local church leadership team of elders, and by Paul himself. Such "official recognition" of a person's call to a task is still practiced in many churches as "ordination."

"Be diligent" (4:15-16). There is nothing more important than a task given us by God. If we're to be successful we need to "give ourselves wholly" to God's work—without neglecting our personal spiritual life.

Chapter summary. Paul now moves on to give Timothy practical advice on many aspects of local church life. In this chapter he focuses on several important interpersonal relationships. Timothy, although a leader, is to show great respect to all members of the church—both older and younger men and women (5:1-2). He is also to oversee the development of "widows' corps." While any woman without relatives to care for her is the responsibility of the church, widows who have earned a good reputation are to be given an official position and an important family-oriented ministry (vv. 3-16).

Outline
Place
Finder

TASK
INSTRUCTIONS
ADVICE

Paul also discusses relationships with elders and the care with which they are to be selected and ordained (vv. 17-25).

Key verses. 5:1-2: Show respect.

Personal application. The way you treat others reveals your character.

Key concepts. Women »pp. 163, 394, 723. Elder »pp. 132, 835.

INSIGHT

Rebuke harshly (5:1). The Gk. term (*epiplesso*) is not the ordinary word for rebuke. It is used only here and means to "strike at." When we correct another person we must do so with an attitude of love. No person who is hurt or offended is likely to respond to instruction or guidance.

Caring for their own family (5:3). Children and grandchildren "honor your parents" by meeting their needs in old age when they are truly destitute. Paul calls this "putting your religion into practice" (cf. 5:8).

The widow who lives for pleasure (5:6). The Gk. word *spatalao* means to live luxuriously. The widow whose lavish lifestyle displays self-indulgence not only requires no help from the church, but is also not qualified to contribute to others in the local body.

"The list of widows" (5:9). Among the truly destitute widows will be some who are older and who have earned a reputation for sterling Christian character. These widows might be enlisted in a widows' corps. In Titus 2:4-5 Paul expands on what was probably the ministry of this widows' corps. They "train the younger women to love their husbands, so that no one will malign the Word of God."

This is a ministry no man could undertake—but that a widow, sharing her own experience, could carry out effectively.

Remarriage (5:11-15). In the 1st century there were few if any jobs offering employment for women, much less for widows. Paul encourages the younger widows to remarry—in part because they still have strong sexual

drives, in part because idleness tends to create busybodies and gossips. Paul applies the general principle that leaders should have matured and demonstrated Christian character over a number of years to the widows' corps by requiring that members of this ministry team be 60 years of age.

"Elders" (5:17). Paul notes that elders "direct the affairs of the church." The Gk. (*proestotes*) means to preside over, to supervise the life of the congregation. Their "double honor" seems in context to be for both respect and financial support.

No accusation (5:19). Deuteronomy 19:15 insists even ordinary people be protected against charges brought by an individual. Why is this repeated here? The elders' public position makes them more vulnerable than others to hostility and false accusations. And if such a charge were believed, it would hinder their effectiveness.

"Those who sin" (5:20). Paul still seems to be referring to the elders here. No one in the church is beyond accountability. In fact, the elder's public position means that if he does commit a fault he must be publicly rebuked. When we protect our leaders from responsibility for their sinful acts, we corrupt the church, for others will *not* take warning.

Hasty ordination (5:22-24). We need to take enough time to discover one's character before advancing a person as an elder. Some folks are so obviously flawed that we would never think of making them elders. Only time reveals the flaws of others.

Outline
Place
Finder

TASK
INSTRUCTIONS
ADVICE

Chapter summary. Paul continues his advice to Timothy about relationships. Slaves are to serve their masters because they want to, not because they have to. And they are not to expect favoritism from Christian masters (6:1-2).

Paul has several blunt things to say about those who look at teaching religion as a way to make money (vv. 3-5). In fact, he warns everyone against a desire to get rich. How much better it is to be content, because every kind of evil tends to spring up where money-love exists (vv. 6-10). Not that Paul views Timothy this way. But Paul does remind Timothy of the need to "flee from all this" and pursue righteousness (vv. 11-16).

Paul then returns to the topic of money, with a word of advice to those who are already rich. Money is something to be used, a resource enabling the well-to-do to do good. If the rich are generous and willing to share, wealth can be a blessing (vv. 17-19). But as for Timothy, his task is to finish his mission and avoid the foolishness which has caused some to wander from the faith (vv. 20-21).

Key verse. 6:11: Run away from sin to righteousness.

Personal application. Value money by the good you choose to do with it.

Key concepts. Slavery »p. 802. Wealth »pp. 124, 125. Righteousness »pp. 124, 734. Good deeds »p. 872.

INSIGHT

More on false teachers (6:3-5). Their content is "false doctrines." Their conceit leads them to a morbid craving for controversy and disputes over mere words. They consider godliness only a means to the end of gaining wealth.

"Godliness" (6:6). Godliness (*eusebes*) is found in the N.T. only in the pastorals and in 2 Peter. It suggests a reverent faith which expresses its awe of God in glad obedience to Him.

Take nothing (6:7). While we leave everything material behind us, we take along a far greater treasure. We take a personality that has begun to experience God's transforming work, a mind more attuned to heaven, a heart that beats closer to God's own, a will that has made choice after choice that glorifies God. What we take with us as we leave this world is a treasure house. What we leave behind is nothing.

Temptation and a trap (6:9). When we desire anything other than, or more than, wanting to do God's will, a terrible conflict is created. Only if we abandon our *desire* for riches can we be free of the danger of making a wrong or sinful choice in hopes of obtaining them.

This does not mean we need to abandon riches, should God choose to give them to us. Riches can be used for good, as can any other resource (vv. 17-19). What we are to abandon is the desire for riches, so that there will be nothing to distract us from our commitment to do God's will.

Flee all this (6:11). "Flee" in its figurative use means to avoid or to shun. Let's turn our back on a desire for anything this world has to offer, in favor of righteousness, godliness, faith, love, endurance, and gentleness. If these qualities are truly what we treasure, then we will be safe from those temptations that drag others down and even plunge them into ruin.

A word to the wealthy (6:17-19). Or, do's and don'ts for Lotto winners. Don't be arrogant or put your hope in wealth. Do shift the full weight of your expectations for a good future to God. Use your money to do good. Be generous and share. And make sure the bottom line is larger each day—but in heaven rather than on earth.

A foundation (6:19). The values we hold and live by today are laying the foundation of our heavenly experience. The more we spend ourselves in service of God and others, the bigger and better the structure we create above.

2 Timothy

After winning release from the imprisonment in Rome reported in Acts and mentioned in 1 Timothy, early tradition tells us that Paul went on to preach in Spain. Later, as official hostility to Christianity hardened, Paul was arrested again. This time he didn't survive. According to the church fathers, both Peter and Paul were martyred in Rome, probably in the late A.D. 60s. And the guidance of the Christian church passed into the hands of the next generation: a generation in which Timothy and Titus were certainly leaders.

This second letter to Timothy was written during Paul's final imprisonment. He looks back over his own life with a sense of deep satisfaction. He has kept the faith and he looks forward to the rewards he is sure to claim. But Paul also has final words of exhortation and warning for Timothy. He must remain totally committed. And he must be ready for mounting difficulties, as new challenges to the faith develop from within.

For those of us who are fascinated by "famous last words," this letter of the Apostle Paul should hold a special attraction. These are his last words, words of wisdom and guidance, as applicable for us today as they were when first read by Timothy, a leader in the emerging church. The values and commitments that Paul shares here with young Timothy are those we can readily adopt and which will surely enrich our lives.

PARALLEL THEMES IN PAUL'S LETTERS TO TIMOTHY

Theme	1 Timothy	2 Timothy
Love and holiness as the goal of ministry	1:3-7	1:3-12
Sound doctrine is important	1:8-11	1:13-14
		4:1-5
Examples of saved sinners provided	1:12-17	1:15-18
Timothy called to ministry	1:18-20	2:1-7
The example set by the leader is vital	2:8-9	2:14-19
	4:11-16	3:10-17
Qualifications and practice of leaders	3:1-15	2:22-26
Dangers from false teachers	4:1-5	3:1-9
Charge to be fully committed	6:11-21	4:6-18

THEOLOGICAL OUTLINE OF 2 TIMOTHY

CONTENT OUTLINE OF 2 TIMOTHY

Outline
Place
Finder

CALLING
COMMITMENT
CHALLENGES

Chapter summary. Paul begins his last letter to Timothy by addressing him as my "dear son" (1:1-2). Memories of Timothy are especially precious now, and Paul longs to see the friend whose sincere faith is rooted in the teaching of his mother and grandmother (vv. 3-5) and whose gifts Paul himself contributed to (vv. 6-7). It may seem strange at first, but Paul urges his dearly loved friend to join him in suffering for the Gospel. Paul is deeply aware that there is no greater privilege for any person (vv. 8-12). And Paul reminds Timothy that his teaching and life provide a pattern to live by (vv. 13-14).

In a personal aside, Paul regrets that so many run for cover now because of his imprisonment—but mentions Onesiphorus as one who risked being associated with Paul by actively asking his whereabouts when he was in Rome (vv. 15-18).

Our calling may not bring us popularity. But the bonds we form with like-minded others are strong and true.

Key verse. 1:8: Best wishes.

Personal application. When you seek the best for your children be sure what you seek is really the best.

Key concepts. Gospel »p. 737. Holiness »p. 879. Grace »p. 789. Holy Spirit »pp. 77, 744, 759. Mercy »p. 880.

INSIGHT

"My dear son" (1:2). The word is *agapatos* and means "dearly loved." It is a term of deep and warm affection. How fascinating, for in this letter Paul urges his "dear son" to follow him in full commitment to a ministry of the Gospel—a commitment which has brought Paul intense suffering and soon will mean his execution. Usually parents want their sons to *avoid* suffering and danger! But Paul is wiser than most parents. He knows that the goal is far more important than the cost and the reward far greater than any pain.

Timothy's gift (1:6). This is not an ordinary spiritual gift, but a special equipping for ministry which was apparently given at Timothy's ordination (cf. 1 Tim. 4:14).

Timidity (1:7). We are responsible to use the gifts God provides. Let's remember that with the gifts God gives us courage. Timidity (*deilia*) is cowardice. If we step out boldly we'll find the Spirit supplies power, love, and self-control.

Salvation (1:9). The Gospel is worth suffering for. It offers a salvation with past, present, and future impact. Salvation past tense is the forgiveness of all our sins. Salvation present tense is the power to live holy lives. Salvation future tense is total freedom from sin's presence and a resurrection to an eternal life to be lived with God. What greater privilege could any person have than to be a "herald and an apostle and a teacher" (v. 11) of such wonderful, good news.

"Immortality" (1:10). Jesus has destroyed (rendered inoperative spiritually) death and so unveiled the possibility of immortality. The Gk. word (*aphthartos*) means imperishable, conveying full immunity to the decay inherent in the material creation. The Gospel brings to light a new unexpected and exciting destiny for humankind.

Jesus' appearing (1:10). The Gk. word is *epiphaneia*. Everywhere else in the N.T. it refers to Jesus' second coming (cf. 2 Thes. 2:8; 1 Tim. 6:14; 2 Tim. 4:1, 8; Titus 2:13). Here, however, it refers to Christ's first coming, in which God appeared to destroy death and unveil immortality.

I know (1:12). Paul has no uncertainties. For years he has experienced God's faithfulness and seen Him work in the lives of his converts. Put God to the test by being fully committed to Him and all your doubts will be gone too.

"What I have entrusted" (1:12). Paul includes literally everything: His own future. The service he has rendered. The results of that service. Repayment and rewards for suffering. Everything Paul cares about has been placed in God's hand, and Paul is sure that it is being kept for him, to be his "that day" when Christ returns.

"Guard" (1:14). We protect our spiritual inheritance by using it, by keeping the pattern of doctrine and life shown us in Scripture.

Outline
Place
Finder

CALLING
COMMITMENT
CHALLENGES

Chapter summary. What will it mean for Timothy to follow the pattern of commitment set by the Apostle Paul and to teach that pattern to others? (2:1-2) Three images provide insight. A committed Christian is like a soldier in his ability to endure hardship (vv. 3-4). He is like an athlete who keeps in training for competition (v. 5). He is like a farmer who works hard in expectation of enjoying the harvest (vv. 6-7).

Paul is very clear that commitment to the Gospel is likely to result in suffering (vv. 8-10). He is also clear on the need to remain fully committed (vv. 11-13). Actually commitment calls for a disciplined attention to service and Scripture that many have been unwilling to give (vv. 14-19). This is not unexpected, for everyone uses cheap dishes as well as expensive chinaware. But it's important for us to "cleanse ourselves" that we might serve the more noble function (vv. 20-21). Finally, commitment calls for the most rigid self-control, not only in fleeing evil desires, but also in maintaining a loving attitude toward those who oppose our teaching, with prayerful reliance on God to change the heart of the lost (vv. 22-26).

Key verse. 2:15: This deserves our best.

Personal application. There are very few causes worth dedicating our life to.

Key concepts. Teach »p. 122. Gospel »p. 737. Resurrection »p. 823. Chosen »p. 897. Holiness »p. 879. Righteousness »p. 734. Repentance »p. 780. Satan »pp. 501, 655.

INSIGHT

Pass it on (2:1-2). Even before the N.T. was complete, basic truths were understood, entrusted to reliable men, and passed on unchanged to the next generation.

The elect (2:10). The word is used here as a euphemism for "Christian." Paul is in chains, but gladly endures that others may hear and respond to the Gospel promise of salvation in Christ.

Suffering can be endured if we are convinced it is for a good purpose. In fact there is a glory in suffering, if the purpose is great enough.

"Disown" (2:11-13). The last two "if" statements here have caused some confusion. The Gk. words for "disown" are also translated "deny." In some places they mean "decisive rejection of Christ" but in others have the sense of "a fall from fellowship." Thus, Peter's denial of Jesus was not a final rejection, but a temporary withdrawal. It is best to take this passage as a warning: If we abandon fellowship with Jesus, His withdrawal of fellowship with us must follow. Even so "He will remain faithful" to His commitment to save us, "for He cannot deny Himself."

Correctly handling the Word of truth (2:15).

Examples of *incorrect* handling of God's Word follow in vv. 16-18. A right handling of God's Word is to teach its truths so that the hearer believes and begins to live a life of love, holiness, and good works (cf. 3:16-17).

"God's solid foundation" (2:19). The image is of a seal with two inscriptions. On one side it reads "God knows those who are His." Only God can look into the human heart and recognize true faith in Jesus. But on the other side, the seal reads "Everyone who confesses the name of the Lord must turn away from wickedness." We can't see into another person's heart. But we should be able to see the commitment to holiness that results when Christ *really* has taken up residence in a life.

Cleanse yourself? (2:21) The choices you and I make each day either tarnish us or polish us to a higher degree of purity and usefulness.

Taken captive (2:26). Satan's influence blinds the lost to the Gospel and holds them captive. There is no use "quarreling" with such persons. Let's be gentle with those who oppose us, realizing that only by God's grace can they escape the terrible trap they have chosen to remain in.

Chapter summary. Paul now turns to the future outlining some of the challenges that Timothy will have to face. The first challenge is the superficiality of the faith of many who will profess Christianity, insidiously corrupted even further by false teachers motivated by evil desires (3:1-7). Also those eager to live godly lives will face increasing persecution, as evil men "go from bad to worse" (vv. 8-14). Timothy, however, has a unique source of strength: He has been well taught, he knows the character of those who taught him, and he has in hand the Scriptures given by God Himself. And the Scriptures contain everything needed to equip God's people for every good work (vv. 15-17).

Outline
Place
Finder

CALLING
COMMITMENT
CHALLENGES

Key verse. 3:16: Something to trust.

Personal application. Don't let anyone undermine your confidence in God's Word.

Key concepts. False prophets »p. 462. Persecution »p. 760. Salvation »p. 841. Good works »p. 872.

INSIGHT

"Last days" (3:1). Many passages in the N.T. indicate the writers were even then living in the "last days" (cf. Acts 2:17; Heb. 1:1-2; 2 Peter 3:3; 1 John 2:18). The phrase views our present age as the final historical stage before the predicted "Day of the Lord" spoken of so frequently in the O.T. prophets (»pp. 413, 541).

"Terrible times" (3:1). This passage, with others, silences the optimistic view of some that the Gospel message is destined to convert the majority of mankind and usher in an era of peace before Jesus returns. In contrast, Paul sees an increase in evil with moral and social conditions trending from "bad to worse." The Christian's challenge is not to usher in universal peace, but to remain true to God in troubled times and aggressively promote the saving Gospel of Christ despite corruption within the church and persecution without.

"A form of godliness" (3:5). The preceding description is of persons who increasingly put themselves and their own desires ahead of every other consideration. "Form" is *morphosis*, which emphasizes *outward* form. People want to keep religion—but they do not want an authentic Gospel which demands they surrender their sins and make a full commitment to true godliness.

Religious charlatans (3:6-9). Paul's scornful description of those who prey on the weak is devastating. As is the critique of those who want to appear learned but at the same time hold on to "all kinds of evil desires." The names of the magicians who opposed Moses (cf. Ex. 7:11) are not given in the O.T., but their description as men of "depraved" (i.e.,

utterly corrupt) minds matches the character and motivation of the false teachers Paul foresees emerging during these last days.

Those who want to live godly (3:10-13). There's really no reason for the wicked to persecute Christians who adopt the world's basic values and seek simply to get along here. "Don't tip the boat" is advice followed by too many modern believers. But the "godly" life Paul encourages is one of *active commitment* to what is right. This means it's impossible to remain silent about evils and injustice in our society. Pornography, abortion, and the erosion of moral standards is something that Christians increasingly resist. It is this, active resistance, that brings persecution.

God-breathed (3:16). The Gk. word describes ships, their sails filled, carried along over the seas. Paul says *every Scripture* is the product of the Spirit's work. He filled the writer and so carried him along that the words produced, though they bear the mark of the writer's personality, remain the true and certain words of God Himself.

The use of Scripture (3:16-17). Scripture is adequate to protect us from false teaching and to strengthen us for persecution. Specifically, the Word of God is useful for: (1) "Teaching" (*didaskalos*), a general word; (2) "Rebuking" (*elegmos*), a word associated with convicting of sin or error; (3) "Correcting" (*epanorthosin*), a term that means restoring to an upright or original condition; and (4) "Training" (*paideia*), rearing a child by training and guiding him in how to live. With this, we have all we need to equip us for good works.

Outline
Place
Finder

CALLING
COMMITMENT
CHALLENGES

Chapter summary. Paul now gives Timothy a direct charge. He must preach the Word, when the time seems opportune and even when it does not (4:1-2). Because hostility to sound doctrine will increase, the time will often seem *not* to be opportune. But even so, Timothy must "do the work of an evangelist" (vv. 3-5). Paul himself has a testimony to add. He has fought his own good fight and now has finished his race. And he knows that there, waiting for him to claim, is the crown God will award him when Jesus comes. And the same is true for all who long for Christ's appearing (vv. 6-8).

The letter now concludes with a series of personal remarks as Paul brings Timothy up to date on his situation (vv. 9-17), expresses continuing faith in God (v. 18), and includes final greetings (vv. 19-22).

Key verse. 4:2: Be ready.

Personal application. Keeping our eyes fixed on the coming of Christ gives us perspective on present difficulties.

Key concepts. Righteous Judge »p. 372. Rewards »p. 759.

INSIGHT

In view of His appearing (4:1). Timothy's thinking and attitude is to be shaped by awesome realities. God and Jesus are present. Jesus will judge the living and the dead and soon will appear to establish His kingdom. These realities are to be ever kept in mind, for it is these weighty truths that compel the believer to serve God and share the Gospel.

But with great patience (4:2). The challenge of faithfully preaching the Word brings the believer into conflict with others. That reality is expressed in the words of Paul's charge. Timothy is to: (1) "correct" (*elenxon*), to convict and reprove; (2) "rebuke" (*epitimeson*), to censure or admonish; (3) "encourage" (*parakaleson*), which here may mean exhort rather than the warmer "encourage." The very choice of these words reveals how resistant people will become to God's Word. Despite this, the Christian is to remain patient and keep on teaching.

"Suit their own desires" (4:3-4). Don't be surprised when people aren't interested in truth. People want to hear what they want to hear—as all too many politicians realize and go on to exploit. But Christian ministry isn't politics. It's presenting God's truth, even when people do not like it, for their benefit and possible salvation.

"A drink offering" (4:6). The O.T. drink offering was added to the sacrifice, not to make the sacrifice effective but to add a sweet smell. Paul sees his coming death as adding nothing to Jesus' one sacrifice for sins. But his death is, to Paul, the final offering he can make to the Lord.

"The crown of righteousness" (4:8). The crown as a symbol of rewards is drawn from both Jewish and Gk. culture. As a reward, a crown symbolizes the honor with which God intends to bless His faithful servants. Three types of crowns are mentioned: a crown of life (1 Cor. 9:25; 2 Tim. 2:5; James 1:12; Rev. 2:10); a crown of righteousness (here); a crown of glory (1 Peter 5:4); and Paul also speaks to his Thessalonian converts themselves as a "crown" (1 Thes. 2:19). Each of these crowns is to be awarded after the return of Christ.

Those who long for His appearing (4:8). If we really long for Christ to return, we're unlikely to become too concerned about the passing things of earth. Keeping one's eyes fixed on Jesus will surely help us fulfill our own charge to live for Him.

"Mark" (4:11). Paul's note is touching, in that years before he had argued violently with Barnabas against bringing Mark on a second missionary journey. Paul has not been reconciled with Mark—and perhaps learned much from the patience and gentleness exhibited by Barnabas in his dealings with the younger man.

Safe (4:18). Nothing that happens to us here on earth can threaten our ultimate security. Heaven is our home, and we will surely enter Christ's heavenly kingdom with joy.

Titus

The letter of Titus, like the second letter to Timothy, was written to a younger leader during Paul's second imprisonment in Rome. Like the letters to Timothy, this is a letter of guidance and instruction.

Titus is mentioned 12 times in the New Testament. A fascinating picture of the man and his ministry can be drawn from the references. Titus was a Gentile, an uncircumcised Greek. He joined Paul's missionary team some time prior to Paul's second missionary journey. Like Timothy, Titus was frequently sent on special missions to deal with difficulties in various churches. Titus was apparently successful in helping reduce the tension that existed between Paul and the Corinthians. Timothy had earlier failed in that particular mission. It is significant that while Paul frequently exhorts Timothy to be strong, or to let no one despise his youth, no such urgings are found in his letter to Titus. Whether settling conflicts or collecting gifts for the poorer churches of Palestine, Titus seems to have enjoyed unusual success.

When Paul wrote this letter Titus was working in another difficult field: Crete. This island, 160 miles long and 35 miles wide, lies in the Mediterranean southeast of Greece. Once it had been the center of a great culture but the Cretans had become known in the ancient world as a depraved and intractable people. In this letter Paul quotes the poet Epimenides, who about 600 B.C. observed that "Cretans are always liars, evil brutes, lazy gluttons" (1:12). Yet Paul expresses no concern for Titus. He simply gives advice, which has been rightly valued by young leaders throughout the Christian era, and expects Titus to successfully lead the Cretan church to "devote themselves to doing what is good" (3:8).

COMMON THEMES FOUND IN TITUS AND THE OTHER PASTORALS			
Theme	Titus	1 Tim.	2 Tim.
Knowledge of the truth is to lead to godliness.	1:1-4	1:18-20	1:3-12
The leader's example is vital.	1:5-9	3:1-15	2:22-26
	4:11-16	3:10-17	
The leader's duties are specified.	1:10-16	6:11-21	4:1-5
Godly life and doctrine are to be applied.	2:1-15	4:11-16	3:10-17
Practical results of our common salvation.	3:1-11	6:11-21	4:6-18

THEOLOGICAL OUTLINE OF TITUS

CONTENT OUTLINE OF TITUS

Chapter summary. Paul greets Titus as a genuine son in their common faith and cannot resist reminding him that this is a faith in which knowing the truth leads to godliness (1:1-4). Paul then quickly reminds Titus why the younger man was sent to Crete. His mission is to "straighten out" affairs there and appoint elders for every town (vv. 5-9). Establishing a recognized leadership is particularly important because of the false teachers who riddle the Cretan church, promoting a distortion of Judaism as true Christianity. These teachers, motivated by greed, are corrupt and detestable and must be withstood (vv. 10-16).

Outline
Place
Finder

MISSION
MINISTRY
RESULTS

Key verse. 1:11: Why silence false teachers?

Personal application. A well-organized church with strong spiritual leaders is safe.

Key concepts. Eternal life »p. 682. Elders »p. 835.

INSIGHT

"**God's elect**" (1:1). The phrase is used in the simple sense of "Christian" (»p. 797).

"**The knowledge of the truth**" (1:1). Christian truth is a revelation of reality. To "know" this truth is to accept its reality and to live by it and thus to be led into godliness. Christian truth can never be isolated from morality, as if knowing God's truth were a mere intellectual exercise. Knowing is actually commitment to realities that must be expressed in our life.

"**Hope of eternal life**" (2:2). "Hope" carries no hint of uncertainty. The Gk. word conveys a sense of settled confidence and expectation. Because we are sure of eternal life we give ourselves freely to live by God's revealed truth.

"**By the command of God**" (2:3). No one calls himself or herself to ministry. It was God who entrusted Paul with his special mission to bring God's word of salvation to light in the Gentile world. Yet while some receive a special call, each of us who knows the Gospel has the same privilege Paul enjoyed of sharing it with others.

"**Straighten out**" (1:5). The Gk. word (*epidiorthose*) means to set things in order. The rest of the letter shows that the Cretan church was in a state of disarray, accepted false teachers and teaching, and was confused about both Christian doctrine and lifestyle.

"**Appoint elders**" (2:5). Parallel passages such as Acts 14:23 show that in the N.T. Age a group of several elders provided leadership for each church. The word "appoint" does not indicate the manner of appointment. Most believe that Paul and his helpers guided the church to select the kind of persons described in 1 Tim. 3 and here in Titus 1:6-9. Then the apostle or his representatives gave them official recognition, probably by laying hands on the elected elders and dedicating them to their task. In view of the disarray in Crete, one of Titus' first tasks was to make sure responsible leaders were clearly established in elder roles.

Elder qualifications (1:6-9). See the parallel passage on p. 835, 1 Tim. 3.

"**The circumcision group**" (1:10). Paul refers to Judaizers, who infiltrated most early Christian communities and insisted that Jewish laws must be followed by believers in Christ. They also promoted fanciful allegorical interpretations of the O.T., which apparently fascinated many, but which unlike God's truth did not promote godly living.

God's raw material (1:12-14). The Cretans were hardly an admirable race. But God has always been in the business of taking sinners and making them into saints!

"**All things are pure**"? (1:15) Purity is a matter of the heart and one's moral character. The false teachers injected the Jewish distinction between pure and impure *things* and missed the point entirely. To a person whose heart is unregenerate, nothing is pure. To the person God has cleansed from within, mere things become irrelevant.

"**Their actions deny Him**" (1:16). Religion without morality is a sham.

Outline
Place
Finder

MISSION
MINISTRY
RESULTS

Chapter summary. Titus' ministry in Crete was essentially teaching, and this chapter contains many different words describing that activity. Yet Titus is not to teach doctrine lifestyle: "What is in accord with sound doctrine" (2:1). In performing this ministry Titus is to instruct older men (v. 2) and women (vv. 3-5) as well as the younger (vv. 6-8). Slaves are to be given specific instruction on how to relate to their masters (vv. 9-10). And all this teaching is to be rooted in the grace of God, for the salvation grace brings makes it clear: believers are to say no to sin and live godly lives while waiting for Jesus to return. This is especially true because Jesus gave Himself to redeem us from all wickedness and create a people eager to do good (vv. 11-14). Titus is to give himself completely to this mission (v. 15).

Key verse. 2:1: Don't stop with doctrine.

Personal application. Christ died to redeem us from sinful ways. No wonder we are to reject ungodliness!

Key concepts. Teach »p. 122. Train »p. 391. Example »p. 867. Grace »p. 789. Present age »p. 777.

INSIGHT

Teaching Christian lifestyle. Lecturing is fine if all a person wants to do is give information. But how does a person teach a way of life that is "in accord with sound doctrine"? A study of the words in this chapter shows us.

"Teach" (2:1, 15). The word *laleo* means to speak, to use words to express.

"Teach" (2:2-3, 9). No separate word is found here. The verse uses the verb "to be" in a common construction which implies an imperative communication of the need to live in the way described. We might say "bid" or "urge."

"Teach what is good" (2:3). The word *didaskaleo* is found only here in the N.T. It means to instruct in what is good; to show, demonstrate, explain.

"Train" (2:4). The Gk. *sophrontizo* means to encourage, advise, urge. It was used in secular Gk. of advice that focused on personal moral improvement.

"Encourage" (2:6, 15). *Parakaleo* implies a close personal relationship, with personal exhortation and encouragement to live a godly life.

"Set them an example" (2:7). Example is *typon*, which is a pattern. We teach Christian lifestyle by showing others how to live godly lives as well as by talking about how to live.

"Teaching" (2:7). The word is *didaskalia*, the act of instructing.

"Teaches" (2:12). Here the word is *paideuousa*. It implies giving parental guidance and daily instruction, as to a child, in order to lead a young person to maturity.

"Rebuke" (2:15). The word is *elencho*, which means to bring to light or expose and in this context to "point out, convince, and reprove" when it is necessary to convict.

Taken together we see that the ministry of teaching to shape lives is not simply repetition of words. Christian teaching calls for an intimate involvement of the teacher with the learner, and involves instruction, encouragement, advising, urging, exhorting, guiding, exposing, convincing, and perhaps most important, providing a living example.

The content of Titus' teaching. A survey of the chapter indicates that the lifestyle "in accord with sound doctrine" that the Christian teacher deals with involves temperance, sound faith, love, honesty, caring for husbands and children, self-control, submissiveness to masters, etc. Christian ministry is concerned with developing godly men and women.

Redemption (2:14). Galatians 4:5 pictures redemption as Christ's act of purchasing the believer by His blood, so that we might be freed *from* our past captivity to sin. This passage reminds us we were redeemed *to* a life of holiness, marked by a dedication to doing what is good.

These you should teach (2:15). Each ministry needs a focus. And the focus that Paul calls for here is one of nurturing believers, to help each become all he or she can be in Christ.

Chapter summary. Titus' ministry is to be one of organizing local church leadership, silencing false teachers, and instilling an appropriate Christian lifestyle. What happens in a church where such a mission is successful? Paul suggests that Christian people will prove to be good citizens of the secular state (3:1-2). They will also be deeply rooted in God's love and in response will "devote themselves to doing what is good" (vv. 3-8). In addition the church will avoid unprofitable disputes and purify itself of warped and devisive individuals (vv. 9-11).

With all this said, Paul closes with a few personal remarks (vv. 12-14) and with greetings to Titus from those who are still with Paul (v. 15).

Outline
Place
Finder

MISSION
MINISTRY
RESULTS

Key verse. 3:8: Show trust.

Personal application. How good it is to show appreciation for all Christ has done for us by eagerly doing what is good.

Key concepts. Love »pp. 351, 529, 680. Holy Spirit »pp. 73, 744, 759. Justification »p. 789. Born again »p. 680. Grace »p. 789. Eternal life »p. 682. Church discipline »p. 761.

INSIGHT

"**Remind**" **(3:1).** There are times when all of us will need to be reminded of what we already know is right.

Submissive and obedient (3:1). The first quality is one of attitude, the second is one of action. It's not enough to obey the government grudgingly. We are to be willingly responsive to secular leaders.

We were (3:3). This verse may well go with v. 2, which calls for the Christian to behave considerately and with humility toward "all men." In fact the Christian has no cause for pride and no basis to feel contempt for the lost. Before our own salvation we too were foolish, disobedient, deceived, and enslaved by all kinds of passions and pleasures. The salvation we enjoy had nothing to do with any supposed merit of our own, but rests completely on God's mercy.

Salvation, past tense (3:5-7). This verse describes what happens when an individual accepts Christ. At that time salvation is applied, and he or she is reborn and renewed spiritually by the Holy Spirit. In addition we are justified—declared innocent of past sins—and adopted into God's family as heirs, certain to inherit eternal life. Salvation also has present and future tenses. Salvation's present expression is seen in the godly life the Spirit enables

us to live. Salvation's future tense looks ahead to resurrection and complete release from every remaining taint of sin.

Good works (3:8). Salvation is to find practical, visible expression in the believer's new devotion to good works. The two Gk. words translated "good" help us understand what this means. One word, *agathos*, views the good as useful or profitable. This is the word typically used when moral issues are involved. The other word, *kalos*, views the good as beautiful as well as beneficial. By a devotion to what is morally right as well as beneficial to others, the Christian's good works make a distinct contribution to society and also bring glory to God.

"**Divisive person**" **(3:10).** The Gk. word *hairetikon* indicates an insistance on one's own opinion to the extent that a person stirs up divisions in the church. The Christian is responsible to warn such persons. But if they persist in propagandizing their unscriptural viewpoint to the detriment of the church, they must be cut off from fellowship.

Daily necessities (3:14). This verse reminds us that one of the "good" things to which Christians are to be devoted is honest work. This theme appears often in Paul's letters (cf. »pp. 28, 823).

Philemon

Most agree that this brief personal letter was written by the Apostle Paul while he was in prison in Rome. It was addressed to Philemon, who lived in Asia Minor, in either Colossae or Laodicea. The letter follows a typical first-century form.

Paul's letter was written to beg a wealthy believer named Philemon to take back a runaway slave, Onesimus, without punishing him as harshly as Roman law permitted. While the details of Paul's relationship with Onesimus remain a mystery, some things can be deduced. The runaway slave met Paul while the apostle was in prison. Paul's appeal suggests that Onesimus may have robbed his master for funds to use in making his escape. Yet Paul describes Onesimus as "faithful" and as a "brother." Apparently Paul led the runaway slave to Christ, and Onesimus had shown evidence that his conversion was real. After his conversion Onesimus had spent enough time with Paul to be "helpful" to him and for Paul to develop an honest affection for him.

With this in mind we can understand why Paul was eager for Onesimus to be reconciled with his master, also a Christian, and to demonstrate his new faith in Christ by rendering Philemon honest service.

We can assume that Philemon acceded to Paul's moving request. There is even speculation that this Onesimus later became the Ephesian bishop of that name the early church leader Ignatius mentions in letters to that city. If Onesimus did rise to become bishop, it shows the stunning impact of the Gospel in Roman society where only the wealthy became leaders of the many voluntary associations and clubs found in society.

OUTLINE OF PHILEMON

Chapter summary. Paul identifies himself as a prisoner as he writes to the "dear friend and fellow worker" Philemon (v. 1). Following a typical first-century pattern Paul extends God's grace and peace to Philemon (v. 3) and outlines the prayer that he offers regularly on Philemon's behalf (vv. 4-7).

At this point Paul launches his plea on behalf of Onesimus, whom he calls "my son" (vv. 8-10). Paul readily admits that as a slave Onesimus had been useless—but states that subsequent to his conversion "now he has become useful" (v. 11).

Paul is sending Onesimus back even though he would have liked to have kept him near. In one sense this was because as the slave's owner, Philemon had a right to his services. But even more, Paul was eager to see Onesimus reconciled to his master as a fellow-Christian (vv. 12-16).

With great delicacy Paul asks Philemon to welcome Onesimus as a brother—well aware that Philemon owes Paul far more than favors (vv. 17-21).

The request made, Paul indicates a hope to visit Philemon personally soon (v. 22) and then closes with typical greetings and a benediction (vv. 23-25).

Key verses. 15-16: One relationship counts.

Personal application. It is better to ask graciously than to demand.

INSIGHT

The church in your home (v. 2). This is one of several references in the N.T. to house churches, a reminder that congregations then were small and intimate (»p. 752).

First-century letters (vv. 4-7). Pagan letters also followed initial greetings with some expression of thanksgiving and a prayer. Paul's prayers, however, are not mere formula. They reveal what the great apostle actually did passionately desire for each recipient (cf. Rom. 1:8-10; 1 Thes. 1:2-5; Phil. 1:3-11; Col. 1:3-8).

Runaway slaves. There was no lower status in the Roman Empire, for runaway slaves were not protected by any law and were subject to all sorts of punishment. When a runaway slave was captured, he was typically seriously beaten and then sold to work as a miner or worker in another occupation with a short life expectancy.

In sending Onesimus back to Philemon, Paul was putting this runaway in a most dangerous position.

"My son" (v. 10). In view of the seriousness of Onesimus' offense, Paul uses every means to influence Philemon in his favor and to assuage his anger. This includes a reference to Paul's own age and apostleship and his affectionate reference later to Onesimus as "him—

who is my very heart" (v. 12).

Humor (v. 11). Paul also uses a play on words which 1st-century readers would have found very humorous. "Onesimus" means "profitable," as does *chrestos*. In this verse Paul says the runaway has been *achrestos* (useless), but now will prove *euchrestos* (useful).

Arguments (v. 15). Paul suggests that Philemon look for a hidden meaning behind Onesimus' earlier flight. Perhaps God worked things out this way so the slave might return home a brother.

Let me pay (v. 18). Paul offered to pay for any loss Philemon incurred through the defection of Onesimus. This would include anything the slave had stolen, but not the price of the slave himself. Apparently Philemon was being asked simply to let Onesimus return to his household as a slave, and if he were willing, Paul would undertake to cover money damages personally.

Freedom? It is notable that Paul does *not* ask Philemon to free Onesimus. The N.T. does not confront the institution of slavery. Instead it undercuts it, by encouraging believers to look at slaves as brothers in Christ rather than property. When this happens, the institution will fall of its own weight.

Hebrews

This is the only New Testament epistle that does not begin like a first-century letter, with a formal salutation and prayer. It does have an epistolatory ending. But because the writer and the recipient were identified in the first lines of a letter, neither the author nor the addressees of this New Testament book are known. What we do know is that the book was written very early. Its references to Old Testament sacrifices presume they are still being carried out, though the temple was destroyed and the sacrifices ceased in A.D. 70. The letter was paraphrased near the end of the first century, and it was well known throughout the church as "the Letter to the Hebrews" by the late second century.

The reason for the name becomes clear as we read the book. Throughout Hebrews Jesus Christ is compared with, and shown to be better than, the Old Testament revelation. Angels mediated the first covenant; Jesus, the Son of God, brought the New Covenant. The Old Covenant had a changing priesthood; Jesus is the ever-living High Priest of the New Covenant. The tabernacle and temple of the Old Covenant were mere symbols of the reality Christ opens up to believers. His one sacrifice for sins won us eternal salvation, while the very repetition of the sacrifices Moses instituted demonstrates their futility. Given this constant comparison with the Old Testament, it has seemed evident to most commentators that the writer was directing his defense of Christianity to the Jewish community, perhaps to unconverted Jews, but most likely to Jewish believers who felt drawn back to the traditions of Judaism, which they rightly loved and revered. But, as the writer of Hebrews might say, while the Old Testament was good, the new that Christ brings fulfills its promise, and is far *better*.

Whoever it was originally intended for, the Book of Hebrews is a treasure for modern Christians as well, for it helps us sense the intimate bond between Old Testament faith and our own faith in Christ. And it helps us appreciate just how great a salvation we have in our Lord.

Date and Authorship. Internal evidence suggests that the author was a second generation Christian (2:3) and that the book was written before the destruction of Jerusalem in A.D. 70. Suggestions that the book was written by Paul or Luke have been discarded, primarily because the Greek style is so different from the writings of either of these two men. Luther argued that Apollos was the author, and some have advanced Priscilla. What we do know is that whoever wrote this epistle was intimately familiar with the Old Testament and particularly with the Pentateuch and Psalms, with 23 of 29 direct quotes coming from these books. It is also clear that the author sees the entire Old Testament revelation as pointing directly to Jesus, who fulfills not only specific prophecies but also the intent of the older revelation. Whoever the author was, he or she was truly a master of the Scriptures, who understood it all through the perspective provided by Jesus Christ.

THEOLOGICAL OUTLINE OF HEBREWS

I. SUPERIORITY OF CHRIST'S IDENTITY	1:1–4:13
II. SUPERIORITY OF CHRIST'S PRIESTHOOD	4:14–7:28
III. SUPERIORITY OF CHRIST'S SACRIFICE	8:1–10:39
IV. SUFFICIENCY OF FAITH	11:1–13:25

CONTENT OUTLINE OF HEBREWS

I. Introduction (1:1-4)
II. Superiority of Christ's Identity (1:5–4:13)
  A. Superior to Angels (1:5-14)
  B. Superior as Author of Greater Salvation (2:1-9)
  C. Superior as True Man (2:10-18)
  D. Superior to Moses (3:1-6)
  E. Warning: Listen to Him (3:7–4:13)
    1. Rebellion keeps God's people from experiencing rest (3:7-19)
    2. Experience God's rest by responding obediently to Jesus' words (4:1-13)
III. Superiority of Christ's High Priesthood (4:14–7:28)
  A. Confidence in Jesus (4:14-16)
  B. Qualities of a High Priest (5:1-4)
  C. Christ's Unique Qualifications (5:5-10)
  D. Warning: Don't Turn Back (5:11–6:20)
    1. Slow progress toward maturity a problem (5:11-14)
    2. Can't lay faith's foundations again (6:1-3)
    3. Can't recrucify Jesus (6:4-8)
    4. So persevere (6:9-12)
    5. Certain God will keep His promise and that our salvation is secure (6:13-20)
  E. Christ's Priesthood Is Superior to That of the Old Testament (7:1-28)
    1. It is modeled on Melchizedek, not Levi (7:1-14)
    2. It is superior because: (7:15-28)
      a. It is permanent (7:15-19)
      b. It was confirmed by God's oath (7:20-22)
      c. It is guaranteed by Christ's endless life (7:23-25)
      d. His ministry was accomplished by a single sacrifice (7:26-28)
IV. Superiority of Christ's Sacrifice (8:1–10:39)
  A. The Covenant Providing for Christ's Sacrifice Is Superior (8:1-7)
  B. The Old Covenant Was Always Destined to Be Superceded (8:8-13)
  C. The Old Covenant Provided Only an Earthly, Symbolic Place for Sacrifice (9:1-10)
  D. Christ Offered His Own, Not Animal, Blood (9:11-14)
  E. His Sacrifice Ransomed Us from Sin (9:15-22)
  F. His Once-for-All Sacrifice Was Sufficient (9:23-28)
  G. His Once-for-All Sacrifice Provides Forgiveness and Makes Us Holy (10:1-18)
  H. Warning: Persevere (10:19-39)
    1. Hold unswerving to our hope in Him (10:19-25)
    2. Deliberate sin always brings judgment (10:26-31)

3. Hold on to confidence in Christ despite suffering and persecution (10:32-39)

V. The Sufficiency of Faith (11:1–13:19)

A. The Nature of Faith (11:1-3)

B. Faith's Hall of Fame (11:4-40)
1. Faith before the Flood (11:4-7)
2. Faith in Abraham and Sarah (11:8-19)
3. Faith in the patriarchs (11:20-22)
4. Faith in Moses (11:23-28)
5. Faith in the Exodus generation (11:29-31)
6. Faith in others (11:32-38)
7. Faith's promise (11:39-40)

C. Faith's Response to Discipline (12:1-13)
1. Consider Christ's example (12:1-3)
2. Remember God loves those He disciplines (12:4-11)
3. Therefore persevere (12:12-13)

D. Faith's Commitment to Righteousness (12:14-29)
1. The importance of personal holiness (12:14-17)
2. The glory of the present revelation (12:18-24)
3. The importance of responding to God with reverence and awe (12:25-29)

E. Exhortations to the Faithful (13:1-19)
1. Keep on loving others (13:1-5a)
2. Keep on trusting God (13:5b-6)
3. Keep on responding to leaders (13:7-8)
4. Keep on praising God (13:9-16)
5. Keep on being responsive to leaders (13:17)
6. Keep on praying (13:18-19)

VI. Conclusion (13:20-25)

A. Doxology (13:20-21)

B. Final Exhortations (13:22-25)

Outline
Place
Finder

IDENTITY
PRIESTHOOD
SACRIFICE
FAITH

Chapter summary. Hebrews begins with a grand affirmation. God, who has spoken to man through intermediaries, has now spoken to us by His Son, a Son who is God Himself in all His splendor and power (1:1-4).

The author underlines the fact that the Son is superior to angels. Jewish tradition held that angels gave the Old Covenant (the Pentateuch, the Law) to Moses. This One through whom God has now spoken is superior for He, not angels, is spoken to by God as "My Son" (v. 5). He is superior, for angels are commanded to worship the Son (v. 6). He is superior because angels are servants, while the Son sits on the throne (vv. 7-9).

The Son is superior not only as Creator of the universe, but as One who in endless life sits at God's right hand (vv. 10-13). Angels are ministering spirits; not masters of the universe, but servants of God's saints (v. 14).

Key verse. 1:3: God, exactly.

Personal application. We cannot honor Jesus too highly.

Key concepts. Last days »p. 843. Revelation »pp. 354, 758. Prophets »p. 131. Angels »p. 521. Father »pp. 140, 663. Kingdom »pp. 380, 605. Creation »p. 430.

INSIGHT

Many times and various ways (1:1). Old Testament revelations came in dreams and visions, through prophets, and in direct messages from the Angel of the Lord (»p. 37). The revelation that comes through Christ continues this tradition, but is a final, ultimate revelation because its agent is God the Son.

The Son's nature (1:3). The Gk. makes the meaning of key phrases clear. The "radiance" of God's glory is *apaugasma*, which is a brightness shining from within, and a brightness caused by an external source. Jesus shines with His own and with the Father's brightness — and the two lights are one.

The phrase "the exact representation of His [God's] being" is the *charackter*. In the 1st century this indicated the imprint of a die, such as the impression on coins. Jesus "bears the stamp" of the divine nature itself.

Jesus' superior name (1:4). The "name" in biblical times summed up all a person was. Though eternally superior to angels as God, Jesus also "became" in accomplishing our salvation. The name "Saviour" was added to His laurels.

"Firstborn" (1:6). The use of this term does not suggest an origin for Jesus subsequent to that of the Father. Rather *prototokos* is frequently used as a technical theological term, applied only to Jesus. It affirms His supreme rank and His unique relationship with the Father and His unique position within the family of God (cf.

also Rom. 8:29; Col. 1:15, 18; Rev. 1:5).

"Flames of fire" (1:7). This verse quotes Ps. 104:4. It is taken by some to refer to forms God's angelic servants may take (cf. 2 Kings 6:17). It is more likely that this phrase, in a passage intended to exalt Christ, contrasts the fiery glory of angels with the awesome radiance of Christ's true deity. Fire is impressive. But not when compared to the awesome power of the sun.

"Sit at My right hand" (1:13). The right hand is the traditional place of power and authority in the biblical world. Christ not only laid the foundations of the earth, and possesses endless life and existence, He also exercises all the power and authority of Deity.

Angels: ministering spirits (1:14). The Gk. word *angelos* means "messenger." It is used 175 times in the N.T. The N.T. teaches that Satan leads a host of evil angels (Matt. 25:41; Jude 6), whom many believe are the demons of the Gospels, dedicated to harm human beings and resist God's purposes. God's angels, on the other hand, are committed by Him to serve and support us, who are the "heirs of salvation" (Heb. 1:14; cf. Matt. 18:10; Acts 12).

While angels have a supportive ministry, and no doubt protect and in other ways help believers, this passage reminds us that Jesus, not angels, is to be the focus of our faith. Paul sternly scolds those who exalt angels rather than Christ (Col. 2).

Chapter summary. The writer now introduces the first of a series of warnings which punctuate this book. If those who disobeyed the older revelation could not avoid God's wrath which was mediated by angels, how could anyone who ignores the "great salvation" announced by the Son of God expect to escape judgment? (2:1-4)

Now the writer returns to the theme of Jesus' superiority. Christ took on humanity, and in the process temporarily became "lower than the angels," even though in Creation God announced a far greater destiny for mankind (vv. 5-8a). But Jesus, who suffered death for us, is now "crowned with glory and honor," and in His exaltation we see our destiny, for now He and we are members of the same family (vv. 8b-15). Christ took on real humanity and through death released us from the fear of death. He did this not to help angels, but to help "His brothers," for whose sins He made atonement (vv. 16-18). In taking on humanity Jesus lowered Himself—that He might lift us up.

Key verse. 2:11: Brother Jesus.

Personal application. Jesus rose to lift us up.

Key concepts. Angels »pp. 521, 855. Salvation »p. 426. Holy Spirit »pp. 73, 744. Dominion »p. 352. Death »pp. 369, 741. Suffering »p. 877. Satan »pp. 501, 655. Atonement »p. 739. Sin »p. 442. Temptation »pp. 655, 871.

INSIGHT

"How shall we escape?" (2:3) In the Gk. sentence the "we" is emphasized. The author is not speaking of Christians, but the present generation, which has heard the message of "such a great salvation" announced by the Lord. In O.T. times those who received the Law and disobeyed it were punished. Today those who *ignore* the Gospel are lost.

The warning surely must have had an impact on Jewish believers also. Turning back to Judaism would have involved neglect of salvation.

Lower means higher—for us (2:5-9). To sense the force of this argument, simply draw a horizontal line. The writer notes that the realm of humanity has been *below* the line and that of angels *above* the line. This is despite the fact that God in creating gave man His own image/likeness and dominion (Gen. 1:26; Ps. 8:4-6). So what God did to fulfill His promise was to send Jesus, to live below the line, that in dying He might be lifted far above the line, above even the realm of angels. In being lifted up and crowned with glory and honor, He lifted us too!

Author of salvation (2:10). The word *achegos* also means one who begins something as the first in a series. Jesus was the pioneer, who marked the trail as well as provided salvation.

How was Jesus made **"perfect through suffering"?** (2:10) Jesus must be a true human being in order to be qualified to save humanity and thus must experience life as we experience it. Christ's suffering as a human being didn't make Him better; it established one vital qualification of a Saviour.

Christ's humanity: brothers in the same family (2:11-18). One of the greatest mysteries of all time is that God the Son entered the human race and was "made like His brothers in every way." To say that Jesus was human "in every way" means that, apart from a sin nature, the Son of God accepted our limitations and lived within them. He experienced hunger and thirst. He grew tired and knew loneliness. He felt the pain of rejection and misunderstanding and yearned for the deep relationships which we find so satisfying. Many passages in the N.T. make it very clear that Jesus truly was both God and man (cf. Matt. 4:1-2; 8:23-24; Luke 2:52; 24:39; John 1:14; 4:5-6; 11:35; 19:28, 34; Rom. 1:2-3; Heb. 2:14, 17-18; 4:15).

He is able to help (2:18). A high priest had to be able to sympathize with those he represented to God. The testings Jesus underwent as a human being mean that He understands.

Chapter summary. As Son of God, Jesus is greater than those supernatural beings known as angels (chap. 1). As a true human being (chap. 2), the writer now tells us, Jesus is greater than Moses (3:1-6). This is a vital point, for no human being was as revered in Judaism as Moses, the giver of the Law.

This point also induces the writer to add another warning. Speaking of the time of Moses, the Scriptures remind God's people that the Exodus generation could not enter the Promised Land because of disobedience (vv. 7-11). Their failure to experience that "rest" was due to hardened, sinful hearts that would not respond to the Word God spoke through Moses. Their failure, and the judgment that followed, is a warning addressed to all who hear God's Word in their own hearts "today." Those who will not believe God's Word, and demonstrate belief by obedience, well never experience "rest" today (vv. 12-19).

Outline
Place
Finder

IDENTITY
PRIESTHOOD
SACRIFICE
FAITH

Key verse. 3:13: Urge obedience.

Personal application. Rest depends on a faith that is expressed as obedience.

Key concepts. Moses »p. 55. Servant »p. 90. Holy Spirit »p. 759. Anger of God »pp. 65, 72. Obedience »pp. 807, 859.

INSIGHT

Moses and Christ (3:1-6). In this passage Moses is praised for his faithfulness as a *therapon*, an honored servant who is high above a mere slave in status. Christ too was faithful, but Christ is far superior to Moses in several respects:

In relation to God's household, Moses was never more than a member of the family, but Christ was the architect who built the family (v. 3).

In relation to role, Moses was an important servant, but Jesus was the Son and Heir.

In relation to ministry, Moses spoke of what would happen; Jesus was the future he foresaw.

In every way Jesus was superior as a human being to Moses, the towering figure most honored in Judaism.

Background (3:7-19). When the Exodus generation led by Moses first approached the Promised Land, they refused to obey God's command to enter. Their rebellion led to a dread decree: the Israelites must wander for decades in the desert until every person over 20 had died. Disobedience demonstrated their failure to trust God in the face of a powerful enemy and doomed those who refused to believe to never see the Promised Land or experience rest there. It is this historic experience that the writer of Heb. looks back on as he utters yet another warning. The spirit of unbelief and disobedience which marked the men and women of Moses' day will surely keep people in the writer's day from experiencing the rest promised in Christ.

"Voice" (3:7). In this passage God's "voice" is any direction from the Lord, delivered through Scripture or through the Spirit's working in another believer. Because the Holy Spirit is the one speaking, true believers will hear and recognize that voice.

"Today" (3:7). This word reminds us that God's voice has a "today" expression. We can know His will and hear Him speak to us today through His Word and through others. The key to our personal relationship with God is to remain sensitive to the Holy Spirit, always ready to respond when He speaks.

"Rest" (3:11). This word is used in a variety of ways in this passage. The model of "rest" is occupation of the Promised Land and the peace and prosperity that were to follow. But "rest" is also an inner experience of peace, which comes from the assurance that we are just where God wants us to be, doing His will. Our task as Christians is to be sensitive to God's voice, respond to it with obedience, and so to experience God's rest.

Unbelief (3:12). A failure to trust God was the root cause of ancient Israel's rebellion. They did not believe and so disobeyed. Faith and obedience are everywhere linked in Scripture, for true faith releases us from our fears and results in obeying God gladly.

Chapter summary. The writer continues his urgent discussion of "rest" from chapter 3. God's Word has come to this generation, as it did to those of Moses' time, with a similar promise of rest. But the promise does us no good unless we hear and respond with faith (4:1-3).

The concept of God's "rest" is rooted in Creation and has vital meaning for us in our "today" (vv. 4-8). When the Old Testament says God "rested from His work" it doesn't mean God is inactive. It means that God no longer works, that in His act of Creation He planned for every contingency. There is no problem we can face that God has not already provided a solution. Our task then is not to find our own answers. It is to listen for His voice, sure He will lead us into His rest (vv. 9-11).

How much trust can we put in God's voice? Total trust, for nothing in our lives is hidden from Him. His Word searches our whole being, not to condemn us, but to sense our deepest, most secret needs. With these laid bare, God's Spirit guides us to His rest (vv. 12-13).

The warning uttered, the writer reminds us of a wonderful truth. Through Jesus our High Priest we have immediate access to God. If we need help to find our way, He will give it freely (vv. 14-16).

Key verse. 4:10: We can find rest.

Personal application. Obedience opens the way to rest.

Key concepts. Voice »p. 857. Rest »p. 857. Today »p. 857. Sabbath »p. 71. Grace »p. 789.

INSIGHT

Effort to enter rest? (4:11) At first the words seem contradictory. But we are not to worry and try to find our own solutions; we are to concentrate on God's voice. Let's not be distracted from the central issue in Christian experience—listening for and obeying God as He speaks to us daily.

Judging (4:12-13). The Gk. word, *kririkos*, means "discerner." The implication of condemnation in the English word "judge" is unfortunate, for these verses are intended to be of great comfort. How wonderful that God's Word reaches into our innermost being, and speaks to all our deepest needs. God's voice is penetrating, and His guidance is based on a complete understanding of us as well as of righteousness.

"Mercy" (4:16). Mercy is *eleos*, a compassion for a sufferer so great that it moves one to help. Here mercy implies failure: we come to God because our sins have led us away from Him and from rest. The wonder of this passage is that, because Jesus understands our weaknesses, we can come boldly to God and find not recriminations but mercy and grace.

Tempted, without sin (4:15). Some have argued that without a sin nature Jesus could not have been tempted as terribly as we are. But consider. Who understands suffering better: the person who when tortured gives in and tells his captors everything, or the person who resists despite the fact that his torture continues? We, who give in to temptation so easily, cannot even guess how strong temptation can be. Jesus, who never gave in, *knows*.

Jesus' high priesthood (4:14-5:10). Jesus takes over all the functions of the O.T. high priest, and completes his mission. Jesus "saves completely" those who come to Him, because unlike O.T. high priests, He lives on to intercede for us (cf. 7:25). What is more Jesus does not need to make repeated sacrifices, providing eternal salvation with the one sacrifice of Himself (7:26-8:2). He fulfills all the imagery of the O.T. priesthood, serving as the Mediator who alone can bring us into full and complete relationship with God.

Chapter summary. The high priest held a unique position in Israel's religion, a position available only to a descendant of Aaron. So the writer is careful to enumerate Christ's qualifications for this role in New Testament faith.

The high priest is "appointed from among men." His commission to represent other men before God requires one whose own humanity makes him sensitive to mankind's needs (5:1-3). This high honor must be conferred by God Himself (v. 4). Christ thus was appointed to the priesthood by His Father (vv. 5-6). Christ also meets the qualification of sensitivity to human frailty: as a man Jesus "learned obedience from what He suffered" (vv. 7-8). Thus qualified He was designated "High Priest in the order of Melchizedek" and became the source of our salvation (vv. 9-10).

With this said, the author launches yet another warning, merited because of his readers' apparent inability to grasp even the elementary truths of Christianity. If they are to go on to maturity, they must use the truths they have been taught as a guide to distinguish good from evil. To be "meat" rather than "milk," truth must be applied and used (vv. 11-14).

Outline
Place
Finder

IDENTITY
PRIESTHOOD
SACRIFICE
FAITH

Key verses. 5:8-9: Fully qualified.

Personal application. Jesus is on our side. He truly understands.

Key concepts. Priesthood »pp. 81, 880. Call »p. 757. Submission »pp. 867, 880. Salvation »pp. 426, 841.

INSIGHT

Dealing gently (5:2). The word *metriopathein* strikes a balance between anger and indifference. We are to take other's failures seriously, but are not to be harsh, realizing our own weakness.

A sinner (5:3). The O.T. high priest was never to forget his own flawed heritage as a sinful human being. Thus on the Day of Atonement the high priest first offered a sacrifice for his own sin offering, before making the sacrifice that atoned for the people's sins (cf. Lev. 16).

Son and priest (5:5-6). The author quotes two O.T. passages. The first establishes Jesus' right as a Son to minister in heaven itself (cf. 8:3-6). The second establishes His right to serve as a High Priest on earth.

The reason why it is important to trace Jesus' priesthood back to Melchizedek is discussed in chap. 7 (»p. 861).

"Obedience" (5:7-8). To obey is to respond in accord with the request or command of another. Both Testaments make it clear that obedience to God grows out of personal relationship with Him and is motivated by love. Two major passages in the epistles examine Christ's

obedience. Philippians 2 focuses on the attitude of humility — of self-surrender — expressed in Christ's incarnation and journey to the cross. This passage in Heb. 5 discusses the significance of Christ's obedience. By "learning" obedience He established His credentials as a true human being, living that life we live here which demands obedience to God. Thus qualified, Jesus "became the source of eternal salvation for all who obey [here, 'believe in'] Him."

"Made perfect" (5:9). The Gk. word emphasizes completion and wholeness. In the biological sense the "perfect" is mature. In the spiritual sense, the "perfect" is complete, having achieved full potential. Here Jesus is "made perfect" in the sense of being fully equipped (through obedience) for the task God set before Him.

Maturity (5:14). The same Gk. word is translated "made perfect" above. These verses show how we achieve spiritual maturity. As we face trials, we constantly seek to understand them in the light of God's Word, and apply Scripture to make wise and godly choices.

Outline
Place
Finder

IDENTITY
PRIESTHOOD
SACRIFICE
FAITH

Chapter summary. The writer continues his warning to those who, though believers, have failed to mature (cf. 5:11-14). The foundation of "elementary teachings" has been laid: We mature by building on them, not going back over them again and again (6:1-3). "Falling away" is not an issue: What would a person who has received the heavenly gift and participated in the Holy Spirit do to start over again? Recrucify Jesus? What a disgrace that would be! (vv. 4-6) Christians are like crop land, on whom God's rain has showered. We're intended to produce a beneficial crop, not thorns (vv. 7-8). The writer is sure that his Jewish Christian readers are not a wasteland—he simply wants to stimulate them to diligence (vv. 9-12).

He also wants to reassure them and so reminds them that their salvation is guaranteed by the promise of a God who cannot lie and that His promise was even confirmed with a sworn oath. What an "anchor for the soul" this provides for we who believe in Jesus, our great high priest (vv. 13-20).

Key verses. 6:17-18: You can be sure.

Personal application. Our salvation is a foundation to build on, not a shaky scaffold to cling to in fear.

Key concepts. Repentance »p. 780. Faith »pp. 35, 740. Baptism »pp. 604, 708, 742. Resurrection »p. 823. Judgment »pp. 372, 724. Fruitfulness »pp. 414, 796. Salvation »p. 841. Covenant »pp. 35, 466. Hope »p. 465.

INSIGHT

Background. The Jewish believers to whom this letter is written were drawn to the rituals and practices of their ancient faith. The writer pictures them constantly reexamining, wondering, rather than accepting the basic teachings of Christianity and growing toward maturity. Like some today, they have accepted Christ, but remain unsure of their salvation and so look back fearfully. This chapter reminds them and us that salvation was won for us by the crucified Son of God and rests on the promise of a God who cannot lie. With this as an anchor, any believer can confidently look ahead and grow to maturity.

Tasting the heavenly gift (6:4-5). Some argue that "taste" here implies the writer is addressing unbelievers. But in O.T. and N.T. "taste" is used of the conscious experience of divine realities. Thus the psalmist says, "Taste and see that the Lord is good" (Ps. 34:8). "Taste" is *not* used in contrast with "partake"; these are true believers.

"If they fall away" (6:6). The Gk. *parapiipto*, "to fall aside," is used only here in the N.T. The writer is posing a hypothetical case for Jewish Christians. If they did return to Judaism, and later changed their minds again, what would they do? Would they crucify Jesus again, as

though His sacrificial death were not enough? How impossible!

Hebrews 6:9 makes it clear that the writer does not view these believers as lost. But he does confront them. If they are to prove fruitful for God they must realize that once trust is reposed in Christ, there's no need to return to basic teachings. They have entered God's "one door" to salvation and have no need to hesitate or look back.

Burned land (6:8). Farmers set fire to the thorns and weeds that grew on unproductive land. The ashes were plowed into the ground to enrich it so that crops might grow. The imagery does not contrast heaven and hell, but the experience of productive and unproductive land.

Oath (6:16). The Gk. word *horkos* indicates a solemn, legally binding pledge guaranteeing that a person will keep a promise. Many N.T. passages speak of God swearing with an oath (Luke 1:73; Acts 2:30; Heb. 3:11; 4:3; 7:20-22, 28). His purpose is to underscore His intentions, and give us a solid basis for believing that all He has promised will come true. Here the commitment is confirmed by God's promise to save those who believe in Jesus. Possessing God's promise, we need not fear or doubt.

Chapter summary. The writer now emphasizes the fact that Jesus' priesthood does not derive from Aaron but from Melchizedek. Melchizedek appears briefly in sacred history, as king of Salem, later called Jerusalem, and as a priest. He blessed Abraham after the patriarch's victory over invading kings, and Abraham gave him a tithe of the plunder (cf. Gen. 14). From this brief account the writer of Hebrews establishes two things: as the greater blesses the lesser, Melchizedek was greater than Abraham. And as Aaron was, in a sense, present in his great-grandfather Abraham, Aaron paid tithes to Melchizedek and thus acknowledged the superiority of his priesthood (Heb. 7:1-10).

As the psalmist quotes God ordaining someone as a "priest forever, after the order of Melchizedek," it is clear that God always intended to make a change in the Aaronic priesthood. And such a change requires a change in the whole system of Mosaic Law of which that priesthood was a part (vv. 11-19).

How is Jesus' priesthood better? It is "forever," and thus rests on a better covenant (vv. 20-22). It is permanent, for Jesus lives and thus can save us completely (vv. 23-25). And it meets our every need, for by the one sacrifice of Himself this High Priest settled forever the issue of our sins (vv. 26-28).

Outline
Place
Finder

IDENTITY
PRIESTHOOD
SACRIFICE
FAITH

Key verse. 7:25: No halfway job.

Personal application. Jesus guarantees our salvation.

Key concepts. Priesthood »pp. 81, 858. Tithe »p. 103. Bless »p. 49. Law »pp. 123, 145, 376, 606, 743, 790. Oath »p. 860. Save »p. 841. Sacrifices »pp. 30, 555, 862.

INSIGHT

"**A priest forever**" (7:3). The writer uses a typical rabbinical argument, based on the fact that neither Melchizedek's birth or death are recorded. Thus in Scripture he is a "timeless" figure, an appropriate type of Jesus, who because of His endless life remains a "Priest forever." Some have taken this verse as evidence that Melchizedek was a theophany—a preincarnate appearance of Christ. It is better to take him, as the text here does, simply as a type of Christ.

A change of law (7:12). The writer's point is that "law" is a linked system. There are commands and obligations, a tabernacle where God can be approached, a priesthood and sacrifices to restore fellowship when men sin, and so on. If we change any part of that system, we affect its other elements as well. Thus the O.T. prediction of a change from an Aaronic to a Melchizedekian priesthood implied from ancient times that God intended to replace the whole Mosaic system. And this implied that that system was flawed: It could not make men perfect, for if it could have, it would not have to be replaced. Christ's ordi-

nation as a priest "after the order of Melchizedek" shows that the old Mosaic system has been replaced—by something much better!

"**Guarantee**" (7:22). The Gk. word *engyos* is found only here in the N.T. It is a legal term which identifies a bond or collateral. It means that the signer of the guarantee pledged his resources as security for the commitment he made. The writer reminds us that Jesus is the living guarantee that the forgiveness God offers us under the New Covenant will surely be ours.

"**Jesus lives forever**" (7:24-25). The high priest represents his people before God. As an ever-living High Priest, Jesus is always available to represent us and thus "He is able to save completely."

Those who worry after accepting Christ that they might be lost again neglect important truths. We were saved by Jesus when we were sinners. If we fall after salvation, He remains committed to save us completely. If it depended on you and me, we *should* worry. But salvation depends on Jesus, so we are truly secure.

Outline
Place
Finder

IDENTITY
PRIESTHOOD
SACRIFICE
FAITH

Chapter summary. Aaronic priests ministered on earth, in a sanctuary which was a copy and shadow of heavenly realities. Our High Priest, Jesus, ministers in heaven itself (8:1-6). The superiority of Christ's ministry is further reflected in the superiority of the covenant which governs it. The old Mosaic Covenant was flawed. The Old Testament itself predicts its replacement by a New Covenant (vv. 7-9). Under the New Covenant that replaces the old, God promises to "put My laws in their minds and write them on their hearts." Under the New Covenant believers will truly come to know God, will be forgiven for all their sins, and will be transformed from within (8:10-13).

Key verse. 8:10: The new is better.

Personal application. God has relegated Mosaic Law to history in order to make us righteous through faith.

Key concepts. Priesthood »pp. 81, 858. Tabernacle »p. 67. Law »pp. 123, 145, 376, 606, 743, 790. Altar »p. 79. Heaven »p. 609. New Covenant »p. 466. Sacrifices »pp. 30, 555. Forgiveness »pp. 357, 633.

INSIGHT

Illustration (8:1-7). *The priests who offered sacrifices under the Mosaic Covenant acted out on earth what Christ would one day do in heaven itself. Services held in the earthly tabernacle and temple were like shadows cast on a sheet: they reflected the reality hidden behind it, but did so imperfectly. Rightly understood, everything in O.T. faith and worship portrays and was intended to prepare Israel for the revelation of heavenly realities in Jesus Christ.*

The first, flawed covenant (8:7). The writer argues the very prediction in Jer. 31:31-34 of a "New" Covenant to replace the one given

through Moses, proves the first was flawed. The writings of Paul have many analyses of the flaws in Mosaic Law. Essentially, what Law could not do was to transform the believer from within, so that righteousness was "written on the heart."

Contrasting covenants (8:8-12). The Mosaic Covenant, or Law Covenant, differed from other biblical covenants. The others announced what God intended to do, irrespective of what men might do. The Mosaic Covenant announced what God would do *if* the Israelites obeyed and what He would do *if* the Israelites disobeyed. The weakness of that covenant lay not in God's ability to do His part, but in man's inability to live an obedient life. The New Covenant is *not like* the Mosaic (v. 9) in that New Covenant promises are unconditional.

The three unconditional promises in Jer. 31 are: God will transform believers from within, planting His Law on our hearts and minds. He will establish an unbreakable relationship which will make Him "our" God and us "His" people. And God will "forgive . . . and remember their sins no more" (v. 12).

The New Covenant Jeremiah predicted was instituted by the death of Christ. Thus in Christ all three New Covenant promises are our present possession, guaranteed by God Himself.

"Remember" (8:12). The word means more than recall. It means to "act in accordance with" what is remembered. Not to remember sins means God will not punish them.

Chapter summary. The writer reminds his readers that every element of the Mosaic Covenant had special significance, for it reflected realities in heaven (9:1-5). But the most significant act of all was performed on the Day of Atonement. Then the high priest entered the inner room of the tabernacle, the most holy place, carrying the blood of an atoning sacrifice (vv. 6-7). The curtain separating this inner room symbolized the fact that under Mosaic Law no one had direct access into God's presence (vv. 8-10).

But our High Priest, Jesus, entered heaven itself, bearing His own blood. By His sacrifice he obtained eternal salvation for us (vv. 11-14). Christ is thus mediator of a New Covenant, activated by His death. This is in fact the significance of Old Testament sacrifices: in cleansing earthly things they symbolize the cleansing Jesus has won for us (vv. 15-22). Animal sacrifices were sufficient for earthly copies, but Christ alone could enter heaven and then with His own blood. When He did He put away our sin once for all, all by the one sufficient and awesome sacrifice of Himself (vv. 23-28).

Key verse. 9:15: Free at last.

Personal application. Never question whether Jesus did enough.

Key concepts. Tabernacle »p. 67. Ark »p. 68. Atonement »pp. 69, 84, 739. Priests »pp. 81, 858. Blood »pp. 85, 766. New Covenant »p. 466. Judgment »pp. 372, 724.

Outline
Place
Finder

IDENTITY
PRIESTHOOD
SACRIFICE
FAITH

INSIGHT

Sacrifice (chaps. 8–10). These chapters focus on the death of Christ as a sacrifice, which instituted the promised New Covenant. Sacrifices were practiced throughout the ancient world, where they were viewed as food for the gods. In the O.T., however, blood sacrifices were not viewed as food. The significance lay in the blood of sacrifice for, as Lev. 17:11 says, "I have given it [the blood] to you to make atonement for yourselves." In essence sacrifice throughout sacred history has graphically indicated that sin deserves death, but that God will accept the death of a substitute in place of the life of the sinner.

Hebrews 8–10 tells us that the system of O.T. sacrifices, structured so as to cleanse articles and persons on earth, were "object lessons," establishing the truth stated above but pointing to Christ's sacrifice. Christ's sacrifice alone was capable of cleansing a lost humanity so that we might have access to heaven itself and stand before a holy God. The teaching of this great section of Heb. is that Jesus' one sacrifice cleanses our conscience (9:14), does away with sin (v. 26), perfects believers, provides a perfect forgiveness (10:11-18), and thus makes all other sacrifices irrelevant. The

O.T. Age truly is past. A new and far better age has dawned.

Approaching God (9:8). The O.T. system permitted the Israelites to come close, but not pull aside the last veil and enter God's presence. What a stunning difference in our relationship with God through Jesus. Through Him "we may approach God with freedom and confidence" (Eph. 3:12; cf. Heb. 4:16). Our approach is characterized as *parresia*, a confident boldness in the presence of a superior.

Cleansed from acts that lead to death (9:14). The O.T. sacrifices worked externally. Christ's sacrifice works internally. With a cleansed conscience we are no longer bound by guilt to our past. We are no longer overwhelmed with a sense of our inadequacy. Our past sins are gone, and we are released to serve God.

"Forgiveness" (9:22). Forgiveness in Scripture is never a cheap, "Oh, forget it," that simply shrugs off sin. Forgiveness is expensive, purchased at the price of blood. The O.T. sacrifices revealed how forgiveness would be obtained. But only the blood of Jesus shed on the cross for us was sufficient to pay sin's penalty. How awesome that Jesus was willing to die that you and I might be forgiven.

Outline
Place
Finder

IDENTITY
PRIESTHOOD
SACRIFICE
FAITH

Chapter summary. The writer continues to identify ways in which the sacrifice of Christ is superior. The endless repetition of sacrifices made under Mosaic Law is proof they could not perfect the worshiper. Similarly Christ's offering of a single sacrifice is proof that He makes men holy! (10:1-10) After making one sacrifice, Jesus "sat down" at God's right hand, signifying that His work was finished (vv. 11-14). And Scripture adds its testimony. It reminds us that under the New Covenant sins are forgiven. Once truly forgiven, no more sacrifice is required (vv. 15-18).

The writer then pauses again. He urges his readers to draw confidence from Christ's High Priesthood and so "hold unswerv-ingly to the hope we profess" (vv. 19-25). There are terrible consequences for anyone who refuses to respond to God's saving act in Christ (vv. 26-31). But the writer knows his audience has made a very different choice—a choice exhibited in their commitment to Christ despite persecution, prison, and confiscation of property. He urges them to hold on to their initial confidence, sure that soon Jesus will come, and we will be ready for Him then (vv. 32-39).

Key verse. 10:18: No more sacrifice.

Personal application. Confidence leads to commitment.

Key concepts. Sacrifice »p. 862. Offerings »p. 78. Holy »pp. 81, 86, 879. Priest »pp. 81, 880. Hope »p. 465. Persecution »p. 760. Rewards »pp. 759, 836.

INSIGHT

Make perfect (10:1). The word is used in the common biblical sense of bringing someone or something to an intended goal.

A reminder of sins (10:3). A person who takes an insulin shot daily has protection from the disease. But each shot he or she takes is a reminder of the illness. In the same way the repeated sacrifices of the O.T. covered the sins of O.T. people—but reminded them that they were still in sin's grip. Christ's one sacrifice has a different message. It does not need to be repeated. Our sins are gone—and we are free.

"Made perfect" (10:14). Christ's sacrifice brings us to the place God has always intended for us.

"Being made holy" (10:14). Christ not only makes us righteous in God's sight. He has power to make us progressively holy in our lives here on earth.

"No longer any sacrifice" (10:18). To "forgive" means, literally, to cancel or to send away. Since our sins themselves are canceled in the death of Christ, and so completely "sent away" that we no longer bear any guilt, there is no need for any further sacrifice. As the hymn says, God has redeemed us "once for all."

"Washed" (10:22). We who hold fast have been cleansed within by God and have made a public profession through baptism.

"Spur one another on" (10:24-25). Here is another brief picture of an early church meeting. Believers met not just to hear preaching, but to encourage each other "toward love and good deeds." Don't overlook such relationships if you expect to live a vital, successful Christian life.

"Deliberately keep on sinning" (10:26-31). Here the writer confronts apostasy, a deliberate choice to return to the old system of sacrifices and so "trample underfoot the Son of God." For such sin there can only be certain judgment.

Perseverance: the consequence of confidence (10:32-39). The word *hypomeno* means to "patiently endure." It involves overcoming difficulties and withstanding pressures. The writer reminds his readers that they have demonstrated this quality, an expression of their confidence in Christ. They stood their ground despite suffering. They remained faithful despite insult, persecution, and even the loss of property. And they took a stand beside those in prison. The challenge now is to hold on, confident, till Jesus comes.

Chapter summary. The theological foundation laid, the author now describes the life of faith he expects his Christian readers to lead. First he reminds them that throughout sacred history faith in God has been the key to the achievement of Bible heroes. Faith has always involved confidence in the unseen (11:1-3). It has also been expressed in action: whether by those who lived before the Flood (vv. 4-7), by Abraham and Sarah (vv. 8-19), by the patriarchs (vv. 20-22), by Moses (vv. 23-28), or by the Exodus generation (vv. 29-31). These and others (vv. 32-38) won commendation for their faith, even though what God has given us is much better than what He provided for them (vv. 39-40). Christ has died for us. We exercise faith—and live for Him.

Outline
Place
Finder

IDENTITY
PRIESTHOOD
SACRIFICE
FAITH

Key verse. 11:6: Please God.

Personal application. How has faith expressed itself in your daily life?

Key concepts. Faith »pp. 35, 458, 740, 872.

INSIGHT

"Faith" (11:1). While the object of faith by its very nature cannot be seen, the writer will go on to remind us that its presence has a vital impact on our lives and character. Real faith produces startling results.

An example (11:3). Creation is one of those things that by its nature cannot be seen (cf. v. 1). No one was there, and no evidence available today can demonstrate origins. Throughout history various theories of origins have abounded, including the modern theory of macroevolution. The believer, however, shapes his or her view of origins by revelation and so understands that all that is came into being by God's command.

It is a peculiar thing that *everyone* holds his or her view by "faith," for no one can adduce proof. Only the believer who trusts God's Word really understands. So the faith that produces heroes is not a subjective thing, but confidence in God and His Word.

Faith orients us to God (11:6). Stripped down to its basics, faith is confidence that God exists, and the conviction that He "rewards those who earnestly seek Him." Only those who know God not only as a power but also as a Person who loves will dare truly seek Him.

Faith exhibited: persistent obedience (11:7-16). The writer goes on to further develop our grasp of this illusive thing called "faith." Noah and Abraham both show us that faith is exhibited as an obedient and persistent response to God's Word. For Noah faith meant a 120-year commitment despite popular ridicule to the construction of a great boat. For Abraham faith meant a lifetime living a nomadic life— and seeing his son and grandson live that same kind of life. Faith obeys God and keeps on obeying.

Faith exhibited: an exalted vision (11:17-23). Abraham, Isaac, Jacob, Joseph, and Moses' parents all looked beyond present circumstances to a future shaped by God's promise. Abraham's vision is most stunning. Told to sacrifice his son Isaac, he was so totally convinced that God would keep His promise to give him offspring by Isaac that he concluded God would raise his son from the dead. Abraham knew that the vision God gave of the future would come true—as he continued to obey God.

Faith exhibited: difficult choices (11:24-28). As "son of Pharaoh's daughter" Moses was in line to inherit Egypt's throne. Yet he chose to cast his lot with the slave people of his parents, valuing God's promises more than earthly treasures. Faith transforms our values and shapes our choices.

Faith exhibited: victories and defeats (11:29-38). Faith is no guarantee of earthly success, though faith has won great victories. What acts of faith do guarantee is that we will please God and ultimately be rewarded by Him.

Faith's fulfillment (11:39-40). It's easy to wonder at the Bible's heroes of faith. Especially when we realize they had relatively little knowledge of God. How motivated we who know Jesus should be to complete what they have begun and live a life of faith today.

Outline
Place
Finder

IDENTITY
PRIESTHOOD
SACRIFICE
FAITH

Chapter summary. Faith is especially needed when we face experiences intended to discipline us. Yet Jesus Himself endured extreme suffering and opposition, setting us an example of perseverance up to the very point of death (12:1-3).

What we must remember when difficulties come is that any good parent disciplines children. Thus hardships are evidence that God is treating us like the sons we are (vv. 4-7). Surely if we respect human parents who discipline us, we must respect God, whose discipline is wiser and directed toward a greater goal (vv. 8-11). So we are not to crumble under difficulties, but proceed with courage and hope (vv. 12-13).

The writer now pauses to introduce a final warning. Faith calls for us to live with others in holiness and peace (vv. 14-17). The first covenant was given to a frightened mob who stood before an earthly mountain that trembled and shook. Our covenant was given by Jesus who opens heaven itself (vv. 18-24). God now intends to shake not just a mountain but the earth and heavens as well, and we alone will inherit the unshakable kingdom of our God (vv. 25-27). How holy our lives should be, and how fervent the worship of our awesome Lord (vv. 28-29).

Key verse. 12:10: Discipline's goal.

Personal application. Struggles strengthen and purify us.

Key concepts. Sons »p. 790. Holiness »p. 879.

INSIGHT

"Cloud of witnesses" (12:1). The Christian life is like a relay race. Persons of faith who have run before us (chap. 11) have passed the baton to us and now watch us carry on.

"Author and perfecter" (12:2). As we run we can look back and see how Jesus ran His race. When we look ahead we can see His exaltation. He is our example as starter and finisher.

Consider Jesus (12:3). The word *analogisasthe* means to "take account of." To "weary and lose heart" were descriptions in classical Gk. of persons who relax or collapse along the way. When we take account of how much Jesus endured we'll realize that suffering and hardships are no excuse for our giving up and dropping by the way.

"Discipline" (12:5ff). The Gk. word is *paideia* and means to bring up a child, or to train, and in this sense to discipline. While God's discipline may often be experienced as hardship, this passage makes it clear that divine discipline is (1) a responsibility God fulfills as a parent toward those who are His true children, (2) expresses love and not anger, and (3) is directed toward a specific purpose, to shape us toward holiness.

"Punishes" (12:6). The Gk. word is *mastigoo*,

and means "to whip." Spanking was one tool a Jewish parent used to train children. But the overall context of the relationship was to be loving and every punishment to be for the child's good.

Bitterness (12:14-15). If we fail to sense the love and the purposefulness that underlie God's discipline we are likely to become bitter and so "miss the grace of God." If we see our trials and difficulties in the perspective provided by God's grace we will accept discipline.

"Esau" (12:16). Esau is an example of the godless in that he saw absolutely no value in spiritual things and so traded his birthright to God's covenant promise for a bowl of stew. If you and I value only the material rather than the spiritual, we too will miss the blessing.

Created things to be removed (12:18-27). Moses gave the Law before a mountain that burned with fire and shook the plain. The terror felt by that generation will be nothing to that felt by those who cannot see spiritual realities and fail to enter the kingdom of Jesus. That kingdom alone will remain when the universe itself is shaken, and this creation disappears. How good to be a citizen of the kingdom of God.

Chapter summary. The Book of Hebrews concludes with a series of exhortations to the readers concerning how to live the life of faith. Believers are to keep on loving (13:1-5a), and to keep on trusting God (vv. 5b-6). Believers are to continue responding to their leaders (vv. 7-8), and the whole community is to keep on praising God (vv. 9-16). After two more exhortations, one concerning leaders (v. 17) and the other prayer (vv. 18-19), the book concludes with a powerful doxology (vv. 20-21) and brief greetings (vv. 22-25).

Outline
Place
Finder

IDENTITY
PRIESTHOOD
SACRIFICE
FAITH

Key verses. 13:5-6: A present help.

Personal application. Faith results in a lifetime of dedicated living for Christ.

Key concepts. Love »pp. 661, 690. Marriage »pp. 26, 801. Adultery »pp. 64, 388. Leadership »pp. 610, 883. Grace »p. 789. Altar »p. 79. Priest »pp. 81, 858. Blood »pp. 85, 766. Praise »p. 380. Obey »pp. 807, 859. Conscience »p. 738. Covenant »p. 35.

INSIGHT

Brotherly love (13:1). Believers are called to "live a life of love" (Eph. 5:2). Christ's "new commandment" is to "love one another. As I have loved you, so you must love one another" (John 13:34). A number of passages describe that lifestyle, and the call to love brothers and sisters in Christ is repeated in every epistle (cf. Rom. 12:9-10; 1 Cor. 13; 2 Cor. 8:24; Gal. 5:13-14; Eph. 5:2, etc.). Here the writer calls Christian love "brotherly," for all Christians are members of God's family. If we extend family love to each other, we will experience unity (Phil. 2:2; Col. 2:2) and be compelled to share material and spiritual resources with others (1 John 3:16-18).

Angels unaware (13:2). Some visitors entertained by O.T. saints were angels (cf. Gen. 18:1-5; 19:1-2).

Identify with the oppressed (13:3). It's one thing to welcome strangers. It's another to go out and look for those who need help. Prisoners were especially needy, for they often had to supply their own food, and many feared being identified with those condemned by the government. Christian brotherly love moved believers to identify with prisoners and try to meet their needs.

A pure marriage bed (13:4-5). Many in 1st-century society considered chastity irrelevant to morals. The Christian community established a high standard, denying believers sexual expression outside of marriage. Within marriage, mutual commitment kept sexuality within God's intended boundaries, and therefore sexual expression was and is pure.

Real security (13:5). The bottom line isn't how much we have in the bank—or the S & L. The bottom line is that God is committed to us and will never leave or forsake us. *That* is real security!

Example (13:7). Leaders are to model a life of faith, which believers can ponder and imitate. Throughout the N.T., teaching and example are linked. Both right doctrine (orthodoxy) and right living (orthopraxy) are required in those who lead the church of God.

Our altar (13:10). Our altar is the cross, our sacrifice Christ, and the blood on that altar is that of the Son of God. The writer makes it clear Judaism and Christianity are not interchangeable. The Jewish believers he addresses have figuratively gone outside the walls of Jerusalem, having left the older faith behind.

"Obey your leaders and submit" (13:17). The original makes it clear that this is not blind obedience, or a surrender of one's personal responsibility to obey Christ as Lord. We can catch the sense of the Gk. in this paraphrase: "Remain responsive to those God has given you as guides and let yourself be persuaded by them." This is appropriate, for leaders are commissioned to watch over us and must give an account to God. Those who prove by their exemplary life and sound teaching to be worthy of respect most certainly deserve it.

James

The Book of James was never rejected by the early church, though it was neglected in favor of the more doctrinal letters of Paul. Luther considered it a "letter of straw" compared with Romans and Galatians. Yet the great Reformation leader quoted over half its verses in his writings, and noted he would not "prevent anyone from including or extolling [James] as he pleases, because there are otherwise many good sayings in him."

Why the debate over James? The book was written by James, the younger brother of Jesus, who became a leader in the Jerusalem church (cf. Acts 12:17; 15:13; 21:18; Gal. 1:19; 2:9). Internal evidence suggests the book was written early, probably in the late A.D. 40s, while the Christian church was still Jewish and still localized in Jerusalem. The theological issues stimulated by the great influx of Gentiles in the 50s had not been raised. James, as a pastor of the Jerusalem church, is thus primarily concerned that believers live a Christian life in the face of increasing local persecution. James speaks often of faith, but in the context of exhortations to live a life that is in harmony with a professed faith in Christ.

As far as doctrine is concerned, those James does express are in fullest harmony with the rest of the New Testament. God is holy (1:13), a giver of good gifts (v. 17), and the Father of His people (3:9). Sin infects human nature (1:14-15) and expresses itself in anger (v. 20), immorality (v. 21), discrimination (2:9-11), bitterness, and passion (4:1-3). Only a faith that works can enable the believer to live a godly life.

Surprisingly, despite Luther's opinion, the word "faith" is found more often in James than Galatians. It is simply that James is interested in the impact of faith on the life of the believer (see chart, below). The Epistle of James is an important New Testament book for any who tend to see Christianity as a matter of just "believing right things." James reminds us "that kind of faith" is worthless, for only a faith that transforms us and our way of life is truly Christian.

DIFFERENT PERSPECTIVES ON FAITH

James writes . . .	Paul writes . . .
To explore how faith finds expression in the life of a believer.	To explain saving faith in relation to the work of Christ on Calvary.
Out of a concern that faith produce fruit, so that no one confuses creeds with a vital Christianity.	Out of a concern that faith be placed in Jesus alone, unmixed with any reliance on Law or on an individual's supposed "works of righteousness."
Shortly after Jesus' resurrection, when the church is still Jewish, and Old Testament truths are known by all.	When the church is primarily Gentile, and their inclusion has raised many theological issues never before explored.

"It is surely not required that all handle the same arguments" —John Calvin.

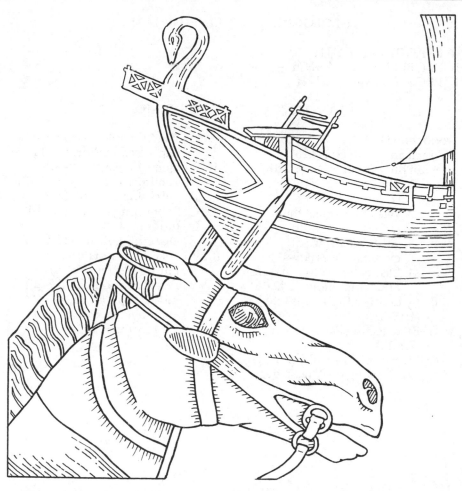

Illustration. *James' emphasis on the practical expression of faith is seen in his imagery. He calls the tongue a "small thing" like a ship's rudder or a bit or bridle which direct the course of the vessel and the animal. The person with faith will control his or her tongue, for unbridled, it can do terrible damage. It is inappropriate that praise for God and curses for others should come from the same mouth. A living faith will be expressed in such a simple thing as the way we talk about others.*

James, the Brother of Jesus

None of Jesus' half brothers responded to Christ's early claims of messiahship (cf. John 7:2-5). But Acts shows us that James and the other brothers did believe after the Resurrection (Acts 1:14). James himself quickly became a person of influence and played a significant role in the Jerusalem council, which he may have chaired (cf. Acts 15). Tradition gives James the nickname "the Just" and tells us his influence extended to Jewish believers throughout the Empire. He was also reputedly called "camel knees," because his fervent dedication to prayer caused calluses to develop on his knees. This pastoral letter written by James gives us insight into the earliest days of the church, when believers "devoted themselves to the apostles' teaching and to the fellowship, to the breaking of bread and to prayer" (Acts 2:42). James was martyred in A.D. 62.

THEOLOGICAL OUTLINE OF JAMES

CONTENT OUTLINE OF JAMES

Introduction (1:1)
I. Practicing Faith (1:2–2:26)
   A. In the Face of Trials (1:2-18)
      1. The purpose of trials
        (1:2-4)
      2. Wisdom to meet them
        (1:5-8)
      3. Attitude toward
        circumstances (1:9-11)
      4. Distinction between trials
        and temptations (1:12-18)
   B. By Living a Righteous Life
      (1:19-27)
   C. By Rejecting Favoritism
      (2:1-13)
      1. Favoritism's folly (2:1-7)
      2. Obeying the law of love
        (2:8-13)

   D. The Principle: Faith Must Be
      Expressed in Works (2:14-26)
II. Problems for Faith (3:1–4:17)
   A. Taming the Tongue (3:1-12)
   B. Subduing the Self (3:13-17)
   C. Submitting to God (4:1-10)
   D. Judging (4:11-12)
   E. Discerning Reality (4:13-17)
III. Prospects of Faith (5:1-20)
   A. Future Redress (5:1-6)
   B. Present Resources (5:7-20)
      1. Patience (5:7-12)
      2. Prayer (5:13-18)
      3. Pity (5:19-20)

Chapter summary. James writes to Jewish Christians everywhere (1:1). He encourages them to greet trials with joy, aware of their potential benefits (vv. 2-4). Anyone who feels a need for guidance in such situations may ask God. But when a person asks, he or she must be willing to do what God directs, rather than waver between obedience and going one's own way (vv. 5-8). As far as financial trials are concerned, rich and poor must each find life's meaning in something other than material circumstances (vv. 9-11).

It is particularly important if we are to persevere to know the difference between "trials" and "temptations." Temptation comes from within and is a response of man's sin nature to circumstances. God has nothing to do with temptation. All that God brings into our lives is a good gift—and that includes trials (vv. 12-18). Whatever happens we must be committed to a righteous life (vv. 19-21) and practicing God's Word (vv. 22-27).

Key verses. 1:3-4. It's easier when you know.

Personal application. Don't blame God or the devil for feeling tempted—or for giving in to temptation.

Key concepts. Joy »p. 803. Wisdom »pp. 387, 873. Prayer »p. 894. Wealth »pp. 124, 125. Poverty »p. 90. Righteousness »p. 734. Humble »p. 259. Father »p. 663.

INSIGHT

Trials and temptations (1:2). The Gk. word *periasmos* is translated by both "trial" and "temptation." Its meaning is rooted in the O.T., where a variety of Heb. words speak of "tests" that God brings into the lives of believers. There the Heb. words (*nasah, sarap,* and *buhan*) indicate a difficult situation as a test devised by God, but intended to demonstrate the quality of an individual's faith or to purify his or her character. Thus tests are shaped by God to enhance our lives.

Periazo and *periasmos,* whether rendered as "trial" or as "temptation" also indicate a test, devised by God, with the intent to benefit His own. It is in view of this reality that James urges his fellow believers to welcome trials with joy, knowing that while they test one's faith, if we persevere they will contribute greatly to the development of spiritual maturity.

"Wisdom" (1:5). In the O.T. and N.T. "wisdom" is a practical, "what do I do next" kind of thing. It's common when we're under pressure to feel deep frustration and be uncertain of what to do. When we are in that situation, James says, "Ask God."

"Doubt" (1:6). The word here is *diakrino,* which when used in the sense of "doubt" is uncertainty about something set forward as an object of faith. In James 1 we ask God what to do. He shows us. But then we hold back, un-

certain whether or not we want to obey. James says that if you are going to hold back, don't bother asking. When God shows you His way, He expects you to take it.

Perspective (1:9-11). Don't evaluate by the world's standards. Poor? Focus on your high position in Christ. Rich? Remember you are nothing but a human being, destined to die, whose only hope is in the Lord. Keep these things in mind and your financial situations will be irrelevant.

Analysis of temptations (1:13-18). The pull toward evil we feel when tested—a pull toward anger, striking out, or surrender to passion—does not "come from" God. That is, temptation is not located in the test but in our sin nature's response to the test. If we realize God intends the test as a "good and perfect gift," our perspective changes. Rather than view tests as temptation and give in, we can welcome tests as blessings intended to help us grow. James reminds us that God has given us a new birth (v. 18). That new life is the source of an inner power that will enable us to triumph not only over the circumstances but our sinful tendencies as well.

Doers of the Word (1:22-25). Just listening to the Word of God won't help us with the tests God sends. But a commitment to *doing* the Word will lead to blessing in all we do.

Chapter summary. The practice of showing partiality to the rich discriminates against the poor and is evil (2:1-4). It is also strange, as the rich rather than the poor exploit Christians and slander that name (vv. 5-7). Worst of all, it is sin, for God's Law calls on everyone to love a neighbor as yourself. Breaking that Law is the same as indulging in the more "serious" sins, for law is like a balloon: Stick a pin in one part and the whole thing breaks (vv. 8-11). We are to speak and act as those who are freed by the law of love from the law of rules. We will be evaluated on this basis: He who has received mercy must show himself merciful (vv. 12-13).

James then moves to evaluate Christian faith itself (vv. 14-26). It is right to be concerned with speech and actions, for a "faith" that exists as mere intellectual assent is no faith at all! Only a faith which produces works, as Abraham's and Rahab's faith produced works, is a real faith. Surely the actions of these two demonstrated that God was justified in declaring Abraham righteous. And Abraham's justification was demonstrated and completed by his works of faith.

Key verse. 2:22: No conflict.

Personal application. A "faith" that is all talk and no actions is no faith at all.

Key concepts. Law »pp. 120, 145, 376, 606, 743, 790. Love »pp. 126, 661, 690. Faith »pp. 35, 458, 740, 790. Righteous »p. 808.

INSIGHT

Why does God choose the poor? (2:5) There is no special merit in poverty. But the poor are more likely to choose God. They sense their desperate need (Matt. 5:3), while the wealthy tend to depend on their riches (Mark 10:23-25). Riches corrupt character, driving the wealthy to exploit the poor and despise the spiritual (James 2:6-7).

Law and love (2:8-13). Mosaic Law is a multifaceted expression of God's will. Violation of any aspect of the Law made a person a "lawbreaker." It follows that no one can dismiss "favoritism" as a minor sin. In fact, it is serious, for it violates Christ's royal command to love. It is even worse when we remember that we have received mercy and thus are to be merciful. Such a sin will surely be brought up at Christ's Judgment Seat (2 Cor. 5:10).

Good intentions (2:14-17). James compares faith without works to expressions of sympathy without giving any help. The latter is totally useless. In the same way a "faith" that exists without works has no value at all. James is not comparing faith and works, but two different kinds of "faith."

Works prove a person has faith (2:18). The verse is better rendered "one person has faith; another has deeds." Neither is right, for faith cannot be demonstrated apart from deeds.

Intellectual acceptance is not faith (2:19). Demons believe God exists. And they shudder. So that kind of faith is not saving faith.

Abraham exemplifies saving faith (2:20-24). What do we learn about saving faith from Abraham? Abraham's obedience demonstrated that his faith was of a dynamic, active nature. It produced an obedience and a trust so great he was willing to sacrifice his son Isaac (Gen. 22). This action pointed back to and demonstrated the validity of God's earlier statement that Abraham's faith was accepted in place of righteousness (15:6). Thus by its very nature Abraham's faith produced righteous works, so that works were an expression of his faith. In that sense Abraham was justified by works: God's claim that he was righteous and any claim Abraham might have made to having faith were indicated by Abraham's acts.

Thus *the kind of faith* that justifies a person before God is a faith that expresses itself in works. Any "faith" which is not accompanied by works is *not a saving kind of faith.*

Chapter summary. Even a faith that produces works will meet many difficult challenges. The first of these problems is with the tongue, which is almost uncontrollable and yet exerts a tremendous influence in everyone's life (3:1-12). Another problem is with the self. The natural man harbors bitterness and ambition in his heart and is moved by a "wisdom" dedicated to helping him achieve selfish ends. But God's kind of "wisdom" directs us into a pure, peace-loving, and submissive way of life (vv. 13-18). How desperately we need to live by the heavenly wisdom, which alone can bring us a harvest of righteousness.

Outline
Place
Finder

PRACTICING
PROBLEMS
PROSPECTS

Key verse. 3:13: Wisdom we can boast of.

Personal application. Not good grades but a good life shows wisdom and understanding.

Key concepts. Teach »pp. 122, 848. Wisdom »pp. 280, 387, 757. Humble »p. 259. Submission »pp. 867, 880.

INSIGHT

"Teachers" (3:1). The Gk. construction suggests that many in the Jewish congregations to which James writes were seeking to become teachers. This is not surprising, for Judaism had a long-established commitment to study and highly valued those who became "teachers of the Law." James discourages this effort, reminding them that teachers are evaluated (*krima*) more strictly. This word does not imply negative rather than positive judgment. It simply refers to a judge's responsibility to examine the facts and render a verdict.

A mark of maturity (3:2). Being able to control what we say is a mark of spiritual maturity and a significant accomplishment. It seems the tongue tells more than we suspect!

"The tongue" (3:3-12). James describes the power (vv. 3-6) and the perversity (vv. 7-12) of the tongue. It has power to inflame passions. It participates in man's wicked acts and even sets our thoughts in their direction, so corrupting our whole lives with an evil whose source is hell itself (vv. 3-6). As a "restless evil" it is almost impossible to control and totally inconsistent in that the tongue that blesses some also curses others.

Blessing others (3:10). To "bless" is to "endue with power for success, prosperity, etc." The Gk. word *eulogia* means literally "to speak well of," to "praise." As Christians we are called to bless others, in the sense of seeking the best for them, no matter how we may be treated (cf. Luke 6:28; Rom. 12:14; 1 Cor. 4:12).

"Wise and understanding" (3:13). These are eminently practical qualities. Each describes the way we use knowlege, not whether or not we *have* knowledge or even whether we are intelligent. The issue is one of showing what an earlier generation called "good sense" in daily life.

Here "wisdom" itself is in a way an orientation to life, a way of making decisions that comes from one of two sources. Our wisdom (approach to making choices) is from above (from heaven) or below (from corrupt human society as dominated by the devil). The wisdom from above is characterized as pure, peace-loving, considerate, and a variety of similar traits that puts blessing others first.

The wisdom from below is self-centered, driven by selfish desires. The one produces righteousness, the other "every evil practice." So be wise in the "wisdom" you use when you make decisions.

"Earthly" (3:15). This adjective specifies the source as well as the nature of selfish "wisdom." It is unable to go beyond the limits of this world to gain the perspective on spiritual realities which guides the believer.

The crop of righteousness (3:18). Farmers who expect a good harvest don't plant in sterile soil. James reminds us that righteousness cannot be produced in human soil characterized by a bitter, selfish spirit. The personality of a person whose goal is peace and harmony is much better soil.

Outline
Place
Finder

PRACTICING
PROBLEMS
PROSPECTS

Chapter summary. James looks at more problems for the person committed to living a life of faith. Faith's lifestyle demands that the believer submit to God, despite the presence of warped desires stimulated by the flesh (4:1-3), the world (vv. 4-6), and the devil (vv. 7-10). Believers must also struggle against the temptation to usurp God's place as a judge, rather than accept our rightful place as a mere citizen in God's kingdom (vv. 11-12). Finally, believers must resist the temptation to distort reality and view the future as though they were certain of being a part of it. We are in fact totally subject to God's will, and it is only by His will that we live or die (vv. 13-17).

Key verse. 4:6: Rely on grace.

Personal application. Living a life of faith calls for strict personal discipline.

Key concepts. Prayer »p. 894. Adultery »p. 85. Pride »pp. 119, 352. Submit »p. 880. Judge »p. 372.

INSIGHT

Desires within (4:1). The word translated "desires" is *hedonon* and means "pleasures." The image is one of the flesh demanding satisfaction, even at the cost of *polemoi* and *machai*, terms used of warfare.

"Quarrel and fight" (4:2). The desires of the flesh are so strong human beings are willing to quarrel and fight in an attempt to satisfy them. That is, these desires lead us into sinful acts.

"Ask God"? (4:2-3) What if we take a "spiritual" approach and ask God to satisfy our *hedonon?* Usually folks don't. But when they do God says no because the motive is not to please God but to satisfy the drive of the flesh for pleasures.

"Friendship with the world" (4:4). The world (*kosmos*) is that complex interweaving of sinful desires that shapes the society of lost humanity. When we surrender to the *hedonon* of the flesh we choose to become friends of the world and are spiritually unfaithful to God.

Envy (4:5-6). Envy here is God's jealous longing for our love. This same theme is seen in Ex. 20:5 and 34:14. God is truly disturbed when we abandon friendship with Him to make friends with the world—and disturbed for our sake. But how does God respond? Not with punishment, but with "more grace" to lead us back into His arms. Only our own pride can keep us from responding to His grace, turning our back on the world, and experiencing blessing.

"Resist the devil" (4:7). However powerful Satan is, if we set ourselves against him he is unable to prevail and will flee from us.

Ten imperatives (4:7-10). These three verses contain 10 sharp commands calling for immediate action. In essence they tell us how to humble ourselves before God, so that we can experience His grace. The 10 commands are: submit, resist (v. 7), come near, wash, purify (v. 8), grieve, mourn, wail, change (v. 9), humble (v. 10). Together they picture a complete reversal of the attitudes that shape the spiritually immature and unfaithful.

Judging (4:11). The original tells us not to "speak against" one another and includes all forms of criticism. The "royal law" that James referred to in 2:8, "love one another," is violated even when what we say is true, if we express it in an unkind manner. No Christian is in a position to stand in judgment on a brother.

One judge (4:11-12). James' point is that a person who takes it on himself to judge, in essence sets himself above the Law. But only the Lawgiver is greater than the Law, and He is the sole judge of how it is kept or broken. What we have to remember is that our role is *keeping* the law, not exalting ourselves as its interpreter or applier.

Carry on business (4:13). Business travel was very common in the 1st century. And it is natural that a good businessman would make careful plans, arranging both sales and purchases far ahead of time. James is not against planning. What James objects to is an attitude toward the future that takes no account of God. We must live each day with the awareness of our mortality and thus of our total dependence on God for all things.

Outline
Place
Finder

PRACTICING
PROBLEMS
PROSPECTS

Chapter summary. James began his letter by encouraging his readers to accept trials with joy, as God has a maturing purpose in permitting them. Now he looks at resources which enable us to endure under severe, continuing persecution. James warns the rich oppressors of the poor. The rich live in luxury now, but face certain judgment for their mistreatment of the innocent (5:1-6). Under such persecution believers are to be patient and stand firm until the Lord returns. The certainty that the "Judge is standing at the door" comforts and encourages (vv. 7-9).

In the meantime believers can take comfort in the example of others, like Job, who have lived through suffering and emerged into an experience of God's mercy (vv. 10-11). As we persevere we are to remain unshakably committed to telling and living the truth (v. 12). Believers also have the resource of prayer. When offered by a righteous person prayer has great and powerful effect on our experience here and now (vv. 13-18). Finally, each of us is a resource for others. When a person strays we are to reach out and turn him or her back to a life lived according to God's truth (vv. 19-20).

Key verse. 5:9: It won't be long.

Personal application. Rather than be discouraged when suffering continues, let's remember that our prospects are good!

Key concepts. Wealth »pp. 125, 838. Poor »p. 90. Second Coming »pp. 581, 827. Prayer »pp. 608, 609. Mercy »p. 858. Oath »p. 625. Sickness »pp. 66, 412, 633, 686, 767. Confession »p. 892.

INSIGHT

Why against the rich? (5:1-6) In Jerusalem, few in the wealthy class responded to the Gospel. As persecution of the early church developed, many believers lost their livelihood and were further exploited by the powerful. The charges James makes against the rich are (1) they greedily hoard wealth when others are suffering, (2) they defraud their employees, (3) they live in extravagance and self-indulgence, and (4) they "murder" innocent men.

Patience (5:7-9). We can afford to be patient even when provoked by the rapacious exploitation of the wealthy. Like farmers, we wait for harvesttime. We know that Christ, the Judge, "is standing at the door."

Job's example (5:10-11). After Job's terrible suffering God blessed him with double of all the good things he had before (Job 42). His example assures us that when the Lord returns we too will experience the compassion of the Lord.

Don't swear (5:12). Why the emphasis on discontinuing the use of oaths? Because our patient waiting requires us to live such an honest life that our integrity rather than an oath will convince others that we are speaking the truth.

Prayer and anointing (5:14-16). This passage

linking prayer, sickness, church elders, anointing with oil, and confession of sins has fascinated Christians throughout the ages.

Several things are clear from the text. (1) Prayer is needed when sickness comes. (2) One role of the elders of a church is to pray for the sick. (3) Prayer is primary, an active verb, and anointing with oil is secondary, expressed as a participle. (4) Oil was the most common ingredient in ancient medical treatments, and the verb describing its use (*aleipho*) means to "smear on" rather than the sacramental "to anoint" (*chrio*). Thus the passage teaches application of both prayer and normal medical treatments. (5) "Confession" is important if sin should happen to be the cause of the sickness, and thus the sickness is disciplinary. (6) Since confession and prayer are associated with good health, it is important for Christians to be sensitive to sin, confess their sins to each other, and pray for each other.

Prayer's effectiveness (5:17-18). The prayer of a person in right relationship with God is truly powerful. Elijah, whose weaknesses are not covered over in the O.T., was effective in prayer because he was righteous and because he prayed earnestly.

1 Peter

As the early decades of the church's expansion through the Roman Empire passed, it grew explosively in numbers. Christians were increasingly viewed as a distinct people—and were seriously misunderstood. Their fierce allegiance to Christ, that kept them from participating in worship of the Emperor and state gods was viewed as a lack of patriotism. Their strict morality, their private meetings for worship, all engendered suspicion, rumors, and a growing hostility. Jewish Christians were often slandered by their old communities, Gentile Christians by their old companions. And in various parts of the empire official persecution developed, to the extent that in some places individuals were executed merely for admitting that they worshiped Jesus Christ.

Against this background of increasing misunderstanding and cruelty by the majority, Peter writes a warmly pastoral letter. He understands their struggle and speaks encouragingly of the hope that will sustain them. And he reminds the scattered communities of believers to which this letter is addressed that living in pagan society calls for humility and submission.

Early tradition tells us that the Apostle Peter wrote this letter from "Babylon," understood as an early Christian code designation for "Rome." Peter had been the leading disciple during Christ's life on earth. He clearly took the lead in the emerging church in Jerusalem and Judea as well. His later years were spent in evangelistic travel, with a special focus on reaching members of the worldwide Jewish community for Christ. Tradition tells us that both Peter and Paul were martyred in Rome in the mid to late A.D. 60s.

SUFFERING IN 1 PETER

Suffering grief in all kinds of trials (1:6).	*Trials demonstrate the genuineness of our faith and will bring praise and glory when Jesus comes.*
When suffering comes we are to fix our hope fully on the grace to be ours when Jesus comes (4:12-19).	*When we hope for what we will receive when Jesus returns, we will then be free to commit ourselves to obedience and holiness, despite suffering.*
Endure unjust suffering "conscious of God" (2:19).	*We are to be obedient to and holy for God's sake, aware of our calling to follow the example of Jesus who also suffered injustice.*
Sometimes, but not usually, we will experience suffering even when we do what is good (3:8-13).	*When we suffer despite doing good we are: (1) not to fear, (2) to remember Jesus is Lord, (3) to remain so hopeful that others will ask about it, and (4) to keep our conscience clear.*
When we live according to God's will we "suffer as a Christian" (4:16).	*Suffering as a Christian rather than an evildoer is a cause for pride rather than for shame. And we must remember that our suffering is only for "a little while," and our destiny is to share "His eternal glory" (5:10).*

Illustration. *Peter's vivid imagery in 1 Peter 3 and 4 likens our salvation to Noah's ancient deliverance by the ark. Like Noah we have been delivered from a world steeped in sin and deposited in a new world where we are to live by the will of God rather than our sinful passions. Living by the will of God will bring suffering here, but in the end earns eternal glory.*

Suffering in Scripture

The Hebrew language contains many different words for pain and suffering. Some express intensity, others are synonyms with slightly different shades of meaning. These may focus on physical pain, on sadness or sorrow, on mental anguish, grief, troubles, or general stress. The New Testament vocabulary is more limited. In general words for suffering in the New as in the Old Testament tend to focus more on mental distress than the physical pain.

In Greek culture suffering was viewed as an evil afflicting humanity that was beyond mankind's ability to control. Thus suffering is a matter of fate, and Greek tragedies typically portray individuals who are victims of life's blind injustice. The New Testament, however, takes a radically different approach. Key words for suffering in the New Testament are frequently used in descriptions of the death of Christ. There the strongest possible language is used to remind us that Jesus suffered by God's express will (cf. Matt. 16:21; Mark 8:31; Luke 17:25; 24:26; Acts 3:18; 17:3; 1 Peter 1:11). In Jesus we learn that suffering, though painful, is not an unmixed evil.

Peter particularly picks up and emphasizes this thought. A person who suffers for doing wrong has no comfort: He has brought his suffering on himself. But whenever a Christian suffers *despite doing what is good* he or she becomes a companion of Jesus, who also suffered despite doing nothing but good. In this case the believer can be sure that God is actively involved in his situation, permitting injustice and suffering for a good purpose of His own. We may not understand that purpose. But looking at the wondrous good God accomplished through the suffering of our Lord and His glorification, we can be sure that when we suffer as Christians both good and glory will result.

THEOLOGICAL OUTLINE OF 1 PETER

CONTENT OUTLINE OF 1 PETER

Chapter summary. Peter writes to Christians scattered through the Roman Empire (1:1-2) who are under severe stress. Yet Peter speaks first of hope: a living hope that comes through the resurrection of Jesus and which promises us a grand inheritance in heaven (vv. 3-5). In view of this we rejoice despite present trials. As a refiner's fire purifies gold, so trials purify our faith and will result in praise and honor when Jesus returns (vv. 6-7). Even here and now our love for Christ stimulates an inexpressible joy, an evidence and an outgrowth of salvation (vv. 8-9).

We are beneficiaries of a salvation the prophets spoke of without understanding it (vv. 10-12). Thus we are to consciously focus our expectations on Jesus' coming and dedicate ourselves to holiness (vv. 13-16). Christ paid for our redemption with His own precious blood. Thus we are to live as strangers to the desires and values of this world (vv. 17-21). Purified through faith's choice of Jesus, we who have received a new, imperishable life from God are to love one another.

Outline
Place
Finder

HOPE
SUBMISSION
SUFFERING
EXHORTATIONS

Key verse. 1:13: The antidote to materialism.

Personal application. Aliens are always aware they do not really fit in the society where they live.

Key concepts. Hope »p. 465. Resurrection »pp. 737, 771. Salvation »p. 841. Faith »p. 35. Joy »p. 803. Prophet »pp. 131, 417, 434. Love »p. 690. Redemption »pp. 791, 848. Blood »p. 766. New birth »p. 680.

INSIGHT

"**Strangers in the world**" (1:1). This theme is important to Peter. A Christian's home is heaven. Our hopes are not centered in what will happen to us in this world, but the inheritance we will receive when Jesus returns (v. 4). Our values are heaven's values and in conflict with the values of human society (v. 14). When we truly orient our lives to heaven we see our trials in an entirely different way, not as unmixed evils but as purifying fires intended to strengthen us and win even greater glory (v. 6). Only if we see ourselves as strangers here will we be sustained by hope and joy.

Shielded by God's power (1:4). God is on double guard. He keeps our inheritance secure in heaven and He shields us here on earth. God will bring us to heaven and heaven to us.

Refiner's fire (1:6-7). Miners refine gold not to harm it but to purify it and make it more valuable. When you experience troubles, don't think, "God is punishing me." Like the refiner, God's intent is to purify your faith, to make you even more valuable to others and to Him.

Joy in the unseen (1:8-9). How many look hopefully for joy in the Lotto numbers printed each week in the newspaper! As for us, we've already won! We have Jesus, and though He is

unseen He brings us inexpressible joy.

Time and circumstances (1:10-12). Old Testament prophets spoke of Jesus, but could not put together the clues in their own writings to understand how the suffering and glory of the Messiah could possibly fit together. Looking back on the Cross and the Resurrection we know. We learn that in our lives too suffering and glories are not at all incompatible. We suffer now. Glory follows.

"**Conform**" (1:14). Strangers refuse to let an alien society squeeze them into its mold.

Holiness (1:15). Old Testament holiness called for Israel to separate from everything ritually or morally impure. New Testament holiness calls for living morally pure lives despite the fact that we must live in sinful human society. We are to be holy in all we do, "abstain from sinful desires," and live "good lives" among the pagans around us (2:11).

Alien (1:17). In the Roman Empire aliens were subject to the state and paid heavy taxes, but were viewed as subject to their own national laws. We cannot expect concern for our "rights" from pagan society. But we can live as citizens of heaven, subject to its laws and protected by God.

Outline
Place
Finder

HOPE
SUBMISSION
SUFFERING
EXHORTATION

Chapter summary. The Christian's quest for maturity calls for cleansing from sin and an eager desire to "grow up in your salvation" (2:1-3). We are "living stones" in a spiritual temple God is constructing on the foundation of Jesus (vv. 4-8). As God's chosen people, called out of darkness to glorify the Lord, we are to live as aliens in this world, such clear examples of heaven's citizens that even the hostile will see our good deeds and when Jesus returns be forced to admit our deeds were good (vv. 9-12).

One way we exhibit our heavenly citizenship is to obey earthly laws, submitting to rulers and doing good (vv. 13-17). Similarly slaves are to submit even to harsh masters, for Jesus subjected Himself to injustice and we are to follow His example (vv. 18-23). Having been redeemed by Jesus we renounce sin and commit ourselves to live for righteousness (vv. 24-25).

Key verse. 2:21: Jesus didn't lead us to Disneyland.

Personal application. Enduring injustice isn't weakness. Often it is strength.

Key concepts. Salvation »p. 841. Priesthood »pp. 81, 858. Cornerstone »p. 375. Chosen people »pp. 124, 797. Submission »p. 867. Freedom »pp. 465, 685. Slavery »p. 802. Example »p. 867. Judge »p. 372. Shepherd »p. 355.

INSIGHT

"Pure spiritual milk" (2:2). Most believe the "spiritual milk" is the Word of God (cf. Heb. 5:11-14). Peter reminds us that as we turn from evil, we will develop a hunger for spiritual truth.

"The living Stone" (2:4). The "stone" here is a gem of great value, a symbol in the O.T. and Jewish thought of the Messiah. "Living" reminds us of the Resurrection, which demonstrated "with power" that Jesus is "the Son of God" (Rom. 1:4).

Believers as a temple (2:5). The N.T. teaches the living personality of the believer replaces the cold stone of the temple as the focal point of God's presence (1 Cor. 3:16). In calling the church a "holy temple" Peter reminds us that God is now present in the world in us — and that together we are to display His beauty in holy lives.

A holy and royal priesthood (2:5, 9). The *Expository Dictionary of Bible Words* notes that "Our identity [as priests] enables us to 'declare the praises of Him who called [us] out of darkness into His wonderful light.' While some take this as mediating Christ to the world, it is more likely that the reference is to worship. We as a holy priesthood are to offer 'spiritual sacrifices acceptable to God through Jesus Christ' (1 Peter 2:5). The other three references — and in Revelation — have a similar emphasis (Rev. 1:5; 5:10;

20:6). With direct access to God through Jesus, we who are God's priestly kingdom are freed to worship Him continually."

Submission (2:13, 18). Submission is subjecting or subordinating oneself to someone or something else. Christians are called on to submit voluntarily to every authority instituted among men (Rom. 13:1). This includes accepting one's role in society, without making judgments about the validity of an institution such as slavery. That is, believers commit themselves to doing what is deemed right according to the norms of one's own culture, assuming of course that what society calls "right" does not require a direct violation of God's commands.

Christ's example (2:20-22). Our natural response to injustice is to fight it, rebelling angrily. This passage deals with "situational submission" (i.e., submission that is mandated by the society in which one lives). In this case we are to do what is right and if, like Christ, we are treated unjustly anyway, we are to submit.

An example of meekness (2:21-25). Meekness is a gentle attitude, shown in patience untainted by malice despite provocation. When we suffer for doing good, we commit our cause to God as Judge and trust Him to bring good out of injustice. He did this for Jesus. He will do it for us.

Chapter summary. Peter concludes his remarks on submission by looking at the marriage relationship (3:1-7). Then he returns to his major theme: suffering unjustly. While this does happen, God is constantly observing us so that He might bless our righteous deeds (vv. 8-12). If suffering should come even though we do good, we are not to fear, being conscious of Christ's lordship, and keep on doing good (vv. 13-17). We are also to remember that Jesus Himself suffered despite doing only good—and that God through Christ's suffering brought us to God. The object of this analogy is to show that when we suffer unjustly, we can expect God to have some good purpose in mind (vv. 18-19). In another analogy Peter reminds us that as Noah was carried through the floodwaters of judgment to be deposited in a new world, so we too have been carried safely past the danger of judgment and, through our union with Jesus, lifted up into heaven with Him (vv. 20-22). Christ's suffering involved injustice, yes. But what glory His patient suffering won for Him and for you and me.

Key verse. 3:14: A strange but real blessing.

Personal application. Trust God to bring good out of your pain.

Key concepts. Submission »pp. 867, 880. Marriage »pp. 26, 801. Fear »p. 363. Baptism »pp. 604, 708, 742. Conscience »p. 738.

INSIGHT

Submission in marriage (3:1-6). Peter includes marriage in his discussion because this too is "situational" submission. That is, wives are to relate to their husbands as is deemed appropriate in the society. This is particularly important where husbands are not believers (v. 1).

Real beauty (3:3). Peter is not launching a tirade against lipstick. He is reminding us that what counts is a person's inner rather than outer beauty. A beautiful spirit in a woman will do far more to win a husband's admiration and allegiance to Christ than a provocative outfit!

Husbands show consideration and respect (3:7). Don't mistake the Bible's references to women's voluntary submission in marriage for divine grant of male domination. Peter reminds us that marriage is a partnership, not slavery.

"Live in harmony" (3:8-13). Peter describes the "good life" that God looks for and blesses—under normal circumstances. The quote of Ps. 34:12-16 describes the usual case: God watches over the righteous and punishes the evil.

"Even if" (3:14). This phrase renders a Gk. "fourth class" conditional clause. It indicates a possible future which is much less probable. Usually no one harms the person who is "eager to do good." Sometime harm may follow. But it is not at all likely.

Response to unjust suffering (3:14-16). What if we are "eager to do good," but still suffer harm? Peter gives these guidelines: (1) Do not fear. (2) Remember Christ is Lord. (3) Remain hope-filled and willing to explain why you are still positive about life. (4) Keep on doing good so you will have a clear conscience, and your enemies will be ashamed. (5) Remember, it's better to suffer for doing good than if we were suffering because we had committed some wrong. It's strange but true. In our faith, the victim is the victor, and the persecuted triumph.

"Christ as Lord" (3:15). We are to remember that Jesus is the sovereign power in this universe. Nothing can happen without His permission. And anything He permits to happen to us is filtered through His love.

Evangelism (3:15-16). The most effective evangelism takes place when people ask wonderingly, "Why are you so different?" And we can say, Jesus.

The proof (3:18). From a human point of view Christ's death was a tragic injustice. The righteous One died, not the unjust persons who deserved death for rejecting the Saviour. But through this "injustice" God brought us to Himself. We can surely trust Him to transform our innocent suffering too.

Outline
Place
Finder

HOPE
SUBMISSION
SUFFERING
EXHORTATIONS

Chapter summary. What does it mean for the believer to be carried through the waters of judgment and, like Noah, deposited in a new world (3:19-22). It means we do "not live the rest of [our] earthly life for evil human desires, but rather for the will of God" (4:1-6). Because the end is near, we are to commit ourselves to loving and serving one another, faithfully administering God's grace (vv. 7-11).

We shouldn't be surprised that such a lifestyle involves suffering (v. 12). In fact we should expect to participate—and rejoice—in Christ's suffering. There is no shame in suffering as a Christian. When we do we are simply to commit ourselves and our cause to God, and keep on doing good (vv. 13-19).

Key verse. 4:19: We *can* "do something."

Personal application. Praise God if you suffer for doing good.

Key concepts. Suffer »p. 877. Judge »pp. 372, 724. Gospel »p. 737. Love »pp. 661, 690. Ashamed »p. 357. Good »p. 849.

INSIGHT

Suffering in the body (4:1). The thought is better, "suffered in the flesh." Christ's attitude of determination to obey God led to suffering and ultimately death. If we arm ourselves with the same attitude, we'll accept any pain caused by denying our own "evil human desires" in order to likewise do the will of God.

Pagans in perspective (4:2-5). Before conversion we had all the spiritual and moral insights that pagans possess—and spent our lives "doing what pagans choose to do." Pagans cannot understand Christian self-discipline and rejection of sinful pleasures, and actually abuse and ridicule us.

But what we understand is that human beings must give an account to God for their moral choices. Our sharing of the Gospel makes their judgment more severe, for their rejection of Christ fully demonstrates that their bent is toward evil.

Our commitments (4:7-11). Peter has described the pagan's choice: to satisfy their human desires. He now describes the lifestyle that pagans can make no sense of, but which reflects the will of God for His people. This includes: self-control, prayer, mutual love, unstinting hospitality, using gifts for the benefit of others, serving wholeheartedly and "with the strength God provides," seeking in all things to win praise for God through Jesus.

Selflessness makes no sense to selfish people. But to those of us who have been taught to love by Christ, it is the only way to be.

Love covering sins (4:8). Love covers sins not in the sense of winning forgiveness for them, but in that our love for others keeps us from either broadcasting other's faults, or being so angry with others that we refuse to accept or forgive them.

Participating in Christ's sufferings (4:13). Jesus suffered for doing the will of God rather than from any fault of His own. When we suffer despite doing good we share deeply in his kind of suffering. This same thought is expressed in Rom. 8:17, 2 Cor. 1:5-7, and Phil. 3:10. How encouraging to sense a closeness to Him and to realize that our suffering too is purposive.

Blessed (4:14). Jesus expressed this in the Beatitudes (Matt. 5:11-12). There is more than one reason for this blessing. In Matt. the source of happiness is the reward such earthly suffering wins for us in heaven. Here the source of our joy is the fact that in our extremity the Spirit of God rests on us in power, to sustain us and give us a sense of the glory such suffering wins.

Suffering as a Christian (4:16). When others persecute and ridicule us for bearing the name "Christian" we shouldn't hang our heads. Not at all. We can lift them up and praise, for we are proud to identify ourselves with our Lord.

Committing ourselves to God (4:19). Why to Him as "faithful Creator"? Because we remember that He is the power who shaped and sustains the universe itself. Trusting ourselves to Him completely, we are free to "continue to do good."

Chapter summary. Peter concludes his letter with a series of exhortations directed to different groups in the church. He urges elders to "shepherd" the flock, watching over them out of love rather than in hope of any gain (5:1-4). The young are to be responsive to the older and remain humble (vv. 5-7). All must exhibit self-control and resist the devil's attempts to discourage or arouse self-pity (vv. 8-9).

With a special word of encouragement Peter assures his readers that "the God of all grace" will restore and strengthen us, to His great glory (vv. 10-11).

Finally Peter says farewell, and sends greetings from his companions in "Babylon" (Rome) (vv. 12-14).

Outline
Place
Finder

HOPE
SUBMISSION
SUFFERING
EXHORTATION

Key verse. 5:5: A source of strength.

Personal application. The Christian life is quiet commitment.

Key concepts. Elders »pp. 132, 835. Shepherd »p. 504. Crown »p. 844. Submission »p. 867. Humility »p. 259. Pride »p. 352. Satan »p. 501. Grace »p. 789.

INSIGHT

Church leadership (5:1-4). Leaders, generally called elders or overseers (bishops) and deacons are to follow Christ's example and function as servants in the Christian community (Matt. 20:25-28; cf. 23:11). Their general responsibility is defined in Eph. 4:12 and in this passage. Leaders are "to prepare God's people for works of service" as ministering members of the body (1 Cor. 3:1-9; 2 Cor. 10:8). And leaders are to "shepherd" (guard, and guide) the local community of faith (cf. Heb. 13:17). Leaders must be men who are equipped for these tasks, in part by gift, but essentially by character (1 Tim. 3:1-7; Titus 1:5-9). Leaders in fact "shepherd" by both teaching (Titus 2) and by modeling, or serving as an example (1 Tim. 4:11-16; Titus 3:10, 14).

The shepherding ministry does not mean leaders exercise *control* of believer's behavior. It does mean they focus on nurture, encouraging maturity so that believers' acts of service will be an expression of love-motivated desire and Holy Spirit enablement. When leaders do shepherd, and do so because they want to serve rather than for financial gain or status, Christians will mature.

Shepherd (5:2). The imperative *poimanate* involves protecting, leading, guiding, feeding, and generally watching out for the welfare for members of the church.

"Be submissive" (5:5). Here as earlier in this letter Peter calls for voluntary submission. But this is interpersonal rather than situational submission. What makes interpersonal submission easy, whether in marriage or in the church, is the respect won by husband or leader through love and example. If we are sure a leader loves us, it is far easier for us to be responsible to his guidance. If we are also confident the leader is a godly person, whose example has won our respect, it is easier still.

Let's apply this in our relationships. Rather than demand children or others obey because of our role, let's win their respect by love and example.

Why be humble? (5:5) Not just because it's right. We should be humble rather than arrogant in our relationships with others because, according to Prov. 3:34, God "gives grace to the humble." If we want to grow, and have strength to overcome despite suffering, we must remain dependent on God.

Casting anxiety on God (5:7). "Casting" is a decisive act. It means to take the load we've been carrying and literally *throw it* on Jesus. What a relief when we do and realize He is willing to be responsible for the things we are anxious about.

Not flight but fight (5:8-9). Firm resistance is the way to deal with Satan's attacks. But we resist in Christ's power, not our own. Revelation 12:11 describes the victory over Satan in these terms: "they overcame him by the blood of the Lamb and by the word of their testimony."

What God will surely do for us (5:10). Four emphatic results encourage us. "Restore" means to make complete. "Make you strong" means to enable to stand fast. "Make you firm" again emphasizes strengthening. And "make you steadfast" means to place on a firm, secure foundation.

2 Peter

This brief letter was not mentioned by the earliest church fathers, but was identified by Origin around A.D. 225 as Peter's. However, early Greek papyrus manuscripts of the New Testament show it was definitely accepted by the church as canonical (having authority as Scripture). There is no compelling reason to doubt the book's own claim to have been written by Peter.

Certainly this book, which looks at the dangers facing the church in the coming decades, reflects the same concerns found in 2 Timothy and in Jude. As the sixth decade of the Christian era drew toward its close, the church faced many dangers (cf. 1:13-14; 2:1-3). In his first letter Peter was more concerned with external pressures exerted on Christians by society. In this letter Peter is concerned that Christians wander from foundational teachings and to false teachers (2:1-22). These immoral and greedy persons may twist and ridicule God's truth, but they rush headlong toward the certain judgment that God will execute when Jesus returns and this universe dissolves in flaming fire.

In the face of this internal danger Peter reminds us of the importance of a growth in goodness and of how confident we can be that Scripture is utterly trustworthy. Surely false teachers are not all that hard to recognize. And just as surely, in view of the certain approach of the Day of the Lord, we are to commit ourselves to living spotless and blameless lives.

Dealing With Heresy

Second Peter, with 2 Timothy, 1 John, and Jude explore the nature of heresy in the early church and show us how to deal with theological aberrations today. The word "heresy" occurs several times in the New Testament, usually in the nondoctrinal sense of "sect" or "party," such as "the party of the Pharisees" (Acts 15:5). The word also may indicate a party within the church which separates itself from others (cf. 1 Cor. 11:18; Gal. 5:20).

But in 2 Peter "heresy" is used in a developed, theological sense (2 Peter 2:1). Here "destructive heresies" deny basic doctrines and are introduced by false teachers who encourage sinful behavior. The early church fathers used "heresy" in this same, theological sense. They used it to denote groups within Christianity which taught errors hostile to God's revealed truth. In church history, the emergence of heresies was a strong impetus to attempts to define the more important Christian doctrines. This was typically done through much debate which led ultimately to the calling of a church council.

How are Christians to respond to heresy? The basic approach is to keep on teaching sound doctrine. False teaching will ultimately be shown to be out of harmony with God's truth. There is no instruction in Scripture for a crusade to purify the church by excluding those with whom we differ, even in important ways. Instead, the writers of the New Testament are confident that when the truth of God is presented with clarity and compassion, God's Spirit will enable Jesus' people to distinguish between the false and the true.

THEOLOGICAL OUTLINE OF 2 PETER

CONTENT OUTLINE OF 2 PETER

Outline
Place
Finder

CONFIRMATION
HERESY
WORLD'S END

Chapter summary. Peter does not mention a particular church as addressees, but rather speaks to all of like faith (1:1-4). If anyone wonders whether he or she really is of like faith, Peter suggests two bases for confidence. First, salvation brings us resources enabling us to live godly lives. We must then "make every effort" to use these resources and develop mature Christian character (vv. 5-9). We confirm our call and election by God when we grow in grace, for we see His work within us (vv. 10-11).

Peter also draws our attention to Scripture. The truths on which we base our hope were delivered by the Son of God Himself (vv. 12-18), and His own testimony about Jesus is demonstrably true, for it is in full harmony with the words of the prophets. And these men "spoke from God" as the Spirit carried them along (vv. 19-21).

Key verse. 1:10: Prove to yourself, not others.

Personal application. Our own changed lives are evidence our salvation is real.

Key concepts. Righteousness »p. 433. Godliness »p. 835. Born again »p. 680. Prophecy »p. 434. Prophet »p. 131. Holy Spirit »pp. 73, 759.

INSIGHT

Participating in the divine nature (1:3-4). Salvation is a stunning gift. It provides a new and dynamic principle of spiritual life. It infuses us with power for a life of godliness. It lifts us beyond our human limitations so we can "escape the corruption in the world caused by the evil one." Yet somehow we often feel weak and powerless. How can we be sure that we are among those whom God has saved? Other passages reassure us by pointing to Christ as the object of our faith and reminding us that salvation depends on what Jesus has done, not on what we do. Peter takes a different, but very practical approach. He says, in effect, step out and *use the resources God has provided!*

Our responsibility (1:5-7). God gives us spiritual resources, but we're responsible to use them. Thus Peter says "make every effort" to develop those qualities God's Spirit will produce in our lives. He won't work if we just sit, lethargic. But He *will* work in us if we do our part.

"Self-control" (1:6). This quality is mentioned often in both Peter's letters. It is self-discipline, a refusal to give in to greed or excess. Like the other qualities here, self-control is both something we "make every effort" to exercise and a fruit produced by the Holy Spirit in us (Gal. 5:22-23). Don't debate what part is the Spirit's and what part is the believer's. Act as if the responsibility were all yours,

knowing that the fruit is all His.

"Make your calling and election sure" (1:10). How do we develop the confidence that we are truly one of God's people? If we grow in the virtues Peter has listed, that growth itself is proof of Jesus' presence in our lives. This internal confirmation of our election is important to us all.

Reminded (1:12-15). Good news bears repeating and being reminded of all we have in Christ can be of great benefit.

"Eyewitnesses" (1:16-17). There is objective confirmation of the truth of Christian teaching as well as internal confirmation. The objective confirmation comes through Jesus' teaching— and Peter can testify as an eyewitness to His sonship and His majesty.

The "more certain" word of the prophets (1:19-21). Peter's point is that the prophets spoke of the same things he witnessed. Thus the Scripture's testimony to Jesus confirms what he witnessed. And the eyewitness reports of the apostles confirm the fulfillment of the prophet's predictions.

Prophecy's origin (1:21). How can the prophets predict with such accuracy events that will not take place for hundreds of years? Peter says that God was speaking through the prophets, expressing in their words exactly what He intended to communicate to humankind (cf. 2 Sam. 23:2; Jer. 1:7).

Chapter summary. Peter predicts that false teachers will infiltrate the church, introducing "destructive heresies." What is more, many will actually follow them (2:1-3). But sacred history shows that God punishes the wicked and rescues the godly (vv. 4-10). Bold and arrogant, these "creatures of instinct" (vv. 11-12) revel in materialistic pleasures with absolutely no insight into the spiritual (vv. 13-16). Their appeal is to "the lustful desires of sinful human nature." The "freedom" they promise is a depravity that enslaves men to a corruption that we escape through Jesus Christ (vv. 17-22).

Outline
Place
Finder

CONFIRMATION
HERESY
WORLD'S END

Key verse. 2:12: The "wise" of this world.

Personal application. Beware of those who promise pleasure rather than self-sacrifice.

Key concepts. False prophets »p. 462. Angels »p. 521. Sin »p. 741. Adultery »pp. 64, 388. Freedom »p. 685.

INSIGHT

Characteristics of false teachers. In this chapter Peter sketches the character, motives, and appeal of false teachers who threaten the church from within. Their character is seen in their bold, arrogant contempt for authority and exploitation of others. Their motives are revealed in their greed and sexual immorality. Their appeal is to man's baser nature, with promises of a freedom that releases all restraint and results in captivity to sin. The false teacher appeals to many because he seems attractive, strong, and confident. Few resent the material prosperity he craves, for he seems to them deserving of God's blessing. And many respond to his promises of health, material blessing, and freedom from the ills that all human beings are heir to in this sinful world. What a contrast with the servant of God, who all too often seems weak and struggling. Rather than a life of ease, Peter calls Christians to servanthood and even suffering.

Lessons from history (2:4-10). In each historic illustration God judged sinners—while at the same time delivering the godly. Let's not be too concerned about any troubles we experience here. It's what happens on Judgment Day that counts.

Illustration. *Old Testament and N.T. refer to predatory animals in a negative way. They are "senseless and ignorant" in that they have no perspective on God and no awareness of the future He has ordained (Ps. 73:22). The animal mind is locked into the present and so responds to situations on instinct alone. This point (2 Peter 2:12) is underlined by Jude, who says false teachers "understand by instinct, like unreasoning animals" (Jude 10). Any who are driven by the passions of the sin nature are indeed like beasts who do not take God into account.*

Outline
Place
Finder

CONFIRMATION
HERESY
WORLD'S END

Chapter summary. The warning about false teachers (chap. 2) is especially important in view of what will happen at Christ's second coming. Peter reminds his "dear friends" of the Old Testament prophet's vision of future judgment (3:1-2). Scoffers today who ridicule the idea of coming judgment forget that the Genesis Flood shows God will surely exercise His responsibility and judge our race (vv. 3-7). The reason for what may seem a present delay is that God is keeping the door of repentance open (vv. 8-9). When the Day of the Lord does come, however, the universe itself will "disappear with a roar" (v. 10). We who understand this ought then to live godly lives, for surely nothing in this world will survive the judgment (vv. 11-16).

Peter concludes with a word of warning: Be on guard, and don't be carried away by "lawless men." If we instead grow in the grace and knowledge of Jesus, we will be secure (vv. 17-18).

Key verse. 3:11: A motive for godly living.

Personal application. Don't pin your hopes for a meaningful life on things which may not exist tomorrow.

Key concepts. Prophecy »pp. 131, 434. Day of the Lord »pp. 413, 541. Flood »p. 29. Holiness »p. 879. Repentance »p. 780. Salvation »p. 841. Last days »p. 843.

INSIGHT

New Testament predictive prophecy. Most O.T. prophets spoke of a distant future in which, after a decisive battle where God personally intervenes, His Messiah will raise up a glorious earthly kingdom. The O.T. prophets also spoke of the creation of a new heaven and earth (»p. 443). New Testament images of the future are in full harmony with major elements of O.T. prophecy but, like the O.T. visions, N.T. pictures of the future are incomplete. Matthew 24 speaks of a coming time of Tribulation and of an Antichrist, as does 2 Thes. 2. First Thessalonians 4 describes a "rapture" when Christians alive and resurrected are caught up in the air to meet a returning Jesus. Revelation 20 describes a time when Satan is bound and Christ with His saints rules the earth. Here Peter speaks of this universe flaming out of existence, while Rev. 21 describes a new universe created after final judgment. We cannot be sure just how all these images of the future fit together. But Peter reminds us that we *can* be sure of one thing. This world is destined to pass away.

Uniformitarianism (3:4). In science this is the name given to the theory that everything seen on earth can be explained by natural laws and processes presently in operation. This notion is reflected in the modern view that evolution can explain the origin of earth, of vegetable and animal life, and of human life as well. Peter reminds us this whole mindset is wrong. Creation was an event: all that is was shaped by God's Word. And the terrible Flood that destroyed early civilization was an event: an intervention that demonstrated God's commitment to judge, and His ability to do so.

Don't be taken in by modern so-called "science." Trust Scripture's portrait of the past—and of the future!

Not slow, patient (3:9). How good to have an answer for those who ridicule the idea of a coming Judgment Day. "God's just waiting for you to be saved!" Delay is another evidence of God's love.

"What kind of people"? (3:11-12) When the Day of the Lord comes God will punish the wicked and deliver the righteous (cf. 2:4-10). Therefore, what kind of people not only "ought" you to be, but do you want to be! Peter's choice is a decisive "holy and godly."

Speeding Christ's coming (3:12). Since God delays sending Christ to permit the ungodly to repent, we can speed that coming by zealously sharing the Gospel with the lost.

"The other Scriptures" (3:15-16). This exhortation to live blameless lives has great theological import, for here Peter gives the writings of "our dear brother Paul" the same status as "the other Scriptures." The early church did recognize our N.T. as the authoritative Word of God.

1–3 John

Tradition tells us that after the destruction of Jerusalem by the Romans in A.D. 70, the Apostle John and a core group of followers moved to Asia Minor. The apostle settled in Ephesus and soon influenced churches in several major cities. Sometime around A.D. 75–80 John wrote his Gospel, which circulated both as a missionary tract and as a report of the Son of God's life and teaching for believers. The Christian church was firmly established by now but, as we know from 2 Timothy, 2 Peter, and Jude, destructive heresies were introduced by false teachers. The letters of John, and particularly 1 John, were probably written around A.D. 85–90 as a response to this internal crisis. John's final work, Revelation, was written near the end of the first century.

These letters of John are warmly personal in character. John does combat heresy. But he does so in a pastoral way, by repeatedly emphasizing basic doctrines about Christ and the Christian lifestyle. Again and again we read that Jesus is the Christ come in the flesh, that righteous conduct is essential in those who have been born of God, and that love is the mark of vital relationship with God. One story about John, reported in Jerome's commentary on Galatians, tells how he was carried into the congregation when he was old and unable to say anything except, "Little children, love one another." When asked why he always spoke these same words, John replied, "Because it is the Lord's command, and if this only is done, it is enough."

There may be no epistles in the New Testament that better remind us of the basic truths which Christians believe and which we are called to live.

WORDS OF WISDOM FROM 1 JOHN

On believer's sins. *"If we confess our sins, He is faithful and just to forgive us our sins and purify us from all unrighteousness" (1:9).*

On knowing God. *"The man who says, 'I know Him,' but does not do what He commands is a liar" (2:4).*

On loving. *"Anyone who claims to be in the light but hates his brother is still in darkness" (2:9).*

On professed believers who abandon their faith. *"They went out from us, but they did not really belong to us. For if they had belonged to us they would have remained with us" (2:19).*

On the impact of salvation. *"No one who is born of God will continue to sin, because God's seed remains in him; he cannot go on sinning" (3:9).*

On the nature of love. *"This is how we know what love is: Jesus Christ laid down His life for us. And we ought to lay down our lives for our brothers" (3:16).*

On assurance of salvation. *"Everyone who believes that Jesus is the Christ is born of God" (5:1). "This is the testimony: God has given us eternal life, and this life is in His Son. He who has the Son has life" (5:11-12).*

Illustration. *The Apostle John was one of the inner circle of three who stayed with Jesus even when the others were absent. John is known as the one for whom Jesus had a special affection and who was "reclining next to him" at the Last Supper (John 13:23). John earned his early nickname, Boanerges, "Son of Thunder," when he and his brother James urged Jesus to call down fire on a Samaritan village that refused them hospitality (Mark 3). What a transformation association with Jesus worked in John, as this Son of Thunder became the warm, caring, and compassionate apostle of love. As John's writings point out, an experience of the love of God in Jesus will move the believer to love Christian brothers and sisters. A growing love for others is one of the clearest marks of an authentic faith in Christ.*

Authorship. The author of the three letters attributed to John does not identify himself at the beginning, as was common in first-century epistles. However, several things point clearly to the Apostle John. First, the author claims to be an eyewitness to Jesus' incarnation (1 John 1:2-3; 4:14). Second, Papias, in the mid-second century, specifically identifies John as the author, as do other church fathers. And numerous quotes or allusions to this letter in early Christian writings show it is a very early document. Third, these letters show many similarities in language, thought, and emphases to John's Gospel. Taken together the evidence for John's authorship is strong enough that one scholar speaks of the "obstinate perverseness" of those who argue for a different author.

THEOLOGICAL OUTLINE OF 1 JOHN

I. LIGHT	1–2
II. LOVE	3–4
III. FAITH	5

Note: First John is the most difficult of New Testament books to outline. Many argue that there is no outline, that John has no logical plan, but simply writes a very personal letter shifting themes as one thought leads him to another. Thus, two possible outlines are included below to show various ways in which this letter might be analyzed.

OUTLINE BASED ON THE NATURE OF GOD

Prologue (1:1-4)
I. God as Light (1:5–2:27)
   A. Communion and Confession (1:5–2:2)
   B. Communion and Obedience (2:3-17)
   C. Warning: Antichrists (2:18-27)
II. God as Righteous (2:28–4:6)
   A. Righteous Children (2:28–3:10)
   B. Righteous Love (3:11-18)
   C. Confidence before God (3:19-24)
   D. Warning: The Spirit of Antichrist (4:1-6)
III. God as Love (4:7–5:12)
   A. True Love (4:7-21)
   B. Centrality of Faith in Christ (5:1-12)
Epilogue (5:13-21)

OUTLINE BASED ON THE DANGER FROM FALSE TEACHERS

Preface (1:1-4)
I. Basic Realities False Teachers Deny (1:5–2:2)
   A. Sin Breaks Fellowship with God (1:5-7)
   B. Sin Exists in Our Nature (1:8-9)
   C. Sin Expresses Itself in Our Conduct (1:10–2:2)
II. Tests of Relationship: Their First Application (2:3-27)
   A. Obedience, the Moral Test (2:3-6)
   B. Love, the Social Test (2:7-11)
   C. Digression on the Church and the World (2:12-17)
   D. Belief, the Doctrinal Test (2:18-27)
III. Tests of Relationship: Second Application (2:28–4:6)
   A. More on the Moral Test: Righteousness (2:28–3:10)
   B. More on the Social Test: Love (3:11-18)
   C. Digression on Assurance (3:19-24)
   D. More on the Doctrinal Test: Belief (4:1-6)
IV. Tests of Relationship: Third Application (4:7–5:5)
   A. More on the Social Test: Love (4:7-12)
   B. A Combination of Social and Doctrinal Tests (4:13-21)
   C. A Combination of the Three Tests (5:1-5)
V. A Basis for Assurance (5:6-17)
   A. Three Witnesses (5:6-12)
   B. Assurance (5:13-17)
Conclusion (5:18-21)

Outline
Place
Finder

LIGHT
LOVE
FAITH

Chapter summary. The prologue (1:1-4) establishes the author's credibility: He is an eyewitness. But even more, it lays the foundation of faith. God the Father has a Son, the source of eternal life. This Son, Jesus Christ, has lived in our world, and those who believe in Him have fellowship with Him even now—and through that fellowship, joy.

But to have fellowship with God a person must "walk in the light." In context and in Johannine theology "light" is utter, absolute truth. To walk in the light is to be honest with God and with ourselves (vv. 5-7). It is neither true nor honest to claim that we are without sin (v. 8). Instead, we are to confess (acknowledge) our sins—and through confession experience both the forgiving and cleansing power of God (vv. 9-10). As we bring our weaknesses to God He will transform us and enable us to become the obedient, loving, and trusting people the rest of this letter calls us to be.

Key verse. 1:9: Our part, His part.

Personal application. The person who excuses himself for his sins is weighted down by them. One who confesses his sins leaves them behind.

Key concepts. Eternal life »p. 682. Fellowship »p. 779. Light »p. 685. Darkness »p. 824. Sin »p. 741.

INSIGHT

"From the beginning" (1:1). In John 1:1 "the Word" (Christ) was "in the beginning." Here is the Gospel John has heard and proclaims is from the beginning. God's plan of salvation is rooted in eternity, although its expression in the flesh is something John himself has witnessed in Jesus.

"God is light" (1:5). To sense the significance of this statement, imagine yourself stumbling through a strange place on the darkest of nights. All you can see is shadows that frighten and confuse. And then, suddenly, a bright light shines on the scene and you can see everything clearly. There are no more illusions, no more imagined fears. Now at last you can find your way safely, for you can see every obstacle for what it really is. In the spiritual realm darkness blinds human beings, forcing the lost to live in a world of illusion. Only if we walk in the light shed by God through His Word can we see things for what they really are—and respond appropriately.

"Live by the truth" (1:6). A basic meaning of both the Heb. and Gk. words translated "truth" is "in full harmony with reality." If we are to have fellowship with God, we must not only see things as they are, but we must live by the reality thus revealed.

Purified from every sin (1:7). Some have taken the "light" as sinlessness. But this verse tells us that when we walk in the light, Christ's blood purifies us from every sin. If we are honest with ourselves and God we will see our sins in the light of God's Word—and will appeal to Christ for purification.

"Without sin" (1:8). Don't ever suppose that salvation makes a person sinless. And don't dismiss anger as righteous indignation, or vindictiveness as justice. Sin is our constant companion and will be, until Jesus comes and we are transformed into His likeness. Only if you and I recognize our vulnerability and are honest about our failures, will we remain in fellowship with God and grow.

Confess sins (1:9-10). The Gk. word "confess" is *homologeo*, which means "speak the same thing," i.e., acknowledge. Confessing sins is not "saying you're sorry." It is agreeing with God that a particular act is sin—and thus taking sides with Him and against yourself. What happens if we confess our sins? Then God forgives our sins and continues the process of purification from unrighteousness the Spirit has begun in us. What happens if we make excuses, or refuse to acknowledge a particular act was sin? We put up a barrier between ourselves and God. In essence, we deny that His word about our sinful act is true and cut ourselves off from His transforming power.

Chapter summary. John has promised that if we confess our sins, God will forgive and cleanse (1:9-10). His motive is not to encourage but discourage sinning! Knowing the full extent of the love God extends in Christ's atonement motivates us to serve Him (2:1-2). Salvation is a transforming experience, and those who truly know God will obey His commands and seek to "walk as Jesus did" (vv. 3-6). Mention of God's commands turns the apostle's thought to Jesus' "new command"—a command which while new is also old. The believer who loves his brothers obeys this command and so walks in the light. The person who "hates his brother" is still stumbling around in the realm of darkness (vv. 7-11).

Again John's thoughts turn, this time stimulated by his mention of darkness. He addresses the whole church, represented as children, young men, and fathers. We can overcome by knowing Christ and appropriating His Word (vv. 12-14). But the believer must not love the world's ways or share its passions (vv. 15-17) or be deceived by antichrists who deny Christ and try to lead us astray (vv. 18-25). The Holy Spirit will enable the true believer to recognize truth and error and to remain in Him (vv. 26-29).

Outline Place Finder

LIGHT
LOVE
FAITH

Key verse. 2:20: God's inner voice.

Personal application. Jesus' people live as Jesus lived.

Key concepts. Christ »p. 646. Atonement »pp. 69, 84, 739. Love »pp. 661, 690. Darkness »p. 892. Antichrist »pp. 522, 828.

INSIGHT

"Not sin" (2:1-2). Some assume that only fear of punishment can keep a person from sinning. The N.T. assumes that the prime motivator of obedience is love. Knowing God will forgive us if we fail helps us sense the depth of His love for us in Christ. We choose godliness because we respond to that love with gratitude and love of our own.

Knowing God (2:4-6, 29). In John, knowing God is not academic, theoretical, nor intellectual. Knowing God is personal, practical, and experiential. To know God is not simply to trust Him, but also to live in daily fellowship with Him. Anyone who claims to "know God" in this personal, intimate way and who is disobedient to the Word or hostile toward other Christians "is a liar."

Walking as Jesus walked (2:6). In the Bible, "walking" is a frequent figure of behavior or lifestyle. Since Jesus lives in the believer, a person who is living close to Him will have a Christlike lifestyle. Christ loved and gave Himself for us. Anyone who hates his brother is still in darkness. Love for others is one way that Jesus expresses Himself in our lives.

Overcoming the evil one (2:13-14). The Gk.

word *nikao* means "to win a victory" or "to conquer." The Christian cannot be victimized by Satan or the world—against his or her will. If we stay close to Jesus we share by faith in the victory He won (cf. also John 16:33; 1 John 5:4).

"The world" (2:15-17). The Gk. *kosmos* when used theologically refers to the "order" or "arrangement" of human society as a system warped by sin, awash with swirling beliefs, desires, and emotions. The world is antagonistic to God (Col. 2:20; 1 John 2:16) and lies under Satan's authority (1 John 5:9).

Worldliness (2:15-17). Given the nature of "world" in the N.T., worldliness is not a matter of some list of do's and don'ts. It is adopting the perspectives (cravings), the values (lust of the eyes), and attitudes (the boasting of status) of man's society rather than the perspective, values, and attitudes of God.

Lost after believing? (2:19) John has a different explanation.

Our anointing (2:20-27). The word *chrisma* looks not on the act of rubbing or spreading, but on that with which one is anointed. Here, this is the Holy Spirit who teaches us (John 16:12-15).

Outline
Place
Finder

LIGHT
LOVE
FAITH

Chapter summary. God's great love has reached out to make us His very children. We do not know our ultimate destiny, except that we will be like Jesus—and that everyone who looks forward to that transformation purifies himself or herself even now (3:1-3).

In fact, continuing in sin is evidence that a person does not know God. Sin can be traced back to Satan, and Christ appeared to destroy the devil's work. It follows that no one born of God will make a practice of sinning: The divine life planted deep in the personality will now prevent it (vv. 4-10).

Again the theme of "doing what is right" turns John's thoughts to love. Evil persons hate righteous ones, and hatred is the source of murder. Surely no murderer is infused with eternal life! (vv. 11-15) Rather than take another's life, the one who loves is willing to lay down his own life for others, even as Jesus laid down his life for us. When this kind of love has practical expression in our lives, we know we belong to the Lord (vv. 16-20). Keep on loving and obeying God and we will have confidence before God and power in prayer (vv. 21-24).

Key verse. 3:16: A living definition.

Personal application. Love does find a way to express itself.

Key concepts. Child of God »p. 790. Sin »pp. 34, 362, 442, 611, 798. Righteous »pp. 120, 808. Born again »p. 680. The Devil »p. 501. Hate »pp. 86, 692. World »p. 893. Obey »p. 691. Prayer »p. 608.

INSIGHT

Purifying hope (3:3). Hope is confident expectation, certainty about the future. If we know our destiny is to be like Jesus, this sense of our true identity will move us to be like Him now.

"Lawlessness" (3:4). John's point is that when we break the law (sin) we rebel against God. Any violation of the moral standards God has revealed is rebelliousness. What we do in the flesh is of real importance!

Lead astray (3:7). False teachers have little concern for morality, as the pressure in some churches to ordain practicing homosexuals makes clear. John warns us not to be deceived. Those who "do what is sinful" are "of the devil," not God.

"Destroy the devil's work" (3:8). The word here is *lyo*, "to undo." All sinful acts reflect the character of Satan. Yet the harm done by Satan can be and is being undone by Jesus. How? Through Christ, God's own "seed" (i.e., nature) has been planted in the personality of the believer. The devil's work in us is being unraveled by God, so surely that "no one who is born of God will continue to sin." This does not mean the believer will be sinless (cf. 1 John 1:7-10). It *does* mean that "he cannot go on sinning, because he has been born of God."

"Cain" (3:11-15). The Gen. 4 story illustrates several truths. The wicked tend to hate the righteous. Hatred expresses itself in evil acts like murder. Hostility itself is diabolical in origin. Thus, "hostile Christian" is a contradiction in terms. One who hates is a murderer in his heart and cannot be one who has eternal life.

Prayer conditions? (3:21-22) Some look at such sayings as "if our hearts do not condemn us" as a condition we must meet before God will answer our prayers. Yet, clearly John intends to encourage us. When we love, and our hearts do not condemn us, we know we are in a relationship with God in which He can answer our prayers. Other supposed conditions should be understood the same way. Disobedience (Deut. 1:43-45), unconcern (Isa. 58:7-9), and injustice (Micah 3:1-4) are signs we are out of fellowship with God. But even (1) two agreeing on God's will (Matt. 18:19), (2) knowing our prayer is in harmony with Jesus' character and expressed will (that is, "in Jesus' name") (John 14:13-14), and (3) sensing an inner, Spirit-taught confidence that we have asked according to God's will (1 John 5:14-15) are not "conditions," but God's gracious indication that He has heard and will answer our prayers.

Chapter summary. John again warns about the "spirit of anti-christ," that corrupting influence which seeks to infiltrate the church. That spirit can be recognized by its denial that Jesus is God come in the flesh (4:1-3). That denial wells up from the world and its evil ruler and is recognized as a falsehood by those who know God (vv. 4-6). But again, the prime directive for believers is to love one another. Love comes from God, is revealed in Christ, and is to be lived by Jesus' people (vv. 7-12). God has given us His Spirit, for we acknowledge Jesus as the Son of God and rely. fully on His love (vv. 13-16). God is love, and as we love the experience of being loved and loving drives out our fears of punishment (vv. 17-18). Again John sums up. Anyone who claims to love God and yet fails to love his brother is a liar. Love for God expresses itself in love for others also (vv. 19-21).

Outline
Place
Finder

LIGHT
LOVE
FAITH

Key verse. 4:16: Living in love.

Personal application. Share God's love, and let love quiet your fears.

Key concepts. False prophets »p. 462. Antichrist »pp. 522, 828. Son of God »p. 896. Incarnation »p. 807. World »p. 893. Love »pp. 351, 529, 680, 690. Holy Spirit »pp. 73, 744, 759.

INSIGHT

"**The spirits**" (4:1-3). In the 1st century it was common for people to claim special inspiration for their teachings, as the apostles claimed the Holy Spirit as the source of their teaching. Now John warns the church to test teachers who claim to give inspired teaching for that teaching's source. And the key test? Whether or not the teacher will say "that Jesus Christ has come in the flesh." Many through church history have praised Jesus as a good man, or a messenger from God. But only those who acknowledge Jesus as God Himself, with us in human flesh, merit any trust.

The Holy Spirit's presence (4:4). The Christian is guaranteed victory over false teachers, whose origins are demonic (cf. 3:8), because while Satan supernaturally energizes the world of lost men God's Spirit, who lives in us, is "greater than he who is in the world."

Demons (4:4). The Gospels speak much of demon possession and oppression. Acts also reports a number of cases of exorcism. Although demons are mentioned infrequently in the N.T., many Christians have been concerned that we might be vulnerable to demonic attack. For those who are concerned, this verse should provide great consolation. It is hard to imagine a demon, or Satan, making himself at home in the life of a person indwelt by the very Spirit of God.

Propitiation: love's atoning sacrifice (4:10). Divine love by its nature is unselfish. It is even more: It is self-sacrificing. John proves this by pointing to Christ's sacrifice as a *hilasmos*. This word in Gk. thought described an act which in some way averted the destructive powers of the gods and, ideally, won their favor. It is used in the Septuagint to translate *kippur*, the word for "atonement." In the O.T. the concept emphasizes the covering of sins by the offering of the life of a substitute in place of the life of the sinner. Jesus' death for us averted the punishment our sins deserve and enables God to shower blessings on us.

Love an ought? (4:11) This ought is not a moral obligation, but a case of simple appropriateness. We have been loved and so it is only fitting that we be loving.

Love made complete (4:12). God's love finds its fulfillment on earth when we love others as He has loved us.

Love and fear (4:17-18). Love and fear are not compatible. When we experience God's love for us our whole attitude toward Him is transformed. We still stand in awe of Him, but that awe is without terror or fear of punishment. The more we live in love—and living in love means expressing as well as receiving love—the more confident we become in our relationship with the Lord.

Outline
Place
Finder

LIGHT
LOVE
FAITH

Chapter summary. John now sums up his message. Those who believe Jesus is the Christ are born of God. We know we are among the reborn when we love God's children, love God, and keep His commands. Only a new birth can provide this kind of victory over the world (5:1-5). John speaks of three witnesses—Spirit, water, and blood—which give authentic inner testimony to Christ as the Son of God (vv. 6-10). That testimony confirms the fact that we have eternal life as a present possession (vv. 11-12). And so John writes that we may know we have eternal life and can approach God with assurance, knowing He hears us (vv. 13-15).

John's letter ends with an appeal to help sinning brothers (vv. 16-17), a reminder that we who are children of God will not keep on sinning, and a promise that God will surely keep us safe (vv. 18-21).

Key verse. 5:13: We can know.

Personal application. It's not presumptuous for a person who believes in Jesus to say "I know I'm saved." Rather, it would be presumptuous to doubt God's Word.

Key concepts. Belief »pp. 35, 458, 740, 790. World »p. 893. Testimony »p. 132. Eternal life »p. 682. Death »pp. 369, 741. Born again »p. 680.

INSIGHT

How we know (5:2). John is not talking about how we know others have a vital relationship with God. He is discussing how a real faith in Jesus expresses itself in our lives. As we experience love for others and for God, and find ourselves choosing to obey His commandments, we realize that we truly have been born again.

"Victory" (5:4). The aorist participle reminds us that victory over the world has been won. And the proof is that our faith in Jesus has worked the transformation about which John writes.

The three witnesses (5:6-7). There is great uncertainty about the identity of the three witnesses. Perhaps the best explanation is that advanced by Tertullian in the 2nd century: The Spirit is the Holy Spirit. The water is Jesus' baptism, in which He affirmed His identity with us as a true human being. And the blood is that shed on the cross, by which He accomplished our salvation. Faith rests on the reality of a historical Jesus, who was both man and God, who died and rose again for us.

The inner witness (5:10). The three witnesses above are objective. The Spirit performed miracles through Jesus. The Father confirmed His identity at His baptism. And the Son died an actual death on the cross, witnessed by dozens. When a person believes the external witness to Jesus, God the Father gives us a witness—"in his heart." Faith serves as its own witness. In believing we somehow know the story of Jesus is true, and our certainty is confirmed by what God then does in our lives.

"Son of God" (5:13). Jesus' sonship was affirmed at His baptism (Matt. 3:17) and "declared with power to be the Son of God by His resurrection from the dead" (Rom. 1:4). In John 1:1-14 we are shown that this name attests to Jesus' unique position in the universe based on His coexistence with and as God from eternity. Many passages use this phrase in' such a way that Jesus' nature as God is make unmistakably clear (cf. also John 5:19-27; Heb. 1; 1 John 4:9-15).

Assurance (5:14). God doesn't want us to go through life fearful and uncertain about our relationship with Him. So He tells us plainly, if you believe in the Son of God you have eternal life. So we need not fear or doubt. We have God's word for it. We are His.

A prayer ministry (5:16-17). John has described the confidence with which we can pray (vv. 14-15). Now he urges us to pray for any brother who slips into sin. John doesn't define the "sin that leads to death," but undoubtedly means physical rather than spiritual death (cf. 1 Cor. 11:27-32). Our prayers will be answered, for "the one born of God does not continue to sin" (v. 18).

2 John

In this brief letter the "chosen lady" John addresses may be a church and its members. Like 1 John, this letter emphasizes the importance of love, and links love to obedience. The letter contains a greeting (vv. 1-3), advice and warning (vv. 4-11), and a conclusion (vv. 12-13).

Chapter summary. John's greeting links truth and love, for those who know and live the truth in Jesus are bound together in a community of love (vv. 1-3). John has been delighted to hear that "some" in the Christian community have been living in accord with God's truth, but urges even greater love and obedience (vv. 4-6). But his exhortation is accompanied by a warning. Deceivers, marked by their denial that Jesus is God in the flesh, abound. Any who come to the church without a clear affirmation of the deity of Jesus are to be refused access to the church (vv. 7-11). In closing, John expresses his desire to visit in person and sends greetings (vv. 12-13).

Key verse. 7: Still the key.

Personal application. The central issue in Christianity is who people say Jesus is.

Key concepts. Choice »p. 797. Truth »pp. 362, 685, 836, 892. Love »pp. 126, 690, 691. Antichrist »pp. 522, 828.

INSIGHT

A promise (v. 3). Most 1st-century letters customarily offer a prayer or wish as the last element of their greeting. Here John departs from custom and makes a promise. How sure we can be that the Lord truly "will be with us in truth and love."

God's command (vv. 4-6). The noun "command" (*entole*) is used four times in these verses. John is clearly showing how we can fulfill the will of God. That will is for us to love and obey God and to love others.

These three are linked in Scripture and in our experience. Love for God stimulates obedience. Obedience indicates love. Love for others is both an overflow of our love for God and an obedient response to His command to love one another.

A deceiver and antichrist (v. 7). All the later N.T. epistles which speak of false teaching and teachers indicate a single doctrine is the key test of heresy. That is the doctrine of the full deity and humanity of Jesus: the conviction

that Jesus was God with us in the flesh.

This is still a vital test to apply to any who claim to be teachers of religion. Anyone who comes to the church without this teaching is not to be welcomed or permitted to minister.

Why this particular doctrine? Because all the central teachings of our faith hinge on the deity of Jesus. The Incarnation and Virgin Birth, the vicarious sacrifice, the physical Resurrection, the Ascension, the Second Coming—all presuppose that the Jesus we know and worship is both God and man. If Jesus were not God, His death could hardly have made a universal atonement. If Jesus were not man, His resurrection could hardly be the "firstfruits" which guarantees our own.

There is only one way to God, only one truth, and only one source of eternal life. Never permit anyone who denies the deity and humanity of Jesus, however urbane or convincing he or she may be, to pass as a teacher of Christian truth.

3 John

John's third letter is written to an individual named Gaius. Like John's other epistles this letter emphasizes love, truth, and obedience. It also indicates some of the tensions and difficulties which made life in the early church much like that of today. They too tried to build their own kingdom and rule over the church, rather than be a part of the larger fellowship of faith. John's letter reminds us that the church truly is one and that we ought to "work together for the truth" (v. 8).

Chapter summary. John writes to a church leader named Gaius (v. 1). John commends him for his faithfulness to God (vv. 2-4). John also commends Gaius for the love he displays in welcoming the itinerant teachers who traveled from church to church in the first century (vv. 5-8). This is in contrast to the practice of one Diotrephes, who rejects John's authority and like a dictator puts out of the church any who disagree with his leadership (vv. 9-10). John urges Gaius to keep on doing good and commends another leader named Demetrius whom both of them know (vv. 11-12). John closes this letter as he did 2 John, expressing his desire to see Gaius soon and talk about these issues at greater length (vv. 13-14).

Key verse. 8: Cooperation.

Personal application. Separation is from sin, not from Christian brothers and sisters.

Key concepts. Joy »p. 803. Truth »pp. 362, 685, 836, 892. Love »pp. 126, 690, 691. Hospitality »p. 37.

INSIGHT

"The elder" (v. 1). While "elder" can mean an old man, it undoubtedly is used here in the sense of a senior church leader. In the 2nd century it was used by Eusebius and Irenaeus of church officials who had been personal followers of one of the apostles. John may speak of himself as "the" elder because he was a personal follower of Jesus.

"Dear friend" (v. 2). The address sets the tone for what is clearly a warm, affectionate letter. John feels and expresses great delight in the faithfulness of this younger Christian leader. How enriching to grow close to others who love the Lord.

Itinerancy in the N.T. world. Travel was common in the 1st-century Roman Empire, both along well kept roads and by the hundreds of ships sailing the Mediterranean. People traveled for business purposes and on religious pilgrimages — the Jews to Jerusalem and pagans to such centers as Ephesus. In addition, intinerate teachers of philosophy and religion went from city to city, teaching in the streets, seeking to gather enough students to support them. It was natural for Christian teachers to travel too. The apostles traveled. Their representatives, such as Timothy and Titus, traveled. And of course false teachers traveled, seeking to infiltrate the church and gain a profit from the untaught and unsuspecting. Yet the world of the 1st century had few hotels. Travelers stayed in private homes, put up by people from their homeland or persons who shared their faith. The traveling Christian teachers of the 1st century visited a church, were usually provided food and lodging by a believer, and often were given gifts of money to help them travel to the next congregation. Second John reminds us that false teachers also traveled and that such visitors were to be questioned and not welcomed if they denied the deity and humanity of Jesus. In this letter Gaius is commended for the hospitality he extended to teachers sent by John, while a leader named Diotrephes is criticized.

Hospitality (v. 8). For more, see Matt. 10:10; Rom. 12:13; 1 Tim. 3:2, 5:10; Heb. 13:2.

Jude

The brief Book of Jude was written by a man who wanted to write a positive treatise on salvation, but found himself driven to pen the New Testament's strongest condemnation of false teachers and teachings. The author identifies himself as Jude, the "brother of James" (v. 1). Of the eight Judes mentioned in the New Testament, one was a brother of James, and this James was a half brother of Jesus and leader of the early church (see p. 868). This identification of Jude as one of Jesus' half brothers is confirmed by the early church historian Eusebius, who tells a story about the grandsons of Jude who was "said to have been the Lord's brother according to the flesh." Jude hesitates to claim such high status, perhaps because like Jesus' other brothers Jude did not believe in Him as the Christ until after His resurrection (cf. John 7:5; Acts 1:14). All Jude will claim is that he is a slave (*doulos*) of Jesus Christ (v. 1). Despite his humility, Jude is far from reticent when it comes to speaking out against false teaching and teachers. His denunciation is blunt and powerful. And, in this day of ours when many seem willing to surrender truth in exchange for the sake of harmony, Jude's words may be especially important for us to heed.

Date. The date of Jude is uncertain, but the theme of teachers who smuggle falsehood into the church fits into the late A.D. 60s and the decades which immediately follow. Many date Jude between A.D. 60 and 80.

THE STORY BEHIND JUDE'S MODEL'S FOR FALSE TEACHERS

Cain (v. 11). *Genesis 4 tells how Cain, although he knew what would constitute an acceptable sacrifice, chose to offer vegetables rather than a lamb. When his offering was rejected, he turned his anger against his brother Abel and killed him. False teachers are rebels who have no concern for true believers, but are delighted to do them harm.*

Balaam (v. 11). *Numbers 22–24 tells the story of Balaam, a seer hired by a hostile king to curse Israel. Although God forbade Balaam to go, the seer was driven by his passion for wealth. He could not curse God's people, but he did suggest they be corrupted sexually and religiously by their enemy. Balaam got his pay, but was killed shortly afterward.*

Korah (v. 11). *Numbers 16 tells how Korah rebelled against God's instructions concerning how He was to be worshiped. He and others tried to force their way into a position of spiritual leadership for which they were not qualified and were destroyed by fire from the Lord.*

Illustration: Jude 12-13. *Jude's dark images of the false teachers not only describe them, but also portray the barren results of their teachings in other's lives. Those who seek rich, fruitful lives and yet abandon Jesus as Saviour are destined to parched emptiness.*

OUTLINE OF JUDE

Greeting (1-2)
   I. Purpose of the Letter (3-4)
  II. Warning Against False Teachers
     (5-16)
     A. Examples of Judgment (5-7)

     B. Doom of False Teachers (8-13)
     C. Enoch's Prophecy (14-16)
  III. Exhortation to Believers (17-23)
Doxology (24-25)

Chapter summary. Jude modestly identifies himself and greets fellow believers (vv. 1-2). He had hoped to write a positive letter about the salvation they enjoy, but instead felt compelled by the appearance of so many false teachers to write a letter of warning (vv. 3-4). History has shown that God punishes the wicked and perverse (vv. 5-7). He will surely punish the arrogant false teachers who reject authority and approach spiritual realities with no more understanding than brute beasts (vv. 8-10). These false teachers follow the example of others in history whom God rejected and punished (v. 11) and are like specters, walking among them without life or the capacity to enrich those who do have life (vv. 12-13). Here Jude approvingly quotes a contemporary Jewish religious tract: The writer is correct in his vision of the Lord coming to judge ungodly sinners—like these false teachers who follow their own evil desires (vv. 14-16). Such persons are sure to infiltrate the church and try to divide the fellowship (vv. 17-19). The best way to resist them is to keep on growing in the faith, to live in God's love, and to show mercy and concern for those who doubt (vv. 20-23). Jude closes with a doxology that expresses his complete confidence that God is able to keep the true believer from falling and will present us "before His glorious presence without fault and with great joy" (vv. 24-25).

Key verse. 4: Two tests for orthodoxy.

Personal application. Growth in faith and love is the best antidote to false teaching.

Key concepts. Salvation »p. 841. False teachers »pp. 462, 887. Judgment »pp. 372, 724. Eternal life »p. 682. Shepherds »p. 504.

INSIGHT

"Secretly slipped in" (v. 4). False teachers do not announce themselves, but infiltrate the church by pretending to be Christians. Jude mentions two things that will identify them as time goes on: they will change the nature of grace and deny Jesus Christ. We change the nature of grace when we take God's promise of forgiveness as liberty to indulge in immorality. We deny Jesus when we refuse to acknowledge Him as God as well as man.

Lost angels (v. 6). Many take this as a reference to angels who abandoned the spiritual realm and came to earth. Intertestamental literature shows Jewish writers interpreted Gen. 6:4 in this way. This interpretation is supported by v. 7, which alludes to a time when God's angels visited Sodom and Gomorrah and were viewed as objects for homosexual rape.

False teachers (v. 8). The link between false teachers and the men of Sodom is immorality: a pollution of "their own bodies" by sexual practices that in context include homosexuality.

"Michael" (v. 9). Michael is identified in Dan. 10:13, 21 and 12:1 as a powerful angel. He is also mentioned by name in Rev. 12:7. Jude's point is that if such a powerful being deferred to God to deal with Satan, how much more ought we human beings to remain humble in our weakness and defer to God too. But false teachers are arrogant. They have no more sense than a mouse who foolishly approaches the snake waiting to devour him.

"Wandering stars" (v. 13). Comets, meteors, and shooting stars were called "wandering stars" in the 1st century. Like the false teachers, they were of no value in guiding a navigator at sea.

"Enoch" (vv. 14-15). Jude quotes this Jewish writing not as an authority, but as a vivid contemporary descripton of a Day of Judgment which is substantiated fully in the O.T. Judgment is coming. Then the false teachers will receive their due—as will those whom they lead astray. But see v. 24.

Revelation

Both Old and New Testaments contain bold images of future events. Armies march, nations rise and fall, and ultimately God Himself intervenes to establish His kingdom on this earth and later still to create new heavens and earth at history's end. Our difficulty is in fitting these images together to form a coherent picture.

When we come to the last book of the New Testament, Revelation, we have another problem. Does the vision John shares deal with future history or is his vision symbolic: a grand and vivid but nonprophetic representation of the fact that God rules over all, that one day God and good will triumph and evil will be set aside?

A History of Revelation's Interpretation

One of the earliest Christian writings we have is the *Didache*, a treatise probably penned around A.D. 100. It shows us how the apostolic church understood the future and the context in which Revelation was understood. The writer of the *Didache* says:

> Watch for your life's sake. Let not your lamps be quenched, nor your loins unloosed; but be ye ready, for ye know not the hour in which our Lord cometh. When lawlessness increaseth, they shall hate and betray and persecute one another, and then shall appear the "world deceiver" as Son of God, and shall do signs and wonders, and the earth will be delivered into his hands, and he shall do iniquitous things which have never yet come to pass since the beginning. Then shall the creation of men come into the fire of trial, and many shall be made to stumble and shall perish, but they that endure in their faith shall be saved from under the curse itself. And then shall appear the signs of the truth, (a) first, the sign of an opening in heaven, the outspreading of the heaven; (b) then the sign of the sound of the trumpet; and (c) third, the resurrection of the dead, yet not of all, but as it is said: the Lord shall come and all His saints with Him. Then shall the world see the Lord coming upon the clouds of heaven (*Ante-Nicene Fathers, Vol. VII*, p. 382).

Shortly after, around A.D. 140–160 Justin Martyr wrote, "I and as many as are orthodox Christians, do acknowledge that there shall be a resurrection of the body, and a residence of a thousand years in Jerusalem, adorned and enlarged, as the prophets Ezekiel, Isaiah, and others do unanimously attest" (*Ante-Nicene Fathers, Vol. I*, p. 239).

Irenaeus, both a great missionary and a church father, who died in A.D. 202, adds this to the picture of the future held in the early church.

> When the Antichrist shall have devastated all things in this world, he will reign for three years and six months, and sit in the temple at Jerusalem; and then shall the Lord come from heaven in clouds, in the glory of the Father, sending this man, and those who follow him, into the lake of fire; but bringing for the righteous the times of the kingdom, that is, the rest, the hallowed seventh day; and restoring to Abraham the promised inheritance; in which the kingdom of the Lord declared

that "many coming from the east and the west should sit down with Abraham, Isaac and Jacob" (*Ante-Nicene Fathers, Vol. 1*, p. 560).

Since the 1,000-year period referred to here, as well as the Antichrist's condemnation to the lake of fire, appear only in Revelation, it's clear that the early church fathers saw this book as prophecy. They integrated its teachings with those of the Old Testament prophets and Christ's own statements about the future found in Matthew 24 and Mark 13. In fact, for some 300 years the Book of Revelation and Old Testament prophecies were understood in a literal sense. The church fathers expected Christ to return and to institute the age of blessing spoken of in the Old Testament before the world came to an end.

But about A.D. 400 a shift took place in the way prophecy and the Book of Revelation were understood. Around A.D. 390 Tyconius, a leader of the African church, wrote a commentary in which he spiritualized the events described in Revelation. His allegorical approach, in which events described were understood to symbolize some hidden, spiritual truth, was generally adopted. In fact an allegorical approach to Revelation was even used later to justify the emergence of the papacy as a political power. Revelation was interpreted allegorically by Primasius (about A.D. 550), Alcuin (A.D. 735–804), Maurus (A.D. 775–836), and Strabo (A.D. 807–959).

It was not until Joachim of Fiore, about A.D. 1130–1202, that this view of Revelation was challenged. Joachim divided history into three ages, the Age of the Father (Creation to Christ), the Age of the Son (Christ to his own day), and the Age of the Spirit (His time until final judgment). He then divided Revelation using this time scheme.

When the reformation movement emerged, Luther, Calvin, and others were quick to adopt the chronological approach. The Antichrist (Rev. 13) and the harlot (Rev. 17–18) represented the papacy and Rome. And the various seals and trumpets of the Book of Revelation were understood as critical events in the history of Western Europe. The Catholics responded to this with a commentary on Revelation written by Francisco Ribera (A.D. 1537–1591) in which he held the Antichrist to be an individual who would come in some future time, not the pope. Other Catholic writers tried to show that Revelation applied only to events before the fall of Rome in A.D. 476.

But strikingly, neither the medieval scholars, the Reformers, nor the Catholic Counter-Reformation writers attempted to relate the Book of Revelation to the writings of the Old Testament prophets and so construct a unified picture of the future.

Today there are two primary approaches to the interpretation of the Book of Revelation. One views this great book as a revelation of things to come in the framework accepted during the first three centuries of our era. The other continues to understand Revelation largely as an allegory, filled with difficult symbolism but conveying with great power the conviction that God is sovereign and that He will triumph in the end.

SYMBOLS IN REVELATION

Symbols Explained in Revelation

Text	Symbol	Interpretation
1:20	Seven lampstands	Seven churches in Asia Minor
1:20	Seven stars	Seven angels (messengers) of these churches
4:5	Seven lamps of fire	The Spirit of God
5:8	Bowls of incense	The prayers of the saints
7:3-4	Great multitude	Martyrs of the Great Tribulation
12:9	Great dragon	Satan
17:9	Seven heads of the beast	Seven mountains on which the woman sits
17:12	Ten horns of the beast	Ten kings
17:15	The waters	Peoples, nations
17:18	Woman in purple	A great reigning city

Symbols Drawn from the Old and New Testaments

Text	Symbol	Interpretation
2:7; 22:2	Tree of life	Symbol of eternal life (Gen. 2:9)
2:17	Hidden manna	Heavenly food, from Ps. 78:24; Heb. 9:4
2:27	Rod of iron	Judgment by Christ, from Ps. 2:9
2:28	Morning star	Reign of Christ, from Dan. 12:3
3:7	Key of David	Power of Messiah, from Isa. 22:22
4:6	Living creatures	Represent God's highest creation, from Ezek. 10:14
6:1	The four horsemen	Carrying out of God's purposes, from Zech. 1:8; Ezek. 5:17; 14:21
10:1	Mighty angel	God's judgment, from Ps. 97:2
	Cloud, rainbow	God's mercy, faithfulness, from Gen. 9:8-17

Many other symbols in Revelation have their roots in other New and Old Testament passages, and this provides a basis for understanding the emphasis of the author.

Generally a person who looks at Revelation as future history will be what is called a *premillennialist*, which means he or she expects Christ to return and afterward set up the kingdom portrayed in the Old Testament. The "millennial" is taken from the reference in Revelation 20:1-3 to a 1,000-year period—the only such reference in either Testament. The premillennialist expects a literal Antichrist to appear, a great tribulation, the return of Jesus to earth, a final rebellion, and then an eternity spent in a freshly created and sinless universe. In essence, the premillennial view is the same as that the early church held for its first 300 years.

Today most who are not premillennial are *amillennial*. That is, they look forward to the return of Christ and a final judgment, but understand references in both Testaments to God's rule on this earth as largely allegorical. It is not earthly blessings but spiritual blessings God has for His people of every age. The earthly is simply a symbolic foreshadowing of spiritual realities we enjoy.

Which prophetic system is right and which should be adopted when reading Revelation? Revelation and other prophetic writings do employ symbolism. But this does not mean it is *all* symbolic, or that prophecy by nature is intended to communicate something other than might be found by taking its words in their normal sense. Premillennialists rightly point out that when Old Testament prophecies have been fulfilled, they have been fulfilled literally. We might not know ahead of time the exact shape of their realization, but when the time has come the description given by the prophets is clearly understood in the fulfillment. Thus premillennialists argue that while Revelation's visions are hard to understand, they nevertheless describe events which will take place—and will be recognizable when they happen.

Yet while sincere believers will continue to disagree on just how to understand Revelation, each school does agree that this book has a unique power. The main message it communicates is unmistakable and overpowering. God does rule. The future is in His hand. And, in His own time, God will judge this universe and all in it. When God does act the world as we know it will end. Evil will be put away. Good will triumph. And those who have put their trust in Jesus will inherit a truly endless life.

THEOLOGICAL OUTLINE OF REVELATION

CONTENT OUTLINE OF REVELATION

Chapter summary. John introduces his book as a revelation given to him by Jesus and pronounces a special blessing on those who read, hear, and take to heart "the words of this prophecy" (1:1-3). The book is sent to the seven Asian churches with which John has special ties (vv. 4-5a) and is dedicated to Jesus as coming Saviour (vv. 5b-8).

John now tells his story. While exiled to Patmos, by the Roman emperor Domitian (A.D. 81–96), John was praying one Sunday, when a voice instructed him to write what he was about to see (vv. 9-11). John turned and was given a vision of Jesus in His full glory, so awesome that John fell to the ground, stunned (vv. 12-17). Jesus lifted him up, identified Himself, and told John to write (vv. 18-20).

Outline
Place
Finder

JESUS
LETTERS
JUDGMENT
RETURN
NEW HEAVEN

Key verses. 1:5b-6: Dedicated to Him.

Personal application. Gentle Jesus is also our glorious God.

Key concepts. Angel »p. 521. Blood »pp. 85, 766. Priesthood of believers »p. 880. Second coming »p. 827. Resurrection »p. 737.

INSIGHT

"The revelation of Jesus" (1:1). In the N.T. *apokalypsis* is always used of a divine unveiling of something that has been hidden. Here Jesus is the one who discloses "what must soon take place" — and in the process reveals something of His own glory.

Blessing (1:3). The "one who reads" and "those who hear" refer to a public reading of the book in church. Because this is "prophecy," in the sense of divine revelation (»p. 131), it merits immediate acceptance as Scripture. Because the revelation comes directly from the risen Jesus, it is of utmost importance.

"The seven churches" (1:4). All seven were in the Roman province of Asia, now Asia Minor. They are listed in 1:11, and a message directed to each is found in Rev. 2 and 3.

"Firstborn from the dead" (1:5a). Christ's resurrection is the pledge that we too will be raised. He was not only the first, He is the one who has supreme authority over the vast family of faith destined to follow Him.

Doxology to Christ (1:5b-6). Here is some of the most powerful praise found in the Bible, celebrating Christ's love, the forgiveness won for us by His blood, and the exalted position to which He has raised us.

John's exile (1:9). Tradition agrees that as an old man John was exiled during the reign of Domitian and that he wrote Revelation from Patmos, an island off the coast of Asia Minor. The book was probably written in the mid A.D. 90s.

The vision of Jesus (1:12-15). Each element in the seven-element description of the glori-

fied Christ has symbolic significance. The white head and hair reflect Dan. 7:9 and symbolize wisdom and judgment. The eyes of blazing fire reflect Dan. 10:6 and may indicate a penetrating gaze or perhaps the fierceness of the judgment to come. The feet of glowing metal reflect a common O.T. symbol of God's glory, found in Ezek. 1:13, 27; 8:2; Dan. 10:6, etc. The voice like rushing waters is a familiar simile in Jewish writings for the power of God's voice, repeated in Rev. 14:2 and 19:6. The doubled-edged sword may reflect Isa. 11:4, which is again a portrait of final judgment. Anyone who has heard a thundering waterfall can sense why. Overall, John's language serves to express the awesomeness of the glorified Christ's appearance and the unity of this book with O.T. prophetic books that describe history's end.

"First and the Last" (1:17). This title granted to God in Isa. 44:6 and 48:12 affirms Jesus as Lord of Creation and Master of history.

"The keys of death and Hades" (1:18). Keys were a symbol of authority. Jesus has full control over every realm.

The key to interpreting Revelation? (1:19) Many understand this verse to provide the key to understanding Revelation. "What you have seen" is John's vision of Jesus, found in chap. 1. "What is now" is reflected in the letters Christ dictates, to be sent to the seven Asia Minor churches, found in chaps. 2–3. And "what will take place later" is a vision of history's end, correlated with the O.T. prophet's vision of that time, found in chaps. 4–21.

Outline
Place
Finder

JESUS
LETTERS
JUDGMENT
RETURN
NEW HEAVEN

Chapter summary. Christ now dictates letters to the seven Asian churches concerning "what is now" (1:19). Each letter is addressed to the "angel," or "messenger" (pastors?) of the church. Each message identifies Jesus in a special way, reveals an intimate knowledge of the church addressed, pinpoints the church's most serious flaw, and then conveys a command intended to correct the problem or warn the church. The letter closes with a promise of reward to the victor who responds obediently. Significantly, each promise is eschatological — and alludes to some element found in Revelation 21–22.

The key elements of each letter found in chapter 2 are listed in the chart on page 909.

Key verse. 2:7: Paying attention.

Personal application. Each of us can be commended in some respect — yet each of us also has areas in which we need to grow.

Key concepts. Wicked »p. 350. False prophets »p. 462. Love »pp. 126, 690. Satan »p. 501. Name »p. 691. Idolatry »p. 433. Adultery »pp. 64, 85, 388.

INSIGHT

"**To the angel**" **(2:1).** The word *angellos* means "messenger" and is used of human as well as angelic agents.

Ephesus: letting go of first love (2:4). Most see this as the initial love of the Ephesians for each other (cf. Acts 20:35; Eph. 1:15). It's all too easy to be both orthodox and active — and unloving. But without an intense and vital love any church will soon also be without light (v. 5).

"**The Nicolaitans**" **(2:6).** The name means "conquerers of the people." But little today is known of this group or movement.

Smyrna: persecuted yet faithful (2:8-11). This city of 200,000 was renowned for its wealth and contribution to the sciences and medicine. It was also a center of emperor worship, having been granted the right in A.D. 23 to build the first temple honoring Tiberius. Each citizen was obligated to burn incense to the "god" Caesar annually and was then issued a certificate of compliance. Christians refused to burn incense and say "Caesar is Lord." As a result, they suffered intensely.

Christ as First and Last (2:8). This designation reminds the persecuted church that Christ is sovereign, the Creator, and also Lord of history.

A crown of life for the faithful (2:10). Garlands of perishable flowers were worn by those worshiping pagan gods and goddesses. Those who persevere in their worship of Christ are given a very different crown — a crown of endless life.

Pergamum: moral compromise (2:12-17).

Pergamum too was a center of emperor worship, but also of Zeus and Aeselepius: truly "Satan's throne."

Jesus' sharp sword (2:12). Pergamum was one of a very few cities with the right to impose capital punishment, symbolized by a sword. The church is reminded that Jesus bears a sword too and has a much greater power.

Moral compromise (2:14). Balaam advised King Balak to compromise God's people by drawing Israel into idolatry by enticing them sexually. A similiar thing is happening in Pergamum, many suggest through the enticement of temple priestesses who practiced prostitution as part of religious rites.

"**I will soon come**" **(2:16).** This is not a reference to the Second Coming, but to divine discipline of those Christians who refuse to repent.

Thyatira: doctrinal defection (2:18-29). This inland city was a center of trade in textiles and leather. The church there is criticized for tolerating a woman, symbolically named Jezebel, who promoted false teaching and also immorality.

Fire and bronze (2:18). These aspects of the glorified Christ, only here named the Son of God in Revelation, are associated in both Testaments with judgment.

Refusing to repent (2:21-23). The accusation is addressed to "Jezebel" rather than the church. This self-appointed prophetess is apparently a believer, destined to be severely disciplined by sickness ("cast her on a bed of suffering") and by the death of her "children" (followers?).

Church	Characteristic	Description of Jesus	Desired Response
Ephesus, the Steadfast (2:1-7)	Works hard, perseveres, rejects the wicked, endures, but left its first love	He walks among the seven lamps (is in heaven)	Return to first love
Smyrna, the Persecuted (2:8-11)	Suffers, is in poverty, endures persecution	He who died, is alive again	Remain faithful
Pergamum, the Morally Compromising (2:12-17)	Remains true, is faithful to death, but tolerates immorality	He holds a sharp, double-edged sword	Repent of evil ways
Thyatira, the Doctrinally Compromising (2:18-29)	Does more than at first, but tolerates immorality, false doctrine	Eyes of fire, feet of bronze	Hold to the truth

Outline
Place
Finder

JESUS
LETTERS
JUDGMENT
RETURN
NEW HEAVEN

Chapter summary. This chapter continues the messages the glorified Christ is sending via John to contemporary churches. The letters in this chapter are addressed to believers in Sardis, Philadephia, and Laodicea (see map, p. 909). Like the letters in chapter 2, these messages have a distinct pattern.

Each letter is addressed to the "angel" or "messenger" of the church. Again each message has a fourfold focus: identifying Jesus in a special way, revealing an intimate knowledge of the church addressed, pinpointing the church's major flaw, conveying a command intended to correct the church. The letter closes with an eschatological promise of reward to the obedient victor with each promise alluding to some element in Revelation 21–22. Key elements in each letter are summarized on the chart on page 911.

Key verse. 3:15: Jesus knows.

Personal application. We can apply the exhortation given to each of these churches to our lives—and win the reward they are promised.

INSIGHT

Sardis: the counterfeit (3:1-6). Sardis lay in an important river valley and was both a trade and military center. Although its greatest significance lay in the past, and in a sense the city was dying, it remained prosperous for some two centuries into the Christian era.

Holding the sevenfold Spirit (3:1). The Spirit is the key to vitality in the Christian life. Remain faithful to Jesus, and He will bring us to vital life. Desert Him and our lives will be as dead as those who lay in the vast cemetery, marked by hundreds of burial mounds, some seven miles from Sardis, but visible from that city.

"Wake up!" (3:2) The call is for constant alertness, just the opposite of the spiritual lethargy which sapped the vitality of the church at Sardis. The situation is so serious that the first order of business is to "strengthen what remains" rather than recapture an earlier commitment. Even their past deeds are "not complete," probably meaning they fall short of the standards of love, faithfulness, perseverance, and commitment required of Christians.

"They are worthy" (3:4). Even in an apostate church or age, God reserves some who are faithful to Him. Soiled clothing in the 1st century kept a person from ceremonies honoring pagan deities. There is likely a touch of irony here. The pagans worried about externals. What Christ cares about is whether a person "walks with" (stays in fellowship with) Him.

Philadelphia: obedient to God (3:7-13). This was an important fortress city on a major highway and an imperial post road. Although devastated in A.D. 17 by an earthquake, the city was quickly rebuilt. Eusebius reports that the church was led in the first half of the 2nd century by a gifted prophetess named Ammia and prospered under her leadership.

Faithful with little (3:8). However weak we are, Christ keeps the door open for us. We can remain faithful, not because we are great, but because He will not let our enemies prevail.

"Endure patiently" (3:10). It's much easier to be enthusiastic when we're winning great victories. But often faith calls for a holding action, and obedience means simply to keep "My command to endure patiently" (cf. 2 Thes. 3:5; Heb. 12:3).

"The hour of trial" (3:10). Most take this as a time of serious, worldwide divine judgment. Some premillennialists see here evidence that the rapture of Christians will take place before the tribulation (»pp. 626, 823).

Laodicea: lukewarm (3:14-21). This city was famous for wealth and medicines, particularly an eye ointment. The Christians of this city took pride in their material well-being, without seeing their spiritual poverty. Jesus warns these believers to spend their funds on the true riches Christ provides.

Jesus is eager to enter and fill their lives and ours. He knocks at the door of our hearts. It's up to us to open up our lives and let Him in, not to save, but to fill and control.

910

Another Approach to the Seven Churches

Some commentators have taken the seven churches of Revelation as contemporary churches which double as symbols of the Christian church through the ages. According to this view each church represents a period in church history, during which Christianity itself is marked by the characteristics specified in the related letter. Usually those who take this view related each church of Revelation 2–3 to the following periods.

Ephesus   The Apostolic Age
Smyrna   The post-apostolic era of persecution
Pergamum   The Catholic era, during which the priesthood developed
Thyatira   The Dark Ages
Sardis   The Reformation
Philadelphia The "true church" of every age
Laodicea   The "lukewarm" church of the twentieth century

Church	Characteristic	Description of Jesus	Desired Response
Sardis, the Counterfeit (3:1-6)	Reputed to be alive but spiritually dead, deeds are incomplete	Holds the Spirit, angels, in His hand	Wake up, obey what they have already heard
Philadelphia, the Obedient (3:7-13)	Has little strength yet has kept the Word, patiently endures	Holds the key of David (messianic authority)	Hold tight to what they have
Laodicea, the Materialistic (3:14-22)	Neither cold nor hot wealthy, but poor spiritually	Ruler of creation	Be earnest, repent under discipline

Chapter summary. John is taken up to heaven to be given a vision of "what must take place after this" (4:1). He sees God in His throne, worshiped by 24 persons identified only as "elders" (vv. 2-6a). The "living creatures" seen around the throne are familiar from the earlier visions of Isaiah (6:2) and Ezekiel (1:5-25; 10:1-22), continuously praising God as Creator and affirming His holiness (4:6b-11). Then John sees an angel, holding a scroll representing judgment, sealed with seven seals, calling for someone worthy to break the seals and open the book (5:1-2). When no one is found, one of the elders consoles John: the Lion of the tribe of Judah will open the seals—and when John looks, he sees a bloody Lamb (vv. 3-7). When Christ as the Lamb takes the scroll, the whole company falls down in worship, affirming His worthiness "because . . . with Your blood You purchased men for God" (vv. 8-10). Unnumbered thousands of angels take up the chorus, praising the Lord as the universe joins in ascribing "praise and honor and glory and power, for ever and ever" (vv. 11-14).

Key verse. 5:9: Salvation's new song.

Personal application. Lift heart and voice and join the chorus.

Key concepts. Heaven »p. 609. Holy »p. 372. Praise »p. 380. Blood »pp. 85, 766. Priesthood of believers »p. 880.

INSIGHT

Two interpretations. The *premillennialist* sees the call to "come up" as the rapture and all that happens after as located in the Great Tribulation. The scroll is related to Dan. 7:13-14 and is seen as the title deed to the kingdom Christ will win through judgment. *Amillennialists* see the vision as a call to worship, with the elders representing O.T. and N.T. saints. The scroll is a symbol of redemption, and thus the vision may be of what takes place in heaven just after the resurrected Christ returned to heaven.

Praise. Whatever the interpretation, it's clear that the focus of these chapters is the five hymns of praise they contain. In chap. 4 God is praised as holy and as Creator. In chap. 5 Christ is praised as Saviour, the Lamb who was slain and thus earned the right to open the sealed scroll.

"The 24 elders" (4:4, 10). The elders mentioned here reappear again and again in John's vision. But who are they? Over a dozen suggestions have been made. Some suggest that they are representatives of redeemed humanity, 12 representing O.T. saints and 12 N.T. saints. Others consider them supernatural beings, like the four "living creatures." This is

supported by the fact that they are never included with "the saints" (5:8; 11:16-18; 19:1-4).

"The living creatures" (4:7-9). See Cherubim, »p. 491.

A seven-sealed scroll (5:1). A scroll that was sealed could only be read when all the seals were opened. Only when judgment has been fully executed will the ultimate intent of God be revealed.

Lion and Lamb (5:5-6). The jolt implied in looking for a Lion and seeing a bloody Lamb is intended. Both "Lion of Judah" and "Root of David" are titles of the conquering Messiah. The vision reminds us that Jesus conquered by giving His life for us. The bloodstained Lamb, still bearing the visible marks of His execution, is about to be revealed as the executor of God's final judgment!

"A new song" (5:9). The song is "new" in that it has never been heard before. At last, the full meaning of the redemptive death of Christ is about to be displayed—both in salvation and in judgment. Soon all will be forced to acknowledge that Jesus, who died a criminal's death, is worthy to rule this universe and the next.

Chapter summary. Jesus, the Lamb, now begins to open the seals on the scroll. As the first four are opened: terrible horsemen representing conquest (6:1-2), devastating warfare (vv. 3-4), famine (vv. 5-6), and plague (vv. 7-8). These bear a striking resemblance to signs spoken of by Christ in Matthew 24:1-35, Mark 13:1-37, and Luke 21:5-33. The fifth seal reveals martyrs, crying out for God to judge and avenge them (6:9-11).

When the sixth seal is opened earth and even the heavens are shaken, as if by a great earthquake (vv. 12-14). Humanity then realizes that this is divine judgment. Rather than repent, king and peasant alike seek to hide from God's wrath (vv. 15-17).

Outline
Place
Finder

JESUS
LETTERS
JUDGMENT
RETURN
NEW HEAVEN

Key verse. 6:17: Too late!

Personal application. Those who reject grace now will not repent when judgment comes.

Illustration. *Detail from "The Four Horsemen of the Apocalypse," a painting by artist Paul Richards, in* The Revell Bible Dictionary, *p. 862.*

INSIGHT

Two interpretations. The *premillennialist* links this passage with Matt. 24:5-8 and sees it as describing events preceding the appearance of the Antichrist. These preliminary judgments are thought to continue from Rev. 6 through 12. *Amillennialists* take this as a symbolic representation of the struggle of the Gospel in a hostile world, to culminate in God's final judgment over sin. The chapter thus is a "nutshell" view of history from the Cross to the Second Coming.

"A white horse" (6:2). Because the horse is "white" some take this rider to be Christ. Others see the rider as the Antichrist, whose instruments are war, plague, and famine.

Food prices (6:5-6). The prices reported show an inflation rate of 1,200 percent over the 1st-century norm. Famine is driving up the cost of

staples needed for survival by the poor, while the rich still enjoy their wine and other luxuries.

The souls under the altar (6:9). Some take these as martyrs who lose their lives in the Tribulation period, while others see them as martyrs from the very beginning of sacred history. "Souls" here means "persons," the normal meaning of the Gk. *psyche.* Why are they "under" the altar? Perhaps because they are covered by the sacrificial blood of heaven's Lamb.

"The sixth seal" (6:12-14). The O.T. "Day of the Lord" is frequently characterized as a time of earthquake, falling stars, and terror on earth. This imagery is very familiar to readers of such passages as Isa. 2:10, 19, 21; 13:10; 34:4; Jer. 4:29; Ezek. 32:7-8; Joel 2:31; 3:15; Zeph. 1:14-18; Matt. 24:29; etc.

Chapter summary. Now there is a pause in the blows that have been striking the earth. The judgments are held back while 144,000 Israelites, 12,000 from each of 12 tribes, are sealed and commissioned as servants of God (7:1-8). When John looks back toward heaven he sees a vast multitude of the saved, standing before the throne and the Lamb—the source of salvation (vv. 9-10). The angels, elders, and four living creatures join the throng in praising God (vv. 11-12), and one of the elders explains the multitude to John. They are those who have believed during the Great Tribulation. Freed from all suffering, they serve God in His temple (vv. 13-17).

Key verse. 7:14: Identity defined.

Personal application. Read Revelation carefully, and many of John's visions can be understood.

Key concepts. Angels »p. 521. Israel »pp. 53, 745. Salvation »pp. 426, 742, 744, 841. Tribulation »p. 626.

INSIGHT

Two interpretations. The *premillennialist* takes the Jewish identity of the 144,000 literally and understands them to be Jewish converts who serve as missionaries during the Tribulation period (cf. Dan. 12:3). The multitude are understood, as the Rev. text states, as those saved through faith in Christ during the Great Tribulation spoken of by Jesus and the Old Testament prophets. *Amillennialists* see the number as symbolic, a "perfect" number, and thus representing the church throughout all history. The careful specification of tribes is dismissed on the basis of Gal. 3:28: that in Christ there "is neither Jew, nor Greek." The multitude are the whole company of the saved in heaven.

"Four corners of the earth" (7:1). This phrase was used in the ancient Near East to mean "the whole world." It does *not* imply a belief that the earth is flat, anymore than our use of "sunrise" indicates we believe the sun revolves around the earth.

Eye of the hurricane (7:2). The great hush that falls on earth indicates a lull in the divine judgments, but their suspension is only temporary.

Sealed (7:3). Commentators argue over the identity of this group that is "sealed" by God. But the seal itself surely represents both God's ownership (cf. 14:1) and His protection from demonic forces (cf. 9:4), although not apparently from human opponents (cf. 13:7; 20:4).

The 144,000 (7:4-8). The specific identification of this number as Israelites, and their makeup from 12 specific tribes, makes it difficult to believe these are "the new Israel" composed of the "completed church composed of Jew and Gentile." Such an allegorical interpretation is made even more unlikely by reference in 7:14 to "the Great Tribulation," which is so significant in O.T. prophecy and predicted by Jesus in Matt. 24.

"Every nation, tribe, people, and language" (7:9). This verse is a favorite text of some missionaries who argue from it that the Gospel must be heard by all peoples before Christ can return.

This application falls short on two counts. Theologians agree that those who die in infancy are covered by the blood of Christ. Thus, those from every nation, tribe, people, and language are *already* represented among the saved. Secondly, the text identifies this "great multitude" as those who "have come out of the great tribulation" (v. 14).

"Wearing white robes" (7:9). In Rev. white robes typically represent the saved, clothed in righteousness by Christ.

The Great Tribulation (7:16). The theme of a period of intense, worldwide suffering from war and "natural disasters," is deeply rooted in the O.T. prophet's vision of history's end. Christ also predicted the appearance of the Antichrist just before His return, and said "then there will be great distress [*thlipsis*: tribulation], unequaled from the beginning of the world until now—and never to be equaled again" (Matt. 24:21). In view of the extensive testimony to such a period in both Testaments, it seems unwise to understand the elder's explanation to John here in an allegorical way.

"God will wipe away every tear" (7:17). Life in every age involves suffering and pain. Yet our destiny is to be shepherded by the Lamb and filled with joy.

Chapter summary. When the seventh seal on the scroll introduced in chapter 5 is opened, a new series of "trumpet" judgments is begun (8:1-6). The trumpet judgments devastate a third of earth's vegetation (v. 7), seas (vv. 8-9), and fresh water (vv. 10-11), as well as a third of the heavenly bodies (vv. 12-13). Yet these judgments that shake the foundations of the material universe seem insignificant compared to what is to follow. Now the boundary between the supernatural and natural universe is breached; locust-like, demonic beings are unleashed to torture humankind (9:1-12). The sixth trumpet unleashes four unspeakably evil powers, with 200 million minions, who kill a third of humankind (vv. 13-19). Yet, despite these terrors, the rest of humanity did not repent but rededicated themselves to idolatry and immorality (vv. 20-21).

Key verse. 9:20: Even horrors don't bring repentance.

Personal application. Stephen King's dark visions are not half as bad as what the future holds for the lost.

Key concepts. Angels »p. 521. Demons »p. 659. Repentance »p. 780.

INSIGHT

Two interpretations. The *premillennialist* takes the terrible scenes drawn in these chapters as descriptions of the initial judgments of the Tribulation period. The demonic enemies of chap. 9 introduce a supernatural yet literal aspect to these judgments. Humanity's refusal to repent, even though what is happening is clearly supernatural in character, is a further indication of how warped sinful human nature really is. *Amillennialists* take chap. 8 as the third of seven parallel representations of divine judgment. No sequence of events is implied. These are simply another way of saying that God as Judge uses natural disasters to foreshadow final judgment. Chapter 9 is taken to represent the present time, and the various beings are demonic, antichristian forces in society.

The prayers of all the saints (8:4). The incense represents the prayers of the believers of all time for vindication, to be won when God judges the inhabitants of the earth and avenges the blood of the saints (cf. 6:10).

The scattering of hot coals and fire from the altar of incense represents God's answer: the time of judgment is now.

"Trumpets" (8:6). Ram's horn trumpets were used in O.T. times to alert the population to imminent danger and to invasion.

Three series of judgments. These series feature seven seals (chap. 6), seven trumpets (chaps. 8–9), and seven bowls (chaps. 15–16). While there are similarities between these judgments, each sequence increases in intensity, and the bowl judgments are called the "last plagues" that complete God's expression of wrath.

How literally are images in these chapters to be understood? This question is raised by John's description of "hail and fire mixed with blood" and of "something like a huge mountain, all ablaze" falling into the sea. Part of the difficulty in interpreting any prophecy rests on the normal limitations of terms and images available to the writer. For instance, how would a 1st-century person ever be able to describe the crowded expressways, the busy airports, the TV, and space shuttles of the 20th century? The very fact that he would have to use the terms and concepts of his century mean that even though describing something quite literal, his explanation simply *could not* convey a clear image of what he saw to his contemporaries. Even if we assume that John is describing actual events that he witnessed, the language limitations alone would make it difficult for us to develop a clear, accurate impression of what he saw.

"The Abyss" (9:1). The *abyssos* is a Gk. term for the underworld, the place of the dead. The N.T. pictures the Abyss as a prison, smoldering with subterranean fires, where demons are held captive (cf. Luke 8:31; 2 Peter 2:4; Jude 6). John witnesses the opening of the Abyss and the release of hordes of demons to torment the lost. Those whom God has sealed, however, are safe from them (cf. 7:3). The size of the horde of demons given in 9:16 has led some to argue the number is symbolic.

Outline
Place
Finder

JESUS
LETTERS
JUDGMENT
RETURN
NEW HEAVEN

Chapter summary. Again John looks away from what is happening on earth. He sees a "mighty angel" approaching from heaven. The angel stands, straddling earth and sea and holds a "little scroll" (10:1-2). The announcement made at his appearance is sealed—kept secret (vv. 3-4). Yet it is no secret that "there will be no more delay": the day of judgment predicted by the Old Testament prophets has come (vv. 5-7). John is then told to take the scroll the angel holds and "eat" it. Thus prepared by appropriating God's Word, John is told to speak out again, describing events as they touch on "many peoples, nations, languages, and kings" (vv. 8-11).

Key verse. 10:6: The end has come!

Personal application. Take advantage of every delay to share Christ now.

Key concepts. Heaven »p. 609. Mystery »pp. 514, 615. Prophets »p. 131.

INSIGHT

Two interpretations. The *premillennialist* sees this as an interlude, intended to prepare John for the final, bitter revelations to come. *Amillennialists* agree this is an interlude, but take it as a promise that God will not abandon His own as they await the judgment that will come at time's end.

The angel (10:1). The angel is not named, but his portrayal suggests he is a very significant being. Some have identified him with Christ, but in Rev. Christ and angels are always distinct and carefully identified.

"Seal up" (10:3-4). The phrase means to keep secret. Some have speculated that the words of the thunders concerned additional judgments. However, this is pure speculation and remains a mystery. God does not reveal everything He intends to do, even in symbolic or masked terms.

Raising the right hand (10:6). When the Jewish people swore an oath they typically raised their right hand (cf. Deut. 32:40; Dan. 12:7). The angel conveys God's promise that there will be no more waiting: the "mystery of God" will be accomplished.

"The mystery of God" (10:7). Here "mystery" does not indicate a revelation of something that has been hidden, but the fulfillment of prophetic visions whose realization has been delayed. Again John specifically links the revelations in this book with the visions of the future reported by O.T. prophets. It is difficult to see how Rev. could be interpreted accurately except within the framework of O.T. prophecy concerning history's end.

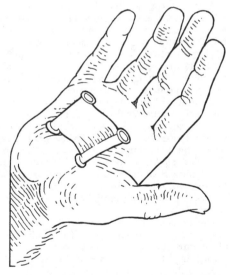

Illustration (10:2, 9-10). The "little scroll" that is open in the angel's hand represents the revelations that John is about to be given. Ezekiel 2:9–3:3 depicts a similar scene, where "eating" the scroll symbolizes receiving and appropriating God's Word—in essence, making what God has said a part of oneself. Only when we so "digest" God's Word will we be able to minister it effectively. In this case, the digested word turns the stomach sour. Many terrors lie ahead.

Chapter summary. John is now given a rod with which to measure the Jerusalem temple and its altar (11:1). He is told that the Gentiles will dominate the city of Jerusalem for 42 months, the same length of time that John says the beast (the Antichrist) will rule (cf. 13:5-7). During this period two witnesses, men given power to bring drought and destroy those who attack them, will serve as God's witnesses in the holy city (11:2-6). At the end of that time they will be killed, and the evil inhabitants of earth will celebrate their deaths (vv. 7-10). Three and a half days later they will return to life and be lifted up into heaven, while the earth quakes and terrified survivors are forced to acknowledge God's hand at work (vv. 11-14).

At this point the seventh trumpet is sounded by an angel, and voices in heaven announce the beginning of the reign of God. The barrier between material and spiritual universe is rent, and lightning can be seen flashing around God's heavenly temple (vv. 15-19).

Outline
Place
Finder

JESUS
LETTERS
JUDGMENT
RETURN
NEW HEAVEN

Key verse. 11:15: Jesus will reign.

Personal application. Defeats today are nothing compared to the total victory which is soon to come.

Key concepts. Temple »p. 283. Gentiles »p. 798. Antichrist »pp. 522, 828. Kingdom »pp. 380, 443, 620.

INSIGHT

Two interpretations. The *premillennialist* takes the two witnesses as real persons, who testify in Jerusalem for a literal three and a half year span before being killed by the Antichrist, at the end of the first half of the Tribulation period predicted in the O.T. *Amillennialists* view the three and a half year period as symbolic. They suggest it is drawn from the story of Elijah and represents affliction. The trampling of Jerusalem represents pseudo-Christianity, while the two witnesses represent the whole church infused by the Holy Spirit. The "death" of the witnesses pictures the church, silenced by tribulation, and their restoration indicates vindication of believers by God.

Altar and temple (11:1). The use of *naos*, which indicates the temple sanctuary where only priests were allowed, and the reference to a measuring rod (cf. Ezek. 40:5), make it more likely the passage speaks of a Jewish temple in Jerusalem, not the believer as the living temple of the Holy Spirit.

42 months and 1,260 days (11:2-3). The times mentioned here in Rev. are so closely linked with numbers given in Dan. 9:27 and Dan. 12 that it seems unrealistic to intepret this passage in any other context than that provided by O.T. prophecy.

The two witnesses (11:3). These individuals are not named. Many writers on prophecy suggest they are Enoch and Elijah, the only two persons in history caught up into heaven without first experiencing physical death (Gen. 5:24; 2 Kings 2:11-12). Jewish tradition predicted Moses and Elijah would return before the Messiah appeared in power.

The city where Christ died (11:6). Jerusalem is the seat of the Antichrist's power at this time. Thus it is "figuratively" Sodom (immorality and rebellion) and Egypt (the world and slavery).

The beast from the Abyss (11:7). This "beast" is further described in chaps. 13 and 17. The phrase "from the Abyss" shows the origin of his powers. Most take him to be the Antichrist, who is empowered by Satan (cf. Dan. 7:21).

The television age? (11:9) Past generations speculated how it might be possible for persons from "every people, tribe, language, and nation" to "gaze on" the bodies of the two witnesses. Today, in a world familiar with TV satellite links, this once thought to be impossible viewing is easily understood.

The seventh trumpet (11:15-19). Voices in heaven now announce that God's final triumph is at hand. This kingdom is not the hidden rule of God over the universe or over the church, but Christ's soon-to-be visible, literal earthly kingdom of O.T. prophecy.

917

Outline
Place
Finder

JESUS
LETTERS
JUDGMENT
RETURN
NEW HEAVEN

Chapter summary. John now sees visions that are clearly symbolic in nature. A pregnant woman is pursued by "an enormous red dragon." The woman gives birth to a son destined to rule the nations with an iron scepter, a clear reference to the Messiah (cf. Ps. 2:9). After God snatches the child up to heaven, the woman flees into the desert, to hide for the 1,260 days mentioned in 11:3 (12:1-6). John also sees war in heaven, with the great dragon, Satan, hurled to earth with his followers (vv. 7-9). This triumph is celebrated by a voice in heaven, which also depicts Satan's fury (vv. 10-12). In frustration Satan pursues the "woman who had given birth to the child" and also makes war on all the saints (vv. 13-17).

Key verse. 12:11: Satan is overcome.

Personal application. Rely on the blood of Christ and treat Satan as a defeated enemy.

Key concepts. Heaven »pp. 437, 609. Blood »p. 766. Satan »p. 501.

INSIGHT

Two interpretations. The *premillennialist* sees the woman as the Jewish people who are preserved from Satan's attacks during the last half of the Tribulation period (1,260 days) foretold by Daniel. Satan's virulent anti-Semitism is redirected toward all believers in these last days of world history. *Amillennialists* also take the woman to be Israel, representing the idealized church of the O.T. The war in heaven pictures Jesus' victory at Calvary, and the whole chapter restates the book's theme using different symbols. Despite Satan's hatred, the church will be preserved and triumph.

"A woman" (12:1-2, 5). The woman represents Israel, from whom Christ came. The later hostility directed toward her reminds us that anti-Semitism is satanic in origin and that God's O.T. people remain precious to Him.

Time frame (12:4-6). The birth of the boy child and his being caught up into heaven are clear references to Christ's incarnation and ascension. Yet John quickly shifts back to the Tribulation period, as indicated by reference to the 1,260 days. However, it is characteristic of all biblical prophecy that little attention is given to sequence or timing of predicted events.

Satan cast out of heaven (12:7-9). No time is specified for the battle in heaven described here. Jewish apocalyptic writings held that the archangel Michael, identified here by name, would cast Satan from heaven in the first great battle to establish the Messiah's kingdom.

Triumph (12:10-12). The foundation for Christ's triumph was laid, and the death knell of Satan's power sounded, at the Cross. Until Christ does set up His kingdom here, we continue to triumph in His name.

Chapter summary. John now observes two beasts come on the scene. The first comes from the sea, his form reminiscent of Daniel 7's description of Gentile world powers (13:1-2). This beast, the Antichrist, is empowered by Satan. He quickly wins a worldwide following that succumbs to his demand for worship (vv. 3-4). Again a 42-month period is mentioned, this time as the period during which the beast rules on the earth. Only those who believe in Christ resist his influence, and many saints will be martyred for their faithfulness to the Lord (vv. 5-10).

John then sees a second beast, who serves the first beast and performs miracles on his behalf. This evil individual sets up an image of the Antichrist to be worshiped and organizes society so that only those who express allegiance to the Antichrist can buy or sell (vv. 11-17). The chapter concludes with a mysterious clue to the Antichrist's name: the number 666 (v. 18).

Key verse. 13:5: Faith preserves us.

Personal application. Miracles may prove supernatural empowerment. They don't prove what supernatural power is involved!

INSIGHT

Two interpretations. The *premillennialist* sees these symbolic "beasts" as specific individuals who have important roles in the Tribulation period. The first beast is identified as the Antichrist (cf. 2 Thes. 2). They believe he will unite the Common Market countries (the ten horns, or governments) and so reconstitute the old Roman Empire. The second beast is called the false prophet. With Satan these three form an unholy trinity, a mockery and counterfeit of Father, Son, and Holy Spirit.

Amillennialists see simply a symbolic representation of Satan's endless attack on the church. The first beast may represent antichristian governments, while the second represents false teachers. The 42 months represents the whole Gospel Age.

"A beast" (13:1-2). This being is mentioned at least 12 more times in Rev. His identi-

fication as the Antichrist appears early in church history and was discussed extensively by Irenaeus about A.D. 190. This view seems supported by Paul's teaching in 2 Thes. 2.

Others, in the past, have identified the beast with Nero, Rome, the Pope, Hitler, and others.

The Lamb's Book of Life (13:8). Faith in Christ protects us from being deceived.

The beast from the land (13:11). In other passages this beast is called "the false prophet" (cf. 16:13; 19:20; 20:10). While he imitates the Lamb, his voice "is like the dragon." Those who take this beast as a movement rather than an individual see counterfeit religion here.

No one buy or sell (13:16-17). The mechanisms needed to instantaneously identify persons by number, and to control earnings and bank accounts electronically, are in place even now.

Outline
Place
Finder

JESUS
LETTERS
JUDGMENT
RETURN
NEW HEAVEN

Chapter summary. The actors in the drama have been introduced in chapters 7, 12, and 13, and the situation on an earth dominated by evil has been clearly drawn. John sees the Lamb on earth, surrounded by the 144,000, who sing His praise. Their work on earth is apparently complete (14:1-5). As John watches he sees three angels fly over the earth calling on mankind to worship God (vv. 6-7), announcing the fall of Babylon the Great (v. 8) and the doom of those who worship and follow the beast (vv. 9-11), as well as the blessing of those who remain faithful to Jesus (vv. 12-13). Then John sees another terrible sight: an angel emerges from God's temple and calls on waiting angels to begin the final harvest of earth's rebellious millions (vv. 14-20).

Key verse. 14:13: Rest at last.

Personal application. Blessing and rest follow for the believer who remains faithful to Jesus.

Key concepts. Judgment »pp. 372, 724, 827. Worship »p. 380. Wrath of God »pp. 65, 72.

INSIGHT

Two interpretations. The *premillennialist* sees here a preview of the ultimate expression of the wrath of God, with details to be developed in the following chapters. *Amillennialists* see yet another parallel restatement of this apocalyptic book's many images of final judgment. The elements in this chapter are understood as representing the purity of the church, despite her association during this age with a secular, pagan society. Babylon represents all the ungodly powers of that society, whose members are destined for destruction.

"Mount Zion" (14:1). Five of the seven references to Mt. Zion in the N.T. quote O.T. passages. There Mt. Zion is a poetic name for Jerusalem as the site of Israel's temple. There too Mt. Zion is the location to which the Messiah will gather the redeemed (cf. Ps. 48:1; Isa. 24:23; Joel 2:32; Obad. 17; Micah 4:1, 7; Zech. 14:10). Jewish apocalyptic writings also placed the Messiah on Mt. Zion. The imagery seems to stress Christ calling His own to Him where He can protect and bless them.

A private new song (14:3-5). The indication that only this group could sing this particular "new song" suggests this is the same 144,000 described in Rev. 7, who have completed the mission for which they were called and sealed.

Defile with women (14:4). As nowhere in the Bible is sex within marriage spoken of as defiling, the reference must be to illicit sex. God's servants of every age must be pure.

Worship Him (14:6). Even on the eve of judgment, lost humanity is invited to turn and worship the Lord. Judgment is sure. But so is grace.

"Babylon the Great" (14:8). Ancient Babylon (Babel) was the first center of human civilization (Gen. 11:1-9) and in O.T. times the center of an autocratic world empire. In Rev. Babylon is a symbol of that world power destined to exist at history's end (Rev. 17–19). Like Nebuchadnezzar's Babylon, symbolic Babylon represents centralized power (cf. 14:8; 17:1, 15-18) which produces great material prosperity (18:3, 11-19). That Babylon is also a corrupt religious system and enemy of God's people. Babylon the Great, in all its expressions, is destined for total destruction.

Forced choice (14:9-13). As events move toward total world dominion by the Antichrist, and he exerts control over humanity by requiring every person's registration with his (the Antichrist's) mark on forehead or hand, it becomes utterly necessary to make a choice between good and evil. A person who accepts the mark of the beast can do business and buy and sell. The person who does not is deprived of even the most basic rights. Thus it "calls for patient endurance" for the living saints to obey God. But even death will be a blessing to those who choose God, for in death they will find rest and reward. Resist evil with everything you have. The day will come when no one will be able to compromise.

Streets filled with blood (14:14-20). We draw back from the overwhelming image of miles of blood flowing from crushed human beings. But the real horror is their sin, not their judgment.

920

Chapter summary. The devastating judgments resume as seven final plagues are launched (15:1), while victorious saints in heaven praise God for His deeds (vv. 2-5). Seven angels emerge from the heavenly temple bearing bowls "filled with the wrath of God" (vv. 6-8), to be directed against those who bear the mark of the beast (16:1-2). Painful sores break out on humans and earth's seas and waters are turned to blood (vv. 3-4), as an angel proclaims the justice of these judgments (vv. 5-7).

The judgments then continue. The sun swells and intense heat scorches the earth (vv. 8-9). All becomes dark, and men twist in agony but continue to curse God (vv. 10-11). Then the waters of the Euphrates dry up, and a vast army is recruited by demonic beings for a last great battle against God at Armageddon (vv. 12-16). When the final bowl is emptied earth itself is shattered: great fissures open, cities crumble and mountains fall as huge hailstones pummel the broken land. Yet the remainder of humankind continues to curse God (vv. 17-21).

Outline
Place
Finder

JESUS
LETTERS
JUDGMENT
RETURN
NEW HEAVEN

Key verse. 15:1: History approaches its end.

Personal application. Read these chapters through for a sense of what God's judgment of sin will mean.

Key concepts. Angel »p. 521. Antichrist »p. 522. Lamb »pp. 38, 912. Wrath of God »pp. 65, 72. Judgment »pp. 372, 724, 827.

INSIGHT

Two interpretations. The *premillennialist* sees these as overwhelming but literal descriptions of what will happen near the end of the Tribulation period. *Amillennialists* see these as symbolic but not literal images of divine judgment.

Preparation (chap. 15). This chapter describes the preparations in heaven for the unleashing of God's culminating judgment. The saints who have been butchered during the Tribulation now stand before God's throne, their faithfulness to death itself a victory over the Antichrist. They praise God for the deeds that will show Him both true to His Word and just (cf. p. 372).

The seven angels emerge from God's temple. In Scripture, visions which place the Lord in His holy temple speak of judgment rather than worship (cf. Micah 1:2; Hab. 2:20).

"Blood to drink" (16:5-6). The angel's pronouncement shows the balance of divine judgment. The followers of the Antichrist have shed the blood of God's saints, and now they are given nothing but water turned to blood to drink. The principle is stated in 2 Thes. 1:6: "God is just: He will pay back trouble to those who trouble you and give relief to you who are troubled." Pay back isn't revenge, it's justice.

Cursing God (16:9). It is typical of sinners to blame others for the consequences of their own choices. Here again we see the extreme grip that sin has on humankind. There is no hint of repentance, no hint of willingness to acknowledge that what is happening to them is just.

"Armageddon" (16:16). The location of Armageddon is uncertain, although many identify it with the valley in Galilee that lies below the fortified city of Megiddo. The name itself, however, may be symbolic, drawn from Heb. roots that might mean "Mountain of Attack," or "Destroying Mountain," or perhaps "Mount of Assembly" (of troops).

The point, however, is that man's armies gather, coming primarily from the lands beyond the Euphrates, that we today identify as Iraq, Iran, and parts of Russia, to battle against God. It is then as the final bowl is emptied that earth itself is shattered and man's army assaulted with giant hailstones.

For a fascinating apparent parallel, read Ezek. 38–39.

"It is done!" (16:17) This announcement makes it clear that chaps. 15 and 16 have provided an overview of the final judgment destined to strike earth. In the next chapters John will go back and examine in detail the impact of these judgments on the corrupt human religion and society, as represented in Babylon the Great.

921

Outline
Place
Finder

JESUS
LETTERS
JUDGMENT
RETURN
NEW HEAVEN

Chapter summary. John again sees a vision whose major elements are interpreted within the text. A "great prostitute" is a city seated on seven hills, who rides the Antichrist to power and then is destroyed by him. John first describes "the great prostitute" (17:1-6) and goes on to interpret the vision (vv. 7-18), identifying the beast, his drive toward power, and his subsequent turning on the "prostitute" when absolute power is his.

Key verse. 17:18: The woman identified.

Personal application. Don't be surprised at society's growing hostility toward Christianty and complacent acceptance of false religions.

INSIGHT

Two interpretations. *Premillennialists* see "mystery Babylon," the "great prostitute," as the religious dimension of future human society. They expect a "one world" religion in the West will accompany political unification under the Antichrist and will support his drive toward power. But when the Antichrist has achieved power, he will overthrow the state church and insist that the world worship him. *Amillennialists* have identified the woman with false religions in the world throughout history and today.

Babylon city? Dr. Alan Johnson (Wheaton College) suggests that Babylon city represents all historic expressions of idolatrous civilizations. He sees their characteristics as splendor combined with prosperity and overabundance and luxury (Jer. 51:13; Ezek. 16:13, 49; Rev. 18:3, 7); as self-trust or boastfulness (Isa. 14:12-14; Jer. 50:31; Ezek. 16:15, 50); as power and violence directed against God's people (Jer. 51:35; Ezek. 23:37; Nahum 3:1-3; Rev. 18:10, 24); as oppression and injustice (Isa. 14:4; Ezek. 16:49; 28:18; Rev. 18:5, 20); and as idolatry (Jer. 51:47; Ezek. 16:17, 36; 23:26, 30; Nahum 1:14; Rev. 17:4-5).

The mystery of the beast (17:7-9). Many commentators have gone to great lengths to identify this beast and have taken the seven hills as Rome. But the "hills" are *ore*, mountains, which in the prophets are symbols of world powers. The point is that the nature of the power that supports the prostitute religion is political, while the spiritual source of that power is satanic. Unlike Christ, "who is, and who was, and who is to come" (Rev. 1:8), the beast "once was, now is not, and will come up (17:8). The beast, like all powers of evil defeated at Calvary, is now an empty shell and yet is permitted a brief time to struggle against God at history's end. The Antichrist and his followers will make war against the Lamb and will be overcome (17:14).

Illustration. *The woman riding the beast is more than an allegory of the relationship between the Antichrist and a counterfeit world religion. It is also a picture of the relationship between the state and religion itself. Secular power is always willing to use religion for its own purposes. But when religion lets itself be used by accepting state support, it seals its own doom.*

Chapter summary. John sees yet another angel who announces the fall of Babylon the Great, the great satanic system of evil that corrupts every human society: a blend of religion and political power, a composite of swirling desires and passions, a web of institutions that befit the powerful and oppress the weak. This system is pictured as a great commercial city, whose fall is celebrated in heaven and bewailed on earth.

Outline
Place
Finder

JESUS
LETTERS
JUDGMENT
RETURN
NEW HEAVEN

First comes the announcement: "Fallen is Babylon the Great" (18:1-3). In a warning intended for John's readers, another angel calls God's people to "come out of her," separating themselves from Babylon in all her forms (vv. 4-8). The viewpoint then shifts. Her fall is lamented by the kings of the earth who tasted her powers (vv. 9-10), the merchants who profited from her passion for luxury and self-indulgence (vv. 11-17), and the seamen who carried her goods (vv. 18-19). But the lament on earth is drowned out by shouts of joy in heaven (v. 20). There, as a parable of the sudden and total destruction to be visited on Babylon, an angel violently hurls a giant boulder into the sea, which swallows it up—and it is gone (vv. 21-24).

Key verse. 18:4: Come out.

Personal application. Don't be caught up in the desires that rule worldly men and women.

Key concepts. Demons »p. 659. Adultery »p. 85. Separation »pp. 87, 761. World »p. 893. Wealth »p. 125. Magic »p. 57.

INSIGHT

Two interpretations. Many *premillennialists* see Babylon as representative of the political and economic powers of the world's nations consolidated under the Antichrist at history's end. This union and all its power is to be destroyed by divine judgment. *Amillennialists* and some *premillennialists* see Babylon as representative of all past, present, and future centers of materialistic human society. Christians must not allow themselves to be seduced.

Babylon's sins (18:3). The verse links spiritual adultery (idolatry) with "excessive luxuries." A focus on material things leads not only to self-indulgence but also to an arrogance which denies any need for God. The worldly person puts his or her hope in possessions and in this sense puts things in the place rightly occupied by God. Idolatry is not just bowing down to images; it is also relying on wealth or power rather than on the Lord.

Sharing in her sins (18:4). The sins of Babylon are sins of worldliness, which 1 John 2:15-17 graphically describes: a craving to satisfy one's passions, a desire to possess the material things seen by the eyes, an arrogance that is based on what a person has and does. When Christians become materialistic and oriented to this world they share in the sins of Babylon—and are in danger of receiving some of her plagues!

An O.T. parallel (18:9-19). Ezekiel 27 is a poem lamenting the fall of Tyre. Both evil Tyre and wicked Babylon are wept over by the people of the world. But the downfall of each is an expression of the just judgment of God.

Bodies and souls of men (18:13). The phrase means "slaves," who are among the luxury items on the list of trade goods in vv. 11-13 coveted by Babylon.

Rejoice saints and apostles (18:20). While others lament the loss of profits the fall of Babylon means, believers are to rejoice that a system so hostile to faith has fallen.

Our American society increasingly has traits in common with Babylon: materialism, a passion for luxury, and growing immorality especially reflected in movies, literature, and contemporary music. Our society too will share Babylon's judgment—perhaps before Christ comes. Let's make sure our allegiance to Christ is so strong that when our Babylon crumbles we will have grace to rejoice.

Chapter summary. Now, truly, the end has come. John hears the roar of a multitude in heaven shouting "Hallelujah!" and praising God for avenging the blood of His servants (19:1-2). The cry is echoed by the worshiping elders (vv. 3-4), and then taken up by the multitude, rejoicing that the ultimate union of believers with the Lord is about to take place (vv. 5-10).

With these announcements made, heaven opens and Christ appears, mounted on a white war-horse, leading the armies of heaven against the nations allied against God (vv. 11-16). An angel calls the carrion birds of heaven to feast on the bodies of the slain (vv. 17-18), but the Antichrist and the false prophet are taken captive and thrown alive into the "fiery lake of burning sulfur" which we call hell (vv. 19-20). The members of their army are slain by Christ's spoken word (v. 21).

Key verse. 19:16: Christ rules.

Personal application. We serve joyfully today for we know that Christ—and we—will triumph tomorrow.

Key concepts. Salvation »p. 744. Punishment »p. 827. Antichrist »pp. 521, 828.

INSIGHT

Two interpretations. The *premillennialist* sees the events described here as the fulfillment of a divine program announced in Dan. 11, Ezek. 38–39, and Zech. 14. Christ will triumph and establish His "rod of iron" (Ps. 2:9) rule. The "marriage supper" is the promised consummation of our salvation. The *premillennialist* believes this battle will actually take place at history's end, and the Antichrist and false prophet will be sent immediately to the place of eternal punishment. *Amillennialists* see here typical apocalyptic symbolism. The intent is to affirm the ultimate victory of Christ and the doom of evildoers. The beast and false prophet are not individuals but personifications of satanic power.

"Hallelujah" (19:1, 3, 4, 6). The word means "praise the Lord" and here introduces a series of brief, jubilant psalms. They reflect the fulfillment of themes seen in a number of O.T. psalms, such as Ps. 113:1.

Bride vs. prostitute (19:7-8). A number of contrasts are implied between Babylon the great prostitute, dressed in purple and scarlet, and the bride of Christ, dressed in white, the company of the redeemed. The wedding supper, which in O.T. society celebrated the union of bride and groom, is frequently used in O.T. and N.T. as an image of the ultimate fulfillment of God's promise to His people of complete salvation (cf. Ezek. 16; Hosea 2:19; Matt. 22:1-14; 25:1-13; Luke 14:7-14; 2 Cor. 11:2; Eph. 5:25-33).

White linen garments are associated in the O.T. with priesthood.

"A robe dipped in blood" (19:13). The blood is not that of His enemies, for the battle has not yet been fought. It is most likely the blood He shed on the cross to redeem humankind.

"The armies of heaven" (19:14). Second Thessalonians 1:7 identifies these as angels. There is, however, no need for them to fight. Christ destroys the Antichrist's army with a word (v. 21).

Three O.T. allusions (19:15). The messianic passages referred to in this verse are Isa. 11:3ff., Ps. 2:9, and Isa. 63:1-6. Each speaks of the establishment of Messiah's authority on earth.

"King of kings" (19:16). Christ has ultimate power, and that power is about to be displayed.

Neither battle nor struggle (19:19-21). Nowhere is the futility of rebelling against God illustrated more clearly. The armies gather to fight, but there is no battle! Christ simply speaks a word, more as a judge than a soldier, and all in the vast host are slain.

Hell (19:19-21). What the average person means by "hell" is neither the biblical "hades" or "gehenna," but the "fiery lake of burning sulfur," also called a "lake of fire" (20:14-15). Jesus said that this place of "eternal fire" was not prepared for man but for "the devil and his angels" (Matt. 25:41). Yet all who reject God's offer of salvation in Christ will be tormented there "day and night for ever and ever" (Rev. 20:10).

924

Chapter summary. With the human host defeated, an angel chains Satan and seals him in the Abyss for a period of 1,000 years (20:1-3). Dead saints are brought back to life in a "first resurrection," to reign with Christ for the 1,000-year period (vv. 4-6). Now comes one of the most stunning series of events to be found in Scripture. After enjoying a 1,000-year era of peace and blessing under the rule of the Messiah, Satan is released and a majority of humanity permits itself to be deceived, and follows Satan in a last rebellion (vv. 7-9a). When the rebel army gathers to attack Jerusalem it is destroyed by fire and Satan is cast into the lake of fire (vv. 9b-10).

Now the material universe itself dissolves, as described in 2 Peter 3, and all the dead from Creation to culmination are assembled for judgment. The dead are judged by their works, and any whose names have not been written by faith in God's "Book of Life" are condemned to the "lake of fire" (vv. 11-15).

Outline
Place
Finder

JESUS
LETTERS
JUDGMENT
RETURN
NEW HEAVEN

Key verse. 20:15: You're either in or....

Personal application. Praise God that your sins have already been judged, and paid for, at Calvary.

Key concepts. Abyss »p. 915. Resurrection »p. 521. Satan »p. 501. Judgment »pp. 372, 724. Hell »p. 924.

INSIGHT

Two interpretations. The *premillennialist* takes these descriptions in their plain sense, and links the 1,000-year period with many O.T. prophecies which describe Messiah's rule on earth. The two resurrections are also taken literally and are considered to be in full harmony with Dan. 12:2 and 1 Thes. 4:13-18. Both the binding and release of Satan are also understood literally, as is the final rebellion that precedes the Great White Throne judgment. *Amillennialists* take this chapter as the seventh in a series of parallel visions, each of which encompasses the whole period between Christ's first and second comings. The "binding" of Satan took place at Christ's death and has made the preaching of the Gospel possible. The 1,000 years is symbolic, and the "resurrection" is the believer's salvation and endowment with spiritual blessings (Eph. 1:3). The last part of the chapter describes a general resurrection which will take place at history's end.

"The thousand years" (20:3). This is the only place where the Bible indicates a specific span of time during which Christ the Messiah will rule. As the introduction to this book indicates, the early church saw this as the period within which God's promises through the O.T. prophets would be fulfilled. The debate is not really about the length of time, but whether O.T. prophecies are to be understood as literal or merely symbolic revelations of God's plans for the future. If the O.T. prophets are taken literally, many prophecies must surely be fulfilled during this 1,000-year span.

"The first resurrection" (20:5). The word *prote* means the first in a series, implying at least two. This first resurrection is to life; the second is for "the rest of the dead" who are not saved and thus subject to what John calls the "second death" (v. 6).

"The second death" (20:6). Hebrews 9:27 reminds us that "man is destined to die [biologically] once, and after that to face judgment." The second death is not biological or spiritual death (»p. 741), but the eternal state of the lost. It is "death" in that it involves permanent separation from God and punishment forever.

"Judged according to what they had done" (20:11-15). Saving faith brings the believer into relationship with God through Christ, whose death is credited as payment for our sins. Thus are names entered in the "Book of Life" by faith, not works. All others can be evaluated only on the basis of "what they had done." On that basis, every human being falls short and is revealed to be a sinner, guilty, and meriting the punishment God as Judge must now mete out.

Outline
Place
Finder

JESUS
LETTERS
JUDGMENT
RETURN
NEW HEAVEN

Chapter summary. John now sees what we call "heaven": a totally new heaven and earth, a fresh creation destined to be the home of God and His people (21:1). John sees a New Jerusalem, the symbol of God's presence, descending (vv. 2-5). He hears Christ proclaim this new creation the home of the godly, from which sin and sinners are forever excluded (vv. 6-8). John is then given a closer look at the vast New Jerusalem, glistening with jewels (vv. 9-21). He realizes that there is no temple in the city, for God Himself is present and provides its light. That city thus serves as a beacon for all humankind (vv. 22-27).

John also sees a river flowing from the city lined with fruit trees. Like the city itself, the land is forever suffused with the light of God's presence, never to know night. There God's servants will reign for ever and ever (22:1-6). As the beatific vision fades John hears Christ speak and promise, "Behold, I am coming soon" (v. 7).

John again falls down before the angel who has shown him the new heavens and earth and again is directed to worship God. John is also directed to share what he has seen—not that the lost will be convinced, but that believers might be encouraged to do right and continue in holiness (vv. 8-11).

Again John hears Jesus promise, "I am coming soon" and urges holiness (vv. 12-16). The church responds, eager for His coming (v. 17). After a final word of warning, John expresses his own deep desire: "Amen. Come, Lord Jesus" (vv. 18-21).

Key verse. 21:3: What heaven really is.

Personal application. Await Him eagerly, welcome Him joyfully.

Key concepts. Jerusalem »p. 451. Temple »p. 283. Holy »pp. 86, 879. Prophecy »pp. 131, 434.

INSIGHT

Two interpretations. The *premillennialist* sees this as a portrait of eternity, the destined home of the redeemed in a freshly created and sinless universe. *Amillennialists* also view this as a portrait of eternity, but insist that the details are to be taken symbolically. Thus the New Jerusalem is not a city, but the church triumphant, while the "new" universe is our present creation cleansed of sin and revitalized.

Heaven. These chapters describe what most Christians would call "heaven." Heaven is not some ethereal realm beyond the clouds, but a completely new universe, created to be the home of the redeemed. The key physical features are the lack of any sea and the suffusion of the universe with light that is not dependent on star or sun. The major feature is a vast city called the "New Jerusalem" (see »p. 927). But the most important aspect of "heaven" is the relationship the redeemed have with God. He is present with us; we will see His face. And be-

cause we are His and He is ours, never again will mankind know death, crying, mourning, or pain. What makes heaven is God!

Old Testament parallels. Both Isa. 60 and 65 and Ezek. 40–48 contain parallels to John's image of the new heaven and earth, and the New Jerusalem.

New and Old Jerusalem. The earthly Jerusalem was intended to be the site of the temple of God, the symbol of His presence among His people and the place where He might be approached in worship. The New (*kaine*: new and superior) Jerusalem fulfills the promise of the old. God is present in reality, and here His people can worship Him freely and enjoy His presence forever.

The jewels (21:18-21). The point of the jewels that encrust the city is not to give an impression of wealth and luxury. Rather, the scintillating light that shimmers and reflects from the city foundations and gates speaks of God's glory.

Illustration. *The holy city called the New Jerusalem is in the form of a jewel-studded cube some 1,400 miles long, wide, and deep. Some scoffers have calculated its capacity and determined that even a city of this size does not have room for enough residents. But they ignore the chapter's report that the city is not heaven itself, but the capital of a vast, newly created universe. We have no real knowledge of what heaven will be like, or how we will serve God there. What we do know is that life there is endless, that it will be lived in God's presence, and that neither sin nor any of its consequences will ever be experienced by us again. If we are impressed at the care with which God created Eden, to give Adam and Eve every opportunity to use each human capacity to the fullest, we can only wonder how His creativity and grace will be expressed in shaping heaven for His glory — and our fulfillment in Him.*

The nations (21:24-26). In the rest of the N.T. the term *ethne* indicates the rebellious pagans of a hostile world. Who are the *ethne* here, since all but God's redeemed are excluded from His new creation? The only possible answer is that they stand for the redeemed, who inhabit the whole earth as well as the holy city. The point of the description is to show that the redeemed are involved in active social and other relationships that bring glory to God.

"The tree of life" (22:1-5). A tree of life grew in Eden, but after Adam and Eve sinned the human race was cut off from access to it (cf. Gen. 3:21-24). Now at last a redeemed humanity has access to this tree which grows profusely along the banks of the river that flows from the throne of God in the New Jerusalem. Christ's sacrifice has brought abundant healing and life to a humankind once ruined by sin, but now restored eternally.

"Soon" (22:7, 12, 20). Three times in this chapter Christ encourages us promising, "I am coming soon." John's eager response is ours as well. "Amen. Come, Lord Jesus" (v. 20).

Index

643, 662, 669, 692, 694,
708, 710, 712, 719, 767,
775, 781, 784, 797, 799,
806, 809, 813, 814, 816,
821–22, 827, 829, 834,
867, 875, 894, 896, 907,
915

Preach(ing) 612, 709–10,
713, 715–16, 720, 724,
728, 751, 770, 806, 836,
844

Predestination 744, 797
Priest/Priesthood 70, 74,
80–81, 83, 88, 103, 108,
170, 182–83, 194, 273,
281–82, 291, 295, 320–21,
460, 464, 482, 526, 533,
652

Promise 32, 197, 223, 271,
280, 352, 357, 419, 468,
517, 520, 559, 646, 790,
833, 860, 897

Promised Land 145, 147,
261, 265, 308, 356, 451,
454, 482, 489, 494, 503,
506, 509, 545, 857

Prophecy 231, 417, 421,
434, 438, 449, 451, 460,
463, 465, 475, 477, 498,
500, 506, 522, 528, 541,
549, 553, 586, 603, 619,
622, 623, 640–42, 645,
652, 669, 689, 709, 726,
767, 769–70, 824, 886,
888, 907

Prophets 131, 182, 187,
208, 210, 212, 221,
230–31, 234–35, 237, 239,
244–45, 256, 259–60, 270,
272, 290, 292–93, 295,
297, 301, 310, 317,
405–08, 412, 455, 457,
462, 464–65, 471, 478,
482, 493–94, 542, 552,
572, 582, 658, 667, 888

Prostitution 45, 135, 146,
223, 231, 494, 497,
525–26

Providence 47
Punishment 65, 89, 101,
114, 149, 209–11, 216–17,
222, 231, 261, 272, 297,
338, 340, 351, 359, 364,
423, 437, 441, 445,
450–52, 454–58, 467, 469,
475, 482, 488, 493, 495,
526–29, 540, 562, 567–68,

782, 784, 827, 866, 901
Purify/Purity 335, 340,
847

Rebellion 103–04, 108,
412, 417, 492, 496
Redeem 432, 436
Redemption 90, 379, 813,
848, 879
Rejection 580, 624, 627,
639, 693, 745–46
Rejoice/Rejoicing 350,
360, 362, 372, 879
Repentance 238, 290, 450,
451, 464, 495, 503, 527,
529, 534, 549, 604–05,
654, 664, 666, 760, 775,
780, 888, 908
Restoration 412, 458, 466,
468, 526, 530, 559, 698,
747
Resurrection 198, 245,
248, 252, 335, 337, 424,
522, 611, 624, 629, 641,
644, 648, 658, 671, 674,
688, 697, 724, 729, 742,
771, 800, 808, 823, 879
Revelation 9, 354, 758,
784
Revenge 169
Revival 233, 259, 319
Riches 390, 399, 838
Righteous(ness) 37, 120,
339, 341, 350–53, 356,
358–59, 364, 371–72, 380,
389–90, 392, 413, 423,
427, 433, 441, 445,
493–95, 528, 534, 539,
563, 604, 606, 608, 627,
739–40, 742–43, 745–52,
778, 800, 806, 836, 838,
844, 872, 880, 894
Roman Empire 699
Sabbath 61, 66, 71, 73,
102, 123, 321, 441, 458,
614, 634, 648, 657,
664–65, 682, 720
Sacrifice 27, 30, 38, 59,
79–81, 88, 97, 107, 128,
165, 217, 223, 235, 253,
272, 280, 285, 309, 399,
509, 527, 543, 554, 739,
748, 778, 863–64, 895
Saints 357, 369, 375, 716,
762, 813, 915, 921, 923,
925
Salvation 353, 363, 372,
381, 418, 424, 426, 434,

437, 442–43, 445, 535,
577, 664, 680–81, 720,
737–38, 740, 744, 746,
779, 797–98, 807, 827–28,
841, 848–49, 856, 860,
863, 879–80, 886, 893,
901, 914
Samaritans 254, 715
Satan 27, 272, 331, 419,
501, 605, 633, 635, 655,
685, 690, 874, 894,
918–19, 925
Saul 186, 188–89, 192–95,
197–98, 200, 265–67
Saviour 271, 354, 432,
436, 438, 709, 855, 907
Scripture 319, 354, 377,
836, 842–43, 886
The Second Coming
581–82, 626–27, 645, 668,
693, 708, 823–24, 827–28,
841, 844, 888, 926–27
Separation 87, 156, 761
Servant 65, 145, 150, 431,
433, 436, 437–38, 504,
622, 624, 749, 759–60,
779, 833
Sexuality 25, 85, 135, 404,
763
Sheep/Shepherd 355,
368, 370, 430, 462, 504,
580, 620, 653, 687, 698,
883
Sickness 66, 211, 257,
412, 655, 659, 686, 688,
807
Sin/Sinner/Sinfulness
78, 87, 102, 149, 189,
210–11, 254, 258, 272,
331, 342, 350, 354, 357,
360, 362, 368, 371, 380,
387, 412–13, 415, 442,
444–45, 450–52, 454,
456–58, 467, 474, 477–78,
482, 488, 494–95, 497,
516, 526–27, 529, 539–40,
543, 611, 614, 620, 634,
656, 666, 668, 681,
685–86, 696, 739, 741–45,
761, 764, 767, 770, 775,
778, 792–93, 798, 815,
827, 833, 837, 859, 862,
864, 872, 880, 882,
892–94, 896, 923
Slave/Slavery 53, 65, 90,
129, 135–36, 150, 228,
245, 281, 791, 792, 801,